Structural Depths of INDIAN THOUGHT

SUNY SERIES IN PHILOSOPHY

Robert C. Neville, Editor

P.T. Raju

STRUCTURAL DEPTHS OF INDIAN THOUGHT

State University of New York Press · Albany

First Published in U.S.A. by
State University of New York Press
State University Plaza
Albany, NY 12246.

TO MY FATHER
POOLLA LAKSHMI NARASIMHAM
AND MY MOTHER
POOLLA SATYA NARAYANA
AND
MY GREAT SPIRITUAL TEACHERS

Contents

"Originally this (universe) was only the Ātman in the form of a Person. He looked around and saw nothing beside him. First he uttered: "I am." Out of it rose the word "I." Therefore, when one is asked: "Who are you?", he says first: "I am," and then adds his other name (like John)."

Bṛhadāraṇyaka Upaniṣad, I,4,1

"So God created man in his own image; in the image of God created He him; . . ."

Genesis I,27

"And God Said to Moses, I AM THAT I AM, and he said, Thus shalt thou say unto the Children of Israel, I AM hath sent me unto you."

Exodus, III,14

Preface

1. SPECIAL FEATURE OF THE WORK

The present work is of a new type. It is said that history is the science of the Germans and economics that of the British. Whatever truth lies or does not lie in this generalization, the German historians of philosophy, particularly J. E. Erdmann and W. Windelband, impressed me so much that I began thinking that to teach Indian philosophy as philosophy—not merely as an accidental, intellectual, incidental addition to some religious practices and dogmas—one had to write it as the Germans had done, i.e., as a critical and constructive exposition of thought struggling to be systematic and comprehensive. Indeed, no writer on Indian philosophy ought justifiably to ignore its major aim to be a philosophy of life and of the spirit.[1] But it should not be meant that he should treat the intellectual content as trivial and indifferent.

During my college days (and even now) professors used to advise the students to adopt the idealistic point of view to examine a realistic doctrine and vice versa; or criticize Plato from Aristotle's point of view and vice versa; and so on. We were not asked ourselves particularly to develop an approach of our own. The result was that students, although often taking sides on philosophical problems, were indifferent to the problems as problems of life and thought which concerned them also. Such an examination of the schools in the various chapters does not philosophically lead to highly fruitful results. There have been a few estimates of the schools from the Advaita point of view; but they do not seem to be systematic, developmental, and comprehensive. To follow fully the plan of Windelband, whom I admire the most, is not possible in the case of Indian philosophy, as it has not been rewritten as a history of thought developing chronologically. All schools and systems grew together. Besides, the element of comparison has also to be added to make Indian thought assimilable to the western philosophical mind. I have, therefore, adapted the method of the Germans to the Indian scene in giving a comparative, critical, and constructive estimate of the schools to the extent to which the boundaries of each school are fairly not lost sight of in the general estimates. These estimates and commentaries are presented in such a way that the estimate of each preceding school in a way leads often to that of the succeeding one; and the critical discussion of the topics such as space, time, cause, existence, nothingness, etc., can be found to be fairly continuous and coordinated. The peculiarity of this work lies in the many comparative and constructive criticisms often being nearly as long as the main expositions. It is also hoped that both the Indian and western readers will find pathways to new insights into philosophical problems, concepts, and aspects of existence. But few of the insights are mine; nor are they new to Indian thinkers. Most of the insights have been culled by me from general and philosophical encyclopedias in Sanskrit and from other original sources.

The doctrines developed in the general estimates are the ones I accept; they represent my philosophy. As they are given in the general estimates, they cannot be given *en bloc* in a coordinated and systematic form. Many doctrines may be found by the reader to have loose ends; but I hope to tie them together (God willing) in a future work on the philosophy of the I-am. Readers may do the same in their own way. The I-am has become nothing or nothingness not only for most existentialists but also to Wittgensteinians and analytic philosophers of the present.[2] But it is more positive to human existence and more valuable to it than nature which man faces. What then has to be revived and made primary in philosophical thinking is the I-am as a self-affirming being; if it is nothing, who is it that affirms its nothingness? The affirmer has to be self-conscious and cannot be himself nothing; he is the I-am. It is hoped that the reader himself of this book will be able, by the time he reaches the end, to relate the objective forms of the world such as time, space, cause, etc., to the I-am. He may await a more systematic presentation—not as an exposition of Indian thought—by the present author. Here the reader can see that structures of time, space, universals, etc., cannot be intelligible without the I-am. The I-am gives meaning to much in the history of philosophy, which has been recently relegated to the sphere of the meaningless.

2. THE NEED AND USE FOR THE WORK

The above mentioned peculiarity of the work constitutes one of the main purposes of writing this book, which is still not fully comprehensive, but more detailed and critical than my *Philosophical Traditions of India*. It aims at being a philosophically and critically discussed presentation of Indian thought, covering epistemology, logic, and metaphysics, which are primary in all philosophy. (For want of space it has not been found possible to include the philosophy of language and grammar, its profound ontological insights, the metaphysics of esthetics of Bharata, Abhinavagupta, and Jagannātha Paṇḍita, and some materialistic vulgarizations of the philosophy of the Supreme Spirit, etc.) The book presents the schemata of the Indian schools of thought prompted by life's urges and ideals. The serious reader, it is hoped, will not only correct the mistaken and one-sided opinions about Indian philosophy, but will also be able to fill in the details in their proper places, if in future more detailed works appear.

My experience of western philosophers and students has disclosed to me the difficulties they encounter in understanding and manipulating many basic concepts of Indian thought presented even by Indian writers, who often use dictionary meanings of Sanskrit terms. The requirement is, therefore, that Indian thought has to be made intelligible to western students and to the Indian students also who have been trying to re-understand their own concepts in terms of the western, which have come to stay in the East because of the long and strong cultural influence and because of the desire of the eastern thinker to be abreast with the world's philosophical thought. For this purpose it is necessary to avoid as many Sanskrit terms as possible, particularly long compounds, which for students not knowing Sanskrit become a great hindrance. I have avoided also Sanskrit quotations, even in the footnotes, which may show the author's scholarship, but may appear pedantic in a work like the present one. The use of certain terms such as *ātman*, Brahman, *Jīva*, *manas*, and *dharma* cannot be avoided, for they stand for definite concepts for which western languages do not have exactly corresponding terms. In my *Philosophical Traditions*, I gave reasons for not completely avoiding Sanskrit terms, for not using the asterisk on the English word in the text and referring the reader to the various synonyms which he may use. This practice is a greater hindrance and more puzzling to the reader than the traditional one. Besides, even the same word has different meanings for different schools and for the same school in different contexts—a feature of language not uncommon in the West—a fact often missed even by many Indian writers.

Another requirement is that Indian philosophies have to be presented as conceptual structures, made clear and intelligible as such, without resorting to scholastic interpretations, which may indeed be very scholarly, but confuse the student who finds it difficult to fix the general nature and central position of the philosophy he is studying. Experience only can tell an author how to meet this requirement, although no philosophy can be made easy for any reader and be understood by him without his making the proper effort of thinking.

To meet the above requirement, I have found that a complicated presentation of a school of thought with all its sub-schools confuses the not well advanced student or reader. A number of books have been written on the history of western philosophy, some elementary, some a little advanced, others still more advanced and so on. I derived some inspiration by looking at the plan of some of them. How much has to be omitted and how much presented depends certainly on the length of the book and the nature and maturity of the reader. The book is meant for students and readers who are philosophical and critical-minded, and who are capable of asking themselves: If this is not the right view, what can the right view be?

A further requirement, I feel, is that the author should constantly bear in mind that a book on Indian philosophy is not merely a book on Indian religion. It is indeed true that Indian philosophy has been essentially spiritual, that it originated in hermitages (*āśramas*), and *its final aim is not only the love of wisdom, but also the life of wisdom*. But it will confuse the philosophical reader if a variety of religious sects is introduced, particularly those whose contributions to philosophical thought is of secondary importance and which do not have a fairly comprehensive conceptual framework. We should not forget that Indian thought is not only religious but also intensely academical and that the student of philosophy has to grasp the latter aspect as clearly as possible.[3] Even Heraclitus, it is said, was a spiritual recluse. The mention of some religious sects may be made whenever their philosophical contributions have to be recognized. But we need not devote to the sects any special attention. They may be mentioned to show the cultural milieu in which they originated or to which they gave rise. In any case, this is not a book merely on Indian culture or Indian religion, but on Indian philosophy, whatever be the conclusions one may draw from it about Indian culture and religion.

The next requirement is more important than any so far mentioned. How is the author of a book like the present one to balance his presentation of the different schools? One may of course answer: "It depends on his own knowledge." But then the total picture he gives of Indian thought may turn out to be a misleading one. We should not forget that Indian philosophy, unlike Greek philosophy, is still new to many western colleges and universities. The reader may think that, since some school received a longer treatment than another, the former is more important than the latter. The author himself may give more importance to it; but then he should justify his preference. Otherwise, one who knows may suspect that the author has a religious bias in favour of a particular school. But religious bias is not justifiable in one who wants to present something like a history of Indian philosophy or Indian philosophy as a whole.

It is true that a school like that of Patañjali has far less literature than one like that of Śaṅkara. But so far as my understanding goes, the basic concepts and doctrines of each are nearly as many as those of the other. In a work that claims to present the basic doctrines, there is no justification for any inordinate difference in length between their presentations. Such difference may mislead one into thinking that the Yoga of Patañjali, compared to the Vedānta of Śaṅkara, contributed little or nothing to Indian thought.

The Cinderellas of Indian thought have usually been the Yoga of Patañjali and the Mīmāmsā of Jaimini. There is justification for a short treatment of the Cārvāka school because of the unavailability of much of its literature. But there is no such justification for a similar treatment of the Yoga and the Mīmāmsā. The Yoga has much to say on the psycho-physical being of the individual and the evolution of the concepts of substance, time, etc., out of process. The Mīmāmsā is a summation of the philosophy of half the Veda—and Jaimini is said to be the earliest of the authors of the aphorisms—and from it the ethical and legal ideas of India are derived. Its contributions to the philosophy of language, to epistemology, and to ethics are very significant. To ignore its importance is to ignore half the life of India, for it is to ignore half the Veda, which is claimed to be the source of all the orthodox philosophies and contributed the atmosphere of the so-called heterodox philosophies also. It cannot be dismissed as a set of rules of ritualism, *for it is the philosophy of the life of action of the Indians*. We may ignore its ritualism, but we cannot ignore its philosophy of action. Otherwise, the picture of Indian thought will be one-sided, and the reader gets the impression that India has had no philosophy of active life. Furthermore, it is in the Mīmāmsā, as in Judaism and the ethical thought influenced by it, that questions such as whether the good or the right is primary, whether action or its result as potency is the more important, what the nature is of ethical merit (*dharma* may be translated as virtue also), and so forth, are raised pointedly. They are all concerned with action and the life of action and are indicative of the life, thought and ideals of the Indo-Aryans in action.

3. POSSIBLE APPROACHES TO THE STUDY OF INDIAN PHILOSOPHY: APPROACH OF THE PRESENT WORK[4]

The philosophies of India may be, and have been studied from different angles, and the chapters arranged accordingly. *First*, they may be studied as religious thought. Then we shall have Jainism, Buddhism, and the orthodox religions with their cults, doctrines, and concepts. Every one of the three may then be divided into its branches. *Secondly*, the philosophies may be studied according to the ways of life they accept and exalt. The most important of the ways are the way of action, the way of devotion, and the way of knowledge. Such a study will cut across all the schools and systems. But then the inter-relationships of some of the sub-schools to one another and to the main school may be lost. *Thirdly*, the philosophies may be arranged according to the values of life they support. These values of life are wealth, enjoyment, ethical merit, and salvation. If this arrangement is followed, we obtain far more philosophies under the fourth than under the others. We get only one, the Mīmāmsā, under the third, and one, the Cārvāka, under the first and the second. Vātsāyana's *Kāmaśāstra* (*Science of Erotics*) may be classed under the second; but it does not deal with all enjoyment, but only of erotic love, and it is not considered to be a philosophy by the Indian traditions, although the founder of the science is considered to be a saint and a sage. The tendency of Indian philosophy, on the whole, is to grade and combine all the four values. In all the three forms of arrangement, we miss philosophy proper and the reader may get the wrong impression that India has had no academical philosophy to which rational and intellectual energies were devoted, but only religion or religious doctrines. If Indian philosophy is not philosophy proper, then applying the same reason, the whole of Greek, Hellenistic, and Medieval philosophy has to be omitted from the history of western philosophy. But if we accept that philosophy, whatever else it ought to be, has also to be the conceptual articulation of the thought-currents of a nation's life and culture, then the presentation of the schools representing the different traditions of thought has to be considered necessary. And in view of the inadequacies of the other ways of approach, it is essential also for the understanding of Indian thought as basic philosophy that it be presented as a critical exposition of the concepts and doctrines distinctive of the individual schools and systems of thought which constitute Indian philosophy as such.

There is still here and there a tendency to mystery-mongering, sometimes wrongly identified with originality and spiritual depth, and of esoterism among some writers. In India religious thought and philosophy were not differentiated, and some religious thought, mythology and literature have an esoteric tendency such as hiding the straight meaning of words by using different words, esoterically interpreting mythological personalities in terms of the concepts of philosophical or spiritual psychology as Philo did for Biblical personalities, and refusing to explain the philosophical texts unless the student becomes a disciple and joins the esoteric sect like that of the Pythogoreans. But as I pointed out, there is an academical side to all philosophical work, and it is not fair to say that the Mīmāmsā and the Cārvāka were esoteric. In this book, I have deliberately avoided esotericism and mystery-mongering. I do not also go all the way with Ganganath Jha, a well-known scholar and translator of many Sanskrit works, in saying that in the 20th century there can be nothing new in Philosophy. Heraclitus is said to be a forerunner of Bergson; but it will be rash to equate the two philosophies. I do not believe also that merely giving old doctrines new names, creating artificial problems, or coining of new names as solutions of problems necessarily constitutes originality. Artificiality ends only in blind alleys and is indicative of lack of true philosophical motive, drive and depth. The touchstone of philosophy is man's life, living and thinking man in search of the meaning of his existence, which cannot be that of a mere stone or animal. The profundity of a philosopher lies in his anxious involvement in the doctrine of human existence—its nature and goals—he develops. Such involvement is attributed to existentialism; but the name ought not to matter. All great religions of the ancient world were anxiously and earnestly concerned with the problems of human existence. Their great philosophers were involved in them with the same anxiety and earnestness as their founders had been. The philosophies they developed were systems of profound and earnest metaphysics and ontology. Artificial philosophies and epochs marked by them will be and will have to be passing phases. For man cannot live, and reality does not allow him to live forever with artificialities of thought, life, culture, and civilization.

4. PRESENTATION OF ETHICS

Another problem that worries me and ought to worry other authors also is the presentation of ethics. Does each school have its own ethics? The answer can be, Yes, if ethics is to be equated to the theory of salvation. *But such an equation gives rise, and has given rise to the impression that Indian thought has no idea of moral and ethical law.* It is not justifiable to equate ethics and the theory of salvation. Here one may notice that my presentation and opinion differ from that of Radhakrishnan by whom some writers have been wrongly influenced. From the ultimate point of view, where there is no "Ought" there is no ethics. Disciplines for salvation consist of different forms of worship, breath-control, etc. Nobody is morally obliged to practice them. Most of the Indian philosophers[5] do not regard such practices as an "Ought" (*vidhi*). But moral law is an "Ought" and the Vedāntins and even the Mīmāmsakas knew the distinction between values which are an "Ought" and values which are only recommended to be good. Obtaining salvation, like obtaining wealth, is not an "Ought." It is, therefore, not justifiable to equate ethics and the theory of salvation.Ethics covers also man's life aiming for the best in this world, his relation to other human beings, and in India in the past it covered also duties of caste (*varṇa*) and of the stages of life (*āśramas*). Even Buddhism observed these distinctions except in its monasteries. Even today many followers of Jainism employ Brahmin priests for their ceremonies. The schools do not differ so far as man's duties in this world are concerned. All philosophies which claim to be philosophies of salvation differ from one another only in their doctrines of salvation. One of the Pundits[6] who taught me Neo-Nyāya used to narrate that his grand-teacher would challenge every one to give him any position to defend or attack, with one exception, namely, the doctrines of ethical codes (*dharmaśāstras*), which he would never criticize. The concept of *dharma* (duty, right action, merit) of these codes is derived from the concept of *dharma* of the Mīmāmsā. My teacher's grand-teacher, to whom I have referred already, would criticize the Mīmāmsā philosophy, its metaphysics, its epistemology, and even its interpretation of *dharma*, but would not reject its idea of *dharma*, its social ethics, its ethical injunctions about sacrifices, and those derived from them and presented in the ethical codes. The Mīmāmsā is the basis and source of the whole of Indian ethics, not only of the interpretative rules, but also of the basic principles and the ideas of morality and positive law. For this reason also, I think that a discussion of the Mīmāmsā should precede the discussion of the other schools. The theory of salvation, according to Indian thought is that of the crowning phase of life coming after ethics. The former may be different for different schools, but the latter is the same for all. A branch of the Cārvāka is the only exception. Then no section may be devoted under each school for ethics, but only for salvation, which is the ideal of life for each individual.

5. MAIN DIVISIONS OF EACH PHILOSOPHY

There rises another problem, viz., the way of the presentation of the schools. What are the topics to be discussed under each of the schools? The historians of western philosophy present the political, religious, and other cultural movements that led up to the schools and systems started by individual philosophers; and under the philosophy of each thinker, they present his metaphysical, epistemological, ethical, aesthetic, religious, and political views so far as they are available. But all the Indian schools originated in the same socio-cultural atmosphere. The Indian philosophers, as philosophers, gave little attention to political thought. Their ethical thought, so far as social ethics—which is ethics in the proper sense—goes, was that of the Mīmāmsā and the ethical codes. Their religious thought, we find, has very little to do with any denominational religion, but only with the ideal of life based upon their conception of the soul and the Supreme Spirit. Every school, including the Cārvāka and the two heterodox ones, can, therefore, justifiably be divided into metaphysics, epistemology, and the ideal of life. The Buddhist and Jaina literature has advices given to kings about the best way to govern their subjects. But one hesitates to call such teachings political philosophy. Similar teachings are found in epics like the *Mahābhārata* and in the clear and definite injunctions of the ethical codes, when they describe the duties of the kings and their subjects. Here and there in the epics, one finds a few good speculations about political thought. The greatest Indian work on what may be called political economy is the *Arthaśāstra* (*The Science of Wealth*) by Kauṭilya, also called Cāṇakya. But the epics, the ethical codes, and Kauṭilya's *Arthaśāstra* cannot be said to belong to any school of philosophy. The epics expound a variety of schools, each epic expounds many. The ethical codes are regarded as the application of the Mīmāmsā concept of *dharma* to different ethical, social, and legal situations, and the *Arthaśāstra* as a further articulation and explanation of a part of *dharma* of the ethical codes, that deals with kings and governments.

In an exhaustive work on Indian philosophy, everything of philosophical interest can be and ought to be presented. But in a work aiming at usefulness for academic philosophy, much has to be omitted, certainly with the aim of balanced presentation of all the important philosophical tendencies. If Kauṭilya's *Arthaśāstra* is regarded as an elaboration of what a king ought to aim at and how to achieve his aim as described in the ethical codes, and if the ethical codes are an application of the Mīmāmsā concept of *dharma* in its metaphysical import to the details of social life, then a work like the present one can only point to the Mīmāmsā concept of *dharma* and its relation to the ethical codes. Indeed, I devoted a chapter to epics and ethical codes in the *Philosophical Traditions*. More need not and cannot be said in this work. The

Mīmāmsā is the only philosophy entirely devoted to an explanation of active life and is also the primary philosophy of action in India. *If the author does not give it its due importance, the reader may wonder how active life could have survived in India at all.*

6. MISUNDERSTANDINGS AND NEGLECT OF THE SUBJECT IN THE WEST

This book may disturb some western opinions and interpretations current for a long time. There are few westerners in this decade who believe or imagine that at every street corner in Bombay one can see a lion or tiger taking a sunny walk. But there are many who still hold some old-fashioned views about Indian philosophy, e.g., that for every Indian the world is unreal, Māyā. It is still unfortunately true that the Indians know more about western philosophy than the western philosophers about the Indian. There have, indeed, been many western thinkers and scholars who are not merely sympathetic, but also enthusiastic about Indian philosophy. But their number is very small—one caustic review of my *Philosophical Traditions* asked whether any academic philosopher of the West took serious interest in Indian thought—compared to those who took up the study for missionary purposes. Even now a few vested interests are present as counteractions to the teaching of Indian philosophy because of the introduction of courses in oriental philosophies and religions and because also of the mystical appeal it has for those persons who are fed up with the artificialities of the western civilization. Indian philosophy is still wrongly taught in many places as something outlandish, sexually oriented, culturally degenerating, unrealistic, quietistic, illusionistic, or undesirable. Such teachers do not even imagine that Indian philosophy has intellectual content, that it does not merely advocate some psychological or sexual sublimation, that it is not para-psychology, invocation of forefathers or merely methods for acquiring super-natural powers. Its intellectual content is as profound as anywhere else. Distortions of true doctrines are not absent even in the West. One not at all interested in intellectual content, but is eager to adopt misunderstood spiritual practices, may as well be in danger of losing his intellectual health.

Now, although Christian missionaries have done real service to Indian thought in bringing its existence to light, their interpretations could not but be biased. And many Indian presentations of Indian philosophy were, consequently, somewhat biased reactions against such bias. But any biased interpretations, favourable or unfavourable, cannot lead to true mutual understanding of East and West. An objective and dispassionate understanding is not possible without philosophical insight into conceptual matters. When mutual understanding is meant for future well-being of the world community, we have to be careful that the insights gained are not coloured by what Bacon called "idols of the mind."

7. SIGNIFICANCE AND USE OF COMPARISONS

I have referred in several places to the views of western philosophers. Such reference does not mean that the concerned Indian philosopher and the western, although they hold the same or similar views about a particular problem, belong to the same school of thought. It is very interesting and may even be surprising at times that the same view is held in a particular context by people belonging to quite opposed schools, e.g., the pragmatism and instrumentalism of Williams James and John Dewey on the one side and the same with an equally deep significance held by the Vijñānavādins and quite a number of other Buddhists and orthodox schools. Similarly, in the writings of the Vijñānavādins, the Sāṅkhya, and the Vedānta, we find very profound and significant phenomenological and existential analyses of consciousness. Yet none of the Indian schools is phenomenology or existentialism in any narrow sense of the terms. In fact, they have no definite meanings, do not even seem to offer general platforms; for while phenomenology makes consciousness central to philosophical understanding, existentialism is somewhat indifferent to it. What we have to note is that such analyses as those made by these schools can be made for different purposes, and different conclusions can be derived from the analyses. What may and should interest a student of comparative philosophy is the question: If different conclusions, for metaphysics and also for a philosophy of life, are drawn from the same analysis, what significance can the differences have for a true metaphysics and a true philosophy of life? What light can they throw on one another? Similarly, if different analyses can be given of the same concept, what is the significance they can have for metaphysics and philosophy of life? Comparisons are not meant for finding out bare similarities, but also for finding out differences and, what is more important, for finding out the significance of these differences and similarities. If bare similarities and differences are not enough to discover the universal in a plurality of individuals, but are only stepping stones for the discovery of something deeper than they, then the discovered similarities and differences ought to be only stepping stones for the discovery of something deeper in man than what the philosophies compared can say. Words such as idealism, realism, phenomenology, and existentialism are not by themselves important. Besides, they are not Indian words. What is important is the significance of those lines of thought found in different contexts in different philosophical traditions and brought together for different purposes. Are the purposes of one culture completely different from those of another? This book, it is hoped, will show the way to the readers of both the East and the West to find out similar strands of thought in dissimilar situations and evaluate for themselves the import of the similarities and differences.

8. "KNOW THYSELF": THE DICTUM

Even if a philosopher is not interested in salvation, philosophies of salvation cannot be unimportant for him. It is such philosophies—even those theologies of revealed religions—that go into the ultimate problems of Being, self, and man more earnestly than others; for such problems are life and death problems for them. One may, for instance, think that the Indian epistemological probe into the ontological status of the illusory object is a vacuous study. But for epistemology, the problem of illusion is and ought to be as important as the problem of Nothingness or Non-being is for ontology. And epistemology and ontology overlap. Just as that the problem of social relationships was not considered to be important by the Indian philosophers does not mean that the problem is not important; so also that the problem of illusory objects was not given importance by the western philosophers does not mean that it is not important. Are the reasons that led the Indian philosophers to attach importance to the illusory object significant? For the Advaita it has an ontological significance, not discussed in western thought. But let the reader answer the question for himself. Indian philosophy, as it now stands, is very small when compared to western philosophy, as it now stands; and modern Indian philosophers have much to learn from western philosophy. Any one who is acquainted well with both has to accept the truth. Yet, the western thinkers, unless they wish to detach themselves from the deeper forces of man's existence, have also to learn from the Indian. The western tradition has ignored some aspects of Being and also of knowing. Mutual understanding leads to deeper understanding of oneself. After all, the Socratic exhortation, "Know thyself," holds true of all philosophies, eastern and western, concerned with human existence. And the East and the West have thrown light not only on some common areas, but also on different ones. As much patience and perseverance and also humility are needed for studying Indian philosophy as for studying the western.

9. ORDER OF THE CHAPTERS AND THE NATURE AND INTERRELATIONS OF THE SCHOOLS

A right presentation of Indian philosophy should start with the Mīmāmsā, because heterodox schools such as the Cārvāka—the Cārvāka is not often mentioned as heterodox, in spite of its materialism and atheism,—Jainism, and Buddhism started as reactions and protests against the rigorous, activistic philosophy of life of the Mīmāmsā; the latter two particularly taught against the primacy of action as taught by the Mīmāmsā; and Buddhism seems to be especially responsible for the introduction of the way of knowledge as against the way of action. The Vedānta is based on the second half of the Veda, which is a later addition and development of the first, on which the Mīmāmsā is based. The other orthodox schools which are fairly independent of the Veda, but acknowledge its authority may come in between the Mīmāmsā and the Vedānta. As in-betweens they may be regarded as helps to logical and rational self-reflection (The Nyāya and the Vaiśeṣika) and to discrimination of one's self (*ātman*) from the not-self (the Sāṅkhya and the Yoga), leading finally to the results of the Vedānta. If they come after the Vedānta, they may be wrongly regarded as reactions to Vedāntic thought. They were rather reactions to the unending life of action and enjoyment of pains and pleasures in heaven, on earth, and in hell than to freedom from the life of such action taught by the Vedānta. The adopted sequence of chapters in this presentation answers also to the general growth of the Vedantic ideal of life out of that of the Mīmāmsā. The picture of Indian philosophy now will fairly be a balanced one.

The practice of presenting Indian philosophy, starting with the Cārvāka and ending with the Vedānta, began with the great philosopher-statesman Mādhavācārya in his *Sarvadarśana Saṅgraha*. He presents sixteen systems of philosophy, each succeeding one supposedly considered by him to be in some way superior to the preceding one. The pattern he follows in introducing the former is to select a point of departure from the latter. But it is not always the case that the point of departure is the most important one that is really representative of the previous systems or even central to them. Otherwise, he would not have given Rāmānuja's system as the fourth and Patañjali's as the fifteenth. Neither can we say that he arranged the systems in a series starting from those which are qualitative pluralisms, out of which qualitative dualisms arose and out of which again monisms developed, although recent writers in English adopted this arrangement. We have also to note that the proponents of many of the systems never accept that any other system is superior to theirs. We cannot also say that the arrangement has a chronological significance. In Indian thought the series of systems do not represent a historical growth of thought or of the ideal of life. All the important schools started almost simultaneously and developed through centuries. A history of philosophy, in the right sense of the term—which has not yet been written, but if it is to be written—may also be a history of each of the systems or schools and their mutual impacts and influences. But at the present, how is an author to present Indian thought as representing the life of a people so as to enable the reader to get a balanced view of the whole?

Certainly, even if one manages to present all the schools given by Mādhavācārya, one may have omitted quite a few others. Even the main Vedāntic schools themselves are now known to be at least ten,[7] out of which Mādhavācārya gives only three, which are perhaps the important ones at his time. There are again sub-schools of the important schools. There are quite a few that represent religious sects rather than philosophies. Moreover, even if an author thinks that Śaṅkara's Vedānta is the highest of all the Indian schools, it has become a common practice to introduce Rāmānuja and Madhva later. But then the reader should not think that the later schools are higher than the earlier and should not mix up the relative importance of the schools with that of chronology.

Regarding the importance given by the author to the Mīmāmsā, one may object that some of the doctrines discussed in the chapter were initiated by the Nyāya and the Vaiśeṣika and so they should be presented before the Mīmāmsā. We should remember that we are not following a chronological order and that in fact nobody has so far followed it. Buddhism and Jainism started before Gautama, the founder of the Nyāya, and before Kaṇāda, the founder of the Vaiśeṣika. But these two heterodox religions and their ideas—the Buddhist and Jaina contributions to logic and epistemology are quite extensive—were reactions to the ritualistic activism of the Mīmāmsā. And many of the doctrines found in the Nyāya and the Vaiśeṣika like those of language and ethical merit were inaugurated by Jaimini himself, who was earlier than Gautama of the Nyāya school—Buddha also was called Gautama, these two names should not be mixed up—and whose doctrines, it is said, predate him. Certainly, the philosophy of action, apart from the term Mīmāmsā (meaning discussion) represented the earliest philosophical outlook of the early Aryans. I do not think that the presentation of the Mīmāmsā before the Nyāya and the Vaiśeṣika will be confusing except for those persons who have already drawn some conclusions from the arbitrary sequence of chapters of the older presentations. Furthermore, my aim in this book is the presentation of Indian thought as embedded in Indian life especially in the past—the present Hinduism is Hindu, not to speak about its being Aryan, in the same sense in which the present Christianity is Christian, not to speak of its being the way of the immediate disciples of Christ—not as mere arm-chair logical analysis of concepts and doctrines.[8] But logical, phenomenological and existential analyses are also given wherever necessary.

A curious tendency has recently appeared of symbolizing everything perhaps including existentialist ideas. For the Nyāya and the Vaiśeṣika, it started with B. Faddagon of Holland and has gripped the minds of a few in the western hemisphere. I have avoided this method as much as possible. As it is remarked, the development of logical subtleties was a mark of the alienation of mind from life in Greece and even of a kind of loss of nerve (J. E. Erdmann), a tendency to engage mind in something for the sake of forgetting the realities of life. Disappointment with, and retreat from life are not necessarily due to political catastrophes, but also cultural failures and life's ennui. It is indicative of the philosopher's loss of contact with, or desire to avoid the current of life and its ideals and of a kind of satisfaction with sophisticated logical analysis detached from realities, to which one can be indifferent then.[9] But even later Nyāya (Neo-Nyāya)[10] and Vaiśeṣika were as much interested in problems of the relation of logic to reality—especially in the hands of its proponents—as any other school. Particularly, my teacher in Neo-Nyāya was fond of repeating a problem like this:

> If time is one, and not spread out like space, and if George Washington and J. F. Kennedy existed in it, they must be contemporaries, if not identical. But are they? It is of no help to say symbolically *TW/A* and *TK/A* are different because *W* and *K* are different. (T = time, W = Washington, K = Kennedy, and A=America.) Should the two persons occupy different points of time simply because their names are different? If we say that they are different because they occupy different points of time, then we attribute extension to time and spatialize it, which will be wrong as Bergson pointed out. This can be our objection. But my teacher would ask: If their times are different blocks of duration, how can we relate them as parts of the same time? Similar considerations apply to space also, if space is one. No reality-conscious mind can be satisfied with mere symbolism, which is no answer to such problems. The Nyāya and Vaiśeṣika were really conscious of such problems.

My teacher, who was an out and out Naiyāyika was also aware of the self-contradictions in thinking and it was for this reason that his grand teacher was able to challenge every one to argue with him on any topic, for or against; for he was aware of contradictions in every theory. His opponents were not always so keen as he to discover them.

Sophistication cannot be avoided completely in any advanced work. I have to introduce it whenever and wherever it was necessary. But it does not always mean originality. So modern attempts to turn the Nyāya into symbolic logic shows Gautama and Raghunātha as second-hand Russells or Quines, as not quite well developed logical minds. But their logic was meant to be metaphysical, reality-or-existence bound (compare the difficulty about time mentioned above); and the Vaiśeṣika claims to explain the nature of *dharma* (duty, "Ought", merit), in the very second aphorism of Kaṇāda.[11]

Incidentally, I should say something about the fallacies in the chapter on the Nyāya. It seems that most of the fallacies recognized by western traditional logic can be found to be recognized by the Nyāya. It has been the practice started by some orientalists to say that Indian logic knew only a few of the fallacies, most of them being material fallacies. But I think that, if one tries to tabulate all the fallacies of traditional western logic, he can reduce them to more or less those of the Nyāya logic. I have tried to show in the concerned chapter that such a task is possible. Besides, writers on Indian logic have not taken into consideration insights of logicians like Bradley, who is a metaphysician as well. Had they done so, they would have formed a different opinion of the Nyāya.

Generally it is the western orientalists to whom modern Indian scholarship is much indebted and who have been interested in Indian philosophy. Western philosophers, except in Germany, were on the whole self-contented, ignored Indian thought, and, if they showed any interest, it was only curiosity to see whether the Indian thinkers said what they themselves have been thinking. But the orientalists are more concerned with the meanings of words, philological and linguistic interpretations—one Belgian orientalist wanted to impress on me that *svapna* and *suṣupti*[12] mean the same as both are derived from the same verbal root *svap* (to sleep); he is right but the two words do not mean the same in the *Māṇḍūkya Upaniṣad*, and for their specific meanings we have to depend on the commentaries, for a word can have many meanings even in any western language—than with the conceptual structures of the schools and systems. This attitude results generally in not seeing in the Nyāya many of the fallacies of the western logic. But a little straining of conceptual thinking, somewhat freeing it from linguistics and philology which indeed have their own use often[13]—will clear the way to a positive recognition of almost all known fallacies of western logic in the Nyāya classification.

The principle I wish to follow is, therefore, neither the importance of the systems nor chronology, but a balanced presentation of Indian philosophy, which is Indian culture raised to the reflective level or rational consciousness. The life of India has not been governed, throughout her history, by any one single philosophical tradition. For a balanced presentation, as the Vedic thought is primary, I start with the Mīmāmsā and end up with the Vedānta placing the other schools in between. In the presentation of the Vedānta, as the other Vedāntins built up their systems mainly through a criticism of Śaṅkara, he will be discussed first and the others next. At the end is given the philosophy of the *Bhagavadgītā* and the philosophies of some of the contemporary thinkers.

10. SIGNIFICANCE OF SUB-TITLES

The significance of the sub-titles may now be explained. The reader can easily see that about half the number of pages of the work is devoted to comparative, critical, and constructive comments on the chapters. None of the standard works so far has given such comment, at least in English. But such a comment is important and necessary. Without it western philosophers, who tend to depend entirely on the writings of men of orientalist and Asian research, have found and will find Indian thought strange, if not outlandish as belonging to another world. Comparisons—not merely pointing out that philosopher in India said what philosopher in the West said, but also using western ideas as elucidating strands in Indian thought and the Indian as elucidating similar strands for western thought, both introduced at the right places, and in a prospective self-development towards ultimate ideas beyond which human thought cannot reach—are needed for giving adequate orientation of the western philosophical mind to the Indian and vice versa. These comments have to be critical in the sense of a constructive analytic of Indian thought, the structures of its theories so that, again, the western mind can react actively, not merely receptively, to Indian theories, which can then become part of the background of the philosopher's mind. Mere comparisons will be insignificant, if we do not have a common philosophical, ultimate goal, or discover one in the eastern and western philosophies. Such an aim cannot be anything else than reaching the point beyond which the philosopher's thought cannot reach. That point is Being itself. It is the innermost, further unfathomable depth of man's own being and thought, the I-AM of the *Exodus* and the Upaniṣads, that in which the universe including man has its roots and by which it is supported.

By "Being" is here meant ontological Being, not classificatory Being. Ignoring this distinction makes ontology confusing. I have explained it elsewhere.[14] Briefly expressed, the distinction boils down to this: Classificatory Being is found—or its concept is formulated—when everything in the universe is classified as *a being*, and is placed under Being as the highest class. But ontological Being is involved or is expressed in the form "That is" or "That exists." The highest form of the ontological Being is "I am," in which if I say "I" the "am" is necessarily implied and vice versa, not merely grammatically, but in actuality and truth. If I say: "That is," the object, whatever it be, may or may not exist. The "is" may be regarded as being implied grammatically, but not in actuality and truth. So in the "I am" both the noun and the verb coincide and are identical. Ontological Being then is the identity of noun and verb, agent and action, Being and Becoming, assertion and its truth.

The true ontologial Being is the God of the *Exodus* and *aham asmi* (I-Am) of the Vedānta. In India the highest ontological developments are found in the Vedānta. So I have attempted to show the drive as directed from the activism of the Mīmāmsā to the ontology of the Brahman of the Vedānta. In between I gave place to the other schools. The philosophy of the Mīmāmsā may rightly be interpreted as pure activism—indicated by the sub-title "sovereignity of ethical law"—and as a philosophy of eternal Becoming of man and his soul. The pluralistic Being of the school constitutes the modes, instrumentalities, accessories of Becoming—cp. the verb in the sentence is primary, according to the Mīmāmsā, and all the rest indicated by the other parts of speech are instrumentalities (*kārakas*), are only secondary to the verb; for Becoming is never pure, as Bergson wishes us to understand, but is determined by modalities expressed by nouns or subjects, objects (of objective case), adjectives, adverbs and so on. In fact, the Mīmāmsā treats both nouns and verbs as primary; but the verb governs the structure, constitution of the agent; and the agent becomes an accessory, though indispensable, to the act or process indicated by the verb. To this extent, only the grammarians are thorough-going activists. For the Nairukta school founded by Yāska maintains that the Ātman is pure activity. However, the rigorous ethical activism of the Mīmāmsā, its literalism becoming in some cases ritualism, was opposed by all the other schools, which placed the good over the right and explained the good each in its own way. The Vedānta taught transcendence of action, but some sub-schools of the Advaita of Śaṅkara spoke of it as though dispensable. But on the whole, the Vedānta accepts life of action (*Vyavahāra*, *Karma*) so long as man lives. It is easy to show that action is a self-contradictory concept. Hegel did it in his *Phenomenology* and Bradley in his *Appearance and Reality*; but it is impossible to make man live a life of no action at all.

The more important reason for my placing the Vedānta at the highest level is that its ontology of Being is the highest and deepest, beyond which thought cannot go. If Being is a plurality, it becomes classificatory. It then becomes empty, unrealistic and powerless. A unitary ontological ultimate is accepted by the latest forms of Buddhism also. But this ultimate is called Śūnya (Void, Emptiness, Nothingness), suggesting to many in the East and the West the idea of Non-being, which is devoid of the whole force or power of ontological Being. Buddhism indeed attributes this creative, dynamic force to the Śūnya. But to call it ontological will be a contradiction in terms. How can an empty something be dynamic? Again, Buddhism started as an analysis of misery and as an analysing away of the self which suffers from it, but not from the self-affirmation of the Supreme or even the finite self as the I-am. This defect is overcome in the Vedānta. So I placed Buddhism in between the Mīmāmsā and the Vedānta.

The ontological ultimate is a consolidated and concentrated unity of Being and Becoming. The "I-Am" is a massive, intense, dense, self-conscious experience, without determinations (*avikalpa*) and without even the possibility of falsity. Even if one swears: "I am not, I do not exist," he exists. Only when we add to the "I am" predicates like professor, strong, etc., as in "I am a professor, I am strong, I am John" and so on, doubt and error are possible. Now, Becoming appears within Being; all that happens to me and in me happens within my "I am" and is observable by my "I am." My "I am" is one with this Becoming and goes beyond. This has to be so with the Supreme I-AM. My Becoming is determined by my life of action, not merely by my thinking. Bradley says that thought has to commit suicide—which means that it has to cease to be thought—if it has to grasp the whole truth including its ontological being. To realize reality, to be fully true, is to become reality; otherwise, the ontological basis of truth remains outside and excluded. But to become reality is not possible without action. Two men can see the same rose without conflict, however the coinciding of the two minds is explained. But it may be that the two men are seeing two different roses or appearances and thinking that they are the same. But when the two act to grab it, the identity of the rose becomes evident. So it is action that strengthens the sense of reality. Realization of the Supreme I-AM is not possible without action, even if action is not the Supreme. At this point, I do not go along with some of the interpretations of the Advaita, as the reader will see. Western philosophers are acquainted with the difficulty with which Kant left his philosophy. In it theoretical consciousness is left in the realm of the hypothetical, the as-if, the if-then, and is bereft of the solid reality accessible, so far as we finite human beings go, to action mainly. Kant left nature and morality, knowing and doing, disparate—a problem his successors struggled to solve. It has to be accepted that action—past, present and future, the actual and the possible—enters cognition just as Becoming enters Being. The comments explain how.

It has to be mentioned that no comment on any one chapter is self-complete. If I adopted the method of making it self-complete, there will have to be many repetitions, as the same comments are applicable to many chapters. The work will have to be far larger than it is even now. Furthermore, the fear of unduly increasing the length of the book is another reason for postponing the applicable comments here and there to succeeding chapters. The reader has to be warned against thinking that he has all that is needed in any single chapter's comments. And the final constructive comments are to be found under the chapters of the Vedānta, in which the import of the ideas of the witness consciousness, space, time, causation, action and so on is given from the side of ontological Being. The discussions can be deeper and wider, but space is limited.

11. SOME CONVENTIONS

Here I wish to stress one point, viz., the use of the definite article, which many authors omit, but which I have been uniformly using in almost all my books and papers. *First*, when the words East and West refer only to cultures, I have not used the definite article. But when they have geographical reference also, I have used the definite article. The reader should not forget that these words in this book do not at all mean communism and democracy, as they mean generally in contemporary political writings. *Secondly*, with regard to the words meaning the Absolute, by whatever approach the concept is arrived at, I think the definite article has to be used, as in "the Brahman," "the Tao," etc. Before the word Brahman, it is necessary to have the "the"; for *brahman* means the ever growing, the ever active. Even in the sense of the Supreme Spirit, the "the" is proper. In the *third* place, I think the "the" is necessary before all the schools of Indian thought, although it has not been the practice. For instance, the word *advaita* means non-duality, the non-dual. In the former meaning, the "the" is not to be used, unless we add "of *X* and *Y*." The word has come to mean non-dualism also; even then the "the" does not seem to be necessary, unless we add "of *X*." But in India and even outside, the philosophy of Advaita is identified primarily with that of Śaṅkara. I feel it, therefore, right to use the "the" when Śaṅkara system is meant. Without the "the" it may refer indifferently to non-duality and to any of the non-dualisms. Similarly, the word *mīmāmsā* means discussion, and we ought to add the "the" to it when it means the philosophy of Jaimini. Again, the word *nyāya* means logic, argument, justice, etc. But when it means the philosophy of Gautama, we should have the "the." Cārvāka is the name of the person who founded the school. But when we use the word to mean the school, we ought to have the "the." So also "the Sāṅkhya" and "the Yoga" mean particular systems of philosophy. It is not easy to lay down rules for every word and its use. But if we give some thought, we can find what is right and useful in each case.

I have uniformly followed the systems of transliteration and diacritical marks adopted by most of the modern oriental scholars, and have given the method used. Sometimes I feel whether it is not right to omit many of the diacritical marks, as I did in my *Thought and Reality* on the suggestion of a Pundit, such as the ones differentiating the different nasals and sibilants; for their tendency is to adjust themselves to the concerned consonant when the words are pronounced. However, I followed the general scholarly tradition. Only in the case of a few Indian words which have become common in English, have I omitted the diacritical marks.

In Indian philosophy, not only the dates of many, but also the identity of persons can be questioned. Not being a historian, I have to depend on historians and orientalists for the dates; and the scholars do not always agree. Nor do I accept the latest article of an orientalist, because it is the latest. Kālidāsa, the great Sanskrit poet said that, simply because a thing or idea is the oldest or the newest, it need not be the best and the truest. However, from about the 8th century on, the dates are fairly reliable. All the dates given in this book are those generally accepted in India. In giving them, I have tried to avoid the prejudices and provincialism of some Indian and western writers and accepted the opinions considered to be sober and objective. In the footnotes I have often omitted the dates, etc., of the references, as they are given in the Bibliography.

I have given a glossary of Sanskrit philosophical terms. But the reader does not have to refer to them too often; for the use of Sanskrit technical terms as such, except in a few cases in which the terms are very common even for the western students of philosophy, has been avoided in the main text. They are generally given in brackets. The advisibility of giving the Sanskrit terms in brackets was suggested by friends who were orientalists, so that they could easily recognize the original Sanskrit terms to which the English translations referred. This book is meant for them also to show the bearings of the doctrines to logic, metaphysics, ontology, etc., as such, apart from linguistic and philological considerations. When an author has the western students in view, it is not necessary to use the Sanskrit terms very often for showing that the book is written on the basis of original sources. The sources may be referred to in the footnotes and their names may merely be mentioned, if the views are too well-known to need reference. It is not necessary to burden the western reader with an unnecessarily large number of Sanskrit terms; and in this book he can ignore almost all the Sanskrit terms if he does not know Sanskrit. It is not meant of course that he can read the book like a novel. I have tried to give the schools and systems as running thoughts and, as one German philosopher, Professor F. J. von Rintelen, advised me sometime ago, not to appear pendatic and display scholarship. For instance, it is not necessary to give references when we mention Plato's doctrine of Ideas or Hegel's concept of the Absolute. Some of the general estimates may contain heavy thought structures; but they could not be avoided. For philosophy has also to disclose unfamiliar content in familiar experiences. Every one knows about time; but what is the structure of time? Augustine is referred to as one of the earliest puzzled philosophers of time. Similarly, what is witness-consciousness, the importance of which was brought to the forefront by Husserl in the western philosophical tradition? It was known much earlier to Śaṅkara, Madhva, and their followers. Śaṅkara and his followers understood its ontological implications also.

12. THE AIM AND ORIGINS OF THE WORK

The book is not meant for undergraduate students in the American colleges and universities. My *Philosophical Traditions* is meant for them. This book may be used as a basic text for intensive philosophical study after undergraduate years of philosophy for the graduate and postgraduate classes. In the colleges and universities of India, the book can be used with profit for B. A. (Hons.) and M. A. and as a pointer to higher research problems. The Indian schools of thought, although they belong to India, are representative of both the East and the West. Both have materialism, activism, process philosophies, idealisms of different kinds, realisms of many kinds and so on. The evaluations of one in the East can be applied to the evaluations of a similar one in the west and vice versa. Thus the book can be a source of philosophical drive and stimulus.

The aim of the work may be summarized thus. *First*, as indicated in the beginning of this preface, the work is meant in its own way to be a counterpart in Indian thought to W. Windelband's two volumes of *History of Philosophy* in western thought. There has been written no book so far on Indian thought with comparative and constructive criticism for making Indian doctrines assimilable, like Greek doctrines, by western philosophers. There is indeed this difference. Windelband could show often how ideas and doctrines developed in time from a philosopher of one generation to a philosopher of the next. For the West for a long time logical and metaphysical development was also a more or less chronological development. I say: "More or less," because particularly after the sixteenth century different traditions could develop simultaneously in different lands like Cartenianism in France and empiricism in England, both of which were brought into some unity in Germany later. However, in India all schools started at the same time and developed through mutual criticisms. The Veda, as the positive and negative source of both the orthodox and heterodox schools and as furnishing their philosophical atmosphere, is generally accepted —and rightly so to have reached its greatest heights in the Vedānta. So the drive of the author's comparative and constructive criticism is directed towards the Vedāntic ontology, which has not yet been fully explicated in English by earlier writers, and the contributions to which by the different Vedāntic schools is clearly acknowledged by the author.

Next, Windelband was not concerned with comparisons between Indian and western philosophers. But I am concerned with many important comparisons to remove apparent outlandishness of Indian thought from the minds of several western philosophers. Besides, these comparisons give depth and new significance to Indian ideas in the light of the western and to western ideas in the light of the Indian. They show also the great academical developments in logic, metaphysics, dialectic and so on, which Indian philosophies went through in spite of their being born in the spiritual experiences of the leaders of hermitages. This work will thus show the implications of the spiritual—although it is called mysticism,—the implications of the background promptings of the spirit in logic and metaphysics or epistemology, phenomenology, existentialism, and ontology. As it is said, even Christian philosophy and theology could not have made any progress without the stimuli of mysticism.

The *second* aim of the work is to furnish a textbook for M. A. and other postgraduate students of philosophy, a textbook that is not merely presentative to be got by heart, but one that stimulates thinking and understanding and makes one's own experience confront the studied concepts and doctrines. Then only can the study of philosophy turn the student philosophical. In the *third* place, these comparisons, which are confrontations of eastern and western doctrines, disclose many new problems for further study and research and can be useful helps and guides to teachers who conduct research. *Fourthly*, and as a consequence of the third, the work will be useful for intensive east-west studies. It is not enough to point out what *X* said in China, *Y* said in India, and *Z* said in Greece are the same or similar. Comparative philosophy should lead first to the pointing out of similarities, and also differences, next to the confrontation of ideas and the background systems, and then to interpenetration of doctrines and systems; otherwise, the subject will have a stunted growth and will lack usefulness. The absorption of world's philosophies into one another, like the interpenetration of cultures, civilizations, and ancient religions—not the modern great religions, which are mistakenly afraid of losing their individuality—ought to be its final aim. *Fifthly*, the present work is meant to be a companion to S. Radhakrishnan's two volumes of *Indian Philosophy*, still used by graduate and postgraduate students as a textbook, and to S. N. Dasgupta's five volumes of *History of Indian Philosophy*. The former is not comparative at all and is hardly critical. The latter is comparative and critical, but only at random, not in a systematic and constructive way. Such are the main five aims which the work attempts to achieve.

If the reader finds here and there differences of interpretation from established previous writers, he can find also reasons for the differences. He can realize that the Sanskrit words meant to the original Sanskrit writers things and concepts different from the hazy ones given by some writers in English. I may have indeed committed some mistakes. As Heisenberg said on one place, not to commit mistakes is not to write, and we may add, not to speak even. It is easy also to sit in an arm chair and criticize persons who write, often without understanding them; and it is equally easy to adopt and adapt somebody's writing without acknowledgement and adding a few more details, publish one's own. I have written much, my interpretations of some of the Indian concepts and some of my philosophical views have been changing. All along, as a human being, I must have committed some mistakes. Nobody is born a living encyclopeadia—which also can be wrong in more than one way—or can become one. But if one has ideas, one feels like expressing them; and what I wrote has been the acknowledged and unacknowledged source of ideas and inspiration for many, right from the publication of my *Thought and Reality* (1937). All along there is a continuous struggle to clarify my thoughts to myself and to others. What is given in the general estimates represents, although under separate chapters, my views as they have deepened and clarified.

The present work is the result of more than fifteen years of reading, thinking, and writing. The idea started with a group in Hawaii of preparing a series of comparative presentations of oriental philosophies, saying that I could make it substantial, short, and comparative. I started the work. But a little later, some members of the group became opposed to the idea of making the volumes necessarily comparative studies and the project was discontinued. But I began collecting ideas and doctrines and had to give up the idea of making the volume "short," whatever the word meant. The present shape and size of the book, and particularly the general estimates and comments on almost all the traditional schools—the estimates are constructive comparisons and criticisms—are all results of my nearly fifty years of teaching, reading, writing, and thinking in India, Germany, and America.

13. ACKNOWLEDGMENTS

Now I should like to acknowledge my indebtedness to my past teachers and friends in writing this book. I owe much to the late Pandit Durgacharan Chatterji of Banaras, who was a saintly Advaitin, for first introducing me, in the traditional way, to the significance of the idea of Being (*sattā*). The recent revival of interest in Hegel, phenomenology, and existentialism has given me new inspiration and encouraged me to bring to the surface the intricate significance of the doctrines connected with the idea of Being in Indian thought. This idea has been relegated till now to the realm of secondary and even tertiary importance because of the attractions of British idealism and the vogue of Anglo-American empirical and analytical schools. But its phenomenological, ontological, and spiritual importance is immense. Even Descartes does not seem to realize that his *cogito ergo sum* has a spiritual dimension, which we find in the *Exodus*. I owe also a great deal to the late Mahamahopadhyaya N. Ananta Krishna Sastry of Calcutta for insights I gained into the Vedānta; to the late Mahamahopadhya Vamacharan Bhattacharya of Banaras, who taught me traditional Nyāya; to Mahamahopadhyaya Srisankar Tarkaratna of Banaras, who taught me Neo-Nyāya; and to Dr. S. Radhakrishnan, who, both as a teacher and a colleague, roused my interest in comparative philosophy. S. N. Dasgupta's many volumes of his *History of Indian Philosophy* are important source books in English, from which I derived much benefit. The followers of Rāmānuja and Madhva have only recently begun to open up the secrets of their philosophies; I have made much use of their published works. Until a few years ago it was not easy for a non-follower of these schools to get the texts explained by their pandits. I thank the College of Wooster, particularly President Henry Copeland and Dean Vivian Holliday for getting, in spite of difficulties, most of the manuscript typed for the press. The names of friends who have been a source of encouragement all along are too many to be included here. But I should here remember the name of the late Dr. Charles A. Moore of the University of Hawaii, who first broached the project, though on a smaller scale, entrusted it to me, and then gave it up. The idea of developing it into what it is now dawned on me. I am thankful also to Dr. W. H. Werkmeister, who has been encouraging me by saying that from my comparative, critical studies something new has always been emerging. I owe thanks to Dr. A. J. Bahm also for similar encouragement.

Wooster, Ohio
January 1984

P. T. RAJU

NOTES

[1]Post-Kantians like Schelling, Schopenhauer, Hartman, etc., were able to develop the idea of ideal life without eschewing intricate systematizations. The term "philosophy of life" is not to be understood in the sense in which W. Dilthey used it, but as the philosophy of human existence as such finding itself in the realm of matter, but oriented toward the Supreme Spirit.

[2]Wittgenstein once said that the I was an error in grammar, something like a grammatical illusion. (He refers to the mistake in several places. But see George Pitcher: *The Philosophy of Wittgenstein*, pp. 145 and 302, Prentice-Hall, Engelwood Cliffs, 1964; and also Wittgenstein's *Blue and Brown Books*, pp. 66–70, (Harper and Row, New York, 1958.) However, Wittgenstein may locate it in the realm of what cannot be

said, which is indeed even more important even for Wittgenstein than the realm of what can be said. But for the personality of both God and man, for their being or existence, the I-am is more important than the world in which it finds itself. The I-am is in the world also.

[3]For instance *Vidyāraṇya* shows great depths of spiritual experience in his Anubhūtiprakāśa and great dialectical and logical skill in *Vivaraṇaprameya-saṅgraha.* He was a saint and pontiff of the Sringeri monastery.

[4]This Section gives the general reasons for the approach adopted by the present work to the presentation of Indian thought, as it differs from the approaches made generally by the works of Zimmer, Radhakrishnan, Dasgupta, and many lesser writers.

[5]For instance, Vidyāraṇya and Madhusūdana.

[6]Sri Sankar Tarkaratna.

[7]See the authors *Idealistic Thought of India* for the ten schools.

[8]In a seminar on Hinduism attended by some teachers, it was proposed that we should adopt the Socratic method to know what Indian philosophy was, even before knowing what it was all about.

[9]The Brahmin ethical ideals are still some of the best, apart from the question whether they are followed.

[10]A sub-school of the Nyāya school.

[11]I, 1, 2. [12]*Svapna*–dream; *suṣupti*–dreamless sleep.

[13]cp. Martin Heidegger who often makes good use of the etymological meaning of words.

[14]See "Being: How Known and How Expressed," *International Philosophical Quarterly*, June 1975. Sections V to VIII.

Introduction

1. THE MEANING OF INDIAN PHILOSOPHY

The term Indian philosophy means all philosophy developed at one time or another in the country called India by people who claimed Indian heritage. It includes the thought of men who belonged to areas lying outside what has been called India since 1947, i.e., Pakistan and even Afghanistan. But even much earlier between the 20th and 15th centuries B.C., the Aryans who entered India from outside, maybe from the Arctic regions,[1] brought with them the accumulated wisdom of their ancestors. The early Indian Aryans were perhaps the kith and kin and even ancestors of the Aryans who stayed back in Assyria, Iran, Afghanistan, and other places. Then some at least of the origins of Indian thought were non-Indian in the geographical sense. But whatever may be said of the remote origins, we may say that roughly all thought developed and funded between Persia on the West and Burma on the East and China and Tibet on the North and Ceylon in the South may be called Indian philosophy.

Indian philosophy should not be equated to the philosophy of Hindu religion. The atheistic and materialistic school of the Cārvākas is part of Indian philosophy, but can hardly be called a religion, as it does not believe in the reality of the soul, God, or any existence beyond. Neither is the word Hindu found in any ancient sacred book of India. The Indian Aryans called their religion *āryadharma* or the Aryan Way of Life. The pre-Buddhist Aryans called it the Vedic Way of Life (*vaidikadharma*) also, as the Veda was their sacred scripture. The word Hindu is a corrupted form of the word Sindhu, which is the name of the river now called the Indus. It is still called the Sindhu in Indian languages. The Iranians and the Greeks pronounced the letter s as h, called the river by the name Hindhu, and the people on its banks and far to the east the Hindus, and their religion by a word derived from the word Hindu. The word does not occur in ancient Sanskrit lexicons also. But later, after the Iranians and the Afghans became Muslims and came to settle down in India, all those who were not Muslims came to be called Hindus. The Buddhists and the Jainas considered their religions reform movements as the Aryan Way and rejected the Vedic Way, as they did not accept the Veda as their sacred scripture. But to the foreigners, the Buddhists and Jainas are still Hindus in a general sense. There is a vacillation between identifying Hinduism with every religion born in India and with a part of what is born in India but distinguished from Buddhism, Jainism, Sikhism and a few minor religions. The difficulty in fixing the meaning of Hinduism is due to its not having a well-defined fixed denominational content when it was first used; it meant to the early Iranians and Greeks 'something that is to be found on the banks of the river Indus and beyond, but we know not what.' For a critical appreciation of Indian thought, the above unsolved and insoluble difficulty has to be kept in mind. The word India itself is derived from the mispronounced word Hindu, but for some reason or other has come to stay. In any case, Indian philosophy includes all philosophies, born and developed in India, whatever be their remote and proximate seeds.

2. HISTORY OF INDIAN PHILOSOPHY

Although India has several schools and systems of philosophy, they do not form a historical or chronological series. The history of western philosophy generally presents one school or system appearing after another in time, although there are several appearing simultaneously also. We find also that later western philosophies can be developments of the earlier ones. Respect for a school or tradition is far less in the West than in India. Every individual philosopher in the West tends to give a new name to his system and to distinguish it from that of his own teachers. Even if he has not done so, the historians of philosophy do so. The history of western philosophy can, therefore, be made to appear like a chronology of doctrines and schools, although they can be presented, if one likes, as detailed articulations of traditions started by the Greek philosophers.[2]

The schools of Indian thought, like the schools of Chinese thought, appeared on the scene almost simultaneously. They developed through mutual criticisms by attempting to be self-consistent and comprehensive. Such developments took place during the course of centuries, each great thinker of the school contributing his own by bridging the lacunae of the argument and expanding it over areas not yet covered. But he would not claim the founding of a new school. On the contrary, he would attribute his own developments to the original founder himself, saying that they were meant by the founder. This way of philosophical development resulted in cancelling the distinction between school and system. Generally the word school means a number of systems built up by thinkers agreeing on some basic principles; such thinkers may live simultaneously or at different times, but differ from one another when the detailed structures of their systems are compared. But the followers of any school in India tend to claim that they only expand the system of the founder, with the result that the difference between school and system vanishes. However, we can discover the differences, the importance of which is generally minimized by the followers. The method of expanding the original system lies in writing commentaries on the original text and gives the impression that the commentary is only an exposition.

However, if a history of Indian philosophy is to be written, it will be a compilation of the histories of the schools, which do not form a chronological series, even if the systems of the commentators do. We may, indeed, do violence to the feelings of each of the system-builders, if we say that he differed significantly from his teacher or founder. But we find acknowledged differences, particularly in the Nyāya, the Mīmāmsā, and the Vedānta. The different systems are generally called sub-schools. However, the common practice has been to present the schools without chronological significance.

When a history of Indian philosophy is written, it will not be right to follow the authors of histories of western philosophy and to show how changes in historical and socio-cultural factors led to the founding of this or that school of thought. Whatever be such factors that obtained in India, the fact that all the schools started simultaneously shows that the factors had very little to do with the differences among the schools.[3] The same factors could not be the causes of all the schools, if they were to be causes at all. The motive of all the schools—theistic, atheistic, and materialistic—was the search for the ideal of life. This search implies that the seekers were not satisfied with the life—material, ethical, and spiritual—they were living day to day. The dissatisfaction was not due to historical and natural catastrophes that overtook the society of the time. The founders of the schools belonged to the Aryan race and the Aryans were at the zenith of their power in India at the time of the founding of the schools; and no more disastrous wars were fought in India then than anywhere else, the ethics of war in India preventing unnecessary bloodshed and destruction. Neither did the power and wealth enjoyed by the Aryans make them accept a self-sufficient humanism. We have, therefore, to attribute this search for a deeper meaning of life than could be found in day-to-day existence to a keen and critical sense[4] of happiness and pleasure somehow developed by the people. Psychologically, the desire for mental and spiritual peace may be the result of too many privations or too much satiation. It is difficult and may even be wrong to trace Indian thought to natural and historical evils. As a matter of fact, the greatest historical evil in the form of destruction of men and culture started with the Muslim invasions; for the destruction of the unbeliever was a sacred duty to the Muslim. The result of Muslim invasions was not the founding of pessimistic philosophies, but the gradual waning of all philosophical activity whatever.

3. CASTE AND STAGES OF LIFE

Whether or not satiation or privation was at the root of Indian thought, the question that all philosophies wanted to answer was: What is man's life? What is its meaning and purpose? How is man to plan his life so that he can attain his ideal? If life is part of reality, how is he to know this reality? The question was, therefore, both philosophical and religious. For answering it, man must develop his reflective abilities. He must have time for reflection. But impartial reflection is not possible so long as man is carried away by the needs, duties, and responsibilities of his daily life in family and society. So man's life was divided into four stages called *āśramas*, about the time of the Aranyaka (Forest Treatise) part of the Vedas (i.e., about the 10th century B.C.).

The first stage[5] (*brahmacarya*) is that of the student. When the boy is about eight years of age, he goes to his teacher's house and lives there until he finishes his studies. The second stage (*gārhasthya*) is that of the householder. When the boy finishes his studies and is grown up, he is asked by his teacher to go home and pay back the three debts. The first debt is to the forefathers and is paid back by marrying and having children, particularly males. In a patriarchal society, only sons prevent the family line from becoming extinct. It was a duty at that time to maintain the line. The second debt is to the teachers and is paid back by educating the next generation and thereby transmitting the learning acquired from the teachers. The third debt is to the gods, who maintain and govern the universe, and is paid back by performing sacrifices. The word sacrifice should not be understood as necessarily involving the killing of animals. A sacrifice may be of butter, cooked or uncooked rice, barley, or wheat. These three duties, called debts, were at that time absolute obligations, the highest categorical imperatives and, even though mythologically conceived, served the objectives of society. They were called debts because meeting those obligations produces no rewards, but violating them produces punishment or unhappiness.

The third stage is called the stage of the forest-dweller (*vānaprasthya*). After leading the life of the householder and paying back the three debts, and after having one's own son married so that he can now start paying the debts, one retires to the forest along with his wife and begins to reflect on the values of life he has been able to realize. This stage is really the stage of self-reflection and self-examination. If one feels still tempted and attracted by worldly values, one is advised to go back home and continue the life of the householder.

The fourth stage (*sannyāsa*) is that of the renouncer of the world or that of the ascetic. If one finds that worldly values have no more attraction, one sends one's wife back to their son and renounces the world. Man then gives up all connections with family and all rights and duties. He spends the rest of his life as a man of God, the holy man. He can own no property, lives by begging, and changes his name so that others do not know his family connections. He may teach spiritual truths to men and women who are eager to know them.

The division of life into four stages is prescribed to all men. But the last two stages are not obligatory. As we can see in the use of the word debt, the first two only are obligatory. Though considered useful, the last two stages are not regarded as necessary for spiritual realization. Some of the greatest spiritual personalities, like the sage Yājñavalkya and the kings Janaka and Ajātaśatru, in the history of Indian thought, were householders. Nor should we think that philosophy originated from men belonging only to the third and fourth stages. It was not necessary for man to be a forest-dweller or an ascetic in order to be a sage. We do not know the personal histories of all the founders of the schools. Jaimini, the founder of the Mīmāṃsā, could not have been an ascetic. Rāmānuja led the life of a householder for a long time. We do not know much about the life of Gautama, the founder of the Nyāya, and of Kapila, the founder of the Sāṅkhya. But they do not seem to be ascetics (*sannyāsins*). Furthermore, many of the sages, like Vaśiṣṭha, were living in forests conducting their schools, which also were called āśramas, meaning hermitages. They were regular householders with wives and children living with them. On the other hand, much philosophical work was done by thinkers living in villages and towns and was mainly what we call academical.

Although the four stages were recommended to all men, women and the fourth caste in general were dissuaded from taking to the third and fourth stages. Old wives of old men accompanied their husbands to the forest. But it was thought that women always needed protection and they were prohibited from going to the forest independently, where no protection was available. Since the fourth stage was hard and its follower had to live by himself or herself, women were not allowed to take to it, even when their husbands took to the fourth stage. There were indeed some exceptions. The fourth caste was prohibited from taking to these stages; it was thought, rightly or wrongly, that members of that caste were not capable of self-reflection, self-examination, and self-control, and were immature both in character and intellect. However, Indian epics, like the *Mahābhārata*, provide instances of men, like Vidura, who were saintly men; and some of them, like Sūta, taught even the higher castes about the nature of God, soul, immortality, ethics, and many other topics. For the sake of social stability and welfare, such saints and sages of the fourth caste did not violate the social injunctions.

The caste system of India was a historical growth,[6] but not a stratification of society according to a preconceived plan. When the Aryans entered India sometime between 2000 and 1500 B.C., and began conquering the land, they found brown and dark-skinned inhabitants, who far out-numbered them. It is rightly thought that the caste system was not the invention of the Aryans, but that they found it in some form among the original inhabitants.[7] One Sanskrit word for caste is *varna*, meaning colour. The Aryans with their white skin could easily be distinguished from the dark-skinned races. But in the beginning, there seems to be no clear idea of what is now caste except that of colour or race. Since the Aryans were far fewer in numbers than the original inhabitants, they found it convenient to establish a social structure with religious sanctions that would safeguard their cultural and political superiority, and adapted what could have been a kind of caste structure of the pre-Aryans. As the religion of sacrifices was the most important for the Aryans, they kept the religious profession to their own people. As they did not want their superior knowledge of the methods and instruments of warfare to be open to the conquered races, they kept the profession of warfare also to themselves. Political superiority needs also that the warriors should belong to the ruling classes. Wealth also is necessary for the strength of the state. So the profession of trade also, at least when and where big money was involved, was taken over by them. But the pre-Aryans (many of whom were Dravidian by race) knew the methods of trade perhaps better than the Aryans, as the excavations of Mohenjo-Daro show.[8] It was, therefore, impossible for the Aryans to prevent the pre-Aryans from continuing their trade. If one compares the facial features of the trading caste in the South with those of that in the North, one cannot but come to the conclusion that the third caste had a mixture of Aryans and pre-Aryans. Along with intermarriages, the third caste also brought about the intermingling of races to some extent.[9]

Agriculture and other forms of manual labour were entrusted to the fourth caste. The priests in charge of religion were called *brāhmanas*, the warriors *kṣatriyaṣ*, the traders *vaiśyas*, and cultivators and labourers *śūdras*. Several sub-castes arose out of the mingling of the four. The division of the four castes became rigid by about the second century B.C., or by the time of Manu, the author of *Manudharmaśāstra* (The Code of Manu). Although these divisions slowly formed themselves in history, the *Bhagavadgītā* rationalized the division, saying that the four castes were created by God according to character and profession. What we should note is that rationalization and theorization followed historical division rather than vice versa. We should also note that from the caste of a man we cannot be exact in inferring his race. Many kings and even emperors in the South belonged to the Śūdra caste. Of the imperial dynasties of historical India, the Nandas and the Mauryas belonged to the Śūdra caste, the Guptas to the Vaiśya caste, and the Śungas, the Kāṇvas, and the Sātavāhanas to the Brahmin caste. Curiously enough, none of the great imperial dynasties of history belonged to the warrior caste. When once a royal or imperial dynasty was founded, whatever be the original caste of the founder, the tendency was to have intermarriages with other dynasties, whatever again be their caste origin. In this way, a large amount of intermixture took place. Furthermore, even men of the Aryan race, if they did not accept the Vedic religion, which was at the time called the Aryan religion, were called fallen Kṣatriyas and even became Śūdras in some areas. But on the whole, we may say, the men of the higher castes have more Aryan blood than those of the lower and the Brahmins have the most. Contributions to the development of Indian culture came from members of all the castes, although those made to philosophies and religious movements came mainly from Brahmins and Kṣatriyas.

4. VALUES AND WAYS OF LIFE

By the time systematizations of philosophies started, viz., by about the 5th century B.C., four main values of life (*puruṣārthas*) and three main ways of life (*mārgas* or *yogas*) for the realization of the values became clear in the minds of the Indian thinkers. The values of life are wealth (*artha*), enjoyment (*kāma*), ethical merit (*dharma*), and salvation (*mokṣa*). Wealth is needed for life in this world for enjoyment and also for ethical activity like charities and performance of sacrifices. Acquisition of wealth by itself is not a sin. But wealth is not meant for acquisition's sake. The miser who amasses huge wealth can have full life neither here nor in the other world. Wealth is for the sake of enjoyment and is, therefore, an instrumental value. But enjoyment also should not be chaotic and unprincipled. The principles of enjoyment are given by the ethical laws of society and religion. Enjoyment has to be canalized according to them; and such canalization brings and accumulates merit (*dharma*). The principles are the laws of duty. Accumulated merit brings more enjoyment in this life and the next. Enjoyment as such is not to be condemned, but only that which violates ethical laws. Again, as such it does not bring merit, but only when it is according to ethical laws. Merit can be obtained through enjoyment and merit itself brings the opportunities for further enjoyment.

The followers of the early Mīmāmsā were content with the third value. But most of the other thinkers introduced the fourth, viz., salvation. Ethical action is meant not merely for further enjoyment, but also for obtaining the highest form of happiness or bliss; it is a pathway to liberation or salvation, which is emancipation from bondage to the laws of the world. It results in purifying our inward being and enables it to receive and recognize the reflection and grace of the Supreme Being.

Thus every one of the lower values was made instrumental and subservient to the higher. In an important sense, the world is a vale of soul-making, not in the sense that the soul is created by it, but in the sense that self-realization is made possible through the realization of the four values in the world of action. As a general rule, it is necessary for man to realize the first three values and the fourth, although the highest, is recommended. After the rise of Buddhism and Jainism, which overemphasized the fourth value, the importance of the first three was lessened and even ignored. For salvation is the highest value; and if it lies in emancipation from bondage to the world of action, then why should man concern himself with the world and be tied down to it? The best way for man to adopt is to renounce the world, give up all duties and rights, and become an ascetic. Thus the life of the ascetic was extolled and came to be more respected than the life of the householder. Such an attitude to life entered the orthodox fold also.

As a historical phenomenon, the life of the ascetic, which is the fourth stage of life, was introduced into the Vedic orthodox way of life only gradually and was not considered obligatory. There was a time when the Aryans were hostile to it and even hunted down people who adopted it. But later they not only reconciled themselves to it, but also accepted it. It is likely that some ascetics of the time were black-magicians and sorcerers, and their renunciation of duties and rights was perhaps regarded as violation of moral law. The early Mīmāmsā explicitly ridiculed and condemned the life of the ascetic and of the life-long bachelor. But gradually as the Aryan religion became more and more inward, the life of the forest-dweller and of the ascetic were introduced into the Aryan plan of life.

It is a peculiarity of Indian culture and thought that it developed philosophies not only combining and reconciling the four values of life, but also for every value of life, the higher ones of course including the lower. The name for both the theory and the art of realization is *śāstra.* The Cārvāka philosophy defended the first two values against the other two and gave a philosophical basis for the former. Vātsāyana (about the 5th century B.C.) in his *Kāmaśāstra* (*Science of Erotics*) did the same for the second, although he was not opposed to the third. We may say that Kauṭilya (3rd century B.C.) in his *Arthaśāstra* (*Science of Wealth*) explained how the first could be obtained. But while the work of the Cārvākas is a philosophy, we cannot with equal justification call the works of Vātsāyana and Kauṭilya philosophies. The Mīmāmsā is essentially a philosophy of ethical conduct and so of the third value; and the ethical codes (*dharmaśāstras*) are elaborations and applications of the Mīmāmsā to practical life in society and politics. All the other well-known philosophies claim to be philosophies of salvation (*mokṣaśāstras*).

The way of life is the way man plans his life for realizing an ideal or value, whatever it be. It is called *yoga* and also *mārga. Yoga* is derived from the verbal root *yuj*, meaning "to join." *Yoga* is that which joins a man to his ideal, i.e., enables him to realize his ideal. *Mārga* means path or way. Many *mārgas* or yogas were recognized by Indian thinkers, of which three are now considered to be important. The first is the way of action (*karmamārga*, *karmayoga*) or the way of ethical action. That the only way of life is the way of ethical action, that through it alone can man obtain happiness in every life, and that salvation is a false idea was enunciated by the early Mīmāmsā. But later when the idea of salvation began to be generally accepted, the Mīmāmsā also allowed it to enter its own philosophy, and maintained that the way of action alone can lead to salvation. To meet the objection that action necessitates the enjoyment of its fruit in the form of pleasures and pains and so binds man to the world, the Mīmāmsā replied that action performed with detachment, without interest in the fruit of action, does not bind man to the world. The categorical imperatives, the payment of the three debts, have to be obeyed. Actions done for the sake of their fruit have to be avoided. When there is no attachment to their fruit, man cannot be bound to them and to the world. At death, such a man will obtain liberation. None can live without action. One desirous of salvation should live a life of action, without any interest in their fruit. This teaching is found elaborated in the *Bhagavadgītā*.

The second way of life is the way of devotion (*bhaktimārga, bhaktiyoga*). This way is advocated by all the theistic schools of philosophy. It is easy to speak of action without attachment to its fruit. But how can the common man act without attachment to and concern about the results? Without a purpose, even the fool does not move. As the way of action is, therefore, difficult, man should completely surrender himself to God in love and devotion. Emotional attachment to God is easier than dry detachment from fruits of action. The former automatically brings about the latter. Man should realize that he is only an instrument in the hands of God and think that he is performing his duties in obedience to the will of God and that the fruit of his actions belong to God, but not to himself. One should, therefore, cultivate love of God and surrender to him. After death, man can then have communion with God and live with him.

The third way of life is the way of knowledge (*jñānamārga, jñānayoga*). Communion with God or realization of the Supreme Being is a conscious process. Life's ideal can, therefore, be attained only through knowledge. So the way of knowledge is primary. Consequently, man should know what his spirit (*ātman*, self) is by discriminating it from the non-self, for the pure self alone can have communion with God. Ethical action purifies our mind and reason. Love of God and devotion and surrender to him enable us to rise above our petty self. The way of action and the way of devotion are, therefore, the means to the way of knowledge.

The controversy over which of the three is the most important and primary has a long history in Indian thought. There have been attempts to combine two or all the three in coordination or subordination to one or the other.

5. DEVELOPMENT OF INDIAN RELIGION

In India, as in Greece, philosophy developed out of religion.[10] Indian religion has its own peculiarity in that it was not founded by any one historical person. It is not a revealed religion in the sense that the revelation is not the prerogative of a particular individual. Although Buddha was the founder of Buddhism, he never claimed that others could not have the same truth. He is even said to have taught that everyone who wants to become a Buddha could become one. Indian religion from the beginning has been a reflective religion[11] and, like the Orphic and Pythagorean trends of Greek religion, contemplative.[12] It is rational and supra-rational, not a development out of some dogmas. Indian religious thought has, therefore, no science of dogmatics and theology. For the religious thinker, religion is generally a search for the ground of our being, it is an ontological and metaphysical search, not through pure thought alone, but also through realization. Although there are several religious sects in India and almost all of them stick to different forms of ritual, worship, and symbolism, their differences are not considered to be essentials. Again, although the Supreme Being of the religious quest transcends reason, the quest was a quest for experience, not merely a matter of faith in the words of some great person. One may say that Indian religion is naturalistic and empirical. Here we should understand "nature" in the broadest sense of the term, but neither in the scientific sense of what obeys determinate laws and so predictable nor in the etymological sense of what has birth. We should understand it in the sense that everything that is, is natural. Then not only physical and biological nature, but also the psychological and the spiritual will be natural. If man's conscious being is natural, then whatever such a being implies and involves is also natural. If it is natural, then it must be capable of being discovered within man's conscious being. But this discovery is a matter of experience, not merely of logic. Then the religious quest belongs to empiricism. The essence of religious experience is communion with the Divine. But communion is experience, although often called mystic experience. There is no *a priori* reason for limiting experience to sense experience, when there are other kinds of experience. The only question that can be and ought to be raised is about the truth-value of the different kinds of experience. For instance, illusions and hallucinations also are experiences, but they are false experiences. We ask ourselves, therefore, when and how an experience is true or false. To determine its truth or falsity, we have systems of philosophy with their branches like metaphysics, epistemology, ethics, etc. Religious experience and the quest for religious experience result in systems and schools of philosophy, provided we do not reduce the experience to the acceptance of some creed on the basis of faith. Such an acceptance leads to dogmatism and fanaticism and makes the quest for the Supreme Being pointless. Nor can we pass judgment on religious experience with standards obtained from experience of physical objects. One may then rightfully ask why we should not pass judgment on physical experience from the standpoint of religious experience. Philosophy cannot dismiss any form of experience as false without thorough self-reflection and without an earnest attempt to be consistent with itself and with the whole nature of man and the world.

The religious quest in India, as it took final shape, consists of three activities:[13] hearing the words of the teacher (as books were not available at that time), thinking over their meaning, and meditation over their truths for assimilating them to one's own experience. Thinking includes reason and discussion. At this stage one may rightly or wrongly come to different conclusions and reject or accept the reality of the Supreme Being and of the spirit in man. In any case, the quest was for the nature of reality, the ideal of life, and the way for realizing it. That is why religion became a way of life for the Indian.

The words used for religion in India are *dharma* and *mata*. *Dharma* is derived from the verbal root √*dhṛ*, meaning to support. Thus *dharma* is what maintains and supports life and the universe. It is the way of life that supports life, which, without the way, will be dissipated and destroyed. *Mata* is derived from the root √*man*, meaning to think.[14] It means opinion, theory, doctrine, view. Thus we may speak of Hindu *dharma* or *mata*, the Christian *dharma* or *mata*, and the Muslim *dharma* or *mata*. It is acknowledged that thinking, reflection, is necessarily involved in religion.

Indian religion has had a gradual growth and development from very early polytheism to impersonalistic monism because of the presence of the reflective element all through. Indian religion can be traced back not only to the beginnings of the Veda but also to the pre-Aryan Mohenjo-Daro civilization,[15] which is assigned to some time between 4000 and 3000 B.C. But we do not know enough about its religion for describing it fully. It had a script, the deciphering of which has not yet been unanimously accepted by scholars. It still belongs to the proto-history of Indian religion. All we know about it is that the Mohenjo-Daro people had a cult of the Divine Mother or Mother-Goddess, which may be some early form of the later Śakti worship or worship of the energy aspect of the Godhead, in a feminine form. There was some early form of the worship of God Śiva also in a yogic posture. It may be that some forms of yoga were known to the people of the time. There may even be some form of the phallus cult (or was it the turning of the energy of the libido to a higher level?) and some animistic faith. Many of the religious cults and beliefs of the Mohenjo-Daro people must have been transformed and absorbed by the invading Aryans.

The Aryans may have invaded India and destroyed the Mohenjo-Daro civilization between 2000 and 1500 B.C. It is difficult to fix the date or even the century.[16] But the history of Indian religion and philosophy begins with the Aryans. Even the earliest forms of their religion, many of which belonged to the Aryans before they entered India, are preserved in their sacred literature, the Veda, particularly, the Ṛgveda. The hymns of the Ṛgveda indicate that their religion was one of sacrifices – not necessarily of animals – addressed to various natural forces like the sun, the wind, the sky, etc., understood as different gods. In the Vedas one can find two forms of worship, worship of the natural forces as animated beings and worship of the deities or spirits living in those forces and presiding over their activities. The presiding deities are called *adhidevatās*. The former type of worship may be called animatism or worship of animated physical forces themselves and the latter animism or worship of the deities living in those forces. It is said that for the early man, the child of the race, it was not easy to draw the distinction between spirit and body even in himself and he could not draw it in the natural forces also. His religion then will be animatism.[17] But when he began to draw the distinction within himself, he would draw it in the natural forces also and address his prayers to the spirits of the forces. His religion then is animism.[18] Both animatism and animism are forms of polytheism.

The second stage in the development of the Vedic religion is called henotheism, or the worship of each of the deities as the Supreme Deity, the others being its manifestations. By this time it must have dawned on the mind of man that the universe is an interrelated whole, and a plurality of independent gods leads only to chaos, not to cosmos; for what any one of them does may come into conflict with what others do. There has, therefore, to be a Supreme Deity controlling the activities of the others. But who was this Supreme Deity? Man wavered in his answers. Since there must be a Supreme Deity, whom all the rest obeyed and whose manifestations or creations they were, the worship of any one, it was thought, would amount to the worship of the Supreme. And henotheism took two forms: Man worshipped on different occasions every one of the deities as the Supreme and the rest as its forms; or for several decades he would worship one god as the Supreme, then dethrone him and worship another in his place. Some of such gods who occupied the highest place was Varuṇa, Viṣṇu, Prajāpati, and Viśvakarma. Varuṇa at one time was the god that surrounded the world and controlled Ṛta or the moral[19] law, punishing the people who disobeyed it. But later he became the god of the oceans.[20] Viṣṇu was originally a solar god, then became God himself, next one of the three aspects of the Supreme Godhead, the Brahman, taking many incarnations for maintaining the world. Prajāpati, the Lord of the living beings, also becomes one of the three aspects of the Supreme Being, viz., Brahma, the creator and custodian of learning and knowledge. Viśvakarma, the maker of the universe, becomes later only the god of the smiths. Thus many gods were enthroned and dethroned until finally the Brahman, the Supreme Spirit, became the Supreme God. We should note that the word *brahman* is neuter, while *brahma*, the name of the creator god, is masculine. The three aspects of the Supreme Being are Brahma the creator, Viṣṇu the sustainer, and Śiva the destroyer. Controversies arose later about who of the three was the most important. Curiously enough—only some mythological reasons are given—no religious sect claims that Brahma is the most important. The followers of Śaivism claim that Śiva is the most important and the followers of Vaiṣṇavism Viṣṇu. However, the three form the so-called the Hindu Trinity. The unity of the three is the Brahman.

The word *brahman* is derived from the verbal root *bṛh*, meaning to grow, to expand. The Brahman is the ever-growing, the ever-expanding, the infinite dynamic Being that has no limits. This dynamism required infinite energy, force, or power. The Brahman is thus not understood as mere abstract Being, but as the root itself of the world. The idea of the dynamism of Being might have been obtained (1) from the food which makes living beings grow, (2) the chant of the sacrificial priests that produces the desired results, (3) the magical formulae that produce results, (4) the power of sacrifices themselves, and (5) prayer. Whatever be the origins of the conception, the Brahman came to be regarded as the Supreme Deity by about 900 B.C. It could be found not outside man high up in the heavens, but deep within and inward to him. We may conclude from the way the Brahman is spoken of—it is the Puruṣa, the Supreme Person—that it was at first regarded as a person or personality. Thus monotheism took the form of the religion of the Brahman.

But doubts about the personality of the Brahman were later raised. How are we to conceive its personality? It is neither male nor female. It is not one among many; on the other hand, everything has its being in the Brahman. It is concrete in the sense that it is, and asserts itself in the form "I am." We can know only that it is. It cannot, therefore, be a person in the sense the word is generally understood. It is, and yet indeterminate, beyond speech and concepts. Thus monotheism became a monistic religion, although we should add, all the religious thinkers did not accept that the Brahman is impersonal, qualityless Being.

This highly abstract conception of the Brahman can be traced to even earlier thought. The Nāsadīya Hymn of the Ṛgveda speaks of the origin of things in something unknowable.

> There was neither what is nor what is not, there was no sky, nor the heaven which is beyond. What covered? Where was it, in whose shelter? Was the water the deep abyss (in which it lay)?
> There was no death, hence there was nothing immortal. There was no light (distinction) between night and day. The one breathed by itself without breath, other than it there has been nothing.
> ....

> Who then knows, who has declared it here, from whence was born this creation? The gods came later than this creation, who then knows when it arose? He from whom this creation rose, whether he made it or did not make it, the highest seer in the highest heaven, he forsooth knows, or does he not know?[21]

The above is a highly abstract idea of creation and Being. The passage wonders whether the origin was out of Being or Non-being, but later it was asserted in the Upaniṣads that Being could come out of Being only, so in the beginning there was Being. When this Being is identified with the Brahman, can we treat the Brahman as a person? Both affirmative and negative answers were given by the Indian thinkers.

When we trace the development of monism out of the polytheism of the Ṛgvedic hymns, we should note that the monistic God was gradually made inward to man. The inwardization started with animism, that worshipped the spirits within the natural forces instead of the natural forces themselves. But these spirits are different from the spirit of man. But in the final stage, the Brahman becomes the Supreme Ātman (Paramātman) and is inward to the individual *ātman* (spirit) and yet transcends it. Historical scholarship is generally content with the classification of gods into gods of the upper world, and of the lower world, or the great gods and minor gods, or the gods of the natural forces and gods of mental functions, and so on. But what is important philosophically is the inwardization of the divinities. When the Supreme Being becomes the Ātman of all the *ātmans* (the Universal spirit residing in all our spirits), all the other gods also are given an inward status. This inwardization is best exemplified in the semi-philosophical and semi-mythological narrative of the *Aitareya Upaniṣad*. The Brahman (Ātman) existed alone. It wanted to create the worlds. It created the upper, the middle, and the lower worlds. Then it wanted to create the rulers (governors) of the worlds. Then it lifted up a person from them and gave him a form (of the Cosmic Person). Then the Brahman focussed its mind on him. Then his mouth burst forth; out came speech and out of speech the god of fire. His nostrils burst forth; out came the life principle and out of it the wind-god. His vision burst forth; out came the eyes and out of them the sun. Similarly, his other senses and organs burst forth, and their functions and their gods came forth. Then the gods were overtaken by hunger and thirst, and begged for food and drink. The Brahman gave first a cow and then a horse. But each time the gods said that it was not enough. Then they were given man. The gods were satisfied. Then the fire-god became speech and entered the mouth of man; the wind-god became life and entered the nostrils; and so on. Then the Brahman created food for the gods; but it began to slip away from them, who became the senses and the organs; that is, by themselves the gods could not eat their food. So the Brahman, after other attempts, thought that, without itself being present in man, nothing could be done. It became, therefore, the spirit in man, the "I," and entered his body.[22] Then food could be grasped and enjoyed and the gods could partake of the enjoyment of man. Thus whatever is enjoyed by man is an offering to gods also. It is sacrifice to gods.

The above narrative is significant in that it shows how man is the microcosm of the macrocosm and how the self, or the spirit in man, corresponds to the Universal Spirit. As the commentators explain, the person lifted from the worlds is the Cosmic Person or the Cosmic Egg (*brahmāṇḍa*), out of which cosmic sound, cosmic taste, etc., as cosmic principles or objectivities, and out of them the gods are born. But when man is created, every one of the gods becomes the corresponding sense and enters man. Thus man is made to be a complete representative of the Cosmic Person. Spiritually, all the gods now become inward to man; and philosophically, the correlativity of the senses of man and their objects is enunciated. Yet nothing in the cosmos, nothing in man works without the presence of spirit. Even the gods cannot work without being sustained by the Universal Spirit, just as my senses cannot work without my "I" being present in my body. We cannot of course press a myth for answers to all the relevant logical and metaphysical problems. But the trend of the narrative and an implicit idealism is evident.

Thus in the Vedic religion, the monistic drive is also a drive towards inwardness.[23] Quite a number of minor gods were placed in charge of very small functions as no more than petty officers in the cosmic administration. Even Indra, who seems to be a tribal god originally became later the king of heaven and the god of clouds and thunderbolt, although now and then we come across his name as meaning the Brahman even. Some of the great gods became aspects of the Supreme Deity, and some others aspects of those aspects. The most important gods became inwardized, for the Brahman itself became the individual's spirit (*ātman*) and in some way the latter was made to be one with the former. By the time of the Upaniṣads, the one-ness of the *ātman* and the Brahman and their inwardness came to be recognized, and philosophical enquiries about the relationship of the Brahman on the one side and the individual and the world on the other started. Thinkers who could not accept the results of such enquiries started their own philosophies. The Upaniṣadic age covering the period between the 10th and the 4th century B.C. was really an age of great philosophical ferment in India.

The Vedic religion thus became not only a religion of sacrifices, but also a religion of the *ātman* (spirit) and of the Brahman (the Universal Spirit). But if the realization of the *ātman* and the Brahman is the highest form of religion and is the only form that leads to the spiritual uplift of man, why should man perform sacrifices and shed the blood of innocent animals? Man wants realization only to rise above the world of imperfections and the sufferings of old age, disease, and death. But the life of action binds man to the world, as he has to enjoy the fruits of his action. If renunciation of action is then the aim, why should religion insist upon the life of householder? Then again, why should renunciation and ascetic life be restricted to the three higher castes and to men only? Such considerations popularized Buddhism and Jainism founded by Gautama and Vardhamāna respectively in the 6th century B.C.

The result of the teachings of Buddha and Mahāvīra was a one-sided overemphasis on inwardness and disregard of the values of outwardness in the general outlook of the Indian people. There was a great depreciation and denunciation of all values of the world. Leaders of thought and action, both men and women, became monks and nuns, and their numbers were swelled by people who could not know their own minds. Age limits for becoming monks and nuns were disregarded. The number of monasteries increased so much that Magadha, the land of the Indian emperors, became Behar, the land of monasteries, *vihāra* being the Sanskrit name for monastery. Imperial and royal treasuries were often exhausted in maintaining them. The political and economic life of the country suffered and India was enervated. For the Mauryan emperors (324–187 B.C.) Buddhism was practically the state religion. There were strong attempts to revive the traditional zest for life and the Vedic religion during the rule of the Śuṅga (187–75 B.C.), Kāṇva (75–30 B.C.), and Gupta (320–500 A.D.) imperial dynasties. But the later Guptas and the Śātavāhanas (100 B.C.–200 A.D.) patronized both orthodox and heterodox religions. By about 800 A.D. the orthodox revolt against Buddhism and Jainism became very strong and effective. Under the leadership of Kumārila, a follower of the religion of sacrifices and a life of action, and of Śaṅkara, a follower of the religion of *ātman*-realization, the leaders of the heterodox schools were finally defeated in controversies; and Śaṅkara, by absorbing all that was considered true in Buddhism made it impossible for it to find any justification for continued existence in India. However, there were no religious wars and persecutions, but only controversies, the defeated party accepting the religion of the winner. Buddhism continued to live in India up to about the 15th century and then practically disappeared except at the country's frontiers. Jainism got geographically contracted and, by reconciliations with the orthodoxy, survived in some parts of western and southern India.

Buddhism and Jainism contributed immensely to the philosophical development of India. The controversies of the religions with one another, which were intellectual and experiential and rarely ended in wars and violence led to the establishment of schools and sub-schools of philosophy, although these branches were often mixed up. Islam began to enter in a militant form from about the beginning of the 8th century and Christianity from about the 16th, although the Syrian form entered much earlier. In fact, the entry of both the religions was far earlier, but then neither entered with conquerors. But their influence began to be felt and feared after their followers came as conquerors. The influence of Islam is noticeable particularly in the Sikh religion founded by Guru Nānak (1449–1538), in one of the sub-sects of Śaivism called the Heroic Śaivism (Vīraśaivism), which was militant also like Islam and eschewed caste distinctions and idol-worship (founded by Basava of the 12th century), and in the Sthānikavāsi sect of Jainism (founded about the 13th century). The influence of Christianity is found in many socio-religious movements of reform like the Brahmosamaj and the Aryasamaj. Islam contributed nothing to the growth of Indian philosophy. Christianity as such contributed little, but the western philosophies which its followers brought to India and the work of the western orientalists have given a new life to India's traditional thought.

6. STAGES OF PHILOSOPHICAL DEVELOPMENT

It is said that, for the West, philosophy is the love of wisdom, but for India it is *darśana* or perception of truth or God. But one should not rely too much on etymologies. Wisdom cannot be had without experience and knowledge cannot arise without encountering negation. If life runs smooth, nobody thinks. Plato wrote his *Republic* after he ran for his life from Syracuse. Man thinks only after he is dissatisfied with actualities. But to acknowledge the imperfections of actualities is not the same as pessimism. Some knowledge may be the result of wonder, but no great philosophical tradition, either in the East or the West, started in wonder. Philosophies written only in wonder are generally shallow[24] and miss the earnestness and depths of life. There is much truth in the view that thought and so logic starts with the negative judgment. Thought is life made reflective, life thrown back on itself; and it does not fall back on itself, unless it meets an obstacle, a disappointment. Modern existentialism is not the result of wonder or of mere love of wisdom. Nor is the life of anxiety which nations even of the West live nowadays in constant fear of nuclear weapons child's wonder and curiosity. The tragic sense of life lies at the core of all religion and serious philosophy.

Nor is Indian philosophy to be equated to the direct perception of the ultimate truth or God. The word *darśana* etymologically means perception; but it means also view. Its synonyms include *mata* and *siddhānta*. *Mata* means opinion, thought, and also what is thought and the conclusion of the thought process. *Siddhānta* means doctrine, theory, philosophy and final conclusion. Philosophy may claim to lead to the direct perception of God, but not necessarily; for a philosophy may reject the reality of God. For example, the Cārvāka, the Sāṅkhya, Jainism, Buddhism, and the early Mīmāmsā rejected his reality. We can say only that philosophy gives a view of reality.

We cannot take the definition of philosophy as the love of wisdom very seriously. Plato did not transmit his philosophy in the sense that he transmitted his love of wisdom. What he transmitted is a system of doctrines. Similarly, the *darśanas* transmitted by the Indian thinkers are not their perceptions, for perceptions like love cannot be transmitted. What they transmitted were their views, their systems of thought. One should not think, therefore, that India had no philosophies, but only perceptions, intuitions.

We have seen that Indian philosophy started with the Vedic religion. Even the earliest parts of the Veda, called the Hymns, contain some highly abstract ideas and anticipated in an incipient form some of the later important doctrines. We have mentioned already the question about Being and Non-being in the Nāsadīya Hymn. There are ideas of Puruṣa (*ātman*, person) and Prakṛti,[25] which play an important role in the Sāṅkhya and the Vedānta, of Māyā,[26] which plays a similar role in Buddhism and thc Advaita, and of the Brahman at several places. The word *ātman* also occurs in the pre-Upaniṣadic parts of the Veda. Originally it meant breath,[27] and by gradual stages came to be identified with self and spirit in man and then even with the Brahman in meaning. It is thought that, in the beginning, the Vedic Aryans, like many other primitive people, did not think of life after death and speak of transmigration;[28] and we may, therefore, conclude that the concept of the *ātman* has had its own historical growth. But when finally the *ātman* was understood as the innermost spirit of man and identified with the Brahman, or the Supreme Spirit, the original Vedic religion of sacrifices gave rise to the religion and philosophy of the Upaniṣads.

But we should not think that the religion of sacrifices was at once discarded; it continued to live, sometimes being made subservient to the Upaniṣadic form on the basis of the four values and the four stages of life and other times in opposition to, and independent of it. In the 6th century B.C., when Jainism and Buddhism appeared with philosophies based entirely on logic and experience and discarding all scriptural authority and yet as developments of the Upaniṣadic ideas, it was felt necessary in about the 4th century B.C., by both the sacrificial and the Upaniṣadic religions to systematize and develop their own ideas into a philosophy. Then the two philosophies of the two religions became different and entered into controversies not only with the other schools, but also with each other. These two philosophical schools are called the Mīmāmsā and the Vedānta.

The Vedaṣ are four in number: Ṛgveda, Sāmaveda, Yajurveda, and Atharvaveda. All the four together are referred to as the Veda in the singular. Each of the four Vedas contains four parts: the Hymns (Ṛks), the Ritual texts (*Brāhmaṇas*), the Forest Treatises (*āraṇyakas*), and the Upaniṣads (also called together the *Vedānta*, as they come at the end). The Hymns are addressed to different gods. The Ritual Texts explain how the ritual is to be performed at the different sacrifices. For the Aryans of the time almost every act, from the time one rises from one's bed in the morning till one goes to sleep in the night, was a ritual; and sacrifice meant every kind of offering to gods, both inward and outward. The Forest Treatises contain reflections of men belonging to the third stage of life and form the transition stage to the Upaniṣads. The Upaniṣads contain mature philosophical ideas, which are, however, not expounded as systems of philosophy. Neither the four parts of the Vedas, nor all the passages contained in any single part of a Veda were composed by any single person or at the same time or place. Often they appear to be inconsistent. Hence interpretations became necessary.

It is difficult to fix the dates of the Upaniṣads and their interpretations. The interpretations must have been begun a little after the rise of Buddhism and Jainism, which, although they grew out of the Upaniṣadic atmosphere,[29] relied entirely on logic and experience and must have demanded systematic argument from their orthodox rivals. In the work of systematization, the Mīmāmsā and the Vedānta used textual criticism and interpretation of the Vedas in order to make them consistent with logic and experience, depending on logic and experience only in their controversies with their heterodox rivals. The word *mīmāmsā* means discussion, interpretation, and so discussion and interpretation of the scriptural texts. As both the schools used the same method, they were called the Mīmāmsās. But what is usually called the Mīmāmsā is called also the Prior Mīmāmsā (*Pūrva-mīmāmsā*), as it is based on the first two parts of the Veda; and the Vedānta is called also the Posterior Mīmāmsā (*Uttara-mīmāmsā*), as it is based on the later two parts of the Veda. Other names for the two are the Action Mīmāmsā (*Karma-mīmāmsā*) and the Mīmāmsā of the Embodied (*Śārīraka-mīmāmsā*) respectively, as the former discusses the nature of action and the latter the nature of that (viz., spirit) which has the body. Now, where the word prior or posterior does not occur, the word Mīmāmsā means only the Prior Mīmāmsā. It is very common to call the Posterior Mīmāmsā by the name Vedānta. According to the Mīmāmsā, the first two parts of the Veda are primary and the other two secondary; but according to the Vedānta, the latter two are primary and the former secondary. The first systematizations of almost all the schools appeared in the form of aphorisms (*sūtras*), which, like telegraphic language, are short, pithy, incomplete sentences. In an age when there were no written books, such sentences were easy to memorize. The *Vedāntasūtras*, also called *Brahmasūtras* for the reason that they propose to discuss the nature of the Brahman, were composed by Bādarāyaṇa during perhaps the 5th century B.C. The *Mīmāmsāsūtras* were composed by Jaimini about the same time or perhaps earlier. As the aphorisms now stand, it is difficult to say who was really the earlier. In any case, the movement to compose the aphoristic philosophical literature must have started around the 4th century B.C. Some aphorisms may belong to about a century earlier or about a century later. It is likely that, as the Mīmāmsā belongs to the earlier parts of the Veda, its ideas, if not the systematized aphorisms, were earlier than the ideas of the Vedānta.

It was thought that, for a proper study and understanding of the Vedas, a number of subsidiary studies were necessary.[30] The main subsidiary studies were six: phonetics (*śikṣā*), ceremonial (*kalpa*), grammar (*vyākaraṇa*), etymology (*nirukta*), prosody (*chanda*), and astronomy and astrology (*ivotiṣa*). In addition, there were four secondary subsidiaries: epics (*purāṇas*, cosmic histories), logic (*nyāya*), rules of textual criticism (*mīmāmsā*), and ethical codes (*dharmaśāstras*). But curiously enough, some of these subsidiaries themselves developed their own philosophical systems, although claiming that, as subsidiaries, they were developing and expounding only the right philosophy of the Veda. Phonetics and ceremonial did not have their own philosophies, and we may say that they got absorbed by the Mīmāmsā,[31] which insisted upon a proper and exact pronunciation of words during the chanting of the Hymns and on the exactness of the ritual procedure. Grammar was started by Pāṇini, who lived sometime between 600 and 300 B.C.,[32] and expressed a number of views on the philosophy of grammar. His views and those of a number of his commentators were developed into a system of philosophy by Bhartṛhari (6th century A.D.). It is a philosophy of Being developed in terms of the significance of the grammatical subject and predicate and of the meaningful word. Yāska (8th century B.C.), the author of *Nirukta*, the first lexicon of the Aryans, developed a distinct philosophy of language, treating the meaning of the grammatical predicate, the verb, as the primary reality, thereby equating Being to activity. He gives several names of earlier philosophers of language. But we do not know anything about their works. Prosody and astronomy do not seem to have definite philosophies, except for the view that they have effects on human life.

The epics do not seem to have distinct philosophies of their own, although we read of epic or historian philosophers (*paurāṇikas*). As the epics now stand, every one of them expounds in an easy, popular way many types of philosophy with examples of lives of heroes of several types. They are meant mainly to propagate and explain in a concrete form the Vedic or the Aryan way of life. Logic developed its own philosophy in the hands of Gautama (5th or 4th century B.C.), the author of the *Nyāyasūtras*. *Mīmāmsā* as textual criticism and interpretation overlaps logic; but as a method of textual criticism, it was expounded by Jaimini and was used by both the Mīmāmsā and Vedānta schools. But the method of textual criticism as such did not become a philosophy. The ethical codes (*dharmaśāstras*) considered themselves as practical expansions of the philosophy of action (*dharma*) of Jaimini. Thus the philosophy of the Mīmāmsā included *mīmāmsā* as textual criticism and the philosophy of the word and sound[33] (*śabda*), or phonetics, and of right action (*dharma*).

Dissatisfied with the religion of sacrifices and the building up of a philosophy of life on mere textual criticism, a number of other schools appeared on the scene. The age of Buddha and Mahāvīra (Vardhamāna) was an age of great philosophical ferment in which individuals began to reflect, independently of the Veda, on the nature of reality, ethics, and meaning of life. There were similar independent thinkers even earlier. Buddha seems to have entered into controversies with the leaders of many schools, whose views have been preserved mainly in the Buddhist and Jaina literature.[34] *First*, there were thinkers who could not accept the doctrine of ethical action (*karma*), although accepted by almost all the well-known schools. According to this doctrine—which will be discussed in detail later—all human action produces its fruit in this life or the next. But action completed is ended once and for all and is dead; how can it then produce any effect in this or the next world after a lapse of time? The fruits of action are the effects of action. The followers of this way of thinking were called amoralists (*akarmāvadins*), while their rivals were called moralists (*karmavādins*). The former were opposed to Buddha's insistence on enquiry into the nature of morality and character (*sīlaparāmārśa*). *Second*, there were those who believed that the soul attains salvation (*nirvāṇa*) through intense indulgence of the senses. They were eroticists and sensualists, but not materialists. We know little about the development of their philosophy. Indeed, one may relate their teaching to the so-called left-handed (*vāma-mārga*) way of Śāktism in which sex intercourse during worship is an essential part. But even this kind of Śāktism is not pure or mere sexism.[35] *Third*, there were agnostics and skeptics, with some of whom the Greek skeptic Pyrrho might have come into contact. Sañjaya seems to be the most well-known of them. Skepticism seems to be not merely epistemological, but also ethical; and ethical skepticism seems to have been intended not to preach moral chaos, but tolerance. As we cannot decide which ethical laws are absolutely right, we should tolerate all ethical views. Sañjaya's[36] position can be seen in the following dialogue:

Question: Do you hold that the view X is right?
Answer: No.
Q.: Do you hold that the view X is not right?
A.: No.
Q.: Do you hold that X is both right and not right?
A.: No.
Q.: Do you hold that X is neither right nor not right?
A.: No.
Q.: Do you hold any opinion?
A.: No.
Q.: Are you without any opinion?
A.: No.

Fourth, there were materialists like Ajita and Pāyāsi, who might have influenced or might have been influenced by the Cārvāka philosophy. *Fifth*, there were eternalists, like Kakuda Kātyāyana and Purāṇa Kassapa, who maintained that all that is, is eternal and is Being, for there is no destruction of Being. Every being came out of Being and re-enters Being; it is, therefore, never lost. *Sixth*, there were annihilationists who maintained that everything will be annihilated and nothing is permanent. In the *seventh* place, there were monists (*ekavādins*) and then in the *eighth*, pluralists (*anekavādins*), perhaps cutting across the other schools.

The *Śvetāśvatara Upaniṣad*[37] (probably of the 6th century B.C.) mentions some views current at the time. Some thinkers held that time was the origin of things; some that it was the very nature of things to be and to be so and so; some that the world was due to necessity or law (*niyati*); some that it was due to chance (*yadṛcchā*); some that the elements (*bhūtāni*) caused the world; some that it originated in a cosmic womb; and the others that it was created by the Cosmic Person.

Out of all such independent speculations, the Cārvāka, the Nyāya, the Vaiśeṣika, the Sāṅkhya, and the Yoga developed into independent and fullfledged schools. Those that could not develop disappeared or were absorbed by others. The full-grown schools seem to have consolidated their positions mainly in the form of aphorisms (*sūtras*) roughly between 500 B. C. (or 600 B. C.?) and 400 A. D. We have already mentioned the founders of the Mīmāmsā, the Vedānta, and the Nyāya schools. The *Vaiśeṣikasūtras* were composed by Kaṇāda (perhaps 6th or 5th century B. C.). The *Sāṅkhyasūtras* were composed by Kapila (perhaps 6th century B. C.), but were lost. But they were collected and recomposed by Vijñānabhikṣu during the 15th century A.D. The *Yogasūtras* of Patañjali were composed during the 3rd century B.C. The Jaina aphorisms were done by Umāsvāti in his *Tattvārthādhigamasūtras* perhaps in the 3rd century A.D. The composition of the Buddhist *sūtras*, which are many, started from about the 5th century B.C. The *Prajñāpāramitās*, the *sūtras* of the Mahāyāna Buddhism began in the 1st century B.C.

If the dates of the aphorisms can be correct only within two or three hundred years, the dates of the epics can be much less exact. The difficulty in fixing the dates or even the centuries is great because the authors never cared to mention their time and many interpolations occurred during the course of centuries. Of the epics, the *Mahābhārata*, the *Rāmāyaṇa*, and the *Bhāgavata* are the most important and popular. Of the three, the first seems to be the earliest, although the story and events of the second the earliest. The story of the *Mahābhārata* might have belongèd to about to 1100 B.C. The author of the *Rāmāyaṇa* was Vālmīki. He is said to have been later than the author of the *Mahābhārata*, who cannot easily be identified. He is called by the name Vyāsa; but the author of several other epics also, which are much later, is called Vyāsa. Either there were many Vyāsas or the name is a title of the composers of epics and means the analyser, the composer, the expounder, the arranger. The story of the *Bhāgavata* also belonged to the age of the *Mahābhārata*, as Kriṣṇa plays an important part in both. The *Mahābhārata*, except in a few places, is written in classical Sanskrit according to Pānini's rules of grammar; its author must, therefore, be later than Pānini. If the *Bhagavadgītā* belongs to the 5th century[38] B.C. and is a part of the *Mahābhārata*, then the latter and the *Bhāgavata* too may be assigned to the same period. But one can never be exact about the dates. However, as pointed out already, the epics are not systems of philosophy, but presentations of different ways of life and their philosophies along with concrete examples, anecdotes, fables, parables, and so forth, suggesting a reconciliation of the different ways of life.

If we take the first two parts of the Veda as the first stage of philosophical development, the later two parts as the second stage, and the period of aphoristic literature as the third stage, the fourth stage may be said to be that of commentaries on the aphorisms. As the aphorisms were pithy, incomplete sentences, they were difficult to understand, although easy to memorize. So commentaries in the form of explanations began to be written from about the 5th or the 6th century A.D. But the commentators began to introduce their own views. Thus differences of view among the followers of the same school began to make their appearance. Along with such differences, there were differences from rival schools. The fifth stage marks, therefore, the rise of polemical literature with discussions on logic, epistemology, psychology, and metaphysics, and may be said to have started sometime during the 10th century A.D. To this period belong also independent treatises apart from commentaries. These stages may be divided in different ways.[39] But what we have to note is that systematic thought began with the composition of the aphorisms, then passed through the writing of commentaries and commentaries upon commentaries, and then reached the stage of polemical and independent works. It should be noted also that every kind of philosophical activity once started does not end when the other kinds start. Even in the 20th century, the fashion of composing aphorisms and writing commentaries has not been given up.

The Muslim invasions and the accompanying vandalism started from the 10th century. But Indian philosophical activity continued up to about the 16th century. From about the end of the 16th century to the founding of the Royal Asiatic of Bengal in 1784 by Sir William Jones, Indian philosophy, one may say, passed through a blank period. Then started the Indian Renaissance to which great names like those of the poet Tagore and the philosopher Radhakrishnan belong. After the Indian universities were founded in 1857, the Indians began studying western philosophy. After a time, Indian philosophy was introduced as a small part of the courses for a philosophy degree. Then comparative studies were started, to which S. Radhakrishnan gave the strongest impetus. Quite a few philosophers in India are well up in both western and Indian thought, and there is an intensive search for comparison and evaluation, and a few attempts at a synthesis of both, a search that has now become world-wide but still in a groping stage.[40] The word synthesis should not be understood as leading to one philosophy and philosophical regimentation or totalitarianism. Every philosophical tradition will have its own synthesis and methods of synthesis; and every philosopher may chalk out his own method. But he should know what he has to synthesize. The first requisite is, therefore, clear mutual understanding.

Philosophical activity in contemporary India is varied. There is, *first*, the work of editing, of translation mainly into English, and of interpretation of ancient classics. *Second*, there is the work of comparative study and evaluation. *Third*, there are philosophers who attempt to develop the Indian positions out of the western—a work made possible mostly by the philosophies of the post-Kantian German[41] thinkers of the 18th and the 19th centuries, many of whom did not hesitate to refer to the Indian doctrines in appreciation and criticism. But most of the western doctrines came to India through the British adaptations and assimilations. *Fourth*, there are philosophers who know only western philosophy and almost all kinds of thought of the West can find representatives in India. But their philosophy, although now found in India, cannot be called Indian philosophy. It is generally lacking in its orientation to Indian theories. And where attempts are made at such orientations they are often far-fetched and artificial, if not wrong.

7. THE DRIVE OF INDIAN THOUGHT

Indian thought, which in essence is spiritually oriented, i.e, oriented towards the attainment of the highest good in life, has naturally to be a drive towards the deepest and highest point in man's being. For this is what he can and ought to achieve. Here, the highest and the deepest are, and have to be the same. The highest in man's being is also the deepest. It is the highest because it is the most desirable; and it is the deepest because it is the ground of his being. This good is variously conceived, as pleasure by the Cārvākas; as eternal Becoming, life after life, through ethical action controlled by ethical law by the Mīmāmsā; as conscious existence beyond the grip of *karma* by the Jainas; as the Śūnya, self-less-ness and so beyond the reach of suffering by the Buddhists; as unconscious existence by the Nyāya-Vaiśeṣika; as conscious existence beyond the clutches of Nature by the Sāṅkhya-Yoga; and finally as the unity of consciousness, bliss, and existence by the different Vedānta schools. But what is ultimate and invulnerable to the ups and downs of Becoming is Being itself that assimilates Becoming to itself; for if Becoming is left out unassimilated, it will assault Being from outside. So unless the quest is an ontological quest, it cannot be said that the goal is achieved by man's thought and practice. The goal is presented in some of the most systematic forms by the Vedānta. The drive of Indian thought then is an incessant one towards ontological Being.

What is it that is ultimately true and real? And what is it that exists ultimately? It is Existence as such, Being itself, *sattā* as such. The rest, names and shapes, are the forms through which Being is known. Such Being may be considered to be an empty concept, unless it is realized that it is the I-AM, the fountainhead of my I-am, as will be shown and explained in the work. To dismiss it as the mere ego (*ahaṁkāra*) is a mistake. As the chapters on the Vedānta show, the ego is not the same as the I-am, but is the latter's deposit as the "me" in theoretical and practical activities. Yet the ego (*ahaṁkāra*) has a deeper relation to the I-am than what the general reader of the Vedānta is led to think. Both are denoted by the word I, the *aham*. The ego as the unitary depository of all the agencies (the experiencing subjects and doers) of theoretical and practical actions, becomes also, through identification with the I-am, the free source of the agency of further theoretical and practical activities. Personality is not an empty, static mask. On the other hand, it is the dynamic source of further activity. It is not a mere bundle of dispositions or of psycho-physical forces working as causal chains. I am not merely a criss-crossing of these chains. I break them up, make myself their meeting point, and freely bend and turn them into processes of my free activity. Without the *aham* (I-am), there is no freedom, no responsibility, no duty. To attain complete liberation from the causal chains, a true realization—which may be understood in different ways by the different philosophies and religions—of full *ahamta* (I-am-ness) is needed. This is found only in the Supreme I-AM. It is the true ontological Being in which cognition and its truth, Being and Becoming, the Is and the Ought, the Supreme I-AM and my I-am, freedom and determinism are reconciled and united. This is the goal theoretically of Indian thought and practically of the Indian religion. A careful study of the comments given in the book, it is hoped, will make the drive of Indian thought clear. Indian philosophy need not be apologetic about its being religiously oriented so long as it is understood that religion is the drive towards the realization of the ontological depths of man's being.

NOTES

[1]See B. G. Tilak: *The Arctic Home of the Vedas*.

[2]Cp. the view that Heraclitus is a forerunner of Bergson. See W. Windelband's *History of Philosophy;* S. P. Latrprechm's *Our Philosophical Traditions*; and J. H. Muirhead's *The Platonic Tradition in Anglo-Saxon Philosophy*.

[3]Albert Schweitzer is right in saying that it was not due to the failure in realizing the good life on earth that made the Indians develop their philosophy. See his *Indian Thought and its Development*, pp. 19 and 24. But his interpretation that Indian thought is life-negating is one-sided. See P. T. Raju: *Introduction to Comparative Philosophy*, pp. 259 fol.

[4]Patañjali says that for a discerning man every pleasure in this world is mixed up with pain. See his *Yogasūtras*, II, 15.

[5]For an account of the *āśramas*, see the author's chapter on Hinduism in *The Great Asian Religions: An Anthology*, pp. 56 fol.

[6]P. V. Kane: *History of the Dharmaśāstra*, Vol. II, Part I, p. 47. See also P. T. Raju: *India's Culture and Her Problems*, pp. 7 fol.

[7]Ibid., p. 5.

[8]See Sir Mortimer Wheeler: *The Indus Civilization.*

[9]Some mythological stories were invented to explain the loss of Aryan features by the trading caste of the South.

[10]F. M. Cornford: *From Religion to Philosophy.*

[11]W. E. Hocking: *Living Religions and World Faith*, p. 95.

[12]W. T. Marvin: *History of European Philosophy*, Chapter VIII.

[13]*śravaṇa*, *manana*, and *nidhidhyāsana*. *Bṛhadāraṇyaka Upaniṣad*, II, iv. 6.

[14]In fact, the English word *man* can be traced etymologically to the Sanskrit root √*man*. Man is the thinking being.

[15]See Mortimer Wheeler: *The Indus Civilization.* Some now think that this also was Aryan.

[16]Many Indian scholars place the date much earlier and some at 1500 B.C., taking some of the incidents referred to in Ṛgveda as the basis. Some think that the Aryans did not come from outside, but migrated to Europe from India. See Ernst Benz: "Address Honouring Sir S. Radhakrishnan" in *Journal for Scientific Study of Religion*, Vol. I, No. 2 Spring 1962. B. G. Tilak thinks that the Aryans came to India from the Arctic. See his *Arctic Home of the Vedas*. See also R. C. Majumdar: *An Advanced History of India*, Chapter III.

[17]A. B. Keith mentions a number of gods under this head. See his *Religion and Philosophy of the Veda*, Vol. I, pp. 63 fol. Philosophically and psychologically, this tendency may be classified as the earliest form of man's religion.

[18]Here Keith refers to the spirits of the dead. Ibid pp. 71. fol.

[19]The English word *right* may be traced to the Sanskrit word *rta*. The word later came to mean practical or ethical truth. See Śaṅkara's commentary on the *Taittirīya Upaniṣad*, the beginning prayer. It means the rightness of right action and also merit.

[20]Cp. Ouranous, the Greek god of the heavens. The Indo-Aryans thought that waters surrounded the world and so Varuṇa later became the god of oceans that surrounded the earth.

[21]Quoted from Max Müller in S. Radhakrishnan: *Indian Philosophy*, Vol. I, pp. 100–101. The hymn is called the first philosophical hymn of the Aryan race. See also Maurice Bloomfield: *The Religion of the Veda*, pp. 235 fol.

[22]See the commentary of Amaradāsa on *Ekdāśopaniṣads*, p. 225. Here I omit some details.

[23]See Maurice Bloomfield: *Religion of the Veda*, pp. 173–75, and also A. B. Keith: *Religion and Philosophy of the Veda*, Vol. I, pp. 124 fol.

[24]Keenness of intellect is not to be equated to profundity of thought or wisdom.

[25]S. Radhakrishnan: *Indian Philosophy*, Vol. I, p. 102.

[26]Ibid., p. 103.

[27]See A. B. Keith: *Religion and Philosophy of the Veda*, Vol. II, pp. 450 fol.

[28]Ibid., pp. 415, 546, and 572.

[29]Ibid., pp. 535 fol. Whether or not the Jainas and the Buddhists accept the view that their

philosophies also are rooted in the Upaniṣads, they have to acknowledge that their doctrines grew in the atmosphere of the Vedic ideas and worked with the Upaniṣadic concepts. Some Hīnayānists, but not the Mahāyānists, asked me whether I was not hinduizing Buddha. But one wonders whether Buddha called his religion Buddhism and what name he gave his teaching. If the Mahāyāna did not contain the original Upaniṣadic ideas, how could it become Vedāntic? And have Mahāyāna ideas nothing to do with the Hīnayāna ideas? See P. T. Raju: *Idealistic Thought of India.*

[30]Bhagavan Das: *Sanātana Dharma*, p. 30.

[31]See G. V. Devasthali: *Mīmāmsā.*

[32]Some place him in the 8th century B.C.

[33]The philosophy of word and sound is more than phonetics, raising questions like: How can a sound have a meaning? and Is sound eternal? Similarly, astronomy includes geometry and trigonometry. These sciences were developed for fixing the time of sacrifices and for raising the sacrificial altars with particular bearings to the constellations and according to exact measurements. After sacrifices were discouraged, the sciences lost further development as interest waned. See G. T. Garratt: *The Legacy of India*, p. 342.

[34]B. M. Barua describes a large number of these schools in his *History of Pre-Buddhistic Indian Philosophy.*

[35]I heard of the advocacy of pure sexism by an acquaintance who related it to the doctrine of Leibniz: This is the best of all possible worlds and heaven lies here. And that is the pleasure of sex. But this way, as the *Bhagavadgītā* says, leads only to the miseries constituting hell. If this world is the best of all possible worlds, we do not need religion, which teaches that there is a higher and better life than here.

[36]Cp. Sañjaya's negations to the Buddhist and the Advaita four-cornered negation and the Jaina doctrine of the sevenfold conditioned predication, and also to Pyrrho's view that he doubts whether he doubts. See the author's article, "The Principle of Four-cornered Negation" in *The Review of Metaphysics*, June, 1954.

[37]The traditional interpretation differs from this interpretation of the passage. I have much respect for the tradition also. Time is the origin of the world, according to the philosophy of astronomers and astrologers (*kālajñas*, time-knowers). But this theory is not found in its developed form, so far as my knowledge goes. The materialists (Lokāyatikas, Cārvākas) maintain that it is natural (*svābhāvika*) to be and to be so and so. This theory sounds theoretically and etymologically somewhat like the doctrine of *tathatā* (Buddhism), meaning such and such, so and so. But the difference seems to be that the former concerns the world around us and the latter ultimate reality. The former does not accept any ultimate reality behind this world. The Mīmāmsakas hold that the world is created by Law (*niyati*, limit, cp. the Greek idea of Fate) resulting from ethical action (*karma*). This is the Mīmāmsaka view that man is the master, controller of his destiny, fate. Some atheists contend that creation is due to chance, no explanation can be given. (*Yadṛccha* is chance, unplanned and uncontrolled.) Some philosophers accept the elements as the origin of the world (cp. the early Greek philosophers like Thales). One school held that the world comes out of a womb (*yoni*). This view is identified by one commentator as that of the thinkers who aspire for salvation through sex-intercourse and also with some Śaktism. But the word womb is explained by some commentators as Prakṛti, beyond which, some philosophers thought, there is nothing. The school may contain one of the origins of the Sāṅkhya system. And if, as the Advaitins and some other Vedāntins say, Māyā and Prakṛti are one and the same and so Māyā is the origin of the world, then we may say that the present view was absorbed even by the Vedānta. Another school holds that the world originated in Puruṣa (Person, Ātman). But this Puruṣa does not seem to be the Supreme Brahman, but Hiraṇyagarbha (the Golden Womb, the Archetype of the self-conscious I-am), whom the Vedānta regards as lower than the Brahman, a higher form of the Logos. But Puruṣa may also be regarded as the finite person. It seems that both views can be traced to the *puruṣasūkta* (Hymn to the Person, Ṛgveda 10, 90). See A. Mahadeva Sastri: The *Śaiva Upaniṣads*, with the Commentary of Upaniṣad Brahmayogi (The Adyar Library, Madras 1950).

[38]For the date of the *Mahābhārata*, see S. Radhakrishnan: *Indian Philosophy*, Vol. I, pp. 479 fol.

[39]See P. T. Raju: *Introduction to Comparative Philosophy*, pp. 177–88.

[40]That is so because very few western academic philosophers are seriously interested in oriental philosophies and so can have little success in assimilating their concepts. The post-Kantian philosophers of Germany and a few Scottish philosophers—particularly the former—were intellectually and psychologically well-fitted for such assimilation; but the extent of Indian philosophy known at that time was not very much. The western orientalists have been very much interested; but their historical, philological, and linguistic approach is viewed with indifference by the conceptually oriented western philosophers. Theologians indeed have their own biases. This situation needs to be overcome before comparative

philosophy can attain any profundity and produce significant results. Another hurdle is the lack of interest of western academic philosophers in what may be called the life of the spirit, which is of primary concern for oriental philosophies.

[41]See Helmuth von Glassenapp: *Das Indienbild deutscher Denker.*

Chapter I

Ideas of the Upaniṣads

1. INTRODUCTION

As already indicated, what is called the philosophy of the Upaniṣads is not a system of philosophy, but several philosophical doctrines brought together, some of which are even mutually conflicting. For example, the statement, "Everything is the Brahman" (*sarvam khalu idam brahma*), is manifestly opposed to the statement, "This is not the Brahman, this is not the Brahman" (*neti neti*), and a system of philosophy is needed to reconcile the two. The Upaniṣads do not belong to the same time or place, neither are they composed by the same authors. The names of many thinkers are not mentioned, although we get some. Since the views are many and disconnected, reconciliations, interpretations, and systematizations of the Upaniṣadic views gave rise to many Vedāntic systems. Many views are repeated by the Upaniṣads in different contexts. The Upaniṣads do not use the same method, and often their method is not what is strictly called logical. They use in their explanations and demonstrations myths, etymologies, analogies, dialogues, etc., which are not really logical proofs.[1] We shall, therefore, give the ideas of the Upaniṣads instead of a system of their philosophy. Systems came in much later through the interpreters and commentators.

The date and number of the Upaniṣads is difficult to determine. It is generally said that there are one hundred and eight Upaniṣads. But some scholars say that there are two to three hundred of them.[2] We do not know how many of them are true Upaniṣads and how many spurious. The orthodox scholars (*pundits*) regard ten, eleven, or twelve of them as the original and important.[3] But they are not always exactly identical. Eleven to them—the *Bṛhadāraṇyaka*, the *Chāndogya*, *Taittirīya*, the *Aitareya*, the *Kaṭha*, the *Īśa*, the *Kena*, the *Śvetāśvatara*, the *Praśna*, the *Muṇḍaka*, and the *Māṇḍūkya*—seem to be the most important and to belong very likely to a chronological order, the first being the earliest. It is said that the *Bṛhadāraṇyaka* belonged to the 9th century B.C. and that all the important Upaniṣads were composed before the 4th century[4] B.C. A few of the others may have been composed before the 4th century B.C., but most of them later. In presenting the ideas and doctrines of the Upaniṣads, the present work follows, on the whole, traditional commentators, who ignored the chronological order of the Upaniṣads and started with the *Īśavāsya*, or simply called *Īśā*.

2. SOME UPANIṢADIC PERSONAGES

The Upaniṣads often mix up mythological persons and deities with historical persons. The names of the upholders of the different views are found mainly in the dialogues and narratives. The greatest among the Upaniṣadic personages is Yājñavalkya,[5] who was the priest and guru (spiritual guide) of king Janaka. Both must have belonged to at least the 9th century B.C. Yājñavalkya taught the doctrine of the Ātman and the Brahman. He held that everything exists in the Ātman, the Ātman pervades everything, it is the ultimate light-giver and light, everything in the world is meant for the Ātman, the Ātman is the highest value, it is sweetness (*madhu*), bliss itself, it is the essence of all, and yet it is beyond all description[6] because as the knower it can never be known. At death it is accompanied by the actions (*karmas*) performed and travels to the next body already prepared.[7] Yājñavalkya entered into a number of controversies with many philosophers, whose names also are given. But they are not of great importance, as they were only testing his knowledge. Maitreyī, one of the two wives of Yājñavalkya, is also an interestingly great soul, who rejected worldly comforts and wealth for the sake of the Ātman; for her husband told her that the Ātman alone was the highest value.

Like Yājñavalkya in the *Bṛhadāraṇyaka*, Aruṇi seems to be the great teacher in the *Chāndogya Upaniṣad*.[8] He taught his son, Śvetaketu, that everything came out of Being (*sat*), for nothing could have come out of Non-being (*asat*). The ultimate Truth is the Ātman itself and "That thou art."

Sanatkumāra[9] taught Nārada that the Ātman is the same as the Brahman. Śāṇḍilya[10] preached that everything is the Brahman (*sarvam khalu idam brahma*), that the Ātman residing in our innermost heart is the Brahman, and that it is smaller than the smallest and greater than the greatest. Perhaps Nachiketas of the *Kaṭha Upaniṣad*, who preferred knowledge of the Ātman to sovereignity of the earth,[11] and Bhṛgu of the *Taittirīya Upaniṣad*, who learned from his father, Varuṇa, that the light of the Puruṣa (Ātman) and that of the sun are the same,[12] were historical persons. The *Śvetāśvatara Upaniṣad* was perhaps composed by a person of the same name, i.e., Śvetāśvatara. In any case, its teachings are attributed to him.

Although the search for the Ātman and the Brahman and their nature and relation seems to be the main purpose of the Upaniṣads, we come across the names of persons who held that the Ātman is something less supranatural. In the *Chāndogya Upaniṣad*[13] we read the discussion between king Aśvapati of the Kaikayi tribe and a few men about the nature of the Ātman and the Brahman. Aupamanyava held that the Ātman is the heavens, Prācīnayogya that it is the sun, Vaiyāghrapādya that it is air, Śārkarākṣya that it is aether (*ākāśa*), Buḍila that it is water, and Gautama that it is earth. But Aśvapati pointed out that the Ātman is the Cosmic Person (*Vaiśvānara*) and that all sacrifice should be made to the Cosmic Person; for all the others that are worshipped as the Ātman are only parts of the Cosmic Person. We may note that the discussion was not between rival philosophers, but between those we were eager to know the true Ātman.

Another king, Ajātaśatru, teaches Gārgya—who was thinking that the Ātman was an external object like the sun, moon, lightning, aether, fire, mirror, echo, space, shadow, and body—that the Ātman is to be found in deep, dreamless sleep, and that the world comes out of the Ātman of deep sleep, just as the web comes out of the spider.[14] One can see that the doctrine of the *Māṇḍūkya Upaniṣad* is an elaboration of Ajātaśatru's view and goes beyond deep sleep. The sage, Kauṣītaki,[15] seems to have taught that the life principle (*prāṇa*) is the Brahman. Jaivali[16] gives a new interpretation of the term sacrifice. He says that everything is sacrificed into something else until all is sacrificed into the Ātman. Pippalāda was a great teacher, who was approached by many enquirers after truth and who taught different psycho-spiritual or metapsychological doctrines.

Other important names of the Upaniṣadic teachers may be mentioned here. Raikva held that air is the ultimate substratum of the universe[17] and is the same as Prāṇa (the vital or life principle) in the macrocosm,[18] holding the parts of the cosmos together and sustaining the whole. Satyakāma Jābāli was taught by the three fires (which every Brahman maintained in his house) the presence of the Brahman in the Earth, the Sun, the Moon, lightning, etc., and by his own teacher that the person seen in the eye is the Ātman (Brahman).[19] The latter teaching has a spiritual meaning, viz., he who sees through the eye is the Brahman and also that in the waking state the Ātman resides in the eye.[20] King Aśvapati of the Kaikayi tribe taught even learned Brahmans that the Cosmic Person was the Fire, Vaiśvānara; he resides in all the parts of the cosmos, not merely in any one of them, he is only about an inch (*prādesamātram*) in size, and he is the same as the sacrificial fire.[21] King Ajātaśatru of Banares taught that the Ātman (Brahman) is to be found in its integrality in deep sleep,[22] thus anticipating the teaching of the *Māṇḍūkya Upaniṣad*. Cākrāyana Uṣasti also held that Prāṇa is the origin of everything.[23] But we should note that the word Prāṇa had a deeper meaning than air and life principle., viz., Hiraṇyagarbha. Prāvahana Jaivali teaches about five sacrificial fires which are not set up by man, but belong to nature or cosmos, and which one after another result in the creation of man.[24] The whole universe is a sacrifice within sacrifice; its creativity is sacrifice, which is not a mere ritual. One should here remember the *Puruṣasūkta* (Hymn to Person), in which the world is created by the self-sacrifice of the Supreme Person. Here we come across the idea of sacrifice raised to high philosophical and cosmic level—a theory reiterated in the *Bhagavadgītā*.[25] We find also Ghora Angīrasa teaching Kriṣṇa (very likely the Kriṣna of the *Bhagavadgītā*) that the whole of man's life is a sacrifice,[26] reminding us of the *Aitareya Upaniṣad* which says that all that man does for his enjoyment is really for the enjoyment of the ruling gods (controlling forces of the cosmos). Pratardana is another discoverer of Prajñātman (self as integral consciousness) as identical with Prāṇa (Life Principle).[27] But Prāṇa, it may be repeated, has to be understood as Hiraṇyagarbha. Sāṇḍilya regards the Brahman as that from which everything is born, that in which it exists, and that into which it re-enters (disappears).[28] Mahācamasya discovered that higher than the three states of waking, dream and deep sleep lies the Mahas,[29] which is generally translated as light (Inner Light), which is a secondary phase of the Logos (Cosmic Person). But many commentators identify Mahas with Hiraṇyagarbha. Among other important names, we should include that also of Pippalāda of the *Praśnopaniṣad*, who answers the famous six questions of his disciples concerning generally the relation of man to the cosmos, and of Varuṇa who taught his son Bhṛgu the doctrine of the identity of the finite self with the Brahman. There are other names which cannot be given here for want of space.

But one point may be noted: the doctrines of all are interrelated, overlapping, and are even repetitions; and it is not always possible to say definitely who is earlier and who is later, although in a general way it may be asserted that persons mentioned in the earlier Upaniṣads are very likely to be earlier than those mentioned in the later Upaniṣads. For some teachers may have lived and taught before others in time, although recognized later than they.

3. CENTRAL DOCTRINES OF THE UPANISADS

Although many names of the Upaniṣadic teachers and inquirers after truth are found, we know little or nothing about their dates and lives. Their names, as already said, are mixed up with those of gods and mythological persons. We are not sure also whether the persons, for instance, who held that water, fire, air, etc., are the Ātman, are actually the founders of the doctrines or only their followers. Which and what is the Ātman and which and what is the Brahman? are the central enquiries, whether the answer is earth, water, air, fire, or aether, or sacrifice or something deep and spiritual. All the views are mentioned in the context of the same enquiry. There can be other enquiries, as for instance those found in the *Praśna Upaniṣad*. In addition, there are instructions about worship and meditation. In the *Bṛhadāraṇyaka* we find even advice about how to have the kind of son or daughter we want. We shall give, therefore, only the main philosophical doctrines of the eleven Upaniṣads, which are generally considered to be the most important.

Īśa Upaniṣad This Upaniṣad starts with a prayer, saying that this and the other world are each full. Even if anything is taken out of the full, the full remains. This teaching is the doctrine of the infinite, to which addition and subtraction make no difference. Regarding the Brahman, the Upaniṣad says that it is the One; it does not move and yet is faster than mind; it is far and yet near; it is outwards and yet inwards to us. Those men who take to the life of action (*karma*) are ignorant and enter the worlds of darkness; but they also who give up action and take to meditation on gods go to the same worlds. One should overcome death through action and attain immortality through meditation. The moral is that through action we purify our minds, when only meditation will succeed. It teaches that everything in the world is pervaded by the Lord and that the Person in the Sun is the same as the "G."

Kena Upaniṣad This Upaniṣad raises the question: What is it that impels the senses and mind to perceive and understand? What is it that sustains all, but which nothing sustains? He who says that he knows it does not really know it, and he who says that he does not know it verily knows it. That is the Ātman, the Brahman. Without it, the senses, mind, and even the gods can do nothing. In this Upaniṣad we come across the idea that Vidyā (Logos or the Higher Reason, personified here as a beautiful feminine angel) is the same as Umā, the wife of Śiva, by knowing which alone one can know the Brahman. Of the gods, Indra (the deity of our intelligence, *Buddhi*, according to some commentators) also was able to see Vidyā and recognize her as such.

KAṬHA UPANIṢAD This is one of the philosophically very important Upaniṣads and teaches that the knowledge of what happens to man after death is more valuable than anything in the world, than even sovereignity of the whole world. Such a knowledge is the knowledge of the Ātman, which is smaller than the smallest and greater than the greatest.[30] The objects are higher than the senses, mind higher than the objects, the individual's reason (*buddhi*) higher than mind, the Cosmic Reason (*Mahān Ātmā,* Logos) higher than the individual's reason, the Unmanifest (*Avyakta*), the same as the goddess Aditi of the Vedas, higher than the Cosmic Reason, and the Puruṣa (Ātman) higher than the Unmanifest; there is nothing higher than the Puruṣa.[31] In the very next stanza, the Puruṣa is spoken of as the Ātman. The Ātman cannot be understood by reason; it has to be grasped only as "Is." It can be realized by withdrawing speech (senses) into mind, mind into reason (*jñāna ātmā*), reason into the Cosmic Reason (*Mahān Ātmā*), and that into the Ātman of Peace[32] (Śānta Ātmā). Here we find reason spoken of as self-as-consciousness (*jñāna ātmā*). Everything else is a branch of the Ātman, and the Ātman is their root. The whole is the Asvattha tree (a big Indian tree), whose roots are above and branches below.[33] That is, the Ātman is above everything and yet is the main root of everything.

PRAŚNA UPANIṢAD In this Upaniṣad the sage Pippalāda answers six questions put to him by six different enquirers. The questions and answers are mixed up with some mythological material. The first question is: How were creatures created? The answer is: Prajāpati (the Creator God) did penance and through it created couples (polar opposites), which in turn created the world of beings. The couples were Rayi[34] (material, stuff) and Prāṇa (the life principle). The life principle is the Cosmic Person (Vaiśvānara). One should realize that this life principle is one's Ātman.

The second enquirer asks: Who are the gods and who among them is the greatest? Pippalāda answers that they are Aether (*ākāśa*), Air, Fire, Water, Earth, Speech, Mind, Eye, and Ear. Greater than all of them is *Prāṇa* (the life principle). We may remind ourselves here that Prāṇa in this context is not mere physical air or physiological *bios*, but the cosmic principle or a person (Vaiśvānara) integrating the part of the universe and the psycho-physical constituent of men. When the life principle leaves the body, nothing remains and none of the other gods can perform their functions. In this answer we see that already the gods of polytheism, who were originally natural forces, were turned into cosmic entities and into man's senses and organs.

The third question relates to the origin of Prāṇa itself. What is the origin of Prāṇa and how does it divide itself into senses, etc., of man? Prāṇa is born out of the Ātman like a reflection and employs its divisions for performing different functions in the body.

The fourth enquirer asks: What happens to the gods (above mentioned) in sleep and who is it that sleeps? In sleep all the senses become one with the god of mind. Only Prāṇa (the life principle) and its activities do not sleep, i.e., the life principle and its involuntary activities continue to work. In dream the agent experiences whatever is experienced in the waking state again and even what is not then experienced. In dreamless sleep he is overpowered by a psychic force (*tejas*) the fire of his conscious being or its intense light and does not see dreams. Like birds resting on a tree everything rests in the Ātman. We may here compare the view of Heraclitus, that the Light of the Logos, Fire, is found only in deep sleep.

The fifth question is about the word *Om* (*Aum*). It is said that the word is the same as the Brahman, both manifest and the unmanifest together.

The sixth question asks about the Puruṣa (Ātman) with his sixteen phases (digits, parts, functions). These phases are Prāṇa (the life principle), Faith (conviction of existence or being (*āstikyabuddhi*), the five elements (aether, air, fire, water, and earth), sense (all the senses taken together, vision, hearing, touch, smell, and taste), mind, food, semen (the generative principle), penance, sacred word, ethical action, the worlds, and name. All of them are fixed in the Ātman like spokes in the axle. That is, the Ātman is the centre and circumference of the universe; it is the source of functions and processes in it, and the consciousness of all of them. It is not empty consciousness, as some interpretations tend to suggest.

In this Upaniṣad we come across the word *māyā*,[35] which later became the name of an important metaphysical principle in the Vedānta of Śaṅkara and Buddhism. The Upaniṣad does not say what *māyā* means, but mentions it along with crookedness and falsity.

MUṆḌAKA UPANIṢAD In this Upaniṣad we find differentiated the two forms of knowledge, the higher and the lower.[36] The former is the knowledge of the Brahman and the lower the knowledge of the empirical sciences and arts including the Vedas and their subsidiaries. Just as the spider throws out its web and withdraws it into itself again, the Ātman (Puruṣa) throws out the world out of itself and withdraws it again into itself.[37] The life of action and sacrifices is as unstable as an unsteady boat and is, therefore, not the highest and belongs to the world of ignorance. In man dwell two spirits, the lower and the higher.[38] The lower performs actions in this world and enjoys their fruit; but the higher remains a pure witness of the lower and its experiences. Because of the rewards and the punishments that follow the merit and demerit of actions, the lower is bound by them and feels unhappy. But it overcomes its bondage and unhappiness when it realizes the higher and its greatness. It then becomes one with the higher. The Ātman cannot be known by study or intellect; it can be grasped only by him who is chosen by it. It cannot be had by the weak, by the deluded, or by mere penance and renunciation; but he who uses penance and renunciation, study and intellect as instruments and strives for it can get it.[39] That is, study, etc., are not ends in themselves.

MĀṆḌŪKYA UPANIṢAD This Upaniṣad is said to contain the gist of all the rest. It teaches that the Ātman has four states—the waking state, the dream state, the state of dreamless sleep, and its original pure state. In the waking state, the consciousness of the Ātman is directed outwards towards external gross objects. It has then seven parts and nineteen gateways. The seven parts are: the forehead, eye, the life principle (*prāṇa*), bodily centre, abdomen, feet, and face. The nineteen gateways are: the five senses (eye, ear, taste, touch, and smell), the five organs of action (hands, feet, the generative organ, the excretory organ, and the speech organ), the five vital principles (*prāṇa*, *apāna*, *udāna*, *vyāna*, and *samāna*),[40] the four inner or internal instruments (mind, ego, reason, and apperception or *manas*, *ahaṁkāra*, *buddhi*, and *citta*). In this state the Ātman is called the worldly or mundane person (*Vaiśvānara*).[41] In dream it has the same seven parts and nineteen gates, but its consciousness is turned inwards towards the dream objects. It enjoys subtle objects, which are dream objects. That is, the objects are not made up of the gross elements, but of subtle elements. In this state it is called the psyche[42] (*Taijasa*), because its experience is constituted by *tejas* or psychic force. In dreamless sleep the Ātman sees no dreams and desires nothing. Its consciousness is its only gate and all plurality becomes one in it. It is then called *Prājña*,[43] because its being is pure, undifferentiated (into objects, senses, mind etc.), solid, unified consciousness. It is the metaphysical Unconscious, out of which everything originates, and into which everything enters. It pervades the other two states and always stays as their background. It is full of bliss and enjoys bliss. But it knows nothing, not even itself. The fourth state is the Ātman in its purity, and is beyond thought and speech. It knows itself immediately and is not overwhelmed by the Unconscious.

The sacred word *Om* (*Aum*) consists of three parts: a, u, and m. The letter a is the Ātman in the waking state, u the Ātman in the dream state, and m the Ātman in the deep sleep. The Ātman in itself, in its original pure state, is beyond the distinct letters, i.e., without their distinctions. It is Om as a whole, the One, Śiva, the Brahman.

This Upaniṣad gives a new idea about the study of the I-consciousness. It has to be studied in its own field, but not in the field of the objects. The four states of the Ātman constitute the specific field of the I-consciousness.[44] They belong not only to the microcosmic personality but also to the macrocosmic.[45] The Ātman is the Brahman.[46]

TAITTIRĪYA UPANIṢAD This Upaniṣad mentions five forms of union: the union of physical elements like earth, water, air, etc. : the union of shining beings like fire, sun, and lightning; the union of knowledge like that in the teacher, pupil, and lectures; the union of creative beings like father, mother, and creation; and the union of physiological parts like the upper jaw, the lower jaw, and speech. The instances here are not important,[47] but is the idea of union as the act of creation. We may, therefore, say that by the time of this Upaniṣad five forms of causal explanation of creation came to be accepted: the physical explanation of the creation of the universe; creation as due to the actions of divine beings; as due to the potency of esoteric knowledge; as due to some cosmic sexes; and as due to the Ātman or man as the centre. The last explanation was, according to the Upaniṣads, the highest.

The Brahman is the Truth, Consciousness, and the Infinite.[48] From the Ātman is born aether, from aether air, from air fire, from fire water, and from water earth. And from earth are born plants, from plants food, and from food Puruṣa (Ātman) or man as "I." He is called Ātman because he eats, swallows, absorbs (*adyate*) the different elements[49] constituting the objective world. Inward to the *ātman* made of food is the ātman made of the vital principle (*prāṇa*). The former is the body of the latter and the latter is the soul of the former. Inward to the vital principle lies the mind (*manas*), inward to mind reason (*vijñāna*), and inward to reason bliss (*ānanda*). Each latter is the *ātman* of the former, and each former is the body of the latter. But every one of them is a form of Puruṣa (Ātman) himself.[50]

The statement of this Upaniṣad that everything was originally born of

Non-being[51] (*asat*) cannot be interpreted literally, for only a little earlier it says that the Brahman should not be understood as Non-being and that one who understands it as Non-being will be condemned to, or become Non-being.[52] So Non-being as the origin of the world means that reality was in the beginning absolutely indeterminate, it was the Unmanifest (*Avyakta*).

This Upaniṣad teaches that that which is in man and that which is in the sun are one and the same.[53] The commentators say that the former is the spirit (self) in man and the latter the spirit (self) of the cosmos.

It is pointed out also that the bliss of the Ātman is infinitely greater than all the pleasures of men and gods put together.[54] It is added also that, although several distinctions among the levels of spirit and body are made, every level is part and parcel of the Brahman and none of them should be looked down upon. Even the material support of the Ātman should be respected and increased.[55]

AITAREYA UPANIṢAD The most important contribution of this Upaniṣad is the semi-mythological account of creation, already given in the previous chapter, according to which the Ātman correlates the microcosm and the macrocosm and the gods become the psycho-physical principles. The Upaniṣad ends up by saying that all the mental functions are only names of our rational consciousness[56] (*prajñānam*) and that our rational consciousness is the Brahman (*prajñānam brahma*).

CHĀNDOGYA UPANIṢAD This is the second largest of the Upaniṣads, the first being the *Bṛhadāraṇyaka*. It says that after salvation man's spirit resides along with the gods and the Brahman in the highest world. This conception is theistic. Yet it adds that "everything is verily the Brahman."[57] It is the innermost to us, it is the smallest and yet the largest, and is reached after death.[58] In the beginning, all this was Non-being, then it became Being, and then the Cosmic Egg. The Egg then bursted and all this came out.[59]

The person seen in the eye is the Ātman and is the Brahman.[60] This passage should be interpreted as meaning the person seeing through the eye. The eye is considered to be the most important of the senses. The idea of the person in the eye is elaborated later, as we shall see. Aśvapati, the king of the Kaikayas, teaches that the Ātman is the Cosmic Person[61]—a story to which reference was already made. This Upaniṣad definitely says that Being cannot come out of Non-being, and so originally there was Being.[62]

Aruṇi teaches his son Śvetaketu that in sleep speech enters mind, mind the life-principle (*prāṇa*), the life-principle the psychic force (*tejas*), the psychic force the Supreme Deity. All these belong to the Ātman and "That art thou" (*tattvamasi*).[63] Just as different rivers fall into the same ocean and lose their self-identity, so everything enters the Ātman and loses its self-identity.[64]

The idea of the person in the eye is elaborated in the last chapter of the Upaniṣad through a story.[65] Vairocana, king of the demons, and Indra, king of the gods, approached Prajāpati, the creator god, for being taught about the Ātman (Self), which is without disease and death. Prajāpati told them that the person seen in the eye was the Ātman. He asked them to adorn themselves and look at their reflections in a pot of water, and said that what they would see was the Ātman. They then started home. Vairocana followed the advice, saw the reflection of his own body in the water-pot, and began to worship himself as the Ātman, indulging in all the pleasures of the body. Indra also followed the advice, saw his own perishable body in the water-pot, and doubted how his perishable body could be the imperishable Ātman. So he returned to Prajāpati for further instruction. Prajāpati said to him that the person of the dream was the Ātman, for when the physical body is hurt the dream body need not be hurt. Even then Indra was not satisfied, for even though the dream person may forget the pains of the physical body and may not be touched by them, he suffers from dream experiences as when a man dreams that he is being clawed by a tiger. Then Prajāpati said that the person in deep, dreamless sleep was the Ātman. But again Indra was not satisfied; for the person in deep sleep knows nothing, is unconscious, and is not a master of himself and, in addition, even deep sleep comes to an end. Then Prajāpati revealed to Indra that the Ātman, the seer of all, is beyond deep sleep; it is bodiless, unfettered, and beyond the reach of pains and pleasures.

We can see that this story is an anticipation of the *Māṇḍūkya* doctrine, pointing out the various stages by which the search for the Ātman has to be carried out and delineating also the field in which the enquiry has to be conducted.

This Upaniṣad mentions also "I am all this" (*ahameva idam sarvam*)[66] and "The Ātman is all this" (*ātmā eva idam sarvam*).[67]

BṚHADĀRAṆYAKA UPANIṢAD This Upaniṣad, being the largest of all, contains much information about different kinds of meditation, besides many philosophical doctrines. In the very beginning, the Upaniṣad says that the sacrificial horse, i.e., the horse sacrificed in the so-called Aśvamedha sacrifice, has to be considered by the sacrificer as the cosmos itself. Only when one sacrifices the cosmos, gives it up, can one realize the Ātman.

In the beginning, there was the Ātman. It did not know anything else and asserted: "I am," and became the "I." Then it felt lonely and was afraid,[68] but wondered why it was afraid. One is afraid of some other, but there was no other. Yet it could not rejoice and wanted an other. Then it became the two, man and woman. Men were born of them. The state of love and embrace is the Unmanifest (*Avyakta*). The Unmanifest becomes the manifest world. The Ātman is the same as the Brahman. He who realizes "I am the Brahman" becomes the Brahman.[69]

The world consists of the three: name, form, and action.[70] Everything has a name given by speech; everything has a form seen by the eye; and all action originates in the Ātman and is full of the Brahman. All the three are Being.

In this Upaniṣad also, in the teaching of king Ajātaśatru to Bālāki, we come across the doctrine that the Ātman is found in deep sleep. Yājñavalkya teaches his wife Maitreyī that nobody wants an object of pleasure for the object's sake, but for the sake of the Ātman; we should, therefore, know what the Ātman is. By knowing it, everything becomes known.[71] Everything is the Ātman (*idam sarvam yadayam ātmā*).[72] When it is realized that everything is the Ātman, where then will be the difference between the knower and the known? How can one know the knower?[73] This Ātman is the Brahman (*ayam ātmā brahma*).[74]

Chapter III presents a famous debate between Yājñavalkya and a number of enquirers after truth. To Ārtabhāga Yājñavalkya says that after death the senses and mind of man become one with their respective deities, who are their sources; but his actions (*karma*, merit and demerit) accompany him and lead him to another life.[75] To Cākrāyaṇa he says that the Ātman lives through the life-principle and works through all the life functions. None can see the seer, none can hear the hearer, none can know the knower.[76] It is not an object of any form of consciousness. To Uddālaka he says that the Ātman is present inwardly in everything (*antaryāmin*)[77] and knows everything, but nothing knows it. It is the ultimate seer, hearer, thinker, and knower. Gārgī, a lady enquirer, is taught by Yājñavalkya that the Ātman is neither subtle nor gross, it is neither the senses nor the life-principle. It is neither inwards nor outwards. It is imperishable. At its command, the sun and moon move, the elements and time perform their functions; everything is founded in it.[78] It is the same as the Brahman, the Brahman is knowledge and bliss (*vijñānam ānandam brahma*).[79]

Yājñavalkya teaches king Janaka that the Ātman is the guiding light of man. But how can man catch it? Janaka asks: "By what light is man guided?" Yājñavalkya answers: "By the light of the sun." Then what is man's light when the sun sets? The answer is: "The light of the moon." But when the moon also sets, what is the light? It can then be the light of fire, e.g., of a torch. But when the fire goes out, what can be the light? It can be the light of speech. For instance, a friend's voice may then guide us. But when there is no such speech also, what can be the light? For example, in dream we act and see things. What is the light that guides us in dream? The answer is: "It is the light of the Ātman." It is through the light of the dream that we can transcend the forms of death or perishable forms.[80] That light itself is imperishable.

This Upaniṣad also teaches that when the "I" is embraced by the Ātman as Prājña in deep sleep, it becomes filled with bliss and knows nothing else, just as a man in the tight embrace of the beloved woman loses himself in the embrace and knows nothing else.[81]

Śvetāśvatara Upaniṣad This Upaniṣad is considered to be a theistic Upaniṣad, as it speaks of the Brahman as a personal being. It enumerates[82] some contemporary doctrines of the origin of the world. The origin was time, nature, necessity, chance, elements, some cosmic womb, or Puruṣa, the finite self or (Ātman). The last also was not to be accepted. (This can be one interpretation.) There are two Ātmans, the perishable and the imperishable. Man is a combination of the two. The perishable is the manifest and is meant to act and enjoy the fruit of actions; the imperishable is the Ātman as the Cosmos, the Lord. The perishable is the Pradhāna[83] (Prakṛti), it is Māyā. The three words, Pradhāna, Prakṛti, and Māyā are technical terms and the corresponding English words may not convey their real significance. The word *pradhāna* literally means the primary, it is the primary state of the whole world of Becoming. *Prakṛti* means the ore, the original, and so the original state of the world of Becoming. *Māyā* means magic, illusion, and so the appearance of something as Being, although it is only Becoming. So the word is interpreted as neither Being nor yet Non-being. What is neither Being nor Non-being is Becoming. As Becoming appears as Being, it is called Māyā. Everything that belongs to Māyā is perishable. The imperishable is the Lord of both the *ātman* and the Pradhāna, called by the two other names also. By knowing the imperishable, Māyā is overcome by man.[84] The Ātman is present in the body like oil in the oilseed or butter in milk.[85] The Brahman is the Puruṣa himself.[86] This Upaniṣad mentions the names of Rudra,[87] Śiva, and Aghora as the names of the Lord; and the names of their consorts are the names of Prakṛti and Māyā. It is, therefore, said to be an Upaniṣad of the Śaiva religious sect. But Śiva is the Brahman itself. This Upaniṣad repeats the Muṇḍaka passage about the two Ātmans as the two birds.[88] It compares the Lord to the *māyāvin* (magician) and calls his power of magic *māyā*. One should know this power of magic as Prakṛti and the great magician as the Lord. The Upaniṣad refers to the sage Kapila[89] (the word *kapila* means the tawny coloured) as the first-born of the Lord. In the history of Indian philosophy, Kapila is said to be the founder of the Sāṅkhya school, many ideas of which are found in this Upaniṣad. But curiously enough, the Sāṅkhya philosophers in their religion do not belong to Śaivism, but to Vaiṣṇavism. The Ātman is neither male nor female.[90] The Lord presides over our ethical conduct (actions, *karmas*), but is accessible to men who have risen above action.[91] He created Brahma[92] (the creator god) first and gave him the Vedas. This idea of creation is mythological and the Upaniṣad incorporates it. The Upaniṣad mentions the name of Śvetāśvatara, who obtained divine knowledge through penance and the grace of God.[93] The divine truths can be known only by him who is absolutely devoted to God and likewise to his teachers.[94] In this Upaniṣad we come across the ideas of grace and devotion. Hence it is treated as theistic Upaniṣad. At least, theism is clearly emphasized.

4. CONCLUDING REMARKS

The ideas of the Upaniṣads are separately given, because students often get confused about the teachings of the Upaniṣads, which contain many nonphilosophical ideas; and many of the translations are biased in favour of one or the other of the Vedāntic schools. It may also be noted that many of the ideas are found in many of the Upaniṣads. But in this chapter the ideas are not generally repeated under every Upaniṣad, but are presented only when the Upaniṣad gives some special treatment to them. And almost all the nonphilosophical teachings of the Upaniṣads are omitted. Often in the same Upaniṣad an idea is repeated or an attempt is made to establish it from different approaches; such repetitions and approaches are in this chapter left out. In addition, a great number of early religious and mythological ideas are found in the Upaniṣads, often with changed meanings and also as steps leading to the same goal, viz., the discovery of the Ātman. They also are omitted, as they confuse the student who is not well advanced.

We can see now that *first* all the Upaniṣads aim at explaining the nature of the *Ātman* and direct the enquirer towards it. That is why the Upaniṣadic philosophy and the Vedāntic systems based on it are said to be Ātman-centred. Their teaching is in accord with the Socratic teaching: "Know thyself." *Secondly*, we find at several places the teaching that the Ātman is the Brahman (*ayam ātmā brahma*)[95] and "I am the Brahman" (*aham* brahmāsmi).[96] *Thirdly*, it is said: "All this is the Brahman" (*sarvam khalu idam brahma*).[97] *Fourthly*, it is said also that all that exists is the Ātman *(sarvam yadayam ātmā*).[98] *Fifthly*, it is asserted that the Brahman is consciousness and bliss (*vijñānam anandam brahma*[99] and *prajñānam brahma*).[100] *Sixthly*, it is said that the Brahman is Truth, Consciousness and the Infinite (*satyam jñānam anantam brahma*).[101] In the *seventh* place, it is taught: "That thou art" (*tattvamasi*),[102] meaning that the "I" in you is one with the Ātman, the Ultimate Truth.

All the above statements, particularly four of them—"That the Ātman is the Brahman," "I am the Brahman," "All this is indeed the Brahman," and "That thou art"—are said to be the essential teachings, the Great Logia, of the Upaniṣads. But we should not ignore the contrary statements that all this is not the Brahman, that it is beyond speech and thought, and that it can be described only in negative terms (*neti neti*).[103] Many Upaniṣads say at several places that he who takes any of the known realities except the Ātman as the Truth belongs to the world of ignorance (*avidyā*). We have seen this teaching in the discussions with Yājñavalkya, king Ajātaśatru, and king Aśvapati. All the Vedāntic schools later strive hard to reconcile these systems[104] and build up their own systems on them.

The number of passages that refer to Ignorance (*avidyā*) is very large and one comes across it almost in every Upaniṣad. But the word *māyā* is used by only a few Upaniṣads. The *Muṇḍaka* uses it once, as we have already mentioned. The *Bṛhadāraṇyaka* says that the Brahman (here called Indra) through Māyā assumes many forms[105] and in this passage anticipates the *Śvetāśvatara Upaniṣad*. This Upaniṣad uses the word more than once and makes it a synonym for Pradhāna and Prakṛti. Its equating to Ignorance (*avidyā*) is mainly a result of the interpretation given to it by the Advaita Vedānta of Śaṅkara, which often speaks of Māyā as Prakṛti also. Then came the identification with the Unmanifest (Avyakta), which is another name for Prakṛti also. These synonymizations interpreted in terms of the *Māṇḍūkya Upaniṣad* gave the idea of the metaphysical Unconscious,[106] which is partly experienced by man in his dreamless sleep. Although the word *māyā* is pre-Buddhistic, it seems to have obtained its logical and metaphysical significance from the hands of the Buddhists, and the significance was later absorbed into the Advaita Vedānta by Gauḍapāda, the grand-teacher of Śaṅkara. The equating of Māyā to Avidyā seems also to have been first done by the Buddhists.

The Upaniṣads make various approaches to the Ātman, of which the levels of the depth of our inward Being as given by the *Kaṭha* and the *Taittirīya* Upaniṣads and the field of the I-consciousness as given by the *Māṇḍūkya Upaniṣad* are the most clear and important. On the whole, one may say that the general trend of the Upaniṣadic teaching is idealistic and ontological or existentialistic.[107] The Vedāntic systems alone attempt to base their teachings on all the Upaniṣads taken together, whereas the other orthodox schools refer only to a few of the Upaniṣadic teachings in support and ignore the rest. The criterion for a system being Vedāntic is that it should be able to furnish a commentary from its point of view on the Upaniṣads and on the *Brahmasūtras*. None of the so-called orthodox non-Vedāntic schools has been able to meet the test till now. Vijñānabhikṣu of the 15th century made an attempt from the side of the Sāṅkhya to write a commentary on the *Brahmasūtras*, but in that attempt had practically to give up the original Sāṅkhya position. The Mīmāmsā of Jaimini developed its philosophy by an enquiry into the nature of right (ethical) action and the meanings of merit and demerit (*apūrva*). As mentioned already it treated the Upaniṣads as subsidiary to the first two parts of the Veda, particularly the Brāhmaṇas, which are mainly concerned with ritual—for ritual also is right action like the performance of family and social duties— and are primary. We should note also that every action, every performance of duty, even every act of enjoyment, was later considered in the Upaniṣads to be a sacrifice, a sacrifice that ultimately reaches the Ātman[108] through the Cosmic Person. He who does not know this truth sacrifices only to the ashes of the sacrificial fire. The Mīmāmsā explains how action finally accrues to the individual *ātman* as merit and demerit. But what is the *ātman*? The Upaniṣads and the Vedāntic systems attempt to answer this question, which they treat as primary and the question about action and merit and demerit as subsidiary.

NOTES

[1]R. D. Ranade: *A Constructive Survey of Upanishadic Philosophy*, pp. 34 fol.

[2]S. K. Belvalkar and R. D. Ranade: *The Creative Period*, p. 87.

[3]One who reads all the Upaniṣads together will say that the essential Upaniṣadic philosophy can be written and has still to be written. The general trend of the Indian writers also, not perhaps excluding even R. D. Ranade, is to follow the western writers in their methods of explanation, which are rightly regarded as historical, philological, and scientific, implying that every other method is not rational, not based on good research. But we should at least allow for the possibility—I think, it is not a mere possibility, but actuality—that the sages and saintly philosophers of the Upaniṣads and some commentators who are equally great, for all of whom the question of the meaning and aim of human life was a question of life and death and to find the answer for which they were prepared for any sacrifice, were aiming at the imitation of science and scientific method, but attempting to say and teach something profound about the depths of man's being. Indeed, we should avoid mystery mongering and mere esotericism, mystifying the readers. But at the same time, the truth of the main Upaniṣadic teaching, even if somewhat amorphous because of its incipient articulation, should be placed before the readers who are eager for it. I hope to undertake such work as an intensive study in the near future, provided God gives me life, health, and facilities. We may, in this connection bring to our mind the interpretation of early Greek philosophers as hylozoists (Max Müller), materialists (Lange and Warbecke), philosophers of religion (Cornford) and ontologists (Heidegger). Aristotle himself spoke of the search for the soul by his predecessors. I think that the Upaniṣadic philosophers were aiming at something the same from different perspectives and in different contexts. As all the Vedāntins maintain, there is an essential unity threading the Upaniṣads together. In this book I have followed the general method of interpretation to make the reading somewhat easy for the reader who may approach the book with the usual interpretations as the background. Besides, the chief aim of the book is what is given in the "General Estimates" of the schools.

[4]S. Radhakrishnan says that they might have been composed between the 10th and 3rd centuries B.C. (*Indian Philosophy*, Vol. I, p. 142), and Ranade between the 12th and 3rd centuries B.C. (*Constructive Survey of Upaniṣadic Philosophy*, p. 12). See also A. B. Keith: *Religion and Philosophy of the Veda*, Vol. II, pp. 501 fol.

[5]*Bṛhadāraṇyaka Upaniṣad*, II, III, and IV.

[6]Ibid., III, viii, 8. [7]Ibid., IV, iv, 3–4.

[8]*Chāndogya Upaniṣad*, VI. [9]*Chāndogya Upaniṣad*, VII. [10]Ibid., III, 14.

[11]*Kaṭha Upaniṣad*, I, i. [12]*Taittirīya Upaniṣad*, *Bhṛguvallī*, X, 4.

[13]*Chāndogya Upaniṣad*, V, x-xviii. [14]*Bṛhadāraṇyaka Upaniṣad*, II, i, 15–20.

[15]*Kausītaki Upaniṣad*, II. In this Upaniṣad we find the god Indra identified with the Brahman. See Chapter III. But the *Kena Upaniṣad* IV, 2, says that Indra is the greatest of the gods, because he was the first to know the Brahman intimately.

[16]*Chāndogya Upaniṣad*, I, vii and ix.

[17]Chāndogya, IV, 3, 3, 2.

[18]Ibid., IV, 3, 4. This air is identified by the commentator with Hiraṇyagarbha or Sūtrātman, the Cosmic Subtle Person holding the parts of the cosmos together. If comparisons are taken to great inward depths, the Upaniṣads will not be disposed of as child's utterances. Indeed, some Upaniṣadic utterances may be those of the children of the race, but not the ones like that of Raikva.

[19]Ibid., I, 7, 5 and IV, 15, 1. [20]Ibid., IV, 10, 15. [21]Ibid., V, 11–24.

[22]*Bṛhadāraṇyaka* II, 1. [23]*Chāndogya* I, 11, 5, and V, 13.

[24]Ibid., I, 1, 8, 1 *Bṛhadāraṇyaka* VI, 2, 1–4.

[25]Chapter IV, 23 foll. [26]*Chāndogya* III, 17. [27]*Kauṣītaki*, III, 6–8.
[28]*Chāndogya*, III, 14. [29]*Taittirīya* I, 5.
[30]I, ii, 20. [31]I, iii, 10–11. [32]I, ii, 13. [33]II, vi, 1.
[34]The word is variously explained.
[35]I, 16. [36]I, i, 4–5.
[37]I, i, 7. [38]I, ii, 7–9. [39]III, ii, 3–4.
[40]It is difficult to identify them. They are said to control the involuntary functions of the body, making life possible. The word *prāṇa* means the general vital principle and also one of its own parts. Of the five parts, *prāṇa* resides in the heart and is responsible for respiration; *apāna* is found in the intestines and enables excretion; *samāna* is in the navel and controls the metabolic processes; *udāna* is at the throat and controls the activities of all parts in the head, e.g., speech; *vyāna* pervades the whole body and coordinates the functions of the bodily parts.
[41]*Vaiśvānara* means also the Cosmic Person. Very likely the gross aspect of the Logos is meant.
[42] I use the word psyche for *taijasa*. The word psychic person has an abnormal ring.
[43]The word *prājña* cannot be translated. It is being as consciousness and consciousness as being. In the dream state, there is dispersion of consciousness among dream objects, but in dreamless sleep there is no such dispersion. Yet there is the veil of the Unconscious, which is not present in the fourth state.
[44]See the author's "Die Struktur des Ich-bewusstseins" in *Zeitschrift für philosophische Forschung*, Band XVI-Heft 4.
[45]The names of the four states of the macrocosmic person are *Virāṭ*, *Hiraṇyagarbha* (or *Sūtrātman*), *Īśvara*, and Brahman.The macrocosmic person includes all the microcosmic persons and interrelates them. As the Cosmic Person works through the finite persons, he also has the four states, the same seven parts and the same nineteen gateways.
[46]2, *Ayam ātmā brahma.*
[47]S. K. Belvalkar and R. D. Ranade: *The Creative Period*, p. 243. I am not giving the liberal translation of the Sanskrit passage.
[48]II, 1.
[49]This is not the only etymological meaning of the word *ātman*. There are many other such derivations. From the point of view of Indo-Germanic philology, the most reasonable seems to be from a word meaning "to breathe," like the German word *atmen*. The Sanskrit root then will be *an* (to breathe). See Monier-Williams: *Sanskrit-English Dictionary*.
[50]The words *puruṣa* and *ātman* are masculine in gender in the Sanskrit language. In philosophy they mean the same. In English the neutral pronoun "it" is used; but when it involves a reference to man, the "he" is used. This difference in usage should not create any confusion: the usage is somewhat like using the word man to mean both man and woman in English.
[51]II, 7.
[52]II, 6 [53]II, 8 and III, x, 4. [54]II, 8. [55]III, 8. [56]III, 1–3.
[57]III, xiv, 1. [58]III, xiv, 4.
[59]III, xix, 1. Here also Non-being has to be interpreted as the Indeterminate or the Unmanifest.
[60]IV, x, 15. [61]V, xviii. [62]VI, ii, 1–2.
[63]VI, viii, 1–7. [64]VI, x, 1–2. [65]VIII.
[66]VIII, xxv, 1. [67]VIII, xxv, 2.
[68]I, iv, 1–3. Like Bochenski, we should not interpret this passage as existential loneliness and anxiety. Fear arises only when the Ātman asserts itself as the "I" without a second, but not before. Fear belongs to *Dasein*, but not to *Sein*. When the Ātman asserts itself as the "I," it becomes a *Dasein*, a *primus inter paris* potentially, and so lonely. See I. M. Bochenski: *Europäesche Philosophie der Gegenwart*, p. 164.
[69]I, iv, 10. [70]I, vi, 1–3. [71]II, iv, 5. [72]II, iv, 6. [73]II, iv, 14. [74]II, v, 19.
[75]III, ii, 13. [76]III, ii, 4. [77]III, vii, 6–14.
[78]III, vii, 11. [79]III, ix, 7.
[80]IV, ii, 1–7. [81]IV, iii, 21. [82]I, 2.
[83]I, 10. Although unborn, it is perishable. Is that an indication that the perishable *Ātman* is the same as Pradhāna, the source of the world?
[84]I, 10. [85]I, 15–16. [86]III, 9.
[87]III, 5. [88]IV, 6. [89]V, 2.
[90]V, 10. [91]VI, 10–11. [92]VI, 18. [93]VI, 21. [94]VI, 23.

[95]*Māṇḍūkya Upaniṣad*, 2 and *Bṛhadāraṇyaka, Upaniṣad*, II, v, 19. [96]Ibid., I, iv, 10.

[97]*Chāndogya Upaniṣad*, II, xvi, 1. See also *Māṇḍūkya Upaniṣad*, 2.

[98]*Bṛhadāraṇyaka Upaniṣad*, II, iv, 6. [99]Ibid., III, ix, 28.

[100]*Aitareya Upaniṣad*, III, 3. [101]*Taittirīya Upaniṣad*, II, 1.

[102]*Chāndogya Upaniṣad*, VI, viii, 7.

[103]*Bṛhadāraṇyaka Upaniṣad*, III, iii, 26, IV, v, 15, and II, iii, 6.

[104]Whatever systems we build on the Upaniṣads, they should not be interpreted as preaching pantheism, for which God is the world and the world is God, but at the most as pan-entheism, for which the world is in God but God is much more than the world. (Cp. the philosophy of K.C.F. Krause.) The doctrine taught is that of both immanence and transcendence.

[105]II, v, 19.

[106]It would be interesting to compare the Vedāntic doctrine of the Unconscious to that of E. von Hartmann, who explicitly refers to the Indian doctrine, and to that of C. G. Jung. (See the author's *Indian Idealism and Modern Challenges*, Ch. XIII, Panjab University Publication Bureau, Chandigarh, 1961.)

[107]It may be greatly rewarding to study how these two trends, the idealistic and the existentialistic, which are considered to be opposed in contemporary thought, could be reconciled by the Vedānta. How could the Vedāntic schools, in spite of their existentialistic bias, develop epistemological doctrines like the idealists and the realists? The existentialists attach very little importance to epistemologies, but not so the Vedāntins.

[108]*Chāndogya Upaniṣad*, V, 19–24. Jaivali interprets even the sex act as a sacrifice (Ibid., V, viii, 1–2). Again, the Puruṣa himself is said to be the sacrifice (Ibid., III, xvi, 1). But this Puruṣa is the human person, who is to sacrifice himself, i.e., surrender himself to the Brahman. Thus the idea of sacrifice and of the polytheistic gods was completely transformed and spiritualized by the time of the Upaniṣads. Jaivali's teaching is repeated again in the *Bṛhadāraṇyaka*, VI, ii. The meaning is that everything in the world is an act of sacrifice. Every transformation is a sacrifice of the transformed. The Ātman also is said to have performed a sacrifice for creating the universe (*Bṛhadāraṇyaka*, I, ii, 6.). cp. also *Hymn to Person* (*Puruṣa-sūkta*).

Chapter II

The Mīmāmsā and the Sovereignity of Ethical Law

1. INTRODUCTION

As has already been indicated, when Indian philosophy is studied not only for its logical and metaphysical doctrines, but also as a philosophy of religion and of a reflective way of life and culture, it is right that the presentation of the Indian philosophical systems should start with the Mīmāmsā, as all the other systems grew and developed out of its teachings or as reactions to its teachings. The Mīmāmsā is essentially a philosophy of ethical action, but more concerned with the supra-sensual nature of the ethical force and the ritual, the significance and workings of which have other-wordly bearings, than with social action, which is concerned with this world and which the Mīmāmsā leaves to the ethical codes (*dharmasūtras* and *dharmaśāstras*) for elaboration and explanation.[1] The ethical codes take for granted and claim to base their teachings on the metaphysics of the Mīmāmsā, which they do not discuss. The commentators on the ethical codes use mainly Mīmāmsā methods for interpreting their texts and for applying them to concrete cases. But as students of philosophy, we are not interested in the different forms of the ritual and their technique, but in the philosophy of action underlying them.

The literature on the Mīmāmsā is very vast. Jaimini composed his *Mīmāmsāsūtras* before all or some of the other *sūtras* (aphorisms). The ideas he expounded must have been older than he; and even if some of the other schools started earlier they must have known many ideas of this school, because they criticized them. Śabara was the first to comment on Jaimini's work in about the 4th century A.D. The two great names that popularized and developed the Mīmāmsā philosophy are those of Kumārila and Prabhākara who belonged to the 7th and the 8th centuries A.D. It is thought that Prabhākara was an older contemporary of Kumārila, who was himself an older contemporary of Śaṅkara, the great Advaitin. All the three belonged to an age of orthodox revival and of the weakening of Buddhism and Jainism. Prabhākara is the author of the great commentary called *Bṛhatī* and Kumārila of *Ślokavārtikā* and *Tantravārtikā*. They wrote other works, which are less important. The works of the former are not even available fully in print. Murāri Miśra is said to be the third great interpreter of Jaimini. But his works are not available and the few available are not in print. The three, Kumārila, Prabhākara, and Murārī Miśra, do not agree with one another always. There are several works of expository nature on this school, of which

Śāstradīpikā of Pārthasārathi Miśra (13th and 14th centuries), *Mīmāmsānyāyaprakaśa* of Āpadeva (17th century), and *Arthasangraha* of Laugākṣi Bhāskara (16th century) are widely read.

The Mīmāmsā is a philosophy of active life and teaches the indispensability and inescapability of ethical action, *as ethical action is the supreme governing force of the universe.* The basic concepts of such a philosophy are, *first*, the agent of ethical action must be real; *second*, action itself must be real; *third*, it must be the controlling and guiding force of the universe and *fourth*, the universe as the field of action has also to be real. The Mīmāmsā expounds and attempts to defend the four theses.

Although the Mīmāmsā is ethical activism, in that, for it, action is ultimate, is the governing force of the universe, and takes the place of God, it is not pure and simple activism; for the individual, as the agent of action, is also ultimately real, although governed by the laws of ethical action. In pure activism, the agent of action is only a mode of action, action only is ultimately real.[2] Such pure activism was advocated by the Nairukta philosophers of India,[3] who did not form an important school. They held, like the Vedāntins, that the Ātman alone is real, but that it is pure activity. The agent, the patient, and the instruments of action are only modes of modalities of action constituting its pattern. The Mīmāmsā could not accept the Nairukta position as such because, although action is important and determines what the agent can attain, the responsibility for action, its merit or demerit, its rewards or punishments, must accrue to the agent, not to action itself. The agent of action must then be as important and real as action itself.

The central concept of the Mīmāmsā is that of *dharma*, for it is *dharma* (ethical potency or the force or power of merit and demerit) that controls the universe and produces for the agent of action what he desires and what his action deserves. It is the governing ethical force of the universe. So Jaimini starts his work with the aphorism (*sūtra*) meaning "now starts the enquiry into the nature of *dharma*." Epistemology and metaphysics are geared to this concept.

2. EPISTEMOLOGY

As the Mīmāmsā accepts the reality of the world and of the individual and his actions, it builds up an epistemology for supporting its realism. Its contributions to epistemology are very important and are accepted even by followers of Śankara so far as this world goes. Other schools also accept much that the Mīmāmsā says.

What are the forms or ways of knowing that have to be accepted as valid, i.e., as revealing the world as it is? For instance, if I hear people say that there is a ghost on the tree, should I accept the knowledge I thereby get as valid?[4] Hearsay and rumour cannot be accepted as valid means of knowledge. The Mīmāmsā accepts six valid means of knowing: perception, inference, comparison, postulation, non-cognition, and word or language.

PERCEPTION Perception is direct knowledge[5] of objects through senses and mind. It is external and internal. The senses come into contact with the objects, mind with the senses, and the *ātman* with mind. Knowledge arises as consciousness when mind and the *ātman* come into contact. Otherwise, the *ātman* is by nature unconscious.

Internal objects, like pains and pleasures, are known by mind (*manas*) coming directly into contact with them without the aid of senses and then coming into contact with the *ātman*. So far, the Mīmāmsā and the Nyāya doctrines, as we shall see later, are alike. But regarding the perception of sound, the Mīmāmsā says that it is due to air particles impinging on the ear,[6] while the Nyāya maintains that it is due to aether (*ākāśa*).

The Mīmāmsā, like the Nyāya, accepts the distinction between the indeterminate (*nirvikalpaka*) and determinate (*savikalpaka*) perception. Indeterminant perception is like the perception of children, the deaf and the dumb. It is the knowledge of a mere That without the What, of a mere being without the universal or essence; in it the individual and the universal are present and known without being distinguished. When a child sees the elephant for the first time, it sees an object; but it does not cognize that the object comes under the class of elephants or that it is called an elephant. According to Kumārila, it is the perception of both the individual and the universal without any distinction. The relation between the two is identity in difference, but the difference is not perceived in indeterminate perception. But according to Prabhākara,[7] the universal, which is comparatively eternal, cannot be perceived then. It is due to distinctions drawn or introduced when the object is perceived a second time and the child remembers the impressions of the first perception and cognizes the similarity between the two. In indeterminate perception, knowledge of the universal is not involved at all; it is the perception only of the individual, everything perceived in it is only an individual. The universal cannot operate in perception, unless there is memory; and there is no memory involved of anything when the object is seen for the first time. But Kumārila argues that, unless the distinction between the universal and the individual is latent in indeterminate perception, it cannot become explicit in the determinate.

Determinate perception is the perception of an object as belonging to a class and as determined by a universal. When I perceive a horse and my perception takes the form, "That is horse", the object in front is determined by the universal horseness (*aśvatva*) and the universal becomes the form (*prakāra*) of the object. This perception involves memory of a horse seen in the past and the distinction between the individual and the universal.

The Mīmāmsakas do not accept the view of the grammarian philosophers that every determinate perception is necessarily associated with the word which means the object. When I perceive a horse, the grammarians say, the object is determined not only by the universal horseness but also by the word horse. The Mīmāmsakas reject the view. They reject also the Naiyāyika view of yogic perception, according to which the yogi can perceive objects both temporally and spatially remote and also microscopic objects like the atoms. For the Mīmāmsakas contend that what cannot come into contact with the senses cannot be an object of sense-perception, yogic or non-yogic.

INFERENCE The Mīmāmsā theory of inference is nearly the same as that of Aristotle's syllogism. In Indian epistemology, the word inference (*anumāna*) does not cover all the thought-processes covered by the word in western epistemology, but only syllogistic reasoning. Again, for all the Indian logicians in general, the major premise has to be accompanied by an example.[8] The mention of the example is considered to be necessary for showing that the major premise is actually based upon an actual instance. The major premise, which is a universal proposition, can then be shown to be a true induction and not a fanciful combination of universals. One may argue

All men are stones;
Socrates is a man;
Therefore, Socrates is a stone.

Here no example can be given, for there is nothing that is both a man and a stone. But we can argue

All men are mortal, like Homer;
Socrates is a man;
Therefore, Socrates is mortal.

The Mīmāmsā accepts the above three parts of the syllogism, but adds that the conclusion may be placed first also, when it becomes a hypothesis. We may then have the form,

Socrates is mortal;
Because all men are mortal, like Homer;
And Socrates is a man.

The universal relationship generally accepted between the middle and major terms is that between cause and effect, whole and part, substance and quality; and class and individual or sub-class.

The Mīmāmsā accepts two forms of syllogism, inference for oneself, in which all the premises need not be mentioned, and inference for another , in which they have to be stated.[9]

COMPARISON Comparison (*upamāna*), according to the Mīmāmsā, is not the deliberating process of comparing two objects,[10] but the *spontaneous cognitive process to be called the observing of similarity*. When an American sees a water buffalo for the first time, he observes immediately and without any effort its similarity also to the bison. It is the similarity that makes him remember the bison; it is not a voluntary or involuntary memory of the bison that makes him observe the similarity. Otherwise, when he sees the buffalo, why does he remember the bison, but not his house or any other object in America? Of all objects, he remembers the bison, because the observed similarity brings it up out of his past experiences. Yet similarity is not an object of ordinary perceptual process, for what is perceived by the senses is the buffalo. Similarity is not an object of inference even, because there is no syllogism. The cognition of similarity is, therefore, a special kind of cognitive process and shows that mind has a spontaneous capacity to observe similarities.

POSTULATION Postulation[11] (*arthāpatti*) is the positing of something for making any unit of cognition self-complete. We accept a fact or principle for explaining an undeniable fact, which otherwise cannot be explained. Newton, for instance, accepted the law of gravitation for explaining why the apple falls to the ground and does not fly upwards. Our understanding of a situation becomes incomplete without accepting the truth of something not seen. Then that something is the object of postulation, *which is a spontaneous cognitive process of mind.* Of course, this spontaneous process may later on be elaborated into a conceptual form or structure.

The Mīmāmsakas contend that postulation is different from inference (syllogism). In postulation there is no major premise. For instance, when we do not even know that there is something called attraction or gravitation of the earth, we cannot form a major premise with it and say

All bodies are attracted by the earth's gravitational force;
The apple is a body;
Therefore, it is attracted by the earth's gravitational force.

So postulation has to be a distinctive cognitive way by which we obtain knowledge of the world. It is, we may say, the framing of a hypothesis. But a hypothesis can also be the result of induction; yet a postulation is not regarded as the same as induction. The principle of gravitation was not obtained by the inductive process. Besides, by induction we always obtain a universal proposition, but we may postulate not only universal laws, but also particular objects. For instance, we postulate the rotation of the earth round its axis for explaining the sequence of day and night. This rotation is a particular fact. We postulate a force in a piece of magnet to explain why it attracts iron.

Generally we postulate something when there is conflict between two accepted facts, although we do it also when we do not find the reason for an event. Instances for the latter are the postulations of gravitation, of magnetic force, of the burning power of fire, etc. An instance of the former is: the fat saint must be eating secretly at night, although he does not eat during the day and claims not to eat at all. If he does not eat at all, he cannot be fat.

Prabhākara says at this point that, before postulation is made to remove a conflict, the latter must have created a doubt about the truth of the opposites and we postulate something in order to remove the doubt. But Kumārila says that the appearance of doubt is not necessary and, in some cases, even leads to doubting what is postulated. For instance, if

Devadatta is alive, but is not in his house,

we postulate that he is somewhere else. But if there is doubt about his being alive, we do not postulate his being alive elsewhere, but only find out whether he is alive. Only when we are sure about his being alive and also his absence from his house, do we postulate his being elsewhere. Indeed, this example of postulation is not a very appropriate one. For we may postulate either alternative, his death or his being present elsewhere, or even both and may remain in doubt. But in the examples of gravitation, magnetic force, and the burning power of fire, there is no question of doubt being at the root of postulation.[12]

Kumārila divides postulation into two kinds: postulation to explain something seen,[13] what is postulated being either perceivable or imperceivable; and postulation of a meaning for making words intelligible.[14] An example of the first is the postulation of a force in the magnet to explain why it attracts iron. The force is imperceivable. Similarly, the Mīmāmsakas postulate as unseen and unseeable ethical potency called the Unseen (*adṛṣṭa*) and the Extra-ordinary (*apūrva*) to explain how ethical actions produce results here and hereafter after the actions are ended. If ethical actions (*karmas*) are the cause of rewards and punishments, pleasures and pains, how can a cause produce the effect if there is a time interval between the two? Causation is a continuous process, but between ethical actions and their results there is no continuity. In order to get over the difficulty, the Mīmāmsā says that ethical actions assume the form of a potential force, called the Extra-ordinary, which waits for the occasion to come when it can become kinetic. This force also is imperceivable. An instance in which the postulated fact can be seen is the saint's eating during the night.

The second kind of postulation is the postulation of the meaning of a word when metaphors, etc., are used in a sentence. In "He is a lion on the battlefield", we do not understand that he becomes the animal lion on the battlefield, but that he is fearless like a lion. We give this meaning to the word lion for making the meaning of the sentence intelligible. Although Kumārila accepts this kind of interpretation as postulation, Prabhākara contends that it is not postulation at all, but that the word lion includes also the meaning of "a fearless being." For Kumārila, the concept of postulation covers a wide field of both cognition and semantics; knowledge by postulation is the knowledge of everything necessary to complete the intelligibility of a fact or situation or the universe itself.[15]

NON-COGNITION Non-cognition (*anupalabdhi*), also called non-apprehension, is not mere absence of knowledge or awareness, but the cognition of the absence or negation of an object. Otherwise, the baby, which is ignorant of many things, has to be said to be aware of the absence of those things. But there is no awareness of the absence of those things in the baby. "I am aware of the absence of the pen on the table" does not mean that I am ignorant of the pen or that I am not thinking of the pen. I expect the pen on the table; that I cognize its absence there means that I do not cognize it there. The absence of the pen is conveyed to me through my not cognizing it. Then non-cognizing is the way by which we cognize absence. The pen (called *pratiyogi* or counter-part of the negation or absence) has to be thought of, and conceptually or mentally posited by me before I cognize its absence.[16]

Kumārila advocated the distinctiveness of non-cognition as a way of knowing, because he thought that, as a pluralist, he had to defend the reality of absence and negation. But Prabhākara rejected it, saying that absence is not a positive entity and that positive entities alone belong to reality and can be cognized. He contends, therefore, that absence is known through inference: When I do not see the pen on the table, I infer from my non-perception the absence of the pen. For defending the plurality of the world, it is not necessary to accept non-cognition as a valid means of knowing.

But Kumārila contends that there is no place for inference—we should remind ourselves that inference always means syllogism for the Indian logicians—in the cognition of absence, but that it is a spontaneous act. There is no inference, because there is no major premise. I have no justification to argue: Whenever I do not see an object, there is absence of the object; now I do not see the pen; therefore, there is absence of the pen. For how are we to get the major premise? How are we to show that the non-cognition itself reveals the absence? If it does, then non-cognition has to be accepted as a distinct means of knowing absence. Otherwise, we cannot explain how we get the idea of absence at all. Again, absence is not limited to perceptible entities; it can refer also to entities known by comparison (*upamāna*), inference, etc. For example, I perceive the absence of similarity between the horse and the elephant. But similarity, as we have seen, is not an object of perception. So the way of knowing negation is not merely non-perception, but non-cognition, although we may use the word non-perception if we take the word perception in the sense of all the forms of cognition. Non-cognition is the non-functioning of every other way of knowing, but is itself a new way of knowing.[17]

Absence is not an object of sense-perception also, because in sense-perception the senses have to come into contact with their objects and they can come into contact only with positive objects like pens and tables. But absence is not a positive object. Besides, as Prabhākara contends, if I am to infer the absence of the pen from my non-perception of the pen, I must have the non-perception first and also know that I have non-perception; and this knowledge of non-perception is the same as non-cognition. As indicated earlier, mere non-perception does not lead to the knowledge of absence. At this moment I am not perceiving hundreds of objects, but I do not have the cognition of their absences. If I have a cognition of my non-perception of these objects, then I have also the cognition of their absences. Prabhākara here misses the central point: if non-perception is necessary for utilization in inferring the absence of the pen, how can I get that non-perception without at the same time cognizing the absence of the pen? And if I have had the cognition of the absence, what is the need for inference?

VERBAL TESTIMONY AND LANGUAGE This way of knowing is also called verbal knowledge or knowledge obtained through words. The knowledge obtained by me when my friend says: "That is a polar bear", is not the knowledge of the sounds he utters, but of the object or the fact referred to by his words. Thus words have a double face. On the one side, they are sounds and are perceived by the sense of hearing. As such, they are only objects of perception. But on the other side, they mean objects or facts other than themselves; and these objects or facts are not perceived by our ear, but yet cognized by us through the words. Indeed, words cannot be understood by a deaf man. But by normal men words are understood not as mere sounds but as meaning objects different from the words. Hence verbal knowledge becomes a distinct way of knowing. It is not inference also. For instance, I do not understand the meaning of the word bear through inference, for there is no major premise here. There is no perceivable invariable connection between the word bear and the object bear, whether the meaning relation is eternal or conventional. The first time we understand the meaning of a word is not by inference, but being told so about the meaning.

It is true that through language we can give false information and mislead a person. That is, verbal knowledge can be false. But the possibility of being false is not peculiar to verbal knowledge. Perception and the other forms of knowing also may be false. Even if the person communicating knowledge to us is honest and truthful, he himself may be mistaken. So the minimum requirement is that the speaker should be authentic.

The contribution which the Mīmāmsā made to semantics and philosophy of language is very great. It believed in the eternity of the Veda, which was originally not written but orally transmitted. It was thought that the Veda consisted of meaning-bearing sounds. As the Veda was considered to be eternal, its sounds also were considered to be eternal. So all the Vedic words were considered to be eternal and their meanings to be eternally fixed. Words other than the Vedic were regarded as conventional, and their meanings as fixed by convention. According to the Mīmāmsā, God did not compose the Veda. The early Mīmāmsā did not accept the reality of God, but only of gods[18] or deities to whom sacrifices were addressed. Out of such a conception of the Veda arose the Mīmāmsā doctrine of verbal knowledge. But however the doctrine arose, it has had profound philosophical importance. Even geometry arose in Egypt for measuring the fields on the banks of the Nile; and geometry, trigonometry, and astronomy arose in India[19] out of the need to erect sacrificial altars according to specific measurements and the positions of stars.

The Mīmāmsā believes that the Veda is infallible and absolutely reliable, as it is not written by any person. Persons are infallible and not always reliable, because they have self-interests. But the Veda has no self-interest. It is the friend and well-wisher of all. It is eternally present in the universe, but is revealed to some persons whose names we come across in the Vedic texts. What is of primary importance is that which is revealed, but not the names of the persons to whom it is revealed.[20] The revelation, the Mīmāmsā believes, took place in Vedic Sanskrit, which is the eternal language. Of the four parts of the Veda, the *Brāhmaṇas* are the most important; and of all the sentences in the *Brāhamaṇas*, those expressing commands leading men to action are primary. For it is only through action that man builds up his destiny.

The word consists of letters. The Mīmāmsakas, as against the Naiyāyikas, say that all letter sounds are eternal and that the Vedic words are eternal. Conventional words are made up of eternal letter sounds, but are themselves not eternal. We cognize a word when all the letter sounds are uttered. For instance, the word elephant is cognized when the last letter "t" is uttered. All the letters cannot be uttered at the same time. Every letter, beginning from the first, produces and leaves an impression on our mind; and when the last letter is uttered, it along with the impressions of the earlier ones makes us cognize the word elephant as a whole.

The Mīmāmsā does not accept the grammarian view[21] that for every word there is an eternal word-pattern or word-universal (*Sphoṭa*). All of us utter the word elephant, but with different intonations, pitch of sound, soft or harsh. So what we utter is not exactly the same. Yet we say that we utter the same word and understand one another. What is uttered by every one of us must then be the same word-pattern with, of course, some variations. We have, therefore, to accept the reality of the word-pattern. Besides, when we utter the word "tan" and the letters "t", "a", and "n" are uttered one after another, why does the hearer not take the word as "ant", which also consists of the same letters? The first letters leave their impressions which get combined with the impression of the last letter. If the hearer's word is a mere combination of impressions, it can be either way, either as "tan" or as "ant." But if we accept the word-pattern, then the letters from the beginning get fitted into the pattern in the particular order and do not get changed. The pattern of "tan" is different from that of "ant". So all the letter and word sounds remind us of the word-pattern, through which we understand the meaning of the word. Just as there are word-patterns for words, there are letter-patterns for letters. That is why we say that we utter the same letter. All the patterns are eternal.

But the Mīmāmsakas say that it is unnecessary to accept that there is a distinct word-pattern apart from the word. The word consists of letters. There is no word apart from its letters and there are no letter-patterns apart from the letter-sounds. We say that we are uttering not only the same letters but also the same words; for the letters are eternal and are everywhere. But they need certain auxiliaries like our throat, tongue, and lips to become manifest. The differences in the way we utter them are due to the differences in the auxiliaries. That we do not take "tan" for "ant" is due to the order in which the letters are uttered by the speaker and the order also makes an impression on the hearer when he hears the word.

As regards the meaning of words, the Mīmāmsā maintains that the word directly means the universal[22] (*jāti*). The individual can be referred to the word only through the universal. The expression, "Bring a horse for sacrifice", does not mean this or that particular horse, but any horse. Indeed, we do not and cannot bring the universal horseness, but only an individual horse. We do so, because the words refer to denotation through connotation. Connotation is the primary meaning of words and is the universal. Kumārila says that the reference to the individual is obtained through postulation; for it is only the individual horse that can be brought and it is meaningless to ask a man to bring the universal horseness. But Prabhākara says that our cognition of the individual is due to the inclusion of the individual in the universal, as no universal can exist except in the individuals. However, both say that the individual is not the primary meaning (*abhidhā*), but brought in (*ākṣipyate*) for completing intelligibility.

As sentences expressing commands are primary according to the Mīmāmsā, Prabhākara says that the meaning of no word can first be understood without being associated with action. It is only in the context of the command, "Milk the cow", that the child can first understand the meaning of the word cow. For completing his doctrine, Prabhākara distinguishes between two kinds of words:[23] words that are directly experienced or heard as in commands and words that are remembered. The former cannot be understood without reference to action; the latter can be understood merely with reference to the universals they mean. In any case, as the remembered word also must have been first understood in association with action, the noun and the verb are understood only after their meanings are already related in a sentence. Thus the unit of meaning becomes the sentence. So, in Prabhākara we find two doctrines: (1) words have no meaning apart from the action they lead to and that the meaning of a word is the action to which it leads, and (2) that a word cannot have its meaning apart from the other words, particularly the verb, of a sentence, and the sentence alone is, therefore, the unit of meaning. The sentence is an expression in which the words have already been related through their meanings.[24]

Kumārila does not accept Prabhākara's views. He says that nouns, even apart from any relation to actions, have meanings. The child can learn the meaning of the word cow, when older people point to the animal and say: "That is a cow." The meaning of "That is a cow" is as primary as the meaning of "Milk the cow." Indeed, in the Veda injunctions are primary and lead to action. But the meaning of all sentences does not imply a command to act. So some sentences express what *is* (*siddhārtha*), others express what *has to be done*(*vidhyartha*). Words can, therefore, have their separate meanings. The meaning of a sentence is a combination of the meanings of the different words forming the sentence, and words do not obtain their meanings as parts of sentences.[25]

The reader can see here that Prabhākara makes the meaning of nouns (substances) dependent on the meaning of verbs (action) and is nearer the Nairukta theory that the noun is only a modality of action than Kumārila, who treats the meanings of nouns as independent of the meanings of verbs. However, Prabhākara's view should not be equated to the Nairukta view for which action is the primary reality and is the *ātman* itself. There is another difference: for both Prabhākara and Kumārila, action (*karma*) is the sovereign of the universe, but is different from the material constituency of the world it governs; but for the Nairukta, action as the Ātman includes everything as its mode, and forms, we may say, the philosophy of an Advaita of the Ātman as Action. However, Prabhākara is closer to the Nairuktas than Kumārila is. We may note also that Srī Harṣa condemns Prabhākara as "a kinsman of Buddha," as he tends to hold like the Buddhists that the primary aspect of the world is activity, process. This controversy makes us think that the Buddhist doctrine of the momentariness of the world as a process is very likely older than Buddha himself. We find it in the earliest speculations of the philosophies of language.[26]

VALIDITY OF KNOWLEDGE It is man who asks himself the question whether what he cognizes is true and whether the object of his cognition is really there before him. Knowing is a process of man's consciousness, the form of knowledge and its nature are both forms of consciousness and concerns also the structure of that form. The object of this knowledge is an object of his consciousness. This consciousness does not belong to the object itself. Man has no other way of knowing objects than through his consciousness. He has to accept the reality of objects as they appear to some form of his consciousness, perceptual, inferential, or verbal. But can he and should he accept everything that appears before his consciousness as real? For instance, imagining and dreaming are conscious processes. But we do not accept the objects of imagination and dream as real. We have, therefore, to determine what forms of the processes of consciousness can be valid forms, i.e., forms reliable for revealing the truth about the world. And we have to accept only as many forms as have each a distinctiveness of its own and is not reducible to any other. For instance, perception and inference have each its own distinctiveness. We classify them, therefore, as immediate and mediate forms of cognition. We should note that irreducibility does not mean unrelatedness. Inference may be based upon perception, yet it is not the same as perception.

The doctrine of determining the different valid forms of knowing is called the doctrine of *pramāṇas* (valid instruments of knowing). The word *pramā*[27] means the exactly measured, and so valid, or exact knowledge or cognition. *Pramāṇa* is the measure, the form that is the measure of reality, and so the ways or the means of valid cognition. The form of cognition, therefore, measures out reality for us. All processes of cognition result in cognition and the result (*phala*) of cognition is a form of our consciousness (*jñānaprakāra*) of the object. Kumārila says that the means of cognition (*pramāṇa*) and the result of cognition (*pramā*) are different. But Prabhākara[28] says that they are the same; for instance, the form of perceiving includes the result of perceiving also, viz., the object as perceived. But Kumārila contends that, if the result is identical with the process, there will be no difference between perception and inference as the object of inference also is an object; again, the object of perception is the actual object and the object of inference is an idea of the object. Or we have to accept that the results of the different ways or forms of the cognitive process are different, in which case we cannot interrelate the results as the cognitive processes are particular processes and separable. But we interrelate them. Only the Buddhist Vijñānavādins do and can accept the identification of the means and result of cognition; for according to them, the object cannot exist independently of consciousness and is a form of consciousness.

If man has to rely on his consciousness, and there is no other go for him to know the world, then reliability of consciousness has to be accepted by all epistemologists.[29] So both Kumārila and Prabhākara maintain—the Advaitins follow the Mīmāmsā at this point—that all knowledge is by itself valid. This doctrine is called the self-validity of knowledge[30] (*svatah prāmaṇyavāda*). But is not knowledge sometimes false? Yes, it is sometimes false; but its falsity is not due to its being a form of consciousness, but to other factors. We rely upon perception, inference, etc., for our knowledge of the world. But they also may misfire. They are false not because they are perception, etc., but because of other reasons. Falsity is due to reasons other than the perceptual processes. This doctrine of invalidity is called the doctrine of invalidity as due to the other (*paratah aprāmāṇyavāda*).

From the above doctrine it follows that the truth of any cognition is revealed through that cognition itself; and the falsity of any cognition, if it is false, has to be revealed by some other cognition, viz., the cognition of the other factor. A true cognition is never made true by any other cognition, but only confirmed. The truth of the first cognition must be revealed by that cognition itself. The second cognition does not confer truth on it, but only confirms it. But the falsity of a cognition is not revealed through that cognition itself, but through a second cognition that contradicts it. Confirmation may be interpreted as coherence. But the doctrine of the self-validity of knowledge does not mean that truth is the same as coherence. One cognition may cohere with another, if both are true; but such coherence is only a corollary of self-validity and is very much limited in scope. For coherence means generally implication, but two true perceptual statements like "This rose is red" and "That marigold is yellow" may not imply each other. So self-validity may at the most mean non-contradiction.

Another implication of the doctrine of the self-validity of knowledge concerns not merely the revealing of the truth or falsity of a cognition, but also the constitution of its truth and falsity. Every cognition, as cognition, is true by itself; but is *made*, not merely revealed as, false by something else, which is, of course, another cognition. A true cognition is not made and cannot be made true by another; its truth belongs to its very nature and constitution. The Mīmāmsakas contend that *although every cognition, as cognition, has to be accepted as true, some cognitions are made false by other cognitions*. But then two questions arise: (1) How can a cognition, true by itself, be made false by another?

and (2) How can a cognition, which is true by itself, be false also even according to another? How can a cognition be both true and false? We shall discuss the Mīmāmsā answers in the next section on illusion.

Doctrine of Illusion[31] The presence of error and illusion in human experience is one of the greatest stumbling blocks for any doctrine of epistemological certainty. In spite of the unavoidability of relying on our consciousness for knowing reality, we encounter errors and illusions even in our inferences and perceptions. The problem is, therefore, why and how do error and illusion arise. Even the valid forms of knowing (*pramāṇas*) present us with objects which are found to be false. If the forms are valid, should we not accept that the objects they present are real and existent? If they exist, why do we treat them as non-existent and false? Do we not mean by falsity non-existence and unreality also? These questions become very important for the Indian thinkers.

The words error and illusion refer not only to the concerned cognitive processes but also to their objects. The object of erroneous inference is due to an erroneous mediating process, which we call a fallacy. Fallacies are formal defects of thinking. So long as we do not equate thought to existence—we do not do it in inference—the problem of the reality or being of the object of erroneous thinking does not bother us. We say that it can have some kind of existence in our mind, like the object of imagination. But erroneous perception is illusion. Mirage is an illusion and yet is an object of perception. Perception lies at the basis of all the other forms of knowing. How then can we treat an object of perception, which is an immediate form of cognition, as false? How can an object of immediate cognition be non-existent? Inference is based upon conceptual consistency, and conceptual non-contradiction can be our guide in it. But since the object of perception is not a concept, but the thing itself, when two perceptions present the same thing as two objects, should we not say that the two perceptions contradict one another? If the objects are things themselves, then do things contradict one another, just as concepts contradict one another? Things are existents and there can be no contradiction between two existent things. If I see an object first as a snake and then as a rope, this school contends, there cannot be contradiction, just as there cannot be a contradiction between two things existing at different places or different times. The Mīmāmsakas are presentationists in their doctrine of perception, i.e., they say that we see the objects directly, and uphold a realistic epistemology.

Both Kumārila and Prabhākara are realists in epistemology and both maintain that our perceptual knowledge of objects is always reliable. They have, therefore, to prove that even the object of illusory perception is a real object. Seeing suddenly a piece of rope, I may mistake it for a snake[32] and say: "That is snake." Certainly no snake exists before me. If so, how can the object of illusion be real? Kumārila says that the snake seen in front is a remembered snake seen some time ago. Illusion is the perception of one object in place of another.[33] It is not mistaking the form (*prakāra*, universal) of the rope for the form of the snake; for forms or universals are above time and space and cannot be seen in time and space except in one of their own individuals. The form or universal snakeness cannot exist in the individual rope; it can exist only in an individual snake. Prabhākara does not accept Kumārila's view.

He says that a remembered snake cannot be seen, as there is no sense-contact with it. Illusion is, therefore, the non-cognition[34] (*agraha*) of the difference between the object in front and the remembered snake. Illusion is thus incomplete perception. Perception, if complete, can never be wrong. Consciousness is absolutely reliable. It confuses neither two forms nor two individuals.

In spite of the bold attempts of Kumārila and Prabhākara to defend realism and the absolute reliability of consciousness, the question still remains how, in Kumārila's view, we can know that we are perceiving the remembered snake and how, in Prabhākara's view, we can know that we have not perceived the difference between the object in front and the snake remembered. Kumārila and Prabhākara have explained, each in his own way, what illusion is, but their explanations do not indicate how we detect illusions.

To the question how we detect illusions, the answers of Kumārila and Prabhākara are the same. We detect them with the help of the criteria of non-contradiction[35] and pragmatism. In the above example, my cognition of the snake is contradicted (*bādhita*) by my cognition of the same object as the rope. The perceptions of other persons also contradict it. In addition to this criterion, we have the pragmatic test. But this pragmatism is not the same as usefulness. The Mīmāmsakas, in fact almost all the schools of Indian philosophy, believe that the world is a field of action, is full of action (*karmamayam jagat*). Everything in the world is meant for action and every action has an end. Even the stinging of the scorpion has an end, viz., producing pain. Then we can test also whether the object serves the end for which it is meant (*arthakriyākārī*) by leading us to appropriate action. The appropriate action, when we see a snake, is to run away from it or to kill it. By running away we cannot test whether it is a real snake. But if we beat it with a stick and do not find flesh and blood, our cognition of the snake is contradicted. In this connection, Prabhākara goes to the extent of saying that the meaning of any cognition includes the action to which it leads us. If I tell you: "This is sugar," the word sugar includes also the meaning that it is sweet to eat. If you eat it and find that it is sweet, then the object is sugar; otherwise, it is some other substance.

In Indian epistemology, we find the difference drawn between the nature of truth and falsity and the nature of the criterion. So far as the criterion goes, there is not much difference among the schools. But on the nature of truth and falsity, there are diverse opinions. The main difficulty in accepting the views of Kumārila and Prabhākara on the nature of illusion is that, in our experience of perception, there is no conscious reference to memory or part cognitions. If there is memory, since the false object is an object of perception, illusory perception has to be of the form of recognition. But there is no experience of recognition in illusion. If one says that all perception involves past experience,[36] that is the result of the reaction of our apperception in which past experience is stored up, then such a memory is not peculiar to illusion and cannot, therefore, explain it. Further, Kumārila's view is wrong as shown by Prabhākara. But Prabhākara's view also is wrong; for we react to an object only when perception is complete and we react to the snake and run away or beat it. So illusion is the cognition of something, but not its non-cognition.

The first of the two questions raised at the end of the above section is answered by Kumārila by saying that, as the nature of cognition is to reveal the existence (*astitā*) of the object and as perception always does so, it is by nature always true. But invalid cognition is of three kinds: perception of one object as another as in illusion, perception of a non-existent object as in hallucination, and doubt. Even if one does not classify doubt as invalid cognition,[37] the two others are certainly invalid. But this invalidity is not due to perception as perception, but to the intrusion of wrong factors. This intrusion is generally of two kinds: defective nature of the psycho-physical factors like the intervention of inappropriate memories as in the perception of a rope as a snake and weakness and defectiveness of senses as in the jaundiced man perceiving everything yellow; and the intrusion of some physical media like light and distance between our physiological sense-organs and the physical object as in the perception of the mirage. Kumārila's answer is so far clear. But there is a difficulty. When I perceive a rope as a snake and say: "That is a snake," the object's existence is revealed through the "is." If so, why do I call the perception false, after I discover that the object is a rope? How can the same perception be first true and later false? If it can become false, how can cognition retain its self-validity?[38] Kumārila does not face these questions. His arguments go only so far as to show that we have to rely, for our knowledge of the world, on the valid means of cognition and that these means of cognition are valid in and by themselves.

Prabhākara's answer is different; but it is more clear than, but equally inadequate as Kumārila's. The latter treats illusory perception as a completed perception. We are, therefore, entitled to ask him why, if all perception is true in and by itself, illusory perception can be false, why perception can become an illusion. But Prabhākara escapes us because he does not regard illusory perception as complete perception. He can say that a completed perception will never be false and is never made false. But the defect in his position is that, for the sake of theory, he is denying one important aspect of illusion. All illusory perceptions are completed perceptions. Our perception of the mirage is a completed perception; so also are the Müller-Lyer illusions. Even the illusory perception of the snake is a completed perception, for either we run away from it or beat it up. Activity generally follows only completed perceptions. All that we can say, therefore, in favour of the doctrine of the self-validity of knowledge in epistemology is that the different forms of cognition have to be accepted as reliable forms of cognition and as capable of revealing the nature of the world as it is, and that nothing other than themselves makes them reliable. The three criteria—the object performing the function for which it is meant (*arthakriyākāritā*), the soundness of the psycho-physical factors and the appropriateness of the media, and coherence or consistency (*samvāda*)—only confirm the truth of cognition. All that the Mīmāmsakas succeeded in defending is that a form of cognition is self-valid means that it is a valid means of knowing reality and that the knowledge obtained through the different means of cognition has to be relied upon as revealing reality. But this general position does not answer the specific questions we have raised.

3. METAPHYSICS

The Mīmāmsā metaphysics is essentially the metaphysics of ethical action. It is, therefore, both qualitatively and quantitatively pluralistic and has to accept almost everything that a pluralistic philosophy has to accept. But its central interest lies in showing the efficacy of ethical action. The importance it gives to this efficacy makes the Mīmāmsā substitute ethical action for God himself. The efficacy of ethical action is a force that creates the forms of the world, although not its being, and its constituents like the physical elements. It is the controller of the world and is its organizer. Yet the plurality of the *ātmans* and of the things of the world is real. The world is meant for action and is created by action; there is no life, no future, for man without action. Man makes or unmakes his destiny, mars it, or escapes the world only through action. Even if he wants to rise above the world of action, he can do so only through action.[39] The nature of ethical action becomes, therefore, the primary problem for the Mīmāmsā.

DHARMA Just as God is the central problem for all theology, *dharma* is the central problem for the Mīmāmsā. *Dharma*[40] is that which supports, and therefore that which supports the universe. It is that which holds the plurality together; without it the manifold will fall apart. It is the grandest conception of the sovereignity of ethical action. Jaimini defines[41] it as the good the characteristic of which is the impelling or the directing of man to action. His definition is accepted by both Kumārila and Prabhākara. Both accept that ethical action must be what answers to a Vedic injunction (*vedapratipādya*). But what is the good that impels a man to action? It is something to be achieved by action and is also *dharma*. On this point also both are in agreement. *Dharma* thus produced brings forth the desired fruit of action. If the *dharma* is ethically right, the fruit it produces brings enjoyment; if it is ethically wrong, the result it produces brings forth suffering and we call it *adharma*.

Now, what is this *dharma*? It is a potential force (*śakti*), which are popularly call merit and demerit. We think that the two are only good and bad qualities attributed to men by God or society because of the kind of actions they perform. Some theistic schools like the Nyāya say that God rewards and punishes men according to the two qualities. But the Mīmāmsā says that merit and demerit are not qualities (*guṇas*), they constitute the potential force, which is the Extra-ordinary (*apūrva*) and the Unseen (*adṛṣṭa*). This force resides in the *ātman* of the agent and controls and determines the future life of the *ātman* here, hereafter, and in the future lives which it takes through transmigration.

We have to accept the reality of this unseen power, because we cannot otherwise explain how action performed now can cause or produce the fruit after a lapse of time. Between the end of action and the appearance of its result, there is a time interval. But there can be no causation with a time interval between the cause and the effect. Causation is a continuous process without any time intervening between the processes of the cause and the appearance of the effect. We have to postulate, therefore, that the action we perform does not end when our activity is ended, but assumes the form of a potential force that can stay as potency until the occasion and opportunity arise for operation. As we do not see this force (*śakti*), it is unseen (*adṛṣṭa*); and as it is not an ordinary kind of force like that of the magnet, it is extra-ordinary (*apūrva*). Ethical activity becomes a force that controls the production of the forms of life we desire. The stuff of the world is not produced by this force, it is eternal; but the forms which the stuff assumes and which the agent of action desires are produced by this force.

In order to remove any possible conflict among the forces generated by the actions of different individuals, the Mīmāmsā postulates a unitary force of activity that controls and guides the forces of different individuals. This unitary Supreme or Universal Force[42] preserves the unity of the universe and performs practically the function of God in theistic philosophies.

So far there does not seem to be much difference of opinion among the Mīmāmsakas. Now, Śabara, the first commentator on Jaimini's *Mīmāmsā Aphorisms*, says that *dharma* is the action enjoined by the Veda.[43] Kumārila says that *dharma* is, therefore, the action enjoined by the Veda and as such is the action (*kriyā*) itself,[44] but not the merit produced by it. He adds that the action is right because it produces good for man. But Prabhākara maintains that the objective (*kārya*) of the Vedic injunction is the production of the Unseen (*adṛṣṭa*), i.e., the Veda commands us to produce the Unseen; and our actions are right because they are in accordance with the injunctions of the Veda, but not because they produce good for man. *Dharma* is the Unseen as the objective of the Vedic command, but not the action. Here Kumārila emphasizes the good, and Prabhākara the right. For Kumārila an action is right, because it produces the good; for Prabhākara it produces the good, because it is right. However, for both it is action that becomes the unseen potency.

The above differences may look more scholastic[45] than substantial. The important ideas of this discussion are: (1) the Veda gives certain commands or commandments; (2) our actions follow the commandments; (3) after our actions are completed, they assume the form of potential force, called the Unseen and the Extra-ordinary; and (4) our actions lie in wait as potential forces and become active when the occasion and opportunity arise. *Dharma* in the sense of merit is that part of the potential force that produces good for the agent of action; and *adharma* in the sense of demerit is that part that produces evil. As the potential force is a transformed state of the action itself, it also is called action (*karma*). Sometimes both *dharma* and *adharma* are called *dharma*; the usage of the word is like that of character. Character means both good and bad character. But when we say: "He is a man without character," we mean that he does not have good character.

For the Mīmāmsā, the doctrine of *karma* or action is the doctrine of *dharma*—which in a general sense may be translated as duty, obligation because *karma* and *dharma* are associated with commandments—and also the doctrine of the unseen ethical force. The Mīmāmsā may be called the metaphysics of ethical action, because ethical action is the central controlling power of the universe. It believes, however, that man is free, although his *ātman* carries within itself the potential forces of his future. His past actions do not deprive him of his freedom, but produce the capital for his future life. He can make whatever use he can of his capital. Furthermore, the effects of evil actions can be countered by good actions and can be prevented through expiatory actions (*prāyaścittas*). The potential force the ātman carries is a mixture (*citra*) of the potentialities of good and evil actions. Sometimes, these potentialities cancel one another. The potentialities of good actions are strengthened by those of other good actions, but counterbalanced by those of evil ones. So it is not necessary that every good or evil act must produce its particular effects.

Actions are primarily of three kinds: (1) Obligatory actions are those that have to be performed by every man only because he is a man, e.g., the paying back of the three debts, already mentioned, by the householder. Their performance supports man, society, and the universe and does not bring any special kind of merit for man. But their non-performance produces demerit. (2) Prohibited actions are those that produce demerit, but their non-performance does not produce any merit. The non-performance of prohibited actions also is obligatory. (3) The third variety consists of those actions the performance of which is optional. The injunctions regarding them are concerned with particular aims of the agent. If one wants to be the king of heaven, one has to perform a certain sacrifice. If one wants to be the ruler of the earth, one has to perform another. But the desire to be the king of heaven or the ruler of earth is not an obligation. To the three we may add a *fourth*, recognized but discouraged by the Mīmāmsā, viz., activities associated with black magic. If one wants one's enemy to die, one performs some sacrifices associated with black magic. Man may choose to perform them. But the Mīmāmsā says that the sacrificer goes to hell. Although this variety comes under prohibited actions, the Mīmāmsā lays down rules for performing them. But it does not lay down rules for performing all prohibited actions that produce demerit, e.g., how to commit murder or theft.

ĀTMAN The Mīmāmsā accepts the reality of the *ātman*, as distinct from mind (*manas*), senses, and physical body. The *ātman* is the same as the I-consciousness (*ahamdhī*) and what the Upaniṣads call the Brahman.[46] Yet there is a plurality of the *ātmans*. We have to accept their plurality, for each *ātman* is responsible for its own actions and has to enjoy the fruits of its own actions. Every *ātman* is an individual, and is infinite. Yet the *ātmans* can be different and exist together. Consciousness is not the essential nature of the *ātman*, but arises in it, when mind (*manas*), along with some information, comes into contact with it. Although consciousness is thus an adventitious quality, the *ātman* is itself the seer, doer, and enjoyer. We cannot attribute the qualities of seeing, doing, and enjoying to mind, senses, or the physical body; for they can never become conscious and our experience is always of the form, " I see, I do, I enjoy."

How do we know the *ātman* and how do we become aware of its existence? How do we become conscious of our consciousness? To these questions Kumārila and Prabhākara give different answers. Prabhākara upholds the doctrine that cognition has three factors (*triputījñāna*). They are the subject knowing the object, the object known, and the knowledge of the object. Every cognition reveals all the three factors simultaneously. Kumārila also says that there are three factors, but contends that all the three are not revealed simultaneously. When I look at the object and say: "That is a pen", I am not conscious of myself or of my consciousness of the object, but only of the object. If I am conscious of all the three factors simultaneously, the form of my experience must be: "I am conscious that I am conscious of the pen." But the experience is not so in the live act of perception. Often we do not care to be conscious of the "I", or the subject. But when we think of it and reflect on it, it is known as the I-consciousness (*ahamdhī*). The "I" can be an object of its consciousness; but the consciousness of the object is not known directly at all, just as nobody can see his eye. Then how do we know that we have knowledge of the object? When we perceive the object, the object is cognized as known (*jñāta*). It thereby gets a new characteristic knownness (*jñātatā*) through our knowing activity. This activity is not perceivable, but inferable, as there can be no perception of the perceptual process. Hence, the action of knowing or consciousness is only inferred. This is the view of Śabara also.[47]

In their account of the knowing process, both Kumārila and Prabhākara are partly right and partly wrong. Kumārila's statement that the middle factor, viz., consciousness, is not an object of sense-perception is a truism. But that we infer its presence from the characteristic of knownness in the object goes against experience. There can be no inference here, because there can be no major premise. Furthermore, we do not observe, perceive, knownness in the object; nor do we infer it. Prabhākara's view that all consciousness and so all knowledge is self-revealing is true and is supported by our experience. But his contention that in cognition all the three—subject, object, and knowledge—are revealed together goes against our experience. In the live act of perceiving the pen in front, there is only the pen before my consciousness or to which any consciousness is tied (*baddha*), but not my consciousness or my "I". Consciousness has an outward direction in perception; it is directed neither to itself nor to my "I." Reflection of my outwards directed consciousness is needed for making the consciousness (of the pen) and my "I" objects. And this reflection involves memory as a moment and the object "pen" becomes an idea. Again, if consciousness can reveal itself, and if the *ātman* is known as the I-consciousness, then the I-consciousness, as consciousness, must be capable of revealing itself to itself. The consciousness of the object does not reveal itself to itself, but to the "I", because it is the "I" that cognized the object. But the consciousness of the "I" can reveal itself only to itself and becomes self-consciousness. Prabhākara's objection that the "I" cannot be an object of itself, since the subject can never become an object, does not hold ground. He himself says that cognition can reveal all the factors simultaneously; then it must reveal also the "I". But to whom can and does it reveal the "I" except to the "I" itself?

There is one difficulty behind this controversy. Both Kumārila and Prabhākara maintain that the *ātman* by itself is unconscious and consciousness is only an adventitious quality of the *ātman*. If so, how can there be self-consciousness (*ahamdhī*)? To overcome the impasse, Kumārila says that the *ātman* is unconscious, but potentially conscious; and this potential consciousness becomes actual consciousness when mind comes into contact with the *ātman*. Prabhākara does not accept even potential consciousness in the *ātman*, but says it is absolutely unconscious. Then to whom does the self-revealing consciousness reveal the three factors? To the unconscious *ātman*? So Prabhākara's position on the nature of the *ātman* becomes weaker than that of Kumārila; for the latter maintains that the desire to know the *ātman* is itself an act of mind and when mind comes into contact with the *ātman*, the latter's potential consciousness becomes actual. However, as both Kumārila and Prabhākara maintain, if mind is an unconscious substance, how can it have any desire, which is a conscious act? Knowledge can be explained, according to the Mīmāmsā, as a spark produced by the impact of unconscious substances on one another—object, senses, mind, and the *ātman*—each upon the next. The I-consciousness cannot be explained.

GOD According to the Mīmāmsā, the problem of God is first taken up in connection with the problem of the meaning of the words of the Veda, which are always true and infallible. According to the Nyāya, which we shall study later, the meaning of the

Vedic words was fixed by God, who was himself the composer of the Vedas. So the information they convey can never be false. But Jaimini was indifferent to the reality of God and did not care to discuss it much. He said that the relation of word and meaning is innate,[48]— which means that God is not necessary to fix the meaning of words. Śabara, the commentator on Jaimini, says that God, as the creator of the world, cannot be proved to exist by any of the valid means of cognition and cannot, therefore, be accepted. Prabhākara adds that the universe had no beginning and will, therefore, have no end; God is not, therefore, needed as its creator. Indeed, the universe has parts, which are brought together in various forms for the enjoyment of the *ātmans*. But this function of bringing parts together is performed by the force (*śakti*) of the Extra-ordinary[49] (*apūrva*), the merit and demerit of the souls. To the argument that the Extra-ordinary is a blind force and needs the supervision of God, the answer is that God is not needed as the force acts according to its own laws, and we cannot think of any motive of God to act as a supervisor even when not needed. Kumārila adds that God cannot be the creator, as he cannot have any purpose in creating the world. If it is said that he created the world, so that the *ātmans* can enjoy the fruit of their actions, the difficulty is not overcome. For there must first be a world in which the *ātmans* performs their actions, which in their turn produce their potencies. Then why did God create the world first? If the world is due to God's desire for sport (*līlā*), then we must attribute the sufferings of men to God's reckless desire. No merciful God would create the imperfections and miseries of men. We cannot understand also how God could act in his act of creation, if he had no material to work with. If there was some material like atoms, we cannot conceive how God could bring them together without having a physical body like us. For only a physical body can handle physical atoms. If he could bring them together through his will, we may as well say that they can be brought together by the Extra-ordinary. So neither the cosmological nor the teleological argument[50] can prove the existence of God. Like the world, the Vedas are eternal and do not need a composer.

Although the early Mīmāmsā is non-theistic and the general trend of the later Mīmāmsā is to reject all proofs for the existence of God, we find some followers of the latter accepting the reality of God on the basis of the Veda. It is said that even Kumārila[51] accepted the existence of God. This opinion is questionable. Some interpreters went even further and said that, according to Kumārila, the state of salvation for the *ātman* is blissful.[52] This interpretation also is doubtful, for it does not agree with the main position of Kumārila that no consciousness, not even that of bliss, is possible without the contact of the *ātman* and mind. And there is no possibility of such a contact in the state of salvation, where the *ātman* dissociated itself from everything including mind. However, some of the Mīmāmsakas who lived after Kumārila and Prabhākara accepted the reality of God. Laugākṣi Bhāskara[53] is one of them.

THE CATEGORIES OF THE WORLD It has already been said that, according to the Mīmāmsā, the world had no beginning and will have no end, and that reality is pluralistic. In categorizing the world, Kumārila and Prabhākara differ from each other. According to Kumārila, the categories are first divided into two kinds, the positive and the negative. The positive categories are four: substance, quality, activity, and generality (*jāti*, *sāmānya*, universal). The negative categories also are four: prior negation (*prāgabhāva*), posterior negation (*pradhvamsābhāva*), infinite or absolute negation (*atyantābhāva*), and mutual negation (*anyonyābhāva*). We thus get the following chart:

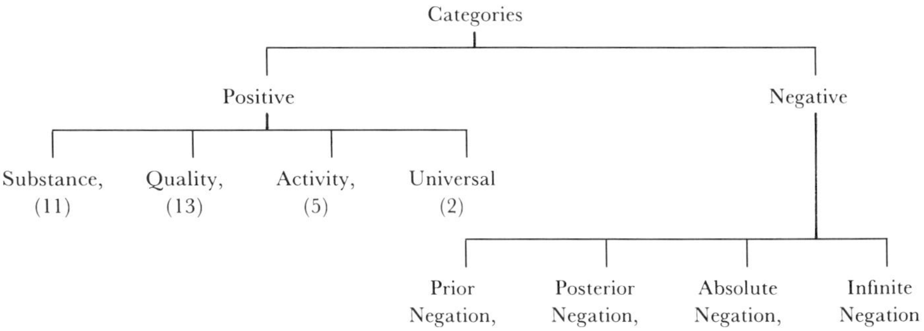

There are eleven substances: earth, water, fire, air, ether (*ākāśa*), space, time, *ātman*, mind (*manas*), darkness, and sound (word, letters). Now, Kumārila treats force (*śakti*, potency) and similarity (*sādṛśya*) also as substances.[54] Then we get thirteen. Darkness is not the absence of light, but a distinct substance, which has the qualities of thickness and thinness. Similarity is a substance, as there can be more or less of it. However, Kumārila's argument is not convincing. While he accepts that mind is infinite (*vibhu*) like the *ātman*, Prabhākara treats it as atomic in size.

The fourteen qualities are: colour, taste, smell, touch, magnitude, separateness, conjunction, disjunction, priority, posteriority, gravity, fluidity, viscidity, and number. Activities are of five types: throwing up and throwing down (or upward and downward movements), pushing aside (side-ward movement), bending or contraction, and stretching or expanding. These five types of activity are the same as those of the Nyāya. The universal is the same as structure (*samsthāna*) and is of two kinds, the higher and the lower. But the distinction between the two is only relative. Man-ness is a lower universal with reference to animal-ness, but is a higher with reference to Englishman-ness. The highest universal, which is not lower than any other, is Being (*sattā*); the lowest is the individual like Socrates.[55]

The Mīmāmsā does not accept the reality of the particular (*viśeṣa*), which will be discussed in the chapter on the Vaiśeṣika. Being a Greek is a universal; but Socrates, Plato, etc., are lower than being a Greek and are individuals. The Mīmāmsā refuses to recognize particulars apart from individuals. It is enough if we have the concept of the higher and lower universals and individuals. It is superfluous to have the particular as a separate category. It is unnecessary to have the individual also as a separate category, for no universal can exist without its individuals and, whenever the universal is referred to, the individual is implied (*arthāt āyātah*).

Prior negation is the absence of an object before it is born. Before my pen was manufactured, it did not exist, it was a non-being. Posterior negation is the absence of an object after it is destroyed. After my pen is destroyed, it becomes a non-being. Absolute negation is not mere Non-being, but the absence of my pen at all places and times except where and when it exists. As these times and places are infinite, comprising beginningless past and endless future and the infinite area of space except the little place it now occupies, this type of negation is called infinite, endless, or absolute negation. Mere Non-being is not a significant negation at all and cannot, therefore, belong to reality. Significant negation is the negation of a possible, positive object and it is the negation of something definite. The negation of what cannot possibly exist cannot be significant. Non-being, as such by its very definition, which is not the non-being of anything in particular, cannot be significant. Further, Being is found everywhere, and it has no possibility of not being found anywhere. So Non-being, as the negation of Being, has no metaphysical significance and cannot belong to reality.

Mutual negation is the negation of two things or two universals of each other. It may be called difference. "This pen is not that pen" means that the two are different from each other. Similarly, "The lion is not the tiger" means that the universal lion-ness is different from the universal tiger-ness, or the class of lions is different from the class of tigers.

Negation is accepted by Kumārila as a category of reality for defending the plurality of the world. If the world is a manifold in essence, then nothing can be the same as another thing and everything exists only in its time and place. So all the four forms of negation have to be accepted as belonging to reality itself.

But Prabhākara does not accept the categorization of reality as given by Kumārila. First, he rejects negation as belonging to reality itself. Reality is, indeed, a manifold, but is always positive, not negative. What we call the absence of the pen on the table is only the table. What we see is only the table. If we say: "The ink is not red", we mean that it is black. Without seeing the black colour, we could not have said that it was not red. So all forms of negation are objects of inference. Indeed, Kumārila asks how inference is possible without a major premise and whether what inference gives is real or unreal.

Prabhākara gives eight positive categories: substance, quality, action, universal, inherence, force, similarity, and number.[56] He would say that Kumārila was wrong in including force and similarity under substance and number under quality. Force and similarity, although found in substances, are not substances; the two are found in qualities and actions also. When ethical action becomes a potency (force), it does not become a substance. If similarity is found between two substances, two qualities, or two activities, it cannot be any one of them. Kumārila holds that inherence is not a distinct category, for it is the same as the entities in which it exists. For instance, quality and action are found in substances and universals are found in substances, qualities, and actions. This kind of being present in something else is called inherence, which is really nothing different from the entities in relation. But Prabhākara says that inherence is the relation of dependence (*paratantratā*). The universal is dependent on the individual, and quality and action are dependent on substance. This dependence is not the same as the object in which it is found. Our experience of it has a distinct character of its own. We have, therefore, to accept it as a distinct category. However, Prabhākara does not accept the Nyāya concept of inherence as an eternal relation. For if the relation between the individual and universal is eternal, then neither can perish. But we see many individuals and universals coming to an end. Many species of animals have become extinct and many individuals are dying every moment, even when their universal is existent. Number also is not a quality, as the Nyāya and Kumārila understand it. If number 2 belongs to two apples as their quality, it must be found in each, just as colour is found in each. What cannot be found in each cannot be found in both. Number must, therefore, be a distinct category. Prabhākara's concept of number is an advance on that of the Nyāya-Vaiśeṣika.

4. LIFE'S IDEAL

We have seen that, for the Mīmāmsā, God as the creator of the world is not wanted, as the world had no beginning and will have no end. He is not wanted also as the composer of the Vedas, for they also are eternal like the world. And he is not wanted as the supervisor of the functions of ethical potency (*apūrva*), for this potency works according to its own laws, whether there is God or not. He cannot alter its workings. All that man has to do is, therefore, to live and act according to the laws of ethical action; and accumulated potency does not bear fruit for another. Such mix-up is possible, if all potencies exist mixed up in God's single mind.

Of the four values of life—wealth, enjoyment, ethical merit, and salvation—generally accepted by Indian philosophers, the early Mīmāmsā, as found in Jaimini and Śabara, accepted the first three; but a little later Mīmāmsā, as found in Kumārila and Prabhākara, recognized the fourth, but did not recommend it; still later from about the 15th century we find the Mīmāmsakas becoming theistic and advocating salvation as the highest ideal. Nārāyana Bhaṭṭa,[57] a commentator on Kumārila and author of *Mānameyodaya*, Nārāyana Bhaṭṭa II, who also expounded the ideas of Kumārila, and Laugākṣi Bhāskara, the author of the popular introductory work, *Arthasaṅgraha*, propounded theism and salvation, making ethical action the means of the latter. Accepting the reality of God on the authority of the Veda and rejecting all other ways of knowing as incapable of proving God's existence, these Mīmāmsakas maintain that, if man performs all obligatory actions till death, avoids all prohibited actions and also all optional actions meant to fulfil particular desires, and surrenders everything he does to God, he will obtain salvation and will not return to the world of births and deaths. And to make the state of salvation the highest ideal, an ideal state of existence in which there is only bliss unmixed with pain, they treat the state as one of consciousness and the *ātman* as essentially conscious and blissful by nature. This view is essentially that of the *Bhagavadgītā*.[58]

The Mīmāmsā was thus turned into a theistic philosophy. But one can easily see that this new interpretation does not agree with the central Mīmāmsā position. It originally looked down upon the idea of salvation. Man lives in a world of action and is meant for action; and beyond man, the world, action, and ethical potency, there is nothing. Ethical potency is the secret of the world; only the Veda knows and understands that secret. Man has, therefore, to follow the Vedic injunctions and build up his ethical potency and, through it, his future. This potency creates the conditions of man's enjoyment and is exhausted through their creation. Man has to live a life of action in every birth, if he wants a life of happiness every time. Man is made for action and enjoyment; it is violation of the nature of himself and of the world to lead a life of non-action and to think that it is the ideal. His ideal is to enjoy pleasure and avoid pain. Heaven is a state of undiluted, intense pleasure and is the reward of the ethically good life. As man alone has the organs to perform actions, he is superior even to gods, who know only how to enjoy a state of happiness, but cannot perform new actions for accumulating new merit. Both heaven and the status of gods have an end. So even gods have to come down and be born as men for accumulating new ethical potency. The status of gods is the reward to men who have the required ethical merit to their credit. The state of salvation is without pain and pleasure, without consciousness, and is, therefore, not to be desired by men, except by those who are like disabled soldiers. It is like that of a stone. Salvation is liberation from everything connected with the world and so from mind (*manas*) also. But when mind is not in contact with the *ātman*, there can be no consciousness and so no bliss. No one desires the state of a stone for ever. Even a life of celebacy cannot be recommended. A man without a wife cannot fulfil the obligations of perpetuating the ancestral line and cannot perform the sacrifices to gods. These sacrifices also are obligatory. The ideal life, according to the Mīmāmsā, is thus a life of continuous ethical activity and enjoyment of its fruits. The ascetic ideal was far beyond the horizon of the Mīmāmsā from the beginning even upto the time of Kumārila and Prabhākara, who tried to give some place to it. But on the whole, there is no life, for the Mīmāmsā, without action.

GENERAL ESTIMATE AND CONSTRUCTIVE COMMENT

(i) Importance of Action

As indicated already, the Mīmāmsā is the most important and well-developed philosophy of action in India; and it is not fair to dismiss it as a borrowing from the Nyāya-Vaiśeṣika, as ritualism which is not of much philosophical interest, or as an incomplete and stunted Vedānta and as, therefore, unsatisfactory as a system of philosophy. Even Hegelianism is unsatisfactory as a system of philosophy, if one expects from a system a constructive inter-relating of all the categories and objects of the world: the advaita dialectic is systematic only in denying all intelligibility—which is done even by some modern idealistics like Bradley and existentialists like Sartre—to such relations.[59] Some later borrowings from the Nyāya-Vaiśeṣika by the Mīmāmsā are due to the demands by later logicians to prove its early primary premises—that the world is a world of action and that that the ethical law of action is the sovereign of the world needs a logic to defend its pluralistic cosmology,—which were more or less tacitly accepted, but articulated in the Nyāya-Vaiśeṣika, which in turn adopted and adapted a good deal from the activism of the Mīmāmsā, however much the two schools differed. The Mīmāmsā contribution to the philosophy of language and grammar—which is not included in this book for want of space—from the stand-point of ethical activism cannot be underestimated. Although Śaṅkara and Rāmānuja give a lower place to ethical action than to knowledge (gnosis) and devotion respectively, both maintain that ethical action purifies mind and prepares for the higher knowledge and devotion, though Śaṅkara speaks of ethical action as dispensable, while Rāmānuja says that one should continue following the Mīmāmsā injunctions until death—which means that for Rāmānuja ethical action is indispensable.

It has become the practice in India—a wrong practice, one should say—to say that Śaṅkara also considered ethical action to be indispensable as he held that one who wants liberation should practice discerning between the eternal and the transient, develop disinclination towards all pleasures, become eager for right knowledge, and practice control of the senses and strengthen the longing for salvation. On the very face of it, these advices—they are not commands, but prerequisites for salvation—are meant only for those desirous of salvation. But as already pointed out, salvation is not regarded as a duty by most of the Indian thinkers; it is not even a categorical imperative; it is not an "Ought" (*vidhi*),[60] and what is required, therefore, for salvation is not ethically binding. Some of the practices prescribed for salvation—such as compassion, non-violence, non-stealing, etc.,—obtain ethical importance in the context of morality also and obtain for ethics only the element of a derivative (hypothetical?) "Ought," not a categorical "Ought." Or in the words of the Upaniṣads, they are not "debts" (*ṛṇas*) which the individual owes to the sages, manes and gods, to which benevolence to mankind and hospitality to guests, etc., were added later.

Furthermore, we may ask: What is ethical action? Leaving aside etymological controversies, we may accept the idea of the *Bhagavadgītā* that it is action according to the structure of the Cosmic Person, the Logos.[61] Such action sets me in the path set by the Logos, lifts me above the pettiness and narrowness of my finite self with its selfish and self-centred desires and ideals to the level of the Universal Person. It is at this level that I can realize my one-ness—in whatever sense the word "one-ness" is understood—with the Supreme Being. Then action in accordance with the structure of the Logos is indispensable—which means again that purification, which is the same as universalization of my mind and self is impossible without ethical[62] action.

One will perhaps say that this universalization can be achieved by the practice of yoga and the following of the advices by the teachers who think that action is dispensable. We may not merely refer here to the *Bhagavadgītā*, which says that it is not dispensable. Mere practice of yoga without experience of ethical action in family and society deprives the person of reality-sense, which abnormal psychology like that of Freud considers to be very important. A normal person is one with a sound reality-attitude and sense. Besides, it is profound ethical conflicts that deepen the person's self and lead him to spiritual depths. We may recall also the Upaniṣadic teaching that objects and senses are polarizations of the gods of the cosmos.[63] My finite self belongs also to this polarization, it becomes one of the poles. I come to grief, fear, loneliness, anxiety, etc., if I forget that I am only a pole of the polarized Cosmic Person.[64] Engrossment in my own inner life may turn me into a mere (abnormal) introvert, instead of leading me to true inwardness, in which the Cosmic Person is to be found. My true inwardness is a correlate of my true outwardness,[65] both of which can be realized only through ethical action which correlate me to the object on which I act and the consequent achievement. Otherwise, I may be mistaking an unreal "I" for my higher "I," which is not what is meant by self-realization. We should not forget that every school of philosophy regards the criterion of truth and reality as "doing what a thing is meant for doing" (*arthakriyā-kāritā*) or "serving the purpose for which it is meant," in which phrase "serving" means "serving in practical activity." We often say that the hard facts of reality dispel our imagination, "bring us to our senses," and so forth. Action is absolutely necessary, if I want my "I" not to belong to a world of fancy. It is my "I" that has to be purified by raising it to the level of universality or the Logos. Otherwise, I may be deceiving myself.

(ii) Merit and Demerit as Forces

There are a few particularly important contributions made by the Mīmāmsā to the philosophy of ethical action. First, merit and demerit, which result from good and evil actions, are given the status of forces (*śaktis*) by this school. The Nyāya-Vaiśeṣika, like the laymen, thinks that they are qualities which the *ātman* obtains by its actions.[66] According to the two qualities, God dispenses rewards and punishments. But there is no God for at least the early Mīmāmsā and so ethical action itself must become a creative force (*śakti*) and produce the results. This force is called, as we have seen, the Unseen (*Adṛṣṭa*) and the Extra-ordinary (*Apūrva*).[67] Indeed the force or power of anything, e.g., that of fire to burn, is not seen; its effect only is seen. Hume would agree on this point. But unlike him, the Mīmāmsā does not deny the reality of force. The Nyāya-Vaiśeṣika tends to refuse acceptance of force as a separate category, saying that the power of fire to burn is the nature, part of the being (*svabhāva*, character, own being) of fire, i.e., its quality (*guṇa*). But if it is the quality or own being of fire, why do we not perceive it when we perceive fire? Such is the Mīmāmsaka contention. But the main drive of the Mīmāmsā is towards treating action as an expression of potency or force as latent activity. Such a theory is needed to explain the working of ethical actions and their results.

The above considerations lead us to raise the question: What is action? The question is important, as mentioned already, for the Mīmāmsā, although we may not get answers to all the possible questions we may raise above the topic from the side of contemporary philosophy. But we may hit upon pointers to some solutions. However, we are told by this school that action performed by the agent assumes the form or condition of potency (*dharma* and *adharma*, merit and demerit, which are *śaktis* or forces) and resides in his *ātman*. Then force (*śakti*), *dharma* (merit and demerit), and action must somehow be one and the same,[68] although we may think of them as distinct. The distinction between them is like the one between potential and kinetic energy, the latter being the potential that has become actual. If the two are the two forms or states of the same thing, then Prabhākara's insistence that force and action should be treated as separate categories does not seem to be justified. Otherwise, force has to be regarded as different from action and as coming into being as a result of action—which seems to be Prabhākara's position. But Kumārila's view seem to be simpler and more rational and straightforward than Prabhākara's which cannot easily explain how this force (*śakti* as *dharma* and *adharma*) turns itself into activity for creating the world for the agent as he deserves. The Mīmāmsā maintains that merit and demerit as latent forces reside in the *ātman* until the occasion comes for becoming active. But how do they reside in the *ātman*? Prabhākara's view is not very clear and definite, and he depends in this context on the sacred Veda too much to make his ideas intelligible. But Kumārila says that action produces an impression (*samskāra*), a kind of an imprint similar to a trauma—we may rather say that action becomes the impression, for the impression is the latent force (*śakti*)—in the *ātman* and sticks to it like an inherent quality[69] till it bursts into activity when the occasion comes.

(iii) Difference between Quality and Action Removed: Karma as Transcendental Will

Here there are two important ideas. The first is that action (*karma*) becomes a quality (attribute?) of the *ātman*, which in the context of the Mīmāmsā philosophy we may interpret as person or personality. For instance, "brave" and "cowardly" are qualities of personality which issue forth, when the occasion comes, in certain forms of activity. Still, we call them qualities which are dynamic and productive or creative[70] and so ontic. Then the Nyāya view that qualities are static, but not dynamic and productive, does not hold. Even at the level of matter some qualities which are constitutive like weight and specific gravity become dynamic in some circumstances. So if qualities can become actions (active) and actions can become qualities, then treating the two as completely different categories will not be justified.[71] The difference is only relative to the state in which we find them. The second is that, as many western writers on ethics like Bradley say, it is not "to do" that is important, but "to be." X aspires to be an ideal person, a committed Christian, a useful member of society and so on. All such ethical ideals are "to be" ideals. What X has to do follows from what he wants to be. In the reverse also, if X continues doing some particular type of actions, say philanthropical, then he becomes philanthropical. Kumārila would say that here "acting or doing philanthropical acts" ends up in "being philanthropical," which results again in doing such acts and so on. But "being philanthropical" is not a mere static quality. At the level of man "to do" becomes "to be" and vice versa.

Now when a quality becomes an act or a dynamic force, latent or patent, what will be the relation between the agent (*ātman*) and that quality or force? Kumārila says that it resides in the *ātman* till it exhausts itself through fructification. Force is of two kinds, natural and imparted. An instance of the former is that of the magnet which by nature attracts iron. An instance of the latter is heat imparted to a piece of iron; such heat exhausts itself after warming up the surroundings. Ethical actions which have become forces are of the latter kind. Yet, when they reside in the *ātman*, their relation to it, Kumārila says, is identity (*tādātmya*) or one in being or the "same self". Personality then assumes a new characteristic, a new dynamic tendency; just as when anger becomes a characteristic of my personality, it moves me forward into some action e.g., of retaliation. This force continues to work until it is exhausted. Exhaustion of the force is important for regaining the original personality and for transcending the change brought about by anger.

The Mīmāmsā,—in fact any of the Indian schools—has no clearly formulated theory of the will. Even the Greeks did not have a clear conception of this. But it is there both in India and Greece in other forms and with other names. The force which action becomes (Kumārila) or produces (Prabhākara) as part and parcel of the agent (*ātman)* is, we may say, its will, but in a transcendental form. It creates the world for the agent according to his desert, so that the nature of his world is not dependent on his mere likes and dislikes, but on the rule of ethical law, which interestingly enough is also called *karma*, regarded as the real sovereign controlling the plurality of *karmas* of the several moral agents without conflict. We may note that Schopenhauer called Māyā the Unconscious, Transcendental Will, because it is a creative force.[72] If we add to his interpretation Rāmānuja's theory that Avidyā is the form which *karma* takes—for even Māyā is, as we shall see, Avidyā with the capital A—we can see how the minds of these Indian philosophers are working in understanding action (*karma*).

Indeed, it is difficult empirically to demonstrate the transcendental processes of this force (*śakti*) of ethical actions. We can only appreciate the possibility and plausibility of the position on the analogy of man's personality and actions which issue from it. Some Mīmāmsakas call this force by the name Fate[73] (*Niyati*, rule, law, limit, that is fixed, *Vidhi*, *Vidhāna*, Vidhi is the name also of the creator god, Brahma), which, however, is produced by man himself through ethical activity. Man is the maker of his own destiny, the process of the realization of which, however, is controlled by the Higher Force (*Śakti*) that transcendentally coordinates other forces into a unity, and rules the world, which is a world of action and is meant for human action and happiness.

(iv) Ātman in the Mīmāmsā and the Nyāya-Vaiśesika

It has become common among Indian writers to dismiss the Mīmāmsā view of the *ātman* as unconscious by itself and its later view of salvation as unconscious bliss as not worth considering. The two views are those of the Nyāya and the Vaiśeṣika also. But we should not forget that even the Vedāntins regard deep sleep (*suṣupti*) as unconscious bliss. From the common man's point of view, we are unconscious in deep sleep. Besides, some later Mīmāmsakas held that heaven (*svarga*) is not a world with flower gardens, rivers, wines, and ever youthful and beautiful girls and boys, but a state of undiluted bliss (*sukha*). Some later Upaniṣads equate *svah* (often identified with deep sleep) with *svarga* (heaven). We find indications of it in *Kauṣitaki* (II, 14) also. Even the *Chāndogya* (VIII, 3,3) says that in deep sleep one meets the Brahman every day, and this meeting is blissful. We shall be wrong, therefore, in thinking that there was no line of thought to interpret the idea of heaven in terms of experience apart from poetic and mythological description, and to assimilate it to a state of one's being—which resulted in equating heaven to rest, peace, and happiness of deep sleep. The Upaniṣads, indeed, say that this is not the highest state of blissfulness and therefore needs to be transcended. But there were many who could not and did not think of anything higher. Patañjali, for instance, speaks of the souls satisfied with merging in Prakṛti (Primeval Nature); but after a time they have to be born again in the world of action and without rest and peace. One may ask: What does it matter if they want to be so reborn? The Mīmāmsakas held that every one had to be reborn after enjoying the fruits of his actions in hell or heaven. Thus this trend of thought and enquiry, search for experience, must have been current at one stage in the development of religion and philosophy and was absorbed and transcended by the Upaniṣads. However, when going beyond the stage of deep sleep and heaven, the Upaniṣads had to give a new interpretation of deep sleep, rejecting the Mīmāmsā and the Nyāya-Vaiśeṣika theory that mind and senses are left out by the *ātman*, and maintaining instead that they are absorbed into the *ātman*, that this absorption is the withdrawing of the world of perceptions, desires, and actions into itself by the *ātman*, and that without such absorption, which is an attainment, bliss or happiness is not possible. Happiness is the *ātman*'s obtaining of everything. But the need for transcending deep sleep is due to our being unconscious of our attainment and still remaining in our finitude. Deep sleep is an image of pure Prakṛti in its state of rest and equilibrium, called the causal body (*kāraṇa-śarīra*) by the Advaita. Prakṛti and deep sleep in its own way are the mythological "mother" of man's being, by obtaining rest on the lap of which man obtains his happiness and regains his exhausted strength. However, these differences of view and controversies indicate, apart from their academical and theological importance, that there was a continuous search to know what salvation as a state of existence was like and also a continuous growth of the idea of the ideal of life from worldly pleasures to those of heaven and thence to complete emancipation from bondage to the laws and vicissitudes of the world of Becoming.

(v) Heaven Like Deep Sleep

One feels that the Mīmāmsā conception of the self (*ātman*) in its discussion of epistemology and salvation is defective and needs further development. Reference has already been made to the idea[74] current perhaps at the time that salvation lies in attaining heaven (*svah* and *svarga* mean the same),[75] that the true heaven is not the mythological heaven, but a state of pure bliss which is the original nature of the *ātman*, and that that state is like deep sleep—Prabhākara is explicit on the point and Kumārila also holds the same view. Unlike the early Mīmāmsakas like Jaimini and Śabara, Prabhākara and Kumārila, as mentioned already, accepted the idea of salvation, but recommended it only to the tired souls because in salvation there is no contact of mind with the *ātman* and so no real, positive bliss, but only absence of misery.[76] For all the Indian schools, salvation lies in regaining the original pure state of the *ātman*; it is so for the Mīmāmsā also. As the state of salvation is a state without any consciousness due to lack of contact with mind, then the natural state of the *ātman* must be without consciousness and the *ātman*'s existence is like that of a stone.[77] So the Mīmāmsakas do not recommend it, although the Nyāya-Vaiśeṣika does. The latter school is open to the objection that no man will aspire for salvation as no one likes to be a stone.[78] Indeed, there is difference between being in deep sleep, merging in Prakṛti, and the Mīmāmsā heaven on the one side and being like a stone and the Nyāya-Vaiśeṣika salvation on the other. In the former position, there is the possibility of coming back to conscious life and appreciating the rest on the "mother's lap;" but in the latter, there is no return from the stone-like existence.

(vi) Ātman Not Unconscious by Nature

But the position creates an impossible situation in epistemology. The *ātman* is said to be by itself unconscious; but when mind (*manas*) with internal impressions like pains and pleasures and external impressions like colours and sounds comes into contact with it, it becomes conscious of the impressions. Consciousness then for this school is adventitious to the *ātman*. But then knowledge becomes impossible. For all cognition involves some kind of memory or recollection. In inference, premises and terms are to be held together by some mental process involving time, even though the relations among the premises and among the terms are not in time. In the cognition of the meaning of a sentence (verbal cognition) memory operates by interrelating the meanings of the constituent words, remembering their meanings and integrating them. In this sense also, all perception is recognition (cp.Plato); for the meaning of every earlier word has to be remembered and recognized in the process unifying it with the meaning of the next later word. When I perceive some object as a pen and say "That is a pen," I recognize the universal or class concept pen in the object in front. In explicit recognition like "He is my friend whom I saw some twenty years ago," the role of memory is unquestionable. There is also what the psychologists call logical memory. There are also intuitive geniuses (those with *pratibhā*, genius), whose thought works spontaneously and makes discoveries. How are these various forms of memory and intuition possible, if the *ātman* is by itself unconscious? Who retains past experiences and who brings them out? Who explodes new ideas? For the Mīmāmsā, as for the Nyāya-Vaiśeṣika, mind is an unconscious and is, for one school, an atom; and one wonders how it can bring out past impressions within itself and contact the *ātman* with them in order to evoke the latter's consciousness, which appropriates them as its own. What prompts the unconscious mind to go through this impossible process? We cannot even understand how an atomic entity which has no size at all and no inward depth even, can retain past impressions. Unlike Prabhākara, Kumārila says that mind (*manas*), although unconscious, is all-pervading. Even so, how can such a mind, so absolutely unconscious, revive past memories? The stone may retain impressions, but does not revive them. *A fortiori*, it cannot select relevant impressions, and disregard the irrelevant ones. How can it contact universals or class-concepts? How can it frame them? How then can mind be in contact with the *ātman* to arouse memory-consciousness? If mind is different from the *ātman* in being, how can it choose the *ātman* to which it can convey the impressions?[79]

If memories belong to the *ātman*, but not to the mind, how can even the *ātman* revive relevant memories if it is not naturally and inherently conscious and self-conscious? It must be conscious because all cognitions are acts of consciousness directed towards particular objects or sets of objects. This directedness, at least in the case of a search for an object is prior to the mind's contact with the object. The objection has stronger force in the case of Kumārila's view that mind is all-pervading. If it is so, is it not then in constant contact with all objects and the *ātman*, thereby making the *ātman* omniscent? To avoid the difficulty, we have to say that the *ātman* must have interest or desire for this or that object, and direct its mind towards it through the relevant sense. But interest and desire presuppose consciousness.

Kumārila indeed says that the *ātman* is conscious, but potentially. But what does "potentially conscious" mean? In his view, it means and can mean only that, when mind with an impression or idea comes into contact with it, it becomes conscious of the impression or idea. But this impression or idea has to evoke many memories, logical and psychological, before the *ātman* can say: "That is a pen." One may say that these memories as conscious past experiences are latently present in the *ātman* and that they now come up to the surface of consciousness. If "potentially" means "latently", then the *ātman* must contain consciousness at least as an attribute, which contains past impressions and experiences latently. Fresh contacts with the objects of the world then do not produce consciousness, but bring it to the surface. When the hearer's *ātman* directs its consciousness through an idea produced by its mind by bringing the words I utter in "Bring the pen from the other room," to the object, it is not the perceived object that draws the consciousness towards itself, but the *ātman* that directs the consciousness towards the not yet perceived object. The consciousness of the object here is not the result of the mind bringing an impression; it is the result of the *ātman* voluntarily directing its consciousness through an idea.

Now, the process involves self-consciousness also, i.e., the *ātman* not only has consciousness which it can direct towards the object of its interest, but can also be self-conscious even patently. All the kinds of memory and intuition and genious involve latent self-consciousness. My memory of my deceased father is not merely the appearance of a mental image, but also of my being involved in my different experiences of him. Similarly, when my logical intuition carries me to some conclusion, I can trace the different steps as being mine. In inspiration, there is welling and expansion of ideas within my conscious being, which I cannot attribute to an external agency like mind bringing impressions from outside. Furthermore, cognitions like "I am conscious that I am conscious of the object," which is reflective consciousness or consciousness of consciousness,[80] will not be possible if I am not self-conscious also. In the above example, the first "I" is conscious of the second "I." Such consciousness is self-consciousness. In this case, there is some memory, however short be the factor of the past. But it implies the possibility of patent self-consciousness without which this experience is not possible.

Potential self-consciousness, when interpreted as latent self-consciousness, may be compared to the state of deep sleep, assuming, against some psychologists who say that there is only a dream state, but no dreamless state, that there is such a state. But deep sleep is not the same as the state of salvation, and so the *ātman* comes out of deep sleep and enters either dream or waking state. In either case, it regains consciousness of a world, the dream world or the real world. For obtaining such consciousness, according to the Mīmāmsā, contact with the mind (*manas*) is necessary. We should not forget that mind is a different entity from the *ātman* for both Kumārila and Prabhākara. The question then will be: What provokes the mind to come into contact with the *ātman*? Mind does not cause itself to act; for as it is an unconscious entity, it may cause itself by chance to come into contact with any *ātman*, not necessarily the particular one to which it is supposed to belong. Nor can the potency of the *ātman*'s actions move the mind to come into such contact; for these potencies also are unconscious and need the direction and guidance of a conscious, purposive principle or entity in provoking the particular mind. In the Mīmāmsā position, the *ātman* also cannot either select the mind or invite it to come into contact; for doing either, it has to be conscious by itself even apart from contact with mind. But the Mīmāmsā denies that such consciousness naturally belongs to the *ātman*.[81] If it is accepted that mind and consciousness naturally belong to the *ātman*, it will be easy to explain why, when I wake up, my consciousness is directed through my mind and my senses towards the object of my interest such as members of my family, friends and properties. What instigates and directs my consciousness and mind can be the potency of my past actions, but this direction can still be controlled by me and by my changing ideals and objectives because I am naturally conscious and know and can know what is happening and can happen without my being entirely at the mercy of the potency (*śakti*) of my actions and an extraneous mind (*manas*). When natural consciousness is conceded to the *ātman*, salvation can be interpreted as a supreme conscious state full of bliss. Correspondingly, the status and function of mind, senses, etc., can be understood in terms of Śaṅkara's, Rāmānuja's or any other of the Vedāntic philosophers who are aware of the difficulties discussed. It is no wonder that the latest of the Mīmāmsakas turned Vedāntins.

The general Mīmāmsā view,[82] that the reality of the *ātman* is not known directly, but through the Veda and postulation, is open to question. Its position is this. The Veda says that by performing certain sacrifices one goes to heaven, and good and evil actions produce good and evil results in this and the next life. This Vedic statement leads us to postulate that there must be an entity different from the physical body which perishes at death and cannot go to heaven or the next life. That entity is the *ātman*. It has to be different from mind (*manas*), senses, etc., as all of them work for something else, not for themselves. That is, the purpose for which they operate does not lie in themselves, but in some other reality. For instance, my eye does not work merely for itself, but for my sake and in the direction I turn it. Besides, we can explain the possibility of memory by postulating a self-identical *ātman* that had the experience at one time and remembers it now.

So far the argument against the Buddhists,[83] who hold that everything, including the *ātman*, is false, holds true. But how does one get the idea itself of the *ātman* at all without some kind of direct experience,[84] vague or definite, incomplete or complete? Like Śaṅkara, the Mīmāmsakas say that it is known in I-consciousness.[85] But while Śaṅkara says that what we empirically know about the I-consciousness is not all that there is to it, the Mīmāmsakas say that it is all that that is why its knowledge does not lead to salvation or happiness, and that therefore there need be no further enquiry[86] about its nature, but only about how to be ethically active and obtain happiness. But how does one obtain this I-consciousness? Kumārila says that the I is known through a kind of inference[87] from the experience, "I know the pen." The existence of the pen is not directly known, but by inference. The pen cognized obtains the characteristic of cognizedness or knownness (*jñātatā*) and from the characteristic we infer the existence of the object to which it belongs. As there is knowledge of the pen, there must be a possessor of that knowledge and that is my "I," the subject of perception. What about knowledge or consciousness itself (of the pen)? That also is not directly known but inferred from the knownness of the object; for consciousness is not an object like a pen.[88]

But Kumārila does not realize that there can be neither inference nor postulation, unless based on something directly perceived. Is the knownness of the pen directly perceived? Are we to classify this knownness into seenness, heardness, tastedness, etc.? Are they not colour, sound, taste, etc.? Or are they different? The position at this point is vague and confusing. Or there is something in it phenomenologically and existentially profound. The Upaniṣads, we may note, accept the idea that the field of sight, for instance, is primary, and colour, the sense of sight and the possessor of sight are its poles. And from the grammarian point of view, as seeing is an activity, then colour, eye, the seer, etc., are the modes of the activity. But neither the Upaniṣads nor the grammarians say that these modes are inferred or postulated. We may say that they are existentially intuited.

Prabhākara does not accept Kumārila's position, but says that the I is not known by inference, but by perception. He maintains that I am directly conscious of my I, but only in the consciousness of the pen in front, but not without an object and by itself. Between any two different cognitions the I, even if potentially conscious, is unconscious as in deep sleep. This position is akin to Rāmānuja's.[89] For Prabhākara then I am conscious of myself only as and in being conscious of the object. This view can be true only if consciousness arises when mind comes into contact with my I, after coming into contact with the object and carrying its impress. But then how are we to explain my consciousness of my consciousness of the pen, for instance? In this instance, the object of my consciousness is the consciousness (of the pen), but not directly the pen in front, but the pen seen a moment ago and remembered. Does mind bring the first (in time) consciousness to the second (in time) consciousness as its object? Does consciousness leave an impression on mind as the pen leaves one on it? Does not mind by itself become conscious then? If so, what would be the difference between mind becoming conscious and the *ātman* becoming conscious? Then why do we need both the mind and the *ātman*? Either by itself can serve the purpose. If consciousness arises only after some interaction between mind and the *ātman*, which by themselves are not conscious, the view comes close to the Cārvāka view that consciousness arises when material particles impinge on one another like one piece of wood or stone rubbing against another and producing fire and light. The more important objection is the one given already, viz., this view cannot explain memory, which, Prabhākara himself says, is involved in all the means of valid cognition (*pramāṇas*). So we have to accept that the *ātman* ("I") is conscious of itself not merely in the consciousness of the object as in "I am conscious of the pen," but also inherently by itself. The I's consciousness of itself is of a different type from its consciousness of the pen. Consciousness of objects as such is never of the form "I am conscious of the pen," but of the form "That is a pen" or more simply "pen," in which there can be no reference to the I, although it is involved. "I am conscious of the pen" is one step removed from the straight perception of the pen and is progressing towards "I am conscious that I am conscious of the pen," in which the prior consciousness becomes the object of the later consciousness. The I and so the *ātman* are always self-conscious even without reference to an object. If we ask a man, "Do you exist?" he may be puzzled or say, "I do" thumping the ground. His behaviour shows that he is conscious of his existence, not merely of the appearance of his body or of his having a body. Consciousness of one's existence is self-consciousness.

Self-consciousness is a puzzle and a mystery for many philosophers and the common man. As Prabhākara says, I am not conscious (aware) of myself—Hume was misled by the difficulty into denying my (I's) existence—in the same way as I am conscious of the pen. Because I admit that the perception of the colour in front is my perception, Prabhākara says that I become conscious of myself in the experience "I am conscious of the pen," and this consciousness is direct awareness. Kumārila rejected direct awareness and maintained that the existence of the I is the result of some kind of inference. We have already examined these two positions. Neither has found any justification for saying that I am conscious of myself, my own existence.[90] One may concede the difficulty they experience in trying to catch their self-consciousness. The truth is that I am not conscious of my self-consciousness with any clear outward intentionality or any intentionality; self-consciousness can have no clear directedness or intentionality towards anything, not even explicitly towards itself. I am not conscious of my pure self-consciousness, not even in (a) my consciousness that I am (b) conscious of the pen. The (a) consciousness is directed towards my previous moment's (b) consciousness (of the pen); and the I in this consciousness is not self-consciousness; its consciousness is directed towards the pen, but not towards itself. One may be prompted to ask here: If the I also is included in the object of the consciousness here, i.e., in the (a) consciousness, and if the I is naturally self-conscious, does not self-consciousness become an object of the (a) consciousness? The answer is: If it were really self-consciousness, it would not be turned at all towards the object but only towards itself. (This turning towards itself is only a way of speaking; literally speaking, it is no turning at all.) There is no self-consciousness even in what the Naiyāyikas call the stream consciousness (*dhārāvāhika-jñāna*) or even the stream of consciousness of the consciousness of the consciousness *ad infinitum* of the pen. For first, there is a big jump from the perception, "That is a pen," to "I am conscious that it is a pen"—which is abridged into "I am conscious of the pen." Secondly, the Naiyāyikas cannot explain how this stream of consciousness is possible; for on their view also, no consciousness or cognition of anything is possible without contact with mind (*manas*,[91] an atom for them also), which cannot bring consciousness as an object of the I, as consciousness is generated in the I but not outside. We have already discussed this point and showed that the I must be self-conscious and retain all the previous experiences for making memory possible. Indeed, the Naiyāyikas do not admit that the stream consciousness is due to any memory, but that it is natural for man to have consciousness of the form "I am conscious of the pen" and "I am conscious of the pen, I am conscious of the pen and so on," and that all the consciousnesses are the same and identical. But if it is reflective consciousness, we have shown that they cannot be the same because the object of consciousness of consciousness is not the same as the object of consciousness, e.g., the pen. On their own admission, if the I is not self-conscious, self-consciousness cannot be grasped even in stream consciousness (*dhārāvāhikajñāna*).

We can, therefore, appreciate the difficulty of the many eastern and western philosophers who either denied explicit self-consciousness, accepting only implicit self-consciousness; or denied it altogether. Then those Vedāntins who accept the reality of the I as self-consciousness (Śaṅkara for instance) say that it is only partly or vaguely known as the I-consciousness.[92] Rāmānuja also, as we shall see, says that the *ātman*'s nature is I-consciousness, but it is fully known according to him. Then he cannot meet the Mīmāmsā objection that if the I-consciousness is the *ātman* and if the whole Vedānta (all the Upaniṣads) aim at teaching the existence and greatness of the *ātman*, then it teaches what every one knows,[93] viz., the I-consciousness. Then the Vedānta would not be needed, and the enquiry into the nature of the *ātman* would be redundant. We have, therefore, to say that the attempt to know the nature of self-consciousness, that I exist in the consciousness directed outwards will end in partial or total failure in the case of the Mīmāmsā and the Nyāya, the Cārvākas and Hume and the Humians. In addition to consciousness directed towards mind, senses, and objects and towards one's own past experiences in the re-cognition of cognitions, there is also self-consciousness, consciousness of one's existence in all acts of self-affirmation. The peculiar nature self-consciousness is, like the Unconscious as in Jung, without dimensions, fathomless. We can only indicate that it is so; fathomlessness cannot be fathomed. Our ignorance of all objectivity in deep sleep is without bounds: we are unconscious of everything, including ourselves, and so of a totality which we cannot encompass intellectually. But when we wake up, we show that the totality is an object in our assertion: "I am aware that I was absolutely unconscious of everything."

It is this self-consciousness—for I was aware that I was present in my totality in deep sleep—that is working in all my epistemic acts. Because of its infinitude it makes stream consciousness, memory, recognition and all the so-called valid forms of cognition possible. It makes possible the cognition of time by its ability to both identify itself with every instant and transcending a succession of them—thereby transcending its own successive momentary pulsations (*spandas*) of existence—and re-collecting them into hours, etc. It makes possible also the cognition of the meaning of the sentence consisting of several words uttered in temporal succession by transcending the succession of the meanings of the separate words and, again, re-collecting them into a unitary whole of the meaning-object. It is difficult to understand how all the above cognitive activity is possible, if for every cognitive act and flash of consciousness mind, which is absolutely unconscious, has to come into contact with the self (*ātman*). Nor can this theory of contact explain my sense of continuity, integrity and integrality (unity comprehending all past experiences in my personality), and being a witness (*sākṣi*) of all. For to make this phenomenon possible, mind has to be in unbroken contact with my self (*ātman*). But unbroken contact means inseparability. "I am aware that I was unaware of everything in deep sleep" implies, in the Mīmāmsā conceptual framework, that mind is inseparable all along from my I—which means again that mind is part and parcel of myself, but not a separate entity and is, therefore, with me in deep sleep also. Similarly, mind must be there also in the undiluted bliss which the Mīmāmsā calls heaven. *Self-consciousness, the consciousness of my existence, is not an existence like that of the pen—the subject of cognition can never be an object—but is the act of self-affirmation and self-assertion, which is the will affirming itself*[94] *as continuous existence.* In my deep sleep also there must therefore be my mind, which, as the Vedāntins say, lies dormant. Yet, it must be mine, not independent of me; otherwise, there is no guarantee that it will come into contact with me always and even in deep sleep or that it will not come into contact with somebody else's self that is handy to it or that many minds come into contact with the same self, as they are unconscious for this school and cannot exercise choice.[95]

NOTES

[1]P. V. Kane: *History of the Dharmaśāstra*, Vol. III, p. 838.

[2]Cp. the philosophy of Bergson. [3]See Yāska: *Nirukta*, p. 56.

[4]Valid knowledge is called *pramā* and valid means of knowledge is called *pramāṇa* in Sanskrit.

[5]There is no correspondence theory involved in this doctrine of perception.

[6]This is so far as sound as mere noise is concerned. But the theory of sound as speech and language is very complicated, and cannot be discussed in this book. See G. V. Devasthali: *Mīmāmsā.*

[7]Prabhākara's view is the same as that of Rāmānuja and may be compared to Bertrand Russell's doctrine of knowledge by acquaintance. But all the Indian theories of indeterminate perception are not the same and are not doctrines of knowledge by acquaintance.

[8]This excludes the universal negative (*Kevala-vyatireki*), as will be shown in the chapter on the Nyāya. This is not the universal negative of Western logic.

[9]G. N. Jha: *Pūrva-mīmāmsā in its Sources*, p. 105.

[10]This is the central point of the Mīmāmsā view. Since the unseen bison, remembered now, also forms part of this cognition, Prabhākara says that the object of similarity is the bison brought into cognition by similarity, and Kumārila contends that it is similarity as determined by the unseen bison or the bison as characterized by similarity. But the similarity is determined by the buffalo also. The two thinkers, in their interpretations of Śabara, perhaps miss the very significance of this distinctive means of cognition. See Ibid., pp. 154 fol.

[11]The use of the word inference in western logic to cover this form of thought process also should not confuse the student in understanding the peculiar meaning of postulation. It is perhaps better explained as "constructive imagination" and "construction of hypothesis."

[12]G. N. Jha: *Pūrva-mīmāmsā in its Sources*, pp. 157 fol. He translated *arthāpatti* by the word presumption. Some writers use the word implication.

[13]*dṛṣṭārthāpatti.* [14]*śrutārthāpatti.*

[15]Western epistemologists and linguistic philosophers may find this expansion of the explanation of hypothesis-formation interesting.

[16]As the term non-cognition (*anupalabdhi*) in the sense of a form of cognition is misleading, much controversy arose on the topic. But compare Sartre's theory of the perception of Nothing or Non-being.

[17]G. N. Jha: *Pūrva-mīmāmsā in its Sources*, pp. 161 fol.

[18]In the writings of the 8th century Mīmāmsakas, even the gods became mental conceptions, necessary for man, but not real: necessary, as otherwise, man will not be earnest in the performance of duties and sacrifices to what he considers to be merely imaginary, unreal entities. What is important is that earnestness which enables man to transcend his pettiness.

[19]See G. T. Garratt: *The Legacy of India*, Chapter on "Science."

[20]This is the general belief of ancient Indians, though hero-worship is not wanting. This belief contrasts with that of the philosophers of revealed or denominational religions.

[21]See K. Kunjunni Raja: *Indian Theories of Meaning* for this controversy, also Bhartṛhari: *Vākyapadīya.*

[22]G. N. Jha: *Pūrva-mīmāmsā in its Sources*, pp. 110 and 151.

[23]Bhīmāchārya Jhalākikar: *Nyāyakośa*, p. 855.

[24]This doctrine is called *anvitābhidhānavāda.* One may compare Bridgman's operational theory of meaning to Prabhākara's, which fits in with John Dewey's theory that the child learns through action.

[25]This view is called *abhihitānvayavāda.*

[26]Compare and contrast the Buddhist doctrine of momentariness with the Mīmāmsā theory of action, and the Nairukta theory of the Ātman.

[27]*Pra* means "well, exact" and *mā* means "the measured" derived from the verbal root *ma* meaning "to measure."

[28]L. Śrīnivāsachārya: *Mānameyarahaśyaślokavārtikam*, p. 276.

[29]Descartes raised this question to himself, whether he could trust his consciousness. The Indian epistemologists would say that, instead of doubting everything known, we should ask what forms of knowing can be relied upon and then ask when we should doubt.

[30]It may be difficult for western thinkers to appreciate this doctrine, as it is reduced by some Indian writers to coherence, correspondence, etc. See the author's *Thought and Reality*, Part III, Chapter VIII.

[31]The doctrines of illusion are called *khyātivādas* in Sanskrit.

[32]Although this is an Indian example and city dwellers of America may never have had such an illusion, I am using it, as it is one of the most classical of examples.

[33]Kumārila's view is called *viparītakhyātivāda.*

[34]Prabhākara's view is called *akhyātivāda.* This non-cognition is not the same as Kumārila's non-cognition as a valid means of knowing. The object of Kumārila's non-cognition is absence or negation, while the results of Prabhākara's is a false positive entity.

[35]Indian epistemologists do not accept non-contradiction or coherence with all the implications of B. Bosanquet's doctrine. Non-contradiction or non-compatibility does not necessarily involve implication. But coherence does. Within limits, coherence is accepted and is called *samvāda*. "This is a pen" implies "It writes"; but it does not imply or entail, the Indian thinkers would say, "The Saturn has satillites."

[36]Cp. Plato's doctrine of reminiscence.

[37]Doubt arises when two different alternatives present themselves with strong reasons in support. Then doubt is valid. If one doubts one's perception without any reason, such doubt is invalid. Invalid doubt is noticeable in abnormal persons.

[38]This question is parallel to the one in Chinese thought: Is human nature good or evil in itself and by itself?

[39]Cp. *Karmayoga*.

[40]It is difficult to find an English word for the meaning given by the Mīmāmsā. It is law in the sense of both the "is" and the "ought." In literary and philosophical works, it is used in a score of senses. In Buddhism it means everything from metaphysical reality to function, thing, quality and category.

[41]*Mīmāmsāsūtras*, I, i, 2.

[42]See the author's "Activism in Indian Thought" (*Annals of the Bhandarkar Oriental Research Institute*, Poona, Vol. XXXIX, Parts III–IV).

[43]See his comentary on the *Mīmāmsāsūtras*, I, 1, 2.

[44]G.N. Jha: *Pūrva-mīmāmsā in its Sources*, p. 173.

[45]In this book it is difficult to go deeper into the scholastic differences. But some parts of the controversy give a keen analysis of the nature of command and action. See the above works.

[46]Mādhavācārya: *Sarvadarśanasaṅgraha*, p. 147.

[47]G.N. Jha: *Pūrva-mīmāmsā in its Sources*, Chapter X. At this point, Murārī Miśra seems to have held that neither the I is an object of inference nor is it given in the first cognition, but in the self-reflection of the cognition, viz., "I know the pen." Ibid., p. 88.

[48]G.N. Jha: *Pūrva-mīmāmsā in its Sources*, p. 43.

[49]G.N. Jha does not mention the difference between the Nyāya and the Mīmāmsā on the nature of *dharma* and *adharma* (merit and demerit). They are qualities for the Nyāya, but forces for the Mīmāmsā, for which quality (*guṇa*) is a different category.

[50]The Nyāya and the Mīmāmsā handle mainly these two arguments, but not the ontological, which is indeed implied by the two.

[51]G.N. Jha: *Pūrva-mīmāmsā in its Sources*, p. 51.

[52]Nārāyana Bhaṭṭa: *Mānameyodaya*, p. 212.

[53]*Arthasaṅgraha*, p. 140.

[54]According to some interpreters, Kumārila tends to treat force as a kind of quality. He could do so by rejecting the Nyāya view that qualities and actions cannot produce effects and be causes. But Radhakrishnan says that for Kumārila *śakti* (force) is a substance. This can be justified when we observe that force can be called a quality and all constitutive qualities can be called parts and parcels of substances. For instance, the burning power of fire may be called a quality. Kumārila says that the relation of fire and its burning power can be identity (*tādātmya*) or oneness in being. All the Advaitins accept this view in explaining the relation between the Brahman and Māyā or the world. Whatever view one accepts, one should realize the tendency of our thought to identify substance, quality, action, and force (power) at certain levels of Being. The fluidity of these concepts will be discussed in the chapters on the Nyāya and the Vaiśeṣika also.

[55]In the categorization of reality, Kumārila and Prabhākara seem to have adopted that of the Nyāya-Vaiśeṣika to their own needs. In fact, we find its influence on all pluralistic cosmologies. But it is hard to prove that the adoption or adaptation is always intentional.

[56]G.N. Jha says that some interpreters of Prabhākara treat number as a quality. *Pūrva-mīmāmsā in its Sources*, p. 65.

[57]*Mānameyodaya*, pp. 171 and 306.

[58]*Yajñārthāt Karmaṇah anyatra lokah ayam Karmabandhanah.* (Man is bound, i.e. remains in bondage by the performance of all action except for the sake of sacrifices.) Here "sacrifice" is to be understood as the payment of the three debts, which are absolute obligations; for obedience to the call of these duties produces no results to be enjoyed, is not meant for rewards.

[59]Cp. *Anaucityam avidyāyāh bhūṣanam natu dūṣaṇam.* (To point to the irrationality of *avidyā* is to point to its merit, but not to its defect.)

[60]See Madhusūdana Sarasvati: *Prasthānabheda* printed with Mādhavācārya's *Sarvadarśanasaṅgraha*.

[61]See Chapter XI.

[62]This is not the same as the Kantian maxim of universalizing one's action. Kant asks: Will you accept if every other person does what you are doing? But the universalization of the *Bhagavadgītā* asks: Rise to the level of the Logos, the Universal Person and act, whether or not any one else acts in the same way. This raises ethics above mere legalism, for the Logos is not merely the structure of the Cosmic Laws, but is more as a person, merciful, just, creative, etc.

[63]See *Aitareya*. The idea is repeated in many Upaniṣads. Every form of experience like sight and touch has three aspects, *adhidaivika*, *adhibhautika* and *adhyātmika*, deity aspect, physical aspect, and human aspect. The first of the three polarises itself into the other two, which thereby become coordinates.

[64]See the discussion between Janaka and Yājñavalkya in the *Bṛahadāraṇyaka* in which the latter says that the cosmic entities like ether and fire are part realities, i.e., without the sense coordinates.

[65]Cp. *Kaṭha Upaniṣad*. The Supreme Being created the senses as directed outwards.

[66]At this point, there is an inconsistency in the Nyāya-Vaiśeṣika. It says that qualities and actions cannot be creative of any qualities and actions; only substances can be causes. Then how can good and evil actions produce merit and demerit even as qualities? Even if it is said that the possessor of such actions produces such qualities in himself, causation has finally to be attributed to actions. Without such causation, neither finite *ātmans* nor God can have any reason for producing those qualities.

[67]There are some differences among the Mīmāmsakas, particularly between Prabhākara and Kumārila on questions like: How is this force known? Is this force a separate category from substance and quality? We need not enter into them in a book of this size.

[68]This interpretation is more in agreement with Kumārilà than with Prabhākara. The former is the more generally accepted interpreter of this school than the latter.

[69]L. Srinivasacharya: *Mānameyarahaśyaślokavārtikam* p. 201. But this conception of quality is different from the Nyāya-Vaiśeṣika *guṇa*.

[70]Here G. E. Moore's objection to treating ethical predicates as natural or ontic fails and can be shown to be wrong. Cp. also Nicholai Hartmann's view that what we call existent, natural, and static qualities at lower levels become ethical ideals at higher levels, i.e., objectives as dynamic forces or values.

[71]Jaimini, the composer of the *Mīmāmsā Aphorisms* denies that action can produce action; but Kumārila, although a follower, differs from him.

[72]Even the Advaitins treat it as Force calling it *Māyā-śakti* and *Mūla-avidyā-śakti*, which controls and transcends the individual *avidyā-śaktis* called *tula-avidyā-śaktis*. Schopenhauer's teaching that this *Śakti* has to be transcended is derogatively interpreted as destruction of will to life. But the Mīmāmsā is absolutely opposed to such a position. We can see why Rāmānuja calls *avidyā* as *karma*. For the potency which my *karma* becomes is not an object of my consciousness.

[73]*Śvetāśvatara Upaniṣad*, I, 2. See the commentaries. Cp. the Greek conception of Fate, which later became Law. One doubts whether the Greeks did not have a similar conception.

[74]See the section of "Life's Ideal." [75]See *Amarakośa* also.

[76]There are a number of differences among the followers. But we cannot discuss them for want of space. We shall be concerned only with the main protagonists. The Naiyāyikas and Vaiśeṣikas also hold the same view and are criticized in the same way by the rival schools.

[77]Cp. Freud's view that the abnormally disturbed soul likes to go back to its materialistic origins—which he relates to the death instinct.

[78]In Sartre's language, no normal man likes to be a mere In-itself, but to be In-and-for-itself. Sartre is so far right, but wrong in thinking that the ideal is impossible.

[79]These observations are applicable to Western materialistic theories of the self and to similar ones of contemporary logicalisms.

[80]The Mīmāmsā position is very varied and indefinite in this context. Jaimini and Śabara hold that consciousness (*buddhi*) of the *ātman* is eternal, which implies that contact with mind also is eternal. The above criticism does not hold against them; for in heaven and deep sleep then consciousness and contact with mind lie latent and centred in the *ātman* and can become patent later. But somehow during the course of about a thousand years, the idea that the *ātman* is by nature unconscious caught hold of the Mīmāmsaka mind.

The Naiyāyikas call "I am conscious that I am conscious of the pen" *anuvyavasāya* reflective consciousness or self-confirmation. There is another form called *dhārāvāhikajñāna* or stream consciousness as in "I see the pen, I see the pen, I see the pen and so on," mere continuity of the same cognition without reflection. The two are confused by some writers.

[81]See the previous footnote.

[82]Following Śabara and Upavarṣa.

[83]We shall study Buddhism in a later chapter.

[84]*Ahampratyayavedya*, Commentary on *Vedānta Aphorisms* I,1,1.

[85]*Ahamdhī* (I-consciousness)

[86]*Ahamdhiya ātmanah siddheh, tasyaiva brahmabhāvatah, tajjñānānmuktyabhāvācca ji jñyāsā nāvakalpyate.* (If the Brahman is the I-consciousness, every one has it, but no salvation. Hence no need for the enquiry into its nature.)

[87]This inference belongs to the perceptual situation, whereas postulation of the eternal *ātman* is an ethical postulation.

[88]Similar analysis of perception is to be found in some forms of phenomenology and existentialism.

[89]The author came across a general Vedānta view that between any two activities of mind, the *ātman* assumes the state of prājñā—a name given to the *ātman* in deep sleep—and yet is conscious of itself only. But Prabhākara says that it is not conscious of itself as an I in such intervals.

[90]Even Descartes had to say: "I think, therefore I am." His interpreters denied all importance to "therefore," and maintained that the dictum was not an inference. Then why add "I think?" It is like saying that I know my existence only when I think. Prabhākara would welcome this interpretation and say that it would be like saying, "I know myself when I see an object or think of an object or idea." But the I-am must be self-conscious even when it does not become "I think."

[91]See the chapter on the Nyāya.

[92]*Ahampratyayavedya* or known as or through the I-consciousness.

[93]Rāmānuja will try to meet the objection by saying that the Vedānta teaches the nature of the I-consciousness (*ātman*, God) that is within each finite I-consciousness. But what cue or clue have we to its existence in our experience?

[94]Philosophers who say that the self is primarily will have their point here. We find the view in Augustine and Schopenhauer also. But more when we discuss Vedānta.

[95]Patañjali regards sleep as a function of *citta*, to which mind belongs as a part. For the Advaita and other Vedānta in general, all functions—mind, ego, senses, and objects—are withdrawn into *citta* like the spider withdrawing the web into itself. The world comes out of *citta* and is withdrawn into *citta*, which can meaningfully be translated as apperception, Reason, and the Logos of the Stoics.

Chapter III

The Cārvāka and Its Anti-Vedic Materialism

1. INTRODUCTION

The school of the Cārvākas may be regarded as one of those schools diametrically opposed to the Mīmāmsā with its belief in the reality of the *ātman*, of ethical potency, and of the efficacy of sacrifices to gods. Even during the time of the early Mīmāmsā, there were men who believed in the reality of God. The Cārvāka was opposed to that belief also. Another name for the Cārvākas was the Lokāyatas, meaning the worldly philosophers. None of the systematic works of this school is extant now, except Jayarāśi's *Tattvopaplavasimha* (7th century) which seems to be a summary of *Bṛhaspatisūtras*, which is lost. We get an idea of this philosophy from Jayarāśi's work, a summary of the views given by Mādhavācārya in his *Sarvadarśana-saṅgraha*, and references made to the Cārvāka by the rival schools.

It is not easy to trace the history of the Cārvāka school.[1] First, they seem to be dialectical iconoclasts of all theories, both epistemological and metaphysical. Perhaps, Bṛhaspati, the composer of the aphorisms after his name, was a dialectician of this type. We cannot determine when he lived; but he was a Vedic personality and must have belonged to a period prior to Buddha's. The Cārvākas maintained that perception alone is the valid means of knowledge and that the processes of the world are due to their own nature, but not to supernatural causation. It seems also that doubts about the absolute validity of perception were entertained, as we find in Jayarāsi's work. But later, some of the Cārvākas seem to have accepted gradually the non-theistic Sāṅkhya position that the world is due to the insentient Prakṛti (primeval material of the world) and that the *ātman* somehow gets enmeshed in it. And there seem to be other kinds of compromises with the orthodox schools.[2]

Tradition is not unanimous about who Cārvāka was. The word may be a proper name. It may also be a title meaning "one speaks sweet words," because Cārvāka is said to have taught that man ought to enjoy his life as there is nothing beyond. He is identified also with Bṛhaspati and also regarded as his disciple. Bṛhaspati is the name of the priest of gods, and he is said to have taught a materialistic philosophy to the demons for misleading them. But some scholars say that the founder of this school is a different Bṛhaspati.

The word *lokāyata*[3] is interpreted as meaning the philosophy for which the world itself is the basis or as the philosophy prevalent among the common people. We have seen that the *Śvetāśvatara Upaniṣad* refers to a set of views, according to some of which the world is due to its own nature, it is due to chance, and it is the result of the contact of cosmic sexes. The Cārvāka, as a system of philosophy, seems to have originated out of these three ideas. Although the theory of cosmic sexes does not seem to be prominent in this system, it seems to have entered it in its Sāṅkhya[4] and Tāntric forms, which are somewhat spiritualized forms of the original materialism. The Sāṅkhya treats the sentient *ātman* (Puruṣa) and the insentient Prakṛti as masculine and feminine respectively; and Tāntric worship, in its left-handed forms (lower, *vāmācāra*) contains a type of the worship of the sexes as creative principles. Indeed, these forms of the Sāṅkhya and Tāntrism were also completely sublimated, purified, and divested of all reference to human sexes. God's creativity and sex-creativity are both creativities. But the difference between the two is, in our view, not one of degree but of kind. However, in spite of the changes, all forms, both the right-handed and the left-handed, continued to exist side by side in different groups of worshipers.

It is difficult to say that the different forms of the Lokāyata school—which we may call the worldly school—originated one out of another in chronological succession. Even during the time of the *Brāhmaṇas*, there were independent thinkers who were doubting the truth of the Brahmanic religion of sacrifices and of ethical potency, for which no perceptual evidence was available. And they must have thought about life's problems and aims without the aid of the Vedic scriptures. The original founder of the Cārvāka[5] school was one of them. There was also the excessive emphasis placed by the Brahmanic religion on ritual, sacrifices, the giving up and away of everything conducive to comfortable life in this world, and the unseen ethical force. Such an emphasis must have alienated many thinkers who thought that the formalities of ritual and belief in the unseen were really meaningless, aimless, and even harmful, though supported by extensive speculative theories. These thinkers developed their own philosophies, diametrically opposed to the philosophers of Brahmanism and its allies.

2. EPISTEMOLOGY

As we do not get the epistemologies of all the Lokāyata thinkers in a systematic form, we shall confine ourselves mainly to the Cārvāka school as presented by Mādhavācārya in his *Sarvadarśanasaṅgraha* and Jayarāsi in his *Tattvopaplavasimha*. Of all the valid means of knowledge, the Cārvāka accepts only perception. Why perception has to be accepted at all is not explained, for it also may present to us illusory and hallucinatory objects. Perhaps in the original *Bṛahaspatisūtras*, it also was doubted as it is doubted by Jayarāsi. However, perception is necessary for practical life and the perception of every man has to be accepted as true for him. Such a view may lead to skepticism; but the Cārvākas were not bothered by its implications.

Inference cannot be accepted as a valid means of knowledge. Its truth depends on the truth of the major premise. But perception can never give us universal propositions and the major premise has to be a universal proposition. This view is like that of Hume in western philosophy. Furthermore, if inference is a valid means of knowledge, it must enable us to know only what is already known in the major premise through perception; then it is unnecessary; but if it gives us a new truth, i.e., if the conclusion gives us information not given by the major premise, then the latter cannot be true; but the conclusion can be true only if the major premise is true. Thus, if the conclusion is true, the major premise is true; but the conclusion can be true, only if the major premise is true. We have then the fallacies of the *petitio principi* and the vicious circle. The Cārvāka does not reject the formal structure of the syllogism, but only its usefulness to obtain imperceptible truths like heaven, the *ātman*, God, and immortality.

If it is said that the major premise can be based on causality, then the Cārvāka answers that every causation assumes the truth of the principle of causality, which is a universal proposition. But no universal proposition can be obtained through perception. No one can prove that the principle of causality obtains in this world. Everything simply happens as it does. Every event is a chance, it is nature.

We often use inference, and often our inference turns out to be true. But all our inferences are guesses. Their truth is accidental. We are able to verify our results only when we perceive the objects of the so-called inference. But if the object inferred is unperceivable, we cannot accept its truth. The *ātman*, God, heaven, etc., are unperceivable and can never be accepted.

Like inference, verbal knowledge (knowledge from speech) also is not acceptable as giving truth. Indeed, we obtain some knowledge from the words uttered by friends. But such knowledge is only perceptual knowledge of the ear. If the words mean perceivable objects, and if we perceive those objects, we think that the words are true. But if the words mean something unperceivable, they cannot be accepted as valid means of cognition. Most of the Vedic words refer to objects that can never be objects of sense perception. The Vedas cannot, therefore, be accepted as authoritative and conveying true information. Besides, they are unreliable because they are self-contradictory. In some places, they ask us not to destroy life; but in other places they tell us that we should kill animals in sacrifices. The Vedas are composed by cunning priests, who make a living by officiating at Vedic ceremonies and by obtaining gifts and who dupe credulous people with false hopes of rewards in other worlds and lives.

As inference and scriptural testimony are unreliable, other forms of valid cognition go with them.

Although the above is a fairly extreme epistemological position of the Cārvāka school, we come across references[6] to some Cārvākas who accepted inference as a valid means of knowledge, provided that the object inferred was capable of being perceived. Purandhara of about the 7th century seems to be one of them. But what cannot by hypothesis be perceived, but can only be an object of inference is rejected as non-sense.[7]

Taking what is not accepted by the Cārvākas to be that which is rejected by them, the rival schools—which are right in their assumption—argue that the Cārvākas themselves are using inference to deny the reality of the imperceptible and are, therefore, contradicting themselves. But the Cārvākas seem to have been great dialecticians interested not in proving,—unlike the Buddhists and some Advaitins, who wish to establish the reality of an indeterminate Supreme Reality,—even the reality of the perceptible world itself. It is very interesting to observe that dialectic was used in India to cut out the perceptible and also the imperceptible, although by different philosophers. However, the aim of the Cārvākas is clear: What cannot be proved to exist has to be treated as non-existent. That is, the inability to prove the existence of something is the same as the ability to prove its non-existence. This assumption gave an opportunity to the rival schools to assail the Cārvākas. Even the view of the Cārvākas that everything is as it is, that everything is due to nature, and everything is a chance and nothing has a cause, contains universal propositions that cannot be supported by perception. So their position also is wrong. We cannot accept inference merely within perceivable limits. All principles are not perceivable; and if principle means an abstract law, then no principle is perceivable. The Cārvāka epistemology remains, therefore, self-contradicted. The aim of the Cārvākas was to cut out the very roots of what they considered to be false and superstitious theories by disallowing inference itself, which helped the rivals to show the reality of the *ātman*, etc. But their criticisms overshot the mark, became a boomerang, and struck the Cārvākas themselves. In attempting to free themselves from the impasse, they dissipated themselves into different sub-schools, made various compromises, and seem to have either gradually got absorbed into the spiritual tradition[8] or degenerated into its absurd imitations.

3. METAPHYSICS

We may call the Cārvākas materialists and naturalists, because they believed in the ultimate reality of only physical nature. Everything else is a form which the natural elements assume. The processes by which the elements assume the forms are also natural, not guided or controlled by any supernatural agency.

Categories Curiously enough, the four elements—earth, water, fire, and air—are given as the categories (*tattvas*) of reality. All the other categories are rejected as not being objects of perception. Indian philosophers generally accept a fifth element, aether (*ākāśa*). The basis for accepting five elements is that we have five senses—smell, taste, vision, touch, and hearing—each of which has its own specific object. Smells are cognized only through the nose, colours only through the eye and so on. The objects of the senses are qualities. Hence, it was thought that the five qualities must belong to five different substances or elements. The Cārvākas accept the sense of hearing, but not the corresponding element, aether, to which sound is said to belong. They say that sound is caused by the movement of air-particles, which impinge upon one another and finally on the ear-drum. In saying so, they are certainly making an inference, which makes them open to the criticism of the rival schools that the Cārvākas are using what they reject. Moreover, it is not also true that we perceive the four elements, but only their qualities. The Cārvāka position contradicts our experience here also. However, they thought that we perceive the four elements, but not aether.

It is doubtful whether the Cārvākas accepted the atomic theory; for the atom is imperceptible and the Cārvākas do not accept the reality of anything imperceptible. They must have meant by atom the smallest perceptible particle.[9]

Man and Consciousness The four kinds of elements come together and constitute everything including man. Man also is nothing but a combination of the four elements. The differences among the types of objects in the world are due to the differences among the patterns in which the four elements combine with one another. What is called the *ātman* is nothing but the physical body of man. But if the *ātman* is the same as the physical body, why do we distinguish between a living man and a dead man? The Cārvākas admit that there is a difference between the two; but the difference is not due to the presence of the imperceptible *ātman*. If the *ātman* is different from the body, nobody will say: "I am fat," "I am tall" and so on. What is fat or tall is the body. The living man is indeed conscious, but consciousness cannot exist apart from the body. It is only a quality of the body. When the material particles of the body come together in a particular ratio and pattern and form a particular structure, the quality of consciousness emerges. It is only an emergent quality. But when the pattern deteriorates and the body disintegrates and is destroyed for some reason, the constituents tend to separate themselves and the emergent quality disappears. We find such emergences in other cases and we cannot explain why emergence of a new quality takes place. It is simply natural and has not super-natural cause. For instance, when yeast is added to grape juice, the latter becomes wine and acquires a new quality, viz., that of intoxicating power, which is possessed neither by yeast nor by grape juice. This power is an emergent quality.

GOD AND ETHICAL POTENCY As consciousness disappears at death, there is no *ātman* that survives death. If there is an *ātman*, it ought to return now and then to earth to visit its family and friends to whom it is naturally attached. We do not need God or ethical potency to create the world and its forms, because the elements naturally come together and produce the forms without any purpose in creating the world. We may call this view of the world mechanistic (*yadṛcchāvāda*) on the whole. But it is not even mechanistic in the strict sense of the term, for even mechanism has its laws, which are universal. We have seen that the Cārvākas do not accept any laws. Their position is a kind of tychism, all events happening spontaneously. But as the Cārvākas speak of the nature of things, one may read a kind of mechanism into their philosophy. But they were unaware of the full implications of a mechanistic view of the universe. In any case, they were opposed to teleology in the universe.

4. LIFE'S IDEAL

As the *ātman* is identified with the physical body itself, pleasure is the ideal of life. Of the four ideals of life,the Cārvāka accepts only wealth and enjoyment. The pleasures are the pleasures of the senses and mind. We should remember that mind, for this school, is consciousness, which is an emergent quality of the body. The Cārvākas are thus eudomonists, hedonists, sensualists, and subjectivists. As there is no life after death, man ought to derive as much pleasure as possible in this life itself. The rival schools treat the Cārvākas as demons and evil persons, who do anything for the sake of momentary pleasure. But it seems that, like Epicurus, they taught controlled satisfaction of the desire for pleasures. It is even thought that they were vegetarians. For even Mādhavācārya, one of their rivals, represents them[10] as teaching

> Live happily so long as you live,
> Borrow money and drink butter.
> When the body is turned to ashes,
> How can you to the world return?

Here the Cārvākas ask men to borrow money, if they do not have it; they do not ask men to steal. They ask men to drink butter (i.e., boiled and clarified), but not wine. They do not ask them to eat flesh. They seem to have preached against all bloodshed. In the *Mahābhārata*[11], we read that one of them was burnt to death for condemning Yudhiṣṭira, who in the great war killed thousands of his kith and kin for regaining his kingdom. He lost also thousands of his own followers, with the result that very few were left alive to congratulate him when he ascended the throne. But Yudhiṣṭira's courtiers caught hold of the Cārvāka for his impudence and burnt him, saying that he was an enemy in disguise. But why should the enemy disguise himself as a follower of the Cārvāka school, if it was in disrepute? He could have disguised himself as the follower of a respected school. However, the Cārvākas, as the story shows, were against bloodshed. Atheists and materialists can also be ethical personalities, however inadequate their metaphysical position may be. The above story is a good illustration.

It looks as though the Cārvākas were not only materialistic and naturalistic, but also humanistic, treating the natural, this-wordly man himself as the *ātman*. The worship of the *ātman* was its full realization; and its realization was the satisfaction of the living, human body.[12] Such a view of the *ātman* is a corollary of the main Cārvāka position that everything is simply what it is, that it is natural, not further explicable in terms of causes, seen, unseen, or unseeable. Man desires pleasures, lives for them; and pleasure is obtained by the satisfaction of desires and urges. Heaven is not anything supernatural, but a state of pleasure, which man obtains from eating good food, from the embraces of beautiful girls, and from fine arts. Pleasure is here and in this world. Hell is the pain we experience with our bodies in this world, not in another. God is the well-known king or emperor, who can make us comfortable and happy. Liberation is death itself. There is nothing supernatural and other-worldly. The way of the sacrificial religion belongs to fools; and the way of asceticism to the impotent. The followers of either attain nothing.

In the ethics of the Cārvākas we find not only hedonism, but also a thorough-going, this-worldly humanism. One can discover in this philosophy not only Protagoras's doctrine that man is the measure of all things, but also that, as he is such a measure, he, as the living body, and his interests are supreme. The Cārvākas were originally, it seems, not mean devils, but were interested in politics and fine arts. According to them, the only book worth studying was not the Veda, but the one embodying the political laws of the country. The orthodox writers interpret the Cārvākas as exhorting their followers to violate every law—if the violation is for pleasure—except that of the state, as otherwise they will be punished. But a charitable interpretation will be that the Cārvākas wanted political stability instead of chaos, so that man could enjoy his life in peace and security. Fine arts like music, dance, and poetry make life pleasant and worth living. It is said that the Cārvākas encouraged all the arts of life and political freedom and stability consistently with their philosophy.

However, it should also be said that their naturalistic and materialistic hedonism supported everything that the ruler could do—a Machiavellian policy and strategy. There is nothing that is objectively right. Jayarāsi at the end of his *Tattvopaplavasimha* says that his book supports every means of acquiring wealth and power, as it rejects and proves to be false all the rival categories. There were several sub-schools of the

Cārvāka, each holding its own views. Some of them must have expounded some doctrines like those of the Greek Sophists: Might is right (Callicles); Accident makes an action right (Thrasymachus). We have already mentioned that Bṛhaspati, the earliest of the Cārvākas, and Jayarāsi, much later, maintained that nothing can be proved, not even perception is invariably true.

Scepticism is an indication that man is struggling to establish indubitable truths and is encountering failure. We have already referred to the sceptics living in the early Buddhist and pre-Buddhist periods. Ajita, Purāṇa Kassapa, and Sañjaya are some of them. But they were not monsters, but simple and enlightened men; some of them were even ascetics. Ajita,[13] for instance, was known for the rough blanket (*keśakambala*), which alone was his possession. Sañjaya could not accept any ethical view as the only right one and wanted to be tolerant of every one. There were some, like Mokkhali Gośāla, who thought that every event happened out of necessity, Fate[14] (*niyati*). All were deeply affected by the evil in the world and by the killings in the name of ethics and religion with super-sensible justifications. It is difficult to say that all such thinkers were Cārvākas, although the orthodox thinkers often clubbed them together.

5. COMPROMISES AND TRANSFORMATIONS IN THE CĀRVĀKA SCHOOL

It was difficult for the Cārvākas to adhere strictly to their sensationalism, scepticism, naturalism, materialism, hedonism, and humanism, which they formulated in the beginning. The terms *cārvāka* and *lokāyata* became terms of abuse, and people did not know what evil a Cārvāka would or would not support in the ethical field of human and social relationships. We can guess that, in the hands of many lesser minds, hedonism became the philosophical support for wine-bibling, licentiousness, and sexual and social chaos. In political theory, the Cārvākas could not furnish any standard for curbing the activities of a tyrant, as they removed the fear of an authority higher than the king or emperor. They could not remove also the conflicts among the different doctrines they preached. So on the one side, a complete degeneration and, on the other, an absorption by different spiritual traditions set in. And the Cārvākas seem to have completely vanished from the Indian philosophical scene. Unfortunately, the history of the gradual transformation is not clear, but can be observed only in the results.

The Cārvākas upheld the doctrine that the physical body itself is the *ātman* and that it is nothing but a compound of different material particles. But they could not hold on to the doctrine for a long time. Later, they divided themselves into four[15] schools: the first maintained that the *ātman* is the physical body itself; the second that it is the senses; the third that it is breath; and the fourth that it is mind (*manas*). Naturally, the problem arose how to realize the *ātman*, if the "I" is any one of these or even the elements of the material world. If I am really the material elements, I should experience this identity. But I do not; I feel that my body is my object. The problem becomes, therefore, how I can realize this one-ness. By the time this question was raised, the Sāṅkhya philosophy of Kapila was current and expounded the doctrine of Prakṛti and the Puruṣa (primeval matter and spirit). Rejecting the reality of the

Puruṣa, the Cārvākas seem to have advocated absorption (*laya*) in Prakṛti, the mistake of which theory seems to have been pointed out by Kapila to one of the Cārvākas by name Asuri.[16] In this context, the Cārvākas preached even detachment (*vairāgya*) from the world, i.e., its renunciation— which is opposed to hedonism. If our *ātman* is the body and the body consists of blood, bones, flesh, and filth, it is something to be detested. Man has, therefore, to become one with the pure elements, the origin of which is Prakṛti. Immortality is the fame which man leaves behind for the good and noble deeds he has performed.[17]

There was another transformation of the doctrine that the body is the *ātman*. Some thinkers did not accept that immortality was possible without the physical body. The body itself has to be made immortal. What can exist is only matter. The immortality of the body is, therefore, the preservation of the living body for ever. Such preservation, it was thought, was possible by taking a drug prepared from mercury. Mercury is Lord Śiva, the Supreme Godhead. Curiously enough, Lord Śiva is represented as teaching the doctrine to his wife.[18] Mercury is Lord Śiva and manganese his wife. The maintenance of the world is due to a combination (contact) of the two. Śrinivasacharya says that this doctrine, according to one Bhāskara, is taught by Buddha[19]—which cannot be true. To attribute the doctrine to Lord Śiva or Buddha is perversity and is indicative of the Cārvāka attempt to ingratiate itself with the orthodox spiritual tradition and Buddhism. It may be indicative also of some forms of degeneration of Śaivism and Buddhism in their religious beliefs and practices and of their compromising with materialistic traditions and physical needs.

Another form of spiritualization of the Cārvāka humanistic religion is the transformation of the worship of the *ātman* as indulgence in bodily pleasures to treating it as the centre of the universe, as the microcosm of the macrocosm. In the Upaniṣads we come across the ideas that the great gods are the senses, the life principle, etc., and that the greatest of them is the *ātman* as the ultimate presiding deity and spirit. We have seen in the *Aitareya Upaniṣad* how the correlativity of the microcosmos and macrocosmos was enunciated. Then the realization of the macrocosmic Universal Spirit can be attained in the microcosm, i.e., the body. The living human body is, therfore, not a despicable object to be shunned, but the locus of the activities of the Universal Spirit. The concept of the living, conscious, human body, thus sublimated, completely transformed and transvalued the original Cārvāka materialistic and hedonistic concept into a spiritual one. The Upaniṣadic philosophy thus gave the Cārvāka concept a dignity that the Cārvākas themselves could not give.

The above sublimation did not prevent a degenerate development also. The idea of the interplay of cosmic sexes led to forms of worship involving the interplay of human sexes. Although sex-worship was prevalent among many primitive people including the pre-Aryans of India and was condemned by the Aryans of the Vedic times, it obtained a new significance in some forms of Tāntrism,[20] whether it involved the idea that the body itself is the *ātman* or the idea that the body is only a vehicle of the *ātman*. Thus arose some of the degenerate and despicable forms of the Kāpālika[21] and Sahajīya sects. It is unnecessary to narrate the view of these sects, which are philosophically unimportant, except the fact that they are based on the idea, in a most perverted form, of the cosmic significance of the human body. It is perhaps not justifiable to attribute all the perverted forms to the original Cārvākas, who seem to be humanistic and law-abiding. They preached against caste distinctions, but they do not seem to have preached the violation of such distinctions in unethical and immoral ways. In any case, the above degenerations and sublimations of the Cārvāka doctrines seem to have resulted in the complete vanishing away of the school from India. If a critical history of the Cārvākas is ever written, it will show why a robust and virile humanism, based upon materialism and this-worldly nature, should not attempt to become a religion and develop cults and rites, which have necessarily to be oriented towards realities behind the world of physical matter. Otherwise, it may lapse into perversities and bring about its own ruin. We can see positivism and worship of man, as taught by Comte in the Cārvāka philosophy and we can find an example also in it of how such a teaching can degenerate. Religion involves the idea of realizing our one-ness with our source. But materialistic humanism does not regard the realization of our one-ness with matter as the life's ideal. On the contrary, it wants man to be distinct from matter and wrench out of the material world as much of the non-material values as possible, even if the values and our life are evanascent and unsteady. Here lies the reason for the inherent philosophical inadequacy of a purely materialistic humanism. This insufficiency led the Cārvākas to various compromises and their final downfall. Non-material values cannot have their basis in matter. If based in matter, they cannot be anything more than what belongs to man with his selfish, biological drives. And if these drives are treated as the highest guides—materialistic humanism cannot but so treat them—man, instead of rising to a higher level, lowers himself; and the attempt to sublimate the drives, on the basis of materialistic humanism, results in perversity. Such a result can be avoided if the values are derived from a spiritual principle. It was self-destructive for the Cārvākas to go beyond human and social welfare.

GENERAL ESTIMATE AND CONSTRUCTIVE COMMENT

(i) Developments of the Cārvāka and the Taittirīya Sheaths

Although the Cārvāka philosophy was generally dismissed as unworthy of consideration, inimical to ethics and religion, and illogical, we have seen in the last section that it is not generally so. It is more appropriate to call it naturalism and humanism than to call it an unethical materialism. Indeed, one may draw unethical conclusions,[22] as some followers of the Cārvāka did; but one may also show that a supernatural justification of ethics and religion may lead to non-humanistic and even anti-humanistic conclusions, as John Dewey[23] in the West has pointed out. Even from the highest type of the Vedānta of Śaṅkara, one may draw harmful conclusions, as it holds that "I am the Brahman"—which may lead one to think that he can do anything irrespective of moral laws. We should not forget that the Cārvāka started as a philosophy of life, which discussed: What is man?, What is his aim in life?, How can he achieve it?, but not as a mere intellectual curiosity or solely with the intention of dethroning the Brahmanic way of life. All metaphysics was meant at that time—and in the author's opinion, it should mean so now also—to elucidate a way of life as an intellectually articulated religion, but not merely as an intellectual exercise in speculative constructions. Even the metaphysics of the Cārvāka or rather its denial of metaphysics was meant to be a way of life and for a way of life.

The attempt to provide an absolute proof for the existence of God, soul, and the moral law have all failed and their failure is acknowledged not only by most of the theologians in the West, but also by most of the Vedāntins in India. All that is possible to offer is a phenomenological and existential analysis of human experience in the realms of nature, ethics, and religion—which may be a different kind of proof, if it is to be called proof—but not a conclusive, syllogistic inference. We may have to accept that ultimatley inference is meant not for any conclusive proof of something absolutely unknown so far, but as an instrument for intellectually articulating the conceptual patterns involved in the several forms of experience in a way not to destroy its integrity and integrality, but to correct its aberrations. In this way, the ideas of our own existence and the existence of the world around us check one another. We may remember also Kant's difficulties in establishing the reality of the soul, immortality, and God, and even the idea of the totality of the world. We may recall furthermore the difficulties of inductive logic, faced and acknowledged by Hume and Mill. We may note the *Vedānta Aphorism*,[24] which says that logic (*tarka*) can be used for proving anything and everything and so cannot reach absolute certainty (*apratiṣṭhānāt*). All the Vedāntins accept this view. We know that not only science, as started by Bacon, but also great philosophers like Spinoza rejected teleology in nature. If God or Nature is the ultimate truth, he or it can have no purpose in creating the world. This is one of the reasons given by a number of Indian schools—the Cārvāka, the Mīmāmsā, and the Sāṅkhya—for not accepting the reality of God. Even Śaṅkara accepts the validity of this reason and says that we should not, therefore, accept the reality of a personal God, but only of an impersonal Absolute (Parabrahman), which is ultimate Being. Aristotle also, in spite of accepting the reality of God as Pure Form, accepts some ultimate tychism. Even if we say that a particular event occurred because of a particular causal law, we cannot explain why the causal law is as it is. In the history thought, some people maintained that the mechanistic view of the world is superior to the teleological and the spiritual. But even they could not explain why the world is a mechanism. And indeed, even the mechanistic view is of late superseded in science also by a kind of statistical view, and chance is a factor in statistics.

Then why were the Cārvākas looked upon with contempt by the other Indian philosophers? A humanism that is limited only to the natural man, man as known only in the phenomenal world, cannot form an adequate basis even for ethics, not to speak of religion. For the objectivity of ethical law requires the reality of the spirit in man as distinct from his body, and as capable of carrying with it merit and demerit and of being virtuous and vicious. The body as such is neutral to such qualifications. And religion involves the idea of the continuity of life after death in some form. That the inadequacy of their idea of the self was realized by the Cārvākas is shown by the gradual transformation it went through in its history—from the aim of life as self-centred interest and licence to do anything, to political stability involving some sacrifice of self-interest, to non-violence and vegetarianism, to the realization that undiluted pleasure is not possible with the body, to the view that the true I (self) that enjoys and enjoys bliss is constituted by the senses, or the life-principle (breath, *prāṇa*), or mind (*manas*)—until the idea of the Vedānta gained ground that man's body is not merely a structure of material particles, but is a microcosm of the macrocosm containing several layers of inward being reaching up to the Supreme Spirit, which can, therefore, be realized by understanding and analysing the being of man himself, thereby making man the clue to the secret of existence and the pathway to the Absolute Spirit. Man's and so humanism's significance is not thereby lost, but is deepened. At this juncture, the Cārvāka must have been completely absorbed by spiritual philosophies.

The transformations which the Cārvāka theory underwent are naturally reflected in the Advaita theory of sheaths (*kośas*) of the *Taittirīya* Upaniṣad[25]—the physical, biological (vital), mental, rational, and blissful—which are not, indeed, given by the Upaniṣad as sheaths, but as *ātmans* (selves), each lying inside the other and controlling it. These are really levels of my existence as man.[26] We find similarly in the *Kaṭha Upaniṣad*[27] seven levels mentioned of existence or of the self, the seventh being the highest, beyond which there can be nothing. This highest level is that of the Puruṣa (the highest Person), the Absolute I-consciousness. We do not know whether the Cārvākas whose ideas reached the highest level were earlier than the Upaniṣads or vice versa. Very likely the Upaniṣads were earlier than they, at least as a school of philosophy; but the ideas of the Cārvākas—without being known as Cārvāka ideas—may be earlier than the Upaniṣads. Anyway, the Cārvākas who reached the idea of the Puruṣa could not have remained materialistic and naturalistic, but must have been absorbed by the Sāṅkhya and the Vedānta. Unconscious nature accepted by the Cārvākas became the Primeval Nature (Prakṛti) of the Sāṅkhya, which is distinct from the Puruṣa (*ātman*); and the merging in Prakṛti,[28] which came to be accepted as the ideal of life by some later Cārvākas, came to be given by the Sāṅkhya a lower place than realizing the identity with the Puruṣa,[29] as mentioned already, Asuri, a follower of the Cārvāka in the beginning, was converted by Kapila to the Sāṅkhya view. Asuri is one of the important names in the Sāṅkhya tradition. This conversion was due to the realization that to become one with Prakṛti does not provide security from rebirth in the world of suffering and death. For birth and rebirth belong to the spontaneity of nature, in the same way in which it belongs to the spontaneity of deep sleep to make the self emerge again with all its senses, organs, and objects.

(ii) Prakṛti as Deep Sleep and as Blissful

It is the general Upaniṣadic belief that deep sleep is blissful and restful. We know that in the *Bṛhadaraṇyaka Upaniṣad*, Indra rejected the self of deep sleep as not the highest self; and Prajāpati, his teacher, had to instruct him on how to know the highest self. That deep sleep is akin to, and is part of Prakṛti—of Māyā, according to the Advaitins, who call it Prakṛti also—is, as already mentioned, a common idea of the Vedānta and must have been a common idea among the later Cārvākas also. All is bliss and peace in it because there is nothing to be desired and no feeling of any lack or want. For the whole universe of the soul—past, present, and future, attained, unattained, and attainable—is all centred in it and absorbed and assimilated into one integrality and massive unity. This absorbtion and assimilation is the same as taking in everything and leaving out nothing to be desired. As Kant and the Kantians would say, it is the fullest satisfaction of the senses, mind, and ego, a returning by them with their objects to themselves and finally to the self. The general tendency, both in the East and the West, to dismiss the idea of deep sleep as not blissful is due to our preoccupation with the world of the waking state and to the wrong conception that deep sleep is like a dark box into which we squeeze ourselves and out of which we come, but not that it is the *ātman* with its mind, senses, and organs withdrawn into itself. In this withdrawal, they rest and get refreshed, and the self feels happy. We tend to forget that the identity and continuity of the self lies through all the three states, not merely in the waking state, and that pleasures do not exist in the objects we enjoy, but in the activity of enjoyment, which is in our case a reflection of the state of attainment characteristic of the highest self.

However, that the Cārvāka conception of the *ātman* (I) reached the stage of deep sleep and Prakṛti (Primeval Nature) is significant and is indicative of the drive of the Cārvāka thought towards the idea that the fullest happiness can be found only in the realization of one's true and full self (*ātman*). We are not sure whether this school developed the idea that the self (*ātman*) in deep sleep—in the complete Unconscious—withdraws its senses and organs into itself, but only that they found their greatest happiness in merger in Prakṛti, which is akin to deep sleep. We may perhaps trace the growth of the theory of the *Taittirīya Upaniṣad* that of the different lower and higher *ātmans*, the lower is the body of higher, and that the lowest is not the self (*ātman*) of anything else and similarly the highest is not the body of anything else, to some conception of the body as the soul, which is the same as that of the Cārvākas. More importantly, we should note that, according to Kasmir Śaivism and some of the late Upaniṣads—perhaps influenced by Kasmir Śaivism—the whole world is my body.[30] This view is implied by and involved in the general Upaniṣadic tradition. For Rāmānuja the whole world is the body of the Supreme Being. If I am in some sense one with the Supreme Being, then in the same sense the world will be my body also. All that the Cārvāka did at first was to stop with the physical body as the highest Ātman (Self) without realizing and accepting that the *ātman* had to be distinct from the body which is its own outward object. As the *ātman*, according to the *Taittirīya* has different levels, the body also has different levels. All through the Upaniṣadic thought and its development, the thinkers, however, always spoke of the levels as the levels of the *ātman* (self), but not as the levels of the body also, as the body was finally to be left back (or absorbed into the *Ātman*). But the bodily levels are implied, as the lower is called the body of the higher. In this line of development of thought, there is involved an interesting and significant philosophy of the body, which is not merely some dumb matter and filth—the physical body becomes so only at death—but much more.

The main shortcoming of the Cārvākas—so far as their writings are known—is their wrong conception of the self as mere consciousness and that as mind. In fact, they did not originally draw a distinction between the self (*ātman*) and mind (*manas*)—an important distinction common in most Indian schools. But curiously enough, the idea that consciousness arises adventitiously when some material particles strike each other or one another or rather when they come together and impinge on one another, sounds a little similar to the Mīmāmsā and the Nyāya view of consciousness arising by a kind of impact of the mind on the *ātman*, both of which are by nature unconscious. There are indeed important differences among the three schools; but the common point is that consciousness is due to some kind of impact on each other of unconscious entities. *What all the three lack or deny is the truth that the ātman is inherently self-conscious, not merely conscious of objects when it perceives them.* As shown in the chapter on the Mīmāmsā, without self-consciousness (I-consciousness) and its continuity, no memory, no experience of happiness or misery, and none of the valid means of cognition are possible; and indeed, neither ethics, nor legal justice, nor religion is also possible. The general argument against the momentariness[31] of the I-consciousness as advocated by Buddhism, viz., that none of the above is possible, applies *mutatis mutandis* to the Cārvāka and the other two schools in different ways.

(iii) Self and Self-consciousness as Distinct from Sense, Mind, Etc

There is further unclearness at this point in the Cārvāka position. Consciousness, they say, appears when some material particles come together, impinge on one another, and get structured. Then does the structure become merely conscious? Does it become self-conscious also? In the former case, consciousness can only be my bodily sense, which is the consciousness of the "I" in "I am six feet tall." Even here the body which is six feet tall is an object, not the subject of the I-consciousness. In the latter case, I can hardly justify my body being self-conscious. If it is self-consciousness, it cannot be an object of my I-consciousness; but it is such an object. No self-consciousness as such can be an object of my consciousness. Moreover, if the body can be self-conscious, then so long as the structure of the material particles which constitute it lasts, it must remain self-conscious. Then dream, dreamless sleep, faint, forgetfulness, etc., will not be possible. Again, if the body is self-consciousness, i.e., consciousness that knows only itself, how then can consciousness of the objects of the world arise? The latter consciousness is directed outwards, not to the body itself. The body as self-conscious can have its consciousness limited only to itself; but to be conscious of other objects, it has to reach out to them.

In the later development of the Cārvāka, we have found that the I, I-consciousness (*ahamdhī, ātman*) was distinguished from the body but was equated perhaps successively, to the senses, breath (life principle), and mind (*manas*). But again, we hardly justify that the senses, life principle, or mind can be self-conscious. We do say that the ear hears, the eye sees, life lives, and mind minds. But we should not be misled by such expressions. They are only descriptions of the functions of the eye, etc. Assuming that the senses are self-conscious, in the easily intelligible example, "The red rose smells nice," the eye that sees the red colour does not smell, and the nose that smells does not see. Then it is absurd to say that my "self-conscious" eye smells the rose, thereby bringing the experiences of colour and smell together. We have already shown that without self-consciousness this bringing together is not possible. I see the rose, I smell the rose; then I know that I see the rose and smell it. Without my ability to transcend instantaneous perceptions—without the transcendental ego or epoche of the "I" in Husserl's terminology—the judgment, "The red rose smells nice," cannot be made. The sense of sight or the sense of smell by itself cannot be self-conscious and cannot rise to the level of the reflection, "I am conscious of the colour or smell", not to speak of "I am conscious that I am conscious of the colour or smell." Neither experience is possible without self-consciousness, which none of the senses possesses. Nor can life be self-conscious. In sleep, fainting, coma, etc., life is present, but is not even conscious. Bergson indeed speaks of life as *elan vital*, intuition, time, etc. But he does not speak of what is here meant by life. Self-consciousness is involved in the intuition of time; for without it, the assimilation of every moment of time consciously to a self-identity is not possible. In the experience of time, there is the experience of the retention of every moment of the past. But there is no such experience in the case of the least lower animals, which have life, but little or no retentive ability, and so no self-consciousness as in "I am conscious of X" or "I am conscious that I am conscious of X."

We cannot justify also that mind (*manas*) is self-conscious and brings the perceptions of colour, smell, etc., together. It is not clear what the Cārvākas who held that mind is the *ātman* (self) meant by mind. It can be roughly what Aristotle meant by "common sense." Generally it is called by Indian philosophers the inner instrument (*antahkaraṇa*), the function of which is to unite all the sensations and present them to the *ātman*—however the relation between *ātman* and mind is conceived, whether mind is a different entity as in the Mīmāmsā and the Nyāya or somehow part and parcel of the *ātman* itself, coming out of it for experiencing the phenomenal world—and also to convey pleasures and pains to it. Generally it is said, "Mind experiences pleasures and pains"; but it is like saying, "Eye sees colours." But really *I experience* colour and smells, pains and pleasures.

Now, this inner instrument cannot be said to be self-conscious. And without being self-conscious, it cannot justifiably be the *ātman*. Even if we do not use the word "instrument," which implies that it is the instrument of something else, we cannot rightly treat mind as self-conscious. We have understood mind as that which performs the function of receiving the impressions of the different senses and uniting them into phenomenal objects and of conveying pleasures and pains to the *ātman* or as the sense for which pleasures and pains are objects. The objects of unified impressions and also of pleasures and pains are conveyed, according to most of the Indian schools, to the *ātman* for enjoyment and suffering and also for appropriation as its own—the process responsible for the experience of "mine," as distinguished from "thine" and the neutral. Thus appears the ego or the egosense.

To the western reader the above explanation is not enough to justify the distinction between the *ātman* and mind and the denial of mind as self-conscious. If mind is self-conscious, it will be the same as the *ātman*, and the difference between the two will only be verbal, a question of terminology. In modern western psychology and philosophy, the word mind is used to mean many things, sometimes written as "mind" and othertimes as "Mind" as in the expression "the Absolute Mind." The term means vaguely everything psychological and spiritual. This makes it difficult for the modern western reader to appreciate the difference, although in the history of western philosophy, distinctions such as *psyche*, *nous*, soul, spirit, etc., have been made. Then is the concept of mind, as distinct from the *ātman* (spirit, I-consciousness) necessary? Why should we not allow the same entity to perform both functions?

There are real difficulties to face, if we treat the two as identical. For the present argument, it is indifferent whether we treat either as atomic or infinite,[32] although we cannot understand how the *ātman* can retain all the past experience in itself if it is not infinite. However, if the two are one and the same, as some Cārvākas wish to maintain, we have to treat mind as infinite; otherwise, we cannot understand and cannot explain how we can experience a star millions of light years away, with which the sense of sight comes into contact, relate it to some past experience, and say, "That is a star." An atomic mind, even if granted self-consciousness, cannot have enough mental space to retain and relate past experiences to the present one. Besides, when I see the star, I locate it far away—whether the star has gone out of existence by the time I locate is not important for the present consideration—and this locating is done by my mind, not merely by my sense of sight, and both have to reach out to that distance. If mind is atomic, it cannot extend that far. It cannot make the judgment, "That is a star." But the more important consideration is, when I am in the act of seeing the star with mind and sense fixed on it, I do not comprehend myself, I cannot know myself also along with the star. That is, I am also struck, bound to the star—which implies that my I-consciousness (*ātman*) also is extended thus far. That is why I am able to say, "I see the star." So neither my *ātman* nor my mind, nor my sense is atomic or even limited to my body.

But why then should we hesitate to identify mind and the *ātman*? If the *ātman* is infinite and all pervasive, then it must be in contact with all objects and must be omniscient; but I am not omniscient. Then there is something between my *ātman* (I-consciousness) and the object that makes the *ātman*'s consciousness directed towards a particular object or objects at a time, and that something is mind, operating and limiting the all-pervasive *ātman* and the all-pervasive senses. That is why some Advaitins say that the Ātman as limited (*avacchinna*) by mind (*manas*, *antahkaraṇa*) is the finite soul. We say now and then: "My mind is dull, it is tired and needs rest." We need not depend on these expressions for establishing the validity of our view; we have to note the drive of the argument based upon self-reflection and analysis of experience. In spite of the infinity and all-pervasiveness of the *ātman*, we see somethings only at some times. Secondly, we remember only somethings at some times; that is, we remember only those experiences which we want to remember and often forget some even if we want to remember them. This experience must be due to a mediating link between the all-conscious *ātman* and the experience. This link fails in forgetfulness to connect my I-consciousness to the object of that experience. Again, we do not remember all things all times. If there is nothing intervening between me and my experiences of those things, I must remember all things all times, and with such plethora of memories no new perception and no organization of experience will be possible. There must be something in me that makes possible my attention to one thing at a time, and relating all things thus attended to. That thing is mind. Again, we experience pleasures and pains only some specific times, not always; and the pleasures and pains are due to the experience of different objects. This phenomenon is possible only if there is something directing or pulling the consciousness of the *ātman* towards such experiences at those times. There has to be something funnelling and focusing the outwards directed consciousness; and this function of funnelling is mind as the inner instrument.

So whether we accept the nature of mind to be atomic or infinite—in the view of the author it is all-pervading, but with limited powers—we have to accept it as distinct from the *ātman*, even if it is not a separate entity, as the Advaitins say. For salvation, if it is at all desired,—as the later Cārvākas did—the reality of the self-conscious *ātman* and its eternity (transcendence of time) have to be accepted. The function of what we call mind—such as forgetfulness, different forms of sleep, pointedness, intentionality or directedness to say something only—can be assigned to it, and through it to the self-conscious *ātman*.[33]

The argument common to all the orthodox schools, including the Advaita, against treating mind and senses as the *ātman*—although they and their activities are subtler than the physical body and its activities—is that their activities are for the sake of something or somebody else. They have no purpose in performing their functions except the purpose of something other than they. Their teleology does not lie in themselves; it is not internal, but external to them. This argument assumes that there is something other than they and that they are instruments and have no being of their own. But there is no reason why they should not function as they do, like the magnet performing its function. It is only the necessity, imposed on us by analysis of our experience, to recognize a self-conscious principle that leads us to the distinction between the *ātman* on the one side and mind[34] and senses on the other. It is not invented syllogistic inferences, which most of the Indian philosophers use, like:

> Whatever acts acts for another;
> Mind and senses act;
> So they act for another;

and that "the another is the *ātman*," that establish the truth of the *ātman*. For counter-inferences can equally be well invented like:

> Whatever acts acts because of its nature, but
> not for any external purpose;
> Mind and senses act;
> So they act because of their nature, not for
> anything else.

Examples can easily be multiplied for and against both the inferences; and so logic of the kind, not based on relevant experience and its analysis, will turn out to be merely artificial.

What is interesting and significant to note as a conclusion or a lesson from the Cārvāka is that no philosophy, however materialistically inclined, can stop with materialism. The imperfections of the being of the natural man force themselves upon every mature, reflective mind and lead it to the recognition of the reality and centrality of the *ātman*, its consciousness and self-consciousness.

(iv) Coherence and Contradiction Imply a Self

We have seen that early *Cārvākas* accepted only perception as a valid means of cognition; but in the history of the school even perception was rejected for the reason that it is not always reliable. Inference also is rejected because we can never get the major premise that is absolutely valid and covers all instances, past, present, and future. And if it covers all instances, the present instance also, which is to be proved, must have been covered and inference will be unnecessary. Furthermore, if inference is to be based upon perception and perception is unreliable, inference *a fortiori* is unreliable.

But this rejection involves the necessity of accepting the continuity and self-identity of the self, the rejecter. We reject perception for lack of coherence and consistency with past and future perceptions. If I look in front and perceive water at a distance, I say: "There is water." When I go near it and find no water, I say: "There is no water, it is a mirage." Now, "That is water" and "That is a mirage" do not cohere or agree. If "water" and "mirage" are not referred to the same That, there can be no disagreement between the two judgments. For instance, between "That is a pen" and "That is a book" there is no disagreement, if the two Thats refer to two different objects. We have to recognize another condition of consistency or inconsistency. If I make the judgment, "That is water," and some one else makes the judgment, "That is a mirage," and we do not compare notes, can there be a contradiction? One may say that the two Thats have to be the same for a contradiction, but the two observers making the two judgments need not be the same. But if the two Thats are to be the same, they have to be the subjects of judgments made by the same mind or observer who has to pronounce that the two judgments are contradictory. If there are two observers, they have to compare notes, and each has to make the two contradictory judgments his own.

So for *knowing* the contradiction the two minds, like the two Thats, have to be the same. Indeed, for the contradiction to exist, it is enough that the two Thats are the same. Propositions like "*X* is *Y*" and "*X* is not *Y*", whether or not any one asserts them, form a contradiction certainly in formal logic.

Whether there can be either contradiction or coherence, whether one perceives it or not, is a question that need not be discussed at present. Philosophers who think that logic is independent of any mind and also of all existence—which is the view in vogue now—may accept that coherence and contradiction are there. If the laws of logic are discovered, but not man-made or invented, they must be capable of existing independently of my knowing or not knowing them. But philosophers who think that the laws of logic are laws of objective thought and are found only in its live activity, and that existence and objective thought cannot be separated—a view which is the result of a long chain of reflection on world and experience—may hold that ultimately, as a final presupposition, we have to accept that unless thought or reason and existence (cp. the Stoics, for instance) are in some way one, no contradiction, no coherence can exist. For "let the propositions, "*X* is *Y*" and "*X* is not *Y*" without any reference to existence float in suspension like the proposition, "*A* is *B*", "*C* is *D*," etc., without being asserted by anybody. Why should there be any contradiction or coherence between any two? Merely floating propositions do not clash or come to an agreement. All have a right to float, if they are apart from existence. If there is contradiction, one at least of the propositions must be false. Without reference to truth and falsity, the idea of contradiction is inane. Blue and not-blue are contradictory because they cannot coincide, but not because they cannot be held by mind and not because they have no meaning at all.

We need not enter into this controversy further. The Cārvākas say that perception is not reliable because it may give two judgments like "*X* is *Y*"and "*X* is not *Y*". But the person who observes the contradiction cannot make the judgment "This is a contradiction," unless he continues to exist through the two moments when the two judgments are made. That which makes the judgment is not the body, but the conscious and the self-conscious self.

It is absurd to think that in a syllogism the first two judgments are retained in the physical body, even the brain matter, and the third judgment is pronounced on their basis by the same physical body or brain matter. Nor is it intelligible to say that the judgment is pronounced by the structure which the different elements of the body obtained when they came together. For such a structure is limited to the body; it is static and cannot be dynamic in guiding the body in its activities on other objects. We can only say that the structure which evolves makes possible the manifestation of the agency of the I-consciousness, but cannot itself be the agency or the I-consciousness. *Evolution may evolve new structures or forms, but the structures or the forms themselves cannot be the new agencies of cognition, thought, action, desire, self-control, and whimsicality. They are only the conditions of higher and higher manifestations of the self.*

It is the presence and continuity of such a self that is a prerequisite of the observation of coherence and incoherence, or any kind of agreement such as the agreement of an idea with an object or with action. It will perhaps be said that the agreement of an idea with an object involves the correspondence theory of truth and the agreement of an idea with action involves the pragmatic criterion, and that both have been found to be defective. In the correspondence theory, the defect is that we can never know whether or not the idea corresponds to the object because the object is, by hypothesis, outside our mind and cognitive apparatus.[35] Besides, to know that my idea corresponds to the object, I have first to perform two acts, the act of getting the idea, and that of knowing the object itself. Then a third act is needed to assert their correspondence. If so, I have to be the same in all the three successive acts. The defect of the pragmatic theory is that it cannot avoid the correspondence theory, unless it accepts that the agreement between the idea and action is to be the agreement between the idea of the object and the idea of the success or failure of the action of the object on the perceiver or on the object by the perceiver. But such an agreement will be the same as coherence.

But the defect of the coherence theory, which has been rightly pointed out,[36] is that we cannot exhaust the number of judgments which have to be made about any perceived object in order to be absolutely certain, and that if, for argument's sake, we accept that they are and can be exhausted, we cannot know how the judgment, "All these judgments cohere with one another," coheres with the group of all those judgments. For example, even a simple judgment like "That is a pot" has to cohere with "That holds water." The latter has to cohere with some other and so on *ad infinitum*. We cannot complete the series. If *per impossible* we complete them, then "All of them cohere with one another" has to cohere with them; and that "It coheres with them" has to have another judgment of coherence and so on *ad infinitum*. This may be an empty and vain objection; but it may be so for practical persons, but not for theory. The impossibility we find in correspondence is found here also in a different form.

But who is it that observes the coherence? Certainly, it is not the physical body, as we have already mentioned. But can I complete the series of judgments which are to cohere with one another? Surely, I cannot complete them as they are inexhaustible.

But can I observe the coherence of even a finite number of judgments at the time the judgments are made? Let us say: the judgments are, "*X* is *Y*," "*Y* is *Z*," and "*X* implies *Z*." When I make one judgment, the others are either not made or already have been made. Next, the fourth judgment, "The three judgments cohere with one another," like the third judgment "*X* implies *Z*," cannot be a perceptual judgment and has to be asserted by thought or reason only. Then thought or reason in me is distinct from me as my self-centred ego, for its assertions have to be objectively valid, not merely for me. Although distinct from my ego, thought or reason has to be in me. It transcends me as this subject of perception, and yet be in me or be mine, as popularly understood.

Indeed, I commit mistakes in thinking, i.e., my thought is now and then erroneous. But so long as I involve myself earnestly in thinking, I claim that I detach my thinking from my subjectivity, my ego—which means that I become or attempt to become impersonal or be one with the impersonal I-am.[37] If and when I am absolutely right in thinking—according to the *Bhagavadgītā* in my conduct also—I am one with Objective Thought, Cosmic Reason, the Logos. (Compare the Pythagorean belief that mathematics takes one nearest to God, the Neo-Platonic idea that the Logos is the nearest to God, and the Upaniṣadic idea that the Mahat or *mahānātmā* as the Hiraṇyagarbha is the first born.)

If we are not satisfied with the Cārvāka answer to the question: "Even though many inferences are wrong, why is inference right often?", which is that if being right often is due to chance or accident or with the modern answer that their correctness is only a probability, we have to say that their correctness is due to the frequent identity of our thought with that of the Logos—we cannot, however, eliminate uncertainty completely—and that our thought and the Logos are the higher reaches of our own self, the I-am at its higher stages, as the *Kaṭha Upaniṣad* says.[38] Life itself becomes impossible if the truths of perception and inference are mere accidents. We can never plan our activities or pursue an idea even for worldly gains.

(v) "Reason" as One's Higher Self

It is important that we do not leave the Logos idea as mystical and mysterious and also as mythological. It is the highest reach of our worldly self and is still worldly, cosmic. The emphasis is on that it is our self at one of its great depths and heights. It is that which observes the coherence or incoherence of judgments and inferences, the observation of which I may miss. My missing them should cause no wonder, as I now and then miss the onslaughts of even perceptual stimuli and make wrong assertions about what I experience. The Logos is the highest observer in me, the witness or witness consciousness (*sākṣi, sākṣi-caitanya*), and the most unaffected witness of my activities. Without being detached and unaffected even when pushed hither and thither by the thrusts of desires and wishful thinking, it cannot observe whether or not the coherence it sees between any set of judgments or premises of an inference is true. Between me as influenced by desires and affections in perception and inference and the highest Logos, my perfected self, there can be various stages. But without a higher stage in my self, coherence or incoherence between any two judgments cannot be noticed or asserted.

The retention of any plurality of judgments for asserting their coherence or incoherence, as mentioned above, needs a higher self. This higher self becomes the reservoir of all our experiences, including the cognitive. It is traceable in our experience: "I know that I asserted that "*X* is *Y*," or abridged, "I know that I know that *X*-is-*Y*" or "I know that I know *X*." If the Cārvāka or any other school, east or west, accepts coherence and consistency as a test of truth, they have to accept the reality of a continuous, identical self in all cognitions and that the self is not the body, or the mind, or the senses. Besides, they have to accept all which the experience implies and is obvious, and all that the self presupposes in its theoretical and practical activity.

In the history of western philosophy, Berkeley, in the later development of his philosophy, accepted what is called theological idealism, viz., that all objects are ideas, but as ideas they exist in the mind of God, and that we know his ideas as concrete objects through the mind of God. But he did not explain how we can know or enter God's mind to know his ideas. We have to enter his mind to know his ideas which are for us the real objects. Spinoza's view that mind knows not only itself but also matter contains a clue to the solution of the problem in Berkeley's theory. But Spinoza does not seem to have noticed the significance of the assertion. For it implies that mind is self-conscious and that in its self-consciousness it includes the consciousness of the object as in "I know that I now *X*." Then our mind would be the same as what Spinoza called Substance, however imperfect and finite it may be at our level. Each one of us is the same as what is called Substance, but are "substances" at lower levels. In Kant's philosophy we find further removal of the mystery of the relation between our mind and God's mind by Kant's introduction of the idea of the Transcendental Ego. But still the problem is not fully clarified, as Kant did not say in definite terms that our Transcendental Ego is the gateway to God's mind. Hegel seized upon the clue, turned Spinoza's Substance into self-consciousness and changed God in Kant—Kant's God included the Transcendental Ego and the Transcendental Object—to the Absolute, Absolute Mind, or Absolute Consciousness. But in Kant's and Hegel's philosophy we miss how *our* Transcendental Ego becomes related to God's. In Husserl's philosophy we get the missing link in his idea of the witness consciousness, which is akin to the witness consciousness (*sākṣi-caitanya*) of the Upaniṣads. The witness here is always of the first I in "I know that I know *X*." There is continuity between the two I's. But there is so much of the continuity in our ordinary waking experience that we hardly notice their distinction. Now, there is continuity between my dream I and my waking I; I remember my dream experiences as my experiences. Sometimes the shock of the experiences lasts for a period even after I wake up.[39] Yet, I try to shake them off as not really there and I try to assume the role of a pure witness and say: "I know that I had those experiences." Thus between the I as a witness and the I as going through the experiences a distinction is recognized in spite of recognizing continuity also between the two.

What is not intelligible then in Hegel is that this self-consciousness can become the Absolute suddenly throwing up the whole gamut or network of categories and their interrelations, and that Hegel's mind could become the Absolute Consciousness suddenly to understand the Absolute Idea and its workings without his passing through levels of the more and more pure forms of the witness consciousness. For instance, the Transcendental Ego of Kant's has to be a witness consciousness, although as my transcendental ego it is polluted by my latent affections and may go wrong in its activities; but the purer it becomes by detaching itself from me as this finite ego, the more and more free from error does it become. There is recognition of Absolute Consciousness in Hegel, but the way to it from my finite subject-object consciousness is not clear in his philosophy.[40]

(vi) The "Other Logo"

In the case of Husserl's philosophy, the way is cleared for the finite I-am to advance to the infinite I-am or Absolute Consciousness through the witness consciousness. But Husserl does not tell us how to advance, how the advance is possible, beyond "I know that I know *X*." In this, the first I-know is the witness consciousness (*sākṣi*), but Husserl does not recognize that even the witness consciousness contains within it the distinction between I-am and I-know or between the knower-consciousness and the knowing-consciousness. Otherwise, he would not have taken this transcendental ego as a flow like Hume did before him. Indeed, there is a flow of consciousness; but a knowing consciousness and a knower consciousness have still to be above the flow for knowing that what is known is a flow and that the flow is continuous, and for supplying the agency to interpret the objective end of the flow as this or that object. Again, one feels that Husserl's deduction of the alter egos, other persons, lacks logic; for we are not enabled to understand how, even as the transcendental ego or witness consciousness, I can become conscious of other persons. To introduce the idea of empathy is to give up the method of transcendental deduction. The witness consciousness in "I know that I know *X*"—which certainly indicates an advance upon Descartes—is *my* witness consciousness and cannot be and has not yet become the Cosmic Consciousness, which can say to itself: "I am all this, I comprehend all this, including both material objects and self-conscious persons." By carrying the method of transcendental deduction further—if Husserl's method can be called deduction is a different question—we have yet to show that the so-called witness has still a higher witness, which is the witness of all the personalized witness consciousnesses and that there is continuity, therefore, between this higher witness consciousness and every other witness consciousness. The higher witness consciousness is really the controller (*antaryāmī*, inner controller) of the whole universe including both matter and minds.

How can a mere witness consciousness be a controller? If he is a controller, does he not cease to be a mere unaffected, detached witness? The reader of the Upaniṣadic literature, when he comes across the idea of a mere detached witness and the explanations of the word by commentators is left with the idea of something empty. But the witness is not a mere vacuum, just as deep sleep is not a mere vacuum; and I do not become a vacuum or nothingness in it. For instance, my waking I-am is the witness of the dream I-am and its dream objects; for it gives witness to what happened in the dream, it remembers the happenings. But it is not an empty consciousness lying in the background of the dream experiences. I am there in my dream with all that constitutes my person in my waking state. In fact, my person of the waking state is the basis, ground, support of my person and objects in my dream.

Similarly, even in Husserl's transcendental epoche, "I know that I know," the first I is not an empty witness, but the support of the second I and its objects. It is immanent and yet transcendent like my waking I in my dream. The experiences of my dream are permutations and combinations, reproductions, deflections, and perversions of those of my waking consciousness. My waking I does not hold itself responsible for the activities and other experiences of the dream and is, therefore, distinct from the dream I; and the waking I later works out complete detachment from it. Similar is the case with the first I in "I know that I know *X*." What we have further to note is, like the waking I somehow comprehending both the dream I and its object by being immanent in both and yet transcending them, the first I in "I know that I know *X*" comprehends both the second I and *X* by being immanent in both of them and yet transcending them. Yet it is my particular transcendental I and has not become the transcendental I of other persons.

So the idea of being the inner controller (*antaryāmī*) does not preclude the higher witness consciousness from being a witness consciousness. Just as my waking I has its own constitution, the higher witness also has its own. The lower witness is a reflection, image, of the higher witness, like the dream I-am is an image of my waking I-am. But an image, by the very fact that it is an image, is not supplied everything which the original contains. To make the situation clear, we should forget the examples generally given of the sun's reflection in a pool of water or my reflection in a mirror, and take only my dream I-am as the reflection of the waking I-am. If the dream I-am is fully what the waking I-am is, there will be no dream and no dream I-am. But there is distinction between the two. We have, therefore, to say that the dream I-am is an imperfect copy of the waking I-am, which in its turn is an imperfect copy of something still higher. That is, in dream, if it is to be a dream, I have to forget[41] a greater part of myself. The dream I-am is an imperfect projection of my waking I-am. It is my imperfect self-projection. What a higher I-am supplies a lower I-am are its basic structures of experience, which the latter utilizes and even distorts and perverts. For example, God or Providence has given us the basic materials like earth, water, metals, etc. What forms we give them in art and architecture, how we combine them, whether we misuse them or use them properly, depends on ourselves. But we cannot change the laws themselves of these materials; they are the capital with which we work and build up our culture and civilization. Thus to the extent to which we cannot change our basic constitutions, we are controlled by the higher witness, who is, therefore, both a witness and a controller.

(vii) Sākṣi and Antaryāmī

Then what basic experience in me leads to my assertion that there are other persons, other I-ams? Empathy may be true, but it does not fit into the method of transcendental deduction. The difficulty in Descartes' philosophy, how mind can know matter at all if mind knows and is certain only of itself, is removed by recognizing that mind knows itself as knowing the object in "I know that I know the table," that consciousness has intentionality or direction pointing outside itself, and that there can be no direction without something towards which consciousness is directed and which has therefore, to fall within consciousness itself. The consciousness which includes the knower and the known is a transcendental consciousness similar to the one in "I know that I know *X*."—which means that my consciousness is necessarily directed towards an object. But can empathy be explained in the same or a similar way? It does not seem to be possible. Or can we say: We have empathy; therefore, other egos exist?

Empathy, like sympathy, is not primarily a cognitive act. If, because of empathy, we accept that the object is a person, analogically we have to accept that because of our sympathy we have to accept the object as a person. Both involve the subject-object relation, but do not necessarily imply *cognition* of a *person*. Here it is not argued that we do not have cognition of persons, but that empathy and sympathy are not the basic cognitive acts for knowing other persons. The cognitive, instinctive assumption that there is action, that we observe action or activity, is basic to the cognition that the object is matter as well as to the cognition that it is a mind. To know that it is matter or mind, I do not, because I cannot, become that piece of matter or that mind. But I can become *as though* I am one with that matter or one with that mind as in indeterminate perception.[42] This "becoming as though identical with" is not what is understood by empathy. Otherwise, "becoming as though identical with" a material object will also be empathy. I perceive Mr. Jones. What I see is indeed his material body, sitting, standing, or moving. These observed acts do not necessarily imply that they belong to a conscious person. A motor car moves, a railway engine moves; children and primitive men, and even we in our imaginative moods, may think or imagine that there is a mind and a will in each of them. But before we do so, we have to know that some of the objects we have seen possess minds and we have to have an idea of "other minds," "other persons," "other egos." The question is not: "How do we know that *X* has a mind and *Y* has a mind?", but more basically: "How do we get at all the idea that there are other minds?", as we get the idea that there are other objects.

We get the idea that there are objects—apart from the question whether the object perceived is true or false—in the experience we spontaneously get in "I know that I know *X*." This is an intuitive experience, not needing any special effort to obtain, and is the root of memory also. There is no point in questioning: "Why do people have memory?" For the only answer is: "They do have it." Similarly, is there a cognitive experience, "I know that I know another mind (person)?" There must be such experience; and it has to be an intuition in which the other mind is still known as an "other." One is still surprised at the refusal of some philosophers to accept this position. They say that, if we know other minds, we enter them, and there will be no privacy of personality. But when we know material objects, do we enter them, and does even the material object give up its secrets to our simple perception? If it does so, Newtons and Einsteins will not be needed.

Man is an ethical animal besides being a religious animal. So by nature man's consciousness is directed towards other persons; ethical consciousness is categoreal (existential as in compunction), although it may have come to the surface in the course of evolution. One may even say that it is instinctive at higher levels like the instincts of animals to love and protect their young, with the difference that man more often violates his ethical instinct than some birds and beasts. But as man's ethical instinct works at a higher cognitive level than in other animals, the general form of the ethical object is included in the cognition. When a tiger directs its love towards its cub, it "knows" that the cub belongs to its own species.

Ethical level is primarily a level of action directly or indirectly concerned with other persons; but this action is conscious action, not like the action of a somnambulist. *This conscious action has at the other end the "other ego," from which I anticipate reaction to me.* Thus the "other ego" is an essential part of my action-reaction consciousness. Communication is one kind of such consciousness, not the only kind, unless we enlarge the meaning of communication to include all kinds of mutual action and interaction. If Jim abuses Dick, Dick pays back in the same coin; even if Dick cries and runs, Jim gets a satisfying response from Dick. Instead of abusing, if Jim beats Dick, and the same thing happens, Jim gets a response which satisfies him and which he anticipates. We may then say that all such activities come under communication. But such communication presupposes that Jim knows Dick as another ego. *Communication confirms the intuitive cognition of the "other ego." It does not constitute the other ego.* For what is it that my ego can constitute, if it does not know, even intuitively and instinctively, what it is to constitute? Why should I communicate in this way, unless I instinctively presuppose that the object to which I communicate is an ego? So communication presupposes the cognition of the other ego, but not vice versa. It may indeed confirm my intuitive cognition that the other is an ego. The idea of the other ego is categorical.

(viii) Knowledge of Other Person

Now, taking up the main thread of our argument which has led us to the idea of the self (I-am) as the inner controller (*antaryāmī*), one may ask: If my I-am is essentially the inner controller of everything including other objects and other egos, if I recognize through this argument that I am that higher I-am, can I become the controller of the universe? I as this person, writing these lines, am certainly not the controller of the universe, although I recognize that essentially and in my truth I am he. He is my deeper I-am. My empirical I-am is in touch with him whenever it perceives, thinks, and acts right. The question: "Do I become the controller of the universe?" is implicitly motivated by finite interests. *If I become the controller, I do not have finite interests; so long as I have them, I cannot become the controller.*

Merely to have contact with something and to acknowledge its existence is not the same as becoming it. This is true in the case of the inner controller also. That is why our knowledge of other things and other persons and the laws of their behaviour is very imperfect and finite. Because we are rooted in the being of this inner controller, we are aware that there are other things and other egos, and that they have their laws of behaviour. What exactly they are and how many they are can be known only through painstaking enquiry. To think that this recognition confers on any one of us the status of the Logos, the inner controller (*antaryāmī*)— except a bit here and a bit there—is to make too large a claim. One's dissatisfaction with philosophers like Hegel and Husserl stems to some extent from their making such a claim overtly and by implication. We find such a claim in Hegel's attempt to deduce the whole categorical structure of the world from the Absolute Idea; we find it lurking in Husserl's assertion that the transcendental ego in the epoche, which we all experience, is the Logos.

All this comment goes to show that the Cārvāka school and other schools like it, eastern or western, have to accept a self (*ātman*, I-am) as distinct from the body, and that it has reaches far beyond the body and its experience, and extends right up to the inner controller, which is also a self (I-consciousness), and even beyond. It has been shown how the idea of coherence and incoherence, which the Cārvāka does and has to accept, involves the ideas of a continuous self. In the future chapters it will be shown that the idea of time, space, and causality also presuppose the existence of such a self. It will be shown also that some of the lacunae in the theory of coherence can be removed only by introducing the idea of apperception and the higher self. Here it has been accepted that the objectivity of the world can be and has to be sought not in the idea of a world completely external to the mind, but in the mind itself at its higher levels. The transcendence of the mind by the object has to be turned into the transcendence of the mind by higher and higher levels of the self-transcendent self. Otherwise, we have to answer the absurd question: *How can we know the object which we can never know, as it is beyond us?* There can be continuity between the different levels of mind and self in its self-transcendence; but such a continuity is denied by this question. It is appropriate to discuss this topic in the chapter on the Cārvāka, as the school started in its understanding of the self of man from the physical body and reached up to mind.

NOTES

[1]D. Shastri: *A Short History of Indian Materialism* and S. Dasgupta: *Obscure Religious Cults*.

[2]Deviprasad Chattopadhyaya: *Lokāyata*.

[3]S. N. Dasgupta: *History of Indian Philosophy*, Vol. III, pp. 514–15.

[4]D. Chattopadhyaya: *Lokāyata*, pp. 51–70.

[5]If the word "Cārvāka" refers to the system, the definite article is used; when it is not used, the word is the name of the person who is said to have founded the school.

[6]D. Chattopadhyaya: *Lokāyata*, p. 28.

[7]This view, though an old one, seems to have some resemblance to logical empiricism. Unfortunately, the works of these thinkers are not available.

[8]The Cārvākas did not remain purely materialistic. According to recent scholarship, they got absorbed also into spiritual tradition.

[9]Ibid., p. 16.

[10]*Sarvadarśanasaṁgraha*, pa. 5.

[11]See D. Chattopadhyaya: *Lokāyata*, p. 34.

[12]Such a doctrine is called *dehātmavāda*, the doctrine that the body itself is the *ātman* and that the realization of the *ātman* is the realization of the perfection of the body. Cp. the story of Vairo-cana in the *Chāndogya Upaniṣad*, VIII, viii. Cp. also to Yang-tzu's philosophy.

[13]D. Chattopadhyaya: *Lokāyata*, pp. 486 fol.

[14]A. L. Bhasham: *The Ājīvikas*, pp. 11 fol.

[15]D. Shastri: *A Short History of Indian Materialism*, p. 39.

[16]D. Chattopadhyaya: *Lokāyata*, p. 61. The mention of the Cārvāka's relation with the Sāṅkhya by a very orthodox pundit makes me believe in this interpretation. See L. Śrinvasacharya: *Mānameyarahaśyaślo-kāvārtikam*, pp. 17–18.

[17]Ibid., pp. 18–19.

[18]Mādhavācārya: *Sarvadarśanasaṁgraha*, p. 61.

[19]*Mānameyarahaśyaślokāvārtikam*, p. 19.

[20]Tāntrism is a form of religious practice aiming at the transformation of the microcosm in macrocosm and at realizing thereby the macrocosmic Universal Spirit or Godhead.

[21]D. Shastri: *A Short History of Indian Materialism*, pp. 43 fol.

[22]Voltaire in France was particularly eager to have an ethics without supernatural justification and was attracted to the Confucian form.

[23]See his *Common Faith* (Yale University Press, New Haven, 1934).

[24]II, 1, II. We can construct a syllogism to prove anything, provided the existence and reality of what is thus proved are not demanded.

[25]Already referred to in the chapter on the Upaniṣads.

[26]In later Upaniṣadic thought the number of levels was raised to sixteen, and even to forty eight, every level being an I-sense or I-consciousness (*aham-abhimānin*). The sheath theory belongs to the Advaita.

[27]See the chapter on the Upaniṣads.

[28]Cp. *Prakṛtilaya* (merging in Prakṛti) of the Yoga philosophy.

[29]Cp. Freud's idea that the troubled mind, in its attempt at suicide, really attempts to become one with matter and be nothing by itself. But the Indian thinkers would say that it would be reborn again and again and take up the thread of suffering.

[30]Cp. Morleau-Ponty.

[31]See the chapter on Buddhism.

[32]See the different chapters for the differences.

[33]Buddhism also seems to have mixed up mind (*manas*), rational consciousness or collected, apperceptive consciousness (*citta*), and *ātman* (I-consciousness) in the history of its development.

[34]In this section, mind (*manas*) is used in the sense of the inner instrument (*antahkaraṇa*). For details, see the chapters on the Sāṅkhya and the Advaita.

[35]Here I ignore, for reasons of space, various modifications of the correspondence theory by writers who want to save it. Similarly, I ignore the various defenses made of the pragmatic criterion.

[36]See Joachim: *The Nature of Truth.*

[37]Cp. the *jñānātman* of the *Kaṭha Upaniṣad*, Mahat, Mahān Ātmā, etc.

[38]It is often necessary to demythologize the ideas of the Upaniṣads not only to understand their philosophy, but also to assimilate them to our experience. Śaṅkara himself did so many times.

[39]Cp. the excitement of persons watching football, wrestling, boxing, etc., on television, although as observers they are witnesses only.

[40]In Hegel's *Phenomenology of Mind*, one may trace the advance of my finite consciousness to higher and higher levels; but the way is cluttered by so many socio-logical and other forms that it becomes unclear. The idea of witness consciousness seems to be alien to his philosophy. However, Hegel's transition from logic to nature and then to Spirit contains the idea that mind as the witness consciousness comprehends both the subject-mind and the object. But the transition to nature need not be from logic alone, although it involves the idea that nature has to be logical, if it is to be real.

[41]This is said to be due to Avidyā by the Advaitins and some others.

[42]See the comments on the Yoga philosophy.

Chapter IV

Jainism and the Ethics of Self-Conquest

1. INTRODUCTION

One of the important schools that developed out of the ideas of the Non-Vedic thinkers, who were called the book-less (*nirgranthas*), is Jainism, founded by Vardhamāna (6th century B.C.). The Jainas do not accept the reality of God, but only of gods, who are treated as inferior to their religious leaders. These leaders are the teachers, who are said to be twenty-four, the twenty-fourth being Vardhamāna. They are called *tīrthaṅkaras* (holy men or men who make their abode a holy place), the first of them being Ṛṣabha, whose name occurs in the Vedas. He preached absolute non-violence and non-destruction of life even for food. If we allow twenty-five years for every teacher and assume that every next teacher was a disciple of the earlier, the concepts of Jainism must have started at least during the 12th century B.C., i.e., before the earliest of the Upaniṣads was composed. Since Jaimini, the founder of the Mīmāmsā, and Bādarāyaṇa, the founder of the Vedānta, belong roughly to the 4th or the 5th century B.C., Vardhamāna was earlier than both. His philosophy could not, therefore, have been a reaction to the philosophies as expounded by either. If the Jaina ideas started in the 12th century B.C., when the earliest of the Upaniṣads was not even composed, then this school must have started as an independent thought and gone into conflict with the ideas of the sacrificial religion based on the first two parts of the Veda, although the ideas of the well-developed philosophy of Jaimini entered the scene later. The Upaniṣadic ideas, except that of the Supreme Spirit or God, must have been only in the making; and even the ideạ of the Supreme Spirit must have been vaguely conceived. We may, therefore, conclude that the origins of Jainism were a reaction against the Vedic religion of sacrifices and the wrong conception that ethical merit could be gained by performing sacrifices to gods, not merely by virtue of self-control. We have seen that sacrifices to gods were one of the obligations; and people perhaps thought that they produced ethical merit also, although it was pointed out that the payment of a debt did not produce any merit while non-payment produced demerit. By the time of Vardhamāna, the *Āraṇyakas* and a few of the early Upaniṣads must have been composed. The Jainism of Vardhamāna was born and developed in the atmosphere of Vedic ideas, which were themselves developing, and Vardhamāna gave Jainism a fairly definite form, although he did not write or compose a book. Up to the time of Vardhamāna, his forerunners were called the book-less.

One may call Jaina philosophy the philosophy of moral self-control. Just as the Buddhists called Gautama by the title of Buddha (the enlightened), the Jainas called Vardhamāna by the title Jina (the conquerer) and Mahāvīra (the great hero). But Vardhamāna conquered only his self, his bodily desires, drives, and dualities like love and hate. He was a hero in the moral battlefield. Although he belonged to the group of independent, book-less thinkers, he accepted the Vedic doctrines of gods, *karma*, rebirth, the reality and infinitude of the *ātman*, and the plurality of the *ātmans* and the world; and like the early Mīmāmsā, he rejected the reality of God. But unlike the early Mīmāmsā, he preached that salvation and liberation from the world of action is the highest ideal of life. Thus he accepted the four values of life. But salvation, he said, could be obtained through absolute, rigorous self-control, absolute detachment from all that belongs to our physical body.

Although Vardhamāna did not put down his ideas in writing, his followers collected his teachings together, expounded and developed them. Thus this school of the book-less now possesses a very vast amount of literature on almost every branch of philosophy. The Jainas first composed many of their works on ethics and religious discipline and practices in the Arthamāgadhi language, which was a spoken language of most of western India and which is a form of Prākṛt, a derivative of Sanskrit. But many of the later important works are in Sanskrit. The Jaina aphorisms were composed by Umāsvāti (also called Umāsvāmi, 3rd century A.D.) and are called *Tattvārthādhigamasūtra* (also called *Tattvārthasūtra*) which may be treated as the basic work for this school. Other important works include Mallisena's *Syādvādamañjari* (13th century), a commentary on *Anyayogavyavacchedikā* of Hemacandra (12th century), the latter's *Pramānamīmāmsā*, Haribhadra's *Ṣāḍdarśanasamucchaya* (9th century A. D.), Kundakunda Āchārya's *Niyamasāra* and *Samayasāra* (2nd century A.D.?), Prabhācandra's *Prameyakamalamārtāṇḍa* (6th century A.D.?), and Yasovijaya's *Jainatarkabhāṣā* (18th century A.D.). These works are widely read and are enough for our purpose. I should repeat that the dates are not always reliable and no two historians agree on all of them.

There are only two main sects of Jainism: the white-clad (*śvetāmbaras*) and the space-clad (*digambaras*). The former wear only white clothes, but the latter wear none. But this wearing or not wearing is restricted only to monks. The space-clad sect believes that women cannot obtain salvation; for obtaining it they have to be reborn as men and are, therefore, not allowed to become nuns. The white-clad nuns wear white clothes. The split between the two sects occurred in the 1st century A.D. It seems that there are eighty-four[1] sects of Jainism differing from one another on very minor details of practice, but holding the same philosophical views. One of such sects is that of the Sthānikavāsis, who do not accept that monks and nuns should do their religious practices in temples but in ordinary places, and who reject idol-worship, very likely under the influence of Islam. This sect is a branch of the white-clad and was formed about the 18th century. The space-clad monks are generally confined to their monasteries and a few holy places in India, and are not allowed by the government to go to all cities or wherever they like.

2. EPISTEMOLOGY

The Jaina epistemology is very elaborate and gives a keen analysis of the forms of knowing. Like the epistemology of other schools, it had a gradual development and final crystallization. But the differences of views among the Jainas are not important, unlike the differences of view among the Mīmāmsakas.

According to the Jainas, consciousness belongs to the essence[2] of the *ātman*, which by nature is omniscient. It knows everything, the nearest and the most remote, past and future. But due to action (*karma*) sticking to it—the Jainas do not speak of the potency (*śakti*) of action (*karma*), as the Mīmāmsakas do, but of action itself—its knowledge gets contracted and limited. It needs, therefore, the instrumentality of mind (*manas*) and senses for obtaining even limited knowledge. Mind and senses are not absolutely separate entities from the *ātman*.[3] For making this identification plausible, the Jainas distinguish between the physical and psychical senses and between the physical and psychical mind, and identify the *ātman* with the psychical, calling the relation identity and difference, or identity-in-difference. As the *ātman* is in essence knowledge, mind and senses are unimportant so far as knowledge is concerned. In the wordly stage, we cannot indeed know objects without their instrumentality. But their instrumentality is dispensable.[4] All knowledge is identical with the *ātman*, yet the two are distinguishable. That is, the relation between the two is both identity and difference. Hemacandra[5] explains the position thus. The senses are born of action (*karma*) and are the indices of the *ātman*. They are only occasions or media of perception, by themselves they cannot perceive anything; the *ātman* alone can be the perceiver. The physical senses have the relation of identity in difference with the physical body; and the psychical senses have the same relation with the *ātman*.[6] Before cognition, there is a veil hiding the object from the *ātman* and the veil is the result of action (*karma*). Cognition is the removal of this veil. The senses are only instruments for removing the veil. Mind (*manas*) is not a sense (*anindriya*, *noindriya*) but is that which cognizes the objects of all the senses. Yet it is not a separate entity from the *ātman*, but the function (*vyāpāra*) of the *ātman* ready to cognize an object. Not only between the *ātman* and mind, and between mind and senses, but also between any one sense and another the relation is identity and difference; for all reveal the same object.[7]

The Jaina classification of the valid forms of knowledge is not unanimous, but in essence the same. Umāsvāmi classifies them into five kinds: opinion (*mati*), verbal knowledge (*śruta*), limited knowledge (*avadhi*), knowledge of other minds (*manahparyāya*), and direct knowledge by the *ātman* (*kevala*). The first includes ordinary sense-perception and inference. The first and the second are fallible, the other three are infallible. A later classification divides the forms of cognition into direct and indirect cognition.[8] Direct cognition is ordinary sense perception and the last three of the above five, which are also direct cognitions. Indeed, these three alone are really direct. Sense perception is not really direct, but is mediated by mind and senses and is called empirical perception (*vyāvahārika-pratyakṣa* or perception for the life of action). Empirical perception is of two kinds: that produced by senses (and mind) and that produced by mind alone. For instance, pains and pleasures are cognized by mind alone and the cognition is fallible; for we cannot know, for instance, where exactly toothache occurs. Now both forms of empirical perception are again divided according to whether the cognition is due to words heard also or without words. For instance, when I am told that the object in front is an elephant, then I cognize it as an elephant. The Jainas like to call such a cognition also perception. Indirect knowledge is of five kinds: remembering or recollection, recognition, induction together with the negative modal argument (*tarka*, *ūhā*, including not only the inductive statement but also the counter-factual conditional), syllogism, and scripture[9] (verbal knowledge). We may note that in the earlier classification, opinion includes not only ordinary sense-perception but also all the forms of indirect knowledge of the later classification. The difference between the two classifications is due to the hesitation of the Jainas to call ordinary perception direct knowledge, as it is mediated by mind and senses.

DIRECT COGNITION Sense perception, which is one of the forms of direct cognition is defined as clear[10] cognition (*vaiśadyam*). This definition resembles Hume's doctrine of clear ideas, but not that of Descartes, for whom clear ideas are also logical and mathematical ideas. When I infer that the earth has a centre, I have no clear image of the object; but if some one draws a circle and places a point at the centre, the object before my consciousness is clear. Clearness is defined as the presentation of an object as "That" (*idamtayā*) without the help of any other means of cognition.[11] If I want to explain the idea of the centre of the earth to a person who has been thinking that the earth is flat, I have to make use of inference. The idea of the centre of the earth then stands before his consciousness only through the instrumentality of inference. His consciousness cannot grasp the idea directly through his senses or mind. To call the inferred idea clear is only a way of speaking. The inferred object, even if it is physical, is never as clear as a perceived object. Mathematical clarity is only clarity of abstract form.

The Jainas would accept the distinction between indeterminate (*nirvikalpaka*) and determinate (*savikalpaka*) perception in their own way. Completed perception is the perception of the object as determined by the universal. Such a perception is determinate perception. But before the stage of determinate perception is reached, the perceptual process passes through three stages, so that completed perception has four stages. The Jainas call the four stages by the same name perception or kinds of perception and treat them, unlike the Naiyāyikas, as valid means of cognition. The first stage is called the approach (*avagraha*), the simple relation or contact of sense and object. Here, two kinds of contact are distinguished: contact with an indication (*vyañjanāvagraha*) and contact with the object itself (*arthāvagraha*). The Jainas say that mind and the eye[12] do not come into contact with the object straight away, but first with the indication processes and through them with the object. This indication is a composite of psycho-physical processes, the form of the object, and the relation between the two. Mind does not touch the object as it is in the physical world, but knows it through the effects, which are the indicators[13] produced by the object on the senses. The eye also, which is part of my body, does not touch the object, but knows it through the influences set in motion by the object. But the other four senses—taste, smell, touch, and sound—come straight into direct contact with the object itself. Unlike the Buddhists, the Jainas do not regard mind as a sense, but as an instrumentality of the *ātman* present in the activities of senses also. Contact with the object does not mean determinate cognition, but a cognition of the object as something, as a being, without knowing its essence, name, universal (class), activity, quality, and even substantiality.[14] It is a mere looking at (*ālocana*) the object.

The next stage is that of expectation (*īhā*), a kind of an effort, a questioning to know what the object is. It is the stage at which perception attempts to fix the qualities of the object and exclude those not possessed by it. We may say that it is an attempt to determine the object, anticipating the object to be something definite. The third state is the fixing (*avāya*) of the object as in the perception, "This is a pen."[15] But as yet the perceptual process does not end. What is thus fixed has to be retained, stabilized. This stage is called the stage of retention or stabilization (*dhāraṇa*). Retention is of three kinds[16] (factors): non-stopping, (*avicyuti*) or the continuation of the same object as the content of the perceptual consciousness as long as the perceptual act lasts; continuation of the idea in (as) memory (*smṛti*) as referring to the same object when the perceptual process is completed; and the impression (*samskāra*) left on our mind and causing such a memory. Perceptual process is completed when retention occurs. In fact, it is complete when the first kind of retention takes place. The second and the third kinds are engendered along with the first and are due to it. All the above analysis shows that the perceptual process is not as simple and instantaneous as one thinks.

We may say that, according to the Jainas, the first three stages of perception belong roughly to the indeterminate stage and the fourth to the determinate. Even the third stage is only the process of fixing the object, not yet the result of fixing. Every later stage is the result of the earlier.[17] The Jainas do not accept the Sāṅkhya view that our consciousness is the *ātman* itself, yet they hold that the *ātman* is essentially conscious. It is revealed in every cognitive act. "That is a pen" is the same as "I know that it is a pen" and "I know that I know that it is a pen." The second is called self-reflective cognition (*anuvyavasāya*)[18] and the third is the same as the second. If the second cognition is not involved in the first, then the first will be nobody's cognition. Since it is my cognition, my "I" also must be involved in it and must have been cognized along with the pen; and since my "I" is conscious, it can be of the form, "I know that I know." All experience is complex (*citra*), we can find and make distinctions in it. All distinctions are both identical with, and different from one another. Similarly, the relation between the knowing *ātman* and its knowledge is both identity and difference. So the *ātman* itself can reveal the object and, in that revealing, reveal itself also to itself.[19] As such, it is the knower (*pramātā*). But it has the power also to know itself alone even when it is not revealing any object. Valid cognition results when the ignorance residing in the *ātman* is removed, which, if the ignorance had not been present, would have cognized everything in the world without the instrumentality of mind and senses. Between the means of cognition (*pramāṇas*) and the result (*phala*) of the cognition, the relation is again identity and difference.[20] Between senses and their objects also the relation is both.[21] Do we cognize in perception substance or qualities? The Jainas answer that we cognize substance, its qualities, and its modes also.[22] Substance is not inferred from the presence of qualities, but is directly perceived along with them.

As the *ātman* is capable of knowing directly everything without the instrumentality of mind and senses, cognition by the *ātman* through the senses is regarded as indirect knowledge and so as fallible. For obtaining absolutely direct knowledge, the veil of ignorance produced by action has to be removed. Consciousness of the *ātman* then gets purified. This purification passes through three stages; and the saint whose consciousness is purified passes, therefore, through three states one after another, the last being the highest and the absolute. The first is the direct cognition of objects with shapes and is called the limited (*avadhi*). At this stage, the *ātman* cognizes one object at a time and its consciousness reveals the object just as sunlight does. The second is the knowledge of other minds (*manahparyāya*). The third is knowledge of everything in the universe and is called the pure (*kevala*).

Auditory cognition (*śruta*), which also is treated as direct perception, is obtained from words heard. Curiously enough, words written also are included as the source of this cognition,[23] perhaps because written symbols are translated by us into auditory symbols and then their meaning is cognized. Still more interesting is the view that auditory cognition, although called direct cognition, is said to belong to mind[24] (*manas*), which is not a sense (*noindriya*). As mind is regarded as a function or process (*vyāpāra*) of the *ātman* itself, we may say that auditory cognition is a direct cognition of the object by the *ātman* through the instrumentality of the auditory sense. The Jainas had to develop this complex theory because the meaning of the sound-symbol cannot be grasped by the ear (the sense of hearing itself). The ear can cognize only sounds, but not their meanings. That the Jainas epistemologists, in spite of recognizing this complexity, regarded verbal cognition as direct cognition (*aparokṣa*) and as perception (*pratyakṣa*) seems difficult to understand.[25] If the nature of the object of perception is clearness (*vaiśadya*), as we cannot say that the object as understood when we hear its name is clear, we cannot understand how verbal knowledge can be classed under perception. Only when an elder points to a horse and tells the child that the object is called a horse, can the object be clear to the child. If an Asian tells his child that the bison exists in America and is like the buffalo, the meaning of the word bison cannot be said to be clear for the child.

INDIRECT COGNITION Indirect knowledge (*parokṣajñāna*), according to the Jainas, is of five kinds: recollection, recognition, induction (including the counter-factual conditional), syllogism, and scripture.

Recollection (*smṛti*) is the cognition that arises through an impression produced in us in the past. It is the result of past experience. Most of the other schools of India do not accept recollection as a distinct means of cognition, because it presents only what was experienced but nothing new. But the Jainas contend that the presentation of something new is not the criterion here, but the removal of the veil of ignorance and the rising of the consciousness of the object. If we do not accept recollection as valid for the reason that it is due to a past impression, then we should not accept inference also as valid, because it is due to, or mediated by the major premise, which also is based on past experiences and impressions left by them. In fact, all determinate perception is thus mediated by past experience held in apperception. If perception is the cognition of the individual as determined by a universal (*prakāra*, form), and knowledge of the universal is a result of past experiences, then perception also has to be rejected for that reason that it is based upon past experience. Remembering is a cognition now of an object seen then and is of the form "that object." Often it is not of the form, "that object seen then", and there may be no reference to time. Remembering my friend in Los Angeles, I may write to him a letter. When I write the letter, I may not have in mind the time and place I met him.

We have seen that the Jainas accept memory as a part of determinate, direct cognition. Now they make it also one kind of indirect cognition.[26] This double classification may be explained as due to memory being the transition stage from the direct to the indirect cognition. Indirect cognition is not possible without memory, spontaneous or voluntary, or as Plato said, recollection, which itself is, again, not possible without knowledge produced in the past. What is important is the instrumentality of the impression in indirect cognition. The impression is that of form, from which the details slowly fade out in time. It is this form that makes indeterminate direct cognition determinate.

The second form of indirect cognition is recognition (*pratyabhijñā*). The Jaina conception of recognition is comprehensive and interesting. It is indeed a combination of perception and memory. I point to the person in front and say: "He is the same man I saw yesterday." This is the first kind of recognition. In the cognition of this sameness, both perception and memory are involved. But also when an American sees a buffalo and says: "That is similar to the bison," both perception and memory are involved; for the American sees in the buffalo many characteristics he saw in the bison. So perception of similarity also is a form of recognition.[27] By thus extending the meaning of recognition, the Jainas reject the Mīmāmsā view that comparison (*upamāna*) is a distinct means of valid cognition. The Naiyāyikas say that comparison is not the cognition of similarity, but a determinate cognition of an object through the knowledge of similarity obtained earlier, as when, for instance, the American cognizes the object as a buffalo through the knowledge of its similarity to the bison, obtained from the words of a friend. But even this view of comparison as a distinct means of cognition, the Jainas say, is unnecessary; for even without the words of his friend the American recognizes the buffalo. He may not remember what his friend told him, sees the object in front, and identifies what he perceives with what he saw at home. The third kind of recognition is found when we say: "That object belongs to the universal horseness or to the class horses." This is not the mere non-classificatory, determinate cognition as when we say: "That is a horse." In simple determinate perception, we do not consciously think of the universal horseness, although the class-concept operates in all determinate cognition. But in this third kind of recognition, we consciously think of the class-concept, which we evoke in our mind through recollection. It is, therefore, a combination of perception and memory. The fourth kind of recognition is the combination of perception and memory through contrast. When we perceive an object, we may remember another that has dissimilar features.[28] When we see a leopard for the first time, we may remember and so cognize the tiger by contrast. Both look alike, but the difference also is striking; and the difference makes us remember the tiger. Similarly, when we see an ugly object, we may remember the beautiful by contrast. Here we do not cognize the contrast consciously first, and then the tiger; the contrast works unconsciously and brings the tiger before our mind. The fifth kind of recognition is referential cognition. It is the cognition of something with reference to something[29] else, without which reference that cognition is not possible. We may say that all recognition is a referential cognition. But the present one is explicitly referential. "The cow is a different animal from the buffalo." In this cognition of difference, there is reference to both the cow and the buffalo. When I look at the cow, I see the difference from the buffalo; and when I look at the buffalo, I see the difference from the cow. "The two are different from each other" means "The first is different from the second and the second is different from the first," and is a combination of two cognitions. Each of the two cognitions involves the perception of one object and memory of the second. Thus the perception of difference and, likewise, of all negation is not a mere perception, but recognition as a referential cognition. Here recognition has to be understood in its etymological meaning. All referential cognition involves a re-cognition, through memory, of something already recognized, whether a moment or long time ago. Number also is cognized through referential cognition. The first apple, for instance, is the first with reference to the second and the second the second with reference to the first. The Jainas did not of course develop a detailed philosophy of number like Russell and Whitehead.

The general tendency of the Jainas is to classify perception of negation not under perception, but under re-cognition and so under indirect perception. If I say: "This is not a pen," the pen, which is a part of the negative object of my cognition, is not perceived, but remembered. Without this reference to the positive, remembered pen, this negation is impossible. In fact, no negation is possible without such reference. Pure negation, which is not the negation of anything, is never cognized. If I say: "There is no pen on the table,"[30] even then the pen is not perceived, but remembered, and the cognition of this negation is not possible without reference to the pen. There can be no perception of pure absence, which is not the absence of something positive. Explaining negation as recognition, the Jainas reject Kumārila's view that negation is cognized by a distinct means of cognition called non-cognition.[31] They reject also the view that absence or negation is a distinct category of reality. Neither the positive nor the negative is real by itself. For everything is relative and is both positive and negative.

The next kind of indirect knowledge is called the cognition of modal relation (*ūhā*, *tarka*), both positive and negative, and includes what is called the counter-factual conditional also. For at the basis of the counter-factual conditional lies an affirmative, universal, categorical relation between the middle and major terms, both of which are universals. In its form as the counter-factual conditional, other schools treat it as distinct from the inductive universal proposition; but the Jaina logicians club them together for the reason that the inductive universal and the counter-factual conditional are two forms of the same relation. It is of the form: "Wherever smoke exists, it can exist only if fire also exists there; and if fire does not exist there, smoke also cannot exist there." It thus becomes a combination of the two propositions: "Wherever there is smoke, there is fire," and "If there is no fire, there will be no smoke." Then if we see smoke, we say: "Had there been no fire, there would have been no smoke." But the other schools, particularly the Naiyāyikas, say that the three propositions—the universal affirmative, the universal negative, and the counter-factual conditional—are different. The first two are propositions about concomitance, are based upon induction, and can be used as major premises of the syllogism. But the third, which, according to them, is the true counter-factual conditional (*tarka*), cannot be used as a major premise, but only to confirm the conclusion of a syllogism and gives an indirect proof, which assumes the truth of the major premise of the original syllogism. To confirm the truth of "Socrates is mortal," we may say: "Had Socrates been not mortal, he would not have been a man; but he is a man; therefore, he is mortal." The counter-factual conditional, which we are using as the major premise, assumes the truth of "All men are mortal." Furthermore, the indirect proof repeats the conclusion of the original syllogism. It says nothing new. Hence, the counter-factual conditional cannot be accepted as an inductive generalization. But the Jainas say that inductive generalization, which forms the major premise, may take any of the forms.[32] Every object has many modes, both positive and negative. The major premise, being the expression of a relation between two kinds of objects, is the expression of the modal existence of the two with reference to each other and can be positive and negative and also conditional.

The fourth kind of indirect cognition is syllogistic inference. It is of two kinds: inference for oneself and inference for another. The syllogism for oneself consists of three[33] parts: reason, the universal relationship between reason (middle term) and consequent (major term), and consequent. It is of the form:

> There is smoke;
> Wherever there is smoke, there is fire; and where there is
> no fire, there is no smoke;
> Therefore, there is fire.

The syllogism for another should explicitly state the relation between reason and the minor term (*pakṣa*) also. It will then be of the form:

> The mountain has smoke;
> Wherever there is smoke, there is fire; and where there is
> no fire, there is no smoke;
> This mountain has smoke necessarily connected with fire;
> Therefore, this mountain has fire.

We see that in the above syllogism the example is not mentioned, which is considered to be essential by the Nyāya. The Jainas say that it is not essential,[34] but have no objection to including it for the sake of immature intellects. As regards the number of parts also, they say that it is immaterial whether we express the syllogism is four, five, or ten parts. The essential parts are the reason (*probans*), the major premise, and the consequent (*probandum*), which is to be proved.

Reason (*probans*) is that by means of which the *probandum* is cognized, which is necessarily accompanied by the *probandum*, and which cannot be found except along with it. The *probandum* is of five kinds:[35] it may be a natural characteristic of the *probans*, its cause, its effect, or an inseparable coadjunct.

The Jainas do not accept postulation (*arthāpatti*) as a distinct means of cognition, but classify it under inference.[36] For, according to them, nothing not directly cognized can be cognized without a major premise.

The last indirect cognition is the scriptural (*āgama*). This is really verbal knowledge, knowledge obtained from words. We have seen that verbal knowledge is included in direct cognition also. The Jainas are not very clear on how verbal knowledge can be classified under both headings. It looks as though ordinary verbal knowledge is direct cognition, and scriptural knowledge is indirect cognition.[37] Scripture is composed by a person, who is omniscient, dispassionate, and beyond ignorance. The words of only such a person are absolutely true and valid. The scriptures of Jainism alone are absolutely true, but not those of others.[38]

The Jaina theory of cognition and of the valid means of knowledge is as keen in its analysis of the different factors as any other's. The fact that they treat every stage of the development of cognition from mere looking at the object (*ālocana*, *darśana*) to syllogistic inference as a valid means shows that a true morphology and evolution of knowledge can be worked out on the basis of their analyses. What appears curious and interesting is the Jainas starting as a sect of the book-less, not accepting the authority of the extant Vedic scriptures, but ending up with regarding scriptural knowledge as the most reliable of all forms of indirect cognition, the scriptures of course being their own. Like the Nyāya and the Vaiśeṣika, the Jainas say that scripture must be composed by some person (*puruṣa*), but unlike them, they say that this person was not God, but the leader of their own religion. Their doctrine of verbal knowledge is, however, interesting, in that they treat part of it as coming under direct cognition and part under the indirect, and of the latter, again, a part as fallible and the other (scriptural) as infallible. But verbal knowledge as direct cognition—as when a man points a pen to the child and says that its name is pen—is not mere verbal knowledge, but a combination of verbal knowledge and perception. One is justified also in saying that what the child here learns is not about the object through the word, but about the word through the object. However, the large number of valid means of cognition accepted by the Jainas and the large number of views among them—all of which cannot be presented here—about classifying those means is due to the fact that the Jainas were aware of the inter-relationship among the different means and of the shading off of some into others, and so expressed different views about classifying[39] them.

THE DOCTRINE OF MULTIPLE MODALITY The idea of multiple modality (*anekānta vāda*) is very important in Jaina epistemology, and they defend it from the attacks of all the other schools. According to this doctrine, every object has an infinite number of modes or modal characteristics[40] in its relations to the infinite number of other objects of the world. So any judgment can be made about it and can be true. We have already come across the Jaina doctrine that the *ātman*, mind, senses, and objects are both identical with, and different from one another. Then every entity is identical with, and different from every other. Identity and difference become two opposed modal characteristics of every object. Similarly, between a thing and its qualities, its activities, its time, its place, its being, its non-being, etc., there are both identity and difference. Thus every proposition about a thing can be true in some modal reference or from some point of view or perspective, and false from another.

Jainism used the doctrine of multiple modality for three purposes. *First*, it wanted to show that every other school was committed to one of the alternate modalities (*ekānta*) and was therefore inadequate. Its view of reality was an incomplete expression. *Second*, it wanted to show its tolerance of other views, by saying that they had some truth, which could be justified from some point of view. *Third*, it thought that it could overcome skepticism and agnosticism by saying that all the alternate views had each some truth and that complete truth lay in understanding the value of the perspectives. If I place my hand first in cold water and then in warm water, the latter appears to be hot. But if I place my hand first in hot water and then in warm water, the latter appears to be cool. But is it cool, warm, or hot? If I say that I do not know and cannot know, I land in skepticism and agnosticism. But if I say that it is cool, warm, and hot also from different points of view, I shall not be a skeptic or agnostic. Similarly, the proposition, "This pen exists," is true with reference to the time and place in which it exists. But with reference to other times and places, the proposition is false. But which of the two propositions, "The pen exists" and "The pen does not exist," is absolutely true or absolutely false? Neither is absolutely true or false, but only relatively to the standpoint. So we should not say: "We cannot know whether the pen exists or does not exist," but "It exists from one point of view and does not exist from another." To recognize that all knowledge is modal does not lead to skepticism; but to take any one modality as absolute is a fallacy.

The Jaina doctrine of modality is not to be equated to the modal form of propositions in western logic. It is not the modality of propositions merely, but of reality itself. It is the modality of knowledge and of the object also; for, the Jainas say, the relation of identity and difference holds between knowledge and the object known.

The Jaina logicians point out that the doctrine of modality is not peculiar to their own school. Many Vedāntins accept that the relation between the Brahman on the one side and the *ātmans* and the world of matter on the other is both identity and difference. Kumārila accepted such a relation between the universal and the individual. The Jainas point to some other views[41] also.

The rival schools ask whether, if truth and falsity are both true of every proposition, the proposition, "The Jaina philosophy is true," must also be both true and false. This is not a fair objection.[42] The Jainas say that every proposition is true from one point of view and false from another. Now, this view about every proposition can be declared to be false either from no standpoint or from some standpoint. If it is from no standpoint, then the declaration cannot be accepted; if it is declared from some particular standpoint, the Jainas have already said that to take that standpoint as absolute is a fallacy. If the relativity of standpoints is accepted, the Jaina doctrine will be relatively false, but may be absolutely true. However, it is difficult to understand how the Jainas can defend the absolute truth of their categoreal scheme, if they succeed in defending the absolute truth of their doctrine of multi-modality.

But a more formidable objection awaits the Jainas. For the doctrine of multi-modality cuts at the very roots of inference.[43] Inference is based upon the major and minor premises and we frame syllogisms like

> All men are mortal;
> Socrates is a man;
> Therefore, Socrates is mortal.

But if either or both the major and minor premises are true and false also, how can we draw any conclusion? If it is said that both the premises are to be accepted as true from that point of view from which they can give a true conclusion, such a procedure implies that we already know the conclusion and that we are interpreting the premises so as to make the conclusion follow from them. It involves then in a *petitio principi* of the worst type, and at any rate it cannot give us any new knowledge. If it cannot give us any new knowledge, inference cannot be a distinct means of knowledge, but can at the most confirm what we know by other means. But the Jainas accept inference as a distinct means of knowing. Furthermore, if the premises are true from some particular standpoint, is the standpoint itself absolutely true or true from some other standpoint? If the latter alternative is accepted, we shall have to raise the same question again and will land in infinite regress. We cannot even be sure that the rose before me is or is not red.

It is, indeed, true that many other schools accept that a relation can be both identity and difference; but they accept it only in a few cases. The relation between the universal and the individual and between substance and qualities may be both identity and difference. But we should not generalize and say that every opposite modality holds true of everything in the world. Each case has to be decided on its own merits. Thus those thinkers who hold that a relation in some cases can be both identity and difference maintain that it will be false to generalize from a few cases and say that this relation must hold true in every case and that, therefore, all opposites like truth and falsity, the positive and the negative, are universal characteristics of all objects and propositions.

However, on the basis of their principle of multi-modality, the Jainas developed two other doctrines: the doctrine of modalities (*nayavāda*), which may be called the doctrine of standpoints, and the doctrine of conditioned predication (*syādvāda*). These doctrines are really parts of the doctrine of multi-modality.

THE DOCTRINE OF MODALITIES OR TROPES These modalities are what in Greek skepticism are called the tropes.[44] The doctrine of the Jainas is not the explanation of a principle, but its application. In fact, it is an attempt to enumerate the possible modalities or one-sided standpoints. The Jainas say that the number of these modalities can be very large, as every object can have an infinite number of them. But they pick up those which they think their rivals adopt in propounding their respective doctrines and commit the fallacy of one-sided-ness. A model statement (*naya*) is the assertion of one part or aspect of an object that has many such parts or aspects, without at the same time referring to the others. *As such it is neither true nor false.*[45] *But it becomes false when the aspects not referred to are rejected.*

Modalities or tropes are at first of two kinds: those concerned with substance (*dravya*) and those concerned with the modes (*prayāyas*) of a substance. The former grasp only the substantiality of objects; the latter only their qualities. The former is of three kinds: the conventional (*naigama*), the summary (*saṅgraha*), and the popular (*vyāvahārika*). An example of the first is: "The *ātman* is consciousness." It is declared so in the scriptures, and it is thought that there is no distinction between the *ātman* as substance and its quality consciousness. It is, therefore, ignored that consciousness can be a quality also. And example of the second is: "Everything is Being." It is thought, therefore, that there is no plurality of beings. The statement is a summary statement on the basis of the most common characteristic treated as the common substance of everything.[46] An example of the third is: "Every object is material." This is a popular idea; common people see the material aspect of things more easily.

Modalities concerned with the modes of objects are of four kinds: the straight (*ṛjusūtra*), the verbal (*śabda*), the etymological (*samabhirūḍha*), and the pragmatic (*evambhūta*). The first takes the momentary, present aspect of an object and equates that aspect to the whole object, as in, for example, "Life is misery." Here is the Jaina attack on the Buddhist teaching. The second modality understands an object literally from the words describing it. For example, in "He sits, he sleeps, and he wakes up," sitting, sleeping, and waking are different acts and are not identical with one another. Then it may be questioned how the same "he" be identical with sitting, sleeping, and waking, and concluded that there are three different "he's" or egos. Here from the verbal expressions of three qualitative states we are drawing a conclusion about the subject of the three states; and as the three states are not identical, we are concluding that the subject that has the three states is not also identical. The Jainas think that this kind of inference is a linguistic fallacy. Even otherwise, we can see that there is a fallacy.[47] It lies in the demand to equate the subject and predicate, or substance and attribute. The third modality tries to determine the nature of the object from the root of its name. For instance, the word man is derived from the Sanskrit verbal root√*man*, meaning to think; we may then conclude that man is nothing more than a thinker and ignore his other characteristics. The fourth is determination of an object simply by what it does or from its function. A cow is the animal that gives milk. Giving milk is a function of the cow. So one may conclude that, when the cow does not give milk, it is not a cow. Giving milk is only one aspect of the nature of the cow.[48]

The above modalities are classified differently into object-modalities or modalities concerned with objectivity (*arthanayas*) and verbal modalities or modalities concerned with words (*śabdanayas*). Then to the first three of the above first classification, the first of the second (concerned with modes) is added, so that the four constitute object-modalities. The rest will be verbal modalities.[49]

Modal fallacies (*nayābhāsas*)[50] arise only when the aspects not referred to by the modal statements are not only merely overlooked, but also definitely rejected. Modality itself is not a fallacy, which lies in the explicit rejection of the other modes. Such fallacies can be of many kinds, but the Jainas consider some as the most important and mention them. *First*, there is the fallacy of grasping only the substance of an object (*dravyārthikābhāsa*) to the exclusion of the modes, denying their reality. *Second*, there is the fallacy of grasping the modes (*paryāyārthikābhāsa*) to the exclusion of the substance, denying its reality. The *third* is the absolute differentiation of substance and its modes (*naigamābhāsa*), rejecting the identity between the two. The *fourth* is the rejection of the plurality of objects, accepting only the unity of their Being (*saṅgrahābhāsa*), as in the Advaita and even in the Sāṅkhya so far as the material world goes. The *fifth* is the acceptance of what appears to be tangible in the everyday world of matter and the rejection of the reality of the soul, or moral law etc., (*vyāvahārikābhāsa*), as done by the Cārvākas, who accept only what is known to common people and reject everything else. The *sixth* is the acceptance of what is immediately experienced at the present and the rejection of everything, past and future (*ṛjusūtrābhāsa*), as in Buddhism, according to which everything is momentary. The other fallacies can easily be imagined and are based on other types of the modalities of existence.

THE DOCTRINE OF CONDITIONED PREDICATION Because of the multi-modality of all existence and because of the truth of every proposition being conditioned by the modalities of existence, predication of different kinds of opposites, separately and in combinations, to objects becomes acceptable, provided we do not take any one predication to be the absolute truth. This doctrine is called the doctrine of "let it be so" (*syādvāda*).[51] The absolute opposites are "is" and "is not" or Being and Non-being. We may take any two predicates also like *P* and not-*P*. What is *P* from one point of view is not *P*, or is not-*P*, from another. In the example of our experience of three buckets of water—cool, warm, and hot—the middle will be hot from one point of view and cool from another. According to the Jainas, the following seven propositions are every one of them true. The relatively true is called by them the conditioned truth, truth conditioned by a standpoint or modality of existence. The expression of conditioned truth is neither a conditional truth like "if it rains, the ground will be wet," nor the statement of possibility like "It may rain," but a conditioned factual truth, a categorical statement of existence like "That figure is vague, because I look from a distance," and "The snow is glaring because of the sun," from which the reasons are omitted. It may be repeated that, for the Jainas, every existence is conditioned by modalities and so every proposition is implicitly a conditioned proposition, whether we know or not the conditioning modalities. The seven conditioned forms of the relation between every subject and predicate are:

1. Let it be: *S* is *P*—The water is cool;
2. Let it be: *S* is not-*P*—The water is not-cool;
3. Let it be: *S* is both *P* and not-*P*—The water is both cool and not-cool;
4. Let it be: *S* is indescribable (or neither *P* nor not-*P*)—The water is indescribable (neither cool nor not-cool);
5. Let it be: *S* is *P* and indescribable;
6. Let it be: *S* is not-*P* and indescribable.
7. Let it be: *S* is both *P* and not-*P* and indescribable.

The seven statements can be made with regard to the existence also of *S*:

1. Let it be: *S* exists;
2. Let it be: *S* does not exist;
3. Let it be: *S* both exists and does not exist;
4. Let it be: *S* is indescribable (or neither exists nor does not exist);
5. Let it be: *S* exists and is indescribable;
6. Let it be: *S* does not exist and is indescribable
7. Let it be: *S* both exists and does not exist and is indescribable.

The Jainas say, and we can see also, that with regard to any predicate and its contradictory, the above seven propositions alone are possible. *P* and not-*P* are contradictories and make two propositions possible. But one may say that we ought to take both the standpoints together if our description of the middle bucket of water is to be complete; for such a thinker the third proposition is acceptable. But another may say that, since cool and hot are opposites and cannot be attributed to the same object, water by itself is neither cool nor hot and that we cannot really describe what water is in itself. For him the fourth proposition will be acceptable. But it is none of the first three. Then some people may like to combine it with each of the first three. If we begin combining them, we get only three in addition to the first four propositions.[52] The first and the second propositions are already combined in the third proposition. There is no use of combining the first and the third, as *P* is already present in the latter. Otherwise, it will be "*S* is *P* and *P* and not-*P*," in which *P* is repeated and the repetition of a predicate adds nothing to the meaning of the proposition. For the same reason, the combination of the second and the third gives no new proposition. So the fourth only can be combined with each of the first three propositions and we get then the fifth, sixth and seventh. There is no point in combining the last three again with each of the first four. For the reasons for which the doctrine of multi-modality is assailed by the rival schools, the doctrine of conditioned predication also is assailed by them. For there can be no conditioned inference; otherwise, we can prove everything and inference will be of no use as a valid means of cognition. For instance, one can infer smoke from fire by adding a condition in the following way:

> There is smoke in the oven;
> Because of fire;
> Wherever there is fire (along with wet fuel[53]), there is smoke;
> This oven has fire;
> Therefore, there is smoke.

In the major premise, the condition, "with wet fuel," makes the major premise true; but it is not mentioned in the minor premise. It can be mentioned only if seen. But when it is seen, the smoke also can be seen, and there will be no need of an inference. Inference requires that, whatever be the number of conditions (provisos), they should be given along with reason (*probans*), and the *probandum* must be an invariable concomitant of the *probans*, without any conditions. Such an inference becomes impossible, if we accept the doctrines of multi-modality and conditioned predication. Furthermore, the Jaina acceptance of the contradictory predicates, *P* and not-*P*, for every subject *S*, makes thinking impossible. Inference assumes the unconditioned truth of the major and minor premises and the former has to be an unconditioned and unconditional universal statement.

VALIDITY OF KNOWLEDGE Validity is the exact determination of an object (*samyagarthanirṇaya*).[54] Determination (determining, asserting, *nirṇaya*) is the cognition that is without doubt, that grasps the peculiarity of the object (*adhyavasita*), and that is unmistaken. An object is that which is to be desired or avoided. Exactness is unmistakability.

The Jainas arrive at this definition from their analysis of the knowledge situation. All cognition reveals not only the object but also the knower, and is self-revealing. As consciousness, it is both identical with, and different from the *ātman*. It is of the form not only of "That is a pen," but also of "I see the pen." As revealing the object it is, again, both identical with, and different from the object. The essence of cognition lies in revealing the knower and the known, but not in its contact with the object, and is due to removing the veil of ignorance produced by action (*karma*) but not due merely to the contact of the sense with the object, as the Nyāya and the Vaiśeṣika maintain.

To the question, whether knowledge is valid by itself or is made valid by something else, the Jainas answer that both the alternatives are true,[55] depending on the situation. All cognition, when it is produced, is produced by the object and is, therefore, valid due to the other (*paratah*).[56] But when it is remembered and when it leads to some action, it may be valid either by itself (*svatah*) or due to something else (*paratah*). The Jainas say that they do not want to take sides with people holding one-sided views. If we are habituated to a particular cognitive situation, then cognition will be self-valid. If a man drinks water to quench his thirst, he does not, and does not have to doubt whether his thirst is quenched. A man bathing in a river does not doubt whether or not he is bathing in water. Inference, which is devoid of fallacies, is valid by itself and does not need anything else to make it valid. In the case of new objects with which we have had no acquaintance, our cognitions are made valid either by the cognition of unmistakability, by repeated cognitions exactly similar, or by confirming cognitions like "This is sweet" confirming "This is sugar." They are confirmed by the pragmatic test that the object performs the function for which it is meant, by the cognition that there is nothing between us and the object, and by the cognition that there is no distorting medium. In the case of verbal knowledge, its validity is always due to something else (*paratah*). If my friend tells me that there is a gorilla in the zoo, my knowledge that there is a gorilla in the zoo cannot be certain, unless I actually go there and perceive the animal. So verbal cognition has to be made valid by perceptual cognition. In the case of scriptural knowledge, it is made valid by its being derived from scriptures, which are infallible.

THE DOCTRINE OF ILLUSION The Jaina doctrine of illusion is not clear, but is akin to the doctrines of the Nyāya and Kumārila. If we see an object that does not merely have a particular form (*rūpa*) and attribute that particular form to it, as if it has that form, we commit the perceptual error,[57] which is illusion. If form (*rūpa*) is taken in the sense of the universal (*prakāra jāti*), then the Jaina doctrine will be the same as that of the Nyāya. Otherwise, it will be the same as that of Kumārila's. But as the Jainas do not mention that the object of illusion is a particular object seen somewhere else, it is likely that the doctrines of Kumārila and Jainism are not exactly the same, although the Jaina writers, like many others,[58] seem to have confused the two. Jainism rejects the views of all the other schools.

3. METAPHYSICS

The Jaina metaphysics is primarily a metaphysics of substance. Everything is a substance. Even motion, rest, space, and action are substances. The Jaina classification of categories may be presented by the chart on p. 120.

In the Nyāya and Vaiśeṣika also, we find space and time classified as substances. But the Jainas include motion and rest also. As we shall see, motion comes under action and rest under quality for the Nyāya and the Vaiśeṣika.

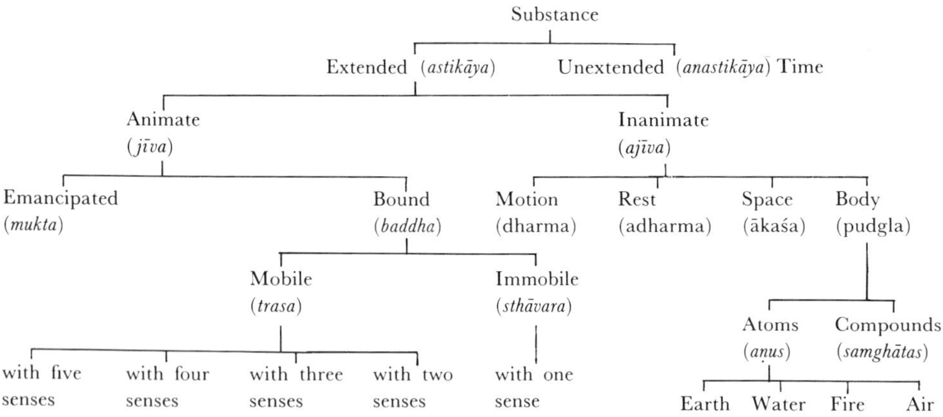

SUBSTANCE According to Jainism, as every object is multi-modal, it has many characteristics. The first distinction is that between that (*dharmi*) which has the characteristics and the characteristics (*dharmas*) possessed by it. The former is the substance. Characteristics were originally divided by the Jainas into two kinds: essential characteristics (*guṇas*) and changing modes[59] (*paryāyas*). But later this division seems to be ignored and both types were called by the name modes (*paryāyas*), of which some change and the others do not. But change and permanence are both real. Furthermore, every object has both positive and negative characteristics. From one point of view, it has the characteristic *P*, and from another, the characteristic not-*P*. Moreover, every object has, again, the three characteristics: origin, duration, and decay. The Jainas reject a Buddhist view that every object is born, lasts, and is destroyed at the same moment. They do not accept also the view that the reality of an object lies in performing the function for which it is meant (*arthakriyākāritā*), i.e., in its causal efficacy—a view advocated by the Buddhists, particularly of the Mahāyāna, and some others.

As we see in the above chart, substance is divided into the extended and the unextended. Time alone is the unextended substance. Even spirit (*jīva*, *ātman*) is an extended substance. Extended substance is divided into the animate and the inanimate. The animate is the soul or spirit, for which Jainism uses the terms *jīva* and *ātman* indifferently. The soul is primarily of two kinds: the liberated and the bound. The bound is again of two kinds: the moving and the non-moving. The non-moving are plants, which have only one sense, touch. The moving are of four kinds: those with five senses like men, those with four senses like bees, those with three senses like ants, and those with two senses like worms.

THE ĀTMAN As mentioned already, the Jainas use the words *jīva* and *ātman* in the same sense, saying that the *jīva* is the same as the *ātman* in the state of bondage and the *ātman* is the same as the *jīva* in the state of liberation. However, consciousness is of the essence of the *ātman* and reveals itself, the *ātman*, and the object. The relation between the *ātman* and its consciousness is both identity and difference and between consciousness and the object also is the same. The *ātman*, not the physical body, is the agent of actions and is also the enjoyer of their fruit. The *ātmans* are infinite in number, and yet they can coexist just as the light of many lamps can coexist. The Jainas reject the Advaita conception of the oneness or non-duality of the *ātmans*. They reject also the reality of God as the Universal Spirit and as the creator of the world; for the world, as the Mīmāmsakas say, is created out of matter by the actions (*karmas*) which the *ātmans* perform. The Jainas reject all the proofs for the existence of God, and declare that God cannot exist and his existence cannot be proved. Here they are one with the Mīmāmsakas except for the fact that they regard action as a substance.

The *ātman*, although not a material substance, is an extended substance. It occupies the space which the body occupies and is only as big or as small as the body. That is, the *ātman* of the ant is as small as the ant and that of the elephant as big as the elephant. However, it does not fill space like matter, but is only present in every bit of the material body. By nature it is infinite; but it can contract or expand, being determined by its actions (*karmas*). It is omniscient also by nature; but its infinite consciousness gets limited by its actions. Action (*karma*) is understood by the Jainas as a kind of dust, the particles of which stick to the *ātman*, which is like a pure white cloth, and veil its consciousness. The Jainas speak of particles of *karma*.

Jainism rejects the Cārvāka view that consciousness is an emergent quality of material elements and that the *ātman* is, therefore, nothing but the physical body. No inference is necessary to prove the reality of the *ātman;* it is directly experienced in every cognition, which reveals not only the object but also the "I" that cognizes the object. It is revealed in experience like "I am happy," and "I am angry." Furthermore, the Cārvākas cannot, on their own hypothesis, establish the universal proposition that consciousness is an emergent quality. For no universal proposition can be established by mere perception and the Cārvākas do not accept inference as a valid means of cognition. Even if they accept it, no concomitant realtion between body and consciousness can be established; for man is not conscious in deep sleep and swoon and also when anesthetized, and dead bodies are certainly not conscious. If it is said that the peculiar structure or pattern of the body is lost in these states, one has still to answer: What is it that produces this structure and controls it? The producer cannot be any part of the body itself. If it is said that it is Nature that produces the structure, we do not perceive her and it is better to say that it is the conscious *ātman* itself, which is different from the material paticles, that produces the structure. We do not see the tendency of material particles everywhere to come together and form the particular structure called the living body. The tendency has to be introduced by an external agent. Besides, the Cārvākas cannot even talk of their consciousness; for they accept only sense-perception and consciousness is not an object of sense-perception.

MATTER The Jaina conception of matter is somewhat peculiar. Indeed, everything is a substance, but every substance is not matter. Matter consists of bodies occupying space and is, therefore, extended. But all extended substances are not bodies and are, therefore, not matter. Bodies (*pudgalas*) alone are matter. The world of matter consists of atoms and compounds. Atoms are of four kinds: earth, water, fire, and air, corresponding to the four senses—smell, taste, vision, and touch. The Jainas do not accept aether as a fifth element corresponding to the sense of hearing. Sound is said to be caused by particles of air impinging on one another and finally on the ear-drum. There are only material elements.

NON-MATERIAL INANIMATE SUBSTANCES Time, motion, rest, and space are unconscious by nature, but not material. Time is of two kinds: real (*pāramārthika*) time and conventional (*vyāvahārika*) time.[60] Real time is continuous duration, one and undivided. We have to accept the reality of time, because without it no change can occur. Yet, time is not the cause of change, but the indispensable locus or ground of change; it is what makes change possible. It is not perceived, but inferred. Again, although real time is indivisible, it consists of an infinite number of particles of time, each of which is indivisible. What the Jainas seem to mean is that the particles of time cannot be divided into timeless points. But we cannot understand how indivisible time can contain particles of time. However, the Jainas say that time does not occupy space, but is an unextended substance. It is eternal.

Conventional time is that which is divided into years, seasons, months, weeks, days, etc. Beginnings and ends are found in it. It is not eternal.

Space is that substance which allows or makes possible all extended substances to exist. It is infinite, indivisible, eternal, and one. It is the indispensable condition for the existence of all extended objects; but it is not the cause of their existence. It cannot be perceived, but inferred. For convenience, it is divided into two kinds: the world-space (*lokākāśa*) and the non-world-space (*alokākāśa*). The world-space is that which is occupied by the objects of the world; the other is what lies beyond world-space. However, the two are really one and continuous. By this division the Jainas mean that there is unoccupied space beyond the world also.

The Jaina conception of motion and rest is peculiar, in that both are called substances. Motion is the condition of all movement and rest the condition of all rest. If a fish moves in water, the motion is certainly initiated by the fish. But given only fish and water, there cannot be motion. So there must be something called motion inherent in the universe. The movement of the fish is made possible by this motion. It is unitary, infinite, formless, eternal, itself non-moving, and fills the entire world-space (*lokākāśa*). For exactly similar reasons, the Jainas accept the reality of rest also as a substance. Its nature also is exactly similar. The Jainas call motion by the name *dharma* and rest by the name *adharma*, which in the usual philosophical terminology mean ethical merit and demerit respectively. The Jainas use the two terms in their ethical meanings also.

4. LIFE'S IDEAL

Although the Jainas do not accept the reality of God, their ethics and religion are spiritual, as they accept the reality of spirit. They accept also the four values of life—wealth, enjoyment, ethical merit, and salvation. The bondage of the *ātman* is due to its being entangled in the world of action (*karma*); and so salvation can be obtained only by lifting oneself above action and eschewing all action. No other Indian school preached more strongly against action than Jainism. Infinity, omniscience, and the original blissfulness are lost by the *ātman* because of action. From the ethico-religious point of view, the Jainas give a new categoreal scheme. This scheme consists of seven categories:[61] spirit (*jīva, ātman*), non-spirit (*ajīva*), inflow of action (*āśrava*), bondage (*bandha*), the stopping of the inflow (*samvara*), exhaustion (*nirjara*), and liberation (*mokṣa*). Of the seven categories, the first two have already been explained. Inflow (*āśrava*) is the flowing in of action (*karma*) into the pure, infinite spirit (*ātman*), as though through a gate. This inflow of action pollutes the *ātman*, veils its infinity and omniscience, and makes it a determinate, finite being. The inflow is the same as joining (*yoga*) or identification of the *ātman* with the actions of body, speech, mind, and senses.[62] We should note that here the word *yoga* is used by the Jainas in a sense different from the ordinary. They use the word in the ordinary sense also. Action is of two kinds, the good and the evil. As action (*karma*) is understood as that which finitizes the *ātman*, life's aim should be to rise above both good and evil actions. Bondage (*bandha*) is the assuming of a physical body according to one's good and evil deeds.[63] The causes of bondage are: false views, non-detachment (attachment), negligence (*pramāda*, error, mistake), passion (*kaṣāya*), and the joining (identifying oneself) with the actions of body, speech, and mind (*yoga*).

For obtaining liberation, man must first stop (*samvara*) all new inflow of action. It can be stopped through restraint (*gupti*), carefulness (*samiti*) in speech, etc., observance of rules (*dharma*, such as cleanliness, truthfulness, non-stealing, penance, non-injury, celebacy, etc.), conquest of one's ailments (*parīṣahajaya*, endurance), and conduct (*caritra*, behaviour). Then one should work for the exhaustion (*nirjara*) of the already accumulated actions (*karmas*) through penance.[64] Penance not only stops the inflow of new actions, but also exhausts the already performed actions. Then when all the accumulated actions are exhausted—that is, when their potency is destroyed—and no new actions enter the spirit, it obtains liberation (*mokṣa*). The path[65] to liberation consists of right views and faith, right knowledge, and right conduct. Right faith is respectful attitude towards all that is rationally established and has itself to be rational. Right knowledge is knowledge found elaborated and explained in Jaina epistemology. Right conduct consists in following the ways recommended for stopping the inflow of new actions into the *ātman* and for exhausting all action already accumulated. Although the Jaina classification of virtues is often overlapping, one can see that all the virtues taught by every other ethics and religion are included. But the Jainas practise these virtues, particularly non-injury, with the greatest rigour imaginable. And their whole philosophy of life is geared to the idea that, unless man rises completely above action and eschews all action, no salvation is possible. He has to rise even above the actions of eating bread and drinking water. In the final stages, the Jaina monk starves himself to death, and creates a legal problem; for such an act comes under suicide. No other school in India, not even Buddhism, preached so rigorous an asceticism as Jainism prescribed.

GENERAL ESTIMATE AND CONSTRUCTIVE COMMENT

(i) Jaina Classification of Categories not Ultimate

Much can be written on the achievements of Jainism as a philosophy. Its epistemology, although in a different way, is as well developed as that of any other school. In metaphysics, it is often naive realism and too much of a common sense philosophy to match the profundity of the Vedāntic schools. It is, indeed, easy to give a new definition of every concept, of even philosophy and its aim as has become the fashion in recent western philosophy; it is easy to justify then one's own metaphysics. In the world of action (*karmamayajagat*), in our pragmatic reality, relativity (*anekāntatā*) as the Jainas themselves say, reigns supreme, and anything can be justified and rejected—which shows the inadequacy of logic when ultimate questions are raised. We came across this possibility in the discussion of the Cārvāka. But there has to be something to which our thought and discussion have to be moored. Otherwise, they will be carried away, blown hither and thither by the winds of empty, unfounded doctrines. In the world of action, action and the agent of action, who is conscious and self-conscious, are the only guides to regulate our thinking; and an adequate study of their structure is, therefore, of primary importance. The Jaina contribution to an understanding of the two is significant and is worth evaluation.

Jaina philosophy is a great defender of pluralism. But as we have seen, that everything is identical with everything else and also different from it—consciousness and its object, universal and the individual, and so forth—leads naturally to a kind of monism, of which the Jainas stopped short. Again, if the *ātman* is identical with everything and also different from it, a kind of monism of the spirit also—as in Rāmānuja's philosophy—is ultimately inevitable. It may be said that the *ātmans* are many; then there will result a position like that of the Sāṅkhya to be discussed in a following chapter. For the Sāṅkhya, Prakṛti (Primeval Matter) is one, not many—all the world is the same for all persons—although presenting different phases[66] to different *ātmans*, with which, the Jainas would say, the plurality of its constituents will be identical and yet be different. Indeed, in the case of the Sāṅkhya, the *ātman* merely throws its reflection into Prakṛti, but never becomes completely identical with it. This, of course, makes an important difference.

The Jaina view that everything is a substance, justifying it by giving a new definition of substance as that which has attributes, as many other philosophers in the East and the West have done, confuses[67] logical and epistemological schemata on the one side with cosmological and ontological schemata on the other. Substance is not merely that to which we can assign a predicate or that which hides itself behind a quality. We may say: "That red is dark;" but our judgment does not make red colour a substance. Even the etymological meaning of the Sanskrit word, *dravya* (*dravati iti*, that which flows, changes, etc.) which distinguishes between that which flows and the flow (change) may be applied to a quality like red, which can fade and so change. The objections of Berkeley and Bradley in the West and of Nāgārjuna and Śrī Harṣa in India, asking who has actually seen anything behind the qualities and activities, dispose of the view that substance lies behind the qualities and activities. The objection applies equally well, the reader may note, to the classification of the categories given by the Nyāya and the Vaiśeṣika schools, which will be presented in a later chapter.

What then is substance? We have seen in the chapter on the Mīmāmsā that the distinction between substance, action and quality is fluid and that even relatively the relation between substance and action is more important than that between substance and quality. Bearing this point in mind, we may say that substance is that from which action starts and that towards which it is directed. Magnet attracts iron. But it is not any quality of the magnet that attracts iron, but the magnet itself, although figuratively, we may say: "It is the quality of the magnet to attract iron."[68] We may say also: "The nature of the magnet attracts iron." Similarly, it is not the activity of the magnet that attracts iron, but the magnet itself. We find figurative uses in this case also. We have also seen that action is energy (*śakti*), and energy passes into substance and becomes one with it. The distinction between the three categories is relative, and we have to conclude that ultimately each can have no ontological status of its own. But in cosmology, they have significance only when the cosmos is considered as a world of action, and only secondarily as a world of thought—which implies that thought has to be based on action and action presupposes a world of objective substances on which we act and which act on us and on one another. The Jainas, like the Buddhists, the Mīmāmsakas, and other orthodox schools, accept that the world is due to action (*karma*) and is meant for action. The categories of the world then have primarily to be the categories of action—which disposes of the Jaina claim that its classification of categories is ultimate. It is not understandable how they can justify adequately their classification of time, space, rest, and movement as substances.[69]

(ii) Ātman not Limited to the Body: Not Finite

What further troubles the reader is the Jaina treatment of the *ātman* (spirit, I-consciousness) as an extended substance. First, it is not a susbstance by itself (in *kaivalya* in its original purity), but only in the world of action as the agent of action. By itself, it is pure consciousness that transcends the world of action, even according to the Jainas. Secondly, it is not an extended substance, as it transcends space and time. In the empirical state of the I-consciousness, as this body or as occupying this body, it may be said to be extended in space and time. But we cannot understand how it can be extended in its transcendental state. In its relation of identity and difference with the physical world if it is to be regarded as extended, it will remain extended forever, as the relation lasts forever; and there will be no point of speaking about its salvation. For salvation is rising above the world of action—which the Jainas advise as the ideal of life.

The similarity between the Jaina conception of time as unextended to Bergson's theory of time does not go very far. Yes, for both time is substantive, but in a sense only. For Bergson would not want the category of substance, which is applicable to the practical world or world of action, to be applied to his *elan vital*, which is time, and is at the same time conscious intuition. Furthermore, we face the difficulty of understanding how the extended *ātman* can be in time which is unextended. For the unextended can be in the extended, but not vice versa. We cannot also explain how a plurality of extended *ātmans* can coexist either in the world of action or in their *kaivalya* or transcendence, salvation.

The Jaina view that the *ātman* can be as small as the body of the mosquito and as big as the body of the elephant, and that it can contract and expand according to the body it occupies is perhaps the reason for saying that it is an extended substance. It may also be an answer to the question: How can the transcendental, infinite—for the Jainas also it is infinite—*ātman* become immanent in a limited finite body? This is, indeed, a question that has baffled all explanations both in the East and the West. But if the above is the answer to the question, it is a very naive answer. For if my *ātman* is limited to my body, then I cannot understand how I can see anything outside my body, not to speak of seeing the star thousands of light years away. The difficulty becomes the greater if we take also into consideration the Jaina view that the relation between the *ātman* and the object, etc., the star, is identity in difference. That is, my *ātman* must be in direct contact with the object; but how can it be in such direct contact if it is limited to my body?

One possible answer is: Although my *ātman* is limited to my body, my senses, my eyesight in the case of the star, can reach that far. But according to the Jainas, the relation between the *ātman* and the senses is again identity in difference. There can be no sense without the *ātman*. Then either the *ātman* also must be infinite or the relation between it and the sense of sight must be something different from identity in difference. Nor can it be said that the sense of sight travels to the star. If this "travel" means that the sight leaves the *ātman* temporarily, the explanation looks absurd—this absurdity applies to all the schools like the Nyāya, which say that sight goes (*prāpyakāri*) to the object—for nobody's sight leaves him in order to reach the star. If it means that my sight is as infinite as the *ātman*, but cognizes the object only when focussed on it through the instrumentality of my mind with its interests and urges directed intentionally or by chance towards the object, then the position that the *ātman* is limited to the body has to be given up or substantially modified.

(iii) Mind and Senses Ray of the Ātman

The Jaina position about mind is not very clear. We have seen that, so far as worldly life goes, the acceptance of mind (*manas*) apart from the senses is necessary. But the Jainas say that what is called mind is only a function of the *ātman*; and no distinct category to be called mind apart from the *ātman* and the senses is, therefore, needed. But if the functions which mind performs—synthesizing the impressions of the different senses into unitary objects and experiencing pleasures and pains—are natural and original functions of the *ātman*, how can the *ātman* ever transcend worldly existence and obtain salvation? Here there is a lacuna in the Jaina argument. Again, if these functions are natural to it, then the so-called pure state is one with them and not without them. Then that salvation lies in regaining the pure state becomes false. If it is said that the so-called mind is a group of some functions[70] and arises as a result of the force (*śakti*) of accumulated ethical activities—which the Advaita would accept, for Māyā or Avidyā contains the causal body (*kāraṇaśarīra*), which is a bundle (*granthi*) of causal potencies of actions (*karmas*)—then mind has to be distinct from the *ātman*, which can arise above them and distinguish itself from them, and so from mind also. That the functions of mind and senses are the functions of the *ātman* needs further clarification, which the Jainas have not given.

There is a function of the senses which has not so much attracted the attention of western psychologists and philosophers as it attracted the Indian. The problem posed by the Indian philosophers may be thought to be somewhat naive in this scientific and technological age, but it has a profound significance even now, if we go beyond some of the common sense assumptions. Usually we think that the senses, i.e., the cognitive senses are limited to the body. When they cognize an object at a distance, do they go, travel to it, and then contact it for cognizing it? If they do not, they must then be infinitely extended, and the *ātman* consequently must be infinite. Here is the problem for the Indian schools.

Before discussing and explaining the question further, we may simply recount what the schools generally maintained. Some schools blurred the question. Again, the followers of some schools are not unanimous. Only representative views will be given here so that they need not be discussed again in other chapters.

We have already pointed out the vagueness of the Jaina view. On the whole, they think that the *ātman* itself, in its purity, is capable of knowing sense-objects by itself without the aid of senses; but in its finite impure state, sense contact is needed to remove the veil of ignorance (this is not the Māyā or Avidyā of the Advaita, but simply absence of knowledge). They think also, like the Nyāya, that there is difference between the physical senses as parts of the physical body and psychological senses—for although the eye, etc., are there in tact, they may not perceive their respective objects, which means that the psychological eye, etc., are not functioning. Of the five senses, the Jainas say that sight does not have to get into contact with the object, which is revealed to it; but the other senses have to get into contact with their objects. For instance, the sense of touch does not reveal the object unless it touches the object. We may make this theory intelligible by pointing to the function of sight extending far beyond the object it cognizes, while the functions of the other senses are not so, although whether such differentiation will stand examination ultimately is a different question.

The Buddhist view is not unanimous. They disagree even about the number of senses. Some of them say that the physical body is the only sense (*indriya*) because everything is cognized by it and without it nothting is cognized. Some say that touch is the only sense, all the others are its forms. There is a third view that mind (*manas*) is the only sense, not the body. Others say that there are six senses, the usual five senses and mind, which is also called sense, the internal sense with its particular function of knowing pains and pleasures. Most of the Buddhists say that, of all the five senses, sight and hearing do not go out to get into contact with the object; others have to contact their objects by going out. Hearing is clubbed with sight because we hear sounds far away, not only one or two but many. The apparent reason is that the objects of sight and hearing can be very extensive like the sky and the resonant drum beats; but those of touch, smell, and taste are very limited, particularly to the areas of the objects we more or less directly contact.

The Nyāya, the Vaiśeṣika, the Mīmāmsā on the whole, the Sāṅkhya and the Yoga, all maintain that all the senses have to go out to contact the objects. They distinguish, however, between the physical and the psychological senses. We can find some argument even in favour of their view. For even in the case of sight and hearing, we see only a certain object and hear only a certain sound—which means that the sense is particularly in contact with it. However, many Mīmāmsakas think that hearing is infinite like space and does not have to reach out for its object.

Another point of controversy is the question whether the senses, like the *ātman*, are infinite or finite. The Nyāya maintains that the senses are neither infinite nor infinitesimal, but finite. So they have to go out to the object. But are the physical senses finite or the psychological finite? We can understand why the former are finite, for they are parts of the finite body. But the psychological ones are not limited to the size of the physical senses; otherwise, the eye cannot see the expanse of the sky and the great Alps and Himalayas. So the Sāṅkhya holds that all senses, although they can cognize only when they come into contact with their objects, are infinite like the *ātman*. Then what is the point in saying that the senses go out to contact the objects? However, the Vedāntins—particularly the Advaitins and on the whole the Upaniṣads—also hold that the senses are infinite.

Generally we miss the crux and significance of the problem in the welter of these controversies, which mix up metaphysics with common sense. Many writers on Indian philosophy ignore the problem or at the most mention it incidentally in a few places, make a passing reference. But it is more important than it appears to be on the surface.

If the *ātman* is infinite, as most of the schools of Indian philosophy maintain, are its mind and senses also not infinite? We have seen reasons for accepting the infinity of the mind and its being somehow a function of the empirical *ātman*, my I-consciousness as I am now. Then are the senses also not infinite? If mind can locate the star thousands of light years away and my I-consciousness is there and my eye fixes it, locates it there, then is my sight not as extensive as my *ātman*? The same can be said *mutatis mutandis* about my sense of hearing also. The fact that my senses of taste, smell, and touch are limited apparently to my body is of secondary importance. We are here not talking of the physical senses. If my *ātman* and mind are not limited to my body, although the last three senses appear to be limited to my body, the inner experience of their objects—tastes, smells, and touches—by the *ātman* through the mind cannot be so limited. In dreams we have tastes, smells, and touches far away from the physical body. The body is spatially limited in size, but not the *ātman* and mind, which are not spatial, although they can touch space. How they can touch space, i.e., contact space, is a different question. It is the experience that is psychological, but not the physical and chemical reactions of the physical senses in the body. We have to say then that it is not the senses that go out to contact the object—although in literary language we say so—but that they cognize the objects when they come to their attention, which is directed by change or by the interest of the *ātman*. The word contact is ambiguous here; for there is always some contact between the sense and the object. But the difference between the two views we are discussing is this: in the one case, the sense goes out, travels to the object and establishes contact; in the other, the contact is established by the object's swimming, as it were, into the sense's ken or by the focussing of the mind through the sense on the object, thereby uncovering the veil, as the Jainas say, that hides the object from the sense. This uncovering of the veil means throwing the light of the *ātman* on the object and removing the intervening darkness. An appropriate example is that of focussing the torch light on an object in the dark. We say that the sight was there at the object, but darkness has to be dispelled by the torch light.

But are the senses independent of the *ātman*? Here we use the word *ātman* in the sense of the empirical *ātman*, this person, this *jīva*, but not in the sense of the transcendental *ātman*. To make the question more intelligible, we may substitute the word I or I-consciousness for the word *ātman* and ask: What is the relation between the I-consciousness and the senses? They must be inherently related to it, as otherwise our experience like "I am conscious of the (visible) pen" is not possible. If the senses are adventitious attachments to the *ātman* like a picture to the wall, we cannot understand how they can be so attached. If and when they are detached—as when I hear a sound and am not seeing and the sense of right is not operating and will have to be considered to be detached from my I—how can I have a mental coloured image of what I once saw, i.e., how can I remember it? If, to avoid the difficulty, it is said that the psychological sense sticks on to the I-consciousness although the physical sense detaches itself, we may ask the same question: Is the psychological sense not inherent to the I-consciousness? If it is not inherent, we shall still be unable to explain visual images and memory. There will also be the question: How can a spatially extended mental image attach itself adventitiously to a spatially unextended reality like the I-consciousness, unless it is part and parcel—not to be spatially understood—of the I-consciousness? How can then the sense of sight attach itself to the I-consciousness? Can the sense exist apart from the "I?" If it does, where does it exist when apart?

The above difficulties lead us to the alternative that the senses are some kind of transformations of the I-consciousness. But "transformation" here has a peculiar sense. In the live act of perceiving the pen before me, I am not cognizing myself but only the colour, etc., of the pen. But in the reflective cognition, "I know that I know the pen," I know myself as having known the pen. That is, the I has the ability to detach itself from its own transformation into the sense of sight, to transcend its own transformations.

In which part of the *ātman* (I-consciousness) do these transformations[71] and re-transformations take place? In the act of perceiving the pen, my I and mind are focussed entirely on the pen. But the focussing cannot mean that the whole being of the *ātman* and mind is changed into, and is lost in the perceptual object. Otherwise, it will not be possible for the reflective cognition, "I know that I know the pen," to arise. This cognition implies that, even when focussed on the object, the I and mind have still a transcendence of themselves towards which they are not directed, but which is receiving and retaining the impression of the object and also of the focussing. That the I retains the impression of the act of focussing also is implied by the reflective cognition. This complex experience in the analysis of which many philosophers have not been and may not be interested is important to clarify—not certainly in terms of any physical relation we know—the peculiar relation between the I-consciousness, mind, and senses. This experience, when generalized, means that without the involvement of the self (*ātman*) there is no experience and without the power of disinvolvement there can be no transcendence and no reflective cognition even.

When my sense of sight is directed towards the pen by my I-consciousness, it is indeed directed through my physical eye. But we have seen the necessity to differentiate between the physical sense and the psychological. The latter is present in the vast expanse of dreams; otherwise, they cannot be perceptual. It is at least as vast as the perceived sky, as extended as the distance of the star from my physical eye, and as huge as the mountain it perceives. Unless this sense also is as infinite as mind and I-consciousness, such characteristics of sight are not possible. As mentioned already, the senses of touch, taste, and smell, as commonly understood, should not be our guides for deciding whether the psychological sensorium, as distinct from mind, is limited like the physical senses. It should be the eye and to a large extent, the ear that should be such guides. They are meant to produce out of the physical and chemical processes, which take place with reference to our bodies, the qualitative conscious aspects of the processes for the use and enjoyment of the I-consciousness. If the senses or sensorium of the *ātman* is unlimited like the *ātman* itself, they do not have to go out (do not have to be *prāpyakāris*) to reach the objects; for nothing infinite has to travel to reach anything else. The processes of sense perception have to be explained differently as focussing by the self, through mind and sense, both of which have to be infinite like the self. Even the senses of touch, taste, and smell can be explained as infinite. Although they are located in a particular part of the body, as the experience belongs to the *ātman*, which is infinite, the experiences also have to be of that infinite magnitude, if indeed the infinity of the *ātman* is a magnitude. The *ātman* is an undivided I; none of its experiences can, therefore, be divided, i.e., they cannot have limits, although some experiences like pains, when referred to the body, are localized and have some vague boundaries.

(iv) Difficulties about Time and Space

The Jaina conception of time as unextended may be true in some Bergsonian sense, but then it is not helpful in measuring the span of life, etc., which have to be regarded as extended. For measuring them, time should be considered as extended into so many hours, days, years and so forth. In fact, the Jaina main definition of time is that which measures one's growth—from childhood to boyhood, to youth, old age, and death—which is the same as the measure of one's span of life. If this is time, then it is extended, even though unlike space. To this objection, the Jainas have an interesting and significant reply: what are called time, space, rest, and movement are not what we observe with our senses, but what make these phenomena possible. Movement, for instance, can be divided into a series of static, observable pictures. But if every picture is static, how can movement come out of them by simply attaching them to one another? So movement, in the sense of what makes observable movement possible, we have to admit, is not observable. Similarly, time, space, and rest, in the sense of the agencies which make the observable time, space, and rest possible, cannot be observed. Then, where are they, as the roots of our experiences, located?

It is difficult to find an answer in the Jaina works. We may surmise that the Jaina answer would be that they are located in action *(karma)* sticking to the *ātman*. This answer is close to the Vedāntic answer that the roots of every plurality lie in Māyā or Avidyā—in whatever sense the terms are interpreted—with of course some differences. We are here pointing only to the drive of thought embedded in experience. We may refer also to the conception of the roots of finitude (called sheaths, mixed creation, etc.,) as given by the Pāśupata and Pāñcarātra traditions.[72] Simply by perceiving or looking out, we cannot observe that there is one time, one space, one rest, one movement—one may say that there is no reason why there must not be one rest and one movement, if there is one time and one space[73]—they are not objects of perception. Almost all schools maintain that time and space are each one and indivisible except by convention and for convenience. Now what are the grounds for saying that each of the four is one and is a unity? But we do say so, particularly with regard to time and space. We may say the same with regard to rest and motion also. Although these two ideas have not attracted very much the minds of philosophers, they are important for Jainism. By rest we do not mean this or that body at rest, but rest as such. Similarly, we mean by motion motion as such. What is rest is not motion and vice versa. They are not negative concepts just as peace of mind and agitation of mind are not mere negations of each other, but are concepts of positive experiences. The Jainas should have said that they belong to the dynamism of the forces which are the seeds of man's finite existence. They can be traced to the accumulated potencies of action (*karma*).[74] Such tracing will not conflict with the general position of Jainism. But the Jainas stopped short of identifying the mass of such potencies with Māyā or Avidyā, misunderstanding, like many others, these two terms of the Advaita. If they did not stop short of the identification, they could have regarded the whole world as the expression of spirit through man. But this would involve the sacrifice of their realism. And one wonders whether their realism is absolute and ultimate at all like the one of the Nyāya and the Vaiśeṣika. But the naive distinction between the two kinds of space, the world space and the non-world space, could have obtained deeper significance as in the Upaniṣads by turning the non-world space into the inner space of consciousness (*cidākāśa*) or the microcosmic space of the inner heart or cave (*hṛdayākāśa* or *daharākāśa*), which is not really the extended space we study in geometry.

(v) The Pronouncer of Relativity has to be Absolute

No other school in Indian thought has carried ascetic rigorism to the degree to which Jainism has. The despising of one's body by smearing it with mud and filth, although it does not seem to be practised now, was common at one time. But Jainism's greatest contribution to ethical practice is its insistence on non-violence and non-injury, the limits of which the Jainas themselves even today have not been able to determine. Nobody can give an absolute answer to the question of limits except death, after which no injury to others is knowingly possible in many cases, but not in all. For if an earning member of a family commits suicide, does he not injure his wife and children by depriving them of their means of livelihood? Again, if one sees a tiger killing a deer, what should he do? If he remains neutral, there is violent death to the deer. If he kills the tiger, there is violence done to the tiger. One may perhaps say that we should allow nature to take its course and allow the tiger to eat the deer. But what is one to do if the tiger attacks another man to kill and eat him? What is one to do, if the tiger attacks the man himself? No absolutely satisfactory answers can be given to these questions; and the Jaina sects are divided on the basis of their answers, but not curiously enough on metaphysical and epistemological issues. But the way they are divided on questions of the treatment of one's body and the application of the principle of non-violence and non-injury shows their concern for detachment from the world, which is of course found generally among their ascetics or monks. Perhaps, they tolerate their divisions with the help of their doctrine of multi-modal predication (*syādvāda*), which may say that each view is true so long as it does not deny the truth of the others.

It is spiritually important for Jainism to prevent the entry of action (*karma*) into the soul and exhaust whatever has already entered. We pointed to the defects of conceiving action as substance. Apart from this defect, we can prevent entry of action into the soul only by not performing any action. But how can one desist from all action?[75] Is suicide the answer? All spiritual schools agree that mere physical suicide does not prevent rebirth, old age, and death, and consequent pains, pleasures, and activities leading to them. Then the answer has to be the stopping of self-centred desires, which are the basic functions of mind[76] (*manas*) as in the expression, "I have a mind to it." It is not the prevention of all action, which is impossible, as suicide also is action, whether it is by means of starvation or some other means. In any case, to perform action or not to perform it cannot be made intelligible if action is a substance and if to perform it is to come into contact with it. For coming into contact with action is another action performed by the *ātman*, and cannot be another substance in the *ātman*, but only the expression or manifestation of a dynamic force originating it. Substance idea is inadequate for action.

Now, what is meant by exhaustion of action (*karma*) that has already accumulated in the *ātman*? It is said that part of it that has already begun to fructify (*prārabdhakarma*) has to be enjoyed through the experience of pains and pleasures, and it exhausts itself through such enjoyment. It is a force that spends itself. What then happens to the other part that is stored (*sañcita-karma*) and has not started to work? The Jaina position is not clear. The Jainas compare the pollution of the *ātman* by action to dust particles sticking to a pure cloth. Then is the exhausting like dusting the particles out? If the particles are substances, what happens to them when they are separated from the *ātman*? Will they not come and stick to it again? And how is this dusting out to be understood? Yes, there are a number of practices of self-mortification and mental purification. But how do they work? It is the *ātman* or *jīva* that acts, performs actions. Physical and mental purification must transform the *ātman*, it does not merely remove patches of dust from it. The activity of purification also is *ātman*'s activity. That the activity of purification is initiated by the same *ātman* as the one determined and made finite by action implies that the *ātman* is self-transcendent. It transcends its own determinateness, which is the form of the limiting force[77] assumed by action (*karma*). Then exhaustion means the realization of one's self-transcendence, the transcendence of one's self as finite or turned finite by the limiting force (*karma* becoming *niyati* as the Mīmāmsakas would say) of one's past actions. If it is accepted that these actions together constitute the forces of Avidyā (cp. Rāmānuja) or Māyā also (cp. the Advaita), the Jaina position becomes more intelligible than it is. But they seem to be working with an inadequate interpretation of the concerned categories. Any exhausting of action should mean liquidating the potentialities created by actions.

The Jainas would regard it as absurd if one applied the seven-fold conditioned predication to salvation (*mokṣa*) also, and said: "It is true, it is not true, etc." But can we ask: Is the seven-fold conditioned predication applicable to the truth of the seven-fold conditioned predication itself? If the predication means relativity, then is relativity relative, i.e., is it only relatively true, but not absolutely? It is said that from different standpoints different statements can be made about the same object, even including its existence. But are the standpoints themselves relatively true or are they absolute?[78] If at least one of them is absolute, then there is something that is absolutely true. If nothing is absolutely true, where are we to end up in tracing the source of this relativity? It is this spectre of relativity that led the great Buddhist dialectician, Nāgārjuna, to say that the whole cosmos is an appearance of Śūnya

(Void). But who is it that pronounced this judgment on the cosmos? The "I", I-consciousness *ātman*, which is present at every point of the network of the relatively true entities and concepts, which do not and cannot have the stability of the pronouncer of the judgment of relativity. The Jaina view, like that of Nāgārjuna, is truncated in this respect.

Indeed, the Jaina theory is at the opposite pole of the Buddhist principle of four-cornered negation,[79] adapted later by the Advaita Vedānta, which will be presented in the respective chapters. The Advaitin could not stop short of this negation, but asserted that the Self (Ātman) is real; for something can be relative only from the point of view of something else which is stable and absolute. Then if the whole cosmos and everything in it is relative, that which makes this judgment must be absolute and transcend the cosmos. It may be written as the Absolute. But the cosmos, because of relativity, is negated by the Buddhists and the Advaitins as neither existent, nor non-existent, not both, nor neither. Considering this position as mere negativism and illusionism, the Jainas advanced their seven-fold predication, confirming every affirmation, negation, their combinations and their joint denials and other permutations as conditioned truths, thereby thinking that realism could be saved. But the Buddhists and the Advaitins do not deny that conditioned truths are relative truths; they deny only that they are absolute truths. They do not see any gain or advantage in proclaiming relativity itself as the absolute truth. Otherwise, salvation itself becomes a relative truth. All that the Jainas could maintain is the reality of relativity—which is no consolation, as what is relatively true cannot have an existence or being of its own. If this relativity applies to the *ātman* also—about the ultimate truth of which the Jainas also are very much concerned—this philosophy reduces itself to that of nothingness; for nothing remains to which our existence can be moored or geared. Who is to pronounce that *X* is relative to *Y*, *Y* to *Z* and so on?

Indeed, questions like: Is relativity itself relative or is it absolute?, are very disconcerting. There are other questions like: Is possibility itself possible? Is necessity necessary? Still more difficult questions are: Does existence exist? Is there Being?[80] Or has Being Being? Such questions have been posed and discussed in the history of western and Indian philosophy. But regarding the relativity of truth and existence of objects, there is one point which perhaps has not attracted the attention of western philosophers as it did that of the Indian. Many idealists think that the argument *a contingentia mundi* establishes the absoluteness of God as the Absolute. The contingent presupposes that there is something non-contingent or absolute; the world and everything in it is contingent; so it presupposes God, who is the Absolute. Even if the argument is not a syllogistic inference, but is only a postulation (in the Kantian and the Vedāntic senses), there is a difficulty here. The argument assumes too much: Every contingent in our experience refers to something else which is again contingent upon a third something and so on; we have, in the phenomenal world, no experience of any object, material or spiritual, that is absolute. "Contingent" here is another name for "relative." If the presupposition of the absolute by the relative is based upon some abstract logic, one may still ask—perhaps some of the followers of Nāgārjuna would ask, if they do not accept that the Śūnya is the Absolute—: Where and what is the necessity in the contingent presupposing the absolute? If, as Kant pointed out, we should not raise questions about the world as a whole existing in space, in time, and as having a cause—as otherwise, we land in antinomies—we should not analogically raise questions about the contingency of the whole world. I may have a mere idea of the Absolute, but the idea is not based upon flesh and blood experience. But my idea of the contingent is based upon such experience. Again, the idea of the Absolute itself is relative to the idea of contingency. With reference to the world of contingency, the Absolute is absolute. Then it is relative to contingency and relativity; it may not be absolute in itself[81] without any reference to something outside itself or within itself.

Now, is the idea of such a non-relative, non-contingent Absolute a mere conceptual construct, the result of a flight of intellectual imagination, of the poetry of the intellect? If it is so, then such philosophy—for true philosophy is concerned with the problem of life, existence, death, and ideals which are to guide our life—may not be taken seriously by me, and may turn into mere dilettantism. In western philosophy a clue to the existence of a non-referential Absolute may be found in something like Descartes' *cogito ergo sum*. His dictum can be interpreted to mean also that the absolute certainty—not referential or relative certainty—is found only in "I am,"[82] without any predicable, the reality of which is always open to the very Cartesian doubt. For instance, "I am tall" and "I am a professor" may be relatively true or even false, but not "I am." We do not indeed call the relation between the I and "tall" referential or relative, but predicative or adjectival. But it is also relational. If the existence of the "I am" is confined only to that relation, then if "tall" is doubtful, the "I am" also will be doubtful. Then the absolute certainty of the "I am" can hold only, when it is considered by itself. But generally we do not have such experience. We have, therefore, to say that it is involved in all experience of the objects of the world. It is also necessary, as pointed out earlier, to accept its involvement and continuity. For without memory, we cannot have any definitive (determinate) cognition, inference and correction of false perceptions. For if I_1 sees the mirage, and I_2 does not see it later, but sees only the earth, no correction of the first perception is possible. So the two *I*'s must be the same, and must be continuous in existence. The certainty of their continuous existence as identical is not dependent on the perception of the mirage or the earth, but simply upon the experience of "I am," which is involved throughout our life, even though with our consciousness directed towards the objects of the world we are unable to grasp the "I am" in its purity and simplicity, and yet are asserting it all the same.

Such pure experience of the "I am" is called spiritual experience in India and mystical experience in the West. It is unfortunate that it is called mystical experience with all the derogative associations of the word mysticism. If we cannot have any experience without it and if all our experiences are and have to be moored to it, it is to be accepted as the root of our lives and is the existential basis of our idea of the non-referential Absolute, which prompts us to declare that everything in the world, and the whole objective world itself, is infected by relativity. The implication of the Cartesian dictum that the "I am" has to be considered apart from any predicate like "tall" indicates the presence of the non-referential, unconditioned, and unconditional Absolute. Almost all the Indian schools—Jainism also is included—speak of salvation as the "lone," the "by itself" (*kaivalya*),[83] which means non-referential, not in any way coordinated or tied down to the world of relativity or relative reality. It is pure consciousness, in which consciousness is not directed towards anything other than itself and so cannot be grasped or caught by our ordinary consciousness, which is directed towards ideas, images, and physical objects. But as the Cartesian dictum indicates, pure self-consciousness or I-consciousness (I-am) is and has to be involved in all our experiences, whether or not Descartes made use of this potent idea.

(vi) Variety of the Ways of Knowing

The Jaina contribution to epistemology—logic is generally included in epistemology by all the schools in India—has not been well recognized. Of the important schools of Indian thought, it is Jainism that seems to have recognized the largest number of the valid ways (means) of knowing or cognition. The maximum number which any of the orthodox schools recognized is six, as given in the chapter on the Mīmāmsā. If we leave out classifications which cross or overlap each other as given by the Jaina logicians, we find about eleven kinds of valid ways of knowing in this school: the three forms of absolutely direct and infallible knowledge—knowing particular objects without the aid of senses (*avadhi*), knowing other minds (*manahparyāya*), and absolute knowledge (*kevala*)—sense perception, mental perceptions like those of pains and pleasures, six kinds of indirect perception—remembering, recognition, induction, positive and negative modals (counter-factual conditionals and pro-factual conditionals),[84] syllogism, and scripture. One can see that the Jainas included some ways of knowing rejected by other schools and excluded some accepted by others.

The reasons advanced by any school for excluding a particular way as valid is that it can be included in one of the ways accepted. For instance, the Jainas do not accept postulation as a distinct way of knowing. They say that it is a form of syllogism. The reason given for including a way of knowing is by showing that it is not covered by any of the others accepted as valid. "Valid" means acceptable, right. For instance, the Jainas include recognition as a distinct form of indirect cognition not covered by syllogism. For there can be no major premise in recognition, which is spontaneous.

How are we to define "valid," "acceptable," and "right" in connection with means of cognition? Does "valid means" mean that which presents objects as they are and is infallible? Even in the history of western philosophy, there is a long controversy about each of the characteristics. Realists claim that true knowledge presents objects as they are, while idealists claim that true knowledge constructs objects by transcendentally synthesizing the impressions (cp. Kant) and that no perception can present the objects as they are. For there are no such objects. Regarding infallibility, nobody can prove that perception, and for that matter any means of empirical knowledge—except in pure mathematics and mathematical logic—is infallible. The view that all empirical knowledge is contingent, never necessary, disposes of any infallibility claim of any of the ways of knowing. Or if we claim with Descartes—the Advaitins will join his ranks on this point—that the only certainty we can have is the certainty of the doubter, the I-consciousness, then its knowledge is not gained by any of the means of knowing the phenomenal world.[85] But we are concerned with the means of knowing this world, as we have to start with its knowledge in our enquiry into the nature of existence. We have, therefore, to determine the means of knowing the phenomenal world and then whatever lies beyond. In philosophical controversy or dialogue, we have to have some mutually accepted ways of knowing to start with; otherwise, dialogue becomes impossible for lack of any common ground. If we want to determine what that common ground is by searching for a valid means of cognition accepted by all the schools, we can find none. Early Cārvākas accepted perception; but some of their later followers rejected it also. Some accepted inference, but inference is based upon perception, the validity of which is questioned. And the dialecticians of Buddhism and the Advaita showed that every form of empirical cognition is self-contradictory, although the latter in a general way followed the Mīmāmsā, and Buddhism also compromised for practical purposes.[86] It looks, therefore, that there is an impasse. For if no form of knowledge is reliable, we cannot feel the ground under our feet.

We have to say then that the definition of "valid means of cognition"—it matters little even if we change the expression into "means of valid cognition" for even perception is not necessarily valid always—as "presenting the object as it is and as infallible" is too demanding to be applicable. We have to agree then that the acceptable or right means of cognition are those which produce in us, each in its own way, its own peculiar form of cognition. Perception and recognition of what I perceive as that which I perceived five years ago present the same object. But the form of recognition is not the same as the form of perception. The Platonic view that all perception involves some recollection and recognition has a different significance; for the view does not refer to the perception of the same object, but to the self-same Idea involved in the perception of the same kind of objects. Now, coming to the present subject, recognition is not syllogistic inference, as there is no major premise. Similarly, the perception of the absence of a clock on the wall is not the same as the perception of the wall. I do not request the administrative office of the college to fix a clock there by merely perceiving the wall, but by perceiving the absence of the clock there. Nor should we say that memory is necessarily involved only in recognition as well as in the perception of absence—though not necessarily of a particular clock. There is some involvement of memory in all cognition. However, in recognition the memory of a *particular* object may be involved; but in the cognition of absence, the memory of a clock in general may be involved except in cases like my perception of my loss of my pen on the table, if some one stole my pen. As memory is involved in all cognition, some overlapping of the different means of cognition cannot be avoided; and we may have to recognize the means as distinct, so long as each has its own peculiarity and leads to the cognition or discovery of something particular and peculiar. For instance, archeologists start digging after they hear some villagers say that some gods lived nearby a few centuries ago and that because of the sins of new generations, they went down—which is a tradition or rumour. Their diggings contribute to historical knowledge and so the hearsay or tradition[87] becomes an acceptable means of knowledge. Similarly, if a man owes five millions and applies for declaration of bankruptcy, the lawyer of the opposite side may point out that the man owns ten millions hidden secretly in a bank and so can pay five million and that the declaration of bankruptcy should not be allowed. This is called the *a fortiori*[88] argument and, like the spatial argument,[89] is not syllogistic. Again, I hear words; and with the help of their meanings, I come to cognize an object or situation. Is this mere auditory perception? The ear grasps only sounds, but not meanings. Is it then a joint perception by ear and mind? Not necessarily. The object may be in Australia, while I am in America; so there can be no perception of the meant object. It is not even inference, because there is no necessary connection between words and meanings. How again, should I interpret my cognition of something by reading (seeing written words) about the thing? What should we say about the meaningful signs and gestures made by men and animals? Are they not also valid means of cognition?

Only a few examples are given here to show that there are in use many more ways of obtaining valid cognitions than those recognized by the well-known schools of India or the West. Or as one thoughtful scholar put it, God only knows how many ways of valid cognition were recognized even in India during the history of the development of its thought. The phenomenal world is very rich both qualitatively and quantitatively. It points also beyond itself. Even our I-consciousness is both within the empirical world and beyond it. Neither can we limit valid cognition to sense perception or to self-intuition. The impact of the variety of existence, so long as we belong to this world, is too great to accept only one or a few of the ways of empirical knowledge. The dialecticians of both Buddhism and the Advaita dismissed every form of empirical knowledge as relative and ultimately false; but the Jainas, who wanted to be positive in their attitude to this world—as shown in the development of their modal logic—should have recognized the peculiarity of the means of cognition they rejected. In some cases, even dreams[90] cannot be rejected; for they may be prophetic, telling us what is going to happen. Indeed, we cannot depend on dreams—our ancients depended on them in making critical decisions—as generally they distort our reality experience.

The objection that if a means of cognition is not always true, it has to be rejected, cannot hold because every means of empirical cognition is fallible. We have also seen that the criterion of "presenting the object as it is" cannot be accepted, as it is not verifiable in any case; for we do not know whether the object is coloured in itself apart from the working of the apparatus of the eye seeing it. The scientists also tell us that colours are "interpretations" by sight and mind of light with different wavelengths. Then which means of valid cognition have to be accepted as really valid and what should be the criterion for accepting them? The answer seems to be: Every means of cognition without which a particular type of experience[91] of an object is not possible, has to be accepted as a valid one.

The object concerned here is not any object, e.g., an object of fancy or imagination, but one belonging to what we call the common world, the world common to all human beings, the one and the same with which every one of us deals in practical life. For whether there is a common world and what it can be, can be established only by using valid means of cognition; but the valid means can be determined only with reference to the world accepted as common. We have then to say that both the structure of the common world and the means of knowing it have to be determined each with reference to the other and that neither can be merely assumed or accepted through a kind of proposal, convenient agreement, or platform, which is called *abhyupagama-siddhānta* by the Nyāya school.

We may remind ourselves of one point here. Although cognition by any valid means of cognition has to be true in itself and cannot be made true, but only false, by another cognition; and although human life, particularly at the level of philosophy and reflection, is necessarily cognitive; the world of cognition is also a world of action, enjoyment, and suffering, and these three—action, enjoyment, and suffering—are, at the human reflective level, also cognitive experiences. Thus the world of cognition is also the world of action resulting in enjoyment and suffering. Then the world of cognition and the world of action being one, have to support each other, confirm each other. This support or confirmation, as some Vedāntins would say, is known reflectively by the witness consciousness (*sākṣi-caitanya*).

(vii) The World as an Idea

But that there is a world in which all of us live and act and that there are ways of knowing it have to be assumed and the assumption has to be one made by all parties of the controversy (*sarvatantra-siddhānta*), not merely the platform of any one party. For instance, an absolute skeptic may reject it, although he has to accept that he who rejects it exists or, if he rejects even that much, he has to accept that he who is rejecting and rejecting his rejection is, or is something, or somebody. If he rejects even that also, we do not know whether we are entering into a controversy, even an insignificant and vacuuous one, with anybody at all, and we should refuse discussion or dialogue. However, it is here not simply a question of knowing, for all cognition of objects—perceptual, inferential, and presuppositional—is open to doubt, as shown by logicians and dialecticians of both the East and West. But this doubt is very largely removed and the truth of one's cognition is confirmed when action with, or on the object leads to the expected result and the subject's (agent of action's) mind is satisfied and thrown back on itself in satisfaction. It is not meant that theoretical possibility of doubt, as Descartes would say, can be removed altogether by this satisfaction. But there is no practical possibility of it, in the literal sense of the term practical. This discussion confirms the view that the world is meant for action, as the western activists and pragmatists say. It agrees also with the view accepted by all Indian schools, except the Cārvāka—who from another point of view support action with any kind of self-interest—that the world is a world of action meant for action, and is created by the potencies (*śaktis*) of actions (*karmas*). It is created for the satisfaction of the agent, soul, that craves for action (*pravṛtti*) and the resulting pleasures.

As Kant said, the world is not an object like the pen in front. Nobody has seen it like the pen in front. He can speak of the pen that is made by Pencil Co., but he has no right to speak of the world and say that it is made by anybody. We always know only a part of the world; yet we have to assume that there is one world of which what we see is a part. So, as Kant said, the world is an Idea, but an indispensable Idea, without which we cannot organize our experience of plurality. The world is, therefore, continually built, constructed by every one of us; it is being organized and expanded as our experience grows and matures. This organization and expansion will be mere dilettantism, what is called speculative in the derogatory sense of the term, if the resulting world is not a field of action. So the ways of knowing which present bits of reality to each of us for building up the world—however partial and incomplete the result may be—are voluntarily or involuntarily, knowingly or unknowingly, controlled by the idea of the possibility of action[92] (*karma*). Indeed, what is known may only be indirectly, but necessarily, connected with possible action.

Thus the ways of knowing—although as repeated already, none of them presenting the empirical world is absolutely conclusive—are in a particular way connected with the nature of world as a world of action, as mentioned in the previous section. Every kind of objectivity, every category, and every way of knowing are spontaneously[93] developed through us and for us, for our activity (*karma*). The ways of knowing, like the methods of scientific investigation—we are told that often great scientists develop their own methods, which can become new ways of knowing—cannot be fixed and stereotyped.

One interesting part of Jaina epistemology is its theory of recognition, which is made to cover many kinds of indirect or mediated cognition; and it is more interesting to note that cognition of absence or negation also is classified under recognition, although called negative recognition. There is no mere absence or negation, which is not the absence or negation of something positive, which has to be remembered and "recognized" as not being there.[94] If I observe the absence of the pen on the table, in the understanding of Jainism, I recognize my pen as not being there. This importance given to recognition shows the unavoidability of acknowledging the importance of memory in all cognitive activity. What perhaps is missing in the analysis of memory given by Jaina scholars is the realization that memory is not mere phantasy, a mere flow of mental images, but also of one's being involved in the past experience remembered. Indeed, my self is not an object of every memory; but so also is my self not directly perceived along with the perceived object. The past experiences do not merely form a flow of mental images as may be in pure phantasy, but have the additional characteristic of being one's past experiences. Indeed, the past cannot be known without memory;[95] and at least for that reason, memory has to be recognized as a distinct way of knowing. There is no other way of knowing one's past, autobiography, and history.

The Jaina explanation that the function of the means of knowing is to remove the veil or curtain of ignorance between the *ātman* and the object—although it sounds somewhat like the Advaita view—does not agree with its own position that ultimate (*kevala*) knowledge is knowledge of the *ātman* by itself. Let us assume that the veil is completely removed in salvation—the Jainas claim that it is removed in the case of perfect souls. But the *ātman* continues to be conscious of all the objects of the world and is, therefore, tied to them (*baddha*) as it is both identical with them and different from them. Then there can be no salvation. The Jainas claim to be realists, and so this conclusion cannot be avoided, as the objects are all real. The Advaita, on the other hand, claims like the Buddhist idealists, that objects have no independent reality of their own and so pure and simple salvation is possible.

The Jaina view that time and space are not directly observed, but inferred goes against both logic and experience. It goes against logic because every inference—we should remember that for all Indian schools inference means syllogism—needs a major premise. But we cannot have a major premise from which we can deduce the existence of time in the form that every change implies time, which is to be the conclusion, but not the major premise. It looks as though Indian schools have not recognized a way for cognizing uninferable existials[96] and were wavering between inference and perception, saying that, if it is not the one, it has to be the other. We cannot say that the means of cognizing time is postulation—not accepted by that name by the Jainas, who say that we have to have the knowledge that there is something called time before we can postulate it. Why they have not used the idea that the past is essentially an experience of memory and is its direct object is not clear. With the past are connected the present, which is experienced as such, and the future is connected with the present as anticipated. I am, as this empirical individual, a deposit of my past in the present and am driving towards the future[97] in anticipation of what I am going to be and experience.

Space also can be similarly explained as an object of direct cognition, not necessarily of sense perception. Kant explains the ideas of time and space with his critical or postulational technique. But he does not tackle the problem how we get the ideas of time and space at all, that is, what the source of these ideas can be. The question is the old Augustinian question: What are time and space? One may say that Kant traces them ultimately to the Transcendental Ego; but he says also that one can conceive of them without objects, but not objects without them. This concession means that we can know them directly also, not merely with the postulational method. Then that which provokes, incites the self to cognize space is the transcendental need for a field of action, action on different objects to convert them into the self's own, or instruments of its satisfaction. And what provokes, or incites the self to cognize time is the presence of itself in the changing experiences as the cognitive and practical activities progress, organizing them as coming one after another, and unifying them in relation to itself. These experiences are direct, temporal, and spatial; time and space are not objects of inference.

In conclusion, a few observations may be made on the Jaina rejection of comparison as a distinct way of cognition and the criticism of Prabhākara's rejection of the negative categories. The Jainas subsume comparison under recognition and deny any peculiarity to the former as a means of knowing. It is true that in comparison, as in recognition, memory is involved; and what is remembered may be seen to be the *same* in recognition and *similar* in comparison. This perception of sameness or similarity is not something necessarily voluntary, but is often spontaneous and involuntary. So far there is something in common to recognition and to what the Mīmāmsakas call comparison, which is spontaneous perception also similarity. But this common element is found in sense perception also like "That is a pen," in which the universal (or class concept) pen is recognized in the object through similarity or sameness—whichever idea one likes to accept. Yet perception of an object or thing is not the same as perception of similarity. In the perception, "The buffalo is similar to the bison," similarity as such is not an object of any of the senses, and yet is spontaneous. This perception is not again the same as recognition as in "He is the same person as the one I saw some five years ago," although some observation of similarity is involved in it. The cognitive structures of the results of recognition, of perception, and of comparison are all different from one another and need acceptance of their peculiarities.

Similarly, the Jaina criticism of Prabhākara's refusal to recognize negation or absence as a category of reality cannot be justified from the point of view of multiple modalities. The motive behind accepting negation as real or as belonging to reality is to defend plurality. If there is no negation, we cannot observe and say: "The horse is not the elephant." The two will be identical,[98] and it follows that everything is identical with everything else. But Prabhākara thinks that plurality can be defended simply by asserting: "*X*, *Y*, *Z*, etc., etc., are there." Furthermore, where the negation of the pen exists—as a matter of fact, if it exists, it will not be negative, but positive, although we may accept it as negative for argument's sake—there can be a negation of a toy, of a photo, etc. Then if I observe the negation of the pen on the table, why do I not observe other negations also if they are there and even if they are the same as the table? Again, no sense comes into contact with negation or absence of the pen; it comes into contact only with the table, which is a positive entity. So negation or absence is an idea only, not a real thing. Such is the motive behind Prabhākara's view.[99]

Now, the Jainas advance the doctrine of multiple modality. An object may be positive from one point of view and negative from another. If so, it is not reasonable for them to reject Prabhākara's position that the absence of the pen is the same as the presence of the table, but from different points of view. Indeed, Prabhākara does not accept multiple modality, as it will justify any and every statement about any and every thing. But the Jainas propound it and so could have accepted Prabhākara's view also as at least one of the many alternatives. However, negation or absence is not an ontological category, but a cosmological and epistemological one. The two points of view should not always be mixed up. It cannot even be defended that the negation of the pen on the table is the same as the existence of the table, or that it is the same as the table; for the contents of affirmation and negation are different. "There is negation in the world" does not mean that negation destroys itself, commits suicide, by becoming affirmation or Being, but that it holds true of the pluralistic world, in which objects exist independently of one another, however relative the conception of independence be. This relativity means that negation needs transcendence, but from a point of view different from the cosmological and higher than it. The cosmological, of course, is through and through relativistic.[100] Kumārila's view that negation or absence is known through non-perception or non-cognition, which has a spontaneity of its own, but is not sense perception, holds within cosmology, and has to be accepted as one of the distinct means of cognition, but not to be identified with recognition. The objection how non-perception can be the perception of negation can be answered by saying that this is not an equation of perception and non-perception, but is the perception of non-perception (of the pen), not by any sense, but by the witness consciousness (*sākṣi-caitanya*). The Nyāya objection to Kumārila's view is due to the absence of the concept of the witness consciousness in both.

The criticisms given here are constructive and are not meant to detract the value of the Jaina contribution to logic and epistemology.[101]

NOTES

[1]S. N. Dasgupta: *A History of Indian Philosophy*, Vol. I, p. 170. See Walther Schubring: *The Doctrine of the Jainas*, pp. 18–73.

[2]Hemacandra: *Pramāṇamīmāṃsā*, p. 10.

[3]Śāntisūri: *Nyāyāvatārasūtravārtikāvṛtti*, p. 77.
[4]Umāsvāmi: *Tattvārthasūtra*, p. 11.
[5]Hemacandra: *Pramāṇamīmāmsā*, pp. 16 fol.
[6]Ibid., p. 18. [7]Ibid., p. 17.
[8]Yaśovijaya: *Jainatarkabhāṣā*, p. 2., and Hemacandra: *Pramāṇamīmāmsā*, p. 7.
[9]Yaśovijaya: *Jainatarkabhāṣā*, p. 8. [10]Hemacandra: *Pramāṇamīmāmsā*, p. 9.
[11]Ibid., p. 10. [12]Yaśovijaya: *Jainatarkabhāṣā*, p. 3.
[13]Cp. Berkeley's Theory of Signs. [14]Ibid., p. 4.
[15]It seems that at this stage the distinction between the That and the What is not yet finalized. It can be grasped only at the next stage, when the impression can be distinguished from the perceived object. The Jaina position does not appear to be very clear here, but can be understood. Here "It is a pen" is not yet a classificatory judgment, but corresponds to Russell's knowledge by acquaintance as in "That pen."
[16]Yaśovijaya: *Tarkabhāṣā*, p. 5.
[17]Hemacandra: *Pramāṇamīmāmsā*, p. 30. Hemacandra says that every earlier stage is a valid means (*pramāṇa*) for grasping the later and each later is the result of the earlier. So the Jainas do not accept the Nyāya view that only determinate perception is a valid means of knowledge, but not the indeterminate.
[18]Prabhācandra: *Prameyakamalamārtāṇḍa*, pp. 98 fol.
[19]Ibid., p. 31. [20]Op. cit. [21]Ibid., p. 18.
[22]Op. cit. The word used for both qualities and modes is *paryāya*. See Ibid., *Bhāṣātippani*, p. 56. It seems that Jainas originally differentiated between qualities (*guṇas*) and modes (*paryavāyas*).
[23]Yaśovijaya: *Jainatarkabhāṣā*, p. 7.
[24]Umāsvāti: *Tattvārthasūtra*, p. 34.
[25]Compare the theory of the word propounded by the grammarians.
[26]Although Yaśovijaya includes memory under both the direct and indirect forms of cognition, Hemacandra mentions it only under the latter. He says that direct cognition ends with impression (*samskāra*).
[27]Hemacandra: *Pramāṇamīmāmsā*, p. 34.
[28]Cp. the view of association psychologists, according to whom ideas can get associated by contrast. Hume, for instance, held this view.
[29]This something else is called *pratiyogi* with reference to the former called *anuyogi*.
[30]The Jaina works do not seem to be very clear about this kind of negation. But the general trend is clear. See Prabhācandra: *Prameyakamalamārtāṇḍa*, p. 346. Śāntisūri says that, as every object has many modes, this negation also is cognized as one of the modes of the object, table, through the instrumentalities of the cognition of positive entities.
[31]See his *Nyāyavātārasūtravārtikāvṛtti*, p. 68. But he does not say whether it is direct or indirect cognition. We have to assume that it is the latter. See also Hemacandra: *Pramāṇamīmāmsā*, p. 34 and Yaśovijaya *Jainatarkabhāṣā*, p. 9. Prabhācandra says that the cognition of negation can be perception, recognition, and inference at different times. See his *Prameyakamalamārtāṇḍa*, pp. 203–16.
[32]Yaśovijaya: *Jainatarkabhāṣā*, p. 11, and Hemacandra: *Pramāṇamīmāmsā*, p. 36 fol.
[33]Ibid., p. 12.
[34]Ibid., pp. 15–16, and Hemacandra: *Pramāṇamīmāmsā*, p. 47. The Nyāya major premise is of the form: Wherever there is smoke, there is fire, as in the kitchen. Here the kitchen, in which both fire and smoke are present, is the example.
[35]Yaśovijaya: *Jainatarkabhāṣā*, p. 42. [36]Śāntisūri: *Nyāyāvatārasūtravārtikāvṛtti*, p. 62.
[37]Yaśovijaya: *Jainatarkabhāṣā*, p. 19. Yaśovijaya says that knowledge obtained from my friend's statement, "There is a pen in the desk," is valid for ordinary purposes, but not for cognizing ultimate truth (*tattvatah*). There seems to be some confusion in the epistemological classification of verbal cognition in Jaina literature.
[38]Śāntisūri: *Nyāyāvatārasūtravārtikāvṛtti*, p. 112.
[39]See *Tippaṇis* on Śāntisūri: *Nyāyāvatārasūtravārtikāvṛtti* and Hemacandra: *Pramāṇamīmāmsā*.
[40]One may compare this doctrine to that of Whitehead's prehensions. If every object, both positively and negatively, prehends every other, then it acquires multiple modality. From one point of view, an object may be *X*, from another non-*X*; from a third *Y*, from a fourth non-*Y*; and so on. The Jainas caught hold of the idea of multiple modality, and elaborated it, but did not go so far as to develop a philosophy of organism. Whitehead also does not seem to have realized that a thing's particularity and individuality are

lost, if it is only a bundle of prehensions. To say that he thought of "the thing and its prehensions," but not of the "thing as prehensions" is no objection; for who knows that there is a thing behind its prehensions?

[41]Hemacandra: *Pramāṇamīmāṃsā*, Section, *Tippaṇi*, pp. 61 fol.

[42]It is interesting to compare this controversy with the solutions of Russell's paradoxes like "The barber shaves all those who do not shave themselves."

[43]This is due to the fact that the Jainas recognize *anekānta* or *anekāntika* as a logical fallacy. Even for those who do not recognize it as a distinct fallacy, the objection holds.

[44]W. Windelband: *A History of Philosophy*, Vol. I, pp. 200–201.

[45]Yaśovijaya: *Jainatarkabhāṣā*, p. 21.

[46]The Jainas are mistaken in confusing ontological Being with classificatory Being.

[47]W. Windelband: *A History of Philosophy*, Vol. I, pp. 89–90. Some of the Sophists committed this mistake.

[48]Yaśovijaya: *Jainatarkabhāṣā*, p. 22.

[49]W. Windelband: *A History of Philosophy*, Vol. 1.

[50]Yaśovijaya: *Jainatarkabhāṣā*.

[51]See Mallisena: *Syādvādamañjarī*. The word *syād* has a double meaning and is often confused even when translated by the compound word "maybe." The first meaning is "It is possible," when it is a declensional form of the verbal root $\sqrt{as}$, meaning "to be." In the second meaning, the word is an indeclinable and means "Let it be," "Let us accept it," "Let it be granted." See the author's article, "The Four-cornered Negation in Indian Philosophy," *Review of Metaphysics*, June 1954.

[52]"*S* is *P* and indescribable" + "*S* is *P*" = "*S* is *P* and indescribable"; for "*S* is *P* and *P* and indescribable" is the same as "*S* is *P* and indescribable"; "indescribable" means "neither *P* nor non-*P*";

"*S* is non-*P* and indescribable" + "*S* is non-*P*" = "*S* is non-*P* and indescribable" for the same reason as above;

"*S* is both *P* and non-*P* and indescribable." this is new;

"*S* is neither *P* nor non-*P*" + "*S* is indescribable" = "*S* is indescribable"; for "indescribable" means "neither *P* nor non-*P*." The proposition then becomes "*S* is neither *P* nor non-*P*, and neither *P* nor non-*P*," which is a tautology.

So only three more propositions, 5, 6, and 7 are possible.

[53]Is there no wet fuel in the mountain of the classical example? Does not the Brahman conditioned by Māyā create the world, as many Advaitins say? Can conditionality be completely excluded from all valid inference?

[54]Hemacandra: *Pramāṇamīmāṃsā*, p. 2.

[55]Ibid., p. 6. See also Prabhācandra: *Prameyakamalamārtāṇḍa*, pp. 149 fol.

[56]Ibid., p. 149.

[57]Hemacandra: *Pramāṇamīmāṃsā*, p. 5. But see also Śāntisūri: *Nyāyāvatārasūtravārtikāvṛtti*, Section *Tippaṇi*, p. 169.

[58]This confusion is present even in some contemporary recognized writers on Indian philosophy.

[59]Hemacandra: *Pramāṇamīmāṃsā*, Section *Tippaṇi*, p. 56. See also Prabhācandra: *Prameyakamalamārtāṇ-ḍa*, pp. 520 fol.

[60]The relation between the two is not clear in the Jaina writings.

[61]Umāsvāmi: *Tattvārthasūtra*, pp. 7–8.

[62]Ibid., p. 135. [63]Ibid., p. 186.

[64]Ibid., p. 210. [65]Ibid., p. 1.

[66]If the same world can offer different phases to different persons, by analogy what is wrong with the idea that the world appears as the world for the unliberated souls and simply disappears for the liberated ones?

[67]One can find this mix up in Aristotle.

[68]There is another difficulty here. If "the quality of the magnet" = "attraction of iron," then to say "the quality attracts iron" = to say "attraction of iron attracts iron," which is a tautology.

[69]Cp. the Nyāya and the Vaiśeṣika also.

[70]Some philosophers like Gilbert Ryle call them dispositions. Indeed, the doctrines of *karma* and Māyā play no role in his philosophy. But if we reduce *karma* and Māyā to bundles of potencies or dispositions, our

objection holds against him. See his *Concept of Mind* for his well-known theory. And cp. the Buddhist theory of aggregates.

[71]Here the Advaitins use the word *vivarta* instead of *pariṇāma*. See the chapter on the Advaita.

[72]See the author's *Idealistic Thought of India*, Chapter II, Section II and III, and *Introduction to Comparative Philosophy*, pp. 241–42. The import of Māyā and Avidyā does not end with their illogicality; they contain the roots of our finite being, forces responsible for our existence. Cp. Ālayavijñāna of Buddhism.

[73]Other schools have not given time, space, rest, and motion as much importance as Jainism. This is particularly true of the last two concepts.

[74]There is a Mīmāmsā view that all action (*karma*) is one.

[75]The *Bhagavadgītā* rightly says that even living becomes impossible, if one desists from all action. Even breathing is action. Suicide is action, although one may think that it puts an end to all action.

[76]In many places in the Upaniṣads, *kāma* (desire) is described as the main function of mind (*manas*), and in a few places the two are given as synonyms even. Cp. for creating the world, the Brahman *kāmo akāmayata manah akarot iti*. (The Brahman desired, has the mind.)

[77]This force, we have seen, may be called the involuntary will in us, producing the world for us. Co. Schopenhauer.

[78]See Satkari Mookerji: *Jaina Philosophy of Non-absolutism.*

[79]See the author's article, "The Principle of Four-cornered Negation" in *The Review of Metaphysics.*

[80]For a discussion of this question, see the author's "Being: How Known and How Expressed," in *International Philosophical Quarterly*, June 1975.

[81]Called *pratiyogi-vinirmukta* or *nispratiyogika* by the Advaitins.

[82]See the author's "Being: How Known and How Expressed" already referred to and "Being, Becoming, and Essence: East and West" in *Idealistic Studies*, January 1976.

[83]Note that for the Jainas, the *kevalas* or pure *ātmans'* are a plurality, but not for the Advaitins. The relative merits of each doctrine will be discussed in the following chapters. The discussions tackle the problem whether the Absolute can be many.

[84]Examples are: Had it not been so, it would not have been so; had it been so, it would have been so; etc.

[85]At this point the Advaitins classify knowledge into non-sense-dependent (*āparokṣa*) and sense-dependent (*parokṣa*) — the latter including mental cognitions like those of pains and pleasures and conceptual knowledge — and regard the latter as ultimately fallible and self-contradictory and relative.

[86]Cp. the Vijñānavāda view that all perception and cognition is false.

[87]This is called *aitihya* (so it was once) in Sanskrit epistemology. Out of it the word *itihāsa* (history) is derived. This means of cognition is generally rejected by the well-known schools, for the reason that it is not always valid. But which way of knowing is always valid? When I mentioned the significance of this in a meeting of the East-West Philosophers Conference, the delegates stared at me, as though I was saying that there was archeology in ancient India. What a lack of historical sense!

[88]Called *sambhava* in Sanskrit.

[89]*A* is to the right of *B*; *B* is to the right of *C*; therefore *A* is to the right of *C*. Cp. Bradley.

[90]Cp. J. W. Dunne: *An Experiment with Time* (Faber and Faber, London 1939).

[91]For example, how are we to determine the means of knowing other persons?

[92]Some Indian philosophers belonging to almost all schools say that, if one withdraws from all action and absolves himself from the potencies of all actions, one does not experience the world at all. Then if no world faces him, how can he be finite?

[93]Spontaneity for the author means more than what it means for Buddhism.

[94]On deeper analysis, even phantasy may not be a mere flow of images, but a flow of images with which I may be very remotely involved or with which my involvement is not sufficiently strong to turn it into a kind of daydream. The problem of the cognition of absence or negation is more complex than presented here. Can there be a significant absence of all time, of all space, of the totality of the world and so on? How can there be absence of the world, when we don't face a world? But who can face the whole world, if it is an Idea, as Kant says? Can we have an absence of that Idea? These questions form further details to be introduced into Kant's transcendental dialectic.

[95]Plato would be very pleased with the Jaina theory of memory and recognition. Indeed, his doctrine of recollection can be interpreted, generalized, and expanded without its mythological association.

[96]The question is how we know that there is something called time, but not where we can locate it. Why do we experience time at all? Cp. Madhva's view that time is the direct object of witness consciousness, which is a very important idea. See the Chapter on Madhva. See my comments on space in the same chapter.

[97]Cp. the views of Bergson and Heidegger.

[98]One may question whether in the perception, "the horse and the elephant," the perceiver takes the two as identical. Here experience is the guide, and its analysis reveals that they are not taken to be identical.

[99]Cp. Kumārila's view.

[100]That all cosmological realities and concepts are permeated by relativism can be shown by reference to Kant's discussions of the cosmological argument and of the World as an Idea; to Bradley's *Appearance and Reality*, and the dialectic of Nāgārjuna and Śrī Harṣa.

[101]For other details, see Vidyabhushan: *History of Indian Logic*.

Chapter V

Buddhism and the Ideal of Enlightenment

1. INTRODUCTION

Buddhism, like Jainism, is more than 2500 years old; but its ideas are older like those of Jainism. It also arose in an atmosphere of great philosophical ferment, in which the ideas of the old sacrificial religion as later expounded and systematized in the Mīmāmsā, the Upaniṣadic ideas as later expounded by Bādarāyaṇa, and the ideas of independent thinkers not owning any allegiance to any part of the Veda, but developing their doctrines each by himself and in controversies with others, relying on his own experience and logical ability, were jostling with one another. But even though logical, dialectical, and independent, their philosophies were all philosophies of life, seeking a way of life according to the reality as understood by them. Except for the Cārvākas and perhaps a few others, all the philosophical sects, even those that preached that there is nothing beyond the world and evil actions produced no sin, were more or less ascetic.[1] Like Jainism, Buddhism arose out of such independent sects, incorporated what it considered to be the best from all, both the orthodox and the heterodox, became one of the world's greatest religions, and contributed one of the highest of philosophies. Its founder, Gautama (6th century B.C.) evoked the admiration of even the orthodox Indians not only by the gentleness and nobility of his character but also by the clarity and simplicity of his teachings, and was absorbed into the Hindu pantheon. His philosophy, in its latest stages, became so similar to the Vedānta that it was eventually assimilated to it; and Buddhism, losing justification for separate existence, gradually disappeared from India, except for a few border areas. One will be justified also in saying that it has not disappeared from India, but forms part of the life-blood of Indian outlook and culture; for Buddha is still venerated as an incarnation of the supreme God-head in its aspect as mercy and compassion (*karuṇa*), and his philosophical and ethico-religious concepts are incorporated into all the great philosophies of spiritual life. If Platonism can be said to be dead in western culture and outlook, then only can we say that Buddhism is dead in India. Throughout its history, Buddhism showed so great a vitality and an earnestness in its search for truth that its followers ignored most of the artificially erected barriers of doctrine, creed, and dogma, and developed their philosophies one out of another. We can say that the history of Buddhist thought is really a history of philosophy that grew out of some ethico-religious teachings of Buddha and, passing through the many pluralistic systems of the Hīnayāna, culminated in the grand idealistic systems of the Mahāyāna. None can escape being struck by wonder at the great philosophical development. Yet every Buddhist school refers to Buddha's original teaching as its basis. This reference is made possible by the simplicity of Buddha's teaching, which can be interpreted as, and supported by alternative doctrines, of which the last phases of the Mahāyāna philosophy must be said to have brought out the full implications.

Gautama, the founder of Buddhism, was called Buddha (the Enlightened) and has other titles also. He did not write any book, but taught his doctrines orally. After his death, his disciples spread over the country and propagated his ideas. But every disciple understood and elaborated them in his own way. Then different interpretations began to appear. In order to unify the teachings, councils were held at different times, attempts were made to remove the diversities, and the unified doctrines were recorded. Through such recordings arose Buddhist literature, which was commented upon, elaborated, and systematized. Every time, there were differences of view and the dissidents formed new schools, each with its own literature. If we take all the Buddhist schools, their number can be about two hundred.[2] The differences among the schools are not always philosophically important, as many of them differed from one another in very minor details.

An error has arisen in the interpretation of Indian culture due to the high degree of importance to which Buddhism and Jainism rose. But they are really protestant movements within the so-called Hinduism (correctly Arya Dharma), although neither has accepted a Supreme Being. But such rejection is found in the early Mīmāmsā and the Sāṅkhya. There were sects other than Buddhism and Jainism, which rejected the authoritativeness of the Vedic scripture. The Ājīvikas,[3] along with whom the orthodox schools clubbed the Jainas and the Buddhists, also rejected the Vedas. The Cārvākas also did the same thing. If the Ājīvikas and the Cārvākas can be Hindus, there is every justification to call Jainism and Buddhism forms of Hinduism. As mentioned already, the word Hinduism has no definite meaning and, we may even say, does not mean a thing. Indeed, the differentiation of Hinduism, with all its amorphous meaning, from Jainism and Buddhism, has continued so long that it is now forgotten that they were originally sects of the same religion, Arya Dharma, the Aryan or Noble Way of Life. At least up to the 15th century, when the Vijayanagar Empire was strong in the South, when Hindus were not calling themselves Hindus, but the followers of Arya Dharma and Vaidika Dharma, the differentiation was made only on the basis whether a man was following the Vedic Way, the Jaina Way, or the Buddhist Way, all of which were forms of the Aryan Way. At that time at least, all the three were equally Hindu for the non-Indian. All were followers of the Aryan[4] Way. Buddhism and Jainism, like Śaivism and Vaiṣṇavism, can be rightly treated as sects of the same religion. In fact, there is evidence[5] to show that all the three sects were mixing with one another in actual life and social relationships and religious practices. Even among the Śaivas and the Vaiṣṇavas, there are sub-sects which do not inter-dine; but there are sects among them, which even inter-marry.

2. THE SCHOOLS OF BUDDHISM

As Buddha did not write out his teachings, attempts were made several times, both in India and outside, to fix his teachings. It is said that four great councils held in India were important, although a few scholars doubt the authenticity of some of them; and some scholars say that all the councils were not general councils, but that some of them were of Buddhist sects.[6] Anyway, the first council was held immediately after the death of Buddha in about 543 B.C., at a place called Rajagṛha, of which Ajātaśatru was the king. The second council was held at the place called Vaisāli about one hundred years after the passing away of Buddha. The third council met under the aegies of Emperor Aśoka in Pātalīputra (now called Patna), the capital, perhaps in the year 249 B.C. That is, it met after two hundred years after the second council. The fourth was convened by Emperor Kaṇiṣka about 100 A.D. The place is uncertain; perhaps it was Peshawar, Jalandhar, or some place in Kasmir. It is believed that practically two thirds of the main Buddhist canon was compiled in the first council. The canon consists of three kinds of literature: *The Basket of Amphorisms* (*Suttapiṭaka*) consisting of the Master's utterances, *The Basket of Discipline* (*Vinayapiṭaka*) dealing with the rules of the order, and *The Basket of Philosophy* (*Abhidharmapiṭaka*) consisting of philosophical doctrines. They were called baskets, as the written manuscripts were carried in baskets. The first two baskets were the work of the first council, and the third of the third.[7] The second council dealt only with some new practices introduced by some monks, who were, therefore, expelled from the order. The third dealt more seriously than the second with some schisms that appeared in the order. It appears[8] that those monks expelled in the second council from the order formed a far larger group than those included; and the larger group was called the school of the Great Assembly (Mahāsaṅghikas) and the smaller group the school of the Elders (Sthaviras, Theras, Sthaviravādins, Theravādins). But again differences arose within each group. Again the attempt was made to fix what the original baskets taught. The discussions were recorded and heretical sects were refuted by Thera Tissa of the school of the Elders in his work, *Kathāvatthu* at the third council. But the expelled monks also were composing their works and attributing their views to Buddha. In the fourth council, eighteen sects were regarded as following the doctrines of Buddha. At that council, Emperor Kaniṣka ordered commentaries (*vibhāṣās*) to be written on those teachings of Buddha that were accepted as authentic.

It is difficult to say which sect arose exactly at which time in India. The eighteen schools recognized at the fourth council seem to belong all to the Hīnayāna. Buddhism is first divided[9] into the Hīnayāna (Lower Vehicle) and the Mahāyāna (Higher Vehicle). These two schools are called the Southern School, as it belongs generally to the southern countries of Asia, and the Northern School, as it belongs to the northern countries, although the Mahāyāna started in the Andhra, which is a part of South India, from among the Mahāsaṅghikas. The basic canon of the Hīnayāna is *The Three Baskets* (*Tripiṭaka*) in Pali, a spoken language of the time derived from Sanskrit; the basic work of the Mahāyāna is the *Prajñāpāramitāsūtras* (*Amphorisms of the Highest Knowledge*). The original teachings of the founder are accepted by both the schools, which interpret and develop them differently. There are many schools of the Mahāyāna also, of which three seem to be philosophically important. Furthermore, there were crossings of the schools of the Hīnayāna with one another and also with one or more schools of the Mahāyāna. Thus several schools of Buddhism arose in India itself. We shall discuss only those schools that are philosophically the main ones. The following chart may give a general idea of them:

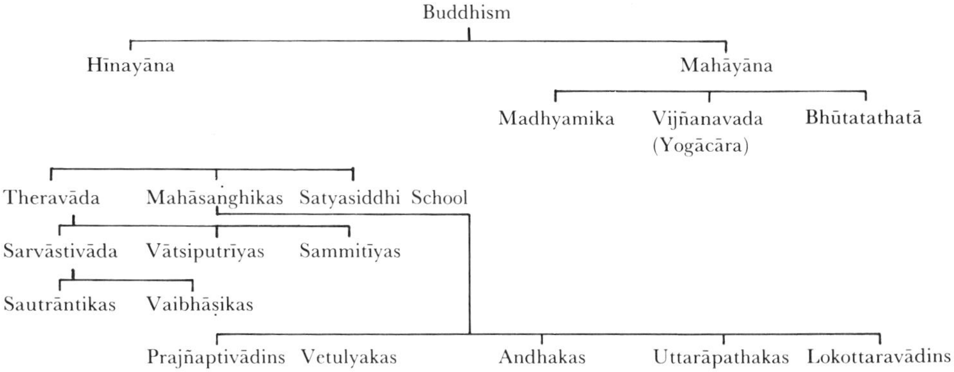

Although Buddhism contributed much to the growth of epistemology, all schools of Buddhism did not have distinct epistemological doctrines. But the contribution of many to the growth of metaphysical thought is significant. We have, therefore, to reverse the order of our presentation and start with metaphysics. Even then, the presentation will be clearer, if we do not club all schools together.

3. BUDDHA'S ORIGINAL TEACHINGS: THE SCHOOL OF THE ELDERS

What are called Buddha's original teachings are those accepted by the school of the Elders,[10] which is the most conservative of the Buddhist schools. According to it, Buddha taught the four Aryan Truths (*āryasatyas*, often translated as noble truths). They are the truth of suffering (*duhkhasatya*), the truth of causation (*samudavasatya*), the truth of cessation (*nirodhasatya*), and the truth of the way (*mārgasatya*). These truths are interpreted as: Everything is misery; everything is caused; if the cause is destroyed, the effect is destroyed; and there is a way to destroy the cause.

Buddha taught the four simple truths so that common people could understand the nature and aim of a true philosophy of life and how to follow the philosophy. But although the truths are simple, their interpretation and exposition gave rise to some of the grandest philosophies and a large number of schools. First, the doctrine of momentariness was developed out of the first truth. There is suffering in every drop of existence, because it is born, decays, and dies. Everything that is born must decay and die. So old age, disease, and death are inevitable. There is nothing in the world that is not subject to change. The world is a continual flux, unceasing becoming; becoming consists of birth and destruction; everything therefore contains suffering.

So far Buddha's conception of the world is that of the Heraclitian flux. No one denies that such a change involves pain and suffering for all living beings. Out of such a doctrine, the Buddhists developed their doctrine of momentariness.[11] Flux or change does not merely mean that a thing is born at one moment, exists for some moments, and dies at another moment. In that case, the thing lasts for some moments. According to the conservative Buddhists, every bit of existence is born, stays, and dies at the same moment, giving place to another bit of existence. Existence or Being is a momentary event and contains its own non-existence or Non-being.

There is, therefore, no being without its non-being. Everything is both positive and negative at the same place and time. This doctrine of flux is called the doctrine of momentariness (*Kṣaṇikavāda*), which, the Buddhists thought, gives the soundest basis for their doctrine that everything is suffering. To be is to suffer. Suffering pervades Being and is basic and universal.[12]

The stability of things is only an appearance. Everything that appears to stay or live for a time is really a series of exactly similar moments of existence. A pattern of events, although dying every moment, passes on its pattern to the next group of events; and we think that the same object continues to exist. But it is really a series of aggregates of events following the same pattern. Apart from the aggregates, the thing is nothing. It is a whole of parts. A chariot is nothing but its parts. Man is nothing but the parts that constitute him. Every ultimate part of man is a momentary event.

But although the events themselves are momentary, the patterns are not momentary, but can continue for a time. *Practically they play the role of universals in Buddhist thought.* But they are neither real nor eternal. The Buddhists do not accept the reality of universals.

Out of the second Aryan Truth, that every event has a cause, is developed the main Buddhist doctrine of causation. Nothing happens without a cause, and the causal relation is fixed between two events. Otherwise, anything can originate out of anything. But the acorn can produce only the oak, but not an apple tree. Yet, since everything is momentary, the cause has to die before the effect originates. The acorn has to perish so that the oak can sprout. There is, therefore, no material cause continuing into the effect. Yet, there must be a material cause; the acorn is the material cause of the oak. There have to be other causes also like water, soil, oxygen, carbon, etc. But the sprout can come out only after they are destroyed. After the sprout comes up, we no longer find the acorn. So we have to say that the effect originates, depending on the cause, but not as a new form of the cause. From the side of the effect, causation is called dependent origination (*pratītyasamutpāda*). From the side of the cause, we have to say that, through self-destruction, it only occasions the effect; or it becomes a necessary occasion for the appearance of the effect. Without it, the effect cannot arise.

The above conception of causation is applied to the problem of suffering, so that it can be overcome by removing the cause. The Buddhists generally accept twelve links in the causal process leading to suffering. (1) Nescience (*avidyā*, Ignorance) is the ultimate cause of suffering and *may be interpreted as the metaphysical Unconscious*. It is not the ignorance or Unconscious of any individual,[13] as it is the cause of the individual himself and cannot belong to him as it is prior to him. It is not clear whether there is an Ignorance for every individual as his ultimate cause or whether it is the same for all and is cosmic. The Mahāyāna is clear in this point and asserts that the Ignorance is cosmic. In any case, the doctrine of Ignorance is as important for Indian thought, as that of the original sin to Christian theology.

(2) Depending on the Unconscious, the forms[14] (*samskāras*) originate. These forms or formative forces also are not those of any individual. They are, we may say, inherent in the Unconscious lying at the roots of the individual and they generate him and are ready to work through him after he appears. (3) Depending on the formative forces, originates the embryonic consciousness (*vijñāna*) of the individual. This is still

an embryonic consciousness without individuality. (4) Depending on this consciousness, arises name-and-form (*nāma-rūpa*). Name-and-form is interpreted as the combination of the mental and physical aspects of the individual. We may say that the individual, the psycho-physical person is formed at this stage.

(5) Depending on name-and-form, the senses—eye, ear, nose, touch, and taste—and mind, which also is called a sense by the Buddhists, come into being. (6) Then depending on the senses, sense-contact with objects arises. (7) Depending on it, arises feeling or sense-experience (*vedanā*). (8) Depending on sense-experience, arises craving (*tṛṣṇā*) for the objects of pleasure. (9) Depending on craving, attachment or clinging (*upādāna*) to objects makes its appearance. (10) Depending on clinging, becoming (*bhāva*) arises. This becoming is interpreted as the tendency to be born. (11) Depending on becoming, birth and rebirth (*jāti*) ensue. (12) And depending on birth and rebirth, old age and death (*jarāmaraṇa*) arise.

Of the above twelve links, every preceding one is the cause in the Buddhist sense or ground of every succeeding one. Every succeeding one can be removed by removing every preceding one. Ultimately, Ignorance itself has to be overcome, when man becomes enlightened. So far as suffering is concerned, the twelve-linked chain of causation explains the second and third truths.

The above explanation of suffering is only a metaphysical explanation. But how are we, in practice, to effect the removal of suffering? To answer the question, Buddha preached the eight-fold Aryan Way as the fourth truth. It consists of: (1) right views (*samyagdṛṣṭi*) or understanding of the nature of the world, the self, and the goal of life; (2) right resolve (*samyagsaṅkalpa*) to follow the truths; (3) right speech (*samyagvāk*), consisting of truthfulness, avoidance of slander, unkind words, and frivolous talk; (4) right action (*samyakkarma*), including non-killing, non-stealing, non-sensuality, non-lying, and non-intoxication; (5) right livelihood (*samyagājīva*) or following a profession that does not involve the performing of prohibited actions as means of livelihood; (6) right endeavour (*samyagvyāyāma*) to overcome the temptations of evil; (7) right mindfulness (*samyaksmṛti*), which consists of constantly placing before oneself one's ideal, without forgetting it; and (8) right concentration (*samyaksamādhi*) or meditation. When meditation becomes perfect, man attains *nirvāṇa*, a state of absolute non-disturbance, equanimity, and peace, and obtains liberation from the world of becoming.

4. THE DEVELOPED DOCTRINES OF BUDDHISM

Through the course of a few centuries, the above doctrines were further developed by the different Buddhist schools. The four Aryan Truths taught by Buddha were recast and were accepted in a new form,[15] though not without a few modifications, by all the schools. The Truths in a new form are: Everything is misery (*sarvam duhkham*); Everything is momentary (*sarvam kṣaṇikam*); everything is self-less (*sarvam nairātmyam* or *anātmam*); and everything is void (*sarvam śūnyam*). The first two propositions have already been explained. The third and fourth follow from the doctrine of aggregates and momentariness.

The whole is nothing but its parts. The self (*ātman*), which experiences itself as "I am," is, according to the Buddhists, an aggregate of psycho-physical aggregates.

These aggregates are five in number:[16] (1) the aggregate of matter (*rūpaskandha*), forming the physical body; (2) the aggregate of feelings and sensations (*vedanāskandha*); (3) the aggregate of ideas (*samjñāskandha*); (4) the aggregate of the formative forces (*samskāraskandha*); and (5) the aggregate of consciousness (*vijñānaskandha*). The last also is called an aggregate, because my consciousness of "I am" is a series of aggregates of drops of consciousness. When my personality (*pudgala*) is analysed into these aggregates, beside and beyond these aggregates there is nothing to be found that can be called the pure self (*ātman*) eternally subsisting by itself. So there is really no *ātman*. I cannot say that I am different from my body, senses, and mind, and that I have my own nature (*svabhāva*) different from theirs. So long as this unity of the aggregates lasts, I am subject to the becoming of the aggregates and their constituents, and experience suffering. But when the aggregates are discriminated and analysed away, my "I" ceases to exist; and there will be no suffering. Then I realize that I do not have my own nature or any nature; I become nature-less (*nihsvabhāva*)., i.e., void. At that stage, there is no becoming, no change, no disturbance: it is *nirvāṇa*, liberation (*mokṣa*).

The experiential being of man is divided, again, into twelve bases or fields of experience, called *āyatanas*. They are the six senses—eye, ear, nose, tongue, skin, and mind, which also is a sense according to the Buddhists—and their six kinds of objects—colour, sound, odour, taste, touch, and the perceived object like the whole pen, the whole tree, the whole mountain, or the whole sun. Senses give only aspects of the object; but mind gives the whole object. The being of man is divided, further, into eighteen elements (*dhātus*). They are the six senses, their six objects, and the six kinds of cognitions also—the visual, auditory, olfactory, gustatory, tactile, and mental.[17] The idea behind these analyses is, again, that if we analyse our being into the bases (*āyatanas*) and elements (*dhātus*), there will be no residue. The analysis sounds like nihilism of our personality and being.

The above concept of selfless-ness (*anātmatā*) and natureless-ness (*nihsvabhāvatā*) was extended to all objects of the world. Not even the objects have a self or nature of their own.[18] The chariot has no self or nature of its own apart from that of its parts, and the parts from their parts and so on *ad infinitum*. As everything is caused by certain causes, it cannot have a self or nature of its own apart from that of its causes. Every one of the causes also cannot have a self or nature of its own apart from that of its own causes. Then nothing in the world can have a self or nature of its own. So everything is a void (*śūnya*), self-less, nature-less. The highest aim of our knowledge is the realization of this truth, in which self-less-ness has become identical with nature-less-ness and voidity.

Although the force of the argument was driving the Buddhists to such conclusions as the above, there were other considerations that checked the drive and that made different thinkers accept different conclusions. If ultimately the void (*śūnya*) is the truth, does the world exist or not? If the aim of life is to transcend the world of becoming and be free from suffering, will there be any consciousness left to experience the freedom from suffering? If there will be some consciousness, is it also momentary and subject, therefore, to suffering? What happend to Buddha, after he entered *nirvāṇa*? Questions like these and the experience of conflicts with the traditionally fixed doctrines gave rise to differences of opinion, expulsion of those men who held such views from established orders, and the formation of new orders or sects by the expelled members.[19]

It is said that Buddha refused[20] to answer questions the meanings of which were not definite. Such questions are: Is the universe eternal or transient? Is it finite or infinite? Is the *ātman* different from the body or identical with it? Does one who enters *nirvāṇa* exist or not? Buddha's silence in answer to such questions was taken by the early Buddhists to be his denial. But a little later the Buddhists began to give different answers to the same questions. To the questions about the universe, we do not find exact answers. But to the questions about the *ātman* and *nirvāṇa* and about the existence of the world we find many answers. *Sarvāstivādins*: The Sarvāstivādins (all-exists-theorists), who branched off from the School of the Elders, maintained that everything, including past and future, exists.[21] They were realists of an extreme type. But the Kassapikas, who broke off from the Sarvāstivādins, maintained that only a part of the past that is preserved in the present exists. Similarly, they held that only that part of the future that is determined by the present exists. The aim of the whole school of the Sarvāstivādins is to show that the world exists and is real. The contention of the school of the Elders on the contrary, seems to be that we can neither deny nor affirm its existence.

Although the Sarvāstivādins were refuted in the third council, they became the most important school during the fourth council under Emperor Kaniṣka. The main work of this school is Vasubandhu's *Abhidharmakośa*.[22] According to him, everything is a *dharma*; and *dharma* is explained as an object, as a category. There are two kinds of objects, the uncompounded and the compounded. The uncompounded objects are three: space (*ākāśa*), which is an eternal, omnipresent substance; the cessation of existence that is not observed by mind (*apratisaṁkhyānirodha*); and the cessation of existence (of observed passions, etc.) which is attained by the knowledge of ultimate truth (*pratisaṁkhyānirodha*). An example of the first kind of cessation[23] is the entering of unconscious impressions into our mind and their disappearing into the past. The second kind of cessation is attained by spiritual practice like meditation.

The compounded objects are of four kinds: (1) matter (*rūpa*); (2) mind (*citta*); (3) the mental (*caitta*); and (4) the non-mental (*cittavipravukta*). Matter is of four kinds—earth, water, fire, and air. The final constituents of these elements are atoms. Mind is the consciousness (*vijñāna*) of all sense-perceptions, substance, quality, etc., and of itself. That is, mind is self-conscious and self-revealing. The mental are the many states of mind such as attention, inattention, conation, hate, love, etc., in short, all the psycho-ethical qualities, which are given as forty six.[24]

The above classification is given from the side of the object, it is a classification of everything that is objective. The Sarvāstivādins give a classification from the side of the subject[25] also; it is a classification of the subject's being, and is the same as that into the aggregates (*skandhas*), the bases of our experience (*āyatanas*), and the elements of our being (*dhātus*) given by the school of the Elders. According to the Sarvāstivādins, although the "I" can be analysed away into the aggregates, bases, and elements and can be shown to be void (*śūnya*), the aggregates, bases, and elements exist and are real, and are therefore, not void. The result of the Sarvāstivādin position is that the "I" alone becomes void, but the rest of the world exists (*asti*).

The Sarvāstivādins were later divided into two main sub-schools, called the Vaibhāṣikas and the Sautrāntikas. It has been mentioned that Kaniṣka ordered commentaries (*vibhāṣas*) to be written on the original aphorisms (*sūtras*) of this school. The Vaibhāṣikas say that they follow the commentaries. The Sautrāntikas contend that the commentaries are not absolutely true to the original aphorisms and that they follow, therefore, the original aphorisms. However, the difference between the two schools does not seem to be very great except in epistemology, which will be discussed in its proper place.

The need to assert that everything exists (*asti*) must have arisen because of some thinkers contending that the world does exist. At least, the contention that we cannot assert that the world exists or that it does not exist must have been understood that it does not exist, i.e., as the denial of its existence; and it must have been felt necessary to assert that it exists. If it exists, then time must exist. As time is one and includes past, present, and future, then everything that belongs to the past, present, or future, must also exist. Such an idea seems to be at the back of the mind of the Sarvāstivādins.

VETULYAKAS We read that one sect called the Vetulyakas held that nothing has its own nature and that by itself it is void (*śūnya*). They belonged to the Great Emptiness School,[26] which seems to be a school of the Elders itself.

Further, the Vetulyakas held the doctrine of Docetism regarding Buddha. He did not live at all in the world. He.had a divine body. The Buddha that lived and taught the doctrine was only an appearance.

LOKOTTARVĀDINS The same docetism was held by the school of Lokρttaravādins, who formed a branch of the Mahāsaṅghikas. They maintained that the body of Buddha was a supra-mundane (*lokottara*). The Mahāsaṅghikas, as a whole, maintained that the bodies of Buddha pervade the whole universe—a view which not only involves the idea of a plurality of Buddhas, but also a distinction between the mundane and supra-mundane bodies. This view later made it possible to identify the true body of Buddhas with ultimate reality itself.

VATSĪPUTRĪYAS In the Sarvāstivādin thought, we found already a divergence from the doctrine of momentariness so far as the positive, objective world went. In some other schools, we find a divergence from the same doctrine even with regard to our inner being. The Vatsīputrīyas maintained that the soul (*pudgala*) is different from the five aggregates.[27] The elders identified the soul with the aggregates, but now the identification is questioned and rejected.

ANDHAKAS The Andhakas, who were a branch of the Mahāsaṅghikas, introduced many new and interesting ideas. They maintained that the objects of mindfulness are the same as mindfulness, thereby introducing a kind of idealism,[28] at least so far as ethical objectives are concerned.[29] They observed that in meditation we keep a single continuous state of consciousness, which is not momentary but lasts for a time. That is, consciousness is not momentary. They maintained, furthermore, that everything is immutable and has its fundamental nature, which it retains whatever be the changes it undergoes. Such a view implies that everything has its own character (*lakṣaṇa*) or nature (*svabhāva*)—an implication that goes against the accepted doctrine that nothing has its own nature (*nihsvabhāvatā*). If everything is itself and not anything else, then it must have its own character. But if it has its own character, how can it be natureless? Again, the Andhakas held that *nirvāṇa* belongs to the aggregate of formative forces (*samskāraskandha*). If it is one of the formative forces of man's being, it is inherent in him and is waiting to be realized. If *nirvāṇa* is spiritual peace, then peace belongs to the very essence of man. *Nirvāṇa* is a force that pulls man towards itself and creates a longing in him for peace.

It is difficult to say that the Andhakas realized the implications of their spiritual and metaphysical discoveries, which they courageously propounded, although getting into great conflict with the doctrines of the Elders and other sub-sects of the Mahāsanghikas. One will not be wrong in inferring the influence of the Upaniṣadic ideas on the Andhakas. Their view that meditative consciousness is continuous and not momentary and that *nirvāṇa* belongs to the essence of man's innermost being must have finally led to one of the Mahāyāna doctrines that ultimate reality is peace (*nirvāṇa*), void (*śūnya*), and consciousness (*vijñāna*). It is believed that the *Prajnāpāramitā*, the main scripture of the Mahāyāna, was originally found among the Andhakas, composed in Pali. They were, again, the first to say that the monks could marry.

UTTARĀPATHAKAS Another sect of the Buddhists, called the Uttarāpathakas, held that there is an immutable "thusness" (*tathatā*, such-ness, so-ness) in all things. The view has a similarity to the one that everything has its own nature (*sarvam svalakṣaṇam*). The Andhakas also held that all things are immutable and retain the aspect of immutability in spite of change. But this own-nature and immutability cannot be further explained. It is only so-and-so or thus-and-thus. The idea of thus-ness (*tathatā*) finally led to the philosophy of Thus-ness of Aśvaghoṣa, who belonged to the Mahāyāna. Thus the Hīnayāna schools, coming between the school of the Elders and the Mahāyāna, furnished a large amount of material to the phenomenology of consciousness, with which the Mahāyāna schools built up their super-structure.

THE SATYASIDDHI SCHOOL Before passing to the Mahāyāna schools, mention may be made of the Satyasiddhi school of Harivarman, who called himself a Hināyānist. He may be considered to be a forerunner of Nāgārjuna's, concerning the doctrine of the Void (*Śūnya*) as the ultimate reality. Harivarman criticizes the Sarvāstivādins for saying that only the *ātman* is void, but the psycho-physical aggregates are real and existent. But really the substratum of everything is void, for every aggregate can be analysed away, just as personality (*pudgala*) can be analysed away, and can be shown to be void in essence. Thus not only our personality in the form of the I-consciousness, but also the objective world is selfless (*ānātmam*) and nature-less (*nihsvabhāva*), and is therefore void (*śūnya*).

We may say that, throughout the philosophy of Buddhism, the two ideas that everything has its own nature (*sarvam svalakṣaṇam*) and nothing has its own nature (*sarvam nihsvabhāvam*) almost run parallel, sometimes separately and other times mixing up with each other in different ways. And the idea of the void is interpreted sometimes as neither what has its own nature nor what is the nature-less, and other times as only the nature-less. Strictly speaking, the Buddhists interpreted the latter as nihilism; but we find also that, for some Buddhists, the former view also was nihilism, in spite of the protests of those holding the view that they did not uphold the doctrine of Nothingness.

MAHĀYĀNA As already seen, quite a number of differences of view were growing within the Hīnayāna, and these differences were crystallized in the Mahāyāna philosophies. But when they were crystallized and systematized, practically new systems of thought and world-outlooks appeared. Apart from the main philosophical differences the views that differentiated Hīnayāna and Mahāyāna are mainly three: *First*, the Hīnayāna maintained that every individual can have only his own salvation. He obtains it when he gets enlightenment and becomes an *arhat*, i.e., a saint who has established his desert for it by following the way to perfection. But the Mahāyāna maintained that one who has obtained enlightenment and becomes an *arhat* could work, without entering *nirvāṇa*, for the salvation of the rest of the world. Such a one is called *bodhisattva*,[30] or one whose being itself is enlightenment or the supreme consciousness. The Mahāyāna brands, therefore, the Hīnayāna as the Vehicle of the Rhinoceros (*khaḍgayāna*), because the rhinoceros lives and dies alone.[31] *Secondly*, the Hīnayāna treated Buddha as only a historical person. But the Mahāyāna contended that Buddha had another body, a divine one, and the historical Buddha was only the apparent Buddha. The true Buddha was identical with the Supreme Reality. *Thirdly*, as a consequence of the second difference, the Mahāyāna maintained that every man, who strove earnestly, could become Buddha. If Buddha's original nature is the Supreme Reality itself and every one who obtains *nirvāṇa* becomes one with the Supreme Reality, then every one can become Buddha, i.e., one with Buddha. But the Hīnayāna rejected this doctrine as a sacrilege and maintained that, although every one could obtain *nirvāṇa*, he could not become Buddha.

As mentioned already, the main text of the Mahāyāna was the *Prajñāpāramitā*, on which commentaries were written and on the basis of which the works of the Mahāyāna schools were composed. The three main schools of the Mahāyāna are the Bhūtatathatā school, the Mādhyamika school, and the Vijñānavāda school. It is difficult to say which of the three schools is the earliest. Aśvaghoṣa of about the 1st century A.D. is the founder of the Bhūtatathatā school, Nāgārjuna of about the 2nd century A.D. of the Mādhyamika school, and Maitreyanātha of uncertain date of the Vijñānavāda school. Some scholars believe that he was earlier than Nāgārjuna and others that he was later. However, the two brothers, Asaṅga and Vasubandhu, of about the 4th century A.D. are the main exponents of this school. Tradition believes that Asaṅga was a pupil of Maitreyanātha and the teacher of his brother, Vasubandhu. If the tradition is true, then Maitreyanātha must be later than Nāgārjuna. We cannot however, be certain.[32]

BHŪTATATHATĀ SCHOOL The philosophy of this school is found in Aśvaghoṣa's *Awakening of Faith*. Aśvaghoṣa is said to have at first been a Vedāntin, later converted to Buddhism. He might have brought Vedāntic ideas into Buddhism and developed its philosophy. All the Mahāyāna schools distinguish between ultimate truth (*pāramārthikasatya*) and empirical truth (*samvṛtisatya*) or, properly translated, between the truth of Higher Reality (*paramārtha*) and the truth within the world of Ignorance (*samvṛti*). Aśvaghoṣa accepts the empirical reality of the five aggregates (*skandhas*), the twelve bases (*āvatanas*), and the eighteen elements (*dhātus*). But their reality is not ultimate. The only ultimate reality is the Such-ness of things (Bhūtatathatā), their very essence. We have to call it "such-ness," because it is indescribable. Even "such-ness" is a descriptive word, but we have to use some word to denote that there is an ultimate reality, and we have to use a positive term because ultimate reality is positive, not negative.[33] Things can be described, but not their essential nature. Such-ness is the same as *nirvāṇa*, enlightenment (*bodhi*), the essential body of Buddha (*dharmakāya*), the *summum bonum* (*kuśalamūlam*, literally the root of all that is good), the perfection of everything that is good, the womb or source of Buddha (*tathāgatagarbha*), and Buddha himself as the one who has become the Such (*Tathāgata*). It is the truth of our inward being, peace, equanimity. It is the conscious conservator (*Ālayavijñāna*), the conserving consciousness of everything that happens and is its source. It is yet void (*śūnya*) of all determinations and is therefore indescribable.

But Aśvaghoṣa is not content with saying that Such-ness is the ultimate reality. He wants also to show how the world of plurality is derived from it. Such-ness is the Absolute and the One. We have to show how plurality can come out of it. Here Aśvaghoṣa utilizes the traditional twelve-linked chain of causation. The plurality arises conditioned by Ignorance (Avidyā), containing the formative forces (*samskāras*) including those generated by our past actions (*karmas*). Then the Conserving Consciousness (Ālayavijñāna), which is the same as Such-ness (Tathatā), is disturbed. Then the original consciousness becomes the action-consciousness (*karmavijñāna*), i.e., consciousness with action-potencies,[34] and next activity-consciousness (*pravṛtti-vijñāna*). That is, the same original consciousness first becomes the potencies and then the activities resulting from the potencies. Next, is born mind (*manas*), next its particularity, next the succession of mental phenomena, the senses, objects, craving, birth, death and so forth.

We see that the Mahāyāna has now become an absolutism like the Upaniṣadic philosophy. Instead of the Hīnayānist pure *nirvāṇa* without consciousness, we have now a conscious *nirvāṇa*. The state of *nirvāṇa* now becomes the ultimate reality as Pure Consciousness. Buddhism has become idealistic, monistic, and absolutistic. Although Aśvaghoṣa treats the Conserving Consciousness (Ālayavijñāna) as the highest reality, he prefers to call it the Such-ness of things (Bhūtatathatā), thereby implying that it is a positive essence of the elements (*bhūtas*, literally the havebeens) of the world, and secondly that it is the essence of things as processions of events. He does not call it That-ness, but So-ness (*tathā* means so, thus) or Such-ness, which refers to activity and change rather than to stability of the objects of the world. Although the events that constitute a process are transient, So-ness itself, as meaning a pattern, is stable. Ultimate reality is a pattern of patterns.

MĀDHYAMIKA SCHOOL Nāgārjuna, the founder of the Mādhyamika school, was not evidently satisfied with the conclusion reached by Aśvaghoṣa. He is said to be the author of many works, but the most important of them is his *Mādhyamikakārikās*.[35] Nāgārjuna wants to show that ultimate reality cannot be described either in positive or negative terms. It cannot have any characteristics, not even that of Such-ness. Not only ultimate reality, but also the phenomenal world cannot be described, because none of the categories we use in describing the world has its own nature. He developed one of the most devastating dialectics[36] ever written in the world and exposed the natureless-ness (*nihsvabhāvatā*) and attacked the view that everything has its own nature or character (*sarvam svalakṣaṇam*). If everything can be shown to have only relative existence, then which thing can have its own nature? And if everything is devoid of its own characters and is, therefore, void, and there is nothing that is not void, then the absolute reality must be the Void. The voidness of everything, both subjective and objective, was held, as we have seen already, even before Nāgārjuna. But it is he who made the voidness philosophy systematic and comprehensive, and turned the Void into the Absolute itself. If everything in the world is essentially a void, the world itself is void. What we see then is only an appearance of the Void, the Absolute. Appearance is the empirical truth (*samvṛtisatya*), the Void the Ultimate or Absolute Truth (*pāramārthikasatya*). So everything that belongs to this world is only an empirical truth. Then, Buddha, his law (doctrine), the aggregates, the bases, the elements—in short, everything that the Buddhists accepted so far—are not ultimately true. Such an assertion was a very bold one on the part of Nāgārjuna, a Buddhist leader, the most prominent and dominating figure of his time. Not only the Buddhist concepts, but also those of the other schools known to Nāgārjuna, were dialectically exploded by him. If the world is not real, it could not have been born and was, therefore, never born. This doctrine is called the doctrine of the non-birth of the world and man (*ajātivāda*), and was taken over by even the Advaita as expounded by Gauḍapāda. If there is no world, there is no ethical action (*karma*), no ethical potency, no bondage, and so no *nirvāṇa*. We find ethos of their view also in Kasmir Śaivism and the Advaita. The world is an Illusion (Māyā), is due to Ignorance (Avidyā); it is like a dream (*svapnatulya*). As the Void cannot be characterized, it is neither one nor many; it is non-dual[37] (*advaya*).

Then should we say that the world is Non-being? We cannot say so. Even to say that it is Non-being is to assert something definite. Furthermore, Non-being has significance only with reference to Being. Ultimate reality, which is the essence of everything, can be neither Being nor Non-being. It cannot be both because they are contradictories. It cannot be neither also, as we have only the two alternatives and there is no third. All that we can say is that we cannot characterize it any way. It is, therefore, that which is devoid (*śūnya*) of all characterizations, all determinations. It is the Void (*Śūnya*).

Is the world of appearance, then, different from the Ultimate Reality? We cannot say that the two are either different or identical. We cannot conceptualize the relation between the world and Ultimate Reality. The relation also is, therefore, voidity. Thus indescribability, inexplicability, expressed as "S is neither P, nor not-P, nor both, nor neither," is the essential meaning of the word "void" (*śūnya*), and the same meaning is given to the words Illusion, and Ignorance. In Nāgārjuna's philosophy, the three words—*śūnya*, *māyā*, and *avidyā*—are interchangeable.

It is not possible to give even a summary of Nāgārjuna's dialectic in the present work. Only a few examples can be given. For instance, he disproved the reality of a causality thus. We say that every event has a cause. Here are we speaking of real events or unreal events? Real events are already real and existent and do not need a cause. Neither do unreal events need a cause. Then what is causality for? Causality is, therefore, unreal. Similarly, he disproves the attainment of *nirvāṇa*. For there is nothing called attainment. *Nirvāṇa* is the goal of attainment. If it is already there, there is no need to attain it. If it is not there, how can anyone talk of it as the goal of attainment? How can he know that there is such a thing? There is no becoming. We say that A is becoming B. But if A has not yet become B, there is no justification to say that it is becoming B. B is not there as yet, so we do not know anything to be B. But if B is already there, there need be no becoming. There are no aggregates; they are unreal. If there are aggregates, is each element of the aggregate also an aggregate? If it is, then there will be infinite regress and each element resolves itself into the void. If it is not, how can it come into being and constitute an aggregate again? How can there be anything without an aggregate as its cause? Buddha said that everything has a cause. If the aggregates are uncaused, they will exist for ever like space, and there will be no end to misery.

Such is the general dialectical method of Nāgārjuna. Yet he protests against being called a nihilist, for reality rejects even negative characterization.[38] The Middle Path taught by Buddha has to be applied to metaphysics also; it will be neither to affirm nor to deny, i.e., it will be to deny both the positive and negative characteristics. Nāgārjuna calls himself the follower of the Middle Path (*mādhyamika*). Reality is neither Such-ness nor consciousness (*vijñāna*); even these two terms are characterizations. It is only Void (*Śūnya*). Indeed, even to call it Void is to characterize it. *Truly, it is neither Void nor Non-void.* In spite of reaching such an extreme conclusion, Nāgārjuna's doctrine is called the doctrine of the Void.

VIJÑĀNAVĀDA SCHOOL The school of Vijñānavāda,[39] also called Yogācāra, is the largest, the most popular and important of the Mahāyāna schools. It has a large amount of literature and many sub-schools. It is difficult to present all of them, but only the central doctrines of all. Besides, its contributions to epistemology, as we shall see later, are greater than those of any other Buddhist school.

Like the other Mahāyāna schools, the Vijñānavāda accepts that the categories and realities of the Hīnayāna have empirical validity (*samvṛti satya*); but it contends that ultimate reality (*paramārthasatya*) is Consciousness (Vijñāna) only, but not Such-ness or Voidness. Ultimate reality is known in *nirvāṇa*, which is beyond misery. But without consciousness, we cannot know that it is beyond misery. As *nirvāṇa* must be an experiential state, it has to be consciousness. But it is pure consciousness without any determinate states. If consciousness identifies itself with any of the determinate states, it will be within the world of becoming and so within the realm of misery. It has, therefore, to be devoid of all determinations. It is the highest nature or law (Dharma), enlightenment (*bodhi*), such-ness (*tathatā*), the womb of Buddha (*tathāgatagarbha*), and everything which the Buddhists treat as the ideal.

Along with the idea of consciousness, the idea of the *ātman*[40] also entered the Vijñānavāda school. As consciousness was regarded as the highest reality, and as the *ātman*, according to the Vedānta, was the conscious spirit, it became easy to identify *vijñāna* and the *ātman*. The Vijñānavādins went further and declared that this reality was the Mahātmā or Mahān Ātman.[41] One who becomes Buddha, i.e., obtains enlightenment, obtains (realizes) the pure *ātman*, and thereby becomes the Great Ātman (Mahātmā).[42] This Mahātman is the same as the Paramātman. This is the womb of the Tathāgata, the source from which objects originate. The idea of the womb of things belongs to the Upaniṣads and the *Bhagavadgītā* also. Yamakami Sogen refers to the latter, in which Kṛṣṇa (as the Supreme God-head) says: "My womb is Brahma as *Mahat*, in which I cast the seed. From that comes the origination of all beings. Whatever mortals are born in all the wombs, the main womb is the Mahat Bhrahma, and I the father giving the seed."[43] The idea of the Supreme Being as the womb of the universe became the idea of the original pure consciousness in Buddhism. The rejection of the *ātman* by the Hīnayāna Buddhists became only the rejection of the ultimate reality of the ego (*ahaṁkāra*) for the Vijñānavādins. But the *ātman* and the ego are experienced as the I-consciousness and assert themselves as "I am", as though they are one and the same. But the former is pure (*śuddha*) and the latter impure (*aśuddha*) being rooted in the Unconscious (Ignorance, *avidyā*) and appearing only like the glistening Himalayan peak out of dark shades and depths. The pure *ātman* is all bright with light like the great sun.[44]

We have seen that the idea of the *ātman*[45] was entering the Hīnayāna itself as if by the back door. The Vātsīputrīyas and the Sammitīyas held a doctrine similar to that of the *ātman* of the Upaniṣads. The former said that the "I" had to be different from the body or aggregates. The latter maintained that the reality of the soul had to be accepted; for the eye does not see, but it is the "I" that sees. Without the "I" or the soul, the eye cannot see. The Andhakas observed that consciousness (*vijñāna*) in meditation lasted for a time and was not momentary. These ideas took a definite, unified shape in the Vijñānavāda, and the ultimate pure consciousness became the *ātman* itself and was enunciated as such without hesitation. Yet, to show their difference from the Upaniṣadic doctrine, the Vijñānavādins declare that the original consciousness is mutable,[46] while the Upaniṣadic *ātman* is immutable. But there is no real difference; for both the Upaniṣads and the Vijñānavādins, the *ātman* is mutable from one point of view and immutable from another.[47] According to the Vijñānavādins, the original consciousness is the repository of past formative forces (*samskāras*) and a depository of all the new ones also; it is continuously changing, expanding (cp. the idea of the Brahman), and creating; and it is the common universal ground of everything.

Such original, pure, absolute consciousness is called Ālayavijñāna. Everything in the world is a transformation (*pariṇāma*)[48] of the Ālayavijñāna, and is, therefore, a form of consciousness itself. This transformation follows the order of the twelve links with the Unconscious (*Ajñāna*) coming below Ālayavijñāna, and assumes the form of the aggregates, bases, and elements. Indeed, the doctrine of the eternal atoms of the Sarvāstivādins cannot agree with the Vijñānavāda position that everything is a transformation of consciousness. However, this transformation is explained in terms of the doctrine of dependent origination (*pratītyasamutpāda*), overlooking the difficulty how dependent origination can be transformation (*pariṇāma*). The detailed analysis and categorization of the psycho-physical world is more or less the same as in the Bhūtatathatā and Sarvāstivāda schools.[49]

The Vijñānavāda should not be interpreted as subjective idealism, but as the objective. Its propounders say that ultimate consciousness is not the consciousness of any individual, but is universal: it is not even *ātmā*—which for them is the ego—but Mahātmā (the Great Universal Spirit). It is the ground not only of all the "I's", but also of everything else. Asaṅga and Vasubandhu further say that that part of the Ālayavijñāna which stores the impressions (*samskāras*) for the individual and becomes the potential state of the evolution of the world for him is *vipākavijñāna*,[50] the consciousness that is ripe for becoming the world. It is lower than the Ālayavijñāna, which itself is lower than pure Vijñāna. For even the Ālayavijñāna, contains the formative forces in their potential state. In pure Vijñāna the formative forces are transformed and transcended into pure, undisturbed consciousness (*nirvāṇa*). In fact, we read that in the Bhūtatathatā[51] philosophy also, a consciousness (*vijñāna*) was postulated and called Ālayavijñāna (the never disappearing consciousness). It is higher than the Ālayavijñāna[52] (repository consciousness) and is equated to Such-ness (Tathatā). We thus see that a few Hīnayāna schools and all the schools of the Mahāyāna mark the different stages by which Buddhism approached through independent thinking and got assimilated to the Vedānta.

SAUTRĀNTIKA-YOGĀCĀRA SCHOOL This school branched off from the teachings of Vasubandhu through Dinnāga and was developed by Śāntarakṣita and his commentator Kamalaśīla.[53] In its main epistemological doctrines, this school wanted to follow the Sautrāntikas, but in its metaphysics it followed the Vijñānavāda (Yogācāra). Like the Vijñānavādins, it maintained that the Pure Vijñāna alone is ultimately real and that everything else is a form of Vijñāna (Consciousness). But it differed from the doctrine of Vasubandhu that ultimate consciousness is stable and permanent. Sāntarakṣita thought that Vasubandhu's position was becoming identical with the Vedānta and wanted to differentiate Buddhism by saying that this consciousness also was momentary. But to say that this consciousness (Vijñāna), which is the same as *nirvāṇa* is momentary is to say *first* that one who attains *nirvāṇa* attains it only for a moment and *second* that this pure consciousness is determinate, for momentariness is a determinant. To meet this difficulty, Sāntarakṣita held that this moment is a timeless moment. We cannot think of the past and present of a timeless moment; it can, therefore, have no end. The indeterminability and indescribability of ultimate reality is applied by Sāntarakṣita to the concept of a moment for saving the absoluteness (unconditionedness) of *nirvāṇa*. As it is usual with the Buddhists, all the terms denoting the highest reality in Buddhism are applied to this absolute moment.

CONCLUSION With the perfecting of Vijñānavāda by Asaṅga and Vasubandhu, Buddhist philosophy entered the phase at which, except for a few differences, it became easy for it to enter the Vedānta and for the Vedānta to assimilate and absorb it. In fact, even its doctrine of causation underwent serious transformation. Taking the whole of Buddhism into consideration, we find four conceptions of causation in it. We have *first* the doctrine of dependent origination, according to which, although the cause is necessary for the effect, it has to die before the effect comes into being and there can, therefore, be no material cause that can constitute the material of the effect. *Secondly*, we have found that, according to the Sarvāstivādins, the effect is an aggregate of the constituents, which continue as the constituents so long as the effect lasts. In the *third* place, the Vijñānavāda introduced the idea of transformation and evolution (*pariṇāma*). In the *fourth* place, we find also a conception like that of Śaṅkara's cause that remains unaffected (*vivartakāraṇa*) in spite of giving rise to the effect. If the highest consciousness (Vijñāna) or Nirvāṇa is eternally present and if out of it the world comes without at the same time affecting its purity, then this cause is the same[54] as that which Śaṅkara accepted.

The development of the doctrine of Buddha's body also led Buddhism into the Vedānta. The Lokottaravādins of the Hīnayāna held that the true body of Buddha could not have been mundane. Then it must be the truth of Buddha's being, *nirvāṇa*, *śūnya*, etc. It must be the Dharmakāya, the body identical with Dharma, the Truth, the essential nature and law of the world and reality.

The concept[55] of *dharma* in Buddhism is so comprehensive that it can mean anything and everything in the universe. We have seen that Vasubandhu in his *Abhidharmakośa* defined *dharma* as anything that can be known, a thing, a category. In the Mahāyāna, when the truth of all *dharmas* becomes the ultimate Vijñāna, Śūnya, the body of Buddha, Bhūtatathatā, etc., the true Dharma becomes all of them. It means also, for Buddhism, the law, the doctrine, the truth taught by Buddha. But what his doctrine pointed to was the ultimate reality. So *dharma* came to mean the highest reality.

In between the historical, mundane body of Buddha and his Dharmakāya (divine body), the Buddhists introduced other[56] bodies, corresponding to different spiritual levels. The highest of these levels was identified with ultimate reality, which can be realized inwardly by mind. Indeed, the ideas of God and the individual *ātman* were rejected; but they were rejected only in favour of ultimate Vijñāna (Consciousness), which was little different from the Brahman of the Upaniṣads. The whole Mahāyāna denied the independent reality of the material world, which was treated by the Bhūtatathatā and the Vijñānavāda schools as ultimately a form of the original consciousness (Vijñāna), and thereby became very similar to the Upaniṣadic doctrine that "All this is verily the Brahman." Only the Mādhyamika stopped short of this result.

Besides, Buddhism from its very beginning accepted all the gods of the orthodox, conservative religion, although rejecting the Supreme God as the creator. And in spite of rejecting the Brahmanic religion of sacrifices, it accepted the Mīmāmsā doctrine of ethical potency as a creator and controller of the world for every individual and made the potency a part of the aggregate of the formative forces (*samskāras*). The Buddhist conception of Māyā and Avidyā, particularly in the Vijñānavāda, is little different from that of the Advaita Vedānta. The Buddhist equation, again, of the two with the Śūnya as that which disappears like a dream at the time of enlightenment made them easily acceptable to the Advaita, according to which the world disappears when the Brahman is realized. The Buddhist definition of every one of the three ideas—Māyā, Avidyā, and Śūnya—as that which neither is, nor is not, nor is both, nor is neither, was bodily incorporated by the Advaita. Even the theistic orthodox schools[57] incorporated the idea of the Void, though in a positive way, saying that it is a state of the Supreme God-head, in which the world is about to be created, but not yet created. That is, the Void is the indeterminate state of objectivity before it becomes the determinate state of plurality. Thus practically every doctrine of Buddhism in its latest phases in India became assimilated in one way or another to some school of the orthodox tradition. But when assimilated, it ceased to appear as Buddhist.

5. EPISTEMOLOGY

Although early Buddhism showed little or no interest in epistemology, later schools, particularly from the time of the Sarvāstivādins, began developing their epistemological doctrines under the pressure of controversies with rival schools. We do not know very much about the Sarvāstivādins themselves; but their two sub-schools, the Sautrāntikas and the Vaibhāṣikas, showed fairly keen interest. In fact, epistemological doctrines with a definite shape could not have started before the 5th or 4th century B.C., to which Gautama, the founder of the Nyāya, belonged. Buddhism could not have been interested in the subject at that time, although it was from the beginning rejecting the Vedas as the scriptural authority and was relying entirely on logic and experience in its controversies with rival schools. However, we find very early attempts at using a form of argument and syllogism in the controversies[58] (3rd century B.C.) among the Buddhist sects. The school of the Elders called itself analytic arguers (*vibhajyavādins*, those who divide a position into alternatives and reject every one of them separately) and used the hypothetical syllogism, dilemma, and in some cases even the syllogism in its simple moods with example (*udāharana*).[59] But there does not seem to be much of an attempt to formulate the forms of argument. Of course, although the Buddhists rejected the Veda as a scriptural authority, they accepted Buddha's words instead. The two forms of valid cognition accepted by them, in their controversies with their rival schools, are perception and inference. But the Buddhists did not think of writing a book on epistemology up to about the 5th century, when Dinnāga wrote his work, *Pramāṇasamucchaya* on the basis of which Dharmakīrti wrote his *Pramāṇavārtikā* (6th century), on which, again, Prajñākaragupta wrote his commentary *Pramāṇavārtikābhāṣya*[60] (7th century). However, the Buddhist schools are not unanimous in their epistemologies, particularly because of the differences among their metaphysical views. The above works belong to the Vijñānavāda school, in which references can be found to the Sautrāntika and Vaibhāṣika views.

Practically all the Buddhist epistemologists accept perception and inference as the valid means of cognition. Although they reject the Veda as a scriptural authority, they accept that language or word is a way of knowing and that it is reliable when spoken by a reliable person, who for them is Buddha. So one cannot be wrong in saying that the Buddhists accepted the word (*śabda*) also as a valid means, indeed, in their own way. They treat verbal cognition or cognition through words as a form of perception.

PERCEPTION Perception is defined as non-illusory sense cognition devoid of determinations (*kalpanā*).[61] Determinations are the characteristics and their relations. This definition of perception is severely criticized by the rival schools. It is the same as the definition of indeterminate perception given by Kumārila. How can such cognition, which is absolutely indeterminate, be perception at all? It can only be a cognition of a mere That, of mere being, without the What. It is not of the form, "That is a pen"; for then the That is characterized by the What, i.e., pen. When thus characterized, the cognition will be a classification of the object under pens. Again, perception for the Buddhists is not also of the form, "That is red", for then "red" is a characteristic characterizing the That. But if the form of perception is a mere That, of what use will such a perception be? The object of every perception is a That and there can be no difference between one That and another. Again, when a man perceives a snake, if he perceives only a mere That, he will neither run away from it nor kill it. But as he does either of the two, his perception cannot be of a mere That. Furthermore, inference is based upon the data obtained from perception. But if perception gives only many Thats, it cannot be a basis of inference and there can be no inference.

The Buddhist doctrine of perception is based upon the view held by many of them that every object is itself and not another and has, therefore, its own character (*svalakṣaṇa*). The object that is itself and not anything else (*svetarabhinna*) is known only in perception. It is a particular. In inference we know the object only as a member of a class, but not as this or that particular object. The Buddhists do not accept the reality either of the category of the particular (*viśeṣa*) or of the universal (*jāti, sāmānya*). The idea of the particular is only that which is not anything else and so of that which is different from everything other than itself (*anyāpoḍha*)[62]. The universal is only either a name (word) or a mental concept (*vikalpa*), and we wrongly think that corresponding to the word and concept there is a real object called the universal. When we observe several men, we tend to use the same name for all of them, as they are similar to one another. Then in our mind, through memory, a common concept (*vikalpa*) is formed. The concept is a product of memory (*smṛti*). Regarding the universal, the Buddhists are not realists, but nominalists and conceptualists.[63]

What the Buddhists seem to mean by saying that all perception is indeterminate (*nirvakalpa*) is not that the object is a mere That and all perceptions give only Thats. When I perceive a horse, I perceive it with its form, size, colour, etc. But the form, colour etc., are not distinguished as characteristics of the horse. The colour patch I see in the space occupied by that animal is that particular patch,[64] but not any other. In the actual process of cognition, in the focussing of the sense, there is no conscious memory of other similar colour patches. Instead of saying that, when my eyes are fixed on the object of perception, there is absence of any cognition of distinctions within the object—as between the substance and attribute, between member and class—and of its positive and negative relations to other objects, the Buddhists said that the object of perception is cognized as different from other objects. Their language is defective.

Then how are action and inference possible after perception, if perception is indeterminate? The Buddhists say that the necessary factors (*sāmagri*)[65] for giving rise to both are present in mind. These factors are the analytic function of mind, memory, and name. After perception, mind makes distinctions within the object, attaches names to the object and its distinctions, and, through the names and concepts so formed and related, makes a major premise and inference. And through the concepts and names associated with action, man acts. For instance, the name and idea of snake are associated with the ideas of its being poisonous, running away from it, killing it, and so on. So man either runs away or kills the snake.

Concerning the relation between the perceptual consciousness and its object, the Sautrāntikas, the Vaibhāṣikas, and the Vijñānavādins differ from one another. The former two, being Sarvāstivādins—who say that all objects are real and existent—contend that, in perception, our consciousness takes on the form of the object; the form of our consciousness and that of the object then become identical. But this identity is coincidence according to the Sautrāntikas,[66] but real identity according to the Vaibhāṣikas. According to the former, our consciousness cognizes only the form (*ākāra*) which it assumes and which coincides with (or becomes similar to) the form of the object; it does not cognize the object and its form. The Sautrāntikas thus accept the representative[67] theory of perception. The existence of the object is only inferred as the cause of the perception; and the inference is mediated by the idea in our consciousness. The object itself is never perceived. But the Vaibhāṣikas ask: If no object is directly perceived, how can we know that there are real objects at all? And how can we know that our idea of the object is true, if we can never see the object? How can we know that there is correspondence between the idea and the object? So the Vaibhāṣikas maintain that there is absolute identity between the form in our consciousness and that belonging to the object, i.e., our consciousness knows the object directly. They accept the presentative theory of perception.

The Vijñānavādins also accept the presentative theory, but say that the object does not have an existence independent of our consciousness. The form which consciousness assumes in perception belongs to consciousness itself, but not to the object;[68] for there is no independent object. The Vijñānavādins are idealists[69] and, as we have seen, accept the reality of consciousness only. In perception, our consciousness puts on the form (*ākāra*) of the object due to the formative forces (*samskāras*)—universal, racial, individual. Essentially, reality is consciousness only. But it takes as though two forms,[70] the form of knowledge (consciousness) and that of the object. The Vijñānavādins accept only the two factor theory of cognition, but not the three factor theory of Kumārila, in which all cognition involves the cognizer, the cognition, the cognized. They say that to think that there is an independent object[71] that is cognized and that there is an independent subject (knower) to whom the cognition belongs is an illusion (Avidyā). What we call the knower is the knowing consciousness[72] itself. The result of cognition is the experience of consciousness of itself as asserting: "That is a pen."[73] The cause of this cognition is to be looked for not in an object existing independently of consciousness, but in the formative forces (*samskāras*) within our consciousness. The causation is from within, but not from outside of consciousness.

The Mādhyamikas accept the reality of neither consciousness (Vijñāna) nor the object, but only of the Void (Śūnya). They say that not only the three factor theory of the Mīmāmsā but also the two factor theory of the Vijñānavādins belongs to the sphere of Ignorance (*samvṛti*) and can have only empirical and pragmatic validity, but not the absolute (*pāramārthika*).

Perception is of four kinds: sense perception, self-revealing perception, mental perception, and yogic perception. Sense perception is the perception of colours, sounds, tastes, etc. Mental perception (*mānaskikapratyakṣa*) is the perception of objects (as wholes, not merely as sensations or senses) and of hate, attachment, etc. How can objects belong to mental perception, if colour, etc., belong to sense perception? The Vijñānavadins say that the perception of the That[74] in "That is red" belongs to mind, but not to the senses. Of the mental perceptions, some, like happiness, are self-revealing (*svasamvedanam mānasam pratyakṣam*[75]), but the That is not self-revealing in "That is red." Yogic perception belongs to the yogis, who are free from all impurities and who can see directly past and future and also objects at any distance.

INFERENCE The Vijñānavādins have an interesting theory of the relation between perception and inference. All perception, according to this school, is indeterminate in the sense that it is without any inner distinctions and is non-relational. But no cognition is valid, unless it leads to successful activity. If the object of my perception is a pen, then the object must lead to writing; if it does not write, then it is not a pen. If the perceived object is sugar, then it must lead to my eating it and experiencing its sweetness. But the object as such does not lead me to action. I am led to action by the idea (*vikalpa*) and name (*nāma*) of the object. The name and idea of the object and the idea of my future activity are related; and I infer that, if I eat that object (sugar), I shall have a particular experience (sweetness). The validity of perception depends, therefore, on this inference. But inference itself depends on perceptual data for its own validity. Hence, perception and inference are mutually dependent.[76] This dependence does not mean that perception is not valid as perception. My cognition of the pen as such is valid as the mere perception of the pen. But simply as perception, it does not lead to action, unless the determinations (*vikalpas*, concepts) arise, leading to my future action based upon the inference of the result.

The Buddhist division of cognition into perception and inference is interesting in that perception is defined as that cognition which is self-dependent (*svatantra*) and inference as every form of cognition that is not self-dependent, but is based on some other cognition. Here the Buddhists interpret inference (*anumāna*) as that valid cognition that follows another valid cognition or occurs after it.[77] An absolutely self-dependent cognition cannot have even the element of memory.[78] If I say: "That is a horse," in which the distinction between the That and the universal horse-ness and a relation between the two is cognized, I am not merely perceiving, but have gone beyond perception. To know the relation is to know that the animal in front is a member of a class. But the class-concept, horse-ness, is a product of past experiences and so of memory. But perception should not include anything except what is immediately present. It cannot then be determinate, but indeterminate. And what is not indeterminate follows upon perception and comes under inference. Inference, for the Buddhists, thus becomes wide and comprehensive and is more than syllogistic reasoning.

The Buddhists speak also of inference for oneself (*svārthānumāna*) and inference for another (*parārthānumāna*). For them, inference for oneself seems to include the whole thought process intervening between indeterminate perception and explicit syllogistic inference as in debate. Thus what are called recognition, cognition of negation, and practical reason—in the sense of Aristotle's, not in that of Kant's—leading to action after perception become inferences for oneself. Yet they are not recognized as separate and distinct means of valid cognition. Verbal cognition or cognition of an object after hearing a word or sentence is the perception of sound and inference of the meaning of the words. Kumārila's non-apprehension (*anupalabdhi*) is, according to the Buddhists, only a means of inference. It is of the form: I do not perceive the pen; therefore, there is absence (*abhāva*) of the pen. Comparison or perception of similarity (*upamāna*) also is a combination of perception and inference. These forms of cognition arise after (*anu*) perception and are based on it. Indeed, in these inferences, the parts of syllogism are not explicit; but they can be made explicit, if wanted. They are all inferences for oneself.[79]

While the Naiyāyikas maintain that the inference for another should have five parts and the Mīmāmsakas that it should have three, the Buddhists say that two are enough. They are the major with the example and the minor term along with the middle term in its relation to the major term. The syllogism will then be:

Wherever there is smoke, there is fire, as in the kitchen;
This mountain has smoke necessarily related to fire.

The Buddhist reject[80] the necessity of the separate mention of (1) the thesis to be proved; (2) reason; (3) application of the major premise to the minor term, pointing out the similarity (*upanayana, upamāna*) of the mountain to the accepted example; and (4) establishment of the thesis or conclusion. Yet they divide inference into two propositions. However, if we analyse the two propositions, we find (1) the major premise with the example, (2) the minor premise, and (3) reason or the middle term. The denial of the necessity to mention separately the reason, etc., seems to be based more on epistemological considerations than on the purely logical. It is indeed true that the conclusion is drawn from the total thought form (*Gestalt*).

Minor term—Middle term—Major term

or

S – M – P

and the conclusion is only the observation of the relation between S and P as "S is P." The parts as accepted by the Nyāya do not play any part separately in the inferential thought process, but only together. Yet from the side of pure logic, if their separate mention is omitted, confusion will result. In fact, the Buddhists themselves give definitions and explanations of these terms.[81]

According to Dinnāga, any true reason (middle term, *probans*) (1) must be present in the minor in which the consequent (*probandum*, major term, the thing to be proved) is to be proved; (2) it must be present also wherever else the *probandum* is present; and (3) it must be absent wherever the *probandum* is absent.[82] He says that the relation between the *probans* and the *probandum* (middle and major terms) is either (1) that of cause and effect, or (2) natural, or (3) inseparability. Natural relationship is what the Buddhists call identity (*tādātmyatā*). For instance we can infer from the object being an oak that it is a tree. The relation between the oak and the tree is called identity. The Nyāya would call this relation the relation of the individual and the universal. But the Buddhists do not accept the reality of the universals. Next, natural relation can also be that of natural succession. For example, night and day follow each other naturally. If it is day time now, we can infer that night will follow. The inseparables may not have any direct or indirect causal relation; yet we can infer the one from the other.

Curiously enough, the Buddhists say that the major premise is obtained from or seen in perception.[83] But if perception is indeterminate as they contend, how can we have a major premise, which is a universal proposition, from perception? A universal proposition expresses a relation between two universals or concepts and cannot, therefore, be obtained from perception. The Vijñānavādins reply that the objection is justified, for the concepts are mental forms and are not true. So inference has only empirical (*saṃvṛti*) or pragmatic (*vyāvahārika*) truth. Only perception as indeterminate is ultimately valid (*pāramārthikasatya*). Then too, it is ultimately valid when it presents no object, but only consciousness (*vijñāna*). In ordinary perception, the object is presented as if it has an independent existence apart from consciousness. But really, only consciousness is ultimately real, the object is false from the stand-point of ultimate reality. The Sarvāstivādins would not accept this reply, because, according to them, the object has its own reality apart from consciousness. On the contrary, they treat consciousness as having no reality, but appearing only as a kind of epiphenomenon. Again, the Sautrāntika branch of the Sarvāstivādins has its own difficulty, as it does not accept that the object is directly perceived by us, but is only inferred. The Sautrāntikas are understood as having rejected perception as a valid means of cognition to be called perception.[84] For them, inference was the only valid means of cognition; for we can know, according to the Sautrāntikas, that the objects exists only through inference from the idea that we have an object.

In spite of the keen analysis of the epistemological situation in perception and inference, the Buddhist doctrine of inference is vitiated by their doctrine of momentariness and their view that the relation between the middle and major terms is perceived. *First*, if all things are momentary, no causal connection can be established among them. And *secondly*, causal relation, being universal, cannot be obtained from indeterminate perception.

VERBAL KNOWLEDGE The Buddhists do not accept verbal knowledge as a distinct means of valid cognition. Hearing the word as a sound is perception, and knowing its meaning is inference. So verbal knowledge is a combination of perception and inference. The Mīmāmsā view that the Veda was not composed by any person cannot be true; for there can be no book not composed by any person. We cannot accept the Nyāya view that the Veda was composed by God; for the existence of God cannot be proved. Here the Buddhists use all the familiar arguments against the existence of God. If we accept the authoritativeness of a book because it was composed by a reliable person, then there is only one reliable person, Buddha. Buddha's teachings (words) ought, therefore, to be accepted. A reliable person[85] is one who has knowledge of the ultimate truth, who knows what is to be sought for and what is to be avoided, and who is infinitely compassionate. He is one who has gone the right way (*sugata*) and who knows and teaches the four Aryan Truths. Such a person is Buddha and his teachings only are reliable. Furthermore, his teachings can be verified by experience and inference.

VALIDITY OF KNOWLEDGE The Buddhists generally accept that a valid cognition and its means are one and the same. That is, they do not distinguish between the process of cognition and the result (*phala*) of cognition. This view holds particularly true of the Vijñānavādins, according to whom the object is only the form (*ākāra*) which our consciousness assumes and there is no object independent of our consciousness. The Vaibhāṣikas say that the form which our consciousness assumes is the same as that of the object, which has, however, an existence of its own, and the validity (*prāmāṇya*) of our consciousness lies in this identity, which becomes the validifying instrument of cognition and which is at the same time not different from cognition. In the sense that the form of cognition and cognition are not different, the process and result are identical. For the Sautrāntikas, according to whom the form of the object and the form which consciousness assumes are similar, but not identical, the result of cognition is the form it obtains and knows (*svasamvitti*). Even then, cognition (*pramā*) and its result (*phala*) are identical, for the result is the form of cognition itself. The Mādhyamikas do not have any objection to accept the Vijñānavāda position at the empirical level.

Regarding the problem whether cognition is valid by itself or is made valid by something else, the view of the Sautrāntikas and the Vaibhāṣikas are not available. But all the schools maintain that truth is known through action, as every object is meant to serve some purpose and we can know whether or not it serves that purpose through activity. The world is created for activity (*karma*) by ethical potency (*samskāra*) generated by activity. So the truth of our cognition, so far as empirical reality goes, can be known finally through activity. This view is common, as mentioned already, to all the Indian schools except the Cārvākas.

The Mādhyamikas and the Vijñānavādins contributed their answers to the question whether cognition is valid by itself, by saying that all cognition by itself is false (*svatah aprāmāṇyam*). According to the Mādhyamikas, neither consciousness nor the object is real, but is only an appearance. Yet, in this world we experience them. They are, therefore, false; and our cognitions presenting objects are invalid by themselves. According to the Vijñānavādins, although our consciousness is real, the object it presents is false; cognitions, therefore, are essentially invalid. Indeed, the Vijñānavādins do not hold that consciousness that knows itself only, but not an object, is invalid. Such a consciousness is ultimate Vijñāna.

But if all cognitions are false, why do we say that some of our cognitions are false and the others true? Why and how do we draw the distinction between truth and falsity? The answer is that those cognitions that lead to expected results in action (*arthakriyākāris*) are true and those that do not are false. This distinction between truth and falsity is only an empirical distinction, not the one made from the absolute point of view. The world of becoming and action consists of Being and Non-being. The nature of Being is to serve the expected purpose[86] and of Non-being to fail to serve that purpose. To be is the same as to serve an expected purpose.[87] This view belongs to the Vijñānavādins and is acceptable to the Mādhyamikas also. The principle of non-contradiction (*avisamvāditā*) is reduced by the Buddhists to the pragmatic criterion (*arthakriyākāritā*), which is regarded as the criterion and definition of Being (*sat*) itself. Since cognitions, which are originally false by themselves, are made valid by their purposeful serving of our actions, it is the success of such actions that makes our cognitions valid. Thus cognitions are true because of something other than themselves (*paratah prāmāṇyam*).

THE DOCTRINE OF ILLUSION There seem to be many doctrines of illusion among the Buddhists schools—the Sautrāntika, the Vaibhāṣika, the Mādhyamika, and the Vijñānavāda—and differences of opinion within every one of the four. But as much of the literature is lost, it is difficult to trace the views to their propounders.[88] Only the most important of them can be presented here. To this topic also the Mādhyamikas and the Vijñānavādins seem to have made the greatest contribution.

According to the Sautrāntikas, the form (*ākāra*) of consciousness and that of the object are only similar, but not identical. Their similarity is due to their being produced by the same causes (*tulyasāmagrī*). By itself, neither consciousness nor the object has any form. The causes that produce the forms are the ethical potencies (*karmas, saṃskāras*). When perception arises, we think that the object is the cause of our perception; but the true cause of perception is the cause of the forms of both consciousness and the object. Sometimes, the forms do not tally and we discover their difference through the pragmatic criterion (*arthakriyākāritā*). The Sautrāntika doctrine of truth is a mixture of correspondence, coherence,[89] and pragmatism. We should remember that according to this school, the existence of even the true object is only inferred, not perceived. The Sautrāntika doctrine of illusion is called the cognition of a form imposed on consciousness,[90] but not on the object. Such a form is the illusory object, from which we draw practical conclusions and experience failures and contradictions (*visaṃvādas*).

The Vaibhāṣika doctrine of illusion is different. The school maintains, as we have seen, that in perception the form of the object and that of our consciousness are not merely similar, but the same. Illusion arises when the form so produced is only an artifact or baseless (*kalpita*[91]). It does not belong to any object; it is objectless and groundless. Illusion is not the mistaking of one object for another, but perceiving a form that does not belong to any object. And this form is not a universal; for universals are not accepted. It can, therefore, be a particular shape. Illusion may, therefore, be called the perception of a non-existent[92] object. If I mistake a rope for a snake, then the snake I perceive has, we think, as its basis (*ālambana*) the rope. But the Vaibhāṣikas say that it is not necessary for a false perception that its object must have a real object as the basis.[93] In dreams and hallucinations we do not mistake one object for another. When we close our eyes and press them, we see some black, white, and reddish form (*kesoṇḍraka*). But it is not a real object, nor does it have an objective basis. What is peculiar to false perceptions is that in them we experience a form that appears[94] as if it is related to an object. We realize the truth or falsity of cognition when we try to make the object an object of practical activity (*arthakriyā*).

The Mādhyamikas accept that illusion is the perception of a non-existent object (*asatkhyāti*), that falsity need not have a real basis (*niradhiṣṭhānakhyāti*), and that illusion is, therefore, without a ground and without an object (*nirālambana*). But they go further and say that what thus appears as an object and the consciousness of the object is only the Void (Śūnya). This aspect of their doctrine is called the doctrine of illusion as the cognition of the void as an object (*śūnyakhyāti*). Indeed, the Void appears not only as the false object, but also as what we consider to be the true object. So far as the world of action goes, we draw the distinction between the true and the false, because the true serves, in action, the purpose for which it is meant. Empirical truth is the same as the pragmatic truth. The reality (*sat*) or being (*sattā*) of an object is the same as the power it has to lead us to successful action. But action itself is not ultimately real. So empirical truth (*saṃvṛtisatya*) is not the same as absolute truth (*pāramārthikasatya*).

The Vijñānavādins also accept all that the Vaibhāṣikas say, except that in true perception there is a real object. Like the Mādhyamikas, they say that all cognition is inherently and by itself false (*svatah aprāmāṇya*). But they reject the Mādhyamika view that it is the Void that appears as the true and false objects. It is the original pure Consciousness (Vijñāna) that appears as the object. This pure Consciousness itself is what is called the Ātman. So all appearance is the appearance of the Ātman (*ātmakhyāti*). Indeed, the original Consciousness (Vijñāna, Ātman) can be called Void, because it is devoid of all characterizations. Like the Mādhyamikas, the Vijñānavādins say that Being (*sat, sattā*) is pragmatic, and the pragmatic criterion distinguishes between empirical truth and falsity. The Sautrāntikas and the Vaibhāṣikas also accept the pragmatic criterion. But as both accept the independent reality of objects, the nature of which includes, but is not merely the same as pragmatic purposiveness, the pragmatic criterion only confirms, but does not make their truth and falsity. But for the Mādhyamikas and the Vijñānavādins, who do not accept the external reality of objects, their empirical being itself is constituted by pragmatic purposiveness and usefulness. Yet, from the ultimate point of view, reality, whether it is the Void or Consciousness, is neither Being nor Non-being. Being and Non-being are correlates and coordinates and constitute the empirical world. They are the determinants characterizing the world of action. False cognition is, therefore, the perception by consciousness (*ātman*) of its own form or a form generated in it (*ātmakhyāti*[95]) without leading to the expected action and result successfully (*arthakriyā*).

6. LIFE'S IDEAL

The Buddhist ideal of life has already been indicated, and the ideas about it may here be brought together. For all the Indian schools of thought, except the Cārvākas and the early Mīmāmsā, the ideal of life is to obtain salvation. Salvation lies in transcending the world of Becoming, which is the world of action (*dharma*). But as Becoming is a combination of Being and Non-being, the Buddhists say that salvation lies in a realm that is beyond Being and Non-being. As that realm cannot be described in terms of Being and Non-being, it is the Void. As the state of salvation does not belong to the world of Becoming, it is absolute Non-disturbance (Nirvāṇa), absolute peace. One can have some experience of Nirvāṇa in perfect meditation, which is the culmination of the eight-fold Aryan Way taught by Buddha.

The Hīnayāna, on the whole, understood *nirvāṇa as individualistic. Every man strives for his own salvation and obtains it for himself. The individualistic ideal is called the arhat* ideal. Although Buddha himself underwent a great deal of self-mortification and ascetic practices, he realized that by themselves they do not lead to *nirvāṇa*, which could be obtained only by enlightenment. Enlightenment lies in understanding and realizing the true nature of man and the world, i.e., in grasping the significance of the four Aryan Truths. He taught, therefore, what is called the Middle Way (Path), which consists neither in extreme self-mortification nor in extreme self-indulgence. What is wanted is proper enlightenment. Because of the emphasis on enlightenment, which cuts away the original Ignorance (Avidyā), the whole Buddhist philosophy may be regarded as preaching the way of knowledge (*jñānamārga*). In fact, Asaṅga, the Vijñānavādin, speaks explicitly of the way of knowledge.[96]

Although the emphasis on the way of knowledge can be found from the beginnings of Buddhism, the idea that the destination also is knowledge (*jñāna, prajñā*) entered a few schools of the Hīnayāna like the Prajñaptivādins and later the Mahāyāna. Although the *Prajñāpāramitās* speak of the highest form of knowledge, wisdom, or consciousness, it is only the Vijñānavādins that speak of Consciousness (Vijñāna) as the ultimate reality and the goal of man. When the destination also becomes conscious, there remains very little difference between Buddhism and the Upaniṣadic theory of the *ātman*. In fact, Asaṅga used the word *ātman* in several places of his work, when he referred to the highest Consciousness (Vijñāna). As mentioned already, this highest Consciousness is not eternal, but a timeless moment, for some of the Vijñānavādins. But the difference between the two expressions, eternal and timeless, is only scholastic, not substantial.

The Mahāyānists introduced altruism into their spiritual ideal and formulated their *bodhisattva*[97] ideal. It is difficult to find a single English word for *bodhisattva*, which means one whose being (*sattva*) is enlightenment (*bodhi*). The *bodhisattva*, although enlightened, does not enter the state of Nirvāṇa and is ready to take as many births as necessary for helping the rest of the world in obtaining the same enlightenment. He is perfect in the practice of the six virtues (*pāramitās*): They are charity, character, endurance, zeal, meditation, and knowledge or wisdom (*dāna*, *śīla*, *kṣānti*, *vīrya*, *dhyāna*, and *prajñā*). He may be a monk or—as the Mahāyāna allowed its monks to marry—a house-holder. He is all compassion (*karuṇa*) for the ignorant, sinful, and miserable human beings, is ready to exchange his merits for their demerits, and suffer for them. Thus was the ideal of vicarious suffering introduced into the original individualistic Hīnayāna ideal.

With the appearance of the Mahāyāna, particularly of the Bhūtatathatā and Vijñānavāda schools, the religious thought of Buddhism underwent a dramatic transformation. The ideal of life, which appeared in the beginning as negative or at least empty because of the idea of the voidness of Nirvāṇa, became gradually positive. *First*, the state of Nirvāṇa, which was a mere void, became the enlightened consciousness (*bodhi*). *Second*, this enlightened consciousness became the self-conscious truth or reality beyond Ignorance (Avidyā). *Third*, it was equated to the essential conscious being of Buddha, to his supra-mundane body. *Fourth*, since ultimate reality, the source of the world, and what Buddha became when he entered Nirvāṇa were one and the same, it was thought that what any one would become when he entered Nirvāṇa would also be the ultimate reality. *Fifth*, it was, therefore, announced that every one could become Buddha, since the essential nature, source, and destiny of every one was the same reality. *Sixth*, as Nirvāṇa is the same as the ultimate reality, the latter is the essence not only of man but also of everything else. In Buddhist terminology, everything in the world is a *dharma*. *Dharma* generally means nature, law, quality. As everything, according to Buddhism, is itself (*svalakṣaṇa*, *svarūpa*), it is its own nature, law, and form. It is, therefore, its own *dharma*, it is a *dharma*. But the ultimate nature of everything is the ultimate reality, which is the *Dharma* of all *dharmas*. It is the Dharmakāya, Dharmadhātu, the way, the nature, the truth of all things. It is everything, it is the reality beyond Ignorance (Avidyā), and all the formative forces (*samskāras*) embedded in it. This ultimate Dharma is beyond all description.[98]

We have seen that *dharma*, according to the Mīmāmsā, is the ethical force that creates the world of forms out of certain eternal elements and that the world of forms is the field of action and enjoyment for man. Buddhism, in its Mahāyāna forms, retains this *dharma* as part of the formative forces (*samskāras*), but goes beyond the Mīmāmsā. For the Mīmāmsā, there are eternal elements on which the ethical force works. But for the Mahāyāna, the objects and their constituents also are products of the formative forces. If at all, we should seek objectivity within the formative forces, but not in the objects we perceive. Some of the formative forces are the ethical potencies engendered by past actions; but the others are universal. It is the latter that are objective and work through every man, not merely through a particular individual. In their universality they can find a place for my ethical potencies also that pertain to me alone. Thus all the forces, both the universal and the individual, have a unity that has cosmic significance. All are *dharmas* and together constitute a unitary Dharma. They are rooted in Ignorance (Avidyā), which also is a *dharma*. But the highest reality is beyond Ignorance and is the Dharma, of which everything else is somehow a part. Thus the Mīmāmsā concept of *dharma* becomes in Buddhism a concept of ultimate reality, with dynamic, but indescribable power or force. The aim of man's life is to realize that he is essentially one with such an ultimate reality.

The above conception of reality and life's ideal is too sublime, abstract, and remote for the common man to understand. Buddhism introduced, therefore, more positive, concrete, and picturesque forms of the ideal in works like the *Sukhāvativyūha* and devotional forms of worship like that of the god or goddess of mercy.[99] It even allowed itself to degenerate into some of the vulgar forms of Tāntrism. But Buddha is not remembered even by the orthodox Hindus and philosophers as having taught any Tāntric doctrines. Some remember him as having misled people into atheism; but others say that he was an incarnation of the Supreme Being embodying infinite compassion (*karuṇa*).[100]

GENERAL ESTIMATE AND CONSTRUCTIVE COMMENT

(i) Body as the Only Sense Organ

Buddhism is undoubtedly one of the greatest religions of the world and one may even say that it is religion *par excellence* in the sense that it is concerned first and foremost with man's spiritual life apart from his social and political life. As a result, it could fit into every society and political structure. It is great because of the freedom of thought permitted to its followers and of the large number of schools it could accommodate and tolerate.

But one wonders whether the grand conceptual and dialectical developments made out of the original simple truths taught by Buddha, in spite of the admiration they evoke, can all be absolutely true. Indeed, some of the great ideas surprise us by their impressiveness and trenchancy; and one wonders why their importance escaped very long the critics belonging to the orthodox schools. But now and then the Buddhists overshot their mark by being too far removed from realities to serve the purpose of their philosophy.

Buddhist doctrines had a development of at least one thousand years. The centres of development belonged neither to the same place nor the same period. So we find the terminology is not uniform. Some very important words such as *manas* (mind), *citta* (mind, reason, apperception), *ātman* (self, spirit, also mind) are used sometimes in the same sense, other times in different senses.[101] In early Buddhism, we find *manas* (mind) treated as a distinct sense, mention of which was made already. But a very interesting—to me it seems important also—Buddhist tradition preserved in some rival[102] schools, takes the body itself as the instrument[103] of both cognition and action, and holds that no other instruments (*indriyas*) need be recognized. In epistemology, then, the body is the means of knowing and may be called the only means of true knowledge (*pramāṇa, pramākaraṇa*)[104]— let it be empirical or pragmatic truth, let it be also that which is made true or simply confirmed by action, which also belongs to the body. There are indeed sense organs like the eye and the ear. But they are parts of the body and are, therefore, only subsidiary means of cognition. For instance, the eye has many parts, the pupil, the rods, the cones, etc. They also are means of perception and so instruments of valid cognition. If we do not give them a separate place as distinct means of perception, we may not, for a similar reason, give a separate place to the eye, ear, etc., but treat the body alone as the one and only instrument of knowledge and action.

(ii) Mind Alone as the Sense Organ

It is not clear what the above Buddhist school means by "body:" it may simply be the physical body, or it may be the psycho-physical body,[105] including the sensorium, mind, and consciousness, which together constitute what they call *pudgala* (individual). In either case, there is much that can be said in favour of this view. Yet, there is a lacuna in the above argument. The body may be accepted as the instrument of both cognition and action; but whose instrument is it? It is a guided instrument, not an unguided one; I guide, direct my body and the senses and organs of action according to my interests. An instrument is utilized and guided by another entity. Even if we interpret the word *indriya* as the Buddhists do, viz., as force, power, it is not an unguided power or force. The I which Buddhism seeks to explain away is missing in the argument; otherwise, it presents an important idea.

One Buddhist school seems to have held that *manas* (mind) alone is the sense organ (*indriya*). Something can be said in favour of this view also. For there is a tradition for which the five senses—eye, ear, taste, smell and touch—are divisions of mind and are supervised and controlled by mind. The view may also agree with the Mahāyāna doctrine that mind alone is real (*manomātratāvāda*).

(iii) Mystery of Samskāra Solved by Buddhism

Credit has to be given to Buddhism for its profound use of the concept of *samskāra*, for which, as pointed out already, no single English word can be found with the exact connotation. The concept is indeed not peculiar to Buddhism; all Indian schools use it. But Buddhism made the most profound metaphysical use, which removes the mystery in the Mīmāmsā doctrine that all actions become potencies in the form of *adṛṣṭa* (Unseen) and *apūrva* (Extra-ordinary, so called because its *modus operandi* cannot be understood), which in some later Upaniṣads was identified with Fate , Limit (*niyati*), the inexorable cosmic law. It removes also the mystery from the

Advaita doctrine of the causal body (*kāraṇa-śarīra* or *bījātman*), so called because it contains all the potential, dynamic forces constituting my empirical personality and responsible for my actions and reactions, and corresponds (or isomorphic) to the Ālayavijñāna (Storehouse Consciousness) of the Mahāyāna. If it is a storehouse, what does it store? Indeed it is a storehouse of *samskāras*, both cosmic and individual. But these *samskāras* are not static impressions like the impressions of a stamp on paper, but dynamic forces. It will be a misunderstanding if they are taken to be static impressions like those made by a seal on wax.

Some scholars translate the term as traces, which is also misleading. They are more akin to the traumas, which do not remain as mere impresses, but as forces which influence our life, knowledge, and action. All my cognitions and actions, both known and unknown, produce impressions on my personality and mould it and they mould it just as the goldsmith's hammer moulds the lump of gold, by beating it and making dents on it, into some shape. But neither my personality nor the impacts (beats) of cognition and action remain static; they become forces constituting the dynamism (drive, force) of my personality. The *samskāras* are, therefore, creative, dynamic. Roughly, they are of two kinds, cosmic and individual, as given in the twelve-linked chain of causation; for *samskāra* is prior to *vijñāna* in the chain. My birth and the equipment with which I am born and which is common to all individuals like me are due to cosmic *samskāras*. The *samskāras* which are peculiar to me—for instance, two sons born to the same parents may become one a saint and the other a criminal, due to each carrying his own *samskāras*—are, almost all Indian schools believe, due to my own actions in my past births. But I may have also acquired new *samskāras* in this life up till now, and they may influence my future activities in this life itself by constantly moulding my personality, i.e., character and conduct.

How do the *samskāras*, according to Buddhism, become constituents of my personality? By being passed on from moment to moment of its duration. Before criticizing this view, we should note the important truth and the explanation it contains of how our ethical actions become seeds (*bījas*) of our future lives, i.e., the explanation of the doctrine that the nature of our future life is due to our actions in this and past lives. We do not have conclusive empirical evidence for the non-empirical (and so called *adṛṣṭa* or unseen and *apūrva* or extra-ordinary by the Mīmāmsā) processes which take place after death in the twilight world before the next birth. But Buddhism explains that the action-*samskāras*[106] are transmitted from moment to moment of my existence, stay in me after my death and become active in producing my next birth and so on. The Mīmāmsakas say that actions become potencies (*śaktis*) of the self (*ātman*) and remain in it; but they do not use the word *samskāras*, which could have been explanatory, as much as the Buddhists do; and so we are left wondering how action becomes a potency and a creative force. But that action becomes a creative force—whether it is called *samskāra* or *adṛṣṭa*—is an idea common to both Buddhism and the Mīmāmsā.[107] Neither school feels the need for God as the creator of the world, apart from action-potencies.

But here comes the hitch in the Buddhist doctrine of momentariness. Even if we go along with the moderate Buddhists—who say that to be has three moments, birth, stay, and destruction—it is not intelligible that the same personality carries the same action-potencies or *samskāras*, if it has only a momentary existence. Yes, we may accept for argument's sake that the *samskāras* are transmitted—or they merely pass on—from moment to moment of consciousness. But if the first moment is a different being (*sat*) from the second, then its suffering or enjoyment for what the first did will be unjustified. The explanation of the consciousness of continuity and sameness of personality becomes impossible. And there will be a mesh of undesirable consequences. For instance, just as in double personality of abnormal psychology, each momentary personality disowns the other. If we take the Buddhist theory seriously, then we have to accept that every momentary personality does the opposite of disowning the previous personality, viz., it claims and appropriates a previous momentary personality by a kind of psychological identification, which is also a possible phenomenon accepted in abnormal psychology. Nothing derogatory is meant by this reference to abnormal psychology. It is a reference to a phenomenon that requires transcending by recognizing one's identity with—and immanence or one's past existence in —the earlier moment of personality in the former case, i.e., of false disownment; and by differentiating oneself, in the latter case, i.e., of false identification, from moments of personality which are not its own past; in either case, it requires transcending by recognizing its own continuity and self-identity. It will be futile to explain sameness in terms of similarity; for one can ask: How can there be similarity, in the case of moments of one's personality, without an element of sameness? To this question one may object: How can two similar red patches be the same when they are numerically different? The answer is that the same person who sees the first red patch gets in his mind the universal red which he recognizes in the second red patch. Recognition involves the cognition of sameness. Furthermore, the person who sees the two red patches, one after the other, has to be the same. If one person sees the first red patch and another sees the second, there can be no sensing of similarity at all. But Buddhism is not prepared to admit this sameness of personality. There will be no protests from the material world if it is treated as nothing but pure Becoming, differing completely from moment to moment, although it cannot be then called even Becoming, but a succession of moments; but it does violence to our experience and is ethically and spiritually dangerous if we apply this momentariness to personality. The Andhakas first protested against this momentariness, saying that in meditation (*dhyāna*) the same consciousness (or mind) has to continue with the same focussing for some time. Again, personality is apperceptive: "I was X" implies—but not explicitly in consciousness—"that I know that I was X." I was a student; now I am a professor. The student is not a professor; but the I in both experiences is the same. Even the awareness of Becoming and its assertion become impossible if the assertor, viz., the I, is not the same . The view is ethically dangerous because, if one I commits a crime, it will be a different I that will be punished, according to this view. It is spiritually dangerous; for who will care for salvation if his I naturally becomes extinct the next moment? If it is said that his *samskāras* (action potencies) of good and evil deeds will produce an I that obtains salvation, what guarantee is there that these blind forces will not continue producing an I and entering it after one obtains salvation? Is there any guarantee that these forces also will become extinct? If it is said that they become extinct when the last momentary I becomes extinct, the position still remains unintelligible. An infinite number of momentary I's must have become extinct before any instant of my existence; but the action potencies have not become extinct with them at that instant. How can we be sure that they will become extinct with the last momentary I? What is the guarantee that the alleged putative last I will really be the last?

The answer may be that the I works for the dissolution of the action potencies (*samskāras*) before obtaining salvation (*nirvāṇa*). But how can it work for their dissolution if it does not remain the same throughout its work? Just as Becoming becomes impossible without a continuous self-same I, action also becomes impossible without it. All action, particularly action for the dissolution of action potencies—even in the sense of *nivṛtti* or refraining from action, which also needs effort—is motivated action, and there can be no motive that can work without the self-same I. Effort needs time, but there can be no time without the I. Time-consciousness[108] needs the presence of the same I at the first instant of any duration and at the last. Otherwise, there will be no sense of duration. Similarly there will be no sense of extensive space, for instance, from the eastern horizon to the western, if the I that observes the two horizons is not the same. In this context, Kasmir Śaivism which seeks to establish the necessary presence and involvement of the same I in every cognition and action is at the opposite pole of the Buddhist doctrine of absolute, all-pervasive momentariness.

It may perhaps be thought that the above objection can be met by regarding every action potency (*samskāra*) not as a blind force, but as a self-conscious or apperceptive force (*prajñapti*). If it is also momentary, the above objection holds here also, and we shall be unable to explain how the same potency is transmitted from one moment of consciousness to another. Again, if every momentary potency is self-conscious, it will be an I-consciousness; and as a large number of such I-conscious potencies are transmitted from one moment of my personality to another, we shall have on our hands the problem of how and on what basis they all submit to unification in my integral, total personality. Why should a certain group of such forces come together to constitute my personality, but not some other, or get mixed up? If they, from the beginning, belong to my I somehow, then my I must have been there all through performing actions and organizing and reorganizing their potencies (*samskāras*). Then we have to say that they do not generate my I, that they do not constitute it in its entirety. Nor can it be maintained that as ideas (*prajñaptis*) they can together become an I or that the I is one of such ideas. We may think of the I as an idea in the third person; but in the first personal experience—which it is essentially—it can never be an idea (*prajñapti*). For the I that maintains the ideas cannot be its own idea at the same time. Nor is the I a coherent whole of ideas, as some idealists of the West seem to think, and philosophers like Plato and Hegel seem to suggest.[109] Then why did Hume, who had a number of ideas, miss it, although he was trying to be a coherent thinker? The I is what asserts coherence, but is not coherence itself. In an important sense, *the I is that which develops coherence, but is not merely what is constituted by coherence*. Nor is it one of the constituents which are made to cohere with one another; for that which makes them cohere has to be distinct from them. For one to say that he is coherent in his thinking does not mean that he is the same as the coherence of his thought. He is the observer of coherence; coherence as such, without the I, is not self-conscious, not an apperception even.

The doctrine of momentariness is the proverbial characteristic of Buddhism as the doctrine of Ideas is that of Platonism. There may be some schools like the

Andhakas who discovered in their experience that momentariness does not hold always and some like the Sarvāstivādins (who hold that everything exists, even the past) who got into puzzles when they attempted to correlate the doctrine of momentariness to other doctrines like those of time and space. But such schools and doctrines were more or less disowned by the orthodox Buddhists and a few were excommunicated by the main tradition. If no adjective is attached to Buddhism, we should necessarily attribute momentariness to it. Any other procedure will only be pedantic. For the early Buddhists the doctrine of momentariness was the basis of their teaching that everything is misery. Plato may have toned down his views in his *Laws*; but the Plato who made history is to be found in dialogues like the *Statesman* and the *Republic*.

But if we take momentariness in earnest, we find it difficult to explain how the same potencies (traces, *saṁskāras*) can be transmitted from one drop of momentary being to another. As Herman Oldenberg has said, we may take the potencies as universals which confer the sameness of form and structure on groups of momentary beings. But we have the difficulty, viz., the Buddhists do not accept that there are universals, but only names and mental concepts, which also are momentary. Besides, if the I's as momentary are all different and form a continuous series of extinctions, then for there being a self-conscious I we shall have only a series of *saṁskāras* which together have to become self-conscious and an I—a process which is unintelligible.[110]

(iv) Buddhist Momentariness Makes Apperception and Historical Consciousness Impossible

There is another difficulty if momentariness is applied to knowledge. Is apperception possible at all on its basis? Apperception is of the form, "I know that I saw the pen," while "That is a pen" is perception. But if the I that makes the assertion, "That is a pen," is not the same I that asserts, "I know that I saw the pen," there is no possibility of apperception. The latter involves self-assertion[111] and includes also the consciousness of the consciousness of the pen. This self-assertion in the past also cannot be explained in terms of momentariness for reasons given above.

If apperception is not possible, is historical consciousness possible? How can I know that there is something called history, if I cannot understand the meaning of the word "past" in my own experience? How can we have any awareness of time? It looks as though it has not been recognized that apperception is essential for the awareness of time. The structure of apperception may not have been grasped at all, although the idea has been used very much by both the Indian and western philosophers who used or emphasized one or the other of its aspects. But its significance is immense,[112] and it constitutes the foundation of the empirical structure of the I or the I-am. Because of it, I am a temporal being, am aware of time, my own past, and history.

If the I and apperception have to be accepted as continuing for at least a time and as not merely momentary, then mind (*manas*) and ego (*ahaṁkāra*) must have a duration longer than a moment. The distinctions between the I, apperception, ego, and mind are more fluid in Buddhist literature than in the Vedāntic. Roughly speaking, mind is the instrument of cognition which presents the object as a unity and a whole, e.g., the pen. The eye perceives only colour, the ear sound, the tongue taste, etc; but the mind gives us the whole object, as a That, as having all those qualities. The general trend of Buddhism is to equate the I to the ego and call it a misnomer or a mere name for nothing; for the unreal ego has to be liquidated in Nirvāṇa and by itself has no nature (*svabhāva*) of its own. However, even apart from the ultimate metaphysical question whether the I is somehow eternal, mind and ego also have to be lasting for a time; for when a man wakes up after deep sleep or fainting, he recognizes his oneness with his past; so his mind and ego have to be the same as before. We have seen how the mere continuity and sameness of the *samskāras* cannot explain the person's awareness of his sameness. Besides, he is the same person, and hence the *samskāras* are his, but not somebody[113] else's. If he is not the same, who knows that somebody else's *samskāras* have not made incursions into what I call mine.

However, we should not treat the Buddhist momentariness lightly and dismiss it. It creates difficulties impossible to remove only when applied to the person or the I. But when applied to the material world or the world of Becoming as a whole, it becomes an intelligible doctrine. We may refer ourselves to the Sāṁkhya doctrine of Prakṛti (Primeval Nature), which will be discussed later, and the constant change which Prakṛti undergoes when animated by the I (Puruṣa). The categories of time, substance, quality, and state (*avasthā*) are forms (in the Aristotelian sense) of pure change, of Becoming, as explained clearly by the sister school of Patañjali Yoga.[114] There are important differences between Buddhism and the Sāṅkhya-Yoga. But we should not fail to see how both traditions attempted to derive stable entities out of pure Becoming. The important difference is indeed that, for the Sāṅkhya-Yoga, the forms of time, etc., are developed, evolved by unconscious Prakṛti when animated—or reflected in—by the conscious I (Puruṣa). But if the Puruṣa himself is made a product, an epiphenomenon of the momentary, unconscious elements as by Buddhism—at this point one may be reminded of the Cārvāka view that consciousness arises when particles of matter come together in certain form of structure—we cannot explain why consciousness or awareness of anything arises at all, and the appearance of the I becomes all the more inexplicable.

(v) Perception Primarily of Particular

There seems to be an element of unfairness in the criticism of the Buddhist doctrine of perception, namely, that what we see is a particular only, not determined by any universal. When I fix my attention on a red object, what I perceive is of the form, "That is red." The That and the red patch on which I focus my attention are particulars. Even if there is another object which is exactly similar to it and which is focussed upon at the same time and so occupies the same field of vision, I do not treat the two red patches as one and identical, even if I have not developed the idea of their difference. There are separate Thats and separate 'reds,' all particulars. Or as a logical question, we may ask: If you have not perceived a particular red patch, how can you bring it under the universal or class concept "red?" There can be a more devastating form of the question: If you have not seen the particular red patch, what are you going to bring under the universal red? And why and when do you bring that "something" seen under the universal red, but not under the universal green? The Buddhists were stampeded into saying that a particular is what is different from everything else, when they were shaken by the Nyāya logicians,[115] who then objected that a perception of a particular would involve the perception of everything else in the world; for it involves the perception of the difference from everything else and so includes a reference to everything else—which is an impossible situation. But actually, when I observe the red patch in front so long as my eye is focussed on the object, there is no reference to anything else in my perceptual experience, neither to a universal nor to any other particular or particulars. Such reference—as in "That is red" and so "That is not green," and "No red object is a green object"—develops later in the morphological development of that perception. Remember even Rāmānuja, a Vedāntin, said that when an object is seen for the first time—for instance, an elephant by an Eskimo—it is seen as an individual, whole form, not merely as a mere something. Some universal, class concept name, etc., are developed later,[116] when other objects of the same kind are observed by the subject. What Rāmānuja[117] says about the perception of an object for the first time in one's life holds true of every perception during the live act of perception. When I see an elephant even for the hundredth time, during the live act of my seeing it, I do not consciously remember other elephants or am aware of their universal or class concept; yet, I am conscious of the whole living elephant. It may be called a spontaneous judgment or an unreflective (or pre-reflective?) one; but these terms are misleading. For they are used also when a crowd spontaneously and unreflectively condemns an innocent person. In any case, what I observe is a particular elephant; and perceptual judgment primarily comprehends what is perceived, not what can be developed even in spontaneous reflection out of that perception.

It is true that perception at the stage when it is that of a particular not brought under a class concept or universal, is not what exactly is communicated and utilized in inference. At least the predicate in "That is red" has to be reflectively brought up to the level of a class concept before we can communicate the perception; for in communication, the word "red" stands for a class and the hearer can next apply it to the That and particularize it. When the "red" is raised to the level of universality, we can also say: "Therefore the colour irritated your eye." For all reds are generally irritating to the eye, though attractive to the babies. But it does not follow from all this that the perceptual judgment even at the lowest levels has explicit reference to universals or class concepts.[118] When the speaker perceives the object as red, the red is a particular; but when he conveys his knowledge to the hearer, he no longer focusses his mind and eye on the colour, but has to raise his cognition to the level of universality; for one's perception in live act cannot be passed on to another.

(vi) Causal Law Presupposes A Continual I-consciousness

The Buddhist theory of causation[119] as dependent origination or as a kind of occasionalism has both merits and defects. In a way, it is consistent with its doctrine of momentariness. Everything is momentary; the cause also is momentary; it dies giving rise to the effect. The cause is the material cause also. It must have perished before the effect is born; for so long as it exists, there is no effect. A good example is the acorn and the oak. Now, if the cause dies before the effect rises, then to what can the cause give rise? We may give up the expression "gives rise," and adopt "occasions." Even then what does it occasion? It can have nothing in view or in its horizon. So what effect it occasions is uncertain. Then predictability is precluded. But can there be a causal law with uncertainty and without predictability, without necessity? The Buddhists accept the necessity of causal law—Nāgārjuna indeed explodes it—but cannot defend it. They seem to have at the back of their minds the idea of the mystery that there have to be causal laws, and accepted them.

Let *X* be the cause of *Y*, and let *Y* arise after *X*'s extinction. We may accept the causal relation between *X* and *Y* for argument's sake, and say that the relation is recognized by us after we observe *X* being followed by *Y* a number of times. But if I am momentary and exist as the observer when *X* exists, I cease to exist when *Y* comes into existence. Then who will establish the causal law between *X*'s and *Y*'s? I have to be the same observer of the many instances of *X* and *Y* for an inductively obtained causal law, whether it is law of probability or necessity. The stability and continuity of the I-consciousness is a necessary implication of any such law. The denial of this nature of the I-consciousness is a defect in the Buddhist philosophy. But the merit lies in the recognition that causation is a mystery. Why should oxygen and hydrogen, when combined, become water? Why does the acorn be the cause of the oak tree, but not of the bananna tree? Or why should it develop into anything at all?

There is another defect. It is said that action-potencies (*samskāras*) come out of Nescience or the Unconscious. But is the Nescience destroyed when the *samskāras* arise? So far as I am concerned, it is still there. Again, the *samskāras* have not produced me by becoming extinct; I have the *samskāras* alive and still working in me and I am rooted in Nescience, the Unconscious . The earlier links of the chain of causation are not dead when the later links are born. Furthermore, unless there is a material cause that continues in some form into the material effect, we cannot establish their causal connection. The acorn does not continue in the form of the acorn into the oak. Yet the acorn has the latent forces in it that work themselves into the huge oak and generate further forces (acorns), which generate more and so on *ad infinitum*. If I hold the acorn in my hand, I do not see the forces; they are latent like the power[120] in the atom. Even then why should life come out of matter? There is no necessity and predictability in this evolution. To call it natural does not remove the mystery.

(vii) Being and Non-being not Coordinates

Next, the Buddhist contention that Being and Non-being are coordinates and so Nirvāṇa (state of salvation, emancipation) has to be neither Being nor Non-being does not stand examination. As I have said in many places, in pure formal logic—one may say, in pure thought above experience of objects—Being and Non-being can be treated as coordinates, although even here one may contend that Non-being is a negative concept connoting a reference to something absent, but that Being is that which does not depend for our grasping it on a reference to its opposite. Generally the corresponding concepts are the "positive" and the "negative", about which also one may make the same contention. For when we think of number 1, we do not think of it as +1 as contrasted with −1, but simply by itself, when it is positive. We may say that to think of something as "positive" need not be the same as to think of a "positive something," as distinct from a "negative something." To think of it as +1, further abstraction is needed, and still more abstraction when we think of it as −1. However, coming to the experience of concrete objects, not abstractions, when I see something as red, I say: "That is red," and may not think of any colour which the object does not have. But when I say: "That is not green," I could not have said it without seeing that it is red or of some colour other than green. So we have to accept that in concrete experience—in philosophy and religion, we are within the realm of concrete experience—Non-being presupposes the positive, and that the two are not coordinates. Where Being and Non-being alternate, as in change or flux, we have Becoming.[121]

Here also arises the necessity for acknowledging the continuous presence of the I-am or I-consciousness. Unless the same I-consciousness makes the two judgments, "That is red" and "That is not green," there is no possibility of the negative judgment at all. If the I-consciousness is momentary and becomes extinct immediately after making the first judgment, the second I-consciousness that is born out of it cannot and will not make the second judgment, that is, the negative one; for it has again to observe the red colour for the purpose. By the time the observation is complete, it becomes extinct before making the negative judgment. Furthermore, if two I-consciousnesses make the two judgments separately, it is like two different persons making two different judgments; and there can be nothing to relate them. Hence the same I must make the two judgments to make them negatively related. The same difficulty obliges us to accept the stability and non-momentariness of the I-consciousness for defending the Buddhist doctrine of perception—if we accept it—as that of a particular object different from all the rest. We have pointed out that this difference to "all the rest" is not necessary for the act of perception. But where the reference is made, if it is made at all, the I-consciousness has to last for more than one moment. For it has to first cognize the object in front and think of its difference from another; at both moments it has to be the same I.

(viii) How is Existence Known?

Now, how does one cognize Being? Non-being is a referential or relative notion and belongs to thought. Without thought intervening, there is no cognition of any negative idea. But Being must have been first known before referential ideas are formed out of it. The eye gives colours and shapes, not existence—using both the words existence and Being in the same sense, as all Indian philosophers do. The ear gives sounds, the nose smells and so on. Then what is the sense or instrument of cognition for existence? Thought may give the idea or notion—whatever word is used, for existence cannot be an idea, universal, or class-concept like that of chair or horse (cp. Kant)[122]—of existence; but unless existence somehow has been directly known, thought cannot form an idea, right or wrong, out of it. Then how and through what instrumentality have I got a direct cognition of existence? One may say: "I see the colour red, and so the colour red exists there." But this is not what the question is directed at. Apart from the possibility that the colour is a phantasm and has no real existence, we assume that what we generally see are concrete objects like pens and roses. What is the instrumentality for the cognition of existence in "That *is* the pen" or "That *is* the rose?" In the case of the existence of a false colour, i.e., of the perception of a non-existent colour as existing, when we realize its non-existence, how do we differentiate existence from non-existence? Is the differentiation made by the demands of a system on the basis of coherence or non-contradiction, as many western idealists think? If it is so made, then the existence we are speaking of hardly differs from mathematical existence, which is what satisfies the requirements of the consistency of a system. The question still presses on us: How do we come upon the idea of existence at all? If non-existence is a referential idea, what is that to which it refers, and how is that to which it refers cognized first? What is meant by "the non-existent pen?" Does it mean that there is a pen that does not exist? This problem troubled many formal logicians even. And what is meant by "the existent pen?" If there is a pen, does it make any difference to it to say that it exists? Indeed, Being and Non-being, Existence and Non-existence cannot be coordinates.

This question is not easy to answer, and the analysis of experience required to answer it is also not an easy one, primarily because western philosophers and theologians have not given much thought to it and, although Indian religious practices and the Upaniṣads gave much thought to it, their thought is not modelled in the way which can easily be cast into familiar conceptual forms. However, it is possible to give indications of the answer or some directions leading to the answer. Kant said that existence can never be a predicate. His view is accepted by a majority of western philosophers. Then no conceptual proof is possible for what can never be a predicate. Before Kant, Descartes had said in his famous dictum that existence is involved in "I think." That is, what guarantees existence or Being is the I or I-am. Then if existence or Being is not grasped through any of the senses, mind, reason, or apperception—here we do not refer to mathematical existence, but to the philosopher's ontological existence—then it can be known only through the I, I-am, or I-consciousness. As we have seen in our estimate of Jainism, the I-consciousness is not limited in size to my body, but is infinite. So in some sense—i.e., in a transcendental way—the existence which is my I-consciousness involves the existence of the objects and coincides and has to coincide with their existence. The crux of the problem lies here and we may obtain more elucidation in later chapters. Descartes's mistake lies in his thinking that the finitude of the I-consciousness means its subjectivity,[123] and so a kind of unreality—non-objectivity in a derogatory sense—and this thought prevented him from making the transition from the subject to the object and he had to invoke God to make our epistemological experiences true. But the I-consciousness is not subjective in the derogatory sense of the term, but is inclusive of the existence of what we call the epistemological subject and object.

Our present concern is to show that Buddhism has no way of showing how we get the idea of Being at all, as it does not accept the reality of the I-consciousness. In that consciousness there can be no place for the presence of Non-being or consciousness of the negative. In the consciousness of the existence of the pure I, there is no place for the consciousness of a non-I. Then Being and Non-being cannot be coordinates. The cognition of Non-being is possible only when consciousness arises with a direction away from the I-consciousness.[124]

(ix) Relativism: Its Positive and Negative Expressions

We should now refer to a related point. Some Indian writers praised *śūnyatā* (the Empty, the Void) in the sense of "neither true, nor false, nor both true and false, nor neither true nor false" and of other four-cornered forms of negation as helpful for the tolerance of all rival views, particularly the ethical, by denying absolute truth to every one. This was the intention of Pyrrho in Greece and Sañjaya in India, who seem to be more or less contemporaries. But the Jainas held the doctrine of seven-fold assertion (*syādvāda*), which has already been discussed in the chapter on Jainism, and which is an opposite of the four-cornered negation, and they claim to show the same tolerance to all theories. It should interest logicians of metaphysical relativism that it can be expressed in both the Buddhist and the Jaina forms, the former denying the truth of every view and the latter conceding the truth of every one. Relativism need not necessarily be negative.

Apart from the logic of the situation, neither position is concretely helpful in critical cases of ethics. It is true that religious wars and violent ideological conflicts can be avoided by accepting that no way of life or ethics is absolutely valid and that every way of life or ethics may be accepted as relatively true. But how does either acceptance guide a person like Antigone in Greek mythology who has to choose between two solemn alternatives? Does it help her to be told that neither alternative is absolutely binding? Or that either alternative is good enough? She has to take a decision; and what should be her guide? Is the guide controlled by any principle? Does tolerance of all alternatives mean indifference or even licence? Certainly not; otherwise, there will be no ethics. There has to be some great guiding principle like self-fulfilment, continuity of the identity and integrality of personality, which has to remain pure and full without the attempt to hide (repress) any part of itself from itself. These expressions may be vague, but cannot be discussed here further. For the purpose of self-fulfilment, etc., the reality of the I-consciousness is indispensable at least in its transcendental depths—which Buddhism explained away and denied. Furthermore, such a crucial decision is not also the free existential decision one has to make, as Schweitzer, for instance, advocates.[125] He says that man has to be like a mariner steering his ship without a compass, untramelled by the directions shown by the instrument. But such a mariner may come to grief, however heroic his end may be. Such an end is unnecessary loss of life, which Schweitzer himself would not advocate. Existential decision is indeed the decision of the I for its fulfilment. But what kind of fulfilment has it to be? In what does it lie? No existing or positive laws are enough. If the guidance is to be found in one self (I-am), then it has to be found in its deeper reaches, the Logos, the Cosmic Person and his nature (law), with which my I has to identify itself, as taught by the *Bhagavadgītā*, Socrates, and the Stoics, and by Christianity in its philosophical renderings. The reality and necessity of the I-consciousness cannot be denied.

(x) Tathatā, Tathyam, Sattā, and Satyam: Their Interrelations

The Buddhist doctrine of Tathatā (Suchness, Thusness) brings to the surface an aspect of truth, reality, and existence, which is generally disposed of as indefinable, but to define the indefinable nature of which thousands of pages have been written.

As the Jainas pointed out, it is often misleading to understand the nature of an object in terms of the etymology of its name. Yet, etymologies, they admit, give some aspect of the nature of the object. Particularly, when we wish to understand ultimate concepts like truth, reality, existence, and Being, etymologies can be helpful. In Indian philosophy, including Jainism and Buddhism, the relevant words are *sat* (existent, existence), *sattā* (existence, Being), *satyam* (truth, reality), *tathyam* (truth), and *tathatā* (truth, thusness, reality). Both *tathyam* and *tathatā* are derived from the same word *tathā*, which means "so" and "thus," and which is adverbial in its significance. *Tathyam* is not generally used in philosophical literature of even the Buddhists, who alone use *tathatā*[126] in its important metaphysical meaning. What is reality? It is that which goes "so and so" and "thus and thus," and which we cannot fix by definitions. What is important is to note that there is implicit reference to the verb, process, activity. Even the word *brahman* of the Upaniṣads means the ever-growing, ever-developing, ever-active, but self-active in the sense of self-producing, although the general trend of the interpreters is to present it as beyond all activity, beyond all process, beyond all Becoming, as a pure noun without a verb. But curiously enough, the words *sattā*, *sat*, and *satyam* are derived from the verb *as* (in English "is," in German "ist", etc.) but not from any noun, thereby supporting the view of some philosophers (Nairuktas) that all nouns are derived from verbs,[127] and the nature of the Brahman itself is activity. Of the words, *sat* is the present participle of *as* ("is"), *sattā* is the abstract form of *sat*, and *satyam* means what is meant for (or agrees with) *sat*. No school, except Buddhism, has an adverbial reference to reality.

Kant and many other philosophers maintained that existence could not be a predicate. Yet the tendency is there—these philosophers could not refrain from it—to use the word existent as an adjective or quality, as though existence is an abstraction from the word existent. Then can we, and should we understand reality, existence, or Being (*Sein*) in terms of substance, adjective, or adverb? For some reason, the Nyāya-Vaiśeṣika, as we shall see later, does not give any place to adverbs in their categorization of reality. (It will be interesting to compare Aristotles categorization to that of the Nyāya-Vaiśeṣika at this point.) But what is the nature of the qualities (adverbs) of action (verb) as distinct from qualities (adjectives) of substantives (nouns)? Why should the classification of Being (*sattā*) be made only into substances (nouns), actions (verbs), and qualities (adjectives)? The Buddhists do not seem to have developed the idea of the adverb as one of the classifications; but their use of *tathatā* raises the question why it should not be so developed. Ultimately, if linguistics can be a guide in this connection, the primary categories ought to be Being and Becoming, or noun and verb. Both again become one in the verb *as* (to be), in which the distinctions of noun and verb, substantive and action, become unified and lose their difference. But in Buddhism there is an over-emphasis on Becoming, as the concept of *tathatā* (thusness) signifies. Nāgārjuna, in his concept of *śūnyatā* (which he refuses to treat as a concept), rejects Being, Becoming, and Non-being even as expressive of reality. (It is not reasonable to use the word reality also according to him.) This shows the impasse to which thought is led in attempting to answer ultimate question and indicates that we can understand it by living or by realizing that we are living the metaphysical truth; we cannot understand it otherwise, if this awareness of truth or its realization can be called understanding at all. Here we find support for the orthodox Indian contention that metaphysical truth is meant for spiritual or religious life and practice, as otherwise it ends up in frivolous bandying of arguments, ideas, and theories. Physical truth is corroborated by application; and spiritual or metaphysical truth is corroborated by living.

(xi) Dharma and the Passing of the Concepts of Substance, Quality, Action and Force into One Another

Another Buddhist idea which set afoot a very significant line of thought is that of *dharma*, to which reference has already been made. This word in Buddhism means everything: elements, categories, qualities, things, law, way of life, form, and even ultimate reality. Buddhists were untramelled, unlike the Mīmāmsakas, in the development of their thought, by any book and so could see through the significance of the concept and reach its depths. Although they themselves did not develop a theory of the development of the meaning of the term or of the interrelations of its meanings, but used it in all its meanings as the occasion rose, we can see why it gets all its meanings.[128] In popular usage, *dharma* means a way of life—as in Hindu *dharma* or the Hindu way of life, the Christian *dharma* or the Christian way of life—ethical law, positive law, like criminal law and civil law, and simply religion. But in the Mīmāmsā the word means action according to the injunctions of the Vedas and also the merit or ethical potency or force created by the action, to which reference has been made in commenting on the concept of *samskāra*, and which becomes the creative power (*śakti*) behind the world of the individual. Now appears a complicated network of questions. Can pure energy, force, create something without belonging to something substantive? If there is no substantive in the world to which forces belong, then a force can create only force. Then can there be any creation or production of anything new? I can understand the force in *X* creating the force in *Y*, which in turn creates the force in Z. But if *X*, *Y*, and *Z* do not exist at all, then there will be no creation, but only the continuation of the original force. If there are *X*s, *Y*s, and *Z*s as substantives, then their forces or energies become adjectival to them. But are the forces mere static qualities like colours? Again, are qualities like colours merely static? If they are the forms of light waves starting from the object, then striking my eye, and then working on my brain centres, they cannot be considered to be merely static; for so long as I see the colour, the product colour is sustained by a dynamic force, the light wave, and is an embodiment of that force, and so a dynamo. Then the concept of substance, action, quality, and force cannot clearly be demarcated, but pass into one another.

What in this context is the status of law, form, or universal? It also cannot have a separate existence from any of the above four. Can the law of magnetism—say, the magnet attracts iron—exist apart from the magnet in action? And can the action of the magnet exist apart from its law, form, or essence? Can there be any action without a pattern and so without a law? Then we have to regard the universe as a system of forces, a plurality of patterns of activity controlled somehow by a supervising pattern of activity—*tathatā* because the pattern becomes the adverb of the activity—the ultimate Dharma or Dharmadhātu, as the Buddhists call it. If substances are regarded as unities of potential activities or forces, the world may be regarded as a system of substances also, provided we do not forget that the unity of the substances is not accomplished conceptually or by a law existing apart and imposed on them, but by a controlling force[129] running through every one of them like the force (law) of gravitation—or whatever else the force is interpreted to be, as for instance by Einstein—binding together the members of the planetary system. The universe must be a pattern of patterns, an active force controlling innumerable active forces—which is a grand idea.

NOTES

[1]A. L. Bhasham: *The Ajivikas*, pp. 11 fol.

[2]See P. V. Bapat: *2500 Years of Buddhism*; Bhikṣu Saṅgharakṣita: *A Survey of Buddhism*; E. J. Thomas: *A History of Buddhist Thought*; Yamakami Sogen: *Systems of Buddhist Thought*; C. N. E. Elliot: *Hinduism and Buddhism*; and for a general survey of important schools, P. T. Raju: *Idealistic Thought of India*.

[3]A. L. Bhasham: *The Ajivikas*.

[4]Cp. Umāsvāmi: *Tattvārthasūtra*, p. 70. The Aryan is a man respected for his character by men who have character. See also *Jaina Encyclopaedia* for the word Arya, which means a man who is truthful, non-violent, and follows the doctrine of Jainism. Cp. also Buddha's four truths called the four Aryan Truths.

[5]P. V. Bapat: *2500 Years of Buddhism*, pp. 340–82. [6]Ibid., pp. 35 fol.

[7]Ibid., p. 110. [8]Ibid., p. 99.

[9]See Bhikshu Saṅgharakshita: *A Survey of Buddhism*. pp. 220 fol.

[10]The main philosophical text of this school is now Aniruddha's *Abhidharmātthasaṅgaha* ed. by S. Z. Aung.

[11]One may compare this doctrine with Whitehead's doctrine of events. The Buddhist doctrine of flux is not alien to contemporary science or philosophy. Cp. Bergson also.

[12]It may be interesting to compare this idea to the tragic sense in Christianity.

[13]Herman Oldenberg: *Buddha*, pp. 223 fol., and P. T. Raju: *Idealistic Thought of India*, pp. 198 fol.

[14]It is difficult to find an exact word in English for *samskāras*. Oldenberg translates it as *Gestaltungen*. In Sanskrit, it means instinctive forces, impressions, urges, habit forming impressions, psychological archetypes, etc. Since forms can be forces, Oldenberg's translation may be preferred. The word is interpreted as *karma* by Yamakami Sogen (*Systems of Buddhistic Thought*, p. 75), thus relating it to the Mīmāmsā doctrine of ethical potency. Bhikshu Saṅgharakshita interprets it as "complexes, impulses, karma-formations or volitions" (*A Survey of Buddhism*, p. 96). See also S. Z. Aung: *Compendium of Philosophy*, pp. 273 fol. The word has a very inclusive meaning like Jung's "archetypes", including even Kant's categories. They can be cosmic, collective, or individual, all at once or separately.

[15]P. T. Raju: *Idealistic Thought of India*, p. 207.

[16]Ibid., pp. 212 fol. See also S.Z. Aung: *Compendium of Philosophy*, p. 182. It seems to me that the word *Samjñā* is better understood as "sign" like in Berkeley's theory of perception. Perhaps the two words have philologically the same root. The perceptual objects first present marks, etc., like colours which signal to us of their presence as, for instance, roses, *Vedanā* or Sensation is the psychological aspect of sign. Their *vijñāna* will be the idea of the object as a rose. This aggregate is that which retains the idea as in memory. For the present I am giving the usually given English terms.

[17]The doctrine of aggregates, bases of our being and experience, and the elements are very elaborately treated by the *Sarvāstivādins*, who were descendants of the School of the Elders. We find them in *The Compendium of Philosophy* belonging to the School of the Elders also. Its author is Aniruddha, who may have lived between the 8th and the 10th centuries A.D. Vasubandhu, the author of *Abhidharmakośa*, a work of the Sarvāstivādins, belonged to about the 2nd century A.D.(?)

[18]Cp. Sartre's views. Sartre allows Being to objects only, but the Buddhists do not. See his *Being and Nothingness*, pp.x/ix fol. The idea is spread over the whole book. See also N. Magill and I. P. Magill: *Masterpieces of World Philosophy*, pp. 1080 fol.

[19]For the different orders and their doctrines, see *Points of Controversy*, Eng. tr. by S. Z. Aung and Mrs. Rhys Davids.

[20]P. T. Raju: *Idealistic Thought of India*, pp. 193 fol.

[21]S. Z. Aung and Mrs. Rhys Davids: *Points of Controversy*, pp. 101 fol.

[22]Edited by Rahula Sankṛtyayana.

[23]See P. T. Raju: *Idealistic Thought of India*, p. 211, and Yamakami Sogen: *Systems of Buddhistic Thought*, pp. 164 fol.

[24]Yamakami Sogen: *Systems of Buddhistic Thought*, pp. 155 fol.

[25]Ibid., pp. 111–112.

[26]P. T. Raju: *Idealistic Thought of India*, p. 222.

[27]Ibid., p. 208.

[28]One may compare the doctrine to the doctrine of the four beginnings of Mencius in Chinese philosophy. For Andhkas, see P. T. Raju: *Idealistic Thought of India*, pp. 218 fol.

[29]For example, anger is the same as being angry. What the Buddhists call *bhāvas* or becomings have this double meaning.

[30]Cp. the Bhagavadgītā's doctrine of *Sthitaprajña* or one whose rational consciousness is steady.

[31]But cp. the ideas of the *Kevalin* (the alone) and *Kaivalya* (liberation).

[32]*Mahāyānaśraddhotpādaśāstra*, Eng. tr. by D. T. Suzuki. The Sanskrit text is not available. See P. T. Raju: *Idealistic Thought of India*, pp. 235 fol. and Yamakami Sogen: *Systems of Buddhistic Thought*, pp. 252. fol.

[33]Yamakami Sogen: *Systems of Buddhistic Thought*, p. 229.

[34]Cp. the Mīmāmsā doctrine of ethical potencies. Aśvaghoṣa attempts to explain how latent stored potencies become active (activated) and become overt-actions or activities or processes. A Kind of *vijñānavāda* seems to be implicitly accepted by Aśvaghoṣa, who speaks of the variety of *vijñānas*.

[35]Edited by Luis de la Vallee Pousin. See also Yamakami Sogen: *Systems of Buddhistic Thought*, pp. 186 fol; and P. T. Raju: *Idealistic Thought of India*, pp. 242 fol. T. R. V. Murti's *Central Philosophy of Buddhism* is in essence a study of the *Mādhyamika*.

[36]F. H. Bradley's dialectic in his *Appearance and Reality*, one may say, was anticipated by Nāgārjuna. Negative dialectic can be traced back to Sañjaya, the skeptic, of the Ājīvika sect.

[37]Neither Nothing nor what cannot be described at all can be a plurality.

[38]The idea can be traced to the "*neti, neti*, not this, not this" doctrine of the Upaniṣads. See Yamakami Sogen: *Systems of Buddhistic Thought*, p. 230.

[39]Ibid., pp. 210 fol.; P. T. Raju: *Idealistic Thought of India*, pp. 256 fol: D. T. Suzuki: Studies in the *Lankāvatārasūtra*; Asanga: *Mahāvānasūtrālankāra* ed. by Sylvan Levi.

[40]Asaṅga: *Mahāyānasūtrālaṅkāra*, p. 37.

[41]Ibid., pp. 37 and 95. [42]Ibid., p. 38.

[43]XIV, 3–4. See Yamakami Sogen: *Systems of Buddhistic Thought*, p. 25, and also D. T. Suzuki: *Studies in the Laṅkāvatārasūtra*, pp. 254. fol.

[44]Asanga: *Mahāyānasūtrālaṅkāra*, p. 38.

[45]See Aśvaghoṣa: *The Awakening of Faith*, pp. 55 fol.

[46]Yamakami Sogen: *Systems of Buddhistic Thought*, p. 237.

[47]The *Īśāvāsya Upaniṣad* says that the *ātman* both moves and does not move.

[48]This word is explicitly used by Vasubandhu. See P. T. Raju: *Idealistic Thought of India*, p. 270.

[49]Yamakami Sogen: *Systems of Buddhistic Thought*, pp. 216 fol.

[50]P. T. Raju: *Idealistic Thought of India*, p. 269.

[51]Yamakami Sogen: *Systems of Buddhistic Thought*, pp. 258 fol.; see also Aśvaghoṣa: *The Awakening of Faith*, p. 61. Note the difference between Ālaya and Alaya.

[52]It will be significant to compare these Vijñānas to the Bījātman, Mahān Ātmā, Mūlāvidyā, and Tulāvidyā of the Advaita. The latter two are the cosmic and the individual unconscious.

[53]The main work of this school is Sāntaraksita's *Tattvasaṅgraha* with Kamalaśīla's commentary. See also Satakari Mookerjee: *The Buddhist Philosophy of Universal Flux*.

[54]Called *sahabhūhetu*, a coexistent cause. See Yamakami Sogen: *Systems of Buddhistic Thought*, pp. 309 fol., for the Buddhist analysis of causation.

[55]P. T. Raju: *Idealistic Thought of India*, pp. 281 fol.

[56]D. T. Suzuki: Studies in the *Laṅkāvatārasūtra*, pp. 208 fol.; and Bhikshu Saṅgharakshita: *A Survey of Buddhism*, pp. 265 fol. If we ignore the many subdivisions, we find three bodies of Buddha: the *nirmāṇakāya* or the mundane body that taught the Hīnayāna doctrine; the *sambhogakāya* or the body of enjoyment that

enjoyed teaching the Mahāyāna doctrine to highly developed souls; and the *dharmakāya* or the body of ultimate reality that is essential nature of Buddha.

[57]P. T. Raju: *Idealistic Thought of India*, p. 142. Cp. the concept of Avyakta.

[58]S. Z. Aung: *Points of Controversy*, pp. xlvii–li.

[59]Ibid., P. L. [60]Ed. by A. S. Altekar. See also T. Stcherbatsky: *Buddhist Logic*.

[61]*Pramāṇavārtikābhāṣya*, p. 245.

[62]Ibid., pp. 262 fol.

[63]What the Buddhists really mean by the object of perception being different from everything else is the non-carrying (*apoha*) of the past (memory) into the present cognition. We have seen that the Jainas meant by *ūhā* and *tarka* the modal or conditioned judgment also, which is based upon memory. The Buddhists want to say that in perception there is absence of this *ūhā*. Thus *apa* means absence and *ūhā* means carrying one into another. But *apoha* is explained as "different from everything else." So the rival schools ask: If in the perception of an object, the object's difference from all other objects is also cognized, there can be no *apoha* in perception as there is reference to all the other objects, which are, therefore, carried into the present perception. The Buddhists missed their own point by thus describing *svalakṣaṇa* and made themselves open to rival criticisms.

[64]Cp. Cook Wilson's theory of qualities. Cp. also Russell's theory of knowledge by acquaintance. For the former, See H. W. B. Joseph: *An Introduction to Logic*, pp. 6–7, p. 80.

[65]Prajñākaragupta: *Pramāṇavārtikābhāṣya*, p. 246.

[66]Prabhāchandra: *Prameyakamalamārtāṇḍa*, pp. 103–110 for an examination of the view.

[67]Cp. Locke's theory of perception and also that of the critical realists.

[68]Prajñākaragupta: *Pramāṇavārtikābhāṣya*, pp. 263–64.

[69]Cp. Berkeley's idealism.

[70]Prajñākaragupta: *Pramāṇavārtikābhāṣya*, pp. 391 fol., and 416 fol.

[71]Ibid., p. 365. [72]Ibid., p. 392. [73]Ibid., p. 392.

[74]Ibid., p. 305. [75]Ibid., p. 307.

[76]Ibid., pp. 216 and 219. Cp. the doctrines of Dewey.

[77]The word *anumāna* is a combination of the prefix *anu*, meaning "after", and *māna*, meaning "measure." All valid cognitions are measures of reality. So *anumāna* is the measure that follows or is derived from another measure.

[78]E.g., perception as interpreted by Plato cannot be perception at all for the Buddhists.

[79]These are immediate inferences different from those of western logic. Cp. the well-known John Dewey's theory.

[80]Prajñākaragupta: *Pramāṇavārtikābhāṣya*, pp. 484–93.

[81]Ibid., pp. 493–95.

[82]The three conditions are: *pakṣe sattvam*, *sapakṣe sattvam*, and *vipakṣāsattvam*.

[83]L. Śrīnivāsāchārya: *Mānameyarahasyaślokavārtikam*, p. 364.

[84]Ibid., p. 345. *Pratyakṣameva nāstīti sautrāntikamukhā viduḥ.*

[85]Prajñākaragupta: *Pramāṇavārtikābhāṣya*, pp. 50–52, 116–18, and 165–69.

[86]Ibid., p. *gha*. For this reason, the Vijñānavādins reject the reality of space, time, God, *ātman*, etc., as they serve no purposeful activity. We should not forget that generally Being is not ultimate for Buddhism.

[87]Cp. the view of Prabhākara.

[88]Many of these views are obtained from the works of rival schools, which are not always sympathetic and might have even misunderstood and misinterpreted them. Some of the interpretations are not even clear.

[89]The word *samvāda* used in this connection may be translated as both coherence and correspondence. The Sautrāntikas know that the object can never be directly perceived. So the correspondence or coherence can only be between the form of our consciousness and the result expected of the activity. *Samvāda* generally means agreement. This agreement is directly experienced, according to all the Buddhists. For purposeful activity is conscious activity, in which the form of the object and the form of the result of activity become the content of the same act of consciousness, which can, therefore, immediately cognize the agreement.

[90]*Arpitākārakhyāti.* [91]*Kalpitākārakhyāti.* [92]*Asatkhyāti.*

[93]*Nirālambanavāda.* [94]*Arthasamsargajākārakhyāti.*

[95]P. T. Raju: *Idealistic Thought of India*, pp. 273–78. Remember the views of Asanga and Śāntarakṣita about the *ātman*.

[96]Asaṅga: *Mahāyānasūtralaṅkāra*, p. 35.

[97]Prajñākaramati: *Bodhicaryāvatārapañjikā* gives a full account of the ideal.

[98]Ibid., pp. 279–91.

[99]Bhikshu Saṅgharakshita: *A Survey of Buddhism*, pp. 348 fol. See also Chou Hsiang-Kuang: *A History of Chinese Buddhism*, pp. 146 fol.

[100]There is a tradition according to which each of the ten incarnations of God Viṣṇu embodies one great emotion such as compassion, anger, love, heroism, wonder, etc. The life of an incarnation is the working out of the emotion and its final subsidence in the Supreme Being.

[101]Cp. *manomātratā*, *cittamātratā*, *vijñānamatratā*, and even *ātman* also in the Mahāyāna.

[102]Called *indriya*, defined by the Buddhists as a power or force. Indra is the god of power, and *indriya* is derived from *indra*.

[103]It may be found in some obscure places of Buddhist works, but has not attracted the attention of interpreters.

[104]I have not found elaboration of this view in any book so far. But we can develop the implications.

[105]Cp. the *Taittirīya Upaniṣad* right from the Reason-body to the physical, all is the body of the *ātman*. The Kasmir school of Śaivism maintains that the world is my body. This school will briefly be presented later.

[106]Another word used by the Buddhists in this connection is *vāsanā* or fragrance transmitted from one layer of cloth to another. But the idea does not contain the element of dynamism in its meaning like the work *samskāra*.

[107]Cp. *karmaiti mīmāmsakāh*. The Mīmāmsakas hold that action (*karma*) is the Lord of the universe.

[108]Early Buddhists treated time and space as *nityaprajñaptis* or eternal ideas, better translated as "eternal cognitive forms." Anyway, how can they be eternal, if everything is momentary?

[109]At this point both B. Blanshard and J. N. Findlay seem to have missed the I by making a fetish of coherence. They can never answer the criticism of coherence made by H. H. Joachim. The I that asserts coherence and the way it observes coherence are missing in their theories. Bradley and Bosanquet also are open to the same objection.

[110]These difficulties have to be considered by western philosophers also who hold that the I is non-existent or is only a series.

[111]This is called *anuvyavasāya* in Sanskrit. It is not the same as *dhārāvāhikajñāna*, the flow of a current of identical cognition, which is not generally possible except in Yogic meditation. There is no empirical perception like "That is a pen, that is a pen, that is a pen and so on;" for the focussing of mind in ordinary perception is instantaneous.

[112]Its relation to *sākṣi* (witness), *sākṣi-caitanya* (witness consciousness) attribute consciousness, and phenomenological consciousness will be shown in the chapters on the Vedānta.

[113]The same criticism applies to Whitehead's theory of the world as constituted by instantaneous events, if the world of events includes my person also, as Whitehead's metaphysics seems to do.

[114]*dravya-lakṣaṇa-avasthā-pariṇāmāh.*

[115]It was a mistake that the Buddhists did not accept the categories of the particular and the universal and were obliged to give such a misleading definition of the particular.

[116]Deeper analysis is needed to determine the value of the view that every percept includes the particular, universal and name also in some way.

[117]He says that *avilkapaka pratyakṣa* or indeterminate cognition is not the cognition of a mere something, which cannot be different from another something, but of a determinate individual, when seen for the first time. Determinants like universals can be found in later perceptions of the same object or objects of the same kind. Cp. Jaina views.

[118]John Dewey holds that all judgment, even the perceptual, is an inference, implicit or explicit. His view can be true only of the higher forms of perceptual judgment. That we call all perception by the name judgment in his sense is misleading; we do not pronounce a judgment, like a judge, in saying, "That is red." It is neither an act of proposing nor of judging.

[119]See the author's *Idealistic Thought of India*.

[120]Here as elsewhere, the Humeans will be wrong by denying the reality of force, energy, or power.

Buddhism may agree with the Humean empiricism; but the agreement is no credit even scientifically, as science now makes use of the concept of energy more extensively than before.

[121]One suspects that in Indian thought Becoming is ultimately confused with Non-being and illusion. Cp. the Platonists also. Becoming is real; and to be real is not necessarily to be Being.

[122]See the author's article, "Being: How Known and How Expressed," for some complexities of the problem. *International Philosophical Quarterly*, June 1975.

[123]How can the I-am, the existence of which is certain, be merely subjective?

[124]This directed consciousness may be called phenomenological consciousness.

[125]One suspects this difficulty in Popper's *Open Society and its Enemies* also. Openness does not mean absence of control by any principle, but the construction of a system with the help of a principle that leaves the system open, not closed and completed.

[126]Dictionaries give the English word *That*, the German *Das*, the Greek *to*, and the Sanskrit *tat* and *sah* as philologically related. If *sah* and *tat* are related, then the English words Thus, So, and That are related at their roots. Then the Buddhist position comes to mean what the Advaitins say: There can be no error in the That (or Thus); error lies only in the predicate. The identity of Thus and That reveals also the identity of noun and verb, substantive and action.

[127]Even for the Mīmāmsakas, what is past (*bhūta*) is a noun and what will be or becomes (*bhavya*) is the verb. This school is in a way supporting the Nairuktas. Cp. the philosophies of Croce and Gentile (and even Marx in some respects).

[128]See the author's *Idealistic Thought of India*, pp. 281 fol., for further analysis.

[129]Cp. the Advaita idea of the *sutrātman* (the thread-self running through everything in the universe and holding all together), which is equated to the life-force of the universe, its *prāṇa*.

Chapter VI

The Nyāya and the Architechtonic of Logic

1. INTRODUCTION

Although Buddhism rejected the Vedic scriptural authority and had to rely entirely upon logic and experience, the credit for formulating the logical principles does not go to Buddhism, but to the Nyāya school, the founder of which was Gautama (about 4th century B.C.). On the one side, the Mīmāmsā was developing not only principles for a correct interpretation of the Vedic texts, but also the principles of logic, semantics, and epistemology; for logic was recognized as an indispensable subsidiary to the study of the Veda. On the other, Buddhism was rejecting all reliance on Vedic authority and was using not very well formulated forms of argument against its rivals. Furthermore, some of the Ājīvikas were dialectically refuting every doctrine without proposing any doctrine of their own. In such a logical and epistemological atmosphere, Gautama felt it necessary to analyse the knowledge situation and fix the forms of argument; for what we know, intend to know, and argue about, depends on the nature of knowledge and the forms of the means of knowledge. As against the dialecticians, Gautama argued that mere dialectical refutation of a thesis, without at the same time offering an alternative thesis supposed to be free from faults, was of no use and could not be accepted as valid criticism. As against the Buddhists, he held that knowledge was not the same as the object known. He accepted the pluralistic position of the Mīmāmsā, its theory of ethical force, but argued for the truth of salvation, rejecting the sovereignity of ethical law in favour of that of a personal God.

Although Gautama's main interest lay in formulating the principles of logic, he did not divorce logic from metaphysics, for what we know depends on the form of knowledge as much as vice versa. For instance, our conceptual definition of an object has to be based upon the nature (*lakṣaṇa*) of that object. Yet the characteristics of the object depend on the forms of cognition that measure out those characteristics for us. But in Gautama's philosophy metaphysics received less attention than that which logic and epistemology did. Although the Mīmāmsā also was developing its logic and epistemology, it relied too much on the Vedic texts for building up its philosophy; but Gautama, in spite of recognizing the authoritativeness of the Veda, followed an independent path and had, therefore, to devote much greater thought to logic than the Mīmāmsā did. To him went, therefore, the credit of being the founder of logic in India. But as his metaphysics was not well-organized and categorized, his followers incorporated the metaphysics of the Vaiśeṣika school of Kaṇāda, which also incorporated in its turn the logic and epistemology of Gautama. This incorporation later gave rise to the hyphonated Nyāya-Vaiśeṣika school. By about the 13th century, the Nyāya school came to be divided into the Old Nyāya and the Neo-Nyāya. In general, the Vaiśeṣika accepts the Old Nyāya and the Neo-Nyāya grew out of the integrated Nyāya-Vaiśeṣika.

The atmosphere in which Gautama's logic appeared was that of controversy or debate, which was at that time mainly oral between rival schools. So he built up his architechtonic of logic with reference to the context of debate, in which two different schools enunciate different doctrines as hypotheses and argue for establishing their truth. Gautama explains the nature of a true debate, the rules of procedure, the nature of fallacious arguments and so forth. For this purpose he composed his *Nyāya Aphorisms* (*Nyāyasūtras*), which were commented upon by Vātsāyana (4th century) in his *Nyāyabhāṣya*. On this commentary Udyotakara (6th century) wrote his exposition (*Vārtika*), on which again Vācaspati Miśra (9th century) wrote another commentary. There are many other works expounding the doctrines of this school. Of them Viśvanātha's *Karikāvalī* (12th century) with his own and several other commentaries is one of the very widely studied, and combines the views of the Nyāya and the Vaiśeṣika. Keśavamiśra's *Tarkabhāṣā* (13th century) and Annam Bhatta's *Tarkasaṅgraha* (16th century) come under the same class. Jayanta's *Nyāyamañjarī* (10th century) is representative of the Old Nyāya. Gaṅgeśa started the Neo-Nyāya with his *Tattvacintāmaṇi*. But Raghunātha, who is said to be a disciple of Gaṅgeśa, is the most famous of the Neo-Nyāya school and is the author of *Dīdhiti* and *Padārthanirūpaṇa*. The Neo-Nyāya flourished from about the 13th to about the 16th century.

Gautama felt that salvation (*nihśreyas*) can be obtained only if the right effort is made. Our effort can be right only if it is in accordance with reality; for life has to be planned according to reality. But then we have to know what reality is. Our knowledge has, therefore, to be right and logically valid. There is no other way to determine reality than experience and logically valid forms of knowing. When the forms and their methods and, through them, reality are properly understood, then only can salvation be possible. So Gautama enunciated sixteen categories[1] of logic, epistemology, and argumentation as means to salvation. They are: (1) the valid means of cognition (*pramāṇa*); (2) the knowable (*prameya*); (3) doubt (*samśaya*); (4) purpose (*prayojana*); (5) example (*dṛṣṭānta*); (6) established doctrine (*siddhānta*); (7) members of syllogism (*avayava*); (8) the negative modal or counterfactual conditional (*tarka*); (9) ascertainment (*nirṇaya*); (10) controversy (*vāda*, discussion, debate); (11) wrangling (*jalpa*); (12) destructive dialectic (*vitaṇḍā*); (13) fallacies of syllogism (*hetvābhāsās*, false appearances of reason, invalid middle term); (14) quibbling (*chala*); (15) futile argument (*jāti*); and (16) grounds of defeat (*nigrahasthānas*).

We see that, except for the second category, all deal with logic and epistemology with special reference to debate. Gautama deals with the sixteen categories one after another on the whole. But in subsequent expository works, these categories are regrouped and reclassified under epistemology, metaphysics, and ethics and salvation. As we can easily see, categories (10), (11), (12), (14), (15), and (16) deal with the nature of debate; categories (5), (7), (8), and (9) deal with the nature of inference and we may add to them category (13); category (1) deals with the valid means or ways of cognition, of which the categories of inference may form a part; category (2) deals with metaphysical objects; category (3) deals with doubt, which prompts all enquiry; and category (4) deals with the general purpose of all enquiry. In fact, categories (3) and (4) can be classed with any of the above classes. We shall, therefore, discuss Gautama's philosophy under the heads: the nature of debate or controversy, theory of knowledge, metaphysics, and ideal of life.

2. NATURE OF CONTROVERSY

All right controversy is an enquiry and every enquiry has a purpose (*prayojana*).[2] The purpose of all enquiry is to obtain something desirable like truth, pleasure, salvation and so forth and to avoid something undesirable like falsity, pain, bondage and so forth. Only when there is a purpose, can controversy become earnest, sincere, and serious. We enter into a controversy when there is a doubt (*saṃśaya*). Doubt should not be an empty one; doubt for doubt's sake is logically unacceptable. A logically significant doubt[3] is one that arises when equally strong reasons are found for two opposed propositions like "S is P" and "S is not P"; when we tend to identify an object through a general characteristic, but find that the object has a new characteristic also; when we hear a word that has two opposed meanings; and when we are not sure that our cognition is true or false. But doubt is not an end in itself. The wavering of mind between two opposites must lead to the determination of truth and is accompanied by the expectation of something special (*viśesāpekṣā*) that will decide the case one way or the other. When two rival parties offer opposed hypotheses, we should not simply stop with accepting or doubting both, but proceed to enquire which of the two is true or whether a third one has to be accepted in preference to both.

An established doctrine (*siddhānta*) is not a hypothesis to be proved, but is the result of a whole system and is accepted as beyond doubt. It is of four kinds.[4] The *first* variety is that which is accepted by all schools (*sarvatantra-siddhānta*) and which also belongs to one's own school. The arguments of any debate should not conflict with such a doctrine. The *second* is that which is accepted by only one of the controverting schools and its friends (*samanatantrasiddhānta*). Then the arguments of that school should not conflict with such a doctrine; but the arguments of the other controverting school may. If the latter points out that the arguments of his rival contradict his own accepted doctrine, then the rival should admit defeat. The *third* is called the ground doctrine (*adhikaraṇasiddhānta*). It is the doctrine on the truth of which depends the truth of the hypothesis to be proved. If the present hypothesis presupposes the truth of that doctrine and yet contradicts it, and the contradiction is pointed out, then one should admit defeat. The rival may point out also that the presupposed doctrine itself is false. The *fourth* is the presumed doctrine (*abhyupagama-siddhānta*). In controversies, each or both of the rivals may make some unexpressed assumptions, wittingly or unwittingly. Such assumptions may be false or unfavourable to a hypothesis and favourable to another. If the falsity or unfavourability of the assumption is brought out by the rival through analysis of one's arguments, then one has to admit defeat.

In a true controversy, the contestants are expected to be sincere, desirous of truth, devoid of passions, without desire to deceive or cheat, and eager to use only logically valid arguments.[5] So a true controversy[6] (*vāda*) is one in which one defends one's position and criticizes the rivals using only the valid means of cognition (*pramāṇas*), the counter-factual conditional (*tarka*), and the five-membered syllogism—all the three will be discussed later—and one never contradicts his own position (*siddhāntāviruddha*). Here the mention of the use of the valid means of cognition, the counter-factual conditional, and the five-membered syllogism is important, for in false controversy they are absent.

The false or unacceptable types of controversy are four. The *first* is wrangling[7] (*jalpa*), in which each of the parties aims only at victory over the other. Here the rivals use not only the valid means of cognition, the negative modal or the counter-factual conditional, and the syllogism, but also equivocation and false or improper analogies for pointing out the grounds of defeat in each other's position. The *second* is that in which one indulges in mere criticism (*vitaṇḍā*)[8] of the rival without one's own position. Here either of the rivals does not have a position of his own and is interested only in refuting the other, but not in truth. Such a debate is not conducive to earnestness of enquiry. The *third* is that which uses an argument that consists of unfair criticism of the rival through a misleading interpretation of his statement (*chala*).[9] The argument is often a kind of equivocation. It is of three kinds. (1) If a word has two meanings, the rival may criticize one's position by taking the unintended meaning of the word. (2) When one makes a categorical (assertorical) statement like "The cow is black", the rival may interpret it as a statement of necessity and ask: "How can you infer from its being black its being a cow?" or "How can you infer from its being a cow its being black?" (3) If a word has both a literal and a metaphorical meaning, when I make a statement using the word in one only of its meanings, my rival may criticize me by taking the other meaning. Very often we use in philosophy and even in science metaphorical expressions for the sake of style. The opponent may criticize us as though we use the expressions in the literal sense, and claim victory.

The *fourth* kind of false controversy consists of futile arguments (*jāti*)[10] generally based upon unessential and accidental similarities and dissimilarities for refuting the rival. If I say, "Man is an animal", the rival may assail me by pointing out that men and horses have no common colour and so man cannot be an animal. If I say: "Man is an ethical being", the rival may object, saying: "Men and the other animals are coloured beings; and as the latter are not ethical beings, men also are not ethical beings." Such criticisms are self-refuting and are, therefore, called futile arguments. They are not based upon necessary relationships. As accidental and unessential similarities and dissimilarities are many, this kind of false discussion is of many types.[11]

The sixteenth category called the ground of defeat (*nigrahasthānas*)[12] may be mentioned here, as it shows how much thought Gautama gave to the problem of controversy and enquiry after truth. The grounds of defeat are mainly defects in one's argument and secondarily the crooked ways one adopts for defeating the rival. When they are pointed out by one's rival, one has to admit defeat or will be declared as having been defeated by the judge. Such defects are many and so the grounds of defeat are many. They are primarily of two kinds: those due to non-understanding (*apratipatti*) and those due to wrong understanding (*vipratipatti*). If one points out that the rival has not even understood one's position and that he yet claims to criticize, then the rival is defeated. Misunderstanding is due to fallacious thinking and argument. One may point out that one's rival is committing one of the fallacies—which will be discussed later—or has wrongly understood one's position. One may also point out that one's rival is indulging in one of the above mentioned unacceptable forms of argument, and the rival will be declared defeated. Although the rival can be defeated by pointing out any of the above faults, Gautama distinguishes between the grounds of defeat and wrangling and other forms of argument. He lists many of the former and leaves many unmentioned. The *first* ground of defeat is what leads to the loss of one's hypothesis or thesis (*pratijñahāni*). For it amounts to giving up one's position, and to accepting the reasons of the rival. The *second* consists in changing one's thesis by giving up the originally mentioned reasons and substituting others for them (*pratijñāntaram*). One's rival will then point out that one has changed his position and is arguing for another. The *third* lies in giving reasons that prove the opposite of the thesis (*pratijñāvirodha*). The *fourth* is the disavowal of one's thesis (*pratijñāsannyāsa*). If one's thesis is disproved by the rival, then in order to get out of the difficulty one may say that he has never held such a thesis. The *fifth* is the offering of a new reason or a modified reason, when the original reason is discredited (*hetvantaram*). The *sixth* is the giving of irrelevant reasons for one's thesis (*arthāntaram*). The *seventh* is the use of meaningless words to confound the rival (*nirarthakam*). The *eighth* is the use of words, which even when uttered thrice, the rival and the assembly cannot understand (*avijñātārtham*). One may coin words with his own meanings and then ridicule the rival for his inability to understand. So Gautama says that they must be capable of being understood by the rival and the assembly. One should then explain the meaning without blaming the rival. The *ninth* is the use, in a sentence, of words which together give no meaning (*apārthakam*). For instance, the sentence, "The tree is hunting rectangles", cannot be understood, although the words separately have each its own meaning. The *tenth* is the violation of the rules of procedure of debate (*aprāptakālam*). If the rules of procedure are violated, one of the parties may wrongly be declared defeated, and so truth cannot be obtained. The rules of the procedure are: first one of the parties enunciates his thesis and gives his reasons; then the rival criticizes him, enunciates his own thesis, giving his reasons; next the first party criticizes the second and defends his own position; afterwards, the second man gets his chance to speak. Only then the judge or the assembly pronounces its judgment. The *eleventh* consists in omitting one or more steps (members) of the syllogism (*nyūnam*). The *twelfth* is the giving of more reasons than one to prove the thesis and more examples than one to support a major premise (*adhikam*). The *thirteenth* is unnecessary repetition (*punaruktam*) as in "That mountain, that mountain has fire". Such repetition is not only unnecessary, but also may lead to confusion. The *fourteenth* is non-reply to the rival (*ananubhāṣaṇam*) even when he has spoken thrice and his words are understood by the assembly. The *fifteenth* is ignorance (*ajñānam*) of the subject. The *sixteenth* is ignorance of the reply (*apratibhā*). That is, there is a ground of defeat when one cannot find an answer to one's rival. The *seventeenth* is the breaking up of the debate through some excuse (*vikṣepa*). The *eighteenth* is the pointing out to the rival that his criticism applies equally well to his own position. Such a pointing out implies acceptance of the criticism. And the rival may not accept that the criticism applies to his position. The *nineteenth* is the failure to point out the ground of defeat in the rival in case it exists (*paryanuyojyopekṣaṇam*). Of course, the party that is unable to point it out may not even detect it; but the assembly can detect and point out the failure of the party concerned. The *twentieth* is the pointing out wrongly the ground of defeat when it does not exist (*niranuyojyānuyoga*). The *twenty first* is arguing in opposition to one's own school (*apasiddhānta*). Then Gautama mentions fallacies (*hetvābhāsas*) and adds "and so forth", meaning that there can be other grounds of defeat.

3. EPISTEMOLOGY

Although the nature of controversy is part of general epistemology and Gautama himself combined what we generally call epistemology in the limited sense of the term with rules of controversy, we have separated the two for convenience of presentation. Gautama accepts four[13] valid means of cognition and the Nyāya school, as distinct from the Vaiśeṣika, follows him. They are perception, inference, comparison, and verbal knowledge.

PERCEPTION Gautama defines[14] perception as the knowledge that arises out of contact between senses and objects, that is non-erroneous, and that may be either indeterminate (*avyapadeśyam*) or determinate (*vyavasāyātmakam*). According to the Nyāya, even determinate perception is not necessarily associated with a name.[15] This view is opposed to the view of grammarian philosophers, who maintain that all cognition is cognition also of the name of the object. According to them, if I perceive a horse, I cognize also the name "horse". As against the Buddhist Vijñānavādins and Mādhyamikas, for whom there is no object and perceptual knowledge arises without the senses coming into contact with the object and yet presents it, the Naiyāyikas maintain that there can be no perception without the contact of the senses with an existing object. The Naiyāyikas are epistemological and metaphysical realists and presentationists. They maintain that the objects as they are in themselves are seen by the senses.

Although Gautama held that indeterminate perception also is perception, his followers maintain, as against the Buddhists, that a completed perception has to be determinate (*savikalpa*). Indeterminate perception (*nirvikalpaka pratyakṣa*) is also called perception, because it is the first stage of the perceptual process. But as such it is neither valid (*pramā*) nor invalid (*apramā*).[16] In fact, Viśvanātha, a later Naiyāyika—he does not belong to the Neo-Nyāya—denies that indeterminate perception is no perception, saying that it does not belong to sense-perception at all (*atīndriya*).[17] Perception has to be of the form, "That is a horse", in which the individual perceived horse and its universal "horse-ness" are clearly distinguished and related. The That has to be seen as being determined (*avacchinna*) by the universal horse-ness, so that the perception becomes the perception of the object as a member of the class of horses. Indeterminate perception is without the form (*prakāra*) horse-ness and is not relational (*sambandhānavagāhi*), i.e., does not relate the individual to the universal and the class. A perception that is without a form and the relation to the class-concept or universal cannot be the basis of inference, which has to get its data ultimately from perception. Indeterminate perception is the cognition of the That only—i.e., without the distinction between the That and horse-ness—and between one That and another That there can be no difference. "That is a cow" is different from "That is a horse", because the first That is determined by cow-ness and the second by horse-ness. When cow-ness and horse-ness are not cognized, the difference between the two perceptions cannot be known. Indeterminateness is therefore useless and cannot even be a valid means of cognition (*pramāṇa*). It cannot have any validity at all, although it is not invalid too.

Perception is of six kinds—the perceptions of the five senses and that of mind (*manas*). All internal perceptions like those of pains, pleasures, desires, volitions, and activities are mental perceptions. Or we may classify perception into two kinds, the external and the internal. The external is of five kinds, because of the five senses. The internal is mental perception. Unlike the Buddhists, the Naiyāyikas do not regard mind (*manas*) as a sense (*indriya*), although they have no objection to calling it, as the Sāṅkhya does, the inner instrument (*antahkaraṇa*).

As a metaphysical realism, the Nyāya insists upon contact with objects in perception. This contact is explained in some detail.[18] It is *first* of three kinds: the four-termed, the three-termed, and the two-termed. In the perception of external objects, first senses come into contact with objects, then mind comes into contact with senses, and then it comes into contact with the *ātman*. The third contact produces consciousness (*buddhi*, *vijñāna*) in the *ātman* and the *ātman* cognizes the object. Here there are three contact relations and four terms. The four are the object, sense, mind, and the *ātman*. In internal perceptions like those of pains and pleasures, senses are not used and mind comes into contact directly with objects. So there are two relations and three terms. In the perception of yogis, mind knows the objects directly without coming into contact with them and the senses also are not used. But mind has to come into contact with the *ātman*. Then there is contact only of the *ātman* and mind.

According to the Nyāya, mind (*manas*) is atomic in size.[19] When I see an orange, which has colour, smell, shape, etc., seen by different senses, these qualities have to be brought together simultaneously into a unity so that I can perceive them as one orange and assert: "That is an orange". This simultaneity is not possible unless mind comes into contact with all the different senses at the same time; and mind cannot do so, unless it is infinitesimal, i.e., atomic in size. That which has no size, but infinitesimal, does not take time in moving from one place to another. It can move with infinite speed. Mind as atomic can move with infinite speed from one sense to another, bring together all the different sensations, and present them to the *ātman*, which sees them as an object. The Naiyāyikas reject the Sāṅkhya and the Advaita view that mind is infinite (*vibhu*); for if it is everywhere, man should know every object. The fact that he cannot and does not know every object shows that mind is not all-pervading.

It has already been mentioned that the Naiyāyikas do not accept the Buddhist Vijñānavāda doctrine that consciousness is the *ātman* itself. Consciousness is the same as knowledge or cognition and is of two kinds: memory (*smṛti*) and experience (*anubhūti*). Memory is not a distinct valid means of cognition; its validity depends on the original cognition, the object of which is remembered. Recognition (*pratyabhijñā*) also is not a distinct valid means, because it involves memory. Only experience (*anubhūti*) is valid, but transient. It is of the four kinds already mentioned: perception, inference, comparison, and verbal knowledge. It arises in the *ātman* like a spark when mind, with some information, comes into contact with the *ātman*. But the *ātman* is eternal and by itself unconscious. By treating consciousness as an accidental and incidental quality of the *ātman*, the Naiyāyikas, like the Mīmāmsakas, differ from the Sāṅkhya and the Vedānta, which were able to introduce distinctions like apperception (*citta*), reason (*buddhi*, *vijñāna*), ego (*ahaṁkāra*), and mind (*manas*) within the inner instrument, differentiating all from the *ātman*. The Nyāya separated mind from consciousness also, treating both mind and the *ātman* as unconscious, consciousness as always transient, calling it at the same time *buddhi*, *citta*, *vijñāna*, thereby depriving reason of every ontological status in spite of elaborate doctrines of inference. The *ātman* is, however, differentiated from the ego (*ahaṁkāra*) as the latter's substrate (*āśraya*).[20] According to Viśvanātha, it is directly known only by mind (*manomātrasya gocarah*). But according to some older Naiyāyikas, it is an object only of inference.[21] But on the whole, the Naiyāyika view seems to be that the *ātman* is an object of mental perception and that, if necessary, its existence can be proved from likes and dislikes, effort, etc., which have to belong to someone and that someone is the *ātman*. But the Naiyāyikas have not realized that the view that the *ātman* is by nature unconscious and is like a stone makes perception impossible. For if I perceive a horse, the perception belongs to me and the consciousness that I perceive a horse is involved in that perception. So the consciousness of my "I" is involved in perception; and its being involved is not possible if the *ātman* is not self-conscious, i.e., if it is unconscious. In the case of the alternative that the *ātman* is an object of mind, mind cannot be the subject of this cognition as it is unconscious. In the case of the *ātman* being an object of inference, no one can say: "I see the horse". If the "I" is inferred, it cannot directly assert itself. But it asserts itself.

The Naiyāyikas analyse the contact between senses and objects into six[22] kinds. As metaphysical realists, they regard every object of cognition as present there in the world. Unlike the Buddhists, they maintain that the universal and negation are real and are perceived by the senses themselves through one of the six kinds of contact process (*vyāpāra*, *pratyāsatti*). The relation, which is a process but is not static, between sense and substance is contact or conjunction (*samyoga*). Thus *first*, substance is perceived by contact with a sense. *Secondly*, qualities (*guṇas*), activities (*karmas*), and universals (*jātis*, *sāmānyas*), all of which inhere in substances are perceived by the combined relation, contact-cum-inherence (*samyuktasamavāva*). *Thirdly*, the universals inhere in qualities and activities—like red-ness and walking-ness—and are perceived through the relation of contact-cum-inherence-cum-inherence. For instance, red colour inheres in the substance of the rose, and red-ness inheres in the red colour. *Fourthly*, the relation of inherence itself—like that between substance and its qualities—is perceived as a characteristic or attribute (*viśeṣaṇa*)[23] of substance. That is, the relation between senses and the relation of inherence is contact-cum-attribute (*samyukta-viśeṣaṇa*). Absences and negations also are perceived in the same way. If there is absence of the pen on the table, then that absence is perceived as an attribute of the table. *Fifthly*, sound is perceived only through the relation of inherence. According to the Nyāya, the substance (element) to which sound belongs as a property is ether (*ākāśa*) and is not accepted as an object of sense-perception. So there is no contact of any sense and the substance ether. Yet, its peculiar quality, sound, is perceived directly by the ear. As a quality, sound inheres in ether. So in the perception of sound, the sense of hearing comes into relation with sound through the relation of inherence. The Naiyāyikas say that the sense of hearing is ether itself as limited by the physical ear (*śrotrāvacchinna*) and sound is perceived as inhering in that limited ether. *Sixthly*, the qualities inhering in sound—like mellowness and harshness—are perceived by the ear through the relation of inherence-cum-inherence. That is, sound inheres in the ear (ether) and "harsh" inheres in sound.

The aim of the Naiyāyikas in enunciating the six kinds of sense-object relational process is to defend that substances, qualities, actions, universals, relations, and negations are all real and objects of sense-perception also. Universals and relations are perceived through the very senses through which the individuals and terms are perceived. If the individual horse is perceived by the eye, then the universal "horse-ness" also is perceived by it. If two books in contact are perceived by touch, then the relation of contact also is perceived by it. The same view holds about negation. If the pen is perceived by the eye, then the negation or absence also of the pen is perceived[24] by the eye.

By making negation or absence an object of sense-perception, the Naiyāyikas reject not only the doctrine of the Buddhists that it is an object of inference, but also that of Kumārila that it is an object of a special way of knowing called non-apprehension (*anupalpbdhi*). The Naiyāyikas admit that the simple perception of the table is not the same as the perception of the absence of the pen on it. For perceiving the absence, the thought[25] "Had the pen been there, I would have perceived it" must accompany the perception of the table. The resulting perception is that of the absence.[26] The Buddhists say that the necessary introduction of the thinking process makes the cognition of absence an inference, although it is a spontaneous inference without explicit reasoning. Kumārila says that here there can be no inference, as there is no major premise. And as it cannot be simple perception also, we have to accept another valid form of cognition to be called non-apprehension.

Another significant point is the Nyāya contention[27] that the universal is perceived through the senses. This significance can be seen in the context of a further classification of the perceptual process (*vyāpāra*). Perception is of two kinds, depending on whether the process is ordinary (*laukika*) or extra-ordinary (*alaukika*). Ordinary perception depends on the six kinds of sense-object relationship, which have already been described. Extra-ordinary perception is of three kinds.[28] The *first* is the perception of the universal through the object (*sāmanysalakṣanā-pratyāsatti*). When I see a horse, I see also the universal horse-ness in the object, for every object is cognized as being determined (*avacchinna*) by the universal present in it as in "That is a horse". But through this universal, —and this is important— all the horses of the world also are cognized in a general way, of course not individually. The Naiyāyikas contend that this kind of perception of the class has to be accepted, for all the members of a class are never perceived individually through sense-contact and we have to explain how we obtain our cognition of the class. The individual is perceived in the ordinary way, but the class is perceived in the extra-ordinary way through the universal. Besides, if we do not accept this kind of perception, we can never have a major premise for inference. When I see fire and smoke together in my kitchen, I doubt whether fire causes smoke or smoke causes fire. This doubt cannot arise, unless I mean by fire the class of fires and by smoke the class of smokes. But how can I get the concepts of the two classes otherwise than by the universal present in the kitchen fire and that present in the kitchen smoke? Through the two universals I perceive the two classes, relate them, and then doubt which is necessarily accompanied by which. The cognition of the class cannot be treated as inference, because it has no major premise, and we are actually in search of the major premise. The class, therefore, is an object of a peculiar kind of perception and the major premise is the expression of a relation of two such classes.

The Naiyāyikas have no separate methods of inductive inference and utilize this extra-ordinary perception for obtaining major premises. They do not say that every hypothetical major premise thus obtained is valid, but that it is only a hypothesis that is formed and doubted. Even a hypothesis can be a universal proposition. For removing doubts and establishing the hypothesis as a major premise, they enunciate certain checks, which will be discussed under inference.

The *second* kind of extra-ordinary perception is what may be called perception by association or perception through an associated concept (*Jñānalakṣaṇā pratyāsatti*). Through my eye, I perceive a rose. Then its fragrance also becomes an element of the content of my cognition and I may say: "I perceive a fragrant rose". Here the fragrance is remembered through the concept of "being fragrant", and my eye sees, as it were, the fragrant rose. Experience like "Fire looks hot" and "Cotton looks soft" may be classed under this kind of extra-ordinary perception. Such perceptions may be called perceptions by association, complication, or transference. The Buddhists would call them spontaneous inferences, but the Naiyāyikas classify them as perceptions.

The *third* kind of extra-ordinary perception is that of the yogis, which has already been referred to. Later Naiyāyikas, like Viśvanātha, divide it into two kinds, the perfect and the imperfect.[29] One who is perfect in yogic meditation can know all things, both infinite and infinitesimal, at all times. One who is not perfect has to make a special effort for concentrating one's mind for knowing particular objects at particular times. In either case, it is only mind that is active; and even sense objects can be known by mind without use of senses and without coming into contact with objects.

The three kinds of extra-ordinary perception are the ways by which man's cognition transcends the directly present. Yogic perception does not belong to the common man, but the other two forms are common. The first explains how classes and universal propositions are known. The second explains how past associations can be determinant factors in present perceptions. Seeing Bill, I may say: "I see the friend of Jim," although Jim himself is not present before me. Recognition also, Like "I see the same Bill", can be explained similarly; but the Nyāya does not accept it as a valid means of cognition. At this point, the Jaina analysis seems to be less inconsistent.

INFERENCE For the Indian thinkers, inference (*anumāna*) means only the syllogistic inference.[30] It is the proof of a statement with the help of a syllogism. We have mentioned that Gautama analysed syllogism in the context of controversy (*vāda*). In it, the thesis to be proved has to be mentioned, then the proof follows, and last the thesis has to be shown as the conclusion of the proof. So the thesis has to be mentioned twice, first as a hypothesis and then as a conclusion. In between the two the syllogistic proof with its three steps has to be given. Thus Gautama gives five steps of the syllogism.

1. Thesis (*pratijña*, enunciation)	The mountain has fire;
2. Reason (*hetu*)	Because of smoke;
3. Major premise with example (*vyāpti* with *udāharaṇa*)	Wherever there is smoke, there is fire, as in the kitchen;
4. Application (*upanayana*)	The mountain also has smoke accompanied by fire, like the kitchen;
5. Conclusion (*nigamana*)	Therefore, the mountain has fire.

Although in the above classical example of Indian logic, there are five steps, there are really only three logical terms[31] —the major term (*sādhya*, that to be proved) is fire; the middle term (*hetu*, reason, is smoke; and the minor term (*pakṣa*, case) is the mountain. One may think that example (*udāharaṇa*) is a fourth term. We have seen that the Buddhist logicians do not insist upon the mentioning of example, but the Nyāya logicians generally insist on it. Example is necessary to show that there is at least one existent object or case in the world in which the middle and major terms co-exist. Such co-existence is the primary condition for obtaining the major premise. How can one, otherwise, know that the two terms are related at all? How can we be sure that the relation is not one of mere imagination? Again, the example had to be one that is acceptable to both the parties in dispute. This condition is generally implied; and it is said also that in the case of well-known major premises, example need not be mentioned.[32] But the rival party has the right to challenge. Otherwise, we may argue

All men are immortal;
Socrates is a man;
Therefore, Socrates is immortal.

But the rival may ask: "What is the example in which "being immortal" and "being a man" co-exist? Example is necessary to give plausibility and possibility to the major premise. Next, there can be other tests.

The step called application (*upanayana*) is in effect the integration of all the logical constituents of the syllogism, example being implicitly admitted as not being a logical constituent. The Naiyāyikas maintain that application is necessary, because it asserts that the minor term (*pakṣa*) has the reason (*hetu*) that is necessarily accompanied by the major term (*sādhya*). It presents the connection between the minor and major terms through the middle so that thought can intuit the connection. Symbolically the Aristotelian inference will be of the form

All M is P;
S is an M;
Therefore S is a P.

Here the connection relates S and P through M. That is

S is M, and M is P *or* S-M-P.

The Naiyāyika application amounts to asserting "S-M-P". This assertion removes all the risk of the ambiguity of the middle. The whole S-M-P is called referring, relating, connecting (*parāmarśa*),[33] which, the Naiyāyikas insist, is the necessary immediate antecedent of conclusion.

The Naiyāyikas did not give separate treatment of the inductive methods, as the western logicians have done. Yet they gave some methods for checking false and hasty hypotheses or universal propositions. We have seen that, according to this school, universal propositions are obtained from perception itself by one of the forms of extra-ordinary perception, i.e., perception of the classes through the universals present in perceived individuals. For instance, after perceiving fire and smoke in the kitchen and seeing their connection, I perceive in general all fires and all smokes through the universals fire-ness and smoke-ness and obtain the proposition, "Whatever has smoke has fire also". But why should I not form the proposition, "Whatever has fire has smoke also?" Hence doubt arises about the truth of the universal proposition. There are here two hypotheses, hence the doubt. If the first proposition is true, then in future inference I can use smoke as the reason for inferring fire; but if the second is true, I can use fire for inferring smoke.

To remove my doubt, I have to find out which of the two terms can exist without the other. The major term (*sādhya*) is the one that can exist without the middle, but the middle cannot exist without the major. In our example, fire can exist without smoke, as in an electrical oven; but smoke cannot exist without fire as in the kitchen of the ancients, forest on fire, the volcano, etc. So I conclude that "Whatever has smoke has fire also" is the true universal proposition, accepting fire as the cause and smoke as the effect. If there is still doubt about the major, the Naiyāyikas recommend the use of the negative modal or counter-factual conditional (*tarka*) to confirm and fortify the major. It is of the form, "Had there been no fire, there would have been no smoke." But unlike the Jainas, the Naiyāyikas do not accept the counter-factual conditional as a valid means of cognition (*pramāṇa*). This negative modal is based upon the positive modal, and that upon a universal affirmative proposition, which is indeed accepted, as we have seen.

The major premise (*vyāpti*) is defined[34] as the proposition meaning the absence of the middle term (reason) wherever there is absence of the major. Although the major premise is generally asserted in its affirmative form, a negative definition is given to emphasize that the middle term should not be found where the major is not found. However, by this definition of the major premise, the major and middle terms also are defined. The middle is that which cannot exist where the major does not exist; and the major is that which exists where the middle exists. Indeed, the major may be found where the middle is not found, just as fire can be present where smoke is not present; but it must be found where the middle is found. We use the word "term" to denote the object, not the word.

The relation between the middle and major terms has to be a necessary relation. Necessary relations accepted by the Nyāya are: (1) the causal relation; (2) species-genus relation; and (3) member-class relation. "Fire causes smoke"; here fire, as the cause, necessarily accompanies smoke, as the effect, and can be inferred from smoke. "Horses are animals"; here the class horses is a species of the genus animals, and we can infer the presence of animals from the presence of horses. "Socrates is a man"; here Socrates is a member of the class of men. We can infer the presence of a man from the presence of Socrates. The Naiyāyikas did not develop special methods for determining these relations in complicated and doubtful cases, although we can find the rudiments of the methods in their definition of the major premise and counter-factual conditional. Even in the West the methods belong to the history of logic after the 16th century. But by that time Indian philosophical activity was on the wane.

Gautama accepts three[35] kinds of inference. The *first* (*pūrvavat*) is the inference of the effect from the cause. We infer rain from thick clouds. The *second* (*śeṣavat*) is the inference of cause from effect. We infer rainfall on the hills from floods. The *third* (*sāmānyatodṛṣṭa*) is inference from the observation of general inseparability, based on the relation of member to class and species to genus. We infer from the object being an oak that it is a tree. We infer also from the animal being a lion that it is carnivorous. The lion is neither the cause nor the effect of being carnivorous. But being a lion and being carnivorous are inseparable.

Viśvanātha, in his commentary on Gautama's *Nyāya Aphorisms* gives a second interpretation also to the three kinds of inference. The *first* (*pūrvat*) is inference (*kevalānvayī*) from a major premise in which reason and consequent are concomitant with each other. The major is then called the purely concomitant (*anvayavyāpti*). The example is the equilateral triangle. We can infer its being equilateral from its being equi-angular and vice versa. The Naiyāyikas give the example: "Everything nameable is thinkable". But inference from such a major premise is not accepted by many thinkers; for each of the terms "nameable" and "thinkable" covers everything in the universe and there is nothing in which the major term is not present and we cannot know that the middle is not present where the major is not present. However, the case of the equilateral triangle becomes a fitting example.

The *second* kind (*śeṣavat*) is inference from a major premise in which the middle and major terms are absolutely non-concomitant (*kevalavyatirekī*). That is, where one exists, the other cannot exist. The major premise then is a negative proposition and the conclusion is negative. For instance, whatever is fire is not cold and whatever is cold is not fire. The major premise is then called the non-concomitant (*vyatirekavyāpti*). The Naiyāyikas use this inference in a way not acceptable[36] to many other thinkers by attempting to prove the reality of earth as an element distinct from the other elements. They argue: "Earth is an element different from the others; because it possesses the property smell; whatever does not have smell is not earth." Indian thinkers generally accept that taste is the property of water, smell of earth, sound of ether, colour of fire, and touch of air. The Naiyāyika argument does not show why the same element cannot have two properties.

The *third* kind (*sāmānyatodṛṣṭa*) is inference from a major premise for which wherever the middle term is present the major also is present, but the middle is not present in some cases where the major is present (*anvayavyatirekī*). An example is the classical one of smoke and fire. The major premise in this case is called the concomitant-non-concomitant (*anvayavyatirekivyāpti*). This kind of inference is accepted by all schools that accept inference at all. For it has cases in which both fire and smoke are not present.

In Vatsāyana's commentary[37] on Gautama's *Nyāya Aphorisms*, we find a third interpretation of the three kinds of inference; and this interpretation as we shall see, agrees with the Sāṅkhya classification of inference. The *first kind* (*pūrvavat*) is the inference drawn from the relation of middle and major terms, which were already seen (*pratyakṣabhūta*). Fire and smoke are objects of previous perceptions, e.g. in the kitchen, and then after seeing smoke again we infer the presence of fire. The *second* (*śeṣavat*) is the inference of what remains (*śeṣa*) by elimination of the irrelevant. This inference corresponds more or less to the method of residues in Western inductive logic. But what is obtained by this inference is not necessarily a universal causal principle but a conclusion about an individual. Vātsāyana gives the example of proving that sound is a quality. In the case of colour, taste, touch, and smell, we easily attribute them to substances like fire, water, air, and earth, as the latter are objects of sense-perception, and we find them also in objects like the orange. But we are unable to attribute sound as a quality to any substance. So doubt arises whether sound is a substance, quality, or activity. Sound cannot be a substance, because it is pervasive and we cannot find its boundaries as we can find those of an orange. It is not activity, because one sound produces another sound like the echo; but no action produces another action.[38] It is, therefore, a quality. The inference that sound is a quality is that of the method of residues, although deductive. Indeed, this inference goes further. Every quality is the quality of a substance. None of the substances we know of can be the substance of which sound is a quality, because they do not possess it. Therefore, there must be another substance of which sound is the property and that substance is ether (*ākāśa*). A similar inference is often made by scientists. An astronomer may ask: What is the deviation of the planet A from its normal route due to? It is not due to the attraction of the known planets M and N. It must, therefore, be due to the attraction of a planet not yet known. Then after some more calculations, the astronomer theoretically fixes the new planet and observes it with his telescope. New discoveries are made by this kind of inference.

The *third* kind of inference (*sāmānyatodṛṣṭa*) is explained in two ways by Vātsāyana. (1) It is the inference, in a new context, of a general characteristic observed previously in a different context. I observe that I appear at two different places if I walk (move). So the appearance of the same thing at two different places implies movement. Now, the sun may appear at 9:00 a.m. and then disappear in the clouds. Then at 3:00 p.m. he appears again at a different place in the sky, as the clouds disappear. Between 9:00 a.m. and 3:00 p.m. I do not see the movement of the sun. Yet from the fact that he appears at different places, I infer, from the experience of my own movement, that the sun moves. Although this example of Vātsāyana violates the Copernican theory, the form of the argument is applicable even when it is accepted that the earth moves and the sun, relatively, to the earth, stands still. We may as well argue that the earth moves because the sun is first seen in the east and then in the west and that without movement this difference cannot be explained. (2) When the relation between the middle and major terms cannot be perceived for the reason that the major term is imperceptible and yet from some general characteristic (*sāmānya*) of the middle term we infer the existence of the major, we have this kind of inference. We have seen that this kind of argument was classified as postulation (*arthāpatti*) by the Mīmāmsakas. Vātsāyana and, following him, all the Naiyāyikas who came later, wanted to treat it as a form of syllogistic inference. Some of the early Naiyāyikas believed that the *ātman* cannot be perceived, although the others accepted that it is an object of mental perception. For the former, its existence is only inferred.

We infer its existence as the existence of that to which the qualities—desire, hate, pain, pleasure, and effort—belong. We observe in general (*sāmānyatah*) that qualities belong to substances. As desire, etc., are qualities, they must belong to a substance, which is imperceptible, and that substance is the *ātman*. One may not accept this argument to prove the reality of the *ātman* and even that desire, etc., are qualities. Yet we often use this form of argument. This form of inference is used by the Naiyāyikas to prove the reality of ether (ākāśa). We have seen that that sound is a quality is proved by the second kind of inference; but that it belongs to a substance called ether is proved by this third kind.

Another classification of inference given by the Naiyāyikas is that into inference for oneself and inference for another. But this division, as given by the Indian logicians, is not very significant. The difference between the two classes lies only in the number of steps. In inference for others, i.e., in actual debate, the Naiyāyikas say, there have to be the five steps previously mentioned. But in inference for oneself, three steps are enough. They are

Thesis	The mountain has fire;
Reason	Because it has smoke;
Major premise with example	Wherever there is smoke, there is fire, as in the kitchen.

INDUCTION It has already been mentioned that the Naiyāyikas had no separate methods of induction, but incidentally indicated here and there how much they knew about induction. We may here bring together what has been said. They accepted as necessary relations (1) causal relation, (2) member-class relation, (3) and genus-species relation. Between (2) and (3) they did not make a clear distinction as the logicians, following Russell, have done recently. They accepted also that, although a universal proposition, i.e., major premise, can be obtained even after seeing a single instance through the universal present in it—that is, through one of the forms of extra-ordinary perception—it generally strikes the mind after seeing a number of instances and we form a universal proposition. In our observations, we see also which of the two terms can exist without the other and make it the major term. We may say also that the Naiyāyikas were aware of what we call the method of residues, although they classified it under syllogistic inference. We may add also that they knew the method of postulation, by which we infer the existence of not only unperceived but also imperceptible entities, as evidenced by the Naiyāyika argument for the existence of ether and the *ātman*. Postulation is really the method of formulating hypotheses. But again, they treated this method as a form of deduction, and refused to accept the Mīmāmsā view that postulation is a distinct valid means of cognition (*pramāṇa*). But the Naiyāyika reduction of postulation to deduction seems to be defective.[39]

Let us assume that sound is a quality and that every quality belongs to a substance. The existence of ether is proved by the Naiyāyikas from its being the substance to which sound belongs through this third kind of inference (*sāmānvatodṛṣṭa*). The Mīmāmsakas say that this argument is postulation, not deduction. We need a major premise for deduction, but we do not have any here. We may accept that wherever there is a quality, there is a substance, as a major premise. But it does not prove that the substance in this case is ether. It may be any of the known substances. So the Naiyāyikas frame an argument like

(1) If ether is not different from earth, etc., it cannot have sound as a quality;
But it has sound as a quality;
Therefore, ether is a distinct substance from earth, etc.

But the Mīmāmsakas argue: How can we get the major negative premise, unless we already knew that an element distinct from earth, etc., is the possessor of sound? A negative statement always implies an affirmative one. To get the affirmative proposition, we need postulation. The Naiyāyikas generally reduce postulation into a disjunctive argument and a negative argument from non-concomitance. The forms will be

(2) Ether is a distinctive element or it does not have sound as a quality;
But it has sound as a quality;
Therefore, it is a distinctive element.

(3) Whatever is not a distinctive element from earth, etc., cannot have sound;
But ether has sound;
Therefore, it is a distinct element (it is not an element that is not distinct).

In both (2) and (3), the major and the minor assume that ether is a substance and that it has sound as a quality. But what is the process of this assuming? The answer is: Postulation. In fact, what the Naiyāyikas call inference from general characteristics is in most cases postulation. Wherever the probandum or major term is not perceivable, we have postulation, for in such cases the reality of the major term itself has to be proved. After it is postulated and accepted, we can have a major premise, affirmative or negative.

However, in addition to the above methods, the Naiyāyikas utilized the negative or counter-factual conditional (*tarka*) not merely as an indirect proof or *reductio ad absurdum* argument but also for confirming a hypothesis by showing that its opposite is false. The opposite is assumed for argument's sake and it is generally given in a negative form. If the original hypothesis is negative, then its opposite, being the negative of a negative, will be affirmative. The negative conditional is not the same as the negative major premise; the former is conditional, but the latter is categorical. The former is an explicit assumption, but the latter is an explicit assertion. So the negative conditional argument should not be confused with a syllogism with the major premise asserting the non-concomitance of the middle and major terms (*kevalavyatirekī*). In the case of the proof for the existence of ether, the negative conditional will be

> Had ether as a substance been not real, sound as a quality would not have been real;
> But sound as a quality is real;
> Therefore, ether as a substance is real.

Or in the example of the saint who claims not to eat at all, but has been becoming fat, the conclusion inferred by the Naiyāyikas according to the observation of general characteristics (*sāmānvatodṛṣṭa*) is that he is eating by night. The modal form given by them is

Had the saint been not eating by night, he would not have become fat;
But he has become fat;
Therefore, he is eating by night.

The counter-factual conditional (*tarka*), as the Naiyāyikas understand it, is only the first step of the argument; it is the assertion of a conditionality. They do not, therefore, accept it a valid means of cognition (*pramāṇa*). But we can supply the two other steps and form a syllogism.

We may say that the Naiyāyikas knew of four[40] conditions for a valid major premise, which are implicitly four valid methods for forming a valid hypothesis. The *first* condition is the concomitance of the major with the middle or the *probandum* with the probans (*anvaya*). That is, wherever the middle is found, the major must be found. The *second* is the concomitance of the absence of the middle with the absence of the major term (*vyatireka*). For instance, the first condition will be wherever smoke is found, fire also must be found; whereas the second will be: wherever the absence of fire is found, the absence of smoke also must be found. The former (*anvaya*) is the concomitance of positive entities, the latter (*vyatireka*) is the concomitance of negative entities, i.e., of the opposites of the former in the reverse direction. The first may be compared to J.S. Mill's Method of Agreement and the second to his Method of Difference. Together they can form his Joint Method of Agreement and Difference. But the Naiyāyikas tell us which conditions are to be fulfilled, without telling us how methodically to fulfill those conditions. Otherwise, they would have given us some full-fledged inductive methods. The *third* condition is the non-observation of a contrary instance (*vyabhicārāgraha*). That is, the middle term *should not have been observed* anywhere where the major term is not observed. The third condition really follows from the first and the second, which are the main logical conditions of a true major premise. The *fourth* condition is the absence of conditionality in the truth of the major premise (*upādhinirāsa*). The major premise asserts the relation between the middle term (reason) and the major (consequent). But if the relation holds true, only under certain conditions, not mentioned, then the major premise (*vyāpti*) cannot be true. So we have to find out whether the major premise can be true without the conditions. Suppose in the kitchen we see fire and smoke and form the major premise

Wherever there is fire, there is smoke.

People generally burn somewhat wet fuel in the old type of kitchens in which wood is the fuel. But if we have an electric oven or even a charcoal oven, we do not have smoke. So we cannot conclude that wherever there is fire, there is smoke. This false major premise can be a true one only under the condition of there being wet fuel. Such a condition becomes conditionality (*upādhi*). Wherever there is such a conditionality, the major premise cannot be true. So we reverse the major premise and assert

Wherever there is smoke, there is fire.

This major premise holds true unconditionally. We may accept also

Wherever there is smoke, there is something that gives out carbon

But we cannot reverse the proposition and say.

Wherever there is something that gives out carbon, there is smoke. For then fire becomes the conditionality (*upādhi*). Thus the concept of conditionality is formulated by the Naiyāyikas to determine which of the terms, smoke and fire, is the middle and which the major. Such determining is necessary, whenever the middle is found without the major, although, in many cases, they are found together.

Had the Naiyāyikas analysed and developed the concept of conditionality (*upādhi*) further, they would have made a great contribution to inductive logic and separated perhaps induction from deduction. But they were content only with saying that, wherever the major premise is only conditionally true, it is invalid and the conclusion drawn from it cannot be valid. Conditionality (*upādhi*) is defined as the necessary relation of something only with the major term, but not with the middle. For instance, in the old example wet fuel is necessarily related with smoke, but not with fire, in the false major premise, "Wherever there is fire, there is smoke." If we have a number of instances like

	I	II
(1)	*ABCD*	*KLMN*
(2)	*ABEF*	*KNOP*
(3)	*AEFG*	*QRST*
(4)	*HBJM*	*XYZS*

in (3) and (4) *A* and *B* are present separately, but *K* is not present in the corresponding (3) and (4) of Group II. But when *A* and *B* are present together, *K* is present. Then do *A* and *B* together form the cause of *K*, or is *K* the cause of both *A* and *B*? Since *A* or *B* can exist without *K*, they are independent of *K*. So we have to say that *A* and *B* together are the cause of *K*, and we can infer the presence of *A* and *B* together or *A* or *B* separately from the presence of *K*. But if we have another instance like

(5) *AVCD* *KYST*

then *A* and *V* together will have to be the cause of *K*, like fire and wet fuel together being the cause of smoke. If we then make a major premise like

Wherever there is *A*, there is *K*,

B and *V* will become, separately or together, the conditionality of the premise. We will then have to proceed further and ask: What is it in *B* or *V* that, along with *A*, is actually the cause of *K*? Thus the determination and analysis of conditionality will lead to the exact determination of the factors of any causation. But the Naiyāyikas have made no contribution to such further analysis.

The Principle of Causality The Naiyāyikas developed their own doctrine of causation, accepting the principle that every compound object has a cause. That is, everything except the eternal realities, which are either infinite like space and time or infinitesimals and particulars,[41] are caused. They contend that the effect is always something new and could not have existed in the cause. Prior to its appearance, the effect is non-being (*asat*). Their doctrine is called the doctrine of the prior non-being of the effect (*asatkāryavāda*), i.e., before it is born. The Naiyāyikas says that, if the effect (*kārya*) is not non-being before it appears, there will be no need of the causal process.

As against the Nyāya, the Sāṅkhya maintains that, if the effect is non-being before it is born, then non-being must be said to have become being when the effect is born. But Non-being can never become Being, for nothing comes out of nothing. We have, therefore, to say that the effect is potentially present in the cause and causation is only manifestation (*āvirbhāva*). For instance, the pressing of oil seeds is the process for the manifestation of oil that is already present in them. But the Naiyāyikas contend that causation is real creation, that we should not generalize from the example of oil seeds, that, even in their case, manifestation is a novelty and was not potentially present in the oil seeds, and that in another example, the figure chiselled out of a stone by the sculptor is not the manifestation of a figure already present in the stone. Another sculptor could have made another figure out of the same stone.

Just as the eternal entities are not the effects of anything, they are not the causes also of anything.[42] The Naiyāyikas do not mean that eternal entities are not involved in the causal process, but that the infinite as infinite does not produce a greater infinite and that the infinitesimal as infinitesimal does not cause a greater infinitesimal. Further, realities like space, time, and atoms are involved in every causal process, and what is involved in every causal process and is common to all need not be considered in any specific causal process. Specific invariable antecedents alone are causes. So cause is defined as that which is not present in any and every case (*anyathāsiddha-śūnya*)[43] and which is the invariable (*niyata*) antecedent (*pūrvavartī*) of an event. That which is present in any and every case is also an invariable antecedent, but is not to be considered. It is of five kinds.[44] The *first* is the universal of the specific invariable antecedent. We may illustrate it by taking the example of the potter making a pot on his wheel by turning it with a stick. In any single instance, an individual potter, an individual lump of clay, an individual wheel, and an individual stick are involved, although causal propositions are of a universal nature like "Pots are made of clay". Now, in any specific instance, every individual involved has, according to the Naiyāyikas, its own universal—the potter potter-ness, the clay clay-ness, the wheel wheelness etc. Yet the universals are not the cause of anything: potter-ness, for instance, does not cause the pot. The *second* is the colour, complexion etc. of the individuals. For instance, the colour of the skin of the potter does not cause the pot. The *third* is whatever is the necessary antecedent of every cause like space, time, etc. The *fourth* consists of the causes of the invariable antecedents. Indeed, every specific invariable antecedent has its own causes. But these causes have nothing logically to do with the present causal process. For instance, the father and mother of the potter are not the causes of the present pot. The *fifth* is what is not the immediate, invariable antecedent, i.e., what is only mediately the invariable antecedent. For instance, the potter brings his clay on a cart or a donkey. But the cart or donkey should not be considered as a cause of the pot. All the five kinds of invariable antecedents are irrelevant for considerations of causation.

Cause is of three[45] kinds. The *first* is the inherent cause (*samavāyikāraṇa*). This corresponds to Aristotle's conception of material cause. Only substances can be material causes.[46] We distinguish between the clay, the material cause of the pot, and the pot, the effect. The pot, in the Nyāya terminology, is said to exist in its clay through the relation of inherence. Similarly, the whole as the effect is said to inhere in the parts. Inherence is an inseparable relation, and the terms cease to be what they are if separated. In this instance, the clay is said to be the inherent cause. The *second* is the non-inherent cause (*asamavāyikāraṇa*). It corresponds roughly to Aristotle's formal cause. It generates the form of the effect. It does not belong to substances, but only to qualities and activities. For instance, the qualities (*guṇas*) of the parts of the pot and their activities (*karmas*) like coming together and sticking together cause the form of the pot. It is called the non-inherent cause, because the effect pot does not inhere in the qualities and activities of the parts, but only in the parts as substances.[47] The *third* type is every other kind of immediate, invariable antecedent except those present in every instance of causation. It is called the occasioning cause (*nimitta-kāraṇa*). Under it are included the efficient cause (the potter), the instrumental cause (his stick meant to turn the wheel), and the purpose for which the object is made (holding water). Although the Naiyāyikas do not give a separate place to the instrumental cause, they have a separate technical term, *kāraṇa*, for it. The instrumental cause (*kāraṇa*) is defined[48] as the cause (*kāraṇa*) through the activity (*vyāpāra*) of which the effect is produced and which is an extra-ordinary (*asādhāraṇa*) cause. The ordinary causes of the pot are the clay, the combination of the parts of the pot which are made separately and the potter. Water, etc., are taken for granted in the material cause. The extra-ordinary cause is, for example, the stick to which the act of turning the wheel belongs. So the stick is an instrumental cause. Similarly, the axe is the instrumental cause for felling a tree and the contact of the axe with the tree is its activity (*vyāpāra*). Activity (*vyāpāra*), in the context of the problem of causation, is defined[49] as that which is born of a cause, but which is also a cause of the effect of its own cause. For instance, the act of felling the tree belongs to or is born of the axe that fells the tree, but the act also is a cause of felling the tree.

We may say that the Naiyāyikas accepted all the kinds of cause which Aristotle accepted, but divided them into three main kinds. Aristotle's final cause is included in the third, but may be included in the second also, for the form of an effect is determined by the purpose for which it is meant.

FALLACIES It has already been indicated that the Naiyāyika interest in logic is for finding out the truth about the existent world, but not merely for finding out the instruments of thought for their own sake. So logic was not formalized and divorced from existence. The fallacies in which the Naiyāyikas were interested were fallacies of the wrong application of the structure of inference and appear as though they are all material fallacies.[50] Indeed, these logicians knew most of the formal fallacies, but made no distinction between them and the material. The forms of controversy in which equivocation (*chala*), futile argument (*jāti*), and many of the grounds of defeat are found can in most cases come under formal fallacies. But the Naiyāyikas did not care to explain how the formal rules are violated in them. The Sanskrit term translated as fallacy is *hetvābhāsā*, which means the false appearance of reason or a false reason or middle term. The Naiyāyika analysis of fallacy is based upon their conception of reason, which is the middle term in the major premise. So some of the fallacies they classify can be shown to be formal fallacies also.

We have seen the four conditions required for a true major premise. The Naiyāyikas lay down five conditions for a true middle term. They are: (1) It must be found in the minor term (*pakṣavṛttitvam*). (2) It must be found in all similar instances (*sapakṣe sattvam*). That is, smoke must be found in all the kitchens, observing which we frame the premise, "Wherever there is smoke, there is fire". If in any kitchen we observe smoke without fire, then smoke cannot be the reason or middle term. (3) It should not be found anywhere where fire is not found (*vipakṣe asattvam*). That is, the middle term should be absent, where the major is absent. (4) The minor term in which it is said to exist should not be impossible (*abādhitattvam*). This condition looks like a material condition, not a formal condition. However, since the function of the middle term is to connect the minor and the major, if the minor is impossible and non-existent, then the middle term ceases to be a middle term as it has nothing with which to connect the major.[51] (5) It should exist in a minor term in which another middle term in necessary relation with the contradictory of the major term is not present. Suppose *A* has two qualities *M* and *N*, and *X* is found wherever *M* is found and the opposite of *X* or non-*X* is found wherever *N* is found. In that case, *M* cannot be the reason for inferring *X*, or *N* for inferring non-*X*. The situation shows that our observation is still incomplete and we have no true middle term. This condition is mainly material, but has formal significance also.

The fallacies are based on the above five conditions. (1) The *first* fallacy is called the indeterminate middle (*anekāntika*, also called *savyabhicāra*). This fallacy prevents us from obtaining a valid major premise. It is of three kinds. (a) An inference is fallacious if the middle term is found to be common to both the major term and its opposite (*sādhāraṇa*). If we infer: "Socrates is a man, because he is mortal," we commit this fallacy; for mortality is found where man-ness is found and also where it is absent. In the Aristotelian form, it will be

All men are mortal;
Socrates is mortal;
Therefore, Socrates is a man.

This will be a formal fallacy of undistributed middle. If we write

All mortals are men;
Socrates is a mortal;
Therefore, Socrates is a man;

then we may call it a material fallacy. But the Naiyāyikas were interested only in pointing out that the middle term is false, may the fallacy be material or formal. Yet the middle term is false because of the violation of a formal condition of its validity.

(b) An inference is false when the minor term has nothing similar to it (no *sapakṣa*) and nothing dissimilar to it (no *vipakṣa)*. Such an inference violates the second and third conditions of the true middle term and cannot give us a major premise or a universal relationship between a middle and major. This seems to be a significant fallacy, the full significance of which is perhaps not noticed by the Naiyāyikas themselves. If I argue

Every thinkable is nameable,
Because it is thinkable,

I commit this fallacy. Here the minor term is "the thinkable" and includes everything I can think of. And I cannot point to anything that is not thinkable. That is, there can be no inference where the minor and middle terms are the same. Another example is: Socrates is mortal, because Socrates is Socrates. This fallacy is called the extra-ordinary (*asādhāraṇa*), because the middle term does not belong to anything else than the present minor term.[52] The definition of this fallacy shows that the Naiyāyikas had at the back of their minds that tautology is no inference. (c) The third is called the inconclusive (*anupasamhārī*) middle, and is committed when the major term is all-pervasive. If I infer: Everything is nameable because it is knowable, there is nothing that is not nameable and I cannot find a place where, because of the absence of the major term, the middle term also is absent. Here the middle term also is all-inclusive. But we can have instances in which the middle term is not all-inclusive. In

> Every physical object is spatial;
> Socrates is a physical object;
> Therefore, Socrates is spatial;

spatiality is all-pervasive and there is nothing in the world that is not spatial. But men are not everything in the world. Even then, this inference is not considered to be valid. Instead of calling it insignificant, the Naiyāyikas call it invalid. What this fallacy means to signify is that what pertains to everything, viz., spatiality need not be proved. Such is the view of the earlier school of the Naiyāyikas. But Viśvanātha says[53] that such an inference may be allowed and is not fallacious.

(2) The *second* main kind of fallacy is that of the contradictory middle (*viruddha*). This does not refer to the inference in which the middle term is found both where the major is found and where it is not found; it is that in which the middle is found only where the major is absent. The middle can be the reason only for the absence of the major term. If I infer the immortality of Socrates from the fact that he is dead, I commit this fallacy. This fallacy affects the validity of the major premise and is a material one.[54] But it can be turned into a formal one also. For instance, we can change the inference into the form,

> The immortals are not those-who-die;
> Socrates is one who-died;
> Therefore, Socrates is immortal.

This fallacy can be expressed in other forms also and it can be shown that what appears to be a formal fallacy can be a material one and vice versa. Ultimately, the fallacy is due to a false middle term. One should hesitate to dismiss the fallacies given by the Nyāya as merely material; for they often rest on the violations of the formal conditions of the valid middle term or reason. The formal fallacies of Aristotle are based on the violations of the formal structure of the whole syllogism.

(3) The *third* fallacy is called the unproved middle (*asiddha* or the unproved, *sādhvasama* or equal to the *probandum*). The middle term has to be that accepted by both the parties as necessarily related to the major term in the minor. But if the middle term itself has to be proved, it cannot function as a reason. Such a middle is unestablished and cannot be accepted. It is of three kinds. (a) The middle term is unacceptable, if the minor term is impossible (*āśrayāsiddhi*); for it cannot be accepted as a characteristic of the minor. For instance, there is a mythological flower, often

found in Indian poetry also, called the sky-lotus.[55] So I may infer: "The sky-lotus is fragrant, because it is a lotus." The Aristotelian form can be

All lotuses are fragrant;
The sky-lotus is a lotus;
Therefore, the sky-lotus is fragrant.

But the sky-lotus is an unreal object and so the inference is fallacious. From the point of view of Aristotelian logic, it is a material fallacy. But what is the formal definition of the minor term? It must be that in which the middle term is present. Similarly, one of the formal conditions of the middle term is that it must be present in the minor (*pakṣa*). But here both conditions are violated. The distinction between formal and material fallacies depends on what we mean by formal conditions.[56]

(b) The second kind of the unproved middle is found where the minor and the middle are contraries (*svarūpāsiddhi*). Here the minor and middle terms are real, but by nature they are never related positively. In the inference, "The lake is a substance, because it has smoke", this fallacy is committed. Smoke, the middle term, can never exist in the lake. Here also one of the formal conditions of the middle and minor terms is violated.

(c) The third kind is found in cases in which the whole or part of the middle term is found where the major term is not found (*vyāpyatvāsiddhi*). In the inference, "The mountain has smoke, because it has fire", fire is found in some places where smoke is not found. Here the whole of the middle term fire is found where smoke is not found. But in "The mountain has fire, because it has bluish smoke", although fire is always found where smoke is found, it is not found wherever the colour blue is found. As it is immaterial whether or not smoke is blue or black, the colour of smoke should be omitted from the middle term. Really, the fallacy in the second example is one of superfluity (*gaurava*).

(4) The fourth main kind of fallacy is that in which the middle term attempts to prove something in the minor in which the opposite can be proved by another middle. Such a middle term is called the contradicted-minor (*satpratipakṣa*). In the same minor term, two different middle terms (reasons) can prove the presence of contradictory majors. Neither of the middle terms then can be valid. Such cases lead only to doubt and further enquiry. All arguments like those for the existence of God come under this class. The classical arguments are

(1) Sound is eternal, because it is an audible quality;[57]
Whatever is not an audible quality is not eternal, like colour.

(2) Sound is not eternal, because it is an effect;[58]
Whatever is an effect is not eternal, like the pot.

(5) The fifth type of fallacy is that in which the major term, that is already contradicted is the *probandum*. In fallacy (4) one syllogism contradicts another, and one middle term proves the opposite of what the other middle term proves. But here the contradictory of the major term is already accepted as belonging to the minor term (*pakṣa*) and so the middle cannot prove the existence of the major in the minor. In the inference

Fire is cold, because it is white;
Whatever is white is cold, like ice.

the opposite of cold, viz., hot, is accepted as the property of fire by perception itself.

COMPARISON Comparison (*upamāna*) is accepted by the Naiyāyikas as a distinct means of valid cognition. But while for the Mīmāmsakas it is the cognition of similarity between an object seen in the past and an object seen now, for the Naiyāyikas it is the cognition of the new object through similarity known by another means of cognition, e.g., through the oral information of a friend. An American may be told by his friend that the Asian buffalo is like the bison in such and such respects. When the American goes to Asia and sees the buffalo, he says: "That is a buffalo". This cognition is mediated by the known similarities. As mentioned already, the Mīmāmsakas do not accept this version of comparison as a distinct means of knowledge, in which the similarity is known through verbal knowledge. In this instance, when the American sees the buffalo, he perceives an object and *recognizes* it as a buffalo. Hence, it is only a combination of verbal knowledge, perception, recognition, and even inference. The inference can be of the form,

All animals with such and such features are either bisons or buffalos;
This animal has those features and it is not a bison;
Therefore, it is a buffalo.

But what is of importance in comparison is the cognition of similarity itself, which is already given by the American's friend. But how did this friend come to know the similarity? The way he cognized the similarity is the true distinct way of cognition. Hence, the Mīmāmsakas reject the Nyāya version. Those who do not accept comparison as a distinct way of cognition either in the Mīmāmsā or in the Nyāya interpretation maintain that it is a combination of perception, etc. The cognition of similarity also may be regarded as the perception of identical characteristics in different objects. The perception of the same characteristic in a second object is recognition, which is a combination of perception and memory.

VERBAL KNOWLEDGE Like the Mīmāmsakas and, to a great extent, following them, the Naiyāyikas gave much attention to cognition obtained through words and sentences, and thus to semantics.[59] Regarding the meaning of words, while the Mīmāmsakas held that the word means primarily the universal (*jāti*), the Naiyāyikas maintained that it means the universal, the structure (*samsthāna*) that goes with the universal, and also the individual. Otherwise, if we ask a man to bring a cow, he will not be able to understand that he has to bring an individual cow. He brings the animal because he understands by the word an individual object characterized by a particular structure (*samsthāna*) and a particular universal (*jāti*), cow-ness. The meaning of the word is grasped in several ways:[60] (1) from grammar, as for instance we know the subject of a sentence from the rules of declension or, as in English, from the placement of the noun; (2) from similarity, as when an American is told that a buffalo is like the bison; (3) from lexicons; (4) from the information of a reliable person (*āpta*), as when we are told that "cavalry" means horse-men in the army; (5)

from practice (*vyavahāra*), as when we understand what "church-service" means by observing the process; (6) from the rest of the sentence in which the word occurs, i.e., from the context, as when we hear: "The captain ordered his infantry to march", we do not understand the captain of a football team; (7) from the explanations (glossaries) of difficult terms; and (8) from nearness to a significant word, as when we hear of "The philosopher's inclination", we understand a mental attitude, but not a physical sloping.

The way a child first learns the meanings of words are generally (4) and (5). An elder brother or sister or parent utters the word "duck", pointing to the bird, and the child learns the meaning of the word. It hears also its mother telling the elder brother: "Bring that glass," observes him going through the act of bringing, and understands what "bringing a glass" means. The Naiyāyikas do not accept Prabhākara's view that the child learns the meanings of words only when associated with action; nor do they accept the doctrine that words have meanings only when they have become parts of complete sentence. The words are understood separately and their meanings are combined after hearing the sentence. The Naiyāyika view is called the doctrine of the relation of the meanings of uttered words (*abhihitānvayavāda*), as against Prabhākara's view, which is called the doctrine of the uttering of words, the meanings of which have already been related (*anvitābhidhānavāda*). The latter view has already been discussed in the chapter on the Mīmāmsā.

Can we rely on knowledge obtained by words as much as on that obtained from our own perceptions and inference? If someone says: "The sun fell on the earth on the 14th March 1963," I cognize the meaning of his words and know what he says. But I do not accept their truth. Hence arises the question of the validity[61] of verbal knowledge. The Naiyāyikas, like all the others who accept this kind of cognition, say that the words must be words of one who is interested in our welfare and is trustworthy. The child trusts the persons who teach it language. The most trustworthy of all persons is God, who composed the Vedic scriptures. Since God composed them, they are absolutely true and reliable. Other persons are reliable to a degree. Some of them may be ignorant, even our parents may be ignorant of other worldly truths; and others may like to deceive us. Accordingly, the Naiyāyikas classify words in two ways. According to one classification, words are divided into those that are of the world (*laukika*) and those that belong to the Veda (*vaidika*). The words of the Veda, being the words of God himself, are absolutely trustworthy. Their meanings are fixed by God and are, therefore, not conventional. While the Mīmāmsakas held that the Vedas are not composed by anyone, not even by God, and are eternal, the Naiyāyikas maintained that God is the author of the Vedas and that they are eternal in the sense that their composer is eternal. The words of the conventional language are not always trustworthy because the conventions are created by ordinary people. However, often the words of the Veda and those of the conventional languages are mixed up in popular usage.

The second classification is that which differentiates words meaning perceivable objects like trees and mountains and those meaning imperceptible realities like God, merit and demerit. About words meaning perceptible and imperceptible objects, the Vedas are always trustworthy. But we trust also prophets and scientists, who speak of the will of God and atomic energy. Regarding perceivable objects, we trust not only the Vedas, prophets, and scientists, but also persons interested in our welfare.

Like many other thinkers, the Naiyāyikas believe that words are not mere sounds, but sounds that have an ability, power (*śakti*) to mean objects. But they do not accept power, force, or energy as a separate category of reality, saying that it is only a property of words and comes under quality. In this respect, they differ from Kumārila. The older Naiyāyikas believed that the power of words to mean was the desire of God (*īśvarecchārūpa*).[62] But the Neo-Naiyāyikas say that, as some words are conventional, this power is the desire of anybody (*icchāmātram*), God or man, that a word should have a particular meaning.[63] The meaning of words is of four kinds. The *first* is the meaning obtained from the word or its parts directly (*yaugika*). The meaning of the word "container" is obtained from the meanings of "contain" and "er". Similar words are "cooker", "school-master", etc. The *second* is the meaning obtained not by combining the meaning of parts, but from the word as a whole (*rūdha*). For instance, the word "shepherd" means one who herds sheep. It is a combination of "sheep" and "herd". But it does not refer to the sheep or the herd, but the man who herds the sheep. Here the meaning of the parts is suppressed or is only implied and the meaning of the whole word is fixed. The *third* is that in which the combined meanings of the parts coincide with the fixed meaning (*yogarūḍha*). For instance, the word "premier" means the prime minister. But according to its parts, it means that which is the first. The prime minister is the first of the ministers. Here the fixed meaning and the meanings of the parts of the word coincide. The *fourth* kind refers to the two meanings which a word may have, one of which is obtained by combining the meanings of its parts, and the other being fixed independently in some particular sense. For instance, the word "Moravian" means any person belonging to the country of Moravia. This meaning is derived from the parts of the word. But the word may also mean a particular, Christian, Protestant sect: this meaning is conventionally fixed. A man belonging to that sect may be a citizen of any country.

All the above kinds of meaning are more or less literal meanings. Besides them, there are unexpressed, intended meanings (*lakṣaṇas*) of words as in "He is a lion on the battle-field" and "The village is on the river". The word "lion" in the first sentence and "on" in the second cannot be understood literally. We have to take only their intended meanings. But we cannot use any and every word to convey our intended meanings. If we use the word "sheep" instead of the word "lion", we convey quite the opposite meaning. The meaning we intend must, therefore, be related to the literal meaning of the word used. The lion is related in our experience with courage and fearlessness. So intended-ness (*lakṣaṇā*) is defined as the relation of a word to a meaning which is itself related to the literal meaning of the word.[64] In the second sentence, the word "on" means "on the banks of" or "at" or "by".

A sentence is a group of words fulfiling certain conditions. Each word is a combination of letters and syllables, and has its own meaning. But the sentence as a whole also has its own meaning based upon the meanings and order of words. According to the Naiyāyikas,[65] a sentence, in order to have a meaning, must fulfil four conditions. (1) The words whose meanings are to be related (*anvita*) should be uttered together (*āsatti*). Instead of saying: "He walked, leading the child", if we say: "He the leading child walked" or "He, I went there, walked, the boys are fighting, leading, the school is open, the, there is no king of France, child", although the same words are uttered in the first variation and occur also in the second, we cannot get the meaning. (2) The meanings of the words uttered must have mutual fitness or suitability (*yogyatā*). Sentences like "Virtue is a triangle" and "Wash the clothes with fire" cannot be meaningful. What is meant is that they are not significant and that the hearer cannot make out their sense. Virtue does not fit any geometrical figure and fire burns the clothes, but does not wash them. (3) The meaning of every word of the sentence must be capable of anticipating the meanings of the other words (*ākānkṣā*). If I say merely: "Goes" the hearer anticipates my answering his questions: "Who goes?", "Where does he go?", "From where does he go?", etc. And the answers given by me must be capable of meeting the anticipation. Without answers to these questions, the meaning of the sentence cannot be complete. Indeed, in many of the sentences descriptive words are often introduced by the speaker, even without which the meaning of the sentence can be complete. What the Naiyāyikas, for instance, mean is that, in case the verb is transitive, there should be an object also. Each part of the sentence anticipates others and what is anticipated must be significant. (4) The meaning of the sentence should convey the intention of the speaker (*tātparya*). For instance, the word "game" means not only those games like football played by people, but also birds and animals protected and hunted by sportsmen. When someone says: "There is excellent game in that reserve", we understand animal and bird life. If we take the other meaning of "game", the sentence becomes meaningless or insignificant. This fourth condition is called a condition, because, if the speaker's intention is not known by the hearer, the latter cannot know what the former wishes to say and will be left undecided and in doubt. After all, communication is to convey a full meaning, and the purpose is not fulfilled if the hearer is left in doubt and confusion. If one says: "Put down the racket", one may have the tennis bat or the racketeers in mind. We generally understand his meaning from the context. Wherever we fail to understand his intention, we cannot understand the meaning of his sentence and remain undecided (without *vyavsāya*).

VALIDITY OF COGNITION According to the Naiyāyikas,[66] cognition is neither valid nor invalid by itself, but is made valid or invalid by the proper or improper functioning of the instruments of cognition. Cognition, according to this school, is consciousness that arises adventitiously like a spark when mind (*manas*) comes into contact with the *ātman*. If this consciousness is by itself valid and, being consciousness, knows its own validity, there can be no possibility[67] of doubt about the truth of any cognition. But that there is often doubt shows that cognition is not by itself valid (*paratah prāmāṇyam*). So the Naiyāyikas reject the Mīmāmsaka view that cognition is by itself valid. For the same reason, they reject the Buddhist view that cognition is by itself invalid. For if every cognition is by itself invalid and knows its invalidity, there can be no doubt about its validity or invalidity. So validity must be due to something else than cognition (*paratah aprāmāṇyam*). When we perceive an object, both mind and senses operate. If mind is distorted through fear, etc., or senses are defective as when a man suffers from jaundice, we see a distorted or false object. Consciousness itself has nothing to do with distortions and defects. But when mind is unperturbed and senses are healthy, the object is seen as it is (*yathārtha*). Similarly, the media of perception, as in the refraction of light, may lead to illusory perceptions.

If the media are normal, we see the object as it is. In this case also, cognition is made valid or invalid by something other than cognition.

But how can we know whether or not the object is true or false? Here the Naiyāyikas take the help of the same pragmatic criterion (*arthakriyā-karitā*) resorted to by the other schools. The world is created by God as a result of our actions (*karmas*) and for future actions. So although the world has a reality independent of our minds, every object is meant to serve some purpose. We can always test whether the object serves the purpose for which it is meant. If it does, we say: it is a true object; otherwise, a false object. Accordingly, our cognitions can be declared to be true or false. Besides, the pragmatic test, which the constitution of the world, which is a world of action, allows, the test of coherence,[68] or consistency (*samvāda*, agreement) is also accepted. Consistency can be observed not only between two cognitions of the same object, but also between a cognition of the object and the action to which the object leads. But the Naiyāyikas give greater importance to the pragmatic criterion than to coherence.

THE OBJECT OF ILLUSION As realists, the Naiyāyikas maintain that the object of illusion exists, but that it is seen in the form (*prakāra*)[69] of something else. In the classical example of the illusion of the rope as the snake, I say: "That is a snake", although it is really a rope. "That is a snake" means "That is a member of the class of snakes" or "That is an object determined by the universal snake-ness." As the Naiyāyikas accept the reality of universals, both interpretations hold true and the first interpretation is true because of the second. Then "That is a snake" is false because of the misplacement of the universal snake-ness in the individual rope. To express the same idea in a different language, illusion lies in wrong classification. In it, all the factors are real—the That is real, the rope is real, and snake-ness also is real, as it exists in a large number of snakes. Only the relation between the individual in front and the universal snake-ness is false. So the cognition of the illusory object is the cognition of one thing in the form of another (*anyathākhyāti*).[70]

The Nyāya view differs from that of Kumārila; for the latter says that the rope in illusion is seen as some individual snake seen in the past and remembered now. Illusion lies in seeing one object as another object, but not in seeing it in the form (*prakāra*) of another object. But the Naiyāyikas contend that the remembered snake cannot be the illusory snake, because the two need not be of the same length, thickness and shape. So what is wrongly present in illusion must be the universal snake-ness, which fits any length, thickness and shape. But Kumārila says that a real universal can exist only in real individuals and snake-ness cannot, therefore, exist in the rope as its determinant (*avacchedaka*). Then it must exist in front separately from the rope in order to be perceived. The illusory snake is observed in space and time; but no universal can be observed in space and time apart from its individuals.[71] We have, therefore, to accept that the rope is mistaken for an individual snake.[72]

4. METAPHYSICS

It has already been said that the metaphysics of the Nyāya school got merged with that of the Vaiśeṣika, as the latter's categoreal classification is more clear than that of the former, and that the Vaiśeṣika in its turn accepted the Nyāya epistemology. There are indeed a few differences, which are of minor importance and so ignored; and the two schools are sometimes treated together as Nyāya-Vaiśeṣika. Further, the Neo-Nyāya grew out of the merger, differing from both on some important points, and will be presented in this work along with the Vaiśeṣika. The whole metaphysics of Gautama, as he conceived it, is given by him practically under the second of the sixteen categories, viz., the knowable. Gautama uses the term "knowable"[73] in the axiological sense of what ought to be known for the sake of knowing the truth about the world and for salvation. The knowable is what ought to be known (*meya*) through exact measurement (*māna*), the exact measures being epistemological instruments. Indeed, Gautama explains how we can know the knowable in the sense of what can be known, e.g., number and the relation of contact (*samyoga-sambandha*). But such knowables are of secondary importance. The important knowables (*prameyas*) are twelve in number—the *ātman*, physical body, senses, objects (of the world surrounding us), cognition (consciousness), mind, activity (*pravṛtti*), imperfection (*doṣa*, defect), life after death (*pretyabhāva*, including rebirth), result (*phala*, fruit of actions), pain (*duhkha*, misery), and final liberation (*apavarga*).

THE ĀTMAN We have already given much about the nature of the *ātman*. According to some Naiyāyikas, it is perceived by mind; and according to the others, it is inferred from the existence of desire, hate, effort, pleasure, pain, and consciousness (*jñāna*). As these six are qualities, there must be a substance to which they belong and that substance is the *ātman*.[74] The body cannot be the *ātman*; for after death the body exists, but the *ātman* cannot be found. It is the basis of the ego[75] (*ahaṁkāra*); and the dead body does not say: "I am here." The senses cannot be the *ātman*; for when a sense is destroyed, who is it that remembers[76] that sense-experience? If the sense were the *ātman*, there could be no memory in such cases. But there is such memory. Mind (*manas*) also cannot be the *ātman*; for consciousness, etc., cannot then be claimed as "mine" by anybody (*anadhyakṣam*). I direct my mind this or that way, if I am the same as my mind, then there can be no director of mind. But I experience that I am the director and controller of my mind. Besides, according to the Nyāya, mind is atomic; so pains and pleasures, which are not atomic, cannot belong to mind. They must, therefore, belong to the *ātman*, which is infinite (*vibhu*). The Naiyāyikas do not accept either the Vijñānavāda view that the *ātman* is the same as a series of momentary consciousnesses or the Advaita view that it is the same as eternal consciousness, but contend that it is different from consciousness, which is transient, although not momentary, and that, as so different, it is by itself unconscious. They do not accept also the contention of the Advaita that the *ātman* is the same as the Brahman and that ultimately there is but only one Ātman. They maintain that the *ātmans* constitute an infinite plurality and that each *ātman* is the knower, doer, enjoyer, and sufferer. God is one of the *ātmans*, but the greatest of them. Although the other *ātmans* are by nature unconscious,[77] God is by nature conscious and his consciousness is eternal and infinite.[78]

GOD Most of the Vedāntins accept that God is the material cause also of the world. But Gautama rejects[79] this view and says that God is only the efficient cause. The material causes are the eternal atoms, etc., which are brought together by God in accordance with the ethical merit and demerit of the *ātmans*. The Naiyāyikas advance four main arguments for the existence of God. (1) The *first* may be called the causal argument. The world consists of composite objects. Every composite object consists of parts and is the result of bringing the parts together. The world is made up of an infinite number of such composite parts brought together according to a plan that agrees with the ethical merit and demerit of the souls. Such a work and plan implies an infinitely intelligent agent as the cause, who is God himself. Besides, for bringing the parts together, one has to start with atoms, which are imperceptible to ordinary beings. It must be, therefore, an infinite intelligence that can bring the atoms together to build up the world. This causal argument is actually a combination of the western causal and teleological arguments. (2) The *second* argument may be called the moral argument.[80] Ethical merit and demerit, according to the Nyāya, are unconscious, blind qualities (*guṇas.*) of the *ātmans*. They are not spontaneous forces (*śaktis*), as they are for the Mīmāmsā. As the *ātmans* are infinite in number and the activities are for each many, an infinite intelligence is needed to guide the creation of the world so that the *ātmans* may receive just rewards and punishments, i.e., pleasures and pains, for their actions. (3) The *third* argument is based upon the authoritativeness of the Vedic scriptures. Every book must have an author. So even the Vedas must have an author.[81] The Vedic scriptures are absolutely valid and teach us truths both about the sensible and supersensible worlds. So the Vedas could not have been composed by an ordinary intelligence, which cannot have adequate knowledge of the supersensible world. Hence, the author of the Vedas must be an infinite intelligence, which is God. (4) The *fourth* argument is based upon Vedic testimony. The Vedas are absolutely reliable and say that God, as the creator of the world, exists. We have, therefore, to accept his existence. The third and the fourth arguments are generally directed against the Advaita, the Sāṅkhya, and the early Mīmāmsā and the first and the second against the Cārvāka, Jainism, Buddhism, and even the Mīmāmsā. In the history of Indian thought, every argument has been refuted; even Rāmānuja, who is a strong theist, does not accept any argument. And we can see also the circularity of reasoning between the third and the fourth arguments: the Veda is absolutely reliable because its author is the omniscient God; but God is omniscient because the Veda is absolutely reliable.

In developing the third argument, the Naiyāyikas advanced the doctrine that sound and so the word cannot be eternal,[82] thereby differing from the Mīmāmsakas. The letter and the word are born when I utter them and then they die. Such is our direct experience. The Vedas, as consisting of words and sentences, are, therefore, not eternal. What we mean by the eternity of the Vedas is the eternity of the truths they teach and of God, as their author. At every creation God composes the Vedas and transmits them to the seers. At every dissolution of the world, the Vedas also disappear. The Naiyāyikas accept that God repeatedly creates, maintains, and destroys the world. As we have seen already, the Mīmāmsakas say that the world was never created and will never be destroyed. So God, as the creator of the world, is unnecessary. The Vedas, as consisting of words and sentences, are also eternal. When two people utter the word "man", they utter the same word, but not two different words. The same word can be uttered at different times and by different persons for centuries. If it is not eternal, it cannot be uttered by many men and many times. We should note that, at the time when the controversy between the Mīmāmsakas and the Naiyāyikas first took place, there were no written books and the Vedas were transmitted orally from teacher to pupil. The Naiyāyikas say that the sameness of the words is due to the similarity of the letters composing them, and the sameness of letters is due to the universal present in them. For instance, when different people utter the letter B, the universal "B-ness" is present in each.[83]

OTHER KNOWABLES Of the other knowables, body is the substratum (basis, *āśraya*) of exertion (*ceṣṭā*), senses, and objectives (*arthas*). Exertion belongs to the physical body, but effort (*prayatna*) to the *ātman*. The distinction between the two is that between the physical and psychological. However, effort is the cause of exertion.[84] The objectives are pain and pleasure. The senses are: nose, tongue, eye, skin, and ear. Their material causes are the five elements: earth, water, fire, air and ether. Smell, taste, vision, touch, and audition are the peculiar functions and properties of the five elements respectively and the five elements are the respective objects (*arthas, viṣayas*) of the five senses.[85] Consciousness is the same as cognition, knowledge, comprehension[86] (*buddhi, upalabdhi, jñāna*). Mind is atomic and is responsible for the simultaneous cognition through all the senses. Activity (*pravṛtti*) is one of two[87] kinds: activity as cause and activity as effect. Activity as cause is that which starts the movement of speech, cognition, and the body with its parts. As effect, it is ethical merit and demerit. Imperfections[88] (*doṣas*) are all those that are the root causes of activity (*pravṛtti*). They are mainly of three kinds: attachment (*rāga*), infatuation (*moha*), and hate (*dveṣa*). Life after death (*pretyabhāva*)[89] is rebirth. Fruit[90] (*phala*, result) is whatever is the result of action. It is of two kinds, pain and pleasure. Pain is what troubles us. Absolute freedom from pain is liberation (*apavarga*).[91]

5. LIFE'S IDEAL

The Nyāya and the Vaiśeṣika philosophies do not present an alluring kind of the deal of life. After recommending an intensive logical and metaphysical training, and in spite of teaching that the world of action is not ultimately desirable and salvation is the highest ideal of life, they present the state of salvation as one devoid of all consciousness like the state of existence of a stone. The early Mīmāmsakas have at least the merit of asserting that there is nothing in reality called salvation and that life is and has to be always a life of action. But the Nyāya and the Vaiśeṣika strongly recommend salvation, and yet present it as dark existence without the light of consciousness. They contend that it is yet a state of happiness not because there is any consciousness to know the state, but because, as there is no consciousness, there can be no experience of misery. In the controversy they carry on with rival schools, they contend that bliss or happiness is only absence of misery, thus treating happiness as only a negative state. They refuse to accept that there can be a neutral state devoid of both misery and happiness, which may be either conscious or unconscious. Their metaphysical basis for this ideal of life is that, so long as the *ātman* is in contact with mind and mind has the possibility of coming into such contact, senses, body, and activity (*pravṛtti*) cannot be transcended; and salvation lies, therefore, in the *ātman* freeing itself from such contact and its possibility. They accept that the *ātman* identifies itself with mind, senses and body, but that such identification is an illusion (*bhrama*).[92]

Knowledge or consciousness (*buddhi*) is finally meant to discover the truth about this identification. It is not merely theoretical knowledge that is necessary for liberation, but also performing all the duties required and prescribed by the Vedas and the ethical codes (*smṛtis*). In fact, the Nyāya, as ethics and religion, did not satisfy even its own followers, who adopted Śaivism as their religion, accepting its philosophy as their philosophy of life. The greatest value of the Nyāya lies in its contributions to logic, methodology, and epistemology. There is practically none in India who follows this school as a philosophy of life. But every student of philosophy studies it for its logic and epistemology. It is prescribed as a necessary subsidiary to the study of the Veda.

GENERAL ESTIMATE AND CONSTRUCTIVE COMMENT

(i) LOGIC NOT WITHOUT METAPHYSICS

Although logic was present in India before Gautama and was regarded as an essential subsidiary to the study of the Vedas—which was the main subject of study at that time—one has to acknowledge the great contribution made by him in his attempt to establish it on solid foundations. We, particularly the western logicians and orientalists, have to remember that logic was developed by Gautama in the context of active controversy—it was not arm-chair logical analysis—and the controversy had the seriousness and earnestness of the discovery of the aim of life and the way of achieving it. Had the Buddhists been more sympathetic to the Nyāya than they actually were, they would have classified it under right views (*samyak dṛṣṭi*) which is one of the eight limbs of the way to salvation. But salvation or no salvation, even the Mimāmsakas insisted on the necessity of logic for the study of the Vedas. But they seem to be more concerned with interpretation of texts than with articulating the structure of argument and fallacies.

But controversy—in fact all logic, if it is to have ultimate validity—has to assume a world of a plurality [93] of thinkables and nameables the reality or unreality of which can be in question. So Gautama assumed the reality of a pluralistic universe, the nature of which he did not discuss in as much detail as the Vaiśeṣika of Kaṇāda did, but concerned himself mainly with logic and epistemology. However, for some reasons, perhaps because of the tradition to which he belonged at the time, he had assumptions which are not essential to his logic and epistemology, and may even be conflicting with his theories, for instance, the doctrine that the *ātman* is by nature unconscious and that mind (*manas*) is atomic in size.

Since Gautama was more interested in logic and epistemology than in metaphysics, we shall discuss mainly the Nyāya-Vaiśeṣika logic and epistemology in this estimate of the Nyāya and its metaphysics in the estimate of the Vaiśeṣika. It is really difficult to separate completely metaphysics from logic and epistemology and there will surely be overlappings in our discussion. The division is, therefore, one of convenience.

In one of the conference in Hawaii, when I repeated Iśvarakṛṣṇa's statement that what can be known (cognized, *prameya*) depends on the means of cognition (*pramāṇa*),[94] it was misunderstood by some members in the Kantian and Hegelian sense of deriving the categories of reality from an analysis of the cognitive processes. Such was not the meaning of Gautama and Kaṇāda, not even of Iśvarakṛṣṇa. What they meant was that any reality, seen or unseen, has to be established by a valid means of cognition. But the implications of the structure of any kind of cognition must not come into conflict with the metaphysical doctrines accepted. So when we examine Gautama's logic and epistemology, we may ask questions such as: Is each doctrine self-consistent? Are they consistent with one another? Are they consistent with the accepted metaphysics? Are they acceptable to reality? In fact, Gautama does not claim that his logic is without metaphysics; his logic is purposely aimed by him to establish a doctrine of reality and is based on such a doctrine.

The very doctrines of his logic and epistemology reject the view that there can be logic without metaphysics or without assuming that anything exists, a view made popular by Bertrand Russell. It is extremely doubtful whether Raghunātha ever intended his logic to be indifferent to metaphysics,[95] whatever his recent followers do. We shall see the way his thought was marching. In Gautama's view, for instance, the counter-factual conditional (*tarka*) is not regarded as inference (*anumāna*) or as a major premise (*vyāptī*), because it is merely negative and is based upon a categorical universal judgment, which is affirmative (existential also in Gautama's sense). The counter-factual conditional by itself is, for him, not even a valid means (*pramāṇa*) of cognition. Secondly, the relation between the minor and the major terms in the major premise has to be a necessary relation; and one of the necessary relations is the causal relation, which is more than a hypothetical relation. Species-genus relation and member-class relation are necessary by implication. That is, if every species of the genus *X* is *P*, then this species *S* also is *P*; and if every member of the class *C* is *P*, then this member *S* is also *P*. One will perhaps say that inference of this type, which is purely formal and hypothetical, need not have any reference at all, implicit or overt, to existence. But the Nyāya insists that the minor term, the species (and in the case of class-membership inference, the member) must exist; otherwise, the inference is fallacious. The fallacy here is called the fallacy of the impossible minor (*bādhita-pakṣa*, opposed to *abādhitatvam*). For instance,

Animals with horn gore their enemies;
The hare is an animal with horns;
So the hare with horns gores its enemies;

is invalid because no hare with horns exists. Similarly, reason or middle term must also exist. This fallacy is of several kinds, but one of them occurs when the reason does not exist in an existent minor. Again, the reason given must be an existent reason, which is generally described as that accepted as true and real by both parties. For example,

Ghosts with five feet attack men;
X is a ghost with five feet;
Therefore, *X* attacks men;

is fallacious because there are no ghosts with five feet, accepted by all.

One will perhaps say that formal logic is concerned with only the formal structure of inference and is based on the principles of contradiction and the excluded[96] middle. But neither Gautama nor any of his followers including those of the Neo-logic was concerned with such pure formal logic; and turning their logic into pure formal logic may even misrepresent them. We may ask: If *X*, *Y*, and – *Y* have no reference to existence, why should a mere proposition, "*X* is both *Y* and – *Y*" be false? *Firstly*, we say that anything that has contradictory predicates cannot exist and is, therefore, false. This statement implies that if *X* does not exist and is, therefore, false, it can have contradictory predicates. Then if *X* has no reference to existence and is indifferent to it, *X* can have contradictory predicates. So reference to existence is necessary for logic. But this existence cannot be the existence in my mind and thought. It cannot be the existence of ideas or images. For in fact, contradictory propositions do exist in my mind and thought and are not impossible to make. They are impossible only as referring to the common existing world. *Secondly*, if logic is indifferent to existence, how can we assume that there is a –*Y*, which is the opposite of *Y*, its contradictory? Russell said that logic is indifferent to monism and pluralism. If it is so, then it may be that *X* is *Y* and *Y* is *X* and there is nothing besides. Then how can there be – *Y* even within the field of logic? Should we not assume then that the field of logic is a plurality? If we do, we give up logic without ontology. *Thirdly*, if everything in logic is hypothetical and is assumed to be so, what is the basis of this assumption? What makes me think of negation, or disjunction, etc.? Yes, there can be multi-valued logics and algebras, multi-dimensional geometries, meta-mathematics, and meta-meta-mathematics and so on. But we have to say that they are abstractions and also abstractions from abstractions from concrete experience, poetry of skeletal intellect from which, as Bradley would say, flesh and blood have been removed. In the *fourth* place, we may ask: If *X* cannot be both *Y* and –*Y*, when we are led to a conclusion that it is both, then is *X* false, or one of the contradictories false, or are both the contradictories false? Generally, we work with the idea that both the contradictories cannot be true or false, and one of them has to be true. But why cannot both be false or both be true? Is it because the principle of double negation will be violated? But is the principle of double negation derived from the principle of contradiction or vice versa? The principle of contradiction is primary, not the principle of double negation. There are many logicians— Rāmānuja is included in them—who deny the validity of double negation. If we say: "*X* cannot be *Y* and – *Y*", or that a concept or theory is self-contradictory, we may not mean merely that *Y* and –*Y* cannot both be true—we may not be concerned merely with denying one of two opposed predicates—but that *X*, the subject of the proposition, does not exist and is not true. Then if it does not exist or is not true, it can have contradictory predicates. That is, if the two predicates are contradictory, *X* does not exist; but if *X* does not exist, it can have contradictory predicates. Then how can we hold that logic does not assume existence? Or taking Russell's example, we may ask: Is it false or true that the present King of France has a beard and also does not have a beard? If some one says: "The present king of France both has and does not have a beard", are we to deny its truth or confirm it? Even if we divide it into two propositions and deny each,

(1) $\sim \exists$ (the present King of France) has a beard;
(2) $\sim \exists$ (the present King of France) has no beard;

we are obliged to deny the existence of the present King of France by the symbol – Ǝ; but we are not obliged to deny his having or not having a beard. Does this not show that logic has to assume existence, directly or indirectly, in order to be meaningful? In the *fifth* place, we have another difficulty: Negations of two opposed predicates can be copresent. Negation we generally say, is not positive, but existence is positive. My pen is black. Then we may have two propositions: "The pen is red" and "The pen is —red". These two propositions are denials respectively of "The pen is black" and "The pen is not red". Now, think of the existence of the black in the pen. Then non-not-red, being red, is also denied. The first is the denial of red, the second is the denial of no-red. Then do not both denials (negations) co-exist? I am giving this example only to show that hypothesized abstractions, not recognized as abstractions, can be misleading. Not-not-red, being negative, is not the same as the positive black. Not-red may be green or any colour other than red; and the positive black is not "any colour other than red". Take another kind of example: There is absence of coins on my table, and there is also absence of flowers there. Now, the space occupied by the coin cannot be occupied by the flower at the same time. So they are opposed. Yet, their absences or negations are not opposed and they do not mind to be co-present. That is, negations as negations can co-exist in the sense of being co-present. But can the negations of the two absences or negations, not-not-coin and not-not-flower, co-exist at the same time and place? If they cannot co-exist, the contradiction must be due to existence, not mere formalization.[97] It is to be noted that many Indian philosophers and some followers of the Nyāya—Raghunātha himself—did not accept the validity of double negation, viz., that double negation is the same as the original affirmation. In fact, none of the Naiyāyikas, neither Gautama nor Raghunātha, wanted their logic to be merely formal; they wanted to decide the nature of the knowable, not merely the abstract concept of the knowable, but also the concrete in flesh and blood of experience. One should think that they were concerned with the elemental foundations of logic, and would avoid the idea of pure formalization, as it would mis-represent them, and could lead to greater uncertainties and fallacies in their metaphysical thinking—some of which will be shown in the general estimate of the Vaiśeṣika—than they now contain.

(ii) Nyāya Perception cannot give Particular Individuals

Yet, one defect, which is both logical and metaphysical, in the Nyāya doctrine of perception is important: its followers cannot show that the particular individual man is different from another particular individual man, on the basis of their doctrine. For them perception is always of the form, "That is a pen", which is interpreted as "That which is determined by the universal penness" or "That which is a member of the class determined by the universal penness". But then any and every pen is determined by the universal penness or is a member of the class determined by the universal penness. *But what I perceive in front is not any pen, but this particular pen.* We came across this criticism when giving the general estimate of Buddhism. While the Naiyāyikas criticize the Buddhists for saying that what is seen is a particular man without seeing the universal therein, they themselves fall into committing the opposite mistake of being unable to explain that what we see is the particular pen.

True, they distinguish between indeterminate and determinate perception and say that at the indeterminate stage we see the particular That. But then what is the difference between one That and another, if all indeterminate perceptions are simple perceptions of Thats? Why does one indeterminate That lead to the determinate perception, "That is a pot"—the favourite example of the Nyāya—and another indeterminate That to the determinate perception, "That is a man?" Is not Rāmānuja, as we shall see later, right and does he not show a stronger sense of reality than the Nyāya, when he says that even indeterminate perception has a form (*prakāra*)? Otherwise, how and why do we abstract the universal potness in the one case and the universal manness in the other, but not promiscuously? We have then to say that the form or universal (*prakāra*) is present in indeterminate perception also, but is present as this particularized form or the universal[98]—or as Plato and Aristotle say, the Idea—as particularized. Furthermore, in the live act of my looking at the pot, I am not thinking of the universal potness or the class of pots. The class is cognized in sense perception, according to the Nyāya, by what they call sense-object contact through the universal (*sāmānya-lakṣaṇa-sannikarṣa*). And the potness is contacted by my sense through the relation of conjunction-inherence (*samyukta-samavāya*), which will be examined below. Now, I have to make a special effort to think of this pot as determined by potness or as a member of the class of pots; and I do not have the experience often of making such an effort.

If the difference between this particularized man and that particularized man is cancelled, not only ethics,[99] but also logic, particularly the syllogism, becomes more insignificant than what has been shown by many logicians. It has been said to commit the fallacy the *petitio principi*, circle in argument, etc. For how can one say that "All men are mortal," if he has not already known that Socrates is a man and is mortal? And if he has had that knowledge, what is the use of inference? The sting of the critics can be blunted a little, if we say that Socrates is a particular—in fact, the term particular is used in modern western logic, but without bringing its full significance to the surface—and is not merely a member of the class of individuals determined by the concept or universal manness. The fact that we are required to enunciate that "Socrates is a man" implies that he is a particular individual man, not any one individual man in general, considered in the context as nothing more than being a member of the class, a mere value of a variable. Every man included in the major premise is considered in general, for the purposes of the syllogism, as a value of the variable; but if he is nothing more than a mere value of the variable, no inference about a particular need be made. So it will be a help for the justification of the syllogism to accept that what we see is a particular.

(iii) Sense Organs do not go out to Objects

The Nyāya-Vaiśeṣika account of the various kinds of contact between the sense and object, though ingenious, is too artificial to be confirmed fully by experience. The school rightly draws the distinction between the physical and the psychological senses; for when one of them works, the other may not. Although the school does not explain how the psychological senses are constituted, it makes clear-cut difference between senses and mind. The school says also that the senses go out to the objects—the senses are treated as *prāpyakāris*, those which work after going out and reaching the objects—and then obtain impressions; then the atomic mind (*manas*) contacts them and carries the information to the *ātman*; the *ātman* then obtains the cognition. That is, when I see a distant star, my psychological eye goes to the star at that distance, of course followed by my mind. But this is a process not intelligible, if we question our own experience. When my sense of sight is in contact with the distant star, has it left me, this man, and am I without sight at the moment? The same question can be asked about mind also. If it is said that the psychological sense of sight is infinite and all-pervading, then why does it have to "go out" to contact the object? If it is said that the sense of sight is not infinite, but the *ātman* is infinite and the object is, therefore, in contact with my *ātman* anyway, then what is the need for the atomic mind to intervene between the *ātman* and the sense to bring the latter's information to the former? It is also not intelligible how the atomic mind can bring non-atomic sense impressions of huge objects like mountains to the *ātman*. We do not find satisfactory answers to these questions in the Nyāya-Vaiśeṣika. But a modern defender of the school may say that all sense impressions—colours, smells, touches, tastes, and sounds—enter the pointed focus of the atomic mind and spread themselves out again on the retina of the eye etc., and reach the *ātman*. *Firstly*, this is a far-fetched explanation. *Secondly*, it is the mind, according to the Nyāya-Vaiśeṣika, that is in contact with the *ātman*, not the sense impression that enters the pointed focus of the mind and then spreads itself out.

Furthermore, how can any atomic mind be focussed—in other words, attend to—an impression or object, if the latter also is not atomic in size? The school accepts the idea of mind being attentive or non-attentive (or absent-minded); it says that mind cannot attend to more than one idea or thing at a time.[100] The idea or impression may be that of a huge mountain. Then attention cannot be explained on the Nyāya theory. It cannot explain even memory. Memory involves the retention of past experiences. How can they all be retained in an atomic mind? Again, it is by itself unconscious. At least, the result (*phala*) of memory is a conscious idea or experience. How can the unconscious mind choose the relevant idea or experience with which to strike the *ātman* so that it can be shaken from its own unconsciousness and become conscious of that past experience or idea? One may say that past experiences are retained in what the Nyāya calls *buddhi*; this seems also to be the view of this school.[101] But *buddhi* is understood by this school as incidental consciousness that appears like a spark due to the impact of mind on the *ātman*. Then how is conscious retention possible at all in such *buddhi*, if continuous contact of mind and *ātman* is not allowed? If there is continuous contact of the mind with *buddhi* as generated by mind—both generation and contact cannot be constant, and it is not right to translate the Nyāya concept of *buddhi* as reason, apperception, or even understanding—how can mind run to other senses for impressions, as it is tied down to one constant *buddhi*? Again if there is continuous contact of mind with *buddhi* and if *buddhi* is a quality, as the Nyāya says, of the *ātman*, then why can the *ātman* be not always conscious, i.e., eternally conscious and even self-conscious?

(iv) Importance of Apperception: not Possible in the Nyāya-Vaiśeṣika and the Mīmāmsā

Again, apperception, and so inference, are, like memory, not possible at all on the Nyāya theory. Apperception is the mass of all experiences presided over and unified by the I-am. This unity of past experiences has to be retained in some form by the conscious I-am. Memory is not only retentive, but also logical; and neither is possible without apperception. Even in the inference,

Wherever there is smoke, there is fire;
This mountain has smoke;
Therefore, it has fire;

there are three propositions—even omitting the other two of the Nyāya syllogism—which are made to oneself or to another in succession; then their consistency or non-contradiction is perceived by grasping the whole in the logical intuition of major-middle-minor unity. This process is not possible without apperception, which is always both consciously and unconsciously present in the *ātman*. Syllogistic process is a conscious process. But neither conscious nor unconscious apperception is possible on the Nyāya theory because on it not even retention is possible. Then what is the function of the atomic mind in the process of inference?

However, the importance of apperception is not clearly grasped by Indian schools, although we can find it to some extent in the Sāṅkhya—Yoga and to a larger extent in the Vedāntic schools, particularly in the ideas of *buddhi* or *citta* and *mahat* or *mahān ātmā*[102] of both the Upaniṣads and the Advaita. In Buddhism also we may find it in the idea of *ālaya–vijñāna* (storehouse-consciousness).[103] But the Nyāya, the Vaiśeṣika, and the Mīmāmsā find no place for apperception.

(v) Kevalānvayī and Kevalavyatirekī

Now, the rules and conditions laid down for any valid inference by the Nyāya are conflicting. In narrating the fallacies, it is said that an inference is invalid if the minor term has nothing similar to it (*sapakṣa*)—that is, if there is only one object of the kind in the universe—and also nothing dissimilar to it (*vipakṣa*)—that is, a term which means everything in the universe, e.g., the nameable. But most of the Naiyāyikas accept what they call unique correlation (*kevala-vyatirekī*), which is opposed to the first condition, and absolute correlation (*kevala-anvayī*), which conflicts with the second condition. We have reinterpreted these conditions before. But the Naiyāyika interpretation and examples are not acceptable. For the former, their example which will be intelligible to the westerners will be:

Any President of U.S.A. not assassinated in Texas is not J.F. Kennedy;
Only one President of U.S.A. was assassinated in Texas;
So he is not other than J.F. Kennedy.

This inference is no inference at all because the relation between J.F. Kennedy and being assassinated in Texas is unique and the minor has nothing similar to it (up to the present time). When there is nothing similar to it, the relation between the minor and major must have been known in advance before any major premise, affirmative or negative, can be formed; and there is the anomaly of the same minor being used as the middle. In the case of "Wherever there is smoke, there is fire," there are many instances where there are both smoke and fire and many instances where there is fire but no smoke (that is, both *sapakṣas* and *vipakṣas*). The two kinds of instances enable us to form the major premise, "Wherever there is smoke, there is fire," and prevent us from accepting "Wherever there is fire, there is smoke." But the present instance about Kennedy is that it is a unique instance and may as well be classified under what Russell would call "knowledge by acquaintance" or "knowledge by description". Or at the most, it may be called the method of residues; but it will be a parody to take its so-called major premise seriously as a major premise. Even to call it "the method of residues" is an undeserved concession; for there is no method at all here as there is no mediation in obtaining the knowledge of the fact.

A somewhat similar criticism applies to absolute correlation also as interpreted by the Nyāya. For instance, the major premise in this context will be: "Every thinkable is a nameable" or "Every nameable is a thinkable". In this case, there is nothing dissimilar to the minor; for even a circular square, which is a common example, is both thinkable and nameable. Remember that similarity and dissimilarity in this context mean having or not having (being governed or not being governed by) a true middle term. Characteristics like nameable and thinkable can be referred to everything, real and unreal, existent and non-existent, true and false. So inference from such universally absolute concomitance has no significance.

One point need be repeated here: inference from uniqueness has very dangerous implications and may result in parodying (*vidambanā*, mockery) of inference.[104] *First*, it turns the particular individual into a universal or at the most into being a member of a class, a value of a variable.

Every one who was the President of U.S.A. in 1962 was assassinated in Texas;
J.F. Kennedy was the President of U.S.A. in 1962;
Therefore, he was assassinated in Texas.

Here the "therefore" is not only redundant, but also a caricature or parody of inference. Kennedy is turned also into a member of a class of Presidents of U.S.A. in 1962. Or as the Nyāya says, there is no other president of U.S.A. in 1962 (i.e., no *sapakṣa*) and no other president of U.S.A. in 1962 who was not assassinated (i.e., no *vipakṣa*). *Secondly*, no merely descriptive characteristics—not in a logically necessary relation on which the Nyāya insists—can constitute the terms of a valid major premise. Their relation is merely coincidence. There is no necessary relation between being the President of U.S.A.—in fact between being the President of any country and at any time—in 1962 and being assassinated. In the *third* place, we cannot treat "being the President in 1962" as even a conditionality (*upādhi* in the Nyāya terminology); for when the condition is added to the middle term, we should still get a valid major premise; the reason is that the original middle term plus the condition can and ought to form a new, but valid, middle term, and the new major premise need not be invalid. For instance,

Wherever there is fire, there is smoke;

> The kitchen has fire;
> Therefore, the kitchen has smoke.

As it is, the syllogism is invalid even if there is smoke in the kitchen. But if we add "wet fuel" as the condition (*upādhi*) to fire, we shall have:

> Wherever there is fire with wet wood, there is smoke;
> The kitchen has fire with wet wood;
> Therefore, the kitchen has smoke.

This is a conditional syllogism or a syllogism with a conditional major premise, but is still valid—if we accept plurality of conditions for the effect—, although not acceptable to the Nyāya. Without the condition (*upādhi*) the opponent's argument is declared to be invalid and he is said to be defeated by pointing out the conditioned nature (*upādhiprayuktatā*) of his major premise; but the declaration does not imply that the conclusion is materially false, but only that the opponent's major premise is inadequately formulated.

But in many discussions of the logical literature of the schools, it is said that the possibility of pointing to the conditionality of an inference makes it both materially and formally false. This idea seems to be encouraged by the dialectics of the Nyāya. But how far can we logically go or not go in pointing to the conditionality governing any syllogism? The importance of this question does not seem to have been recognized so far; but we have to raise it if we are to grasp the full significance of the idea of conditionality. It seems that in the phenomenal world there is nothing unconditioned, no law is absolute by itself without being related to other laws of the universe—whether or not we are able to discover all—and that it is the inter-relatedness and inter-conditionedness of everything in the universe that led to the seven kinds of conditioned statements (*syādvāda*) of Jainism and to the destructive dialectic of Nāgārjuna and Srī Harṣa in India and to Bradley and others in the West, declaring this phenomenal world to be an appearance. But we need some guidance in formulating our inferences and answering the question we have raised, even for the sake of practical logic or logic workable so far as our practical living and thinking go. The answer to the question can be given in a general way: We can logically continue adding conditions to the middle term so long as we do not thereby turn the inference into a parody or a mockery (*vidambanā*). Let me give as an example a case—privately condemned—of the President of university who had to appoint a professor in a department. It seems he advertised that "All those who have the qualifications *A*, *B*, *C*, *D*, and *E* are eligible for the post." This statement looks innocuous. But it was rumoured that the qualifications apply only to his nephew. Let us see. *A* stands for Ph.D. in Botany, *B* for M.A. First Class; so far there is nothing to object. Then let *C* stand for twenty five years old, neither more not less, *D* for being born on the 31st of March, and *E* for being born in the country of the Presidents's only sister. These conditions are fulfiled only by that particular nephew. Now, if we view it from our present context, the conditions turn this universal proposition into the description of a particular individual and of no other; conjointly they have lost their universality. We may say, the major premise is killed as a major premise. Logically, if the distinction between the individual—each with his own particular status—and the universal is removed, then there will be neither universal nor individual, and inference becomes a mockery.[105]

(vi) Verbal Cognitions not Possible on the Atomic Theory of Mind and Unconscious Ātman

The Nyāya theory of cognition which makes an atomic mind intervene between the externally obtained sense information and the unconscious *ātman* renders verbal knowledge—cognition produced by a sentence uttered by another person impossible. Now, a sentence consists of words; but all the words cannot be uttered simultaneously, but only one after another. Then how is knowledge of the meaning of the whole sentence produced? Let us take a simple example, "Jim is walking." Words consist of syllables; and all the syllables cannot be uttered simultaneously. For argument's sake, let us take only the three words as units, of which the sentence consists. Mind has to take the word sounds separately to the *ātman*; for they are not available simultaneously to the mind. Then it has to take the first word, Jim, to the *ātman* and contact it; it then comes back and takes the second word similarly; then it does the same with the third word. But if, as the Nyāya maintains, the *ātman* is by nature unconscious and becomes conscious only when in contact with the mind, there are intervals when the mind and the *ātman* are not in contact, when the *ātman* becomes unconscious. Then what happens to the cognitions of earlier words before and when the later words are brought in by the mind? They must have disappeared. If they are to be retained as impressions in the *ātman*, it has to consciously and apperceptively—in one sense of the term, "self-consciously" also—retain them so that it can relate them to the new word which its mind will bring; and it has also to expect, anticipate (*ākāṅkṣā*) some word to complete the meanings of the words it has retained. Anticipation is not possible without consciousness and self-consciousness. At this point we have to use "self-consciousness" also, for there can be no anticipation for bits of separate objective consciousnesses, if there are such unrelated bits not belonging to any self (I-am), which unifies them with itself. It is the I which anticipates something, if someone says: "John killed," asking itself or that someone: "Whom?" The mere consciousness of the word "John" or of "killed" or even of both together does not anticipate anything. If in all these contexts, the *ātman* can be and has to be conscious and self-conscious apart from contact with mind, we do not see any reason for accepting that it is unconscious apart from such contact. Anticipation involves also a spontaneous will, a desire to know more than what has been heard.[106]

(vii) Nyāya Syllogism not Psychological

Quite a few contemporary philosophers tend to think that the introduction of the idea of the self (I-am) into logic and epistemology turns them into psychology. In fact, there are a few western philosophers who think that epistemology itself is psychology[107] and that logic has to be without metaphysics and ontology, and even without epistemology and without psychology. But none of these disciplines can be completely demarcated from the others. It was not the intention of the Nyāya to separate them. However, if we separate logic from the other disciplines, then we can have no reason for X and $-X$ being opposed, except by some proposal. Then one has a right to ask why he should accept this or that proposal, but not its opposite. He may be replied that he must be mad not to accept it. But why should he be mad not to accept it? Is he mad because there is nothing in the world to which both predicates can be assigned? Then at the very foundation logic is not without ontology; it is applicability to the real world that determines the validity and meaningfulness of logic. And along with applicability epistemology comes in; for we have to determine the right way of knowing the real world to which logic is to be applied. One can say that logic also is one of the means of knowing the real world. True, but the objection only shows that logic, epistemology, and metaphysics are interdependent, which is what is here contended. But epistemology involves some psychology—call it philosophical psychology, if you like—and a continuous self (I or I-am) in whom or in whose mind inter-relations within each discipline and among disciplines take place. Such an I or I-am, the *ātman*, cannot be by nature unconscious. This criticism of the Nyāya doctrine applies *mutatis mutandis* to similar contemporary philosophies including those for which the I-am, the self, is the material body or even a name without corresponding reality.[108] The ultimate interrelatedness of the sciences should set us rethinking whether absolute separation of formal and material fallacies is in the end justifiable.

(viii) Sense-object Contacts and Relations Arbitrary

It is perhaps the artificiality of the explanation of the cognitive process—with its so-called naturally unconscious *ātman*, atomic and unconscious mind, and the incidental nature of consciousness—that led the Naiyāyikas to posit the many kinds of sense contact with objects, universals, negations, etc. We have seen that the concept of apperception is beyond the horizon of the Nyāya-Vaiśeṣika thought. The formation and development of universals, negation, etc., is possible within apperception and by it only. As this school has no concept of apperception, it says that the universals, etc., are found in the world outside, and the senses come into contact with them. If it is asked: How can any sense come into contact with objects which have no existence (*sattā*)—for according to this school, universals, particulars, the relation of inherence (other relations[109] like separateness, contact, etc., which we tend to regard as relations, are called qualities, *guṇas*, by this school) and forms of negation have no existence—the school answers that there are different kinds of contact of sense and object, and classifies them into six. These six contacts are combinations mainly of conjunction (*sanyoga*), inherence (*samavāya*) and *adjectivality*[110] (*viśeṣaṇatā*). The eye, according to this school, is directly in contact—understood literally—with substance (*dravya*). But if we ask: Which sense is in contact with it, we cannot find an answer in experience. The eye gives colour, shapes, but not substances. In western thought, "How do we know substances?" is a crucial question for Locke, Berkeley, and Hume. None of the other senses also is in contact with substances.[111] If the knowable (*prameya*) is determined by valid means of cognition[112] (*pramāṇa*), which is given priority in this school, then what is it that determines the existence of substance? No contact of my eye with substance is observed by me. Even if we accept that colours exist there in the world and the eye reflects them—no modern psycho-physical theory will accept such a view—there can be, if at all, contact with the colour, but not with substance. The answer we sometimes come across that substance is that which produces the idea of substance in me is no answer. For we have many false ideas (*vikalpas*) without corresponding realities. The Nyāya-Vaiśeṣika, as has been mentioned already, has no place for apperception and so can hardly explain how we experience substantive objects. Accepting for argument's sake that my sight comes into contact with substances, is the contact perceived or inferred? I can see the object either after the contact or during the contact. If we are speaking of determinate perception (*savikalpaka*), it can arise only after the contact. Indeterminate perception (*nirvikalpaka*) only can arise during the contact. In the former case, contact can be known through memory or some kind of inference. But I have no memory of contact between my eye and the pen in front; then the contact has at the most to be an implication, a postulate, a presupposition (known through *arthāpatti*) or a guess, but not inference, as there can be no major premise. But postulation is not accepted by the Nyāya. In the case of indeterminate perception, we can have no cognition, according to this school, of substance as substance—in the form "That is a substance" or "That is what is determined[113] by the universal substanceness (*dravyatva*)"—but only of "something" which may be anything like quality or activity. Even then, how is contact known? When I am cognizing an object, I am not cognizing the contact of my eye or sight with it, but only the object; so contact cannot be cognized during the contact itself.

Again, is contact a quality or activity (*guṇa* or *karma*)? Sense contact is defined by this school as a *vyāpāra*, which may be translated as instrumental cause (*kāraṇa*), which is other than substance, and which produces the same effect.[114] For instance, the activity of the axe in the hands of the wood-cutter is such an instrumental activity. It produces the same effect as the axe itself. But contact is classified by this school as a quality,[115] which is produced by activity[116] (*karma*). In any case, how is it cognized?

The contact of my eye with the object cannot be known at all even on the basis of the doctrines of this school. As a quality (*guṇa*) it exists in both the objects in contact.[117] How can I cognize it as a quality of my sight? My sight works when it is seeing an object like the pen; there is no more seeing of the sight by itself. This difficulty is present even when we regard contact not as an activity, but as a quality; for the quality of my sight (and also of the pen) can be cognized only when my sight is cognized. But there is no cognition of sight by itself; otherwise it would be self-conscious.[118]

In fact, there is no category of relation as such for this school except inherence (*samavāya*). But curiously enough, it says that the relation between substance on the one side and qualities, activities, and universals on the other is the relation of inherence (*samavāya-sambandha*) and defines this relation as inseparable.[119] This had led to a number of misunderstandings—we find them in western logic and metaphysics also in taking the literal meanings of expressions like "John as qualified by man-ness," as though it is similar to "John as qualified by red hair," or "John as qualified by fear, white complexion, etc.,"—for the determination (*avaccheda*) of John by man-ness is not similar to the determination of John by his complexion. The complexion may change if John lives in a hot country, but not his being a man. I have several times pointed out that universals like man-ness are constitutive of each of the individuals; they are not mere qualities like colours which are not constitutive—even the red colour of the rose is not constitutive of the rose—but adjectival. Similarly, activities like walking and running are not constitutive. Of the qualities, only properties like specific gravity of substances in chemistry can be called constitutive qualities and eternal (*nitya*) in the sense that so long as the substance X remains X, it must have that specific gravity Y. In that sense the relation between X and Y is eternal (i.e., necessary). But every quality is not related to its substance in this constitutive way; and so the Nyāya idea that the relation between substance and its quality is inherence (*samavāya*), which the school calls eternal, is questionable.

Now, if Y constitutively determined X and so constitutes it, can there be any relation, in the proper sense of the term relation, between the two? For a relation to relate, there must be two terms having their separate existence. But X and Y are so absolutely inseparable; how can they be two terms to be brought together by a relation, except in thought's analysis? Here we can appreciate the view of some rival schools (e.g., the Mīmāmsā), which say that the relation is some kind of identity (*tādātmya*) which is not the same as pure identity or equivalence as in

"$X \equiv Y$" or "$X = Y$ and $Y = X$",

but which is often misunderstood as pure equivalence. Does man-ness reside through the relation of inherence (*samavāya*) in John, who is not already a man or who is already a man? If John is not already a man, then man-ness cannot find any place in him; but if he is already a man, then it does not have to get into him to make him a man. Here we have a peculiar logical and metaphysical situation; and so the relation between the universal and the individual should not be treated on a par with qualities and activities on the one side and substances on the other.

Now, how is the relation of inherence cognized? This school maintains that this relation also is cognized by sense. That any relation, all the more so in the case of inherence, is cognized by sense is not easily acceptable. Even the relation of inherence of the red in the rose is not cognized by sense. It is true that a red rose is differently cognized by sense from a white rose. Even if, for argument's sake, we accept that red and rose are cognized together and that similarly white and rose are cognized together by sense, there is no sense cognition of the relation as such between the red and the rose and the white and the rose. The question of relation arises only when we reflectively analyse the percepts "red rose" and "white rose." At that time, we think of the relation of inherence of rose-ness in each of the roses. But there are other qualities (*guṇas*) and universals like smell and flower-ness. Then how many inherences does my sense of sight perceive when it perceives the red rose and the white rose? To say that all are perceived by my sense at the same time is against experience and will only be an artificial explanation. For sense perception is always spontaneous, immediate; but the cognition of relation is not immediate.

One may object: If the sense has not perceived the relations when it perceived the object,—leaving aside the question whether the relations are inherences or some others—are they created by the intellect (*buddhi*) arbitrarily? If they are arbitrary, why and how do they come to have objective validity? If they are not there, but invented, they cannot be objective. But to accept that they are objective does not imply that they are objects of mere sense, as such a conclusion violates experience.

On the other hand, we have to change our view of perceptions of the form "That is a pen" or "That is an object determined by the universal pen-ness." The latter makes it obvious that perception is not a mere sense act, but is more complex than what this school makes us think.

As I have pointed out, this school suffers for want of the concept of apperception. Instead, it introduces two kinds of perception called perception by association (*jñāna-lakṣaṇa*) and perception through the universal (of the class, *sāmānyalakṣaṇa*), which are inappropriately described as forms of sense contact (*pratyāsatti*). What kind of sense contact is it? What is it that comes into contact (has *pratyāsatti*) with the associated quality and with the universal? Now, association belongs not to sense, but to apperception. Past sense impressions are retained in memory, which is a function of apperception. This school assigns memory to *buddhi*, which is consciousness (understanding, if we stretch its meaning) for this school. But it arises only when the atomic mind comes into contact with the *ātman*. But as mentioned already, neither the atomic mind nor the *ātman*—both of which are unconscious for this school—knows which relevant past impression is to be revived at a particular time. So there is no ground in the Nyāya-Vaiśeṣika to make *buddhi* of the school perform the function of apperception, without which perception by association is not possible. When I see the "soft bed" with my eye, although "soft" is not an object of the eye, its experience is revived and added to the percept by apperception.

Perception through the universal (*sāmānyalakṣaṇa*) is not perception of the universal, but perception of the class—like "all pots" or "all pens"—via the perception of the universal in the perception "That is an object determined by the universal potness." Then how is the universal perceived? The answer of this school is: "It is perceived as that which inheres in the object pot." It is one thing to say that the universal potness is cognized—but not as an object of my eye—through the instrumentality of my eye, for the colour and shape of the object are known through my sight. But it is another thing to say that the universal potness is an object of my eye. For instance, "all pots" or "the class of pots" is not an object of the eye for the simple reason that my eye cannot come into contact with all of them. It is no answer to say that the contact (*pratyāsatti*) here is not conjunction (*samyoga*), but contact through a universal (*sāmānyalakṣaṇa*). But what is this contact through a universal? This is a very artificial explanation; for no sense comes into contact with a class, determined by a real universal, with the help of any relation. This is quite evident in the case of classes determined by universals like man-ness, for the membership of the class is indefinite. The relation of the universal with the class is that the former resides in each member of the latter. Now, is that relation also cognized by the sense? Can it be so cognized?

Perhaps, the Naiyāyikas do not mean that any sense is capable of such a complicated contact (*pratyāsatti*). Here is the contact between the eye and the physical pot; then contact between the eye and potness; then contact between the eye and the relation of inherence by which potness resides in the pot; then there is the contact between the eye and the indefinite, open class of pots through the universal potness; and then contact between the relations and relations which relate the terms; and so on *ad infinitum*. This looks like a maze through which any sense can hardly go.

The Nyāya here introduces a new kind of relation called adjectivality (*viśeṣaṇatā*).

But what is this adjectivality? It is not a quality (*guṇa*), as it is not like colours, tastes, etc. It is not activity. If we translate the Sanskrit word as "qualification," we may relate the idea surreptitiously to activity; but the Nyāya-Vaiśeṣika does not mean any activity, direct or indirect. If some indirect activity is meant in the sense that a quality, qualification, or adjective qualifies an object and "qualifies" is a verb denoting activity, then this school has not only to give greater importance to activity than it has done, but also has to turn all relations into relatings or activities, and say that the so-called relations are one kind of noun-forms or names for activities.[121]

We have already noted that the relation of inherence between a universal (potness) and the individual (pot) is a constitutive relation, but not a mere quality that qualifies. One may question even the appropriateness of the word relation in this context; but we use it knowingly, as we distinguish in thought between the universal and the individual. An adjective like the red colour of the pen-holder is a mere qualifying relation, not a constitutive one. Any change of colour does not change the constitution of the pen-holder. But this school mixed them all up.

When cornered by the question, what exactly adjectivality is that is seen in the relation between the pot on the one side and the relation of the inherence of potness in the pot on the other, the Naiyāyikas say that it is "own-form" (*svarūpa*).[122] The so-called "own-form" relation has misled many students into thinking that it is the result of acute intellectual analysis or that the concept has in it something very profound; but it means simply the "relation as a phenomenon" or the "relation as an appearance." Let me explain. I see the red pen in front as "The pen is red." Why do I call this pen a red pen and the other one a black one? It is because the first *appears as* red and the second *appears as* black. So the Nyāya would call the relation between the pen and red in the first and the pen and black in the second *appearance relations*, for such are the appearances as I see. In fact, this school calls this relation inherence (*samavāya*), which we have examined already, and the relation between the relation of inherence and the pen adjectival (*viśeṣaṇatā*). But when cornered, they turn both relations into "appearance relations" (*svarūpa-sambandhas*). True, red is not the same as the pen; and the pen appears as red or the object appears as the red pen to my sight. But to turn these "appearances" into relations is artificial intellectuality or intellectual artificiality. The truth is that most of these appearances which are called relations[123] by the Naiyāyikas are not relations at all; and certainly, "own form" or appearance is not a relation. It is the result of the activities of the senses and mind and takes on the appearance it does. But because of the eagerness of the Nyāya-Vaiśeṣika to treat not only everything of the cosmos but also every result of intellectual analysis as real and out there in the objective world as a distinct entity—which does not seem to be the original aim of Gautama or even Kaṇāda—the school had to introduce many artificial concepts, and for the purpose turn substantives and appearances into relations.

Take again the relation of *nirūpaka-nirūpita-sambandha*, which is translated as describer-described[124] and conditioner-conditioned[125] relation. These translations are not only confusing but also misleading. In western logic the term description covers much more than what the Naiyāyikas mean by the verb "*nirūp*," which means to mark, to fix, to determine and in a general sense to indicate, to define. The first translation is therefore confusing. Next, to translate it as the conditioner-conditioned relation is misleading. For *upādhi* also is a condition. Conditionality in western logic is related to the "if-then" and "because-therefore" sense. Of all the possible translations, the term indicator-indicated relation seems to be the best and the least inappropriate. Indeed, there is always a difficulty in selecting the right English technical terms. Now, coming to our present problem, is the indicator-indicated relation objective in the sense in which the colour of the pen is objective? The colour of the pen, if it is red for me, is red for every one: this is a meaning of its being objective. But is the indicator-indicated relation objective in that sense? The cause may indicate the effect to one; but the effect may indicate the cause to another; but to a third there may be no indication at all. Let us take the example of the pen on the table. The table is called the substrate (*ādhāra*) and the pen superstrate (*ādheya*). Does one see the substrateness of the table in the way he sees the colour of the table? Similarly, does one see the superstrateness of the pen in the way he sees the colour of the pen? No, we may say, in this case we do not think that the pen is the substrate and the table is the superstrate; and we may accept that the substrateness of the table is *indicated* by the superstrateness of the pen when we analyse the form of the content of the percept, "the pen on the table."[126] But what is it that indicates that the table is the substrate and the pen is the superstrate? The Nyāya maintains that the superstrateness of the pen indicates (*nirūpayati*) the substrateness of the table. But I do not see with my eye either the superstrateness or the substrateness. And who or what indicates the superstrateness of the pen first, before it indicates the substrateness of the table? It is I who indicates which is which by action. For instance, I can lift the pen without lifting the table, but I cannot lift the table without lifting the pen. And what is this substrateness and this superstrateness? They are not called real universals like horseness, but *akhaṇḍopadhis*, which can be freely translated as conceptual forms like spaceness, absenceness, etc., which are indivisible unlike white-horseness, which is a product of whiteness and horseness.[127] If they are not real universals, but imposed conceptual forms, by whom are they imposed? Or even indicated? Not merely by each other—which they do only so far as they are correlated by me—but by me and my activity, actual or possible. And which is which of even the correlates is determined by my apperception containing the potencies of action and cognition.

(ix) Substances Turned into Relations

How otherwise can we explain the Naiyāyika conception of temporal relations and spatial relations? To the western student there seems to be nothing strange in treating time and space as relations. But remember that for the Nyāya and the Vaiśeṣika, time and space are substances and each is infinite, eternal, and one, and the divisions like past, present and future, and like right, left, up and down, are relative and conventional. We shall make a rather extensive examination of the concepts of time and space in the next chapter. Here we ask the question: *How can substances be turned into relations?* The answer is: Everything *appears* to be temporal and *appears* also to be spatial; and so time and space are included in the appearance (*svarūpa*)—not to be confused with the appearance in "appearance and reality"—of everything. Even if, for arguments's sake, we concede the truth of everything appearing as temporal and spatial, we still ask how this appearance can be a relation. And really, when I perceive a pot, I do not see its temporality, but at the most its spatiality, or extension.

What would Kant say to the question: How is a category or a form of intuition related to the sense-content? And also, how is this relation, if there is one, again related to the category or form of intuition on the one side and the sense-content on the other? He tried the artificial schematism of the categories, but the attempt was a failure. He could have said that they are all included in the appearance (phenomenon, *svarūpa*); but is appearance a relation? There is a trend among the Kantians to interpret categories and forms of intuition themselves as relations. For example, the category of substance-attribute may be treated as a kind of relation relating different sensa into, say, the rose and its colour. But is substance a sensum? Then what do these relations relate? How does a relation relate a content that is not a sense datum? And is there a datum that is not an appearance? If the datum is an appearance (*svarūpa*), it must have already included the relations, about which the same question can be raised again. If the datum, on the other hand, is not an appearance (*svarūpa*), who can know anything about it? Bergson's view is perhaps nearer the truth in this context than Kant's. The former says that the appearance produced is produced as a unitary object through some kind of activity of mind, senses, and whatever acts as a stimulus—for Bergson, this is an activity of intuition—and the rest of it is our intellectual analysis which can go to any artificial lengths. He gives the example of the imprint of the palm on a heap of fine iron filings; How many kinds of relations can produce the imprint if we start with arranging and re-arranging the filings? The object is the result of integral activity, not of relations.

(x) Artificiality of Many Relations

We may accept the contention that the appearance (*svarūpa*) of negations, for instance, to the eye is different from that of the positive. Gangese seems to have made the right use of this distinction up to a point. The table as seen by itself or as such in the form, "That is a table" and as seen qualified (*viśeṣaṇaviśiṣṭa*) by the absence of the pen on it in the form, "That is a table without the pen on it," form different kinds of content of the acts of perception. But is the table as qualified—unfortunately English does not have different words for the qualifying activity by a quality like red colour and for the qualifying activity by an adjunct or adjectivality like absence, negation, and relation—by the absence of the pen not the same as the table with its original colour? If it is not the same, we may say that a blue lotus is not the same as a lotus and a red rose not the same as a rose; and to take the famous example of the "white horse"[128] in Chinese philosophy, a white horse will not be a horse. Then if, in the case of positive qualities like blue, a blue lotus is a lotus, we may as well say that a table qualified by the absence of the pen is as much a table as when qualified by a positive quality like red, or even by the presence of the pen. It may be asked: Is there is no difference between the table with the pen on it and the same without the pen on it in the appearance (*svarūpa*) of the content? Yes, there is difference. But the question which the rival philosophers like Prabhākara raise is not about appearance (*svarūpa*) of the content of the cognitions, but about ontology. Many of the controversies in

Indian and western thought between rival schools or philosophers are due either to misunderstanding each other or intentionally misrepresenting each other and then attacking the strawman. Does the Nyāya, new or ancient, assign Existence or Being (*sattā*) to negation in any of its forms? It says that Being is possessed only by Substance, Quality, and Activity, which also is questioned by later Nyāya. Then not only negation, but also universal, and particular have no Being. If so, what are the Naiyāyikas fighting for in defending negation? Not for its ontological status, but only for its logical and cosmological status.[129] But such a status is not denied by rival schools. They use the words and concepts of negation and the negative as many times as the Nyāya-Vaiśeṣika uses them.

Now, the negative (*abhāva*) is seen as being related to the table by the relation of adjectivality. Suppose I ask a student to bring a table from the other room. If it has lots of books on it making it too heavy to carry, he removes them and brings the table. These books are in conjunction (*samyoga*) with the table; and this conjunction is seen as related to the table by the relation of adjectivality (*viśeṣaṇatā-sambandha*).[130] Now, if the table is without any books on it and so with the absence of each of the books on it, but I want it with the books on it, will he remove all these absences—in the way he removes all the books, by pushing the absences also related to the table adjectivally? We say, he is mad if he attempts to push aside the absences as he pushes aside the books. Now, the more crucial point. How many absences—absences of books, absences of toys, of horses, of elephants, tigers and what not—are not present on the table? Even according to the Nyāya, absences are not positive entities (*bhāvas*). Adjectivality is a positive form. How can it qualify a negative entity like absence? Absence is conceptual; adjectivality belongs to the table which is a substantive object independent of the mind; then how can the latter qualify the former? This qualifying activity must at least be different from the qualifying activity of inherence (*samavāya*) which is positive, although not ontological. It is difficult to think of relations between entities which have no ontological status, although positive; the difficulty becomes the greater when we think of relations between entities which are merely negative. It is a misnomer even to call them entities; for the word has an ontological meaning in its roots. If two absences like that of the pen and that of the inkstand can be present on the same table, how are they related on the table? Are they related only in my mind or thought and are, therefore, conceptually valid? In fact, all absences coincide except where the objects of which they are absences are present. When I look at the table, I do not see all the absences present there; for there is no spontaneity in the contact (*pratyāsatti*) of my sight with the absences as there is in the conjunction (*samyoga*) of my sight with the table or at least with the colour and shape of the table, as the Nyāya explains.

(xi) Contact of Sense and Object

Western students are acquainted with the problem left over by Descartes, viz., how can mind or spirit, which is non-spatial, come into contact with matter, which is spatial. This problem arises in a slightly different form about this sense-object contact also in the Nyāya. For how can my sight, which is non-spatial, come into contact with the table, which is spatial? This question does not seem to have been raised in Indian thought, but we can raise it. One possible answer is: The sense and its corresponding object—sight and colour, tongue and taste, etc.,—are made up of the same element, and so parts of the same element can come into contact. But then how can every sense come into contact with the same "substance?" And why is one part of the element psychological and the other physical? And if the element is physical, how can one part become psychological and the other remain physical? How can the physical be transformed into the psychological? Now, coming to our present question of the contact of the sense with relations, are the relations also made up of elements (*mahābhūtas*)? The more we carry on this analytic enquiry into the Nyāya-Vaiśeṣika theory of perception, relations, and the negative, the larger will be the number of unintelligibilities we encounter. The safest answer seems to be that we see an appearance (*dṛṣya, savarūpa*, not illusion); and later intellectual analysis needs the acceptance of some relations within the object which appears and among the objects which we see or cognize in other ways. But the Nyāya-Vaiśeṣika has carried its realism too far to make it intelligible and avoid self-contradictions.

(xii) Difficulties of Presumed Doctrine

It is hoped that this comment will remove the mystification surrounding the terminology of the Nyāya logic, a source of confusion to many earnest students, by throwing light on some of its artificialities. Not only the Nyāya, but also some other schools often say: "This is what we accept." We came across this idea in the concept of "presumed doctrine" (*abhyupagama-siddhānta*), which corresponds to what is generally called "the platform of the school." The followers of a school may say: "This is our platform; this is what we accept to start with; and this is final." But such a position is not philosophical. If the postulates of a system can be theorems of another, it is and must always be possible to question a presumed doctrine. For instance, we raised the question: If the absence of the pen and the absence of the inkstand are both present on the table, and my sight can come into contact with both, how are they related then on the table?[131] The answer given is: We do not accept that one absence can be present in another absence, which is the same as that two negatives are not by themselves related. But "we do not accept" is no philosophical answer. If the two absences are there on the table, my eye cannot but have contact with them; and when it has the contact with them, it cannot but see the relation between them, for they are there. In fact, if I do not anticipate a pen there, I do not perceive its absence; and if I anticipate both the pen and the inkstand, I see the absences of both. Because anticipation is the act of apperception (as memory) provoked in some way, generally by need, and because there is no mere absence, but absence of some object, many philosophers say that negation, although objective, is the result of an intellectual process and is, therefore, not perceived by every one, but only by those persons in whom the stimulus for the intellectual process occurs. Because of its objectivity—i.e., if the pen is not there on the table, every one who looks for the pen must observe its absence, but not those who do not look for the pen—Kumārila said that non-perception of the anticipated object is a distinct source of cognition. Of course, mere non-perception without the anticipation does not result in any cognition. The difference between the perception of the pen on the table and perception of its absence on the same table lies in this: If one looks at the table with the pen on it, one perceives the pen, whether or not one anticipates it; but one has to anticipate it before one perceives its absence on the table. Then where are the absences of the pen and of the inkstand related? In the mind of the person who anticipates them. The activity of mind or thought then is as important as the so-called non-perception to determine the constitution of negation; and it is more important than it is for determining the constitution of the positive, existing object.

(xiii) Need of Apperception for Verbal Cognition

It has been pointed out a few times already that the absence of apperception in the Nyāya-Vaiśeṣika makes much of its epistemology unintelligible. It is due to the same defect that an answer from this school is not available to the question: Why does the word uttered by the speaker produce the idea of an object in the mind of the hearer? Many sounds I hear do not signify anything else than themselves. But if something creeps on my back, I say: "The fly is moving on my back." That is, this touch sensation is interpreted by me as or as due to the movement of the fly, although I do not see the fly with my eye. The Nyāya may explain this cognition as cognition by association or associated cognition (cp. *jñānalakṣaṇa–sannikarṣa*) of the sense of touch with the fly. Should we say then that the cognition of the word-sound is associated with the cognition of the object, conceptual or perceptual, in the same way? But perception by association is regarded as sense perception by this school. Then, is the cognition of the object meant by the word, say, "sun," the object of perception of the ear or hearing? One can understand that, in the case of the perception of the "soft bed"; for softness is the object of touch and the bed is the object of sight, and "soft" as a quality is *seen* as though it is an object of sight. But the connection between the sound "sun" and the object sun is different. The "sun" is heard, but the object is cognized as the meaning of the sound and as seen sometime ago. But "soft" is not meant by the word "bed."

Perhaps the inability to answer this question is not peculiar to the Nyāya-Vaiśeṣika. The mystery that is the word—or the wonder that is the word—led Indian thought to a mysticism of the word and meaning, as it did so in some other countries. But the roots of this mystery lie deep within our perceptive being, in which the pattern of the word sound and the pattern of the object get related. But as both the patterns do not lie within my sense of hearing, the object is not cognized by simple sense association with the word sound (i.e., by *jñānalakṣaṇa*). The two patterns do not mix, while the pattern of "soft" and that of "bed" can mix.

One may think that there is too much of critical estimate of the Nyāya and the Neo-Nyāya given here, while an account of the latter is given in the next chapter. This procedure has to be followed to make the critical estimate of the Nyāya as a whole almost self-complete and both the old and the new Nyāya devoted much of their thought to epistemologies. The estimate of their metaphysics will be more or less self-complete in the next chapter.

These sections should not be taken as a depreciation of the Nyāya-Vaiśeṣika philosophy, which has an important place in the development of Indian thought, both academical and religious. Without Gautama, Indian thought would perhaps be mere schwarmerei, self-hypnotism, sexual sublimation and what not, which it is taken to be by some western thinkers, wrongly indeed, even today. But the Nyāya-Vaiśeṣika overshot its mark in its realism to defend which it invented numerous artificial, logical relations, turning many things, even results of intellectual analysis, into objective entities and relations, claiming them to being observed by the senses, and developed a technique of defending and refuting anything. My own teacher in Neo-Nyāya, Sri Sankar Tarka Ratna, used to take pride in his grand-teacher challenging every one to give him any position to defend or refute, even including his own Nyāya. As a student, I felt it was great. But it was not the aim of Gautama, the founder of the school.

(xiv) Definition of an Object not a Proof of its Existence

Like the attempt to prove the truth of a conclusion with the help of a one-member class forming the major premise, the idea took shape in the mind of the Naiyāyikas that we can prove the reality of anything by giving its definition (*lakṣaṇa*). But the definition of any questionable reality is that which is unique to that alone; i.e., it is the definition of a one-member class. In mere wrangling, this method works; for then there is no eagerness in knowing the truth. To say that if something is real or exists its definition must be possible, is one thing; but to say that because I can give a definition, whatever I define must be real or must exist, is another. Even the first alternative may be questioned: for what is the definition of the knowable (*prameya*)? Even without regard to Aristotle's definition of definition—which requires reference to a higher genus— a true definition must not apply to those to which it is not applicable, i.e., the characteristics it includes should not be found in them, and must be found in all to which it is applicable. But there is nothing that is not covered by the term knowable; for we know the unknowable as the unknowable in the same way in which we understand the meaning of the meaningless, or give the name nameless to what cannot be named. If absolute, universal concomitance (*kevālanvaya*), as we have seen, is not acceptable as a major premise in inference, why should this definition be accepted as a definition? Furthermore, in the Vedānta the Brahman is said to be indefinable. Is the implication then that it does not exist? But it is called Existence, Being (*sattā*) itself. And what is the definition of existence or Being? Should we say that these terms are to be defined as indefinables? Then what is the point in demanding the definitions of reals?

One can easily see that the definition of a one-member class has to be a universal proposition and can, therefore, be the major premise of an inference. With it one may try to prove anything, even if unreal, either an individual or a class, as real. But as already shown, this procedure is risky in earnest philosophy. The whole polemical and logical literature of this school contains innumerable examples of adding conditions (*upādhis*) to conditions limiting the definition's applicability to exactly what is wanted to prove or define. It is difficult to give the translation of definitions running to between five and ten lines (some of them like the proverbial German and also Sanskrit compounds) in length with modifications, qualifications, or provisos—in fact *upādhis* are provisos—and discuss them. Let me give one example of the definition of the major premise in my own way to make it fairly perspicuous. Let us start with the definition:

> A major premise is a statement asserting, "wherever the middle term is found, the major also is found.
> All cases of the Md. (middle) are cases of the Mj. (major) term.
> Wherever there is smoke, there is fire."

But suppose smoke is wafted by wind over a lake, and one sees it there. Then one can infer fire in the lake? No, the smoke on the lake is wafted by wind, not caused by fire in the lake. So we modify the major premise by adding the proviso in the form.

> Wherever there is smoke not wafted to the place by wind, there is fire.

Now, suppose that one smokes, keeps the smoke in his mouth, even after throwing away his cigar, then should we say:

> There is fire in his mouth, for there is smoke not wafted by the wind?

Or should we say:

> There *was* fire in his mouth, because there is smoke now?

Will not the introduction of the time factor, destroy the necessary relation? We can go on adding conditions to the middle and major terms for avoiding such difficulties. We have seen that this practice amounts to adding negative and positive limitations (*upādhis*) or conditions. But by adding the required number we can prove or disprove anything. As we have also noted, in this world in which everything is somehow related to everything else, every major premise must ultimately be conditioned and can never be absolute. For instance, we say that all other conditions remaining the same, water boils at 100 degrees Centigrade. And as J.S. Mill speaks about the causal law, the negative and the positive conditions remaining the same, fire causes the gunpowder to explode. But these negative and positive conditions include the whole of the rest of the world. The Nyāya tries to exclude this assumption by saying that these conditions are present even otherwise (*anyathāsiddhas*), assumed to be present, but not relevant to the present definition of cause-effect relation. But are they really irrelevant? If they are not irrelevant, but have to be recognized, such a recognition is not the same as a licence to prove or disprove anything. Because the Nyāya-Vaiśeṣika does not treat the inter-relatedness of things in the universe as a primary recognition[132] (as either *abhyupagama, samānatantra,* or *sarvatantra siddhānta*), it was obliged to introduce numerous relations and limiting qualifications—like "provided it is so" and "provided it is not so"[133]—to defend the absoluteness of the major premise,[134] which goes against the view that no empirical truth is absolutely necessary.

There is also another difficulty, not generally pointed out, viz., this school finally defines the major premise in negative terms.[135]. Here again, let me express it in my own words to avoid a cumbrous translation. The major premise expressing invariable concomitance is of a simple form:

> Wherever there is the middle term, there is the major term.

The general concrete example is:

> Wherever there is smoke, there is fire.

But if the concrete example is:

Wherever there is smoke, there is reality or existence (*sattā*),

can anything particular be proved by this major premise? Nothing exists that is not real. So we have to accept that, for inference to be significant, there must be things other than those meant by the major term, and the middle term should not be present in them. Then we have to say:

Wherever there is absence of the major, there must be absence of the middle. But this expression does not indicate any positive relation between the middle and the major. We cannot draw a positive, definite conclusion from such a major premise. In the instance,

Where there is no major, there is no middle,

or

Wherever there is absence of fire, there is absence of smoke,

how is the absence of fire related to the absence of smoke? Can absences by themselves be related? The relation of absences, if there is one, is not one of the three forms of necessary relation accepted by this school—genus-species, class-member, and cause-effect relations. Absenceness (*abhāvatvam*) is no universal (*jāti, sāmānya*) for this school, and so there cannot be a class determined by it. And can one absence be the cause of another absence? Causality belongs to positive, existent realities, but not to artificial concepts. If there is any causality in concepts at all, their effect also can only be a concept. But here we are talking not of mere concepts, but of existent realities.

One perhaps will say that the major premise represents only a cognition through which our mind refers to objects. Then the person who makes the major premise cognizes by perception the causal relation between fire and smoke, or between the absence of fire and the absence of smoke, and then makes the conceptual premise. But no one can observe all instances of fire and all instances of smoke. According to this school, one instance, viz., the kitchen (of the old type using wood as fuel) is enough; for that particular smoke gives rise to the idea of all the instances of smoke and that particular fire to the idea of all instances of fire;[136] and the two classes become necessarily related in our mind. But then how are we to eliminate the possibility of the mere coincidental occurrence of smoke and fire in the kitchen? To remove the possibility, negative formulas like

Wherever there is absence of fire, there is absence of smoke,

are needed. Then the negative formula is only a help, but cannot be the primary major premise.[137] Why does the Nyāya define then the nature of concomitance in negative terms? It rejects the negative counter-factual conditional (*tarka*) as concomitance—the Jainas accept it—but accepts it as a help in grasping concomitance and in the removal of doubts. A negative formulation of concomitance is unjustified then, and ends up in the Nyāya contradicting itself.

NOTES

[1]Gautama: *Nyāyadarśana* with Viśvanātha's commentary, I i, 1.
[2]Ibid., I, i, 24. [3]Ibid., I, i, 23. [4]Ibid., I, i, 26–31.
[5]Ibid., p. 23. [6]Ibid., I, ii, 1.
[7]Ibid., I, ii, 2. [8]Ibid., I, ii, 3. [9]Ibid., I, ii, 10–17.
[10]Ibid., I, ii, 18. This *Jāti* should not be confused with *jāti* meaning universal, genus.
[11]Ibid., I, ii, 19–20. [12]Ibid., V, ii, 1–24.
[13]Gautama: *Nyāyadarśana*, I, i, 3. [14]Ibid., p. 7.
[15]Jayanta Bhatta: *Nyāyamañjarī*, pp. 73–82, (Chowkhamba Sanscrit Series, Benares 1936).
[16]Viśvanātha: *Kārikāvalī*, p. 118. [17]Ibid., p. 43.
[18]Jayanta Bhatta: *Nyāyamañjarī*, p. 70.
[19]Viśvanātha: *Kārikāvalī*, p. 96.
[20]Viśvanātha: *Kārikāvalī*, p. 38.
[21]Jayanta Bhatta: *Nyāyamañjarī*, Part II, pp. 7 fol. Gautama says in his *Nyāyasūtras*, I, i, 10, that likes, dislikes, pain, pleasure, and cognition are indices of the *ātman*. The work index (*lingam*) is interpreted by some of his followers as reason, middle term.
[22]Viśvanātha: *Kārikāvalī*, p. 44.
[23]We should note the distinction between quality (*guṇa*) and attribute (*viśeṣaṇa*) in the Nyāya technical terminology. Quality can always be an attribute, but not vice versa. *Guṇas* are sounds, tastes, smells, colours, etc. and are positive; but anything can be an attribute, an absence, a substance, or even a whole thing. The distinction is ignored in literary language.
[24]Viśvanātha: *Kārikāvalī*, p. 47. [25]*pratiyogi-prasañjana.*
[26]For details, see Jayanta Bhatta: *Nyāyamañjarī*, pp. 46 fol.
[27]Cp. the doctrines of Plato and Aristotle.
[28]Viśvanātha: *Kārikāvalī*, pp. 47 fol. [29]Ibid., p. 50.
[29]Ibid., p. 50.
[30]The Indian logicians have no separate place for immediate inference. At the most, we may say that it is implied in the means of cognition called *sambhave*, which is a kind of a *fortiori* argument. Examples are: "A has a million dollars, therefore, he has a thousand" and "A man of seven feet can pass through this door, therefore a man of six feet can pass through it." It is an argument from more to less. But the Naiyāyikas reduce it to syllogism and reject it as a distinct means of cognition. See Jayanta Bhatta *Nyāyamañjarī*, pp. 59–60.
[31]See Y. V. Athalye and M. R. Bodas: *Tarkasangraha of Annambhatta* for comparison between the Nyāya and Aristotelian syllogisms. (Bhandarkar Oriental Research Institute, Poona, 4, 1930)
[32]Gautama: *Nyāyadarśana*, p. 19. [33]Viśvanātha: *Kārikāvalī*, pp. 50–51.
[34]Ibid., p. 53. The Naiyāyikas are great conceptual analysts and devoted much thought to the definition of the major premise. The definition given here, although good enough for general understanding, is not logically adequate. For instance, in the inference, "The horse has Being, because it has horse-ness", the major premise is: "Wherever there is horseness, there is Being". According to our definition of the major premise, there must be absence of horse-ness wherever there is absence of Being. But there is nothing in the world in which there is absence of Being. So our definition becomes inapplicable and has to be changed We cannot here enter into logical subtlities. The interested student may refer to Viśvanātha: *Kārikāvalī*, with the commentaries *Dinakarī* and *Rāmarudrī*, pp. 216–30 (Chowkhamba Sanscrit Series, Benares, 1951). Five different definitions have been given, for which see Mathuranatha: *Vyāptipañcakarahaśyam* (Chowkhamba Sanscrit Series, Benares 1928) and D. H. H. Ingalls: *Materials for the Study of Navyanyāya Logic* (Harvard University Press, Cambridge, 1951).
[35]Gautama: *Nyāyadarśana*, I, i, 5. Viśvanātha, in his *Kārikāvalī*, (p. 125), accepts the three kinds of inference, *kevalānvayi*, *kevalavyatirekī*, and *anvayavyatirekī*, and two kinds of major premise, *anvayavyāpti* and *vyatirekavyāpti*. The first two of the earlier classifications are defective; for instance, there may be no rain even when dark clouds are present, and no inference from effect will be valid, if there is a plurality of causes, and all the plurality is not mentioned.
[36]The extreme forms of *Kevalānvayi* and *Kevalavyatirekī* are not unanimously accepted, as will be seen later.

[37]Vātsāyana: *Nyāyabhāṣya* on Gautama's *Nyāyasūtras*, I, i, 5.

[38]This is the Nyāya view.

[39]See the author's "*Arthāpatti*: Its Logical Significance" (*Proceedings of All-India Oriental Conference* (Benares Hindu University, 1942).

[40]Viśvanātha mentions only two conditions: cognition of concomitance and non-cognition of any contrary instance. *Kārikāvalī*, p. 121. He adds that the counter-factual conditional can, in some cases, remove doubt.

[41]Viśvanātha: *Kārikāvalī*, p. 10. The nature of the particular will be explained in the chapter on the Vaiśeṣika.

[42]Ibid., p. 10. *Pārimaṇḍalyabhinnānām kāraṇatvanudāhṛtam. Evem paramamahatparimāṇam atindriyasāmānyam viśeṣāsca bodhyāh.*

[43]The word means that which is present even otherwise. See *Dinakarī* and *Rāmarudri*, pp. 80–81. Bosanquet says that the whole universe is the necessary condition and cause of every event. (*Essentials of Logic*, pp. 164 fol. Macmillan and Co., London, 1914).

[44]Viśvanātha: *Kārikāvalī*, pp. 12–14.

[45]Ibid., p. 11. [46]Ibid., p. 14.

[47]One may ask: why not?

[48]*Vyāpāravadasādhāraṇakāraṇam.* [49]*Tajjanyatve sati tajjanyajanakattvam.*

[50]See Y. V. Athalye and M. R. Bodas: *Tarkasaṅgraha of Annambhatta*, pp. 193 fol.

[51]This also shows that the Naiyāyika logic is not meant to be mere formal logic, which does not care whether any minor exists or does not exist.

[52]This can be turned into an example of the extreme form of *kevalavyatireki*.

[53]Viśvanātha: *Kārikāvalī*, p. 79.

[54]The major here may be called a self-contradiction, equivocation, etc.

[55]The milky way is called the heavenly river in which, as in the Indian rivers, lotus flowers are said to bloom.

[56]We may remind ourselves that much of Aristotle's logic is regarded as psychological and metaphysical by the recent formal or symbolic logicians.

[57]Other kinds of fallacies also can be pointed out in this inference.

[58]For instance, the effect of clapping hands.

[59]The best work on the subject is Jagadīśa's *Śabdaśaktiprākāśa*. (Chowkhamba Sanscrit Series, Benares, 1934).

[60]Viśvanātha: *Kārikāvalī*, pp. 83 fol.

[61]There is an ambiguity here between the correct understanding of the meaning of a sentence and the truth value of the meaning. It is the latter that is meant here.

[62]Ibid., p. 82. [63]Ibid., p. 83.

[64]Ibid., p. 88. [65]Ibid., pp. 92–95.

[66]Jayanta: *Nyāyamañjarī*, pp. 146 fol., and Viśvanātha: *Kārikāvalī*, pp. 118 fol.

[67]Ibid., p. 119.

[68]The Naiyāyikas would not go all the way with idealists like Bradley and Bosanquet in the use of the idea of coherence.

[69]For a detailed discussion, see *Dinakarī* and *Rāmarudrī* on *Kārikāvalī*, pp. 475–79. See also Jayanta Bhatta: *Nyāyamañjarī*, pp. 161 fol.

[70]Jayanta uses the word *viparītakhyati*, which is used by Kumārila. But Viśvanātha makes the difference from Kumarila's view clear by saying *tatchūnye tanmatiryā syāt apramā sā nirūpitā*. See the above references. Many recent writers in English mix up *viparītakhyāti*, and *anyathākhyāti* and the positions of Kumārila and the Nyāya. It is a mistake. Kumārila's theory is *viparītakhyāti* and the Nyāya theory is *anyathākhyāti*.

[71]Often the views of Kumārila and Nyāya are confused, as the difference is very subtle. In very elementary works, they may even be treated as the same. In any case, both wanted to be realistic.

[72]S. N. Dasgupta treats them together. See his *History of Indian Philosophy* Vol. I.

[73]Viśvanātha's Commentary on *Nyāyadarśanam*, p. 9.

[74]Gautama: *Nyāyadarśana*, I, iii, 10. [75]Viśvanātha: *Kārikāvalī*, pp. 31–38.

[76]This applies to dispositions also. For who remembers and says: "I had this disposition sometime ago, but not now?"

[77]This view is not accepted by the Neo-Nyāya, which, basing itself on the Upaniṣadic statements, regards every *ātman* as conscious.

[78]Jayanta Bhatta: *Nyāyamañjarī*, p. 184. [79]Gautama: *Nyāyadarśana*, IV, i, 19–21.

[80]Note the difference from Kant's moral argument.

[81]Jayanta Bhatta: *Nyāyamañjarī*, pp. 213 fol.

[82]Ibid., pp. 188 fol. [83]Viśvanātha: *Kārikāvalī*, pp. 139–40.

[84]Viśvanātha's Commentary on Gautama's *Nyāyadarśana*, p. 10.

[85]Ibid., p. 11. [86]Ibid., p. 11. [87]Ibid., p. 12. [88]Ibid., I, iii, 18. [89]Ibid., I, iii, 19

[90]Ibid., I, iii, 20. [91]Ibid., I, iii, 22.

[92]Viśvanātha: *Kārikāvalī*, p. 116.

[93]Bertrand Russell thought that logic made no such assumption. Cp. also the modern view that logic should be divorced from all metaphysics.

[94]*prameyasiddhiḥ pramāṇāddhi*. (Iśvarakṛṣṇa: *Sāṅkhyakārikā*, 4.)

[95]It is a pity that some recent writers on the Nyāya think that by symbolizing Gautama's and Raghunātha's logic, they can make it more intelligible and make it more valid than it is. Except in mathematics, so far as I can see, symbolization is not as helpful as these writers think. We can symbolize even existentialism. Even in the case of the Nyāya, we have to understand what we are symbolizing. Besides, we should not forget that most of the relations which the Nyāya has introduced are and are based upon the perceptual, not hypothetically accepted relations. This consideration is relevant to western logic also.

[96]Perhaps contemporary logicians who do not accept the validity of the excluded middle may have different objections. But then the exactness of inference vanishes and such logic may not be much different from the logic that presupposes the existence of the world.

[97]There is perhaps no philosopher of importance from any of the leading universities of Europe and America, who advanced these criticisms. However, truth is not the monopoly of any country or university. If that is ignored, philosophical thinking becomes empty, intellectual gymnastics. One may consider other fallacies, other kinds of syllogism, the introduction of *vitaṇḍa* and its context, in short, all the points of defeat (*nigrahasthānas*) to be convinced that the Nyāya did not mean its logic to be merely formal.

[98]See the discussion of the universal in the general estimate of the Vaiśeṣika for further development of the implications of the theory of the particularized universal.

[99]See my paper on "The Problem of the Individual" in *Review of Metaphysics*, Sept., 1963.

[100]This indeed conflicts with the feats of attending to eight and even a hundred things at a time (*aṣṭāvadhāna* and *satāvadhāna*) practised by some savants of the ancient tradition. This phenomenon also cannot be explained if mind is an atom. I attended the former a couple of times.

[101]*Kārikāvalī* with *Muktāvalī* and with the commentaries *Dinakarī*, etc., p. 319 (Chowkhamba Sanscrit Series, Benares 1951). But memory as one of the forms of *buddhi* is assigned also the *ātman*. See p. 155, Ibid.

[102]See my article, "The Logos and the Mahān Ātmā", in the *Ohio Journal of Religion* July 1973. The Logos may be explained as the Reason of the Cosmic Person.

[103]The Buddhists, however, do not seem to have made much use of it, not even as much as the Advaitins did. They were more concerned with its being creative—which is also the main concern of the Sāṅkhya-Yoga and the Advaita. It has cosmic significance like Reason in Stoic philosophy.

[104]I mentioned this a few times in my papers, but western logicians seem not to be impressed by it for some reason. But the reason is not clear to me.

[105]Some Indian philosophers actually used this name, cp. *mahāvidyāvidambanā* (the mockery of great knowledge). I have said many times that this is involved in the idea of one-member class and the individual as the value of the variable.

[106]King Bhoja says that the consciousness that cognizes the meaning of a sentence is the *Śabdabrahman* (the Brahman as the Word), the highest stage of the Logos, which is both Word and Rational Consciousness. Put in more intelligible terminology, it is the highest form of Cosmic Apperception, which can be related to the Logos, the *Natura Naturans*, Mahān Ātmā etc. These concepts and the concerned literatures have to be intensively studied for extracting their deep spiritual and philosophical significance.

[107]Husserl was criticized in the same way and his phenomenology was called psychology.

[108]Wittgenstein's language often seems to imply this view.

[109]Do relations have *sattā*? Or are they mere intellectual formations?

[110]I do not use the word quality; and the Nyāya term *guṇa*, which means a distinct category, is

translated by the word quality. Nor is it intelligible to translate it as qualifier, for that also brings to our mind *guṇa*. In using this term, the Nyāya depended more on the grammarian philosophers than on their categories. English translations, which are literal and dependent on dictionaries are confusing.

[111]None of the contemporary philosophers seem to advocate such a view.

[112]Cp. *Nyāyasūtra* with Vṛtti, I, 1, 3 and *Kārikāvalī*, 134.

[113]Translation of the word *avacchedaka* as limitor may be etymologically correct, but logically confusing, as western logic uses the word determinant, which also etymologically means limitor.

[114]*Vyāpāratvam ca dravyānyatve sati, bhāvatve sati, tajjanyatve ca sati tajjanya janakatvam*. This means that both qualities and activities can be causes. Then what happens to the restriction that qualities and activities can only be relational causes (*asamavāyikāraṇas*)? Is contact in perception *asamavāyikāraṇa*, and the result cognition?

[115]*Kārikāvalī*, 89. [116]Ibid., 96. [117]Ibid., 89.

[118]In the language of the Nyāya, it would be its own *adhyakṣa* (president, supervisor). But the school proves the reality of the *ātman* by saying that senses and mind cannot be their own *adhyakṣas* and need an *adhyakṣa*, which is the *ātman*. But how can the *ātman* be a supervisor of mind, if it is unconscious and depends on mind for being conscious?

[119]The word used is *nitya* (eternal), which may be interpreted as inseparable in one direction, i.e., the individual is inseparable from the universal, but not vice versa.

[120]"I am the Brahman" is also misunderstood similarly. In the present case, *tādātmya* may be translated as "identity of being".

[121]As we shall see in the next chapter on the Section on Neo-Nyāya, Raghunātha was already heading towards such a view. But he was still unable to disentangle himself from the maze of the artificial schemata of the Nyāya and was wavering between the Mīmāmsā and the Vedānta on the one side and the Nyāya-Vaiśeṣika on the other.

[122]*Svarūpa* in Vedāntic terminology means Being (*sattā*). The Nyāya usage should not be confused with it. Cp. the ideas of *svarūpa-lakṣaṇa* (constitutive or existential characteristics), *svarūpaikya* (oneness of Being), and *svabhāvaikya* (oneness in nature) of the finite and the infinite *ātmans*. See pp. 199, etc., of my *Philosophical Traditions of India* (George Allen and Unwin Ltd., London, 1971 and Pittsburgh University Press, Pittsburg, 1971), and also "Existential and Phenomenological Consciousness in the Philosophy of Rāmānuja" in *Journal of the American Oriental Society* (Oct.-Dec., 1964).

[123]Western readers who are curious about these techniques may see: H. H. Ingalls: *Materials for the Study of Navya-Nyāya Logic* (Harvard, Cambridge, 1951); Karl Potter: *Padārthatattva-cintāmani of Raghunātha Śiromaṇi* (Harvard 1957); C. Goekoop: *The Logic of Invariable Concomitance in Tattavācintāmaṇi* (Humanities Press, New York, 1967); and B. K. Matilal: *The Navyanyāya Doctrine of Negation* (Harvard, 1968), which is based only on a few pages of Gaṅgeśa's and Raghunātha's works.

[124]Ingalls.

[125]Matilal. The difficulty with the Nyāya is that it does not advocate an organic theory of the universe, in which everything must have some kind of objective relation with everything else like the prehensions in Whitehead's philosophy. Hence the artificiality of the Nyāya technique.

[126]There is a parody of the relation's objectivity in an example generally given. A Nyāya teacher sent his pupil with a pot to the market to buy and fetch some clarified butter, which is liquid. On the way to the teacher's house, the pupil began to doubt which the substrate was, the pot or the butter, as he could not see the substrateness in either. Then he turned the pot upside down to find out the truth, the butter fell to the ground, he got rebukes from his teacher, and his doubt was not cleared. But we may ask: Is not action or possible action the determinant of substrateness and superstrateness?

[127]The word *upādhi* has more than one meaning in Indian thought. Its literal meaning is "That which is placed near (an idea or object)." Generally it means condition, conditionality. But it may also mean a conceptual form, which, according to some logicians, may be a real universal, but generally a concept that is not a real universal. For the definition of a real universal, see the next chapter. Some universals and conceptual forms are indivisible like Being (*sattā*) and knowableness (*prameyatva*). But the distinction between divisible and indivisible is questioned in many cases. For instance, spaceness—although space is regarded as one—may be a combination of this-spaceness and that-spaceness and so forth. Is this all right? The Nyāya may say that it is its *abhyupagama-siddhānta*.

[128]The discourse on "White Horse" is attributed to Kung-sun Lung. See my *Introduction to Comparative Philosophy*, p. 119.

[129]See my article, "Being, Existence, Reality, and Truth," in *Philosophy and Phenomenological Research.*

[130]Conjunction (*samyoga*) is itself seen as residing in the table on the one side and the books on the other by the relation of inherence, and inherence is seen as an adjective. This type of conjunction is called *ādhāra-ādheyatā-sambandha*, substratum-superstratum relation or simply holder and the held relation.

[131]If two absences can be present at the same place and time, can their counterparts, i.e., the objects of which they are absences, be also present at the same place and time? If they cannot coexist at the same place and time, but their absences can, here is another reason for emphasizing that affirmation and denial, the positive and the negative, are not complementaries, and also not coordinates. Formal logic may work with their nature as coordinates, but logic concerned with existence cannot.

[132]One need not start with "everything in the world is inter-related" as a dogmatic assertion, but should at least treat it as a realization.

[133]The language often covers up the proviso-nature of the adjectives. But it is easy to find out the meaning. For instance, smoke exists in the lake through temporal relation, i.e., both smoke and the lake exist in time or at the same time. Then can we have: "There is smoke in the lake, so there is fire in it". And should we add: "provided the relation of the smoke and its locus is not temporal?" But this is an *upādhi*, and all *upādhis* vitiate the validity of the major premise.

[134]Even "water boils at 100°C" is not absolute.

[135]Not only the famous *simhavyāghra-lakṣaṇa* (lion-tiger definition) (See p. 64, C. Goekoop: *The Logic of Invariable Concomitance* for the translation), but also the ordinary one is negative in form (see *Kārikāvalī* with *Muktāvalī*, p. 53) "Necessary relation is the nonrelatedness of the middle with any term that is not the major term."

[136]through *sāmānyalakṣaṇa-sannikarṣa* (contact of the sense and object through the universal).

[137]The tiger-lion definition is blatantly negative. See Goekoop's work for the English translation.

Chapter VII

The Vaiśeṣika and the Doctrine of Particulars

1. INTRODUCTION

The Vaiśeṣika school has already been referred to in the chapter on its sister school, the Nyāya of Gautama. It is generally believed that this school was earlier than the Nyāya[1] and its founder Kaṇāda was earlier than Gautama. It seems that the Vaiśeṣika developed out of some independent and, probably, materialistic speculations, which were gradually assimilated[2] to the Upaniṣadic ideas of salvation and the reality of the spirit (*ātman*). However, by the time Kaṇāda composed his *Vaiśeṣika Aphorisms* (*Vaiśeṣikasūtras*), the group of thinkers to which he belonged acknowledged the authoritativeness of the Vedic scriptures and became an orthodox school. We know little about the Vaiśeṣika thinkers before Kaṇāda, who is recognized as the founder of this school.

The philosophy of this school underwent much transformation, and it is likely that many aphorisms were added to the original ones. Praśastapāda (5th century A.D.), the first great commentator on Kaṇāda, introduced his own ideas and practically resystematized[3] the original system. Udayana (10th century) wrote a commentary called *Kiraṇāvali* on Praśastapāda's commentary, but wrote also a commentary on Vācaspati's commentary on Udyotakara's indices on Gautama's *Nyāya Aphorisms*. So one may say that by the time of Udayana, who commented on both the Nyāya and the Vaiśeṣika works, the two schools began merging.[4] Another great commentary on Praśastapāda's work was Śrīdhara's *Nyāyakandalī* (10th century). Śaṅkara Miśra's *Upaskāra* (16th century) is a direct commentary on Kaṇāda's *Vaiśeṣika Aphorisms* and differs from Praśastapāda's on some important points. Almost all the later works on either the Nyāya or the Vaiśeṣika are syncretistic, although the authors show preference to either Gautama or Kaṇāda on some minor details.

Like Jaimini, the founder of the Mīmāṃsā, Kaṇāda proposes to explain the nature of *dharma* in the very first aphorism of his work. But while Jaimini explains *dharma* as the action commanded by the Veda, Kaṇāda explains it as that from which happiness in this world (*abhyudaya*) and the supreme good of salvation (*nihśreyas*) result. In this definition, we see the attempt to reconcile the ideals of life of the early Mīmāṃsā and of the Vedānta by making the word *dharma* include both ethical obligation and salvation. The word is thus made to include in its meaning all proper actions turning man towards the world (*pravṛtti*) and also that which makes him withdraw from the world (*nivṛtti*). By performing ethical actions, one obtains happiness in this world; and by following the way to salvation, one obtains eternal bliss. Both ethical duties and the way to salvation are given by the Veda. Therefore, says Kaṇāda, both are to be called *dharma*. Indeed, salvation is the highest ideal, and there is nothing higher than salvation.

But whether one wants pleasures and happiness in life after life in this world or to obtain salvation, one has to know the truth about the world and reality. Knowledge of reality is knowledge of the categories of reality. Kaṇāda says that knowledge of the Vaiśeṣika philosophy is essential for salvation.

As the Vaiśeṣika holds the views of the Nyāya on God, creation, and life's ideal, they will not be presented again, as they have been dealt with in the chapter on the Nyāya.

2. EPISTEMOLOGY

It has already been mentioned that the Vaiśeṣika school practically incorporates the epistemology of the Nyāya. However, Kaṇāda thinks that there are only two primary means of valid cognition, perception and inference.[5] He accepts the authoritativeness of the Veda for the reason that it is the word of God;[6] otherwise, knowledge obtained from words is only a combination of perception and inference.[7] We perceive the sounds that constitute speech and infer their meanings from them. Kaṇāda contends that verbal knowledge need not, therefore, be given a separate place. For the same reason, he does not accept comparison (*upamāna*) as understood either by the Nyāya or the Mīmāmsā. Like the Nyāya, he rejects postulation (*arthāpatti*)[8] and non-apprehension (*anupalabdhi*),[9] which are accepted by the Mīmāmsā.

Although Kaṇāda accepts mainly two means of valid cognition, he seems to have no objection to accept memory[10] also (*smṛti*). As he accepts Vedic testimony for his own reasons, commentators like Praśastapāda and Śaṅkara Miśra say that the Vaiśeṣika school accepts four valid means of cognition: perception, inference, verbal knowledge (Vedic testimony), and memory. As we have seen, the Nyāya does not accept memory because it is only a cognition of a past cognition and is, therefore, a cognition of what has already been cognized. Furthermore, the Vaiśeṣika, unlike the Nyāya, does not treat doubt (*samśaya*) as an error (*bhrama*), but as a cognition that produces no impression (*samskāra*) of the object and that leads to no decision (*vyavasāya*) about the object, but leaves us in suspense. It comes, therefore, under absence of knowledge (*avidyā*), which has four forms:[11] doubt (*samśaya*), error (*bhrama*), indeterminate cognition (*nirvikalpakajñāna*), and dream (*svapna*). But these distinctions were ignored by writers after the Vaiśeṣika got merged with the Nyāya. Before the merging took definite form, there were different classifications of true and false cognitions. But these classifications are not of great value. The confusion in the epistemology of the Vaiśeṣika is due to Kaṇāda's main interest being metaphysics and to his discussion of the epistemological problems being incidental to metaphysics and so disconnected. So far as the problems of the validity of knowledge (*prāmāṇyā*) and the nature of illusion and its object go, the Vaiśeṣikas, on the whole, follow the Naiyāyikas. The problems need not be discussed again.

3. METAPHYSICS

It is in metaphysics, particularly in laying the foundations of an ultimate pluralism, that Kaṇāda shows his genius. His discovery and formulation of the category of the particular (*viśeṣa*) as the final differentiator of each of the ultimate entities of the manifold world prevents any attempt to reduce the manifold to a monistic unity. And the school got its name from the term *viśeṣa* (particular). There is a tradition, according to which the founder of the school obtained his name Kaṇāda from the particulars, which were thought to be ultimate particles (*Kaṇas*). *Kaṇa* means particle and the root *at* means "to eat." So *kaṇāda* means one who eats ultimate particles. The ancient Sanskritists would call Bertrand Russell and the other logical atomists "the eaters of logical atoms." According to another tradition, Kaṇāda was a great ascetic and was living on grain particles (*kaṇas*) that fell from plants. In addition, he was the foremost exponent of the atomic theory. He had two other names, Ulūka and Kaśyapa.

The number of categories originally enunciated by Kaṇāda are six.[12] He says that by understanding the similarities and dissimilarities of substance (*dravya*), quality (*guṇa*), activity (*karma*), universal (*sāmānya*), particular (*viśeṣa*), and inherence (*samavāya*), one obtains the Supreme Good. Praśastapāda[13] explains that such understanding enables man to seek the good and avoid the evil. These six categories are called the meanings of words (*padārthas*), but what is meant by a word need not be a thing (*vastu*) in the ordinary sense. Nor do they cover the meanings of all words, which are many. They are the main categoreal meanings or the categories of reality. That is, they are the central nameables or thinkables in terms of which we think of the objects of the world. They are the key concepts of intelligibility. Yet, they are not the categories of Existence or Being (*sattā*). They are not forms of Being or kinds of Being. The kinds of Being are only three and are called *arthas*, which may be translated as beings or existents.[14] *Artha* may mean thing (*vastu*), entity (*ens*). The three kinds[15] of Being are: substance, quality, and activity. Words refer to these three directly, to the others indirectly, i.e., through the former. These others are: universal, particular, and inherence. Their nature is dependent on thought and is relative to it (*buddhyapekṣyam*).[16] The six categories are positive (*bhāva*) and concern Being. In fact, the former three alone have Being (*sattā*), but not the latter three, although all the six are positive. The category of Non-being also is accepted[17] and mentioned in the IX Chapter of the *Vaiśeṣika Aphorisms*. It is not mentioned in the beginning, as the negative is dependent on the positive. All subsequent writers mention seven categories, and include the negative also.

The Vaiśeṣika school seems to have had a history in which the number of categories was different at different times. But we do not know much about the history. H. Ui gives us an English translation of a Sanskrit work called *Daśapadārthaśāstra*, in which the categories given are ten.[18] We get three categories besides the above seven. They are potentiality (*śakti*), non-potentiality (*aśakti*), and common-ness (*sāmānya*). Potentiality is the capacity (power, force) of the cause to produce the effect. It exists in substance, quality, and activity—the three categories comprising Being (*sattā*). Non-potentiality is the opposite of potentiality. For instance, fire does not have the power to cool anything. Potentiality (*śakti*), accepted by the Mīmāmsā, was rejected by the later Nyāya-Vaiśeṣika as a distinct category. Non-potentiality was rejected with it. By common-ness is understood what we call genera and species; for example, substanceness (*dravyatva*), quality-ness (*guṇatva*), action-ness (*karmatva*, the universal of actions) and their species like pot-ness, red-ness, and throw-ness are regarded as coming under this category. Common-ness is distinguished from the universal, which is Being (*Sattā*) only. Being is the real universal, for it is universally present. But later the distinction between common-ness and universal was given up. Finally only the seven categories were retained. But the list of ten categories shows that at one time the Vaiśeṣika was under the influence of the Mīmāmsā.

The reader may be struck by the way the categories are classified in terms of Being and Non-being. The first six categories are called positive, but Being is not found in all of them. It is found in only the first three—substance, quality, and activity. Although it is not found in the other three—universal, particular, and inherence—, they are not forms of Non-being, but are positive. According to this school, the first three are objects of our knowledge and are independent of our thought (*buddhi*); the other three are objects only relatively to our thought. Again, the latter three belong to the first three, which are forms of Being, but not to Non-being. They are, therefore, called positive. Non-being can have neither a universal nor a particular; nor is anything, positive or negative, related to it through the relation of inherence. Non-being or negation also is relative to thought; but unlike the second group, it is negative, not positive. Yet in controversies with rival schools, the Nyāya and the Vaiśeṣika defend the reality of all the seven categories. Such defence may confuse the student, who will ask: "If four of the seven categories cannot have Being, how can one defend their reality?" And what can one mean by such defence? The answer can only be: Being[19] is not the same as reality, and not even the same as the positive. Reality[20] includes everything, positive and negative that thought has to accept for the purposes of understanding the cosmos; but Being is only part of the positive. Everything that is not Being is not the same as Non-being. The universal, the particular, and inherence are neither kinds of Being nor kinds of Non-being. These distinctions are not clearly explained by the Vaiśeṣika, but are implied by its categoreal scheme.

SUBSTANCE Substance (*dravya*) is defined as that in which qualities and actions inhere (*samaveta*). Qualities and actions cannot exist except in a substance. It is thus their substratum (*āśraya*). The relation between substance and its qualities and actions is the inseparable relation of inherence (*samavāya*). There can be no substance without qualities and activities and vice versa. Substance is also the material cause. It can be defined also as that which can be the material cause of every causal process and can constitute the effect (*samavāyikāraṇa*). Clay and the parts of the pot constitute the pot, which as the effect (*kārya*) inheres in them. Qualities and activities cannot be material causes. Now, the effect, pot, can be produced when its parts are brought together into contact (*samyoga*); such parts can be substances only, but not qualities and activities. So another peculiar characteristic, which can also be a definition of substance is that it alone can come into contact (*samyoga*) and there can be contact only between substances.

There are nine kinds of substances: earth, water, fire, air, ether (*ākāśa*), time, space (*dik*), spirit (*ātman*), and mind (*manas*). The first five are generally called physical substances (*mahābhūtas*) and each of them has its own peculiar quality or property. Smell is the property of earth, taste of water, colour of fire, touch of air, and sound of ether. Each[21] divides itself into, and assumes three forms: the corresponding cognitive sense, the corresponding physical sense organ, and the corresponding physical object and its quality. Thus there is a psychological sense and the physical sense organ, which is a part of the physical body. There is the physical nose and the sense of smell; the physical tongue and the sense of taste; the physical eye and the sense of vision; the physical skin and the sense of touch; and the physical ear and the sense of hearing.

Of the five substances, only the first three—earth, water, and fire—are perceptible; air[22] and ether[23] are inferred from the qualities, touch and sound, respectively. For every quality must have a substance as its substratum, and the substances here concerned are air and ether. Perception is taken as visual perception. Kaṇāda thinks that, as air is not perceived like the cow, it is to be inferred,[24] and we have come to talk of it as perceptible because the Veda and popular tradition speak of it. The Mīmāmsā does not accept ether, and many Indian thinkers treat air as an object of perception cognized by the sense of touch and do not limit perception to sight. The Vaiśeṣika lays down two conditions for a substance to be an object of perception: (1) it must be big enough, i.e., it must have molecular dimension (*mahatva*); and (2) it should have manifest colour or form (*rūpa*). Of course, neither air nor ether has manifest colour and so it does not satisfy the second condition. Perhaps, what Kaṇāda meant was that, for an object to be perceived, it must have a definite form or shapes (*rūpa*) like the cow; air and ether do not have such forms or shapes.

According to both the Nyāya and the Vaiśeṣika in general, none of the nine substances, except the first three, is perceptible. The existence of all the other six is inferred. Time[25] is inferred from the ideas of past, present, and future; and it is the universal common generator of everything that is born. Space[26] is inferred from the ideas of near and far. The *ātman* has already been discussed in the chapter on the Nyāya. According to Kaṇāda, it is not perceived even by mind, but only inferred.[27] He gives more indicators than the Nyāya does for inferring the *ātman*. They are the different vital principles (*prāṇas*), the movement of the eye, life, mind, bodily movement, the activities of senses, pain, pleasure, desire, hate, and effort. All these presuppose the *ātman*, which is their guide and controller. Mind[28] (*manas*) is inferred from the fact that, even when there is contact of the *ātman*, senses, and the object, there will be no cognition if there is no mind or if mind is absent. To understand this argument, we should remember that, according to both the Nyāya and the Vaiśeṣika, cognition of external objects involves four terms and three relations connecting them. The four terms are: the *ātman*, mind, senses, and objects. If any of the terms is absent, there can be no cognition. We know that sometimes objects are within our vision; our *ātman* also is there; but we are not aware of the objects. We explain this lack of cognition by saying that our mind is absent or that we are absent-minded. The Nyāya-Vaiśeṣika says that such experience is proof of the reality of mind as distinct from the *ātman* and senses.

Atomic Theory and the Externals Of the nine substances, the first four are constituted by atoms. That is, earth, water, fire, and air have atoms. Mind (*manas*) also is an atom; it is atomic in size. Its nature and function have already been explained in the chapter on the Nyāya. The other four substances—ether, time, space, and spirit—are infinite in dimensions. The atom is conceived by the Nyāya-Vaiśeṣika as being without any dimensions and so as infinitesimal. As the infinite and the infinitesimal are indivisible, they cannot be destroyed and are, therefore, eternal. Time and space are indivisible; and divisions, like past, present, and future, of time and like the east and the west of space, are conventional and artificial. Time and space are, therefore, each infinite, indivisible, and eternal. As mind is infinitesimal, it also is indivisible and eternal. But it is many; every man has his own mind. Spirit (*ātman*) is also a plurality; every person has his own spirit. Yet each *ātman* is infinite and indivisible. All *ātmans*, all minds, and all the atoms of each of the four elements—earth, water, fire, and air—are exactly alike. That is, qualitatively there is nothing to differentiate one *ātman* from another, one mind from another, one earth atom from another, one water atom from another, one fire atom from another, and one air atom from another. Of course, qualitatively the *ātman*, mind, earth atom, water atom, fire atom, and air atom are different from one another. Yet within the class *ātmans*, each is different from every other; and similarly within the class of every other, each member is different from every other. Such differences are possible because each individual *ātman*, each individual mind, and each individual atom have each its own particular (*viśeṣa*). *Leibniz's doctrine of the identity of indiscernibles is avoided and would be denied by the Nyāya-Vaiśeṣika through the category of the particular.*

Space and time also have each its own particular. The principle enunciated is: all ultimate (*antya*), eternal (*nitya*) substances (*dravyas*), both infinite and infinitesimal, have each its own particular.[29] Non-substances do not have particulars. Different kinds of qualities, activities, universals, particulars, and negation do not have particulars.

Of the four kinds of atoms, each group differs from another qualitatively.[30] The earth atoms, although infinitesimal, possess the quality of smell, water atoms taste, fire atoms colour, and air atoms touch. All of them are imperceptible except to the yogis. For us, ordinary men, their existence is proved by inference. All the objects we perceive are composed of parts and are, therefore, divisible. Next, each part is again divisible. If we carry on this division, we have to stop at some point, where further division is not possible. Then we reach the atom. The division cannot be *ad infinitum*. Otherwise, if everything can be divided *ad infinitum*, it must contain an infinite number of parts. And if everything contains an infinite number of parts, then all objects must be equal in size and even the mustard seed has to be considered to be as big as the Himalayas, as both have equal number of parts. We have, therefore, to say that the mustard seed has fewer parts than the Himalayas.

The atoms are imperceptible, as they have neither length, nor breadth, nor thickness. Their qualities also are imperceptible because they are not manifest (*udbhūta*). They become manifest when first two atoms combine and become a dyad and three dyads combine and become a triad. The triad alone possesses a manifest quality and is itself manifest. It is said to be of the size of a mote in the sunbeam. Since according to the Nyāya-Vaiśeṣika originally, perceptibility belongs only to earth, water, and fire, but not to air, the perceptible triads belong only to the first three, but not to the fourth, although the qualities of the four are perceptible at the triadic stage. The experienced world of matter is built up of such triads. However, the objection that, if the atom has no size, even an infinite number of such atoms cannot produce any size, did not bother the Nyāya-Vaiśeṣika.

DIFFERENCES AMONG SUBSTANCES There is another difficulty. Perceptibility of substances is accepted only as visual perceptibility. Thus, air was excluded. Then if the atoms, even after they come to form triads, have only their different properties, earth and water must not be perceptible, as their triads do not have colour, which belongs to fire atoms. To overcome the difficulty, the Nyāya-Vaiśeṣika says that all the three have colour[31] also, although colour is the specific quality of fire. Thus a distinction is drawn between specific qualities and common qualities. A quality may be both specific and common. Colour is the specific quality of fire, but a common quality of earth and water. Touch is a specific quality of air, but a common quality of all the others including ether.[32]

Specific qualities are possessed only by the *ātman* and the five elements[33]—earth, water, fire, air, and ether—but not by the other three substances—time, space, and mind. The specific qualities of the five elements—smell, taste, colour, touch, and sound—and of the *ātman*—pain, pleasure, desire, hate, cognition, and effort—have already been given. Now there is a difference[34] between the specific qualities of the *ātman* and ether on the one side and those of the first four elements on the other. *First*, the specific qualities of the latter are pervasive in their substrates, e.g., colour is found wherever fire is found. But those of the former are non-pervasive; e.g., if sound is found in one part of ether, it is not found in another, although ether is all-pervasive (*vibhu*). Similarly, if cognition is found in one part of the *ātman*, it may not be found in another, although the *ātman* is all-pervasive. *Secondly*, the specific qualities of the *ātman* and ether are momentary; while those of the other four elements need not be momentary. That is, the specific qualities of the former occur one after another; but they can be simultaneous in the latter. For instance, the same pot can have two smells at different parts; but the same *ātman* cannot have two cognitions simultaneously and ether cannot have two separate sounds at the same location of the ear. The first cognition has to disappear before the second appears in the *ātman*; and the first sound has to die out before the second can arise in the ether of the ear. In case of the *ātman* and ether, if two qualities arise simultaneously, they get mixed up; but they need not be mixed up in the case of the other material substances. Momentariness here should not be understood literally. And regarding the impossibility of the simultaneous appearance of two sounds, the position is not very tenable. It is mainly meant that our ear cannot take in two sounds simultaneously, without their being mixed up.

QUALITIES Before giving the nature of each of the substances in terms of their qualities, it will be convenient to know about the qualities, which the Nyāya-Vaiśeṣika accepts. Quality is defined as the being that is different from substance and activity and that is itself without qualities and activities. The school gives a list of twenty-three[35] qualities. They are: colour, taste, smell, touch, number, magnitude, distinctness (*pṛthaktva*), conjunction (*samyoga*), disjunction (*vibhāga*), nearness (temporal and spatial), remoteness (temporal and spatial), cognition (*buddhi*, consciousness), pleasure, pain, desire, hate, effort, weight, fluidity, viscidity (*sneha*), tendency (*samskāra*), unseen merit or demerit (*adṛṣṭa*), and sound. Some give the number of qualities as twenty-four, separating merit and demerit and treating them as two.

Of the above, cognition, as mentioned already, is an adventitious, though a specific, quality of the *ātman*. Viscidity is the oily nature of some of the liquids. Tendency (*samskāra*) is not only what is left in our spirit by our ethical actions, but also the tendencies produced in physical objects by our actions, e.g., the tendency of a spring to regain its original form after it is stretched or pulled. The unseen merit and demerit produced in us by ethical actions are treated by the Nyāya-Vaiśeṣika as qualities, distinct from tendencies (*samskāras*), which are also qualities whereas the Mīmāmsā would treat tendencies and ethical merit and demerit as the same and as potencies (*śaktis*). The Buddhists, particularly of the Mahāyāna, follow the Mīmāmsā. However, according to the Nyāya-Vaiśeṣika, tendency is of three kinds: velocity (*vega*), mental impressions (*bhāvanās*), and elasticity. The first keeps things in motion, the second enables us to remember, and the third enables a physical body to regain its original state or position. Sound is of two main kinds: noises like the sound of a drum and words which have meanings. Another quality that interests us is number, which, instead of being treated as quantity, is called quality. The idea of number originates out of referential cognition (*apekṣābuddhi*) and disappears when its origin is destroyed. We refer the quality "two" to two apples, when each is taken along with, or with reference to the other. It is not understandable, therefore, why it is regarded as a quality at all; for quality is a form of Being, while number is dependent upon thought; and for being dependent upon thought, the universal, particular, and inherence are not regarded as forms of Being. Magnitude is recognized, but only as a kind of quality with four subdivisions: the atomic, the infinite, the small, and the large. It is interesting to observe that quantity as a distinct category is not found in the Nyāya-Vaiśeṣika. There are further subdivisions of the qualities, such as different colours, tastes, smells, etc., which the reader can easily visualize.[36]

QUALITIES OF THE NINE SUBSTANCES[37] Of the above twenty-three qualities, air possesses nine—touch, number, magnitude, distinctness, conjunction, disjunction, nearness, remoteness, and one of the three tendencies, velocity. Fire possesses eleven—touch, number, magnitude, distinction, conjunction, disjunction, nearness, remoteness, colour, velocity, and fluidity. Water has fourteen—touch, number, magnitude, distinctness, conjunction, disjunction, nearness, remoteness, velocity, weight, fluidity, colour, taste, and viscosity. Earth also has the same fourteen qualities as water, except that it has smell instead of viscosity. The *ātman* has fourteen qualities—cognition (consciousness), pleasure, pain, desire, hate, effort, number, magnitude, distinctness, conjunction, disjunction, mental impressions (one of the three kinds of tendency), merit, and demerit. The last two are here separated. Time and space has each the same five—number, magnitude, distinctness, conjunction, and disjunction. Although time and space are the grounds of our cognition of nearness and remoteness, the two cannot be the qualities of anything all-pervasive, and so of space and time also as wholes. These two qualities can belong only to finite and infinitesimal objects. Ether has the same qualities as time and space with the addition of sound. Thus it has six qualities. Mind (*manas*) has eight qualities—nearness, remoteness, number, magnitude, distinctness, conjunction, disjunction, and velocity. By conjunction and disjunction one should understand the contact of two separable substances and the breaking up of that contact.

ACTIVITIES Action belongs to finite substances and is the cause of conjunction and disjunction. Like quality, it can only be a formal (*asamavāyi*) and an instrumental (*nimitta*) cause, but not a material cause, which only a substance can be. Actions are of five kinds: throwing upward, throwing downward, contraction, expansion, and locomotion. Some actions cannot be perceived, e.g., the action of mind. The actions of perceptible substances—earth, water, and fire—can be perceived both by sight and touch. There are subclasses of each of the five.

UNIVERSALS The definition of the universal (*sāmānya*, *jāti*) is that which is eternal (*nitya*) and inheres in many.[38] Although the Nyāya-Vaiśeṣika is opposed to any form of idealism, it accepts the reality of the universal.[39] The universal is not a kind of being, although real. And although real, it is dependent on our cognition (*buddhyapekṣyam*).[40] It exists in substances, qualities, and activities. It is first of two kinds, the higher and the lower. The higher beyond which there is nothing higher (*para*) is Being (*sattā*) itself. As it is present in substances, qualities, and activities, they are cognized as beings (*sats*). But Being does not exist in Being again; it is meaningless to ask: "Has Being Being?", but only "Has substance Being?" Again, it does not exist in substance-ness (substantiality, *dravyatva*), etc., it does not exist in any kind of universal, but only in individuals. Substance-ness, quality-ness and action-ness are universals lower than Being (*sattā*). Man-ness, redness, throw-ness, etc., are lower than substance-ness, etc. The individuals are never universals and Being is never an individual.

The Nyāya-Vaiśeṣika insists that simply by adding "-ness" to a word we do not get a real universal. Otherwise, we can have universals like man-ness, man-ness-ness, man-ness-ness-ness, etc., *ad infinitum*. In such cases, all except man-ness are false universals; they are not real but conceptual (*upādhis*). This school lays down, therefore, six conditions which a real universal has to satisfy. (1) It should exist[41] in a plurality of individuals. This condition is found in the definition itself of the universal. Because of this condition, space-ness (spatiality) and time-ness (temporality) are not real universals. For there is only one space and one time. Space-ness and time-ness are only conceptual forms (*upādhis*). (2) If two supposed universals refer to the same class of individuals,[42] they are not two universals, but only one. We may have two words, two definitions of the same class of objects or two connotations having the same denotation. Man and human being refer to the same object; so "man-ness" and "human-being-ness" cannot be two different universals. If man is defined as a political animal and also as a rational animal—which Aristotle does—then "political animal-ness" and "rational animal-ness" cannot be two different universals.[43] (3) If a universal leads to cross-classification or hybridity (*saṅkara*)—neither the Nyāya nor the Vaiśeṣika is unanimous at this point nor has either analyzed this condition well—such a universal cannot be a real universal. For instance, "two-legged-ness" cannot be a real universal. For men are two-legged and swans are two-legged; but the former belong to the class of animals and the latter to the class of birds. "Two-legged-ness" belongs therefore to hybrid universals, leading to cross-classification. But we may retain the idea as a concept. (4) A universal cannot be real, if its formation by our mind leads to an infinite regress. This condition is laid down for avoiding universals like man-ness-ness, etc. (5) A universal is not real, if it is not capable of being positively related to the individuals. This condition is laid down for excluding the universals of Non-being. For instance, in front of me on the table there is the absence of water and there is absence of water on the floor also. We cannot, therefore, conclude that the absence-ness of water is a real universal. It is trivial and insignificant to think that the universal absence-ness of water exists in different absences of water. The universal exists in the individuals by being related to them through the relation of inherence, which will be explained later. Now, any relation can exist only between positive entities, but not between negative entities. So there can be no relation between the universal absence and the different absences. Furthermore, in front of me there is absence of water, absence of fire, absence of the tree, absence of the mountain, etc., on the same table at the same time. I cannot perceive any differentiating characteristic among them, except in my mind. Now, in which of these absences can the absence-ness of water exist? All of them are there as one object on the table. No kind of Non-being can, therefore, have a universal. (6) No universal can be a real universal, if its presence in the individuals destroys their very nature. This condition is very important for the Nyāya-Vaiśeṣika to defend its ultimate pluralism, and can best be explained under the category of the particular.

PARTICULARS The particular is defined as that which is ultimate and exists in eternal substances. That is, it does not exist in anything except substances, then too only in ultimate, eternal substances. They are the four kinds of atoms, ether, the *ātman*, space, time, and mind. The particular is the ultimate differentiator and is different from that in which it exists. All the earth atoms are alike; yet they are differentiated from one another as each has a particular in it. So also are the water atoms, fire atoms, and air atoms to be understood. The *ātmans* also are ultimately alike and are differentiated from one another by each one having a particular. So also are minds differentiated from one another. Ether, space, and time are differentiated from one another by each of them having a particular, although all are all-pervasive. One ordinary object can be differentiated from another ordinary object, as each has different qualities or occupies different spaces or times. But when and where none of the ordinary differentiators is available and yet objects, infinite and infinitesimal, exist as a plurality, there must be a particular that is the ultimate differentiator residing in each and every one of them. Such a differentiator is a positive entity, not a negative one.

Now, the question arises: If there is a particular[44] for each of the ultimate entities and there is, therefore, a plurality of such particulars, must there not be the universal, particularity (*viśeṣatva*, particular-ness), that resides in every member of the class of particulars? The answer is that particularity cannot be a real universal. For instance, every *ātman* has the same characteristics as any other; the characteristics cannot, therefore, differentiate one *ātman* from another. So we postulate a particular in every one to function as the ultimate differentiator. But if every particular is similar to every other particular,—and it becomes similar to the others, if all have the same universal particularity,—then it loses its power as the ultimate differentiator. For the particulars to have a universal is to destroy themselves. They cannot have a universal, called particularity, which, however, can be retained as a concept.

INHERENCE Inherence (*samavāya*) is defined as the eternal relation.[45] But by the word "eternal" the Nyāya-Vaiśeṣika means a kind of inseparability. Yet every kind of inseparability is not inherence. For instance, the leaf of a book has two sides and they are inseparable; but the relation between them is not inherence. Each side of the page does not inhere in the other side. But the whole leaf inheres in both the sides. Inherence is found between the whole and parts, between substance and qualities, between substance and activities, and between the universals on the one side and substances, qualities, and activities on the other. The whole inheres in its parts, qualities and activities inhere in substances, and universals inhere in substances, qualities, and activities. But no higher universal, as mentioned already inheres in the lower universals, but directly in the individuals. In any individual man, Being (*sattā*), substance-ness (*dravyatva*), and man-ness[46] (*mānavatva*) inhere together. Being is higher than substance-ness because it is found not only where substances are found, but also where qualities and activities are found. For the same reason, substance-ness is higher than man-ness. But that it is higher does not mean that it inheres in the lower.[47] The old Nyāya and the Vaiśeṣika held that there is only one relation of inherence in the world, just as there is only one space.

NON-BEING For Non-being, non-existence, absence, and negation the Sanskrit word used is *abhāva*, but occasionally *asat*. Non-being is defined merely as what is not, or as different from the six positive categories: substance, quality, activity, universal, particular, and inherence. As all the six categories are positive, Non-being is the negative reality. The Nyāya-Vaiśeṣika thus accepts that reality is both positive and negative. However, Non-being is real only with reference to our thought (*buddhyapekṣya*); it is neither a form of Being nor what is positively related to any form of Being. Yet, the Nyāya-Vaiśeṣika holds that Non-being is perceived; but it is perceived only when accompanied by the thought, "Had the object been there, it would have been perceived." Hence, the Advaitins dismiss it as only a thought-product. Even in the Nyāya-Vaiśeṣika doctrine there is no Non-being or Nothingness as such. It cannot even be conceived. Every non-being is a negation, and every negation is always the negation of something positive such as the negation of a pot and the negation of a pen. There can be no negation, if there is nothing positive to be negated. Similarly, there can be no absence, if there is nothing positive that is absent. Now, in perception, what is negated, e.g., the pot, is only remembered or thought of, but not perceived. If so, how is the Nyāya-Vaiśeṣika justified in holding that negation is an object of perception? Again, if the absence of water, of fire, and of a pot are all together on my table at the same time, with which of the three absences does my sight come into contact when I look at the table? Contact is a relation between two positive entities or substances. But absence cannot be a positive entity. So my sight cannot come into contact with it. Then perception of absence is impossible. But the Nyāya-Vaiśeṣika brushes aside these objections, saying that the absence of fire, for instance, must be seen by the eye as fire is seen by the eye. And to support its view, this school, as we have seen, posits different kinds of sense-object relationship.

Non-being or negation is primarily of two[48] kinds: relational absence (*samsargābhāva*) and difference (*anyonyābhāva*) or mutual negation. Relational absence is the absence of something at or on or in something else, like the absence of the pen on the table. Difference or mutual negation is the difference between two individuals or universals. Jim is different from Bill: that each is not the other means that they mutually negate each other. Mutual negation exists in the two, not merely in one. Similarly, the lion as a class is different from the tiger as a class and lion-ness is different from tiger-ness.

Relational absence is of three kinds: prior negation (*prāgabhāva*), posterior negation (*pradhvamsābhāva*), and absolute or infinite negation (*atyantābhāva*). Prior negation is the absence of an object before it is born. The pen with which I write did not exist before it was manufactured. Prior negation has no beginning, but an end. It disappears at the moment the pen is made. Posterior negation is the absence of the same pen when it is destroyed. It has a beginning, but no end. Absolute or infinite negation is the absence of an object in time and space except when and where it exists. Since the time and space in which it does not exist are infinite, this negation is called absolute or infinite.[49] But there is another interpretation of absolute negation. It is that which exists in all times and places. An example is the absence of colour in air. The Nyāya-Vaiśeṣika did not know of coloured gases like bromine. We do not see colour in ordinary air and this school thought that air is absolutely uncoloured. But then there is no positive relation between air and colour. The upholders of the first interpretation say that, when there is no such positive relation at all, this negation becomes the negation of the non-natural or even the impossible and so insignificant. But the others maintain that absolute negation must truly be absolute; it must be the eternal, natural negation of all relation between two entities.[50]

Śaṅkara Miśra, the author of the commentary, *Upaskāra*, on the *Vaiśeṣika Aphorisms*, raises some doubts about treating difference (mutual) negation, (*anyonyābhāva*) as negative (*abhāva*) and distinctness (*pṛthaktva*) as a quality and as positive. He thinks that the two ideas are the same. That Jim and Bill are distinct individuals means also that they are different individuals and mutually negate each other and vice versa. He reduces the negative mutual negation to the positive quality of distinctness.

APPENDIX TO THE NYĀYA-VAIŚEṢIKA

THE NEO-NYĀYA

1. INTRODUCTION

The Neo-Nyāya[51] grew out of the merger of the Nyāya and the Vaiśeṣika schools. Its founder is generally regarded as Gaṅgeśa (12th century), the author of *Tattvacintāmaṇi*. The greatest commentary on it is the *Tattvacintāmaṇivyākhyā* of Vāsudevasarvabhauma (15th century). The most renowned logician of this school is Raghunātha (16th century), the author of *Dīdhiti*, and *Padārthatattvanirūpaṇa*. Jagadīśa and Gadādhara (16th, 17th centuries) are also great exponents of this school, but they are more inclined towards the combined Nyāya-Vaiśeṣika than towards the new school, particularly in their metaphysics.

This school, in spite of attempts to break down its boundaries, does not seem to be very much interested in metaphysics and its contributions to the subject are few and generally not considered to be very important. They are often ignored and not discussed. Its main interest is in logic, particularly definitions of logical and epistemological concepts. Its followers worked with the conviction that an object could be accepted as real if an exact definition could be given to it. And if an object is real, it must have an exact definition. So it tried to formulate elaborate definitions of everything it accepted as real—definition of definition, definitions of the ways of knowing and of their factors, and definitions of the categories and their sub-classes. The presupposition seems to be: To have a definition is to have a clear idea; and we cannot have a clear idea, unless there is an object of which it is the idea. If an exact definition cannot be given—a definition that covers everything that belongs to the same class and does not cover anything that does not belong to the class—of an object, then the object cannot be real.

2. EPISTEMOLOGY

In epistemology, the Neo-Nyāya accepts practically everything that the earlier Nyāya-Vaiśeṣika accepts. Its contributions lie, however, in the great clarifications and definitions it gives to the ideas by bringing out their full implications through analysis. The works of this school are studied mainly for understanding the analysis of concepts through definitions. For the same reason, viz., that the work of the school is merely an analysis of concepts and definitions, the other schools regard the Neo-Nyāya as a futile labour. But one has to admit that the school shows extraordinary skill in conceptual analysis; and its methods and ways of expression are followed by the other schools in their polemical works.

3. METAPHYSICS

Although logic and epistemology formed the main field of interest for the Neo-Nyāya, its followers differed considerably not only from the main Nyāya-Vaiśeṣika tradition, but also from one another. Gaṅgeśa followed the traditional Nyāya-Vaiśeṣika metaphysics, but Raghunātha not only saw the difficulties in the categorization by Kaṇāda, but was also influenced by the Mīmāmsā school. In fact, the followers of the Neo-Nyāya, who lived mostly in the Navadvipa of Bengal, were practically isolated from the other schools and showed very little interest in them. But the ethical codes (*dharmaśāstras*) and the Mīmāmsā, on which they were based, could not be ignored by them, as together they governed every form of daily life and action. At several points they differed from the Mīmāmsā position; but its doctrine of the importance, if not of the sovereignty, of ethical law could not be ignored by any orthodox Indian. The followers of the Navya-Nyāya were, therefore, well acquainted with the Mīmāmsā. Thus Raghunātha was influenced by its philosophy.

Kaṇāda's classification of the categories into the positive and the negative and the subsuming of only three of the positive under Being created a difficulty. Raghunātha denies, therefore, Being to all categories except to substance and activity—a view which agrees in general with the Mīmāmsā position and that of the grammarian philosophers. He treats all the rest as indivisible, imposed properties (*akhandopādhis*)—which means that they are conceptualizations due to the ways of our thinking. Mind (*manas*) is not accepted as a distinct substance; it is identical with a triad of any of the four elements. Time and space are not distinct substances, but are identical with God. Ether also is not a distinct substance; God, but not ether, is the inherent cause of sound. At this point, Raghunātha seems to have been influenced by the philosophers of the Word (*śābdikas*), according to whom the original Word, out of which the world issued forth, is God himself. Early Mīmāmsā did not accept the reality of God. Raghunātha rejects the reality of atoms and dyads and says that the triads are the ultimate constituents of the material world. This view is the same as that of the Mīmāmsā, for which the so-called atoms are the ultimate perceptible molecules. He goes even so far as to say that Being (*sattā*) as the highest universal (*sāmānya*) is by itself not real at all, because nobody can cognize it. We know only what are called the six categories, which are positively presented to our cognition, which may, therefore, be called positive. Of the six the primary categories are only substance and action, which may be called beings.

To substance and action, Raghunātha adds (1) having (possession, *svatva*), (2) force (*śakti*, potentiality, capacity, which is a Mīmāmsā category), (3) cause (*kāraṇa*), (4) effect (*kārya*), (5) number (cp. Prabhākara), (6) qualified-ness (*vaiśiṣṭya*), (7) objectivity (*viṣayatā*), (8) moment (*kṣaṇa*), and (9) the relation of inherence, which is one according to the earlier Nyāya-Vaiśeṣika, but many according to Raghunātha. That is, the relation of inherence between man-ness and Socrates is not the same as that between the same universal and Plato. If it is the same, then when Socrates dies, Plato also must die; or when one man dies, all the other men also must die. For the relation between the universal and all the individuals coming under it is the same. So we have to accept many inherences.

Other followers of the school gave other re-classifications, making some additions and omissions.[52] But they have not been very seriously taken by the writers on either the Nyāya or the other schools. Raghunātha seems to be a genius, in that he noticed that the categorization of reality should not be confined to the objects of the world and their inter-relations, but also include the relation of object to subject. So he made objectivity (subject-object relationship, *viṣayatā*) an important category. He seems also to have realized that the Nyāya-Vaiśeṣika, if it is really to be one of the orthodox systems, should accept the Upaniṣadic view that the *ātman* is by nature conscious and self-conscious; he rejected, therefore, the original view that the *ātman* is unconscious and that consciousness is only its adventitious attribute. In the state of salvation, the *ātman* does not, therefore, lose its consciousness. Thus the Neo-Nyāya in the hands of Raghunātha was adjusting itself to the Mīmāmsā and even to the Vedānta. But further development of his divergence from the traditional Nyāya-Vaiśeṣika—which is more or less a rebellion—do not seem to have occurred. For one who is interested in tracing the general growth of the philosophical thought of India, such development would be of greater interest than the exercises in the formulation of definitions and the great eagerness to pick up defects in them as given by opponents and also in the intellectual energy spent in discovering defects. A sharp eye can see that many of the important defects pointed out by the Nyāya logicians are adaptations of the dialectic of Buddhism and the Vedānta extant so far. However, the Neo-Nyāya gave a new twist to thought and expression of these two schools also in return.

GENERAL ESTIMATE AND CONSTRUCTIVE COMMENT

(i) Motives behind Realism

Like Jainism, the Nyāya-Vaiśeṣika is an earnest attempt at realism. Although the Jaina doctrine of "let-it-be-so" (*syādvāda*) is generally said to be due to the charitable attitude of the Jainas, it does not seem to have been realized that it is really the opposite of the four-cornered negation of the original skeptics like Sañjaya, who said: "*S* is neither *P*, nor not-*P*, nor both, nor neither." Then, what is *S*? If it is none of the predicates, it is merely void (*śūnya*). This was the conclusion drawn by Nāgārjuna, the greatest of the Buddhist dialecticians, perhaps a product of the Andhaka Buddhist movement, which is said to have brought out the first *Prajñāpāramitā* text in Pali. The Jainas could not deny the argument that led to the four-cornered negation, but wanted to defend the reality of both Spirit and matter. So they said: "Let *S* be *P*, not-*P*, both, neither, etc." When "neither" is added to *P*, not-*P*, and both, we get three more alternatives and the total including "neither" by itself, makes the seven-fold affirmation or assertion.[53] It attempts at making affirmation, negation, combined assertion of both, rejection of both, and assertion of their combinations always true; for there is always a point of view from which each of the seven predications can be made with justification. For instance, Berkeley said: If we have three pots of water,—the first cool, the second warm, and the third hot—and if we place our hand first in the cool one and then in the warm, the warm appears hot; but if we place our hand first in the hot and then in the warm, the warm appears cool. But is the water by itself cool, warm, or hot? He concluded that it is none of them, and so all qualities are mind-dependent ideas. As nobody sees the so-called substance behind these qualities—which by themselves do not exist—substance also is an idea. Then all objective reality disappears for Berkeley, who still retains the reality of the spirit. Hume rejected the reality of the spirit also, and turned everything into an idea or pure phenomenon. But Buddhist Nāgārjuna would take up the thread here and argue that, as the ideas have no basis (support) and cannot therefore exist even fleetingly, they also are not truly there; we merely imagine them (*kalpanā*) and we ourselves are the products of our own imagination (*kalpanā*). What is true is pure Void (*Śūnya*).

Here the Jainas would join issue and say that everything that is affirmed or rejected is true, depending on our point of view.[54] The Jaina realism is not mere common-sense realism. In fact, there is and can be no common-sense philosophy, and no common sense-sense realism, for all philosophies which started as common-sense philosophies and common-sense realisms ended up with such uncommon theories, concepts, and formulae that even trained philosophers do not find it easy to interpret them. Very often the followers of such schools of thought think that, by giving a definition of something which they accept or by formulating a long formula or equation, they establish the reality of what they accept. The formulae and the equations become hard nuts to crack for the critics, who may exhaust themselves in attempting to meet the challenge and may be overcome by its glamour. Such activity is often a mere hiding behind technicalities artificially invented, and evades the main questions and arguments which the rival schools advance. The Nyāya-Vaiśeṣika realism comes more or less under the second class of realisms.

In the philosophical atmosphere of ancient India, we may say that there were three motive forces behind the realistic attitude. The *first* was the conviction that logic is necessary to understand reality and determine what it is. But logicians will have no jurisdiction over reality if reality is all one. It has to be a plurality, and to defend the validity of logic we have to defend the validity of a pluralistic reality. The Nyāya and the Vaiśeṣika have mostly this motive. The *second* driving force is the idea that man can control his destiny through ethical action (*dharma*) and action necessarily implies the reality of plurality. The Mīmāmsā attitude comes under this type. The *third* motive force is a kind of inalienable feeling in our minds that, in spite of the arguments against the reality of plurality, it must be real; and therefore, the arguments against plurality can be true and those for plurality also can be and must be true. Summed up, the Jaina attitude seems to be of this type. To reconcile the arguments, pro and con, it developed the doctrine of view points and the seven-fold predication.

If we consider the etymological meaning of the term realism, there is no philosophy that is not a realism; for every philosophy tries to establish the reality of something or other—the Śūnya, Absolute Nothingness, Relativity of the World, Pure Phenomenologism, Mentalism, and so on—except in rare instances like those of Sañjaya and Pyrrho, who were not sure that they were even skeptics. But the term realism is reserved by convention for the philosophy that upholds the absolute and independent reality of what we consider true and real in this world. It has also to be noted that none of the above three classifications can be found in its pure form. The Vaiśeṣika, for instance, claims to be primarily interested in explaining the nature of the "Ought" (merit, *dharma*),[55] which is also the primary aim of the Mīmāmsā. The difference is that the Vaiśeṣika regards working for salvation (*mokṣa*) also as an "Ought," while the early Mīmāmsā rejected even the possibility of salvation, accepting only ethical perfection, although the later followers first ridiculed the idea of salvation and then accepted it, still maintaining that ethical activity without selfish desire and for the sake of the good of the universe was absolutely necessary.[56] However, the Vaiśeṣika allied itself with the Nyāya and with its logic and epistemology, and the two schools got hyphonated, as mentioned already. We may note that the Mīmāmsā also developed a pluralistic metaphysics and epistemology, but gave greater attention to the analysis and explanation of action and to the working of its potencies than any other school did; for ethical action was sacrosanct and ultimate for this school, just as Being or the Brahman is ultimate for the Vedānta. Again, although Śaṅkara, the Vedāntin, is said to have totally rejected action (*karma*) as important for salvation, he does not emphasize the rejection of action as strongly as Jainism did. Jainism formulated its way to salvation as a technique for the liquidation of the potencies of action (*karma-samskāras*) and the prevention of every action, good or bad, from entering (or leaving a *samskāra*, potency in) the *ātman*. All salvation philosophies of India preach going beyond action and life of action. But the literatures of some schools show a kind of obsession. Like the Mīmāmsā, Jainism has to devote, in its own way, a good deal of thought to an analysis and working of action. Hence also, it has to be realistic.

We have seen also that the Nyāya-Vaiśeṣika in the hands of Raghunātha was marching away from the original or ancient Nyāya-Vaiśeṣika. Had his movement of thought been continued and developed, it would have ended in a form of *Vedānta* similar to the Advaita (Non-dualism) of Śaṅkara with the difference that the plurality of categories would have been turned into forms of force (*śakti*, energy), which is Becoming (Bhāvanā) for the Mīmāmsā. In fact, his thought was leading him towards the Mīmāmsā. Let us see whether the categorical plurality of the Nyāya-Vaiśeṣika can be justified ultimately.

(ii) Analysis of Relations

We should remind the reader that giving a definition or formalization of a concept or category is no answer to the question whether the concept or category is ultimately valid. Taking F.H. Bradley's attack on relations, his argument is: if A and B are related to each other by the relation R, how is R related to A on the one side and B on the other? Note that this question arises only if one contends that R is objectively there like A and B and is not the result of the observer's intellectual analysis. Now, if r_1 relates A and R, and r_2 relates R and B; how is r_1 related to A and R_1 and r_2 related to R_2 and B? To answer these questions, the number of relations posited has to be infinite. Then do I follow the infinite number of relations before I grasp that A and B are related? One may say that we may express the relation by a formula:

$$A - r_1 - R - r_2 - B.$$

Has he answered Bradley then? How can there be an infinity of relations between A and R? Following Russell, one may ask: Is there no infinite series between the number 1 and the number 2, and between 1 and 3? Yes, because there is some mathematical space between 1 and 2 or even between 1 and 1.1. But there is no physical space between my book and the physical table on which it rests. Between the two the relation is said to be conjunction (*samyoga*), or contact. Similarly, there is no physical space between the individual and the universal, or between the colour and the thing to which it belongs. It matters little what relation we take: Bradley's objection is not answered. It is of no avail to say that the relation is "own form" (*svarūpa*); but this is what we do not observe, and we have already discussed this concept. One will perhaps say that there is intellectual or thought space between A and B. Yes, this is what Bradley would want you to admit. Relations are our thought products and constitute a network which we throw on what surrounds us to catch it and assimilate it. Remember, the simile is not to be carried on all fours; the fish we catch with a net are not marked actually by the lines formed by the lines of the threads of the net, we can remove the fish from the net and observe them. But we cannot remove reality from the thought structure, the net that holds the reality thus known. There is no other way of cognizing what we call the objective world or reality. *And if the reality thus known through the mesh of thought is objective, then thought must be objective*, not subjective or psychological as most contemporary Anglo-American philosophers think. *And what is important to deduce from this situation is that, if objective reality apart from thought's net is to be known, we have to seek it, not where thought's net has full sway, but deep inside thought and beyond it in the activating force which prompts thought but which is not prompted by thought.*[57]

The Nyāya-Vaiśeṣika is loath to make such an admission. It resorts to several kinds of expedients like introducing new kinds of relation,[58] and ultimately falls back on the concept of "own form" (*svarūpa*, own shape, depending on the context). Now, what is the significance of this concept with reference to the plurality of the world? It means that everything is as we see it, except in illusions; it is as it shows itself; it is that which creates the idea (*buddhi*) of itself in our mind. This view also does not answer our enquiry: Is everything as it appears to us? Or is everything as we know it? Very often this school regards it as the ultimate answer to say: "*X* is that which is the object of the idea of *X*" and "I could not have got the idea of *X*, if there were no *X*." But this attitude practically ignores the fact of epistemological illusions and errors—in which there are no objects answering to our ideas—but also the importance of the enquiry into the nature and validity of the categories we pick up in our everyday activities.

The idea of "own shape" (appearance, *svarūpa*) has its difficulties. Does the appearance or shape of an object as perceived by me belong to the object (*sva*, own)? This is the question raised, for instance, about relations by thinkers like Bradley. It is no answer to say that common sense affirms that the appearance belongs to the object. The whole complex of questions raised by the idealists has first to be answered before we can give an affirmative answer. The vogue of saying that we have a platform, that we regard such and such propositions and theories as sacrosanct and axiomatic (*abhyupagama-siddhāntas*) is little less than being dogmatic and is philosophically unsatisfactory; for philosophy attempts and has to attempt to probe right down to the existential foundations.

Now, coming back to the idea of relation, which is basic to both modern western logic and the Vaiśeṣika and the Neo-Nyāya, we have seen that the only answer possible to Bradley's dialectic is that relation is a thought-product. Even then, two questions arise. First, is any relation, even as a thought-product, the result of joining an infinite number of relations to one another, and then joining the two objects, *X* and *Y* with their product? We may say that this is old Zeno's paradox in a different context. It takes me an instant to cognize the relation of contact between *X* and *Y*; but it is said to be due to my joining an infinite number of relations to one another and then to the two objects. How could I have finished such an addition in one single, finite instant? It may be said that my mind or intellect passes from the integer 1 to the integer 2 in a single instant; and in the same instant it must have passed through an infinite series of decimal numbers or fractions. So the same instant may be viewed as single and finite, and also as consisting of an infinite series. Note, that we are at the intellectual sphere, not the physical or mental (i.e., the image of completing the images of an infinite series). Now, it has been asked: Is it meant that the single, finite instant is *infinitely divisible* or that it originally existed as *infinitely divided* and I add up the divisions in a finite instant? The latter alternative seems to be impossible; but the former is plausible in the mathematical sense like $1.9\ldots = 2$. We may put the same question in a common sense form: Which is primary in passing from 1 to 2, the single finite instant or its infinite number of divisions? It looks that it is against all experience, mathematical and perceptual, to say that I first pick up an infinite number of ready-made divisions, which I add up and constitute one single, finite instant. *So all that can be meant by the relation being intellectual is that it has its source in thought, and thought can think of the possibility of infinite division after asserting the relation between X and Y.* But actually we carry out the division only so far as we want for meeting some purpose. The relation is posited by thought itself, which can carry out the division so long and so far as it likes. There is only a *possibility* of unending division, which can never be carried out actually.

The *second* question is: If the relation relating the two objects in thought has its source in thought, can the objects related have their source outside and independently of thought? It looks that the relation of contact or conjunction—both are the same except that conjunction is viewed as taking place after disjunction or separation—obtains between two objects *X* and *Y* existing independently of each other and of thought, and that thought, when comprehending the two together, introduces a relation from outside. Such an idea may agree with the theory of external relations, which we shall examine a little later. But relations are not limited to contact, conjunction, and disjunction, that is, to a mere "and." Are the relations between the universal and the individual, substance and quality (or adjective), and substance and activity, and activity and its modality (adverb) external to the entities they relate? How can horseness and the individual object we call a horse be external to each other? At least the Nyāya-Vaiśeṣika accepts that the relation is inseparable (*nitya*) and is not conjunction (*samyoga*), but inherence (*samavāya*). We have pointed out that universals like horse-ness are constitutive, and we objected to their being used as qualifications. Similarly, when *X* is running, *X* is not conjoined to the act of running. So also the colour of any wood (not its external paint) inheres in the wood, and yet is not constitutive of wood as such. Similarly, in "*X* is running fast" fastness is not an entity added externally to the act of running. True, *X* may not be running; and when he is running, he may not be running fast. But when he runs and runs fast, running and fastness are inherent to *X*. There is no running that is added to *X* who is sitting quietly, like adding paint to a wall. Similarly, fastness is inherent to running which is inherent to *X*. But inherence here is not an eternal relation—as manness is to man—but temporarily constitutive. Manness belongs to man as long as he lives;but running is not constitutive of his being in a similar way, and fastness also does not constitute running in a similar way.

So if the relation between the horseness and the individual horse, the act of running and the person running, is our thought product and yet is inherent to the horse and the person, how can the terms related by thought be external to thought, if the relation constituting them is internal to it? Then the things which are related have also to have their source in thought. The conclusion seems to me to be inescapable, if we accept that relations are thought products; and there are no alternatives to "relations are thought products" if objections like those of Bradley have to be met satisfactorily.

Now, as regards the relations of contact and conjunction, which appear to be mere "ands," we should ask ourselves: Is there any object that is not in contact with something else? Is there any conjunction without disjunction? If my book is on the floor first, and then is lifted and placed on the table, the first contact is broken and there is disjunction, and then there is conjunction or contact with the table. So the relations are interdependent. But is not my book also dependent on something or other for resting? It cannot hang in mid air or vacuum. Does not this mutual dependence make the relation of even "and" internal to things? Even the "and" cannot escape mutual dependence. Still, the residual realism and pluralism at the back of our minds prompts us to ask: Are we not handling things individually and independently apart from things on which they are dependent? For instance, when I take my book from my office, I do not take the table also or the floor also on which it is resting. Yes, the book is independent of the floor or the table; but is it independent of the necessity of the relation of resting—the Nyāya calls it the relation of *adheyatā*—on something? That is, the relation of dependence covers the whole universe of objects, for no object can be without dependence on something else.[59] If we use the term "and" in the sense of absolute independence of objects from one another, the term will not and cannot find anything corresponding to it in reality. But in the pragmatic or activistic sense that I can pick up the book apart from the table or the floor and carry it home, holding it in my hand or placing it in my hand bag, the book is independent in existence. But action, possible or actual, is my action, with my purpose towards which I guide my action. Then I and my thought cannot and should not be ignored in determining the extent of the independence of the object and the significance of the "and." Again, there are prepositions, relative adjectives, etc., to which there is something corresponding in the world and is fixed by our action and thought. So there seems to be no escape to the alternative that both things and their relations have their source in thought.

Then there is another aspect of reality we have to notice. Every relation has its counter or reverse relation. Every relation has two directions. If we speak of "*X* and *Y*," we imply also "*X* is not *Y*." If "and" implies "not" and "not" is, as we have seen, a thought product, then "and" also has to be a thought product. If *X* is related to *Y* by the relation of resting, then *Y* is related to *X* by the relation of being a rest or support. If *X* has the relation of being a quality of *Y*, then *Y* has the relation of being qualified by *Y*.[60] The universally present mutual dependence precludes absolute independence of things from one another and from thought.

It is a truism to say that even in perception no object is seen separately from everything else, although the Buddhists say that every perception is that of a particular. We have already examined the Buddhist view and have given the support it has to be given. But certainly, they do not mean that, when I see two volumes of the same work, one on the other, I see only one volume. We should also bear in mind that the Buddhists, so far as this world goes, are thorough-going pragmatists (*arthakriyākāritā-vādins*) and activists, who hold that our perception is determined by the possibility of action (*bhāvi-kriyā*) on the object perceived; they do not mean that I cannot pick up one of the volumes by itself, if I am not interested in the other. But when I see the two volumes, one on the other, my percept is one and particular. So the independence of the objects is dependent on my interest and on the possibility of my action in accordance. The "and" even in perception does not denote absolute independence. If there are two books, each of two volumes, all piled up on one another, I may say: "This book (with two volumes) and that book (with two volumes)" or "This volume and that volume and that volume and that volume" referring to each of the four. There is only one "and" in the former expression, but three "ands" in the latter. Then this separation depends on my interest. Furthermore, we even say: "The thing and its form," "The thing and its structure," "The thing and its quality," and "The thing and its movement." Can the "and" in each of these cases separate the two terms and make them independent?

Now, there can be the objection: The above discussion leads to the conclusion that all relations are internal to the terms related; but if the relation between the book and the table is internal to them, how can the book be detached from the relation and placed on the floor? It is, therefore, foolish to say that relations are internal to things, if things are external to thought. If things, say the book, carries with it the relation of inherence—i.e., if the universal or form of the book is inherently related to the book and the book cannot exist without it—and if the relation is a thought product, then the book also, as mentioned already, is a thought product. If the "and" relates the book to the table, then the "and" also must be a thought product. As we have seen, even the "and" does not imply absolute independence. Now, if the book carries the relation of inherence wherever it exists, it carries also the relation of "having to rest on" wherever it goes. We cannot see how anything can exist without depending on something else; and resting is one of the forms of dependence. "Depending on" and "being depended on" are the same relation viewed in opposed directions.

(iii) Objective Thought

This time another objection may be raised. Thought is generally considered to be psychological and finite; it belongs to the finite man. How can finite thought be the source of the infinite world, containing an infinite number of things and their relations? This objection generally seems to dispose of the philosophical importance of all discussions and results like the above. But the objection seems to play fast and loose with ideas of the finitude of man and of his thought and the infinitude of the world. When we speak of the infinitude of the world, do we have the world as an object before our minds like I have the object book before me? The book has a definite shape, contour, size, occupies some fifty cubic inches of space, was brought out into existence in the year 1890. Can I describe the world, even the physical world, in any similar way? What are its shape, size, and contour? We know the difficulties which Kant raised in his "Transcendental Dialectic" about the world being in time and space, and being caused and so forth. The world is then an Idea, a principle;[61] it is indeed not a mere working hypothesis, as some philosophers tend to interpret it. It is a necessary Idea, because we live and work in what we call the world. It is really what I see, experience, and am able to think about—even including the idea of the finitude of space-time—and as going far beyond. So the infinitude of the world—however this infinitude is explained—has its origin in the thought of the thinker. If this infinitude has its source in thought, then thought cannot be finite.

Still one residual doubt bothers the objector. Can I now think of everything that is there in the universe? This inability is the index of the finitude of my thought. Even then, whatever is thought of has its source in thought. This capacity to think and project reality is the infinitude of thought. If the world is its Idea, then somehow everything that the world contains, its objects and their relations, must have their source in thought. Then if the whole world is in thought, why do we not find the parts of the world, their relations now? Here we are again caught up in the problem of relations; and we have pointed out that the so-called "whole world" here is not held by my thought as an object like the book in front. It is safer to say that the Idea of "the Whole" works through *my thought*; but as an Idea that is active, dynamic in all thinking, it must be inherent to thought. We have to say also that this thought is the Cosmic Thought,[62] the Logos, which works through my erratic and groping thought, regulating and correcting it. Still the Logos is mine and yours also when we think correctly; but my erratic thought is mine and your erratic thought is yours. Man is not finite in every sense of the term. Yes, my existing body is finite; but my deeper conscious being, as we have already shown, reaches up to the stars millions of light years away. Even my finite thought which accompanies my perception expands itself to the distances and even beyond them. Where am I, where is my conscious being, when I am immersed in the perception of the star and its beauty? Often when such immersion is intense, I am not attentive to anything nearby. The focus of my being is not in my body then, but far away. My being at the base is extended up to the star and beyond it; it is infinite.

Thus we can see that my thought, as studied by the psychologists, the thought that gropes around for understanding the world, may be finite; but the thought which it becomes when correctly understanding the world and which prompts it to understand the world—which we may call meta-psychological, transcendental—is ontological and confers ontological validity on my empirical thought.[63] For this reason, my thought also is said to be essentially ontological.

(iv) Relations Spontaneously Discovered

One objection may yet be advanced against relation being regarded as a thought product. In the above section, we have shown that, instead of speaking of the source of the world, its plurality of objects, and the relations among them in a world external to our thought, we should seek all of them in thought itself. To answer the question, how the finite, psychological thought be the source of the world, we have said that we should revise our ideas of thought and man, although his body is finite. Relations belong to the structure of thought only in its infinite aspect, and for that reason the things related also belong to that thought structure. There seems to be no other way to remove the difficulties in our understanding the situation. Since we have approached the position held here by an examination of relations, the objector may say that, to avoid what appears to be a psychological explanation, he would regard relations as *simply found* spontaneously between things, but not as simply constructed by thought, not also as relating terms, but as acts simply existing as such. Similarity, we have shown, has to be prior to comparison, and we preferred the Mīmāmsā view of comparison as a valid means of knowing to the Nyāya view. Just as similarity *does not make* things similar, but is found spontaneously discovered, relations do not relate things, but are found spontaneously discovered. Then realism in the popular sense of the term can in a way be defended.

We have emphasized that thought here is not what the psychologists study, but is ontological; and we need not repeat what has been said. Although we have said that similarity is prior to comparison, even as an involuntary process, *it is not something that is spontaneously perceived by the senses as they perceive the colour of a red rose.* When discussing what are called the valid means of cognition in the estimate of Jainism, we pointed out that to be a valid means does not imply that whatever is cognized through any of the means is incapable of being erroneous. Every valid means including perception is prone to error. For what we call spontaneity or immediacy in even perception is not absolute spontaneity or immediacy, and whatever has an element of mediation can result in at least some slight error.[64] So similarity, although perceived in the object, is not even direct perception, but *an unconsciously mediated perception*, and is one step removed from even the so-called immediacy of ordinary perception. For instance, if I see an object as red, every one else, except some colour-blind persons, sees it as red. But when I observe the similarity of the water buffalo to the bison, another may observe their dissimilarity. Again similarity is not of one type. My brown pencil and the brown horse are similar in colour; but the brown horse and the grey burro may be similar in structure. Here what one person sees as similarity may not be seen by another. At higher levels of thought, Newton could see the similarity of the relation between the falling apple and the earth on the one side and the relations among the planets and the sun on the other. So observation of similarity depends far more on our interests, practical and intellectual, than in the case of sense perception. What cannot be observed at least as spontaneously as in sense perception can hardly be said to be out there in the world independently of my thought. Nobody observes relations like he observes colours.

(v) Form of Contact not Perceived by Senses

From the view-point which has so far taken shape, we can hardly justify the Nyāya-Vaiśeṣika realism of the relations between substance and quality, substance and action, the universal on the one side and the three—substance, quality, and action—on the other, the relation of inherence and all of them, and the various other types of relation between negation and all the others. To confer independent, objective reality on these six entities—or categories, as there may be an objection to call negation an entity—the Nyāya-Vaiśeṣika holds that all of them and their relations are objects of perception. (The particular, *viśeṣa*, may be left out for the present as it is not an object of perception for us, but for the yogis.) Now, if our above discussion has arrived at any truth, these relations cannot be objects of perception, as perception of them does not even have even that much of immediacy as the perception of colours. This school calls each of these relations by the term contact (*sannikarṣa*), which is explained again as activity (*vyāpāra*) of the senses.[65] Now, how can quality be activity and activity be quality, if the two are ultimately two different categories? For the present, we only raise the question, which will be discussed below. Our present concern is about whether these contacts are perceived by the sense by which the concerned substances are perceived. I do not even perceive the activity of perception, but only the result of that activity, e.g., the colour red. One may even question whether any activity is an object of sense perception at all,[66] although this school generally holds that it is. For what we call movement or action is constituted by a series of static pictures which our eye records and our mind interprets as action. Now, if I cannot perceive the contact of my eye with the colour red, it is pointless to say that

I perceive the contact of my eye with the relation between colour and substance, horse and horseness, etc. Perception has a certain immediacy, although not absolute, which these relations, contacts, activities—whichever term one prefers here—do not possess. There is some absurdity in saying that I perceive the absence of the book on the table. As mentioned in the previous chapter, I do not "see" the absence of the book if I am not interested in the book, but may see the absence of the coffee flask, if I am interested in my coffee. How can the relation of the absence of the book to the table be seen by my eye with the immediacy with which it sees colours? The relation of the absence of the book to the table is called adjectival relation (*viśeṣaṇata-sambandha*) by this school. If it is adjectival and objective, it is so because of my interest and thought structure.

We have to say that the objectivity of these relations—which means that they have to be recognized by every thinking person, if his thought is to have cosmic validity—has only cosmological significance, not the ontological. And because the schools did not distinguish between cosmology and ontology, they carried on endless controversies.

We may raise one more question about relations. If these relations are all objective and are there in the world, as this school maintains, they must all be related among themselves and with everything else like universals, particulars, negation, substance, qualities, and activities. What is the relation between two universals like horseness and elephantness, between a universal and negation and so on? These may be awkward questions; but if the relations are out there and all these possible terms are also out there in the world, they ought to be related.[67] And what is the relation between two particulars and between a particular and a universal? What, for instance, is the relation between a particular in an atom, in time, in space, or an *ātman*—the *ātman* constitute a plurality for this school—and the universal *ātmanness* or horseness?

(vi) Estimate of the Classification of Categories

Although the whole of our discussion so far seems to have centred in the doctrine of relations, the reader may have noted that we have introduced several other concepts or realities, which will be discussed along with still other realities in a different setting. Much space has had to be devoted to the discussion of relations because the Nyāya-Vaiśeṣika in its later developments overawed the philosophical scholars with new terminology, formulation of new concepts of relations, and long technical definitions by which the other schools were overwhelmed, fascinated and challenged, and as a result incorporated the new methods of argumentation to pay back this school in its own coin and to confuse and defeat one another in controversies. One may rightly anticipate that such artificial development of thought, although challenging and engrossing our minds, leads us away from basic realities and makes us forget them. All the development of the Nyāya-Vaiśeṣika was necessitated by the desire to defend absolute realism and pluralism and defeat all rival schools. The school that started with the aim of clarifying and controlling our thought and controversy ended in inventing cumbrous methods to defeat the rivals apparently logically.

In this estimate and the estimate of the previous chapter, we have already raised the question whether relations are activities, and whether there is absolute difference between qualities and activities. We asked also whether substances can be relations; if they can be relations, we may ask now whether qualities and activities cannot be relations. If substances can be converted into relations, and relations into qualities and activities, will any ultimate difference remain between substances, qualities and activities? Then can universals be reduced to qualities and activities? How then does the particular (*viśeṣa*) be related to them? Is the world possible without energy or force (*śakti*), which this school rejects?

We generally think that universals are abstract nouns; but to think so is a mistake in philosophy. We are misled by the practice of calling them abstract nouns[68] in grammar and by deriving them by adding "-ness" to the substantives. What is horseness? It is "being a horse." But does this mean "being an individual that is characterized by the universal horseness?" Then we have the universal horseness again and we are using the very word about the meaning of which we are questioning. We have shown also that a universal like horseness is not a characteristic like colour or smell, but is constitutive, and forms the very structure of the animal. What is constitutive cannot be a quality or characteristic. The Nyāya-Vaiśeṣika is right in calling the relation between the horse and horseness inherence, thereby meaning that it is inherent. Is it not a tautology to say that horseness is inherent in every horse? This school failed to see that this is not a relation between two entities; but for the sake of understanding, our intellect introduces a particular relation after intellectually making distinctions within the same unitary, perceived object. The entities only intellectually distinguished cannot be perceptually and factually different.

Can we justifiably reduce the universal then to a propositional function governing all members of the class or determining the class? This point concerns the philosophy of some contemporary logic. Yet, the discussion is important. *First*, for those who hold this view, a propositional function is an intellectual function and an artificially formed one. "To be a horse" is as good a function for them as "to be a book with a red cover," "to be a unicorn," and "to be the President of the U.S.A. in 1962." But all are artificial and arbitrary functions except the first; the second is purely artificial, governing a purely artificial class; the third has nothing corresponding to it in reality; and the fourth is not a function governing any class as it refers only to one individual. All that this view brings to the forefront is that the so-called universal is essentially intellectual; but the view ignores the truth that real universals have an existential or ontological or at least cosmological reference also, and that our intellect or thought cannot arbitrarily frame rules and regulations, when we are concerned with discussion about reality. *Secondly*, what again this view fails to notice is that the function, when expressed in words, is of the form "to be a horse," which is the same as "being a horse." That is, it fails to notice the significance of the use of the word "to be" or "being," which has ontological or existential reference. One may object that this is only a linguistic form without reference to existence or Being. We say: "Number 3 exists between 2 and 4." But in discussing the categories of reality, we are not considering abstractions as in mathematics, but realities like horses and elephants. We do not consider universals as merely common features of a number of individuals arbitrarily selected. A merely common feature may be a superficial feature belonging to all, but not essential to the structure of their being.

Then if "being a horse" is the significance of horseness, every real universal is a continuity of the same act of the formation or structure.[69] "I drink tea" is an act, and "I am a man" is an act, but the two acts are of different kinds.[70] The first is an act originating from me and ending in a short time. But the second constitutes my empirical I and ends only at my death. Again, like "drinking tea," "being a man" also is a patterned act. But the pattern, in the latter case, constitutes me and turns me into a patterned act of being.[71] Here the objection may be raised: "Does not 'being a man' use the word man as a universal or even as a substantive again?" The answer, as before, is that the word man here is adverbial. For instance, in "He is running fast," the "fast" is not a characteristic added to the act of running, but constitutes a factor in its pattern or it is an essential constituent. Similarly, the "man" means the pattern of my being, and my being cannot be differentiated from the pattern. There is no being in the cosmos without a pattern, every object is something definite like the horse or the elephant. We may intellectually distinguish between an act or process and its pattern. But considered by themselves, they will be abstractions, not realities.

Now, a universal is said to determine a class and the individual; similarly, even the propositional function is said to determine the class, even if arbitrary. In the former case, "determining" has to be a real act in the world. For instance, horseness determines what is a horse and what is not a horse. *Real objects cannot be determined by abstractions, if universals are mere abstractions.* They have to be real. How can the universal perform all this unless it is a force (*śakti*)? We have pointed out that my "I" is the act of "being a man," in "I am a man." It cannot be differentiated from this act. Similarly, can we differentiate the force (*śakti*) of an act or process from the act or process? The act or process is the expression of the force (*śakti*), the kinetic, acting state of the force. Force is the potentiality of action; it is the consolidated, inactive state, we may say here, of action or of force itself. Force is the potential state of action itself. We may here think of the atom, which is immense energy or force centred in a minute nuclear form. Release the energy, we see action. Then is the atom a substance, force, or an unexpressed, unmanifest action? It is all of them, depending on how we look at the atom and speak about it. We may say: "The atom has energy," "The atom is condensed or concentrated energy," "It is the source of such and such action," and "It has such and such qualities."[72]

If the form or pattern of action, which we generally denote by an adverb, is the pattern in which the force—we generally speak of the force inherent in that activity, as the Nyāya-Vaiśeṣika speaks of the universal inherent in the individual—is inherent in action, and the force is really the same as the substance to which it is spoken of as belonging; then is not quality the same as force and so the same as action? Then substance, quality, and action—which only are said to *have existence* (*sattā*) by this school—must be different forms of expression of energy or force (*śakti*). So far as this world goes, force (*śakti*) has to be the primary category, but not the other three. We have seen also that the so-called universal, which is said to have no existence (*sattā*), is action in one form and so is a form of the expression of force. Personality also, which also is a pattern of force—every pattern is also a universal and is the source of action,[73] both mechanical and ethical, both voluntary and involuntary—is a universal in the sense that I am this person and am existent[74] and controlling the patterns of my conduct and behaviour.

One may here question whether qualities such as colours, sounds, tastes, smells, and touches are activities at all. In the popular parlance, they are referred to as static qualities. But why are they said to be produced by the objects? Why do they last so long as the objects are producing them, and not afterwards (except as echoes of the so-called qualities, after-images and so forth)? The answer is that they are patterns of activities (*karmas*) of the objects on the senses and of the senses on the objects. The objects supply light rays which are transformed by the eye supplying the life processes—this is the expression of the Upaniṣads, psycho-physics speaks of nervous processes—into colours. Which means that colours are the patterns of the mutual interaction of the processes of the eye and light, which originally belongs to the sun and which is his activity of heating and lighting. Similarly, all the other qualities are patterns of the combined activities of the senses and the corresponding objects. Sight is the same as seeing, and there is no seeing without seeing some colour or form, which is therefore a pattern of seeing. Audition is the same as the act of hearing, and there is no hearing that is not the hearing of some sound, and so sound is the pattern of hearing. Every sense has its own echo, although the word is used particularly with reference to hearing. In the case of sight, we have the term after-images. In the case of the other sense, our language does not seem to favour us with technical terms, but we have the experiences. For instance, I and some other persons also have a sense of beautiful smells, even when there are no corresponding flowers. Which means that these experiences of echoes are a stage in the process of their originals getting into man's memory, through it to the structure of his personality, and through it to his grounding in his Unconscious and the Cosmic Basis.[75] However, our present concern is to show that all the sense qualities also are forces and forms of their activity.

Here we may take up the contradiction in this school, to which we have already referred. The three categories—substance, quality, and activity—are said to have existence or Being (*sattā*); but the universals are said not to have Being (*sattā*). In holding this view, this school seems to have confused itself. Raghunātha tried to see through this difficulty, but did not realize all the difficulties in the traditional Nyāya-Vaiśeṣika position. *First*, how can *sattā*, which is Existence or Being itself, lack Existence or Being? If it lacks Existence, how can it confer existence on the others? It is a universal; and as a universal lacking existence, can it inhere in something that is existent? "Does Existence have Existence" must be equal to "Is Existence Existence?" In fact, the question in terms of "have" should not be answered with an Yes or No, as it is pointless.

Secondly, *sattā* or existence is said to be the highest universal. Then the lower universals must be patterns and sub-patterns of Existence. So it is absurd to say that they lack Existence. In the *third* place, can Existence be a pattern or universal at all? Horses and elephants have patterns (structures), and they exist. Then horseness and elephantness are patterns of Existence and Existence itself is not a pattern which horses and elephants possess.[76] In the *fourth* place, we have seen that the universal is not an abstraction, but activity or force, and so a form of Becoming. Then Existence, as universally present in all existing objects, has also to be a force (*śakti*). It is not *a universal*, but is *universal*, *all-pervasive*. Every becoming has a form, there is no becoming without a form; so Becoming, covering all these forms, is diversified into a plurality of becomings, which are processes, activities, and which, we say, are controlled by a pattern, a universal, an essence.[77] But we have seen that the pattern of a process as inherent in it, constituting it, is not different from the process. The force, the drive of the process, is also inherent to the process. All of them can be distinguished in our thought, but cannot be separated at all. Then the universals are these forces as so many becomings in the same continuous form which we call stable and substance. The form that is changing is called by us process, activity, action. Now, substance, noun, and Being are the stability of Becoming and Becoming is the process of or belonging to substance, noun, and Being. We are not here discussing the ultimate Being or *sattā* of my self, the *ātman*—which is *nirvāṇa*, *mokṣa*, emancipation from the process of Becoming, which is the sphere of Death—but only Being and Becoming as we experience them in this world so that we can clarify our categories of thought and the world. Now, Being and Becoming are so inseparable in this world that the force in both—for starting a process and for fixing a pattern—has also to be one with them. Then Being or Existence—we may remind ourselves that there is no difference between the two in Indian thought—is force, power energy; it is not merely lifeless Being, as many thinkers, eastern and western, seem to understand. That is why the word *sattā* is used in the sense of power, strength (*śakti*), even bodily and financial strength.

Although Raghunātha was wavering and did not push his analysis of the categories to the farthest limits even so far as the ontological basis of the world is concerned, the two ultimate ontological categories of the cosmos are really Being and Becoming, Substance and Force, Substance and Activity, or noun and verb. The last Dyad is significant from the linguistic point of view. If we want to combine the other two sets, we may get Being, Becoming, Force, and Activity. If Force and Activity are the potential and kinetic stages of Becoming, then we are left with two categories, Being and Becoming. Hence it is futile to fight for the absolute plurality of the world and independence of the categories and the forms of reality they stand far from one another and from thought that discloses them by reflecting or analysing its uniform unitary experience.[78]

(vii) The I-am and Thought not Psychological but Ontological

If my thought is the source of the categories and obtains them—which I mistake for being independent of one another and from my thought—by analysing its unitary experience; as I and my thought are finite and psychological is not the view of the world resulting therefrom merely psychological and a finite being's idea? We already came across this objection. But in times of materialism, in both its gross and subtle aspects, and its all-pervasive fashionableness, this question or doubt crops up off and on, in spite of the results of earnest analyses of experience. *What is required is a complete reversal of the attitude that the I-am is finite and the world is infinite, and that thought is less than the world of which it thinks and which it posits.* We have already noted that the world or the universe is not a definite object like my book, the spatial and temporal boundaries of which are fixed and can be fixed. The more space and the more time our thought covers, the more is anticipated of them for covering. We call the world and its unitariness an indespensable working idea, the boundaries of which no one has seen and no one can describe, not to speak of giving even an intellectual definition. Then where do they end up? They cannot end up in discursive thought, which always works with the ideas of space, time, causation and so on, always anticipates something beyond, but cannot go beyond that beyond it anticipates with the categoreal structure—whatever it be, Kantian or Hegelian or something else—inherent to it. But the I-am can go beyond thought. It is present wherever thought is present.Thought is my thought; the I-am is present not only in it, but also above and beyond it. We have already seen that my mind is where my sight locates the star, and my I-am is there where my mind and sight are. It may give one a shock to know that the I-am is infinite; but there seems to be no escape from the acceptance of this conclusion. This school accepts that the *ātman* (I-am) is infinite and all-pervading (*vibhu*); but we do not understand how this school can still hold that the senses are finite and travel all the way to the object (*prāpyakāris*) like the star. It takes only an instant for my mind and the psychological eye to locate the star. But this school does not hold that my sight also is atomic. If it is atomic, the school could have said that it travels with infinite speed to the star. But if it is atomic, it becomes unintelligible, how atoms without any size—according to this school, they have no size—can come into contact with anything that has size.

Now, if the I-am is infinite and thought is relatively finite, as it is structured by a categorical scheme, then the loose ends of space and time in all their directions—which disturbed Kant and generated his dialectic—must end up or rather be lost[79] in the I-am. The loose ends of the chain of causation also must end up in the I-am and be its will.[80] As focussing and controlling my thought I am above and beyond my thought, but not in any spatial and temporal sense, but as transcending space and time. For just as space and time originate in thought, thought originates in my I-am.[81] That the far ends of space and time end up in my I-am is due to their ultimately originating in it. The pure I-am is neither spatial nor temporal; only our bodies are spatial and temporal. I perceive myself as spatial and temporal only so long as I identify myself with my physical body. But we have seen that their identification does not stand examination. Again, my body is a product of thought,[82] which starts differentiating between the self and the other, the subject and the object—all within itself—and imposes the rest of the categoreal scheme of cognitive and action (*karma*) processes, which it assimilates[83] to itself and finally to my I-am. All the experience I have is within my I-am; and experience includes everything that I perceive, think, and act upon; it includes the whole world and what is beyond.

We should not, therefore, think that there is any parallelism between the I-am and the world or that the I-am and the world are two sides of the same reality.[84] The I-am is not a passive counter-part of the world, but the source of the world, comprehends the world, and goes beyond it and beyond thought through which it posits the world. Remember that this transcendence of the I-am is not to be understood in terms of time and space; for the I-am transcends time and space also.

One mistake, or rather a wrong lead made by the Nyāya-Vaiśeṣika is to say that the *ātman* is all-pervasive (*vibhu*) like ether (*ākāśa*) and space (*dik*) and time (*kāla*). But "all-pervasive" may mean merely "to be found wherever any object is found" or unending. It is this unendingness that perhaps makes Raghunātha say that time and space are identical with God, who is an *ātman* for this school also. If its infinity means transcendence of time and space, then they cannot be identical in any constitutive sense with the *ātman*, not even with God.

Now, if the I-am is infinite, one may ask: Why can I not do anything I like and get whatever I want? The question is self-contradictory. For if I am infinite and everything is within me, why have I to do anything? What can I do, as there is nothing besides me on which to act? And what is it that I still want? This answer may be irrefutable, but is only an intellectual answer. Factually, as sitting at this table and writing, I need many things and have to work hard for obtaining them. The infinity of my being, discovered by analysis of my experience, does not help me in getting the things I need.[85] Then how and why does this finitude come out of thought which comes out of the I-am? Finitude in thought and action, in cognition and life, lies in being dependent on forces, on acting according to their own laws not dependent on my will, which are all independent of my wishes. I do not take the initiative willfully to start them, set them in motion, like my I in the dream, in which I am simply carried away by the happenings. But the dream I and the waking I are continuous, I often remember what I did in my dream, although I do not take any moral responsibility for those deeds. Similarly, the transcendental I-am which, through the forces of thought, splits itself up into the waking I—what we call the true empirical I, calling the dream I a false I—and its objects, is continuous with the waking I and is discovered as the necessary basis of the waking I by examination and analysis of experience. Such is the factual description of the stages of the I-consciousness discovered by analysis. The question why there should be these stages of the I-am, why there is this finitization, has never been answered satisfactorily by any philosophy or religion. The modern fashionable answer which asks us either to shelve the transcendental I-am or live with unsolved questions is neither satisfactory nor healthy. For without concern for man's transcendental nature, without it as a motive force, his life tends to be unethical and rankly this-worldly and selfish, at the most guided by the fear of laws of the political constitution. We leave out then the essential spiritual significance of human life. No one has answered the question satisfactorily why the world is as it is, if it has its roots in the transcendental I-am, which is infinite. But it can be shown that "man is not alone" and he is not what he appears to be, a tiny creature helplessly thrown into an alien world.

(viii) Universals as Patterns of Assimilation to the I-am

If real universals, as we have seen, are forces, patterned forces, not mere abstractions, how are they related to my I-am? They are cognitively patterns of assimilation[86] to the I-am so that I can see in my own way my own being in the object, e.g., the horse in front. The being of my empirical I-am and that of the world of objects are rooted in the same Being. The horse is known by me as having a particular form—which may be very imperfectly known to me and may be identified merely with the spatial shape, but which still is known as a form, structure, universal, genus. The form is discovered by me, not created by me out of my mind or nothingness. But we have seen that the world of reality, of objects, has its source in my thought, which is yet transcendental to me as this person, although working through my thought which gropes for grasping reality that has cosmological standing. It is my groping thought[87] that discovers horseness and it is my transcendental thought that actively frames the universal and assimilates it to my I-am. When I see the horse in front, my cognition of the object is not complete and my thought is not satisfied unless I assimilate the object to what I already knew and can remember. What I already knew and remember is what I have already assimilated. This process may be involuntary and spontaneous. The function of the universal then is the assimilating, which is transformation into my own being of the forms and shapes of objects I confront in my experience. Perception is an early stage of the transformation of the object into the constitution of my self. All the patterns of objects are assimilated to the total pattern of the world, which is one of the active patterns of my thought, which along with its world is assimilated to the being of the I-am. This assimilation is absorption.[88] We have already seen that the loose ends of time and space, their mirage-like bounds, lead up to and end up in the I-am. That is, space and time and the world said to be located in them, come out of my I-am and are absorbed into it. Similarly, the universals originate in my being through my thought when I confront an object and make it form one with my being. In popular language, this process is called making the object familiar. Because it is a process, it is Becoming. As pointed out already, my being is not *essentially* finite, but infinite and thus includes the being of the horse in front.[89]

How can my being include the being of the horse in front? If it does so, does it not lead to the absurd conclusion that one who sees a horse becomes the horse, or the horse that is seen by a man becomes a man? This is not the right way of understanding the position which is being developed here. To know that I am the whole world, that the being of the world is my being, does not and cannot mean that I am merely the objects belonging to the world. If I am the objects, I cannot know them as my objects; for then I will be merely they. To know an object involves at the same time the capacity to transcend even that knowledge situation as in "I know that I know the object."[90] *On the other hand, to know the world as belonging to my being and thought is to know myself as determined by the complicated structure or constitution of the world,*[91] *and as being made finite by the necessity of following the laws of the world, if I want to attain worldly values*. These two sides of the situation are equally important to recognize. But my finitude does not mean that my being is basically finite, limited to my body. Here also we may remind ourselves again that I am able to transcend this apparently parallelistic situation. The position developed here does not advocate parallelism.

How does the assimilation of everything that is experienced take place? Assimilation is absorption into what is called apperception in modern philosophy[92] of the West and into Nature, Reason, Logos, etc., in the Hellenic and Hellenistic philosophy. When I perceive an object like a horse, the physical horse is not assimilated to me as the physical body or even as the subject distinct from the object. The object as experienced and its subject experienced as the experiencer are together assimilated into "I as knowing that I know the object." But the peculiarity here is that the I as knowing the object and as different from it and the I as knowing the I which cognizes the object are continuous. The former I may be called the *apperceptive I* and the latter *perceptive I*. We may say that we have the experience of the perceptive I being assimilated to, absorbed into the apperceptive I. But the object also is assimilated through the process of being molded into its universal; that is, the horse is assimilated to the apperceptive I through horseness.[93] The horse we see has two aspects; its existence and its form. Its existence or being is the same as my existence, the existence or being of my I, which, we have seen, is infinite. Existence or Being is not a plurality; otherwise, it becomes a predicate—a result which both Kant and Russell rejected.[94] Then there is really no question of assimilating the existence of the horse to the apperceptive I, but only of assimilating the form of the horse. The form, we may remember, is not merely the spatial shape, but the structure also. We have seen that both belong to the world, which belongs to thought, the apperceptive I in its objectivity as comprehending itself and the world.[95] The particular spatial form and structure of the horse then are assimilated to apperception through the universal horseness,[96] which is the subtle (*sūkṣma*) state of the horse. When a new horse is perceived, this universal (horseness, *aśvatva*) is actively projected into the object,[97] which is fixed, decided in perception as "That is a horse." But this active projection of the universal horseness does not occur when I see a cow. So there has to be a receptive, passive[98] side also, belonging to my apperception; and this reception is met half way by the active projection. This is the basic function of apperception, although there may be errors in the process leading to perceptual illusions. The whole apperceptive mass becomes my being as belonging to this world of action and cognition, and constitutes my ethical capital[99] and character also.

Here we have to note one important distinction. There is the Cosmic Apperception working through my finite, error-prone apperception. The former is the basic categoreal structure of the cosmos, which, although it is in every one of us, is not presented to us like a chart on the board. Its structure has to be discovered through analysis and reflection by living. As it has cosmic objectivity, it is not prone to error. But the latter, i.e., the finite apperception, is formed, grows, and changes, and is prone to error both in cognition and action because of the intrusion of my idiosyncrasies, motives, and interests into it. Kant introduced the idea of transcendental apperception; but he did not see that there are two levels of it, and did not enunciate that it is an "Ought" for the lower to be one with the higher. The lower is transcendental in the sense that my I as the subject cannot make it my object as it can make the horse an object or even as in "I know that I know *X*." Yet, it constitutes my I in cognition and action, giving a bent to both. The higher is much more so as forming the basic structure of the lower, thereby accounting for the common features of the processes of cognitions and actions of all individuals of the race.

Kant does not seem to have made use of the distinction between active and passive intellects and of the implications of his philosophy that, if the world is an Idea, then everything belonging to the world, including horses, is part of that Idea. It is difficult to understand how we can escape the conclusion, unless we introduce arbitrary distinctions and relations, which, we have seen, will not stand examination. Had Kant made use of the implications of his view that every object is part of the world and that the world is an Idea, he would have been able to answer the question why categories and forms of intuition conform to or fit into the sensations received by the mind and vice versa. The objects then will be thought-constituents over which of course I, as this empirical being, have no control—we have noted that this is my finitude—and my thought then will have to be passive in receiving the impressions, and active in assimilating them. But all this—the individual object in its own location, the passive process of thought in receiving the messages from it, and its active process in assimilating it to apperception—takes place spontaneously within my thought by which my active life is controlled and guided.

So much is involved in the theory of the universal. But most of it was outside the philosophical horizon of the Nyāya-Vaiśeṣika, which thought that a pluralistic realism could be defended by introducing a complicated theory of relations, and which confused ontological Being with Being as an abstraction, and the universal as potency and force with the universal as an abstracted common feature of a group of objects. If we say that the universal determines a class (*avacchinatti*), this determining, in the case of objects like horses, is an objective activity; and in the case of the red colour or books with red covers, it is the abstracting activity of my thought. In either case, it is activity. The universal is thus not a dumb and static entity. Here we find a justification for Plato calling the universals Being and forces or powers.[100] Activity is the transformation of a potency into an actuality.

However, the so-called eternity of the universals except in the case of Being—if we accept ontological Being as a universal, which the present author does not do, as otherwise it will be a predicate—cannot be accepted in the sense in which Plato and the Nyāya-Vaiśeṣika have done. The latter says that, even during deluge, when there is no world, the universals exist in the mind of God, who produces the next cycle of creation according to the previous patterns. Maybe, even the patterns—such as those of horses, elephants, men, trees, and oceans—will continue to exist in the mind of God. But this hypothesis forgets that such universals belong to the realm of Becoming and so undergo process and change like the forms of the mammoth and the ape becoming the forms of the elephant and man. Even if one accepts fundamentalism, it will be difficult for him to explain satisfactorily why elephants and men came into existence at a particular time, but not at the beginning of creation itself, when everything was a ball of fire. If one answers that the universe was not a ball of fire even in the beginning, but was like as it is now, we may accept that the world will be as it is now for ever—which is of course the Mīmāmsā view. There may be deluges; this planetary system may disappear; but another crops up somewhere else, and man will always be present in the world. But for the reason that the world is there for ever, the Mīmāmsā rejects the reality of God as a creator. It accepts the reality of force, energy (*śakti*), but stops short of saying that the universal is a force; it is only the structure (*ākṛti, samsthāna*)[101] common to the individuals of the class. But this structure is derived from the father and the mother of the individual; whatever is derived and is active, grows, is a formative force.[102] We see the acorn as a minute, static object; but place it in the right soil, it becomes a dynamo of force that develops into the huge oak.[103]

(ix) Particular not Non-being

Our discussion so far shows that the two main categories of reality are forces and substantives or things continuing in the same form for some time. What we call substances are forces with patterns stabilized for a period—from an instant to thousands of years—from which issue forth again activities, which are the kinetic forms of some of the inherent forces. Substance is not a mere loose collection of forces, but a consolidated (*ghanībhūta*) unity of forces. The magnet, for instance, is a consolidated force with a horizon of influence, which we call its field. The magnet acts within that field, and after a time, may exhaust itself, unless it acquires more magnetic force in some way. Man is similarly a consolidated force stored in his apperceptive[104] mass—conscious and unconscious, but always latently conscious and self-conscious as in deep sleep—from which issue forth cognitive and physical activities. He also may exhaust himself unless new forces are substituted for the exhausted ones. We may say, therefore, that the primary categories of reality in which we live are Being and Becoming.

Now, if the universal is a force, how are we to make the category of the particular intelligible in the Vaiśeṣika philosophy? The school got its name after this category, which is therefore very important for it. Plato understood it as Non-being, assigning both Being and force to the Ideas. But Aristotle called it potentiality; the particular must have the power, force, to develop into the object having the form of Idea. Now, Plato cannot explain how mere Non-being is susceptible to, conform to a particular form. Non-being is nothing, and the question of conforming or not conforming to anything does not arise with regard to it. Aristotle is, therefore, on a firmer ground than Plato with regard to this question; the particular as potentiality can become actual by taking on the pattern (form). But is every potentiality the same as any other potentiality? There is this particular horse and that particular elephant. Now, can the particular, as the potentiality of the horse, take on the pattern of the elephant and become actual as an elephant? Hybrids indeed are being produced; but the constituent seeds as potencies are different. We cannot conceive that the seed of the horse can become an elephant. Then the potencies also, even as potencies, must be patterned. That is, the potency has already the universal in it. The mere particular, as Plato says, must then be nothing. Then, have we reverted to Plato's position? The answer will be in the negative if we mean only that there is nothing to be called a mere particular. The difficulty with Plato is that he speaks of the realm of Being (Ideas) and the realm of Non-being, and says that the world of Becoming is a combination of the two. This is the general interpretation of Plato. Then besides the dualism of the realm of Being and that of Becoming, there is then a second dualism of the realm of Being and that of Non-being, as though there is something called the realm of Non-being. There is to be the realm of particulars, and so the realm of Non-being; then we get into the self-contradictory position that *there exists Nothing*. The position developed here does not advocate either the realm of pure unpatterned potency or the realm of Non-being. Potentiality is the potential state of the universal and is a latent patterned force. Then what is the status of the particular in the Vaiśeṣika philosophy?

The answer is that critical examination reveals that it has no status, as this school understands it. If the particular as potentiality is a latent patterned force, and if the universal also is a patterned force, what is the difference between the two? There is very little; the particular is like a noun *in inaction* and the universal the same noun *as action*. That is, the difference is like that between a magnet when not attracting iron and the same in attracting iron. This conclusion may astound the devotees of the Nyāya-Vaiśeṣika and similar forms of realistic pluralism in the West. But how can the conclusion be avoided? It can be avoided only by stopping to think peremptorily where we like—which is unphilosophical and even superficial. Such arbitrariness can be neither spiritually nor intellectually profound.

This school introduced the category of the particular for defending the uniqueness and plurality of the *ātmans*, of all pervasive and unitary entities like space and time, and of the absolutely same kind of infinitesimal atoms of earth, water, fire, and air. Now, the particular is a hypothetical entity without Being (Existence, *sattā*), accepted for preserving the separateness of the absolutely similar atoms of the same class, and of the *ātmans* of the same class; its acceptance is the opposite of Leibniz's principle of the identity of indescernibles—which itself is open to doubt. But if the particular is not existent, how can it perform any function? A red pencil is differentiated from a black one by the colour; but colours exist, while the particulars do not. If the particular is only an intellectual, hypothetical concept, then the plurality of independent atoms of the same class has to be accepted prior to our accepting the particular for hypothetically explaining such a plurality. There is a kind of vicious circle here: atoms of the same class are independent of one another because of the particular each possesses; and the particular must be real because the atoms are independent of one another. Apart from this vicious circle—which shows that the category is artificial—a particular that has no existence cannot perform any function independently of thought; and a thought product has no jurisdiction on anything that is independent of thought. The particular becomes a concept; but the atom is independent of thought for this school.

This school contends that particulars, although alike in performing the same function or absolutely similar functions, constitute a plurality. And although a plurality, they do not embody a universal called particularity (*viśeṣatva*). For the possession of a common characteristic—the universal is said to be a common characteristic, which we have rejected already—by the particulars destroys their nature as particulars. But if all particulars perform the same function, it is difficult to understand how they do not have anything in common, even apart from what we have concluded, namely, the universal is constitutive of the plurality. The same universal constituting many particulars is possible in the sphere of thought, subjective or objective, but not in the sphere of material reality independent of thought.[105] The universal is again a force; and because the particular is a force and the universal also is a force, they can conform to each other.

As a force (*śakti*), the particular cannot but possess Being (*sattā*) or Existence in our sense of the term. There is no being that does not possess some force or power (*sattā* is the sense of *śakti*). And if the universal and the particular are powers, dynamic functions, they must possess Being in the sense of Existence. But the Nyāya-Vaiśeṣika deprives the two categories of Being. Even if we accept the contention, for argument's sake, that no universal can possess another universal—the contention cannot be true at all, if there are higher and lower universals, the higher residing in the lower—we cannot understand why the particular cannot possess Being (*sattā*). Again, this school contends that no universal possesses Being; then Being cannot be a concept of existence, but an empty abstraction, a mere concept, for the universal can possess Being as a concept, but not ontologically. Then if substance, quality, and activity possess Being, and if *sattā* as a universal is an empty abstraction, how can it make the three possess concrete existence?

The dialectical analysis goes like this: Does Being have Being? Does Existence have Existence? Does Non-being have Non-being? Does negation have negation or negativeness? The questions can be differently interpreted and may be called ambiguous. Or they may be called tautologies. The first question may be interpreted as: Is Being Being? Or it may be: Does Being[106] possess Being? This question is definitely puzzling. Or should we say that we should not and logically cannot raise such questions about Being?[107] If the term is used in the ontological sense—this school must be using it in that sense when it attributes Being to substance, quality, and activity[108]—the question is non-sense; for Being is ultimate. If it is used in the classificatory sense, then the universal can only be conceptual; and if it is not ontological, it can hardly confer ontological status on substance, quality, and activity. It is the intention of this school to maintain that they are ontological.

Next, the negation of negation is accepted by many philosophers—not by every one of course—as affirmation. But what is the affirmation of an affirmation? Can it be negation? It ought to be, if affirmation and negation are coordinates. But it cannot be, if we examine our experience. Does the second affirmation make any difference to the first affirmation? One may call the difference by the name emphasis; but the content remains the same, but not so in the case of negation for those who accept the principle of double negation. What is the reason for this difference between double negation and double affirmation? Few philosophers seem to have raised this question. But the answer seems to be: While thought is forced to move from or out of negation altogether by the second negation, i.e., away from the content of the first negation to the content of affirmation, it is not so forced away from the content of the first affirmation by the second affirmation. In fact, negation itself is movement of thought away from the content of an implicit or explicit affirmation, and the negation of negation is a counter movement back to the content of the original affirmation. *But as the negation of negation is a negation and is conceptual, it cannot be affirmation, which has a strong ontological element.*

That Being is affirmation has to be accepted as ontologically primary. The particular, as we have seen, is really force in inaction. Then how can it be different from Being? It may be said that the particulars are many. Then should we say that the particulars are beings? For while Being is one, beings are many. But ontologically considered, can Being be many as beings? Take the example, "Horses are beings." A corresponding statement is: "Horses are existences or existents." Now, if existence cannot be a predicate, can being be a predicate? Here many confuse the use of the terms Existence and Being as ontological with their use as classificatory terms. But really there can be no classificatory sense of beings and existents as distinct from non-beings and non-existents. The term existent includes everything that is and does not, therefore, distinguish a real class of existents from a real class of non-existents—if the two are real classes present out there in the world. *The class of non-existents is no class at all, as it does not exist.* Then there is nothing from which the so-called class of existents is to be distinguished and the latter is, therefore, no class at all. Then as there is no class of beings or existents, Being or Existence cannot truly be a classificatory term and has to be one and indivisible in itself. And if the particular is Being, then there cannot be a plurality of particulars; there can be only one particular, and that is Being or Existence.

One will perhaps object that the two classes, Beings and Non-beings, are out there, the former as ontological and the latter as only conceptual. But the two cannot constitute two classes on the same footing; for the latter depends on the former for its content. The class of beings will be a real class then, but not the class of non-beings.

Here also we have an astounding and unanticipated conclusion. But how can we escape it? If Existence is many, it becomes a predicate; but it cannot be a predicate and is, therefore, one. If the particulars are many, they will have a universal called particularity or particularness and the particular becomes a predicate. But particulars cannot have a universal and the particular cannot be a predicate and must, therefore, be one. We have seen that the particular cannot be mere Non-being—even then since there can be only one Non-being, all the particulars must be one—but a force or energy, which conforms to the activity that is the universal.

But do we not say: "This horse is a particular, that horse is a particular?" Here we are confusing between the real particular and the individual.[109] The individual, as we see, is a combination of the universal and the particular. It gets its particular aspect from the particular that is Existence or Being in the ontological sense. How then can Being, which is one and indivisible, become the spatio-temporal many as particulars conforming to the many as universals, is one of the ultimate metaphysical questions, which will be taken up in the chapters on the Vedānta. But this present one is the conclusion to which we are led inexorably. Temporarily and tentatively, we shall have to be satisfied with the answer that an analogue to the situation can be found in our spiritual and psychological processes, and that it is the nature of the Spirit to create the world and control it in that way. My being a particular is my "to be" itself; I am primarily the self-conscious particular. I do not find a particular as distinct from my being and related to it by any relation whatever, although this school thinks otherwise. There are many horses; what is the particular aspect of this horse apart from being that horse? "To be a particular" is "to be" and vice versa. But "to be" is one act, viz., the act of being; so the particular also is one.

(x) Necessity in Negation

Some space has already been devoted to the discussion of negation and its forms in the chapters on the Nyāya and the Mīmāmsā. In the former, we examined them in the context of epistemology; and in the latter, we pointed out that the difference between Kumārila, who follows the Nyāya, and Prabhākara was due to the difference between the cosmological and ontological points of view. The controversies are due to the confusion between the two points of view. The sphere of cosmology is my world of knowledge and action; the sphere of ontology is the sphere of Being that supports me and the world. We should not understand the term "support" as though Being lies beneath my feet; it is what makes me and the world of cosmology real and existent. Now, the world of knowledge and action is a world of plurality. I am here along with other persons, and the objects I see are many. The idea of "many" cannot be explained without the use of negation. I am not you, and neither of us is he; and we are not the things we see and on which we act.

The forms of negation are forms of Non-being. Just as pure Being cannot be a part of the cosmos and cannot be seen or experienced as one of the entities in it, pure

Non-being also cannot be experienced by us.[110] We experience beings (in the classificatory sense) like horses and elephants, and non-beings (negations) like "There is no book on the table" and "That horse is not this horse." But while beings have ontological element in them, non-beings have none. We say indeed: "There is absence of the book on the table," but the "is" in the proposition does not signify ontological status. Even the Nyāya-Vaiśeṣika does not confer Being (*sattā*) on "no." However, the school fights for the reality of negation and, we have seen, even Gangeśa accepts it as an adjective (*viśeṣaṇa*) or qualifier of that which is. Yes, I do distinguish between the table with the book on it and the same table without the book (with the absence of the book) on it. But what kind of qualifier is the "absence of the book?" There are hundreds of other absences on that table. Do I perceive all of them? If all are together, are all the same and identical? No, we say that the absence of the book is not the same as the absence of the pen. Why so? Because the first absence is qualified by a "possible book," which I expect to be there but is not there, and the second is qualified by a "possible pen," which I expect to be there, but is not there. Here, in addition to the idea of the pen and the idea of the book, there is also the element of my anticipation or expectation and the possible activity of using the object. Otherwise, my mind has a number of ideas—of pens, pencils, books, letterheads, etc., etc.—the corresponding objects of which may not be there. But I do not "perceive" all their absences. It may be asked: Even if I do not experience them—which is a psychological question—are the absences not there? But if they are there like positive books and pens, they also have to be positive entities, not negations and absences. Then what is the significance of the objectivity of the absence of the book on the table in "There is no book on the table?" Is negation merely imaginary? Any explanation of negation has to avoid the two extremes, viz., that negation is an ontological "is," and that it is merely psychological.

The objectivity of negation, *which is the factor of necessity in it as it is in mathematics*, lies in what Kumārila says my inability to perceive a book where it does not exist. He called it non-cognition or non-perception; but he should have called it also *the impossibility—which is a necessity—of perceiving the book not only by me, but also by others.* Negation has the activistic aspect also. It has been said already that the cosmos is the world as presented for my thought and action, and that negation is a cosmological[111] concept, not an ontological one. The necessity in negation is not only due to the structure of my thought concerned with the cosmos, but also due to the factor of necessity in activity. If I want to ride my horse, I cannot take another's horse; so one horse is different from another, is not another. If I want to give a person a dollar in charity, I cannot take one away from him. Just as I am obliged to say: "That horse is not my horse," I am obliged to say in action: "That is not good, but evil." Even in the case of actions which are not tangibly ethical or unethical, e.g., making as much money as possible without harming any one and without violating the laws of the country and humanity, I have to make choices like choosing the table with the book on it for picking up the book and ignoring the table without the book even when I see it. The necessity in negation is, therefore, the necessity in thought and action.

We have already referred to one peculiar difference between negation and affirmation, viz., the affirmation of affirmation does not change the content, but the negation of negation often changes the content. We may note another difference. The being we perceive is the being of something like the book on the table; similarly, the negation or absence we perceive has also to be of something like the book on the table. While there is pure ontological (not the classificatory or cosmological like that of the book) Being, there can be no pure ontological Non-Being. Even to be cosmologically significant, it has to be qualified by something. Absence to be cognized has, for instance, to be the absence of the book. In the case of the Being of the book, we may say: "Being is qualified by that book in front." Here both the being of the book and the book are at the same place and are identical. But can we say the same thing in the case of the non-being (or absence) of the book? Without the qualification by the book, absence is insignificant, as there is no experience of pure absence of Non-being. But if the book is there where the absence is for qualifying it, there will be no absence of the book. Then how does the book—let us for the moment consider my particular book, not any book in general—qualify absence to make it definite? So it cannot be the physical book, but the book as remembered by me and expected there that has to qualify the absence. But then again, what I remember and expect to see is that particular book, not the idea or image of the book—what I remember is not an idea like I remember a theory, and if, for instance, I miss seeing the book although it is there and later see it again, I did not miss an idea and later discover it, but missed and discover the physical book—and that book is somewhere else. Then how can it qualify the absence here? So we have to emphasize that negation has no ontological status; the book which has an ontological status, cannot qualify the absence here. Then as what and how does the book qualify the absence?

There seems to be an inherent contradiction in the idea of negation or absence. One escape seems to lie in saying that the absence of the book is everywhere except where the book is; and so it can be perceived not only on my table but also in all other places except where the book is. But why is it that I do not experience the absence except where I expect the book? Then we have to say that negation or absence is a category of thought, but with the element of necessity in it. But it is a category one step removed from the category of Being or of the positive, provided we do not treat the positive as merely conceptually positive. For always negation or absence has to be qualified to be significant by something that is positive. But the positive like the book does not have to be qualified by the negative. For the purpose of knowing that the object in front is a book, it is not necessary to know that it is not a pencil. That it is not a pencil is a cognition derived from the affirmative cognition that it is a book, but not in the reverse way.

What has been said about negation, taking the absence of the book as an example, can be applied *mutatis mutandis* to the other forms of negation accepted by the school. For none of these forms is significant when not qualified by a positive being or beings, which are negated. It is always questionable how they can qualify their own negations. (It makes no difference to the criticism even if the positive beings negated are called counterparts.)[112] The difficulty is the most obvious in the case of what this schools calls mutual negation.[113] "*X* is not *Y* and *Y* is not *X*;" this is mutual negation. But where does it exist or is present? The answer is: "In *X* and *Y*." *X*'s absence exists in *Y* and *Y*'s absence exists in *X*. Now comes the difficulty. *X* and *Y* are to be taken together for consideration in asserting mutual negation. But if taken together, how can their own negation exist in them? It taken and considered separately, then *X* is *X* and *Y* is *Y*, and there is no question of negation. I see *X* and say: "That is *X*;" I see *Y* and say: "That is *Y*." I may not care to think of them as different. If I do, then their mutual negation is a product of my thought. But again, we have to warn ourselves: to say that negation is a product of our thought does not mean that it has no element of necessity. It belongs, as it is generally said, to the cosmos controlled by the laws of cause and effect, purpose and means.[114]

(xi) Time and Space: Their Analysis

We have already made references to the Nyāya-Vaiśeṣika concepts of time and space, how on the one hand, the school calls them substances and on the other, treats them as relations. If time is a substance and all-pervading, it can never change. If it cannot change, it cannot have divisions of past, present, and future, and cannot also have other divisions like hours, days, years, etc. These divisions cannot be treated even as characteristics; for these characteristics can be had only if time as a substance changes; at least the characteristics of past, present, and future have to follow one another and have to replace one another; nor can the divisions of hours, days, etc., occur without replacing one another. This replacement implies change and we cannot understand how these occurrences are possible without change. Then what kind of change can time have, if it is one and all-pervading?

If the divisions are incidental, not inherent to time, then time stays the same without change. If time is essentially one and without divisions—even without those of past, present, and future—then Plato will be a contemporary to Queen Elizabeth II. For changeless time is contemporaneous or the eternally present. Then how is it different from space? We have seen that Gangeśa and Raghunātha do not accept space, time, and ether (*ākāśa*) as different from God; and they seem to have some truth, if one says that each is one and all-pervading like God.

Now, to safeguard Plato's being earlier than Queen Elizabeth in time, if we say that the divisions of past, present, and future are real, not identical, how are we to determine that one is earlier than the other, if the determination is not against a common background or in terms of a common denominator, which is time again? We cannot have separate unrelated blocks of time if we are to place historical individuals at different points of the same time.

The followers of this school, as we noticed, use the ideas of the oneness of time and of its divisions also loosely as and when the usage suits them. But therein they have not seen the significance of the self-contradiction involved. Furthermore, they give another definition of time, viz., "it is the father (creator) of all that is created." If time is the creator of all that is created—an idea found in many schools—it has to be active, a force, a power. This idea may fit well with Bergson's conception of time and Croce's conception of history and even Raghunātha's identifying it with God. Then how can time be conceived as holding all things (*jagatām āśrayah*) like the table holding my book? There is indeed a popular conception that all things exist in time, as they exist in space; and time and space are external to things and are their relations; they are realities indifferent to things. If time is indifferent to the individual who exists at a particular point in it—as though the same individual could have existed at any point of time like my book existing on my table or in my bag—then Plato could have lived and written his Dialogues in the year 1979 and Elizabeth II could have ruled England in 1000 B.C. This is an absurd conclusion that follows from the idea of time's indifference[115] to the objects in it, it does violence also to our historical sense and memory and autobiography. Of course, "time holds everything in its bosom," means that nothing is lost in it, and can be interpreted as that it is the projector and withdrawer of everything. But then time is not a mere support of everything like my table or my book.[116]

A similar criticism applies to space (*dik*). In western philosophy there are two—excluding Einstein's—conceptions of space: *one*, that it is a simple vacuum, empty extension, in which extended objects exist; and *two*, that it is one with matter, which is extension itself and that individual objects are configurations of that extension. The idea that it is a constitutive form (of intuition, Kant) may be included in the second. The first is generally associated with Hume and the second with Descartes. The more popular and common sense view of the two is the first. Generally we do not think that a change of place for my book from one end of the table to the other will make any difference to the book. And space, which is thought to be place with boundaries knocked out, is indifferent to the nature of the book. But what is the status of the extension of the book? It has a volume 10″ × 6″ × 4″. If the book changes its place from the left to the right of the table, does not the book release 240 cubic inches of space on the left and consume the same amount on the right? *Is not space then the possibility of give and take in the movement of configuration or that which makes physical movement possible*? Kant seems to have thought that space can be conceived without objects and as a stable form. But it cannot be so stable as we think. *It is what releases and absorbs configurations, which are again configurations of itself* (*its mūrtas*).

The Nyāya-Vaiśeṣika defines space primarily as the ground for the idea of nearness and distantness, and secondarily (viz., incidentally) as divided into directions (east, west, etc.) by some conditions (*upādhis*) like the rising of the sun, etc. But is the primary definition really primary? Is not the characteristic of near-far a relative characteristic? For one in New York, the Atlantic is near and the Pacific is far; but for one in San Francisco, the Atlantic is far and the Pacific is near. So the characteristics which make space space are relative to the individual; he is the point of reference and space is a product of his mind or, as we have been saying, of his apperception (*buddhi*). It is an aspect or law of the organization of all objectivity considered as distinct from mind.

(xii) Kāla, Ākāśa, and Dik Formative Forces of Apperception

Time and space are then forms of activity of my apperception; they have no being apart from it. They have some deeper aspects, which cannot be discussed in this estimate, which is already very long, but in the chapters on the Sāṅkhya and the Yoga. But one important question may be raised in the present context: How does any mind know the infinity of time and space? Who has cognized it? If their infinity means all-pervasiveness in the sense that whatever I see, I see as temporal and spatial, as having a past and a future and as having extension, we can accept the word infinity. But it is often understood as though my mind cognizes the endless expansiveness of the world of space and time, which is somehow located in them with its own boundaries. To cognize endless expanse is to go beyond it; and to go beyond it is to give it boundaries and so ends. But this is a self-contradiction. As some Vedāntins would say, the web and woof of the world is fitted into time and space.[117] But the loose ends of the past and future of time and the directions of space are tied together in my apperception. Kant does not seem to have mentioned and stressed this idea, but his profound thought needs this supplementation. There seems to be no escape from its acceptance except arbitrarily.

For there seems to be no way of solving the problem of infinite divisibility of time and space, and the infinite synthesis of the parts supposed to be obtained in any finite time or extension, which gave rise to Zeno's paradoxes, than by accepting that the ends of time and space are tied together in apperception. My apperception is the source of both time and space constituting the world. They issue from my apperception, are projected by it, end up in it, are absorbed and assimilated by it. My apperception does not project, in constituting the world, infinitesimal static points of time and space and then synthesize them. It projects temporal objects or groups of temporal objects, and spatial objects and groups of spatial objects, synthesizes them and analyses them, but never carries the synthesis and analysis to the logical end in a concrete way, but only in an abstract way as in mathematics[118] and—depending on interests and possibilities—as in the nuclear sciences. Synthesis and analysis are the powers of apperception *to perform those acts, but are not the completion of the acts.* They are forms of apperception's activities, its potentialities. No other view can succeed in explaining Zeno's paradoxes.

For when I see the book, I see the whole length of the book, viz., ten inches. My mind may then divide the length into ten parts and each part again into another ten; and later it may combine all and see the whole length. But it never starts with infinitesimals, nor does it continue the division into infinitesimals empirically. (One may say, in the Kantian language, that the work with infinitesimals in analysis or synthesis, is a transcendental activity, which Zeno mistook for empirical activity. Zeno succeeded only in showing that they are not empirical activities. One may add also that the activities of apperception cannot be merely results of sense perception.) As it is said, given the letters of the alphabet and all possible combinations of letters, nobody can produce Shakespeare's plays; but given the plays, he can analyse them into all kinds of parts and derive laws which may have guided Shakespeare's mind in writing the plays. Time and space are aspects of action, process, growth, and action is primary. *They are part and parcel, ingredients, constituents, of the force (śakti) of Becoming.* As such only can they be and have to be understood. The activities of analysis and synthesis are elements of the processes of time and space. It is absurd and fruitless to understand them as existing outside apperception by themselves in space and time as having been empirically completed. Apperception contains, among other things, the inexorable and unending process of Becoming, the inexhaustible power (*śakti*) of projecting and assimilating or absorbing.[119]

The concept of ether (*ākāśa*) in the Nyāya-Vaiśeṣika school is that of a substance the specific quality of which is sound (*śabda*). The *ākāśa* of this school is generally translated by the word ether, which does not seem to be quite correct. Ether in physics is considered by scientists who accept it to be the medium of sound, but not as a substance in which the quality (*guṇa*) called sound[120] inheres. This school, as we have noted, accepts rightly the difference between the psychological and the physical ear. It says that the ear is only a condition (*upādhi*) imposed upon *ākāśa*, which is one and infinite.[121] That is, what we call the ear is constituted by *ākāśa* within the area of the individuals's ear.

Indeed, my physical ear is made up of skin, flesh, blood, and bones. It cannot be said to be constituted by *ākāśa* or be of the same substance as *ākāśa*. (We better not translate the word here.) Then if the ear meant is psychological and is part of *ākāśa*, then *ākāśa* must be psychological.[122] Is not sound, as a sensum, then psychological? Then this school should treat *ākāśa* as a transformation of subtle sound (*śabda-tanmātra*), as the Sāṅkhya and the Vedānta do; for both, sound and *ākāśa* are of the same substance,[123] even though the former is called a quality and the latter a substance. There thus seems to be some real basis for the Mīmāmsakas calling sound a substance. Are not both transformations of the subtle element of *ākāśa*, called *śabda-tanmātra* by the other schools? And does not this school also regard the psychological ear as part of *ākāśa*, and what is the psychological ear but the sound heard? However, no school called all the other perceived qualities by the name subtle substances (*sūkṣma-dravyas*), although so much is implied in the Sāṅkhya-Yoga and the Vedānta accepting the doctrine of subtle elements (*sūkṣma-bhūtas, tanmātras*). Unless we want to cloud the term subtle element in some mystery, what else can it be than what constitutes my psychological being or my personality—we should remember that my I is not limited to my body—as distinct from my physical body? Unfortunately, except in the case of sound, the Mīmāmsā also seems to be guided by unreflective common sense in its theory of elements and their qualities.

When and how the term *ākāśa* came to be associated with the ear and sound is not easy to answer. All that we can say, on the basis of the Upaniṣads, is that both space (*dik*) and *ākāśa* are associated with the ear and sound. Often, it is space (*dik*) that is associated clearly with the ear (*śrotra*). But *dik* here means generally direction, such as right, left, up, down, east, west and so on. We know by experience that our ears can recognize the directions from which sounds come. Animals are particularly capable of detecting such directions and they turn their physical ears towards them. Śaṅkara here and there in his commentaries combines *ākāśa* and *dik* and associates them with sound. He says that sound is the quality of *ākāśa* as guided (presided over) by *dik*.[124]

What then is this *ākāśa*? Etymologically, it means that which shines in all directions or everywhere.[125] Shining or appearing is the primary meaning and "from or on all sides" is the secondary. The second etymological meaning is that of scope, place, room, etc.; that is, in the sense of "There is no place or scope for anybody else or anything else," "There is room enough for twenty boxes here," and "He gave no opportunity (room) for the critic to speak." Roughly, it means that which makes any occurrence possible.[126] In our present context, we may say that *ākāśa* is that which makes the appearance possible on all sides of the object facing me. This is certainly not ether. Nor is it the scientific concept of space, which does not have the connotation of appearing or shining. In Kant's idea of space as an intuition, the factor of appearing or shining can be detected; but generally his interpreters ignore this factor, and some have branded his philosophy as not merely epistemological, but psychological. But from the point of view here developed, to brand him so is a mistake.

Now, sound that is heard by the ear, even if it starts from a drum, cannot be treated as a quality of the drum like we treat its colour. The ear cannot catch or see the physical drum. Sound is heard as spread out through the distance between me and the drum and also beyond. Take for instance the echo of sound in a valley. Even if the sound originated in my throat, the echo is heard as if it exists all over the valley, not merely in my ear, but all round and over the tops of the hills and mountains. Even a blind man has this experience. Then "all round and everywhere" turns out to be not myself as the subject, but an object for me, in calling which the Upaniṣads wavered between the names of *dik* (space) and *ākāśa* (ether).[127] Provided we keep in mind that *dik* and *ākāśa* are not mere physical substances existing independently and in separation from my personality, but constituting its real base—which they do—we ought to identify and equate the two. How far and for what reason they ought to be merged with the concept of time, which also is a factor of the real basis of my personality—not the imaginary or pseudo-personality—will be discussed later. A little clue to how the three are at the basis of my personality is to be found in the idea, indicated already a few times, that my personality in its depths is not limited to my so-called body, but comprehends the whole world and goes beyond.

A few points relevant to this chapter remain to be discussed, showing a few more self-contradictions in the concepts of space, time, and ether. Are the locations of space, time, and ether grasped by the senses? Regarding time, this school maintains that it is not perceived by any sense,[128] but is inferred. How is it inferred? If inference is to be based on some perception and if there is no perception at all of time, then what is it that we infer or can infer? If Jim is older than John, do we base our inference on Jim being taller or stouter than John? This is an uncertain inference, for John may be taller and stouter than Jim. Then if I know of Jim's birth and of John's birth, I can know that one is temporally prior to the other. But his temporality is based on my memory, but not on the physical features of Jim and John.[129] Although memory may be assimilated to inference—cp. logical memory and the formation of universals already discussed—it is not any of the kinds of inference which this school has in mind. It is the postulation—which this school calls a kind of inference—of a feature of reality as experienced by me—it is a categoreal feature—divided by me into past, present, and future and given a kind of proper name—a technical name—like time. But this postulation is based upon a direct experience of occurrences assimilated to my apperception (*buddhi*). The occurrences need not be sense perceptions, but mental occurrences like the passing, in succession, of images. In any case, the source of time experience is apperception,[130] and is grasped as a feature, ingredient, modality, of a process that is taking place within me, even in cases where it is produced by external objects. So the Mīmāmsā is right in saying that time has no reality apart from activity, although its extreme view that time and activity are one and the same may be questioned. But the Mīmāmsā does not seem to have recognized that there can be no time without the activity taking place within me, without my experiencing it, and without my going through the process of Becoming[131] (*bhāvanā*).

Where then is time located? It is not really seen in the objects I perceive with my senses, but in the constructive and assimilative process of my apperception which moulds the objects, and through the same moulding process assimilates them to itself.[132] The object can rightly be called known only so far as it is fully apperceived.

That is why, although we do not perceive time by any sense, we are able to make time an adjective of the objects as in "ancient mountains." Thus history becomes objective.

How are next space (*dik*) and ether (*ākāśa*) located? My eye is able to locate the star at a distance or my mind locates it or I locate it. We say so because there is a light seen by the eye. But where are the so-called film colours located? They have no fixed boundaries and may extend to infinity. But when physical objects are seen, my sight seems to locate their colours. Space does not seem to be an object of sight. The eye may see[133] extension of objects and empty spaces between objects, but it does not see infinite space, just as it does not see infinite time. But if the object seen is the result of constructive and assimilative processes of my apperception, then space, like time, must have its origin in my apperception. This school thinks that the inference of space is based upon the cognition, "*X* is farther away from *Y*." But is this cognition simple sense perception? If we did not already have the concept of space or distance, we could not have applied the concept of "farther." This means that space, like time, is an intuition—one may call it an existential. The being of my apperception includes both as constituents. It should be noted that the use of the word inclusion does not imply that my apperception itself is spatial and temporal. The source of space and time cannot be spatial and temporal; it is beyond both. The two then are its powers, forces, *śaktis*,[134] which create worldly forms we see and we think that we see.

Somewhat similar considerations apply to the idea of *ākāśa* (ether or the basis and source of sound). Where is sound located? If I see the drum from which the sound originates, I can trace it to the drum. A blind man can trace the direction of the sound and may even reach the drum. But direction is space, not ether. In the case of the echo, the sound is pervasive and in a way corresponds to the so-called film colours. The echo is heard not only by the man who shouts, but by many others. It seems impossible to define the boundaries of sounds and film colours. Besides the difficulty of explaining why *dik* and *ākāśa* should be differentiated, we face the difficulty of explaining how far our psychological ear can extend, like the difficulty of explaining how far our psychological sight can extend. As pointed out in a previous chapter, they are infinite and are powers (*śaktis*) of my apperception.

A few contradictions present in the way qualities are assigned by this school to time, space, and ether also show that their roots must be in apperception; and that through active involvement of apperception in my cognitions the differentiations within time, space, and ether are made possible. One may say that sound is known by the ear, whereas direction or space is known by touch and eye (cp. Berkeley); so ether or the basis of sound must be different from space. But cognitions of direction and distance are due to acquired habits; and also space and direction are cognized by the ear, particularly by animals. So there is a strong reason to identify space and ether (*dik* and *ākāśa*). Again, if ether is one and indivisible, and if the only divisions possible are those introduced by my ear and the ears of others, how can there be any contact and disjunction (*samyoga* and *vibhāga*)[135] with ether? We cannot understand how physical objects like tables and books can have contact or separation with something that is all-pervading. Nothing can be separated from anything all-pervading and so nothing can be brought into contact with it. If ether is the inherent cause (*smavāyikāraṇa*) of sound, there can be no question of conjunction and disjunction of anything with ether. We cannot understand also how sound inheres in anything that is not *spatially* divisible. For sound is said to have both conjunction and disjunction. Ether (*ākāśa*) is not spatially divisible. But a very important consequence of the argument is that, if ether is one and sound inheres in it, then it is the same whole ether that constitutes my sense of hearing as that which constitutes the hearing of others. This line of thinking and investigation ought to lead us to the idea of one world for all, like the Prakṛti (Primordeal Nature) of the Sāṅkhya, on which the being of the personality of every one is grounded or rather in which it is rooted. It is a mistake to think that I, this person, is apart from the world in which I live.

Similar arguments apply to the idea of the qualities assigned by this school to space and time. For there can be no conjunction and disjunction (*samyoga* and *vibhāga*) with anything that is one and all-pervading (*vibhu*).

We may here raise the question: What do we mean by all-pervading (*vibhu*)? I can appreciate why people, although wrongly, say that space is infinitely extended and is physically there apart from me. But in what sense are time and space all-pervading? Generally we think that we know their all-pervasiveness; but we ought to examine ourselves. What is the all-pervasiveness of time? Does it mean that time is found everywhere where space is found? If it is so found, it has to be extended like space. But is time extended like space and does it coincide with space? To think of time as being extended like space is a non-temporal and so a false conception of time. The primary empirical conception of time is that it is extended towards the past to infinity and towards the future[136] also to infinity. What is the length of the present then? Is it one minute or one second?[137] Thus approached, the problem has become knotty. What do we mean when we say: "There is past and there is future?" Does the word "is" in both parts of the sentence mean the present? If it means so, it will lead to contradictions; for the past and the future will be identical with the present. The contradiction cannot be removed, unless we say that all the three *are* one, and are present, in my apperception,[138] which is "I am." In fact, when Kaṇāda, the founder of the Vaiśeṣika school, says that time is found in transient objects, but not in eternal objects, he is paving the way for the difficulties in thinking of time as all-pervasive. If it is all-pervasive, it must be found in all-pervasive objects. If it is found only in transient objects, it is limited to them and cannot exist beyond them. He may merely intend to say that transient objects are temporal, but the all-pervasive and eternal objects are not temporal. But how is the difficulty about the one-ness of time removed?

Now, what is meant by the all-pervasiveness of ether[139] (*ākāśa*)? The amorphous nature of the concept of *ākāśa* and the difficulty of differentiating it, in critical examination, from space (*dik*) makes the discussion somewhat a mix up and difficult. According to this school, ether and time are not objects of sense perception. We infer the existence of ether as the substance to which sound as quality belongs. But how do I know that it is infinite or all-pervasive? Again, does its all-pervasiveness coincide with that of space and that of time? Further, if *ākāśa* is all-pervasive, why should its specific quality, sound, be finite (*avyāpya*)? We cannot understand a specific quality not existing where its substance is existing. Or should we say that sound is eternally existing in eternal *ākāśa*, but becomes manifest to my ear as transient in the shapes and forms it takes through vocal organs? The reason given can be that the ear and the vocal organs are transient. If my sense of hearing is not merely physical but also psychological, then *ākāśa* must also be psychological.[140] And if *ākāśa* is infinite, why should we not accept that the elements—air, fire, water and earth—are also infinite? Should we not consider their specific qualities also to be infinite?

It is really tempting to ask the question: Why have some schools associated sound and *ākāśa*? There seems to be given no sound reason in the literature of the schools for differentiating *dik* (space) and *ākāśa* (ether). The reason given by Kaṇāda to differentiate the two is that sound is heard by the ear, but the specific qualities of space are not heard.[141] But sound indicates direction and so does space. One may uncritically say that space is cognized by sight and also touch. But may we not accept that it is cognized by the ear also?[142] When we once accept what is called *dik* (space, direction) is not merely the empty space between two extended objects—for they also are spatial or configurations of space—but a formative force (*śakti*) of apperception, we can accept that sound also is one of its manifestations (this school calls them qualities, *gūṇas*) and is cognized only by the ear. The infinity of *ākāśa* then can be explained like the infinity of space.

There is a spiritual tradition[143] in India, according to which *ākāśa—śūnya*, but in the sense of pure homogeneity—is a pure vacuum, the first manifestation of the Supreme Spirit, the possibility of appearance of all shapes and forms (*mūrtas*), not merely of sound. As such a pure possibility, we may equate it to the formative force (*śakti*)—call it a category, if you like—of space. The first shape that appears is that of sound (*śabda*). It is this sound that transforms itself into definite names and forms of things including myself (I-am). But for some reason, this original *ākāśa* splits itself into *ākāśa* as the origin of sound and *dik* (space), particularly in the schools of pluralistic realism. But a few schools retained their unity.[144]

But in any case, the idea that time and space, and *ākāśa* can exist independently of my apperception, with their own objective, physical infinitude cannot stand examination.

NOTES

[1]S. Radhakrishnan: *Indian Philosophy*, Vol. II, p. 177.

[2]H. Ui: *Vaiśeṣika Philosophy*. Feddagon thinks that this school built its philosophy on the basis of grammar (*The Vaiśeṣika System*, p. 11). But this can be said of most other schools. All the categories of this school do not belong to grammar. One may say this of Aristotle also.

[3]A. B. Keith: *Indian Logic and Atomism*, pp. 25 fol.

[4]Kaṇāda: *Vaiśeṣikasūtras*, pp. 3–6. (Eng. tr. by Nandalal Sinha) The English words chosen by the translator for some of the Vaiśeṣika technical terms are not happy, and tend to mislead. Feddagon follows this translation. The Sanskrit editions are: (1) *Vaiśeṣikadarśana* with the commentaries of Praśastapāda, Jagadīśa, Padmanābha, and Vyomaśiva and (2) *Vaiśeṣikasūtras* with the commentary of Chandrānanda. There are differences in the numbering of the aphorisms in the different editions.

[5]Ibid., X, 4. [6]Ibid., I, i, 3.

[7]Eng. tr. of *Vaiśeṣikasūtras* by Nandalal Sinha, IX, ii, 3. In future this edition will be referred to as Nandalal Sinha: *Vaiśeṣikasūtras*; otherwise, the reference is to the Sanscrit editions.

[8]Ibid., IX, ii, 5.

[9]Ibid., IX, ii, 5 and IX, i, 8. [10]Ibid., VII, i, 1.

[11]A. B. Keith: *Indian Logic and Atomism*, pp. 60 fol.; and S. Radhakrishnan: *Indian Philosophy*, Vol. II, p. 181.

[12]Nandalal Sinha: *Vaiśeṣikasūtras*, I, i, 4.

[13]Praśastapāda: *Padārthadharmasaṅgraha*, pp. 16–17 (Eng. tr. by G. N. Jha).

[14]The Vaiśeṣika has nothing to do with existentialism, in terms of which these words should not be understood.

[15]Nandalal Sinha: *Vaiśeṣikasūtras*, VIII, ii, 3.

[16]Ibid., I, ii, 3. [17]Ibid., IX, i, 1 fol.

[18]Same as *Vaiśeṣika Philosophy* already referred to.

[19]Indian thought makes no distinction between Being and Existence—a distinction newly made by existentialist philosophies.

[20]See the author's article, "Being, Existence, Reality, and Truth," *Journal of Philosophy and Phenomenological Research*, March 1957 and "Being: How Known and How Expressed," *International Philosophical Quarterly*, already mentioned.

[21]Nandalal Sinha: *Vaiśeṣikasūtras*, IV, ii, 1.

[22]Kaṇāda: *Vaiśeṣikasūtras*, II, i, 17.

[23]Nandalal Sinha: *Vaiśeṣikasūtras*, II, i, 27.

[24]Cp. the western epistemological doctrines, according to which all substances are inferred, only qualities are perceived.

[25]Viśvanātha: *Kārikāvalī*, p. 30. [26]Ibid., p. 31.

[27]Kaṇāda: *Vaiśeṣikasūtras*, III, ii, 4. [28]Ibid., III, ii, 1.

[29]Viśvanātha: *Kārikāvalī*, p. 7. But one may question: If qualities have no particulars, how can the red colour of one rose be different from that of another rose?

[30]Cp. Empedocles and Democritus.

[31]Viśvanātha: *Kārikāvalī*, p. 17.

[32]Ibid., p. 15. Cp. *Pancīkaraṇa* of the Vedānta. [33]Ibid., p. 18.

[34]Ibid., p. 16.

[35]Ibid., p. 5.

[36]The Nyāya-Vaiśeṣika gives several cross-classifications of qualities. See Ibid., pp. 98–101.

[37]Ibid., p. 18.

[38]Ibid., p. 6.

[39]In western thought it is the rationalists and idealists that accept the reality of universals. But in Indian thought most of the idealists reject their reality.

[40]Kaṇāda: *Vaiśeṣikasūtras*, I, ii, 3. [41]Viśvanātha: *Kārikāvalī*, p. 6.

[42]Some scholars prefer the word "subsists" to "exists." But as Being (*sattā*) is also a universal, and as substance, quality, and action are kinds of Being or beings, the preference does not make much difference. Besides, if Being is a universal, why not substance-ness, etc.?

[43]Cp. the problem of synonymity.

[44]It may lead to confusion in thought if the word *viśeṣa* is translated as particularity, which is an abstract term.

[45]Ibid., p. 7.

[46]One cannot be idiomatic and keep to the peculiarity of the English language by translating *mānavatva* as humanity, manliness, humane-ness, etc., as they do not mean "to be a man," which is a function of Being, but not one of the functions of man. It is better to translate such Sanskrit words by adding "-ness" to the English substantives and other words, as the case may be.

[47]So there can be no classification of universals as we find in platonic classification of Ideas.

[48]Ibid., pp. 8–9.

[49]The Neo-Nyāya says that even prior negation and posterior negation are absolute negation, and does not accept the distinctions. Ibid., p. 9.

[50]Ibid., p. 8.

[51]See *The Cultural Heritage of India*, Vol. III, Part I, Chapter VI, ed. by H. D. Bhattacharya; D. H. H. Ingalls: *Materials for a Study of Navya'-Nyāya Logic*; and Karl Potter: *Padārthatattvanirūpaṇam of Raghunātha Śiromaṇi*.

[52]See *The Cultural Heritage of India*, pp. 146–47. It is interesting to note that one of the Neo-Naiyāyikas, Rakhaldas, distinguishes between non-inhering universals, which are only concepts, and real universals. What are called *upādhis* by the early Nyāya-Vaiśeṣika are non-inhering universals, as they do not inhere in the individual objects, but belong only to our thought. But this distinction is not the same as that given by the *Daśapadārthaśāstra*.

[53]Some western students wrote to me that none could explain to them the significance of the seven-fold predication. It is hoped that this "General Estimate" and the one on Jainism will make the doctrine more intelligible than before. It is an attempt to get over skepticism and the blind alleys to which thought often leads us.

[54]One may here be reminded of the proverbial difference between the pessimist and the optimist, the former saying that the glass is half empty and the latter countering that it is half full.

[55]Kaṇāda's *Vaiśeṣika Aphorisms*, I, 1, 2.

[56]This is what is called *niṣkamakarma* in the *Bhagavadgītā*.

[57]One may call it the Logos, the Cosmic Apperception, Hiraṇyagarbha, Vijñānātman, Alayavijñāna etc. It is already pointed out that the Nyāya-Vaiśeṣika has no concept of apperception.

[58]Like the adjective-qualified relation, pointer-pointed relation etc., which are all artificial and do not answer Bradley's questions.

[59]Compare Whitehead's philosophy of organism, Hegel's philosophy of the Absolute, the Buddhist concept of Ālayavijñāna, and the Upaniṣadic concept of Vijñānātmā.

[60]The Nyāya-Vaiśeṣika calls it *viśeṣaṇatā-nirūpita-viśeṣyatā* and its opposite. Its terminology in all these cases is different. But the essence is the same.

[61]It seems to me that what the medieval philosophers and, before them, Aristotle called "active intellect" is the regulating intellect.

[62]This is the Ālayavijñāna of the Buddhists and the Vijñānātman of the Upaniṣads, to which we already referred, and which is akin to apperception, and which also has two levels, the individual and cosmic. I hope this discussion will remove the mystery and outlandishness of the concepts. One should compare the ideas of *natura naturans* and *natura naturata* also with them.

[63]Here is the difference between *vijñānātmā* and *mahānātmā*. Relate it to the difference between active intellect and passive intellect.

[64]Here the Nyāya view that error and truth are dependent on proper functioning of perceptual facts has a point.

[65]See *Kārikā* 89 in *Siddhānta-muktāvalī*. Here it is called a quality (*guṇa*).

[66]Prabhākara holds that it is inferred because it is an object of no sense.

[67]One is tempted to discuss these projected, possible relations. But already the estimate of relations has become very long, and there are other topics to be discussed in this section. But the reader can now free the discussion from the Nyāya-Vaiśeṣika context, and examine possible answers.

[68]In Sanskrit grammar, the universal of the horse is called the *bhāva* of the horse, i.e., "the becoming, the activity of being a horse."

[69]There is much to be said in favour of the Nirukta view that all nouns are derived from verbs, all substances from activities. The world is a world of process or Becoming; so there is nothing strange in this view. Cp. Bergson and Whitehead.

[70]Cp. the significance of the verbs and so of the acts of "to be," "to become" and "to do." The distinctions are very important.

[71]One can notice that the former is a transitive verb, and the latter an intransitive one. But all intransitive verbs or their corresponding acts do not constitute "me" in the same way.

[72]It is not my intention to appear modern by bringing in the atom. The significance of the distinctions was known to many Indian thinkers, who knew, however, little of the modern theory of the atom. We may remember J. S. Mill's idea that substance or thing is a source of action, although expressed in a different context. As Bosanquet says, extremes of philosophy have to meet, if they deal with the same reality.

[73]The concept of will belongs to this context.

[74]Here is a relevant question. If personality is existent, are its qualities like courageous, gracious, and merciful, existent or non-existent? If they are existent, are they not natural? Here G. E. Moore's famous and, in many cases, fashionable naturalistic fallacy about ethical qualities can be questioned. Besides, there is no clear-cut meaning of terms like natural, empirical and so on.

[75]Cp. the idea of the Ālayavijñāna of the Buddhists, Vijñānātmā and Māhān Ātmā of the Upaniṣads, and the Logos and the Unconscious of Jung's. For Jung, the Logos is higher than the Unconscious; but for the Upaniṣads, we may say that the individual unconscious is lower than the Logos and the cosmic Unconscious (Māyā) is higher than the Logos, but lower than the Brahman.

[76]Cp. Kant who says that Existence cannot be a predicate.

[77]See my article, "Being, Becoming, and Essence: East and West."

[78]Even Wittgenstein was obliged to say that languages are the nets for catching and knowing whatever reality could be known. He could have used "thought" instead of language. However, this is not the place for a critical appreciation of his theories.

[79]Bradley's drastic solution that thought must at this point commit suicide may be remembered here. But note the difference of the position being developed here from his.

[80]Had Kant noticed the significance of this, he would not have been troubled by the dichotomy of the necessity of nature and freedom of the will.

[81]Hegel is wrong in taking the Cartesian I as thought. Unknowingly, he is identifying himself with the Vijñānavādin Buddhists for whom Vijñāna is the ultimate reality. In fact, in their later developments, they identified Vijñāna with the Ātman. This identification is refuted by Śaṅkara. See his Commentary on the *Bṛhadāraṇyaka Upaniṣad.*

[82]Descartes missed the point that the object outside has its source in thought itself, and in the I-am. Treating the object as something absolutely outside the I-am, he started the insoluble dualism of mind and matter.

[83]This is the function of what is called in the West apperception, which is of the form, "I know that I know the book." Spinoza practically recognized it when he said that mind not only knows the object but also itself as knowing the object. But philosophers later bypassed it in preference for the stereotyped parallelism.

[84]G. F. Stout in western philosophy held this view; but it is not the position developed here.

[85]Religion tells us that existential, not intellectual, discovery of the Infinite Being, gets the things the finite needs. The way is the way of religions.

[86]I formulated this idea of assimilation sometime in 1973. It struck me as the right view of the universal when I was groping for a solution of the many problems raised by the different theories. Its import seems to me to be very wide and deep. Recently I was struck by a similarity to a view of Śaṅkara that the eye (the psychological, not the physical) is not something that is there creating colours and shapes, but that these are there independently of the eye and that the eye (the psychological) is the way (pattern, function) of assimilating them to the *ātman* and its *buddhi* (thought). However, Śaṅkara and his followers do not accept the reality of universals and give little positive thought to them. But the position developed here ought to be acceptable to both Advaitas of Śaṅkara and Kasmir.

[87]Here also one can find the significance of the difference between passive intellect or thought and active intellect or thought.

[88]Cp. Spinoza's intellectual love of God to the process of assimilation and absorption of the finite self and its experiences into the transcendental I-am. According to Spinoza, I have to consider myself and my experiences as being logically or mathematically derived from God. My dream I is derived from my waking I, but not logically or mathematically, as a Spinozist may say. It is an image, reflection, not a mathematical entity.

[89]Descartes was not able to show this identity and so landed in dualism and its problems.

[90]This is what is called *vimarśa* in Kasmir Śaivism. It is the recognition of myself as involved in the cognition of the object, a cognition in which the self-transcendence of the cognizer is experienced.

[91]Cp. Vijñāna, or simply *buddhi*, *vijñāna*, and Mahat.

[92]This is an aspect of the phenomenological consciousness, identical with the phenomenal world.

[93]Even Śaṅkara says that all objects enter the Unmanifest (Avyakta), which is the darkened state of the apperceptive mass, by becoming the respective universals. Fire becomes fireness, water waterness and so on. But the agent of action (*karta*), in our case the empirical I or the I of the world of action, does not become agentness (*kartrtva*), but remains as such in the Unmanifest. See his Commentary on the *Bṛahadaraṇyaka.* This shows also that the agent is a particular, not a mere universal or value of a univeral.

[94]This also is a point which Descartes missed. He was thinking that there were two disparate existences and so got stuck with subjectivism.

[95]Cp. Spinoza's idea that mind comprehends both mind and matter. Hegel turned the idea into Self-consciousness, often misunderstood.

[96]Śaṅkara calls horseness the subtle being of the horse.

[97]Cp. Aristotle's active intellect. [98]Cp. Aristotle's passive intellect.

[99]Called the causal body (*kāraṇa-śarīra*, *bījātman*) in the Vedānta. But this term is not often come across in Buddhism; but its doctrine of *samskāras*, as we have shown in the chapter on Buddhism, leads to it. It is the finite *ālayavijñāna*.

[100]He should not have stopped with treating the universals as Being, but should have worked out the transcendence of the universals by Being.

[101]*Ākṛti* is generally translated as shape or form (not in the Platonic sense) and *samsthāna* as structure. That this school uses both words as if they are synonyms shows that "form" is not understood as merely the common feature.

[102]This is made clear in the Mīmāmsā philosophy of language, in which everything else becomes a constituent of action. We cannot go into the theory here.

[103]Cp. Mīmāmsā, the Nyāya-Vaiśeṣika, Whitehead and Husserl. The latter two call it essence. This is not a book on the various problems of comparative philosophy, but mainly on Indian philosophy, indicating possible significant comparisons. Yet, it is not out of place to refer to some important points. (See my paper on "Being, Becoming, and Essence: East and West.") Let us consider Whitehead first. *Firstly*, it is not clear whether, like Plato, he considers the world of Ideas, the conceptual nature of God, his primordeal nature as Being, or the world of events, which is really the world of Becoming, as Being. Interpreters drew different conclusions. *Secondly*, he gives the impression that he separates the world of Being and the world of Becoming, as Plato did before him. In the *third* place, the world of Being as a system of conceptual forms, looks like a world of abstract concepts, not of forces, and his philosophy looks like committing the fallacy of the bifurcation of nature (or reality), to which he is opposed. But all this may be due to the archetechtonic of his presenting a system part by part, and may be a wrong a criticism. For he speaks of the world of forms *determining* the empirical world, of conceptual feelings, conceptual prehensions and so on, all of which have to be activities, forces (*śaktis*). But there can be an activity only of that which is, which is a being; empty conceptual forms cannot have force or power over events, which, according to Whitehead, constitute Becoming. But this distinction between the force of Being and the events of Becoming is only a way of speaking; for there can be no event as a constituent of Becoming if it is not itself a potential activity and so force. Then what is called the conceptual or primordeal nature of God cannot be a mere empty framework, but dynamic structured force. Hence between the so-called two natures of God, between actuality and concepts, Being and Becoming, and so on there can be no separation. The reader will find further that deeper comparisons will be quite illuminating. Most of the distinctions are due to our finite thought when it does not care to reflect deep; the deeper it reflects the more of its distinctions will lose their validity. It is very important to think deep for man to know what he is and what the world is in which he lives. Where and what are his roots?

If we take Husserl's method of reduction seriously, we find that he wants the essences to be the results descriptive analysis. It is a contemporary vogue to call one's philosophy descriptive and empirical to get for it a kind of prestige. But if man wants to uncover the roots of his being, a descriptive, empirical method will not be enough. The roots of my being are deep down beyond my empirical consciousness. Even the structure of my personality, which is my finite I-am as this individual looking around, cannot be present to me as an objective chart, but is discovered bit by bit through analysis of my cognitive and active life. Husserl 's example of grasping the essence of the house by, turning it round and round and up and down in mind reminds us of Spearman's colleagues trying to get the universal of a bird by turning its picture in different ways. (Cp. Aveling's experiments.) They can be helps, but do not give the essence of the nature of the universal. Husserl's method of reductions has its forerunner in experiments like the above. It is difficult to say that his method is confined merely to such procedure. For it becomes transcendental as in Kant and it is not easy to differentiate it from the latter's critical method. Consider, for instance, his obtaining the transcendental ego in the IVth Chapter of his *Cartesian Meditations*. Is it removed far from Kant's transcendental deductions? Little or not at all, except in language. Now, is the transcendental ego obtained as a mere function, a transcendental activity or as existing also? How can anything that does not exist perform any function? It is not a mere algebraic function, which is a skeletal form, according to which I am obliged to think; it is a being with a life, functioning in actively projecting forms (universals) into which some forms like those of horses and elephants are passively received. We may call the latter forms empirical, but the former have at least to contain non-empirical forms (universals) projected out through remembered (recollected, cp. Plato) empirical forms in cases where the objects are not new; but in other cases, in which the object is new they are projected in a gradually changing formative process so as to accommodate the form which is passively and empirically received. But Husserl seems completely to ignore the processes of what was called in early western philosophy active intellect. The universals generated by it are active forces (*śaktis*). The universals actively projected and the universals passively formed and obtained can conform to each other because both are universals engendered by the same reality. Plato ignored the function of passively obtaining the universal of the horse, and was obliged to call the particular a non-being. Kant could not answer the question why the categories conform to the sensations because he gave little or no importance to the passive universals, which are changes of concrete perceptions of objects into forms assimilable to active universals. The Nyāya-Vaiśeṣika mistakenly thought that the transformation of the percept into the passive form is a new kind of sense-object contact. The understanding of the epistemological mechanism by this school, as already indicated, is naive and defective. The answer to the question, why should there be any conformity between the processes of active intellect and those of the passive, is that they are not really two different intellects or realities, but one and the same. The active belongs to my transcendental being, and the passive to my empirical being; or in other words, they are in an important sense, *my own* transcendental and empirical beings, which are the same continuous being and which, so far as continuity is concerned, are like my waking I-am and the dream I-am. They are my apperceptions. We have distinguished between the higher and lower apperceptions, the higher being the Logos. When we remove from the universals as forces their popular misconceptions that they are lifeless abstractions, we can understand the great role they play in constituting the world. For the purpose, we have completely to revise Husserl's purely phenomenological doctrine of essences; for there can be no real essence without existence. To ask me to bracket out my existence and the existence of the object for fixing the structure of essences is to ask for the impossible; for everytime I do something with an essence or for obtaining an essence, I do so as existing, I am always with my existence; I cannot abstract myself from myself or turn myself into an abstract essence. This is not merely an intellectual objection. One who thinks that it is so, may try the abstraction in his experience and see whether it is possible. The I that does the bracketing, which is holding something in suspense, cannot be kept out of the bracketing. It will be very useful for the reader to carry on this comparison and enquiry; he will realize what true philosophy and philosophical thinking imply and involve.

[104]Cp. the Upaniṣadic ideas, *prāṇabandhanam hi saumya manah*, Mahat and Hiraṇyagarbha. Mind (here apperception, *buddhi*) is (the consciousness) bound, tied, to life. Mahat or the Logos is the soul of Hiraṇyagarbha, who is bound to cosmic life. Cp. also the Christian idea that God is Life and is the force of life. Then does life, in these contexts, mean merely the biological life, present in worms and insects? The Upaniṣadic ideas of life and death need deeper study.

[105]The objection of the rival schools how the same universal can exist in many particulars and other allied objections are potent if the universal and the particular, in short the world, is accepted as outside my thought. It is the power of thought to be one and be present in many just as I am one and can be present in a plurality of sense activities.

[106]I referred to two meanings of Being, the ontological and the classificatory. In which meaning does this school use the term? See my paper, "Being: How Known and How Expressed."

[107]See the above paper to find out whether we can raise any such questions. Should we not say: *sākāṣṭā sā parā gatih*, that is the limit, that is the highest (*Kaṭha Upaniṣad*).

[108]Should we say that the three are existentials? The question needs further analysis.

[109]See my article, "The Problem of the Individual," *The Review of Metaphysics*.

[110]Cp. Bergson's interpretation of Nothing and contrast it with Heideggar's and Sartre's ideas of Non-being.

[111]Phenomenological, not existential.

[112]*pratiyogis*. [113]*anyonyābhava*.

[114]*niyati*, measure, limit (Plato). *Kārya-Kāraṇātmakam* or *sādhya-sādhanātmakam jagat*.

[115]If time is not really a simple holder, receptacle of everything, mere support of everything, it is a mistake to call it *anyathāsiddha* in the explanation of causation as it cannot be the same for everything.

[116]Cp. the view referred to in the Upaniṣads that Time is the origin of the universe as a whole, not merely of the individual objects.

[117]*otam ca protam ca*.

[118]The problems connected with this infinite analysis and synthesis are *perhaps* solved in contemporary mathematics. But I am not competent in that field. But are all mathematicians satisfied with the solutions? Why is mathematics called the science of the possible? Is 1.99, etc., as equal to 2, the same as completing the infinite series empirically?

[119]It is interesting to note that *Vijñānātmā* is now and then called Death (*mṛtyu*), for it withdraws, swallows whatever it projects. We have already mentioned that the universals are forms of assimilation and in the process the individual is swallowed by the universal and finally by the Vijñānātmā.

[120]See *Muktāvalī*, 44.

[121]Why should we not treat the other senses and the corresponding agents or causes as limiting conditions of the corresponding elements? The Advaita can accept such a theory.

[122]This argument applies *mutatis mutandis* to the other senses like smell and taste and to the other elements like earth and water. The senses are the elements themselves.

[123]It looks as though the *tanmātras* or subtle elements become the specific qualities of gross elements.

[124]*digdevatādhiṣṭitah ākāśaguṇah.* [125]*ā smantāt kāśate prakāśate iti.*

[126]Other senses will be presented in the chapter on the Vedānta. They have a profounder connotation, including logical space and the whole apperceptive.

[127]I think that "ether" is an unexamined translation of the word *ākāśa*. The word is good enough for beginners, but is a cheap translation. I still use it to maintain continuity with the indological tradition. Etymology here will be very helpful to bring out the full Upaniṣadic connotation.

[128]not *pratyakṣa*.

[129]although scientists can determine their comparative ages by examining bone structures etc. But in their work they assume the existence of time; they do not prove that there is time. The question is how we come to get the idea of time at all.

[130]Cp. the doctrine of witness consciousness in the chapters on the Vedānta.

[131]In reconstructing history, I go through this Becoming in imagination, called historical imagination. The same is true in reconstructing the biography of myself or of another person.

[132]Note the difference from Kant, for whom time and space are sense intuitions. But time at least cannot be said to be seen in the percept.

[133]Provided we ignore Berkeley's view that distance is the result of acquired perception, which is a combination of sight and movement.

[134]Śaṅkara uses the word *digdevatā*, the deity of space, which means it is a force or power. Cp. also the words *kālaśakti* and *dikśakti*, the force of time and the force of space.

[135]See Praśastapāda's Commentary on the *Vaiśeṣika-sūtras*, pp. 308–359 ed. by G. N. Kaviraj (Chowkhamba Sanskrit Series, Benares, 1924–31.) The qualities are assigned by this school to ether.

[136]If "future" means the possibility arising out of the present, then time and causation are essentially interrelated.

[137]This is to be discussed more in the chapters on the Sāṅkhya and the Yoga. The later Buddhists may call it the eternal moment. Nāgārjuna denied the reality of the present. But Zen Buddhism seems to hold that the infinitesimal and apparently contentless present is the root of everything and the laws of self-realization. The eternal present is the eternal Self. It may appear as *Mahāśūnya* (the Great Void), but is absolutely full and overflowing.

[138]Descartes should have known this. He made use of the I-am for the certainty of cognition, but not for examining the other concepts like time and space. In fact, space does not have its origin in the I-am in his philosophy.

[139]We continue using the English word ether for want of a better term, although, as we have noted, it is not an exact translation.

[140]I use the word psychological, for want of a better word. But I wonder whether it is not misleading to use it in the contemporary sense of the term psychology. The Indian philosophers use the word "subtle."

[141]*Śrotrapratyakṣāt-caṇa dikkālayoh*, II, 1, 25, *Vaiśeṣikasūtras* with Chandrānanda's Commentary (Gaekwad Oriental Series, Baroda, 1961).

[142]In fact, the synonyms given by this school are *nabhas* and *antarikṣa*, meaning sky, heavens etc. These words mean pure empty space in modern scientific terminology.

[143]This is only one of many others. We shall have occasion to refer to them in later chapters.

[144]It should be noted that the term *ākāśa* is used for the Brahman and also for Māyā in its original potential state, when it is equated to *śūnya* or void. In some places, the mythological waters out of which the world issued forth are interpreted as Māyā and so as śūnya. But note that the word *śūnya* even in Buddhist philosophy cannot mean vacuity, emptiness; for it is the source of all that we are and experience, the source of configurations of the object of every sense.

Chapter VIII

The Sāṅkhya and the Ideal of Self-Discrimination

1. INTRODUCTION

The word *sāṅkhya* is derived from the word *saṅkhyā*, generally meaning number. But the verbal root √*khyā* means "to know," and the prefix *sam* means "exact." So *saṅkhyā* means exact knowledge. As the most exact concept is number, the word has come to mean in literary language number. Since exact knowledge includes discrimination, *sāṅkhya*, the name of this school, means that which gives exact knowledge of reality. And as this school counts the number of categories it accepts, the word has come to mean also the philosophy that gives an exact number of categories. In another sense, the Sāṅkhya is the philosophy that enables man to discriminate exactly his real self from the not-self.[1]

The Sāṅkhya is one of the oldest philosophies of India. Like the ideas of the Mīmāmsā and the Vedānta, the ideas of the Sāṅkhya are found even in the Ṛgveda and certainly in the Upaniṣads, particularly in the *Kaṭha* and the *Śvetāśvatara*. In the latter Upaniṣad, even the name of Kapila, which is also the name of the founder of this school, is mentioned. Indeed, there were many Kapilas in the history of the Indian religious literature. The word may also mean the colour tawny or red. But it is generally believed that the Kapila of the *Śvetāśvatara* is the founder of this school, as he is described as a sage (ṛṣi). However, as the *Śvetāśvatara* is a theistic Upaniṣad, we shall have to say that Kapila was a theist. But the most important of the Sāṅkhya works now available, the *Sāṅkhyakārikās*[2] of Īśvarakṛṣṇa, is atheistic or at least non-theistic. The word *kārikās* means explanatory verses. But what is the book of which they are the explanations? We have no satisfactory answer, as we do not know the original work, which was perhaps the *Aphorisms* (*sūtras*) of Kapila himself. But Kapila is generally regarded as a theist and to have accepted the reality of God.

Thus we get two kinds of the Sāṅkhya, the theistic and the atheistic. In its narrow philosophical reference, it is generally regarded as atheistic or non-theistic. Kapila is said to belong to about the 6th or the 7th century B.C.,[3] but Īśvarakṛṣṇa to about the 3rd century A. D.[4] There is thus a difference of about nine centuries between the two. If we consider the tradition that Āsuri, a disciple of Kapila, was originally an Ājīvika and a kind of materialist, we may guess that atheistic Sāṅkhya of Īśvarakṛṣṇa was a kind of compromise between the theistic Sāṅkhya of Kapila and the materialism of the Ājīvikas through Āsuri. We come across the theistic Sāṅkhya in the epic *Mahābhārata*, in its two parts, the *Bhagavadgītā* and the *Anugītā*.

Kapila is said to have composed the original *Sāṅkhya Aphorisms* (*Sāṅkhyasūtras*), which are lost. Āsuri is said to be a disciple of Kapila and Pañcaśikha of Āsuri. But the works of neither are available, except in references by others. Hariharānanda recently made a collection of twenty-one aphorisms, said to belong to Pañcaśikha and other sages.[5] Though very short, this work gives us good insight into some of the basic ideas of the Sāṅkhya. Vijñānabhikṣu (15th century) wrote a commentary on the *Sāṅkhya Aphorisms*, alleged to have been composed by Kapila himself. But scholars do not believe in the authenticity of the *Aphorisms*, as they contain references to views held much later than Kapila. The suspicion is that Vijñānabhikṣu collected most of them from different sources and, after adding a few composed by himself, attributed all to Kapila and wrote a commentary on them. These *Aphorisms* are not as atheistic as the philosophy of Īśvarakṛṣṇa. Vijñānabhikṣu wrote a commentary on Bādarāyaṇa's *Vedānta Aphorisms* also. We may surmise, therefore, that he wanted to turn the atheistic Sāṅkhya of Iśvarakṛṣṇa into a theism for making it a form of the Vedānta, which was perhaps the teaching of Kapila. In fact, all the categories of the Sāṅkhya find mention in the Vedāntic schools, though given more or less different interpretations. The Yoga philosophy of Patañjali—which we shall study in the next chapter—is also called by the name theistic Sāṅkhya (*seśvarasāṅkhya*), for Patañjali explicitly accepts the reality of God and the only main difference between the two schools is the rejection or acceptance of God. Just as the Nyāya and the Vaiśeṣika got merged and formed the Nyāya-Vaiśeṣika school, the Sāṅkhya and the Yoga were combined and formed the Sāṅkhya-Yoga school, to which metaphysics and epistemology were mostly supplied by the Sāṅkhya and the practice of meditation for the final discrimination of the self from the non-self was explained by the Yoga.

So far as the general practice goes, it is customary to present mostly the views of the atheistic Sāṅkhya of Īśvarakṛṣṇa as the main Sāṅkhya; for his work is the main authoritative one now available. This chapter will follow the general practice.

2. EPISTEMOLOGY

In the chapters on the Mīmāmsā, Jainism, Buddhism, and the Nyāya, all the important epistemological doctrines of the Indian philosophers have been given and certain differences also indicated. It is not necessary, therefore, to discuss now every problem of epistemology, except when necessary. The Sāṅkhya accepts three valid means of knowledge—perception, inference, and verbal testimony.[6]

PERCEPTION The doctrine of perception expounded by this school is, in many respects, the same as that of the Nyāya. According to both, there is difference between indeterminate (*nirvikalpaka*) and determinate (*savikalpaka*) perception. There is, as the Sāṅkhya also wants to be realistic in epistemology, the contact between sense and object, and then between sense and the inner sense (*antahkaraṇa*), and then some kind of relation between the inner sense and the *ātman*, which the Sāṅkhya calls generally by the word Puruṣa, before knowledge of the object becomes a full cognition. But there are some differences also between the two schools.

The inner sense consists, according to the Sāṅkhya, of three distinct, but not separate, ontological forms—mind (*manas*), ego (*ahaṁkāra*), and reason (*buddhi, citta, vijñāna*, *sattva*, all of which are used as synonyms by this school). This conception of the inner sense is different from that of the Nyāya, according to which mind (*manas*) alone is the inner sense and there is nothing like reason (*buddhi*) as an ontological form, but only consciousness (*buddhi, jñāna*), which is an adventitious quality of the *ātman*. The ego (*ahaṁkāra*) is only an experience based (*āśrita*) on the *ātman*, which is itself unconscious. For the Sāṅkhya, the *ātman* is by nature conscious. Mind (*manas*), according to the Nyāya, is atomic: but according to the Sāṅkhya, it is not atomic,[7] it is not without parts, and yet is not eternal or infinite. It is both a sense organ and an organ of action.[8] The five senses—sight, audition, taste, smell, and touch—and the five organs of action—hands, feet, the organ of speech, the excretory organ, and the generative organ—are only different kinds of the energy (*śakti*) of mind. Again, unlike the Nyāya, the Sāṅkhya holds that the senses are not only one of the forms which the elements take,[9] but of mind. One should understand these ten as psychological, but not as physical; for instance, we act in dreams, but our physical organs are at rest then. Vācaspati says that these ten organs are presided[10] over (*adhiṣṭita*) by the same mind, but that they are not its powers (*śaktis*). Thus there is a difference of view within the Sāṅkhya. The function of mind is analysis and conceptualization (*vikalpa*) and decision and determination (*saṅkalpa*).[11] Mind distinguishes the object of perception into the individual and the universal and then unites them and decides or makes an assertion (an act of will in cognition) as in "That is a horse." Vācaspati attributes this function to mind itself, but Vijñānabhikṣu attributes it to reason (*buddhi*). The ego (*ahaṁkāra*) is that part of the inner sense which appropriates all experiences to itself as in "I see the horse" and "I ride the horse." While mind is regarded by the Sāṅkhya as a sense—and so as the sixth sense—the ego is not so regarded. It is that which possesses the senses, presides over them; they originate out of it and it appropriates them as its own (*mama*).[12] Reason (*buddhi*) is that part of the inner sense which decides, makes decisions, determines, fixes. It determines not only what has to be done, but also what the object is.[13] It has ontological significance, as it has for the Stoics.

According to Vācaspati, when the senses—not the physical, but the psychological—come into contact with the objects and assume their form with the help of mind, reason (*buddhi*) becomes transparent and receives the form (*ākāra*) and the form becomes lighted up by consciousness, which is, and belongs to the *ātman*.[14] Cognitions, pains, pleasures, etc., are, for the Sāṅkhya, unconscious. They become parts of conscious experience only when lighted up by the consciousness of the *ātman*. That is, the *ātman*'s consciousness is reflected into the reason (*buddhi*), which has taken on the form of the object. The knower then becomes reason itself, which function is appropriated by the ego in the form "I know the object." But according to Vijñānabhikṣu, the lighted up object of reason is reflected back into the *ātman*, which is the real knower.[15] Vācaspati thinks that to be a knower would imply some kind of self-transformation (*pariṇāma*) of the *ātman*, which, according to the Sāṅkhya, never undergoes transformation. But Vijñānabhikṣu says that such transformation belongs only to reason (*buddhi*), the *ātman* merely receives the reflection of the lighted up reason. For instance, heat makes iron red-hot and also soft; but this softness, if it can be reflected back into heat, does not make heat soft. Or fire may be reflected into water, but water does not become fire or hot thereby. The *ātman* has to be the knower, although an unaffected knower (*sākṣi*); and it cannot become a knower, unless it receives the reflection of the reason. Vijñānabhikṣu seems to be nearer the truth.

INFERENCE Inference is understood by the Sāṅkhya mainly as Gautama, the founder of the Nyāya, understands it. The difference lies in that, while the commentators on Gautama classified the three kinds mentioned by him in several ways, the Sāṅkhya kept to the three main divisions. (1) Inference from past experience (*pūrvavat*) is the inference of fire from smoke, in which the relation between fire and smoke has already been observed. (2) Inference of what remains (śeṣavat) is the method of residues. And (3) the last is the inference from the application of general characteristics observed in one situation to a new one (*sāmānyatodṛṣṭa*). In explaining these three kinds of inference, Vācaspati generally follows Vātsāyana, the commentator on Gautama and even quotes him.[16]

The Sāṅkhya rejects comparison, postulation, and non-apprehension as distinct means of cognition and gives the same reasons for the rejection as those given by the other schools that reject them. Comparison is only a combination of verbal cognition and inference. Vācaspati does not refer explicitly to the Mīmāmsā view and the view rejected is that of the Nyāya. He says that the cognition of similarity between the bison and the buffalo is only perception; and we may, therefore, conclude that he rejects the Mīmāmsā view also. Postulation, as the Naiyāyikas say, is a kind of inference only. There is really no Non-being (*abhāva*). It is only a transformation (*pariṇāmaviśeṣa*) of a form of Being. All beings, except the ātman, change every moment.[17] Non-being is only one of the forms of this change and is perceived by the senses themselves. So no separate form of cognition called non-apprehension need be recognized.

VERBAL KNOWLEDGE Verbal cognition is regarded as a valid means of knowledge. The Sāṅkhya accepts nearly the whole doctrine of the Nyāya. But it maintains that the Veda was not composed by any one person (*apauruṣeya*), but embodies the insights of many great seers (*ṛṣis*). Yet although not composed by God—the Sāṅkhya rejects all arguments for the existence of God—the Veda is not eternal as the Mīmāmsā contends. No sound, not even the word of the Veda, is eternal. This part of the view is the same as that of the Nyāya.

VALIDITY OF COGNITION To the Sāṅkhya is attributed the doctrine that all true cognitions are true by themselves (*svatah prāmāṇya*) and all false cognitions are by themselves invalid (*svatah aprāmāṇya*). Cognition (*pramā*) is the form which reason (*buddhi*) takes, when from the side of the senses it receives the form of the object and from the side of the *ātman* the reflection of consciousness. It is a function of reason. If it is true, nothing else makes it true; another cognition can only confirm its truth. If it is false, nothing else makes it false; another cognition can only reveal its falsity. Whether true or false, the form which reason takes is its own transformation and is known to itself. It is a transformation of Being, of what is. But how do we know whether a cognition is true or false? We know it through the pragmatic test (*arthakriyākāritā*). Indeed the cognitions obtained from the Veda are always true and so also are the teachings of Kapila, the founder of the Sāṅkhya.

There seems to be another line of thought leading to the view that a true cognition is true by itself and a false one false by itself. Cognition is a power[18] of reason to present a determinate object, whether true or false. When a truth is confirmed, it is reason itself that grasps the confirmation; similarly, when falsity is discovered, it is discovered by the same reason. It seems that the controversies over the problem of knowledge being valid by itself or invalid by itself is due to different meanings given to the terms.

THE OBJECT OF ILLUSION Vijñānabhikṣu rejects the views of other schools, and says that the object of illusion has both Being and Non-being, and is both real and unreal (*sadasatkhyāti*).[19] It cannot be non-existent; for the non-existent, like the horns of a hare, can never be perceived. But we perceive the illusory object. It cannot be existent; for what exists is never contradicted. But the illusory object, which first appears as existent, is later contradicted and declared to be non-existent. It is not the perception of one object as another—a view held by the Nyāya-Vaiśeṣika. For no object can be perceived as another object. We have, therefore, to conclude, that the illusory object is both existent and non-existent. The water we see in the mirage is existent; there is water in lakes and rivers. But when we see it in the desert mirage, it is non-existent. The primeval matter (Prakṛti)—which we shall explain later and which is the stuff of the universe—consists of both Being and Non-being (*sadasadātmaka*).[20] So the existent can be non-existent and vice versa.

The above explanation of the object of illusion is neither logical nor epistemological. How can anything be both existent and non-existent? The question is at least as important as: How can an object appear as another? Water may exist in rivers, lakes, etc., but is it the same water as that which appears in the mirage? If it is the same, why should it be non-existent there? Vijñānabhikṣu rejects the Advaita doctrine—which we shall study in another chapter—that the object of illusion is neither existent (*sat*) nor non-existent (*asat*), but a third something that is neither both or neither and which has, therefore, to be an inexplicable being (*anirvacanīyasat*). He argues[21] that what is not existent must be existent and vice versa and that there can be no third alternative. His argument will be valid if the existent and the non-existent are contradictories. Then how can they be unified in the water of the mirage? If the Primeval Stuff (Prakṛti) is both Being and Non-being and every one of its products is, therefore, of both kinds, then how is the water of the mirage, which is both, different from the water of the lake, which also is both? If practical activity, like moistening our feet, distinguishes the two, then why should not the Sāṅkhya say explicitly that the pragmatic criterion distinguishes the true from the false and that the true is that which leads us to successful practical activity; and also add that the false is not merely what is both Being and Non-being? Such an answer will agree also with the general position of the Sāṅkhya that the Primeval Stuff (Prakṛti) is meant for the enjoyment (*bhoga*) of the Puruṣa (*ātman*).

3. METAPHYSICS

It is in metaphysics, particularly in the explication of the conscious nature of the *ātman* that the Sāṅkhya shows a great advance on the Mīmāmsā and the

Nyāya-Vaiśeṣika. Like the philosophy of Descartes, the Sāṅkhya is a qualitative dualism of spirit and matter, Puruṣa and Prakṛti. By matter we should not understand the matter of contemporary physics, but the *physis* of the Greek thinkers, for whom it meant some primeval stuff or material, that is a becoming, and that constitutes everything from inorganic matter to mind, all of which constantly goes through change. Even our mind and reason (*buddhi*) are not above change. The world of change or transformation is one, not many, and is called Prakṛti (ore, the original). By itself it is absolutely unconscious. Opposed to it is the Puruṣa, who is pure consciousness. We may say that the Puruṣa is conscious or that he is consciousness which is also an existence: both mean the same for the Sāṅkhya. Somehow the Puruṣa comes into contact with Prakṛti and throws the reflection of his consciousness into it. Although Prakṛti is one, the Puruṣas are many and infinite in number; there is, therefore, an infinite number of reflections in the same Prakṛti. As soon as the reflections are thrown into it, Prakṛti begins to evolve the world. And since Prakṛti is the same and has its own structure, the objective world it evolves for all the Puruṣas is the same. Thus communication between one Puruṣa and another is made possible through the identity of Prakṛti.

EVOLUTION OF THE WORLD Prakṛti evolves the world through its three[22] Attributes (*guṇas*, Qualities) called the Transparent (*sattva*, Pure), the Active (*rajas*), and the Static (*tamas*, Dark). Just as Spinoza calls mind and matter the Attributes of God or Substance, the Sāṅkhya calls the three aspects the three Attributes of Prakṛti. We generally think that attributes or qualities are static characteristics; but these three are forces (*śaktis*) also, which try to separate themselves from one another and combine in various degrees, every one trying to dominate the others in the creation of the world. We may, therefore, treat the three as factors or constituents of Prakṛti also. The original nature of the Transparent is pleasantness (*prīti*), of the Active drive, and of the Static depression and dullness. Everything static is fixed and, therefore, bound. Whatever is found fixed and bound is due to the preponderance of the Attribute called the Static. But none of the Attributes is found alone without the other two. In the different forms of the world, one or the other of the three Attributes dominates over the other two. In the original state of Prakṛti, they remain in equilibrium (*samatā*), when there is no world of forms. But when somehow—we cannot explain why and how—the reflection of the Puruṣa is thrown in Prakṛti, the latter becomes disturbed. The disturbance is the breaking up of the original equilibrium of the three Attributes,[23] which then try to dominate over one another. Through the struggle of the three Attributes, the world evolves out of Prakṛti by various stages, which will be explained below.

What makes the originally pure Puruṣa throw his reflection into the originally undisturbed Prakṛti is an ultimate mystery in this school. A few unsatisfactory explanations are given. Īśvarakṛṣṇa[24] says that the seeming contact—for it is only seeming, there is no real contact between two disparate substances—between the Puruṣa and Prakṛti is effected by showing Prakṛti to the Puruṣa, "who could not have had any desire to see it," so that he will see it with all its evils and will then be without any desire to see it at all. He will then long intensely to exist in his separateness. This bringing them together is like the burning of the finger of a child so that in future it will not like to go near fire. It seems that the occasion for the contact between Puruṣa and Prakṛti is adventitious and accidental; for there is no third to bring about the contact. According to Vijñānabhikṣu,[25] the contact is beginningless (*anādi*) and is of the nature of the relation between the proprietor and his property (*svasvāmibhāva*) and is strengthened by the life of action. According to Pañcaśikha,[26] it is beginningless and due to ignorance (*avidyā*) viz., of the fact that the Puruṣa is really different by nature from Prakṛti. According to Sadānanda, it is due to the subtle body (*liṅgaśarīra*).[27] But according to all, the contact has no beginning. Consequently, we may conclude, the Sāṅkhya, like the Mīmāmsā, believes that the world is beginningless. Such a conclusion agrees with the atheistic Sāṅkhya. If the world is not created but eternal, there is no need of a creator.

The Sāṅkhya in its atheistic form generally gives twenty-five categories (*tattvas*, ultimate Thats, Thatnesses). They are not meanings of words (*padārthas*) as in the Nyāya-Vaiśeṣika, but ontological entities, to which we can point to as Thats. However, the two words are used interchangeably. In the theistic Sāṅkhya, there is God in addition to the twenty-five. They may be given in the form of the following chart:

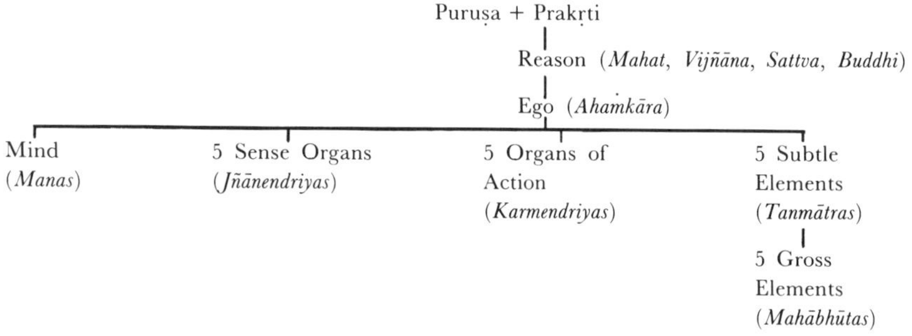

We should remember that the contact between the Puruṣa and Prakṛti is only a seeming contact (*abhimāna*, mine-ness), but not real characterization as in that of the rose by red colour. Prakṛti becomes characterized by the reflection of the Puruṣa just as water may be characterized by the reflection of the sun.[28] That is, it embodies consciousness or I-consciousness. Water by itself and by nature cannot light itself up; neither can the sun have the ripples of the water in which he is reflected. Yet the sun's reflection in water appears to be moving with the ripples. If that reflection were the reflection of consciousness, not merely of light, it would think that it is moving. It would think that the affections of the water are its own affections. But the Puruṣa does not really get involved in the fortunes of Prakṛti like the sun who does not get involved in those of the water. He remains only the mere knower (*sākṣi*, *kūṭastha*), not the doer, enjoyer, or sufferer.

When Prakṛti receives the reflection of the Puruṣa, it becomes animated or conscious and then agitated. This agitation disturbs Prakṛti's equilibrium and its three Attributes start their struggle. First, the Transparent becomes dominant, and the category, Reason[29] (*buddhi*), appears. Out of Reason, the ego (*ahaṁkāra*) issues forth. The Transparent is less dominant in the ego. The ego is of three kinds, depending on which of the three Attributes is dominant: the transparent ego, the active ego, and the static ego. In fact, the three are aspects or phases of the same ego. The Sāṅkhya distinguishes the three egos, as from each different evolutes follow further. According to Vijñānabhikṣu,[30] mind evolves out of the transparent ego, the five senses and the five organs of action out of the active ego, and the five subtle elements out of the static ego. The reason for this view is that mind is a pure sense, the senses and organs of action are active, and the elements are unconscious and static. But Īśvarakṛṣṇa[31] says that both mind and the ten organs originate in the transparent ego, the five subtle elements in the static, the active ego supplying the required energy to all.[32]

Reason is placed next to Prakṛti and is called also the Great (*Mahat*), because it has cosmic significance. Although it belongs to me, whatever it fixes rightly is objective and true not only for me, but also for all the others. In other words, it is the individual's Logos. But the ego is personal and whatever follows or is derived from the ego is also personal, mine. The difficulty with the Sāṅkhya is that Reason, although said to be cosmic and above the ego, is still individual; there are as many Reasons as there are individual egos. Then if each Reason is cosmic, why do they not coincide and be one and the same? Or like the *Kaṭha Upaniṣad*, why does not the Sāṅkhya accept a unitary Logos (*Mahān Ātma*), of which the individual Reasons are parts and become cosmic so far as they partake of it? The Sāṅkhya leaves a lacuna in its explanation of Reason as having cosmic significance.

As the ego (*ahaṁkāra*) is limited relatively to Reason and introduces subjectivity, it is lower than Reason. Reason works always with the reference to someone, some ego that appropriates its work. Reason with its function of decision (*niścaya*) always asserts in the impersonal form, "That is." But this decision is appropriated by the ego, which says: "I assert that That is."

The five gross elements issue out of the five subtle elements. The former are called also the Great Elements (*mahābhūtas*) and the latter Thats-only (*tanmātras*). The term Thats-only for the subtle elements indicates that the Sāṅkhya and the Vedāntic systems, which accept it, understand by it the five kinds of pure objectivities presented by the five senses. These objectivities are presented not only when we are awake, but also when we are dreaming. The stuff constituting the objects of dream is said to be of subtle elements. The Sāṅkhya and the Vedānta do not accept the atomic theory of the Vaiśeṣika. But the Sāṅkhya does not accept the Vedāntic theory that the elements originate one out of another. According to the *Taittirīya Upaniṣad* accepted by all the Vedāntins, air comes out of ether, fire out of air, water out of fire, and earth out of water. But the Sāṅkhya maintains that all the elements originate simultaneously. It rejects the Nyāya-Vaiśeṣika view that space (*dik*) and time (*kāla*) are substances different from either[33] (*ākāśa*). Ether is all pervasive (*vibhu*) and so also are space and time. Space is extension and time is succession, both of which are only characteristics (*guṇas*) of ether. The differences within space, like east and west, and within time, like past, present, and future, are conventional and due to adventitious conditions.

CHARACTERISTICS OF THE CATEGORIES So far the evolution of the categories and the role which the three Attributes play in their evolution has been explained. To that extent the nature of the categories also has partly been explained. The Sāṅkhya assigns certain other characteristics also to them.

(a) *Puruṣa*: As mentioned already, Puruṣa means the same as the *ātman*[34] (spirit). He is a pure knower (*draṣṭā*), but not a doer (*kartā*). For actions belong to the ego along with mind and the ten organs, all of which are the products of the three Attributes. The Puruṣa exists by himself (*kaivalya*), separate and unrelated to everything else. There is a plurality of Puruṣas and the plurality has to be accepted for several reasons.[35] *First*, birth, death, and the eleven organs (including mind) are separate for each individual. If the Puruṣas are not many, when one man is born all the others must be born at the same time; if one man knows an object, all the others must know it; if one man acts, all the others must act. Similarly enjoyment and suffering, good and evil, must be the same and simultaneous for all. Even though Puruṣa is a pure witness and never the doer, that there are different egos implies that they are due to the reflections of different Puruṣas. *Secondly*, everything that is a product of the three Attributes can be traced to the single material principle, Prakṛti. But Puruṣa is that which is in every way opposed in nature to Prakṛti. So if Prakṛti is one, Puruṣas must be many.[36]

The above arguments do not stand examination, as the Advaitins have shown. That the egos are many may be accepted and the reflections also out of which they originate may be a plurality. But from a plurality of reflections it does not necessarily follow that that which is reflected has to be many. The same object can have many reflections like the sun in many mirrors. The argument proves neither plurality nor unity. Again, that the Puruṣa is absolutely different from Prakṛti does not prove that, if Prakṛti is one, the Puruṣas must be many.

The essential nature of Puruṣa is consciousness (*cit*) only. According to both Īśvarakṛṣṇa and Vijñānabhikṣu, it exists[37] also. It is generally accepted that the Sāṅkhya conceives the *ātman* as existence and consciousness,[38] but not as bliss[39] (*ānanda*), thereby differing from the Vedānta, which generally accepts all the three—existence, consciousness, and bliss (*sat-cit-ānanda*) as the constitutive qualities (*svarūpalakṣaṇas*) of the *ātman*. The Sāṅkhya contention is that, as the Puruṣa is only a witness (*sākṣi*) and is not actually involved in the processes of Prakṛti, he cannot be by nature blissful. Bliss (*ānanda*) is a form of pleasure; and pleasures and pains arise for the men of action, but not for the mere witness or knower of the activities of the ego. The witness stands always aloof and remains indifferent (*madhyastha*) like the witness who watches two men fighting. The Puruṣa's thinking that he is happy or miserable is due to lack of discrimination and to false identification with the ego, which is a product of Prakṛti; it is like the colouring of a pure, colourless, transparent glass by the reflection of some colour.[40] Just as the glass, if it has consciousness, would say: "The colour is mine," the Puruṣa thinks that pleasures and pains are his. They are the ego's.

The above argument is not really convincing. For the reason for which bliss is excluded from the Puruṣa, consciousness of the objects also can be excluded from him. The consciousness of the ego may be due to his reflection in the ego. For instance, the ego knows the rose. Then for the reason that pleasure derived thereby is not attributed to the Puruṣa, we should not attribute the cognition of the rose also to him. But the Sāṅkhya attributes the agency of knowing to him. If, without being the doer, the Puruṣa can think that he is the doer even though the ego is the doer, the former can still think that he is the knower, even though the ego is the true knower.

The consciousness of the objects, activity in life, and the enjoyment of the fruits of that activity need not necessarily be dependent on the Puruṣa himself being consciousness and active, when we accept the doctrine of reflection. We have, therefore, to accept the view that the *ātman* is consciousness not on the basis of the consciousness of objects, but on the basis of self-experience. If we do not, the resulting position can be nothing different from the Nyāya-Vaiśeṣika, according to which the *ātman* is unconscious by itself. And if consciousness can constitute the very being (*svarūpa, sattā*) of the *ātman*, bliss also can constitute it. For pleasure is the regaining of one's self and is self-realization in the literal sense of the term. But like the Nyāya-Vaiśeṣika, the Sāṅkhya defines pleasure as the absence of pain (*duhkhanivṛtti*).[41] Then why should we not define consciousness as the absence of ignorance (*avidyā*)? There is absence of ignorance in the stone also; nobody attributes ignorance to it; it is attributed only to conscious beings. That the consciousness of the ego is due to the reflection or image of the consciousness of the Puruṣa can mean only that the consciousness of the Puruṣa is the source, the well-spring of the consciousness of the ego; similarly, the activity of the ego can have its source in the potential power energy of the Puruṣa. For instance, the consciousness of the dream I has its source in the consciousness of the waking I.

Unlike some Vedāntins like Rāmānuja, the Sāṅkhya does not treat pleasure as a form of consciousness.[42] There is, indeed, no pleasure without consciousness; but to have pleasure is not the same as to be conscious and vice versa. There is in our experience no pain also without consciousness. And I may be conscious, but may not have either pleasure or pain. But when I have pleasure or pain, my consciousness is divided (*sakhaṇḍa*) into subject and object. But the consciousness of the Puruṣa is undivided (*akhaṇḍa*). There can, therefore, be no positive pleasure in it, according to the Sāṅkhya.

The above analysis also is not convincing. For even if bliss is taken as a constitutive characteristic of the Puruṣa, it can form an all-pervasive, constitutive characteristic as in "I am happy," unlike that in the experience, "I have a tickling sensation."

However, to show that the arguments of the Sāṅkhya for proving that the Puruṣa is not blissful by nature are not valid is not the same as proving that it is blissful. The Sāṅkhya asserts that ordinary pleasure is due to the transformation of Reason (*buddhi*) when the Attribute, the Transparent, predominates. When the Active predominates, the drive towards activity becomes strong; and the drive is due to a felt lack of something and is, therefore, pain. When the Static predominates, depression and dullness appear without the drive to fill the lack; it also is pain. But what happens when the external conditions make the Transparent dominate over the rest? It appears when there is a feeling of fulfilment. Reason is then peaceful, undisturbed and unclouded, and is able to reflect the Puruṣa clearly. This reflection is experienced as pleasure. If so, if such a reflection is the experience of pleasure, the original, viz., the Puruṣa, must have had that pleasure which is reflected. If the reflection itself is pleasure, the original, Puruṣa, must be immensely so. There can be as much difference of degree between the Puruṣa and his reflection as between the sun and his reflection.

Again unlike some Vedāntins like Rāmānuja, the Sāṅkhya does not accept that the Puruṣa is atomic in size. He is all-pervasive and infinite, without any internal divisions or distinctions. He is different from the body, mind, senses, etc., because they are the products of Prakṛti,[43] whereas he is completely independent of it. All of them undergo change (*pariṇāma*), but not the Puruṣa. Even mind and reason undergo transformation as in cognitions, pleasures and pains. But the "I" remains constant as the onlooker. All the transformations are known and knowable; but they are known by the same knower, who has to be distinct from all of them. We speak of "my body," "my mind," "my reason," and so forth. All such expressions imply that there is something to which they belong.[44] We cannot say that these expressions are metaphorical[45] like the expresssion, "the hands of a statue," because the statue has no knowledge of its hands as I have of mine.

(b) *Prakṛti*: Prakṛti is the world of change (*physis*) in its unmanifest state. For this reason, it is called also the Unmanifest (Avyakta). Another name for it is the Primary (Pradhāna), because it is the source, origin, of everything in the world. It has the three Attributes[46] and everything in the world is their product. It is absolutely unconscious, and is always an object, but never a subject. Even its evolutes such as Reason, ego, and mind, are objects. Reason and its processes are observable and the observer is the Puruṣa. The ego and mind and their states are similarly observable. We generally think that the ego itself is the observer, the knower. But for the Sāṅkhya there is still the transcendental observer, and he alone is the ultimate knower (*sākṣi*). The knower of truth has to be unaffected, undisturbed, and uninvolved. But he cannot be a doer, for a doer gets involved in what he does, while the Puruṣa does not get so involved. Such a knower is the Puruṣa. But the truth is, as the Advaitins say, that the Puruṣa, even as the knower, if he is really the *de facto* knower as in "I see the rose," gets involved in the experience. If this involvement is only apparent, then involvement in activity also can be treated as apparent. The observer of wrestling, boxing, or football on the T.V. often gets agitated by the happenings; he may even take sides. So even a witness (*sākṣi*) may not be indifferent to what he witnesses. Later, he may shake off his agitations. The same can be said of practical activity. The Puruṣa, as transcending the ego, is neither the real doer nor the real knower, if knowing means particular acts of cognition like "seeing the rose" and "seeing the book." He is only the supplier of consciousness for knowing and of consciousness and energy for doing to the ego. However, for this school, the womb of the world, its birth-giver, is Prakṛti. The world evolves out of it and also enters it when dissolved. What we call destruction is only dissolution.

(c) *Reason*: Reason, called the Mahat (Great) is the first evolute out of Prakṛti. Its function, as explained already, is to decide,[47] make decisions, both cognitively and ethically, both in cognition and action. It is cosmic and covers the whole world. The world comes into being out of a cosmic assertion or decision, "The world is," or "That is." This cosmic decision is identified with the Cosmic Person.[48] Though cosmic in significance, it is separate for every individual. In it either the Transparent or the Static may predominate. If the former predominates, it exhibits the qualities of merit, knowledge, detachment (ethical), and power (*aiśvaryam*, lordship, capability); and if the latter predominates, it exhibits the opposite qualities. If Reason, however, can exhibit both groups of qualities, we cannot identify it with the cosmic Logos (Mahān Ātma), which can have only the higher qualities. Or we have to say that, according to the Sāṅkhya, Reason in its highest aspects is the cosmic Logos and in its lowest the reason of the meanest individual; and there can be many degrees of gradation between the two. By not introducing a distinction between the higher and the lower Logoi as the *Kaṭha Upaniṣad* has done, the Sāṅkhya has left a difficulty unsolved.

(d) *Ego*: The sense of the "I" in experiences such as "I know this," "I do this," and "This is mine," is called the ego (*ahaṁkāra*). Its function is to appropriate all experiences to itself; otherwise, they become impersonal.[49] As mentioned already, mind, the five senses, the five organs of action, the five subtle elements, and the five gross elements, which constitute the factors of the world of experience, issue out of the ego. It comprehends and covers the entire world and is not merely a point of reference. There is no experience that is not the experience of the ego. Even if I speak of "objects not known to me," they are still my unknown objects. Neither mind nor the senses work without being accompanied by the ego as in "I think" and "I see." They work only in unison with, and as belonging to the ego (*ahaṁkārābhimāninah*). If the ego is not present, mind does not think and senses do not see. Yet the ego is a product of Prakṛti.

(e) *Mind*: Mind (*manas*) has already been explained. It has also been pointed out that, according to the Sāṅkhya, all the three—Reason, ego, and mind—together constitute the inner sense (*antahkaraṇa*, also translated as internal organ and inner instrument). The five senses and the five organs of action are called the external organs or instruments. But one peculiarity of this school is that, although along with Reason and the ego mind forms the inner sense, it is classified also along with the ten external organs as one of the eleven senses. Thus mind seems to be the connecting link between the inner sense and the outer senses and organs. Vijñānabhikṣu regards the ten organs as the different powers (*śaktis*, forces) of mind. He says also that the inner sense is one and it is called Reason, ego, and mind, just as we call the same thing seed, plant, and tree, depending on the stage of development,[50] and that for that reason mind (*manas*) and Reason (*buddhi*) are used often as synonyms. The differences among the three are only differences among the functions of the same reality. As both the senses and elements are derived from the inner sense, the Sāṅkhya refuses to derive them from the elements, as the Nyāya-Vaiśeṣika has done. Of the two kinds of sense, the inner and the outer, the inner can grasp past, present, and future; but the outer can grasp only the present.

(f) *The Vital Principle*: In many of the Upaniṣads it is said that the vital principle is the origin of the senses. The five kinds of the vital principle are often misleadingly spoken of as the five kinds of air. Vijñānabhikṣu explains that they have really nothing to do with the element air, that they are not kinds or forms of that element, but that because they move in the body freely as air moves in space, they are called airs. They are actually functions of the inner sense.[51] This view does not agree with that of the *Taittirīya Upaniṣad*, according to which the *ātman* as the vital principle is distinct from the *ātman* as mind. But the Sāṅkhya has some Upaniṣadic statements in support, which Vijñānabhikṣu quotes in his commentary. He says also that the vital principle (*prāṇa*) does not originate the physical body, which can be seen even without life.[52] According to the Nyāya-Vaiśeṣika, the life principle (*jīvanayoni*) is an effort (*yatna*) of the *ātman* to make the vital airs (*prāṇas*) function properly.[53] At this point, we see a distinction between the life principle (entelechy) as an effort or a force and the vital airs which seem to belong to the element air. We see also the distinction between the vital principle as a function of the inner sense and the vital principle as an effort (energy) of the *ātman*. But both the concepts of the vital principle and vital air are combined by the Sāṅkhya and attributed to the inner sense.

PROOFS FOR PRAKṚTI AND THE PURUṢA We have seen that the Nyāya-Vaiśeṣika uses inference from an observed generality (*sāmānyatodṛṣṭa*) to prove the existence of the *ātman*. The general principle observed was: All qualities belong to substances and there can be no qualities without substances. We observe qualities like pain and pleasure, but not the substance to which they belong. We infer, therefore, the substance *ātman* to which they belong, although it is unseen.[54] The Sāṅkhya also uses the same kind of argument to prove the reality of both the Puruṣa and Prakṛti. All realities that are imperceptible are to be proved by the kind of inference called inference from observed generality. If some imperceptible realities cannot be proved by this kind of inference, then they have to be accepted on the basis of the Veda.[55] For instance, the categories—Reason, ego, and mind—and the fact of their evolution out of Prakṛti cannot be proved and have, therefore, to be accepted on the basis of the scripture. The Sāṅkhya thinks that the Veda teaches the Sāṅkhya philosophy.

Prakṛti cannot be an object of perception, because it is too subtle to be so. But it can be inferred from its effects. The inner sense, the outer senses, and all the objects around us are its effects.[56]As nothing can come out of nothing and as everything comes, therefore, out of Prakṛti, Prakṛti is Being, not Non-being. The Sāṅkhya does not accept that the world of objects is Non-being. The cause of the world must, therefore, be Being (*sat*). The Sāṅkhya gives the following[57] reasons for accepting Prakṛti. (1) We see that all effects come out of something and, when destroyed, enter it. For instance, objects like pots are made up of clay and, when destroyed, become clay again. So also the world of objects, which is an effect, must come out of something and again enter it, when destroyed. That something is Prakṛti. (2) Every effect functions because of the power, force, or energy conferred upon it or transferred to it by its cause. So the power by which the objects of the world change must have been conferred upon them by something, which is called Prakṛti. (3) Every object that has a definite form originates out of something that is comparatively indefinite, as for instance the pot out of clay. Hence that out of which the whole world of forms originates must be absolutely indefinite. Such an indefinite cause is Prakṛti. (4) Every object in the world has a capacity to produce pleasure, pain, or stupefaction. This capacity is their common characteristic. Pleasure, pain, and stupefaction are due to the three Attributes, which are, therefore, common potentialities of all objects. The cause of all the objects must, therefore, have the three Attributes; and that cause is Prakṛti.

Vijñānabhikṣu tells us why Prakṛti must be the uncaused cause of everything and why it must be infinite and all-pervasive. The ultimate cause of everything cannot itself have a cause; otherwise, it cannot be the ultimate cause.[58] For this reason, Prakṛti is called the Primary (Pradhāna),[59] the Root Cause. Although the Upaniṣads declare that ultimately the cause of the world is the Puruṣa himself through his ignorance (*aviveka*), as he does not transform himself into the world, and as Prakṛti alone is capable of so transforming itself, we have to stop, in our search for the ultimate cause, with Prakṛti only.[60] We have to treat Prakṛti as infinite, *first*, because it is the cause of everything,[61] *secondly*, because, as everything finite is itself caused, nothing finite can be the ultimate, uncaused cause,[62] and *thirdly*, as causation is present everywhere, Prakṛti, as the ultimate cause, must be present everywhere.[63].

We find four[64] arguments given for the existence of the Puruṣa. (1) Everything that is a compound is found to be meant for the use of another. All objects, including Prakṛti, are compounds; even Prakṛti is a compound of the three Attributes. Then the whole world must be meant for somebody who is not a compound; otherwise, he also will be included in the world of compound objects and be meant for something else. Such an uncompounded reality is Puruṣa. (2) Everything that is capable of producing pleasure, pain, and stupefaction is guided[65] and controlled by an intelligence. Such an intelligence is Puruṣa. (3) There must be an enjoyer of pains and pleasures produced by objects. And he is the Puruṣa. That is, the Puruṣa not only guides and controls objects that produce pleasures and pains, but also enjoys[66] those pleasures and pains. There can be no pleasures and pains without somebody enjoying them. (4) The scriptures speak of men striving for salvation. It is meaningless to speak of salvation for the unconscious Prakṛti. So salvation must be for the conscious Puruṣa alone. He must, therefore, exist.

DERIVATION OF PRAKṚTI AND THE PURUṢA The above proofs for the reality of the Puruṣa and Prakṛti lead one to think that the Sāṅkhya arrived at the two conceptions through syllogistic and speculative reasoning. Particularly when an imperceptible reality is proved with the help of some observed generalization (*sāmānyatodṛṣṭa*), what is so proved may at the most be accepted as a good hypothesis. Even if this method of inference is regarded as the method of postulation, the Sāṅkhya will still be regarded as mainly speculative. But the early history of the Sāṅkhya—which is, however, not yet available in a connected form—shows that the concepts of the Puruṣa and Prakṛti were not at first arrived at by mere inference, but through a kind of self-analysis—which is akin to the existential, phenomenological analysis—, and then the attempt was made to prove their reality through syllogistic reasoning, which by itself cannot appear to be conclusive. One can see throughout the history of Indian philosophy a confusion between inference, postulation, and phenomenological and existential analysis. Indeed, even in the West, the last two have been brought to the foreground in the 20th century. Simply because the Sāṅkhya attempt and claim to prove the reality of the Puruṣa and Prakṛti are found to be defective, we should not throw out the ideas as false or superstitious. For behind its avowed method of syllogistic proof lies another method by which they were led to the acceptance of the two ideas. The main difference between a system like the Vaiśeṣika and one like the Sāṅkhya is that in the reflection of the former the self of the reflector is not involved, whereas the Sāṅkhya appears to be absurd, not merely unintelligible in one of its main doctrines—the doctrine that the whole world evolves out of the ego—if such involvement is overlooked. We see that the Sāṅkhya was originally a philosophy of self-involvement and that it derived its concepts from self-analysis, when we consider the few remnants[67] of the works of Pañcaśikha and others. There are available only twenty-one aphorisms.

In the above aphorisms, as in those of the *Sāṅkhyadarśana*, we find that the Puruṣas, in spite of their plurality, are regarded as quality-less (*nirguṇa*, attribute-less). The statement of the Upaniṣads that the Brahman is quality-less is here made applicable to every Puruṣa in his purity. Nothing more is mentioned about him, except that he is a pure witness (*sākṣi*) and conscious. Out of the Puruṣa comes "I am." This "I am" is every man's experience, but is not the Puruṣa as such. It is Reason (Mahat, the Great).[68] It is the first self-affirmation. It is absolutely subtle and infinitely potent. When one realizes its existence, one's experience will only be "I am." Everything in the world is the result of the transformation (*pariṇāma*) of this "I am." It is the self-objectification of the Puruṣa. The experience is such that in it the Puruṣa identifies himself with the "I am" and yet knows[69] it as his object. But from where does this principle of objectivity come in, if the Puruṣa is only the pure witness? It is thought that it comes from Prakṛti, the nature of which is to be pure objectivity.[70]

The above account shows that the Sāṅkhya started originally out of an analysis of the "I am." When the question: "Who am I" or "What am I"? is raised, there can be no answer except through self-analysis. I am not certainly anything that is around me. I can make even my body an object of my consciousness, and detach and suspend my being as "I am." Even then, there is something in the "I am" that knows the "I am," and must, therefore, be distinct from the "I am." That something must be my pure nature, of which the "I am" is an object.[71] But if the pure witness-consciousness also is identifying itself with the "I am," which is its object, how does this objectivity intervene? It cannot belong to the pure witness, which is always a witness and never an object. It must, therefore, be due to Prakṛti, an insentient principle and something that has characteristics opposed to the pure witness consciousness. But how can such opposites combine in "I am"? Hence arose the doctrine that the "I am" is only Prakṛti animated by the reflection of the Puruṣa, but not the Puruṣa himself. Thus animated, Prakṛti is Reason (*buddhi*, Mahat) out of which the rest of the categories of the Sāṅkhya follow. At the starting point we can detect a form of the phenomenological and existential analysis. But later the Sāṅkhya thought that it could present itself as a rationalistic system.

When we appreciate the starting point, we can appreciate also the Sāṅkhya view that the whole experience and the world originate in the ego. We can understand the significance of the origination in two ways. *First*, the so-called origination is a phenomenological derivation of all the factors of experience from the "I am." The "I am" first appears as the ego, the finite "I." But this "I" cannot remain stable, unless it ends up in something like "I see the rose." And this seeing involves, when further analyzed, the presence of mind and senses. As we started from the "I am," the latter factors become derivatives. If again I, as the ego, go back to the "I am," all the derivatives are withdrawn and assimilated to the "I am." This analysis is conscious and reflective, not involuntary or intuitive. *Secondly*, when we naturally wake up after a quiet sleep without any psychological disturbances that violently make us conscious of the objects, the first thing one becomes conscious of is one's "I am," a pure, placid state of one's being. Then appear the ego and all its ramifications and objects. If the Sāṅkhya is not understood thus, its so-called doctrine of the evolution of the world out of the ego will look absurd.[72]

EVOLUTION AND CAUSATION When once Prakṛti receives the reflections of the Puruṣas, the process by which it creates the world of experience is of the same type for all. This process is called evolution or transformation (*pariṇāma*). If some of the Puruṣas obtain salvation, then the world of experience disappears for them, but remains only for the others. For Prakṛti withdraws, like a dancing girl, from those who are not interested in it. Here, we have only a simile to explain why Prakṛti withdraws from some Puruṣas. This withdrawal is effected through what is called involution; that is, each lower category is withdrawn into its higher and finally everything is withdrawn into Prakṛti, which regains its original equilibrium (*sāmyāvasthā*) of the Attributes and loses the reflection of the Puruṣa.

Evolution, it may be said, is a form of causation. The Sāṅkhya holds the doctrine that the effect is existent (*sat*) before it is born.[73] This doctrine has already been referred to, when the Nyāya doctrine of causation was explained. In consonance with the doctrine of momentariness, the Buddhists maintain that the cause must perish before the effect is born and, for this reason, agree with the Naiyāyikas in saying that the effect (kārya) is non-being (*asat*) before it is born. But the Sāṅkhya rejects this view and says that, if the effect is originally non-being, since non-being cannot become being, a non-existent effect cannot become an existent effect. The Sāṅkhya gives four reason for its view. (1) Non-being can never be the cause of anything, for it cannot have the power to become anything, even another kind of Non-being.[74] The effect is always a being and cannot be the transformation of a non-being, just as the pot is a transformation of clay. The Sāṅkhya rejects the view of some Buddhists and Vedāntins who say that the objects of the world are Non-being; for whatever is perceived by us as a being cannot be, without sufficient reasons, rejected as a non-being and there can be no sufficient reason for rejecting the whole world as a mere Non-being. (2) We see that every effect is related to a particular material cause. Oil is produced out of oil seeds, but not out of sand; the pot is produced out of clay, but not out of air; and so on. But if an effect can be produced out of Non-being, but not out of something positive and definite, then anything can come out of Non-being and there can be no causal law. (3) The cause can produce only that which it is capable of producing; it is not capable of producing anything and everything. This capability is directed towards that which can be produced. But if that which can be produced is only Non-being, how can the capability be directed towards it? So the effect must be a being.[75] (4) The being of the effect must be the being of the cause. For instance, the being of buttermilk is the same as the being of the milk out of which it is made. So if the being of the cause is admitted, the being of the effect also must be admitted.

In fact, the Nyāya does not reject the necessity of a material cause or of the being of the cause. What it rejects is that the form of the effect, e.g., the pot, is already there in the clay before it is turned into the pot. If the form of the effect is already there in the cause, there will be no need of any causal process. If it is there, why do we not see it? Furthermore, if it is there, then the cause will be the same as the effect and vice versa. In answer, the Sāṅkhya says that cause and effect are both identical and different. They are identical, as their being is the same. They are different, because the effect is a form, state, of the transformation of the cause (*pariṇāmāvastha*). This transformation is only manifestation (*abhivyakti*) of the effect already potentially present in the cause, just as everything in the world is a manifestation of what is already contained in Prakṛti.

But is not this manifestation a novelty? Again, if Prakṛti can manifest everything in the world, should we say that everything in the world, which is part and parcel of the same Prakṛti, can cause anything and that there is, therefore, no fixed causal relation in the world? To the first question the answer is that manifestation, although new every time, belongs to the very being (*svarūpa*)[76] of things, is their constitutive characteristic, and does not, therefore, originate out of Non-being. The second question is answered by saying that actually all the objects of the world have common features and must have originated, therefore, out of something that is their common ground. So in an ultimate sense, anything can originate out of anything. Even in this world of experience, we see that the same seed can produce different kinds of fruit under different conditions.[77]

We see that the Sāṅkhya accepts practically two kinds of causation for defending its doctrine that every effect is a being, but not a non-being, even before it is born: (1) anything can come out of anything; and (2) the causal relation is fixed and so everything cannot come out of everything. But we have to understand that the former view is metaphysical in terms of Prakṛti, the unitary source of everything in the world, and of its three Attributes; and that the latter is cosmological. We may call the former the view of vertical or linear causation and the latter that of horizontal causation.

There is still an unsolved mystery in the processes of Prakṛti, in its evolution and involution. It is said that Prakṛti is one and unconscious, and its processes are mechanical and spontaneous. Yet, it evolves the world only for those Puruṣas whose reflections are thrown into it and who have not yet discriminated themselves from it. As soon as a Puruṣa realizes his separateness, Prakṛti withdraws from him and withdraws its own evolutes into itself. But if it is an unconscious entity, how can it manifest its evolutes to some Puruṣas and not manifest them to the others at one and the same time? Has it a mysterious power and a sense of discrimination? If it has them, how can it be called unconscious? The Sāṅkhya resorts to the simile of the dancing girl, who withdraws from such men as are not interested in her blandishments. But how can Prakṛti which is unconscious and material and works in fixed ways, be as delicate, sensitive, and prudent as a self-conscious dancing girl? The only reasonable way in which we can understand this view of the Sāṅkhya is that the Puruṣa himself withdraws from Prakṛti like a bored spectator from the dancing hall. Even then there is no question of the Puruṣa withdrawing; for he is always separate from all that takes place. But does he withdraw his reflection? He has himself not thrown it into Prakṛti and the reflection is not he himself. Then why should he bother about withdrawing his reflection? The sun is not worried about the vicissitudes of his reflections in water. Then the reflection itself of the Puruṣa, which animates and identifies itself with Prakṛti, should be the soul that worries about the vicissitudes. If so, we approach the general Vedāntic position, which again, as we shall see, has its own variety of interpretations and explanations. For the reflection need not be unreal. A daughter may be the reflection of her mother, but need not be unreal.

GOD It has already been said that there are two kinds of the Sāṅkhya, the theistic and the atheistic, and that Īśvarakṛṣṇa, the author of the *Sāṅkhyakārikās*, alone is generally understood to be atheistic. Between the two kinds of the Sāṅkhya, the main difference is the acceptance and non-acceptance of God; other differences are of minor importance. Between the two again, there are a few positions like that of Vijñānabhikṣu, who says that the Sāṅkhya does not hold that God does not exist,[78] but only that his existence cannot be proved. Sophisticated and conceited philosophers (*prauḍhavādins*) think that they can prove the existence of God and the Sāṅkhya destroys their conceit. Although Vijñānabhikṣu does not tell us on what basis he accepts God, we may say that he accepts him on the basis of the scriptures.[79] The arguments advanced against the proofs are the usual ones.[80] However, if God is accepted on the basis of the scriptures, why Vijñānabhikṣu, who refers to the scriptures very often in his commentary on the *Sāṅkhya Aphorisms*, does not allow God to play an important role in the system itself—he does so to some extent in his commentary on the *Vedānta Aphorisms*—can be explained, it seems, by the original Sāṅkhya being developed out of phenomenological and existential self-analysis, but not through an interpretation of the Vedic scriptures. Yet, one should say that, in the Sāṅkhya, on the whole—except in the Sāṅkhya of the *Bhagavadgītā*—and even in the Yoga system of Patañjali, which is regarded as a theistic Sāṅkhya, the idea of God looks like an after-thought added on to the system.

4. IDEAL OF LIFE

Although the Sāṅkhya does not emphasize as strongly as Buddhism the suffering aspect of existence, by the time of Īśvarakṛṣṇa at least it offered its philosophy as showing the way out of suffering. The aphorisms alleged to be those of Pañcaśikha and others do not start with the enunciation of suffering in the world. They start, on the other hand, with the ignorance (*avidyā*, *aviveka*) of the Puruṣa, who, identifying himself with Prakṛti and, enjoying the pains and pleasures it offers, does not suspect that he is something higher. However, both the *Sāṅkhyakārikās* and the *Sāṅkhya Aphorisms* start with the enunciation of three kinds of suffering and say that we have, therefore, to enquire and find out how to overcome suffering. One may object that these sufferings may be removed by means known in this world itself, e.g., fever can be cured by some medicine. Such an antedote to suffering is not final, and one may get fever again. We have, therefore, to understand the ultimate cause of suffering so that we can overcome it once for all by destroying the ultimate cause.

Suffering is of three kinds: personal, environmental, and supranatural. Personal suffering is either bodily suffering like fevers and aches or mental like fear, anxiety, and nausea. Environmental suffering is due to environmental causes like scorpions and stones. Supranatural suffering is due to supranatural causes like ghosts and displeased gods. All the forms of suffering are due to the Puruṣa falsely identifying himself with Prakṛti and its evolutes, thinking that their vicissitudes are his own. Mind, body, and every other means of enjoyment are the modifications of Prakṛti and its three Attributes. The Puruṣa is by nature different from all, although entangled in them. This entanglement is the root cause of suffering. Birth, decay, and death are characteristics of the processes of Prakṛti. But the Puruṣa, in identifying himself with Prakṛti, thinks that he is born, becoming old, and dying. This identification is due to ignorance, which is lack of discrimination between himself and Prakṛti. The way to overcome suffering is to develop this discrimination (*viveka*), which is the highest knowledge. When this knowledge dawns and becomes perfect, the Puruṣa is liberated and obtains salvation.

Liberation (*mukti*) is of two kinds:[81] liberation in the body when still alive (*jīvanmukti*) and liberation at death when detached from the body (*videhamukti*). Even though discrimination dawns upon the Puruṣa and remains stable when he is alive, the ethical potency of past *karmas* that started his present life may not have exhausted itself; he will then continue to live until it is exhausted. When it is exhausted and the body is left by the Puruṣa, he obtains absolute liberation. Salvation, as pointed out already, is not a state of bliss, but a complete removal of every kind of pain; it is the destruction[81] of pain. However, the ideal of life presented by the pure Sāṅkhya—not the Sāṅkhya of the *Bhagavadgītā*—with its idea of the *ātman* as pure consciousness without positive bliss, is a kind of escape from Prakṛti and is without the love and protection of a merciful God. It did not, therefore, satisfy its followers, who became the followers of the Vedāntic Vaiṣṇavism, as evidenced by the Sāṅkhya of the *Bhagavadgītā*, which is a part of the *Mahābhārata*, originally a Vaiṣṇava epic. Just as the followers of the Nyāya and the Vaiśeṣika became Śaivas in religion, the followers of the Sāṅkhya and the Yoga became Vaiṣṇavas.

GENERAL ESTIMATE AND CONSTRUCTIVE COMMENT

(i) Assimilation of "Image" and "Reflection" to Experience: Prakṛti an Ingredient of Puruṣa

The first point that needs comment for becoming intelligible is that of the Puruṣa throwing his reflection into Prakṛti. Something has already been said about this idea. Throughout the Vedāntic philosophy, Buddhism, and even Christianity, the spirit throwing its reflection and man being an image[83] of God are common ideas. But what does the idea of reflection mean and how can we make it intelligible to ourselves? How can I, this particular person with all my affections and imperfections, be a reflection of the spirit, which is pure and unagitated? And how can spirit remain pure in spite of, and during the agitations within me, if it identifies itself with me even falsely, as the Sāṅkhya, the Vedānta, and Buddhism assert in their respective philosophies? The sun being reflected in different pools—some muddy, some pure, some placid, and the others rippled and disturbed—, I reflected in various tinted mirrors, and other examples are material, objective examples, which I cannot assimilate experientially to my experience of my own person; and so they remain only helpful examples. The idea of the spirit (Puruṣa) being only a witness (*sākṣi*) also cannot be assimilated except as a theory, unless pointed to as not an absolutely uncommon experience. Do we even remain detached witnesses of our own experiences? Do we even in our normal experiences realize that we are agitated, but unnecessarily, and then detach ourselves from the agitations and become placid? Nobody is an unagitated witness of the joys and sorrows of others, and even if he does not and cannot do anything about them.

When the question is put thus, the idea of reflection makes us think that we often do so. Often we relive our past, frightful experiences with a background knowledge that those experiences are now no longer actual. When we shake ourselves off from such re-living, we regain our placid state.[84] As having the background knowledge, I become a witness of this reliving; but the peculiarity of the situation is that often even in this reliving I get agitated and forget and so become ignorant of my being a witness only at the time, as in observing wrestling or boxing. But when this ignorance is removed, the agitation ceases. This is so in many cases of fantasy also. Take the example of the pedler who built castles in the air, for whom the glass ware he was peddling was valueless in his fantasy, and so kicked and broke it. Without identification with himself as living in the castle, he would not kick at the glass ware. But when he came to his senses and became sorry, he realized that he was not the rich man with a castle in the air, and this realization was possible because he was a witness also at the time of his identification with the rich man.

Even in imagination in which I imagine that I am acting or have to act in such and a such a way in a situation, I identify myself with the I in that situation and become affected and agitated.[85] But when I come back to the situation in which I am actually living, the agitation slowly fades away. The I as living in the actual situation is the background witness of the I in the imagined situation. In the imagined situation I may not be conscious that I am the I of the actual situation; but the latter, although remaining in the background, must have been conscious of the I in the imagined situation.

The relation between the two "Is" is more impressive and illuminating when we consider the relation between the dream I and the waking[86] I. The dream I has no knowledge of the waking I; but in the dream I itself the waking I remains as a background witness, a real spectator, although identifying itself with the dream I as shown by its memory of the dream experience which it later disowns calling itself the true I and calling the dream I a false I. Then what is the relation between the I which is disowned as a false I and the I which is acknowledged as the true I? The former is called the reflection of the latter; and the vicissitudes of the reflection do not factually affect the original. This realization comes as soon as the identity of the two is recognized as false or illusory.

The above explanation is an attempt to bring nearer home the idea of reflection and that of pure witness (*sākṣi*). We can then fairly understand how in our experience we can be pure witnesses (*sākṣis*) of our experiences and also be involved in them and be affected by them—which means that splits within the I-consciousness are possible and yet the I-consciousness can remain a whole and integral[87] and be not fragmented into bits.[88] Using another terminology, we may say that the I of the waking state, although immanent in the I of the dream, transcends it. *Thus the ideas of reflection and of transcendence and immanence are related.*

It is thus that the Sāṅkhya idea of the Puruṣa being reflected in Prakṛti and—although actually unaffected by it—falsely thinking that he is affected comes near our experience and understanding. But as we mentioned already, the same Puruṣa can have many reflections like the same sun being reflected in many pools. The Sāṅkhya argument that the Puruṣas have to be many does not, therefore, hold ground. Besides, the similarity between the sun's reflections and the Puruṣa's reflection in Prakṛti is not strong. I am reflected in the dream not as a mere subjective point, but as having sight, hearing, smell, the organs of action, etc. The material objects of the dream may not be the same as the material objects of my waking. But still the forms and structures of the dreamt objects are to a large degree similar to those of the objects of waking. This is what is meant by my entering the dream not as a pure point or an empty consciousness, but with all the potential paraphernalia of the world, and with such potentialities in me I create the dream world. I should then expect that the potentialities with which Puruṣa creates the world belong to him not merely to Prakṛti.

But the Sāṅkhya separates the Puruṣa from Prakṛti and assigns all such potentialities to Prakṛti alone, but not to Puruṣa as carrying Prakṛti as an essential part of his being. Here is the question: How can the Puruṣa, who is so absolutely different from Prakṛti, as this school maintains, get reflected in the latter? I am reflected in the dream because my dream body and the dream objects are all constituted by the potential forces of the waking I and its objects—remember these potential forces are called subtle forms, subtle elements, *sūkṣmabhūtas*, *tanmātras*, etc.—which in the waking state are controlled by *niyati* (limit, measure), but in the dream state are not governed by the same controlling force. The example of the sun's reflection in many ponds, and of my reflection in many mirrors[89] does not explain why the reflection becomes active, an agent in the case of the Puruṣa's reflection. It can become an active agent if it carries with it the potentiality of being an agent—which it can do if the Puruṣa who is reflected is a force like a dynamo. Otherwise, the reflection ought to be merely passive, being carried away by the natural forces of Prakṛti without holding itself responsible for the happenings. Yes, the Vedāntins and the *Bhagavadgītā* also place the idea of the passive onlooker before man as the ideal. But why does the reflection of the Puruṣa consider itself to be the active agent of all actions, cognitive and ethical, unless it derives this potency from the original? So the word passive is not to be understood as inert and dull like the passivity of mirror receiving my reflection, but as the one with the ability to activate, get involved, and yet get disinvolved.

It is said that it is the nature of Prakṛti to supply this ability to the reflection to regard itself as the agent. Then how is the supplying possible? Maybe, Prakṛti is rich in such potencies. But how can a reflection, which is purely passive, become active in accepting any of Prakṛti's riches? If it is passive, how can it actively appropriate any of the offerings of Prakṛti? The solution of such problems lies in accepting that the Puruṣa carries in himself all of Prakṛti, sometimes keeping its forces latent and other times as patent, and identifying himself with its manifestations. I am not merely the passive consciousness of objects, but also the "consciousness that I am conscious of objects" or "I am an active possessor of the consciousness that I am conscious of objects." The status of the first I is similar to that of the witness consciousness. In activity I am not merely led by the forces of Prakṛti to do this or that act like a puppet, but am the real agent of actions. Even to detach myself from the processes of Prakṛti, I have to be an agent of the activity of detachment. After waking, I detach myself from the activities of dreams; but this waking is not a voluntary act of mine, but a natural involuntary process. But religion and spiritual ideals exhort me to actively realize that I am not the true agent of activities. This exhortation seems to be given by the Sāṅkhya and some other schools the extreme interpretation that the Puruṣa has really nothing to do with Prakṛti. But does he know that there is something called Prakṛti? If he does not know it, his becoming involved in Prakṛti becomes a passive affair and he is to be treated as pure passive consciousness like light revealing objects. We cannot then explain how it is possible at all for a purely passive being to become active later in freeing itself from the embraces of Prakṛti. Besides, if he does not know Prakṛti, if his consciousness is not directed towards it, how can he throw his reflection in it? To throw his reflection, his consciousness must have a direction towards the object into which his reflection is to be thrown.

In terms of the Cartesian system, mind (spirit) must be able to know that there is matter (Prakṛti); and this consciousness implies conscious activity directed towards matter and the consciousness of the consciousness of matter. Even Descartes cannot deny that mind knows that there is matter. *If the two substances are so disparate as he thinks, then mind cannot even know that there is matter.* Even if we accept, for argument's sake, that mind comes into contact with the body at the pineal gland, the contact is not enough to explain how mind knows matter unless mind's consciousness is directed towards matter and grasps[90] it. Otherwise, mind will be pure consciousness turned into itself and this contact will matter little either to matter or mind. For neither can have concern for the other. Hegel was, therefore, right, like Spinoza, in treating mind and body together, but going beyond Spinoza by turning Spinoza's Substance into name Spirit and Self-consciousness. Or in Husserl's language, I must know that my consciousness is directed towards the object—which means that I know the directionality also or my consciousness of the object includes my consciousness of the directionality and the object also towards which the direction obtains.

In the Sāṅkhya we do not find the above implication discussed; otherwise, it could have elaborated the idea of the *Śvetāśvatara Upaniṣad* that Prakṛti is an ingredient of the Supreme I-am. As indicated already a few times, this directionality or intentionality has its orientations within existence; but if both subject and object of consciousness fall within consciousness as in "I know that I know *X*,"—which refers to the I transcending itself—the subject-object poles of cognition need not be two disparate, not even separate, existents as in the philosophies of Descartes and the Sāṅkhya, but the same Existence or Being into which a split is introduced somehow, but with a directionality. We cannot answer why it is or was introduced, but that we experience it now, and that the experience cannot be explained without assuming transcendental implications pointing to the ultimate unity of Existence or Being.

(ii) Being and Becoming: Becoming Self-Propulsion of Being

From the point of view of ontology, the split is due to Becoming issuing out of Being, which is the transcendental I-am. There is no Becoming without Being; for Becoming implies that something, a being, is becoming something else. The heart-beats, pulsations, vibrations of Becoming have to occur within a field, self-consciously stable, in order to be recognized as pulsations of Becoming. If Becoming is a mere procession of instants, without anyone watching a pure change as Heraclitus apparently thought, we cannot even say that it is Becoming (*bhāvanā*); for there has to be something stable in the background or all round with reference to which the progression or succession of instants assumes the status or character of Becoming. But there can be no Becoming without a drive or force (*śakti*) behind; and this force must be operative in Being itself, as there can be no other source. It is, therefore, a mistake to think of Being as something static and powerless. If according to this school, Prakṛti is a dynamo of forces—for what are called the three Attributes (Guṇas) are dynamic, creative—and is still a Being, then Puruṣa also as Being can be dynamic. If the two are ultimately to be one as shown above, then the dynamism of Prakṛti must be a derivation from the Dynamism of Puruṣa, and Prakṛti must belong to Puruṣa.

Now, the persons interested in salvation may ask: If Being is essentially dynamic and by nature creative, and if salvation means rising above the realm of Becoming and to be one with pure Being (*sattā* or *brahmasattā*), then how is salvation possible? For Being then will again be Becoming. The answer lies in Being and Becoming not being separate entities, but in Becoming being a self-propulsion or self-projection of Being without losing itself as Being at the same time. In every moment of a becoming, for instance, if that belongs to a being, then that being is "reflected." It is the same being as observed and as it is at that moment. If water becomes ice, for instance, it is the *same* water that is present at every instance of its becoming ice. Otherwise, the statement, "Water becomes ice," cannot be understood; no connection between the two can be established except the spatio-temporal. And one may even say that God or the Devil placed ice in the place of water and that the two are different objects. Similarly, "John is becoming a youth" cannot be understood if the same John is not present at every instant of the process. Now, salvation, one aspect of which is the realization that I am pure Being above Becoming, is similar to John's realization that he is the same person, ignoring of course the vicissitudes through which he is passing. It is the nature of Being to be itself, to be apart from Becoming by swallowing (cp. the idea of *attā*, the Braham as the swallower) it and making it a part of itself, but not by separating itself from Becoming—which is impossible. The possibility of salvation lies in this peculiar nature or power of Being—which, in different terms, is its power of self-transcendence—which is not to be understood in the classificatory sense.

If it is the nature of Being to propel itself as Becoming, will it not again create me and make me a part of the world of Becoming? No. When I become one with pure Being through moral and spiritual perfection, the conditions of my ego-hood (*ahaṁkāra*) and finitude are dissipated and lost. What may be thrust out of Being later after my salvation will not have any numerical identity with me. I can be eternally emancipated without creation itself coming to an end at the same time. The same Being can be the origin of several forms and loci of Becoming. More will be discussed in the next chapter on the relation between Being and Becoming. But what has to be emphasized here is that the Puruṣa (or Being) is not pure passive consciousness as concluded by this school from the statement "He throws only his reflection into Prakṛti." For throwing is activity, not passivity. And he need not be many, but the same Supreme Spirit as in the Vedāntic systems; for even though he is one, his reflections or images can be many. Prakṛti is not a different Being opposed totally in its nature to the Puruṣa, but is the inherent force, energy of the Puruṣa, his inherent dynamo, the foundation, well-spring, or potential state of Becoming. If Being and Becoming can be reconciled in Prakṛti—which, the Sāṅkhya says, can remain in its original stable, balanced form as unity and yet be many for the many souls, making advances to some and withdrawing from the others—they can be reconciled more justifiably in the Puruṣa. "More justifiably" because only a self-conscious I can project itself into many situations,—as we have seen in the explanation of the reflection theory with the help of dream experience etc.—, identify itself with the projections and also withdraw itself from them. Such identification and withdrawal are possible because the identification is not absolute like the identification of myself with my reflections in convex and concave mirrors, but is still identification. In the case of non-sentient objects, such reflections, identifications, and withdrawals are pointless. They can have no conscious desire to withdraw themselves from the identifications.

The Sāṅkhya may find support in the *Bhagavadgītā* exhorting man to develop detachment regarding all activities, pains, and pleasures as due to and belonging to the Attributes (*Guṇas*) of Prakṛti with which the *ātman* is not really one. This detachment, it may be said, is possible if the *ātman* (Puruṣa) is not factually one with Prakṛti. Then why does the Puruṣa feel pleasure and pain? The answer is: Through false identification which is the same as the Puruṣa throwing his reflection only in it. Detachment is the realization that that which suffers and enjoys is only a reflection.

Although reflection is a good example to help understanding the situation, it is not adequate. For if Prakṛti is insentient and, without some contact with the Puruṣa, cannot be active, how can a mere reflection set it in motion? My reflection in the mirror cannot move the mirror; it cannot be active, unless I am active. Or should we not say that, like the Puruṣa's reflection setting Prakṛti in action, the sun's reflection sets the water of the pool in action? It will not be true. If it is said that the heat of the reflection can introduce some motion into the water of the pool, it will be an admission that the Puruṣa, through his reflection, actively transmits his dynamic energy to Prakṛti. The reflection theory only helps us in understanding how the Puruṣa can remain unaffected, even when his reflection is affected.

We have to conclude, therefore, that there is some primordeal intention,[91] inherent potentiality (*śakti*) in the Puruṣa, to set Prakṛti in motion; that that potentiality is the potentiality of Becoming; and that Prakṛti is really his inherent nature with the drive to become the world and also to return to him as Pure Being. But the outward movement of manifesting the world and the return movement to himself are the two directions of his Becoming. The two forms of the activity of Prakṛti, called evolution and involution, are really two forms of Becoming founded in Being.

(iii) Space, Time, and Ether

In this school we find that time (*kāla*), space (*dik*), and ether (*ākāśa*) are identified and are not given separate places. We have already commented on the relation of the ideas of ether as the source of sound and of space as the source of our sense of directions. We pointed also to the Upaniṣadic idea that hearing is the source of our cognition of space and that ether and space can be one and the same. But this school identifies time also with ether (*ākāśa*) as the source of sound. The metaphysics of Patañjali, the founder of the Yoga school, seems to differ from the Sāṅkhya on this point, which will be discussed in the next chapter.

Now, how is it possible to justify the identification of time and ether? Even if space-time is one, the concepts of time and space are generally different. It should be noted here that commentators and followers of this school differ in details in explaining this identification.[92] The general trend and the underlying conception are fairly clear. Eternal time, which we call one and which is divided into past, present, and future, is really the basis of the divisions. Even if it flows, it cannot but be the same as the divisions of past, present, and future. Now, if these divisions are different, how can time be one? So what makes the time concept possible and lies at the base of the divisions, has to be above the divisions. What can it be? *It is eternal time, ever present and is, therefore, always the present.* The need for the division lies in activity,[93] which is a series of activities and activity moments in succession. And succession is made possible by time; for it takes place in time, although succession is not the same as time. Yet the idea of succession involves the ideas of past and future; and time enables us to relate the different moments as succession. Without time, succession will not be succession, but a series of unrelated moments.[94]

Space also is what makes divisions and directions possible, such as right and left, and east and west. But these divisions and directions do not constitute a succession, but imply simultaneity. Space then is not the same as these divisions and directions, but is what makes them possible and lies behind them.

Now, it is easy to understand the plausibility in identifying space and time. Their manifestations as past, present and future, and as left and right and east and west are all essentially related to activity, which is succession of movements and goes often from one direction to another; or the object within which the movement occurs has to have extension. If activity like cooking is one act, then time and space, which are its essential ingredients, have somehow to be one; and they have also to originate in the same principle or entity.

So Vijñānabhikṣu thinks that such a principle is the original Darkness (*Tamas*, not one of the Attributes of Prakṛti, but what is often identified with Māyā, Avidyā, and even Prakṛti itself), which is both the original time and space and the source of what we experience as time and space. That Darkness is often called also the original space (*ākāśa*) or space in its transcendental form, which is an Upaniṣadic idea. That it is also time is not new to the Upaniṣads. The source of everything is that original Darkness (*Tamas*).

But curiously enough, this Darkness in the Upaniṣads[95] is the same as *citta* or Reason—to be understood in the meaning given by the Stoics—in deep sleep, and is called causal body (*bījātman, kāraṇa-śarīra*) in the Advaita, according to which the whole world, including the constituents of personality, is withdrawn into *citta* (also called *vijñānātman*) or Reason and lies dormant, the state which Reason assumes then.[96] This Darkness, so far as I in my deep sleep am concerned, is my Unconscious, in which the directionality of the relation from the subject to the object and the one of the opposite relation are withdrawn. Then it is really what we have in our apperception in its inactive and dormant state.

Now, both the Sāṅkhya and the Yoga schools maintain that space and time have no existence apart from *citta* or apperception. That is, they are two of its forms or modes of activity. So we can appreciate the Sāṅkhya-Yoga view that we should be content with the idea of transformation (*pariṇāma*) of Prakṛti and do not have to accept the separate reality of space and time. Activity, movement, or transformation is basic to time and space, and they are artificially derived or abstracted from it. But how are we to understand that the two are identical with ether (*ākāśa*) as the source of sound (*śabda*)? Yes, they may be identical with Prakṛti and its transformation process; but how can they be identical with ether (*ākāśa*), the source of sound? Is sound the primary derivative of Prakṛti?[97]

One reason may be that the source of sound is called *ākāśa* and the source of everything also is called *ākāśa* in its transcendental nature. This is only a linguistic explanation; for in both cases, the word *ākāśa* is used. But for a philosophical reason, we have to turn to the philosophers of language like Bhartṛhari, who maintain that meaningful sound (word) is the origin of the world and its source is *ākāśa*. We have made references to the idea that hearing and space are related, that we know the directions through hearing, and animals use the sense of hearing to locate the source of sound. Such cognition is not possible, if sound is not spread out. Then the medium through which sound is spread out and which is space has to be identical with the entity which is the source of sound and which is ether. As such, again, it has its origin in transcendental space, which we have seen, is identical with Darkness (*Tamas*), and which is the same as Prakṛti.[98] We have to note also that space and time are not and cannot be different from the objects said to be occupying them.

(iv) Attributes, Prakrti, and Causal Body

It has been pointed out that the word *guṇas* should be translated as Attributes using Spinoza's terminology, but not as qualities after the Nyāya usage. There is the feeling that Spinoza used the word attributes to indicate that, if they are qualities, they depend for their existence on God, who is called the Substance; and for methodological purposes the concept substance-attribute was utilized by him to solve the mind-matter problem. Even if Spinoza's purpose is such, we do not generally think that mind and matter are merely qualities or characteristics, but substantive entities whatever they be; and their substantiveness stays with our thinking and their being ineffective qualities recedes from our mental horizon. In addition, the Sāṅkhya treats the Attributes as constituents—not like the Nyāya as inert qualities, but like the strands of a rope—and as forces each trying to dominate the other two. They make Prakṛti a dynamo of creative activities. In fact, the Attribute *Rajas* (Activity) is responsible for the evolutionary transformation of Prakṛti into the subject-object world.

This transformation should be understood in terms of or in the light of the causal body (*bījātman*) lying dormant in deep sleep, assuming the form of personality and its world. The existence or being of everything is that of Prakṛti as manifested through the presentations and combinations of the three Attributes. As the I-am (Puruṣa) is reflected in Prakṛti, of which the world is a manifestation and, if, as contended above, Prakṛti as so reflected in, is part and parcel of the I-am, then the manifestations are the manifestations of the I-am.

(v) Subtle Elements; Correlation of Senses and Objects

Another point that puzzles both the Indian and western students of philosophy is the idea of subtle elements (*tanmātras*) or mere Thats (objectivities). The idea may leave in their minds the impression that the concept is something outlandish. In fact, there was a controversy even in India about whether they are not realities.finer than the atoms of the Nyāya, which themselves have no dimensions. We have explained that they are the stuff of objects seen in dreams.[99] This explanation also may not be enough for appreciating the idea. For can there be any stuff in dreams? If there is real stuff, it ought to be available even after the dream. It ought to be, because the Vedāntic schools and the Sāṅkhya-Yoga hold that the stuff of the gross elements which we see in tables, stones, etc., is a transformation of the stuff constituting the subtle elements.[100] As the constitutive (material) cause of the gross elements, the stuff by which the dream objects are constituted has to be there objectively for physical experimentation. But we do not find it. Then where does the rationality or justification of the theory lie?

The justification of the theory lies in the acknowledged central Vedāntic tradition that the senses[101] (not the physical, but the psychological) and their respective objects are the polarizations of the subtle forms of the elements (sometimes called gods and deities, *devatās*); and the subtle elements as such are the manifestations (rays, *rasmis*, *amsus*) of the potentialities (*śaktis*, powers, energies)—here it should be remembered that one should get rid of the idea that the *ātman* is empty consciousness and that Being is an empty concept as Hegel thought—of the Ātman and are co-extensive, if this word can be used, with the Ātman. They are the potential senses as powers or potentialities, not the senses of this or that person, but patterned, potential, forces of the cosmos—also called the Cosmic Person, the Logos, tending to create my person and my horizon of experience—ready to embody themselves in this person, me, as my senses and their fields of objects. Language fails to express the idea of impersonal seeing—unless we take the Cosmic Person into consideration—without some eye to see and a colour to be seen. Why should the eye see colours and not hear sounds? The reason can be that the eye and the colour are polarizations, splits, of the impersonal sight-force and enter me as soon as my finite *ātman* is created out of the Cosmic Person or the Supreme Ātman.

Now, that which polarizes itself thus is called the subtle element. These elements are the infinite potencies of polarization lying latent in me, my person, my I-am. The general Vedāntic position is that these elements are derived one out of another, air out of ether, fire out of air, water out of fire, and earth out of water; or in different words, touch out of sound, colour out of touch, taste out of colour, and smell out of taste, all of them being *tanmātras* or subtle elements. They, as impersonal qualities—for they are the Thats (*tats*), do not inhere in substances, but substances in their gross form are formed out of them—lie in wait for each created person to be appropriated by him as his potentialities.

The Sāṅkhya does not accept this derivation,[102] but maintains that the subtle elements evolve out of the ego (*ahaṁkāra*) independently of one another and get transformed into the gross elements. And instead belonging to the Cosmic Person—for whom the atheistic Sāṅkhya has no place—they belong to Prakṛti. But in the Sāṅkhya it is not, however, clear that the same subtle element bifurcates itself into the senses and their corresponding objects; rather all the subtle elements along with the senses originate in the ego (*ahaṁkāra*) in its *tāmasic* or insentient aspect (*bhūtādi*). The Sāṅkhya seems to have viewed the subtle elements in a somewhat physical way like invisible particles constituting a stone. But this interpretation also is not absolute; for the subtle elements are derivatives of the I-am as the ego. In any case, the controversy about their being the atoms or finer than the atoms of the Nyāya is due to misunderstanding the spirit of the Sāṅkhya-Yoga and the Vedānta (Upaniṣads).

Whatever the Sāṅkhya says, unless we are thinking of compounds and constituents—which thinking becomes pointless in this context—the idea of subtle elements becomes meaningless, if they are not taken as the potentialities or latent forms of the different senses or sensation possibilities. Furthermore, these potentialities have to be taken as belonging to the *ātman* and our senses have to be taken as the channels of the manifestations, rays, expressions of the *ātman*. Remember by senses here we do not mean the physical senses or even any person's psychological senses, but the fields of the sensations including my psychological senses, the objects of the senses, and the fields of their correlations. Or rather they are the impersonal sensation-potentialities or sense-fields of the Cosmic Person (Virāt), of whom every finite person partakes. We may here remember Plato's idea of the physical object partaking of the Idea; similarly the finite person partakes of the Logos, the Cosmic Person, of whom he is an image, a reflection.

Then what are called subtle elements are really what can be treated as the transcendental grounds of the substance-quality or substance-property manifestations. That is why they are called mere Thats-only (*tanmātras*), although identified and named with the help of the specific qualities (*viśeṣaguṇas*) such as *śabdatanmātra* (sound-That), *sparśatanmātra* (touch-That) etc. These qualities are the potentialities of the activity of the self-manifestation of the *ātman* or Puruṣa as the experiencer of this or that object. The objects are the objective ends or poles—the resting and stopping places of the activities of mind and senses—of the *ātman*'s manifestations.[103] And what we call senses like my sight and hearing are the instrumentalities and channels by which I sense objects, or the instrumentalities by which the objects reveal and manifest themselves, and more significantly, they are the channels of the manifestation of my self, the *ātman* and also the channels through which I withdraw and assimilate my manifestations to my self.

But the deeper implications of the correlation of senses and objects are not brought out by the Sāṅkhya except saying that both originate in the ego (*ahaṁkāra*). However, the subtle elements are evolutes, the potential evolutes from the Attributes for the Sāṅkhya, not constituents of the senses like atoms of the stone. So the Sāṅkhya justifies itself in its contention that the senses are not the transformations of the elements (*bhūtas*, significantly the word means "have-becomes" or the ends or results of becomings), if the word *bhūtas* means gross elements constituted by atoms. But they have to be transformations of subtle elements as we have said; for otherwise, the correlativities like that between hearing and sound cannot be explained. In the reverse direction, the correlativities point to their unitary origin in the ego and finally in the *ātman*.

(vi) Prakrti cannot be Both Being and Non-Being

We came across the idea of Vijñānabhikṣu that Prakṛti is both Being and Non-being. This view conflicts with the tradition that, for the Sāṅkhya, both the

Puruṣa and Prakṛti are beings. It is not very easy to justify that Prakṛti is both Being and Non-being. If it is inherently a plurality or inherently a change, it may be said to be both Being and Non-being. For both plurality and change involves the concepts of Being and Non-being. In the case of plurality, *A* is not *B*, *B* is not *C* and so on. In the case of change as Becoming, *A* becomes *B*; but when *A* exists as *A*, *B* does not exist, and when *B* exists as *B*, *A* does not exist. But we have seen that for the Sāṅkhya the effect, even before it is born, exists in the cause. Then should we not say that in all cases of causation, which involves change, cause and effect co-exist, although in the two states of actuality and potentiality? When the existence of the cause is actual, the existence of the effect is potential; and when the existence of the effect is actual, the existential of the cause is potential. As an illustration of the latter case, my past [104] exists in my present and influences my future; but it exists only as a potency or potentiality.[105] Such also is the case with the effect existing in the cause.

Then should we say that the whole manifested plurality exists potentially as unmanifested in the unitary Prakṛti? And is it as such a plurality that Prakṛti is both Being and Non-being? Then this potential plurality and change are its very nature like attracting iron is the nature of the magnet. Then Prakṛti being constantly in motion and the reflection of the Puruṣa being passive like the reflection of the sun in the water, we cannot understand, how the reflection can be an active agent in order to decide that it has had enough of Prakṛti and then to vanish. My reflection in the mirror cannot decide that it has had enough of the mirror; even my reflection in dream cannot decide that it has had enough of the dream. So it is not intelligible how Prakṛti can be one and also many, or Being and Non-being, at one and the same time without a self-conscious nisus or drive lying inherent in it. Then if such a nisus is admitted, Prakṛti will not be separate from the Puruṣa; as self-conscious, it will be the same as the Puruṣa. Self-discrimination, the realization of the self as the self, need not be numerical separation from Prakṛti, but the realization that the true self or the *ātman* has everything in it and that the drive for satisfaction and pleasure by going after an object different from the *ātman* is really running after will-o'-the-wisp. Earnest and real analytic understanding of the nature of consciousness is not deep enough in the Sāṅkhya. However, we cannot blame this school very much. It is a common sense idea that consciousness is like empty light and this idea is found in many contemporary philosophies.[106] The example of the light of a lamp revealing the objects to elucidate how consciousness reveals its objects is too often superficially understood to guide our thought in the right way. The active, creative aspect of consciousness is often ignored.

NOTES

[1]Vijñānabhikṣu: *Commentary on Sāṅkhyadarśana*, p. 7. Another commentary by Brahmamuni on *Sāṅkhyadarśana* has recently appeared and is avowedly theistic.

[2]It has been published with Vācaspati's commentary called *Tattvakaumudi* with G. N. Jha's English translation and notes.

[3]S. Radhakrishnan: *Indian Philosophy*, Vol. II, p. 254. This is another instance of confusion about dates. Is Kapila then earlier than Jaimini, Bādarāyana, Kaṇāda, and Gautama? Was he an older or younger contemporary of Mahāvīra and Buddha?

[4]Ibid., p. 255.

[5]*The Sāṅkhyasūtras of Pañcaśikha and Other Ancient Sages* edited by Jagneswar Ghosh.

[6]*Sāṅkhyakārikās*, 4 and 5, and *Sāṅkhyadarśana*, I, 87.

[7]Vijñānabhikṣu: *Sāṅkhyadarśana*, V, 69–72.

[8]Ibid., II, 26.

[9]Ibid., II, 20 and V, 84.

[10]*Sāṅkhyakārikās*, 27.

[11]Op. cit. Vācaspati explains *sankalpa* in the *Kārikā* as the changing of the original indeterminate perception into the determinate, in which both the individual and the universal are distinguished and unified. He accepts the Mīmāmsā view and actually quotes Kumārila. But Vijñānabhikṣu explains *sankalpa* as desire and *vikalpa* as doubt or error. He says that determinate knowledge, which decides what the object is, cannot belong to mind but to reason (*buddhi*), according to the *Sāṅkhya*. He seems to be right. (*Sāṅkhyadarśana*, II, 30).

[12]The senses and organs are called *ahaṁkārābhimāninah*.

[13]Vācaspati understands it only as that which determines what has to be done (*Sāṅkhyakārikās*, 23). But Vijñānabhikṣu takes it in the cognitive role also (*Sāṅkhyadarśana*, II, 30).

[14]*Cetanāśakteranugrahah tatphalam pramābodhah*, see *Sāṅkhyakārikās*, p. 10.

[15]Vijñānabhikṣu: *Sāṅkhyadarśana*, I, 99.

[16]*Sāṅkhyakārikās*, p. 11.

[17]Ibid., p. 16.

[18]Vijñānabhikṣu: *Sāṅkhyadarśana*, V, 51.

[19]Ibid., V, 52–56.

[20]Ibid., p. 183.

[21]Ibid., V, 54.

[22]*Sāṅkhyakārikās*, 2.

[23]This doctrine of Attributes is generally compared to Plato's doctrine of the three parts of the soul and is very important in Indian thought as a whole. It is applied to the explanation of the differences among the characters of men and of women, the differences among plants and animals, and also the differences among the forms of the world—matter, life, and mind.

[24]*Sāṅkhyakārikās*, 21.

[25]*Sāṅkhyadarśana*, VI, 67.

[26]Ibid., VI, 68.

[27]It consists of everything constituting the individual, except the physical body, the physical senses, the physical organs, and the gross physical elements; i.e., it includes everything beginning from the reflection of the Puruṣa and ending with the subtle elements. *Sāṅkhyadarśana*, III, 12–16.

[28]Ibid., VI, 28.

[29]*Buddhi* is often translated as intellect and understanding. But intellect and understanding have no ontological status, which *buddhi* has in the Sāṅkhya. Reason has an ontological status in the Platonic tradition, in medieval philosophies, and modern idealistic systems; and it is even the Logos. So I use the word Reason.

[30]*Sāṅkhyadarśana*, II, 18.

[31]*Sāṅkhyakārikās*, 25.

[32]This view seems to be the better of the two; for mind also is active like the organs of sense and action.

[33]*Sāṅkhyadarśana*, II, 12.

[34]In Sanskrit, both the words, Puruṣa and *ātman*, are masculine in gender. Puruṣa literally means the person and *ātman* the "I." So in English, Puruṣa may be referred to as "he" and the *ātman* as "it."

[35]*Sāṅkhyakārikās*, 18.

[36]*Sāṅkhyadarśana*, VI, 54.

[37]Ibid., VI, 1.

[38]Consciousness is not a quality of the *ātman*, just as red is a quality of the rose. This view is accepted by the Advaita also, which, as the expression, "The *ātman* is conscious," is not tautological, calls consciousness a constitutive quality (*svarūpalakṣaṇa*). See ibid., I, 145–46.

[39]Ibid., V, 66–74. [40]Ibid., VII, 27. [41]Ibid., V, 67.

[42]Ibid., V, 66. [43]Ibid., VI, 2. [44]Ibid., VI, 3. [45]Ibid., VI, 4.

[46]*Sāṅkhyakārikās*, 11. [47]Ibid., 23. [48]*Sāṅkhyadarśana*, II, 13.

[49]We have to accept that what we call impersonal and objective experiences and cognitions fall within

personal experiences and cognitions. Otherwise, there will be no door open even from initial or tentative subjectivism to reach the objective world. This is the essential meaning of all things issuing from the ego.

[50]Ibid., II, 16.

[51]Ibid., II, 31, also see *Sāṅkhyakārikās*, 29. This is an important idea.

[52]*Sāṅkhyadarśana*, V, 113.

[53]Kārikāvalī with *Dinakarī*, p. 510.

[54]For Mīmāmsā, this is postulation.

[55]*Kārikāvalī*, p. 6. [56]Ibid., 8. [57]*Sāṅkhyakārikās*, 15.

[58]*Sāṅkhyadarśana*, I, 67. [59]Ibid., I, 68. [60]Ibid., I, 68.

[61]Ibid., I, 76. [62]Ibid., I, 77. [63]Ibid., VI, 36. [64]*Sāṅkhyakārikās*, 17.

[65]Is not guidance activity? How can the Sāṅkhya then defend its position that the Puruṣa is never a doer?

[66]The same question can be asked about Puruṣa's enjoying of pains and pleasures.

[67]*The Sāṅkhyasūtras of Pañcaśikha and Other Sages* with Hariharananda's Commentary.

[68]Ibid., p. 104.

[69]Ibid., p. 97. *Asmītirūpā ātmabuddhih yena pratisamviditā bhavati sa puruṣah.*

[70]Ibid., p. 101.

[71]Cp. Sartre's *pre-cognito*, or better with Husserls' witness. Cp. also the *Bṛhadāraṇyaka Upaniṣad* in which Prajāpati is described as having first said: "I am."

[72]In any case, it has little to do with the doctrine of evolution of Darwin's and evolutionary philosophies of Alexander and Lloyd Morgan.

[73]*Sāṅkhyakārikās*, 9.

[74]This point is not very much elaborated by the Sāṅkhya. E.g., the absence of the pen on my table cannot be said to be the material cause of any other absence.

[75]Cp. Aristotle's idea of potential being.

[76]*Sāṅkhyadarśana*, I, 123.

[77]It is believed that a bamboo seed produces a banana tree after a forest fire. I do not know how much truth this belief contains.

[78]Ibid., I, 1 and 92. Even then he accepts the reality of God only to the extent to which the Yoga of Patañjali accepts it. He wants to show that a spiritual philosophy of life can be justified on the basis of the Sāṅkhya, even in face of the arguments of the materialists.

[79]Ibid., I, 87. He mentions Viṣṇu, one of the Hindu Trinity, as omniscient and says that his cognitions are not dependent on the means of cognition.

[80]Ibid., V, 1 fol. [81]Ibid., III, 78–84 and V, 120. [82]Ibid., VI, 10.

[83]See the author's *Concept of Man*, pp. 140 ff., and the article, "Being: How Known and How Expressed," *The International Philosophical Quarterly*.

[84]Confession and atonement are meant for the purpose. But more often than not, they become a mere ritual.

[85]That is, even in imagination we often lose ourselves. There seem to be degrees of difference also between imagination, fantasy, day dream and real dream.

[86]See the author's "Approaches to the I-consciousness: Its Depths, Normal and Abnormal" in *The Problem of Self.*

[87]Relate this to the experience of the relation between "I know *X*" and "I know that I know *X*," and find out the similarities and differences.

[88]Cp. the idea of the two birds of the *Muṇḍaka Upaniṣad.*

[89]Mahesvarananda, more popularly known as Gorakhnath, in his short book, *Mahārthamañjari*, asks the significant question: "If my face is reflected in the mirror, where is the mirror reflected?" How can I know that the face reflected is my face?

[90]Here is a point in favour of Husserl's idea of directionality or intentionality of consciousness.

[91]Cp. *icchāśakti.*

[92]The differences are listed in Kumar Kishore Mandal's *A Comparative Study of the Concepts of Space and Time in Indian Thought*, pp. 116–27. (Chowkhamba, Benares, 1968)

[93]The relation between activity and time will be discussed in the estimate of the next chapter.

[94]Compare the Bergsonian idea that time is an intuitive drive with the load of the whole past thrusting

itself forward which is called future. Compare Croce's idea of history also, which may be referred to here for obtaining some useful insights.

[95]Here we are not justifying these conceptions, but pointing to their relationships and plausibility. Some day, some scientist philosopher may justify them.

[96]Cp. the Heraclitian idea that the Logos is present in deep sleep. What is the full significance of the idea with reference to the being of man?

[97]We have already said that ether is an inadequate translation of *ākāśa*, which may or may not be the ether of the physicists. For the Indian thinkers, it is not only the medium, but also the source of sound and has transcendental functions also. It is pure Reason or Rational Consciousness also, in which all meaningful words are related and spread or laid out. Cp. Heidegger's Logos. Cp. also *khecara*, one who moves in pure space or sky, which really means Cosmic Reason, the sphere of Hiraṇyagarbha or Mahān Ātmā, but popularly misunderstood as flying through space.

[98]Vijñānabhikṣu calls transcendental *ākāśa* as causal (*kāraṇa*) *ākāśa*, and the *ākāśa* which is the source of sound as effect (*kārya*) *ākāśa*. In the Vedānta we come across the idea that the transcendental *ākāśa* is Cosmic Reason, Māyā, Prakṛti, the Logos, and even the Brahman according to context.

[99]Śaṅkara gives this explanation.

[100]In appreciating this concept, the newcomer to Indian philosophy may start with the idea that the subtle elements are the mental side and the gross elements the physical side of objects we perceive. The subtle elements then will be mediating links between mind and the physical objects.

[101]Vijñānabhikṣu clearly denies that the senses are transformations of subtle elements through polarization. See his Commentary on *Sāṅkhyadarśanam*, II, 20. But then we cannot explain why there is the fixed conformation between particular sense and particular objects.

[102]The position of the Sāṅkhya is not very clear. S. N. Dasgupta, following Dr. B. N. Seal, attributed the derivation theory to the Sāṅkhya. But the tradition in the Southern India is different. Although *Tattyakaumudi* accepts the mixing of subtle elements in the gross objects, it does not seem to advocate a derivation theory. This derivation theory, called *pancīkaraṇa* may or may not apply to the origin of the subtle elements. The *Taittirīya Upaniṣad* clearly enunciates the derivation of the elements in the order given in the text.

[103]Spinoza could have used the word manifestations instead of the mathematical term deductions.

[104]This idea gave rise to many puzzles in the history of philosophy. If the past exists, how can it be past? If it does not exist, how can there be any past? If there is no past, how can there be any present and any future?

[105]We should not overlook the fact that in my personal history and also in the history of any people, the past exists in the present, but it exists as a potency, a power, a force, actively influencing my activities and the activities of the people. The past is not dead in the absolute sense. It stays like *kārmic samskāras* or potencies.

[106]Cp. the idea of *tabula rasa* of Locke.

Chapter IX

The Yoga and Self-Realization Through Psycho-Physical Practice

1. INTRODUCTION

The practice of *yoga*, which is control of body and mind for the sake of self-realization or realization of one's pure self, must be older than the Vedas themselves. There are indications of the prevalence of such practices even during the Mohenjo-daro civilization. We shall not be wrong in thinking that some *yoga* was current throughout the prehistoric world, as evidenced by the Orphic cults of Greece, which are wrongly dismissed as oriental in origin as if the occidental man in the beginning of civilization had no intimations of his inward being. Even the Dionysian cults at their best are attempts to draw man's inward being to the surface or drive man's outward being to the inward core. Whenever man felt its intimations, he tried to dive inward to catch and understand them. Had Pythagoras not been struck by their reality and their autonomy, the rationalism of the western civilization would not have started so early. We can only think that some other person would have been struck by their presence. The Pythagoreans may have made too much of the inwardness of reason as being akin to God (Theos) himself and founded esoteric circles. Yet it is still a mystery that reason, apart from the observation of the empirical world, can disclose rules and laws that are applicable to some at least of the important aspects of reality, a mystery that still awaits final solution. Reason may be inward; yet it is not mere lawless imagination. For understanding the workings of reason, the human mind has to go through strict self-control, which we notice in any book on logic and mathematics. Whatever is inward is not merely subjective, false, and unreal; otherwise, our very being has to be treated as unreal. Since it is my consciousness that discovers reality, if my inward consciousness itself is unreal, then one wonders whether what an unreality discloses can be real at all. To say that the world is a real object of an unreal consciousness seems to be a self-contradiction.

Obviously, the realization of the inward through the outward-looking senses is impossible. Since mind and senses are by nature outward-looking, special discipline is needed to develop the power to look inward. To look inward is not the same as introspection. In western psychological terminology, introspection is the looking of mind into itself. It then catches whatever passes in it and becomes its object. But for the inward look, the object is the mind itself, but not what passes in the mind; one may call it roughly self-consciousness of mind without other-consciousness. Although we use the expression self-consciousness quite often, we do not realize that mind can never be self-conscious, because mind is not the self but always the object of some consciousness, which is the self. This ultimate consciousness, which is the seer, the on-looker, the witness of everything that happens in me and outside me is my self. How can I catch it?[1] Is it the same as my rational consciousness? Can I catch even my rational consciousness? Much of what we experience and know of the ordered world seems to originate from it. To catch and grasp it is to grasp not only my higher being, but also the source of the intelligibility of the world. By grasping it, I accomplish two things: my own spiritual uplift, when I, as a man, realize the higher or deeper level of my being; and explanation of the intelligibility of the world.

Such were the motives of all the inward-looking religions and philosophies, whether in India or the West. How far they succeeded in their aims is a different question. When Yoga first started, it must have started with either or both motives. As Yoga is essentially inward-looking, it is both metaphysics (in the modern but not the Aristotelian sense of the term)[2] and metapsychology; for the inward is as real as the outward and the approach is from the outward to the inward depths and vice versa, all forming a continuity. It must have become a recognized philosophy, a metaphysics of practice, when its basic empirical and trans-empirical ideas obtained definite shape. The Sāṅkhya met the requirement by supplying the metaphysical ideas, and Patañjali based his teaching of practice on them. It is difficult to fix his date; he might have lived anytime between the 4th and the 2nd century B.C. But the 4th century B.C. is the period characterized by the general appearance of important aphoristic literature.

The word *yoga* is derived from the Sanskrit verbal root *yuj*, meaning to yoke, to join. In fact, the English word is traced back to the Sanskrit word *yuj*. Thus *yoga* is the method that joins. But what are thus joined have to be understood according to the context. It may be the joining of the finite spirit with the Supreme Spirit; or of the apparent spirit to the real spirit, if the reality of the Supreme Spirit is not accepted; or of an individual to his ideal, in which case *yoga* is self-realization in the widest sense of the term, even the ethical ideal as distinct from the religious, being understood as self-realization. Not only this joining, but also the methods or practices leading to the joining are called *yoga*. If the methods are divided into the main and the subsidiary, then even the subsidiary methods are called *yoga*.[3] So no school of spiritual philosophy would ignore them and all thinkers pay respect, to that extent, to Patañjali, whatever be the metaphysical differences.

Yoga may be used for many purposes. Many of its physical practices may be utilized, even if one does not believe in the spiritual teachings, for keeping the body healthy and agile, for reducing its weight and controlling the functions of the different physical organs. The breathing exercises it recommends, which can be practised by oneself only within limits beyond which they need the guidance of an expert, help us in clearing our lungs and in controlling even the involuntary functions of the body, which are regarded generally as the functions of the life-principle, and which the Yoga thinks are the functions of mind (*manas*) itself. The mental practices it recommends purify our mind, clear it of all dross, and enable it to receive the reflection of the spirit in its purity. Physical control is subservient to the vital (*prāṇa*) and control of the vital principle (*prāṇa*) to the spiritual. The methods of control of the voluntary and involuntary functions of the body are classed together separately under *haṭhayoga*, although its followers[4] claim that by itself also it results in spiritual realization. But Patañjali makes *haṭhayoga* only a means to mental control and self-realization.

Patañjali composed the famous *Yoga Aphorisms* (*Yogasūtras*). He may have systematized the ideas and practices of the time on the basis of the Sāṅkhya metaphysics. Vyāsa (4th century A.D.) wrote a commentary on Patañjali's work and Vācaspati (9th century A.D.) wrote a commentary on Vyāsa's commentary. This Vyāsa cannot be the same as Badarāyaṇa, the composer of the *Vedānta Aphorisms*, who was also called Vyāsa. The *Yoga Aphorisms* have other commentaries, the most well-known of which are those of King Bhoja (10th century) and Vijñānabhikṣu (15th century).

As mentioned already, Patañjali adopted the Sāṅkhya metaphysical theory. His epistemology also is, in general, the same as that of the Sāṅkhya. But the practical side of philosophy developed by him gave him greater insight into some of the problems; we may, therefore, say that he has his own contributions to make, which throw extra light on the Sāṅkhya ideas. For this reason, some of the commentators in explaining some of the Sāṅkhya ideas refer to Patañjali; and as Patañjali adopted the Sāṅkhya metaphysics, they refer to the Sāṅkhya in explaining Patañjali. But his main contribution to spiritual thought lies in showing how and by what methods the spirit, involved in the world of matter, can withdraw from it and attain absolute freedom by first transforming matter into its original state of Prakṛti and thereby realizing its own pure nature.

2. EPISTEMOLOGY

SOURCES OF VALID COGNITION Like the Sāṅkhya, Patañjali accepts three sources of knowledge—perception, inference, and verbal testimony, which is mainly the Veda. But in his explanation of cognition, he recasts the Sāṅkhya position. As we have seen, cognition is a transformation, modification, of Reason (*buddhi*, Mahat). In fact, everything, even the objects of the world, are modifications of Reason. Patañjali classifies these modifications as the five[5] functions (*vṛttis*) of Reason: the sources of valid knowledge (*pramāṇas*), false knowledge (*viparyaya*), empty concepts (*vikalpas*), sleep (*nidrā*), and memory (*smṛti*). What we have to note is that even sleep is regarded as a modification of Reason (*citta*, Mahat); it is that experience which is based on mere absence (*abhāva*).[6] We have noted in the previous chapter that Darkness (*Tamas*) was regarded as transcendental space and was identified also with time and ether, all the three being identified again with *citta* or Reason, the Logos. In Patañjali we do not find these identifications clearly mentioned. It will be interesting also to examine the hypothesis that space or even transcendental space is the same as pure nothingness, which gives room (*avakāsa*) for definite, positive shapes to occur. The reason for this conception may be that, if it is something positive, where it occurs nothing else can occur.[7] Another idea of interest is that of empty concepts (*vikalpas*).

We should remember that, according to this school, Reason is not the ratiocinative process or reasoning, but the all-pervasive metaphysical principle out of which everything "that is" originates. Even the ego originates out of it. The essential nature of reason is "I am (*ahamasmi*) or "am-ness" (*asmitā*). The "I" here is not the ego, but something higher; it is impersonal and yet experiences itself as "am." To say that the world is rational is to say that it is the assertion of the impersonal Reason that is in me and, nevertheless, transcends me and with which I feel my identity, accepting its assertions as mine. The above mentioned five functions are the modifications of the impersonal Reason in me.

Empty concepts are also modifications of Reason. Cognition through an empty concept is defined[8] as the cognition that follows upon a word and that has nothing objective corresponding to it in reality. For the Sāṅkhya-Yoga, the *ātman* is consciousness itself. But we speak also about the consciousness *of* the *ātman*. Here the meaning of the word "of" has no meaning of possession and yet it may lead one to think that there is an *ātman*, which by itself is not consciousness, but possesses it as a quality, just as the rose possesses its colour. Similar misconceptions arise when the main constituents of an object are spoken of as possessed by that object, when we use the possessive preposition "of." The idea of empty cognition is an indication that language can mislead us. *Vikalpa* generally means the ideational, the conceptual, the imaginary, the fanciful, or what is only mentally created. The Buddhists regard all universals as *vikalpas*, or conceptualizations. The Naiyāyikas regard man-ness-ness, space-ness, etc., as *upādhis*, or mere concepts, but not as real universals. Mind has the power to form concepts without corresponding realities. Patañjali calls such concepts *vikalpas* (perverse or distorted mental creations) and warns us against them.

By sleep is meant deep, dreamless sleep. It also is a modification of Reason.[9] As such, it is conscious, not unconscious. It is not the consciousness of absence (nothingness), but the consciousness that persists when all other functions are absent. There must be consciousness in sleep, because when a man wakes up from sleep, he says: "I slept well, I did not have even dreams." He could not have remembered how he slept, if his consciousness were not present in sleep.

ILLUSION A slight difference may be noticed between the Sāṅkhya and the Yoga in their doctrine of illusion (*viparyaya*). It is defined by Patañjali as false knowledge, which is due to the perception of a non-existent form (*atadrūpapratiṣṭham*).[10] The object perceived in illusion is a non-existent[11] form. But the Sāṅkhya would say that it also is existent and that it is only a modification (*pariṇāma*) of the real object and is, therefore, both existent and non-existent. This is the view, as we have seen, of Vijñānabhikṣu. But Patañjali would say that the false object could not be a real modification of a real object, as it is contradicted by the object of the true cognition. We see then that in the Sāṅkhya-Yoga tradition, there are three distinct views of the illusory object: the atheistic Sāṅkhya maintains that the illusory object is real; the Vedāntic Sāṅkhya of Vijñānabhikṣu holds that it is both real and unreal; but the Yoga of Patañjali holds that it is an unreal object.

Illusion is caused by five impurities—ignorance (*avidyā*), false identification of oneself with objectivity (*asmitā*), attachment (*rāga*), hate (*dveṣa*), and self-attachment (*abhiniveśa*), which is accompanied by the fear of death. These impurities will be explained later. The rest of Patañjali's epistemology is the same as that of the Sāṅkhya.

3. METAPHYSICS

The addition which Patañjali makes to the metaphysics of the Sāṅkhya lies (1) in his deeper analysis of the nature of transformation (*pariṇāma*), (2) in the acceptance of God, which is ignored by the Sāṅkhya, and (3) in showing in detail the relation of the ontological Reason to ethical action.

Moments of Transformation The word moment is used in the sense of factor or element. The Sāṅkhya does not discuss the relation between substance and attribute. It says only that everything undergoes transformation (*pariṇāma*) and that transformation belongs to the very being of objective reality. There is no instance when there is no transformation. But such a doctrine resembles the Buddhist doctrine of momentariness, according to which there is no stable substance to which change belongs and we cannot rightly speak of something to which change belongs, but only of change as such. Change is observed when one quality becomes another. But if there is no identical substance to which the first and the second quality belong, we should not even speak of change, but only of succession of qualities. The Sāṅkhya-Yoga is committed to the view that all change belongs ultimately to Prakṛti, which is stable and eternal, and that change is a modification of its Attributes. Proximately also, every finite object is stable relatively to its qualities (*dharmas*) and the object is the possessor (*dharmī*) of the qualities. But if change is present every moment of time, how are we to distinguish between substance (*dravya, dharmī*) and its qualities (*dharmas*)? So Patañjali tries to explain how within continual change, we can make the distinctions—substance, quality, and their changes.

Transformation is modification. We may take the example of water. The transformation of water into ice is a modification. This modification has three aspects—modification of substance, modification of quality, and modification of the mode of quality. In the example, water, which is originally liquid, obtains the quality of hardness when it becomes ice. *So what we call the change of substance is really the change of one quality into another (dharmapariṇāma). This is a change within the same substance.* Now, taking the quality hardness into consideration, it was not there when the substance was a liquid. It belonged, therefore, to the future at the time of its liquidity; then it becomes the present when the substance is ice; and next when the substance becomes liquid again, hardness becomes the past. The passage through the three moments—future, present, and past—constitutes the change within the quality (*lakṣaṇapariṇāma*). But the three moments of qualities have their states (*avasthās*) also. For instance, if the zero temperature remains long, i.e., ice remains as ice for a time, then hardness, which is a mode or state of ice continues for that time and dominates or suppresses liquidity. It should not be understood that so long as hardness remains, the present also lasts. The three moments are only instants and at every instant there is the process of change. The continuance of hardness for more than one moment means that the force behind the change is the same and pulsates similarly at every instant of that period. This continuity of the same force is called the mode, state (*avasthā*) of the moment. It is not meant that there is no change during the moment, but that the process is the same *avasthāpariṇāma* or a procession of similar states. What we call an enduring state or mode is a succession of instants of similar pulsations of change.

Each state has, again, three moments, strong, weak, and submerged. When strong, it is clearly observed; it becomes weak when about to be overwhelmed by the next state; and when fully overwhelmed, it is merged (in the moment of time) and the next state becomes strong. We see that these states have to be overlapping and do not allow intervals of nothingness (*śūnyatā*). In all the three kinds of modification, the same substance is present. But only the modifications of its qualities and the modes of their modifications are observed by us, because substance is too subtle[12] to observe. We do not have sufficient reason to say that, when the qualities change, one substance becomes another or that what is called substance is only a group of qualities. Substance is that which performs the function for which it is meant (*arthakriyākāri*);[13] qualities merely accompany substance and are not the causes of anything. It is water, but not its colour, that quenches our thirst. A substance may change into another, as when the elements change back into Prakṛti. The transformation which substances undergo and by which they become other substances (*dravyāntarapariṇāma*) is not the same as the transformation within any substance,[14] which can remain the same in spite of transformation.

In the above account of the three kinds of change, we find a new approach to the concept of substance. Substance is the individual (*vyakti*), so far as our observable experience is concerned. It constitutes the element of stability in the object observed. It accompanies the change of one quality into another (*dharmāntarapariṇāma*), of the change of one moment of quality into another (*lakṣaṇapariṇāma*), and of one mode or state of a moment into another (*avasthāpariṇāma*). All the three kinds of change are changes within the same substance, and the sameness is observable. *Change is not within time; on the other hand, time is constituted by, and is none other than the three moments of the changing quality*. Space also is only the extendedness of substances and has no reality of its own. Both time and space are only forms of ether (*ākāśa*), which is the ground of the possibility (*avakāśa*) of the change of objects and their extendedness. It may be derived from subtle sound (*śabdatanmātra*), or the subtle element of ether, but is essentially the same as time and space. To say that objects exist and change in time and space is only a way of speaking. Time and space are only aspects of the transformation of objects. When we say that wax changes its quality of solidity into liquidity when heated, we do not think of wax as a group of qualities—as the Buddhists and Berkeley say—and say that the group of qualities exists in time and space, and that one of the group,[15] solidity, is changing bit by bit into liquidity. We think also that there is something that is continuously the same through the change of qualities. Space is the extendedness of the wax; and time is constituted by the moments of the change of the qualities of the wax. We may call the substance by the name wax or by some other; but there must be a substance. It is true that the wax apart from its qualities is not observable. The reason is that by itself it is too subtle and is observable only through its qualities, which are forms of its constant change and which are not separate from it. Yet we should not say that either the substance or any of its qualities is unreal. For both are experienced by us as existing (*sat*). Substance is not separable also from its change (*pariṇāma*), which is its very constitution (*svarūpa*). By its very constitution, substance generates the qualities and their change. It has to be understood as dynamic, not as static. Its staticity is a mode (*avasthā*) of its constant dynamism. Substance, as the individual (*vyakti*, that which is manifest), is the generator or manifestor of qualities, including time and space. Time is only a name for the three moments of the change of qualities.

The above concept of substance is the contribution of Patañjali, who accepts at the same time incessant change taking place in everything. Then, we may give the other conceptions of substance with which we have already come across. The second will be that substance is the support of qualities, the third that it alone is the material cause of effects, the fourth that it alone can come into contact with other substances. But we should remember that substance is not really different from its qualities. Thus Patañjali tries to preserve the reality of substance in spite of constant change.

God Patañjali accepts the reality of God, although the general tendency of all theistic Sāṅkhya, including the Yoga, is to give very little part to him in the creation of the world. For the potencies (*saṁskāras*) left by ethical actions of the individuals in their Reasons (*buddhis*) are themselves capable of creating the world through corresponding self-transformations of the Reasons.

Yoga is defined[16] by Patañjali as the stopping of the five functions of Reason (*citta*, *buddhi*), which have already been explained. But the stopping of the functions is a difficult task; for the nature of Reason is to be constantly active, and when it cannot perform any other function it tends to sleep, which is also its function. Then if it is to function, let the function be meditation on God, which also leads to salvation,[17] and is, therefore, the easier way. God is omniscient and there is no knowledge greater than his.[18] He is untouched by the five afflictions[19] (impurities)—ignorance, egoity, desire, hate, and fear of death—, by the results of ethical actions (*karmavipākas*), and by the potencies left by ethical actions (*karmāśayas*). He is a Puruṣa, but of a special kind (*puruṣaviśeṣa*). He is the teacher of even gods, and is not bound by time.[20] His name is the sacred syllable OM[21] (*Amen*, *omni*). Meditation on God consists of repeating his name and thinking of its meaning.[22] Then our mind becomes inward-looking, and all hindrances to meditation[23]—such as disease, lethargy, doubt, inattention, heaviness of body and mind, attachment to objects, error, inexplicable failure to obtain trance (*samādhi*), and unsteadiness of mind—are removed.

Patañjali does not give any proofs for the existence of God, but only his description and the advantages of meditating on him. But commentators like Vijñānabhikṣu read some arguments into the descriptions (1) The scriptures say that God exists and they are absolutely reliable. So God exists. (2) Men have different degrees of knowledge, some having more and some less. The law of continuity requires that, wherever there are degrees of more and less, there must be an upper and a lower limit. For knowledge, the upper limit is that possessed by God, greater than whose knowledge there is nothing. (3) God is needed for effecting the association and dissociation of the Puruṣa and Prakṛti. The two are absolutely independent and disparate principles. The Puruṣa is never a doer and does not come into contact with Prakṛti; and Prakṛti is an unconscious principle and knows nothing about coming into contact with anyting. There must, therefore, be an independent principle that knows both and brings them into contact. Similarly, the Puruṣa and Prakṛti do not and cannot know how to dissociate themselves from each other. But their dissociation is needed for salvation, which is also true. Then God must be the person who effects the dissociation.

Reason and Action How do ethical actions change the character of our personality and effect the dynamic forces creative of our future births? As a spiritual philosophy, the Sāṅkhya-Yoga, like the Mīmāmsā, accepts the doctrine of *karma* and reincarnation, but answers the question in a slightly different way. The Mīmāmsā, as we saw, maintains that ethical actions become creative potencies (*śaktis*), remain in the *ātman* until the opportunity comes, and produce their effects either in this life or some future one, although by themselves the potencies are blind forces. The Nyāya-Vaiśeṣika says that ethical actions produce merit and demerit, which become qualities (*guṇas*) of the *ātman*. But as they are blind inactive qualities, God creates the future lives of the *ātmans* according to their merits and demerits and sees that the doer of actions receives proper rewards and punishments in this life or some future one. But the Sāṅkhya-Yoga asserts that ethical actions leave their potencies (*samskāras*) in the Reason (*buddhi, citta*), and these potencies become the modifications of the creative energy of Reason. Thus the Reason of each individual man is modified in a different way according to the actions he performs. As the world issues forth out of such modified Reason—we may remind ourselves that Reason for this school is ontological—it appears with different aspects in different men. Even our bodies are evolutes of Reason and are, therefore, not agents of enjoyment (*bhoga*), but its instruments. The enjoyer is the "I" as the ego. The Puruṣa is really the onlooker (*sākṣi*) only of the enjoyment.

Reason then has two aspects or parts. One aspect creates the world common to all individuals, i.e., the common world. The other makes the world different in its enjoyability to different individuals. The same object may produce agony in some and pleasure in others. Such differences are due to the differences among the ethical actions of individuals. The potencies (*samskāras*) of ethical actions reside together and constitute the reservoir of potencies (*karmāśaya*) like the potent libido or the Unconscious of depth psychology. This reservoir becomes one of the afflictions (*kleśas*) of Reason, which creates the world as coloured and distorted by it. This part of Reason is called the Reason of Action-potencies (*karmacitta*). Some of these potencies are known in this birth[24] itself, the others only in future lives. These potencies produce their results (*vipākas*) in the form of birth, duration of life, and enjoyments,[25] the three of which really constitute the capital with which man starts his life. What he makes of them, whether he performs new actions to cancel them or improves upon them, is left to his freedom. The potencies can produce their effects only so long as the original ignorance of the difference between the Puruṣa and Prakṛti lasts. When, through yoga, discrimination dawns and ignorance is dispelled, only those among the potencies that have started the present life continue to bear fruit, until their force (*śakti*) is exhausted; the others become like dried and dead seeds. During the period in which the former potencies continue to work, the actions which the yogi performs are neither good nor evil (*aśuklākṛṣṇa*)[26] and cannot become fresh potencies.

Thus the doctrine of *karma*, which appears more or less mechanistic in the early Mīmāmsā, becomes a teleological doctrine in the Sāṅkhya-Yoga. Accepting the idea of salvation, the Nyāya-Vaiśeṣika also tells us that the unexhausted action-potencies—the word potency is used, although understood as a quality by this school—cease to have effects after salvation, but only because God so decides. But the

Sāṅkhya-Yoga explains their cessation without reference to God by making Reason ontological, creative, and teleological. If there is nobody to enjoy or suffer, then actions do not produce their effects.[27]

4. THE PRACTICE OF YOGA

MEANING OF SAMĀDHI It may be misleading to translate the word *samādhi*. It is generally translated as trance, ecstacy, rapture, concentration, and so forth. But trance conveys the meaning of morbidity, ecstacy at its best exalted[28] feeling, and rapture a kind of being carried away by being attracted, and concentration the mental process of fixing one's mind on something. But *samādhi* is not exactly any of these psychological states or processes. Etymologically, the word means the settling[29] down of Reason (*citta*, *buddhi*) on something. Settling down implies peace and steadiness. It is the settling down of Reason in itself.

Yoga is defined as the stopping or the damming of the functions of Reason. When they are stopped, the disturbances, the agitations, and the out-going activities of Reason disappear. As we have seen, sleep also is an activity of Reason and has, therefore, to be stopped. Then Reason stays in itself. But as Reason is conscious and its consciousness is due to the reflection of the Puruṣa, the reflection, having nothing objective to know, stays in its original nature[30] (*svarūpa*). This staying of rational consciousness in itself is the *samādhi*, which is the aim of yoga. When this rational consciousness does not stay in itself, the knower (*draṣṭa*) in it identifies itself with the functions (*vṛttis*) of Reason and assumes their forms.[31] The final *samādhi* is the staying of the Puruṣa in himself, not even as the knower. This is the stage of final liberation[32] (*kaivalya*). The earlier *samādhi* is only the beginning, the gateway[33] to the later. In the final stage, the three Attributes of Prakṛti stop their work, as they have no purpose to fulfil.

PREPARATION It is wrong to think that this final *samādhi* or even a lower one can be had by going merely through physical and mental exercises, although they are useful by themselves. The most important preliminary is the purification of one's Reason, which in the Sāṅkhya-Yoga is the "I am," and so the purification of one's personal being. So long as the "I am" is activated by inner drives and functions, it cannot be pure and attain stability. It can be made steady by practice (*abhyāsa*) and detachment (*vairāgya*). Practice is repeated effort. Detachment is the control one obtains over objects through non-longing, i.e., equanimity. For obtaining equanimity or placidity of mind, one should practise[34] friendliness with those who are happy without being envious, compassion for those who are afflicted by sorrow, pleasantness instead of jealousy towards those who are meritorious, and indifference towards the evil of evil-doers. One should practice also five kinds of self-control: non-injury, non-stealing, truthfulness, celebacy, and non-acceptance of gifts. All the above virtues are worth practising even by those who do not care for salvation.

All ethical virtues are mentioned by Patañjali with reference to the obtaining of the steadiness of mind for the sake of yoga. That he has not discussed the social importance does not mean that he was unaware of their importance for society. His purpose was not to explain the virtues as social virtues, but only to point out their importance for yoga.

STAGES OF STEADINESS Fortunate people may obtain the steadiness of mind very easily. But others have to make more or less effort. One easy method is to meditate on God. Or one may practise measured inhaling and exhaling[35] (*prāṇāyāma*). Irregular inhaling and exhaling is a correlate of mental agitation,[36] which can be controlled by regularizing the breathing process. When mind is fixed on the measures of breathing, its agitation ceases. Or by removing all attachment from mind, one can make it steady. Another alternative is to meditate on the consciousness present in dream and deep sleep. It is not the meditation on the objects of that consciousness, but on that consciousness itself, the very essence of which is the "I am," the ontological Reason (Mahat). Or let one fix one's mind on the objects one likes the best; for example, a devout Christian may concentrate on the picture of Christ, which is charged with religious emotions.[37]

When the effort is made to fix one's mind in any of the above ways, it passes through five stages (*bhūmis*) or levels. By mind here we understand Reason (*citta, buddhi*, Mahat), the nature of which is to change at every instant. (1) When the attempt is first made to make Reason steady, it becomes agitated and restless (*kṣipta*). (2) When then we exert greater force to fix it, it becomes torpid (*mūḍha*), which is a tendency to fall asleep. (3) When still we make greater effort, it becomes distracted (*vikṣipta*). (4) If we do not give up our attempt even then, it becomes centred or concentrated (*ekāgra*) on the object of meditation. (5) And finally when we make a steady effort to keep our mind at that level, it becomes restrained (*niruddha*) and its functions stop. The last two levels are conducive to *samādhi*.

THE EIGHT-FOLD YOGA The practices recommended so far are not really easy. Our mundane being is the being of Prakṛti, the nature of which is to change constantly. We are practically asked in practising meditation, to go against what apparently is our very nature. So Patañjali recommends eight steps or limbs (*aṅgas*) to be practised generally one after another. It is not meant that the earliest steps are to be discarded when the later steps are practised or that the later should not be practised until the earliest ones are perfected. But some kind of steadiness is presupposed in the earlier before the later can have any steadiness. Generally the earlier has to be started before the later, and the later makes the earlier perfect. The eight limbs are:[38] self-control (*yama*), regulation of life by rules (*niyama*), bodily postures (*āsanas*), breath-control (*prāṇāyāma*), withdrawal of senses from objects (*pratyāhāra*), fixing the mind on an object (*dhāraṇa*), meditation (*dhyāna*), and *samādhi*.

(i) *Self-control*: Self-control[39] is of five kinds: non-injury, truthfulness, non-stealing, celebacy, and non-acceptance of gifts, which means mainly the refusal to accept instruments of pleasure.

(ii) *Rules for Regulating Life*:[40] They are (1) purification of the body through washing and the taking of only pure food, and of mind by practising friendliness, kindness, cheerfulness, and indifference to the vices of others, (2) contentment, (3) penance by practising austerities, (4) regular study of sacred books, and (5) meditation on God.

(iii) *Bodily Postures*:[41] The main purpose of bodily postures is to keep the body comfortably steady during meditation so that no discomfort may distract the mind. Some of the postures are meant also as exercises for keeping the body healthy and prevent the yogi from falling ill, as illness also is a hindrance to meditation. The number of postures are many, and one is advised to choose those that suit him best.

(iv) *Breath-control*:[42] This control is the regulation of inhaling and exhaling. It is of several kinds, and perfection in the practice is believed to give one control over one's involuntary functions also. Irregular breathing is a result of mental agitation, which can be overcome by regularizing breathing. Further, the Sāṅkhya-Yoga believes that the life-principle (*prāṇa*, the principle of life that works involuntarily in our bodies) is a function of the inner sense, and breathing is a function of life. We live through the involuntary muscular and nervous activities that take place in us. For instance, the assimilation of food to our body is an involuntary activity. So by controlling breath, it is thought, we can control our involuntary activities also. And since life is a spontaneous activity of the inner sense, by controlling breath the inner sense also is controlled.

Breathing generally consists of two parts, inhaling and exhaling. Two more parts can be added to it, retention of the inhaled air in our lungs and keeping the lungs empty[43] for a time by not inhaling immediately after exhaling. We can regulate these four parts according to some measure of time. All the four parts may be made equal or different. It is said that, by proper practice, inhaling can be stopped for great lengths of time without dying and thereby we gain control over the life-principle. But the higher levels of breath-control are not recommended for ordinary people. It is dangerous to practise them, unless one can devote oneself entirely to yoga and then goes through the practices with the help of experts. But they are very rare.

(v) *Sense-withdrawal*:[44] The withdrawal of the senses from their respective objects is a difficult task to accomplish. But through careful effort, the senses can be turned inward. Such an effort does not result in the destruction of the senses. Their withdrawal is uniting them with their source. As objects also issue out of the inner sense, we have to say, they also are withdrawn when the senses are withdrawn. At this stage of yoga, the senses assume the form of Reason itself. Then the senses are completely conquered.

(vi) *Concentration*:[45] Concentration is the fixing of the inner sense upon something, especially a desired object. It is the activity or process of centring the mind. The object upon which mind is fixed may be an external object, an idol or image of God, or any part of one's own body, or the inner sense itself. It will be easier to start with an external object or image of God.

(vii) *Meditation*:[46] Meditation is the steadiness or unbroken continuity of concentration. In this state of Reason, the cognition of the object that is fixed upon by mind becomes continuous like the flow of oil, in which drops are not distinguishable.

(viii) *Samādhi*:[47] In the above stage, Reason, knows itself as knowing the object; the distinction between the object and cognition persists. But in *samādhi*, Reason is so completely absorbed in the object that the object only stands and cognition (consciousness), as it were (*iva*) disappears. There is no sense, no awareness, of being *aware* of the object. Then the inner structure of the object reveals itself completely, whatever be the object, a physical object, one's own mind with its layers of the Unconscious, or another's mind.

Of the above eight limbs of yoga, the last three are said to be inner[48] (*antaraṅga*) and the first five outer or external (*bahiraṅga*) to yoga. But *samādhi* may be that in which the potencies (*saṁskāras*) of the world are left (*sabījasāmadhi*) or that in which they are destroyed (*nirbījasamādhi*). The last three steps are, in their turn, external to the latter kind of *samādhi*. That is, the practice of the first five limbs leads to the last three, which end up in the *samādhi* that retains the seeds (*bījas*) of worldliness; but this *samādhi* leads, in its turn, to the higher kind of *samādhi*.

5. THE METAPHYSICAL BASIS OF PRACTICE

The aim of man who is intent on yogic practice is to obtain salvation, which is liberation or freedom from entanglement in Prakṛti. This entanglement is of the form of identification with the forms of Prakṛti and with the functions of Reason (*buddhi*, Mahat), which is its first evolute. Thus I am my Reason, I am my ego, I am my mind, I am my senses, I am my physical body, and the objects are *my* objects and belong to *my* experience. I am entangled in all of them. My liberation lies in disentangling myself from all of them, as all can be my objects. We have seen that all of them are evolutes and transformations of Prakṛti and Reason (Mahat). If bondage is due to this evolutionary process, freedom can be obtained through a corresponding involutionary process, starting from the gross physical objects and ending up with Reason and Prakṛti, when the Puruṣa realizes that he is really separate from everything with which he has been identifying himself in one way or another. Evolution and involution are corresponding processes in opposite directions; but involution has to be effected voluntarily by man's own effort. In explaining the stages of involution, which are to be reached through meditation, Patañjali follows the Sāṅkhya metaphysical derivation.

Every lower stage of the Sāṅkhya categorical scheme is transcended and the higher stage attained, according to Patañjali, through concentration (*dhāraṇa*), meditation (*dhyāna*), and *samādhi*. That is, at every stage there is a *samādhi*, in which I, as this consciousness, become one with the object at that level. And this *samādhi* at every stage, except the highest, is of two kinds—one in which the distinctions of the nature of the object, the consciousness of the object, and the name of the object are still experienced; and the other in which these distinctions disappear and the object alone remains. In the former, the distinctions persist because of the apperceptive mass in our mind working as memory.[49] When I perceive a cow, my cognition is of the form: "That is a cow," which contains the distinctions, the object as such, and its form (*prakāra*). At the level of "That is a cow," my "I" is kept in the background. In the former kind of *samādhi*, these distinctions are retained, as memory brings in the form (*prakāra*) dissociated from the perceived objects of the past. According to Patañjali, the name of the object also is brought in along with the form. But when Reason (*Mahat, Citta*) is purified and such influences of memory are cleared out, the content of *samādhi* will simply be the object without any distinctions. However, in both the forms, the object is an object as known; for the "I" is still there, although kept in the background and the object is an object for the "I's" consciousness. This kind of *samādhi* is called the *samādhi* in the known (*samprajñātasamādhi*). But there is a final *samādhi* in which there is no object as known and only the consciousness of the Puruṣa is presented. It is called the *samādhi* without the known[50] (*asamprajñātasamādhi*).

The stages of concentration are graded according to the grossness and subtlety, concreteness and abstractness, of the evolutes of Prakṛti. It is more difficult to concentrate on one's own mind than on physical objects. It is recommended, therefore, that one should start with gross objects and reach more and more subtle stages. The *samādhis* thus attained are given different names. For a quick comprehension, they may be charted as follows:

Samādhi in the Known
(*Samprajñātasamādhi*)

	Objects of concentration	With Distinctions	Without Distinctions
Inner Sense	1. Reason or with ("I am") the go transcended.	*Sāsmitā* (with the object as "I am") → Attribute of the Transparent suppressed	*Nirasmitā* (without the "I am")
Inner Sense	2. Mind or with ego in the background	*Sānanda* (with bliss as object) → Attribute of the Transparent predominates, others suppressed	*Nirānanda* (without bliss)
	3. Subtle elements	*Savicāra* (with subtle elements as objects) →	*Nirvicāra*
	4. Gross elements	*Savitarka* (with gross elements as objects) →	*Nirviṭarka*

At every stage, there is a progress from the left to the right kind of *samādhi*, and the general progress is from the bottom to the top. When the *samādhi* on the right side at every lower stage is attained, then the *samādhi* on the left side of the next higher stage may be attempted.

It is difficult to find exact English words for some of the above Sanskrit terms. *Sāsmitā* and *nirasmitā* may be translated as "am-ful" and "am-less"; *sānanda* and *nirānda* as "blissful" and "non-blissful"; *savicāra* and *nirvicāra* as "with formation" and "without formation";[51] and *savitarka* and *nirvitarka* as "determinate" and "indeterminate." The words used for the third and the fourth stages are not different in their significance. But as the objects concentrated upon are subtle and gross, different sets of terms are used.

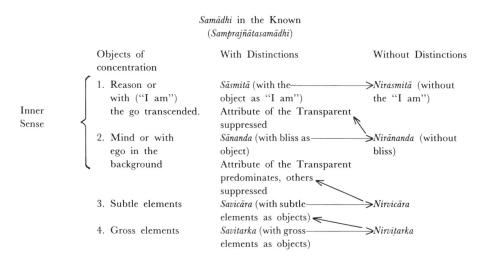

In these distinctions, *we come across a new significance of the concept of indeterminate knowledge*. Indeterminate knowledge is knowledge, whether of gross or subtle objects, in which the distinction between the consciousness knowing the object and the object is not present. As soon as the distinction is present, the other formations like the name (word) and concept (universal) make their appearance. In ordinary perception, the stage of indeterminate knowledge is assumed, but is never caught; *but the indeterminate knowledge of which Patañjali speaks is something attained by voluntary effort*. It is said that we can never catch the indeterminate stage of perception; but the Sāṅkhya-Yoga maintains that we can and should catch it, if we want to rise to the higher levels of yoga. As indeterminate perceptual knowledge is not of use for mundane purposes, we do not care to know what it is. But it reveals our very being that is entangled and dispersed in the objective world.[52] The identity of our being with the objective world is the intuitive basis of our cognitions. At the stage of the "formation-less" (*nirvicāra*, without formation), our knowledge is full of truth only (*ṛtambharā*). For then we must have known intuitively, through self-identification in the form of "being the whole subtle objectivity, which is the root of gross objectivity," everything of the world.[53] At that stage, the inner sense must have become completely pure,[54] and capable of concentrating on its own essential aspects.

After *samādhi* in the known (*samprajñātasamādhi*) is attained and perfected, *samādhi* in the unknowable or without the known (*asamprajñātasamādhi*) can be attained. Even in the former *samādhi* in its highest stage, there is the knower and the known, although the distinction is not observed in the *samādhis* mentioned on the left side of the chart as when I often identify myself with my body. But at the highest stage transcending all the *samādhis* in the known, all the potencies (*samskāras*) that form the root cause of the false identification of the Puruṣa with Prakṛti become purposeless and become inactive, i.e., transformed into Prakṛti; and the consciousness of the knower directed to the object settles down in the knower, for whom there will be nothing then to be known. So this *samādhi* is called the known-less *samādhi*, *samādhi* in the knower himself, (i.e., his consciousness directed towards, and merging in himself), who is never an object of knowledge and, in that sense, the unknowable. Philosophically, it reminds us of Hartmann's *Philosophy of the Unconscious*.

But the absence of the known may be due to more than one reason. It may be due to our consciousness having settled itself down in the knower, i.e., in the Puruṣa and become as if identical with him; or to its being merged in the unconscious Prakṛti. In either case, there is no object facing the knower for him to know; and both are, therefore, known-less *samādhis*. But the latter is not liberation. The yogis who have reached the second stage, i.e., the blissful (*sānanda*) and the non-blissful (*nirānanda*) may like to stay there itself and are called the bodiless (*videhas*),[55] as they no longer identify themselves with their bodies constituted either by the gross or subtle elements. Some yogis may like to stay at the first stage, i.e., the "am-ful" (*sāsmitā*) and the "am-less" (*nirasmitā*) and are called the Prakṛti-merged (*Prakṛtilayas*), as they do not identify themselves with the knower himself, i.e., the Puruṣa himself. But in the truth, the latter alone ought to be called Prakṛti-merged, as the former still retain their am-consciousness. Neither the bodiless nor the Prakṛti-merged yogis are liberated, as the root cause of their worldly existence, viz., the lack of discrimination of the Puruṣa from Prakṛti, is not removed. The *samādhi* attained by the yogis who are liberated is of a higher kind[56] obtained through conviction (*śraddhā*, faith) about the truth sought for, zeal (*vīrya*) for realizing it, the continuation of the consciousness of the stages attained (*smṛti*), the power of concentration, and the cognitive power (*prajñā*) to discriminate the truth sought from all else that is mixed up with it. In the lower yogis there is a lapse of the consciousness of the ideal and the temptation to identify oneself with an object, though of a higher type, and a false fear of losing one's being or this "I am."

One can realize by now that the explanation of *samādhi* given by Patañjali cannot be that of any mental transformation that may be produced by drugs or by self-hypnotism. One may not care for the ideal placed before us by Patañjali. But we can see that the explanations given by him are based on an analysis that combines the phenomenological and the existential. Where is my "I" present in my act of perception? Even when I see a mountain miles away, my consciousness must be present where the object is perceived. Let it be the projection of my idea by my mind, as the subjective idealists contend; even then my mind has to reach the end of its projection and must, therefore, be present there where the mountain stands. Let the object be a real one independent of my mind, as the realists contend; and let my perception be due to the light rays that start from the object and impinge on my eye; and let my seeing the object be due to the projection of the sensation in my brain to that distance; or let us assume that there is a sensum at the place where I perceive the object; or let any other explanation be given: in every case, my consciousness must be as extended all the distance of the object from me. One term of this reference in "I see the mountain" may be my comparatively tiny body. But how extensive is my consciousness, and where I am with reference to my consciousness are a mystery that has to be resolved. Patañjali gives his own explanation. I am wherever my consciousness can be and, whether I know or not, my "I" must, therefore, be at every possible place. It is identical with the whole Prakṛti, because the reflection of the infinite Puruṣa received by Prakṛti is and has to be as infinite as Prakṛti itself, just as my consciousness of my personal being is at least as extensive as my physical body. The "I" that identifies itself with the physical body is the ego, a poor evolute of Prakṛti. The original Puruṣa can be realized only after the infinite reflection is realized. This realization is the end of a series of identifications with, and dissociations from the lowest to the highest evolutes of Prakṛti; and the series of *samādhis* (also called *samāpattis*, attainments) explained by Patañjali are such a series.

6. EXTRAORDINARY POWERS

If really, as the Sāṅkhya-Yoga implies, my being, as that of a particular individual, is identical with the whole world of nature (Prakṛti), and if I realize that identity just as I realize my identity with my physical body, I can have as much control over the world as over my body. The extraordinary powers resulting from such a control will not then be even supernatural,[57] but natural. So long as I am identical with my body without knowing and realizing the distinction from it, I am carried away by its vicissitudes and cannot control their flow like the water that is being carried by a current cannot control its flow. I have, therefore, to distinguish myself from every aspect of Prakṛti, realize my separateness from it, then enter it and be one with it without at the same time losing my discriminatory power attained, and then control its movements from within. The first requirement is, therefore, a kind of detachment (*vairāgya*) from Prakṛti, which results in the control (*vasīkāra*) of Prakṛti. As the final realization of such discriminatory one-ness with the evolutes of Prakṛti, at every stage some extraordinary powers are attained. But Patañjali advises the yogi, if he is intent on final liberation, not to be tempted by those powers. To be tempted by them is to be attached to them; and to be attached to them is to be lost in them without rising higher. To be lost in them is also to forget the truth about oneself.

We have already noted that at the end of the second stage of *samādhi* from below, i.e., at the end of the "formation-ful" (*savicāra*) and the "formation-less" (*nirvicāra*), the cognition of the yogi, which is neither ordinary perception nor inference nor verbal knowledge,[58] is always truth; it is direct intuition of anything in the world like my intuition of the existence of my body. How much of the universe can be known thus depends on the perfection of this *samādhi*. But one can obtain other powers (*siddhis*) by following other methods of concentration, all of which can become temptations and hindrances to yoga. Some men obtain them simply by birth and they must have made necessary efforts in their past lives. Some obtain them through drugs, some through incantations, some through penance, and the others through *samādhis*.[59] By concentrating on the three moments of change (*pariṇāmatraya*), explained already, one can obtain knowledge of the past and future.[60] By concentrating on the relation of the word, the object, and the cognition of the object, one can obtain the power of knowing the meaning of words and sounds made by any living creature.[61] By concentrating on the potencies (*samskāras*) of one's own Reason (*citta*), one can know his past births.[62] By concentrating on the relation between the expression on a man's face and his mind thus understood, one can have knowledge of that man's mind.[63] By concentrating on the form of one's own or another's body, the body can be made invisible.[64] By concentrating on objects as they appear, as they are in themselves, on the subtle elements that constitute them, on their qualities, and on their enjoyability, i.e., affective nature, one conquers all the elements and obtains the important powers often spoken of[65]—becoming infinitesimally small (*aṇimā*), becoming infinitely large (*mahimā*), becoming infinitesimally light (*laghimā*), becoming infinitely heavy (*gurutvam*), the power of touching anything at any distance (*prāpti*), obtaining anything desired (*prākāmya*), lordship over everything (*īśitva*), and control over everything (*vaśitva*). Patañjali mentions many other kinds of powers and methods for obtaining them. It is difficult to prove or disprove Patañjali. One rarely comes across a yogi, who has these powers; and one who has the powers does not care to exhibit them. What should interest a student of philosophy is the rationale which Patañjali offers as the theory of the practice, which throws immense light on our being. We should also remember that Patañjali does not insist that one should practice the yoga he has described at length, but says also that one who leads an ethically good life and meditates on God obtains the same salvation.

7. TRANSITION TO THE VEDĀNTA

The Sāṅkhya and the Yoga philosophies logically, but not chronologically, constitute a kind of metaphysical transition to the Vedānta schools from the Mīmāmsā, the Nyāya and the Vaiśeṣika, which are both qualitatively and quantitatively pluralistic. The Sāṅkhya and the Yoga uphold qualitative dualism of matter and spirit, quantitative and qualitative monism of matter, and quantitative pluralism of spirits. The Yoga and the other theistic forms of the Sāṅkhya accept the reality of God also. We have then the Universal or Supreme Spirit, a plurality of other spirits, and the unity of the unconscious Prakṛti. Both the Sāṅkhya and the Yoga fail to explain the relation of the three to one another. The Vedāntic schools attempt to do what the Sāṅkhya-Yoga failed to accomplish. Furthermore, the Sāṅkhya-Yoga introduced the concept of the pure witness consciousness (*sākṣi*), which is transcendental and is identical with the Puruṣa (*ātman*). The ego (*ahaṁkāra*) is only a product of matter (Prakṛti) with the reflection of the Puruṣa. The conception of the inwardness of the Puruṣa as the inwardly transcendental witness, to the ego and even to Reason changed the Nyāya-Vaiśeṣika conception of the relation of the ego to the *ātman* from a naively mechanical view to that of some existential and phenomenological depths. The conception of *buddhi* as only an incidental consciousness of the *ātman* and as arising out of it like a spark from a stone when rubbed, found in the Nyāya-Vaiśeṣika, changed into that of *buddhi* as the Mahat (the Great) or Mahān Ātmā (the Great Ātmā, the Great Ego), as the ontological Reason,[66] the experience of which is "am-ness" (*asmitā*), or "I am." Such developments—which are not historical developments, as their basic ideas are found in the Upaniṣads themselves, but a regrasping of the original ideas as differences from the Nyāya-Vaiśeṣika and the Mīmāmsā— are of tremendous importance to Vedāntic thought, which also is not a historical development out of, but a different line of thought from the Sāṅkhya-Yoga. We shall find in the Vedānta many important doctrines of the Sāṅkhya-Yoga, which are incorporated, assimilated, and unified by its different systems.

GENERAL ESTIMATE AND CONSTRUCTIVE COMMENT

(i) Substance, Time and Space with Reference to Transformation

The two main problems on which Patañjali has thrown a good deal of light so far as philosophy goes, are first that of time and space and their relation to transformation (*pariṇāma*) and second the phenomenological and existential significance of the levels of *samādhi*. His contributions for these two problems are generally ignored and he was and is treated as a teacher of yogic practices only. Radharkrishnan has said very little or nothing on the philosophical significance of these points. Dasgupta dealt with the former in an extensive, but not philosophically very clear, way in his book on Yoga (*not his History of Indian Philosophy*). The reason is obviously that they had written their works before the importance of phenomenology and existentialism was recognized in India; and so the significance of the levels of consciousness for a true philosophical analysis of consciousness did not strike them. The ideal of self-discrimination[69] on which the Sāṅkhya emphasizes is the ideal of self-analysis, which is both phenomenological and existential. Such analysis does not imply that the Sāṅkhya is not meant for spiritual realization, but that self-realization at every step or stage of its progress involves genuine, not fanciful and artificial, self-analysis. It is generally self-analysis that can lead to genuine phenomenological and existential self-analysis, resulting in reaching the core of the self, which is the authentic self (*ātman*). The reverse also is possible, if undertaken in earnest. The different levels of *samādhi* are different levels of the *ātman* itself leading ultimately to its pure, essential being.

We have discussed the problem of time and space in our estimates of the Vaiśeṣika and the Sāṅkhya schools and referred to their identification with ether or the source and medium of sound. The grounds for the identification of the three were also pointed out: one being the tradition of the philosophers of grammar or linguistics elaborated by Bhartṛhari, for which the Sound Brahman, or Word Brahman (*Śabda-brahman*), is the Logos, Mahān Ātmā, and is the origin of everything, and for which the universe is a manifestation of the Word; and the other being the Upaniṣadic tradition which relates space (directions like east and west, and up and down) to the sense of hearing (*śrotra*) and, as there is no hearing without sound, to sound itself. As *ākāsa*, which is the source of sound, is the origin of all elements according to the Upaniṣads, it is the source of everything.[68] Thus the view of the linguistic philosophers does not seem to be totally unrelated to that of the Upaniṣads. But the peculiar point to note in these two philosophical traditions is that time seems to occupy a lower place than that of space. (Reference is made, we noted, in the *Śvetaśvātara Upaniṣad* to a view that time is the origin of everything, but the view is rejected[69] by the Upaniṣad itself. Nor does it accept space as the highest.) But in their transcendental states, we have to conclude, they are identical.[70]

The only ultimate material substance, for both the Sāṅkhya and the Yoga philosophies, is Prakṛti, which is a state of equilibrium of the three Attributes (forces, *Guṇas*). But if the three are forces, is the substance Prakṛti merely a unity constituted by the forces? Or is there something called Prakṛti, which is the Substance *having* the three forces like the wall having a colour? If Prakṛti is an equilibrium of forces, it is really the unity of forces in a stable condition and is, therefore, force itself lying latently and ready to act if an occasion arises. As force, it is dynamic by nature. As forces, the three—Transparence, Activity, and Darkness—are active[71] by nature. Their latency in Prakṛti means only that the three are in a state of equilibrium, and so there is no occasion for any one of them to assert itself over the others. It is like Lao Tze saying that, if in a society every person lives according to his or her own God-given nature, there need be no law-givers, as there will be no turmoil. *The stability of any object or any society, not merely of Prakṛti, can mean that the forces inherent in it are in a state of equilibrium, none becoming dominant over the others, all being equally active and the activities of each force being harmonious with the activities of the others.* Stability then need not mean inactivity, lethargy, but harmony in activity. This idea of stability is implied in the Sāṅkhya-yoga conception also of stability and equilibrium and the so-called inactivity of Prakṛti. What is essentially and by nature force cannot but be active; and what we call its inactivity may really be its pulsations of activity under the same conditions and in the same circumstances and pattern, so that we do not observe any change occurring in them. Then the stability of an object can be the sameness of the pattern of the pulsations (vibrations) of its activity. This sameness is not possible unless the concerned context also remains the same, and unless the environment of that context also remains the same.

Now we can appreciate Patañjali's concept of substance as an aspect of the continual transformation of Prakṛti. The word substance refers here to substances like tables and chairs also, not merely to Prakṛti. We have discussed the three aspects of transformation, also called the three kinds of transformation: transformation as and of substance (*dravya-pariṇāma* or *dharmi-pariṇāma*,[72] or simply *dharma-pariṇāma*): transformation of quality as *lakṣaṇa pariṇāma* (meaning characteristic, not a happy word to use here) into the three moments of past, present, and future, for before it arises it is future, when it arises it is present, and after it is changed into another quality it is past; and transformation of states (*avasthā-pariṇāma*) in which each moment goes through the three sub-moments of strong, weak, and submerged.[73] Here Patañjali and his commentators seem to imply that time belongs to and is a succession of the states of a changing quality. They retain the idea of substance because there has to be something the same as the background of the change of any quality so that the successive moments—past, present, and future—can be attributed to something remaining the same through the three moments. That is, the same has to be of the future, the same has to be of the present, and the same has to be of the past. While these moments concern quality, quality lies within substance, which has to be the same through the three moments of the change of its quality and so remain stable; something else cannot take its place during the three moments. Then it is not that same something, but its quality or qualities which have to go through change; that is, they can become some other qualities, provided of course the old and new qualities can be attributed to the same something. This same thing is the substance of the qualities, which pass in their change through the three moments of future, present, and past.

Now, substance also, to which the changing qualities, and the moments of time and states belong, goes through constant change. One substance can become another as mercury can become gold, or hydrogen and oxygen, which are gases, become water. Such a change is not generally called by us a mere change of qualities; it is called a "substantive," or "substantial" change. Now, it is not clear why Patañjali attributes time—as the succession of states—to qualities, but not to substances also. The reason may be that he accepts the change of one substance into another as due to the change of all the qualities—one after another—of the former into another group of qualities; and that substance as such is not perceived, but is known only as possessing a group of qualities, which are, relatively to it, constantly changing and passing through the three moments of future, present, and past, which necessarily imply a relatively unchanging substance.

The above view contains two new ideas: *first, there is no absolute substance except Prakṛti,* and *second the idea of time necessitates the idea of substance.* We have seen that, for the Sāṅkhya-Yoga, even Prakṛti is not a substance *having* forces—although this expression is used—but the equilibrium of the forces themselves. The three categoreal forms of cognition—substance, quality, and state (*avasthā*)—are aspects of transformation which Prakṛti undergoes. They are the modes of the process or its modal forms, adverbial to Prakṛti's activity. That Prakṛti undergoes transformation is also a way of speaking; for it is the equilibrium of forces that changes or is in constant motion or activity—which means that the equilibrium, which is another name for stability, ceases and the forces begin to work in different ways with unstable permutations and combinations.

If there are no really absolute substances like they are in the Nyāya-Vaiśeṣika theory, why do we think of substance at all? How do we get at all the idea of substance? Patañjali and his commentators do not seem to have raised such a question. But we may guess what their answer will be. As all the qualities of the so-called substance do not generally change simultaneously, but only one or a few at a time, the rest remaining recognizably the same, we think that there is something stable and that the stable qualities attach themselves to it. *But the main argument for the epistemological and metaphysical necessity of the idea of substance is that the idea of time implies the idea of substance*, although, viewing the problem from a different angle, we have to say that there is no absolute substance having qualities and forces, but that there exists an equilibrium of forces and that in that equilibrium the forces are apparently inactive and so latent. In any case, Patañjali would say, time is an aspect or modality of change (*pariṇāma*), depends on it, and cannot, therefore, be a separate metaphysical category. Nor is time a substance, unlike the Nyāya-Vaiśeṣika view.

(ii) Self-Identical Self in Time-consciousness

There is still a missing link in Patañjali's explanation of time. We may accept that time is the succession of the three states—past, present, and future—of a changing quality with reference to something stable called substance. But Prakṛti, which ultimately is going through this transformation, is unconscious, non-sentient, and consequently all substances derived from it must be non-sentient. Now, for the past, present, and future to be referred to the same entity which is to relate them to itself, the entity has to be self-consciously continuous. When reference is made to the past, present, and future of a table, I, myself, have to make the reference; the table itself is indifferent to the moments and does not, and as insentient, cannot relate them. Their being moments of a continual, unbroken entity belongs to my apperception, and is not an aspect of the being of the table by itself, which has no mind, and so no apperception. There can be no time, no history, no biography, no autobiography, but only unrelated succession or beats of occurrences, without some conscious being to whose apperception the moments or pulsations belong or whose apperception interrelates the moments or pulsations belonging to another person or physical object *in a pattern called by the technical name time.*

But the recognition that without a conscious being interrelating the moments of the transformation of Prakṛti, there can be no time is an idea not patent in the Sāṅkhya-Yoga philosophy. It may be said that apperception (*Mahat, citta*) as holding the reflection of the Puruṣa is conscious and that time and time-experience are one in it. But the reflection is that of an inactive, passive Puruṣa, according to the Sāṅkhya-Yoga, and activity belongs to Prakṛti only. It is not, therefore, intelligible how a passive reflection can interrelate the moments in the pattern of time and how the pattern of time into which it fits the moments can belong to its constitution. If the Puruṣa is a mere unaffected, unconcerned witness (*sākṣi*), then its reflection also will be such. Even the agitation of the reflection of the sun in rippled water is only an apparent agitation, not real. Even if the sun is active, his reflection is passive; its activity is only apparent. If the sun acts, the reflection appears to act. Besides, the reflection of the Puruṣa in Prakṛti has to take initiatives in deflecting Prakṛti's transformations and in channelling them to suit its good or evil ends. If the reflection is absolutely passive, as this school contends, how can it take the initiative even in desiring salvation? As passive, why is it not eternally carried by the more or less mechanical currents of the transformatory forces of the insentient Prakṛti? If it is carried away thus, there is no justification for attributing ethical agency and responsibility to the reflection, and salvation will be out of question. If a man commits murder, his image in the mirror is not hanged.

Then Prakṛti must belong to the Puruṣa himself and has to be the latent power or force (*śakti*) in him, as the *Śvetāśvatara Upaniṣad* contends. It is an inexplicable force and we cannot explain why the Puruṣa exercises it now and then, but not always. We cannot explain even why the magnet attracts iron at all, why hydrogen and oxygen together become water. If some natural explanation is given, we press the questioning further. To say that it is all nature is to admit that we cannot answer the question. We may say then that Prakṛti is the nature of the Puruṣa[74] himself, and that he evolves himself through his nature (Prakṛti) into the world without losing his fulness and identity at the same time. Nobody can answer why there are Being and Becoming.

(iii) Vivarta and Pariṇāma

The above transformation, generally called evolution also, does not mean that Puruṣa, a indicated, exhausts himself in creating the world, which is also his manifestation. Even the Sāṅkhya-Yoga maintains that Prakṛti can remain in its equilibrium for those Puruṣas who are liberated and yet it can be evolving the world for those who are not liberated. Then in terms of change and time, transformation implies the transformation of something which yet remains the same. Change, transformation, and time necessarily imply something stable to which they are referred and without reference to which they become at the most a mere correlated—but what is to be the agent of correlating?—procession of instants and moments. As Prakṛti is ultimate, it has to be, in fact, a stable entity and be the inherent power or energy of the Supreme Puruṣa himself. Then the power of remaining the same and yet be transformed can be assigned to him. This is what the Vedāntins did in their interpretations of the Upaniṣads and development of their systems of thought. To change and yet be itself can belong to the self or the I-am only, but not to Prakṛti, which is independent of the Puruṣa and is insentient according to the Sāṅkhya-Yoga. For the recognition of sameness in change, a self-conscious self is needed.

It is this kind of change, the transformation of something without in any way affecting that something, that Śaṅkara and his followers called by the term *vivarta*. The dictionary meanings of both *vivarta* and *pariṇāma* are often the same, viz., change or transformation. But in their technical usages, they are different. *Vivarta* means change without being affected by change.[75] Perhaps, the word modification is still less appropriate than change. *Pariṇāma* means change in which the object is affected by the change and can no longer be available in its original form. The difference is explained by the classical writers using examples such as gold or wax and milk. Gold and wax can be given many forms, but we can obtain the original lumps again by melting. But when milk is turned into buttermilk or yogurt, we cannot get back the original milk. Whatever be the examples, the difference in the meanings of the two terms, *vivarta* and *pariṇāma*, is evident.

(iv) Samādhi: Existential and Phenomenological Analyses

The next important point to consider is the contribution which Patañjali would make, through his discussion of the levels of *samādhi*, to the phenomenological and existential analysis of our conscious being. It should not be thought that Patañjali was a phenomenologist or existentialist. He was primarily a philosopher of the spirit and of salvation through yoga; but his discussions of the ways of obtaining ultimate spiritual realization includes and is based on an analytical understanding of the levels of our psycho-physical being. Unless this understanding is earnestly undertaken, our striving for salvation will miss the mark. Buddha included true views (*samyak-darśana*) in the eight-fold limbs of the path to salvation. The emphasis on true views is common to all the schools of Indian thought. True understanding of man and his universe enables him to chalk out the right conduct he has to follow. But "true views" implies a true analysis of man's self-conscious being until the greatest possible depths are reached. Such an analysis is given by Patañjali in his description of the levels of *samādhi*. Note that *samādhi* is not merely concentration of mind on an object or idea or getting lost in self-hypnotism; its essence is the concentration or centring ("centrifugalizing") of man's diversified being as such. Now, the levels of *samādhi* are more or less common to all the schools. There can be and there are other kinds of analysis of man's conscious being; but that given by Patañjali, from the point of view of the depths of human existence, is more important and illuminating than most of the others, although the context makes one think that Patañjali's is not philosophically important, but is useful only for the practice of yoga. But such thinking is mistaken.

We have seen that Patañjali divides *samādhi*, which is the concerted state of my self-conscious being—in a sense my absolutely original state as it is the reflection of the pure state of the Puruṣa—into two primary kinds: *samādhi* in the known[76] or with the known as being known as an object, and *samādhi* in the unknown[77] or without the known as an object. That is, the former has the consciousness of the object as an object and the latter is without such consciousness. He divides the former into four kinds, each of which is again of two kinds; and he divides the latter into two kinds. The former is based on the constitution of the empirical personality, which consists of the inner sense or inner instrument (*antahkaraṇa*), the subtle elements, and the gross elements. Interestingly enough, in this division there is no mention of concentration on each of the three factors of the inner sense, viz., mind, ego, and reason (*buddhi*), but only on two, viz., mind and "am-ness" (*asmitā*). We have noted that in the Sāṅkhya tradition *mahat* (*vijñāna*, *buddhi*, *citta*) is described as pure I-am or am-ness (*asmitā*). That is, the ego or *ahaṁkāra*, the nature of which is to appropriate objects and experiences as mine, but not yours or his, is transcended, submerged or rather transformed into the pure "am-ness" which is still first-personal, but not egoistic (cp. the reduction by which the transcendental ego is obtained by Husserl, and note the differences also). For instance, in reason even in the sense of ratiocination or discursive thinking, we say: "I am lost in thought," when we are not aware of a friend's approach. I may be lost in thought, yet my I is not destroyed as it comes back when I stop thinking. We may say that the I, as this ego, is transcended, but not destroyed. The Upaniṣads say that it is absorbed, submerged. The Sāṅkhya-Yoga agrees with us. We use also the expression, "he is absorbed in thought." Patañjali would say: "The ego, which is also a pattern of similar pulsations of Prakṛti, is *niruddha*, stopped, checked, and merged in *mahat* (rational consciousness, *asmitā* in its pure state)."

Ontologically and basically, reason, in which the I as the ego is absorbed, is the pure I-am or "am-ness." *It is am-ness but not merely "is-ness," which is third-personal and may not have the significance of self-conscious being.* Patañjali here omits concentration on the ego[78] or on the I in its ego-form as such, for the aim of Yoga includes the removal of egoity or egoism. One can strengthen his ego by continuing to do more and more egoistic deeds, and Patañjali's yoga is not necessary for him.

Indeed, when I am in deep thought, the experience is not pure I-am or am-ness, but also of many ideas jostling against one another, confronting one another, issuing out of one another and so on. The ideas are in my consciousness, in my awareness; but my ego is not in it. If I am aware of my ego then, I will not be aware of my ideas and vice versa. That I am not aware of my ego does not mean that I am not present then, but that I do not have such experience as "These ideas are *my* ideas; I am thinking, but not you, this thinking belongs to me, but not to you," and so on. This pure thinking without the I is possible because what is present then is the pure I-am or am-ness. For the Sāṅkhya-Yoga we have then to say that this am-ness, undetermined by the ego (*ahaṁkāra*) is reason (*buddhi*, *mahat*) in its potentiality, but with ontological and cosmological significance, for everything else, including the ego, is derived from it.[79] It transcends the ego and everything else, which get merged in it, the am-ness, in the involutionary process of my universe becoming one with the unitary Prakṛti. What is called the transcendental ego then is, for the Sāṅkhya-Yoga, pure am-ness. Although this tradition holds that *mahat* (reason, am-ness) is different for different individuals, it is difficult to prove its plurality as it transcends the egos, which are numerically different. We have to accept the Upaniṣadic view[80] that there are two levels of reason, the individual and the cosmic, called respectively *vijñāna* (*buddhi*) and Mahat or Mahān Ātmā, the latter explained as the soul of the Cosmic Person,[81] the Logos, the first-born.[82] The individual's reason may go wrong, even when his ego is lost in it; for his own innate and unconscious tendencies may interfere with his thinking and deflect the process; but when he identifies himself with Cosmic Reason, his reason works correctly in accordance with the structure of the cosmos. Of course, as we do not know in detail the content of Cosmic Reason, we have to say that, when we are right in thinking, we are at one with Cosmic Reason. The main test we can apply to ourselves is to ask ourselves the question: Is my egoity, self-interest, involved in my thought and its conclusions?[83] And is my thought contaminated by wishful thinking, selfish interests, which also, not merely psycho-physical defects, are personal factors, to avoid which scientists take every humanly possible precaution? It has already been pointed out that the Sāṅkhya, in the narrow or atheistic form, ignored the distinction between the individual and the cosmic reason. Patañjali also does not seem to have made this distinction.

(v) Perception and Samādhi

The distinction between concentration on gross objects and subtle elements (objects) has already been explained. We have shown also the difference between "determinate" and "indeterminate" *samādhis*. The determinate is that which has a shape, a form, a formation. Even subtle objects like those of dreams have forms or shapes. Furthermore, even our abstract mathematical thinking like $(a + b)^2$ has a form and to that extent determinate. Then the indeterminate is that in which no shapes are perceived as objects. In the case of the *samādhi* on gross objects, there can be the difference between concentration on a pot made up of clay or earth, resulting in at-one-ness (*samādhi*) with the pot as a pot and the concentration on earth as such resulting with at-one-ness with earth. The latter will be *relatively* without form or shape, and yet marks a progress from the former and gives the power of control over the whole element. In the former, according to Patañjali, the distinction between the knowing consciousness, the known pot, and the word or sound "pot" remain but in a stable form or as strands of a continuous, uninterrupted flow.[84] But it seems that this stage may better be interpreted[85] as that in which the distinctions between the knower, the known (the pot), the universal (form, potness), and the name of the object ("pot") constitute a continual flow. But in the *nirvikāra* and *nirvicāra* states, they recede to the background and only the known (object, pot) stays, as if (*iva*) the yogi's consciousness has become the pot. This is the point at which the indeterminate stage of perception can be caught. It is generally thought that we cannot catch it. We certainly have it, but cannot stay at it except through this kind of meditation. But almost always the tendency is to detach ourselves from the object and not be one with it. So we say in explaining ordinary perception that the indeterminate stage is presupposed and cannot be caught, and perception is always of the form, "That is a pot."

So this kind of *samādhi* is not really unfamiliar to us. We have it in our everyday perceptual activities, although it is so momentary that it eludes us if we try to catch it. The person who aims his gun at a bird is absorbed in his sight fixed on it; then he is having indeterminate perception of it. Himself, the form (universal, birdness), and the name of the object ("bird"), are not present before his consciousness, although they are not lost and are regained. When he finishes the act, whether he succeeds or fails in it, they return to him and he will say: "I have got the bird" or "I failed to shoot the bird." The experience of these distinctions may precede and may also succeed the act of shooting. In the ordinary experience of perceiving the pen also, if I search for the pen, they precede the contact of my sight with the pen; if suddenly my sight happens to contact it without any effort on my part, the experience of the distinctions succeeds the contact, as when I say: "I see the pen." Almost all the schools accept the distinction, in one way or another, between determinate and indeterminate knowledge and perception.[86] But Patañjali has the insight into it, which he used in explaining the development of the stages of *samādhi*. In terms of the distinction, we may say that *savitarka* and *savicāra samādhis* are determinate *samādhis* and the *nirvikarka* and *nirvicāra samādhis* are indeterminate *samādhis*. These *samādhis* should not be confused with *samādhis* in the unknown, which also are indeterminate.

(vi) Concentration on Subtle Elements

Now, can there be concentration on subtle objects? It has already been explained that the best example of subtle objects is the stuff constituting the objects of the dream. They are not to be explained as constituting the objects of imagination, which are dependent on my conscious will and desire. According to the Sāṅkhya-Yoga, the subtle elements are the correlates of mind and the senses and yet independent, both mind and senses on the one side and the subtle objects on the other independently having their source in the ego (*ahaṁkāra*). We may, however, say that they are the potentialities of the gross objects, which we perceive in this world, and which are correlated to our senses. We explained this correlation already. To repeat: colours and shapes are correlated to the eye in the field of sight; and the potentiality of the objects as visible is constituted by a corresponding subtle element.

The subtle objects also have forms and shapes and names like the mountain I see in the dream. So at this level also there can be determinate *samādhi* (*savicāra*) and the indeterminate *samādhi* (*nirvicāra*). Here also at higher stages, the power of control over elements is obtained. Patañjali says that at the level of indeterminate *samādhi* in the subtle elements, our apperception (*prajñā*) is full of truth (*ṛtambharā*); for at this stage the knower becomes (as if, *iva*) one with subtle objectivity without his instincts and drives in any way deflecting the process of cognition. Subtle objectivity is the potentiality of the objects of the world being there at all.

We should remember that at every one of the stages the Sāṅkhya-Yoga insists on discrimination, which is self-analysis in the sense of discriminating the real self from the apparent self in the several identifications. This self-analysis is not to be understood in the psycho-analytic sense, but in the sense of discriminating whether the self, Puruṣa, is really that with which it identifies itself. Remember that Puruṣa's image, reflection, in Prakṛti identifies itself with all the happenings of Prakṛti and its salvation lies in dis-identification with the happenings, which is discrimination. The ability of the self, developed through practice of identifying itself totally with the object of meditation and then detaching itself from the object when the self comes out of *samādhi*, suddenly or through the determinate stages, produces the realization that the self is not the same as the object meditated upon and that the realization of the self is still remote.[87] It produces also an insight into the secret of the original identification of the reflection with Prakṛti. Besides, the practice enables the self to understand how to detach itself from the vicissitudes of Prakṛti. Patañjali's use of the term "as if" (*iva*) at these stages of the identification in *samādhi* indicates that even the identification of Puruṣa with Prakṛti is only an apparent, "as if," identification, which leads the forgetful Puruṣa to think that the happenings of Prakṛti are his own. Then if the "as if" holds true at the highest level and can be explained by saying that it is only the reflection that enters Prakṛti and becomes identical with it, then even at the different levels of *samādhi* it is the knower's reflection that is thrown into the object meditated upon. We may say then that my self, which enjoys and suffers in dreams, is also my reflection; and as the dreams and dream objects are many and unrelated, we have to say that the reflections can constitute a plurality, not interrelated directly, but only through me by their being my reflections. I remember many of my dreams; but my reflections in my dreams, as a general rule, do not remember me, as otherwise the dream will not be a dream, but a continuation of my waking consciousness or its fantasy; and moreover, the reflections do not know one another and do not remember my earlier reflections, just as I remember what I did and what happened to me yesterday in my waking state.

(vii) Copresence of Phenomenological and Existential Consciousness

The above and the following, based upon Patañjali's description of the *samādhis*, is a phenomenological analysis, an analysis of my phenomenological consciousness,[88] i.e., consciousness concerned with the phenomenal world including my own phenomenological existence. The phenomenological consciousness covers, comprehends, all phenomena, including my empirical person. But it should not be thought that this phenomenological consciousness can work alone in cognition and action without being activated or propelled by existential consciousness, which is the I-am and which is present in both the real (as such) and apparent (as if) stages. It has been mentioned already in a few places that there is no Becoming without Being; for Becoming becomes meaningless without Being lying in the background and will be a mere unrelated procession of events. Similarly, the phenomenological consciousness becomes disunited and falls as under without the existential consciousness being present in all the forms of the former and without its interrelating and uniting them. As Patañjali insists, when I meditate, I become "as though" one with all the indeterminate forms of *samādhi*, which are indeterminate because of the as-though identifications of my self with the various forms of Prakṛti, which constitutes the phenomena. Patañjali is, in a different terminology, saying that my existential consciousness has to be present in all stages through an "as though" identification.

Patañjali resorts to the expression "as though" because of the Sāṅkhya-Yoga separation of the Puruṣa and Prakṛti. But we have pointed out that the two cannot be so completely separate and disparate, and that Prakṛti has to be part and parcel of the very nature of the Puruṣa. If our argument is valid, then the "as if" has to be reinterpreted as the activity of the Puruṣa to be immanent in Prakṛti and also transcend it. If the latter belongs to the very nature of the former, it cannot have a separate existence. The phenomenal world, also, which it reveals or becomes—both the terms can be used now—, cannot have a separate existence from the Puruṣa. Then Existence or Being will be the Puruṣa himself, and Prakṛti will be his peculiar nature and power.[89] By this power he can be immanent in his derivations and also be transcendent to them. Then the factor of Existence or Being in our phenomenological or empirical cognition of the existence of things is really the Existence or Being (*astitā, sattā*) of the Puruṣa himself. All of us are then his "reflections" or "images." Such a Puruṣa is the Supreme Puruṣa; and our existence and the existence of the objects are borrowed from him. When Prakṛti assumes the form of objectivity, it drags with it the consciousness of the Puruṣa like the baby in its birth dragging the umbelical cord from the mother. This consciousness thus dragged becomes the phenomenological consciousness. The whole structure of existential consciousness, phenomenological consciousness, and the objectivity of the world is reflected in the experience of every one of us in form, "I know that I know *X*." The first I knows the second I and also its consciousness of the object. This is what Spinoza could have and should have meant when he said that mind comprehends both mind and matter.[90]

(viii) Concentration on Antahkarana

The stage which is the next higher than the *samādhi* in the subtle elements is the *samādhi* in mind (*manas*). Mind here, as already explained, is not to be understood in the western sense, but as one of the parts of the inner sense (*antahkaraṇa*.) Here there seems to be a gap in the explanation of the ascent from the lower to the higher stage of *samādhi*. If both mind and the subtle elements originate in the ego, then indeterminate *samādhi* in the subtle elements must lead to determinate *samādhi* in the ego, but not to any *samādhi* in mind, unless it is accepted that the subtle elements issue out of mind itself. The derivation of mind out of the ego, the ego out of apperception (*citta*), and the subtle elements out of mind seem to be logical in view of the clubbing together of mind, ego, and apperception as the inner sense (*antahkaraṇa*).[91] However, it may be noted that the Sāṅkhya is clearer than the Yoga in the explanation of *antahkaraṇa* (inner sense, inner instrument). And again, although the senses and the organs of action also issue forth like mind from the ego, no *samādhi* or even concentration is mentioned in the senses and the organs of action.

At the level of mind, one feels very happy and blissful (*sānanda*) in the *samādhi*. The reason is that the inner sense at this level begins to reflect on itself after withdrawing its whole world through the subtle elements into itself. The pleasure is due to the factual gaining of the whole world of that person. At our level the pleasure we derive generally by getting what we want is a small part of that pleasure. But this attainment is not unconscious, but begins shining like the sun, moon, and the precious stone.[92] That is, mind shines like them; and the pleasure is not like our ordinary pleasure, but extremely intense. Mind is transformed into something like shining pleasure, the brilliance of which is perfected at the level of am-ness, *asmitā*. The state may appear mystical; but the analysts' explanation of why we derive pleasure and of its intensity is not mystic.[93]

Patañjali thinks that pleasure is experienced in the determinate *samādhi* in mind; but in the indeterminate there is no experience of pleasure. It should be noted that the word mind (*manas*) is used loosely by the commentators and we should interpret the term according to the context. At this point it is not simple *manas*; it includes *citta* (apperception), but perhaps not the ego (*ahaṁkāra*) as such, for the whole process of *samādhi* is obviously to get over the ego or liquidate it. However, it is to be remembered that throughout the stages of *samprajñānata-samādhi*, classified as the original determinate *samādhi* or *samādhi* in the evolutes of Prakṛti, all the *samskāras* (the potential, innate forces) remain as such, the seeds of man's particular personality are not destroyed.

But why Patañjali says that there is no pleasure in the stages beyond the determinate *samādhi* in mind is not clear. The only explanation seems to be that at the determinate stage the knower experiences himself as distinct from the known, which is pleasure, and so knows pleasure; but in the indeterminate stage he becomes (as it were) one with pleasure and so there is no pleasure as an object. But the explanation is not satisfactory. When I come out of the stage of one-ness, I remember that I was all blissful; and this remembering is not possible unless there was pleasure in that state. This would be the Vedāntic view, which seems to agree with experience. To be one with bliss is not to be deprived of the experience.

From this level onward, one will not be wrong in saying that all states are blissful; for in all, the absorption of the world into one's mind and inner sense is involved and so a sense of satisfaction and attainment fills the inner sense. But Patañjali does not mention pleasure or bliss in the higher states, but even says that at the indeterminate *samādhi* in mind, it is *nirānanda* (non-blissful). There is the Sāṅkhya tradition that pleasure, the aesthetic also, belongs to *citta* or apperception, and that the *ātman*, (Puruṣa) is by nature not blissful, while the Advaita maintains that the *ātman* is by nature blissful (cp. *sat-cit-ānanda*) and the bliss of apperception is a reflection of the bliss of the *ātman*. It is likely that Patañjali adopted the Sāṅkhya view and stopped the experience of pleasure with *samādhi* in mind—*citta*, *mahat* is of the nature of I-am or am-ness into which the whole world in its subtle form is absorbed, then it also has to be immensely blissful, which can be a reflection of the bliss of the Puruṣa—which Vācaspati in his commentary[94] explains as *buddhi* or cognition involving the factors of the knower, known, and name in the determinate stage. It seems then that what is called *buddhi* by Vācaspati is the basis of what we call the basis of discursive reason, intellect, apperception; and the stage next higher, viz., *samādhi* in *asmitā* or am-ness is the non-discursive, integral reason. The latter indeed has to be present in the former, as otherwise the unitary background of the three factors—knower, knowledge and the known—will be lost and I shall not be able to recognize that the cognition is my cognition.

The above Sāṅkhya view seems to be related to the idea that pleasure, pain, and other experiences belong to the transformations of Prakṛti and so the Puruṣa by himself has no such experiences. But as we have pointed out, if Prakṛti is to be the essential nature of the Puruṣa himself—for Prakṛti by itself is unconscious and there can be no pleasure without conscious experience—the Vedāntins are right in maintaining that all the pleasures we experience in the phenomenal world are different degrees of reflection of the bliss of the Puruṣa (Brahman).

The stage next higher than the indeterminate *samādhi* in mind is the determinate *samādhi* in I-am or am-ness (*asmitā*),[95] which is not egoity, but the pure experience of I-am, which is equated by Pañcaśikha to Mahat (reason, apperception) and which is higher than the ego. We may remind ourselves again that the I-am is the first self-assertion of the first-born, the Cosmic Person. Now, at the determinate stage, we have to say that the form of the experience is "I know that I am," as the three distinctions of the knower, known; and word flow evenly. But at the indeterminate stage, the knower becomes one with the known and so only the pure am-ness (*asmitā*) remains.[96] But it cannot be unconscious, but is consciousness itself, from which the cognitive acts at the mundane level borrow their consciousness. It is at this stage that the equilibrium of the three forces—*sāttva*, *rajas*, and *tamas*, or transparency, disturbance, and lethargy—begin to appear, although the force *sattva* remains absolutely dominant. For without transparency, the Puruṣa's reflection of consciousness cannot be received. Indeed, we may ask here again: If the brilliance of the state of am-ness is due to it, why must this state also be not full of pleasure or bliss?[97]

We may remind ourselves again that in all the above levels, both the determinate and the indeterminate, the distinctions between the known, the knower, and the name of the known obtain, patently in the determinate and latently in the indeterminate. But after the *samādhi* in am-ness is perfected and the three forces attain their complete equilibrium, there are two courses open to the knower. He may merge himself in Prakṛti—and that experience also must be blissful, although the Sāṅkhya-Yoga does not admit it—and attain relatively eternal, not absolutely eternal, sleep, which, for the Vedāntins, is full of bliss, or he may realize that he has nothing to do with Prakṛti and regain his original form as the pure Puruṣa.

Now, according to Vyāsa, both these *samādhis*—the one in Prakṛti and the other in the pure Puruṣa—are called *samādhis* in the unknown or uncognized (*asamprajñāta*-

samādhis). But Vācaspati ignores Vyāsa's statement and says that the souls merged in Prakṛti, i.e., who have attained *samādhi* in Prakṛti, are all those who have perfected their *samādhis* in both Prakṛti and in its manifestations. Bhoja here says the same. One may interpret all the three as meaning the same.[98] For perfection in all the indeterminate forms will ultimately be the indeterminate one-ness with Prakṛti. But one may say that perfection in the determinate forms—unless it leads automatically to indeterminate forms and their perfection ending up in Prakṛti—is of a different type and cannot be *asamprajñāta samādhi* or *samādhi* without a known or without facing an object or without discursiveness. It is hoped that the point is clear.

Patañjali says rightly that both the *samādhi* in the known and that in the unknown are not still without traces (*samskāras*) i.e., latent traumata. That is, in the latter also the traces or the impressions of the *samādhi* in the known *samprajñāta samādhi* remain.[99] But in the *samādhis* in Prakṛti and the Puruṣa there is really nothing particular (*ālambana*) on which consciousness hangs or in which it is centred. We can easily see how it is so in the case of the *samādhi* in the pure Puruṣa; for there I concentrate on myself. In the case of the *samādhi* in Prakṛti also, my consciousness is not fixed on anything in particular and determinate; I am overwhelmed by the unconscious Prakṛti, like I am overwhelmed by the darkness of deep sleep. It is a common experience that, if I try to concentrate on deep sleep by making it an object of consciousness, I may not get any sleep at all. Now, neither *samādhi* is complete liberation; for even the one in the pure Puruṣa enables me to become one *as it were* with him, and so the traces (*samskāras*) of my empirical existence remain. They can be destroyed by constant practice of the latter and by leading an ethically pure life.

Here we may raise some questions of explanation. If Prakṛti is an object of the Puruṣa, may it not be an object also of I or I-am as a reflection of the Puruṣa? Then should not *samādhi* in Prakṛti be called that in the known? The *samādhi* in it seems to occupy a place between the *samādhi* in the known and that in the unknown. Remember, Īśvara as the highest Puruṣa—accepted by Patañjali—treats Prakṛti as an object of his consciousness without being overwhelmed by it. We are not completely conscious—because we identify ourselves with it—of our nature within us and belonging to us; but not so Īśvara.

The ideas which phenomenology and existentialism can get here are that the knower (I-am) can not only make gross and subtle objects the objects of his consciousness (cp. *grāhya-samāpatti*), but also his own senses and the three factors of the inner sense (cp. *grāhaṇa-samāpatti*), and his I-am or am-ness (*asmitā*), and Prakṛti and his self (cp. *grahītṛ-samāpatti*). To make Prakṛti one's object means that there is a way by which my consciousness is directed towards objectivity as such; not consciousness for this or that object, but a general consciousness that there is objectivity[100] which is not myself, and through which the ontological status of myself and all the separate objects can be ascertained. It is the experience next lower than that of the I-am and is nearly as certain of existence and truth as the experience of I-am. A thorough-going dualism like that of the Sāṅkhya and Descartes cannot explain why at all the I knows any object. For if it is conscious of only itself, how can it know of any object, as its consciousness is not directed towards that object? if it is directed outwards towards the object or objectivity as such—if there is an out-going consciousness—how can it shut itself up always and by nature only in itself? The out-going consciousness can arise only, if the objective also belongs potentially to the I; and the subject-object situation is an unfurling of what is furled and potentially retained within. The attempt of Descartes and Vijñānabhikṣu to bring in God to relate the two disparate beings, mind and matter, Puruṣa and Prakṛti, not only brings in *deaux ex machina* solutions very naively and evades the problem, but also cannot explain how God can bring the two together, if they are independent of him and of each other. If they are not independent of him, then they are not disparate and cannot be disparate—as matter must have some affinity with God who is Spirit and so with mind also—and have finally to be, as the *Bhagavadgītā* says, his innate Prakṛti. Spinoza made them dependent on God, but turned them into merely passive qualities, which they are not, ignoring a possible solution lying in his conception that mind knows not only itself but also the object (matter). This possible solution involves that the consciousness of mind is not merely centred in itself but is also directed towards objectivity, and that this peculiar activity is not possible unless the objectivity is a part of mind itself in some sense. As it is an apparent part of myself, this finite self, the mind of which it is to be a part has to be a higher mind (I-am), which as the Supreme I-am confers its am-ness on my ego and I say that I am. In that sense, my I-am is a reflection, an image, of the Supreme I-AM.

(ix) Mediation on the Consciousness of Dream and Deep Sleep

One point needs explanation. Sleep, according to Patañjali, is a function of *citta* (reason, apperception).[101] But if sleep is a function of apperception, is the latter then completely overwhelmed in the former? Patañjali says that it is not completely overwhelmed and does not also become extinct. Sleep is also a kind of cognition[102] of the absence of cognition. Patañjali's language, literally translated, means "the cognition dependent (hanging) on pure absence."[103] For nothing is known in sleep; and man coming out of sleep says that he "knew" nothing. *This knowledge is not possible, unless the knower was conscious of nothing, pure absence.*

Now, as sleep is a function of apperception (*citta*), and all functions of *citta* have to be stopped[104] in *samādhi*, the yogi has to stop the function of sleep also; i.e., he should get rid of sleep. When all the functions are stopped, the Puruṣa's reflection in its purity is caught in *citta*. Yet Patañjali recommends concentration on the "consciousness of sleep" to obtain steadiness of mind in meditation.[105] He recommends also at the same place concentration of mind on the "consciousness of dream." Vācaspati here refers to the Vedāntic view that the consciousness in revealing the objects of dream is the consciousness of the Brahman itself—constituting the Being of the Brahman—or of the Supreme I-AM.[106] But Patañjali does not refer here to the consciousness of God, although he accepts his reality. As I remember my dream, my consciousness and my I-am must have been present there and the objects must have been transformations of my own consciousness, which transforms itself also into the senses and the sense-fields of sight, hearing, etc. Vācaspati here rightly recommends that the consciousness in both dream and deep sleep should be one in which *sattva*, the Attribute of placidity, transparence, predominates, not the one in which the Attribute of *rajas* or of activity and disturbance and even misery predominates. For otherwise the peacefulness needed for steady meditation will be lacking. We may add that, although this advice is helpful so far as dream goes, it seems to be redundant for deep sleep as sleep cannot be deep unless *rajas* is completely submerged. What is interesting to note here is that *sattva* can dominate over the others in dream and deep sleep as, otherwise, placidity cannot be had. But in deep sleep, although I am conscious, I am conscious within the Unconscious or *tamas*, for I am overwhelmed by it, though not made extinct.

Here Vācaspati refers to the above Vedāntic (Advaita) view,[107] but does not discuss the difference between the Yoga and the Vedānta. The Yoga, like the Vedānta, accepts the presence of consciousness in deep sleep; and Vācaspati says that the Puruṣa in deep sleep is called "inward consciousness" (*antah-sañjñā*)[108] The Vedāntins generally call the Puruṣa (*ātman*) in dream *antahprajñā*, which means generally the same. But they treat deep sleep as the causal body—for it is enveloped in Darkness, *Tamas*—of the individual, the unconscious state of the whole personality, including the normal and the different grades of the abnormal, even though the Vedāntins showed no interest in discussing the abnormal.[109] According to the *Māṇḍūkya Upaniṣad*, the soul (*ātman*) in deep sleep is the gateway to the pure existential consciousness of the Brahman. But Patañjali makes no mention of the philosophical and metaphysical significance of sleep. Again, the Advaita Vedānta does not accept[110] that deep sleep is consciousness of pure absence,[111] i.e., that it is a function of *citta* (apperception), which is the result of (hangs on, *ālambanā*) its being tied down to absence as the object. They maintain that deep sleep is not a negative entity,[112] from which everything is absent, but a positive entity in which all objectivity becomes a unity and is submerged in *tamas* (Darkness, or the darkness aspect of Māyā). The so-called absence (*abhāva*) to which Patañjali refers is a misnomer for pure undifferentiated objectivity, i.e., in which no distinctions can be made. It is like not perceiving the individual objects in a moonless and starless night.[113] Some schools refer to it as *śūnya* (void, but, not that of the Buddhists), but in which *samskāras* (potentialities, traces) lie latent, but are not lost, and which is, therefore, not mere nothingness. Now, that we do not perceive anything is also a perception, a perception of something which we are unable to describe or define. Yet this is not doubting, in which we are unable to determine whether something like *A* is *X* or *Y*; it is a certainty into which we cannot probe in that state and in which we do not get the desire to probe because all the functions and the derivatives of our apperception, which have to be used for probing, are merged in it and unified into a solid mass (*prajñānaghana*), which is conscious.

Another difference between the Yoga and the Advaita in this context is that for the former sleep is a function of *citta*, but for the latter it is a state of the *ātman*. This difference may perhaps be treated as apparent only. For even for the Advaita, deep sleep is due to the withdrawal of everything into *citta* or apperception and the veiling of the *citta* by *Tamas* or darkness, which is one of the powers, forces (*śaktis*) of Māyā and Avidyā, and is called *āvaraṇaśakti* (the veiling, concealing, enveloping—like the original waters of mythology—possessing force).[114] For both the Sāṅkhya-Yoga and the Advaita, the person in bondage or bound to determinateness or cause-effect dominated world (*kārya-kāraṇa* and *kārya-karaṇa prapañca*) is only the reflection or image of the Puruṣa. But for the former, as we have noted, there is no Supreme Puruṣa and the Puruṣas form a plurality. For the latter, the Supreme Puruṣa is one and is everything. Prakṛti for the Advaita then must belong to the very nature of the Supreme Puruṣa and is his creative energy; and because inexplicable, it is called Māyā. As it has no being of its own ontologically and apart from that of the Puruṣa—here lies the difference from the Sāṅkhya-Yoga which treats the Puruṣa and Prakṛti as dual realities with separate existence or being—it is described as neither Being, nor Non-being and so on. But this description is secondary to the idea that Māyā belongs to the very nature of the Supreme Puruṣa as the power, force (*śakti*) of burning belongs to the very nature of fire and has no separate existence from that of fire.[115] That is, fire and its burning power cannot be two separate existing entities or beings; similarly, the Supreme Puruṣa and his Māyā cannot be two separate beings. And as we cannot say that because the burning power of fire has no separate existence from that of fire, it cannot, therefore, be a being: we cannot say also that Māyā, for the reason that it has no separate being of its own, cannot be being. Since it is being and cannot be a separate being, its being is identical with that of the Supreme Person. That is, it is his inherent nature.

Now, if deep sleep is finitized Māyā and the causal body of man (his *kāraṇa-śarīra*), is the container of the seeds of his personality, then it cannot be a function of *citta*, but *citta* will be a function of his causal body[116] or rather is its derivative. My causal body is always in the dark (*tamas*) for me, for although I think about it, as a finite person I cannot make it my object like I make the book my object of perception. If forms the basis of my existence or being. Then concentration on the cognition or consciousness of deep sleep (its *pratyaya*) should not be and cannot be concentration on deep sleep itself constituted by my causal body, but on the consciousness of deep sleep. But now, the question is: If my finite I-am, as this ego, or as the consciousness belonging to this Puruṣa, is merged in *citta* or apperception, how can I be conscious of deep sleep even as pure absence? But I am now still conscious that I was not then conscious of anything in that state. Then the consciousness that is conscious of my unconsciousness can be mine only in my transcendental level. This is called *ultimately* the Consciousness that is the Supreme Brahman. Vācaspati says that the Vedāntins regard the consciousness of deep sleep as *similar* to the Brahman. Yes, it is similar, but much more. It is a stage, not a mere example, of the transformation of my being and consciousness into those of the Brahman. That is why the I-consciousness of every person is called the gateway[117] to the Supreme Brahman.

Reference has already been made to the fact that the I-consciousness cannot be a mere point of reference, even though the Upaniṣads give that impression for the purposes of the methods of explanation. No individual is born simply with an I, but with all the more or less latent, complex structure of his personal being and that of the world. For there is a correlation between the structure of the world and the structure of the psycho-physical individual. The structure innate at birth may or may not be perfect and complete, may later develop fully, or may be retarded in its growth; but one way or another, it must have been there potentially as a latent structure of forces (*samskāras* or even instincts). Otherwise, we cannot explain why the world of the worm is different from that of a dog, and that of a dog from that of man. The evolution of mind from the lowest to the highest stage of which we so far know is not merely the evolution of the mere I-consciousness as a point or atom, but of self-consciousness with memory and historical consciousness and of the potentialities of cognition and action upon more and more complex structures of the world, of which the lower forms of consciousness are ignorant. These potentialities belong to the I-consciousness, they are not merely attached to it by accident. They belong to and constitute the structure of the phenomenological consciousness, which cannot exist separately from the existential or ontological I-consciousness. The idea of their ultimately belonging to the I-consciousness reveals its significance when we remember what has been said, viz., that Prakṛti is and has to be part of the nature of the Puruṣa and cannot have an independent existence. In a different terminology, phenomenological consciousness cannot have its being or existence apart from existential consciousness. The Puruṣa is not empty Being.[118] As the potentialities, e.g., of the senses, of the phenomenological consciousness are necessarily directed towards their corresponding objectivities, which also have to form structural unities, the objectivities also must have been somehow potentially incorporated in the phenomenological consciousness, which is part and parcel of the I-consciousness. The potentialities on the subjective and objective sides are parts, bifurcations of basic potentialities which are the fields like the field of sight, the field of hearing, etc. This idea of fields agrees with the Upaniṣads.

(x) Avoidance of Subjectivism through Self-transcendence

Generally, except perhaps in psycho-analysis, the epistemological and metaphysical aspects of sleep are ignored in western thought. This observation is particularly true of Anglo-American philosophy, which is motivated by the idea that by becoming a hand-maid to science and mathematics and by ignoring the I-consciousness and its centrality to philosophy, it avoids psychologism and subjectivism.[119] Yes, there is a sense in which psychologism and subjectivism are detrimental to the objective validity of every philosophical and religious theory. In philosophy we should not be led to the conclusion that the world is as this finite, selfish individual makes it to be, and whatever he sees and thinks need not be or must be true to every other individual. Otherwise, there need be no philosophy. In religion similarly no man as such should place himself in the position of the Supreme Being, who is the Supreme Being for everyone. But objective Being, as indicated in the previous general estimates, cannot be found, when we raise questions about the world apart from everybody's consciousness. If it has to retain its objectivity and yet be in the consciousness of persons, then that consciousness must somehow be in me also, and yet not be my monopoly.[120] These two conditions can be satisfied only if we can admit a transcendental consciousness which is immanent in everyone of us and is identical with us only in the self-transcendence of each one of us. It is this self-transcendence that philosophy has to teach intellectually and we in our religion have to realize experientially.

Furthermore, if I have to say that the objective world exists and yet my I that makes this assertion is merely psychological, even if not false, how can psychologism be avoided by those realists who wish to regard the I-am as a mere psychological entity? It is really the philosophy of such realists that is to be branded as psychologism. Again, if the I is false, how can what is false asserts be true? The contemporary Anglo-American philosophical vogue, for which even Descartes' starting point also is psychological,[121] does not see that not only has it lost all moorings in its searches for philosophical truths, but also that its starting point itself is self-contradictory. For it is not philosophy hovering in some vacuum that makes the assertion of an objective world, but the philosophers who have each his or her own "I." For if that I is merely psychological, they can assert nothing objectively true. A recent tendency to accept some tentative, initial, or methodological subjectivism,[122] etc., is also based upon the wrong assumption that the I-consciousness in every respect is necessarily subjective.[123] The trend in existentialism, following Kierkegaard, which revived the importance and value of so-called subjectivity, although important by showing that the being of the subjective is of primary value for man and religion, is also based on the wrong assumption that the I or I-am is necessarily subjective. Perhaps, his opposition to Hegel prevented him from realizing the importance of the I's self-transcendence; for self-transcendence, not merely intellectually but also experientially or existentially, is also a jump into the dark *until it is committed.* However, Kierkegaard thought that the I is subjective in the sense of mental or psychological, as opposed to the objective, which is necessarily logical and real. This is how Kierkegaard is generally understood. We find this attitude in Sartre also, who calls the material world Being and the I Non-being.[124] But at the basis of these positions and teachings lies some form of the dualism of mind and matter, whether both are regarded as real or one of the two is condemned as a false.

But if I am essentially a part of the objective world and I have to declare its objectivity, how can the world be understood without me? If the I also has to be understood, how can an analysis of the I-consciousness be avoided and the objective world alone be taken as real without concern for my declaration, unless we are content with partial solutions of this or that problem arbitrarily limited in scope? After all, it is the I that has to understand the world and has to pronounce also that it is such and such. At what level then can the pronouncements of the I have objective validity? The I in some moods and states, we know, cannot be trusted to make objectively valid judgments. In such cases, we say, the I is subjective. Then what should be the state or level at which the I can be objective? So a philosophical inquiry into the problems of how the world can be known as it is, not as imagined by us, involves the question, when and how can the I have an objective stance or state, for the I as consciousness is part of the world. My I is part of the world, not merely as this body. My body does not make any pronouncements on the world: on the other hand, my I makes pronouncements on my body. One may call the study of world-consciousness and of I-consciousness phenomenology or existentialism or both. Whatever be the name, such a study is central to philosophy and it was central to it when it first originated.[125]

Philosophically, it is such a study which the Sāṅkhya-Yoga and the Vedāntic systems make. Then spiritual practices and their intellectual studies are based on each other or are mutually dependent. We may say that at certain points in the history of thought, the practices led to deeper intellectual articulations and vice versa than at others. Let us not forget that even mathematics, the highest intellectual discipline, originated in the mystic experiences of the Pythagoreans. Indian philosophy is life at its reflective depths. Meditations are not merely intellectual reflections on some philosophical problems of the world—cp. Husserl's *Cartesian Meditations*—but also on the levels and stages of the depths of one's own self, at which it is objectively one with the world. Without the I's objective one-ness with the world, the objective truth of the world can neither be known nor be asserted. Without such identity, we could not have even known that there is a world. That identity is indeterminate cognition. In an important sense, we are in constant *samādhi* in our body and the world. This is a philosophically important lesson which Patañjali can teach the intellectuals, who, whether they care for *samādhis* or do not care for them are in one of them, which they can realize through meditation.

NOTES

[1]This may look like Sartre's *pre-cognito*, Husserl's transcendental consciousness, and Heidegger's *Sein*. There are similarities, but differences also, which are worth grasping.

[2]For Aristotle, even psychology is physics in the Greek sense of the term as the science of all becoming (*physis*).

[3]Cp. every chapter of the *Bhagavadgītā* being called a *yoga*, although the book aims at teaching one philosophy. Apparently it teaches eighteen *yogas*.

[4]See *Haṭhayogapradīpikā*. Some philosophers include spiritual practices also in *haṭhayoga*.

[5]*Pātañjalayogasūtras*, with the commentaries of Vyāsa, Vācaspati, and Bhoja, I, 6.

[6]Ibid., I, 10.

[7]Cp. Kant's idea that, if we think away all objects of the world, what remains will be pure space. But how does it differ from empty being or empty nothing?

[8]Ibid., I, 9.

[9]Note the difference from Heraclitus, for whom the Logos is found in deep sleep. But for Patañjali sleep is a function of the Logos.

[10]Ibid., I, 8.

[11]For this reason, Patañjali's doctrine is called *asatkhyāti*.

[12]Ibid., Vyāsa's commentary, p. 128.

[13]Ibid., Vācaspati's commentary, p. 127.

[14]In the above interpretation of Patañjali's doctrine, I have tried to be free from the technical terminology of Patañjali, which, otherwise, will need its own use and explanation.

[15]Other qualities remain the same and so we think that there is something stable. Each of the other qualities also may change without the rest not changing. So we think there is a substance or something substantial.

[16]Ibid., I, 2. [17]Ibid., I, 23. [18]Ibid., I, 25. [19]Ibid., I, 24.

[20]Ibid., I, 26. [21]Ibid., I, 27. [22]Ibid., I, 28. [23]Ibid., I, 30.

[24]Ibid., II, 12. [25]Ibid., II, 13. [26]Ibid., IV, 7.

[27]One can now see why Reason in the individual can be a logos in its ethical aspects also. Its workings do not depend on the sweet will of the ego.

[28]The modern existentialists have given the word the meaning of self-alienation from one's Being.

[29]*Samyak ādhīyate asmin iti samādhi.*

[30]Ibid., I, 3. [31]Ibid., I, 4.

[32]Ibid., IV, 34. [33]Ibid., IV, 24.

[34]Ibid., I, 33. [35]Ibid., I, 34.

[36]Cp. *prāṇabandhanam hi saumya manah* (Oh good one, mind is tied to, or based upon, *praṇa*, life or breath).

[37]Which, spontaneously centred by him in Christ, do not drag him hither and thither.

[38]Ibid., II, 29. [39]Ibid., II, 30. [40]Ibid., II, 32. [41]Ibid., II, 48.

[42]Ibid., II, 49. [43]Many works omit the fourth.

[44]Ibid., II, 54. [45]Ibid., III, 1.

[46]Ibid., III, 2. In popular language concentration and meditation are mixed up.

[47]Ibid., III, 3. [48]Ibid., III, 7. [49]Ibid., I, 43.

[50]Even if we are not interested in *samādhi*, we ought to appreciate the wonderful phenomenological analysis given by Patañjali, which goes much deeper than the analyses of Descartes and the

phenomenologists and even the existentists. Meditations even in the ordinary sense like that of Husserl's, not exactly those of Patañjali's, will be helpful for phenomenological and existential analysis.

[51]Since *vicāra* is explained as *vikalpa* by Bhoja. Ibid., I, 47., one may translate them as "discursive" and "non-discursive." But the difference between *vitarka* and *vicāra* seems to be in the former being concerned with gross elements and the latter with the subtle.

[52]Curiously enough, the Sanskrit word for object is *viṣaya*, which etymologically means that which ties down our consciousness to itself. When I am actually in the process of perceiving the object, I am not conscious of myself or of the distinction between the universal and the individual. When I have such consciousness, I must have freed myself from the actual object, risen to the level of thought, and appropriated the whole experience as mine.

[53]Ibid., I, 48–49. [54]Ibid., I, 47.

[55]Ibid., I, 19. Interpretations differ. The bodiless are called the deities or gods (*devas*) by Vyāsa. They are satisfied with merging in the elements, gross and subtle, the senses, and the three forms of the inner sense. We referred to the Upaniṣadic view that the senses and their respective objects, like sight and colour, have a common foundation that appears (shines) as the eye and its object. It is also the field, or medium in which the two rise. The appearing or shining foundations are called *devas*, *devatās*, which, translated as deities, seem to lose the primary meaning.

[56]Ibid., I, 20.

[57]In ordinary parlance the word "natural" seems to apply only to my I-consciousness as identified with this body. But if it is identical with the whole "nature" or "World" or Prakṛti, is the word not applicable to it? And in truth, is my I-consciousness to be identified only with my little body?

[58]Ibid., I, 49. [59]Ibid., IV, 1.

[60]Ibid., III, 16. [61]Ibid., III, 17.

[62]Ibid., III, 18. [63]Ibid., III, 19. [64]Ibid., III, 21. [65]Ibid., III, 44–45.

[66]Remember the Stoic conception.

[67]Which is not an ideal for the Mīmāmsā.

[68]We have already said that the concept of *ākāśa* in the Upaniṣads is very complicated and the complication has to be kept in mind and utilized according to context.

[69]However, in the Pāśupata and the Pāñcarātra traditions, the followers of which commented on the Upaniṣads, time is given a higher place than space, which is generally equated to *ākāśa* as the origin of sound. See my *Introduction to Comparative Philosophy*, pp. 241–42.

[70]Perhaps in their identity, they come closer to Einstein's theory of space-time. Scientists well-trained in both physics and philosophy may explain this very interesting theory of the Sāṅkhya-Yoga and the apparently contradictory statements like the infinity of space and the contraction of space at great distances. Has the structure of our apperception anything to do with these paradoxes?

[71]It may sound contradictory to speak of the Attribute of Rajas as both active and passive. But compare the principle of *prāṇa* being divided into five classes, one of which is again *prāṇa*. The so-called passive state is its latent state.

[72]Vyāsa says that in truth there is only one *pariṇāma*, viz., of the *dharmi*, *Yogasutras*, I, 3, 13. The changes are the manifestations of the same *dharmi*, a substance.

[73]Although I have abstracted the metaphysical or ontological aspect of Patañjali's idea of time from his conception of transformation (*pariṇāma*), his commentators' main interest seems also to be to show that the Buddhist view that the cause becomes nothing (*śūnya*) in the cause-effect transition or that it becomes extinct before the effect is born, is false. The common factor between Buddhism and the Yoga is that the world is a continual becoming, a process, a flow, and a transformation. Now, in apperception (*citta*) the three moments—the idea *X* is born, *X* stays, and *X* disappears—constitute transformation. But this disappearance of *X* is not its extinction, but entering the being of apperception. We have said that the Yogic concept of *citta*, the Buddhist concept of *Ālayavijñāna*, and the Vedāntic concept of *bījātman*, *kāraṇaśarīra*, *citta*, or *vijñāna* perform the same functions. But neither Patañjali nor the Vedānta accepts that whatever disappears is destroyed, but is only submerged (*niruddha*). Patañjali explains the situation in terms of the Yogic practice of meditation in which one finds that his mind tends to change from idea to idea.

Now, the three moments of arising, staying, and merging belong not only to apperception (*citta*), but also to senses and objects. But in the case of apperception and the senses, personal effort is needed. In meditation in the case of apperception, I first try to stop, check (*nirudh*) a *samskāra* (the impression or imprint of a previous experience, which lies latent like a trauma) from arising; this effort of mine constitutes the stopping moment of transformation which is constantly taking place in my apperception and is called *nirodha-pariṇāma* (stopping or checking moment of transformation). But apperception contains many ideas and *samskāras*, and it passes by nature from one to another constantly. Through my effort it fixes itself on one of these ideas, and the rest of them disappear (get submerged and stay submerged as *samskāras*). This rising of the moment of fixing or concentration is called *samādhipariṇāma* (transformation as concentration or concentration within transformation). But remember that all along, transformation, Becoming, process, is incessantly taking place. Even when this concentration arises, apperception is going through some process; it never becomes static and the process never stops. But the difference lies here: In our ordinary recognizable transformation *A* arises first, then goes down giving place to *B*. But when concentration on the same idea (*pratyāya*) is stabilized, *A* arises first, then goes down giving place to another *A* only. The two *A*'s are called similar ideas (*tulyapratyayas*), but not *ekaparatyaya* (the same idea) because similarity in this context permits *pariṇāma*, but sameness implies cessation of *pariṇāma* (transformation) Cp. The Andhaka Buddhists said that the same idea (*pratyaya*) and consciousness continue for a time when meditation is perfected —which violated the Buddhist doctrine of momentariness. Patañjali indeed accepts the sameness of Puruṣa and of Prakṛti also, the latter in spite of transformation and its processes taking place within it. So the above explanations are to be taken to apply to me at the empirical level. Furthermore, if Prakṛti is ultimately the substantive and all the processes are taking place *within it* and all of them are the processes of the three Attributes which are constituents of Prakṛti, should we not say that all, at least, constituent qualities and activities lie *within substance*, and that substance is not *behind them* or *underlies them*? This aspect of experience and reality gives another conception of substance, as *that within which properties and activities lie*. This *pariṇāma* in which exactly similar *A*'s arise and get merged one after another is called single-pointed transformation (*ekāgratā-pariṇāma*). In this process nothing becomes mere *śūnya* or extinct, but is only stopped, checked, i.e., submerged. (It is better not to use the terms "suppressed" and "repressed"—although they can be English equivalents of the term *niruddha* in a general way—as they are associated with abnormal psychology.)

These three moments, stopping, fixing on one element in a succession of dissimilars, and fixing on a succession of similars (*nirodha-pariṇāma*, *samādhi-pariṇāma*, and *ekāgratā-pariṇāma*) can be clues to the explanation, in case of the processes of the senses and the physical objects also, of the constant transformations of quality (*dharma*, characteristic), temporal moments (*lakṣaṇas*), and states (*avasthās*). I have explained in the text how these kinds of transformation take place in the physical objects. In the case of the senses also, e.g., the eye or sight, the arising or appearance of the red (of the perceived red rose) and the disappearance of the green (of the green leaf first perceived) constitute the process of stopping the green or losing the green and the arising of the red or having the red. This is transformation of quality (*dharma*) of the eye or sight. This arising of the red has its three moments of future, present, and past: past also because my eye may be turned towards some other colour later. When some other colour arises, the impression of red, which is strong in the present, becomes weak first, and then disappears. These "strong," "weak," and "disappearing or merging" are the three states (*avasthās*) of each of the three moments of time, called *lakṣaṇas*, also of the eye or sight.

What is to be noted here is that red, etc., are called qualities (*dharmas*) of the eye also, for when nothing is seen there is no seeing and so no sight; and that the senses and their objects, according to the Sāṅkhya-Yoga, are functions of apperception.

This analysis of transformation (*pariṇāma*) given by Patañjali in the context of meditation—in which the involvement of the individual's effort brings out the incessantly changing aspect of his empirical being—can be fruitfully applied to epistemological processes for obtaining a profound understanding of their import. It discloses some inward identities of the self, apperception, and the processes of perception. The commentaries on the *Yoga Aphorisms* I, 3, 9–15 need to be thoughtfully and carefully studied—more so than many writers in English have so far done—for insights into one's psycho-physical nature. Here a kind of summary is given, and further elaboration is not possible. Note also that the flow of succession (transformation) concerns *dharmas* (qualities, properties, characteristics), which exist in the *dharmi* (the substantive, substance, that which remains the same through change and has the *dharmas*); the temporal moments of future, present, and past, which belong to each of the changing qualities; and the states of strong, weak, and vanishing or merged, which belong to each of the temporal moments. The three successions of change—of *dharma*, *lakṣaṇa*, and *avasthā*—are of different types. The *dharmi* or substantive accompanies all (*anupatati*) and cannot be perceived by itself by the eye. Note further that the transformations (*pariṇāmas*) all belong ultimately to Prakṛti and that it can remain the same in spite of the transformations. (Cp. the Advaita view of *vivarta.*) All of them are patterned processes within patterned processes within patterned processes and so on, all happening within Prakṛti; and that they are patterned processes of subject-object and sense-object unities. There are no processes of the subject, sense, or object by itself the object being understood not merely as the gross object, but also as subtle, as explained already.

[74]Cp. the statement of Lord Kṛṣṇa in the *Bhagavadgītā*, according to which he has three kinds of Prakrti within him, belonging to his being.

[75]We have related ideas in the concepts of substance, which remains the same while its qualities change, and of transcendence and immanence, in which *X* as immanent in *Y* goes through the transformations of *Y*, but yet as transcendent it is free from those transformations. Cp. also the idea of the two birds in the *Muṇḍaka Upaniṣad*. Another concept is *vikāra* or affection. The drunkard has it and is transformed for a time by the effects of alcohol; after a time he comes to his senses, but may or may not remember what happened. A particular type of weather also may change our mind or mood; here also we have *vikāra*, affection, which may also be translated as modification in many contexts. When man recovers from it, he may remember he had it—which means that his self retained its transcendental aspect also like the waking self in the dream self. This leads us to the idea of witness (*sākṣi*) consciousness. *Sākṣi* consciousness stays the same in spite of the changes and vicissitudes of the lower self and these vicissitudes are transformations of the unities of subject-object experiences; that is, they are transformations of correlated subject-object experiences. These transformations are witnessed by the witness-consciousness, which has to remain the same to witness the transformations. So it corresponds in the world of experience to substance in the realm of physical matter. But material substance cannot know that it remains the same through the changes of its qualities, but the witness-consciousness can do so. And it is the witness-consciousness, again, that has to posit and recognize the presence of substance in material objects.

So there is much to be said in favour of the view that Substance, which is the constant in a changing object, is the same as Being, as distinct from Becoming, which belongs to qualities, etc., and that the witness-consciousness supplies the factor of Being in the objects perceived and mind (*antahkaraṇa*) supplies changing qualities, etc. Note that none of the subjective poles of experience can exist without its objective pole.

[76]*Samprajñāta*. [77]*Asamprajñāta*.

[78]Cp. the view of Kasmir Śaivism, according to which the I is the gateway to the Brahman, which is the fulness of I-ness (*pūrṇāhamta*). Here we have pure existentialism, but at a far higher level than that of Sartre, Heidegger, etc. Note also how in the Sāṅkhya-Yoga the ego gradually becomes one with the Puruṣa, who is at least the source of am-ness.

[79]Cp. Descartes' "I think, therefore I am." The I with thinking is the I with am-ness. Here arise many complications.

[80]Cp. *Kaṭha Upaniṣad*.

[81]The *jiva* or soul of Hiraṇyagarbha.

[82]It seems to me that there is a mistake committed by some translators and interpreters of Vijñānabhikṣu of the Vedāntic Sāṅkhya, who said that the first-born brings the Puruṣas and Prakṛti into contact. The first-born is explained as though he is an individual among individuals. The Upaniṣads say that Prajāpati or Hiraṇyagarbha, the Cosmic Person, who first said "I am," is the first-born, and started the creation of male and female. He is also called *mṛtyu* and Yama (Death and the God of Death); for in the consolidated unity, called the Cosmic Egg (Brahmāṇḍa), of all the cosmic processes of Becoming, the same Hiraṇyagarbha, who is that Egg, not only creates, but also absorbs, swallows, every moment of Becoming. Cp. the Zoroasterian (Avastan) conception of Yama and Yami as the first-born.

[83]I think that the idea of the avoidance of the personal factor is not merely of methodological importance in science, but has also ethical and religious significance. It implies the sacrifice of the ego and what pertains to it at the altar of the Cosmic Person and the Supreme Being.

[84]Patañjali does not seem to accept the *sphoṭa* doctrine held by grammarian philosophers.

[85]According to King Bhoja's interpretation.

[86]The Jaina epistemology, in its own way, recognizes the indeterminate stage mainly in what it calls *avagraha* in the process of perception. Anyway, this concentration should not be thought to be alien to man. We live within Prakṛti and are reflections of the Puruṣa. As the *Bhagavadgītā* says, even a little success in this field saves one from great fear (*Svalpamapi asya dharmasya trāyate mahato bhayāt.*)

[87]Cp. Yoga Aphorisms, I, 3, 7.

[88]Rāmānuja would call it *dharmabhūtajñāna*. See my article, "The Existential and Phenomenological Consciousness in the Philosophy of Rāmānuja" (*Journal of the American Oriental Society*.)

[89]It is unnecessary for Rāmānuja to make Prakṛti independent of the *ātmans* and adopt a kind of Sāṅkhya dualism.

[90]The advisability of comparing the analyses at the different levels of *samādhi* to those of Husserl's reductions has already been mentioned. It may be repeated that Patañjali's aim is not to give an intellectual, phenomenological analysis, but help man in rising to higher and higher stages of *samādhi*, which is really catching, grasping, and staying in one's own true self. (Think about whether this idea helps in understanding how man, as Spinoza said, can realize that he is a derivation from God, the Substance and also in understanding how man's mind, as Berkeley said, can know the objects as ideas in the mind of God.) This ought to sound like, and be similar to catching the transcendental ego, although it goes beyond as it exhorts man to remain, stay, at the highest transcendental level. It is also, as has been pointed out, an existential analysis, but goes beyond mere analysis as it asks us to stay at the level of Being itself. The Being or Existence of everything in the world would be a reflection of the Supreme, an "as if" independent existence, if our development and criticism of the Sāṅkhya-Yoga dualism is true.

It is not possible to discuss satisfactorily the complementary nature of the possible contribution of the above estimate of Patañjali's ideas to the phenomenological reductions of Husserl's; we can only indicate them. As they are complementary, they are distinct, and considered with Husserl's may lead to a deeper understanding of the forms of consciousness involved in I-am and I-know, *sum* and *cogito*. First, if, as Husserl thinks, ontological Being even of the objects can be found only in the transcendental "ego," which can be found only in eidetic reduction, then this reduction does not and cannot bracket out the existence of factual objects, but assimilates them to the transcendental ego and incorporates them in it. (Cp. the ideas of active and passive genesis in Husserl and of active and passive intellect in medieval philosophers.) *Secondly*, the transcendental "ego" or, as in our case, the transcendental I-am, does not leave Existence or Being back in the factual world; for it is the transcendental I-am that lent existence to the world. It cannot, therefore, leave back existence, but withdraws the primary and potential forms of existence into itself through eidetic reduction. *Thirdly*, the eidetic form or universal is, for that reason, ontological—cp. Plato who maintained that the Idea is Being—and that it is so is confirmed by the withdrawal of the object and its existence through eidetic transformation, which is not mere abstraction, but assimilation of the object as perceived to the I-am. *Fourthly*, Husserl does not seem to recognize the I-am's oneness with the object. Without this oneness—however it is interpreted, as a mere "as-if" or as the ability to be immanent and then transcend its nature and constitution at the time—perception, which involves merging (cp. the indeterminate stage) with the object, becomes impossible. *Fifthly*, even in the highest state, the transcendental subject, for Husserl, remains a pure flow of consciousness and is temporal. But we have noted that time cannot be time unless with reference to something which transcends the mere flow of time. Who can know the flow as flow, unless he is above the flow? Husserl does not seem to have extricated himself from I-know and to have reached the I-am. I-know contains process, flow, history; but without the I-am, it will not be the I-know and its history. From our point of view, the transcendence he has reached is not the highest possible. If the highest is not accepted, the stability and even the continuity of any object for a time will not be possible. It will be a mere procession of unrelated events. Even to say so, I as the observer have to be the same all through. *Sixthly*, we may say that what are merely transcended through assimilation by the self or I-am are the fields of its diversified consciousness, to which we referred as sense-fields etc. But Husserl does not seem to have introduced and elaborated the idea of fields in any significant way. Other differences from Husserl's philosophy can be worked out and a unified ontology of the I-consciousness can be developed. This difference from Husserl should in no way be meant to lessen his importance. It means only that his philosophy needs further development. For instance, if the I-know *implies* the I-am, as Descartes himself said, and there is no mere knowing without the I as in I-know—Husserl seems to ask us to omit the I even in the I-know by asking us to bracket out existence—then the implied I-am cannot be merely inactive in the processes of consciousness. Then in what ways is it active in the different contexts?

[91]The commentaries mix up the terms and exactness in interpretation is not easy, but has to depend on the logic and experience of human nature. It seems to me that mind here is not merely *manas*, but *manas* plus apperception (*citta*). It is the general position of the Sāṅkhya-Yoga that bliss (*ānanda*) belongs to *citta*, *buddhi*, not even to the *ātman*. Then *manas* as such cannot be blissful, without activation by *citta*.

[92]*Yoga Aphorisms*, I, 136. *Visokā vā jyotismatī* (without pain and full of light. See Vyāsa's commentary. He adds that *samādhi* in "am-ness" is absolutely peaceful and brilliant (*jyotiṣmatī*).

[93]There are detailed explanations in the commentaries on the mystic aspect of the stages. It will be very fruitful to study them in depth. In the present work we cannot find space for those explanations.

[94]*Yoga Aphorisms*, I, 36. One should be careful in translating these terms.

[95]*Asmitā* means also egoity, egotism, see *Yoga Aphorisms*, II, 3. But it is not egoity here. Mere dictionary translations should be avoided.

[96]These distinctions can be helpful in understanding the logical and ontological explanations of Descartes' *cogito*. Descartes may not be a saint or Yogi, but he touched upon a point that is important both for philosophy and religion.

[97]In the interpretation of these stages there are differences between Vācaspati following Vyāsa and King Bhoja. Our interpretation does not follow either completely. Nāgojibhaṭṭa also has his own explanations. See commentaries on I, 17–20, *Yoga Aphorisms*.

[98]For perfection in the lower indeterminate forms may be the same as becoming *as if* one with Prakṛti. It seems that there can be a determinate form for this *samādhi* also. The Advaita says that for Īśvara (so at the Īśvara stage) Māyā (Prakṛti) is a powerless object.

[99]Bhoja's explanation here is clearer than Vācaspati's.

[100]Simple *idamtā* (thisness) as in Kasmir Śaivism.

[101]I, 6. It will be interesting and useful also to note that for the Stoics Reason is Nature also. Then it is the ultimate ontological truth also for them. In our context, it is an important point that Nature and Apperception are one or that Prakṛti with its total involved structure is inherent in apperception.

[102]Cp. Kumārila's explanation of the cognition of absence or negation.

[103]*Yoga Aphorisms*, I, 2 and Vyāsa's and Vācaspati's commentaries on I, 10.

[104]See *Bṛhadāraṇyaka Upaniṣad*, discussion between Janaka and Yājñavalkya. Here lies the difference between the Vedānta and the Stoics, who have nothing higher than Reason or Nature.

[105]I, 38.

[106]See Footnote 4 on previous page. The light guiding one to the objects in dream is the light of the *ātman* itself.

[107]*Yoga Aphorisms*, Commentary I, 38.

[108]Ibid., I, 10, see commentary.

[109]See my paper in *The Problem of the Self*.

[110]Rāmānuja may, however, accept it.

[111]*abhāva-pratyayālambanā vṛttiḥ nidrā.* [112]*abhāva-padārthah.*

[113]*bhāva-padārtha*. From another point of view, viz., that of Māyā, of which the *avidyā* of deep sleep is a part, the Advaitins may say that deep sleep is neither positive nor negative. Here the followers of Kasmir Śaivism (Advaita) may object to the view of Śaṅkara's followers and say that, if Avidyā as deep sleep is positive (*bhāva*), then Māyā, of which *avidyā* is a part, must be positive and so real, in spite of inexplicability.

[114]There is a line a thought which is not generally pursued in the literature of this school. If both the concealing power (*tamas*) and the projective power (*rajas*) belong to Māyā, it is essentially the unity of all the three attributes, including the transparent (*sattva*). Then it is a unity of all the forms of its manifestation like *citta*, ego, mind, senses, etc. And if Prakṛti has to belong to the Puruṣa, as we have shown, then Māyā as Prakṛti must somehow belong to the Brahman.

[115]This is generally the example given by the Advaitins. Even if the scientists and their technology discover fire without any power of burning or even making things cold, this example is to be understood for the purpose of what it is meant to serve and the analogy should not be pressed too far in the light of contemporary and future scientific discoveries.

[116]If, on the other hand, the causal body is identified with apperception, Mahat, as *asmitā* or *ahamasmi*, Reason and Nature of the Stoics, the interpretation can be different. The so-called unknownness of the causal body is due to its being a constituent of my I-am, which cannot be made an object.

[117]Cp. *Aitareya Upaniṣad* saying that the Brahman descended into man as his I or I-consciousness. The reference to the *Bṛhadāraṇyaka* has already been given a few times. Here is the real meaning of the Judo-Christian conception that man is the image of God. It cannot mean that man's hands and feet are reflections of God's hands, etc. What can be the full implication of the God of the Bible telling Moses that the I-Am "is my memorial unto all generations?"

[118]Hegel thought that Being is an empty category and distinguished it from the concept of Self-consciousness. We may form an empty concept of Being; but true Being cannot be empty. It is the

highest state of the I-consciousness, which also cannot be empty. An empty concept of Being cannot be Being itself.

[119]The present writer has examined this claim at several places. Here only the main difficulty is repeated.

[120]which means that the avoidance of the so-called personal factor in observation and thinking can be achieved only by self-transcendence.

[121]The author heard it from the lips of many teachers even.

[122]Cp. for instance C.I. Lewis.

[123]Many senior philosophers have made this assertion. Some even said that the I is a false entity. Gilbert Ryle's criticism that philosophers think of mind as a bird in a cage and have committed a category mistake is also based upon the wrong opinion that philosophers are necessarily thinking of two realities like mind and matter, mind being encaged in matter. An unprejudiced starting point for philosophy is to realize that all experience starts with subjective and objective poles taken together and to suspend the judgment that the subject or mind alone or the object or matter alone exists, and then analyze the subject-object unities of experience and dig up the implications.

[124]Even the idea of transcendental subjectivity cannot express the ultimate I-consciousness. It is not subjectivity at all, if it transcends both the subject and the object as this finite I and as this world. In the relatively transcendental stages of my self, in which my complete one-ness with the objective world is not realized, the stages may be mine, not those of the others and only to that extent may be called subjective, although transcendental. Transcendental stages are more than one.

[125]Cp. Aristotle's view that even the pre-Socratics were in search of the soul.

Chapter X

Introduction to the Vedāntic Schools

The word *vedānta* means the end of the Veda and, therefore, the Upaniṣads. The philosophy based upon the Upaniṣads is also called the Vedānta. As the Upaniṣads are many, not composed by the same person or at the same time, they hold apparently different views. As mentioned already, it was found necessary to systematize their views and Bādarāyaṇa attempted the systematization in his *Vedānta Aphorisms*, also called the *Brahman Aphorisms* as they expounded the nature of the Brahman. His philosophy is called also the Posterior Mīmāmsā and the Mīmāmsā of the Spirit, or of that which has the body.

We may repeat that Bādarāyaṇa's *Aphorisms*, being pithy and incomplete sentences, themselves required explanations and systematic interpretations. Through such interpretations arose about eleven schools of the Vedānta. As the *Vedānta Aphorisms* were based upon the Upaniṣads, to show that the interpretation of the *Aphorisms* was not at variance with the Upaniṣads, commentators on the *Aphorisms* had to comment on the Upaniṣads also, thus interpreting both in the same way. As the *Bhagavadgītā*, a very popular book, was regarded as teaching the same philosophy as that of the Upaniṣads, the commentators on the *Aphorisms* and the Upaniṣads were expected to agree with the teachings of the *Bhagavadgītā*. So the attempt was made to comment on this book also for making all the three commentaries agree. Thus for all the Vedāntic philosophers, the three texts—the Upaniṣads, the *Vedānta Aphorisms*, and the *Bhagavadgītā*—became the basic (starting, *prasthāna*) triad (*prasthānatraya*) for building up their systems. As the *Bhagavadgītā*, which is a part of the epic of the Mahābhārata, is regarded as a scripture that is remembered (*smṛti*), but not as a scripture heard (*śruti*)—all the epics are called remembered scriptures—the commentators felt free to use whatever epics suited them in support of the doctrines introduced by them through their commentaries, although the epics were not non-sectarian unlike the principal Upaniṣads.

Besides the general Vedic tradition represented by the different parts of the Veda and the independent philosophical traditions represented by Jainism, Buddhism, Nyāya-Vaiśeṣika, and the Sāṅkhya-Yoga, there were three important religious traditions—the Pāśupata, the Pāñcarātra, and the Śākta—which had their origins partly in the Vedas and partly in some popular religious cults, and the literature of which, called the Āgamas and also the Samhitās, seems to have started about the 1st century B.C., or A.D. The founder of the Vedāntic schools, except Śaṅkara and Bhāskara, belonged to the first or the second of the three traditions (*sampradāyas*) and commented on the three basic texts in conformity with their traditions. There seems to be none from the Śākta tradition, who commented on them. The Pāśupata tradition treats the Vedāntic Brahman as Śiva and is, therefore, called also the Śaiva tradition. The Pāñcarātra treats the Brahman as Viṣṇu and is called also the Vaiṣṇava tradition. *Śakti* (force, energy, power) is the creative, maintaining, and destructive power of the supreme Godhead and is considered to be its inseparable, feminine aspect, with which we are immediately in contact and the transformation (*pariṇāma*) of which is the world. In popular religion, Śakti is regarded as the consort of the Godhead. For the Śākta tradition the energy aspect of the Godhead is primary. It developed its own philosophical literature and even composed its own Upaniṣads. But it did not furnish commentaries to the three basic Vedāntic texts. Even if it composed them, they are not available. At least I have not come across any. All the three traditions have their own Upaniṣads, called them parts of the same Veda, and furnished commentaries also on them. A few Upaniṣads are even common to all the three. As mentioned already, about ten of the Upaniṣads are said to be the primary ones. The Śākta tradition could not become Vedāntic, as it could not furnish commentaries on the *Vedānta Aphorisms*, the primary Upaniṣads, and the *Bhagavadgītā*. The very orthodox Vedāntins do not regard the Śākta Upaniṣads are genuine.[1]

Although the Vedānta is the philosophy based upon the Upaniṣads, in practice it has come to mean the philosophy developed by commenting on the *Vedānta Aphorisms* of Bādarāyaṇa, who is considered by all as the authentic interpreter of the Upaniṣads. It seems that there were interpreters of the Upaniṣads even before Bādarāyaṇa, who mentions the names of some such as Āsmarathya,[2] Auḍulomi,[3] and Kāśakṛstna.[4] But their works are not available. We cannot be very sure also about what views they held, as the commentators on Bādarāyaṇa attribute to them different views according to their convenience. The earliest commentary available on Bādarāyaṇa is that of Śaṅkara of the 8th century. It seems that there were earlier commentaries, but we do not have them. By the time Śaṅkara wrote his commentary, the ideas of the Mahāyāna Buddhism and of the Sāṅkhya-Yoga got mixed up with the Upaniṣadic ideas and the philosophical development of the Vedānta took a richer shape than before. Indeed, none of the Vedāntins accepted Buddhism and the Sāṅkhya-Yoga as such, and made it a point to criticize and reject them along with the other schools. But they were in fact incorporating and developing many of the important ideas of the two schools into grander systems, without of course acknowledging any debt to them. We have seen that very early the Sāṅkhya developed the idea of the witness consciousness,[5] which has been put to great use by the Vedānta. The Buddhist concept of Māyā was utilized by the Vedāntic schools in one way or another, by identifying it with the Unmanifest (Avyakta) and Prakṛti of the Upaniṣads. So when it is said that the Vedāntic schools reject Buddhism and the Sāṅkhya-Yoga, we should not understand that every doctrine of these schools is rejected, but that it is either transformed or incorporated into a more comprehensive structure.

The Upaniṣads assert in some of their passages that the Brahman is everything, including the individual spirits and the material world; but in some other passages they assert that the Brahman is none of them and is different from all. They thus maintain both unqualified monism or nondualism (*advaita*) and unqualified pluralism. The primary task of the commentators is to reconcile both groups of passages with each other. There are here three kinds of reality—the Supreme Spirit, the individual spirits, and the material principle. There are, therefore, three kinds of relationship—the relation of the Supreme Spirit to the individual spirits, the relations of the individual spirits to matter and of matter to the Supreme Spirit. Each of the three terms is related to the other two, and so each relationship has two directions. Then a number of questions arise. For instance, are all the relations of the same kind? Are they of the same kind in each of the directions? If the three relations are of different kinds, what is the nature of the differences? If each relation is different in each of its directions, what is the nature of this difference? The Vedāntins have to answer these questions, which constitute the second problem they have to tackle and they are not unanimous in their answers.

There is a third problem which the Vedāntins have to solve, viz., the nature of creation. Creation is a causal process. Then what part does God, as the Brahman, play in it? Again, the answers vary.

In solving the above problems, it did not matter whether a Vedāntin belonged to the Śaiva or the Vaiṣṇava tradition. A Śaiva may give the same solutions as those of a Vaiṣṇava. And two Vedāntins belonging to the same tradition may give different solutions. So far as the Vedāntic philosophies are concerned, it is immaterial whether a particular Vedāntin belongs to the Śaiva or the Vaiṣṇava tradition. Thus there are different sub-schools of Śaivism and Vaiṣṇavism, and the Vedāntic schools cut across them.

In the Vedāntic thought, the two extreme positions are called non-dualism (*advaita*) and dualism (*dvaita*) and are held by Śaṅkara and Madhva respectively. While non-dualism means that non-duality obtains between the Supreme Spirit and the individual spirits, and between both on the one side and the world of matter on the other, dualism does not mean that there are only two qualitatively or quantitatively different realities, but that the Supreme Spirit, the individual spirits, and the world of matter are three qualitatively different realities and also that the second and the third kinds are each pluralistic. What Madhva has in mind, when he teaches dualism, is the duality of the Supreme Spirit and the individual spirit; the former is not at all the same as the latter. On this point, Madhva is uncompromising and is, therefore, called a dualist. Otherwise, he is a real pluralist and a mono-theist.

In between the positions of Śaṅkara and Madhva, there are a number of intermediary views. Śaṅkara attempts to explain the passages in the Upaniṣads teaching the difference between the Supreme Spirit on the one side and the individual spirits and matter on the other, by taking the plurality as a manifestation of the underlying unity. Madhva thinks that Śaṅkara explains away plurality and so himself explains away the passages teaching the reality of the underlying unity. But the other Vedāntins, taking both passages seriously, introduce different kinds of relationship that can preserve both unity and multiplicity. Thus arose different Vedāntic schools. But all along, the primary interest of all lies in the relationship between the Supreme Spirit and the finite spirit. The interest in the principle of matter is secondary and subsidiary.

One of the *Vedānta Aphorisms* says that the Brahman is realized as one's own *ātman*.[6] Such a realization is accepted by all, but interpreted differently. The Supreme Spirit is of course not an object of our senses. It is not an object at all. It is not, again, the subject in the ordinary sense of the term. The subject of my experience is myself; but I am not the Supreme Spirit. As it cannot be experienced outside me, it has to be experienced within me. The word "within" should not lead us to think that this Spirit is something in our mind like an idea or feeling. The gate leading to the Supreme Spirit is my very self, which refers to itself as "I." As the Supreme Spirit is never an object, it has to be understood as an "I," within my "I," as the witness (*sākṣi*) of my "I," and as transcending it, though within it. We may say that it is an "I am" within my "I am." We may say also that the Supreme Spirit's "I am" is deeper, higher, greater, or more comprehensive—spatial meanings are really inapplicable here—than my "I am."

The above relationship is difficult to comprehend and is susceptible to a variety of interpretations even without reference to space and time. Śaṅkara said that the Vedāntic aphorism referred to has to be understood literally. The Brahman (Supreme Spirit) is my spirit itself (*ātman*). My apparent "I" is only my ego (*ahaṁkāra*). There is an absolute, transcendental identity between my *ātman* and the Brahman. Madhva took the opposite view and did not take the aphorism literally. Indeed, the Brahman is realized as "I am," but not as an object in the form, "That is." But there is only similarity between my "I am" and the Brahman's "I am"; yet they are absolutely different. The other Vedāntins say that the Brahman is the Ātman of my *ātman* and is within me as the root of my being, and that both the passages teaching identity and difference are equally true. But in reconciling identity and difference, opinions differ again. Rāmānuja maintains that the Brahman is the Spirit of my spirit, which constitutes a part of the former's body. Others maintain different forms of identity-in-difference, which will be explained in their proper places.

Corresponding to the different interpretations of the above aphorism, which is crucial, though simple, from the religious or spiritual point of view, the Vedāntins had to develop different metaphysical views and teach different methods for realizing the Supreme. They maintained also different epistemological doctrines, although some of them can go with more than one metaphysical position. Practically all of the Vedāntins were epistemological realists and were opposed to the epistemological idealism of the Vijñānavāda Buddhism, which attained a fully developed form even before Śaṅkara; yet the Vedānta could become in their hands absolutism, idealism, realism, pluralism, and so on in different forms. Such a phenomenon shows that, although metaphysics is dependent on epistemology in that it has to use the epistemological methods, the same epistemological position can be consistent with different metaphysical systems and that, therefore, metaphysics is guided also by methods and considerations other than merely the epistemological. These other guides may be factual, religious, and existential. Because of the preponderant spiritual interest of the Vedāntic systems and of the association of most of them with Śaivism or Vaiṣṇavism, both the Nyāya-Vaiśeṣika and the Sāṅkhya-Yoga philosophies later became Vedāntic, the followers of the Nyāya-Vaiśeṣika becoming Śaivas and of the Sāṅkhya-Yoga Vaiṣṇvas. The purely pluralistic systems of the Vedānta tended towards assimilating the Nyāya-Vaiśeṣika with some modifications, and the rest towards assimilating the Sāṅkhya-Yoga. Such assimilations, though not systematic and not of the same type, are found in both the Śaiva and the Vaiṣṇava Vedānta.

From the point of view of religion as spiritual life, all the Vedāntic schools are philosophies of self-realization. Their common exhortation, like that of Socrates, is: "Know thy self." This exhortation is not meant merely for ethical self-realization, but for spiritual self-realization and salvation. Salvation is not possible without the realization of the Supreme Spirit, which can be known not through senses and mind, but through one's own self. So man should first know his true self or spirit. At the deepest level of our being, the spirit of man and the Supreme Spirit are transparent to each other. The realization of one's spirit spontaneously and automatically leads to the realization of the Supreme Spirit. Furthermore, immortality, as existence beyond time, is not possible for our body and even mind, both of which are in constant flux and are within time. It is possible only for that in us which is beyond time. Only the spirit in us, which is a constant witness of all that is historical, can be that which is immortal. Hence the interest in spirit in the Upaniṣads and the Vedāntic systems is keen, primary, and very strong; and they take very great pains to understand and explain its nature. Yet the schools differ from one another in their developed doctrines.

Of all the Vedāntic schools, those of Śaṅkara, Rāmānuja, and Madhva are the most important. They have the largest following and the largest amount of literature in the form of commentaries, independent treatises (*prakaraṇagranthas*), and polemics against one another. In their writings, we find some of the most illuminating analyses of epistemological, metaphysical, and spiritual ideas. The present work, although it cannot deal with much of such analyses and is not intended to deal with them, will discuss the three schools in some detail, and some of the rest in a general way.

NOTES

[1]Cp. the Śaiva, Vaiṣṇava, Śākta, and the general (*sāmānya*) Vedānta Upaniṣads.

[2]*Vedāntasūtras*, I, iv, 20.

[3]Ibid., I, iv, 21. [4]Ibid., I, iv, 22.

[5]Cp. Husserl's idea of the transcendental ego as the witness consciousness, but note the differences also.

[6]IV, i, 3.

Chapter XI

The Vedānta of Śaṅkara: Non-Dualism

1. INTRODUCTION

Although Śaṅkara is regarded as the founder of the non-dualistic Vedānta, which developed mainly through his commentary on Bādarāyaṇa's *Vedānta Aphorisms*, the line of thought is at least as old as the Upaniṣads themselves. A few centuries before Śaṅkara, the Vijñānavāda and the Mādhyamika Buddhists began calling their ultimate reality non-dual (*advaya*). The Prajñāparamitā literature, which is perhaps earlier than the birth of Christ, repeatedly uses the word non-dual. Bhartṛhari (6th century), the author of *Vākyapadīya*, which is perhaps the first great work on the deeper philosophical basis of grammar, developed his philosophy along non-dualistic lines. It is said that he became a Buddhist before he became again a Vedāntin. About the same time, Gauḍapāda, the grand teacher (teacher's teacher) of Śaṅkara wrote his *Māṇḍūkya-kārikās* and used a language very reminiscent of Vijñānavāda Buddhism, and even incorporated some of its ideas. The logical significance of Māyā was already clarified by Buddhism in terms of the four-cornered negation. Gauḍapāda and after him the whole Advaita tradition incorporated it. Nāgārjuna maintained that, from the ultimate point of view, the world is neither born, nor exists, nor disappears (*ajātivāda*). Gauḍapāda incorporated it into his Vedānta developed out of the *Māṇḍūkya Upaniṣad*. The forms of the world are like hallucinations, due to the principle of the Unconscious (*avidyā*, Ignorance). They are forms of mere flux appearing as Being, like the circle of fire that appears when a fire brand is moved in a circle with great speed. All such ideas are Buddhist, the only difference being that they have no ontological basis at least for the Mādhyamika Buddhism, while they are all rooted in the Being of the Brahman for Gauḍapāda.

But Gauḍapāda did not develop his ideas further, and the only work left by him seems to be his *Māṇḍūkyakārikās*. The task of developing the system, of entering into controversies with other religious and philosophical schools, and of commenting on the three basic works of the Vedānta—the Upaniṣads, the *Vedānta Aphorisms*, and the *Bhagavadgītā*—were left to Śaṅkara. On almost every count, Śaṅkara was a genius. His life lasted only for about thirty years. During this short span of life, he wrote not only the above commentaries, but also several other works, called his *Minor Works*; he is even said to have been the author of *Prapañcasāratantra*, which is a Śākta monistic treatise, the teachings of which do not according to some scholars, agree with much of the Vedānta and which is yet not proved conclusively to have been written by another person of the same name, so that the tradition can be discounted. He travelled by foot almost to every part of India, entered into controversies with every rival school and defeated and converted their greatest leaders to his philosophy. Till then, Buddhism and Jainism, particularly the former, were in the ascendant. But Śaṅkara defeated their leaders, converted most of them, and revived the orthodox religions and philosophies. He showed his genius also for organization by dividing the whole of India into four regions, placing each under one monastery, the one in Sringeri being the most important.[1] To each of the monasteries, he appointed a pontiff, whose duty it was to travel through the region, administer to the spiritual needs of the people, and supervise their socio-ethical relationships. And he was a fragile ascetic. No wonder, therefore, that his personality, in spite of his short life, came to be admired by all the intellectuals of India, whether or not they accepted his views. Every subsequent philosopher, whether or not he was a Vedāntin, had to reckon with the views of Śaṅkara.

Śaṅkara's own commentaries and other works were commented upon by several of his followers, the greatest of whom, known for developing his philosophy further, are Vācaspati (9th century), Sarvajñātman (9th century), Padmapāda and Prakāśātman (12th century), Śrī Harṣa (12th century), Citsukha (13th century), Vidyāraṇya (14th century), Madhusūdana (16th century), and Appaya Dīkṣita (16th century). Śrī Harṣa and Citsukha are the greatest dialecticians of this school and perhaps of the world also. Appaya Dīkṣita is well-known for his work in bringing together all the sub-schools of this school. Vidyāraṇya (also known it is said, as Mādhavācārya) was a great statesman and prime minister of the Vijayanagar Empire and it is said that the city of Vijayanagar (originally called Vidyānagar) was founded after his name. It is even said that he acted as the commander-in-chief of the army. His *Pañcadaśī*, Sadānanda's *Vedāntasāra* (15th century), and Dharmarāja's *Vedāntaparibhāṣa* (16th century) are three of the standard, systematic, introductory works. This school has had a vigorous and systematic development in the hands of many more thinkers and scholars. One of Rāmānuja's followers, Vedānta Deśika (13th century), wrote a book called *Śatadūṣanī* (*Hundred Defects*) to disprove Śaṅkara, to which an answer is given by M. M. Anatakrishna Sastry during the last decade of the last century in his book called *Satabhūṣanī* (*Hundred Jewels*) — which is an indication of the interest which the Indian intellectuals still have in the philosophy of Śaṅkara.[2]

2. EPISTEMOLOGY

Śaṅkara's main works being commentaries, it is difficult to say how many kinds of the means of valid cognition (*pramāṇas*) were accepted by him. He is said to have accepted three main sources — perception, inference, and scripture or verbal testimony. But his followers accepted all the six sources accepted by Kumārila, the Mīmāmsaka. It was natural also for them to accept all the six sources, because Kumārila's Mīmāmsā is the Prior Mīmāmsā and the Vedānta is the Posterior Mīmāmsā and is supposed to be a continuation of the former. Whatever be the reasons, it is generally considered that the Advaita as a whole recognized the validity of all the six sources of knowledge. However, the Advaita dialecticians, like Śrī Harṣa,[3] do not accept any of the six, but only the ultimate, indeterminate intuition of the Brahman, which is Being itself. They show that every one of the six means of knowledge is self-contradictory.

It is difficult in this short work to give any place to Śrī Harṣa's dialectical destruction of all the epistemological doctrines. His *Khaṇḍanakhaṇḍakhādya* with even one of its commentaries devotes nearly one thousand pages of very terse language to exploding the epistemological doctrines alone. But we may give some idea of the method, which consists in showing the self-contradictions innate in every doctrine.

First, we cannot know what valid cognition (*pramā*) means. Some logicians define it as the knowledge of the real (*tattvānubhūti*).[4] But what is that reality apart from how it is known? This definition involves the self-contradictory idea of having a knowledge of the object before even knowing it. A second definition may be that it is the experience of the object as it is (*yathārthānubhava*).[5] But do you mean by "as it is" the real itself or something like the real? The first alternative has already been disposed of with the first definition. Regarding the second alternative, even an illusory object has some similarity to the so-called real; then knowledge of the unreal also may have to be called valid. So when we talk of valid knowledge, valid means of knowledge, or means of valid knowledge, we talk of something the meaning (i.e., the truth) of which is not all clear. We cannot, therefore, say that there is what is called validity of knowledge. Then the validity of perception also becomes an empty idea. If perception is defined as the cognition of an individual object that is different from the other objects of the same class and from all the others of all the other classes, it becomes impossible;[6] for the other objects of the same class and the other classes do not become the content of that cognition. If they are all excluded, then we cannot say that the perception is, for instance, "That is a horse," and the question of its validity does not arise. For the cognition is then confined to the perceiver's mind only. Many of the objections raised by contemporary western epistemologists against the validity of perception are raised by Śrī Harṣa also. If perception goes, inference and the other forms of cognition go with it, as it is their basis.

The above destructive dialectic is not followed by most of the followers of Śaṅkara. Their explanation of the different means of valid cognition is the same as that of the Mīmāmsā and is realistic. But the analysis of perception, which is based upon a new theory of the mechanism of knowledge, is on the whole different from that of the Mīmāmsā. According to the Advaita, perception is a function (*vṛtti*) of the inner sense (instrument) which consists of four[7] parts or levels — mind (*manas*), ego (*ahaṁkāra*), reason (*buddhi*), and apperception (*citta*). The function of mind is analysis and synthesis of whatever is perceived by the senses. When I see an apple, my mind first gets all the impressions of colour, shape, taste, etc., synthesizes them and separates the total unified object thus built up from other objects. The function of the ego then is to appropriate the object as its object as in "I see an apple." Reason then makes the object an existing object in the form, "That is an apple." Until reason does its work, the object is an object of my experience, not an object of the common world. The function of reason is to make it an object of the objective world through an assertion or decision. "That is an apple" is the result (*phala*, *Ergebnis*) of the decision of reason. But the inner instrument goes further in its work. In turning the sensations into a unified object, the inner instrument brings in past experiences also into the unity, relates the apple to the tree, to my eating, its price and so forth. This relating is the function of apperception (*citta*, that which gathers or collects), which collects different ideas about the object and relates them. These four functions of the inner sense are nearly the same as in the Sāṅkhya, which speaks of only three. But even in the Advaita, there is the tendency to speak of only three or even two, clubbing mind with ego, and reason with apperception.

To the above analysis, the Advaitins add another factor from their doctrine of the Unconscious (Avidyā). Before the perceptual cognition of the apple arises, I am ignorant, unconscious of its existence. The darkness of this Unconscious has to be lighted up for the cognition to arise. It is lighted up by the consciousness present in the senses and mind coming into contact with the object. When the light in my consciousness, reflected in mind and senses, lights up the area, the objects of that area are disclosed. And this disclosure is effected by my mind, which acts through the senses and takes the form of the object. The object has its own reality, its own place in the cosmos. But my mind also has the power to take on exactly the same form, and then abstract the mental form later, if necessary, for instance, when it remembers the object.[8]

As the Advaitins generally follow the Mīmāmsā in their explanations of the other forms of the valid means of cognition like inference, they need not be discussed again.[9] But we may note that what the Advaitins insist upon in the case of perception is that it reveals, along with the forms, Being (*sattā*) that is common to every existent and without which the forms cannot be real and cannot have objective status. In "That is a cow" and "That is a horse," along with the forms of the cow and the horse, Being also is revealed through the "is," whether or not we express our cognition in words. The Advaitins reject the grammarian view that the name is necessarily involved in all cognition and that when I perceive a horse, the word horse also is an object of cognition. This Advaita view is the same as that of the Mīmāmsā. In the analysis of verbal knowledge, both reject the grammarian doctrine of the eternal word (*sphoṭa*).

There is one doctrine peculiar to the Advaita. If there is conflict between perception and inference, the Advaitins say that we should accept inference and reject perception. Similarly, if there is conflict between inference and scriptural testimony, we should accept the latter and reject the former. The other Vedāntins, although they give scripture the highest place, do not want to reject any of the valid means of cognition, and say that, in cases of conflict, they should be reconciled and none of them treated as false. If perception tells us that the object at a distance is water, and inference from the place being a desert tells us that it is a mirage, the Advaitins say that the former is false and latter alone is true. But the other Vedāntins want to regard both as true — which, the Advaitins think, is unjustified. Again, accepting the principle of self-contradictoriness as the mark of falsity, if dialectical reason shows that the world of the manifold is self-contradictory, we have to accept its ultimate falsity and the truth of the Brahman. But none of the other Vedāntins is prepared to deny ultimate reality to the world and does not want to reject any of the valid means of knowledge at any level. The Advaitins retort that, in that case, the very basis for the distinction between truth and falsity, reality and unreality, existence and non-existence, will be destroyed.[10]

VALIDITY OF KNOWLEDGE So far as the validity of cognition goes, the Advaitins, except their dialecticians, go with the Mīmāmsakas.[11]

THE OBJECT OF ILLUSION Regarding the status of the object of illusion, the Advaitins reject the Mīmāmsā doctrines of Kumārila and Prabhākara and come very close to the doctrines of Mahāyāna Buddhism, incorporating its view that the object of illusion is neither real (*sat*), nor unreal (*asat*), nor both, nor neither. The Advaitins mean that the illusory object is inexplicable (*anirvacanīya*) in terms of reality and unreality, or of existence and non-existence. But there is an important difference from the Mādhyamika Buddhists, for whom the basis of the illusory object is the Void (Śūnya), which also is explained in terms of the four-cornered negation, i.e., as inexplicable. Thus the ultimate inexplicable, viz., the Void, is seen in illusion as the proximate inexplicable. Such an explanation cuts at the very root of the distinction between truth and falsity, as both are inexplicable. The Advaitins say that this distinction is primary for all epistemology and that we have to say, therefore, that something that is true and real is the basis or the locus (*adhikaraṇa*, *adhiṣṭhāna*) of the object of illusion. In illusion we mistake one object for another object, e.g., a rope for a snake. We have then two perceptions in the form, "That is a snake" and "That is a rope," and for several reasons we treat the former as false and the latter as true. But what is false is the predicate "snake" in the former judgment. The That is never false and is the same as the That in the latter judgment. We have to accept that both the Thats are the same, as, otherwise, there will be no contradiction between the two judgments and contradiction alone can make at least one of the judgments false. If I say: "That is a pen" and "That is a pencil," and if the two demonstratives are different, there is no conflict between the two propositions and neither of them need be false. But if the two Thats are the same and point to the same object, one proposition at least has to be false. We can of course find out whether the object is a pen or pencil by writing, i.e., action (*arthakriyākāritā*).

Thus falsity applies only to the predicate and the subject to which the predicate belongs remains comparatively undisturbed. In the rope-snake example, the subject is later discovered to be a rope and we have, therefore, to say that the rope, which is the real object, is mistaken for the snake. That is, falsity has its foundation in truth, and unreality in reality. The Advaitins do not, therefore, accept the Vijñānavāda doctrine that the real basis of illusion is pure consciousness (*vijñāna*) or the Mādhyamika view that it is pure Void (Śūnya). For even if the pure consciousness or the Void is accepted as the ultimate reality, it forms the ground or basis of everything, both true and false, and cannot explain their distinction. One may object that the Advaitin's Brahman also forms such a basis. Besides, both the real world and illusion are Māyā to both schools, and Māyā is the same again to both. But the Advaitin would ask: "Then how and where do we get the ideas of truth and falsity?" We get them in empirical reality. In it an empirically true object forms the basis of an empirically false one.

Indeed, both the Advaitins and the Buddhists accept the pragmatic criterion (*arthakriyākāritā*) so far as the reality of this world goes. But here also there is a difference.[12] Even when there is conflict between the two propositions, "That is a snake" and "That is a rope," we do not know which of them is false. We can decide one way or another by testing whether or not the object performs the function for which it is meant. We find that the object performs the function as a rope, but not as a snake; and we treat, therefore, the latter proposition as true. Here the Buddhists say that *reality is, therefore, the same as the capacity to perform that function.* But the Advaitins say *that reality has that capacity, but is not the same as that capacity.*[13] Indeed, the capacity has no existence apart from that reality. The rope has its own existence and also performs its function; but when it has no occasion to perform that function, even then it is a rope and has its being.

The Advaitins reject all the other views on the object of illusion, using the arguments of each against the rest. Their doctrine is called the doctrine, according to which illusory cognition is the cognition of an inexplicable object (*anirvacanīyakhyāti*) in terms of reality, existence, or truth. We cannot say that the illusory snake is existent, for its existence is contradicted by the later proposition; we cannot say that it is non-existent, for a non-existent object, like the son of a barren woman, is never perceived, but the snake is perceived; we cannot treat it as both existent and non-existent, for then we violate the principle of contradiction; and we cannot say that it is neither, for there is no third alternative. The snake faces us, Being (Existence[14]) shines forth through it, it is not imaginary. The imaginary leads to no activity, but the snake makes us either to run or to kill.

THE PRINCIPLE OF INEXPLICABILITY The inexplicable then is not actually the non-existent, the unreal, the false, although these terms are used in popularized expositions. It is what faces us, and yet what cannot be explained as existent or non-existent. It is what contains within itself the element of self-contradictoriness. So far as our perceptual experience goes, which is really the basis for our distinction between truth and falsity, there is no self-contradiction in existence as such or in non-existence as such. The object before me is a pen, it is not a pencil; the pen exists, the pencil does not exist. There is no self-contradiction in either or both the statements taken together with an "and" (as a conjunctive statement), and we discover none even later. But in the illusory object, which we perceive, we discover self-contradiction in terms of the very basic ideas of existence and non-existence. When we discover that the object is really a rope, we say that the snake not only does not exist now, but also did not exist even when we actually perceived it. What we perceived when we perceived the snake is now known as the perception of the self-contradictory. The snake, unlike the circular square, is not a self-contradictory concept, but a self-contradictory percept, a percept that contains its own contradiction.

So far, the thought of the Advaitin is moving within the world of ordinary experience, the world held together by the ideas of space, time, causation, substance, attribute, etc. But are all these ideas self-consistent? If they are not, how can the world be self-consistent? If it is self-contradictory, it also has to be treated as inexplicable (*aniryacanīya*), as having a falsity or truth similar in logical significance, but not exactly the same as that of the snake. We have so far taken the rope as an existent object. But it exists in space and time; it is caused by something, made by somebody, and is the cause of something; and it is a substance with attributes. If none of these categories is self-consistent and every one of them self-contradictory, then the rope also must have a self-contradictory being. At this stage, the Advaitins use much of the destructive dialectic found in Western thought and also in Buddhism to show that none of the categories is self-consistent. Space is extension and is divisible. If the ultimate parts of space are extension-less, even an infinite number of extension-less points cannot produce extension, just as a hundred zeros cannot produce 1. If the parts have extension, they must be further divisible. Then how can an extension of one inch have an infinite number of parts? If both one inch and one yard have each an infinite number of parts, they will have equal parts and must, therefore, be equal. The same argument *mutatis mutandis* is advanced against time. Similarly, causation is inexplicable. We say that *A* is the cause of *B*, after *A* has changed into *B*. But before *B* appears, there is only *A*; and when *B* appears, we do not see *A*. When we see *A* only, we cannot say that it is the cause of *B*; and when we see *B*, there is no *A*, which is to be its cause. Furthermore, *A* is the cause with reference to *B*; *B* is, therefore, the ground for *A* being its cause. Then *B* causes *A* to be its cause. But if *A* cannot exist when *B* exists, how can *B* have any influence on *A*? And also, how can we point to *A* as the cause of *B*? How can we say that *A* *is* the cause of *B*? We cannot say also *A* *was* the cause of *B*, for when *A* existed, *B* was not there. Hence, causation is a self-contradictory idea. It is neither existent nor non-existent.[15]

Likewise, substance and attribute are self-contradictory ideas. Who has ever seen substance? We perceive only qualities like colours and sounds. But if objects are groups of qualities, how can objects interact? When I break a stone, do I break a group of qualities? Qualities are passive beings; they neither come into contact nor act on one another. So the categories of substance and attribute also are self-contradictory. Besides, if substance and attribute are related, what is the nature of their relation? Any relation is said to exist between two terms. But how is the relation related to the terms? If it is related by other relations, and they again by other relations, we end up in an infinite regress. If it is not related, we cannot understand how it can pull the terms together. If it is related eternally to the terms, we cannot explain how terms change their relations.

With the help of dialectic, the Advaitins attempt to destroy[16] the ultimate validity of the categories of all the schools. The aim of their dialectic is not to establish acosmism—although some philosophers may draw such a conclusion—but to show that there is something, viz., the Brahman, higher and deeper than the world and not explicable in terms of any category except that of Being (*sat*, *sattā*). The categories of the world are not themselves Being, but concepts meant for the world of action (*vyavahāra*). The Advaita thought works according to the principle that every thing that is self-contradictory and so false must have as its basis something that is relatively nonself-contradictory and true. The Brahman is the ultimately and absolutely nonself-contradictory (*abādhya*) and true, because it is non-conceptual, indeterminate Being. It is Being itself, in which Being and consciousness are identical. They must be identical, because Being is posited by our epistemological consciousness (*jñāna*). If it is different from consciousness, the latter will again form concepts about the former, and self-contradictions will again creep in with conceptualizations. But everything that is self-contradictory presupposes something that is not self-contradictory; it is self-contradictory with reference to something, whether clearly or vaguely apprehended.

LEVELS OF REALITY The idea of relative nonself-contradiction brought into the Advaita the doctrine of levels of reality or existence, which are not degrees of truth—the mistake of calling them degrees of truth has been committed by some writers—as they do not contain a graduated measure of more and more of truth. One may call them levels of Being (*sattā*). The Advaita propounds four levels of Being, known through whatever corresponds to the "is" in our expressions. The lowest of them is insignificant Being or existence (*tucchasattā*). It is the merely imaginary, the fanciful, the accepted as self-contradictory. Examples are the horns of a hare, the lotuses of the heavenly river (sky-lotuses), the son of a barren woman, the circular square, etc. They may belong to imagination or thought, but are acknowledged as having no place in reality. Their being is said to be insignificant, because it has no significance for epistemology. Still it is a kind of being, for we say: "The son of a barren woman *is* a baby born to a woman who never bears any children." This is an obvious self-contradiction in definition and description. The Advaita logicians have not drawn a distinction between what is logically impossible like the son of a barren woman and what is factually not true like the horns of a hare. What they have in mind is our recognition, without doubt, that the object, whether of imagination or thought, is false. Yet it is an object; otherwise, we do not say that it is false. The subjective side of the cognition of such objects is not false; that I have before my imagination a hare with horns is not false and that I am thinking of a circular square is not false. As objects in my mind or thought, they have being, but only insignificant being; *my reason (buddhi) does not make the assertion or decision that they belong to objective reality*; on the other hand, my reason makes no assertion at all. Logically speaking, falsity arises only when reason makes the assertion, as in the case of the perception of the snake.

The next higher level is that of the illusory being (*prātibhāsikasattā*) or apparent being. An example is the perception of the illusory snake. Here reason makes the assertion, "That is a snake," and then discovers that its assertion has to be contradicted. The level higher than that of the illusory being is that of the pragmatic being (*vyāvahārikasattā*), often inadequately translated as empirical reality. This is the being that conforms to our activity. It has often been misunderstood, because of the fine shade of difference between the Advaita and Buddhism on this idea. It is the product of our past ethical actions (*karmas*) and is meant for future actions.[17] While the illusory being is contradicted by perceptual experience within the world itself and also by the experience of action, the pragmatic being is not contradicted either by perception or action, but by dialectical reason and intuition of the Brahman. The innate and ultimate self-contradictions of the pragmatic world are revealed to the light of reason by its own self-reflection. *That is why, even if I am convinced dialectically of the rational incoherence of the world, when I look in front of me I see the same objects existing and not contradicting my active life; whereas when once the perception of the illusory snake is contradicted by the perception of the rope, I can no longer see the snake with the same eyes, and my active life also contradicts the being of the illusory snake.*[18] However, just as illusory being presupposes pragmatic being, the latter also, because of inherent self-contradictions, presupposes the ultimate Being (*pāramārthikasattā*).

Each of the above lower levels presupposes and is superimposed (*adhyasta*) upon the higher. Śaṅkara does not actually say that the imaginary object is superimposed on the illusory, but we may say that it is superimposed on, (projected by) our mind.

If, for the reason that at this level being is not asserted at all, this level is left out of consideration as insignificant for epistemology, we may say only that the snake is superimposed on the rope and the rope on the Brahman.

MĀYĀ AND AVIDYĀ Of the above four levels of Being, the lowest, as we have said, is not worth epistemologically discussing at all, since nobody raises the question of truth and falsity about what every one regards as having no existence. Significance attaches to the other three levels. When the illusory object, e.g., the snake, is contradicted and negated, it exists nowhere as an independent object. Only objects not so negated are assigned by us existence independent of our minds. When negated, some of us say that they are fabrications of our imagination or thought. Indeed, the illusory object appears as having independent existence so long as it is perceived and before it is negated. What is so negated and whatever can be so negated is regarded by us as false.

Then, although for a different type of reason, we declare the world to be self-contradictory, should we regard it also as false? The illusory snake is self-contradictory, for it is first declared to be existent and later as non-existent. Otherwise, it cannot be illusory. For instance, the son of a barren woman is not called an illusion, because he is never declared to be existent. He is not even a false object. Then if we accept the characteristic of falsity or illusion to be self-contradictoriness in terms of Being and Non-being and if the world also is shown to be similarly self-contradictory, should we not declare the world also to be false and illusory? Indeed, there are two kinds of difference between the illusory snake and the world. *First*, the snake is illusory from the standpoint of the pragmatic world, but the pragmatic world is illusory from the standpoint of ultimate Being. *Secondly*, the snake is contradicted perceptually and through action, but the world is contradicted only dialectically.[19] But whatever be the difference, both are contradicted. Then should we call the world also an illusion?

The general tendency of the Advaita as a whole is to use the word Māyā, meaning falsity, for both the types. The word falsity is a relative term, and we have always to ask: "With reference to what is something false?" The snake is false with reference to the rope, but the rope is false with reference to the Brahman. The rope is not false with reference to any object at its level, e.g., to the cow that is tied by it to a pole. Again, if we do not have the cognition of the rope, the cognition of the snake cannot be false. But when it is forgotten that falsity is a relative term, the Advaita may be accused of placing the world on the same level as the snake's.

Indeed, it may be objected that what is dialectically false should not be called false, but by some other adjective. But unfortunately, we generally use two-valued logic (truth and falsity), and two-valued metaphysics and ontology (real and unreal, existent and non-existent, and Being and Non-being). The Advaitins did the same and had no other means.[20] But it should be clear now what the Advaitins mean by the four levels of Being. We can also understand why the Advaitins say that inference and scripture have to be accepted and perception rejected in cases of conflict; for the Brahman is established by the scripture and dialectic, which is a form of inference, and the world by perception. We can see, furthermore, why the other Vedāntins object to rejecting perception in such cases and advocate reconciliation. For instance, why should we not treat the perceptual world as real and treat it and the other lower levels as depending on the higher? Cannot the idea of dependence, which Madhva introduces, solve our difficulty? The Advaitins accept the idea, but say that it does not solve the difficulty; for the idea of self-contradictoriness as the mark of falsity has still to be accepted. If we accept it, the world has to be regarded as illusory and false, although relatively to the Brahman.

The Advaitins use the word Māyā to mean the appearance of the object as an existent and its non-existence at a higher level. It is a mystery that the snake should appear as an independent and individual object, although the real object is a rope; and equally mysterious is it that we are living and acting in a world the forms of which are ultimately self-contradictory and having no being of their own. What is self-contradictory cannot have a being of its own, i.e., it cannot be real. The word Māyā expresses this mystery. Again, if the world is an illusion, it is an illusion for every human being. Every human being experiences it. But the snake is not experienced by every man; out of a group of men looking at the rope, only one or some may see it as a snake. The world is, therefore, a cosmic illusion, whereas the false snake is an individual illusion. For drawing this difference, some Advaitins call the individual's illusion Avidyā (Unconscious). By nature, both Māyā and Avidyā are the same; Avidyā, we may say, is only a part[21] of Māyā, just as the individual's reason is a part of the Logos. But the word "part" should not be understood, as if Māyā can be divided into parts. However, many Advaitins do not like to draw any distinction between the two and they treat them as synonyms. We may understand that Māyā is what corresponds to the cosmic Unconscious, the creative force behind the cosmos; and Avidyā is what corresponds to the individual Unconscious.[22] The latter is rooted in the former. Māyā and Avidyā should not be treated as mere falsities in the sense of properties of propositions, but as creating and constituting false experiences at different levels in different ways. One may not accept the Advaita doctrine of the four levels of Being, in which the second and the third are falsities; but one will not understand the Advaita if one does not keep in mind that the words Māyā and Avidyā mean dynamic forces (*śaktis*) creative of the mysteries at both the levels. The two are identified with the Upaniṣadic Avyakta (Unmanifest) and Prakṛti; and the significance of the identification is missed, if Avidyā is understood as only negative ignorance. It may be ignorance too in some contexts, but it is much more besides.

So long as Māyā or Avidyā lasts, man can know the Brahman only as a presupposition of the discovered self-contradictory nature of the world. To realize the presence of the Brahman, just as I realize the presence of my body, requires meditation and transcendence of the ordinary means of valid cognition. The highest kind of knowledge, in which knowledge and Being are one, will be discussed next.

Higher and Lower Knowledge Although the pragmatic criterion (*artha-kriyākāritā*) enables us to distinguish what is empirically true from the empirically false, the criterion itself is not without its defects. Śaṅkara and his followers are aware of the defects and refuse to accredit the criterion with absolute validity. *First*, what is false also may produce the results that can be produced by the true. A man may tread upon a thorn in the dark, think that he is bitten by a snake, and die of shock, as though a real snake had bitten him. *Secondly*, the cognition that the object meets the pragmatic criterion is itself a judgment and needs further verification, if questioned. And this process of verification has to be carried out *ad infinitum*. So we can never have final certainty about any cognition at the empirical level. *Thirdly*, mere coherence (*samvāda*) leads to infinite regress, as every validating judgment has, in its turn, to be validated by another. Only that cognition which is uncontradictable (*abādhya*)—not merely the uncontradicted (*abādhita*)—can be known as absolutely true. The others are only approximations to truth, they are practical truths. What is uncontradictable is a cognition that is integral experience, in which there can be no distinction between subject and object, and subject and predicate. Wherever the former distinction is found, the latter distinction is unavoidable. Higher knowledge is the experience of the Brahman, of Being as such; it is intuition, integral experience. All the valid means of cognition are forms of lower knowledge and lead only to such forms. Even knowledge of the Vedic scriptures is lower knowledge; for it is only verbal knowledge, knowledge about the Brahman, but not direct knowledge or intuition of the Brahman. Such direct knowledge is experienced, as the *Vedāntic Aphorisms* say, as the cognition of one's own Ātman, as one's own "I am." Our reasoning also, along the lines of the four levels of Being, shows that integral experience has to be such, viz., the final intuition of the Brahman. The criterion for higher knowledge is non-contradictability (*abādhyatvam*).[23] For lower knowledge, one may use the criterion of the agreement (*samvāda*) of two cognitions about the same object or agreement of the object and the action to which it leads (*arthakriyākāritā*). Indeed, the doctrine of higher and lower knowledge is as old as the Upaniṣads. But the Advaitins have given it a systematic explanation. We find it in the Mahāyāna distinction between worldly truth (*samvṛtisatya*) and ultimate truth (*paramārthasatya*). But the Mahāyānists do not like to include in their conception of ultimate truth any reference to Being (*sattā*); for Being belongs, according to them, to the world of becoming, which is a combination of Being and Non-being, and Being is the capability (potency, *śakti*) to serve the purpose meant and Non-being is the incapability to serve it. But according to the Advaitins, Being can exist apart from Non-being, though becoming cannot exist without Being.

3. METAPHYSICS

The metaphysics of Śaṅkara is devoted to the establishment of the reality of only the Brahman, to showing that the world cannot have an independent being of its own,[24] to demonstrating that its being is the Being of the Brahman itself in which it is rooted, and to pointing out that the causality of the Brahman in creating the world is such as not to effect the plenitude and perfection of its Being. For the purpose, Śaṅkara found the concept of Māyā the most suitable. Full and complete demonstration of the Advaita position is not found in Śaṅkara's writings in a connected way. His followers right up to the 16th and even the 20th century, analyzed, developed, and systematized his concepts and doctrines through controversies with rival schools, particularly those of Rāmānuja and Madhva. In this systematization, they brought to light many implications and explained them.

THE BRAHMAN Śaṅkara accepts the reality of the Brahman primarily on the basis of the Upanisads. But in his controversies with the schools that do not accept the Vedic authority, he develops independent arguments. The Brahman is described in different ways by the Upaniṣads, and the descriptions boil down ultimately into three constitutive characteristics: Being (*sattā*), Consciousness (*cit*), and Bliss (*ānanda*). The first two are relevant to epistemology and metaphysics, and the third to aesthetics and the life of salvation. Śaṅkara would show, so far as metaphysics is concerned, the ultimate truth of the Brahman in terms of Being and Consciousness. But actually in his writings, the discussions are mixed up with other considerations.

We have seen, in the discussion of the four levels of Being, the highest or the fourth is presupposed by the third and this presupposition is based upon the epistemological principle that every falsity presupposes a truth. We may say that even the imaginary, like the horns of a hare,[25] which we consider to be below the realm of truth and falsity, is called imaginary, because we have experience of objects, like the rope, that cannot be produced by our sweet will, while the horns of a hare can be produced so in our imagination. Now, if the snake is false and yet appears as a being, its appearance, as independent of our mind, is due to the fact that it has the borrowed being of the rope. Similarly, the world of forms, in spite of their being self-contradictory and false, appears as being, because the Being of the Brahman or Being that is the Brahman shines through the world. When we say: "That man exists" or "That is a man," the meaning of the expression is "Being shines through the form of man there." Without Being shining or gleaming through the form in front of us, there can be no perception, but only imagination. In perception Being reveals itself and through itself reveals the object (the particular form or shape) man. If and when Being does not shine through that form, the form, man, is called a mere idea or mental image and we say: "That man does not exist." So the appearance of the forms of the world as existing presupposes the truth of Being.

But this Being is Consciousness itself. Consciousness accompanies all our cognitions. When I see a mountain at a distance, my consciousness is there where the mountain exists and it is also there where my "I" stands. It is present in imagination, in perception, and in inference. And unless it knew the nonself-contradictoriness of Being, it could not have called the world self-contradictory.[26] It is present wherever Being is present. Furthermore, Being that is present to consciousness at the highest level cannot be different from that consciousness; otherwise, Being becomes an object. But objectivity, as in the case of the world, is vitiated by self-contradiction. Nor consciousness at that level is the epistemological subject. For the subject also, as set over against the object, becomes another object with the same self-contradictions. So the Being, which my consciousness at my level postulates is the root of the being of my consciousness and is, therefore, the same as the Being that shines through the world. The consciousness that knows the world has as much falsity as the world itself has. So through both my subjective consciousness and the objective world, the same Being shines. I think, therefore, that I, as this finite being, exist and that the object also exists. The ultimate Being that is consciousness also is the Brahman itself.

THE BRAHMAN AND THE EGO We have already introduced a distinction between my "I," as my conscious ego, and the Brahman, as both Being and consciousness and as the root of the being of myself and of the world. I am able to say that "I am," that I exist, that I am a being, only because my "I am" is rooted in the Brahman, which is the ground of all existing objects. When I want only to assert my existence, I stop with saying that "I am"; but I say also that I am so many feet tall, have such a complexion, am a professor and so on. But the Brahman does not say anything of that kind, but only "I am." It shines through me as the witness of my self, my actions, my cognitions, my states. In cognition, I am able to say that I know that I know the pen,[27] which is a cognition of cognition, due to the presence of consciousness that accompanies me and my activities and which is continuous with my particular I-consciousness, and yet higher and deeper than it. It is called the witness-consciousness (*sākṣicaitanya*), an idea first found in the *Muṇḍaka Upaniṣad* and later elaborated by the Sāṅkhya.

But is this witness-consciousness[28] the same as the Brahman? The Advaitins are not unanimous in their answers. Śaṅkara seems to have followed the general trend of the Upaniṣads and to have been content with showing the ultimate identity of the ego with the higher witness-consciousness, treating the latter as the Brahman and the former as an appearance. But his followers found difficulties in equating the witness-consciousness to the Brahman and gave, therefore, different answers.[29] The witness-consciousness witnesses, in an undisturbed and unaffected way, all that I do and know and also all that I dream. But if this witness is the same as the Brahman, then it must be the witness-consciousness of all the other egos also, for the same Brahman is present in all egos. Then just as my ego is continuous with my witness-consciousness, the other egos also must be continuous with it and be able to know all that I do and know. But they do not. So some Advaitins identify the witness-consciousness with the I-consciousness (*prajñā*) in deep sleep, according to the *Māṇḍūkya Upaniṣad*, and give it a lower place than to the Brahman. Some say that it is one form of the Brahman as the personal God (Īśvara)—which will be explained later—witnessing everything I do and enjoy. For every ego then, there will be a separate witness-consciousness, which will be one of the forms of the personal God. Then there will be the Brahman, the single personal God, and his different forms as witness-consciousness. Others do not care to introduce the idea of the personal God, but say that the witness-consciousness, as the root of everything, reveals the ego-subject, its object, and the consciousness of the object through the instrumentalities of mind and senses. In each of the above main views, there are differences also and the plurality of views shows the difficulty of the problem, which is at the same time important for understanding the I-structure.

In the above discussion, we find that between the Brahman and the "I" as the ego, two levels have been introduced, viz., those of the Īśvara-consciousness and the witness-consciousness. The ego-consciousness is continuous with the three higher levels. But for all the Advaitins, except a few, the ego is not the same as the higher levels. Even for the few exceptions, the ego can at the most know its identity and continuity with the witness-consciousness, but none at all with the personal God and the Brahman. The realization of one's continuity with the latter two is an ideal. The continuity with them exists, but is forgotten and lost, due to the veiling power of Māyā (Avidyā, the Unconscious).

THE BRAHMAN AND THE PERSONAL GOD Just as my ego (*ahaṁkāra*) is continuous with the Brahman, the personal God (Īśvara) also is continuous with it. Śaṅkara uses the term Brahman for both, calling them the Higher Brahman (*parabrahman*) and the

Lower Brahman (*aparabrahman*). The lower Brahman is not ultimately real. It is the same as the Higher Brahman as facing the world of objectivity, i.e., with reference to the world or Māyā. Indeed, it is not overwhelmed and overpowered by Māyā, just as the witness who witnesses people fighting is not overpowered by what he witnesses. It is, therefore, not in bondage, i.e., within the power of Māyā. Finite souls only are so overpowered.

We now get two ideas of the Divine: the Absolute (Brahman) and God (Īśvara). But how can the Brahman, which is perfect, become God, the less perfect? The concept of God is full of contradictions. If God is the final truth and is, as the concept is understood, the creator of the world, which is full of evil and misery, how can such a perfect, omnipotent, omniscient, all-merciful God be the creator of evil and misery? How can we prove the existence of God? Śaṅkara examines the usual arguments for the existence of God and offers the usual criticisms. We can show only that the Brahman, which is Being and Consciousness, must be true. We cannot show that the concept of God is a true concept. We may teach that God exists as only a popular concession.

Then what is the ontological status of God? He is the Brahman with reference to the world. Although thought leads us to the idea of pure and indeterminate Being, it wants also to relate this Being to the empirical world. It thinks of Being as perfect, as having all the best qualities which, as human beings, we possess, but raised to the power of infinity. Being, as indeterminate, is quality-less (*nirguṇa*), but our thought attributes to it all the best qualities and makes it full of qualities (*saguṇa*). Thus while the Brahman is known to thought as beyond itself, God is only a thought-product.[30] The idea of God is valid only so long as the world lasts. *Sub specie aeternitatis* God has no reality; but *sub specie temporis* he is as real as the world.

GOD AND THE INDIVIDUAL SOUL Both God and the individual thus belong to the phenomenal world and have no ultimate reality. But God, unlike the finite soul, is not bound by, and is not subject to the laws of the world. The soul (*jīva*)—it is better to use the word soul for *jīva* and spirit for the *ātman*—is the same as the *ātman* and so the same as the Brahman, according to Śaṅkara. There can be no difference between the two; for difference—as we shall see—is not a valid category. The soul is the Brahman as limited (*avacchinna*) by, or reflected in (*pratibimbita*) in Avidyā (Unconscious). It consists of the Ātman (Brahman) as its basis, the internal organ, the senses, and the subtle elements. The so-called subtle body (*sūkṣmaśarīra, lingaśarīra*) is the same as the jīva, except for the Ātman present in the latter. What transmigrates is the soul, not the Ātman as such; it is the subtle body without the gross body, which is given by the parents. God (Īśvara) is the Cosmic Soul, the Cosmic Person; the *jīva* is the individual soul.[31]

The difference between God and the soul is explained by some Advaitins in terms of the distinction between Māyā and Avidyā.[32] The main position of Śaṅkara himself is that God is the Brahman itself facing or witnessing Māyā, the Cosmic Unconscious. So some of his later followers said that the soul is the Brahman with reference to Avidyā, the individual Unconscious, which is a part of Māyā. But then difficulties arise. God, as the witness of Māyā, is not involved in, and overpowered by it; then the soul also, if it is only a witness of Avidyā, must not be involved in it. But the soul is involved and indentifies itself with the processes and laws of Avidyā. Should we then think analogically that God also is involved in the Cosmic Māyā? If he is involved, how can he, like a suffering God, be a pure witness of Māyā and be the lord of its processes?

To overcome the difficulty, several ad hoc doctrines were developed by the Advaitins, to which, however, they did not attach much importance, saying that the doctrines were intellectual and contained, anyhow, inescapable contradictions. Some maintained that God is a reflection in Māyā and the soul a reflection in Avidyā. The agitations of the reflection do not affect the reflected. But the soul gets involved in Avidyā because of greater ignorance than God has. God, because of his nearness to the Brahman, does not get involved and retains his lordship. Some Advaitins who do not accept that Māyā has parts and who identify, therefore, Māyā and Avidyā, say that, as Māyā is the same as the Prakṛti of the Upaniṣads—but not exactly the same as the Prakṛti of the Sāṅkhya for the reason that Māyā, unlike Prakṛti, has no being of its own, independent of the Brahman—it has the three Attributes, the Transparent, the Active, and the Dark. God is the reflection of the Brahman in the Transparent, and the soul the reflection of the Brahman in the other two Attributes. As a reflection in the Transparent, God can remain a pure witness and retain his lordship; but as a reflection in the Active and the Dark, the soul is bound and gets involved. But there are some Advaitins who do not like the reflection theory, for it is difficult to understand how the formless Brahman can be reflected in anything. The sun is reflected in water, because he has a round shining form. So these Advaitins advocate what is called the limitation theory (*avacchedavāda*). The Brahman as limited by Māyā is God, and as limited by Avidyā is the soul. Limitation is the same as determination, qualification, characterization. Again, some Advaitins who do not differentiate between Māyā and Avidyā say that God is the Brahman limited by Māyā and the soul is the Brahman limited by the inner instrument (*antahkaraṇa*), which is a product of Māyā. There are some Advaitins who do not think that the Brahman, which is infinite and unlimited, can be limited by anything and revert to the reflection theory. They say that the soul is the reflection of the Brahman in Māyā; God is not really there as even a phenomenal being. But as every reflection must have a prototype, the Brahman *considered by our thought* as the prototype of the reflection is God. The Brahman appears to our logical intellect as God.

Because of the difficulties in both the reflection and limitation theories, some Advaitins say that both God and the soul are appearances (*ābhāsās*) of the Brahman due to Māyā. The Brahman appears as God and God appears as the soul (*jīva*).[33] These appearances cannot be explained, as they are due to Māyā, the inexplicable principle. All these differences of view show the great difficulties experienced by the Advaitins themselves in their attempt to explain the relation of the Brahman, God, and the soul with the help of Māyā. It was easy for their critics to pin them down at this point; and the Advaitins tried to escape by saying that to say that the inexplicable Māyā cannot be explained is to point to a virtue, but not to a defect.[34] Mystery is a mystery. How can the principle of inexplicability be explicable?

THE BRAHMAN AND MĀYĀ Let us, for argument's sake, accept that God, soul, and the world are all due to Māyā. But Māyā is described as an unconscious principle, the principle of the Unconscious, and, unlike the Prakṛti of the Sāṅkhya, as having no being and reality of its own. As unconscious, it cannot be the same as, or even a part of the Brahman, which is described as pure consciousness, indeterminate, and so as having no divisions within itself (*akhaṇḍa*). Then how does Māyā arise, and from where does it come? As the Brahman is the only reality and as it is pure undiluted consciousness, Māyā could not have originated in the Brahman; and it could not have come from anywhere else, for there is nowhere else. The Advaitin's answer is that the question is an ultimate one and cannot be answered. That it cannot be answered is implied in the very nature of Māyā, the essence of which is inexplicability. It is neither Being nor Non-being.

The above answer of the Advaitins does not satisfy many intellects. So the answer is advanced that it is the very nature of the Brahman to use Māyā as its power (*śakti*). Then does it belong to the Brahman? Does the Brahman contain the principle of the Unconscious within itself? How can pure undiluted consciousness contain the Unconscious as a factor? The answer again is: It is a mystery.[35] Yet the Brahman is not the same as Māyā. If Māyā is what is neither existent, nor non-existent, nor both, nor neither, then the Brahman is a negation of all the four negations, a fifth negation. But if Māyā is thus different from the Brahman, should we not say that Māyā has its own being? No, it cannot have its own being; its being is the same as the Being of the Brahman, just as the being of the power (*śakti*) to burn is the same as the being of fire. Then does Māyā remain in the Brahman just as the power to burn remains in fire, whether or not the fire is burning something? Yes, it remains in the Brahman, but not as the Unconscious; we may, therefore, say that it does not remain in the Brahman. How can we understand such a self-contradictory idea? The idea is certainly self-contradictory; it has already been said that it is inexplicable.

MĀYĀ AND AVIDYĀ We have seen that the relation between Māyā and Avidyā has been variously conceived by the Advaitins. Some identify them completely; some treat Māyā as the Cosmic Unconscious and Avidyā as the individual Unconscious and as a part of Māyā; and others say that Māyā is the Attribute, Transparent, and Avidyā the combination of the other two Attributes of Prakṛti. The last group does not separate Māyā and Avidyā, but treat them as two aspects of one and the same principle, using either word indifferently. Māyā is understood not only as ignorance but also as power, energy, force (*śakti*). In the creation of the world, it uses its two Attributes, the Active and the Dark, which also are regarded as two forces. The Dark Force veils the Brahman from us and is called the Veiling Force (*āvaraṇaśakti*); and the Active Force projects the forms of the world and is called the Projecting Force (*vikṣepaśakti*). The forms of the world are thus the projected objects and are known through the attribute, the Transparent. But often, the Advaitins speak only of the Veiling and Projecting Forces; but here and there we come across the third Force also.

THE BRAHMAN AS THE CREATOR If the Brahman is either logically or ontologically prior to everything, then it itself has to be regarded as the origin of everything. In fact, the *Vedānta Aphorisms*[36] define the Brahman as that to which the birth, maintenance, and destruction of the world have to be attributed. The Brahman is, therefore, the creator, the sustainer, and destroyer of the world. Then it must be the personal God. But Śaṅkara is not prepared to accept a personal God or attribution to the Brahman of the characteristics or qualities of being the creator, etc. For such an interpretation conflicts with the position that the Brahman is without qualities (*nirguṇa*). He reinterprets the aphorism, therefore, as meaning that the Brahman is the *ground* of everything. As we have seen when discussing the four levels of Being, each higher is the ground (*ādhāra, adhiṣtāna*) of the lower and ultimately the Brahman is the ground of all the lower levels and the world.[37] As it is the ground or basis, the Brahman is called the cause (*kāraṇa*), in the ordinary sense of the term, of the world. (The Sanskrit word *kāraṇa* means ground, support, reason, and cause also.) The aphorism is, therefore, not given by Bādarayaṇa as a causal argument for the existence of God or the Brahman. The Brahman is only the supporting Being of the forms of the world. The stuff of the forms of the world is Māyā.

Although the above view seems to be the intention of Śaṅkara, some of his later followers found difficulties with certain Upaniṣadic statements asserting that the Brahman is the cause of the world.[38] They introduced, therefore, certain modifications into the original theory, viz., that the Brahman, as the ground, remains unaffected and Māyā undergoes transformation (*pariṇāma*) for producing the objects of the world. Then why is the Brahman called the cause of the world? It is an indirect cause as Māyā has no existence apart from the Brahman. Besides, the Brahman also can be a cause, but a different type of cause, a cause that produces the effect without being affected in the process (*vivartakāraṇa*). Thus there are two kinds of material causes, the self-transforming cause (*pariṇāmakāraṇa*) and the nonself-transforming cause (*vivartakāraṇa*). An example of the former is milk as the cause of buttermilk. When milk is transformed into buttermilk, it is no longer available as milk. An example of the latter is a piece of pure glass into which colours are reflected. When red colour is reflected into it, it appears red; when green is reflected, it appears green. But all along it has never changed and is available as pure glass. The Brahman is the material cause of the world in the sense of the nonself-transforming cause. It is the material cause of everything also, because it supplies Being to all. Māyā supplies the forms. The Brahman is the efficient[39] cause also, because there is nothing else that can be such a cause. The idea that there are two kinds of material cause and that the Brahman is the efficient cause also belongs to Śaṅkara himself. However, when cornered again with the question whether the Brahman thereby does not get characterized by the quality of being some cause, whatever be the nature of causation, he would say that all such ideas and questions belong to the level of the intellect and are, by their very nature, self-contradictory.

Some of the followers of the Advaita introduced other distinctions in explaining the creativity of the Brahman.[40] The idea that the Brahman remains the nonself-transforming cause keeps it aloof from the world, whereas it is immanent everywhere as Being, though transcendent also. So some Advaitins say that the Brahman, as Being (*sattā*), is the material cause, but Māyā is only a subsidiary cause as responsible for the rising up of forms. But some others say that Māyā alone is the material cause, as the unconscious stuff of the world cannot originate in the Brahman. Still others say that the Brahman along with Māyā is the material cause,[41] as both

Being and unconsciousness are present in the world. Māyā then veils consciousness and shows only Being in the object perceived.

The above doctrines and the difficulties to solve which they have been propounded are interesting in that they show what a complicated problem the Advaitins had to face when, from the four ontological levels, they attempted to derive a cosmology or cosmogony. Unable to find a satisfactory answer, some Advaitins, like the author of *Saṅkṣepaśārīraka*, say that the four levels and cosmogony are propounded for immature minds, which ask, when told that God created the world, "Who created God?" In fact, for the consciousness that is able to rise to the highest level, there is no experience of the world, and the question of relating the world to the Brahman in any way does not arise. We may conclude by saying that the truth behind the above explanations and discussions is that the four ontological levels based on considerations of truth and falsity are not meant to demonstrate that the world is created or caused by something. The idea of causation or creation belongs to the world of objects; to carry the idea over to a realm beyond the world necessarily leads to self-contradiction. One may even ask: "What is the cause of causation? and Who created causation?" And who created truth and falsity? What is their cause? Are truth and falsity cosmological problems?

Critique of Negation and Difference Śaṅkara does not accept either the plurality of spirits (*ātmans*) or the duality of the Brahman and Prakṛti. His followers made strenuous efforts to prove the falsity of plurality and duality. Plurality and duality can be true, if negation is true, and duality can be true, if difference, and so negation, is true. Truth always means the nonself-contradictory. If we say that something is real, we have to show that it is not self-contradictory.

Difference is a form of negation, as we have seen in the chapter on the Nyāya. "*A* is different from *B*" means that *A* is not *B* and *B* is not *A*. Difference is thus a combination of two negations. But what do we mean by saying that negation is real? Do we mean that it exists? Colour exists; but does negation exist similarly? I say: "The ink is not red." Then does non-red exist? Can we say that the ink is not red, without looking at it? Certainly, we cannot. But if we look at the ink, what is it that we see? We see only black colour. It may be objected that black colour is the same as not-red and so what I see is not-red. But black is not green also; and why do I not say that it is not green? The question is not about the words red and green, but about perception or cognition itself. Why is not my cognition, at that time, of the form, "The ink is not green?"

The answer can then be that I want or have in mind the red colour and say, therefore, that the ink is not red. That is, I expect or am interested in red colour and so perceive not-red. Then, is the perception of not-red a true perception, if it is the result of expectation also? There is no sense contact with either red or not-red and "The ink is not red" cannot be a perceptual proposition. Furthermore, there is nothing corresponding to the "not" in the object before me. Negation is, therefore, only conceptual and is not a part of Being. It cannot be real in the sense in which red colour is real.

One may say that negation and affirmation, the negative and the positive are complementaries. If the ink is black, it is not red, green, etc. Yes, but if a thing is not red, can we say that it has necessarily to be black? Black implies that it is not any one of the other colours. But not-red does not imply that it is black or any other one particular colour. We cannot say what it is, unless we see it. It may be green, blue, white, or black, etc. *If negation and affirmation are complementaries, just as we say that it is black implies that it is not red, we must be able to say that it is not red implies that it is black.* But we cannot say so. So they are not complementaries. To see that the ink is black, we do not have to hold the idea that it is not red; but to see that it is not red, we have to *float* before our mind the idea of red, but *directly perceive* black. With so much difference, affirmation and negation cannot be at the same level and cannot, therefore, be complementaries.

Then in perception, can we say that the ink is not red, if we have not seen that it is black? We cannot. The perception that the ink is not red, which is a negative judgment, presupposes the perception that it is black. But the perception of which negation is presupposed by the affirmative judgment that it is black? By itself, it presupposes nothing in particular. If I expected red, then it presupposes that the ink is not red; but if I expect green, then it presupposes that the ink is not green. Without my expectation, it does not presuppose any negative judgment in particular. Then what justification is there to say that negation belongs to the objective reality itself? We are wrongly attributing what is only conceptually elaborated, i.e., true only for our thought, to objective reality itself. Reality is, therefore, pure Being (*sat*); it is positive (*bhāva*) only, not negative.

It may be asked: "Do we not say that there is absence of the rose on the table"? Absence is a form of negation. If absence can exist or is even perceived by me on the table, the negation has to be accepted as belonging to reality itself and therefore as existing. But if the absence of the rose is a definite object of perception and is objectively there, it must be different from other absences like the absence of water, of mud, and of the glass. And where one is found, the other must not be found.[42] If there is one object in one place, then no other object can exist in the same place, because they are definite objects with definite forms. If the absences also are definite objects, they must not exist in the same place and time; and if they exist, they must all be perceived at once, when any one of them is perceived. Now, on my table, there is absence of the rose, absence of water, and absence of mud. They can be found together, because they are concepts, not beings. But if one of them is perceived, the others are not necessarily perceived. Negation has, therefore, no place in Being; and ultimate reality is Being. Being does not shine directly through the negative, which is only a thought-product.

If negation is only a thought-product, then difference also is a thought-product. One may say: "I perceive the difference of *A* from *B*," just as I perceive the absence of the rose on the table. We have seen that even the perception of absence is no perception. Furthermore, is the difference between *A* and *B* identical with *A* and *B* or different from both? If it is identical with both, then my perception of both must be the same as the perception of their difference. But the two perceptions cannot be the same, for the latter includes negation, while the former is purely affirmative. Next, if the difference is different from *A* and *B*, does it exist in *A* alone, or *B* alone, or in both? It cannot exist in *A* alone or in *B* alone, as it has reference to both. It cannot belong to

A alone or *B* alone. Then, how can what does not belong to either *A* or *B*, belong to both? One may say that a bank account in the names of wife and husband meant to be operated by both only, although it cannot belong to either taken separately, has to be said to belong to both. Yes, it is so, because it is conventionally arranged. We are not talking of conventions, but of the being of difference.

It may be objected that "*A* is different from *B*" means "*A* is not *B* and *B* is not *A*." Here is raised a very basic question by the Advaitins about negation. *They distinguish between the logically significant and empty (insignificant) negation.* If I say: "The ink is not red," I make a significant negation. For I am negating what could have been or what is possible; it is possible for the ink to be red. But if I say: "Virtue is not a square," I am making an insignificant negation. I am negating what nobody thinks is possible. We have seen that no negation is possible without expectation or interest. Negation is always the negation of something; there is no negation as such that is not the negation of something. And that something has to be a possible something, not an impossible something. It must be something capable of being expected. When nobody thinks or expects virtue being a square, it is insignificant and purile to negate their identity. Then to say: "Jim is not Bill" is equally purile,[43] for who thinks that the two are identical? Similarly, "Red is not green" is equally purile. But "The ink is not red" is not purile, because it could have been red, but red could never have been green. We have seen that even significant negation has only conceptual validity, but not metaphysical validity. Difference, being an insignificant negation, *a fortiori* has no place in reality. Negation has no reality of its own, its reality or being is that of positive entities, to which it is attributed. The truth of "The ink is not red" is the same as "The ink is black," which is a positive perception and is the basis of the former.

Having dismissed negation and difference, the Advaitins find it easy to dismiss the plurality of the *ātmans* and the duality of the Brahman and Māyā. No difference or negation is possible at the highest level of Being between one *ātman* and another and between the Brahman and Māyā. Besides, the Brahman, the *ātmans*, and Māyā are all infinite. But how can there be many infinite Beings, except in thought? Thought, which contains self-contradictions, may entertain whatever concepts it finds useful; but the same thought reveals their self-contradictions and yet wants to attribute reality to them. Thought is able to realize its own self-contradictions because of its continuity with intuition or integral experience, in which it is rooted and which is aware constantly of the nonself-contradictory Being. This Being is the Brahman and is alone the ultimately true.

THE PRINCIPLE OF CAUSALITY It is wrong to think that Śaṅkara denies that the world is a cosmos. The world is an ordered whole in which the laws of space, time, and causation hold true. But we should not think that the world is a self-contained and self-consistent whole. The self-contradictory nature of every aspect of the world—spatial, temporal, causal—shows that it is not so. Yet, what lies beyond the world is not a chaos, but Being itself. The Being of the world we experience is that of the Being beyond the world, the Brahman. It is the nature of that Being to support the world in spite of self-contradictions. The self-contradictory has always a direction pointing to something that is at least relatively nonself-contradictory. And in spite of its self-contradictory nature, causality holds true in the world.

We have seen that Śaṅkara accepts two kinds of causation with reference to the material cause—"material" should not be understood in terms of physical matter, but in terms of the stuff, whatever that be—, causation in which the cause is self-transforming (*pariṇāmakāraṇa*) and causation in which the cause is nonself-transforming (*vivartakāraṇa*). He is opposed to the Nyāya-Vaiśeṣika doctrine that the effect is Non-being before it is born. It is in the state of its cause and is identical with it; but the cause is not Non-being. Before the pot appears, it is in the form of clay; and clay is not Non-being. The Nyāya-Vaiśeṣika may say that the pot is not the same as the clay and is, therefore, Non-being before it is made. But the effect is not different from the cause;[44] if it is different from the cause, we must be able to have a pot without the clay. What is new is only the form of the pot. We have then to say that the form of the pot does not have its own being before it is made, for its being is the being of the clay. As the form does not have its own being, we are justified in saying that it has no reality of its own. We may then generalize and say that no effect has a reality of its own; relatively, the cause has reality. This line of thinking leads us to the conclusion that ultimately the Brahman alone is real, all else is relatively unreal. With the same argument, Śaṅkara dismisses the view of the Buddhists that the world comes out of the Void, but not out of Being; for relatively to the effect the cause must have Being. His doctrine is called the doctrine, according to which the cause alone is real or Being (*satkāraṇavāda*). The Buddhists say also that the cause must first become Non-being, out of which the effect arises. But Śaṅkara contends that, if the cause becomes nothing first, then nothing can come out of nothing.

THE STAGES OR LEVELS OF THE COSMIC PERSON It is well known that the Advaita accepts and propounds the absolute identity of the spirit in man (*ātman*) and the Supreme Spirit (Brahman). *But this identification is not a native identification or a coinciding like that of two equal triangles. It is not even merging, although that word is often used; for there is no separate ātman to be merged in the Brahman.* It is the realization that I, as the consciousness asserting and affirming itself in the world, am a finitized appearance of the Brahman. This realization is possible through the realization of my unity with the Cosmic Person or God (Īśvara), that I am essentially the same as he, the Cosmic Person.

In terms of the *Māṇḍūkya Upaniṣad*, the Advaitins say that there are three levels[45] of the Cosmic Person corresponding to the three states of the individual—dream, waking state, and deep sleep. The three cosmic stages are called Virāṭ for the waking state, Hiraṇyagarbha or Sūtrātman for the dream state, and Īśvara (God) for the state of deep sleep. Only in the fourth state, the state above deep sleep, the distinction between the individual person and the Cosmic Person is cancelled.

The three stages of the Cosmic Person are explained further. All the three are indeed the Brahman, but in three successive stages. It has been mentioned already that Māyā is the Advaita interpretation of the principle of the Unmanifest (Avyakta) of the *Kaṭha* and the *Śvetāśvatara* Upaniṣads. The Brahman as related to Māyā—the relation may be reflection, appearance (*ābhāsā*), or conditioning, as explained already—in its undifferentiated and unmanifest state is Īśvara (God). He is the Brahman about to create the world and with all the potential forces necessary for creation and without being overwhelmed by them. He is the causal state of the world.

This causal state then becomes a subtle manifest state and is Hiraṇyagarbha. He is the lord of all the subtle elements and preserves the inter-relationship of all dreaming persons to their physical bodies, through the life-principle (*prāṇa*).[46] Cosmically, he is the lord of life, every individual using his subtle elements and producing the dream objects in his own way. The third stage is that of Virāṭ,[47] who is the lord of all the gross objects of the waking state. He presides over the totality of the world of the objects of the waking state. The Advaitins accept also, corresponding to Īśvara, a causal body, (*kāraṇaśarīra*) for each individual. This is the ātman in deep sleep with all the potentialities of the dream and waking states held in a unity. Deep sleep is not mere absence of knowledge, but the individual Unconscious. This idea corresponds to the Ālayavijñāna of the Vijñānavādins.

SOME ADVAITA EXTREMISTS Śaṅkara, compared to the philosophers of the time, was an extremist. Yet in epistemology, he accepted, on the whole, the Mīmāmsā position and, in ethics, its doctrine of *karma*. He propounded four levels of Being, without saying that the lower levels are absolutely without Being; and he tried to give a place to the ways of action and devotion, though making them secondary to the way of knowledge. But some non-dualists, Guaḍapāda before him and few others after him, drew more extreme conclusions than he did and developed extreme positions in non-dualism, which may have a strong intellectual appeal through astounding novelty, but perplex our life's ways.

Guaḍapāda,[48] who was a grand-teacher of Śaṅkara, was a Vedāntin, who, according to a tradition, became a Buddhist, before reverting to the Vedānta again. Whether this tradition is true or false, it is certain that he was greatly influenced by Mahāyāna Buddhism.[49] In his work, *Māṇḍūkyakārikās*, he maintains *first* that the stability of the objects we see is due to the forms through which the flux flows. If man moves a torch in a circle, we see a circular flame. But it is really a series of movements and positions of the torch. So a series of events is mistaken for a thing. *Secondly*, the pragmatic criterion cannot establish that the object concerned belongs necessarily to the empirical world; for the water we drink in dream quenches the thirst we have in dream. The implication is that there is really little difference between dream and waking states. *Thirdly*, the world is never created (*ajātivāda*) for it is unreal, and an unreal object is neither created nor destroyed. This doctrine was first propounded by Nāgārjuna. *Fourthly*, the world is, therefore, a projection of mind (*citta*). Mind only can be the phenomenal reality. This position roughly corresponds to the Vijñānavāda. But we cannot understand how mind itself is created. From these ideas a few later Advaitins drew the conclusion that, if everything is unreal, then ethical action, bondage, and liberation also are unreal. Believers in such doctrines as Guaḍapāda's may be top-ranking saints, just as some of the greatest ethical personalities are atheists. But lesser minds, not understanding the full significance of such doctrines, may justify unethical behaviour on their basis.

We have seen that the Advaita epistemology is, on the whole, realistic. But Prakāśānanda (16th century), in his *Vedāntasiddhāntamuktāvalī* maintained what apparently is a pure subjective position. He maintains that the object comes into existence when it is perceived (*dṛṣṭisṛṣṭivāda*). For an object to be seen is to be created. If the Brahman is the only reality, and cognition results only when the veiling power (*āvaraṇaśakti*) of Māyā screens the Brahman and the projecting power (*vikṣepaśakti*) projects the object out of the veil, then the object lasts only so long as the cognition lasts. Thus the object becomes the result of the function of mind (*antaḥkaraṇa*).

But the idea that the function of mind or cognition and the object are simultaneous could be, and was interpreted differently also. Some Advaitins held that the appearance of cognition and of the object is only simultaneous; neither is the cause of the other. But some others maintained that the creation of the object is the same as its perception but logically the former is prior to the latter. The objects are not created by our minds, but by God.[50] If we add that these objects can stay for a time without being perceived, we get the usual epistemological realism.

Another extreme position taken by the Advaitins is that of Sarvajñātmamuni (9th century) in his *Saṅkṣepaśārīraka*. He says that the doctrine of the four levels of Being is meant only for immature intellects. For mature minds, there is only one level, viz., that of the Brahman. He notices also the difficulty in calling the world and the Brahman also inexplicable (*anirvacanīya*). The world is inexplicable, because it is self-contradictory in terms of Being and Non-being. But the Brahman is inexplicable not in terms of Being and Non-being, but in terms of any concept applicable in the world. Thus not only negative ontology but also the Mādhyamika position that both the world and the Void are inexplicable in terms of Being and Non-being is avoided. The Brahman is Being as such; that is why we call it indeterminate, indescribable and so on. Thus there are two kinds of inexplicability—inexplicability in terms of Being and Non-being, reality and unreality, existence and non-existence, and truth and falsity; and inexplicability in terms of any determinate concepts such as cause and effect, space and time, substance and attribute and so on, which are applicable to the objects of the world.[51]

Another extremist position is that the soul (*jīva*) also one,[52] just as the Brahman is one, and that this soul takes on many bodies. Śaṅkara does not seem to have given any support to this view (*ekajīvavāda*), but maintains that there are as many souls as there are living beings (*anekajīvavāda*). However, there seem to be minor differences of opinion within the single-soul theory. This single soul is identified by some of these extremists with a lower Logos (Hiraṇyagarbha), and the apparently many souls are said to be its reflections or semblances in bondage. Thus God (Īśvara) is the higher Logos, the creator of the world, and comes next to the Brahman. The single soul (Hiraṇyagarbha) becomes the lower Logos. But some other extremists hold that the soul for all living beings is one and has several bodies; there are no reflections or semblances coming in between. The bodies are only numerically different. But if the soul is one, why does not every man know every other man's experiences? Nature (Prakṛti) prevents them from knowing others' experiences. We have forgotten the experiences of our own past lives; there is something like a screen coming between our present life and past lives. There is a similar screen between one man's experiences and another's. But just as we can remember the experiences of our past lives if we make the necessary effort, we can know another's experiences if we make a similar effort.

4. LIFE'S IDEAL

The ideal of man is to realize his self (*ātman*). As the *ātman* and the Brahman are the same according to Śaṅkara, realization of the *ātman* is the same as the realization of the Brahman. Śaṅkara takes the great logia of the Upaniṣads—"I am the Brahman," "That thou art," "The *ātman* is the Brahman," and "All this is the Brahman"—in their literal sense, and accordingly reinterprets the statements declaring the difference between the Brahman on the one side and the individual and the world on the other. Indeed, he does not mean that trees, mountains, and men as they are, are the Brahman. We have seen that the Being of the Brahman is the ground for our saying that objects exist; their existence is the Being of the Brahman shining through their forms. The Brahman is, therefore, immanent in the world we see around us. Our consciousness of these objects is due to the Brahman's consciousness shining through our "I's" and egos. The Brahman is thus immanent in the whole world including ourselves, and without it there can be no existence of ourselves or the world around us. In the sense that the Brahman is immanent, the world is the Brahman. Yet though immanent, it is transcendent also: the Being of the Brahman shines through the forms of the world; but the forms themselves are not the Brahman; they are constituted by Māyā and are subject to the laws of space, time, and causality and also the laws of change—birth, decay, and death. The Being of the Brahman is not subject to any of those laws, because it is constantly present and accompanies everything.

To be subject to the laws of Māyā produces fear of death, fear of the other, pain, and misery. Being is above all, it has no death and no other. It is one, not many. The highest ideal of man is, therefore, to realize his true being, which is his *ātman* or the Brahman. We may write the word *ātman* in Śaṅkara's philosophy with the capital *A* as Ātman, as it is the same as the Brahman. But how can the realization of the Brahman—we should remember that realization is not intellectual conviction—free us from the laws of Māyā? Māyā is such an entity as to vanish when the realization dawns. The nature of Māyā is to screen or veil us from the Brahman, and then produce the forms of the world we perceive. The nature of ignorance is such as to disappear altogether when knowledge dawns. Śaṅkara takes the example of the illusory snake and asks: "Where does this snake, we have seen, exist when we realize that the object in front of us is a rope?" It vanishes, it is nowhere. Similarly, as soon as the realization of the Brahman dawns on us, the world disappears along with our egos; we realize that we are no longer our particular egos, but the Brahman itself. Śaṅkara wanted a concept meaning a power that appears as the world and yet vanishes altogether when higher knowledge dawns; and he found it in illusion and called it Māyā and Avidyā, adding to it all the connotations said to be necessary for explaining the world.

Śaṅkara used the word Prakṛti as a synonym for Māyā, but did not accept the Sāṅkhya interpretation.[53] Prakṛti for the Sāṅkhya is eternal and has its own independent being and reality. But if it exists even after liberation (*mukti*), what guarantee is there that it will not again enslave the liberated *ātman*? It must vanish altogether for such an *ātman*. The Sāṅkhya deprives Prakṛti of its mysteriousness by bestowing independent reality on it. *First*, Prakṛti should vanish completely for the liberated souls. *Secondly*, it must be capable of being the same and many for the different souls—the same for the souls in bondage, and many when we take both the liberated and bound souls into consideration—those liberated, those being liberated, and those in bondage. The Sāṅkhya conception does not satisfy these two conditions. *Thirdly*, its nature should be such as not to affect the nature, purity, and perfection of the Brahman. Its nature can be such, only if it does not have a being of its own apart from the Brahman.[54]

When we understand what Śaṅkara means by the Brahman and the significance he gives to Māyā, we can appreciate why he teaches that the way to salvation lies in knowledge. Bondage is subjection to the laws of Māyā, and is due to the forgetting of our original being and becoming ignorant of it. Salvation lies in overcoming ignorance and forgetting. Our finite being is rooted not only in the Being of the Brahman, but also in ignorance, the latter has to be destroyed. Destruction of root ignorance (*mūlavidyā*) is the destruction of finitude and the attainment of infinitude. Śaṅkara places, therefore, the way of knowledge (*jñānamārga*) over all the others. We should remind ourselves that the way of knowledge is not the way of intellectual convictions or beliefs, but that which reveals the deeper levels of our being itself, of our finite "I am," and so of our existence. This knowledge is existential or ontological in the literal sense of the term, not merely rationalistic. The deeper levels are those explained by the Upaniṣads, particularly the *Kaṭha*, the *Taittirīya* and the *Māṇḍūkya*, all of which are the basis of almost every Vedānta philosophy, although interpreted differently by the different Vedāntins.

As the deeper levels of realization are not mere intellectual convictions, strict ethical preparation is necessary. One may know what is ethically right and may violate the law, because he does not care to be what the laws wants him to be. I may know that charity is one of the virtues and is so regarded by society. But I may pretend to be charitable to obtain social prestige or I may not care to be charitable. But if I want to be charitable and do not care to be known as charitable, then I really want a self-transformation of my being from the non-charitable to the charitable. The ethics underlying such an idea is often called the ethics of self-realization. I want to realize myself, i.e., to be a charitable being, whether or not others know my charities. The realization of the deeper levels of my being is also self-realization. *The emphasis on this realization, which is self-transformation to higher or deeper levels, is not on what I know, but on what I become.* In the process of realization, I become the deeper and deeper levels of my being, until I become the same as the Brahman, the deepest Being.

As the emphasis is on what I become, but not on what I do or know, Śaṅkara gives less importance to ethics than to self-realization. Ethics is the means, although necessary, but not the end of self-realization. It belongs to the world of self-contradictions, but self-realization leads to the realm of the nonself-contradictory Being. It presupposes plurality—myself as the moral agent, my action, the object on which my action works, and merit and demerit as the fruits of my action. It involves a reality governed by the laws of space, time, and causality.[55] But all this plurality has been shown to be self-contradictory without any being of its own. So self-realization alone is the aim of life and that alone can lead to truth and salvation.

But man's finite being, as the *Kaṭha Upaniṣad*[56] says, is turned outwards, towards the world of plurality; but the self (*ātman*) is inward. The presence and depths of the inward being cannot be recognized, unless mind is purified, unless man becomes unselfish, and non-ego-centred. We have, therefore, to start with ordinary ethics, which lifts us to a level higher than that of our petty ego. When I act according to a universal ethical law, I place my ego at the level of a universal ego and lift myself to that level; I do not *merely think* of a universal ego. *In ethics I universalize my ego.* This universalization is not expansion in external space, but expansion in the inward dimension, in which the petty interests of my particular ego are transcended. Śaṅkara recognizes the spiritual significance of ethical actions and says that they are wanted for the purification[57] of mind (*antahkaraṇa*). But he tells us that man's destiny and ideal do not merely lie there. There is something more which he can become, viz., the Brahman.

Śaṅkara includes in ethical actions some disciplines for the realization of the Brahman. He has no objection to utilize the eight-fold yoga taught by Patañjali. But he says that there are four important disciplines to be followed: (1) discrimination between the eternal and the non-eternal, which enables us ultimately to grasp the eternal Being; (2) detachment from all selfish pursuits, both worldly and other-worldly; (3) cultivation of the six virtues—tranquility (*śama*), restraint (*dama*), renunciation (*uparati*, withdrawing from worldly activities), endurance (*titīkṣā*), meditation (*samādhi*), faith (*śraddhā*); (4) desire for liberation (*mumukṣā*).

Śaṅkara has no objection to practising the way of action[58] (*karmamārga*) and the way of devotion or love (*bhaktimārga*), but says that both lead to the way of knowledge (*jñānamārga*). For the nature of the Brahman is consciousness; the realization of the Brahman can, therefore, be through consciousness, i.e., knowledge. The way of action can purify our mind and make us non-egoistic, only if the actions are performed without egoistic motives (*niṣkāmakarma*), i.e., without the desire to appropriate the fruits of action. But there is always a danger in remaining at this level, because of the risk of the ego intruding into non-egoistic actions. I live in the world of plurality; and even if I make a gift of all the results of my actions, I may still feel that I am the great man who has been so charitable. The way of devotion also purifies our mind. If I am devoted to God and surrender everything, including myself, to him, my ego becomes liquified and liquidated. But devotion implies the difference between the devotee and God. The ego of the devotee, therefore, persists. So long as it persists, salvation is not obtained. The way of devotion should, therefore, lead to the way of knowledge before salvation can be obtained.

Like the Sāṅkhya, Śaṅkara accepts both liberation in the body (*jīvanmukti*) and liberation after death (*videhamukti*). The latter is final. One who has obtained liberation in the body continues to live and act so long as his body lasts. The explanation is the same as that given by the Sāṅkhya.

Śaṅkara believes, on the basis of the Upaniṣads, that the Ātman or the Brahman is not only Being (*sat*) and Consciousness (*cit*), but also Bliss (*ānanda*). At this point, all the Vedāntic schools are unanimous, and differ from the Mīmāmsā and the Nyāya-Vaiśeṣika, according to which the *ātman* is only being (*sat*), and from the Sāṅkhya-Yoga, according to which it is only being and consciousness. As mentioned already, both these schools generally interpret bliss negatively as absence of pain. But the Vedānta treats both pain and bliss (pleasure) as positive, saying that where both are absent we have only indifference or a neutral state. The *Bṛhadāraṇyaka Upaniṣad*[59] speaks of the *ātman* as the honey (*madhu*) and as the "honiest" of all the honeys. The *Taittirīya Upaniṣad* [60] teaches that the bliss of the *ātman* is infinitely more intense than the essence[61] (*rasa*) of everything in the world and that man becomes blissful by gaining his *ātman*. This essence (*rasa*) is interpreted by writers on aesthetics as the aesthetic pleasure in its perfection, the aesthetic pleasure derived from dance, drama, music, poetry, etc., being only a reflection[62] of it in our inner instrument (*antahkaraṇa*) or mind. The *Bṛhadāraṇyaka* says also that the *ātman* in its original unity is like a man in the embrace of his beloved.[63] This idea is elaborated in the *Māṇḍūkya Upaniṣad*, which says that the *ātman* in the state of deep sleep, in which there is no distinction between subject and object, desire and the desired, and in which all objectivity and the *ātman*, dispersed into the ego, mind, and senses, are brought together into a unity, lives on bliss and is bliss (*ānanda*) itself. Bliss is the collecting together of our dispersed and divided being into an intense unity; *it is the intensity of Being*. As such, the state attained in salvation is Bliss itself.

But Being, Consciousness, and Bliss are not qualities of the Ātman or the Brahman, which is quality-less (*nirguṇa*). But we say that the Brahman exists, is conscious, and blissful. Then they are qualities. Then how can the Brahman be quality-less? The Advaitin's answer is that they are constitutive qualities (*svarūpalakṣaṇas*), not attributive qualities (*taṭasthalakṣaṇas*).[64]. We have seen that the Sāṅkhya speaks of Prakṛti as *having* three Attributes, and most of the Advaitins also regard Māyā as *having* them. But the Sāṅkhya does not mean *that Prakṛti has the three Attributes, just as the rose has the red colour*. Prakṛti is the unity of the three Attributes; that is, they are constitutive and may even be called parts. Similarly, the Brahman has the three attributes, which are not qualities that it possesses, but which it is. To say that the Brahman has Being, Consciousness, and Bliss may sound like saying that the earth has existence. It is a way of our expression. Existence is not a predicate of the earth and the three attributes are not the predicates of the Brahman. So they are called constitutive qualities. But attributive qualities do not constitute the substance of which they are attributes. The red colour of the rose is indifferent (*taṭastha*) to the being of the rose; it is a mark of the being of the rose, but is not itself the being of the rose. The rose could have been white. But the Brahman is nothing other than the three attributes—Being, Consciousness, and Bliss. Indeed, according to the Advaita, the Brahman is not a substance, which is a category of the world.

GENERAL ESTIMATE AND CONSTRUCTIVE COMMENT

(i) Advaita No Acosmism, Negativism, Etc.

It is unfortunate that, although the Advaita of Śaṅkara enjoys the highest prestige among traditional philosophies, it is regarded as acosmism, negativism, illusionism, super-duper monism, etc., in different philosophical and religious circles of the West. But one or the other of these characterizations has been made of one or the other of western philosophers also, not excluding the great names of Plato, Spinoza, and Hegel. But primarily and basically, Śaṅkara is an ontologist of the Spirit—a fact which is often forgotten even when interpreting the Upaniṣads, which equate the Brahman not only to Consciousness and Bliss, but also to Being (*sattā*, existence). If the western or the eastern reader wants philosophical justification, intellectually presented, for the view that our being, in short, the being of the world which includes that of the thinker, is rooted in the Being of God or the Supreme Spirit, also called the Supreme Being, he can find the best in Śaṅkara's Advaita.[65] It is true that some extremist interpretations and popularizations have turned his philosophy and religious practice into negativism and illusionism by treating Māyā as illusion in some cheap, derogatory sense. Perhaps, the times of Śaṅkara and the influence of Buddhism as understood by the masses did not make people of the time react to his idea the way we do, as we are obliged to take the world really seriously as a matter of life and death. But the etymological roots of the word Māyā[66] that it is a measure, something that makes the object we experience determinate through spatial, temporal, and causal laws (corresponding to Plato's idea of the Limit), and the *Śvetāśvatara Upaniṣad's* idea that it is a kind of net thrown on Being making it look like the world fixed by some laws (constituting the structure of the net) ought to make it clear that Māyā is not *mere* illusion and that the use of the idea of illusion by some early writers of this school was only to use a paradigm or model, a conceptual instrument for explanation. For the object of illusion, like that of dream, disappears later, whatever fright it may have created in the experiencer. The idea of God creating the world, which is not there in its own right, through his will, involves something like the idea of illusion. Now, salvation is freedom from determinateness, whether it is the life of lust and pleasure or of pain and misery; it is the same as freedom from Māyā. This freedom, again, is not the knowledge that we are determined, which is simply the consciousness of the consciousness that we are determined—which Hegel and some of his followers and the Marxists tend to think, and which has some truth in the fact that the transcendence of consciousness in its realization of its determinateness contains a factor of freedom—but complete ontological transcendence of determinateness like our transcendence of dream and its horrors when we wake up.

That the Advaita is not acosmism can be shown by bringing to the attention of the critic that, while the determinate world—called also Māyā and the product of Māyā in different places—is transformed for the liberated soul into the pure Being of the Brahman, it continues to exist for the unliberated souls. If, for saying the same, the Sāṅkhya is not acosmic, the Advaita also cannot be acosmic. It is also not negativistic. It does not say that the world or Māyā does not exist. It says, like Nāgārjuna when challenged to define, that Māyā neither exists, nor does not exist, nor both, nor neither. Other forms of the expression are: "It is neither real, nor unreal, nor both, nor neither," and also "It is neither true, nor false, nor both, nor neither." In contemporary philosophy, although Wittgenstein and some others accept only two truth-functions in logic—relying on the principle of the excluded middle—others have accepted more truth functions. Even in Wittgenstein we find propositions are either true or false or without sense, i.e., non-sense, the first two having sense. But those propositions also that have sense can be neither true nor false. There can be questions like: Is life the same as matter, or is it not identical with matter?[67] It is difficult to say Yes or No in the categorial sense. We cannot say that it is both; for if identity means absolute sameness, we shall be wrong; if the No means absolute difference, we shall again be wrong. We find life in matter, it is matter alive; so it is not neither. It cannot be either or both; for to say "Either" means indifference;

and to say "Both" means to assert a self-contradiction. Then what is life? There is only one categorical answer: It is life. Why should I explain it in terms of matter? Yet, I find life only in matter, although not wherever there is matter. When forced to explain life in terms of matter, I may use the four-cornered negation.

True and false are applicable only within any single realm of discourse. But when another realm also is involved, to say that proposition *p* is not true, does not mean that it is necessarily false. In the above example neither alternative is true; but also neither is false.[68] The question falls within the realm of matter, but one of the terms of the question, viz., life, transcends that realm. Still the question is not sense-less or non-sense; for there is something towards which it is directed. If I ask: "Is a triangle the same as bravery?" I ask a non-sensical question.

Where two realms of discourse are mixed, the principle of contradiction also does not hold. For to say that one of the alternatives is false does not necessarily mean that the other is true. I may ask: "Is that a stone or turtle?" If one alternative is true, the other has to be false; but if one is false, the other need not be true. For both may be false, if the object is a tree stump. Classical logicians called such negation contrareity. In all such cases, the principle, "Double negation makes an affirmation," does not hold. It stays as a double negation. In the Nyāya estimate, we referred to other reasons for not accepting this principle. This kind of negation does not agree also with the principle of the excluded middle. Other cases like the traditional example, "He is either a fool or a knave," are related to this. Fools are different from knaves and one may say by definition: "A fool is not a knave." But actually in application and experience we may find that some one is neither and some one else is both. So negation as pure contradiction cannot be a universal logical principle, if, as Wittgenstein said in his *Tractatus*, that logic represents the structure of reality. Whether or not it does so, if logic is to have ontological foundations and is to be applicable to reality, contradiction cannot be the only, and even the basic form of negation and of opposition. One may say that negation is one of the forms of opposition and may develop a theory of the forms of opposition. It may be useful; but in the present context we can only say that such work will result in mere change of terminology.

The implication of the above discussion is that Māyā as represented by the principle of the four-cornered negation precludes the idea that it leads to negativism or acosmism. On the other hand, it is those philosophers who treat negation as basically contradiction and demand that pure logic based on it should be the measure of reality, become acosmists; for the world does not meet the demands of such logic and ceases, according to their philosophy, to be the ordered cosmos; order is structure and it has, according to them, to meet the requirements of pure logic.

(ii) Levels of Being and the Paradox of Reality and Unreality

The Advaita is again not super-duper monism; for what it considers to be one or non-dual is the Brahman which is pure ontological Being or Existence (*sattā*) — not forgetting that in Indian philosophy Being and Existence are one and the same. Now Being cannot be many; otherwise, it becomes a class and the word becomes the name of the class. *But when I ask questions about how and where my being is rooted, I am not asking what class of things it is, but what is "to be."* These two questions are different. Since ontological Being cannot be many, or rather the question whether it is one or many does not arise for it—for one may reasonably say that *to be one* is to be one among many, but ontologically "to be" is the act of being or existing — all duality both within and without Being is rejected. (If "to be" is many, then the "is" in "he is" and the "am" in "I am" or even the "is" in "that is" should have different meanings, which they do not have.)

That it is ontological Being that is in question, but not epistemological truth or cosmological reality when the four levels of Being—insignificant Being, apparent Being, pragmatic Being or the Being of the world of active life or what we call the real world, and ultimate Being—are propounded by the Advaita is missed by many western and even by Indian writers. For Śankara does not mean that the cosmos is not the cosmos or is not a real cosmos. As mentioned already, he describes it as the realm of cause and effect (*kārya-kāraṇa prapañca*) and as the realm of means and ends (*Kārya-kāraṇa prapañca*) or of instruments and effects. But ontologically, the being of the cosmos is rooted in the Supreme or Ultimate Being. Now, the world of instruments or means, causes and effects, is the world of process, action (*vyavahāra*). The term "the world of action" (*vyāvahārika-sattā*) is generally translated as "empirical reality" and also as "empirical being"—which may mislead one into thinking that it is a matter simply of experiencing. But dreams also are experienced; yet they do not come, for the Advaita, under what we call empirical reality. For this school, empirical reality is meant to be a realm of action (*karma*), is the result of past actions and *samskāras,* and is changeable through present actions controlled by the laws of causes-and-effects and ends-and-means.

The world of dreams and illusions, which we experience as confronting us (*gegenstehend*), but which one cannot relate generally to the world of action through causal laws, etc., is called apparent being (*prātibhāsika-sattā*); for the objects in dreams and illusions, as faced by us as existing so long as those dreams and illusions last, are not wilfully created by us. They are apparent also in the sense that the dreamer and the perceiver of the illusion themselves reject them as unrelatable to the objects of the cosmos or the world of action.[69]

Although the objects of the real cosmos have also "appearance" (shining, *shein* for our consciousness) like the objects of dreams and illusions — as otherwise, we cannot see, cognize them at all — the word "apparent" is applied only to the objects of the latter. In the former case, appearance means "observability," "perceivability," (*dṛsyatva*). As observed, they are meant for action, and meet the conditions of action. The objects of dream also are observed, not merely imagined; but they do not meet the requirements of action, one of which is my will or desire to act on it and turn it into a shape which I like and which it does not now possess, or into an instrument (*kāraṇa*) of some other action as when I shape a lump of iron into an axe. This is evident in the use of the word insignificant Being (*tuccha-sattā*) for objects like the imaginary and the self-contradictory. In this case, we do not act at all on such objects. Indeed, one may wish that the Advaita logicians could have distinguished between the imaginary and the self-contradictory and also a few others. But they did not do so.[70] Now, the imaginary and also the self-contradictory also are experienced by us. I can imagine a unicorn or a hare with horns, even though they are empirically not real.

Imagination also is experience, and the object of imagination has "appearance" also. Yet, this appearance is entirely dependent on my will, and the object does not satisfy the conditions of action. Then, do I experience the self-contradictory? I understand what it means to say: "*X* is both *Y* and not *Y*" is self-contradictory." But is not understanding experience? Does experience go only so far as imagination, but not up to understanding and pure reason? I cannot imagine many things like $(a+b);^{925}$ but it is neither imaginary nor self-contradictory. I cannot imagine also what universals like "horseness"[71] are, or even precisely and fully the class of horses. But I can act on it or make it an instrument of action. But I cannot act on the image of the unicorn or the self-contradictory except that I avoid or ignore it in my actions. This excepting is not positive action.

We can see then that Śaṅkara did not really mean that the world does not exist or that any object in the world is the same as any other object. His main interest is ontological and ontology is spiritual for him. Spiritually speaking, only at the highest ontological level is man free from the restrictions, limits, and the laws of cause and effect, birth and death, etc., in short of determinateness. To say so is not necessarily that the world is not there. To teach that one ought to be free from determinateness implies that there is a world of determinateness from which one has to be free. But when this world is man's cosmological Being, he has to be free from his own cosmological Being and realize his one-ness with the ontological. Then what happens to his cosmological Being? It disappears for him. But ontological Being is eternal and is the support of the cosmological — we have shown that it is the support of everything. Then from that point of view, one may say that the cosmological Being has eternally not been there. Here lies the explanation of: "The world is not real, and yet is not unreal; it is Māyā." In other words, determinateness is there and yet is not there from the highest ontological point of view. And the difference also between the four levels is not merely epistemological, but ontological, and the distances between them are also ontological.

(iii) Pramāṇa, Prameya, and Māyā

That the word Māyā does not mean absence of order, that it is not magic, ought to be fairly clear from the above discussion. It is indicated also by the use of the word *pramāṇa* for the means or ways of cognition. *Pramāṇa* means the instrument for measuring; and *prameya*, which is generally translated as the object of cognition, means that which is measurable or even measured. Note that measuring is not possible without determinateness in the measured.[72] *Pramāṇa* means also standard, rule, evidence. Almost all the schools in the East and the West accept perception and inference as ways of knowing. Now, our question is not how many such ways are recognized, but what is meant by "way of knowing."[73] The term "means of knowing" is less indefinite than "way of knowing," although both are meant by epistemologists to be the same. Now, the means of knowing is somewhat like "the means of catching fish" or a little more appropriately like "the means of measuring a pure undivided expanse by placing a transparent squared paper on it," and then counting the squares. It is actually throwing the network of thought, mind, and senses on pure objectivity[74] as such. The structure of the network conveys to us the structure of objectivity after actually determining the structure of objectivity transcendentally. There is no other way of knowing what objectivity is than through the network, which is called the instrument of cognition and is of different forms like perception and inference. *Pramāṇa* is the way of measuring reality; it is more also: it is the way of determining reality. The Nyāya-Vaiśeṣika speaks as though the *pramāṇas* convey to us what is there outside existing by itself. But this view leads logically to the conclusion that not only mind, but also the senses merely reflect, like blank mirrors, what is there outside and that each of them is made to reflect one type of object; this is a doctrine of *tabula rasa* in another context.

It is significant that the three words — *pramāṇa* (means of cognition), *prameya* (object of cognition), and Māyā are derived etymologically from the same verbal root $\sqrt{m\bar{a}}$, meaning "to measure." The world of cosmology is what is measured and is called Māyā[75] and also the product of Māyā. The Supreme Being, Ātman, Brahman, is beyond speech and means of cognition — although, in a sense and as some condescension, the Veda (*Śruti*) is often given as a *pramāṇa* — and cannot, therefore, be measured. If what cannot be measured is Being, then what can be measured is Māyā and is not exactly Being. But do not forget that what is not Being is not Non-being for this school. For instance, it is a mistake to think that because Becoming is not Being, it must be Non-being — a mistake committed by Plato and some of the popularized versions of the Advaita.[76] At this stage of thought, the principles of contradiction, excluded middle, and double negation do not obtain; they hold and have application only within the realm of pure logic, not even necessarily within the realm of concrete plurality. Where there can be no Becoming without Being[77] and where we are driven to think of Being only by noticing Becoming, the two cannot be treated even as contraries, although they are not the same[78] and yet are true.

In spite of the misleading popularizations of the idea of Māyā, it means that the world is an ordered whole according to measures. But what is the Being of the objects obtained by this measure? Here are given the four levels of Being as the answer. The highest, the Supreme Being (*paramārthasattā*) is not an object obtained through this measure; for it is that which does the measuring and lies behind the act of measuring. The others are the results of measuring. The highest of the three, the world of action (*vyāvahārika-sattā*) or the Being for action (inter-course, inter-communication, etc., all come under action) is determined by the accepted means of knowing. But this is the world primarily meant for action; the being of the objects of the world is meant for action and is determined by past actions of the souls. The being of the objects of dreams and illusions is an imperfect reflection of the being of the world of action and is called apparent Being (*prātibhāsika-sattā*). The last, the insignificant Being (*tucchasattā*) belongs to mental images like those of unicorns and self-contradictory ideas like that of the son of a barren woman (born to her). The objects of mere fantasy also belong to this realm.

All except the first belong to the realm of Māyā or the measure. How are the last two the results of measure? They are so indirectly, not directly. The dream objects are permutations and combinations of the objects of the world of action and are produced by the impressions (*samskāras*) left by the latter, which are objects of measure (*pramāṇa*); but their permutation and combination are not done by us voluntarily and knowingly. If I can create the dreams I like, I always create the most pleasant; but quite often they are very unpleasant and even horrid. So long as the dream objects last, I take the objects and experiences to be real. The objects of the fourth level are known to be unreal even when they are imagined and thought of. Indeed, the credulous and children may believe in a number of them. Unless simple belief is accepted as a means of knowing (*pramāṇa*) — no school accepts it — they cannot be called the results of measure. Yet, those ideas which are non-empirically combined like that of the unicorn and those which are the compounds of contradictories like "*Y* and not-*Y*" have components which are ideas of objects resulting from measure. So the Being of the compounds is called insignificant in the sense that it is only the Being of the ideas of the components which have Being.The difference from the third level lies in the activities of permutation and combination being voluntary in the fourth.

Often students of Indian thought are confused by the use of the word truth (*satyam*) for these levels and by the statement that there are four levels of truth. The Sanskrit word needs to be translated as "the four levels of Being or Existence," but is often translated also as "the four levels of reality," and "the four levels of truth."[79] But the word *satyam* has always in its import Being or Existence as the major element; it is used because in every live, concrete, and true knowledge situation, the cognitive and the ontological aspects of the object known have the same-self-ness (*tādātmyatā*, identity) like that of the being of substance and the being of its essential, inherent property, e.g., fire and its burning power. But the word *prāmāṇyam*, derived from the word *pramāṇa* or means of knowing is not used in this context,[80] not even the word *prameya* or that determined by the *pramāṇas*. It is absurd to translate *pramāṇas* as "true means of knowledge" but only as "valid means of knowledge" although it is done so. Even superstitions are true in the sense of "There are superstitions" or "Superstitions exist in the world," but they are not *valid*. In western logical and philosophical literature, "true" means the "existent" and also the "valid." The four-fold classification of Being given by the Advaita is given from the point of view of ontology, and the classification of the valid means of knowledge is given from the point of view of logic and epistemology.[81]

(iv) Sāksicaitanya and Antaryāmi (Witness Consciousness and Inner Controller)

In the pure undifferentiated Brahman, what is the nature of the differentiation which takes place in creating the world out of the Brahman without its being affected by its creative activity? The clue to the answer lies in the idea of the witness consciousness (*sākṣi* or *sākṣi-caitanya*), which witnesses that it is knowing, cognizing, willing, experiencing urges and emotions and so forth. The western philosopher may get the cue to this idea in Husserl's idea of the witness and even Spinoza's idea of the mind knowing both itself and matter. In Spinoza's thought also, the knowing mind he speaks of is the witness. But it is certainly not my mind, which is only a mode of the Attribute, but the Cosmic Mind, which is the Attribute itself. However, my mind also is similar to it as its reflection or mode;[82] for there is, within it also, the distinction between the witness and witnessed consciousness. We have noted that, when I come out of the dream, I know that I experienced the objects of the dream, but try to shake off the identity of the waking I with the dream I and absolve myself from, and be unaffected by the responsibilities of the actions of the dream I.

The popular conception of any division in the undivided Brahman is, that of a drawing a line in it and separating the subject from the object,[83] and then getting into the difficulty of explaining how the subject knows that there is an object at all. But the so-called split or division is that of the I-am descending into the unity of the subject and object in the form, "I know that I know That," thereby comprehending both the I and the That. The first I then becomes the witness of the second I and its object; and as a witness, it is said to be unaffected (and free in some contexts).

But the witness consciousness has several levels. In the above example, the witness is at the empirical level. Although it often dissociates itself easily from itself as experiencing the dream objects, it has to make as often some special effort for the purpose, and then forgetfulness helps in blotting out the dream experiences. But at the deeper or higher levels of the witness consciousness, the dissociation[84] is more and more spontaneous and obvious to oneself. These levels are variously described by the different schools. For the Advaita there are roughly three[85] levels before reaching the Brahman: Virāt (Cosmic Person), Hiraṇyagarbha (the soul of the Cosmic Person), and Īśvara (the Personal God). All the three are higher forms than the finite I-consciousness, but are continuous with it and the Supreme Brahman. According to this school, it is only God (Īśvara) who is eternally and spontaneously detached from the drama of the world. The literature of the school mentions only that he keeps Māyā as his object without being overwhelmed and enmeshed by it. But it does not explain the structure of his consciousness in terms of what we can experience. One may say that the three are three levels of the Logos or the Cosmic Person understood in a general way; and all may be called cosmic personalities.[86] But the distinctions within are important. The Logos is a kind of Unity in Trinity.

Virāt corresponds roughly to *natura naturata*, which cannot really exist apart from *natura naturans*, which corresponds roughly to Hiraṇyagarbha. In the history of western philosophy, the Logos is not equated to either *natura naturata* or *natura naturans*[87] or both uniformly; but we can understand how the conceptions fit into related philosophies and theologies. It comprehends all that stands between me and the Supreme Being, or in philosophical terminology, between the beginning of the finitization of the Supreme Being for forming the finite person and the finite person. However, these distinctions made by this school are not absolute differences, but pass into one another by the presence of the witness consciousness at various levels. *Virāt* is generally explained as the gross form of the Logos; he is the Logos manifest in the world. The word *virāt* means the king, the shining one, the controller of the whole gross universe or the manifest universe or the universe as patent, not latent, and so the great and the grand. Hiraṇyagarbha literally means the golden womb (occasionally the golden foetus), but in philosophy, the soul of Virāt, his Reason (in the Stoic sense), and is identified by this school with the Mahān Ātmā[88] of the *Kaṭha Upaniṣad*, which is often called by the simpler term Mahat, the Great. But as the soul of Virāt, Hiraṇyagarbha is attached to him and in a way is stuck to him, enmeshed in him. (For instance, I know my body as my object, but cannot detach myself like a mere witness from it.) But Īśvara (personal God, or the lower Brahman), although related to Virāt and Hiraṇyagarbha and is continuous with them, is not overwhelmed by the principle of objectifying and limitation-producing Māyā, but is able to detach himself from it completely, though not completely unconcerned with it. That is, his consciousness is directed towards it, but is not affected by it. He is really the fully unaffected witness (*sākṣi*). The others also are witnesses, but not so completely detached and unaffected as Īśvara. Even I, as pointed out above, am the witness of my dreams, illusions, and cognitions according to the valid means of cognition. But my being a witness is realized after I have been involved. But this involvement becomes less and less until it ceases completely in the case of Īśvara. At the stage of the Supreme Brahman, the I-consciousness is completely unconcerned with Māyā; for in it Māyā becomes part and parcel of the Brahman's self-transparent I-consciousness.[89] The vanishing of Māyā means that it has become part and parcel of myself and is not controlling me, but is being controlled by me. Just as I cannot find myself as an object distinct from me as even like a mental image, I cannot, when Māyā becomes a part of my self, make it my object or feel its limiting and constraining power. I am in full command of it, as it becomes part of my person.[90]

Now, one should be able to understand how each of these stages is the so-called Inner Controller (*antaryāmi*). Even in my case, which is that of a limited, finite individual, my I-conciousness is the inner controller of the activities of my senses and my organs of action. Even in the case of ethical activity, my character, which constitutes the nature of my personality, is the inner controller of my conduct. Generally we say that character determines conduct. The idea of control becomes meaningful when it is realized that my I-consciousness is the witness consciousness also, and as such it guides my activities. Even the activity of an arsonist or a bank robber, during the live act, is controlled *spontaneously* by his I-consciousness; for he is watchful, even when committing the act, that the police are not observing him, that nobody is aiming a gun at him and so on. After the act is completed, he begins to reflect how he could be so successful and then can realize that he is also his own witness consciousness. Similarly, with different degrees of detachment the three stages of the Logos also become inner controllers, each higher of the lower. Generally we club the three together and say that the Logos is the inner controller (*antaryāmin*) and witness (*sākṣi*); and also that God is the eternal inner controller and witness. Just as they are levels of witness consciousness (*sākṣi-caitanya*), they are levels of the inner controller also (*antaryāmin*).[91]

(v) Being and Becoming: Their Relation to Witness and Inner Controller

The ideas of the witness consciousness (*sākṣi-caitanya*) and the inner controller (*antaryāmin*) are closely related to those of Being and Becoming. We have noted that so far as this cosmos goes, there is no Becoming without Being and no Being without Becoming, and that Becoming is always patterned.[92] If there is no pattern that enables us to say that it is the same *X* that is becoming *Y*, the instants of Becoming will be disconnected and Becoming will be a disconnected plurality. The pattern confers the unity needed[93] on the different instants, and among the different instants. That is why Plato called the Idea by the name Being.[94] That is, without something the same running through the different instants or moments of Becoming, Becoming cannot be Becoming, change cannot be change, but merely unconnected events.

It was indicated previously that Becoming is truly applicable only to self-conscious beings; for it is they that can know that they are becoming, that they are going through the process of Becoming; and it is applicable indirectly to inanimate objects through the observations of self-conscious beings. For it is the self-conscious being that remains the same through the observations of Becoming in inanimate objects, although the structure and content of the observations, in their turn, go on changing. The observer then is the witness consciousness (*sākṣi-caitanya*) so far as the Becoming in the inanimate object is concerned. But he may or may not be the inner controller (*antaryāmin*) of that Becoming. Here the inner controller is the Logos, the World-Person, of both the observer and the inanimate object. For, as already said, the basic structures and potentialities of both, which put certain limits on their activities and processes, are supplied or constituted by the Cosmic Person, which is also the witness-consciousness of both. But so far as my self-conscious being is concerned, it is, within its own limits, both the witness consciousness and inner controller of its becoming. Thus although Being and Becoming are ontological categories, they are applicable to, and are involved in the cosmological implications of epistemology. Only when we understand this, can we appreciate the relation between the Brahman and Māyā or between the Brahman and the world. And unless this relation is appreciated, the student of the Advaita may think that the philosophy is acosmic and negativistic.[95]

(vi) Action and Self-Realization

One lacuna in the exposition of the Advaita philosophy by the great Śaṅkara is his frequent dismissal of action as unimportant, although he commented on the *Bhagavadgītā*, which successfully persuaded Arjuna, the hero of the work, to act, but not to renounce the world and not to avoid his duty. But Śaṅkara's writings apparently imply that action is to be eschewed completely, ignored altogether. This creates the impression that his philosophy is not constructive,[96] does not positively lead from a life of ethical activity to one of spiritual renunciation and detachment—explaining the significance and inner meaning of both activity and detachment to the I-consciousness—but that it is destructive like Buddhism. For besides some belittling of ethical action, we find lack of any significant analysis of ethical action. It may be that Śaṅkara was satisfied with the analysis given by the Mīmāmsā, which also is based on the Veda, and that he encouraged the idea popularized by Buddhism—or spread by popularized Buddhism—that man may and should kick the ethical ladder by which he ascends to spiritual heights. But one feels that Śaṅkara is misinterpreted and misunderstood when he said that ethical action, however good and noble, does not itself lead to emancipation from the world of determinateness; for all action is patterned, and the patterns of action produce patterns of *samskāras* which become potential wordly drives in the depths of the person. But it is not openly and explicitly discussed that these drives and potentialities at the higher ethical life can become identical with those of the Cosmic Person, who contains the gateway to the Supreme Being and emancipation in him.[97]

According to the *Bhagavadgītā*, action in agreement with the nature, law, and processes of the Cosmic Person is the same as renunciation. Now, how is this possible?

How does any explanation elucidate the law of ideal life for man? Now, both Śaṅkara and Rāmānuja, as the latter's commentary on *Brahmasūtras*, I,1, shows, hold that ethical action[98] purifies mind (*antahkaraṇa*) and makes it possible for man to develop the supreme gnosis (*jñāna*) according to Śaṅkara, and the highest form of devotion (*bhakti*) according to Rāmānuja. But while Śaṅkara gives the impression that the purification of mind can be obtained by means other than ethical action—e.g., desire for liberation and non-attachment to the values of the world—Rāmānuja gives the impression that such purification can be attained only through positive ethical action. Otherwise, there is no point in the latter insisting on doing one's duty till death.

It is indeed said that by the practice of yoga as explained by Patañjali, our inner sense (*citta*) is made pure and transparent (*sāttvika*); and that it then reflects the highest consciousness, which is equivalent in a way to salvation. But we have seen the defects of the Sāṅkhya-Yoga metaphysics and indicated that liberation is not escape from Prakṛti or Māyā, but absorbing it and then becoming one with the Supreme, in whom it is transformed into his Being (*sattā*). Patañjali's yoga may lead to such a state of mind, but is not the safest and the truest way, as it is based on ultimate dualism. When it is asked: Which is the real self (*ātman*)?, the Sāṅkhya-Yoga answer will be: That which you are apart from Prakṛti. But one may mistake an illusory self or I-consciousness of himself as apart from Prakṛti. The reality attitude to one's self, or the being of one's self, may be perverted in this practice. Meditation by itself may lead one to a dreamland, a world of fantasy. Action restores the reality sense; if we embrace fantasies, we may come to grief in the world of action, which we can realize if we are in any sane mind. That is why the *Bhagavadgītā* preaches a combination of meditation, ways of gnosis, of devotion, and self-less action, and even the ways of selecting the right foods and so on. Ethical action is not merely doing something good and forgetting about it: every action becomes a *samskāra*, a potency, and transforms the individual.

Let us enquire. What is meant by purity of mind (*citta, antahkaraṇa*, etc.)? It may be said that it is pure and transparent mind. But what does this mean? Is such a mind placid like a mirror, a *tabula rasa,* and so empty? Is it possible for any mind to be empty? If it is empty, it does nothing. On the other hand, it should be directed towards the Supreme Being and reflect the Supreme Being. This reflection means being a perfect image, not the clean mirror. So it cannot be empty. And the stages through which one has to pass in order to be such a reflection are the stages of the Logos or Cosmic Person. So to be pure means to be one with the Cosmic Person and act according to the processes (laws) of the Cosmic Person, who is not a simple static being, not a mere *tabula rasa*. Simply put, it means: Develop a universal point of view, rise to the level of the universal law.[99] We have seen that reality, objectivity, as the Upaniṣads conceived it, is the law of the Cosmos or the Cosmic Person. So it contains the factor of necessity, logical, empirical, practical, ethical, and even aesthetic. To be pure is to cancel one's ego, and be one with the processes of the Cosmic Person. This is the state of what the *Bhagavadgītā* calls *sthita-prajña* or one with steadied rational consciousness, one whose enlightened mind is steady and not wavering; or in other words, rational consciousness marks his steadied character. This may sound like merely floating in a current, namely, of the processes of the Cosmic Person; but no, only a dead body floats in a current, a living body swims with it.[100] So to be one with the law guiding the processes of the Cosmic Person—for all processes are patterned and so are controlled by, or are the manifestations of the law of all laws—is to act according to that law. It is action controlled by the cosmic law that confers the proper reality attitude both to the world and to one's real self. There is no life without action; or as the *Bhagavadgītā* puts it, no one can live without action, even breathing is action. None can condemn it; even condemning it is action.

Again, we have to remember in this connection what has already been said that even in ethics "to be" is the aim of "to do" and is, therefore, more important than the latter. That is, every ethical action results in transforming my personality; and repeated ethical activity, like the hammer of the goldsmith, moulds my personality, i.e., my being. The ultimate result of this moulding is my becoming one with the Cosmic Person.

Thus action strengthens my reality sense and lifts me to the level of the Logos. As this empirical person, I feel my reality only with reference to, or taken along with the objective world. I am part and parcel of it. Without my active connection with the object, I may live in a world of fantasy, abstractions, etc. The object concerned has to be a real object, not an imaginary one. And the reality of the object is made less uncertain in action than in cognition, imagination, etc. The differences may be matters of degrees only; but even those differences are important for life. Practical life involves not only the reaction of inanimate objects to my action on them, but also the reaction of other persons to my actions towards them and affecting them. These activities tend to correct one another and shake me out of my fantasy about myself. The objects of imagination and artificial mental constructions like the unicorn are entirely dependent on my imagination. The objects of dream and illusions are dreamt as reacting to me and existing independently of my desires and imagination; but then when the dream is over and the illusion is corrected, they are found to have no spatio-temporal and causal relations with the objects of my waking self. Their difference from the objects of imagination lies in their reaction to my actions and in their existence independently of my desires and imagination. This independence is experienced in the objects of my waking consciousness; for they exhibit necessary spatio-temporal and causal relations (laws), which are not exhibited by the objects of dream and illusion.

These necessities are discovered by man through action on the objects and the observations of their reactions. My action on them and their reaction are patterned according to laws of necessity, and this necessity reveals the objectivity and reality of both myself and the object. Action should not have been dismissed as unimportant by any school. For it is through action and the expected reaction that my own reality sense is confirmed, my own real being apart from my being in the world of imagination and fantasy is repeatedly established, and true satisfaction, pleasure, and happiness, apart from those of dream and fantasy are realized. For as an empirical person, I have no being apart from the world of action. I am in the world and am a part of the world.

(vii) Levels of Being and Assimilation of Objectives

The Advaitins, we have noted, have spoken of four levels of Being, which are mistakenly interpreted as levels of truth in much of recent writing.[101] Each higher level transcends the lower. But this transcending is not by abstracting, but by assimilating, absorbing. The Supreme Brahman is described as the swallower, devourer (*attā*)[102] of the universe; for just as he creates and maintains it, he destroys it also. But where does it go when it is destroyed? One answer may be that it simply vanishes. But the Upaniṣads are opposed to such an idea of destruction. Only the forms and shapes of the world are gone, but not the being of the world, which is the Being of the Brahman. Then what happens to the world? It is absorbed, assimilated to the Brahman. The Brahman swallows, absorbs, assimilates the world to itself.

We can appreciate the idea, if we ask: What happens to the objects of imagination, when we stop imagining and start doing something else? They are absorbed into our own mind. The being (*sattā*) of the object of my imagination is the being of my mind into which the object disappears. The being of the object of my dream is the being of my empirical, waking self into which the dream disappears. That is why I can remember my dream, which sometimes accidentally comes up to my consciousness years later. Thus I am the retainer of the objects of my imagination and of dream in some form (potencies, seeds (*bijas*) which can sprout up again); in a sense, I am the swallower, devourer[103] of those objects. Have I devoured only the objects of my imagination and dream or am I also the devourer of the subjects (the I-consciousnesses) of them? If every object is necessarily related to a subject, then what is absorbed by the I of the waking state are the worlds of imagination and dream, of which my I also, in a transformed state, is a part. I remember what I did in my dream. Thus the transcending of the lower level by the higher level of Being is not by abstraction, but by assimilation. The world of imagination and dream, of which I am a part, is transcended through the process of assimilation to my world of action or waking, of which also I am a part. As belonging to the three worlds, I retain the objects of the lower worlds in myself and become part of the world of waking without interrelating the objects of the lower world to the objects of my waking.

We can now understand what it is for the Brahman to transcend the world of waking and action. The transcending takes place through me, my I-consciousness, by making it absorb the world of action. Or one may say that the world of action transcends itself, transforms itself, into the I-consciousness that is the Brahman. Thus, it seems that what is called Māyā, which is the force behind the appearing, issuing forth of the lower worlds, is not something apart from the Brahman, but is part and parcel of the Brahman's essential nature.[104]

Ontologically thus, the I-am is central for considerations of Being (*sattā*), as my action is central for truth and falsity of the world of action, which is to be called the cosmological world from the same standpoint, i.e., of Being. Falsity within the cosmological world is indicative that the Being of the object is only apparent Being (*prātibhāsika-sattā*), not meant for the observer's activity on it. Insignificant Being (*tuccha-sattā*) is what I knowingly project out of my mind, without losing myself in the object. We have already mentioned in a few places that in both true and false perception, the object is experienced as independent of the subject and that the subject in all perceptions becomes one with the object in the live act of perception, and forgets its own being. But in imaginating, the subject does not lose consciousness of himself, although in some cases of fantasy he forgets his real self and may pass into a day dream. And there can be several degrees of difference between imagination and dream.[105] But Being in all the states is to be found and traced to the different states of the I-am, which for the reason becomes central.

(viii) Advaita and the Austrian Theory: Wittgenstein

The Austrian (Brentano and Meinong) theory of Being is not to be confused with the four levels of Being in which even imaginary objects are said to have Being, although called insignificant. Again, the Neo-realists of America introduced the idea of subsistence for imaginary and false objects; and subsistence was to be distinguished from Existence. Such Neo-realists want to be thorough-going realists and want also to defend the independent reality of even illusory objects. But in the Advaita view, both the illusory and imaginary objects are absorbed into the self, the I-am, and can have no independent existence. For the same reason, they cannot have their independence or independent Being, which the Austrians accept. The self is all-absorbing and it absorbs both kinds of objects. In ordinary language, we say that they have disappeared, vanished. But if they vanish, why do we remember them? Why and how are they retained? One may say that they are only remembered, that they are produced by imagination prompted by memory. But memory refers to past experiences and objects, not to new experiences and objects. How are we to explain the experience of sameness in this connection? Are not the objects in some way the same? *Furthermore, do we not have to say that imagination exists, illusions exist, dreams exist? If they also exist, what is the nature of their existence or Being* (*sattā*)? This is the question which the Advaita can answer through its theory of the four levels of Being. But these levels are not set apart, they are inter-connected; and the connecting link is the I-am, to which they pertain, in which and to which they belong, and which absorbs all of them.

Because of this inter-connection, these four levels are not like four different realms of discourse or language game, as some admirers of Wittgenstein may tend to think. As some of his critics point out, Wittgenstein showed no way for inter-connecting different language games—man is, therefore, torn asunder—which cannot be done without a self-same person who plays them in different situations. And the person, although a member of society, is an individual with his own private life also, which Wittgenstein's philosophy apparently tends to ignore. The individual is the empirical I-am, the I-consciousness, in which not only the different language games, but also the different levels of Being are interrelated. Society is not a mere network of impersonal entities, but of persons, not a mere machine of life-less parts, but a cooperative and coordinated whole of free wills. So no analogy with Wittgenstein's theories will be appropriate in interpreting the Advaita theory.

(ix) Theories of Illusion and Means of Knowing: Their Significance

In the Vedānta particularly, and in all the other schools of Indian thought in general, the two questions form important branches of epistemology: (1) What is the metaphysical constitution or status of the object of illusion; and (2) Is every cognition valid or invalid by itself, i.e., by being a cognition or is it made invalid by something else? That they are important is significant of the general trend of Indian thought.

The discussion of these topics covers a large area of the literature of all the main schools. In the West, the Neo-realists and the Austrians, to whom we have referred already, were concerned with the first question. Even in F. H. Bradley we find the attempt to answer the question; for he held that falsity is a low type of truth in his theory of degrees of truth and reality, and that ultimately, "somehow," all falsity and unreality would be incorporated into the Absolute Reality. But the question, How?, has not been answered by him. The Advaita can answer; it is through the assimilation to the I-consciousness, which is the devourer (*attā*); but Bradley thought that the self was a falsity and rejected the only way open.

Now, how can a false object like the snake seen in a rope (in the illusion of mistaking the rope for the snake) become the rope, which negates it? If the snake of the illusion does not become the rope, what does it become when absorbed by the Absolute? There seems to be no answer in Bradley. But from the point of view here developed, the absorption or assimilation takes place through my I-consciousness, the perceiver of the illusion. The whole illusory experience, "That is a snake," is taken in as part of myself like taking in the dream experience into my waking person; it becomes "me." Another experience with the same That (subject) is now made objective in the form, "That is a rope." In this process the predicate form of the snake in "That is a snake," is made to vanish by making it part of the being of myself, which is my apperception; it is retained in my apperception and can be brought up when I remember my illusion.

Indeed, the Advaitins were content with saying that the snake vanishes, and that because it was experienced as something objective, it was neither Being, nor Non-being, and was therefore Māyā. But if the snake vanishes, where does it go? There is ultimately nothing but the Brahman, the Supreme I-am; and so it has finally to become one with the Being of the Brahman. But as it has become manifest through my experience, it becomes unmanifest (*avyakta*) also through my experience; for my being is representative of the Being of the Brahman; my I-am is the image, reflection, of the Supreme I-am. There is no realm beyond Being to which falsity goes; for there is no beyond, there is no Non-being, no Nothing.

The same idea as the above is implied in Bradley's theory that falsity is somehow absorbed by the Absolute, although he could not see how. In the drive of his thought towards Hegelianism from the side of the British empiricism, but not from the side of the Cartesian *cogito*, he started with the That as the object of perception, but not from the side of the I-am, which is the subject of perception, and dismissed the self as a mere appearance. But there is no discussion, certainly not an elaborate one, of why the That also is not a mere appearance. This step, combined with his doctrine of coherence, led him to the conclusion that the Absolute has to be an objective (excluding the subjective), organic whole. Then what happens to the consciousness of which the That is an object? Is the Absolute an unconscious organic whole? Bradley does not seem to be inclined towards such a view. If, on the other hand, it is conscious and is also an organic whole such an organic whole can only be an apperceptive mass, which is the same as objective thought, the Logos, Cosmic Reason. Then thought does not have to commit suicide in order to become the Absolute Reality. If thought cannot become reality without committing suicide, then what it becomes after committing suicide must be something above apperception, which is the Supreme

I-am or the Self. It is into the being of such a self that falsity of various types is absorbed. Without the recognition of the Absolute Self, there can be no satisfactory and intelligible explanation of the assimilation and absorption of all falsity into ultimate reality. We can now appreciate the significance and import of the doctrine of the four levels of Being. Coherence is not important here; it is only a method of the process by which the self constitutes the world of action and of waking consciousness and it is unending. To treat it as an accomplished fact, presenting a closed system of structure, will be a mistake. The liquidation of the object of illusion occurs in the self of the perceiver. Some explanations found in the literature of this school suggest that the being of the false object and that of the true object, e.g., of the snake and of the rope in the classical example, is given in the That in "That is a rope" and "That is a snake." The snake in the predicate form, though a particular, vanishes into nothingness. But this view of the school conflicts with the other view that there is no nothingness; and so nothing can disappear into it. Besides, as Nāgārjuna, the Mādhyamika Buddhist, questions: If the That and the "snake" are never perceived by me as distinct and separate, and if, as such, they cannot exist also as distinct and separate, if the "snake" disappears, the That also must disappear. So the fact must be that the whole experience, "That is a snake" is absorbed into my self[106] and a new experience, "That is a rope," is posited, indeed by projecting the same That. If the That is not the same, there can be no opposition between "That is a rope" and "That is a snake."

The above explanation of the illusory object with its own ontological foundations looks like idealistic; and so the realists in India gave other explanations to preserve the independent reality and being of the object. There is no doctrine of subsistence, as we have noted, or something like the ontology of the Austrians for the Indian realists, who maintain that the object of illusion is a real object seen somewhere else and remembered (the Mīmāmsā), or it is the same That as determined by the universal of something else which is real (the Nyāya). In either case, when falsity is realized, we recognize that the false object is constituted by real elements which we later trace and assign each to its proper place. But if the I-am is central to philosophy—which we have attempted to prove in the general estimates of the different philosophies so far—then the so-called real factors constituting the false object must disappear into the I-am. We cannot understand how an object seen somewhere else can be seen as the That in front with its new contours, size, etc. Besides, we shall then have not perception, but explicit recognition in the form, "This snake is the same as the one seen then or before." Nor can the false object be a misplacement of a universal. For even according to the Nyāya, the first contact[107] of the senses is with the object, and through it with the universal *present in it*. Then how can another universal come in to determine (*avacchid*) the object? These theories cannot stand by themselves without the centrality of the I-am.

The second question concerns the valid ways of knowing. We have already discussed the question, "How many valid means of cognition should be recognized?" Our answer was: "Every one recognized by the Indian schools and many more besides." But what has to be emphasized is that *pramā* (valid cognition) is not exactly the same as *satya* (literally, cognition tied to Being), although they often overlap in literature and can be made to overlap completely by analysis and criticism of the concepts. *Pramā* is cognition measured by a limit ($\sqrt{ma}$ means to measure, to limit), whereas *satya* is what is "agreeable to Being." We have already referred to these meanings. *Pramāṇas* or valid means of cognition are different measures (like bushels for measuring corn, etc.) of cognizing reality by fixing limits; they are the ways of limiting, of measuring reality, or rather the ways by which cosmological reality is obtained, established, and accepted.

As already pointed out, these ways are not foolproof, but generally correct and substantiate one another and are finally substantiated by, and substantiate action. But why are some valid ways accepted at all, or why is any valid way of knowing accepted at all? For instance, why should even perception be accepted as a measure of reality? Is the acceptance arbitrary? Is there a logical necessity for accepting it? What is the source of that necessity, if it exists? What is it that makes any means of knowing valid?[108] Is there any independent criterion or standard for validating their validity?

The Advaita, following the Mīmāmsā, maintains that every accepted means of knowing is valid in itself. That is, all cognition obtained by the accepted means of knowing is valid in itself (*svataḥ prāmāṇya*). A less sophisticated expression is: If you do not depend on cognition to know what an object is, on what else can you depend? Yes, cognition now and then goes astray; then it is corrected by another cognition or action and is therefore shown to be erroneous (unreliable) by something else (*parataḥ aprāmāṇya*). Then is not its erroneousness shown by another cognition—let it be another perceptual cognition or cognition of the result of action—which has of course to be valid and which produces the realization that the first cognition is invalid? Then the Sāṅkhya would say that the validity of the second cognition is known by itself and the invalidity also of the first is known by itself, when it comes up through memory and held together with the other in apperception. (Perhaps the introduction of apperception or *mahat, buddhi*, here meets the objection that no perceptual cognition can make another perceptual cognition its object and so both the valid and invalid cognitions have to be raised to the consciousness constituting apperception in other words, to witness consciousness, *sākṣi-caitanya*.) This theory is called the theory of cognition being valid by itself and also invalid by itself (*svataḥ prāmāṇya* and *svataḥ aprāmāṇya*). The Nyāya maintained that because the validity as well as the invalidity of any cognition are discovered by another cognition, cognition by itself is neither true nor false, but is made so by something else. This theory is called the doctrine that a cognition is made true or false by something else (*parataḥ prāmāṇyam* and *parataḥ aprāmāṇyam*). The next extreme view is that of the Vijñānavāda Buddhists, who maintained that all cognition is invalid by itself (*svataḥ aprāmāṇyam*) and made valid by another (*parataḥ prāmāṇyam*). There are other views coming in between these combinations and they have already been explained before. We have repeated some to suit the present context. Here the main alternatives are given to bring out the significance of measured cognition (*pramāṇa*), in which to be measured according to the accepted measures[109] is the same as to be valid. *Since these measures belong to the constitution of man, then man in the Socratic, not in the Protagorian, sense becomes the measure of the cosmos.*[110] That is, the whole cosmos falls within the consciousness of man, taken both in its depth and width, and is not something alien to him.

Here one may refer us back to the previous section and ask again: Why should we not call the four levels as levels of reality and levels of Being at the same time? For if the Buddhists say that all cognition is invalid by itself, they mean cognition in the world of action or empirical cognition. Then there must be a cognition above the empirical with which action has nothing to do and that is called *pramā* (valid knowledge). But first, the highest kind of knowledge—called *prajñā*, *ālayavijñāna*, etc., by this school—does not seem to be called *pramā* (measured knowledge). Even if in some not very famous work or in some places in the famous works even, it is called *pramā*, the writer does not use the term in the sense of measured knowledge or consciousness in the exact sense of the word *pramā*, but in the sense of the infinite, timeless consciousness. It is only a generalized, inexact use of the word. For any measure, like a mould, fixes many of the measureds, which are not beyond *pramā* and the result cannot be the immesurable (*aprameya*). The Buddhists also say that ultimate reality is *aprameya*. *Secondly*, it is absurd to call apparent Being (*prātibhāsika-sattā*) and insignificant Being (*tuccha-sattā*) by the names reality and truth by any classification, because they are called apparent and insignificant for the reason that they are other than reality and truth, which is decided at the cosmological level. There the apparent Being is called falsity and the insignificant as unworthy of classifying as even falsity. For the same reason, we should not use the terms "apparent reality" and "insignificant reality."[111] For the objects of these two levels are assigned to these levels only because they are found to be unreal.[112] Indeed, "apparent existence" and "insignificant existence" may be used, as Indian thought makes no distinction—perhaps rightly so—between Being and Existence. As many western philosophers have pointed out, Existence cannot be a predicate, so also Being cannot be a predicate; what cannot be a predicate cannot be finite, limited; it has therefore to be identical with Being;[113] so Being and Existence must be one and the same. We need not go very much into the question: If Existence is infinite, why do we say, "*X* has existence"? Such statements need to be rightly interpreted to avoid confusion. Russell and some others have wrestled with the problem.

We have to note also another point. At the highest level of the Absolute Being, the three distinctions—Being (or Existence), Reality, and Truth—collapse and become one. The highest Being is the Absolute, Transcendental Self (I-am). It is also the Absolute Reality, because it not only satisfies the criterion of noncontradiction, but also is non-contradictable and meets the highest criterion of logic, at the level of transcendental dialectic.[114] Such a dialectic even raises the question whether the so-called valid means of cognition (*pramāṇas*) are valid in the absolute sense. But what we call cosmological reality, or the second level of Being, accepts these valid means of cognition as final—each school accepting its own number of them and in its own way—and is decided to be what it is through them. That is, from the cosmological point of view, the world really has colours, sounds, smells, shapes, forms and so on. It is because the question is raised about what exactly is valid cognition (*pramā*) and what exactly is the valid means for it (*pramāṇa*), and it is found that the Absolute Self alone in a negative way (non-contradictability) meets the standards of such questions; it is also called Reality. There is absolute objectivity in it, not mere subjectivity as some existentialists think, although it is approached through finite subjectivity and its self-transcendence.[115] In fact, it cannot be reached without the finite self somehow merging, or becoming one with the Absolute Self (according to the Vedāntic schools); without thought committing suicide (according to F. H. Bradley); without leaping into the irrational or making an irrational leap (according to Kierkegaard); and without some kind of a shipwreck (according to Jaspers, Sartre,[116] and even Heidegger). Self-transcendence in a sense is irrational, not rationally accomplished—transcendence is not logical expansion, higher degree—as for example, we do not build up the world of waking consciousness by elements of the dream world, we jump out of the dream; but we should not forget that in this jumping or leaping, we carry our I-consciousness forward to higher and higher levels or, we may say, we carry the lower worlds through assimilation to our I-consciousness. We generally take the world of action to be the Reality; but the world is a self-contradictory idea, as Kant and others have shown. Or as Bradley says, the world is something hung on its sides from chains the ends of which are fixed to something we know not what.[117] So the idea of Reality also is self-contradictory, that is, it is not self-sufficient, self-standing.

Because we struggle to fix Reality through the valid means of cognition with the help of valid cognitions (truths), and for the reason that ultimate Reality is the self-conscious I-am and so consciousness, we call the Absolute by the name Absolute Truth also. It is what comprehends the knowing consciousness and the known object, that is, it is consciousness that is its own object, often called intuition, integral knowledge and so on. Simply because it is consciousness, it should not be identified with subjectivity as opposed to objectivity. At every transcendental level, as pointed out already, the opposition between subject and object at the lower level is overcome, and what transcends and covers both cannot be a mere subject[118] of the lower level. So there is some reason to call the highest I-am by the name the highest Truth. Yet to prevent drawing misleading conclusions and forming false opinions, we have to keep in mind the important distinction in meaning between the two questions: "Do dreams exist?" and "Are dreams true?" The answer to the first is: Yes; but to the second, it is: No. Apart from literary and popular usage, so far as philosophically technical usage goes, we have to differentiate between Being, Reality, and Truth.

(x) Space and Time

The Advaitins have not devoted much thought to space and time for the same reason that they have given little thought to action. It may be said that the general Mīmāmsā position—in spite of internal differences within the school into which we cannot enter here[119]—is that space and time, even if real, are adjuncts of action. They are two of the modes of all action. For that reason, it is the verb that has conjugations of past, present, and future, but not nouns. We have attempted, through the general estimates of the previous chapters, particularly those on the Nyāya, the Vaiśeṣika, the Sāṅkhya, and the Yoga, to show that their views have still to be transcended; for roughly put, time and space belong to action and to the world action, and action belongs to man, a self-conscious being, but not to mere material objects to which only process, which cannot be, apart from the observer, even Becoming, belongs. The difference between action and process and the necessity of consciousness for the being of time and space have already been shown. Now, some other problems connected with the two concepts will be discussed.

Which of the two, space and time, is the higher of the two? We raised this question already in an earlier chapter. For Kant the two are on the same level. For

Bergson time is the higher of the two. In the Pāñcarātra and the Pāśupata systems, time is higher than space, a higher significance[120] of which seems to be ignored by both the traditions. The Advaitins ignore the question, but not we.

Now, the present is the experience of the aspect of I-am in apperception. Apperception is not something different and separate from the I-am. It has no being of its own, when not activated by the I-am.[121] *The present then of time is the presence of the aspect of I-am in apperception*, which collects together past and future into the present. This collecting is done by the memory and anticipation aspects of the I-am in apperception. It is said that time belongs to action, the verb, but not to the noun. The I-am is a noun (pronoun as it is called). *But there is no action unless initiated by the I-am as in "I am walking."* In the experience of the I-am, part of the action of walking is past, part is being gone through, and part has still to be completed. There is a point in the I-am's action at which the action is completed and yet is not part of the past, which is actually the I-am's presence of itself as in action or as acting. That is why the I-am is called the eternal present. In the act of walking, as in cognizing an object, the I-am and the I-know are together; they have what may be called *tādātmyatā* (same-selfness). In the reflective consciousness, "I have walked," which implies "I know that I have walked," the I-am recedes and makes the experience of walking its past, when its present lies in itself as falling back (receding). The anticipated experience of, for instance, taking rest after the walk, will be the I-am's future with reference to its present. But the past is remembered and the future is anticipated, not as mere floating independent ideas, but as the I-am being involved in each. Memory and anticipation are interrelated through the I-am and so also are the past and the future. The past is of the form, "I-am remembering the I-am-as-walking"[122] and the future is of the form, "I-am anticipating the I-am-as-taking-rest." The experience of the involvement has always to be there in memory and anticipation, if they are to be memory and anticipation, even though such experience may be very weak sometimes. The nature of apperception is such as to be swaying between the I-am and the I-know,[123] the latter having an intentionality or directedness towards objectivity, directly experienced, remembered, anticipated, inferred, or imagined, with a tendency to make the object concrete as a sense[124] object. That is, mind does not rest—except in a way when it is doing higher logic and mathematics—until the directedness, which is also attending or fixing,[125] ends up in an object of sense, which is for the time stabilized. Even a mental image has sense content. There are no visual mental images for the ear and no auditory mental images for the eye and so on in ordinary experience.

Thus the source of time-consciousness and, according to the position developed here, of time is apperception. Similarly, the source of space and space-consciousness is apperception. Space is what makes the act of locating the objects possible. But the objects may be physical or imagined entities, universals like horseness and class concepts, remembered, anticipated or even abstract entities like those of logic and mathematics. All objects as known need location.[126] And do we not have any justification for raising the question: "Where is the directedness of the I-know consciousness located?" Where is apperception located? The I-am may be above space and time; but is the I-know also above space and time? Indeed, as we said that apperception is the source of space and time, to ask where apperception is located is to ask where space[127] is located and where time is located. What sense does it make to ask: "Is time within time?" or in a little less puzzling way, "Is time created in time?" or "When was time created?" Augustine said that time was created along with the world. We may accept the view in the sense that time is a constituent of the world. But when did that grand event occur, if there was the act of creation?

The upshot of the questioning is that space should not be conceived only as the physical space.[128] The physicists and the mathematical physicists may be concerned with it only; but philosophers ought to go beyond. There is the dream space as infinite for me as the physical space, psychological space in which the objects of my imagination exist, and logical and mathematical space in which logical and mathematical realities exist. *When we think of a + b, there must be some kind of space between whatever the two letters a and b stand for.* Apperception is the source of time and space and contains them in its constitution; it is, therefore, both time and space.[129] Physical space is a concretization of the apperceptive space; the process of concretization works through intentionality into the space of sense objects. That is why the Upaniṣads speak of several kinds[130] of space, which are really levels of space. The highest, if the Brahman also is to be regarded as space (*ākāśa*) for the reason that all things exist in it, then, has to be above time.[131] The question, "Which of the two is the higher?" cannot be answered with a simple Yes or No.

(xi) APPERCEPTION

We have seen that apperception is always of the form that it collects (*cinoti*) the past and the future through memory and anticipation into the present. As a collecting instrument, it is a means in the hands of the great swallower (*attā*), the Supreme I-am, into which everything finally enters. That is why questions like: "Does the past exist or is there a past?" and "Does the future exist?" or "Is there future?"—in which past and future are turned into the present—become meaningful to us. In and through this apperception the I-am is connected with the I-have-known and the I-shall know. But neither is the former merely retentive memory, nor is the latter merely wishful imagination. In both processes the laws of pure logic and mathematics and of the empirical sciences retain their control. And the logic of the laws also belongs to apperception. But in dreaming, fantasy, and wishful thinking, such control becomes weaker and weaker, until even the laws and logic of the empirical sciences become absent as in some very absurd dreams. In dreams memory is working, but only as retentive memory; then what we call logical memory is inactive. What makes us dream is some emotion (surge, motion) within, prompted by some desires or some weak or strong traumata which get reenacted generally for self-exhausting, for emptying themselves, and for becoming slowly merged and transformed into the general constitution of the self.

What is important to note here is what we call logical memory or the forces of pure logic and mathematics operative in apperception are closer to the pure, undifferentiated being of the I-am than the forces of the retentive memory. But even retentive memory is retentive only because of the stability and permanence of the base, the I-am, in which they are retained. The difference between the two kinds of memory is analogous (but not the same) to that between *natura naturans* and *natura naturata*, and that between the active intellect and the passive of the Neo-Platonists and the medieval thinkers. In the case of the retentive memory, so far as the laws of the empirical logic are operative, what we remember may not be mixed up; and when we fail to remember something, we struggle to remember it with the help of the laws of logic together with those of psychological association. But there is also pure logical memory. The forces of pure logic still remain discursive, in which whatever is represented by letters and symbols like *A*, *B*, and *C* and =, +, −, and so forth, remain distinct but transparently interrelated in the undiversified and undifferentiated light of the consciousness of the unitary I-am. That is why logic and mathematics are said to function beyond time and space. Although we cannot utter all the sounds and symbols simultaneously, but only in time, and we write them in extended space, what they represent exist near the I-am above time and space. Without the presence of the undivided I-am, the unity of every inference, which necessarily contains different elements, is not possible. Had Kant raised the question, Why is logic true ultimately?, he would have struck upon the undivided (*advaita*) I-am. He raised the question, Why do objects conform to my ideas?, but not, Why is logic true? And how is it known to be true?[132] This will be an ontological consideration about logic. If the *cogito* is indisputable, if I cannot question my existence when I am in my senses, the same indisputable element must be present in any inference (that is, its structure, not its empirical content) in any observation of coherence and consistency to confirm the truth of what is observed. As Bradley said, I have to make the three propositions of inference separately, hold them together, and observe their consistent unity (not merely holding the three letters and the three propositions as one group before my mind, but also as being consistent with one another with the relations of implication in between) for asserting the conclusion to be true. I make the first proposition, then I make the second, and next I make the third. In all the three the I has a special relationship to its assertions. When there is consistency, the special relationship remains uniform and identical; when there is inconsistency, the I realizes that its universality and identity are disturbed, and there is a jar in its being. The I as making an assertion inconsistent with the other two assertions feels a dividedness in its being. What divides the I-am then cannot be logically true. It may be objected that this is only a psychological explanation, not ontological. But if ontology is to be traced to the I-am,[133] none should dismiss the *cogito* as psychologism. Otherwise, no true ontology would at all be possible. The I-am is central to Being and is not opposed to it or even to the cosmological world.

We have to recognize then that apperception has levels within it. It is the source of both time and space. But part of it is above time. It has cosmological, objective significance, the significance becoming greater in its higher parts or levels. At its lower levels, it is merely mine and is motivated in its workings by my motives. That is why the Sāṅkhya[134] describes apperception (*citta*, *buddhi*) as the function of cognitive and ethical decision (*adhyavasāya*) and also knowledge, merit, non-attachment, which is described by Patañjali as self-control or self-conquest, and different kinds of extraordinary and supernatural powers. But apperception has two levels—the higher, which is the pure (*sāttvika*) form to which the above characteristics belong, and the lower (*tāmasic*) form to which the opposite characteristics belong. The middle Attribute (*rajas*) activates both. Now, the lower ones belong to the finite individuals who are selfish, lazy, stupid and so on. But by possessing the higher, the Vedāntins would say, we partake of the Logos or Cosmic Reason, for whom the Sāṅkhya, as we pointed out earlier, has no place, but ought to give a place. The Vedāntins will have no objection to absorbing the Sāṅkhya by going beyond. And we have shown that apperception (*buddhi*, *citta*) is not merely what the Sāṅkhya and the Yoga say it is, but contains much more besides.

(xii) Ontological Causation and Cognition of Being

Śaṅkara's contribution to the theory of causation has already been referred to. It is the concept of cause as that which produces the effect without itself being affected in the process (i.e., *vivartakāraṇa*). It is a separate concept from that of the cause which is affected and is lost as such in the process (i.e., *pariṇāma-kāraṇa*). When for instance, the seed becomes the tree, we cannot get back the same seed. But when gold is made into a ring, we can get back the gold. When examples like this are given by the Advaitins, the readers think that Śaṅkara is referring to what Aristotle calls the material cause as distinct from the other kinds. But the interpretation is a half-way house at the most to the right meaning, but generally a mistake. *We can best understand Śaṅkara as referring to the ontological cause.* He himself says that similarities should not be carried on all fours between the explanatory examples and the concept to be explained, but should be taken only as helping guides leading to proper understanding. When he says that the Brahman is the cause of the first type (*vivarta-kāraṇa*) for the world and explained it with the example of a lump of gold, he does not mean that there is somebody who transforms the Brahman by beating it with a hammer. He means that the being of everything (i.e., its "to be,") lies in its being rooted in the Brahman; and that in that sense, the Brahman is the support of everything that is. The other aspect of this causation, viz., that the world is due to the mysterious power of the Brahman which throws out of itself the shapes and forms of the world, makes the Brahman the efficient[135] cause also. But because ultimately, the stuff of the universe is the Being of the Brahman, it is the ultimate material cause also. This idea simply means that the Supreme Spirit (I-am) is everywhere, in all things, just as the gold made into a ring is everywhere in every part of the ring. But there is this difference: gold is unconscious matter, while the Supreme Being is the consciousness itself. If as Being and consciousness, God is everywhere, then the worry of many theologians that God cannot be the material cause of the world will be pointless. Just as I am everywhere both in my I and every part of every object of my dream, the Supreme Being is everywhere both in my I-am and in every part of every object I experience. God in many religions is the Supreme Being, the Supreme Consciousness, and the Supreme I-AM. As the ultimate ontological Being, he is the foundation of all our beings (to-bes). He is the support of my being, not like the table with the books on it, but like the ocean of the waves, like the sun of its reflections, like my face of the many images in mirrors. The significance of these metaphors and similes has already been explained.

It has also been explained already that the Supreme Being is the Supreme I-AM.[136] The I-am at various stages is the Being at those levels. It is only the I-am that can cognize Being as such. The senses cognize colours, tastes, sounds, etc., not the being or the existence of the object; mind cognizes forms, pains and pleasures, not again the being or the existence of the object. Then how do I get at all the idea of the existence of the object? It is only the I-am that can cognize existence or being.[137] As the ego (*ahaṁkāra*) or as present in the ego function,[138] the I-am only appropriates the given experience and so the cognition of existence has to be by apperception (*citta*) in which the I-am is present at a higher level than in the ego, and which splits up into the subject (ego) and the object, thus conferring existence on both. We can now appreciate the Hegelian contention that Reason confers existence on objects—a view that can be traced to the Stoics and Neo-Platonists—which we perceive and the Sāṅkhya view that mind and its objects are derived from Mahat (apperception, *citta*) through the ego[139] (*ahaṁkāra*). But Reason can do the conferring only if itself is ontological, which it can be again only by being a higher I-am. Reason in the sense of a mere structure of inference or a mere network of bloodless categories ends up only in giving us a lifeless concept, but not an object with full-blooded being.

NOTES

[1]Situated in the state of Mysore, now called Karnataka.

[2]For a detailed exposition of the Advaita of Śaṅkara, see the author's *Idealistic Thought of India*, S. Radhakrishnan's *Indian Philosophy*, Vol. II and S. N. Dasgupta's *History of Indian Philosophy*, Vols. I and II.

[3]See his *Khaṇḍanakhaṇḍakhādya*. G. N. Jha translated it into English.

[4]See his *Khaṇḍanakhaṇḍakhādya*. G. N. Jha translated it into English, p. 239.

[5]Ibid., p. 397. [6]Ibid., p. 530.

[7]See the author's article, "Nature of Mind and its Activities," in *The Cultural Heritage of India*, 2nd edition, Vol. III, and S. Radhakrishnan: *Indian Philosophy*, Vol. II, pp. 485 fol.

[8]There are differences of view on the perceptual process among the Advaitins, which I cannot explain here. See Appaya Dīkṣita: *Siddhānta-leśasaṅgraha*, pp. 146–80.

[9]Dharmarāja: *Vedāntaparibhāṣā*.

[10]Rāmānuja: *Śrī Bhāṣya*, Vol. I, pp. 18 fol., and 50 fol.

[11]Dharmarāja: *Vedāntaparibhāṣā*, pp. 153–57.

[12]Mādhavacārya: *Sarvadarśanasaṅgraha*, p. 163. The object is created by cosmic Māyā for purposes of our action, but is not constituted by its potentiality to be an instrument of our action.

[13]Interpretations can still differ.

[14]The Indian epistemologists did not have a word for subsistence. Even then, to use a new word is only a verbal escape without solving the problem raised.

[15]Such dialectic is found in Bradley's *Appearance and Reality*.

[16]For a detailed discussion, see Śrī Harṣa: *Khaṇḍanakhaṇḍakhādya*.

[17]According to Vidyāraṇya, empirical reality is a product of Māyā and the illusory snake is a product of *Avidyā*. See his *Sarvadarśanasaṅgraha*, p. 163.

[18]The distinction between ultimate and pragmatic Being supplies the philosophical reason for the advice of Berkeley and Hume to think with the learned and act with the common man.

[19]and by the intuition of the Brahman.

[20]We may consider using a multi-valued logic and multi-valued ontology, or a two-valued logic and multi-valued ontology, or a multi-valued logic and two-valued ontology. The Advaitins did not have these possibilities before them.

[21]See Appaya Dīkṣita: *Siddhāntaleśasaṅgraha*, pp. 71 fol.

[22]Cp. Jung's theory of the collective and individual Unconscious, which can throw some light on this Advaita doctrine. Cp. also Schopenhauer's use of Māyā in his philosophy of the will and E. von Hartmann's idea of the Unconscious.

[23]See Madhusūdana: *Advaitasiddhi*, Chapter I, for a discussion of ultimate truth and falsity.

[24]See Śaṅkara's commentary on the *Vedāntasūtras*, II, i, 21–23 and 26–29.

[25]Poetic fancy and imagination can build up unicorns, damsels bathing in the divine river (the milky way is called so), etc., and the expressions are understood. But we cannot construct in imagination the

meanings of expressions like "the son of a barren woman," "circular square," "crooked straightness," etc. So even of admittedly nonexistent objects, there are kinds. Strictly speaking, nothing should be pronounced false, unless understood. To understand is to know the meaning. But often we call the above expressions meaningless.

[26]This analysis removes the purely speculative nature of arguments like that of a *contingentia mundi.*

[27]Appaya Dīkṣita: *Siddhāntaleśasaṅgraha,* pp. 182–83.

[28]The analysis of this idea by the Advaitins and Sartre (other existentialists also) throws extra light on each other's ideas.

[29]See Śaṅkara's commentary on the *Vedāntasūtras,* III, iii, 34; Appaya Dikṣita: *Siddhāntaleśasaṅgraha,* pp. 182–209; the author's *Idealistic Thought of India,* pp. 114 fol., and *Indian Idealism and Modern Challenges,* Chapters XI and XIII.

[30]See S. Radhakrishnan: *Indian Philosophy,* Vol. II, pp. 533–61.

[31]Śaṅkara's commentary on *Vedāntasūtras,* II, iii, 41–53.

[32]Appaya Dīkṣita: *Siddhāntaleśasaṅgraha,* pp. 79–123.

[33]This idea corresponds to the idea of the Logos, or Prajāpati (Virāt, Hiraṇyagarbha, etc.). That is, my soul is a reflection, image, determination, etc., of the Logos, which in its turn is a reflection, image, determination, etc. of the Supreme Brahman.

[34]See the author's *Idealistic Thought of India,* pp. 114 fol., and his article on "Post-Śaṅkara Advaita" in *History of Philosophy: Eastern and Western,* Vol. I. See also S. N. Dasgupta: *History of Indian Philosophy,* Vol. II, Chapter IX.

[35]I should say that this controversy is wrongly carried on from an external point of view (*bāhyadṛṣṭi*). But from the human and experiential point of view, both the Brahman and Māyā are experiences (*anubhūtis*). They are not like physical light and physical darkness.

[36]I, i, 2.

[37]Compare and contrast with Vijñānabhikṣu's view.

[38]See the author's *Idealistic Thought of India,* pp. 111–14.

[39]Ibid., pp. 409 fol., and 416 fol. [40]Ibid., pp. 106 fol.

[41]I still think that the authorship of *Ānandalahari* and *Prapañcasāratantra* cannot be denied to Śaṅkara; for as the commentaries say, they agree with the Advaita view that the Brahman creates the world with the help of his mysterious power, Māyā.

[42]That is, they have spatially to exclude one another at all places and times. But they do not do so.

[43]Except in some indirect sense in answer to questions like, "Why is Jim not bold like Bill?"

[44]Śaṅkara's commentary on the *Brahmasūtras,* II, i, 14–20.

[45]Raṅgarāmānuja identifies them with the *vyūhas* or pure creations of the Pāncarātra school. See my *Idealistic Thought of India* for the Pāncarātra.

[46]He is called also the Primary Life (*Mukhyaprāṇa*) of the cosmos.

[47]Even the followers of Rāmānuja identify Virāt, Hiraṇyagarbha, and Īśvara with Brahma, Viṣṇu, and Rudra, the three cosmic levels of the Logos, corresponding to the gross sense objects, subtle objects, and the undifferentiated mass of Māyā.

[48]See S. Radhakrishnan: *Indian Philosophy,* Vol. II, pp. 452 fol.; S. N. Dasgupta: *History of Indian Philosophy,* Vol. I, pp. 420 fol., and Sacchidānanda Sarasvati: *Māṇḍūkyarahasyavṛtti,* the latest and best work on Guaḍapāda in Sanskrit.

[49]He was influenced also by the *spanda* (vibration) doctrine of Śaivism. (See the author's "An unnoticed Aspect of Gauḍapāda's Māṇḍūkya kārikās, "*Annals of the Bhandārkār Oriental Research Institute,* Vol. xxvi, Parts III-IV, 1946.)

[50]Cp. occasionalism and allied doctrines.

[51]Indeed, the principle of inexplicability can be extended further. Is matter explicable in terms of life or vice versa? Life is not matter, but yet it cannot exist without matter. So it is neither matter nor not matter. The explicable, the significant, the true, and their opposites seem to have a logical connection. But this methodological question has not been worked out by the Advaitins.

[52]This view may not look strange if we take Hiraṇyagarbha as the first born *jīva or jivottama.*

[53]See Saṅkara's commentary on the *Vedāntasūtras,* I, i, 5–11, I, iv, 1–7, and II, i, 1–2.

[54]Śaṅkara, according to Radhakrishnan, makes six significant uses of the concept of Māyā. (1) It means the self-contradictory nature of the world. (2) The Brahman is known to our thought as the ultimate Being, due to which the world appears as existing, in spite of its self-contradictory world nature. Yet, the

same thought wants to know how the self-contradictory world can be related to the nonself-contradictory Brahman. The relation is a mystery, and Māyā is an expression of this mystery. (3) As the Brahman is everything, we think that it is the cause of the world. But a cause transforms itself in producing the effect, whereas the Brahman is posited in the doctrine of the four levels as the perfect Being that remains always perfect. This kind of causality that can be attributed to the Brahman, if we wish to attribute it, is that of Māyā. (4) The Brahman is said to appear as the world through the instrumentality of Māyā. (5) Māyā is the power of Īśvara, through which he expresses himself as the world, the Brahman remaining undisturbed. This connotation of Māyā is found in the views of those Advaitins who accept that Īśvara may be conceded some reality. (6) Māyā is the unmanifest state (*avyakta*) of the world before it is born. These significances have already been explained. (*Indian Philosophy*, Vol. II, pp. 573–74.) In addition, Māyā makes liberation possible in Śaṅkara's philosophy.

[55]The laws of negation and difference also may be added to them; for like space, time, and causality, the forms of negation and difference constitute the structure of cosmological Being.

[56]II, iv, 1–2.

[57]Rāmānuja: *Śrī Bhāṣya*, Vol. I, pp. 5 and 11.

[58]See his commentary on *Vedāntasūtras*, III, iv, 26–27, *Bhagavadgītā*, II, 47, and *Vivekacūḍāmaṇi*, II, 47.

[59]II, v. [60]II, viii. [61]II, vii.

[62]See K. C. Pandey: *Abhinavagupta*. [63]IV, iii, 21.

[64]The term *taṭastha-lakṣaṇa* literally means a characteristic indifferent, aloof, to the being of the object. The other kind forms the very being of the object. The term "constitutive" also may be misleading, perhaps "apposite" may be better. *Svarūpa* means in this context being. We may write, "Brahman = Being + Consciousness + Bliss." *Svarūpalakṣaṇa* translated as "existential quality" may perhaps be well understood because of the vogue of existentialism and ontology. *Sat, cit* and *ānanda* may, for practical purposes, be explained as the constituent attributes of ontological Being, or as its substantive qualities.

[65]Cp. the famous verse, "Being (Existence), appearance (glittering, shining) and pleasantness, and form and name: these are the five factors (of everything in the world). The first three belong to the Supreme Spirit, the other two to the world." But what is to be emphasized is that the world cannot be apart from the other three. The position of Maṇḍana Misra in his *Brahmasiddhi* (Govt. Oriental Manuscripts Series, Madras, 1937; ed. by S. Kuppuswami Sastri) is essentially ontological and is called by the editor ontological monism (*ens-monismus*). Maṇḍana is a pre-Śaṅkara Advaitin.

[66]The verbal root is *ma*, from which the word *māyā* is derived meaning measure.

[67]Another intriguing question is the proverbial: "Have you stopped beating your wife? Answer Yes or No." See whether this comes under contradiction, contrareity, or a third something. Formalized logic, divorced from life and experience, is led to ignore many forms of opposition. The man questioned may have never beaten his wife or he may have no wife at all. See whether the question can be related to: "Has the King of Utopia a beard or has he not? Answer only Yes or No."

[68]For a time I thought that the opposition in the four-cornered negation is contrareity. But in contrareity, both alternatives can be false; but here both cannot be false also. So this opposition is neither contradiction or contrareity, but of a third kind (*tṛtīya-prakāra*).

[69]Indeed, they can be related psychologically as being impressions of past experiences projected into the status of independent objectivity. But the point to note is that I relate myself to the subject of dreams and illusions, but not the objects of my waking consciousness to the objects of dream and illusion through cause-effect, identity, space, and time relations.

[70]Wittgenstein and his followers make several distinctions such as compound propositions, atomic propositions, sense-less propositions, nonsensical propositions, and corresponding facts, most of which fall outside the real world, and statements about it. Modern followers of this school can do something similar.

[71]Cp. Bradley's difficulties in his attempt to fix which part of the mental image is the idea or the universal. Compare it with the theory developed in this book, viz., in both its passive and active forms it is the form of positing the individual and the form of assimilation to the self, that is, the transcendental one. The universal is the name for the activity of the inner sense (*antahkaraṇa*) in both the processes.

[72]Rāmānuja misunderstood and misinterpreted Śaṅkara at this point. Śaṅkara does not deny that every object has its own structure and determinateness at the cosmological level. But at the ontological level, all is one or indistinguishable. There determinateness is transcended. Rāmānuja confused the two levels and asked: "If all is one, why should one interested in buying a cow, not buy a buffalo?"

[73]W. P. Montague: *Ways of Knowing*.

[74]Mythologically called the egg (*aṇḍa*), cosmic or individual, i.e., the universe in its latent, unmanifest, integral form. It is called also *bindu* (seed, like the acorn of the oak) in Śākta and Śaiva literature. (*binduh vedyasya samskārah*)

[75]For Kaśmir Śaivism, Māyā is the original force, power (*śakti*) of the Brahman (Śiva), which inserts itself between him and a projected objective world, the determinants of which are generally regarded as derivatives from Māyā. The word has several important meanings in Indian thought.

[76]Deeper questionings about the nature of the ultimate categories like Being and Becoming lead to severe complications. They cannot be raised here.

[77]The relation between the two is generally said to be *tādātmya* (same-self-ness), often translated as identity, here a very inadequate term.

[78]"The world is not Being" and "The world is not Non-being" are not as such contraries; but "The world is Being" and "The world is Non-being" are contraries because both of them are false and a third something is true. What we have to note is that the opposites of two contraries are not themselves contraries, for both of them are true. This does not exactly correspond to the square of opposition of the classical logic. But even there, we have to note that the contrary opposition to a contrary opposition (double negation) does not necessarily lead to affirmation. It looks as though there are here different kinds of logic, e.g., formal logic in which contradiction is the primary form of negation, concrete logic, in which contrareity is primary, and a logic that transcends both. Here we have one topic of transcendental logic.

May we regard the first opposition as sub-contrary opposition and the second contrary opposition? But here the subject of all the four propositions is the same, while the sub-contraries of traditional logic have "some" as their subject and one of them is affirmative. Or should we say that sub-contrary opposition has deeper implications which have to be worked out?

[79]*Sattā* and *sat* mean Being or Existence. The former is an abstract noun from the latter, but means the same, as there cannot be Being-ness or Existenceness. *Satyam* means that which is "meant for," "favourable to," "form of," "nature of," or "bound to" (*baddham*) Being or Existence. Falsity is called abaddham (that which is not bound to Being or Existence). The words *pramāṇa*, *prāmāṇyam*, and *prameya* and *prameyatvam* are not used in this context at all. Being or Existence is beyond all *pramāṇas*.

[80]For instance, there is no expression like *vyāvahārika-prāmaṇyam*, *prātibhāsika-prāmāṇyam*, or *pāramārthika-prāmāṇyam*. All *pramāṇas* are *vyāvahārika* and so no adjective is needed. The second is opposed to all *pramāṇas*, and the third is beyond *pramāṇas*.

[81]*Satyam* is heavily weighted by *satta* or Being, *pramāṇa* by the empirically cognitive reference, and *ṛtam* by reference to ethical activity. Often the three words are interchanged, but technically have different meanings.

[82]Mode, reflection, and image perform the same functions, even if they do not have the same connotation, in this context.

[83]See how it is associated with the misunderstood parallelism of Spinoza.

[84]That is why the exhortation to practice detachment. It is for the purpose of dissociation from the lower and identification with the higher.

[85]Some Upaniṣads give up to sixty levels from one point of view. Here is the positive significance of *vairāgya*.

[86]Cp. these levels with the levels of what is called pure creation in the Pāśupata and Pāñcarātra traditions. See my *Introduction to Comparative Philosophy*. Compare similar levels in the philosophy of Aurabindo Ghosh.

[87]Cp. the philosophies of the Stoics, Philo, Plotinus, Origen, and John Scotus Eregina, and see how they fit with or into Spinoza's.

[88]This is explained also as the soul of Hiraṇyagarbha.

[89]Here the traditional Advaitins may disagree with me. The point will be further discussed later in the general estimate of Rāmānuja's philosophy. I think that it is a mistake to treat the witness (*sākṣi*) as different from the latter; the witness absorbs, swallows (*atti*) what he witnesses and what is witnessed enters his being and loses itself or its distinctness in it. We can then explain also where Māyā comes from and what it enters when it vanishes.

[90]Māyā, as the Unconscious, has no separate existence of its own. There is no Unconscious in the absolute sense. In this sense, some existentialists who deny the reality of the Unconscious seem to be right. Even Jung thinks that the Unconscious can be turned into the Logos.

[91]These ideas are generally left as mystic and mysterious in the Vedāntic thought and even in Christian theology. But their elucidation is necessary for an earnest grasping of one's personality.

[92]See the author's article, "Being, Becoming, and Essence: East and West."

[93]We may find here the justification for Plato calling his Ideas substances; for it is "substance" that supplies the needed factor to the nature or structure of Becoming, which is, for Plato, this empirical world.

[94]Remember that *ens* and essence come from the same root.

[95]Which is unfortunately strengthened by the doctrine that the world is not even born or created (*ajātivāda*) in its popular interpretations. It is one thing to say that, when I realize that the I and everything else are the Brahman and ask: Where is the world as different from the Supreme I-consciousness?; but completely another thing to say that because the world has no separate existence at that stage, it is not born at all for me even at my stage. This extreme view is found *mutatis mutandis* in the Advaita, Mādhyamika Buddhism, and Kasmir Śaivism also, although the last is more constructive in explaining its philosophy than the others. But unfortunately, it got enmeshed in some popularized, undesirable, *tañtric* forms of worship and spiritual practice.

[96]Indeed, there is a leap from one state of the *ātman* to another, from one transcendence to the next. But this leap has to be a self-conscious one from one stage to another in the progress towards self-realization and the consciousness should be realistic. See *Tripād-vibhūti-Mahānārayāṇa Upaniṣad.*

[97]Sureśvara in his *Naiṣkarmya-siddhi* (Establishment of Non-action) took the extreme view that salvation cannot be obtained through action, not even by combining it with knowledge (gnosis). He thereby goes not only against the central teaching of the *Bhagavadgītā*, but also against the teaching of Maṇḍana Miśra (simply called Maṇḍana), the author of *Brahmasiddhi* (Attaining the Brahman). The orthodox tradition identifies the two persons, the latter being the name of the former before he was converted to a monk's life (*sannyāsa*) by Śaṅkara. Some moderns believe that the two are different persons, as their views are completely opposed. But note that Maṇḍana, although a great Mīmāmsaka, was a upholder of the Advaita, called by the latter group as pre-Śaṅkara Advaita — and Vācaspati Miśra is said to be influenced by it. However, I think that it is the most constructive of the available works of this school in presenting how man can realize the highest.

Maṇḍana says that verbal knowledge like the words "Thou art the Brahman" cannot produce the gnosis-experience of the identity of the finite and infinite spirit or I-consciousness without proper meditation (*prasankhyāna*) and actively good ethical life. But Sureśwara says that it does, and actions are unnecessary and are even hindrances. But in my opinion, the two views are not necessarily opposed. For the former is speaking of verbal knowledge at the level of the ordinary man, who has not yet attained the needed pure state of mind, while the latter is speaking of it at the level when man has attained the level of purity at which the sentence can produce the experience of the identity of the finite *ātman* and the Brahman. Maṇḍana is more practical than Sureśvara in that no amount of shouting, as he says, that the *ātman* is the Brahman can produce the realization in ordinary minds. It is like telling a little boy that loving girls is more enjoyable than eating candy. Besides, knowledge conveyed by language is indirect knowledge, and indirect knowledge of the Brahman is not enough to lead to salvation. For obtaining direct knowledge (*aparokṣānubhūti*) or experience of the Brahman, one has to go through all processes and activities which liquify the hard knot of the ego and lead to its sacrifice or identity or merging in the Supreme Being. What also is the significance of declaring that the Brahman is beyond speech, if the words of a sentence can produce the experience of the Brahman?

In any case, the full implications of ethical action do not seem to have been recognized and worked out in the Advaita works. But one can trace them in the discussions of Maṇḍana's work. The main point is that ethical action, good or evil, is not an unconsciousness process like the attraction of iron by the magnet; it is *sākṣivedya* or witnessable and witnessed by the witness consciousness. It becomes a *samskāra*, a latent potentiality, and then a part of the agent's personality; it transforms his personality and goes on transforming it through good and selfless deeds until the personality becomes one with the World Person. It becomes *Sāttvika*, pure, opening the gateway to the Supreme Being, the gateway to the realization of the indentity.

These ideas—they have further implications like even pure personality does not push aside its content, but assimilates (*atti*, bhakṣati), swallows it and transforms it; and that purity of personality is not emptiness, but equilibrium, balance, *sthitaprajñatā*—do not seem to have been seriously taken into consideration by the later Advaitins. If Prakṛti is the *sāmyāvasthā*, equilibrium, peace, of the turbulent Attributes, then the Brahman is the equilibrium, peace of all the activities of the world of Māyā or

Becoming. He is not a *tabula rasa*, not empty consciousness. At this point also Maṇḍana seems to me to be more consistent than Sureśwara and Vimuktātman, all of whom reached the greatest spiritual heights. For while Maṇḍana maintains that the Brahman is positive Being uncontaminated by any kind of Non-being, i.e., without any reference to it—his philosophy is called *bhāvādvaita* (the Advaita of pure positive Being)—the others are worried about how to relate the negation of the world to the Brahman; and they call the negative relation a fifth kind of negation (*pañcamaprakāraka-abhāva*)—that is, it is neither Being, nor Non-being, nor both, nor neither, nor all the four together. But does the new concept—it looks like artificial fabrication—not mean that the Brahman is both Being (of consciousness) and Non-being (of Māyā) at one and the same time? And what happened to the two important doctrines that the negative has no ontological validity but is only the underlying positive, and that the positive ontologically needs no reference to the negative, but the negative needs reference to the positive? Why should the consciousness of the Brahman need any negative reference to Māyā? It will be rewarding to study the three works: Maṇḍana's *Brahmasiddhi* (Superintendent, Govt. Press, Madras, 1937), Sureśvara's, *Naiṣkarmyasiddhi* (University of Mysore, Mysore, 1965), and Vimuktātman's *Iṣṭasiddhi* (Gaekwad Oriental Institute, Baroda, 1933).

[98]As prescribed by the Vedas and the ethical codes. But in the present age we need not limit ethical action to these books.

[99]Often expressed as the law of the Veda, law of Buddha, law of Christ, etc.

[100]One should see that this goes against the modern general existentialist teaching that man ought not to be guided by any law above him, as it violates his freedom. But freedom does not lie in going against the law of the Cosmic Person, but in being one with him. To go against him is self-destructive, and true freedom does not lie in self-destruction.

[101]We have explained that the levels are primarily ontological, not even epistemological. There is epistemology involved in fixing the ontological levels, but is not primary in this context.

[102]Cp. *Vedānta Aphorisms*, I, 2, 9.

[103]When many classical writers derive the word *ātman* from the verbal root $\sqrt{ad}$ which means to eat, some western scholars think that the derivation is artificial and I also was guided by them. Now, we see the reason for this derivation, for the *ātman* is that which absorbs everything else. This gives a justification, viz., for occasionally calling it Death.

[104]The same is the way by which Becoming is absorbed into Being, and the past is absorbed into the *ātman*, projecting itself into the future.

[105]It may be worthwhile to carry out a detailed phenomenological analysis of the different degrees of difference between imagination in which one is conscious of one's true being and dreaming in which one projects a false being of oneself and loses touch with his true being.

[106]Indeed, Nāgārjuna does not accept the reality of the self also, but only of the Śūnya.

[107]Cp. the different kinds of sense-object contact (*sannikarṣa*) propounded by the Nyāya school.

[108]Here one may be reminded of Wittgenstein's theory of the difference between "saying" and "showing." But "showing" the validity really means that it is valid by itself, as the Mīmāmsakas say. Or as some logicians say about the validity of the principle of contradiction, to prove that it is valid, we have to use, assume its validity. Its validity lies in its inescapable use, it shows itself.

[109]These measures are really manifestations of the Supreme I-am; Māyā then is the means of the Supreme's manifestation, and also its veil when we are confined to the manifestations and miss the Supreme, as in Plato's allegory of the cave.

[110]Cp. the Buddhist view that the body is the only *pramāṇa*.

[111]This author committed such a mistake in his *Thought and Reality*. See also his paper, "Being, Existence, Reality, and Truth" which also commits some mistakes.

[112]Some Indian writers thought that the four are degrees of truth and reality. This is a mistake as there is no question of degree, "how much," here.

[113]When I once asked Heidegger whether Being was finite or infinite, he replied it depends on what we understood by the word. Perhaps he was thinking of his idea of *ex-sistere* or *Dasein*. In a way, the Hegelian category of Being, which is empty, is to that extent finite.

[114]As found in Śrī Harṣa and also Bradley.

[115]We should note that self-transcendence is not that of a mere point called the I, but the I as including its whole world at the level, as assimilating and transforming it to itself.

[116]Sartre and Heidegger have different conceptions of the finite's failure and frustration. For Sartre, consciousness, which for him is Non-being, can never become Being, and the ideal of the identity of the two

can never be reached. This is his well-known position. For Heidegger, Dasein is destined to end up with care and Nothingness and cannot realize the underlying Being. These philosophical structures and schemata have to be translated into the Vedānta for understanding the essence of all the patterns of human thinking, which will be the same for all philosophies of human existence. Has not Bosanquet said that the extremes would meet?

[117]Cp. Kant's transcendental dialectic.

[118]As indicated already, this position overcomes the so-called parallelism of Spinoza and the pre-established harmony of Leibniz. The highest transcendental I-am cannot be merely one among many.

[119]Interested students who know Sanskrit may consult *Mīmāmsākośa* (Mīmāmsā Encyclopedia). There has been no meaningful presentation of the Mīmāmsā philosophy in English so far.

[120]The set of categories which are called mixed (pure and impure) may be said to belong, for both the schools, to what is called my transcendental apperception, not my finite or lower apperception.

[121]See the author's paper, "Self and Body: How Known and Differentiated" in *The Monist.*

[122]In this experience, the I-am, as the present, transcends its past by absorbing it into itself. It is the eternal present, eternity present in time as the present, swallowing both the past and the future. Time with its three moments is an aspect of eternity, its image in a sense.

[123]Early Sāṅkhya equated apperception (*mahat*) to the self-assertion of the I-am, but omitted recognizing the I-know factor. It should be noted that even the combination of the two is above the ego (*ahaṁkāra*).

[124]Husserl does not seem to have stressed the point that intentionality works through the senses, which belong to the individual.

[125]They may be voluntary or involuntary.

[126]It is worth reflecting on the idea that everything is a (its own) spatio-temporal contour. Then we have to say that every object has its own space and time. If every object is a posit of the transcendental ego, then this ego posits every object with its own space and time. Where objects do not have spatio-temporal contours (*mūrtis*) as in logic and mathematics, we have to think of a different kind of space and time.

[127]The question, "Is *Mahadākāśa* located in a different kind of *ākāśa*?" does not make much sense. As it originates in Māyā, Māyā also is described as *ākāśa* in some Upaniṣads. Even the Brahman is described as *ākāśa* in some places, as everything, both physical and non-physical, is located in it.

[128]A mistake committed by some Indian systems also.

[129]Cp. the idea of *daharākāśa*, the space of the cave (*dahara*). *Dahara* is explained as *hṛdaya* (heart), which is explained as *citta* (apperception). This is what we become in deep sleep, although enveloped by Darkness.

[130]In some places five and in some others even eight kinds of space are spoken of.

[131]But cp. The *Śvetāśvatara Upaniṣad*, which says that for some philosophers time is the origin and cause of everything, but not the Brahman or the Ātman. Then time has to be above space. Some scholars say that time here refers to the time of astrology, which is said to determine every occurrence. But it is doubtful whether such a view will be presented as high philosophy.

[132]See the explanation of *sākṣi-caitanya* (witness consciousness) in the estimates of the later chapters.

[133]See the author's article, "Being: How Known and How Expressed."

[134]*Sāṅkhyākarikās*, 23.

[135]See my *Idealistic Thought of India*, pp. 416 fol.

[136]Which follows even from Descartes' *Cogito.*

[137]In the general Advaita tradition, the being or existence of the object is said to be due to, or cognized by the I-am, the qualities of the object and its unity, etc., by the senses and *antahkaraṇa* (inner instrument). There is also a line of thinking that the being of the object is cognized by *sākṣi-caitanya* (witness consciousness). Both can be reconciled, for the object as distinct from the subject is cognized within *sākṣi-caitanya*.

[138]See the author's article "Self and Body: How Known and Distinguished."

[139]Indeed, the differences between these philosophies are not to be ignored. But the necessary underlying pattern has to be appreciated.

Chapter XII

The Vedānta of Rāmānuja: Non-Dualism of the Qualified Brahman

1. INTRODUCTION

After Śaṅkara, Rāmānuja (11th century) is the most important Vedāntin. Like Śaṅkara, he is the author of many works, the most important of them being his commentary, *Śrī Bhāṣya* on Bādarāyaṇa's *Vedānta Aphorisms*. Some of his other works are his commentary on the *Bhagavadgītā*, *Vedāntasāra*, and *Vedāntadīpa*, both being shorter commentaries on the *Vedānta Aphorisms*, and *Vedārthasaṅgraha*. Pillai Lokācārya (13th century) wrote his *Tattvatrayam* expounding the philosophy of Rāmānuja. Vedānta Deśika, also called Venkaṭanātha, is the greatest dialectician of this school. He pointed out approximately one hundred defects in the Advaita of Śaṅkara in his *Śatadūṣaṇi*. Śrīnivāsācārya's (Śrīnivāsadāsa's) *Yatīndramatadīpikā* (17th century) is a valuable introductory work. Atreya Rāmānuja (13th century) is the author of *Nyāyakuliśa*, which is a logical exposition of this school. Raṅgarāmānuja (18th century) wrote commentaries on many of the Upaniṣads from the stand-point of Rāmānuja's philosophy. Much of the work done by the followers of this school is a systematic attack on the Advaita.

The school of Rāmānuja had its origins in the Pāñcarātra religious thought, which was known to Śaṅkara, who rejected it as non-Vedic and unacceptable. The school as such, particularly its *samhitā* literature, seems to have started about the 1st century B.C., or A.D.; but it can be traced to the early Ṛgvedic hymns.[1] Its religion is devotional and theistic. But there is another tradition in South India, which is like the Pāñcarātra, the leaders of which are called Ālvārs, and which is perhaps of pre-Aryan, i.e., of Dravidian, origins. It is said that the earliest Ālvār belonged[2] to 4203 B.C. We may, therefore, say that the Pāñcarātra, as it appeared later, was a combination of the Vedic and non-Vedic elements. That is why the sacred literature of this school is called also Double Vedānta (*ubhayavedānta*), meaning that it is based on the three basic Vedāntic works—the Upaniṣads, the *Vedānta Aphorisms*, and the *Bhagavadgītā*—and also the Tamil work called the *Prabandham*. Rāmānuja mentions Bodhāyana, Taṅka, Dramiḍa, Guhadeva, and Kapardin as the forerunners of his way of thinking. Rāmānuja's teacher was Yādavaprakāśa, who held that the Brahman, the individual souls, and the world of matter are all real and yet they are both identical with, and different from one another.[3] He did not see that the same relation could not be both identity and difference, his reason being that it was natural and that our theory should accord with facts, but not facts with theory. He held also that the Brahman transforms itself into the world (*brahmapariṇāmavāda*) and yet can remain perfect and pure. Rāmānuja could not accept his teacher's view.[4] He was, however, indebted to another thinker of the tradition, Yamunācārya, whom he does not seem to have met, but whose book, *Siddhitrayī*, he read. Yādavaprakāśa and Yamunācārya were, therefore, older contemporaries of Rāmānuja and are generally placed in the 10th century.

As already mentioned, Pāñcarātra is another name for the Vaiṣṇava religion and philosophy, for which the Brahman is the same as the personal God (Īśvara) and the individual souls and the material world are both real. This view is accepted by both Yamuna and Rāmānuja. But they do not accept that the relation between God and the world, including the individual spirits, is both identity and difference. It is the relation of body-spirit (*dehātmasambandha*). The body may undergo transformation, but the spirit remains the same. I say: "I was a child, a boy, a youth, and now a man." But in all these changes, the "I" remains the same; the body alone changes. We should note that the "I" in Indian thought is not the same as the ego, which is part of the material world (*physis*). Similarly, the Brahman, as the Supreme Spirit (Soul) of the world, remains the same, while the world undergoes transformations, which do not affect the Brahman. This school advocates the way of devotion to God and complete self-surrender to him, and says that he takes full care of such men of devotion and self-surrender. During the 13th century, schism arose in the school in interpreting God's protection of men of devotion. One sub-school held that God takes every care of man, just as the mother cat catches hold of the kitten and removes them from danger (*mārjālakiśoranyāya*), and that men have to do nothing but rely on God; but the other held that man, through his own effort, should hold on to God and would then be out of danger, just as the baby-monkey holds on to its mother and remains out of the reach of danger (*markaṭakiśoranyāya*). The two sub-schools[5] are called the Teṅgalai and the Vadagalai, the proponents of which are Lokācārya and Vedānta Deśika respectively. The former relies more on its Dravidian (Tamil) scriptures than the latter and is called also the Southern School of Rāmānuja Vaiṣṇavism, in distinction from the other which is called the Northern school.

2. EPISTEMOLOGY

Rāmānuja and his followers accept only three valid means of cognition—perception, inference, and scripture (verbal testimony). Like the Sāṅkhya, they say that the other means accepted by the Mīmāmsā and the Advaita can be included in one or more of the three. *Perception*: Rāmānuja's theory of perception agrees mostly with that of the Mīmāmsā. But his distinction, to which we already referred, between indeterminate cognition (*nirvikalpakajñāna*) and determinate cognition (*savikalpakajñāna*) differs from that of the Mīmāmsā. For the latter, as well as for the Nyāya-Vaiśeṣika, Sāṅkhya-Yoga, and the Advaita, indeterminate cognition is the cognition of an object without reference to its name and class characteristics; it is cognition of the object as only a being. But according to Rāmānuja, there is no cognition that is not the cognition of something with an attribute.[6] Even indeterminate cognition contains the distinction between substance and attribute. It is cognition of the individual (*vyakti*) for the first time, into which memory of past experiences does not intrude. As past experiences do not enter it, we do not classify it and draw the distinction between the individual and the universal or class. If we perceive the same individual for a second time, we relate our present perception to the past, distinguish the individual from the universal, and relate the two. Then our perception becomes determinate; it becomes the perception of an object as characterized by its universal and so as a member of a class.[7]

Rāmānuja accepts extra-sensory perception and the perception by liberated persons and God, who do not depend on the instrumentality of the senses.[8] Regarding inference and verbal knowledge, the views of this school are more or less the same as those of the Advaitins, except for the fact that, for this school, there is no cognition of an object without its attributes.

VALIDITY OF KNOWLEDGE Valid knowledge (*pramā*) is the consciousness (*caitanya*)[9] of the *ātman*. Consciousness is of three kinds—consciousness as limited by the inner instrument (*antahkaraṇāvacchinna*), consciousness as limited by the function (*vṛtti*) of the inner instrument, and consciousness as limited by the object. When the three are identical or coincide, perceptual cognition (*sākṣātkāra*) arises. These three consciousnesses arise, when the senses come into contact with the object, mind with the senses, and the *ātman* with mind.[10]

The epistemological definition of valid knowledge given by the school of Rāmānuja is peculiar. Valid knowledge is knowledge that is conducive to the practical interests of life as they are.[11] This definition has no explicit reference to objects as they are, although they are involved in our practical life. The definition is committed only to the reality of practical life with its actions, pains, and pleasures,[12] but not to the independent reality of the objects of the world. But practical life with activities, pains, and pleasures is found also in dreams and illusions. So Rāmānuja says that all are valid forms of knowledge. He interprets self-validity (*svatahprāmāṇya*) of knowledge in a very extreme form. Cognition of every object arises when the three forms of consciousness (*caitanya*) above mentioned coincide. They coincide when we perceive a mirage, a dream, or a true object. Cognition can, therefore, be never false. The falsity of cognitions is due to other factors (*paratah-aprāmāṇya*),[13] i.e., an object is made false by its not conforming to practical life, when it does not serve the purpose for which it is meant (when it is not *arthakriyākāri*).

The Advaitins also accept that all cognition is self-valid and its falsity is due to other factors. But they speak explicitly, in their definition of perception, of the independent existence of objects. Rāmānuja's epistemology also implies the independent reality of objects, but it is not a factor in his definition of validity. The cognition of the illusory snake is false, according to the Advaita, because of the rope. "That is a snake" and "That is a rope" are contrary propositions, and the former at least is, therefore, false. But Rāmānuja says that both are true propositions, that they are two different propositions occurring at different times, and that the That in the former is different from the That in the latter. So there is no conflict between the two propositions. The snake in "That is a snake" is true, because it has frightened me and made me run and bring a stick; and the rope in "That is a rope" is also true, because it enables me to tie the cow with it. The purpose of Rāmānuja in maintaining such a view is to defend the self-validity of cognition in each and every case, and shift falsity on to the side of the object.[14]

But Rāmānuja did not see the difficulty in the attempted shift. If the illusory snake has existence (*sattā*), why is it called false? We have to say, and he admits also, that it is false because it is contradicted (*bādhita*) by the rope. But two objects, if they have existence, do not contradict each other. There can be contradiction only between two judgments and then, again, only if the conflicting predicates refer to the same That. Then the cognition in one of the two judgments can be false and its object unreal. Otherwise, we have to say that, while validity belongs to cognition, invalidity belongs to objects—which is absurd. If they are real objects (*sats, satyas*), they cannot be invalid.

THE ILLUSORY OBJECT The illusory object, according to Rāmānuja, is real and existent. His doctrine is, therefore, called the doctrine of the reality of the illusory object (*satkhyātivāda*). Both the real snake and the illusory snake are beings (*sats*); the difference is that the snake has non-worldly being (*alaukikasat*) and the rope has worldly being (*laukikasat*). Both have pragmatic significance. The snake is created for us by God to frighten us and make us miserable for the time; the rope is created by the same God for another purpose. Even the dream objects have their pragmatic significance; they also are created by God to produce pains and pleasures according to our past actions (*karmas*).

Rāmānuja's epistemology can be appreciated perhaps from the standpoint of man, his consciousness, his actions, pleasures, and pains. But he fails to offer an adequate distinction between truth and falsity, reality and unreality. Why do we draw the distinction between the objects of dream and illusion on the one side and the objects of the waking world on the other? Rāmānuja may say that illusion or error (*bhrama, apramā*) lies in taking a worldly being (*laukikasat*) for a non-worldly being (*alaukikasat*) and vice versa. But how are we to know that something is a worldly being and something else is a non-worldly being? According to Rāmānuja, both satisfy the pragmatic test. Then why do we not call the illusory snake or an object of dream a worldly being and the rope or the pen in my hand a non-worldly being? Both are objects of my direct experiences when they are experienced. What is the criterion to distinguish the worldly from the non-worldly? Without giving a criterion for it, Rāmānuja assumes the distinction.

It is a peculiarity of our experience that both truth and falsity fall within our experience. The false has to be an experience; otherwise, we cannot know that something is false. The unreal has to be experienced as independent of our mind and sweet will; otherwise, we call it the imaginary, which will be the proper adjective then. The object as known is experienced always as an object that has an existence independent of its being known. That our experience is such is itself a fact, not an illusion. Yet within that experience itself, the distinction between truth and falsity has its source. There can be no other source. Every perception, as an act of perception, is a fact. But the objects of some perceptions are not facts in the sense that they do not belong to the real world; and we know their falsity, when their existence is contradicted. Without this contradiction, which Rāmānuja's theory tends to ignore, there can be no distinction between truth and falsity. To say that, only because we experience an object, it must be real and have being (*sattā*) cuts at the very root of the epistemological distinction. If the object is false, we have to say that its cognition also is false. Even for Rāmānuja, the distinction between truth and falsity arises at the level of determinate knowledge; and cognition at that level has to be of the form of judgment, like "That is a horse." Thus Rāmānuja's theory of validity and illusion is inadequate.

However, Rāmānuja's robust realism rejects the Advaita view that, if there is conflict between perception and inference, and between inference and scripture, the latter alone in each case has to be accepted and the former rejected. In some cases, as in the example of the mirage, the Advaitin seems to be right. But when he says that, when perception and scripture are in conflict, the former has to be rejected, Rāmānuja's contention[15] that, since both are valid means of knowledge and if both are true, then both have to be accepted and the apparent conflict reconciled, appeals to us as reasonable. The ground for Rāmānuja's contention is that the scripture, even as verbal knowledge, is based upon the perception of sounds, and if perception is to be rejected, scripture also has to be rejected. If both perception and scripture are true, then their conflict must only be apparent and has to be reconciled. If one side of a medal appears yellow and the other white, we reconcile the conflict, but do not say that the medal is neither yellow nor white or that it does not exist at all.

Similar reconciliation has to be made when there is conflict between one perception and another and also between perception and inference. Here Rāmānuja overshoots his mark when he says that, through such reconciliation, we should consider both the illusory snake and the real rope to be real and existent. In support of his epistemological doctrine, he does not give an epistemological reason, but a metaphysical one. According to the Upaniṣads, all the objects we see are constituted by the five elements—earth, water, fire, air, and ether. They are present in different objects in different proportions. So even the mirage has the element of water in it and is, therefore, real in the form of water also. But this reason does not explain the difference between truth and falsity; it tells us only that there are grounds for similarity among all the objects of the world, both real and unreal. We have already seen that the Sāṅkhya gave a similar argument and said that Prakṛti is present in both the true and false objects.

3. METAPHYSICS

Rāmānuja's Vedānta is called the philosophy of the Non-dualism of the Qualified Brahman (Viśiṣṭādvaita). Some writers call it simply Qualified Non-dualism. The term does not mean non-dualism with a proviso, but that the Brahman is non-dual and is yet qualified or characterized by the world and the individual spirits, both of which form its body (*śarīra*). For instance, the height of my body forms a quality or attribute of my I-consciousness, when I say: "I am so many feet tall." Really the I-consciousness is not so many feet tall and the adjective is not applicable to consciousness at all; yet nobody can know me except through my body. Rāmānuja says that I cannot even know myself except as qualified by an activity or state of consciousness. Similarly, even the Brahman cannot be known except as qualified by something; it can be known only as a substance qualified by some attributes. There is no knowledge of anything except through its attributes. At this point, Rāmānuja differs from Śaṅkara, who says that the Brahman can be known without any qualities and that Being is without qualities,[16] and is and can be cognized as such.

THE CATEGORIES The categorization of reality, according to Rāmānuja, may then be made into substance (*viśeṣidravya*) and attribute or quality (*viśeṣaṇa, guṇa*). Everything in the world is either a substance or an attribute, and what is substance from one point of view can be an attribute from another. If I say: "Please call the gentleman with the umbrella," although the umbrella is a substance from the standpoint of its own colour, it is a qualifying characteristic from the standpoint of that gentleman.[17] As in the Advaita, in the writings of this school also we come across the categorization of reality into the knower and the known (*draṣṭā* and *dṛṣya*) and the enjoyer and the enjoyed (*bhoktā* and *bhogya*). The former categorization is epistemological and the latter ethical. The two categorizations are practically common to all the Indian schools. But that into substance and attribute is peculiar to Rāmānuja's school.

But the categorization of reality into substance and attribute cannot take us very far in understanding metaphysics, except in finally pointing out that all the plurality is an attribute of the Brahman. So the followers of Rāmānuja developed different classifications[18] of categories for understanding reality. One is the division into three[19]—God, spirit (*ātman*), and matter (Prakṛti). This division is found in Rāmānuja's own writings. Another, which is a little more elaborate, is the following one.

First, all categories (*padārthas*) are divided into the means of cognition (*pramāṇas*) and the objects of cognition (*prameyas*). The means of cognition are three only—perception, inference, and scripture. Memory (*smṛti*) is valid; but since it is a cognition of what is already cognized by perception, it comes under perception and does not need separate mention.[20] The objects of knowledge are of two kinds, substance (*dravya*) and non-substance (*adravya*). Substance is of two kinds, the conscious and the unconscious. The unconscious is of two kinds, Prakṛti and time. Prakṛti itself is divided into the twenty-four categories as in the Sāṅkhya. The conscious is of two kinds, the inward (*pratyak*) and the outward (*parāk*), i.e., the inwardly directed and the outwardly directed. The inward is of two kinds, the *ātman* and God. The *ātman* is of three kinds—the bound, the liberated, and the eternal. The outward consciousness is of two kinds—the eternal force (*nityavibhūti*) and the attribute consciousness (*dharmabhūtajñāna*).

God has five states (*avasthās*)—the Transcendent, the Supernal (*vyūha*), Incarnation (*vibhava, avatāra*), the Immanent (*antaryāmi*), and the idol (*arcāvatāra*), which is God incarnate for worship. The Transcendentent is the Brahman itself. The Supernal is of four kinds: Vāsudeva, Saṅkarṣaṇa, Pradyumna, and Aniruddha. According to the Pāñcarātra, which Rāmānuja follows, the four are the descendent stages of the Brahman before it manifests the world.[21] Vāsudeva is the same as the Brahman itself. Saṅkarṣaṇa, Pradyumna, and Aniruddha correspond cosmically – that is, they are the states of the Cosmic Person corresponding to—the soul (*jīva*), mind (*manas*), and ego (*ahaṁkāra*). Rāmānuja explains that the three are the rulers of the individual souls, individual minds, and individual egos.[22] The Incarnations are generally given as ten – Fish, Tortoise, Boar, Lion, Half Lion and Half Man (*Narasimha*), Dwarf (*Vāmana*), Parasurāma, Rāma, Balarāma, Buddha, Kalki—in the mythological epics. They represent the actual descent of the Brahman in various mundane forms into the world, when evil prevails and good is about to be destroyed. The Immanent dwells in all souls and accompanies them in life and death. It is the Brahman residing in the spirit (*ātman*) of man like lightning in a cloud.[23] The Incarnate as worshipped is the idol of God in various forms presentable to ordinary people.

The non-substance is of ten kinds—The Transparent (*sattva*), the Active (*rajas*), and the Dark (*tamas*), which are the Attributes of Prakṛti, sound, touch, colour, taste, and smell, which are the properties of the five elements, the relation of conjunction (*samyoga*), and force (*śakti*). These are mere attributes or qualities that always remain qualities, and never become substances, whereas some substances can become qualities also. What we have to note here is that consciousness is regarded as a substance by this school, while the Nyāya-Vaiśeṣika treats it as a quality.

PRAKṚTI Prakṛti is one of the six substances – Prakṛti, time, the Pure Transparent (*śuddhasattva*), attribute consciousness (*dharmabhūtajñāna*), spirit (*jīva*, *ātman*), and God. While the Sāṅkhya conceives Prakṛti as the state of equilibrium of the three Attributes, Rāmānuja maintains that the three Attributes are the qualities of Prakṛti, which is their substance.[24] That is, the Attributes are not the constitutive qualities of Prakṛti, but its functions. Rāmānuja does not accept the Nyāya-Vaiśeṣika classification of categories, and says that everything, except substance, comes under non-substance. He rejects the relation of inherence (*samavāya*), saying that it is only an adjective (*viśeṣaṇa*). To say that the red colour inheres in the rose is the same as to say that it is an adjective or quality of the rose. The universal (*sāmānya*, *jāti*) is not accepted, because it is nothing but the structure (*samsthāna*) of the individual. Action is only movement, which can be understood in terms of conjunction (*samyoga*). Movement is only a series of conjunctions.[25] The particular (*viśeṣa*) does not have to be accepted, because it is nothing but the atomic nature of the atoms and the all-pervasive nature of infinite entities like God and time. Then only the six substances and the ten qualities remain and they come under the two categories of substance and non-substance. There is nothing like absence or negation; for the negation of something is the same as the presence of something else.

Prakṛti is eternal and is called by many names, the Non-transient (*akṣara*), Avidyā, Māyā, etc.[26] It evolves the world of plurality. The twenty-four categories of its evolution are the same as those of the Sāṅkhya except for one difference. According to the Sāṅkhya, the five elements – earth, water, fire, air, and ether – originate in the ego simultaneously. But according to Rāmānuja, they originate in the ego in succession – air out of ether, fire out of air, water out of fire, and earth out of water. This view belongs to the Upaniṣads. All the five have subtle and gross forms.

First, out of the subtle element of ether, gross ether comes; out of gross ether, subtle air; out of subtle air, gross air; out of gross air, subtle fire; out of subtle fire, gross fire; out of gross fire, subtle water; out of subtle water, gross water; out of gross water, subtle earth; and out of subtle earth, gross earth. Although the cosmic gross elements are created thus out of one another, every object in the world around us contains all the five elements, but in different proportions. Every element is divided into two parts; the presence of one half, for instance, of water, constitutes water as water. The other half is divided into four parts and each part is added to one half of each of the other elements. Thus the water we drink is half original water and one eighth of each of the other four elements.[27] This doctrine of every object containing five elements is called quintuplication (*pañcīkaraṇa*), and is common to all the Vedāntic systems. It is doubtful whether this doctrine can have a scientific basis. Even the doctrine of the five elements is based upon the doctrine of the five senses, and is not scientific in the modern sense of the term.

Rāmānuja rejects the Nyāya-Vaiśeṣika view that space is different from ether. So space is not separately given. Unlike the Sāṅkhya, he does not equate time to change, but says that it is independent of Prakṛti.

ETERNAL FORCE The conception of the eternal force, energy (*nityavibhūti*), is peculiar to the Pāñcarātra.[28] It is the same as the Pure Transparent (*śuddha-sattva*) and is called also the Pure Essence. As distinguished from it, the impure Transparent is one of the Attributes of Prakṛti and is never found unmixed with the other two Attributes, the Active and the Dark. But the Pure Transparent is not mixed at all with any of the three Attributes of Prakṛti. It is by nature unconscious (*acetana*),[29] and yet thoroughly self-revealing, i.e., transparent. Its very nature is bliss (*ānandātmika*). It constitutes the bodies, the means of enjoyment, the objects of enjoyment, and also the process of enjoyment by God, the eternally liberated souls, and the liberated souls. God's body has the six attributes – knowledge (*jñāna*), power (*śakti*, capability), strength (*bala*), lordship (*aiśvarya*), the heroic quality (*vīrya*, enthusiasm), and splendour (*tejas*). It is wrong to think that the liberated souls have no body; they have bodies made up of the Pure Transparent (*śuddhasattva*), but not of Prakṛti.[30]

The above description of the Pure Transparent shows that Rāmānuja was as much a theologian in the western sense of the terms as a metaphysician. The liberated souls enjoy the constant presence of God, but enjoyment is possible only if the enjoyer has a body, mind, and senses. Rāmānuja himself does not seem to have discussed this question,[31] and to have expounded the doctrine of the Pure Transparent. But his followers felt the need for a concrete theological conception of the highest heaven, in which the spirits live and move in the medium of love, which is the same as bliss. And they wanted the conception to be metaphysical also. So they formulated the idea of the Pure Transparent, in which the differences and distinctions are preserved and yet everything becomes transparent to everything else. If we asked from the point of view of western philosophy: "Is the Logos a concrete, substantial being or only a unity of the abstract structure of the world?", Rāmānuja would answer: "The Logos is a concrete, substantial being and its substantiality is due to the Pure Transparent." God (Īśvara) for Rāmānuja is not merely pure Being (*sattā*), but structured and qualified Being, and every part of the structure is transparent to, and is known by every other part, except by Prakṛti.

ATTRIBUTE CONSCIOUSNESS The concept of attribute consciousness (*dharma-bhūta-jñāna*) is another important contribution of the Rāmānuja school. The Buddhist Vijñānavādins maintain that the knower (*jñāta*) is nothing but the consciousness of the object. The distinction that appears between the knower and his knowledge is false; and the object also is unreal. Through this view they concluded that the *ātman* (not in the sense of the Vedānta, but as pure consciousness) alone is real and is the knower; and the object is real. But the knower is nothing but the knowledge or consciousness of the object and is impersonal. The view boils down to that the consciousness (*vijñāna*) alone is real, but the knower and the known are unreal. The Nyāya-Vaiśeṣika wants to defend the reality of the *ātman* that knowledge (I-consciousness) belongs to it, which by itself is unconscious. The Advaita[32] also wants to defend the reality of the *ātman*, but by saying that the consciousness of the object is ultimately the same as the consciousness that is the *ātman* and is the *ātman*'s constitutive quality (*svarūpalakṣaṇa*). But in this view, Rāmānuja would say, not only is the distinction between the *ātman* and the knower and its knowledge of the object overlooked, but also the *ātman* seems to be equated to a quality (*dharma*), as in the Vijñānavāda. For consciousness directed to the object is a quality (*dharma*) of the *ātman*. So felt Rāmānuja and made a severe attack on the Advaita view with the help of the concept of attribute consciousness (*dharmabhūtajñāna*), or consciousness that is only an attribute.

My perception of the pen has three factors – myself as conscious of the object, my consciousness of the object, and the object of which I am conscious. My consciousness of the object reveals itself to me, but not to itself. If it reveals itself to itself, it will be a person, an ego, an "I". To say that I know[33] that I know the object is, for this school, the same as saying that I know the object. Cognition and the cognition of that cognition are the same, because cognition is self-revealing; no other light is needed to reveal the presence of a light. Now, my "I", as the knower, reveals itself to itself, but not to the consciousness revealing the object. Thus we have here two consciousnesses, one that reveals itself to another, and the other that reveals itself to itself only. The former belongs to the latter and is called its attribute (*dharma*). Its name is attribute-consciousness (*dharmabhūtajñāna*).[34] The other is called the being-consciousness (*svarūpajñāna*) or existential consciousness or consciousness that is existence (*sattā*). It is the I-consciousness (*ahamdhī*). Here Rāmānuja says that the I-consciousness can never be known by itself apart from the attribute consciousness. And as the attribute consciousness does not arise except when it reveals an object, the "I" can know itself only when it knows an object. As knowledge at the highest level of salvation is also the same attribute consciousness, every *ātman*, even in the world of the Pure Transparent, (*śuddha sattva*) knows itself only when it knows some object, e.g., God. Thus there is no consciousness without distinctions either in this world or in the other.

We have seen that there is another distinction made by Rāmānuja, viz., between the consciousness that is turned inward (*pratyak*) and that which is turned outward (*parāk*). These two are the existential and attribute consciousnesses. They are inseparable and neither can work without the other. Then existential consciousness, which knows itself, knows itself only when the attribute consciousness also works, i.e., knows some object. The former knows itself, when it knows itself, only as the knower (*jñāta*), and the knower is always the knower of some object, which is other than the knower.[35] In deep sleep, the attribute consciousness does not work, as there is no object. And as the attribute consciousness does not work then, the existential consciousness also does not know itself.[36] Yet it is present in deep sleep. At this point, Rāmānuja differs partly from Śaṅkara, who does not accept the distinction between the existential and attribute consciousness, except at the empirical level. Both agree in saying that existential consciousness exists in deep sleep, as otherwise we cannot explain how we can say that we slept well. There must be an experience then of sleeping well. But we say also: "I did not know anything, not even myself in sleep," Śaṅkara explains my not knowing myself as being due to the consciousness of the existential consciousness being overwhelmed by the positive Unconscious (Avidyā)—which is further explained as the consciousness knowing only the Unconscious, which is a kind of darkness (*Tamas*) covering up our mind and senses. But Rāmānuja explains it as due to the absence of attribute consciousness. For Śaṅkara, to be overwhelmed by the Unconscious means to have the Unconscious as the object also. But for Rāmānuja, to be unconscious of everything, including oneself, means the absence of the attribute consciousness.

According to Rāmānuja, both the existential and attribute consciousnesses are eternal; but the former is atomic in size (the *ātman* is atomic), and the latter infinite. Although attribute consciousness is eternal and infinite, it has the power to contract and expand like the coil of a serpent.[37] When it contracts completely, we know nothing; when it contracts partially, our knowledge is finite,; but when it expands completely, our knowledge will be infinite. It spreads through mind and senses, and comes into contact with objects. In the case of God and the liberated souls, it always remains infinite.

The attribute consciousness, although an attribute of the *ātman*, is a substance (*dravya*). It is the same as reason (*buddhi*, *mati*, etc.). Here there is a difference from the Sāṅkhya, for which reason (*buddhi*) is the same as the first evolute of Prakṛti. But *buddhi* and *mahat* are not synonyms for Rāmānuja; the latter is the first evolute of Prakṛti but the former is not. Yet strangely enough, mind (*manas*) is also called by the names *buddhi*, *ahaṁkāra*, *citta*, etc.[38] Why this school calls what is above Prakṛti and what is below it by the same name is not understandable. Does this school mean that there is a higher and a lower reason or rational consciousness, as in the *Kaṭha Upaniṣad*? Or does the higher reason enter the forms of Prakṛti and appear as they? The answer seems to be affirmative to both the questions.

It is said that the same attribute consciousness[39] appears in different contexts and under different conditions as pleasure, pain, desire, hatred, effort, etc. We say generally that desire, will, doubt, conviction, etc., are mind (*manas*); but they are really forms of the attribute consciousness when it is in contact with mind.[40] Every conscious experience, including the valid forms of cognition, are states of this consciousness. It seems that, according to Rāmānuja, the *ātman* gets really bound by Prakṛti, identifies itself with its forms and laws. This identification means that the *ātman*'s attribute consciousness gets involved in Prakṛti and its forms. The *ātman* itself experiences, therefore, pains and pleasures. And as the *ātman*, its attribute consciousness, and Prakṛti are all real, the *ātman*'s experiences also are real. Self-realization lies in the *ātman* realizing that it and its attribute consciousness are not the same as Prakṛti and its forms.

AVIDYĀ Rāmānuja has a peculiar conception of Avidyā, which, as we have mentioned, means ignorance, the Unconscious, and Nescience. He says that it is not the Māyā of the Advaita, but action (*karma*).[41] That Avidyā keeps the spirit in bondage means that action keeps the spirit in bondage. We have seen that Avidyā, according to this school, is another name for Prakṛti also.[42] Then is Prakṛti the same as action? By action (*karma*) may be meant the actions we are performing and have performed in this life and also the potentialities (*dharma* and *adharma*, merit and demerit) of actions performed in previous lives. These potentialities are called by the Mīmāmsā, for which Rāmānuja has greater respect than Śaṅkara has, the Unseen (*adṛṣṭa*). Is Rāmānuja identifying the Unseen with the Unconscious? If actions (*karmas*) are responsible for the conditions limiting the attribute consciousness, which is originally blissful in the realm of the Pure Transparent (*śuddhasattva*), then what is the need for accepting Prakṛti as having an independent reality of its own? Or if Avidyā is different from Prakṛti, how can it be the same as action (*karma*) and also be a synonym for Prakṛti? We receive no clear answer. Atreya Rāmānuja[43] says that the word *avidyā* may be interpreted either way according to context. But in either case, it will be a positive entity, not a negative one. Yet the same author says that in the context of cognition it is absence[44] of knowledge, which is a negative entity. Then this meaning will be a third one. We may, therefore, conclude that the school of Rāmānuja is not interested in giving any importance to Avidyā.[45]

THE ĀTMAN This school, like Jainism, calls the *ātman* by the name *jīva* (soul) also. It is inward consciousness (*pratyakcetanā*). Inwardness means the revelation of oneself to oneself only. The attribute consciousness is not inward, because it reveals its being to another, viz., the *ātman*, but not to itself and is directed outward (*parakcetanā*). The *ātman* is by nature atomic (*aṇu*), but its attribute consciousness, which is inseparable from it, is infinite. It is, however, dependent on God and is subsidiary (*śeṣa*) to him, as my body is to my spirit. It is eternal, different for each individual, and by nature blissful.[46] It is the knower, doer, and enjoyer (*jñātā*, *kartā*, and *bhoktā*). Rāmānuja does not accept the Advaita position that the *ātman* is only an on-looker (*sākṣi*), while the ego (*ahaṁkāra*) is the real knower, doer, and enjoyer. If the ego is the agent of all these functions and if it is to disappear in salvation, why should it try for salvation, if salvation means its self-destruction?[47] Rāmānuja accepts the distinction between the *ātman* and the ego, and says that the latter is only a product of Prakṛti.[48] But the nature of the *ātman* is to be the I-consciousness (*ahamdhī*), but not mere consciousness (*jñāna*) or mere witness consciousness (*sākṣicaitanya*). The "I" is always the I-consciousness. As the "I", the *ātman* itself is the agent of all the functions. But when it identifies itself with the ego, it suffers the vicissitudes of Prakṛti; it has, therefore, to realize that it is not the ego, but the pure I-consciousness. The ego, as a product of Prakṛti, cannot be the knower, the doer, and the enjoyer; for it is unconscious like Prakṛti.[49]

The *ātman* is of three kinds — the bound, the liberated, and the eternal. The bound are the souls living in the world of Prakṛti. The liberated are those souls that have freed themselves from Prakṛti. The eternal are the eternal servants of God, who live with him and have never done anything against his wishes. The liberated and the eternal souls live with God, enjoy like him, and are similar to him. They are not identical with him, and do not have his powers of creation and destruction of the world.

GOD The Brahman is the same as God. It is personal and has all the auspicious qualities. It is the primary Being, the controller of all, the final object of worship, the creator, sustainer, and destroyer of everything. The whole world including the *ātmans* is the body of God. He has two states, the subtle and the gross. But the two states really belong to his body, which consists of both the conscious beings and the unconscious matter. His Being (*svarūpa*) remains the same in both the states. The subtle state of his body is called the destruction of the world, and the gross state its creation. Creation and destruction are only transformations of states (*avasthāntarapariṇāmas*). There is really nothing that is absolutely new or that vanishes altogether. In his subtle state, God is the material cause (*upādānakāraṇa*) by his desire to create the world, he is the efficient cause (*nimittakāraṇa*); and as time and the immanent spirit (*antaryāmī*), he is also the instrumental cause.[50] Non-duality is thus said to be preserved even in the cosmological and cosmogonic sense. Reality, although it consists of God, souls, and Prakṛti, is non-dual. For in both the subtle and gross states, the souls and the world constitute God's body, which is inseparable from him.

To the question, how God, who is inseparable from the transformations of his body, can remain pure, perfect, and unaffected by them, Rāmānuja's answer is that what happens to the body does not happen to the spirit. But Śaṅkara asks how I can be unaffected by the changes. If my body is hurt, I feel pain. If we cut a goose into two, and eat one half, can the other half lay eggs? Either we have to say that God is separable from the world and can remain perfect without being affected by its evil or we have to admit that God, in being inseparable from the world, is affected by its changes and becomes a suffering God. Here lies a weak point in Rāmānuja's conception of the Brahman.

Rāmānuja maintains that causation belongs only to the self-transforming cause (*pariṇāmakāraṇa*) and rejects the Advaita view that God is the non-self-transforming cause (*vivartakāraṇa*). But then he encounters the difficulty pointed out by Śaṅkara and his followers, which he has not been able to overcome.

Rāmānuja does not accept any of the arguments for the existence of God. He rejects all the arguments as if he is an atheist, and finally says that God's existence has to be accepted on the basis of the Veda. If the Brahman is to be known as one's deepest self, its existence is not amenable to rational proof. At this point, Śaṅkara and Rāmānuja are in agreement.

CRITIQUE OF ŚANKARA'S MĀYĀ AND AVIDYĀ Rāmānuja shows great dialectical skill in his criticism and rejection of Śaṅkara's interpretation of Māyā and Avidyā. His commentary on the first *Vedānta Aphorism* is longer than one hundred pages, and most of it is an examination of the Advaita position. Whatever be the reasons that led up to the final position of Śaṅkara, it holds (1) that the Brahman alone is real, (2) that it creates the world with the help of Māyā, (3) that the nature of Māyā is inexplicability in terms of Being and Non-being, and (4) that the Brahman, as limited and veiled by Avidyā, is the soul (*jīva*). As we have seen, there is no essential difference between Māyā and Avidyā; the latter is the former in its veiling aspect.

Some Advaitins consider Avidyā as part of Māyā; but often the words are used as synonyms. It has been the practice of every follower of Rāmānuja to attack the doctrine of Māyā and Avidyā. Vedānta Deśika, as already mentioned, wanted to advance about one hundred arguments against it. Only the central points of the criticism can be given here.

(1) Māyā or Avidyā is said to be of the nature of ignorance. But ignorance resides in some one, it must belong to some one. To whom does it then belong? It cannot belong to the Brahman, which is of the nature of pure consciousness. It cannot belong to the soul, for the soul itself is a product of Avidyā and Avidyā must first exist before it can produce the soul. The Brahman becomes the soul when veiled by Avidyā. So it must be prior to the soul. But if Avidyā can have no existence without the soul, then the soul must be prior to Avidyā. We have, therefore, a vicious circle.

(2) Avidyā is said to veil the Brahman, before the Brahman becomes the soul. But as the Brahman is of the nature of pure self-consciousness, it can be veiled only if it forgets itself. But it can forget itself only if it is veiled by the Avidyā. This is another vicious circle.

(3) We cannot understand the nature of Avidyā. Is it positive or negative? If it is positive, how can it be destroyed by knowledge, as the Advaitin contends? Knowledge only recognizes the existence of the positive, but never destroys it. If it is negative, how can it combine with the Brahman to produce the world? As negative, it is only absence of knowledge, but absence causes nothing. Nothing comes out of nothing. And to say that Avidyā is both positive and negative will be a self-contradiction.

(4) Māyā is defined by the Advaitin as neither Being, nor Non-being, nor both, nor neither. This definition is self-contradictory. If something is not Being, it must be Non-being; and if it is not Non-being, it must be Being. Indeed, it cannot be both and neither; it must be one of the two. In this definition, the Advaitin violates the principle of contradiction.

(5) The presence of Māyā cannot be established according to any of the recognized valid means of cognition. Ignorance is absence of knowledge; and absence can never be perceived. That I perceive the absence of the rose on the table is the same as my perceiving the table, which is a positive entity. Māyā cannot be inferred. How can anybody infer anything that lacks any peculiar characteristic? If it has a characteristic, then Māyā must be a real entity. But the Advaitin says that it is not. It cannot be proved on the basis of the scripture; for the Veda says that Māyā is the mysterious power of the Brahman. But the Advaitin says that the Brahman has no characteristic and so it cannot have the mysterious power also.

(6) If the Advaita understanding of Avidyā is to be accepted, then it cannot be removed even by knowledge. For what is this knowledge? It must be the knowledge of the Brahman that removes the ignorance that is responsible for the knowledge of the world. Now, does this knowledge of the Brahman have the Brahman as an object or is it the knowledge or consciousness that is the same as the Being of the Brahman? The first alternative is not possible for the Advaita view; for the Brahman, according to it, is never an object of my knowledge, but the same as my *ātman*. The second alternative also does not make the removal of the knowledge of the world, which is due to ignorance, possible. For knowledge of myself does not contradict the knowledge of the world. Again, if the Brahman is an object of my knowledge, then likewise the world

also is an object of another act of knowledge. We have two different kinds of objects and two cognitions. How can the knowledge of the one cancel the knowledge of the other and show it to be due to ignorance? Hence there is no possibility of the knowledge of the Brahman removing the knowledge of the world.

(7) If Avidyā is a positive entity, then its removal by knowledge is not possible. If ignorance means the absence of knowledge of an object, then knowledge of that object removes that ignorance. But if it means a positive entity, then knowledge does not remove it. But the Advaitin says that Avidyā is positive.[51]

The Advaitin answer to all these questions and objections is that Rāmānuja and his followers are shooting a dead horse by demanding that the inexplicable must be explicable. Furthermore, when Rāmānuja is speaking of knowledge, he is thinking only of the attribute consciousness, but not of the existential consciousness (svarūpa-jñāna), which also is accepted by him. My Unconscious is what grips my own being, but is not unawareness of an external object. I cannot explain how my Unconscious originates as it is the root of my very being. I am what I am because of it. But I can be more than what I am, if my Unconscious becomes my Conscious. Even if the Brahman has become my "I" through self-forgetfulness, which is due to the power of the Unconscious, this self-forgetting is not the forgetting of an external object, but of my own true being. But there is reason to accept the first and second arguments. For the force or power (*śakti*) of Avidyā, if it does not belong to the Brahman, cannot in anyway screen it, as Rāmānuja says; for if Avidyā cannot belong to, or originate in the Brahman, there is no way of explaining how it originates. To say that it is an inexplicable mystery is not enough. If it is positive, it must somehow belong to the positive Brahman. Otherwise, it must come out of nothing—a view not accepted either by Śaṅkara or Rāmānuja. Śaṅkara will then be obliged to accept the Judo-Christian doctrine as popularly interpreted that God created the world out of nothing and add that, so soon as man realizes God, the world vanishes into nothing.

DEFENCE OF DIFFERENCE Śaṅkara, like Parmanides and Zeno, rejects the ultimate plurality of the world and, for the purpose, rejects the validity of the concept of difference. But Rāmānuja accepts God, Prakṛti, time, and the plurality of souls, etc., as different entities, though together constituting the non-duality of the Brahman. He and his followers have, therefore, to defend the reality of difference. Indeed, by interpreting the negation of something as the affirmation of something else, they rejected negation (*abhāva*) as a reality. Even then, reality is pluralistic for them. Hence, they have to defend the reality of difference.

The Advaitin rejects difference by reducing it to two negations. "*A* is different from *B*" means "*A* is not *B* and *B* is not *A*." As there is no bare negation, but only negation of something, and as that something negated is not the object of perception, but only a concept, the Advaitin argues that negation has no being or reality. It is not really perceived, but conceived. Again, he says that difference is either the same as the terms differentiated or different from them. If it is the same, then it has no being of its own; and if it is different, there has to be another difference between the first difference and the terms. This analysis may be continued *ad infinitum*.

To the above dialectic of the Advaitin, Rāmānuja answers that difference is given in perception itself. If the difference between *A* and *B* is not given in perception, how do we know that *A* is different from *B*? Why does a man who wants to purchase a cow not purchase a horse? The Advaitin says that perception gives only Being, the rest is only ideational. What is perceived in the two propositions, "That is a cow" and "That is a horse" is only Being. Then why does the man not treat both the perceptions as the same? So Rāmānuja[52] says that the forms of the cow and the horse also are given in perception. The fact that the man milks the cow and rides the horse shows that he perceives their difference. Practical activity (*vyavahāra*) here proves that the man perceives it.[53] All known objects lead to action; and contradiction by action indicates that cognition is false and that there is absence of true knowledge (*avidyā*).

To Rāmānuja and his followers, the argument that difference is a combination of two negations is not acceptable. Difference may be so according to the Nyāya-Vaiśeṣika.[54] But according to the Rāmānuja school, it is a constitutive form (*svarūpa*) of the object. No object is cognized without a form or quality. So difference also is cognized along with the being of the object. The Advaitin argues that, if the form or quality of an object is different from that object, then difference also as a form of the object must be different from the object. Then we have a second difference, which is different from the first difference and also from the object. And there will be a third and so on *ad infinitum*. But Rāmānuja says that the first difference is a constitutive form (*svarūpa*) of the object and does not need another difference.[55] Other differences are conceptual formations. Just as we cognize, "That is a cow" and "That is a horse," we cognize that each object is different.

The above attempt of the Rāmānuja school to turn difference from a negative to a positive concept, in which the referential aspect of the idea is excluded, is bound to fail; for there is no difference that is not the difference of something from something else, just as there is no negation that is not the negation of something. If difference is a constitutive feature (*svarūpa*) of the object, we should be able to perceive it, as we perceive the object's being. We may at the most say that the positive conception of difference, for this school, can be the Nyāya-Vaiśeṣika conception of distinctness (*pṛthaktva*), about which also there are difficulties; for even distinctness also cannot be understood, if it is not a distinctness from something. If positive, it can hardly be different from the particular.[56] But for the school of Rāmānuja, distinctness is the same as separateness, which is defined as the absence of conjunction (*saṃyoga*).[57]

When the Advaitin is asked how, if difference has no reality, we come across the idea at all, he answers that our cognition of difference is due to a false, innate psychological tendency. But this school answers that the reason given is invalid. If difference is false, then we can say that the innate tendency is false; but if the innate tendency is false, then difference is false. Because of the vicious circle in the argument,[58] we have to accept both the tendency and difference as true.

One of the other important arguments is that, if difference is false, there can be no action, no thinking, and no speech. Action involves plurality—the agent of action, the object that is acted upon, and action itself. Thinking involves the thinker, the object thought of, and the thought of the object. Speech involves the speaker, the hearer, different sounds, and the objects about which the speaker speaks. If all these differences are one and the same and there is only one reality, there will be no action, no thinking, and no speaking. Even the scripture, which consists of different words, has to be false; and if it is false how can it teach truth? The Advaitin's reply is that, although the scripture as scripture is false, it can teach truth. An unethical man can teach ethics. But Rāmānuja asks how falsity can teach truth. How can we trust a habitual lier? How can what a dream person tells us be accepted as true? If the world is not different from God, where is the point in exhorting man to rise above the world and realize God? Here Rāmānuja seems to have scored against Śaṅkara. Inexplicability is not exactly the same as unreality and illusoriness, and self-contradictoriness is not necessarily the same as falsity, although very often we have to treat the inexplicable as unreal and the self-contradictory as false. However, the controversy between the Advaitins and the Viśiṣṭādvaitins (the followers of Rāmānuja) has followed a long course. We may, however, say that these concepts need further analysis.[59]

Although Rāmānuja wants to retain both identity and difference between the Brahman and the world including the souls, he does not accept the relation of identity-difference (indentity-cum-difference, or identity in difference) between them. For it is self-contradictory for a relation to be both identity and difference.[60] He says that, as identity-cum-difference is self-contradictory, we should accept the relation as that of spirit-body. In this relation, we find both identity and difference; but the relation itself is not identity in difference. We should not say that, because we find in the rose colour, smell, and form, the rose itself is the same as the three.

4. LIFE'S IDEAL

As a realist, Rāmānuja accepts that action is real and insists that man should continue performing ethical actions till death,[61] although strangely enough he says that action is the same as Avidyā. Here his teaching is more in accordance than Śaṅkara's with the *Bhagavadgītā*, which says that there is no life without action and that man has to be ethically active till death. But like Śaṅkara, Rāmānuja does not accept that action by itself leads to salvation; both say that it purifies our mind and makes it transparent (*sāttvika*) and pure so that truth can be received clearly[62] by it. Without purity of mind, God cannot be known.

But Rāmānuja does not accept that ultimately the path of knowledge leads to salvation. Certainly, when mind is purified, knowledge of the Brahman dawns upon it. But such knowledge by itself cannot lead to salvation. It has to be steady and constant like the uninterrupted flow of oil (*dhārāvāhika*), which is the same as devotion or love of God. The Pāñcarātra school has made a very interesting and keen analysis of love, which can form a useful study even apart from religion. Love is effortless, but knowledge can be retained only with effort. Love does not exist without knowledge, for when we love a person we are conscious also of that person. Where there is real love, it is constant also. Love is, therefore, more than knowledge. When a girl falls in love with a boy, the consciousness of the boy grips her whatever she may be doing or thinking. Such consciousness is effortless. So Rāmānuja says that the way of action leads to knowledge; and knowledge perfected, made steady and constant, becomes love. Hence love only can lead directly to the realization of God and salvation.[63] Besides, knowledge may only be *about* an object and so indirect; but knowledge of the Brahman has to be absolutely direct. That is why, meditation and concentration of mind (*dhyāna*) and the different kinds of yoga are recommended by the Upaniṣads, which are not content with imparting mere verbal knowledge.[64]

Rāmānuja's conception of knowledge is related to the kind of the way of love he teaches. Knowledge is understood by him always in terms of attribute consciousness (*dharmabhūtajñāna*), although he accepts existential consciousness (*svarūpajñāna*) also. But the latter can know itself only when the former knows an object; and the object here is the Brahman. At our level, knowledge of the Brahman is only knowledge about the Brahman; it is indirect knowledge obtained through the scripture. Words need not convey direct knowledge; and particularly when they are about a transcendental object, they convey only indirect knowledge. For being convinced of the truth of even this indirect knowledge, our mind has to be made pure by the performance of all the ethical actions prescribed by the Mīmāmsā. Next, this conviction has not only to be turned into direct knowledge, but also this direct knowledge has to be made constant and steady. Such an ideal can be achieved only through love and devotion to God.

Unlike the Sāṅkhya and the Advaita, Rāmānuja does not accept liberation in the body[65] (*jīvanmukti*). To be alive and to be liberated is a contradiction in terms. So long as we are alive, we have to perform ethical actions; there is no freedom from them in life. In the liberated state, there are no ethical actions, there is no choosing between good and evil, everything is the good only; and the liberated souls, like God himself, have their being in the Pure Transparent (*śuddhasattva*), which is untouched by the two Attributes, the Active and the Dark. But so long as one's body belongs to the world of Prakṛti and so long as one has to perform actions, it is false to think that one is liberated. Liberation comes only with death for the souls possessing knowledge and devotion. It lies in being completely severing oneself from Prakṛti, when one takes on the body of the Pure Transparent. In that state, the soul, which is by nature blissful, realizes its original bliss; and its attribute consciousness (*dharmabhūtajñāna*) is uninterrupted.

Love, which is defined as the uninterrupted flow of knowledge, is very difficult to practise, as mind by nature is fickle and moves from object to object. To strengthen the love of God, several types of yogic practices, meditations, forms of worship, initiations, etc., are recommended; but they also are difficult to practise. Strict observance of ethical laws and self-control are equally difficult. Action, knowledge, and devotion throw man on himself, and require absolute self-reliance. But as a finite being, man cannot be perfect in action, knowledge, and devotion. He has, therefore, to surrender his self to God, instead of relying upon himself alone. Self-surrender includes in itself doing what is in conformity to God's will, not doing what is against his will, the faith that he saves men, and surrender to him as the protector. This is true renunciation[66] (*nyāsa*, *prapatti*). The followers of Rāmānuja insist that both devotion and self-surrender are essential for salvation, and that the two are not opposed to the way of knowledge, but are its consummation.

GENERAL ESTIMATE AND CONSTRUCTIVE COMMENT

(i) Rāmānuja's Main Contribution to Vedāntic Thought

There are many important elements in Rāmānuja's contribution to the Vedāntic philosophy. His formulation of new concepts like those of the attribute consciousness (*dharma-bhūta-jñāna*), eternal force (*nitya-vibhūti*), the Pure Transparent (*śuddha-sattva*), his new interpretations of Avidyā (the Unconscious) as action (*karma*), his equating Avidyā to Prakṛti (Primeval Nature), his division of consciousness into two kinds, the inward (*pratyak*) and the outward (*parāk*) are potent with significance which perhaps many have missed. Again, his idea that attribute consciousness (*dharma-bhūta-jñāna*) works *through* mind (*manas*) and senses and perhaps the later development of this idea that it is, or is constituted by mind and senses, and that everything except the unconscious Prakṛti is attribute consciousness itself, reveals more about the structure of the I-consciousness than what Rāmānuja and his followers themselves explicitly disclosed. That is, they were perhaps unaware of the potential importance of these ideas for a constructive philosophy. The following sections will attempt to elucidate the ideas.

(ii) Māyā as the Force and Potency of the Supreme I-consciousness

Here we shall underline the importance of one objection of Rāmānuja's to the traditional interpretation of the Advaita, which says that Māyā as the creative force is foreign to the Brahman. The trend of the development of thought in our successive estimates of the systems may have already indicated that Māyā cannot be foreign to the Brahman and that the whole universe as a manifestation of the Brahman—let it be through Māyā —enters the Brahman and becomes part and parcel of his Being just as everything that I absorb and assimilate enters the structure of my being and forms my character and personality. If it is asked what happens to all that is absorbed into my personality, one may answer either that it disappears, or that it has no being of its own when it is absorbed, or that it is retained within my personality in a subtle state and, to that extent, it transforms and enriches my personality. Indeed, it will be objected that there is no point in saying that the Brahman, which is already full, will be enriched by repeated absorptions of his Māyā.[67] The objection is valid; for there can be nothing new to be added by this assimilation and absorption. But because there is nothing new, it seems also that it is not unreasonable to say that Māyā neither exists, or does not exist, and so on. And there is nothing new in the Brahman that can be the result of the transformation which takes place in his nature by the absorption of Māyā; the Brahman will be only what it eternally has been. In a sense, what is absorbed into my personality, into my I-am, is not available to me as an object to be observed; for I cannot observe my I-am as an object of my mind like I observe a mental image. So Hume was mistakenly led to denying the reality of the I-am altogether, and Edward Hartman was led to calling the Absolute by the name Unconscious. We can appreciate the traditional Advaitins denying all being to Māyā. For instance, what is absorbed into me has no being of its own left for itself. My character has no being of its own apart from one. But when we realize that what is assimilated to the I-am cannot be made an object—even the I-am cannot be made an object—we may think that it does not exist. That there is an I-am is known only in reflective consciousness as in "I know that I have seen *X*," "I know that I have done *Y*," etc. But this reflection is possible only in time. But when and where time and space and so Becoming are completely transcended, i.e., transcended without reference to what is transcended, the I-am cannot even reflectively be objectified. It can only be lived, but cannot be cognized as an object.[68]

There are a few points to be underlined here. There is no reflective doing, there is only reflecting knowing. "I know that I know *X*" is meaningful, but "I do that I did *X*" is non-sense. I do *X* by living the act of doing *X*; it is not, properly speaking, living *through* the act, although this expression is used. For I do not differentiate myself from the act of doing *X*, when I am doing *X*. I am the act then.[69] It is in experience akin to *asamprajñāta samādhi* or *samādhi* in the unknown or without an object and in cognition it is akin to indeterminate knowledge. That is, in action which automatically—without a special effort of controlling my mind—lasts for a time, my cognition of my action during that action is due my being one with it and is indeterminate; but my cognition of an object, as the knowledge of it, is one step removed by being the cognition of the cognition by being one with the object. It is like by cognition of my having performed an action and now taking rest. In cognition of objects, unless we put forth special effort like meditation, our being one with the object is only momentary; there is greater chance of our being mistaken both about the object and about ourselves as involved in the cognition than in the cognition or consciousness of action. Action produces, therefore, a healthier reality-sense than cognition, although cognition is involved both in performing action and in merely cognizing objects. After the act is over, there is only *reflective knowing* of the act, not a *reflective doing* of it; but in the case of mere cognition of an object, there is a *cognizing* of the object and also a *reflective cognizing* of the object. When I am knowing *X*, I am living the act of knowing it; I am the act of knowing it. There is again a difference here from doing: I can know that I have known *X*; but substitute seeing (visual perception) for knowing, there is no "I see that I have seen *X*" in which the first "see" is distinct from the second "see," but both are used in exactly same sense of visual perception. For "see" can be used in the sense of "realize" also, in which neither is used in the above sentence. If they are used in exactly the same sense there can be no reflection, and no transcendence will be involved. The implication seems to be that seeing, hearing, touching, etc., are acts like doing; but knowing has a different structure. Again, "I see *X*" and again "I see *X*"—this repetition—does not affect *X*; but "I do *X*" and again "I do *X*" affects *X*. This difference enables knowing to be nearer unchanging Being, while doing remains nearer Becoming and change. So "reflective doing" sounds absurd.

The second point to be noted is that in the life of the I-am, taking its whole depth into consideration, there is transcendence with reference to what is transcended, corresponding to what we have called witness consciousness, and transcendence without such reference, corresponding to the pure Absolute I-am. This distinction corresponds to Being with reference to Becoming and Being without such reference. The former corresponds to reflective consciousness, the latter transcends all reflection, all thought. The former contains the element of time and time-consciousness, the latter is beyond time as it is beyond Becoming. There Becoming is absorbed into Being.

What Rāmānuja could have noticed but, it seems, did not, is that there is a stage of the Absolute in which Becoming is absorbed and assimilated to pure Being, the Supreme I-am. At that stage there can be nothing to characterize the Supreme Being, whether we take the term in a religious or metaphysical sense. Rāmānuja says that before creation everything exists in a subtle state. But what does "subtle state" mean?

And where does it exist? Indeed, in the Brahman, as Rāmānuja says, as its body, i.e., subtle body. But can what becomes one with my personality be distinct from it and be its body? My constitutive character is not something attached to me and it is not even like the colour of my skin, which I, as this living body, distinguish from myself. Rāmānuja himself says that God with the world as his body is one unity, one person. What sort of unity can it be except of the form of I-am, which is a personal experience? If there is characterization, if God as the I-am, is known with a predicate, Hume and others like him could not have said that the I-am, the spiritual substance for them, could never be found. They are right to the extent that it has no characteristics or qualities as distinct from its Being.

The controversial point, which cannot be decided one way or the other easily, is whether the Absolute is a person. For the word person is not an elementary word, denoting an elementary experience. But the term I-am is different. Every man uses it and knows, without objective reference, what it means. But person, in our context, is a philosophical term, not understood by ordinary men.[70] if we ask a person: "Are you reading?", "Are you eating?", he answers using the first personal pronoun.[71] But ask him: " Are you a person?", he will be puzzled and may say: "What do you mean? I am a first person." Much has been made of Rāmānuja's insistence that the Absolute is a person. But is he a person among persons? How can he be one among many, if he is inclusive of all? Then there is no point in calling him a person. But there is another side to the question. When asked: Is there any indication that there is *ātman* (self) at all?, even Śaṅkara answers[72] that it is what manifests itself as the I (*aham*) in our experience. And all the Vedāntins, including Rāmānuja, accept that the Brahman is realized as the I-am (*ātman*).[73] Indeed, Rāmānuja explains this experience of realizing the Supreme I-am as meaning its inwardness to my I-am, that is, the Supreme is the highest transcendental I-am. Nor does and can Śaṅkara mean that it is not transcendental, but my finite I-am, as this author. Then what can be the ultimate difference between the two philosophers, whatever they and their followers say? If the Supreme I-am cannot be one among many even for Rāmānuja, and if even for Śaṅkara it is of the nature of the I-am, then we have to say that the essential experience of the transcendental, Supreme I-am,—because it is of the nature of the I-am which is its cue and clue—is personal living consciousness, conscious of its being only. It has to be continuous with my finite I-am in experience and being. But to prevent drawing wrong conclusions, we may have to say that the experience of the I-am is or is like that of personal being, but not that of knowing a person. The difference is between "being a person" and "knowing a person." It may perhaps be understood in terms of "am-ness" which involves self-consciousness, but not in terms of "is-ness" which need not involve it. That is, the Supreme Being, even in ontological[74] terms, is a first (the most intimate) personal experience (*uttama-puruṣa*), but not that of a (particular) person, leave aside the second and third persons. So much is actually implied in Rāmānuja's acceptance that the Supreme is an I-am within my I-am. Indeed, this experience transcends all thought, but not all experience. But what is there surprising in what transcends thought not being amenable to thinking? What transcends thought is *eo ipso* not amenable to thought.

(iii) Existential and Phenomenological Consciousness

The distinctions drawn by Rāmānuja between existential consciousness (*svarūpa-jñāna*) and phenomenological consciousness (*dharma-bhūta-jñāna*) in a clear-cut fashion focusses our attention on the two forms of consciousness which are important for the clarification of the knowledge situation,[75] although he makes the distinction too rigid to be ultimately true. The general style of the Advaita literature slips over the distinction and renders the epistemological situation not easily explainable. Indeed, it seems to draw a similar distinction by making *jñāna* and *samvit* correspond to the two; but the practice is not uniform and the terms are used interchangeably.

The phenomenological consciousness is described as working through mind and the senses. More exactly put, it is everything that is said to be internal except the *ātman* and mind.[76] The *ātman* is indeed internal to us, as ordinarily understood; but what should we say about mind (*manas*)?

The conception of mind (*manas*) in this school is not very clear. It calls phenomenological consciousness by the name *buddhi* (Reason in the Stoic sense or Mahān Ātmā of the *Kaṭha Upaniṣad*), but says also that mind is a synonym for *buddhi*, ego, etc.[77] *Darśanodaya* also says the same. So it is not intelligible how, if *manas* is a synonym for *buddhi*, and *buddhi* for *dhī*, and *dhī* for *dharmabhūtajñāna*—here the situation is unavoidable which troubles the western student with Sanskrit terms, for there are inconsistencies in their use—the last can mean everything internal except the *ātman*. If only the literary and popular usages are referred to, then it should be said that *dharmabhūtajñāna* includes everything except the *ātman* (which is *svarūpajñāna*) and Prakṛti. Because the internal instrument (*antahkaraṇa*, which includes *mahat* or reason of the finite individual in this case, and the ego, and mind) is an evolute of Prakṛti, it must exclude the whole of *antahkaraṇa*, including reason also; what then is this phenomenological consciousness?

The intelligibility we accepted in what this school says does not imply experiential justifiability of what it says. It is true that this school makes empirical consciousness intelligible by giving two separate names to existential and phenomenological consciousnesses, and maintains that the latter works through the inner instrument and the senses and that it is directed outwards towards the object. We have then to understand that the inner instrument and the senses are the patterns supplied by Prakṛti and that the phenomenological consciousness flows through the patterns like water through pipes and takes their forms. But according to this school, even the phenomenological consciousness by itself is unconscious,[78] but self-revealing like light, which reveals also its source, the flame of the lamp. By self-revealing, this school and all the other schools also mean that nothing else is needed to reveal its existence. Indeed, to know the presence of light we do not need another light as help or instrument. But can a blind man know the presence of light? So some consciousness is needed to know its presence. Then some consciousness is needed even to reveal phenomenological consciousness, and it will be absurd and a contradiction in terms to call it consciousness that is unconscious. Then this revealing consciousness must either be phenomenological consciousness itself—in which case, it cannot be unconscious (*jaḍa*, *acetana*)—or be existential consciousness (*svarūpa-caitanya*), which is the *ātman*. But this school holds that phenomenological consciousness reveals not only itself but also the *ātman* and that the *ātman* cannot know itself except when phenomenological consciousness reveals it.[79] Then there will be no possibility of the *ātman*'s consciousness revealing the phenomenological consciousness, which is by nature unconscious like a stone.

We can get over this impasse only if both the existential and phenomenological consciousnesses are in essence one and the same and also can be distinct as in the reflective consciousness "I know that I know *X*." When I see a star, it is not merely my phenomenological consciousness that becomes one (as if)[80] with the existence of the star. In the live act of perception, the two consciousnesses unite, but in reflection the existential can transcend the identity and make it its own object. The phenomenological consciousness is only the outward going force of the existential consciousness and is part and parcel of it and can be absorbed and assimilated to it. The complete disappearance of the phenomenological consciousness—the disappearance would be called "contraction" by this school, but what does a fully contracted entity enter?—in deep sleep can be explained as complete withdrawal into, or assimilation to existential consciousness as structured by our finitude. Even if we, for argument's sake, accept the contention of this school, it should be realized that the phenomenological consciousness does not reveal the existential, at the time that it reveals an object; but that the presence of the existential in the act of seeing and locating the object is revealed in the reflective consciousness through the transcendence of the witness consciousness (*sākṣi-caitanya*). In fact, the light which reveals the object through the phenomenological consciousness is the borrowed light of the existential; or in other words, it is the light which is the existential consciousness, that reveals the object through the phenomenological consciousness, which is a form of activity of the existential consciousness (*ātman*). It is for this reason that we do not know ourselves when we are focussed on the object and know the object. And although "phenomenological consciousness" is a noun and appears to denote something substantive, it is essentially the form of the activity of the *ātman*, one of the types of its Becoming. This aspect of our cognitive experience does not seem to have been given importance, not to speak of having been noticed, by this school.

Another point to be examined is the exclusion of Prakṛti and its evolutes from the phenomenological consciousness. The above discussion shows that the *ātman* as existential consciousness cannot be excluded from the phenomenological, but rather that the latter is a function, power, force (*śakti*) of the former. Now, the phenomenological has a directedness, an intentionality. But there can be no directedness without something towards which the direction points, and that something is to be the object, gross or subtle, or even an idea, or a mental image. Now, direction has necessarily two terms, that from which and that to which it points. Then the two terms must have been included in the direction of the phenomenological consciousness or rather have to be inseparable from it. This direction or directedness is not that of an empty, life-less relation, but that of a concrete, living process. It is a case of the concrete, factual, experiential, not merely that of an abstract symbol as in formal logic or mathematics. Indeed, the phenomenological consciousness in a sense "flows" through the inner sense (*antahkaraṇa*) and the senses; but they are not patterns external to it, but constitute its own form or format. They are inherent to it, constituting its patterns of active directedness, which is not to be understood as something static, inactive. Thus the independence of Prakṛti from the phenomenological consciousness (*dharmabhūtajñāna*) of either the Supreme Spirit or the finite *ātman* is not ultimately tenable.

If the whole phenomenological consciousness can be absorbed into the existential, the I-know into the I-am, then Rāmānuja's contention that the *ātman* is atomic in size—indeed he does not accept the atomic theory of the Nyāya-Vaiśeṣika, but seems to mean only size whenever he says that something is atomic—while the attribute (phenomenological) consciousness, with its power of contracting and expanding, is infinite, cannot be accepted. For how can something that is atomic absorb something that is infinite spatially, temporally, and potently? For instance, does the attribute consciousness in deep sleep contract to nothingness or a point? If it contracts to nothingness, it vanishes, destroys itself, and cannot appear again. If it does not disappear, it must be absorbed into the *ātman* which throws it out again in dream and waking. If it is reduced to a point or an atom, then also it becomes identical with the *ātman*. And are we to take this contraction in the spatial sense like pressing cotton into a small lump? This is too physical an idea to be applicable to non-physical realities. Even then, where does such consciousness, pressed to a point, rest? In the *ātman*? Then the *ātman* can absorb its attribute consciousness and must have infinite power or potency to do so. This is what we mean by saying that the directed knowing (I-know) can be absorbed into Being (I-am), the phenomenological into the existential consciousness. That the latter is atomic has no significance and applicability here.[81]

Now arises the question whether the individual *ātman* as existential consciousnesses (*svarūpa-jñānas*) can ultimately remain independent of one another. Undoubtedly, empirically in the world of action, they are very often independent, i.e., separate, although dependent on one another in practical life. But are they and can they remain separate and be many all through the transcendental stages? If the Logos and its various levels are the same for every individual, and if they are the stages of his higher self, how can we escape the conclusion that at these transcendental stages all the *ātmans* are one?

In Indian philosophical literature, the question whether something remains so and so ultimately is answered by considering what it will be in liberation; for in the liberated state, everything assumes its absolutely original form. Now, this school holds that, in spite of the infinity of the attribute (phenomenological) consciousness of the *ātmans*, these consciousnesses can remain separate from one another and from that of the Supreme Being.

Now, if the attribute consciousnesses are each infinite by nature, overlapping, interpenetrating, conscious, and conscious of one another, how they can be separate is not intelligible. If I can know whatever is happening in another's mind, his thinking, his pains and pleasures and so forth without his telling me, then there is nothing to separate him from me and I must be the same person as he or, as the yogis say, I must be able to identify myself with his person through some super-natural power. Much has been written on the privacy of experience after Wittgenstein raised the problem in "I do not know another's pain" and similar expressions writers interpreting him differently.[82] If John says: "I am in pain," and I know and the doctor also knows that John is in pain, it does not mean that I and the doctor are having the same pain.

Unfortunately, "to know" has so many meanings that it can mean "understand" also and not necessarily "to experience." Even the word "privacy"[83] has many meanings. Yet the significance of the word can be over-worked. When I and John see the colour red of a book cover, and use the same expression, "I see red," and even if the same colour appears on different books and we use the same word, it may be doubted reasonably whether we are seeing exactly the same colour or even a similar one, even if we use the same word consistently whenever the colour is presented to us, whatever it actually be. So regarding sensations and sense-data, one may say, there is privacy of experience. However, we cannot be so sure about the privacy of sensations or sensa as we can be of pains, pleasures, and mental images, illusions, and dreams, although all are experiences. When my perception is "That is red" and John's perception also is "That is red" and we both point our fingers to the same location, *do our sensations or sense of red coincide or are they numerically identical?* Although we cannot decide, merely through cognition and verbal expression, whether our sensations are or are not numerically identical, our pointing to the same location and, if necessary, pointing it with pointers that meet, can decide that we are referring to the same substantive object (not colour). That is, when simple cognition cannot decide, action decides. Suppose the object is a rose and both I and John want to have it and try to snatch it before the other can. Naturally we have to say that we are contending for the same object.[84] Even then one may say that the way—or whatever term we have to use in this context—its colour appears to me may not be the way it appears to John. Yet whatever it is in itself, it pleases me as it appears to me and it pleases him as it appears to him; and so we both want the same object.

We should not overlook the lesson that can be drawn from this aspect of experience. Even if the same colour, whatever it is, appears to both me and John differently, our visual senses locate it at the same place and so overlap there. It seems to me that it is difficult to say that the spaces also overlap and so may be different; for there must be something common at the base for two entities to overlap there and that must be the common space. Now, in spite of this overlapping, the sensations and the senses are different as belonging to different persons. So it may be concluded that, although the *ātmans* are each infinite in size, or as in Rāmānuja's philosophy, even though the attribute consciousnesses (*dharmabhūta-jñānas*) of each are infinite, they can overlap and be different. We have shown that the *ātman* cannot be atomic in size and has to be infinite like its attribute consciousness. Now, although the sensations may be different and yet overlap without becoming numerically identical, for the reason that the way the colour appearing to each of us may be different; how are we to account for the numerical identity of the object—e.g., the rose for which both I and John contend—for which there is competition? If our object is not numerically identical, there will be no competition. If the senses present sensations (or sense data), mind their unity as an object as a whole, then what is it in us that presents the numerical identity? Taking the inward structure of the self as given by the Upaniṣads—senses, life, mind, individual reason, Cosmic Reason, and the *ātman* in ascending order—we have to say that it is the Cosmic Reason, which has to be the same, numerically identical, in all of us. It is what finally confers existence on all the phenomenal objects in so far as they are real. Rāmānuja and his followers call it the Pure Transparent (*Śuddha Sattva*), but it must have a function even at the empirical level, although clothed in a theological and mythological garb. It is called Eternal Force, Power, Splendour, Love,[85] etc. (*Nityavibhūti*). For this school, although attribute consciousnesses are different for the different *ātmans*, the Pure Transparent is the same, for in it all souls and God live and move. But our consideration that the Cosmic Reason in all of us must be the same and also must be above the impurities of individual reasons leads to the conclusion that the Pure Transparent or Eternal Force has to be the higher aspect or dimension of the individual reason and has also to be its deeper aspect or dimension. The numerical sameness of the object we contend for can be made possible only by something numerically the same for all in our inner beings. Hence the contention that, in spite of overlappings of experience, we can be different persons[86] cannot be carried all the way to the *ātmans*; it ends even at the stage of Cosmic Reason, the Logos.

(iv) Consciousness as Inward and Outward

We have called attribute consciousness (*dharmabhūta-jñāna*) by the more philosophically intelligible modern term phenomenological consciousness. This school classifies consciousness into the inward (*pratyak*) and the outward (*parāk*). We may remind ourselves of the reason for renaming attribute consciousness as phenomenological consciousness. This consciousness, which is not bare and empty light, although compared to it by this school, is structured and directed—i.e., it has intentionality—and as such is responsible for the way the phenomenal world of objects is experienced. The structure of the phenomenal world is also due to the structure of the phenomenological consciousness in so far as it works rightly. This phenomenological consciousness is said to be outward (*parāk*) like the Eternal Force (*Nitya-vibhūti*). Yet this school maintains that the *ātman* (self) knows itself only when knowing an object; otherwise, it has no knowledge (cognition) of itself. It has already been shown that this is a mistaken view. However, accepting it for argument's sake, we may ask: What is the nature of the I-am's (*ātman*'s) cognition of itself when knowing an object? The two forms of consciousness—of the *ātman* and of God—are said to be inward (*pratyak*); we have been calling them existential (*svarūpa-jñānas*). Now, in the *ātman*'s act of cognizing an object, how are the two forms, the inward and the outward, get related? And how are they to be related? One pulls itself inward, and the other pulls itself outward. No wagon can go forward even if one horse pulls to the right and the other to the left. We have to say, therefore, that the same phenomenological consciousness, when it reveals an object, reveals itself to the *ātman* and, for this school, also reveals the *ātman*. Then for revealing itself to the *ātman*, which is inward, it must have inward directedness and for revealing the object, it must have outward directedness. Then the so-called inward or inner (*pratyak*) and the outward or outer (*parāk*) are not absolute distinctions, but are two intentionalities of the same consciousness, viz., the phenomenological.

It will perhaps be objected that Rāmānuja does not mean by inner and outer the inward and the outward, but what is within, viz., within the phenomenological consciousness and what is without, viz., outside the existential consciousness. They are to be spatially understood like the flame which is within the light which it emanates and the light which the flame emanates. But are the *ātman* and the phenomenological consciousness spatially located, are they within space? The source of space cannot be within space. So the words inner and outer cannot be understood spatially in the context. Again, how does the *ātman* know that the phenomenological consciousness is external to it, if by itself it is not conscious and if the other consciousness is not its own power or force like heat of fire? If the phenomenological belongs to the existential, this "belonging" must be consciously recognized by the latter; and so it has to be self-conscious by nature. We have then to conclude that the other-consciousness, i.e., consciousness of the other, is a power of the *ātman* or existential consciousness itself.

Then we have to say that, so long as the distinction remains between the existential and the phenomenological, the so-called inner has significance only because of the inward (*antarmukhatā*) directedness of the phenomenological and the so-called outer has its point only because of the outward (*bahirmukhatā*) directedness of the existential. We may remind ourselves in this context also that in this reversing of the directions, the existential does not lose itself, does not get lost, as explained in the distinctions between the two forms of causation, the ontological (*vivarta*) and the cosmological (*pariṇāma*). Becoming may enter Being and be held in a tight grip and be lost in it; but even when Becoming is let loose, Being is not lost in it, but remains in the background as the basis. Without Being in the background, Becoming cannot be Becoming; without the existential in the background, the phenomenological consciousness cannot be phenomenological consciousness. Another consequence of this discussion is that the existential consciousness is not revealed only by the phenomenological when it reveals an object, but is cognized by itself; and its cognition of itself is not like revealing an object by the phenomenological consciousness; existential consciousness is not an object of the phenomenological like the book in my front. The phenomenological is known as an other to the existential consciousness, but also as being covered, comprehended and within my existential, like my body being an object of my consciousness, but my consciousness extending beyond my body.

(v) External Force and the Pure Transparent

What has been said of the phenomenological consciousness holds true of the Eternal Force (*nitya-vibhūti*) and the Pure Transparent (*śuddha-sattva*). The latter two are identified by this school itself. The function of the two is to form a medium for the movement, embodiment, and enjoyment, and perfect knowledge of the *ātmans* in the liberated state, which is their pure state unpolluted by Prakṛti. And because the Attribute (*Guṇa*) of transparence (*sattva*) of Prakṛti is impure, Rāmānuja introduces the Pure Transparent as the medium of existence in heaven. But if phenomenological consciousness is the potency, force (*śakti*) of the *ātman* and can be pure in its higher[87] functions, and is also inseparable from the *ātman* and is infinite, then there is no need for introducing these two new concepts. Even at the empirical level, all emotions, pleasures, pains, and states of rational consciousness and mind[88] belong to the phenomenological consciousness. We have to infer, therefore, that it has higher and lower states. These two new concepts then can refer only to the higher levels and states of the phenomenological consciousness.

In spite of what appear to be adverse comments on Rāmānuja's philosophy, his contributions to the Vedāntic thought should not be undervalued. The tendency of the Advaita, like that of Buddhism, is simply to cut away the whole phenomenological experience as irrelevant to ultimate reality and existence, thereby creating a puzzlement—except in the minds of the most mature who can easily adapt themselves to both realities—about how one has to conduct oneself in the empirical world of action. Rāmānuja's categories can show how our mundane world contains categoreal forms leading up to the Supreme, which is not to be understood as mere empty Being. Rāmānuja has not given up the inwardness of the Supreme Being to my being, both empirical and transcendental, although at the highest transcendental level, in which the words inwardness and outwardness are pointless, my *ātman* is one with the Supreme Ātman. Rāmānuja pinpointed the higher spiritual aspects of man by raising them to the level of independent realities—which is misleading only because they are certainly the higher dimensions of my being and are one with it. The Pure Transparent and the Eternal Force are not separate realities. He could have seen that these are really the potencies, forces (*śaktis*) inherent to the Supreme Being and can have no being of their own when assimilated and absorbed. He could have seen that Prakṛti,[89] the impure, cannot remain impure when absorbed by the Supreme Being. The distinctions of pure and impure have their significance only for me at this level of finite personality, at this mundane level. All is pure when it enters the Being of God. Rāmānuja also says that the whole universe is within the Being of God (Īśvara) and constitutes his body. As his body, it can have no impurity; or the distinction between purity and impurity can have no meaning from God's point of view. Rāmānuja could have seen also that Being is one and cannot be many; that, although the senses of Jim and John overlap when they locate the colour of the same rose, their locating its existence raises the problem: How can existences overlap? Existence can only be one, for Jim and John contend for the same. This leads us to the conclusion that ontologically all existences, all beings, of both God and the *ātmans* are one; only empirically in the world of action, they are different.

(vi) Māyā, Avidyā, Adṛṣṭa, and Karma

In the estimates of this and the previous chapter, we have emphasized the importance of understanding Māyā in the etymological sense of the word as measure and treating it as a methodological concept. It should not be understood in the popular sense, which says that I, as this particular person, is real, but the objective world is unreal and even suggests that even I am unreal and so it matters little whatever I do, good or evil. If I, as this particular person, am a part of the world, then I am also not real. This conclusion was certainly not intended by Śaṅkara, who wanted to teach that the I-am in its greatest depths as the Absolute Consciousness and Being is real, and conversely the Absolute Consciousness is of the form of the I-am.

Now, if Māyā means measure, how are we to explain its aspect as Darkness? As identified with Prakṛti of the *Śvetāśvatara Upaniṣad,* it has all the three Attributes, although the Advaitins generally emphasize its veiling (*tamas*, Darkness) power and the projecting (*rajas*, positing definite, limited, bounded, shaped, objects of the world) power. (Note that although the Sāṅkhya calls them *guṇas* or Attributes, they are powers, forces, *śaktis*. Spinoza also should have called the two Attributes, Mind and Matter, by the name also of Forces, Powers, of God, the manifestations of his inherent creative forces.) But when the world is projected, it has also to be "known," and knowledge or consciousness of the limited or limited consciousness—for every object has, besides its other aspects, the aspect also of "being known" (*jñātatā*)—is made possible by Māyā's force of the Transparent, which is called by other schools by the name *jñānaśakti* or the force of consciousness, which splits up into the subjective and objective poles. Now, how does the idea of measure fit in? It fits into the concept through the principle of limit (*niyati*); for to be measurable is to be limited. We cannot measure what is unlimited and infinite like space considered as one and time considered as one.

In this connection, it will throw a great deal of light on this concept and on Rāmānuja's view that Avidyā is only *karma* (potency of past actions), if we note that *niyati*[90] (limit, determinant, limiter) is explained by commentators on the *Śvetāśvatara Upaniṣad* as the potency of past actions, which forms the capital, the fixed environment of the individual, and in Husserl's terms, the individual's horizon of experience, his world. We have explained that, because this potency forms part and parcel of the being and character of the person, it cannot be made an object by him to be faced. Its existence can be known only by its results. It can, therefore, be said to constitute my Unconscious (*avidyā*). Because it acts from behind me as it were, and limits my capabilities of knowing and acting, it becomes the force veiling my original infinity. Unless my infinity is veiled, hidden from me, I cannot find myself as a finite person in the phenomenal world. Māyā becomes also the principle of measure, the forms of measure being the valid means of knowing, and the means of acting and enjoying. We can thus see that Rāmānuja is right in saying that *avidyā* is only *karma*,[91] but he took Māyā in the popular sense and hence the unending controversy.

We may make the additional comment, namely, that Māyā or Avidyā does not remain as the Unconscious for ever for all individuals. To be liberated is to overcome the Unconscious that determines, limits, measures one's being. When it is overcome by being made part and parcel of one's conscious being, it loses its veiling and limiting power. So the Advaitin says that for the liberated souls, Māyā and Avidyā do not exist, and the souls become infinite, and reach the realm of the immeasurable, unlimited.[92] The Advaitin can agree with the two trends of thought in western psychology one accepting the existence of the Unconscious, and the other denying its existence; but he will say that the views are true at different levels. However, we have to keep in mind that this Unconscious is both cosmic and individual. For a total dispelling of the Unconscious, the cosmic also has to be overcome.

NOTES

[1]S. N. Dasgupta: *History of Indian Philosophy*, Vol. III, p. 12.

[2]Ibid., p. 64.

[3]S. Radhakrishnan: *Indian Philosophy*, Vol. II, pp. 671–72.

[4]Nārāyaṇārya: *Nītimālā*, pp. 31–37.

[5]See K. D. Bharadwaj: *The Philosophy of Rāmānuja*, pp. 234 fol. The philosophical position is, on the whole, the same for both the sects. The differences concern mainly the methods and implications of self-surrender.

[6]Śrīnivāsadāsa: *Yatīndramatadīpikā*, p. 9.

[7]Rāmānuja's distinction between indeterminate and determinate cognition corresponds to Russell's distinction between knowledge by acquaintance and knowledge by description.

[8]Ibid., p. 10. [9]Ibid., p. 19. [10]Ibid., p. 9. [11]Ibid., p. 5.

[12]L. Śrīnivāsāchārya: *Darśanodaya*, p. 212.

[13]Ātreya Rāmānuja: *Nyāyakuliśa*, p. 39.

[14]Rāmānuja: *Śrī Bhāṣya*, Vol. I, pp. 49–50.

[15]Ibid., pp. 18 fol. [16]Ibid., p. 26.

[17]Śrīnivāsadāsa: *Yatīndramatadīpikā*, pp. 89–90.

[18]Ibid., p. 2 fol. I find the simplest and clearest account of the categories in this book, which I am following.

[19]Cp. *Tattvatrayī*.

[20]Śrīnivāsadāsa: *Yatīndramatadīpikā*, p. 11.

[21]See the author's *Introduction to Comparative Philosophy*, p. 241.

[22]Rāmānuja: *Śrī Bhāṣya*, Vol. II, II, ii, 41.

[23]Radhakrishnan: *Indian Philosophy*, Vol. II, p. 690.

[24]Śrīnivāsadāsa: *Yatīndramatadīpikā*, p. 52.

[25]Ibid., p. 51. [26]Ibid., p. 53.

[27]There is another doctrine called triplicating (*trivṛtkaraṇa*) in the *Chāndogya Upaniṣad*. (V, ii and iii). The elements here are three only—fire, water, and earth. Still another doctrine is mentioned, vix., seven-folding, in which reason (*mahat*) and ego are added to the five. Ibid., p. 66.

[28]Ibid., p. 78. *Vibhūti* means power and *nityavibhūti* means eternal power. But this power is, for this school, a substance; *Śakti*, which also means power, is a quality. As the words force and energy have the connotation of substantiality also, *nityavibhūti* may be translated as eternal force or energy. *Śakti* also may be translated as force, provided we understand that it means, for this school, only a quality.

[29]Ibid., p. 80. It is unconscious according to the Tengalai school, but conscious according to the Vadagalai. See K. C. Bharadwaj: *The Philosophy of Rāmānuja*, p. 236.

[30]Śrīnivāsadāsa: *Yatīndramatadīpikā*, pp. 82–83.

[31]K. D. Bharadwaj: *The Philosophy of Rāmānuja*, p. 241.

[32]Most Advaitins accept the three factor (*tripuṭi*)—Knower, Knowledge, and the Known—theory of cognition, but do not accept the ultimate distinction between the *ātman* and *dharma-bhūta-jñāna*.

[33]Śrīnivāsadāsa: *Yatīndramatadīpikā*, p. 88, and Atreya Rāmānuja: *Nyāya-kuliśa*, p. 70.

[34]It is this consciousness that can be studied phenomenologically and may be called the phenomenological consciousness.

[35]Rāmānuja: *Śrī Bhāṣya*, Vol. I, p. 38.

[36]Ibid., p. 39. [37]Op. cit. [38]Ibid., p. 54.

[39]Ibid., p. 90. [40]Ibid., p. 91.

[41]Rāmānuja: *Śrī Bhāṣya*, Vol. I, p. 12. It may be the potency (*samskāra*) also of action.

[42]Śrīnivāsadāsa: *Yatīndramatadīpikā*, p. 53.

[43]Atreya Rāmānuja: *Nyāyakuliśa*, p. 122. [44]Ibid., p. 124.

[45]In Indian thought, Avidyā seems to have played different roles. It is even regarded as the material (non-conscious) energy (*śakti*) of the Godhead. (See L. Śrīnivāsāchārya: *Darśanodaya*, pp. 111 fol.) *Vidyā* (knowledge) becomes his conscious energy. Both are spiritual energies (*citśaktis*). This school throws out a number of suggestions, but does not work them out into a theory.

[46]Śrīnivāsadāsa: *Yatīndramatadīpikā*, p. 105.

[47]Rāmānuja: *Śrī Bhāṣya*, Vol. I, pp. 45–46.

[48]Ibid., p. 47. [49]Ibid., p. 43.

[50]Śrīnivāsadāsa: *Yatīndramatadīpikā*, pp. 122–23.

[51]These seven arguments are supposed to point to the main seven defects in the Advaita doctrine of Avidyā: (1) lack of support for Avidyā (*āśrayānupapatti*), (2) impossibility of veiling the Brahman (*tirodhānānupapatti*), (3) beinglessness of Avidyā (*svarūpānupapatti*), (4) self-contradictoriness of inexplicability (*anirvacanīyānupapatti*), (5) lack of any means of knowing Avidyā (*pramāṇānupapatti*), (6) lack of the cognition that removes Avidyā (*nivartakānupapatti*), and (7) impossibility of removing Avidyā (*nivṛttyānupatti*).

[52]Rāmānuja: *Śrī Bhāṣya*, Vol. I, p. 46.

[53]Ātreya Rāmānuja: *Nyāyakuliśa*, p. 58. [54]Cp. its *pṛthaktvam* (separateness)

[55]S. M. S. Chari: *Advaita and Viśiṣṭadvaita*, p. 35. See also Nārāyaṇārya: *Nītimālā*, p. 20.

[56]*Viśeṣa* in Madhva's philosophy seems to be hardly different from *pṛthaktva*; for he says that every object has a *viśeṣa*, which means that it is distinct.

[57]Śrīnivāsadāsa: *Yatīndramatadīpikā*, p. 152.

[58]Nārāyaṇārya: *Nītimālā*, p. 17.

[59]For example, we know that circularity and mutual implication in an argument are not fallacies when they apply to a system. Hegel was emphatic on this point. They are, on the contrary, virtues.

[60]Rāmānuja: *Śrī Bhāṣya*, Vol. I, pp. 27 and 97.

[61]Ibid., p. 11. [62]Ibid., p. 149.

[63]Śrīnivāsadāsa: *Yatīndramatadīpikā*, pp. 95 fol.

[64]Rāmānuja: *Śrī Bhāṣya*, Vol. I, pp. 7 and 149.

[65]Ibid., p. 148. [66]Śrīnivāsadāsa: *Yatīndramatadīpikā*, p. 99.

[67]Both Śaṅkara and Rāmānuja accept that the Supreme Being is *attā* (swallower).

[68]that is, it becomes *asamprajñāta*, as Patañjali would say.

[69]See my "Self and Body: How Known and Differentiated."

[70]They may understand the grammatical use, first person, second person, and third person about pronouns. But note a very significant difference between Sanskrit and English grammars. For the former, I is the "best person" (*uttama puruṣa*), You is the "middle person" (*madhyama puruṣa*), and He is the "first person" (*prathama puruṣa*). Why is the I the "best person?"

[71]It is an important question whether the I should be called a pronoun at all. When I use it, it does not stand for anything else than itself. See my article, "Being: How Known and How Expressed."

[72]*Vedānta Aphorisms*, I, 1, 1. [73]Ibid., IV, 1, 3.

[74]See my "Being: How Known and How Expressed."

[75]See the author's paper, "Existential and Phenomenological Consciousness in the Philosophy of Rāmānuja."

[76]L. Śrīnivāsāchārya: *Darśanodaya*, p. 211.

[77]Śrīnivāsadāsa: *Yatīndramatadīpikā*, p. 54.

[78]*acetanadravya*, (*Yatīndramatadīpikā*, p. 86).

[79]This discussion has much bearing on Husserl's ideas, and can throw light on their deeper aspects.

[80]Remember Patañjali's insistence on *iva* (as if), which from our point of view applies necessarily to our experiences in this world, although it may take a different significance at the transcendental levels.

[81]Rāmānuja interprets the Upaniṣadic statement that the *ātman* is more atomic than the atom itself and is greater in size than the greatest by referring to the two forms of consciousness as understood by him. But the Upaniṣad does not speak of two realities, but only of one. The confusion is made worse by this school calling soul, God, attribute consciousness and the Pure Transparent by the name consciousness (*jñāna*). But cp. the ambiguity in Western philosophy also. See *Darśanodaya*, p. 210.

[82]See Ludwig Wittgenstein: *Philosophy and Language* by Alice Ambrose and Morris Lazerowitz (George Allen and Unwin, London, 1972) Chapters 3 and 10.

[83]My toothache is private, my property is private, the president of a state has a private life of his own and has also a public life. In these expressions, the word private does not mean exactly the same.

[84]This gives another cue to the Vedāntic theory that existence (*sattā*) is one and is common to all and the *sattā* of objects is known by the self, and their qualities etc., by mind and senses, which are private.

[85]It seems to correspond to the *Śuddha Vidyā* (Pure Gnosis or Knowledge) of the Śaiva and Pāśupata schools. Its acceptance indicates that before realizing the Supreme Being, one has to reach the stage of the Logos.

[86]It has also to be explained why, if I cannot know another's pain, I know that there is another, and that he has pain.

[87]St. Thomas also thinks that the liberated souls acquire a new body, which is devoid of impurities. But the conception is mythological.

[88]*Darśanodaya*, p. 211.

[89]It seems to me that Prakṛti can intelligibly be interpreted as the mass of the potencies of the individual's actions residing in him. Then there will be two levels of Prakṛti also, the cosmic and the individual. Relate the ideas of the causal body, Avidyā, and Māyā, Prakṛti, and Avyakta.

[90]In the Śaiva and Pāśupata tradition, *niyati* is explicitly said to be an offshoot of Māyā; but the explanation that it is *karma* and *avidyā* belongs to the *Śvetāśvatara Upaniṣad* and Rāmānuja.

[91]I have not found any traditional follower of Śaṅkara explain Māyā this way clearly. But it is implied by all that they say.

[92]Consider the fact that when the mental patient knows why he is having the trouble, he overcomes the trouble, the trouble ends. That is why I suggest explaining the *samskāras* (translated as impressions generally) of actions as weak and strong traumas, a term easily understood in modern thought.

Chapter XIII

The Vedānta of Madhva: Dualism of God and the World

1. INTRODUCTION

Madhva is generally assigned to the 13th century. His original names were Nārāyaṇa and Vāsudeva.[1] Later he assumed two other names, Pūrṇaprajña and Ānandatīrtha. Madhva is the name he took last, and he is generally known by it. He was the author of many works, the most important of which are his commentaries on the three basic works of the Vedānta—the Upaniṣads, the *Vedānta Aphorisms*, and the *Bhagavadgītā*—, his commentary on the great epic, *Mahābhāgavata*, and his twelve monographs (*prakaraṇagranthas*). Jayatīrtha (14th century?) and Vyāsarāya (16th century) are the greatest dialecticians of this school. The former's *Nyāyaśudhā* and *Vādāvali* are important polemical works. The latter's *Nyāyāmṛta* is a dialectical attack on Śaṅkara's Advaita. His *Bhedojjīvana* is a dialectical defence of the reality of difference and of plurality from the attacks of the Advaitins. His *Tarkatāṇḍava* shows the points of similarity and difference between his school and the Nyāya-Vaiśeṣika.[2] For to defend the plurality of the world, Madhva made elaborate use of the categories of the Nyāya-Vaiśeṣika.

Madhva, like Rāmānuja, is a follower of Vaiṣṇavism and the cult of devotion or love of God. Yet he was not satisfied with the philosophy of Rāmānuja. For the latter made the world the body of the Brahman and became open to the charge that he made the Brahman suffer the change and vicissitudes of the body. If the Brahman suffers from them, it cannot be perfect. Hence Madhva wanted complete difference between the Brahman and the world, and said that the non-duality referred to by the Upaniṣads had to be interpreted as that found between the king and his subjects, between one who is independent (*svatantra*) and one who is dependent on the former (*paratantra*).

The school of Madhva counts several predecessors to him, but many of them seem to be mythological persons. We may say that this school had very ancient origins, for the idea that man is a servant of God is as old as religion itself. The love of God that Madhva teaches is that of a devoted servant to his master. As Madhva rejects all relationship of being between God and the world, his philosophy is called dualism (*dvaita*). It means primarily the dualism of God and the individual spirit and then the dualism of God and the world. The world of matter (Prakṛti) is different from both God and the individual spirits. Madhva's philosophy is metaphysically qualitative dualism and quantitative pluralism.

2. EPISTEMOLOGY

Madhva accepts three valid means of cognition—perception, inference, and scripture (verbal knowledge). Like Rāmānuja, he says that the others can be subsumed under one or more of the three. Valid cognition[3] is defined as the cognition of the object as it is, thereby retaining explicit reference to the object. It is of two kinds:[4] cognition as knowledge itself (*kevalapramāṇa)* and cognition as an instrument of true knowledge (*anupramāṇa*). In the former, there can be no distinction between valid cognition and valid means of cognition. In fact, the definition itself overlooks the distinction. However, the former kind of valid cognition is again of two kinds—valid cognition which is the consciousness belonging to the knower (*sākṣijñāna*) and valid cognition which is the consciousness belonging to the functions (*vṛttis*) of mind and senses. The former is infallible (*svatahprāmāṇya*), but not the latter, which is of three kinds—perception, inference, and verbal testimony. Memory (*smṛti*) is valid, although a form of perception.

PERCEPTION The doctrine is practically the same as that of the Nyāya-Vaiśeṣika, except that the followers of Madhva[5] do not accept the six-fold contact relationship and also the distinction between indeterminate (*nirvikalpaka*) and determinate (*savikalpaka*) perception. The six-fold contact of the sense and the object cannot be accepted, because Madhva rejected the relation of inherence (*samavāya*) for reasons which will be shown later. The distinction between indeterminate and determinate perception also is not accepted, because, according to Madhva, all cognition is that of a determinate object. According to the Nyāya-Vaiśeṣika, the determinants of an object of perception are eight—(1) quality as in the "red rose"; (2) substance like the umbrella in "the man with the umbrella"; (3) action as in "the moving car"; (4) class concept or universal like horseness in "That is a horse"; (5) the particular (*viśeṣa*) like the particular in space, which differentiates it from time; (6) inherence (different from that of the Nyāya) as in "The body inheres in the organs" and "The whole inheres in its parts"; (7) the name as in "That is a horse" (sometimes, but not always, the name also characterizes the object); and (8) negation as in the "table that is not red". The Mādhvas (the followers of Madhva) say that the particular *(viśeṣa)* as understood by the Nyāya-Vaiśeṣika is not acceptable as belonging to only ultimate realities. It is present everywhere as a constitutive characteristic. The relation of inherence also cannot be accepted, because it is only a form of "being determined (*viśiṣṭa*)." We always see some determinant in every perception, for no object can be perceived without some determinant such as colour or shape. The Mādhvas are not prepared to accept even the kind of distinction accepted by Rāmānuja between indeterminate and determinate perception.

INFERENCE AND VERBAL TESTIMONY Regarding inference, the Mādhvas differ little from the other Vedāntic schools. Scripture is of two kinds[6]—that which has an author and that which has no author. The epics (*purāṇas*, *itihāsas*) and the ethical codes (*dharmaśāstras*) — both of which are called *smṛtis* (the remembered texts) — belong to the first class; the Veda belongs to the second. Unlike the Nyāya-Vaiśeṣika, this school says that the Veda is eternal. At this point, it agrees with the Mīmāṃsā.

However, both kinds of scripture are infallible. Of course, as a Vaiṣṇava, Madhva would not regard the Śaiva epics as equally reliable.

VALIDITY OF KNOWLEDGE On the topic of the validity of knowledge, Madhva has something new to contribute. Like all the other Vedāntins, he maintains that knowledge is self-valid (*svatahprāmāṇya*) and its invalidity is due to other factors (*paratah aprāmāṇya*). But he raises the question:[7] How can knowledge which is valid in itself, become invalid sometimes, even if due something else? If valid in itself, what can anything else to do it? How can anything else make it false? If it knows that it is valid, how can anything else make it know that it is false? So long as I see the mirage as water, I know that my knowledge is true; but later I realize that it is false. Thus it is possible for any knowledge to become false later. So when it is said that some knowledge is self-valid, it means, according to Madhva, first that it is the knowledge obtained from scripture or, secondly, it is knowledge that is the consciousness of the witness (*sākṣi*), which is the *ātman* itself. But knowledge obtained through the functions (*vṛttis*) of mind and senses is liable to be false and is not self-valid. Thus Madhva gives a new interpretation to the idea of self-validity.

We now see why Madhva distinguishes between direct knowledge obtained by the *ātman* without the instrumentality of mind and senses and knowledge obtained through their instrumentality. The former knowledge is not only uncontradicted, but also uncontradictable. Madhva gives the example of pain and pleasure.[8] If I have a toothache, I never doubt it. Even if the pain is psychological and has no physical cause, as in the case of psychic patients, the experience of pain can never be doubted. In such experiences, the witness consciousness (*sākṣicaitanya*, also called *jīvasākṣi*) not only cognizes the pain, but also the truth of the cognition of pain. In dreamless sleep, it is this witness consciousness that is awake[9] and says later that it slept well. The other kind of consciousness, viz., functional consciousness (*vṛttijñāna*) is absent in deep sleep, because there are no mind and senses then and nothing objective is known. This witness has two aspects;[10] its aspect as a being (*svarūpa*), as constitutive of the *ātman*, and its aspect as an instrument (*indriya*) of knowing some object like pain. But the distinction between the two aspects is relative and referential; in fact, both are one and the same. Yet the aspects have to be recognized; each is a particular (*viśeṣa*) and has its own peculiarity and function. We can understand this distinction, if we remember Rāmānuja's distinction between existential consciousness (*svarūpajñāna*) and attribute consciousness (*dharmabhūtajñāna*). But Rāmānuja's attribute consciousness covers also functional consciousness.

Madhva has seen a very important complexity in the Vedāntic idea of the self-validity of knowledge. If knowledge is self-valid, why does it become invalid at any time and in any circumstances? As this question cannot be answered easily, Madhva draws a distinction between witness consciousness and functional consciousness. For argument's sake, we may accept the distinction and also the self-validity of witness consciousness. Then has functional consciousness no self-validity? Is it made valid by something other than itself? Should we then accept the Nyāya-Vaiśeṣika doctrine, so far as functional consciousness goes, that cognition is by itself neither valid nor invalid? If we accept it, can we trust our functional consciousness at any time? We may say that functional knowledge is valid or invalid by itself, but that its validity or invalidity is *known* by something else—a position held by the Sāṅkhya—or that it is neither valid nor invalid by itself, but is made so by something else—a position held by the Nyāya-Vaiśeṣika. Which is Madhva's position? There is no clear answer.

Again, Śaṅkara explains the memory of deep sleep, saying that even the consciousness of the *ātman* is overwhelmed in it. Rāmānuja explains it by saying that the attribute consciousness is absent in it and, as the existential consciousness can never know itself without the functioning of the attribute consciousness, our experience of deep sleep is of the form, "I did not know even myself." But Madhva cannot explain this aspect of the memory of deep sleep, viz., "I did not know even myself." He cannot say, as Rāmānuja does, that I know myself only in knowing an object. For knowledge of the object, according to Rāmānuja, is a function of the attribute consciousness. For Madhva, it has to be a function of the functional consciousness. He cannot say that the witness consciousness cannot function without the functioning of the functional consciousness; for he says that pains and pleasures are known directly by the witness consciousness and that whatever is known by it is uncontradictably true. If the witness consciousness is present in deep sleep, why do we not know ourselves in deep sleep? The only alternative then left for Madhva is to say that it is present in deep sleep only as a being (*svarūpa*), but not as an instrument (*indriya*) of knowledge. Then if part can be present and part absent, how can the two be identical and how can we maintain that the distinction between the two is only relative and referential? How can my being be my instrument also? Of whom is it an instrument, when it becomes an instrument? There seems to be nothing. Thus although Madhva has noticed an important difficulty in the conception of the self-validity of knowledge, the solution he offers raises greater difficulties than before.

Madhva does not seem to accept that the pragmatic criterion[11] (*arthakriyākāritā*) directly confirms the validity or invalidity of cognition belonging to functional consciousness. He seems to say that validity or invalidity is grasped through correspondence, coherence,[12] etc. He seems also to say that all valid knowledge, even of functional consciousness, is grasped and is known also as valid by the witness consciousness. But in the case of invalid knowledge, it grasps only the bare being (*svarūpa*) of the functional consciousness and its content, while its invalidity is known by tests like coherence and correspondence. But how can we know whether the witness consciousness knows, in any particular instance, only the bare being and content of the functional consciousness or its validity also? We do not get an answer.

THE OBJECT OF ILLUSION In explaining the status of the object of illusion also, the Mādhvas want to strike a new path. They call their doctrine a new form of the doctrine held by the Nyāya-Vaiśeṣika and Kumārila, viz., that the illusory object is something other than the real (*abhinava-anyathākhyāti*).[13] We have seen the difference between the doctrines of the Nyāya-Vaiśeṣika and of Kumārila. In fact, the Mādhvas are having in mind the doctrine of Kumārila, from which they show their difference. But they mention the name of the Nyāya-Vaiśeṣika; for, as mentioned already, the two doctrines are often confused. According to Kumārila, in the illusion of the snake a particular rope is mistaken for a particular snake, which was seen somewhere else and remembered now. The Mādhvas argue that, if both are individual and real objects, why is either of them called illusory and unreal? When the cognition, "That is a rope," arises, the cognition, "That is a snake," is contradicted. Without this contradiction, there can be no illusion. And the contradiction means that the snake, even during the time of perception, was not existent, not real. So we cannot contend that a real object seen somewhere else and remembered now exists in front and is seen now. If that were the object seen, it would not be contradicted. So what we see in illusion is a non-existent (*asat*) snake. Illusion lies, therefore, in perceiving a non-existent (*asat*) object as an existent (*sat*) object. By propounding this doctrine, the Mādhvas say, they combine the important aspects[14] of the doctrine that the object of illusion is non-existent (*asatkhyāti*, but really *viparītakhyāti*). They reject every other view for the reasons for which it is rejected by its opponents.

By propounding the above doctrine, although the Mādhvas removed one difficulty, they introduced others. How can a non-existent object be seen as an existent object? If it is said that such a perception is due to the similarity between, e.g., the rope and the snake, the difficulty then will be that the snake, before it is seen is non-existent. How can there be any similarity between a non-existent and an existent object? How can we see any similarity between existence and non-existence? It may be said that the similarity between the rope and some snake already seen in the past is known. Yes, but it is the similarity between two existent objects, but not between an existent and a non-existent object. Are non-existent objects individuals? Or is the illusory snake, as in the Nyāya-Vaiśeṣika, the That in front of the perceiver and characterized by the universal snakeness? But snakeness is real, not unreal. How can it characterize a non-existent object? In this problem also, the Mādhvas have seen a difficulty; but their solution lacks adequacy.

3. METAPHYSICS

While Rāmānuja makes use of the Sāṅkhya in the development of his metaphysics—in fact such a use is found in the Pāñcaratra, which he follows—but very little use of the Nyāya-Vaiśeṣika, Madhva uses both equally well. It is more an adaptation and incorporation of their doctrines, so far as they are useful, for developing a pluralistic theism than following them that we find in the philosophy of Madhva. The Sāṅkhya has to be utilized, as the idea of Prakṛti is retained. And as a pluralist, Madhva needed a category that preserves ultimate pluralism. He found it in the Vaiśeṣika doctrine of the particular (*viśeṣa*), but changed its connotation very greatly.

THE CATEGORIES The classification of Madhva's categories also may be given in different ways. As we have seen, some of them are common to all and others to some Vedāntins. Madhva's main division of the categories is into the independent (*svatantra*) and dependent (*paratantra*).[15] The only independent reality is God. The dependent, i.e., the reality that is dependent on God, is of two kinds, the conscious and the unconscious. The conscious are the individual *ātmans* and some supernal beings like the consort of Viṣṇu, called Lakṣmi. The supernals are eternally liberated and perform certain cosmic and divine functions. Here Madhva follows certain traditional mythological epics and the Pāñcarātra, as Rāmānuja does, in giving the supernals theological meanings. He classifies the individual *ātmans* into four kinds—those that are released, like Hiraṇyagarbha (the Cosmic[16] Soul), who is called the Highest Soul (*jivottama*), those that are capable of obtaining salvation (*muktiyogyas*), those that are always transmigrating (*nityasamsāris*), and those that are eternally damned (*tamoyogya*, those that deserve only Darkness), viz., the beings of the underworld like demons. This classification involves the doctrine of pre-destination, which is not accepted by many of the Vedāntins. The unconscious reality is of three kinds: Prakṛti, space, and time.[17] Unlike Rāmānuja, Madhva gives an important place to space also.

ANOTHER CLASSIFICATION We come across in the writings of the Mādhvas a cross classification also of all the categories. First, the categories are said to be nine—substance (*dravya*), quality (*guṇa*), action (*karma*), universal (*sāmānya*, *jāti*), particular (*viśeṣa*), the characterized (*viśiṣta*) or the whole (*amsi*), force (*śakti*), similarity (*sādṛśya*), and negation (*abhāva*). If we take the characterized and the whole as separate the number of categories will be ten. The whole may be said to be characterized by the parts or vice versa. We can easily see that these categories are very similar to those of the Mīmāmsā and the Nyāya-Vaiśeṣika, if taken together. Substances are said to be nineteen—God, his consort (Śrī, Lakṣmi), innate forces (*samskāras, vāsanās*), the *ātman*, space, Prakṛti, the three Attributes (the Transparent, the Active, and the Dark), mind (*manas*), the senses, the elements, the subtle elements (*tanmātras*), ignorance (*avidyā*), word-sounds (*varṇas*), darkness (*andhakāra*) as in the night, time (*kāla*), reflection (*pratibimba*) like a face in the mirror, Cosmic Reason (*mahat*), ego (*ahaṁkāra*), and individual reason (*buddhi*). In this division of substances, we see that some of categories treated as qualities by Rāmānuja are treated by Madhva as substances. We find also that space, time, and Prakṛti are separately mentioned. But their separate mention may or may not mean that they are really separate, for even the evolutes of Prakṛti find a separate mention.

QUALITIES AND ACTIONS The Mādhva list of qualities includes not only those given by the Vaiśeṣika, but also mental and ethical qualities such as self-control (śama), mercy (*kṛpā*, grace), endurance (*titīkṣā*), gravity (*gāmbhīrya*, depth, dignity), beauty (*saundarya*), courage (*śaurya*, heroism), fear (*bhaya*), liberality (*audārya*), strength (*bala*), and shame (*lajjā*). Actions (activities) are practically the same as those in the Nyāya-Vaiśeṣika. The actions of creation, sustaining, and destruction, which belong to God, are eternal and are constitutive of his being.

THE UNIVERSAL AND SIMILARITY The Mādhva school differs partly from the Nyāya-Vaiśeṣika in its doctrine of the universal. According to the latter, all universals are eternal. The universal horseness is eternal, although there were no horses in the universe once upon a time. But Mādhva says that the universal of eternal entities, like the *ātmans*, are eternal; but those of non-eternal entities are not eternal. The Nyāya-Vaiśeṣika says that, if smokeness and fireness are not eternal, then the universal proposition, "Wherever there is smoke, there is fire," cannot be eternally true. And unless it is eternally true, we cannot have valid inferences. The Mādhvas reply that, for inference, similarity (*sādṛśya*) along with the negative instances is enough for the truth of the major premise.[18] Similarity is objectively real, it is not a mere mental concept.

THE PARTICULAR In the philosophy of Mādhva, as in that of the Nyāya-Vaiśeṣika, the particular (*viśeṣa*) plays an important role. But while in the latter, it belongs only to the eternal infinite and infinitesimal entities, in the former it is present everywhere. Again, in the Nyāya-Vaiśeṣika, the particular is different from the entities to which it belongs; but for Mādhva it is a feature of their very being[19] (*svarūpa*).

According to Madhva, the particulars are found everywhere and exist in all things, eternal and transient, conscious and unconscious, God and the World. In conscious beings, the particulars are identical with their substrata. But in unconscious beings, if the particulars are essential properties of substances, they are identical with their substrata; otherwise, they are both identical with, and different from the substrata. For instance, in chemistry every substance has its property. We cannot, therefore, say that the property is different from the substance. Madhva says that the relation between the two is "colourful identity" (*saviśeṣābheda*), i.e., an identity that retains the differences of the two terms. The two cannot be separated, there is no difference, but the identity is not bare identity, but an identity of two particulars, substance (*dravya*) and property (quality). What we have to note is that both substance and quality are particulars (*viśeṣas*). Unlike in the Nyāya-Vaiśeṣika, the particular is not an entity different from the substance in which it inheres. Yet any substance and any quality are each a particular. In a "red rose," the red colour is not a property of the rose; the rose could have been white. Furthermore, the colour changes as the rose dries up. The relation between the red colour and the rose is, therefore, that of both identity and difference. Here substance and quality are different, because they can exist without each other. The rose may exist with white colour and the red colour may exist with another kind of flower. But when the red and the rose exist together they cannot be separated; they are, therefore, non-dual (*abhinna*) or identical.

The particular (*viśeṣa*) is the name of the power of everything to be itself.[20] Every object is a unity of many differences; it is one and yet has qualities, activities, and so forth. Still it is an entity by itself. It is, therefore, a particular. But every quality, activity, or a part it possesses is also an entity by itself; so it also is a particular. Thus particulars are found everywhere and everything we see and think of is a particular. The world is, therefore, an infinite plurality. Every unity is a particular and is made up of particulars.

THE CHARACTERIZED, THE WHOLE, AND POWER The Mādhvas recognize the characterized, the whole, and power (*śakti*) as separate categories.[21] The characterized is that which is determined, qualified, or limited by a characteristic or adjective (*viśeṣaṇa*). The characteristic is not necessarily a quality, but an adjective, which may be anything. As we have seen, in "the man with an umbrella" the umbrella is a characteristic or attribute. Thus the characterizer (*viśeṣaṇa*) may be a substance, quality, universal, particular, etc. Just as we distinguish between substance and quality, we have to distinguish between the characterizer and the characterized. The latter also may be a substance or anything else. If the characterizer is coeval with the characterized, it is identical or non-dual with the latter. For instance, the great attributes of God such as omnipotence and omniscience are identical with him. If the attributes are not coeval with the substance, they are both identical with, and different from it. Even in the former case, the identity is not absolute, but modified by the characteristic (*viśeṣaṇa*). For instance, in the "red rose," the identity is characterized by "red." It is non-difference (*abheda*) with a characteristic or a particular type of non-difference (*saviśeṣābheda*). What Madhva seems to mean is that this identity between a substance and its characteristic does not make the former the latter or the latter the former, but is a particular type that holds between a substance and its characteristic and that preserves the substance as substance and the characteristic as characteristic.

The whole is that which is made up of parts. The Buddhist dialecticians like Nāgasena argue that the so-called whole is unreal, as it is nothing but its parts. The chariot is nothing but its wheels, axle, seats, top, etc. But nobody, Madhva would say, would pile these up and use the heap as a chariot. So the reality of the chariot, as distinct from the reality of its parts, has to be recognized. Madhva insists, therefore, that we should recognize the concept or category of the whole (*amsi*), as distinct from its parts (*amsas*), as true of reality. In the case of the category of the whole also, Madhva distinguishes between the parts that are expressive of the being of the whole (*svarūpāmsas*) and the parts that are not so expressive and are, therefore, different from the whole (*bhinnāmsas*). He uses this distinction with reference to conscious beings like the *ātmans* and divine beings like God. The power (*śakti*) of God is a part of God and is expressive of his being, i.e., it is constitutive. Similarly, the consciousness of the *ātman* is constitutive. The power of fire is a constitutive part of fire and specific gravity is a constitutive part of substances. Of course, very often we find the ideas of part and characteristic overlapping.

Power (*śakti*) is accepted as a distinct category, for it can be distinguished from that which has the power, e.g., the power of burning from the substance fire. They cannot, indeed, be separated, but only distinguished, as each has its own particular. In Madhva's philosophy, whatever can be distinguished or thought of as distinct from others, even when not separable from them, has a constitutive particular (*svarūpaviś-eṣa*) and, we may say, is a particular. Power exists in two forms and is of four kinds. Its two forms[22] are the latent state and the manifest state. Its four[23] kinds are: (1) the mysterious power (*acintyaśakti*) of God, called Māyā; (2) the causal power of things, which is natural to them (*kāraṇaśakti, sahajaśakti*), e.g., the burning power of fire; (3) the power imparted to a thing from outside, which may be a caused power, but is not natural, e.g., the power of one billiard ball imparting movements to another[24] (*adheyaśakti*); and (4) the power of words, which are by themselves mere sounds, to mean something (*padaśakti*).

NEGATION Like the Nyāya-Vaiśeṣika, Madhva accepts the reality of negation, but with a difference.[25] We have seen that, for Rāmānuja, difference cannot be reduced to negation; it is a positive, constitutive feature of the object itself. Madhva treats differences similarly. We then have only three kinds of negation left: prior negation, posterior negation, and absolute negation. Madhva's views on prior and posterior negation are the same as those of the Nyāya-Vaiśeṣika. But his views on absolute negation are different. According to the Nyāya-Vaiśeṣika, absolute negation is the negation of an object at all times and places except when and where it exists. Such a negation is what Kant would call infinite negation, for the times and places in which the object does not exist are infinite. It corresponds in a way to what we call the contradictory term like non-colour, which refers to everything except colour. But some ancient Nyāya-Vaiśeṣikas included under absolute negation even negations like the negation of the son of a barren woman. We have shown already that this negation cannot be a logically significant negation and is similar to the negation in "Virtue is not a square." So later Naiyāyikas did not include such a negation under absolute negation.

But Madhva calls only such a negation absolute negation. He reduces what we call infinite negation to either prior negation or posterior negation. The absence of a pot on my table means either the prior negation of the existence of the pot there or its posterior negation if the pot has been removed from there. But can such a negation as the negation of the son of a barren woman[26]—"The son of a barren woman does not exist"—be significant, if there is no possibility of there being the son of a barren woman? Similarly, can "Virtue is not a square" be significant, if "Virtue is a square" is not significant and is not even possible? Madhva answers that the question of the possibility of the object or the concept that is negated, is irrelevant to negation. What is negated may be imaginary, possible, impossible, real, or unreal.[27] Its purpose is only to help us in forming the idea of negation, which is always the negation of something. So whatever can be thought of—we think of the circular square and the son of a barren woman— is capable of being the counterpart (*partiyogi*) of negation or of being that which is negated. Such a negation is significant, for we say that "Virtue is not a square" is a true proposition, although we do not say that "Virtue is a square" is true at any time or place.

SUBSTANCE Substance is understood by Madhva as the material cause of change and also as that which comes into contact with other substances. However, God, the supernals, and the *ātmans* do not undergo change (*pariṇāma*), but only manifest themselves in different circumstances (*abhivyajyante*). So we may say that change in some cases is only manifestation. Or we may define substance as that which changes or manifests itself. It is also that which comes into contact with other substances.

THE ĀTMAN Madhva identifies the *ātman* with the witness consciousness (*sākṣi, jīvasākṣi, sākṣicaitanya*). It is of the nature of I-consciousness (*ahamdhī*), which is, as in Rāmānuja's philosophy, different from the ego (*ahaṁkāra*), an evolute of Prakṛti. It is the knower (*jñātā*), doer (*kartā*), and enjoyer (*bhoktā*) of the fruits of actions. The *ātmans* are atomic and constitute a plurality, each having, in Madhva's own way, a particular (*viśeṣa*). They are absolutely dependent (*paratantra*) on God, who alone is self-dependent (*svatantra*) or independent. By nature, every *ātman* is existent, conscious, and blissful (*sat-cit-ānanda*). Through ignorance (*avidyā*) of its original nature it becomes entangled in Prakṛti. This entanglement is bondage. Every *ātman* is entirely different from God, Prakṛti, and the other *ātmans*. The Upaniṣadic statement that the *ātman* is the same as the Brahman is to be interpreted as meaning that the *ātman* is similar to the Brahman, just as the reflection of a face in the mirror is similar to the face. Here Madhva introduces the idea of the image, reflection (*pratibimba*), adding that the *ātmans*, although they are images of the Brahman, are not destructible like the ordinary images. They are real. The *ātmans* are by nature reflections of the Brahman; their being reflections is not due to any external conditions (*upādhis*). So we cannot say that, when the conditions are destroyed, the reflections disappear. For instance, if the mirror is taken away or is broken to pieces, I do not see any reflection. But the *ātmans* are not reflections of God in some material, but reflections as such. Here Madhva differs from the Advaita, according to which the souls are images, or reflections, of the Brahman in Māyā or Avidyā, which forms the condition or material receiving the reflection, and when Māyā or Avidyā disappears the reflection vanishes and the Brahman alone remains. The *ātman* is by very nature an image of the Brahman, just as the son may be the image of his father.

The *ātman* is self-conscious, self-revealing, self-luminous; that is, it reveals itself to itself. Yet its consciousness is distinct from itself, just as the specific gravity of a substance is distinct from that substance. That is, the *ātman* is its own particular and its consciousness is its own. As the two are thus particulars, one of them can be overwhelmed by ignorance. The Mādhvas say that, as the Advaitins do not recognize the particulars, they cannot explain how the *ātman*, which is always self-luminous, can become unconscious of itself in deep sleep.[28]

MĀYĀ AND AVIDYĀ Although Māyā and Avidyā are often equated to Prakṛti, they are treated as separate from Prakṛti in the philosophy of Madhva. Like Rāmānuja, Madhva rejects the Advaita conception of Māyā and Avidyā. He regards Māyā as the mysterious will of God (*īśvarecchā*) and Avidyā as the ignorance of the *ātman*, or as belonging to the *ātman*. Yet, as in the Advaita, this ignorance is not a negative[29] entity— which it is in Rāmānuja—but a positive one that bears fruit. The locus of Avidyā is the *ātman*, but not the Brahman, which is always omniscient and self-luminous. Avidyā has a two-fold function: it conceals the true nature of the *ātman* from itself and it conceals the Brahman (God) from the *ātman*. Although the *ātman* is by nature self-luminous, Avidyā enters it and becomes part of its nature due to the peculiar will of God. The *ātman* then gets entangled in Prakṛti and its modifications. No one can say when Avidyā entered the *ātman*; its relation to the *ātman* is beginningless (*anādi*). When the *ātman* obtains its liberation, it sheds Avidyā and frees itself from Prakṛti.

The second function is to veil the Brahman from the *ātman*. Then the latter thinks that it is self-dependent or independent of God. It can free itself from this function of Avidyā by realizing its dependence on God. The two functions of Avidyā are spoken of also as two kinds of Avidyā or two Avidyās. We thus see that Madhva's conception of Avidyā is different from that of Rāmānuja and also from that of Śaṅkara. But his conception of Māyā is similar to that of Rāmānuja, but different from that of Śaṅkara.

GOD AND THE BRAHMAN Like Rāmānuja, Madhva identifies the personal God with the Brahman and rejects the doctrine of Śaṅkara that the Brahman is without any qualities (*guṇas*). The Brahman possesses all the auspicious qualities and is the personal God himself. He is the creator, sustainer, and destroyer of the world. Madhva's God is the same as Rāmānuja's, except for the view that he is completely different from the *ātmans*, Prakṛti, space, and time; for Madhva also is a follower of the Pāñcarātra. God is absolutely independent and self-dependent. The idea that God is completely different from the rest brings in other differences from Rāmānuja's conception. For Rāmānuja, everything forms the body of God, and so creation can be interpreted as the self-transformation of God from the subtle to the gross state and destruction as the opposite process. Rāmānuja can, therefore, say that God is the material, efficient, and instrumental cause of the world. But Madhva argues[30] that such self-transformation affects the perfection of God. God must be independent of all such transformation. He cannot be the material cause. He is the efficient and instrumental cause only. He has eight cosmic powers, according to Madhva—the powers of creation, preservation, destruction, control over the world, enlightenment, obscuration, bondage, and release.[31]

PRAKṚTI AND CAUSATION Madhva does not accept the Nyāya-Vaiśeṣika doctrine that the effect does not exist before its appearance and is, therefore, Non-being. There is nothing absolutely new even with regard to its being.[32] Every causation is a change from the subtle to the gross state and vice versa. Transformation (*pariṇāma*) means such a change. But this kind of change obtains only in the case of Prakṛti and its evolutes. What Prakṛti evolves is already contained in it in a potential stage. But God and the souls do not undergo such a transformation; they become manifest or unmanifest. In the case of God, manifestation is due to his kindness. But if Prakṛti shows what is already contained in it, it is difficult to draw a distinction between change and manifestation. Madhva perhaps means that there are two kinds of manifestation, one of which is change.

The creation of the world by God does not mean that the world came into existence at a particular time. It is not true that God first existed and then created the world. He is God and creator at one and the same time. That the world is created by God means that it is always dependent on him. Creation is continuous creation, which is continuous dependence on God. To be created by God means to be dependent on God for one's being a particular (*parādhīnaviśeṣāpatti*).[33] Causality means dependence; for the effect is dependent on the cause.

Madhva's conception of Prakṛti is practically the same as that of Rāmānuja's, except that the former according to some of his followers, treats time as an evolute of Prakṛti along with reason (Mahat). Out of Reason the other evolutes issue forth. Another difference is that, while Rāmānuja does not distinguish between two levels of reason—the Great or Cosmic Reason and the individual reason—, Madhva draws the distinction.

TIME AND SPACE Madhva's conception of space[34] and time has its peculiarities, and is not the same as that of Rāmānuja. The latter thinks of time along with Prakṛti and as distinct from it; but Madhva thinks of it as an evolute of Prakṛti along with Cosmic Reason[35] (Mahat), out of which all the evolutes come and exist in time. Thus while the Sāṅkhya rejected the reality of time, saying that it is nothing but change, Madhva says that it comes out of Prakṛti.

Again, while Rāmānuja rejects the reality of independent space, saying that it is the same as ether (*ākāśa*), which is the origin of sound, Madhva argues that space is and must be different from ether. Space (*dik*) is that which offers place for things to exist and move. Ether, as the origin of sound, is something else; it is one of the five elements (*bhūtas*). Even Prakṛti needs space to exist. (It is not clear how it can be prior to Prakṛti, if it is its evolute.) Space is, therefore, a distinct reality independent of Prakṛti and so of time also. It is great and unmarked (*avyākṛtākāśa, mahākāśa*), i.e., without any form.[36]

Furthermore, Madhva differs from the Nyāya-Vaiśeṣika and Rāmānuja by saying that, although both time and space are infinite, they are divisible infinitely and the divisions also are as real as the infinite wholes. The question whether we can carry out an infinite division is irrelevant; we can conceptually think of it. The parts into which time and space are divided are also times and spaces, but not durationless and extensionless points. Moreover, time and space are not merely inferred. For there can be no major premise from which they can be inferred. They are perceived. But they are not perceived by the functional consciousness (*vṛtticaitanya*) of mind and senses. Functional consciousness can perceive only concrete objects and concrete forms like colours and mental images. But time and space are formless. So they are perceived, we have to say, by the witness consciousness (*sākṣijñāna*), i.e., by the *ātman* itself. For the *ātman*, its consciousness, which is its own being (*svarūpa*), can also be the means (*indriya*) for perceiving time, space, pain, and pleasure. The *ātman* intuits space and time directly. In the philosophy of Madhva, witness consciousness plays as important a role as attribute consciousness plays in the philosophy of Rāmānuja.

DEFENCE OF DIFFERENCE The other categories do not need explanation, as they are the same as those of the other orthodox schools. The idea of darkness (*andhakāra*) is the same as that of the Mīmāmsā (*tamas*). The idea of innate forces (*vāsanās*) is found in all schools that accept the doctrine of *karma* and includes the idea of the impressions left in the form of potencies (*samskāras*) by ethical actions and also the cosmic drives imparted by Prakṛti to the individuals. In treating word-sounds as substances, Madhva follows the Mīmāmsā of Kumārila.

Like Rāmānuja, Madhva was concerned with the reality of difference. One may say that he was more concerned than Rāmānuja. The latter wanted to give more substance to the idea of non-duality (*advaita*) than the former, who wanted absolute pluralism and more or less explained away non-duality in terms of dependence. However, the dialectic used by Madhva and his followers is the same as that of Rāmānuja and his followers. It lies in rejecting that difference is mutual negation and in redefining it as a constitutive feature (*svarūpaviśeṣa*) of every object and as lying at the vary basis of every negation, including mutual negation. That is, difference is prior to mutual negation; if two objects are not different from each other, they cannot negate each other. Indeed, the critics of Rāmānuja and Madhva will then say that this new interpretation of difference will lead to the Buddhist view that the object of perception is the individual as different from every other.

Madhva insists upon five[37] kinds of difference: (1) difference between the *ātman* (*jīva*) and the Brahman (God); (2) difference between all that is unconscious (Prakṛti, time, and space) and the Brahman; (3) difference of every *ātman* from every other; (4)

difference of every *ātman* from all that is unconscious (Prakṛti, time, and space); and (5) difference of every unconscious entity from every other unconscious entity. Thus all the evolutes of Prakṛti are different from one another from time and from space. Madhva accepts not only the difference of every member of a class from every other member of the same class (*sajātīyabheda*) and also of every member of a class from every member of every other class (*vijātīyabheda*) but also the difference of every element of the content of a whole from every other element in that whole and from that whole[38] also. He says that every element is a particular (*viśeṣa*) and is not merely distinguished but differentiated from the others. How such a view agrees with the idea of non-duality of a particular with its substrate (*saviśeṣābheda*) and with identity-cum-difference (*bhedābheda*), which Madhva accepts in certain cases already mentioned,—e.g., between substance and qualities that are not coeval—is difficult to understand.[39] One may say that Madhva tried every way possible to defend ultimate plurality and difference. But wherever he found difficulties, he introduced modifying concepts, which are left unreconciled with the original thesis. After all, reason cannot work with mere difference without aiming at the unification also of our conceptual knowledge, which needs the recognition of underlying unities and a unity of unities. But Madhva wants to dismiss the ultimate unity and explain it as ultimate dependence (*paratantratā*). But if the world is dependent on God and if God is the monotheistic God and the creator at one and the same time, he cannot be understood apart from the world—this has been recognized by the Mādhvas who say that creation does not mean that God first existed and then created the world, but that it is dependence of the world, as a particular, on God (*parādhīna-viśeṣāpatti*)—and to that extent at least God is dependent on the world for his being a creator. And what can be meant by God sustaining the world, if there is no metaphysical basis for the dependence of the world on God and if the two are so different as Madhva maintains? However, Madhva has made one of the grandest attempts to expound a monotheism that is to be at the same time a thorough-going pluralism.

4. LIFE'S IDEAL

Life's ideal, according to Madhva, is nearly the same as in Rāmānuja's philosophy. Both say that action leads to knowledge, and knowledge to love of God and self-surrender to him. Both insist upon leading a life of action. Madhva says that the souls, after liberation, live in the same world with God (*sālokya*), live near God (*sāmīpya*), become like God (*sārūpya*), and enjoy together with God (*sāyujya*). They never become one with God. He holds that there are various levels of salvation, depending on how strenuous an effort the soul makes to attain it. Rāmānuja does not seem to be particularly interested in such levels, although he accepts that the *ātmans* in the state of salvation do not become one with God. For Madhva, they do not form the body of God, whereas they do so according to Rāmānuja.

Madhva says that bondage is due to Avidyā, which, as mentioned already, is positive for him. This Avidyā has two functions, the veiling of the *ātman*'s own original nature and the veiling of God. The former conceals the consciousness of the *ātman*'s original nature as pure self-consciousness, thereby making it ignorant, and its original blissful nature, making it miserable. But Avidyā does not veil the original existence aspect (*viśeṣa*) of the *ātman*, which always knows its existence. Avidyā can veil even the constitutive differences or particulars (*viśeṣas*); for even the *ātman* consists of particulars, e.g., its qualities. When this Avidyā is overcome, the screen between the *ātman* and God is also removed. Or rather, both veils are removed simultaneously, for Avidyā cannot be overcome without the love of God.

God himself is responsible for the Avidyā in the *ātman*. He has, therefore, to be loved and worshipped so that Avidyā can be overcome. When the *ātman* is once limited by Avidyā, it goes on adding other limitations to its being. They[40] are the subtle body (liṅgaśarīra), which transmigrates, the potencies of past actions that have begun to bear fruit (*prārabdhakarmas*), and desire (*kāma*) for the pleasures of the world. These limitations are imposed on the *ātman* by Prakṛti, with which it identifies itself. It has, therefore, to free itself from Avidyā and Prakṛti.

Like Rāmānuja, Madhva says that love is the continuous flow (*dhārāvāha*) and perfection of knowledge. Its ultimate aim is to have direct, unmediated experience of God (*aparokṣānubhūti*). When such experience dawns, man becomes liberated. Here Madhva differs from Rāmānuja, by accepting salvation with the body also (*jīvanmukti*),[41] and agrees with Śaṅkara. The body will continue to live even after the experience of God arises; for the potencies of actions that have started their work will not stop until they are exhausted. Later, when the body dies, the liberated man will have no return, no future re-incarnation.

GENERAL ESTIMATE AND CONSTRUCTIVE COMMENT

(i) The Concept of Difference

The defence of the concept of difference is more important for Madhva than for Rāmānuja. (Remember nobody denies difference at the empirical level, but those who deny it do so at the ontological level or they deny its ontological status and significance. The latter want to bring out the full import of "Not is not the same as Is" or "No is not equal to Yes.") However, Madhva wants absolute difference between God and the souls and between the two on the one side and the material world on the other. For the defence of ultimate difference, he rejects the Nyāya-Vaiśeṣika interpretation that difference is mutual negation and maintains that difference is not a form of negation at all. Madhva, like Rāmānuja, says that difference is a positive category (*bhāvapadārtha*). But if it is positive, which sense—eye, ear, or nose—perceives it? As there is no separate sense organ to perceive difference, Madhva said that it is perceived by witness consciousness (*sākṣi-caitanya*), which for him is the *ātman* itself. Here he differs from Rāmānuja who says that difference is given in perception itself. Madhva maintains that it is not perceived even by functional consciousness (*vṛtti-caitanya*), not to speak of the senses.

Now, functional consciousness belongs to the inner instrument (*antahkaraṇa*). Generally in perception, mind (in the wide sense of inner instrument) takes over what is given to our senses. But now, if the witness consciousness perceives differences, does this consciousness transmit its experience to mind, just as the senses transmit their experience to mind? That the witness consciousness, which is the *ātman* itself for Madhva, cognizes difference without the intermediaries of mind and the senses is unintelligible. After all, difference belongs to the objective world, which can be known only through the mediating activities of mind and senses.

Indeed, it is one thing to say that the *ātman* as witness consciousness perceives difference directly, but another thing to say that in the elaboration, appreciation, and assimilation of the cognitions given by senses and mind, the *ātman* "construes" the experiences as different from one another. But this constructive process, as we noted in the earlier chapters, is done by apperception, which in effect Madhva equates to the *ātman*. It is indeed true—a fact noticed by us already—that without the activation by the *ātman*, neither the inner instrument (*antahkaraṇa*) nor the senses can act. But we should not equate the *ātman* to either or both.

So if difference is a positive quality like colours and smells, one of the senses must perceive it. But there is no sense set apart for perceiving difference. Nor can it be that every sense is capable of perceiving it. Senses can perceive a plurality, but they cannot perceive that every item of the plurality is different from the rest. Madhva's attempt to show that difference is knowable and known by the witness consciousness (*sākṣi-caitanya*), which for the purpose is treated by him as a sense also, is strange. The *ātman* itself is not a sense in any ordinary sense of the term sense. Senses are the instruments of cognition for the *ātman* (self). But can the *ātman* become an instrument of itself even for knowing difference? Again, if the *ātman*, as Madhva says, is atomic, —here he agrees with Rāmānuja—how can it perceive even a single difference, which has to hold between two entities and so cannot be atomic? Or is the *ātman*, as witness consciousness, infinite, while atomic at the same time? Then the relation between the two aspects or dimensions must be like that between the *ātman* and the attribute consciousness (*dharmabūta-jñāna*) in Rāmānuja's philosophy.

Strictly speaking, witness consciousness must be reflective consciousness as in "I know that I know the pen" and, as covering both past knowledge, and the object, it cannot be atomic. If the object is as distant as the star I perceive, my witness consciousness has to be as extensive as the star's distance from me. And what is not perceived in this instance, by the second, i.e., the lower I, cannot be perceived by the higher, i.e., the witness consciousness. So if the lower I cannot perceive difference as a positive quality, the higher I also cannot perceive it. It may be said that in reflection on experiences, we can come to realize that every item of the plurality we experience is different from every other. But then it amounts to admitting that difference is a category of reflection, developed by reflection, and is therefore conceptual, not ontological as Rāmānuja and Madhva claim. It may be objected that unless there is some basis in the experience, the concept of difference cannot arise. One may say the same in favour of negation and reduce difference to mutual negation. But the basis itself may not be experienced as difference. If, as Madhva says, witness consciousness sees only existence of objects, as for instance in illusion, and is, therefore, never erroneous, then it cannot see difference, but only existence in the plurality of objects. And pure existence or Being cannot be many, as we have previously seen. One may even suspect that, when Madhva says that difference is seen as a positive reality by the witness consciousness, he had in mind only the conceptual positing of difference among plurality by apperception (*citta*).

(ii) The Particular as Force or Centre of Force

A follower of this school may still say that every object *has* a particular (*viśeṣa*), and the particular is a force (*śakti*). We can appreciate this idea and its usefulness for understanding difference. Every stone of a heap has its own force, for instance, to lift a particular weight in a balance, and so we may say that it has its own existence. But this idea of equating existence to force and to a particular is a cosmological idea, not an ontological one. First, existence or Being cannot be many, each stone cannot have its own existence in the ultimate sense. The force it gets and is said to be inherent in it does not have isolated reality and function, but is dependent on many other things, e.g., the gravitational force of the earth. To say that it has a particular is only a way of speaking; for the particular it has is an endowment by many other things like the earth, which itself has a particular that is an endowment by the rest of the solar system.

Furthermore, there seems to be some confusion in the writings of this school between a thing "being a particular" and a thing "having a particular." We can understand everything being a particular thing, which generally means that it is an individual. The words particular and individual are used in the same sense in literary language. But what can be meant by saying: "Everything has a particular?" This question applies *mutatis mutandis* to the Nyāya-Vaiśeṣika view also that the atoms and the infinites (*vibhus*) *have* particulars. If the word particular is interpreted as a force (*śakti*), not merely as an indication that every particular has a force, even then this question obtains. If it is said that a particular is ultimately the "own being" (*svarūpa*) of the object, then no object can exist apart from its "own being" and it will be only a way of speaking, not to be understood in the exact sense of the terms, that every object *has* its own being; for every object really *is its own being*, but not "*has its own being*." The object and its "own being" are not even distinguishable except in literary usage. And if particular, own being (*svarūpa*), and force (*śakti*) are equated, then Being or Existence cannot be empty, but is force (*śakti*). Since Being, as we have seen, cannot be many and is ultimately the highest transcendental I-consciousness, the plurality of beings of the cosmos have to be understood as derived by the diversifications of the supreme transcendental force.

We can now appreciate why this controversy has arisen. It is due to the mixing up of ontological and cosmological stand-points. We should not mean that these stand-points must not be related; *my I-am, as we have seen in our discussion of the four levels of Being, belongs to all the levels, and can understand itself only when it realizes that it belongs to all of them and that all of them are related to one another through it.* But confusion and unending controversy arise when, for instance, negation, individuality, particular, difference, etc., which are cosmological categories, are assigned ontological status. The Mādhva classification of force (*śakti*) shows the mix up of the cosmological and the ontological. Cosmological categories are not self-sustaining.[42] We are all familiar with the self-contradictions involved in the concepts of negation, space, time, and so forth. But ontologically, there cannot be a plurality of Beings, for then Being or Existence will become a predicate and will lead to further self-contradictions.[43] We have, therefore, to say that the ideas, particular, difference, etc., have only cosmological validity, validity in the world of action, cognitive and practical. If this much is admitted, there should be no quarrel among the Vedāntic schools. But philosophers committed to pluralism will not make the admission. But they have either to accept that Existence or Being is a plurality and can be a predicate—thereby going against the views of Kant and quite a few modern logicians and becoming open to all the absurdities they pointed out—or make the admission that the ontological and the cosmological levels are different and should not be mixed up always.

(iii) Self-validity of Knowledge

The explanation of the self-validity of all knowledge as given by this school offers an important clue to a true understanding of the distinction between the ontological and the cosmological. Madhva accepts, like Śaṅkara and Rāmānuja, that all cognition is valid by itself, i.e., as such. This view is defended by asking: If you do not depend on cognition for knowing the truth, on what else can you depend? Indeed, truth pertains to cognition, and if we are to know truth at all, we can know it only through some cognition. This reason is practically a truism. But then, why are some cognitions false? And how are we to be sure that a particular cognition is true? For there is always a chance of a cognition being false. All the Vedāntic schools say that practical activity confirms or disconfirms the truth of all empirical cognitions, for the general trend of all the schools is to regard the empirical world as a world of action (*karmamayam*).

Then if it is action that enables us to confirm the truth or falsity of a cognition, should we say that all cognition by itself, apart from the consequences of action based upon it, is true, or that some cognitions are true and the others are false, or that their truth or falsity is disclosed by action? The writings of the schools mix up these questions and their answers become vague and inconclusive.

Certainly, no school could have meant that all empirical cognitions are necessarily true. If they were true, the experience of falsity could not have arisen at all. Yet we have to accept that, because we depend on cognition to know the truth or falsity of cognition, cognition has to be trusted and we have no other go. Taking the example of seeing the rope as the snake, "I see the snake" is false; but "I know that I have seen the snake," in which the first I becomes the witness of the second I as seeing the snake, can never be false. It is never false not only as immanent in the live act of seeing the snake, but also in treating it as a past experience as in "I know that I saw a snake." In fact, the conflict between perceptions and the consequent rejection of one of them as false arises only in the reflective consciousness, i.e., the witness consciousness. "I know that I saw 'That is a snake' " and "I know that I see 'That is a rope' " are held in and by the same witness consciousness, one of the contents of which "That is a snake" cannot agree with "That is a rope," and is therefore rejected. The rejection takes place in the witness consciousness.[44]

But unless the That in the two judgements is the same, as mentioned before, there can be no conflict. But who can certify that the two Thats are the same? The Advaitins indeed say that the two Thats have to be the same and that there can be no falsity about the cognition of the That. Falsity can arise only with regard to the predicate as in "That is a snake."[45] But who can certify about the That? The Advaitins do not seem to have discussed this question pointedly. The credit goes to

Madhva for tackling it. He says that the identity of the two Thats is known to the witness consciousness (*sākṣi-caitanya*), which knows or cognizes the existence aspect of the perceived objects. By implication, what this school calls functional consciousness (*vṛtti-caitanya*)[46] cognizes the form of predicate. Witness consciousness, as cognizing only existence, can never be wrong; but functional consciousness as cognizing the form (predicate) may be wrong. It is the truth of the cognition by functional consciousness, that is, of the predicate, that is confirmed or disconfirmed by practical action and other cognitions. Do not forget that human action is not an un-conscious process, but action of the type in which I know that I am acting by being that action.

One wonders whether Madhva is here elaborating the Advaita view or striking a new path for its own sake. But the implications of this profound analysis do not seem to have been fully recognized. For one thing, the Advaitins say that in all perception the existence or the "is" aspect is the Brahman, the Eternal Truth; and name and form are not ultimately true. They say also that all forms (shapes, colours, sounds, etc.) of the objects of cognition are the functions of the inner instrument (*antahkaraṇa*)—which comes to the same as saying that they are the results of, and cognized by functional consciousness. But they do not seem to have answered the question in the epistemological context: Who knows the existence aspect of the perceived objects?[47]

Now, if the existence aspect is known by the witness consciousness, which is the same as the *ātman*, and if the existence of the object, as Madhva claims, is separate and different from that of the *ātman*, how can the *ātman* know the existence of the object? Descartes, in the history of Western Philosophy, landed in difficulties by treating spirit and matter as two separate existences. (We often forget and historians of philosophy overlook the implication of his idea that these two substances are dependent on God, they are only relative substances and that God only is the absolute Substance.) It is philosophically not helpful to say that God can bridge the gaps. Rāmānuja distinguished between existential consciousness (*svarūpa-jñāna*) and attribute consciousness (*dharmabhūta-jñāna*) of the *ātmans*. We find a similar distinction between existential consciousness (*svarūpa-jñāna*) and its witness consciousness (*sākṣi-caitanya*) in the philosophy of Madhva. Now witness consciousness witnesses and is, therefore, directed towards the experiences it witnesses; so it is directed outwards, while existential consciousness is not so directed and knows only itself. As we pointed out in the estimate of Rāmānuja's philosophy, the attribute consciousness which is directed towards the object must include or comprehend the object for knowing its existence; similarly, witness consciousness must be directed towards, and include the existence of the object. For directedness as a relation has to include both the terms of the relation. Then witness consciousness knows the existence of the object, true or false, as its own existence and the existence aspect of the object are one and the same. Thus the empirical split between the subject and the object must have been based on a transcendental unity to which the power (force, *śakti*) of the creative split must be inherent. If that much of the implication is recognized, the controversies among the Vedāntins will have little for which to contend.

(iv) Māyā and Avidyā

The controversy about Māyā and Avidyā, if so much of our above estimate is accepted, will then be more about definition of the terms than about accepting the concepts in principle. Even the Advaitins speak of them as forces (*śaktis*); even Nāgārjuna, the Buddhist, spoke of it as creative; and what is creative is a force, a patterned force. Then the question is: How are we to relate Māyā to the Brahman? The Advaitins say that Māyā can have no being of its own, ontologically it has no separate existence of its own. The example of the burning power of fire and the being of fire is given in this connection. Māyā becomes then, as we interpreted it, a constitutive quality, character, power, energy, of the Brahman—which the Advaitins are not prone to admit. But philosophy requires its clear admission. If by nature, Māyā and Avidyā are the same—we have noted that the Advaitins use them often as synonums—Avidyā also as a creative force belongs to the very Being of the Brahman. If we accept that Māyā belongs to the Brahman and Avidyā to the finite *ātman*—"belongs" is only a way of speaking, only in the sense that my I or my character belongs to me, although I am my I-am and am my character—the latter is the constitutive character of the *ātman* as Māyā is of the Brahman. We have given support to Rāmānuja's view that Avidyā is the same as *karma*, the potency of past actions, the unseen force (*adṛṣṭa*), which is explained as fate (*niyati*, determinant), the capital with which the life of the individual starts.

Madhva, influenced perhaps by a branch of the Advaita, draws a distinction between Māyā and Avidyā. But unlike the Advaita, he regards both as different from Prakṛti; for this school treats Prakṛti as being material, non-sentient, while Māyā, as in Rāmānuja's philosophy, is treated as the mysterious will of God in creation etc., and Avidyā as only the veiling aspect similar to the Advaita interpretation. That is, Avidyā shrouds the *ātman*'s true nature from itself and it shrouds also its relation of dependence on the Brahman, and even the presence of the Brahman. However, it is positive, while Rāmānuja's view is both negative, in so far as it means lack of cognition, and positive, in so far as it means the potency of past *karmas*.

If Māyā is the mysterious will of God,[48] then Avidyā can be treated as the will of the finite *ātman*. This will agree with Rāmānuja's interpretation of Avidyā as the potency of *karma* acting in the form of the creative drive in me as a finite *ātman* and constituting my "fate" (*niyati*), so far as it determines me and my environment with which I start my life. But Madhva treats it merely as a veiling power. Then what makes the *ātman* interested in Prakṛti? Why does not the *ātman* simply go to sleep instead of becoming actively identified with Prakṛti and its modifications? Is there a separate will in the *ātman* that moves it into activity? The general tendency of this school to regard everything as having a particular and as being different from everything else stands in the way of properly understanding the external and internal relationships of the categories, which can be and have to be recognized at the surface and at depths. Does the will of the *ātman* lie lurking somewhere to pounce on the *ātman* made ignorant of its true nature by Avidyā? There is no will apart from my willing, my own act; I am my will so long as I am willing.[49] When I am not willing something, my so-called will disappears as an act or as actual, and becomes part of my character or potency, my I-am. My character and its force are constituted by the potencies of my past actions. Then Avidyā is my will and is the drive of my character, nature, structure, inherent to my I-am. Thus if Māyā as a force, power (*śakti*) belongs to the very constitution of the Brahman, then Avidyā must similarly belong to the very constitution of the *ātman*. And as we pointed out, because they belong to their very I-ams they cannot be experienced by the I-ams as distinct objects. If the two I-ams are ultimately one, the higher being the transcendental state of the lower, then Māyā and Avidyā have similarly to be one. The immanent and the transcendental, the dependent and the independent, are referential terms. In the spheres of cosmology and ontology, their referential nature implies underlying unities, which can be understood and explained better in terms of Śaṅkara's philosophy than of any other.

The present context can be utilized to explain one philosophical shortcoming in the Buddhist conception of Māyā (and Avidyā), extensively used in Buddhist literature. The Mahāyāna interprets Māyā as Śūnya and equates the two. Everything is simply Void. I erroneously think that it is there. But the I also is Void. If so, how does it come about that there is something responsible for erroneous thinking? Even in the Hīnayāna or earlier Buddhism, Nāgasena, for instance, teaches king Milinda (Menander) that just as there is no chariot apart from the wheels, yoke, etc., there is no I apart from the psycho-physical constituents; it is only an error to think that I am something distinct from them. But if originally there was nothing besides the psycho-physical constituents, and the I-am was nothing, was not there, how has it come about that an "I" arises and thinks, rightly or wrongly, that it is something distinct from them? To think is an act, and presupposes a power or force (*śakti*). Or even as Descartes says, even erroneous thinking, as an act of the spirit (I-am), presupposes a thinker, the I-am. Thinking is not an instantaneous act, but is an act that endures for a time, may be a few seconds. This continuity or duration is possible only by the same I continuing through the different moments of the thinking process. The I-am as well as its thinking act could not have come out of nothing. And who is to assert even that the I-am is nothing but the psycho-physical elements bundled together by chance or anything with momentary existence? He who says so, affirms himself in asserting it, and cannot deny his existence.[50]

(v) Necessity of Indeterminate Perception

The Mādhva school denies that there is indeterminate perception at all. The Nyāya-Vaiśeṣika and Śaṅkara accept it in one sense, Rāmānuja accepts it in a difference sense. But Madhva denies it altogether, because every perception is of a determinate object.[51] Rāmānuja also said that even indeterminate perception is that of an individual as a determinate object; but unlike what is called determinate perception, it has no reference to its universal explicitly. Madhva accepts the reality of the universal. Then does he mean that in the live act of perception, when I and my mind and my eye are fixed on the object, the distinction between the universal, individual, and particular is also cognized? Then he goes against all common experience. To say that they are involved or implied is one thing; the self also is involved in it. But to say that all of them are cognized along with their differences is another and is not true. Madhva goes also against the pronouncements of Patañjali, who gave great importance to the development of indeterminate cognition—which has already been explained. Madhva rejected indeterminate cognition because its acceptance may pave the way of the ultimate unity of the Brahman, the *ātman*, and the world. But he is also against the essence of Yoga, and no serious attempt seems to have been made to reinterpret and utilize Yoga. There have been reinterpretations of the Yoga from the side of the Advaita and of the Advaita from the side of the Yoga.

All living experience, actual experience, or experience in act requires the acceptance of indeterminate cognition, which is "cognition by being," but not "cognition by facing or opposing." In the act of experience, whether it is the perception of a pen, the feeling of pain, or going through abstract and even imageless thinking,[52] the processes take place in an indeterminate way, although it may look as though all is quiet and at rest. In it are involved the epistemological subject and object, the logical subject and predicate, the individual object and name (whatever be the language), and the individual and the universal. But their distinctions are not experienced in the live act, and the whole is experienced as a unity at rest or equilibrium, true or false. Their distinctness is not experienced just as the distinctness between the waking I present in the background of the dream and the dream I in it is not experienced. But in the reflective consciousness, "I know that I experienced *X* and *Y* in my dream," the distinction creeps in. Similarly, in the reflective stage of perception following upon indeterminate perception, the distinctions between the universal and the individual, the logical subject and the predicate come in; and in further reflection like "I know that I saw *X*," the other distinctions also come to the surface. By refusing to recognize indeterminate perception Madhva violates the very nature of perceptual experience.

Yet in understanding the structure of indeterminate perception, there seems to be some misunderstanding among modern writers on Indian epistemology. As has been said, the Nyāya-Vaiśeṣika and the Advaita accept the reality of indeterminate perception. For instance, in the visual perception of the pen, indeterminate perception is the first stage and is of the form, it is said, "That is something." The Nyāya-Vaiśeṣika denies that this is full perception which can be accepted as a valid means of cognition (*pramāṇa*) because it is not useful for extracting from it the major premise for inference. The indeterminate perception of the pen, the pencil, the book, etc., are of the form, "That is something," and no inference can be drawn from mere somethings. This view is accepted by the Advaita (following the Mīmāmsā). But it has led to the misunderstanding[53] that at the indeterminate stage nothing definite is seen, that my mind and sight are fixed on a something without form and shape, without outline even. It is this misunderstanding that Rāmānuja corrects. For instance, when my mind and eye are fixed on the pen in front, they are fixed on (bound to, *baddha*) the length, thickness, shape, etc., of the pen; they are fixed on something definite, with a borderline, not on something like the film colour of the sky. They are fixed, therefore, on a particular colour, shape, length, etc. Yet at that stage the perception has not yet been developed into the reflective perception in which all these distinctions and the distinctions between the individual and the universal, subject and object, subject and predicate, and name and object are made. They arise only when the witness consciousness penetrates the perception intermittently. It is only in the witness consciousness as reflective consciousness that the major premise is formed and inferences are made.[54]

Hence indeterminate perception is not without form; but the form is a particular shape, a particular colour sensum, etc. Yet it is still perception; that it is not useful for inference as such, is a different question. It can lead to some action. For instance, one who sees an elephant for the first time may still run away from it. Many animals tend to run away from strange creatures; or their perception may lead to some behaviour of curiosity. However, whether or not indeterminate perception leads to inference or action is not a question of present importance. What is of importance is that, in this cognitive act, my I-am, mind, and sense of vision are involved and they cut out a specific contour out of the cosmos. They are involved by being identified (as though) with the object. Then indeterminate perception, when it is completely indeterminate, is not even of the form, "That is something," as though a distinction is drawn between the That and "something." There is no such distinction at all. Even the subject of perception, my I-am, is stuck in (*baddha*) the object; and unless it starts to free itself from the identification or boundness, reflection does not begin. Then it is that the distinction between the That and "something" appears and the universal pen-ness and the distinct word "pen" supervene on the "something."[55]

(vi) Witness Consciousness and Time and Space

There is an important element of truth in the Mādhva view that time and space are perceived by the witness consciousness (*sākṣi-caitanya*), but not by the functional consciousness and the senses. It is also important that various levels of witness consciousness are recognized, although it is not shown or indicated by Madhva how they can be related. Leaving aside many mythological (*paurāṇic*) souls (*ātmans, jīvas*) accepted by the school, we find three grades—God, the Cosmic Person (Hiraṇyagarbha, called Jīvottama or the highest soul), and the finite *ātman*. We may have to say that each of these souls or selves has both existential (*svarūpa*) consciousness and witness (*sākṣi*) consciousness. Then how are their existential and witness consciousnesses related? Or do they not have to be related? If not related, how do I know the objective world of the Cosmic Person, and he of God? Do they and can they inter-penetrate? If they cannot inter-penetrate, mutual knowledge becomes impossible. If they inter-penetrate, how can they inter-penerate without God and the Cosmic Person being the higher, transcendental forms of the *ātman*? Their number may be more or less. But the two forms of consciousness—whether or not they are understood in terms of the divisions given by Rāmānuja and Madhva—the existential and the phenomenological, have not only higher and higher transcendental forms, but also they have, as we have shown, to become unified at the highest stage, namely, that of the Supreme Being or the Brahman. For my phenomenological consciousness in the final analysis is my rational consciousness with directions outwards and inwards, and is finally to be absorbed, assimilated to, and made part and parcel of my being, my I-am, which will be the true indeterminate consciousness (*jñāna*), infinite, without contours, and fully restful.[56]

Now, the witness consciousness perceives, according to Madhva, time and space. Truly, functional consciousness working through mind and senses cannot perceive time and space. The senses are capable only of seeing their specific objects and, time and space are not included in them. Yet time and space are not objects of inference;

for inference needs a major premise—we do not have any about space and time—and is based on perception, and the perception of time and space has still to be established. For the purpose, Madhva treats the witness consciousness as an organ of perception (*indriya*). It is strange to treat witness consciousness as a sense or sense organ—unless it is done metaphorically, which does not seem to be Madhva's idea. Witness consciousness is a reflective function of the I-am; otherwise, it cannot be a witness. It has to be a witness of itself also. That is, it witnesses the object and it witnesses its witnessing the object. Surely, it has an instrumental function, and we may as well say that time and space are perceived through the instrumentality of the inner instrument (*antahkaraṇa*) or mind in the general sense of the word. Only because there can be no inference in the cognition of time and space, we should not think that there is only one alternative left for cognizing them, i.e., perception. Indeed, the word perception does not mean necessarily visual perception; and in the general sense of the word we may say that time and space are perceived, not inferred. But Madhva does not seem to have used the word perception in the general sense, but in the sense of sense perception. Because there is no sense for the perception of time, he turns witness consciousness into a sense (*indriya*).

But really to prove that time and space are not inferred, but *directly experienced*, it is not necessary to say that they are perceived by a new kind of sense organ. Even pains and pleasures are not perceived by any of the five senses generally accepted as senses. They are directly perceived by mind, for which reason some schools include mind (*manas*) in the class of senses. But as we have pointed out in the previous chapter, time and space are two of the formative processes of apperception (*buddhi, citta*) the functions of which are performed by the attribute consciousness in Rāmānuja and by witness consciousness in Madhva. The mistake of both is to treat them as different and as having their own existence apart from that of the existential consciousness (*svarūpa caitanya*). But we should note that Madhva regards the witness consciousness as the *ātman* itself; but then can they each have its own particular? If they can, their existences have to be different, but their difference cannot be defended.

What may have to be noted, at the final stage of the discussion of the concepts of space and time, is that time consciousness involves the element of recognition. This is the recognition of the presence of one's self in the first and at every succeeding moment of any span of time and, in the objectification of time, the recognition of every previous moment in every succeeding moment. The recognition of course may not be explicit. But without the implicit recognition—when questioned, it becomes explicit—we cannot get the idea of time as one and continuous; without it, even objectively, time cannot be one. I have to be there at every moment as the witness of the moment. Suppose that there are five moments, *m*1, *m*2, *m*3, *m*4, *m*5, in a particular span of time. And the subject of the perception of *m*1 is *S*1, of *m*2 is *S*2, of *m*3 is *S*3, of *m*4 is *S*4, and of *m*5 is *S*5. At every succeeding moment my I becomes a reflective consciousness as in "I know that I perceive *m*l", and so on. It is this reflective self-recognition, which is the nature of the witness consciousness, that enables me to collate all the five moments or instants and becomes the time-consciousness, the objectification of which becomes time. One may call this my subjective time, but I can relate its moments to the moments of an objective process like those of the movement of the sun (or the earth). In any case, whether it is the collating of events or moments within my consciousness or of the events taken to be outside my consciousness, the collation has to be done within and by my witness consciousness for the cognition of time and necessarily involves recognition, which is impossible without presence of the same self throughout.[57] Then we can appreciate also what truth there is in the view that time is perceived by the witness consciousness.

A similar consideration leads us to the appreciation of the view that space is perceived by the witness consciousness. Is space something in which extended objects are located, or is it something which is the extension itself of the objects and their intervals, or is it the function itself of locating, which involves extension? Descartes spoke of matter as extension without limits. Or should we say that extended objects are placed in some empty extension? The contemporary theory that objects are spatio-temporal contours lends support to Descartes, who indeed does not think of time in this context. Nor does he think of empty extension. It is full and there is no empty space for him. However, to think of extended objects being placed in empty extension is redundant; for if the objects are by themselves extended, they do not need to be placed in some empty extension as we place tables and chairs in some empty room. It may be asked: If the room is not empty but full, how can we place anything in it? But here the question is not about placing extended objects in some empty room, but of space itself, whether empty or full. If space is extension as such, it has to be the same whether it belongs to the objects themselves or their intervals. If both are extensions, they are continuous and adjacent, and become one, if overlapping. We think of this one as being extended *ad infinitum* or as being divided *ad infinitum*. But as neither the process of extension nor division is carried out in act *ad infinitum* (except in a mathematical formula), we have to think of either infinite as conceptually possible, not as actual. The division and extension of time also *ad infinitum* refers to conceptual possibility, not actuality. But the process in either case involves the idea of uniformity. Similar to the concept of the smallest extension of space—which is not possible to conceive—every moment of time may have in it many events compressed. We can also think of some moments full and some intervening moments empty.[58] But for the sake of uniformity, we accept some process like that of the sun as a standard succession of events. In the case of space, we invent the yardstick or the meter rod. So in the cases of both time and space, we ignore fullness and emptiness and the time intervals and the space intervals. In the case of time, there is recognition of myself in every succeeding event and also the recognition through me of every earlier event in every succeeding one. Similarly, in the case of space, there is recognition of myself in every successive placing of the yardstick and also of every earlier placement of the yardstick in every succeeding one. Thus time is involved in the conception of space. But is not space involved in the conception of time?

To answer this question, we have to raise another, viz., can we measure absolutely empty time and empty space? If no events are occurring anywhere, not even mental events or even imageless thoughts, can there be any time consciousness or time at all? If there is no passage of events, if nothing is happening, I may be myself in eternity, timelessness, without time and time experience. So some process, some succession of events, is an absolute condition for the reality of time and for time consciousness. But can any event occur without its being located? It may be located in the external world, in my mind, or even in my imageless thought. But locating is a "spacing" function, a placing function. Even in abstract imageless thought, there is placing, the idea or concept is in me (my higher apperception). So there is reason for the Upaniṣads treating apperception or even the Supreme I-am as a higher *ākāśa* (space). But if nothing occurs, there is no locating and so no space; likewise, there is no time then. So without action or activity, there can be neither space nor time. And if locating is a space-function or placing function, there can be no time also without space, if we carry our questionings to their ontological depths.

The discussion leads us to the idea that time and space are not necessarily out there, but are functions of apperception, whether understood as Rāmānuja does or as Madhva does. The objective space and time may not be the voluntary functions of my finite apperception as I have it now, but the spontaneous functioning of my apperception in its transcendental aspect[59] (the Mahān Ātmā of the Upaniṣads). Their necessity lies for me in their belonging to my inescapable transcendental depths. If time and space then have their roots in my transcendental apperception, and Prakṛti also is covered by apperception as phenomenological, attribute, or witness consciousness—attribute consciousness and witness consciousness as defined by Rāmānuja and Madhva respectively are not exactly the same, but functionally they play the same role, as we have shown—then time, space, and Prakṛti need not be treated as three different entities, but as functions and forms of the same witness consciousness, and as overlapping one another. For Prakṛti also is a form of consciousness;[60] *even the Unknown cannot be known as the Unknown, unless it is a block of consciousness known as the Unknown.* Only the conscious can be known as the object of consciousness; cognition of insentient matter has really to be consciousness of a block of consciousness (not necessarily personal) as veiled. It is not necessary to treat Prakṛti as inherently unconscious[61] and lying there outside us. The inherently insentient cannot react to the approaches of consciousness. A log of wood in popular conception is indifferent to our actions.

(vii) Tamas or Darkness in Self and Cognition of Objects

The phenomenological and existential significance of *Tamas* (Darkness) has not been properly explained or perhaps understood by writers on Indian philosophy in English. The Mīmāmsā accepted it as a positive reality; and Madhva followed suit. The Nyāya-Vaiśeṣika treated it as absence of light and as only a negative entity. The Advaita view as well as that of the Upaniṣads is not clear-cut, but is inclined towards the Mīmāmsā and will be presently discussed. Prabhākara also gives it a positive import calling it the base or locus of the absence[62] of light. It is seen also as blue or black by the eye. Maṇḍana says that it is the shadow of the earth (eclipse), which we may generalize and say that it is the shadow of something seen positively when light is obstructed or removed. The point is that *it is seen*; it is not the absence of perception, in which case we get only non-cognition (cp. the Mīmāmsā) and negation (cp. the Nyāya-Vaiśeṣika). We should note that Maṇḍana was a Mīmāmsaka, according to tradition, at one time. The Upaniṣads also say that just as air is without colour but has touch, darkness (*tamas*) is without touch, but has colour. That is, we do not see air with our eyes, but touch it or know its presence through the sense of touch; on the other hand, we see darkness with our eyes, but cannot make it an object of the sense of touch. Thus positive entities have their own peculiarities.

But there is darkness not only for the senses but also for the *antahkaraṇa*, the inner instrument and its parts, and for the self even. The senses are limited to the cognition of some specific qualities such as colours, smells, touches, tastes, and sounds; every sense cannot perceive every quality. Mind's specific objective qualities, as generally accepted, are pains and pleasures; and its specific functions are the unification and differentiation of groups of qualities into groups of unitary objects. Of the ego, the function is the appropriation of experiences as mine and not thine and so on. Of reason, the function is the organization of the totality of experience. There is, in addition, the I-consciousness pervading and activating all functions. Now, darkness can darken, veil, any or all of these functions. We generally think that "darkness" refers only to physical darkness, as when there is no light of the sun, the moon, and fire.[63] We forget or do not realize that absence of speech in the human race deprives it of one of the important sources of cognition. The source of light in any one of these cases may be veiled, but they can be veiled also in the case of the senses, speech, mind, ego, reason, and I-consciousness.

In deep sleep and when a man faints, he does not know himself also. This is a peculiar experience. For if he is totally absent in those states, how can he *know* that he did not know himself? This can be explained only by accepting that his finite person is not there, but its transcendental being, as witness (*sākṣi*), is there. His being, transcendental or immanent, is self-conscious. For instance, my waking I-am is there in my dream; otherwise, I cannot remember any dream. My dream I-am experiences the pains and pleasures of the dream. If my waking I-am is aware of itself as the waking I-am in dream also, there will be no dream. Such is the peculiar power of darkness that it results in complete or partial forgetfulness of all or part of my I-consciousness, —one or more of its levels or depths—my personality, and its true identity. Similarly, it may withhold, hold back, or impair, partially or completely, the functions of the inner instrument and the senses. In the earlier chapters we tried to show that, since the specific objects are correlated to specific senses and mind, the correlates have no existence separate from each other, but are ultimately functions of the witness consciousness, the results of its formative processes.[64] Generally we do not even realize that there is darkness concerning senses other than the eye. If a man's hand is numbed, but the hand performs other functions, what does he feel there? Take the case of the dentist numbing the tooth. The patient may still feel something, but not pain. We may compare the experiences to perceiving darkness as something positive.

Then darkness is not merely negative. It works as forgetfulness, as absence of light, and as an essential condition of the malfunctioning of the I-consciousness, ego, mind, senses and their objects. It is a force (*śakti*). It is not Non-being in the negative sense.[65] Whatever is, is Being or its manifestation. Non-being as negative "cannot be." But it "can be" as a manifestation of Being. For instance, when a man is afraid of death when on the edge of a precipice, he is afraid of becoming Non-being. But there is really nothing like Non-being, and Being can never become Non-being. The fear of the person is like that of the little child who is afraid of the dark room. When asked by its father what it is afraid of, it says that it is afraid of Nothing. But is the room really

Nothing or Nothingness? Is the darkness of the room Nothing or Nothingness, without content in the objective sense? The room may contain hundreds of objects. The darkness of Non-being (*tamas*) is positive Ignorance; we are afraid of death because we are ignorant of what happens then. My cognition of my death is my cognition of my Non-being. But what about the cognizer of the cognition of death? He is still there in the background. He cannot perish; and if he perishes, there will be no actual cognition of death and of Non-being. As all sacred books teach us, only when we die, can we know what happens at death, but not when we are alive.[66] For example, we do not generally know what dreams we shall have and we are unaware now what happens in deep sleep. This is the important point: the transition from one state to another is a leap like that of the frog. When I leap into the dream state from the waking state, I do not consciously carry my memories of the waking state; if I do, there will be no dream. And when I go back to my waking state, the transition is similarly a leap, but the dreams can be remembered. Thus the transition from immanence to transcendence and vice versa has to be explained as a leap with the proviso that the higher, when it regains its transcendence from its immanence, carries the experiences of the lower as though it is only a witness of the latter's experiences. Indeed, the experiences at the stage of the Logos (Mahān Ātmā) and the higher ones, in which the privacy of the individuals is lost and every bit of experience is an object and is open, the transcendentals know the experiences of the individuals and at the same time know themselves in a special way. It is like correct reasoning showing itself in the gropings of my finite reason to know the truth and also knowing the gropings. It is also like the judgment, "It is a rope, but not a snake," in which the judgment, "it is a snake," is recalled also, but is also denied.

The above explanation and discussion are needed to show how darkness (*tamas*) works positively in the lives of all of us. It is a force (*śakti*), and so not a mere negation. Mere negation or absence produces nothing. But this darkness constitutes my ego, for without darkness penetrating the essential being of the I-am, I will be infinite. When constituting my ego, it constitutes also the being or existence aspects of the manifold objects. In one sense, they are ripples of my ego, and also ripples of the darkness (*tamas*)[67] constituting my ego. Yet, their existence is impenetrable to the existence of my ego as this finite being. However, I am aware of the "existence" of the external objects at all, I get the idea of external existence at all, the idea that any object exists at all, only because inwardly their existence and my existence are one, but the oneness also is veiled by darkness, in which my transcendental ego is split into my finite ego and the object, the existence of each being hidden in different ways. I know that the object exists, but there is no sense organ that reveals its existence. I know that I exist; but I cannot make my existence an object like the pen in front.

However, darkness (*tamas*) is not the whole of Māyā or Avidyā. It is an essential prerequisite for the bubbling up or the bursting forth of the manifold of the objective world, the cognitive instrumentalities like reason, mind, and senses, and the instrumentalities of practical activities. This bubbling up and practical activity are the results of the dynamic, creative (*rajas*) aspect of Māyā or Avidyā. The cognitive aspect of our life, the cognitions of our activities and of the objects towards which our activities are directed are due to the pure, conscious (*sattva*) aspect of Māyā or Avidyā. And because the whole works in presenting the world—we do not know how and why—to us, we tend to treat the whole of Māyā or Avidyā as Darkness.[68] And this Darkness, which cannot be explained, as Advaitins and the Buddhists say, in terms of Being, is mistakenly taken to be Non-being, absence of light, and so on. The main test of real Non-being is to be incapable of producing anything; nothing comes out of nothing. But Māyā or Avidyā is so obviously creative!

If the idea of self-transcendence, with all its import, is accepted by Madhva, there will be no need for his differentiating, in the way he does, Māyā and Avidyā, the finite and the infinite I-ams, and the conscious *ātman* and the unconscious Prakṛti. Māyā can be regarded as the cosmic aspect of Avidyā and Avidyā as the individualized aspect of Māyā. Furthermore, Māyā does not have to be given a separate being of its own from that of the Brahman; for as forgetfulness or stupor, it becomes absorbed when it is overcome. Even physical darkness or even a shadow disappears when it is completely lighted up. It is not staved into another place, but absorbed by light. What is absorbed must be capable of becoming one with the being of the absorber (absorbent); it has, therefore, to be of the same nature as that of the absorbent. The Advaitin and the Buddhist interpretations of Māyā and Avidyā as four-cornered negations, although correct ontologically, is misleading in that it creates the impression that the schools teach that Māyā and the cosmos have no reality also, do not have even cosmological status. To say that the cosmos has no cosmological status sounds meaningless; it is like saying that the cosmos is not the cosmos—which violates the principle of identity.

But since the Being of the cosmos is the Being of the Brahman, Madhva's principle of absolute difference cannot be applicable. One wonders why he teaches that difference is a positive quality, while teaching that absolute negation, the opposite of which is never possible as in "Virtue is not a red-haired person," is a form of negation, differing from the Nyāya-Vaiśeṣika in the explanation of the concept of absolute negation. "The Brahman is not Māyā"[69] is not a negation of the type "The tiger is not a lion." Cosmologically, the tiger and the lion are not one and the same. Even if, like Rāmānuja, we treat this negation as positive difference, it is not the nature of the relation between the Brahman and Māyā. They are one in Being, when ontologically considered; but in nature or as understood in their functions or roles in the cosmos, they are different. Or as some Advaitins say, the same Brahman performs both functions. Even from the common sense point of view, absolute difference and infinity of the number of particulars cannot be defended in the way Madhva does. For instance, one lump of wax is different from another lump of wax, and one may say that each has a particular. But when melted together, they become one. What then has happened to their particulars and their positive difference? Particulars which can so easily disappear cannot be truly particulars.

But one point has to be accepted: Creativity is negativity. Māyā is accepted as the creative force. But there is no creativity, unless there is a leap from one state to another. Even in the case of ordinary change, there is a leap from one moment of the process of change to the next. There is a leap from waking to dreaming, and then to deep sleep, and back again to the different states. But the leap does not mean complete destruction or negation, as the Buddhists interpreted causation. I am not completely destroyed and I do not become extinct, when I pass from the waking to the dream and vice versa. This is what is implied by the statement that Being never becomes Non-being. There is continuity of Being, but change of form, one form succeeding another. So negativity cannot mean negation in the sense of destruction or absolute Non-being. It is this aspect of negativity that the Advaitins seeks to express by the four-cornered negation, which is ingenious, but cumbrous and puzzling to many. This remark applies to Buddhism also.[70] Māyā is not something static waiting somewhere ready to pounce on the Brahman; it is the Brahman's own power of negativity, of creative self-differentiation, of immanence and self-transcendence.[71]

But what is it then that makes me forget my waking state when I pass into dreams? Dream is a new creation, which is not possible if I remember my waking state in it. We call it sleep, but it is really darkness (*tamas*) that partially overcomes me in dreams and completely overcomes me in deep sleep. The process of entering deep sleep through that of dream is the gradual thickening of darkness, call it spiritual darkness or the psychological. As physical light can become physical darkness, and at the time the light of the eye becomes the darkness of the eye, the light of my self-consciousness also, which is existential consciousness, becomes darker and darker when I enter the dream state and then deep sleep. One may call it existential Darkness or unconsciousness. And just as when our eye lids are closed we see a network of light, colours, and darkness (*kesoṇḍraka*), we see objects in dream. In both cases, we are not fully overtaken by darkness; and just as the light of the eye and the field of sight are operative when the eye lids are closed in our waking state; apperception, mind, ego, the senses, their fields and objectifications are operative in dream. But then the cosmic forces of the Logos (as Virāṭ) are not fully operative and we are comparatively free from their control; and so what we see in dream cannot be related to what we know in the waking state. But in deep sleep, all operations cease; all are fully overcome by darkness; only my transcendental ego, as an I-am, limited to my causal[72] body (*kāraṇa-śarīra*) as the Advaitins call it and to the storehouse (of impressions and action potencies) as the Buddhists call it, remains awake,[73] to tell me and others, when I wake up, that I slept well.

But this overtaking of me by darkness in deep sleep has another aspect to it. It is complete forgetfulness of even my finite being along with my own experiences. But where do the experiences go, when they are forgotten? We came across this question previously. They do not become extinct. If they become extinct, how can I later remember them, bring them up to the surface of consciousness? They are absorbed into my person, character, apperception, my finite being, my finite I-am. As they enter the so-called subject side, they are not available on the object side. This unavailability also is the same as entering darkness (*tamas*).[74] As Freud, Jung, and other psychologists say, much that is passed into my being and made part and parcel of it can be brought up, sometimes by myself making the attempt, and other times with the help of some psychological techniques. But everything in my finite being cannot be so brought up to the surface of consciousness. My person, my I-am, cannot be pulled inside out and be made a clear object; for something has to be in the background to know the object. The cosmic structure that is reflected in my being and appears as my finite I-am cannot be made an object so long as my finite person lasts; but whatever I added to it through my actions and idiosyncracies can be brought up to the conscious level. Indeed, when the finite I-am realizes that it is a reflection, image, of the Cosmic Person and identifies itself with it, all is revealed, but my finitude is dispelled.

The function of darkness (*tamas*) cannot be underestimated. It makes all my experiences enter my person and disappear behind a veil *as it were*, but not become extinct, in it; and when the need and opportunity arises, it comes out with all those experiences—and we may say, as the phenomenological consciousness, which is inherently permeated by darkness and appears as the vast panorama of the subject-object scene—and takes on the form of the world including myself. In this sense, as performing this function at the cosmic level, it is Māyā.

Even in ordinary causation, in a physical object *A* becoming *B*, we can see how the principle of darkness (*tamas*) works. The Buddhists interpreted the causal process as a combination of affirmation and negation, of Being and Non-being, saying that the two are coordinates and that neither can exist without the other. First, there can be no question of the existence of negation or Non-being; if it exists, it will be affirmation or Being, but not negation or Non-being. Secondly, what they say can be true in a way of the cosmological realm, but not of the ontological, which has only to be that of Being. Even in the cosmological realm, we negate something because something else *is there*, i.e., because of our affirmation of something else.[75] Negation implies the affirmation of something else; and in perception this implication is unmediated pre-supposition. But affirmation does not imply any particular negation. So even at the cosmological level, and in the epistemological realm also, affirmation and negation, the positive and the negative, Being and Non-being, cannot be coordinates.[76]

The Buddhists interpreted the causal process in the above way and concluded that the effect comes out of nothing or Non-being. For instance they say that unless the acorn is destroyed and becomes nothing, the oak does not sprout out. But if some-one destroyes the seed by burning it into ashes, can he produce the oak out of them? So the Buddhist interpretation is not satisfactory. When *A* becomes *B* through the stages of *A*1, *A*2, *A*3, and *A*4, we have to say that at the stage of *A*2, *A*1 enters darkness (*tamas*) and so on.[77] If there is complete destruction, *B* will not appear at all. So some philosophers like the followers of the Sāṅkhya say that causation is the manifestation of what is already there. Thus *B* is already there in a potential form *A*. But this view belonging to the other extreme precludes creativity and novelty in the causal process, and we cannot deny them. Then we have to say that the cause "creates" the effect by itself entering darkness (*tamas*) to acquire the necessary force (*śakti*), and this creation is the cause becoming[78] the effect. The cause's entering darkness is similar to our entering deep sleep for gaining freshness and new strength. To enter darkness is to become a potency. Thus *A*1, *A*2, etc., enter a potential state for constituting the being of *B*. Here we are dealing with material causes like the acorn of the oak.

But in the material causal process, there is no remembering of the earlier stages, although there is continuity of being throughout. That is, there is identity and also continuity of sameness from *A* to *B*, but the identity is not conscious or self-conscious. However, I, the observer, have to be conscious of the continuity; otherwise, I shall have no ground for saying that *A* has become *B*; and it may be that what we call the moments of the causal process are separate unrelated events and causation has no objective validity. The presence or absence of self-conscious identity makes the difference between a mere (unconscious) process and time-consciousness also. The defect of the theories that reduce time to a mere process or succession of events lies here: there is self-conscious identity throughout the succession of events in time and time-consciousness. Even this identity in succession is not to be equated to time. For I may be conscious of the succession of events without the consciousness that they are in time. For example, in any particular dream that I am visiting a temple, walking up the steps and so on, or even in observing a series of events like watching a football game, I may be conscious of a succession of events without any idea of the lapse of time. Yet the conditions mentioned constitute the pre-requisites for the rising of the time-consciousness or consciousness of time, and for turning the succession of events into moments of time. *Or time is a pattern of the relation of succession and is the act of correlating the events in succession to the presence of the identity of my self-consciousness as the eternal present.* Time, as Bhartṛhari says, is a drive in my being, a force, a power (*śakti*) which introduces the order of succession (*krama*, order) into the process of Becoming.[79] Every occurring event is correlated to my presence, and then turned into my past and its past and so on, and retained as such in me. Every anticipated event is considered to be a future; it enters my present or my presence, and then enters my past and its past.[80] It is not lost just as I am not lost; my past is my darkness (*tamas*) and its past also is darkness. The future springs out of darkness. It is future to me as my projecting myself into the not yet present and not the past, but a kind of surge, a drive to be something which I am not now. This also is an indication of a power, force (*śakti*) within my being, and this force pushes my being into a becoming. The rearrangement of the succession into past, present, and future is also a condition for the generation of time and the idea of time. Time then is a primary pattern of force innate to the generally outwardly directed consciousness (attribute consciousness, phenomenological consciousness, witness consciousness, or witnessing consciousness), positing the events of succession as objective and independent of existential consciousness. *In a way, time can be defined as the act of correlating a succession of events to my I-am as the eternal present; in another way, it can be defined as the act (or the force behind the act) of the ordered (sakrama) projecting of the eternal present into what we call the moments of time.* Thus time is a patterned force of activity. Prakṛti is the system (pattern of patterns of patterns and so on) of objectified events considered as apart from the existential consciousness or the I-am. But as mentioned before, time is not really independent of the I-am at the transcendental depths.

Space and space-consciousness are also to be interpreted likewise. Space is the pattern of force inherent to the phenomenological consciousness for locating an event or a package of events one by the side of another, i.e., simultaneously. This locating is the space force (*śakti*) or space function and generates the idea of space as the pattern of an inherent function of apperception. *In a way, like time, space may be defined as the correlating of many events to the I-am as eternally present.* The correlation of one event even as out there among others involves both time and space, but their ideas may not be clear. Any point event may not produce the idea of space, although it is involved in locating it. The idea is brought out to the surface of consciousness when the locating of one event by the side of another is involved.[81]

When time and space are taken as patterns of the functions of apperception, it is not necessary to take them as independent of Prakṛti. Space is a patterned act of locating done by apperception,[82] which we identified with witness consciousness in the function of the form "I know that I know *X*." Locating is at the same time cognition, it is known; and the act of "space" or "spacing" is realized as such by the witness consciousness (*sākṣi-caitanya*), as Madhva says. This is the "I know" that projects itself out of the "I am;" but the two are not separate entities; for the I-know, as the phenomenological consciousness, can become part and parcel of the I-am as the existential consciousness. Now I-know and the act of locating cannot be objectless. I do not perform the act locating or knowing unless there is something to locate or know. So the object, which is Prakṛti, has to be an ingredient of the phenomenological consciousness and does not, ontologically and at the transcendental level, have its own existence. As this finite person, my problem then is to realize that the object I cognize is congnized, as Berkeley puts it, through the mind of God. Or in the terminology of the theory which is being developed here, my problem is to realize that the object I see, if real, is identical with the object which is part of the cosmos, the Cosmic Person who is my transcendental I-am. Berkeley's theological idealism gets its intelligibility only in this way.

Similarly, time is the apperceptive act of remembering or re-cognizing onself through change, causal or otherwise, or a series of cognized events, and the act of turning past and future into the present or what has happened and what is to happen into what is happening. This is a characteristic of time in addition to what we have noticed. My finite ego or I-am, as passing through the live cognitions of the series of events, is divided into instants or moments which are culled together by my witness consciousness, which transcends the moments. But this witness consciousness is my own apperception transcending my ego. This is the force of culling these instants together into the present, which is the I-am or rather correlated to the I-am, which is my existential consciousness. Thus, time and space in one sense are the meeting points of the I-am and the I-know; but they disappear, made part and parcel of the I-am, when the I-know enters it. Such also is the relation between Being and Becoming: there is no Becoming without Being, but Being can absorb Becoming and then there is only Being without Becoming. Transcendentally viewed or in their transcendental significance, they are distinctions we draw within the processes of the Spirit.

Enough has been said to indicate that Darkness, as positive Non-being, Śūnya (Void, Nothing, Nothingness or Śūnyatā, etc.), and Māyā, although Being, is not different from the Being that is the Brahman or the transcendental I-am, which in deep sleep, is said to be the Śūnyadṛk (seer of Śūnya) and the Draṣṭā (seer) of Māyā. It is important that we keep in mind that Being, ontologically, is not a plurality or even a duality, but is one without a second. Yet, Non-being as Darkness has to be treated as Being, as different from the negative Non-being, for the reason that it is an experience (*tamorūpa-anubhūti*),[83] experience in the form of Darkness in oneself, which hangs on (is dependent on) an object (*ālambana*). It is a shadow (*chāyā*) of the transcendental I-am within itself and has no separate Being of its own.

NOTES

[1]B. N. K. Sharma: *A History of Dvaita School of Vedānta and its Literature*, Vol. I, p. 104. This work seems to be reliable so far as the presentation of the theories go. But on the criticisms of other schools and the use of western terms, there can be a difference of opinion.

[2]S. N. Dasgupta: *A History of Indian Philosophy*, Vol. IV, pp. 150–204.

[3]B. N. K. Sharma: *The Philosophy of Śrī Madhva*, pp. 82–85.

[4]S. N. Dasgupta: *A History of Indian Philosophy*, Vol. IV, p. 161.

[5]Ibid., pp. 182–84.

[6]B. N. K. Sharma: *The Philosophy of Śrī Madhva*, p. 89.

[7]Ibid., pp. 100–15.

[8]Ibid., p. 109. [9]Ibid., p. 114. [10]Ibid., p. 115.

[11]S. N. Dasgupta: *A History of Indian Philosophy*, Vol, IV, pp. 183–84.

[12]B. N. K. Sharma: *The Philosophy of Śrī Madhva*, p. 102.

[13]Ibid., p. 134. [14]Ibid., p. 132.

[15]Mādhavācārya: *Sarvadarśanasaṅgraha*, p. 49. Also S. N. Dasgupta: *A History of Indian Philosophy*, Vol. IV, pp. 150 fol., and B. N. K. Sharma: *The Philosophy of Śrī Madhva*, pp. 43 fol.

[16]According to Madhva, the world-soul is one of the liberated souls, but not the supreme Godhead in one of the stages of descent. Note the difference from the Advaita.

[17]S. N. Dasgupta says that time is the first evolute of Prakṛti. (*History of Indian Philosophy*, Vol. IV, p. 156). But B. N. K. Sharma speaks of space and time as independent of Prakṛti. (*The Philosophy of Śrī Madhva*, pp. 72 fol.) In fact, in the Pāñcarātra, which both Rāmānuja and Madhva follow, the views on space and time do not seem to be unanimous. So the Mādhvas also do not seem to be unanimous. If time is an evolute of Prakṛti, it as well as the other evolutes should not find a place along with and by the side of Prakṛti.

[18]S. N. Dasgupta: *A History of Indian Philosophy*, Vol. IV, p. 151.

[19]B. N. K. Sharma: *The Philosophy of Śrī Madhva*, pp. 50–52.

[20]Ibid., p. 51. [21]Ibid., pp. 67–70. [22]Ibid., p. 68.

[23]S. N. Dasgupta: *A History of Indian Philosophy*, Vol. IV, pp. 154–55.

[24]Madhva mentions the power of an idol to do good to its worshippers. This power is imparted to it by the ritual of installation (*pratiṣṭhāpana*).

[25]B. N. K. Sharma: *The Philosophy of Śrī Madhva*, pp. 80–81, and S. N. Dasgupta *A History of Indian Philosophy*, Vol. IV, p. 155.

[26]Cp. Russell's ideas on existential negative propositions like "The King of Utopia does not exist."

[27]But contrast the experience of absolute Darkness, in which the witness consciousness experiences Nothingness.

[28]B. N. K. Sharma: *The Philosophy of Śrī Madhva*, p. 186.

[29]Ibid., p. 181. But remember that for Rāmānuja, it is also *Karma*.

[30]Ibid., pp. 165–76. [31]Ibid., p. 254.

[32]Ibid., p. 154. [33]Ibid., p. 155. [34]Ibid., pp. 72–77.

[35]In Indian philosophy, the ideas of Mahat as the Mahān Ātmā (the Great Soul), Cosmic Reason, Objective Reason, Mahākāśa (the Great Space) Mahākāla (the Great Time), Māyā, Avidyā, Prakṛti, Mahāmāyā, Avyakta, and even Śūnya are so mixed up in the non-systematic original works that the later schools interpreted them each in its own way. The student has, therefore, to be careful that he does not attribute the view of one school to another. The same word may be used, but the meanings or connotations in the different schools may be different—a phenomenon not uncommon in western philosophy also. However, what we call time and space are regarded as eternal and all-pervading (*nityasarvagatas*). As such, they cannot be evolutes of Prakṛti, but stand on the same level with it. (P. Nagaraja Rao: *Vādāvali*, p. 14).

[36]We have referred to different levels of *ākāśa* in the Upaniṣads. Is there a confusion among the Mādhvas between the physical and the transcendental space?

[37]Madhavācārya: *Sarvadarśanasaṅgraha*, p. 54.

[38]B. N. K. Sharma: *The Philosophy of Śrī Madhva*, pp. 58–59.

[39]See S. N. Dasgupta: *A History of Indian Philosophy*, Vol. IV, pp. 178–80, and S. Radhakrishnan: *Indian Philosophy*, Vol. II, pp. 749–51.

[40]B. N. K. Sharma: *The Philosophy of Śrī Madhva*, p. 181. [41]Ibid., p. 329.

[42]Bradley exposed almost all of them, but unfortunately he could not think of a better self-sustaining category than the world as a whole, which is, again, a cosmological category. Even before him, Kant exposed the self-contradictory nature of the idea of the world as a whole.

[43]as noted by Kant and Russell, to whom we have already referred a few times.

[44]Cp. the Sāṅkhya view that cognition is, and is known to be both valid and invalid by itself.

[45]*Dharmyamse sarvam abhrāntam prakāre tu viparyayah.* In illusion there is no question about the falsity of the subject, only the predicate can be false.

[46]All *vṛttis* or functions belong to the inner instrument and the senses, according to the Advaita. They are not merely static, reflecting mirrors.

[47]We have already referred to the view of Sureśvara that the That of the object of cognition is due to existential consciousness and its predicates like qualities are due to *antahkaraṇa* (inner instrument). But the view is not worked out in detail.

[48]Schopenhauer interprets Māyā as the cosmic will in his *World as Will and Idea.*

[49]See the author's article, "Self and Body: How Known and Distinguished."

[50]As pointed out earlier, in the philosophy of Asaṅga and some other later schools of the Mahāyāna, there is a considerable trend towards the affirmation of the *ātman.*

[51]One reason may be that every object, for Madhva, is and has a particular.

[52]Cp. Külpe and Bühler.

[53]The present author also was so misled for a time.

[54]Although John Dewey says that perception is judgment, and judgment involves inference (or is potential inference), there can be no inferential process, unless and until the witness consciousness detaches itself from the object in reflection. See his *Logic* and *How We Think* for his well-known theory.

[55]Some of this interpretation can be read into the Jaina theory of perception.

[56]That is, without traces of Becoming (*bhāva*).

[57]This explains why the Supreme Person says: "I am Time," in the *Bhagavadgītā.*

[58]The author is not competent to relate this theory to the theory of Einstein's. But it looks that for him also, there is no empty time and empty space. And if time is fast or slow depending on the velocity of light or vice versa, then it seems that it is possible to interpret the travelling light as the disclosure of time and space.

[59]Ontologically considered, they are ecstasies of my transcendental being, results of its inherent force (*rajas śakti* or *kriyā śakti*), as in existentialism, they are the forms of overflowing of the fulness of Being as in Neo-Platonism. They are also the formative processes for the assimilation of objectivity to the functions of apperception.

[60]Even Māyā, the Dark Maiden, is said to contain *jñānaśakti* (the power of consciousness, cognition, knowledge). Cp. also the idea of *prajñānaghana*, solidified massive consciousness of deep sleep.

[61]It is also the personified will of the supreme spirit in creation, according to the Ṛgveda.

[62]*tejohīnādhikaranam tamas.*

[63]Note that speech also has revealing power like light. The labour of most of the western philosophers of language, including Wittgenstein, becomes inconclusive because they want to explain the power (*śakti*) of language without reference to its revealing power, which they seem to shun as a superstition. But like light, speech is meant to reveal objects which are there. (cp. *Bṛahadāraṇyaka Upaniṣad*). Yes, it is known in its use like mind and senses. Without use, except in action, they do not reveal anything. It is also worth considering that the Heraclitian and the Stoic fire as reason is the revealing power of consciousness, which is not lost even in deep sleep (cp. *prajñānaghana*), of which again fire is said to be the presiding deity. It is a mistake to interpret the Heraclitian and the Stoic Fire as physical.

[64]In the Upaniṣads, even the light of the sun and fire is said to be a correlate of the eye and to be the origin of the eye of man.

[65]Cp. the Ideas of Sartre's and Heidegger's.

[66]Yogis are exceptions.

[67]Cp. the Sāṅkhya conception that the physical world evolves out of the *tāmasika* or darkness aspect of the ego (*ahaṁkāra*).

[68]In many of the Upaniṣads the word *tamas* is used for Māyā. The original waters (cp. Thales) out of which the world arose are also interpreted as *tamas* and Māyā and Avidyā. Padmapāda says that the terms,

nāma-rūpam, avyākṛtam, avidyā, māyā, prakṛti, agrahaṇam, avyaktam, tamas, kāraṇam, laya, śakti, nidrā, akṣaram, and *ākāsam* are used in the Vedas and other literature in the same sense. (*Pañcapādikā*, p. 20, Vizianagaram Sanskrit Series, Benares 1891). See *Tattvāloka* December 1978, Madras.

[69]Not accepting that darkness is absorbed by light and Māyā by the Brahman, some Advaitins introduced a fifth negation adding it to the four alternatives of the four-cornered negation. But this is unnecessary, when reference is made to experience. And really the highest experience is non-referential (*pratiyogi-Vinirmukta*). It has no negation aspect.

[70]Then the Buddhists ought to say that the so-called destruction of every moment of the causal process is not becoming Non-being, but entering Māyā, which is neither Being nor Non-being. Of course as positive it ought to be Being for both the Buddhists and the Advaitins.

[71]The Brahman's own creative will as in the *Ṛg Veda*, 9, 10. *Prakṛti* is so regarded by Madhva also. See B. Jhalakikar: *Nyāyakośa*.

[72]This was explained on the chapters on Buddhism and the Advaita.

[73]This is the *sākṣi* (witness, witness consciousness). For instance, of "I know that I know *X*," the first "I know" stays awake, but, "I know *X*" tends to become Nothingness, Darkness (Tamas, Śūnya, Māyā).

[74]For this reason, ontological tamas (Śūnya, Māyā), even though positive, has no Being separate from the Being of the I-am. The shadow has no Being apart from the Being of the object of which it is a shadow.

[75]Interpreters of Wittgenstein rightly say that both the affirmative proposition "*S* is *P*" and the negative "*S* is not *Q*" describe the same positive state of affairs and that there is no negative state of affairs. They hold that negation is a kind of truth-function of affirmation and is a compound, a molecular proposition. Primary or elementary propositions have all to be affirmative, although it is questionable whether all are propositions at all.

[76]They may be so in artificially constructed formal logic. The confusion and unending controversy are due to the mixing up of these levels and treating them as though they constitute one level.

[77]This will agree also with the Buddhist view that the Śūnya, Māyā, or Avidyā is not negative.

[78]This view may not agree with the contemporary scientific view of causation. It may not also be acceptable to the analytic philosophers. But neither is sacrosanct in even the sense of having universal applicability. From the ontological and existential points of view, what is said here seems to me to be correct.

[79]Interested students who know some Sanskrit may read his works and compare the view presented here to his theory of time-force (*kāla-śakti*). It is also worthwhile studying the theories of Kasmir Śaivism. Neither can be discussed in this book for want of space.

[80]This aspect of time led the Sarvāstivādin Buddhists to say that both past and future exist. But the orthodox Buddhists of the centre repudiated them, for they thought that to enter the past is to enter nothingness. And if the past *exists*, does it become the *present*? The same question arises with regard to the future also for the orthodox Buddhists. But if the past and future do not exist as parts of my present, we remove two essential constituents of the process of time, and time and time-consciousness disappear.

[81]Space and time are basic concepts and cannot be explained in terms of others. So we have to use them in explaining them.

[82]Note the difference from Bergson's theory, according to which space is static. But for the Upaniṣads, on which the theory developed here is based, space is a force which is an ingredient to Becoming. Time also is a force which belongs to Becoming. Being plays little or no part in his philosophy.

[83]*Nṛsimha-uttara-tāpinī Upaniṣad*, IX, 4.

Chapter XIV

Other Vedāntins, Kasmir Śaivism, and Śaktism

1. INTRODUCTION

Of all the interpreters of the Vedānta who founded their own schools, Śaṅkara, Rāmānuja, and Madhva are considered to be the most important. Others like Vallabha also have their following and their own schools, but their literature is not as extensive as that of the three and their epistemological and metaphysical doctrines are not as well developed. We shall, therefore, be content with giving their main metaphysical positions. As mentioned already, some of these Vedāntins are Śaivas, and the others Vaiṣṇavas. But their metaphysical positions cut across their Śaiva and Vaiṣṇava leanings, so that a Śaiva and a Vaiṣṇava may have the same metaphysical position. Kasmir Śaivism occupies a special place, as it propounds a non-dualism (*advaita*) without at the same time accepting Śaṅkara's interpretation of Māyā. In fact, it was practically dead up to the 8th century, when Śaṅkara revived it. In Kasmir, until Śaṅkara visited that land, Buddhism was the dominant religion. But Śaṅkara in his controversies convinced the Buddhists that they were wrong and the thinkers of Kasmir revived their original religion, Śaivism, under the influence of Śaṅkara's non-dualism. But they did not call themselves Vedāntins and did not rely only upon the three basic works—the Upaniṣads, the *Vedānta Aphorisms*, and the *Bhagavadgītā*—for expounding their doctrines, but mainly upon their own traditional works called Āgamas. They did not at the same time say that they were opposed to the teachings of the three basic works and even used them, now and then, when it suited them. They even wrote a commentary on the *Bhagavadgītā*.[1] However, commentaries on the *Vedānta Aphorisms* by Śaiva writers other than those of Kasmir Śaivism are available and are important. Śaṅkara seems to have encouraged them to develop their doctrines in their own way. Their contribution particularly to Indian aesthetics is one of the best that is made in India. They gave the subject one of the best and the soundest metaphysical bases.[2]

The Śāktas are mostly non-dualists and claim Śaṅkara himself as one of their great leaders. But their approach to the problem of Being and their terminology are different from those of Śaṅkara's Vedānta. Although their philosophy is not as popular in the academical circles because of its association with some of the prohibited practices of one wing of its followers and because also of its emphasis on religious practice rather than upon rational exposition of its doctrines, it has really something important to teach about the depths of our being.

The Śaivas, the Vaiṣṇavas, and the Śāktas composed their own Upaniṣads[3] to support their own doctrines. But many of those Upaniṣads are not regarded as genuine. Some of the ordinary Upaniṣads also are utilized by them.

2. THE OTHER VEDĀNTINS

As mentioned already, the central and common idea of the Vedāntic schools is that the Brahman is realized as our *ātman*, but not as an object facing us. But this idea may be interpreted in different ways. The Brahman may be our own *ātman*, not different at all from it. This is the interpretation of Śaṅkara. But those Vedāntins who are shocked by the idea that our own finite spirit can be the same as the Supreme Spirit say that the Supreme Spirit is the spirit of our spirits, it is the Supreme Ātman (*Paramātman*) residing in every *ātman*. Then what is the relation between the Supreme Ātman and our *ātmans*? If there is any difference or even distinction between the two, does a similar relation obtain between the Supreme Ātman and the world of matter? We have seen that Rāmānuja says that the finite *ātmans* and Prakṛti constitute the body of the Supreme Ātman; and in bondage Prakṛti constitutes the body of the finite *ātman*, but becomes separated from it in the state of salvation. We have seen also that, according to Madhva, the three—the Supreme Ātman, the finite *ātman*, and Prakṛti—are absolutely different from one another. The other Vedāntins give other answers to the question about this ultimate relation.

BHĀSKARA Bhāskara[4] (9th and 10th centuries), like Śaṅkara, is a commentator on the *Vedānta Aphorisms* and does not follow any of the sectarian Āgamas. He does not, however, accept Śaṅkara's doctrines of Māyā and of the quality-less Brahman. The Brahman is the personal god (Īśvara). Bhāskara does not accept that Prakṛti is not real, as it is the power of God. Both are equally real. But the *ātman* is the Brahman itself as limited by Prakṛti. As Prakṛti is real, the *ātman* also has to be considered to be real. Yet the *ātman* is identical with the Brahman, and this identity is natural (*svābhāvika*); but the difference is not natural (*asvābhāvika*) and is due to the incidental limitations (*upādhis*) imposed on the Brahman by Prakṛti. Since Prakṛti is the power of the same Brahman, we have to say that the Brahman imposes upon itself the limitations and appears as the finite *ātman*. The Brahman has two kinds of power (*śakti*): one is Prakṛti and takes the form of the object of enjoyment (*bhogyaśakti*) and the other is the power of entering Prakṛti and of becoming the finite *ātman* as the enjoyer (*bhoktṛśakti*). But as Prakṛti is real and yet a power of the Brahman itself, there is identity between the two. And as the Brahman is conscious and Prakṛti unconscious, there is difference also between the two. But in this case, both identity and difference are natural (*svābhāvika*).

Bhāskara contends that, as the world is due to the transformation (*pariṇāma*) of Prakṛti, which is only a power of the Brahman, the transformation belongs to the Brahman itself, which can, therefore, be said to have transformed itself into the world. But if the Brahman transforms itself into our world, how can it remain unaffected by the process and by the evil of the world? To meet the objection, Bhāskara draws a distinction between transformation that is a change of states only (*avasthāntarapariṇāma*) and transformation that is a change of being (*vikāra*) or that is a constitutive change. The Brahman's becoming a finite *ātman* is only a change of states. The change of Prakṛti also, as in the Sāṅkhya, are changes of states, of the latent into the patent and vice versa. The change of being (*vikāra*) is observed in some instances in the world, e.g., in the change of milk into buttermilk.

The suspicion that Śaṅkara was too strongly influenced by the Mahāyāna Buddhism, which he along with Kumārila controverted and worked peacefully to drive away from India, made a number of Vedāntins think that his defect lay in an over-emphasis on the Upaniṣadic idea of non-duality. They wanted, therefore, to give equal emphasis to the idea of duality and struggled hard to reconcile the ideas of identity and difference by positing the complex relation identity-cum-difference. But it is easier to say that the relation between the world and the Brahman is identity-cum-difference than to explain in detail how much a relation holds between the two. Besides, the problem is complicated by the world including the finite *ātmans*, which are conscious beings like the Brahman. Because of the complexity, each Vedāntin explained the relation in his own way. However, the first important Vedāntin to introduce the idea of identity-cum-difference is Bhāskara. Even before Śaṅkara, Bhartṛprapañca[5] introduced the idea and Śaṅkara knew about it. But it seems to have been lost and its protagonists completely eclipsed. In the chapter on Rāmānuja, we have referred to Yādavaprakāśa, who also held a similar view; but he came after Bhāskara. Rāmānuja could accept neither Bhāskara nor Yādavaprakāśa, but following Yamuna, developed the doctrine of spirit-body relation.

Śrīkaṇṭha Śrīkaṇṭha[6] (13th century) wrote a commentary on the *Vedānta Aphorisms* and was mistakenly taken by Appaya Dīkṣita (16th century) to be a follower of Śaṅkara. In fact, Śrīkaṇṭha was expounding the same system as that of Rāmānuja, viz., non-dualism of the qualified Brahman (Viśiṣṭādvaita) and spirit-body relation, although from the side of Śaivism. There is little difference between the philosophies of Rāmānuja and Śrīkaṇṭha except that the former identified the Brahman with Viṣṇu and the latter with Śiva. It is likely that Śrīkaṇṭha was influenced in his views by the philosophy of Rāmānuja, that of Kasmir Śaivism, and perhaps also by some Pāśupata Āgamaic literature of both the north and the south of India.

Nimbārka Nimbārka (13th century) was a Vaiṣṇava commentator on the *Vedānta Aphorisms*. The relation of identity-cum-difference is purely conceptual and Rāmānuja rejected it, as he could not understand how two contradictory concepts like identity and difference could hold together. But the relation of spirit and body is experiential and experience shows that what happens to the body affects the spirit. So Nimbārka could not accept it, for it could not preserve the Brahman in its perfection and freedom from the evils of world. The two ideas, body-spirit and identity-cum-difference, continued, therefore, to struggle with each other and also with the ideas of non-duality and the Māyā of Śaṅkara. Nimbārka accepted the relation of identity-cum-difference rejecting the views of both Śaṅkara and Rāmānuja. He could not accept a view like Madhva's at all, as it does violence to the Upaniṣadic text declaring non-duality.

But Nimbārka[7] did not accept Bhāskara's philosophy, for it leaves no essential difference between the *ātman* and the Brahman. He propounded therefore, the relation and identity-cum-difference between the Brahman and the *ātman*, between the Brahman and Prakṛti and between the *ātman* and Prakṛti. But this identity-cum-difference is only of nature (*svabhāva*). All the three are identical in nature, because they have common features. The *ātman* and the Brahman are conscious; the *ātman* and Prakṛti are dependent on God; and Prakṛti, as the power (*śakti*) of God, has something in common with him. But they are different also, as they have different natures. But this double relation does not hold in each case regarding the constitutive being or existence (*svarūpa*). As beings, they are different from one another, they are not always identical.

Creation is explained as the transformation (*pariṇāma*) of the Brahman. But this transformation does not affect the being of the Brahman, because what undergoes transformation is not Brahman's being (*svarūpa*), but his power (*śakti*) in the two forms, the conscious and the unconscious. The former creates the individual *ātmans* and the latter is Prakṛti, which produces the forms of the material world. Creation is the throwing out of the Brahman's power, its projection (*śaktivikṣepa*). For Nimbārka, the Brahman is the same as God and possesses auspicious qualities; God is not quality-less.

VALLABHA Vallabha (15th century) is another Vaiṣṇava Vedāntin, who propounded the philosophy of Pure Non-dualism (Śuddhādvaita) through his commentary of the *Vedānta Aphorisms*. He distinguishes his non-dualism from that of Śaṅkara, by calling the latter's non-dualism impure (*aśuddha*), as Śaṅkara used the concept of the impure[8] Māyā. Like Rāmānuja, Vallabha rejects the doctrine of Māyā and says that the Brahman has a mysterious power, through which it can create anything. There is no difference between the creator and the created, for there is no difference between cause and effect. Yet the cause undergoes transformation (*pariṇāma*) to produce the effect. Then if the Brahman undergoes transformation to produce the world, how can it remain perfect? It can remain perfect, because transformation is only manifestation; it is rendering an already existent object capable of being experienced. The world is not different from the Brahman; the former is the latter's quality, attribute (*dharma*). There is no difference between substance and attribute. The *ātman* issues out of the Brahman like a spark out of fire. It is the same as the Brahman, just as the spark is the same as the fire. The Brahman is not without qualities; it is full of auspicious, supra-mundane qualities (*saguṇa*). Yet, as the qualities are identical with the Brahman, it is non-dual; there is nothing that is a second to it. It is the personal God. But if I am so identical with the Brahman that there is not even a distinction between us, why do I know that I am the Brahman? I do not know the identity because of my ignorance (*avidyā*, *māyā*). But ignorance in Vallabha's philosophy has no metaphysical significance; it is the absence of the knowledge of my identity with the Brahman. In fact, as the Upaniṣads say, the Brahman is everything. We can realize this identity through absolute surrender to God and love of him.

VIJÑĀNABHIKṢU We have already come across the name of Vijñānabhikṣu (15th century) in connection with the Sāṅkhya and the Yoga. He was more inclined towards the theistic Sāṅkhya than towards the atheistic. And he wanted to confer prestige on it by turning it into a Vedāntic system.[9] He wrote, therefore, his own commentary on the *Vedānta Aphorisms*. For turning the Sāṅkhya into a Vedānta, he had only to add God and equate him to the Brahman of the Upaniṣads. We have seen that, according to him, the Sāṅkhya, is not really atheistic; it says only that God's existence cannot be proved by any rational proof, but has to be accepted on the basis and authority of the Veda.

It is a Himalayan task for Vijñānabhikṣu to relate God to the *ātmans* and Prakṛti as explained by the theistic Sāṅkhya. If the *ātmans* and Prakṛti are so independent of God as the Sāṅkhya maintains, how can the Brahman be the creator of the world? To find an answer to the question, Vijñānabhikṣu introduces a new concept of cause, viz., that of support or ground (*ādhāra, adhiṣṭāna*).[10] The Brahman (God) does not undergo transformation at all to create the world. He is not the material cause of the world. He is not even the efficient cause (*nimittakāraṇa*). The efficient causes of creation, of the transformation (*pariṇāma*) of Prakṛti, are the potencies of the actions (*karmas*) of the *ātmans*. God is, only the ground, the support of all that happens and is. He is that in which we move and have our own being. Yet, all the three—the Brahman, the *ātmans*, and Prakṛti—are real and have their independent being.

Then does God contribute nothing to the world? Yes, he contributes time[11] (*kāla*). Time is the dynamic agency of God and he introduces through it motion into the *ātmans* and Prakṛti. Both the *ātmans* and Prakṛti are static by nature. We have seen that the Sāṅkhya does not accept the reality of time. But it becomes real in Vijñānabhikṣu's Vedānta. Yet his conception of time is not definite. It seems to be another name for dynamism. The time that is introduced by God is one and eternal and has no distinctions of past, present, and future. These distinctions obtain within the world of change and are posterior to it. But what is change itself due to? It is due to eternal time, the pure principle of dynamism itself. While the Sāṅkhya attributed dynamism to Prakṛti itself, Vijñānabhikṣu, as a Vedāntin, treats Prakṛti as static and as in need of dynamism, which can be supplied by God. Even according to the Sāṅkhya, Prakṛti is able to obtain motion when it receives the reflection of the Puruṣa. So it is Puruṣa that introduces dynamism along with its own reflection into Prakṛti. Now Vijñānabhikṣu attributes this function to God.

Vijñānabhikṣu accepts a kind of identity-cum-difference between the Brahman and the world, in which difference is primary and identity has to be explained as that between father and son or whole and parts. But we cannot push the similarity very far; for identity seems only to be inseparability as that between whole and parts. Even then, while the parts constitute the whole, the *ātmans* and Prakṛti do not constitute God. Yet if we move and have our being in God, we cannot be separated from him.

CAITANYA AND BALADEVA Caitanya[12] (15th century) is the founder of the Bengal school of Vaiṣṇavism, but himself did not write a commentary on the *Vedānta Aphorisms*. One of his followers, Baladeva (18th century), wrote the commentary, thereby making the school Vedāntic. This school maintains that the relation between God (Brahman) and the world is that of inconceivable identity-cum-difference (*acintyabhedābheda*). The relation is inconceivable; for we cannot conceive how it can be the two contradictories, identity and difference. Yet we have to accept both, for everything must be one with, and yet be different from God.

The Brahman has three kinds of power (*śakti*)—the supreme power (*parāśakti*), the lower power (*aparāśakti*), and the power of the unconscious (*avidyāśakti*) or Prakṛti. Through transformation (*pariṇāma*) of the second power, the Brahman creates the souls; and through that of the third, it creates the material world. But through its supreme power, it controls both. Through the second and the third powers, God is the material cause (*pariṇāmakāraṇa*) of the world; but through his supreme power, he is the efficient cause. All the three powers are identical with him and different from him. The souls forget their identity with God because of ignorance, which is only absence of knowledge and has no metaphysical significance. But through love of God and self-surrender to him, the souls can regain the knowledge of their original relationship to God. This school teaches love in some of its most rapturous forms.

ŚRĪPATI Śrīpati is a Śaiva Vedāntin[13] of the 16th (?) century. He wrote a commentary on the *Vedānta Aphorisms*, making the philosophy of Heroic Śaivism (Vīraśaivism) Vedāntic. This religious sect of Śaivism gives little importance to caste, saying that initiation into spiritual truths is enough to make a man a Brahmin. So all the followers of this school claim to be Brahmins. It makes also no discrimination between sexes so far as spiritual training goes. Although some other sects also claim to make no such discrimination, this school goes farther than any of them in the practice. There is a difference of opinion about whether Śrīpati is a true follower of Heroic Śaivism. But he claims to be one and his work is that of a great scholar.

Śrīpati maintains that the relation between God and the world is that of identity-cum-difference. We have seen that Bhāskara accepts this relation in one way, Nimbārka in a second, and Baladeva in a third. Both Bhāskara and Nimbārka attempt to explain how the relation is identity and in what sense it is difference. Baladeva regards it as inconceivable and inexplicable, and leaves it at that. But Śrīpati tries to explain it and differs from both Bhāskara and Nimbārka. Nimbārka maintains that both identity and difference between the Brahman and the world are of nature (*svabhāva*, essence), but not of being (*svarūpa*).[14] But Śrīpati maintains that both identity and difference are both of nature and of being. And this complex identity-cum-difference holds between the Brahman and the world of nature and between the Brahman and the *ātmans*. The world of nature and the world of the *ātmans* are due to the transformation (*pariṇāma*) of the two powers (*śaktis*, forces, energies) of the Brahman. The power of the Brahman is both identical with, and different from the Brahman. The power of fire to burn is not the same as fire and yet is identical with fire. Similarly, the characteristics of power and of that which has the power are identical with, and different from each other. The heat of the power of fire is the same as that of fire; but is different also, because it is not the same as the colour of fire, which also is a characteristic of fire. When the Upaniṣads say that the Brahman and the world are both identical and different, they do not mean merely identity in essence or nature alone, but also of being. For the Brahman is ultimately the Being of all.

Śrīpati is a Śaiva theist and identifies the Brahman with the personal God, calling him Śiva. He combines the three ways to salvation, but gives a higher place to knowledge than Rāmānuja and Nimbārka do, although he says that all are of equal value. Like Śaṅkara and Madhva, he admits the possibility of salvation in the body (*jīvanmukti*). And he gives a greater significance to the idea of identity than the other Vedāntins, except Śaṅkara and Bhāskara. For the reason that he treats the world of matter and *ātmans* as the powers (*śaktis*) of God and calls power an attribute (*viśeṣaṇa*) or form (*prakāra*) of God, Śrīpati's system is called also "non-dualism of the Brahman as qualified by power" (*śaktiviśiṣṭādvaita*). But some Vīraśaivas (Heroic Śaivas) question such an interpretation. In fact, we may call all the Vedāntic systems, except that of Śaṅkara, by the name "non-dualism of the Brahman as qualified by power;" for according to all of them, the world of the *ātmans* or at least the world of matter is the transformation, in one sense or another, of the power or powers of God. But the differences among them are also important.

3. KASMIR ŚAIVISM

As mentioned already, the Śaivism of Kasmir occupies a peculiar position in Indian philosophy. For although it is sectarian in origin, it developed its philosophy under the influence of Śaṅkara's Advaita and is very much akin to it, although maintaining that Māyā is a real entity and is not what Śaṅkara and Buddhism understood it to be. It is, however, not considered to be a Vedāntic school, but is almost like one. In fact, one of its greatest exponents, Abhinavagupta, even shows indifference to the reality of Māyā, although he did not definitely reject its reality.[15] All that this school wants to defend is the reality of Śiva and of Śakti as his power, figuratively understood as his consort. The world is due to the transformation (*pariṇāma*) of this power[16] (*śakti*) and is, therefore, the transformation of Śiva himself. *It is a transformation within him, but not of him.* Many transformations take place within my consciousness every moment, but my conscious being, my I-am continues to be, and remains the same. The world we experience consists of such transformations, which are vibrations (*spandas*)[17] in the being of Śiva. For holding the view of vibrations, this philosophy is called the vibration philosophy (*spandadarśana*). The finite *ātman* is one of these vibrations and forgets that it is the same as Śiva. Salvation lies in the *ātman* recognizing (*pratyabhijñā*) its true and original nature. The doctrine of recognition gave this school the name recognition-philosophy (*pratyabhijñādarśana*). But as the *ātman* is essentially the same as Siva, there is non-duality between the two Even the relation between Śiva and his power (*śakti*) is non-duality (identity). This doctrine gave this school the name of Śaiva non-dualism (Śaivādvaita). The difference between Śiva and his power is due to the different standpoints from which we view the same reality. From our point of view, Śiva is different from the world; but from the ultimate, i.e., Śiva's point of view, the world is not different from him. Some pictures, which, when seen from one side, appear as horses and from another side as elephants, are given as examples.

Vasugupta (8th century), Utpala (10th century), and Abhinavagupta (10th century) are the greatest names of this school. The last is undoubtedly the greatest and the most well-known of the three. Vasugupta is the author of *Śivasūtra* and *Spandakārikā*, Utpala of *Pratyabhijñāsūtra*, and Abhinavagupta of more than forty works including *Paramārthasāra* and *Pratyabhijñāvimarśinī*. He is one of the greatest writers on aesthetics.

Śiva may be viewed as personal or impersonal, depending on what we mean by person. He is the only reality. But he appears as the world through his wonderful power. He remains perfect in spite of the world. His power has five aspects—consciousness, bliss, will (*icchā*), knowledge (*jñāna*), and activity (*kriyā*). When the power is pure consciousness, Śiva remains as pure Śiva and as the only reality. In the bliss aspect, Śiva appears as Power (Śakti). In the aspect of will, he appears as Sadāśiva; in the aspect of activity, as Īśvara; and in the aspect of knowledge, as Śuddhavidyā. These words cannot be translated, but the nature of the states of Śiva, the Supreme Godhead, in these aspects is understandable. However, these states are appearances of the same Śiva and are his transformations. These four stages are called Supernals and constitute pure creation.[18] They are described also as the experiences of "I," "I am," "I am this" without the clear distinction of the "I" and "This," and "I" and "This" as separately experienced without identity with each other. Out of Śuddhavidyā is born Māyā, which is unconscious, but real, and which is the root of everything and includes everything, including the finite *ātmans* and the world of matter. In Māyā originate the five principles—limit (*niyati*) or necessity, time, attachment (*rāga*) or the principle of identification of the self with other objects, limited cognition (*vidyā*) that is dependent on mind and senses, and limited ability (*kalā*). These five along with Māyā are called the six shackles (*ṣaṭkañcnkas*) and constitute the mixed creation, which is a combination of purity and impurity. They are prior to the individual souls. Man is born into them, he does not create them. As they are prior to individual souls, they are pure principles; but as they are the cause of the soul's bondage, they are impure.

After these six principles and out of them, starts the impure creation. First, the Puruṣa and Prakṛti appear. The rest of the process is practically the same as that given by the Sāṅkhya.

4. OTHER ŚAIVA SCHOOLS

The Śaiva schools are so many and there are so many differences of view on many topics that it is difficult to present all of them. It is possible only to mention a few of them and give their most common features. The philosophy of the *Pāśupatasūtras*, which is perhaps the original text of all the Śaiva schools, seems like an absolute pluralism of spirits (*ātmans*), all of which are Śivas. This view sounds like the Sāṅkhya in the garb of Śaivism. King Bhoja in his *Tattvaprakāśa* maintained a position that lies between the absolute non-dualism of Kasmir Śaivism and the pluralism of the *Pāśupatasūtras*. He said that every *ātman* becomes a Śiva, but the Śiva it becomes is not the Supreme Śiva but one like him. And he accepted the forms of descent from Śiva and the evolution of the world as expounded by the Kasmir school. And as Paśupati is another name for Śiva, all the Śaiva schools taken together are said to belong to the Pāśupata tradition, which has some degenerate forms also. Almost all the Śaivas accept liberation in the body.

Heroic Śaivism (Vīraśaivism), which is a branch of Śaivism, has already been presented. The South Indian school[19] of Śaivism is called Śaivasiddhānta and is older in origins than perhaps the advent of the Aryans, although we do not know whether it had any literature at that time. Many of its followers later became Vedāntins. Śrīkaṇṭha and Śrīpati are two of them. Originally the literature of this South Indian school was in Tamil, some of it in very ancient Tamil. But later it appeared in

Sanskrit also. But this particular school that calls itself Śaivasiddhānta depends mainly on Tamil works, also called Āgamas like the corresponding Sanskrit Śaiva Āgamas. But it is clear by now that Śaivism is not one philosophy, but contains pluralism, dualism, monism, and some modified forms of monism. The Śaivasiddhānta is on the whole pluralistic. It works with the three concepts—the Lord (*pati*), the animal (*paśu*), and the bond (*pāśa*, rope, bondage). The other Śaiva schools also mention these words, but transform their concepts into the Vedāntic. The souls are the cattle belonging to the Lord and find themselves in bondage due to ignorance (*avidyā*), action (*karma*), and Māyā, the material cause of the world corresponding to Prakṛti. The soul can free itself from bondage through love of God, when the shackles are broken.

The process of creation is more or less the same as in the Kasmir school, except for a few differences. The power (*śakti*) of Śiva is not identical with him, but mediates between him and the material world. The souls also are not identical with him, even in the state of salvation. Or they are identical with him only as belonging to him. It is not the power (*śakti*) of the Lord, but Prakṛti, that transforms itself into the world.

5. ŚĀKTISM

Śāktism[20] is the philosophy and religion that give more importance to the energy (*śakti*, power, force) aspect of the Godhead than to the transcendent Godhead himself; for we are in direct contact with the forms that the energy has taken. As God has the energy aspect according to many schools, Śākta philosophy also has many forms. That is, it can be detected in Vaiṣṇavism also. But usually when Śāktism is spoken of, it means the philosophy of the energy of Śiva and is associated with Śaivism. It is generally non-dualistic. Śaṅkara's name also is associated with it; his work *Prapañcasāratantra* is regarded as one of the classics of this school and was commented upon by the famous Padmapāda, who was a follower of Śaṅkara. Bhāskara (date uncertain, but much later than Śaṅkara and different from Bhāskara, the Vedāntin) and Lakṣmīdhara (date uncertain again) are two of the great names of this school. Even Abhinavagupta of Kasmir Śaivism was a great follower of this school. Sir John Woodroff (Arthur Avalon) made the significance of this philosophy known to English readers and translated and expounded many of its works. But the school thus presented by him is a form of non-dualism, very much akin to Kasmir Śaivism, in which Māyā is treated as real and as identical with Śiva. But this school is so full of symbolism that it is difficult to present it in two or three pages. Furthermore, as Śāktism can be associated with almost all schools and as the energy aspect of the Godhead is understood differently by them, there are several schools of Śāktism, including that of a later school of Buddhism, called Vajrayāna. But the school that enjoys the greatest prestige is that associated with the name of Śaṅkara. We can give here a few central ideas of his work for presenting the rationale of this school.

First, this school accepts that the world is a transformation (*pariṇāma*) of the energy (*śakti*) of Śiva. We are all forms of this Śakti. The more remote the result of transformation, the more removed the result will be from Śiva. So realization of Śiva can be attained by re-transformation reaching back to the stage at which Śakti and Śiva are identical. We have found a similar idea in the Sāṅkhya also. *Secondly*, this realization is the same as the merging (*laya*) of Śakti in Śiva. To become identical with Śiva means to merge our finitude in his infinitude. So the yoga or path that this school teaches is called the Yoga of Merging (*layayoga*). *Thirdly*, the creation of us by Śakti is the process of emotional disturbance—we may remember here the idea of vibration (*spanda*)—that takes place in Śiva. Śakti is this emotive power that creates its objects. Behind all creation, ours or God's, lies emotion that moves. We can understand this idea in terms of depth psychology, according to which repressed emotions, when they begin to act in dreams, produce their own objects and, when they work themselves out and subside, our ordinary being is regained. Emotions are not states of mind, which we can watch undisturbed; they are outward pulls of our being. All emotions have an admixture of pain; even love has it in the form of longing. So intensity of bliss (pleasure) is obtained when, after some emotion produces intense disturbance and subsides, our being regains its original placidity and harmony. But this intense disturbance is necessary, for then only are we close to our being and gripped by it; otherwise, we may be living an imaginary or conventional being—not our own or authentic being—, thinking that we are husbands, wives, rich, poor, happy, or miserable. Such thinking is false self-identification. Śiva is the true underlying Being of everything and has to be realized, if we are to realize our true being. The method of realization lies in arousing some intense emotion in ourselves—not necessarily the fear of death, in face of which we realize our existence according to existentialism—and overcoming it by rising above it. *Fourthly*, our nervous system is attuned to the structure of the cosmos. If we realize how it is attuned, we can know the truth about the cosmos. But the cosmos is embedded in Śiva. Our knowledge of the microcosmos, therefore, leads to the knowledge of Śiva. *Fifthly*, as the nature of Śiva is consciousness, Śakti, which belongs to, and is Śiva, is also conscious. One may compare it to the Logos, which is both Word and Reason. Many Śāktas give all importance to the Word. The world is a transformation of the Word.[21] This Word is originally distinct and pure and is the highest Sound (*paranāda*). It is like the voice of silence or void (*śūnya*) and may be called the Void (Śūnya) also. It is intensely blissful and is the root of the pleasure of music. Then the all-pervading sound of the Void or emptiness is focussed and becomes like a drop (*bindu*). This drop then splits or is differentiated into three—drop (*bindu*), seed (*bīja*), and sound (*nāda*). According to this school this sound (*nāda*) is known as the Sound Brahman (*śabdabrahman*) or the Word Brahman. Through further vibration (*vimarśa*, *spanda*) the Sound Brahman evolves the world. Śiva himself is present in the drop (*bindu*) aspect; Śakti in the seed (*bīja*) aspect; and both equally in the sound (*nāda*) aspect. We may understand the distinctions thus. The drop (*bindu*) is the whole about to become the world. The sound of silence is like diffused water, and the drop is like the point of a powerful vortex created in the expanse of water and about to burst forth into a manifold. The dynamic seed (*bīja*) of creation is the energy loosened from the drop. The sound is the transcendental sound (*nāda*) that later becomes the names of all beings and of their activities, yet retaining in itself the wholeness of Śiva and the dynamism of Śakti. This school believes that everything in the world has its original name, although the conventional names are different. The evolution of the world of plurality out of the original sound (*nāda*, Word Brahman) follows mostly the stages found in Kasmir Śaivism. This school of Śāktism is also a mysticism of the Word.

GENERAL ESTIMATE AND CONSTRUCTIVE COMMENT

(i) The Supreme Being as my Deepest Ātman

It is often thought by some traditionalists that the most important of the *Vedānta Aphorisms*, which divided the Vedāntic schools from one another, are the ones explaining the causal relation between the Brahman and the world. Causality is explained by Śaṅkara as *vivarta* or change without the cause being affected in the process and as transformation or change by the others[22] in which the cause is affected by the process. We have distinguished the two as the ontological and the cosmological conceptions. Almost all except Śaṅkara hold that the Brahman is the latter type of cause of the world. Most of them are divided in interpreting the aphorism that the Brahman is realized as one's own *ātman* or self (spirit, I-am).[23] It is more reasonable to take this aphorism as basic, and as the bone of contention. For much grammatical and etymological gymnastic is needed for explaining this aphorism in a way agreeable to one's own system. The aphorism also expresses the supreme experience, viz., that the Supreme I-am is experienced as my I-am at the stage of realization. The causal theory that my finite I-am, as this person, is a *vivarta* of the Supreme I-am, that it is a transformation of the latter, its *pariṇāma*, that transformation is only a state (*avasthā*), that it is a substantial change, and so on, comes in mainly to support the explanation of the primary transcendental experience.[24]

The general tendency of man is to think of the material, non-sentient world, whenever the word world is uttered. But there can be no world for me except as my mind and senses can *present it*.[25] I am not created merely as a point, but with potential realms or fields of perceivable qualities and objects. Then the idea that the Supreme I-am creates the world means that it creates my finite I-am and the horizons of its actual and potential experience, which is my world. We have shown in the previous estimates that objectivities are part and parcel of myself in my transcendence, and that my I-am is not really limited to my body in size, but extends as far as my mind and senses can reach, and that it is not spatial, but transcends both time and space. Thus the world has its roots, its origins, in something that is beyond time and space. The world cannot be merely material, but hangs from a chain as it were (cp. Bradley) the two ends of which are stuck to my I-am and disappear in it. Time and space are two patterns of Becoming of the world that issues out of my transcendental I-am. They are again patterns by which I assimilate the world of Becoming to myself, absorb it, withdraw it into myself. When the assimilation is complete, I realize that I am no longer the finite I-am facing (which is really positing, extending through my forms of time and space) a world, but the transcendental I-am, the Supreme I-am. The realization of the Supreme is the realization that it is my own I-am, Ātman, Self, Spirit. Then this aphorism, even though the commentators did not write much on it and the traditions give only a passing look at it, is the most important, in the sense that it is basic to all the other aphorisms.

To make this idea more intelligible, we should remember that Becoming is not an unpatterned process, but is a pattern of patterns of patterns and so on; and that the patterns are the limits, limitations (forms of *niyati*, limit, as Plato said). Every becoming is temporal and spatial, provided we do not understand space merely as physical space and time as merely physical time. Then time and space are patterns of Becoming. Causation also occurs according to patterns, which are limits, laws. We are unable to prove any empirical law of causation with absolute certainty; yet we cannot accept that everything can become everything else in the empirical world; if it does, there will be no cosmology, no order in the world. So causation is another limit. But again, these patterns are patterns of the coming out of the world from my transcendental self; and they are also patterns of assimilating the world of Becoming to my transcendental self. When Kant said that we could think of space and time as apart from objects, we should not understand him as holding that there could be empty time and empty space (cp. his antinomies) into which objects are dropped or which are ready to receive sensations and spread them out in themselves. *On the other hand, we have to think that space and time are projective and assimilative forms through which the objects, all of which belong to the realm of Becoming, are posited or projected out of Being and absorbed into it.* The objects become spatio-temporal contours (*mūrtas*) or chunks of Becoming. It is generally represented that time is the devourer of all things; but space also is such a devourer. Both are devourers (*attās*), because they are assimilators, absorbers of all objectivity. Ultimately, the Ātman as Being is the absorber of all objectivity, or all Becoming. As we said previously, all universals—all those belonging to the individual, racial, and cosmic minds fabricated as tools for the purpose of creation and absorption, which are the processes of Becoming—are in a sense devourers.[26]

Then if the world comes out of me, not as this empirical person, but in my transcendence, and if, as such, space, time and causation are forms of limit coming out of my transcendental I-am; then the aphorism containing the relation between my finite I-am and my transcendental I-am is more important as expressing the basic fact of our existence than the one's devoted to the problem of causality, whether of the Brahman or of the material objects. The relation of transcendence-immanence is basic to all philosophy of existence, to all ontology. This relation, which would elucidate Berkeley's problem how our minds partake of the mind of God, is explained by the Vedāntins in four main ways. *First*, Śaṅkara interpreted it straightly, identifying my finite *ātman* with the Supreme Ātman or the Brahman, the difference between the two being the immanent and the transcendent, the image or reflection and the original, that which is limited (*avacchinna* or even *upahita*) by the functional mechanisms of apperception (*citta*), reason (*buddhi*), ego (*ahaṁkāra*) and mind (*manas*) and the senses and the organs of action and that which is not so limited.[27] *Second*, Rāmānuja interpreted the relation as that of soul and body which are inseparable, but not completely identical. *Third*, Nimbārka interpreted the relation as that of both identity and difference, which is explained as identity-in-difference. And *fourth*, Madhva interpreted it as complete difference, explaining away the word *ātman* (thinking perhaps that it does not mean self) as the devourer (*attā*), the word meaning for Madhva the God Viṣṇu who creates, sustains, and destroys the universe. This explanation looks artificial—for *attā* (the eater) can mean also, as we have explained, the *ātman* as the I-am, which is the usual meaning—but raises the important problem whether the word *ātman* primarily means the self (spirit), tracing it to the German word "*atmen*" which means "to breathe" or devourer, deriving it from the Sanskrit root *ad* = to eat, and Greek "*adein*." So far as the Upaniṣadic literature goes, the primary meaning of *ātman* is self or spirit, and secondarily because of the functions of assimilating and absorbing which it performs, it is the devourer, in both the senses of the finite and the Supreme Spirit. Following Madhva, the Śaiva dualists and pluralists would identify the *ātman* of this aphorism with Śiva and defend their dualism and pluralism.

(ii) Difficulties of Identity in Difference, of Identity and of Difference

Both identification and differentiation, and even their combination as identity-cum-difference or identity-in-difference have each its own difficulties. For the commentators of the Upaniṣads and the *Vedānta Aphorisms*, the question was also a question of interpreting the Upaniṣadic sentences with the help of grammar and etymology. But along with the question of interpretation, the philosophical, religious, and experiential aspects of the problem were equally important. And for us, who cannot entirely rely on grammatical and etymological analyses—all of which are possible, but may land us in confusion—the experiential are more important than the others. If the finite and the infinite are absolutely identical as Śaṅkara maintains, are we to regard this world as unreal, in which the finite finds itself struggling? Can Rāmānuja's concept of body-soul relationship preserve the perfection of the Brahman, if its inseparable body is going through the travail of Becoming? Śaṅkara can say that the Brahman can be perfect because the travail of Becoming is only apparent for it and the creation of the world is only *vivarta*, but not transformation; but Rāmānuja cannot say so. Bhāskara said that the relation between the finite and the infinite spirits is both identity and difference. But how can two contradictory or even contrary relations hold true between any two realities at the same time? And if the opposition is neither contradictory nor contrary, what else is it? Bhāskara had no clear answer. Nimbārka and Śrīpati followed Bhāskara in the main, and had to face the same difficulties, particularly so because, unlike Bhāskara, they accepted the causal theory of real transformation, but not of *vivarta*. Bhāskara holds that the creation of the finite *ātman* is only the effect of incidental or accidental limitation (*upādhi*)—a view of causation which sounds like *vivarta*. But yet he calls it transformation (*pariṇāma*); but it is not transformation of his Being, but of his energy, force (*śakti*), which, unlike Śaṅkara, he regards as positively real.[28] But one feels that this view is closer to *vivarta* than to pure, real *pariṇāma* (transformation). For this transformation of energy (*śakti*) only makes the infinite Brahman *appear* (disguised) as finite.

But while the Brahman is said to appear as the finite *ātman* when circumscribed by the limitations (*upādhis*), it does not appear as the material world. It is the energy (*śakti*) by itself, as distinct from the Brahman, that takes on the form of the material world through transformation (*pariṇāma*) and can re-transform itself into the original state of energy (*śakti*). But in the case of the finite *ātman*, to become the Brahman again it does not face the task of re-transformation, but of knocking out the limitations (guises) which obscured its original infinitude.

Nimbārka and others do not accept the kind of distinction made by Bhāskara between the creation of the finite souls and that of the material world. They seem to be opposed to Bhāskara's, as well as Śaṅkara's, view of the Brahman appearing as the finite *ātmans*. Even this kind of creation will impair the perfection of the Brahman. The finite *ātmans* have, therefore, to be different from the Brahman and yet have to be its creatures in some way and be dependent on it. So these Vedāntins say that the Brahman transforms (*pariṇāmata*) itself into the finite *ātmans* and the material world. But then how can he retain his eternal purity and perfection? He can retain them because he is infinitely powerful, he has mysterious powers. But this is not a philosophical answer. What seems to be a philosophical answer, in spite of many differences of view, is that the transformation belongs to the energy (*śakti*)—let it be of one, two or three kinds—of the Brahman. That the world, including the souls, is a transformation of the energy of the Brahman rather than of the Brahman itself sounds more intelligible than all the other doctrines, which appear abstract and far-fetched. For I am present in my dream, my dream I forgets the waking I, and the dream objects along with the dream I are created by, or are transformations of the potencies (energy, *śakti*) of my waking I and its activities. The potencies are activities in a latent form, waiting for elaboration into experiences, waiting for materialization. The primary idea is then that it is the energy of the Brahman that takes on the forms, but activated always from within by the Brahman. The question of the relation between the Brahman, its energy, and its forms is subsidiary. It is interesting and important to note that both the *Bhagavadgītā* and the school of Caitanya speak of three kinds of energy, the supreme (*parā*), that which creates the finite souls, and the one that creates the material world. Even in Śaṅkara's system, we have noted that Māyā is energy (*śakti*). Although Śaṅkara rejects any relation between it and the Brahman, we may ask: Whose energy is it? Why is it compared to the burning power of fire? True, this power can have no being apart from that of fire; ontologically then, Being is one and the same. When the opportunity and occasion appear, it is the power that works, acts. Fire enters the object it consumes through its power. So Bhāskara seems to be right in thinking that the material world is the transformation (*pariṇāma*) of the inherent energy of the Brahman; and when the Brahman appears through the forms of his transformed energy by entering those forms, he appears as though limited or he appears through the limitations of those forms, which then become his forms. Bhāskara has certainly the *Aitareya Upaniṣad* to support him, which says that the Brahman entered as an I-am into the forms and forces constituting man. For without the Brahman as the Supreme I-am, none of the forms can work. And the power of entering the forms is also a form of his energy (*śakti*); and we can introduce, for purposes of understanding, several ramifications of the single energy of the Brahman, and also ramifications of these ramifications. The three ramifications of the energy of the Brahman in the *Bhagavadgītā* are of this type.[29] The ultimate identity (*abheda*) of the Brahman and his energy is accepted also by Kasmir Śaivism. There is no way of understanding the Vedāntic position and of making it intelligible to others than by accepting the reality of the I-am and the reality of its character and constitution, not as an ineffectual quality like the colour of wood, but as potency and power (*śakti*).

The above discussion of the difficulties faced by the Vedāntins in identifying the Brahman, the finite *ātman*, and the material world, may have thrown some light on the difficulties of the view of complete difference between them. If there is complete difference between God and the rest, the former can have little or no control over the latter, and there is no point in calling the latter the power or energy (*śakti*) of God. I have control over my powers, they are mine, and I am a free being, with the freedom to use or not to use my power. (By the way, the word power has to be understood in the concrete, ontological sense, like the power of the magnet to attract iron, but not in the derivative sense like the power of the President of U.S.A. over his army.) Similarly has to be understood God's power. Rāmānuja is, therefore, in a better position to explain how God can use his power over the souls and the material world; for they constitute his body; and every one, as many philosophers understand, has power over his body. But the inexplicable point in Rāmānuja is how the souls and the material world can have their own, eternal being apart from that of God.

Nimbārka and the others also who accept both identity and difference, cannot be free from the above difficulties. For how can the finite *ātmans* (souls) and the material world have their own being different from that of God, if they are only his energy (*śakti*)? A logical window of escape from the difficulty may be to maintain that God and his energy have their own different beings, and that similarly fire and its power to burn have their own different beings. Madhva would accept this answer and add that each could have its own particular. However, for him the world does not consist of one or a few particulars, but of a infinite number of them. Every stone in a heap has its own particular, and the heap also has its own particular. Accordingly, the energy (*śakti*) of God must consist of an infinite number of particulars and also all the possible future particulars of bits of stones into which I can break them. Such an idea looks too unreasonable to accept. We may reasonably and intelligibly say that God's power is one and it can take on an infinite number of forms without violating its inherent self-limitations (*niyati* and *māna*, limit and measure). Besides, it is not logically and ontologically reasonable to say that fire and its power to burn are, or have two different beings. Where fire exists, there is power to burn; if the fire is removed to another place, its power also is removed to another place. Although "fire causes burning" is a correct statement with reference to the object burnt, it is absurd to say: "Fire causes its own burning power."[30] Fire and its burning power are identical in being. Similarly, God and his energy (*śakti*) have to be identical in being. God does not cause his character or nature or power; if he does so, there has to be another energy to cause this energy and so on *ad infinitum*. There is a sense in which we can say: "I cause my character," through repeated actions of good or evil; but God does not cause his character, nature, or power, as it is God's eternal nature.

(iii) Being (Existence) and Nature (Essence) with Reference to Identity and Difference

Most of the Vedāntins from the time of Bhāskara have been concerned with the problem whether identity and difference can obtain with respect to Being (*sattā*) only, or with respect to nature (*svabhāva*) only, or with respect to both. Can insentient matter and the Brahman, which is the Supreme Intelligence be identical in Being? Can they be identical in nature? Again, can the finite *ātman* and the Supreme Ātman be identical in Being? If matter and the Brahman are identical in Being or nature, then the latter becomes insentient. If the *ātman* and the Brahman are identical in Being, the former cannot be finite; if they are identical in nature, the former will have infinite power. But none of these consequences can be accepted, and our experience is otherwise. These questions do not concern Śaṅkara, for there is nothing ultimately insentient and finite for him; all is essentially the Brahman ontologically or in Being. Yes, they may be different in nature, if by nature we do not understand anything eternal, but only names and forms (*nāma-rūpas*), non-essential for the Brahman, but essential for the world with its limits and measures. By "in Being" and "by Being" we have generally to understand "ontologically;" by "in nature" and "by nature" we have generally to understand "cosmologically."[31] Basically the question is, how is the cosmos—and if we treat it as alive, how is the Cosmic Person, the Logos—related to the Brahman? Śaṅkara would say that in Being they are identical, but by nature they are different, with the proviso that the Brahman shines through all the differences or objects of the world as their being and that they have no being of their own. But in explaining how the names and forms (*nāma-rūpas*) appear at all, the general Advaita tradition holds that they come from nowhere. As we have been trying to explain, they have to be regarded as the throwings up, belchings of Māyā like the belchings of fire, gases, and other material by a volcano from the bosom of the earth. They are the discharge of the energy (*śakti-vikṣepa*) of the Brahman. This explanation does not hurt the perfection of the Brahman; for the workings of his energy (*śakti*) do not result in the transformation (*pariṇāma*) of the Brahman, but only in his *vivarta*, as explained before. Even in the case of the finite person, his actions may result, it may be said, in the transformation of his personality, or more exactly, his character. But the change (*pariṇāma*) cannot be absolute; for the I-am has to remain the same through all the change. For without its self-identity throughout, there can be no change even, but only a procession of unrelated events. The idea may raise another question: Does the energy transform itself into names and forms or does it also undergo *vivarta*? In the former case, it gets exhausted in its work and cannot be full to repeat and continue the work. We may, therefore, say that at that level causation is always a *vivarta*, somewhat similar to that part of my being, which is unaffected by the working of my mind in dreams. The main point to consider here is that Māyā can never completely detach itself from the Brahman—the Being of both is the same—and create the world of names and forms. So the statement that Māyā creates the world and the Brahman remains unaffected cannot be taken literally. But the ability to be completely detached and at the same time to be involved is perfect in the case of the Supreme Spirit.

What we should note as a difficulty in Bhāskara's view is that his explanation of the manifold world as the transformation of the energy (*śakti*) of the Supreme Being does not allow the Supreme Being to be both completely detached and at the same time involved. At this point he is open to Śaṅkara's objection that we cannot eat half the chicken (hen) and allow the other half to lay eggs. If the Brahman's energy is transformed into the world, to that extent he is affected. Even if, as Bhāskara says, the world is a state, condition (*avasthā*) of the energy (*śakti*) of the Brahman, the difficulty pointed out cannot be removed.[32] What is required here is the concept of the Brahman with his power or energy throwing up the forms of the world like the subconscious and the unconscious in dream, and yet knowing, witnessing all the process with detachment. This throwing up or ejecting the forms—which erupt as though from a volcano—includes also the ejecting of the plurality of the finite *ātmans* by the Brahman out of itself. We may use any other metaphor or simile to explain this process. But the essential nature or structure of the process should not be falsified. The Brahman has not only to be the creator, but also the absolute witness (*sākṣi*) of the world process. What is wanted is the concept of the witness of all (*sarvasākṣi*) and of the eternal witness (*sadāsākṣi*), which, to the degree that it is only a witness, is unaffected by what it witnesses.

The above difficulties cannot be overcome even in the philosophies of Nimbārka, Śrīpati, etc., who accept both identity and difference between the Brahman, the finite *ātman*, and the material world. Nimbārka hesitates to accept the identity of Being between the Brahman and the *ātman*; for if they are identical in Being (*sattā, svarūpa*), there will be no difference left in the state of salvation, but some difference is important for Nimbārka. As a follower of the devotional tradition, he is not prepared to accept complete identity in the state of salvation as Śaṅkara and Bhāskara do. But if it is not accepted, what is there to prevent the emancipated *ātman* to start the world process again? Have we to say that the Supreme Spirit has always to be on the watch that its energy does not enmesh the liberated *ātman* again? This will be too much of a burden to place on the shoulders of the Brahman to keep an eye on the infinite number of liberated *ātmans* and the infinite number of the unliberated. But if, as Śaṅkara and Bhāskara say, the *ātman* becomes one with the Supreme Being by recognizing that it is its own original I-am, the finite is merged in the Supreme like the wave in the ocean. And when the energy of the Brahman creates another *ātman* like the water expanse a new vortex, appropriating experiences like the vortex swallowing water, the one created will no longer the one emancipated.

But Nimbārka accepts identity by nature between the Brahman and the *ātman* (*svābhāvika-abheda*). This identity is, in plain words, only similarity. (Here we may think of *kalā* and *vidyā*, limited powers of action and knowledge which somehow percolate into the nature of the finite *ātman* from the infinite power of the Supreme Being.) Between the Brahman and the material world, both the relations hold true. But one point may not be intelligible. How can there be identity of Being between the material world and the Brahman, if it cannot be present between the *ātman* and the Brahman? If there has to be identity of Being between the material cause and its effect, as between clay and the pot made out of it, then it ought to be present not only between the material world and the Brahman, but also between the *ātman* and the Brahman. Both the *ātmans* and the material world, according to Nimbārka, are eruptions from the Brahman, eruptions of his energy (*śakti-vikṣepa*). How can eruptions be transformations (*pariṇāmas*)? And how can eternal realities like the *ātmans* and Prakṛti be results of transformations? Such questions cannot find satisfactory answers in Nimbārka's philosophy. The fact or truth is that for the Vedānta—this ought to be true of any philosophy of the Spirit—the Being of everything is the Being of the Brahman; all forms, all things of the world, including the finite *ātmans*, are rooted in the Being of the Brahman or in the Being that is the Brahman. How are we to interpret this truth? The best way to explain it is to say: The material world and the *ātmans* are identical in Being (i.e., ontologically), in *svarūpa* as we interpreted the term, with the Brahman, for they have no separate Being of their own; but in form (*svabhāyena*) or by nature they are different from each other and from the Brahman. But are they not, as modifications or transformations of the energy (*śakti*) of the Brahman, identical in form, by nature (*svabhāyena*) also with the

Brahman? We have to answer in the affirmative; for in the re-transformation of the forms, or their absorption, they become one with the energy (*śakti*)[33] of the Brahman; and the energy of the Brahman is part and parcel of his Being. But as forms, as phenomena merely, they cannot have any place in the Brahman. My actions enter me as my character and its potencies, but not as explicit actions.

Śrīpati went further than Nimbārka and said that, in the case of both the *ātmans* and the material world, their relation to the Brahman is both identity and difference in Being as well as in nature. But he is open to the above criticism, and cannot overcome the difficulties. It is indeed possible to find some aspect of the *ātmans* and the material world to be akin to the Being and nature of the Brahman—remember that Being is never empty Being, if it is Being at all—and some other aspect different. But we have also to explain the difficulties discussed above. We have to note that no simplified logical concepts like identity and difference can have straight application to this ultimate relation. *More basic than such concepts are those of transcendence and immanence, which are essential to interpret the Vedānta Aphorisms above mentioned.*

The Caitanya school, as presented by Baladeva, accepts both identity and difference; but when confronted with the difficulties, it takes shelter behind the adjectival concept of "unthinkable" or "inconceivable." That is, as mentioned already, the relation between the Brahman, the *ātmans*, and the material world is inconceivable or inexplicable identity-cum-difference. Really, inexplicability pervades the whole spatio-temporal-causal world. I cannot explain why I have come to be at all. Why and how did I start to be a finite being and when did the event occur? Why are there any finite beings? Is there any necessity in their coming into being? If the relation mentioned is inexplicable, how can we justifiably ask the rival schools to accept our truth, as the justification will be inexplicable? If the relation is like Māyā, which, besides being a force, energy (*śakti*), is regarded as the principle of inexplicability, then this identity-cum-difference will be absorbed into the principle of Māyā as two of its patterns of its activity; and the whole system of Baladeva can be absorbed into that of Śaṅkara as we have finally interpreted it, that is, by not viewing Māyā as merely a negation of negations, but taking into consideration its positive aspect also—which the Advaita itself did—and regarding it as the potency of Being that is the Brahman. Otherwise, this ultimate, inexplicable identity-cum-difference becomes a dogma or only a platform (*abhyupagama-siddhānta*) of this school.

It is not necessary to say much about Vijñānabhikṣu's position. There is the mystery of creation, which is best expressed by the word Māyā, the inexplicable force (*śakti*), which because of its inherent factor of limit (*niyati*) and measurability (*māna* and *meya*) produces the urge in us to explain it (*nirvacana*). The urge is essential for practical activity (*karma*); for the world which Māyā creates is the world of action (*karma-mayam jagat*), although called the world of the manifold of names and forms. But these names and forms are not empty names and forms, but vortexes of forces, acting on one another and on us, and they can be controlled only by our acting on them. As practical activity, even if evil, is patterned and so controlled by limit (*niyati*, *vidhi*, *vidhāna*) and measure, we have to know what exactly the nature and structure of the limit and measure are of the centres of the forces with which we have to deal. The supply of this knowledge is explanation. But this is an explanation within Māyā, but not of Māyā. However, we want to push our explanation beyond limits, beyond the source of the limit (*niyati*) itself and so get into difficulties. Kant showed in his "Transcendental Dialectic" how we land in contradictions when we attempt to explain the totality of the world in terms of what lies within the world. Similarly, many Vedāntins landed in difficulties when they attempted to offer us explanations—which are forms of the limit (*niyati*) supplied by Māyā—of what lies beyond the limit, to the source of the limit itself. "What kind of cause is the Brahman with reference to the world of souls and matter?" is a question that uses the idea of cause to explain what transcends the world of cause and effect (*kārya-kāraṇa-prapañca*). But the question was raised and the spiritual leaders attempted answers. I cannot answer even the question: How does the waking self witness the actions of the dream self, if the two are different as shown by the former shaking off even the effects of the dream after waking, and if the waking self itself is not dreaming? To be the dream self in some way and yet be different from it is not logically explicable. But we all live through the experience. *Or should we not here make transcendence-immanence a logical concept? Should not logicians accept and incorporate it into their discipline?*[34]

Thus Vijñānabhikṣu also lands in contradictions. He treats the soul and matter as two forms of energy (*śakti*) of the Brahman, but says that the Brahman is only a support-cause (*ādhāra-kāraṇa*) of creation. But if the souls and matter are the energy of the Brahman, i.e., his potency, how can anybody accept that the Brahman is only the arena on which the drama of creation takes place? How can we separate the Brahman and his energy and allow the former to keep aloof and the latter to create the world? This may satisfy the demand that the Brahman should be unaffected by what happens in creation; for my table, as the support of my books, is unaffected by the wear and tear of the books. But this view goes right against the teaching of the *Aiteraya Upaniṣad*, according to which the Brahman enters every soul (person) as its I-am, without which the physical body does not work. Even the cosmos (the Logos) does not work without the activation by the Brahman as an I-am. This view of the support-cause violates also logic and experience. It violates logic because, as we have already discussed, the being or the power of any object cannot be different from the being of the object itself; ontologically, they are the same. It does violence to our experience because what we call our power, energy, or potency originates in our character, our structured being, and cannot have an existence of its own. We enter into all our activities and acknowledge them, saying: "I do this, I do that," and so on. How I do it, whether completely involved and egotistic (*sakāma-karma*) or both involved and detached[35] (*niṣkama-karma*) as the *Bhagavadgītā* says, is a different question. The Brahman has somehow to be both immanent in the world and yet be transcendent. What kind of support can the Brahman be to the world? The being of the world is the Being of the Brahman; he supports the world by supplying its being, by entering it. The names and forms of the world will be mere sounds and lifeless skeletons or sketches with no power or efficiency without the immanent Brahman like the stars a drunkard may see. It may well be noted that the Sanskrit word *sattā* (Being) means also *śakti* (power, energy, capability, etc.).

(iv) Nature of the Supreme Witness

Some explanation is needed of the idea of witness consciousness (*sākṣi-caitanya*), the importance of which has not been noticed even by Indian writers so far. In the

West, its significance has been brought to the forefront recently by Husserl. But it can be traced to even Descartes, and more so to Spinoza. How can Descartes posit two absolutely disparate substances like mind and matter? For if they are so disparate as he thought, how can the mind of Descartes know that there is matter at all? To have this knowledge, mind must be able to know not only itself, but also matter—which means that mind is the witness (*sākṣi*) of itself as knowing matter. In the live act of cognizing matter, mind's being a witness of itself as knowing matter may not be recognized; but after the act, and in the reflection of consciousness, it appears as "I know that I know *X*." It then comes to the surface.

The act of cognizing matter, the aspect of mind knowing itself as cognizing matter and thereby comprehending both itself and matter, is more or less explicitly accepted by Spinoza—although one may say that even Descartes had the idea in the background of his mind when he said that these two are only relative substances and that God only is the absolute substance. When the relationship between mind—I am using the word in the western sense—and matter is tacitly or overtly accepted, there is no real place for occasionalism or parallelism. For if the I-am, as the witness consciousness, covers both the I-am as the subject and matter as the object of any perception, and if the witness I-am is the same as the subject I-am of perception as shown in "I know that I know *X*," then there is direct perception of matter and whatever is happening in it. The important question is not of occasionalism or parallelism but, how can the I-am detach itself from the subject cognizing the object and become the subject cognizing itself and the object? We can answer only that it is the peculiar nature, power, or energy of the I-consciousness (I-am). This experience is so common and familiar in our waking state that we do not notice it, not even ask about its significance. But this is the beginning of the appearance of the witness consciousness (*sākṣi-caitanya*), the deeper aspects of which assume spiritual significance as in the Upaniṣads. It is absurd to say that the first I in "I know that I know *X*" is all that has to be realized for the highest spiritual realization; otherwise, every one may be expected to be emancipated without even attempting to be moral. Husserl's idea of the witness consciousness stops here. But when the Vedānta speaks of God as the eternal witness, it does not refer merely to the kind of witness of which Husserl speaks. What he recognizes is the earliest stage of the higher witness, the gateway, as it were, to the experience of the higher. The higher witness is more like the waking I witnessing the dream I and its experience than the first I in "I know that I know *X*." The former comes out of the dream as though by a leap and disowns all that the dream I did. Indeed, there are some similarities between the two. The waking I is identical with, or immanent in the dream I; similarly, the first I and the second I are one in "I know that I know *X*." In the latter case, the first I cannot be so much detached or free itself from the second as the waking I from the dream I. But as one goes more and more into the transcendental depths of the I-consciousness, this detachment does, and has to become more and more pronounced until it becomes complete in the pure Brahman. Yet, without the involvement or immanence of the Brahman, nothing can happen in the world.

Except at the deepest level of the pure Brahman, the witness consciousness is, as we have previously explained, of the nature of apperception (*citta*), individual or cosmic, and functions as such.[36] Pure reasoning takes place in the witness consciousness (*sākṣi-caitanya*). Even in the abstract reasoning processes of pure mathematics, in which what we call imageless thought works, there is process, agitation, movement, disturbance (*calanam*) like unnoticeable ripples in a pool. Or they are like agitations due to movements of deep water fish. If we are in the state of correct reasoning, if we are one with the stage of cosmic apperception (the Logos); even then there is process and movement.[37] For even abstract reasoning belongs to apperception. But we have to remember that at the deepest level of the I-consciousness, i.e., the pure Brahman, apperception is absorbed, withdrawn into the I-am; witness consciousness (*sākṣi-caitanya*) which is directed outwards, and which is phenomenological consciousness in our terminology, is absorbed into the existential consciousness (*svarūpa-caitanya*).

The witness consciousness or attribute consciousness, as we have interpreted the concept, is a tremendously important concept for elucidating many doctrines. It is this consciousness that certifies that I see or cognize an object, not that the object is really what I see, but that I see an object facing, and other than, the subject of perception. It is again this consciousness that knows pure space and pure time, for they are constituents of its structure. Furthermore, it is within this consciousness that the concepts of coherence, correspondence, the criterion of pragmatism, the criterion of satisfaction and enjoyment (*tṛpti, bhoga*, or enjoyment which is also a sense of accomplishment) are realized. We have already explained how they are realized. To repeat: taking the concept of correspondence between the idea and the object, we cannot explain, so long as we remain within the domain of the dualism of mind and matter, how the correspondence can be verified at all. But then we are ignoring the basic question: If mind and matter are so completely outside each other, how can the mind know at all that there is a material object outside, with which its idea is said to correspond? It knows that there is an object outside; and this knowledge is possible because of the witness consciousness witnessing both the subject and the object of the original cognitive act. The witness consciousness can then find out whether the idea and the object correspond to each other, for it comprehends both. In the case of coherence, if *S*, the subject, sees *A, B, C,* and *D*, then to see the coherence of the four, *S* must assume the form of *W*, the witness consciousness, retaining the cognitive experience *S–A* (*S* knowing *A*), which is brought successively into the cognitive experience of *S–B*, *S–C*, and *S–D*, and next relating *A, B, C,* and *D* and later absorbing *S* into itself (i.e., *W*). Without *S* rising to the level of *W*, cognition of coherence is not possible. We should not forget that *S* is not a different entity from *W* except in function. Similarly, the confirmative cognition that the bottle of white crystals is sugar, obtained by tasting the substance, belongs to *W*; for *S* tastes the sweet substance and the cognition that it is really sugar arises in *W* after the perception and enjoyment of sweetness. Without the acceptance of witness consciousness, one cannot explain how the idea of these criteria arises at all, and how they can be applied or even taken to be verifiable. The witness consciousness or the phenomenological consciousness covers both the subject and the object, mind and matter, and is more complex than what it is generally taken to be. To say, however, that it *covers* both mind and matter is to over-simplify the situation; for neither matter nor mind is simple.

NOTES

[1]Rājānka Ramākaṇṭha: *Commentary on the Bhagavadgītā.*

[2]See K. C. Pandey: *Abhinavagupta*, and *Comparative Aesthetics* 2 vols., and P. V. Kane: *History of Sanskrit Poetics.*

[3]See *Śaiva Upaniṣads, Vaiṣṇava Upaniṣads, Yoga Upaniṣads*, and *Śākta Upaniṣads.*

[4]See P. N. Srinivasachari: *The Philosophy of Bhedābheda*, Book I, and P. T. Raju: *Idealistic Thought of India*, pp. 150–54. See also L. Śrīnivāsācārya: *Darśanodaya*, pp. 188–91.

[5]P. N. Srinivasachari: *The Philosophy of Bhedābheda*, pp. 179 fol.

[6]See S. N. Dasgupta: *A History of Indian Philosophy*, Vol. V, Chapter XXXVI.

[7]See S. N. Dasgupta: *A History of Indian Philosophy*, Vol. III, Chapter XXI, S. Radhakrishnan: *Indian Philosophy*, Vol. II, pp. 751 fol., P. T. Raju: *Idealistic Thought of India*, pp. 158 fol., and P. N. Srinivasachari: *The Philosophy of Bhedābheda*, pp. 183 fol.

[8]See P. T. Raju: *Idealistic Thought of India*, pp. 166 fol., S. N. Dasgupta: *A History of Indian Philosophy*, Vol. IV, pp. 320 fol., and S. Radhakrishnan: *Indian Philosophy*, Vol. II, pp. 756 fol.

[9]P. T. Raju: *Idealistic Thought of India*, pp. 173 fol., and S. N. Dasgupta: *A History of Indian Philosophy*, Vol. III, pp. 445 fol.

[10]Cp. Śaṅkara's view.

[11]Ibid., p. 446.

[12]P. T. Raju: *Idealistic Thought of India*, pp. 170 fol., and S. N. Dasgupta: *A History of Indian Philosophy*, Vol. IV, pp. 396 fol.

[13]P. T. Raju: *Idealistic Thought of India*; pp. 163 fol., and S. N. Dasgupta: *A History of Indian Philosophy*, Vol. V, pp. 173 fol. Dasgupta places him in the 14th century.

[14]One has to be careful in translating the words *svarūpa* and *svabhāva*. Literally translated, *svarūpa* means "own form" and *svabhāva* "own being." But the meanings they acquired in philosophical literature are just the opposite. *Svarūpa* means one's constitutive form and so one's own being. *Svabhāva* means one's nature, essence, form, character, characteristic.

[15]P. T. Raju: *Idealistic Thought of India*, p. 139.

[16]Ibid., pp. 135 fol., S. Radhakrishnan: *Indian Philosophy*, Vol. II, pp. 731 fol., and S. Radhakrishnan: *History of Philosophy: Eastern and Western*, Vol. I, pp. 381 fol.

[17]*Spanda* corresponds to agitation, disturbance in the pure *ātman* of the Vedānta, and in Prakṛti of the Sāṅkhya.

[18]See P. T. Raju: *Introduction to Comparative Philosophy*, p. 242.

[19]S. Radhakrishnan: *Indian Philosophy*, Vol. II, pp. 722 fol., S. N. Dasgupta: *A History of Indian Philosophy*, Vol. V, Chapter XXXIV, and Violet Paranjyoti: *Śaiva Siddhānta.*

[20]See S. Radhakrishnan: *Indian Philosophy*, Vol. II, pp. 734 fol., S. Radhakrishnan (editor): *History of Philosophy: Eastern and Western*, Vol. I, pp. 401 fol., and Bhaskararāya: *Commentary on Lalitāsahasranāma.*

[21]Bhartṛhari, the great philosopher of grammar, regards the Word itself as the highest Brahman, calling it the Sound Brahman (*śabdabrahman*). But the Śāktas give it a lower place than that of the highest Brahman and use a different terminology. However, both the grammarians and the Śāktas believe that there is an essential relation between names (words) and things, whatever be the language used and whatever be the names given to things. The relationship, according to them, has spiritual roots.

[22]*Vedānta Sūtras*, II, 1 and 2 chapters. [23]Ibid., IV, 1, 3.

[24]In fact, the commentators themselves, including Śaṅkara, wrote longer comments on the causality aphorisms than on the realization aphorism, which mislead us into thinking that the latter is not primary. But what for are the Upaniṣads, on which the *Aphorisms* are written, except for *aṇubhūti* or realization or experience?

[25]Cp. also Wittgenstein's view that the world is my world, which in a way supports the theory of Mead and Dewey that even animals are created with specific, limited cognitive potentialities. Their world is limited to their potentialities. All this means that the subject of experience is part and parcel of the world and that the horizons of the world are limited to the spread of the subject's cognitions and actions.

[26]Cp. the picture of the Cosmic Person by the *Bhagavadgītā*; creating, sustaining, and destroying are the three basic features of the universe which cannot be gainsaid. Only in pure Being are they transcended.

[27]The sub-schools of the Advaita adopt different explanations, but we cannot enter into them here for want of space.

28One does not understand why the Advaitins explain Māyā Śakti of the Brahman in terms negative (cp. the four-cornered negation), while regarding it as positive (*bhāvapadārtha*) in deep sleep and as the creative force. However, Bhāskara's view is more like *avacchedavāda* and the *upādhivāda* of the Advaita sub-schools than *pariṇāmavāda*.

29Cp. *Śvetāśvatara Upaniṣad*, 6, 8. *ekaivaśakti vividhaiva śrūyate* (the same *śakti* is heard of as many)

30One should not be misled by the Nyāya-Vaiśeṣika terminology with reference to causation (*kāraṇatvam, hetutvam*, etc.). They have, for instance, the concept of *ādhāra-kāraṇa*, support-cause. The table on which my book lies is the support-cause of my book. For some philosophers this idea is absurd. Indeed, for a philosophy like Hegel's, in which the whole reality is one organic whole, everything can be the cause of everything else in different ways. But the Nyāya-Vaiśeṣika is not a philosophy of organism, but of rank pluralism. Cp. also the meanings of the terms, cause, reason, ground, occasion, etc., in western logical and philosophical terminology. Vijñānabhikṣu, for instance, may say that fire is the *ādhāra-kāraṇa* of the burning power; even the Nyāya-Vaiśeṣika speaks of substance as the *samavāya-kāraṇa* of its qualities, it is the cause of the inherence of qualities, but still it is a type of *ādhāra-kāraṇa*.

31The Indian and also the western readers who know Sanskrit should understand the word *svarūpa* as Being and *svabhāva* as nature. I have referred already to the confusion which the literary use of the words creates. I was myself at one time in this confusion and depended on the general translations. For *rūpa* means colour, form, etc., and *bhava* means being, becoming, etc., in ordinary language; and the translators did their work without right insight into the structure of the system. The same difficulty about identity and difference "in Being" and "in Nature" arises with the idea of Trinity in Christian theology, and very few theologians seem to have given an adequate explanation. The real Trinity in the Vedānta is the Brahman, the finite *ātman*, and the material world. This idea raises a more serious problem than that of the unity of the Trinity of Brahma, Viṣṇu, and Śiva, the three aspects of creation, maintenance, and destruction in and of the universe, which constitute the flow of Becoming in which we find ourselves. For how can the same unity be both Life and Death? Or are Life and Death the same? This also is a serious problem.

32Remember the *Maṇḍūkya Upaniṣad* speaking of the three states (*avasthās*)—waking, dream, and deep sleep—of the *ātman*. But these states are the *vivartas* of the *ātman*, not its *pariṇāmas*.

33*Śakti* itself has to be regarded as being included in the *svarūpa* of the Brahman, just as my character and capabilities have no being of their own separate from me. Or in the terminology of the Advaita tradition, at the stage of the Brahman which is the all-inclusive I-am, even *tatasthalakṣaṇas* of the worldly stage have to become or enter the state of *svarūpa-lakṣaṇas* and be merged in them; for there is nothing outside the Being of the Brahman.

34It looks that transcendental logic ought to start here.

35This is the same as being both immanent and transcendent in my activity, the ideal kind of action, or life of works, taught by the *Bhagavadgītā*.

36Reasoning to be correct has to be detached from all egoistic involvement and will then be a function of witness consciousness.

37The Advaita accepts three stages of the I-consciousness with reference to internal disturbance or activity. (a) The pure Brahman is the completely undisturbed Being; (b) The Antaryāmin (Inner Controller) who controls and coordinates all the activities of the individual souls, the active Logos, is only slightly disturbed; and (c) The Kṣetrajña, the knower or the subject of the individual's horizon of experience, which constitutes his body, is the most disturbed or agitated. This agitation or disturbance is due to activity. The activity of forming theoretical ideas even at the level of abstract logic and mathematics is also activity. One can experience for oneself in abstract thinking that some process is going on, in him or his being. One may call it *spanda* or vibration of being, as Śaivism does, or agitation or disturbance as the others do.

Chapter XV

The Philosophy of the Bhagavadgītā

1. INTRODUCTION

The *Bhagavadgītā* is the most important, the most beautiful, and the most widely read of the popular philosophical works of India. It is a part of the great epic, *Mahābhārata*, and as such belongs to the Sātvata, also called the Bhāgavata, branch of the Vaiṣṇava religion. Another great epic, the *Bhāgavata*, belongs to the same sect and gives an account of the life of Kṛṣṇa, who belonged to the clan of Yādavas. The *Mahābhārata* gives the story (history) of the clan of the Bharatas. Both clans belong to the same period, and Kṛṣṇa of the Yādava clan and Arjuna of the Bharata clan were not only friends, but also relatives, Arjuna marrying Kṛṣṇa's sister. But the Bharata clan was divided in itself. Dhṛtarāṣṭra and Pāṇḍu were two brothers belonging to the Bharata clan. As Dhṛtarāṣṭra, the elder brother, was born blind, Pāṇḍu became the king, but died earlier than his brother. The sons of Dhṛtarāṣṭra, called Kauravas, became jealous of the sons of Pāṇḍu, called Pāṇḍavas,[1] and through intrigues and phony gambling, sent them to exile for fourteen years. But when the period of exile was over, the Kauravas refused to return the possessions of the Pāṇḍavas, who were ready to accept much less than was their due. Hence a war ensued, in which the Aryan tribes of the time took either side. The war was so destructive and devastating that it is said that it brought about the downfall of the Aryan supremacy in India. We can say that it was at least the beginning of the downfall.

The Pāṇḍavas were five brothers, of whom Arjuna was the third. As the story of the *Bhagavadgītā* goes, Arjuna, when he saw his own cousins, kinsmen and friends on the other side, ready to exchange blows with him and get killed, and when he realized that he had to destroy them, felt so dejected that he wanted to throw his bow and arrows, retire to the forest, and be a recluse. Kṛṣṇa was his charioteer, saw Arjuna's mental and moral condition, taught him the truth about the world, man, and ethics, and finally persuaded him to fight. The ethical question is not whether the men on the other side are our kinsmen, but whether we are doing our duty. But why should we do our duty, if it requires the killing of our own kinsmen? For duty is not based upon our sentiments, likes and dislikes, but upon the nature of reality. By not performing our duty, we cut ourselves off from reality and become unreal or untrue to ourselves; we shall be strangers to our own being; we surrender our selves to our likes and dislikes, but not to our real being.

The *Bhagavadgītā*, often called simply *Gītā*, came to be known to the West towards the end of the 18th century as an important philosophical poem. It was perhaps known much earlier, even during the Roman times, but attracted little attention. Wilhelm von Humbolt said of it that it was the most beautiful, and perhaps the one truly philosophical poem of all known literature, and thanked providence for giving him life long enough to come to know about the book.[2] Its importance for the Indian thinkers can be gauged from the fact that it is regarded as one of the three basic works (*prasthānatraya*) of the Vedāntic schools and is commented upon not only by the Vaiṣṇava schools, to which it originally belonged, but also by the Śaiva[3] and even by Śaṅkara, who, so far as his Vedānta goes, refused to accept the Vaiṣṇava and Śaiva Āgamas as authoritative for the reason that they were not Vedic. Then why did he accept the *Gītā*, which is a part of the *Mahābhārata*, a Vaiṣṇava work? The only reason seems to be that it was the most popular, accepted by all as teaching the essence of the Veda, and it could hardly be ignored by any one, if he wanted to spread the truth which he considered to be in his philosophy. Hence, Śaṅkara, Rāmānuja, Nimbārka, Vallabha, Madhva, Ramākaṇṭha, Jñāneśvar and a host of others commented on it, reading into it their own philosophies. Even in this century, B.G. Tilak wrote his *Gītārahaśya* (The Secret of the *Gītā*), showing that the book did not teach quietism, but an active life. Mahatma Gandhi also gave *Gītā* his own interpretation and called it his solace and guide, which he would open whenever confused.

It is difficult to fix the date of the *Gītā* or that of the *Mahābhārata*. It may be assigned to the 5th century[4] B.C. In presenting its philosophy also, one encounters a great difficulty, in view of the many commentaries finding different philosophies in it and interpreting the many technical terms in different ways. Then, what does the *Gītā*, apart from the commentaries, teach? The only way to answer the question is to accept the direct meanings of its words, forgetting for the moment the philosophies of the commentators. We have also to keep in mind that it is part of the *Mahābhārata*, a Vaiṣṇava work, and that its whole teaching in the mouth of Kṛṣṇa is meant to persuade Arjuna to act and to dissuade him from renouncing action.

The *Gītā* is meant to teach yoga; but every chapter of the book is called a yoga. Even the first chapter describing how Arjuna became dejected is called the "Yoga of Arjuna's Dejection." As we have seen, the work yoga can mean and has been made to mean any kind of achievement, the object achieved, the process or method of achieving it, the teaching of the achievement, and also the subsidiaries to that achievement. How Arjuna got dejection, how he "achieved" it, is also a yoga. If the practice of meditation is a yoga, then the procuring of the kind of food that contributes to the fixing of mind and to its steadiness is also a yoga. If that food is the best from the spiritual point of view, then the discovery of the best in each of the classes—foods, men, animals, trees, mountains, and every other class—is also a yoga. Then all the topics on which the *Gītā* speaks are yogas.

Kṛṣṇa is regarded as a historical person like Arjuna. His name occurs in the Upaniṣads.[5] But his historicity is mixed up with so much mythology that it is difficult to separate the two. In Indian mythology, imagination runs riot and in the *Bhāgavata* the idea of Kṛṣṇa as the embodiment of divine love was turned into making him the husband of thousands and the lover of other thousands of women, mysteriously spending his nights with all of them simultaneously. Is not the loving God present in the hearts of all his devotees simultaneously? But in the *Bhagavadgītā* little of the amorous rapture is found, and Kṛṣṇa becomes the teacher of stern duty and shows not his loving nature, but the dreadful, destructive aspect of the Logos or the World-Spirit (Viśvarūpa). Kṛṣṇa's teaching in essence is: Follow the path of the World Spirit; if it has the creative, sustaining, and loving aspects, it has also the destructive aspects; you cannot follow what you like, and shrink from what you dislike; as part and parcel of the World Spirit, you have to follow every one of its aspects, even the destructive; if you flinch from your duties because of likes and dislikes, you separate yourself from the World Spirit, in whom you have your being; in fact, there is nothing like destruction, for everything comes out of Being and re-enters Being, nothing comes out of Non-being and nothing enters Non-being; and when you realize this truth, there is no fear, no sorrow, no dejection.

The *Bhagavadgītā* is said to give the quintessence of the Vedas and the epics. The systems may quarrel with one another about the ways of salvation and about the nature of the Brahman, God, man, and the world. But the *Gītā* wants to reconcile all the schools and systems, showing each its place in a total philosophy of life and each yoga (*mārga*, way) its own usefulness. It is a book for inspiration and general guidance in all contexts of life. To dismiss it for the reason that it upheld caste duties would be like dismissing Plato and Aristotle for upholding slavery, Judaism and Islam for insisting on circumcision and prohibition of pork, and Christianity for its inquisitions. It is because of the catholicism of its teachings that the Vedāntins of diverse views found it not only useful and necessary, but also possible to write commentaries.

2. THE DOCTRINES

THE BRAHMAN AND GOD The *Gītā* is essentially theistic in its teachings,[6] although Śaṅkara thought that it taught his own supra-personal non-dualism. The Brahman is personal and Kṛṣṇa calls himself both the Brahman and God. The world including the *ātmans* is only a part of him, for he transcends[7] the world. This position is pan-entheism, advocated by K. C. F. Krause[8] in German theology; and he was acquainted with the *Gītā*, the Upaniṣads, and Indian philosophy in general. Kṛṣṇa adds that the Brahman or God is not to be found in the objects of the world, but they are in him.[9] Foolish people think that God, who is originally unmanifest (*avyakta*) has become manifest (*vyakta*); but in spite of his manifestations, God is far above them.[10] These people do not know God's highest nature (*param bhāvam*). He is not visible, because he is shrouded by his Māyā (*yogamāyā*)[11] which expresses his yogic power. God is the unmanifest (*avyakta*) from our point of view, but he is manifest to himself, as he is self-conscious.[12] He is really one and undivided, yet appears to be divided into the objects.[13] All the living objects, even the non-living (as Prakṛti is his own power) are only his parts.[14] He fills everything. Here we find it necessary to reconcile the two statements, viz., that God is not in the world, and that he fills everything and everything is his part. The *Gītā* intends to say that God is not only transcendent, but also immanent. There is nothing other than God. It is to explain such contradictions that Śaṅkara introduces the concept of Māyā. However, we should not identify the *Gītā* with Śaṅkara's Advaita.

There are two kinds of *ātmans* (Puruṣas)[15] in the world, the transient (*kṣara*) and the intransient (*akṣara*),[16] which is also called the Unmanifest (Avyakta). The transient is all the living creatures (*bhūtas, jīvas*) and the intransient is the onlooker (*kūṭastha*, one who sits in the group, the collection of mind, senses, etc., and is also called *sākṣi*). But the highest Ātman (Puruṣottama) is other than the two. In explaining what the intransient *ātman* (*akṣara*) is, the commentators differ from one another. It may be the witness consciousness (*sākṣicaitanya, Jīvasākṣi*) of Śaṅkara and Madhva, the World Soul (*jīvottama*) of Madhva, the Logos (*Mahān Ātmā*) of the *Kaṭha Upaniṣad*, or the unmanifest stage of God ready to create the world, as in the Pāñcarātra. The word unmanifest is used in two meanings. In one meaning, it is masculine[17] in gender and means God himself in a logically prior state to the manifest (*vyakta*). In the second meaning, it is neuter[18] in gender and means Prakṛti, as in the Sāṅkhya. Now, what this passage means is that God in his pure nature, without reference to the manifest world, is higher than he himself as the unmanifest. This concept has meaning only with reference to the manifest manifold.

Then what is God as different from himself as the Unmanifest? If the source of beings is he as the Unmanifest, and if this Unmanifest is, therefore, Being, what is God as different from it? He cannot be Being; yet, he cannot be non-being, for Non-being cannot do anything, whereas God is ultimately the creator of everything. So God by himself is neither Being nor Non-being.[19]

MĀYĀ AND PRAKṚTI As in the philosophy of Caitanya and Baladeva, we find in the *Gītā* three energies or powers of God, which Kṛṣṇa, as God, claims to be his own. Māyā is the highest of the three, it belongs to God's very being and his power of lordship (*yogamaiśvaram*), through which he rules and controls the world. It is called also the mystery of his yoga (*yogamāyā*),[20] by which he can be many and yet remain always the one, pure, and perfect. It is through this Māyā that he conceals himself from the world and the *ātmans*. In addition to Māyā, God has two powers, both called Prakṛtis,[21] the higher (*parā*) and the lower (*aparā*).[22] The finite *ātmans* constitute the higher. The lower produces the objects of the material world through the three Attributes—the Transparent, the Active, and the Dark (*sattva*, *rajas*, and *tamas*). The evolution of the world out of this lower Prakṛti is the same as in the Sāṅkhya. It is not clear in the Gītā whether this Prakṛti undergoes self-transformation as Rāmānuja says or a non-self-transforming process (*vivarta*) as Śaṅkara says. We are told only that, through this Prakṛti as the cause, the world arises (*viparivartate*).[23]

THE THEORY OF ETHICAL ACTION As the *Bhagavadgītā* is meant to persuade Arjuna to take to a life of action, it gives a fairly significant analysis of ethical action. Action is divided into two kinds: that which is motivated by some personal benefit (*kāmyakarma*) and that which is not so motivated (*niṣkāmakarma*). As the Sanskrit word *kāma* is generally translated by the word desire, the two kinds of action are translated as "action to fulfil a desire" and "desireless action" and also as "motivated or motived action" and "unmotivated or unmotived action." But these translations may be terribly misleading. For how can there be any desireless action, unmotived action, for it may then be aimless action? Man does not act without a purpose. Even the ass does not move without a purpose, without a desire to eat hay. Is the teaching of the *Gītā* then unnatural? If we are led by the words "desireful" and "desireless" and "motived" and "unmotived," we turn the *Gītā* teaching into an absurdity. To understand the distinction made by the *Gītā*, we have to take into consideration the traditional distinctions made by the *Mīmāmsā* and also the explanations given by the *Gītā* itself.

Traditionally the distinction refers to two kinds of action—the non-obligatory and the obligatory. The non-obligatory actions (*naimittika* or *kāmya karmas*) are those which a man performs for enjoying the fruit of those actions. They may, indeed, be ethical, not necessarily unethical. If a man performs some worship of God or prays to him for obtaining children or wealth, he is performing a non-obligatory action. But if he prays to God or does some charities without any reference to the results, his actions are obligatory; for prayer and charities are obligations. The Mīmāmsā enjoined certain sacrifices to gods, to ancestors, to the teachers, and to all living beings of all the worlds, and also the duties pertaining to one's caste and stage of life as obligatory; for the performance of such sacrifices and such duties sustains the universe and society. But it recommended certain other sacrifices including certain charities, etc., for men who desired many sons, wealth, and so on. But it is not obligatory to have many sons, to become wealthy, etc. These are called desireful actions or actions with a desire. We may think also of two men helping the police to catch a murderer. Both of them are doing what is ethical. But one may do it for the reward it fetches, promised by the police. The other may do it as a social obligation; he would do it whether or not there is a reward. He does it for sustaining society, for social welfare. Similarly, all duties for sustaining the world and society are obligatory and are called actions without desire (*kāma*), desire meaning one's own personal desire. And all actions meant for enjoying their results are called actions with desire. Thus which English words we use to explain the distinction is important. I prefer the words which are often used and which are the least misleading, viz., selfish and egoistic actions (*sakāmakarmas*) and self-less and non-egoistic actions (*niṣkāmakarmas*).

In the absolute, unconditional sense, there is no desireless action. Even the desire to do the right action is also a desire. Absolutely desireless action belongs to the machine, the inorganic world. Desirelessness, in the ethics of the *Gītā*, means the absence of the desire to enjoy oneself the results aimed at. Otherwise, the action is an egoistic action. The *Gītā* makes the point clear in two ways. *First*, it says that God himself is the desire (*kāma*) in men that is not opposed to the law[24] (*dharma*) of reality or the universe. If God himself is desire that is in accordance with the law of the universe, there can be no way of escaping every type of desire, just as there is no way of escaping every type of action, e.g., breathing and eating. Thus desireless action means non-egoistic action, the desire behind which is the law of the universe. So it is better that the term desireless action is not used. The kind of desire that is one of God's forms is the law that is the support of the world and society; and without action according to that desire men and the world will be destroyed.[25] *Secondly*, Kṛṣṇa says that mean folk act only when they desire the result for themselves and that Arjuna should, therefore, take shelter in reason[26] (*buddhi*). He should act in accordance with his rational dictates and do that action with all the skill needed, *for yoga is skill fulness*[27] *in action*. The rational is only of one type, but the irrational is of many,[28] that is, those who are motivated by rational desire act in only one way, but those who are motivated by egoistic motives act in different ways. For instance, there is only one answer to the question: What is 2+2? But wrong answers are infinite in number. One who performs actions with the law of the universe as the guide will not be bound by the results of those actions.[29] All actions except those of sacrifice (*yajña*) keep man in bondage.[30] But the word sacrifice is given a new meaning, which we have already noticed in the chapter on the Upaniṣads. It is giving away, it is offering to gods, beasts, plants, ancestors, and even the spirits of the lower world, so that all remain satisfied and work for the welfare of man and the world. Living beings are born of food, food out of rain, rain out of sacrifice, sacrifice out of action, action out of Brahma (one of the Hindu Trinity), and Brahma out of the non-transient Puruṣa (*akṣara*). Thus the Brahman, which is all-pervading, is installed in sacrifice[31] (*yajña*). God himself is eternally active, but not with any motive or desire; and he is active, although he has everything he wants.

One should understand what is right action, what is wrong action, and what is non-action.[32] Wrong action is the prohibited action. The wise man is he who sees non-action in action and action in non-action. Non-action does not mean non-movement of limbs; for then even life (*sarīrayātrā*) becomes impossible.[33] Ethical non-action is action without any egoity. Merit and demerit, the results of action, do not accrue to the agent of such an action. For he knows that he is doing the action for the sake of law (*dharma*), not for his own sake, and that it is not he, as the *ātman*, but as the body, which is a product of Prakṛti and its Attributes, that does the action. Man should perform all actions as skillfully as he can and surrender the fruit to God, saying: "Lord, thy will is done."

Renunciation (*tyāga*) is of three[34] types—sacrifice, charity, and penance (*tapas*). All the three are actions. They purify the soul. They are obligations to every man, who has to perform them without any attachment to the fruits (merit) that may result. One who gives up actions through ignorance is under the influence of the Attribute of Darkness (*tamas*). One who gives them up because of the trouble they involve is under the influence of the Attribute of the Active (*rajas*). Neither is right. But one who performs them without desire for their fruit is under the influence of the Attribute, the Transparent (*sattva*). He is the true renouncer of action, the true knower, the truly wise (*jñānī*).

The three initiators of action are the knower, the known, and knowledge; and the three factors of action are the agent, action, and the instruments of action.[35] Of these, the agent, action, and knowledge are of three kinds, according as they are determined by the three Attributed.[36] The knowledge that sees unity in multiplicity, the unmanifest Brahman in the manifested differences, is determined by the Transparent (*sattva*). That which sees only the differences as separate from one another is determined by the Active. And that which leads man to action without any thought is determined by the Dark. That is, the first leads man to act with the idea of the welfare of the whole universe in view; the second with the idea of the immediate result and its relevance to the agent in view; and the third without any idea of the result or as a blind need, e.g., in animals. The agent in the first, as he has no egoistic motive, is untouched by the results of action; but not the other two. Correspondingly, the agents and actions also are classified into three kinds.

In another place, action is classified into five[37] kinds, according to the kinds of causes that produce it. It may be produced by the body, the agent (*ātman*), different types of instruments, different kinds of biomotor and vital functions, and even fate as the unknown factor. The will of the agent alone cannot produce what is aimed at. All have to cooperate in the right way and all have to be favourable. Action is classified also into the three[38]—bodily action, speech, and thought (mental action). All the three have to be pure and under the guidance of the Transparent.[39]

DHARMA We have seen that the word *dharma* obtained different, but not unrelated connotations in the Mīmāmsā and Buddhism. For the Mīmāmsā, it meant either action itself or its potency, as enjoined by the Veda and as creative of the world for man. For Buddhism, it meant not only the law but also the substance of the universe and is ultimately the reality itself. In any case, it is the law, the support, the ideal of the universe; it is that which makes the universe what it is. The *Bhagavadgītā* is not particularly interested in the metaphysical problem of the ultimate dharma, but only in the *dharma* of man and society. Both Arjuna and Kṛṣṇa are eager that the law of society is preserved in any case. For the purpose, Arjuna is prepared to give up fighting, retire to the forest as an ascetic, and allow his cousins to have his kingdom. For if the rulers are killed, who else will maintain the social order?[40] The castes will then mix up, men and women become promiscuous,the foolish, the incompetent, and the vicious will become the lawmakers. The caste and tribal laws will go to the winds, and all men will go to hell. But Kṛṣṇa points out that Arjuna is indulging in psychological rationalization. In the name of preserving social order, he is going to violate that very order, by refusing to perform the duties of a warrior and defender of justice. Every man should perform the duties incumbent on his station in society. Even Kṛṣṇa, the Absolute, has his duties. He performs them, although he has nothing to gain. If he does not perform his duties, men will imitate him and the worlds will go to naught.[41] He will then be responsible for disorder, promiscuity, and ultimate destruction of the world. It is only for maintaining and defending order (*dharma*) that he, as the Brahman, takes on incarnations and punishes the wicked and destroys disorder.[42] Arjuna should, therefore, follow Kṛṣṇa and perform his duties. Here the *Gītā* shows the intimate involvement of God and his interest in the world.

There is, indeed, an opposition in the *Gītā* to the original *Mīmāmsā* philosophy of life and action, which did not include the ideal of salvation. Kṛṣṇa says that his noble teaching may be controverted by people who are engaged merely in Vedic disquisitions and who are attached to heaven, actions, their fruit, and their enjoyment.[43] They cannot meditate on God and cannot obtain salvation. They do not realize that actions are performed by the body, which is a product of Prakṛti and its Attributes, but not by the *ātman*. But as the *ātman* is different from Prakṛti and its Attributes, it should overcome its self-identification with them; yet so long as the *ātman* is within the realm of Prakṛti, it should continue to perform dutiful actions.[44] So non-egoistic action is natural, has its basis in the very nature of reality. The theory of action as enjoined by the Vedic Mīmāmsā belongs to the realm of Prakṛti;[45] man has to transcend it, because the nature of the *ātman* points to such transcendence. Kṛṣṇa's criticism of the Veda has to be interpreted as a criticism of the original Mīmāmsā as taught by Jaimini or as a criticism of the original Vedic religion of sacrifices and gods, but not as a rejection of the Veda itself. Otherwise, he would not have said that he is the Sāmaveda[46] among the Vedas and even all the Vedas.[47] As mentioned already, he gives a new meaning to the word sacrifice (*yajña*), which is a part of *dharma* according to the Mīmāmsā. Arjuna has to perform the duties of his station in his society, even if they involve the killing of his kinsmen. If he does his actions, realizing that he is doing them to fulfil his obligations, but not in personal interest, the demerit that results will not accrue to him. It goes to, and dissolves itself in the Cosmic Person. Such action is surrender to the Cosmic Person. Everything, even Arjuna and his actions, belongs to the Cosmic Person, and to the Absolute (Brahman). This surrender to God is itself sacrifice, in which the oblation is man and his actions. The sacrifice of surrender is performed in various ways.[48] Some yogis—all those who make this surrender are called yogis—surrender everything, saying that they and their actions go to the Brahman and are the Brahman. This is one-ness (*samādhi*) with the Brahman's activities, the placement of one's self in the Brahman. *We get here a new interpretation of samādhi.* Some worship sacrifice itself which is, as mentioned already, God himself. Some perform sacrifices and offer those sacrifices themselves as oblations to the Brahman. Some offer the senses as oblations to self-control; some the activities of the senses and of life also in the fire of self-control; some perform sacrifices with substances like food, some with the practice of yoga, and some with study; and others, devoted to breath-control, offer their breath to the life principle.[49] All such people are performing sacrifice, which purifies their soul. The purpose of sacrifice, as given by Kṛṣṇa, is the purification of mind and soul, not enjoyment and pleasure as given by the Mīmāmsā.

What then is *dharma*? It is all the above mentioned. It is yoga, not merely the one described by Patañjali, but all that which is mentioned by Kṛṣṇa. Thus the words *yoga* and *dharma* are given the widest meaning possible. The philosophy of yoga and *dharma* is the philosophy of the whole of life. It covers all the duties of social ethics as understood at that time and also the surrender to God. Not even one's personality can be kept back; it also has to be surrendered. It belongs to one of the Prakṛtis of God; we have to give him back what belongs to him. We have to consider ourselves to be instruments (*nimittamātras*)[50] or occasions of the processes of the Cosmic Person, not independent agents.[51]

THE WORLD SPIRIT It is for showing that we are instruments of the cosmic process that Kṛṣṇa reveals his cosmic form (*viśvarūpa*). We have seen that the Logos or the World Spirit is depicted as having different states—waking, dream, and deep sleep—in the Upaniṣads and as having different stages by the Vaiṣṇava (Pāñcarātra) and Śaiva (Pāśupata) thinkers. The *Bhāgavata* describes him in its own mythologically symbolic way as the Spirit of Love and its embodiment. The *Gītā* presents the World Spirit in its destructive aspect. The world has three aspects—creative, sustaining, and destructive. The last is found on the largest scale on battlefields. Besides, Kṛṣṇa has another reason for appearing as the devourer of every thing. He wants to demonstrate that most of the heroes on the battlefield are going to die, whatever be the feelings of Arjuna. If so, why should Arjuna, with his own personal sentiments, try to cut himself off from the World Spirit? His attitude merely strengthens his egoity, but does not stop the world process.

So Kṛṣṇa says that he, as God, is time that has grown immensely (*pravṛddha*, also means extremely old) with the intent of destruction.[52] Arjuna should, therefore, rise to the occasion, kill his enemies, and gain name and his kingdom. Really, the figure that Arjuna saw must have been terrible, the whole cosmos in its destructive aspect. But we should not draw the conclusion that God for the *Gītā* is only a destroyer and devourer of everything. We should remember that the *Gītā* is only a small part of the *Mahābhārata*, which, in its turn, is one of the group of epics of the Bhāgavata (*Śātvata*) branch of Vaiṣṇavism, some of the others being the *Bhāgavata* and the *Harivamśa*.

WAYS TO SALVATION On the face of it, the *Gītā* is not biased in favour of any one way—action, devotion, or knowledge. Its aim, like that of the whole epic literature, is to explain every one of them and to reconcile them. In fact, it speaks of many yogas (ways); but any impartial reader can see that, according to the *Gītā*, no way by itself is possible without the others. The way of action, which has to be self-less, or non-egoistic, is not possible without knowing why it has to be non-egoistic. Similarly, devotion is not possible, without knowing why we should practice self-surrender and love. Knowledge also will be useless, unless our mind is attached to God; for attachment is identification expressed in the determined effort to follow the path of reality or God. Kṛṣṇa says that the yogi who is always contented, who has self-control, who is determined and resolute, and who has surrendered his mind and reason to God, is his true devotee.[53] But such a yogi is and can be resolute, when he knows what reality is. We do not find specific mention of any one of the ways in preference to the others.

Kṛṣṇa's advice[54] in the above connection is illuminating. He asks Arjuna to fix his mind and reason on God and live in him. If Arjuna is not capable of doing so, let him desire realization through practice (*abhyāsayoga*) like the yoga of Patañjali. If he cannot go even through such practice, let him perform all ethical action for the sake of God. If he cannot perform non-egoistic actions, let him perform them as he can and renounce all the fruits of action. Knowledge is higher than the practice of yoga (Patañjali's), meditation is higher than knowledge, renunciation of the fruits of action is higher than meditation, and finally at the end peace (*śānti*) is higher than even such renunciation.[55] We may interpret this passage as meaning that every former leads to the latter, until ultimately absolute peace of mind is attained.

THE YOGAS IN THE GĪTĀ What are the ways of salvation, or yogas, taught by the *Gītā*? To answer this question, we have to leave out certain chapters like the first, called "The Yoga of Arjuna's Dejection," and "The Yoga of the Three Kinds of Faith," which deal really with some details. We shall then be left with the usual three. In fact, all the eighteen chapters, except the first, are instructions about the different topics current at the time. Chapter II, called "Sāṅkhyayoga," teaches the basic concepts of the theistic Sāṅkhya, saying that there is really nothing that vanishes at death and every being comes out of Being and re-enters it. So none need be sorry for the death of anybody. Chapter III, called "Karmayoga," teaches that every man should perform actions, and explains that those actions should be non-egoistic. Chapter IV, called the "Yoga of Knowledge as the Renunciation of Action," explains that renunciation of action is the same as the realization that the *ātman* is not really the same as Prakṛti, which is the true doer of actions and the enjoyer of their fruit, and with which the *ātman* falsely identifies itself. What is called renunciation is the performance of actions with such knowledge. Chapter V, called the "Yoga of the

Renunciation of Action," shows that knowledge and ethical action are not different, knowledge here meaning knowledge of the ultimate truth. Chapter VI, called the "Yoga of the Control of Oneself," explains how meditation can be practised. Chapter VII, called the "Yoga of the Higher and Lower Knowledge," shows how the lower forms of knowledge embody or partake of the higher. For the best[56] or the highest in every object of empirical knowledge is a form of God himself. He is the light in the sun, the best of fragrance in the earth, the life-principle in all living creatures, reason (*buddhi*) in man, etc. Chapter VIII, called the "Yoga of the Non-transient Brahman," explains that the Non-transient is the same as the unmanifest Brahman (avyakta in the masculine gender), and out of it originate all the souls. Chapter IX, called the "Yoga of the Kingly knowledge and the Kingly Secret," tells us that God pervades everything and every soul, and all objects reside in him. He creates the world by presiding over his Prakṛti and its activities. Fools think that Kṛṣṇa is a man with a physical body; they do not know his higher nature. God is impartial to all; he does not show favours to some and disfavours to others. He is in all who are devoted to him, and they are in him. The immanence of God in the world is the kingly, or royal secret; and the discovery of him is the kingly or royal knowledge.

Chapter X, called the "Yoga of Exaltations," (or *vibhūtis*), shows where the presence of God can be felt even in the objects of the world. He is the best, the highest, and the noblest of all beings—beasts, birds, men, angels, deities—and he is manifest in them. Chapter XI, called the "Yoga of the World Person," has already been described, in discussing the nature of the World Spirit. Chapter XII deals with the "Yoga of Devotion." Chapter XIII, called the "Yoga of the Field and the Knower of the Field," explains that God himself is ultimately the knower of the field, the field being Prakṛti. The finite *ātman* is the knower of the field that is the body. The *ātmans* also are forms of God, for they are forms of his higher Prakṛti. Ultimately God is the knower of everything. Himself undivided, he appears as divided, as the many. Chapter XIV called the "Yoga of the Division of the Three Attributes," shows how the three Attributes of Prakṛti can be detected not only in objects, but also in character and qualities. Chapter XV, called the "Yoga of the Supreme Person," says that the Supreme Person is God himself and that he is higher than the Non-transient (*akṣara, avyakta*). Chapter XVI, called the "Yoga of the Divine and the Satanic," gives the difference between the divine and satanic qualities in men in their ethical and spiritual relevance. Chapter XVII, called the "Yoga of the Three-fold Division of Faith," classifies faith (*śraddhā*) according to the three Attributes. *But faith is defined as what makes man become that in which he has faith.* It is not mere intellectual conviction, nor irrational belief. The warning is that one should have faith in the divine, not in anything less. Chapter XVIII, called the "Yoga of Liberation as Renunciation," explains the nature of ethical action—which has been given above—, saying that renunciation does not lie in giving up all action, but only egoistic action. One who is not attached to the fruit of one's actions attains the state of non-action.[57] Thus it is difficult to prove that the *Bhagavadgītā* is biassed in favour of any one way of salvation.

THE IDEAL MAN The ideal man, according to the *Bhagavadgītā*, is one who has realized his rational being (*prajñā*)[58] and whose reason has become steady (*sthitaprajña*).[59] He preserves his equanimity under all conditions, whether they are favourable or unfavourable, whether in grief or in joy. He does not have any egoistic desires and looks upon all events that happen without being disturbed. He does not have any attachment or longing for the objects of his senses and can withdraw his mind and senses from all objects. Attachment to objects is the destroyer of reason. For attachment breeds desire, desire leads to anger when anything unfavourable happens to the objects of desire or desire is frustrated, anger clouds mind, such clouding destroys memory, and then reason is destroyed. For reason and memory are intimately connected. So the ideal man is neither attached to the objects nor hates them. He performs all actions without any egoity and attains peace and Nirvāṇa. Such an ideal, we may say, is that of Socrates[60] and the Stoics. It answers also to Kant's conception of duty for duty's sake and Bradley's idea of "my station and its duties," irrespective of feelings and consequences. Indeed, Kṛṣṇa did not raise the question whether caste system, to which the duties he was speaking about were relevant, was ethically right or wrong. Yet he tried to give the rationale behind it. The four castes were created by God, according to character and profession.[61] We do not find any passage in which Kṛṣṇa maintains that birth is the main factor; in fact, birth is not mentioned in this stanza, though mentioned at other places. But it is taken for granted that it is included. However, we should keep in mind that, in ancient India, it was the caste system that prevented the massacre of the non-Aryans by the Aryans, although the system has outlived its use till very recently, when the Government of India abolished caste system. But the rationale of caste given by Kṛṣṇa is well worth comparing with the class system advocated by Plato. In fact, all advanced ancient societies had a caste structure, whether or not caste was determined by birth. In any case, Kṛṣṇa says that not only men but also women[62] of all castes are eligible for salvation, if they perform their duties in the spirit advocated by him. All can be ideal persons.

NOTES

[1]The Pāṇḍavas also were Kauravas, or descendants of King Kuru; but generally the sons of Dhṛtarāṣṭra are described as Kauravas, although often called Dhārtarāṣṭras.

[2]Helmuth von Glassenapp (editor): *Bhagavadgītā: Das Lied der Gottheit*, p. 9.

[3]Rājānaka Ramākaṇṭha: *Commentary on the Bhagavadgītā.*

[4]S. Radhakrishnan: *Indian Philosophy*, Vol. 1, p. 524. There is much controversy about the date, for which see also S. N. Dasgupta: *A History of Indian Philosophy*, Vol. II, pp. 549. fol.

[5]*Chāndogya Upaniṣad*, III, 17.

[6]For a detailed study of the *Gītā*, see S. Radhakrishnan: *Bhagavadgītā*, and *Indian Philosophy*, Vol. I, Chapter IX, S. N. Dasgupta: *A History of Indian Philosophy*, Vol. II, Chapter XIV, P. T. Raju: *Idealistic Thought of India*, pp. 178 fol., Franklin Edgerton: *Bhagavadgītā*, 2 vols., Aurobindo Ghose: *Essays on the Gītā*, and Mahadev Desai: *Gītā according to Gandhi.*

[7]*Bhagavadgītā*, X, 42. The reader may use any edition, Sanskrit or English.

[8]H. von Glassenapp: *Das Indienbild deutschen Denker*, pp. 61 fol.

[9]*Bhagavadgītā*, VII, 12.

[10]Ibid., VII, 24. [11]Ibid., VII, 25.

[12]That is, manifest to himself as consciousness that is Being also.

[13]Ibid., XII, 16. [14]Ibid., XV, 7.

[15]Ibid., XV, 16. [16]Ibid., XIII, 31.

[17]Ibid., II, 25 and VIII, 21, and XV, 16.

[18]Ibid., XIII, 5. Corresponding roughly to Virāt and Hiraṇyagarbha or to *natura nāturata* and *natura naturans*.

[19]Ibid., XIII, 12. This idea needs careful interpretation, as the Brahman is said to be Being itself. Note also that the term inexplicable is applied to both the Brahman and his Māyā.

[20]Ibid., VII, 25. [21]Ibid., VII, 4 and 5.

[22]In the text, (VII, 5) the word *aparā* is used for the higher Prakṛti, but it means the "other ," but not the "lower."

[23]Ibid., IX, 10. The word *viparivartate* can be analyzed into *vi* + *pari* + *vartate*. *Vartate* means "exists"; *vi* means "particularized," "formed," "much," and "differently"; *pari* means "round about" and "much." *Parivartate* means "exchanged ," "changed." Śaṅkara can make much of this word and contend that the *Gītā* teaches his *vivarta* causality.

[24]Ibid., vii, 11. Here lies the difference between Kant's "duty for duty's sake" and the *Gītā* 's "duty for duty's sake." For the latter, this duty is to be one with the law or nature of the Supreme Person, one's highest self and so to attain the good. We find the Greek and the Jewish ethics reconciled here.

[25]Ibid., II, 23. [26]Ibid., II, 49. [27]Ibid., II, 50.

[28]Ibid., II, 39 and 41. We should not interpret *buddhi* here as the way of knowledge; for Kṛṣṇa explains yoga as skill in acting and asks Arjuna to acquire that skill.

[29]Ibid., II, 51 fol. This idea is repeated several times.

[30]Ibid., III, 9. [31]Ibid., III, 14–15.

[32]Ibid., IV, 17. [33]Ibid., III, 8. [34]Ibid., XVIII, 4–6.

[35]Ibid., XVIII, 18. [36]Ibid., XVIII, 19 fol. [37]Ibid., XVII, 14. [38]Ibid., XVIII, 15.

[39]The analysis of action given by the *Gītā* is from the side of ethics and in terms of the three Attributes of Prakṛti. For a logical and metaphysical analysis of action, the interested student should study the Mīmāmsā doctrine of Dharma and the analysis of the verb in the philosophy of grammar, which we cannot discuss in this book.

[40]Ibid., I, 40–46. [41]Ibid., III, 23–24.

[42]Ibid., IV, 7–8. [43]Ibid., II, 42–43. [44]Ibid., II, 45.

[45]Op. cit. [46]Ibid., X, 22. [47]Ibid., IX, 17.

[48]Ibid., IV, 24–32.

[49]One explanation seems to be that this life principle is *mukhya-prāṇa* equated to Hiraṇyagarbha, the Logos holding together the divisions of the Universe.

[50]Ibid., XI, 33.

[51]Cp. the early Greek idea of justice, which lies in becoming one with the source of the universe, i.e., surrendering one's own being to it. This sacrifice is justice, *dharma*, *drvit*, the right, and the good.

[52]Ibid., XI, 32. The word *pravṛddha* may be interpreted as a mere adjective in the sense of "Time, the old man," or in the sense that Kṛṣṇa, as God, was fed up with the evil which the Aryan tribes were perpetrating and perpetuating and that he had grown old with the sense of evil and the intent of destruction. It is said that Kṛṣṇa, although he knew that the Aryan tribes would destroy themselves in the war, did not prevent it, as he felt that the evil resulting from the civilization of the time could be checked only by the destruction of that civilization. Otherwise, as God, he could have stopped the war and nobody could have dared to fight, if God was determined against fighting. However, such interpretations belong to the apologetics of the epics.

[53]Ibid., XII, 14. [54]Ibid., XII, 8–11. [55]Ibid., XII, 12.

[56]See *Bhagavadgītā*, Chap. X (Vibhūtiyoga) also.

[57]Ibid., XVIII, 49.

[58]The word *prajñā* may be translated as reason, or rational being. One of its synonyms is *buddhi*, which, both for the *Gītā* and the Sāṅkhya, is ontological.

[59]Ibid., II, 55–72. Cp. the idea with the Buddhist idea of the Bodhisattva.

[60]Cp. *Phaedrus*.

[61]*Bhagavadgītā*, IV, 13. [62]Ibid., IX, 32.

Chapter XVI

Contemporary Indian Philosophy

1. INTRODUCTION

Contemporay thought in India is very varied. Many old schools of thought, particularly the Vedāntic, are still quite strong, as they are religious philosophies with strong spiritual bearings. Most of the great philosophical scholars are born into them, trained in their ways of thinking, and more or less committed to them. But many schools of western thought also have made their inroads, as India was closely associated with England and the British educators introduced western philosophy into the Indian universities even before Indian philosophy was given a place. Of the western philosophies, the British, particularly the Oxford philosophies, influenced the Indian academic circles the most.[1] Of the Oxford philosophies, again, the Neo-Kantian and the Neo-Hegelian thought of T. H. Green, J. F. Caird, F. H. Bradley, and B. Bosanquet have had the strongest influence, so much so that even now metaphysical idealism, which was considered dead in the west through the efforts of the school of analysis and of logical positivism and empiricism, is a living thought in India. The reasons are simple. *First*, Oxford had its prestige for all the Indians, who were subjects of the British. *Secondly*, the attack on Indian religious thought in terms of philosophy was made mostly by missionaries trained in some form of idealism, which is the philosophy best suited to express religious experience. And philosophically trained Indians could pay back the criticisms in terms of the same idealism. The conviction of educated Indians that India's spiritual philosophies are as great as any other spiritual philosophies made them re-understand and re-interpret their own philosophies in terms of western idealism, the prestige schools of the time. And for studying western idealism, they had to study realism also and along with it all the other schools that have been critics of idealism. The work of understanding and interpreting western thought in terms of the Indian and of the Indian in terms of the western became, therefore, very important; and educated Indians, who felt a responsibility to their own culture and spiritual life, thought that such a task was an absolute necessity. Hence arose Comparative Philosophy, the protagonist of which was S. Radhakrishnan, a late President of India. However, comparative philosophy was not new to the West. Paul Deussen in Germany, and before him F. Max Müller in England, and also Paul Masson-Oursel in France did significant work in the field. But it was Radhakrishnan who brought the importance of the subject to the largest philosophical public through his works and lectures.

As may be anticipated, comparative philosophy is a very large and comprehensive field and, being a new subject without definite boundaries, aims, and methods, ends up in the hands of many in very naive forms. Radhakrishnan's aim is to show that man is basically the same in the East and the West, that human thought runs along basically the same lines, and that man everywhere is a creature in quest of his spirit, although the cultural forms to which he belongs may be different in their super-structures. Some thinkers in the field were satisfied with pointing out bare similarities[2] Their work has a particular appeal to those who are disgusted and shocked by the acrimonious and even bloody and brutal religious conflicts, particularly between Islam on the one side and the other religions on the other. But such comparisons do not have much academic value, although they point out many basic common factors. Some academic philosophers, instead of directly criticizing and rejecting western views, attempted to show that the Vedāntic position can be reached by properly developing the philosophy of a western philosopher. The work of K. C. Bhattacharya[3] is particularly of this kind. He reopens the Kantian problem that metaphysics is impossible for the reason that thought ends up in antinomies or in opposed and mutually contradictory doctrines, if it makes the Absolute or any ultimate an object, and answers it by saying that the consciousness that knows the ultimates is not ordinary thought, but the transcendental. It is what the Vedāntins call intuition, which is clearly explained by Radhakrishnan, as we shall see later. The present writer's *Thought and Reality: Hegelianism and Advaita* was also a similar work.

But there are others, like S. N. Dasgupta, who refuse to bring in any comparisons with western philosophers and say that such comparisons will be misleading. However, Dasgupta himself, in one of his latest works, *Religion and Rational Outlook*, did not avoid considering western thinkers also. For we are no longer living in isolated worlds, but in one world, in which thought currents are crossing one another too frequently to segregate them; and such thought currents are not only religious, but also scientific, sociological, and ethical. The idea of segregated study, although not dead in India, can no longer be considered to be very important.

Again, there are academical philosophers in India whose acquaintance with Indian thought is superficial and remote and who are trained mainly in western philosophy. It is some of them that raise the cry against all traditional Indian philosophy.[4] They belong to different western persuasions—logical positivism, empiricism, Marxism in one or the other of the latest forms, linguistic analysis, etc. But one does not know how earnest such people are about what they talk and to what end they will lead Indian philosophy. They do not get any inspiration from within India, but from outside. One may say that for all of them, except for those influenced by Marxian thought, philosophy is not a philosophy of life.[5] But the general trend among the younger philosophers is to study the western movements, examine them, and either reject them as not leading to the end for which philosophy is meant or incorporate them into one of their own traditions. Of late, phenomenology and existentialism also have attracted the younger generation. As these schools have much in common with the Vedāntic thought, one may expect further developments of the Vedānta and a falling back on the grand tradition of India. After all, neither the dialectics of the new positivism, empiricism, and the linguistic schools, nor phenomenological and existential analyses are absolutely new to Indian philosophical literature, although, they are not called by those names and appear without their banners, but under the banners of some of the Indian traditions. This statement is made not with any arrogance and not with the idea that the Indians have nothing new to learn from the West, but only to show that man thinks and can and should think alike both in the East and the West. Indeed, the rigour with which a method like the phenomenological, the existential, the linguistic, or the logical is carried out in the modern West is not found in the same form and in the same context in Indian philosophical literature; and the Indian students of philosophy have much to learn from the western schools. But the spiritual bias of the Indian philosopher in general and the idea that philosophy is and has to be a philosophy of life and guide to life are still quite strong, and supply the right moorings to philosophical thinking.

Besides the Greek, Christian, modern western, and the classical Indian traditions, some elements of Islamic Sufism also have influenced contemporary Indian thought. Islamic contribution to the growth of Indian thought is almost nothing; for it was not the Shia tradition of Iran (Persia),[6] but the conservative and unprogressive Sunni that was dominant in India. The Aryan Muslims of Iran, with their Shia tradition, are, like the Greek and Indian Aryans, philosophical and rational in outlook and can generally tolerate and encourage a philosophical understanding of religion. But the Sunnis saw to it that the Shia sect and their kings did not prosper in India. However, Sufism[7] thrived well, and got new impetus from the Vedānta. It did not produce any philosophy worth mentioning in India, but in this century it found an interpreter in the person of Muhammad Iqbal, who towards the later part of his life became a communalist and an advocate of the separation of India into India and Pakistan. He had a number of admirers among the non-Muslims, including Hindus; but the massacres (said to be initiated by M. A. Jinnah) that preceded and followed the partition of India deprived him of much of the respect he earned. It is doubtful whether he commands much respect even in Pakistan now. For in spite of his philosophy of aggressiveness, which is reminiscent of Nietzsche and which suited the Muslim temperament in India, it is doubtful whether his philosophy can be called orthodox Islam.

Another factor in the development of contemporary Indian thought should not be ignored. All the great philosophers in the last few decades in India are products of the Indian Renaissance[8] and Enlightenment. The Renaissance is the revival of ancient learning in literature, fine arts, religion, and philosophy, thanks to many western orientalists particularly the German, who drew the attention of the world to the greatness of the ancient Indian cultural achievements and who expounded and even interpreted them. The names of men like Friedrich Schlegel, Alexander Hamilton, Wilhem von Humbolt, Max Müller, Paul Deussen, Herman Oldenberg, La Vallée Poussin, Sylvan Levi—to mention only a few—stand out foremost among such scholars and thinkers.[9] The importance of Sanskrit culture impressed men like Goethe, and its philosophies influenced such thinkers as Schopenhauer and Edward von Hartman. In fact, the post-Kantian idealism and romanticism of Germany wove up many currents of Vedāntic thought,[10] although British idealism, which was an offshoot of German idealism into which the British empirical thought was incorporated, never recognized the significance of the Vedāntic elements in her thought, although Britain was ruling India. However, the western recognition of the depth of Indian thought shook the Indian themselves from a kind of cultural, pathological slumber in which they began to forget their past and began to imitate the British. Nationalism gave a new incentive for the revival of the past, and ancient philosophies reappeared not only in their old forms, but also in the clothings of new western concepts. The Renaissance produced an Enlightenment (*Aufklarung*), which enabled the Indian thinkers to re-interpret to themselves and to others the significance of their spiritual concepts. This Renaissance is of ancient philosophies, but the Enlightenment is in terms of western, rational, scientific methods and concepts. However, we should not think that Indian philosophers had no idea of methods and logic. We have seen that they have had them since at least the 4th century B.C. The study of western methodologies started also a re-study of the Indian, and comparisons and evaluations of both.

We have to say that all the contemporary great philosophers of India are products of the Indian Renaissance and are greatly influenced by the East and the West. It is said, not without truth, that all the great philosophies of India originated in forests and hermitages, but not in what we generally call schools and universities. Their founders were all saints and sages. But their philosophies were later developed in academic circles, which would correspond to our schools and universities. Such a tradition of philosophical development in India may be one of the reasons for important philosophies not originating in the universities as yet,—arm-chair philosophers are not lacking—although some of the philosophers are really great thinkers. In this chapter, the philosophies of only a few of them will be presented, viz., of the outstanding ones, who are not merely scholars, but also thinkers.

2. CONTEMPORARY PHILOSOPHERS

S. Radhakrishnan Of all the contemporary Indian thinkers, S. Radhakrishnan (born 1880) is undoubtedly the greatest and is so recognized all over the world. He is recognized also as one of the greatest thinkers of this century. He is not merely a scholar, a historian of Indian thought, but also a thinker who can handle concepts as concepts, whether Indian or western, religious or academical. His great contribution to the growth of world-philosophy, in my opinion, lies in his interpreting the East to the West and vice versa, in showing that man and his philosophy, whether eastern or western, are basically the same; in his oft repeated conviction that intuition is the basis of all the other forms of cognition; and in his teaching that the spirit in man is as real as his body and that without the recognition of its reality, there will be complete displacement of humanity, there can be no democracy, no freedom, no morality, and no religion. Such a teaching is neither merely eastern nor merely western, but both. As a thinker, not merely as a scholar of Indian thought, he expounds his ideas in his different works, which are many.[11]

The final position of Radhakrishnan in philosophy is a non-dualism (*advaita*) like that of Śaṅkara, but does not seem to be exactly Śaṅkara's. In his *Reign of Religion in Contemporary Philosophy*, he showed more bias toward Hegel and Rāmānuja than towards Śaṅkara. But in his *Indian Philosophy*, he is more inclined towards Śaṅkara than towards Rāmānuja. In his *Idealist View of Life*, he tries to reconcile Śaṅkara and Rāmānuja. For Śaṅkara, the Absolute (Brahman) is non-dual, without external and internal differences and relations; for Rāmānuja, it is the personal God with external and internal differences, although all external differences become ultimately internal differences. Radhakrishnan says that both views are true, but from different standpoints. From the standpoint of our thought, the world we see is certainly not the Brahman, which appears as the creator-God, the ground and the cause of the world. So Rāmānuja is right in saying that the Brahman is personal and different from the world, although identical with it in the sense of being inseparably related to it. These distinctions hold true for our discursive, logical thought. But as the support of thought and as its ground and basis stands integral experience—a higher and deeper consciousness—that holds together all the distinctions and their relationships in a fluid unity. Such an experience is intuition. From the standpoint of intuition, which is the higher knowledge, the difference between God and the world cannot exist. When such intuition is reached, there can be neither God nor the world, but only the Brahman without a second. It is a unitary, non-dual experience like "I am."

Naturally the question arises: What is this intuition? In answering this question, Radhakrishnan does not depend merely on ancient texts, but uses modern western concepts. He means by intuition much more than insight gained by intellection. The subject knows the object; but there is also a consciousness that knows that the subject knows the object; it comprehends both, both fall within it. Yet the subject is continuous with it. Intuition is continuous with, and is the basis of thinking, imagining, feeling, perceiving, and sensing. It is something like the higher bird of the *Muṇḍaka Upaniṣad.* It is not a mere subject or a mere object, but the integrality of both. It grips the being of both and transcends them. One may call such an idea mystical and misty; but one should examine one's own experience, analyse it, and ask it questions. In view of the modern existential analysis, which has disturbed the conceptual schemes of ratiocination so far as man's existence and its knowledge go, we should not find anything strange in Radhakrishnan's theory. He called himself an idealist for a long time; but he lately said that existentialism is not a new philosophy, but is found in the ancient Upaniṣads,[12] which he follows. The philosophy of the Upaniṣads is both existentialism and idealism. A reconciliation can be made, as both can be spiritual philosophies.

Radhakrishnan thinks that many of the forms of existentialism, materialism, and positivism are revolts against contemporary religions, which failed in their purpose by being reduced to dogmas, creeds, and formulae. True religion is a spiritual quest, a quest for the spirit in man and for the Supreme Spirit. Man has, but should not have lost himself in the externals. As true religion is lost sight of, several types of atheism, naturalism, materialism, etc., have arisen with ultimate humanistic or socialistic goals. But neither humanism nor socialism can be self-justifying without spiritualism. Democracy, the most cherished form of government in the world today, will be impossible as a philosophy without the reality of freedom. But freedom cannot be justified without the reality spirit. It is spirit that is free, not the body. And it is religion, in which man's spirit, as a being, is in private communion with the Supreme Spirit, that has recognized the reality of spirit and its freedom from society and nature. In all anti-religious philosophies, man becomes spiritually displaced. Radhakrishnan is not opposed to the existence of many denominational religions; but they should recognize the essential truth of religion as such, viz., that it is a spiritual quest.

Radhakrishnan holds the view that ultimate salvation is not possible, unless it is the salvation of all humanity. This view is not the result of a merely humanistic sentiment. The individual, as part of the world, may be enlightened; but he cannot become one with the Absolute, so long as God exists as God. But as the rest of humanity is not enlightened, the world stays; and so long as the world remains, God also has to remain as God and cannot become the Absolute. The individual soul has, therefore, to remain with God, until the latter becomes the Absolute. Such individuals are the great souls (*mahātmas*), who, remaining with God, work for the uplift of humanity. Thus the distinction between God and the Absolute, which was originally an epistemological distinction, becomes now an ontological distinction.

The evolution of matter out of God and of spirit out of matter, as found in the Upaniṣads, particularly the *Tattirīya*, is accepted by Radhakrishnan. The levels found in the *Taittirīya* are exhaustive enough—matter, life, mind, reason, spirit—to denote the ascent from matter. The cosmic descent is not the mere reverse, but that of cosmic elements—ether, air, fire, water, and earth. However, Radhakrishnan has not given much thought to the cosmic descent, perhaps because it is a matter of pure speculation without verifiability in experience. But for the ascent, we find examples in the world, in man's own psycho-physical being, and in the many philosophies of evolutionism. We may even find support for the descent as the reverse process of the ascent in the *Kaṭha Upaniṣad*, the Sāṅkhya, the Pāśupata, and the Pāñcarātra. The world comes out of the over-flowing fullness of the Absolute Being. One may find a strain of Neo-Platonism here.

SRI AUROBINDO Like most of the other great philosophers of India, Aurobindo (1872–1950) is a mystic. All of them assert that the experience of God is above perception and ratiocination, yet it is knowledge. Aurobindo is a non-dualist, but his non-dualism is different from that of Śaṅkara. As in the philosophies of Śaivism and Śāktism, to which his ideas can be traced and which he follows but with a different terminology, Māyā is the real power of God and, even as Ignorance (Avidyā), it is part and parcel of consciousness. Māyā is the creative power of God, who descends through it to the world of matter. So there is nothing that is not permeated by God, and everything is real. All that is the Conscious is permeated by an element of the Unconscious and vice versa. Both the Conscious and the Unconscious are powers, forces (*śaktis*) of God. These ideas are not foreign to the Vedāntic systems.

Aurobindo Ghose[13] is a scholar of the Vedas and particularly of the Śaiva and Śākta philosophies, and is a prolific writer. He was at first one of the leaders of the secret and violent revolutionary nationalist movement of Bengal against the British rule, then was arrested by the British who could not prove the case against him, was discharged, and fled to the then French possession of Pondicherry, where he devoted all his life to study and practice of yoga and became an ascetic. He was one of the few Indians who had the best English education of the time in England itself, and for sometime taught philosophy. One may say that his ambition to re-conquer India from the British turned him ultimately into a yogi, who conquers the world of matter by becoming divine. Such a man is, for Aurobindo, a superman, yet not the one as taught by Nietzsche.

Aurobindo is acquainted with the evolutionist philosophies of the West, but is dissatisfied with them, for they cannot explain why mind evolved out of matter at all. The nisus from matter to spirit can be explained only if there is in the very being of matter something to which the nisus belongs as its very nature. The nisus then will be the attempt of that something to regain its original nature. Then the original nature must be spirit. If so, why does it hide in matter at first? Why has it become, and why does it appear as, matter? To become matter must be something natural to it. The movement from spirit to matter and matter to spirit belongs to the very nature of the Absolute; it is Māyā, the power of the Absolute. If spirit is conscious and Māyā is unconscious, then both the Conscious and the Unconscious are not separate from each other, but belong to each other. The movements of descent and ascent constitute a circular movement, as in the philosophy of Plotinus. Man belongs to a stage in this circular movement.

Aurobindo gives nine stages of the descent of the Supreme Spirit into matter, which are also the nine stages of ascent in the reverse direction. They are: Existence, Consciousnessforce, Bliss, Supermind, Overmind, mind, psyche, life and matter.[14] The stages from mind to matter belong to the empirical world. The stages from Supermind above are Supernals and divine. The Overmind is the mediator between mind and Supermind through the veil of Māyā that separates the two. We may say that the Overmind corresponds roughly to the witness consciousness (*sākṣicaitanya*) of the Vedānta. The first three levels beginning with Existence together constitute the Brahman, which is Being-Consciousness-Bliss (*sat-cit-ānanda*), and which splits itself into the three forms, as in some Śākta philosophies, before evolving the world. Māyā stays between the mind and the Supermind, and it and the Overmind belong to each other.[15]

The aim of man's life is to follow the path of the ascent and rise to the levels of the Supernals one after another, first to the Overmind, next to the Supermind and so on. At the higher levels there is no possibility of falsity at all; for there Ignorance and Consciousness are not separated. The Overmind now and then passes on to mind some great truths; and they appear like some occult truths, inspirations, intuitions, which cannot be accounted for by mind. When man rises to the level of the Overmind and becomes one with it, he becomes a Superman. But the Superman of Aurobindo is a yogi, who has surrendered his mind and ego to God for becoming one with him. He has little or nothing in common with the Superman of Nietzsche. For those who have risen to higher levels, there is no conflict, no strife. Even if the differences are seen there, their unity also is transparent. At the highest level, differences are not seen at all. Experience there is all one, every part of which is completely transparent to every other. Such an experience is integral knowledge according to Aurobindo.

Rabindranath Tagore Tagore (1861–1941) is not an academical philosopher, although trained in philosophy, particularly the Upaniṣads and Bengal Vaiṣṇavism. He is first and foremost a poet. But like the great epic poets of ancient India, he has a philosophy to teach. Yet he felt that epic poetry is unsuitable to the present age.

Nevertheless, he drew his inspiration from the ancient epics, caught their rapture of divine love, and presented his ideas not only occasionally in the ancient garb, but often also in modern clothing. If we do not mean by an epic poet one who writes long epic poems, like Valmīki, Vyāsa, and Kālidāsa of ancient India and Homer, Dante and Milton in the West, but one who has a world view and succeeds in conveying it in numerous poems, dramas, stories, etc., so that we can get a total picture of the world and the life of man as the poet conceives them, then Tagore is a modern epic poet. Besides, like some other great poets of the world, he has written prose works expounding the philosophy of God, man, and the world.

Tagore is a non-dualist,[16] but not like Śaṅkara. He thinks that the Absolute in its perfection, living away from all that happens in the world, is of no interest to man.[17] It is the picture with all the richness of its colours, shades, and forms that interests us, but not the canvas on which it is painted. The author of the picture must be a person. The Absolute is and must, therefore, be a person. Tagore humanizes the Absolute and calls it Creative Personality. Personality is that which acts and creates. We can love God, because he is a person. Tagore gives a higher place to love than to knowledge. He says that in knowledge the distinctions are either kept separate or completely dissolved in a bare unity. But in love, the terms, the lover and the beloved, are distinguished and yet united. The consciousness of love retains both unity and difference. Love is the consummation of knowledge. True knowledge is not ratiocination, but a knowledge of things in their relation to the universe, a knowledge that retains the distinctions and yet grasps them in their unity. God is everything, but everything is not equally God. To realize God as the Supreme Person is our destiny, our *dharma*, that which supports ultimately our being. We fulfil it only when we know our true nature, which is one-ness with God. But if we are really one with God, why do we not know this one-ness? We do not know it because of Avidyā, Māyā, Ignorance, which we can overcome only through love of God.

MOHANDAS KARAMCHAND GANDHI Gandhi (1869–1948) is known throughout the world as a fighter for the independence of India and as the father of the Indian nation. He is not an academic philosopher and never claimed to being one. But he is a religious man, called even an incarnation of Christ for his gospel of peace and non-violence even in political action. We may call him at least a follower of Christ in the true spirit, not merely in word but also in thought and action. But he is also a follower of Mahāvīra, the founder of Jainism, in his teaching of non-injury, of Buddha in his teaching of peace and compassion and uplift of the downtrodden, and of both Christ and Buddha in his teaching of active love; for between the teachings of Christ and Buddha, the difference is one of shade, but not of colour. He is a follower of Hinduism, particularly of the philosophy of action of the *Bhagavadgītā*. He refused to become a Christian and insisted on remaining a Hindu; for he found that all religions teach the same truth, the essence of all is the teaching of non-violence, compassion, and love, and also he was born a Hindu and found no reason why he should become a Christian.[18] Change of religion does not bring one nearer to truth, for such a change will only be a change of name.

The teachings of great religions—non-violence, compassion, and love—are meant to be expressed in action. But in the contemporary world, these virtues cannot fully be expressed merely in the individual's life, although every individual ought to embody and express them. They will be ineffective, unless they are embodied in political and social life. The life of the individual is now entwined with that of the community, society, nation, and even humanity. Gandhi's aim was, therefore, to show how they could be worked in the spheres of both the individual and social life. As an Indian, he found India the proper field in which their working could be demonstrated. Furthermore, he was convinced—and in his convictions he used to rely, like Socrates, on an inner voice for guidance—that the methods of action dictated by the three virtues are the only right methods in all spheres of life—family and communal relationships, internal politics of a nation, and international relationships. His conviction was so strong that he even threatened that he would isolate himself from his party and retire to the forest if the members did not follow him, thereby assuming that all other methods involving violence and hatred were wrong. He even said that he would meet Hitler and his army, if he invaded India, with an army of non-violent, compassionate, and loving souls—which looked noble, but quite unrealistic to all those concerned. But he was, like Mencius in China and Socrates and many idealists in the West, of the conviction that man is essentially good, that good, because it is the truth in man, will always prevail over evil, and that even the most evil person cannot resist the appeal of love and non-violence. But the training in love and non-violence requires as rigorous a discipline as training in war. The non-violent soldier cannot be a coward. For the courage required needs absolute self-discipline, which is the highest kind of self-rule. In this context, Gandhi interpreted self-government (*svarāj, svarājya*) in the most comprehensive and basic sense as not only government by oneself, but also government of oneself. Nobody who cannot govern or control one's self, is entitled to govern, rule other selves. In the individual, the two governments must coincide. In the nation and society, they branch out from each other. If man is not good in the government of one's self, he will fail in the government of others. The society of men who are good in both will be the true welfare society. The philosophy of Gandhi is, in a true sense, a combination of the philosophies of Paine and Mazzini.

Gandhi calls his philosophy the philosophy of *satyāgraha*, a word we may use as such, as it is known throughout the world. This word has been translated and interpreted variously as "passive resistance," "non-violent resistance," "civil disobedience," and so on. But these interpretations convey only aspects, results, and corollaries of what Gandhi meant. *Satyāgraha* means "passionate adherence to truth." When Gandhi was asked to say what he believed God to be, he said that God is the same as Truth. For we may reject any other definition of God, but we do not and cannot reject Truth. As Truth is the law of the universe, its support (*dharma*), man should follow Truth under all conditions. There is no other way of life for man than passionate adherence to Truth, and that is *satyāgraha*. Truth, as the law and support of the universe, is love, of which non-violence and compassion are two aspects. Gandhi does not say much about compassion; but in his practice and in the time, thought, and energy he devoted to the uplift of the lower and downtrodden classes and castes of India, one can easily discover it. But he repeatedly speaks of love and non-violence. Non-violence without love is only a body without life; and love without non-violence is only a disembodied and ineffectual spirit. Non-violence is only a minimum expression of love. Thus *satyāgraha* connotes passionate adherence to love and non-violence.

Satyāgraha is identified with civil disobedience, because Gandhi said that unjust civil laws should be resisted or disobeyed, but not criminal laws. He exhorted also that, when once a civil disobeyer was in jail, he should obey all its laws and regulations. As the man who follows *satyāgraha* is non-violent, he appears to be passive. But resistance cannot be truly passive. It is resistance to evil, a non-acceptance of, and a non-surrender to it under all conditions and a facing of the consequences even if they end up with one's death. But Gandhi believes that, if one is sincere and earnest in following *satyāgraha*, the enemy is bound to yield, because love is unconquerable and love and truth admit of no defeat. But should we not use violence in punishing the wrong-doer and destroying evil? Such punishment and destruction should be left to God, who, in love and without hatred, knows how to punish an incorrigible evil-doer. We are finite beings; and for us hate always goes with violence. We should not hate even our enemies. If they are wrong and do not yield to truth, God will punish them.

The application of such a high idealism in social, political, and international fields of action is not very easy, and requires many provisos. Gandhi himself was aware of the difficulties and limitations, and towards the end of the British rule came to the conclusion that his philosophy could be practised only by individuals in their individual capacity. The Hindus asked him how they could practise non-violence against Muslim rioters, who attacked their women and property. Gandhi had to say that it was the duty of such Hindus to defend the honour of their women even with the sword. They would then be doing their duty not in hatred of the Muslims, but for doing their duty to their women. Another example was that of the calf, which he killed by poison, as he found it in immense and incurable suffering. How could his killing the calf be justified, if non-violence includes non-killing? He had to save the poor calf from its misery.[19] Furthermore, the Hindu-Muslim riots and killings at the time of the partition of India showed that he was too idealistic for humanity to accept and follow his teachings. And he himself had to lay down his life by the bullet of a person who thought that his idealism was dangerous, although sublime.

Yet no one will and can question the sublimity of Gandhi's philosophy of action. Unfortunately, the realistic world is not what Gandhi thought it to be. Nobody will question also how useful his philosophy can be for humanity. But what is needed is to find out the limitations imposed on its effectiveness by the nature of man, society, and politics, both national and international—limitations which Gandhi would say are due to Māyā. But they cannot be dismissed as unreal. If they are not recognized, the result of the application of his sublime philosophy may be quite the opposite of the result aimed at. Men are not wanting who think that the independence attained through Gandhi's teaching, which costed the lives of about two millions in the Hindu-Muslim riots, could have been attained by sacrificing the lives of about one million in a violent struggle with the British, if India was willing to go through it a long time ago. But others say that independence through peaceful methods, even if they involved the lives of more men, is better than that obtained through violence but involving the lives of fewer, for the latter leaves in its train acrimony and bitter memories. But whichever line of thinking is true, both show that the application on a wide scale of even the most sublime method needs foresight, calculation, and analysis[20] of the conditions under which it can work and under which it is risky. Even Christ's sermon on the Mount and his doctrine of love have to be moderated by the ideas of justice and welfare of society. We can say at least and in a general way that the Gandhian principle works only if both the parties in dispute are earnest about each other's welfare, although Gandhi thought often that it would work even if only one of the parties is so earnest. But if one of the parties thinks that its own welfare lies in a partial or total extermination of the other, when the other adopts the principle of non-violence, the former can become the hangman of the latter the more easily. The future applicability of the principle depends on how much every group or nation of the world realizes that its own welfare and security depend on the welfare and security of every other. However difficult and complex the application of the sublime principle be, it offers a great hope to mankind.

The central ideas of Gandhi's philosophy of action may now be reduced to a few principles. (1) God is Truth. This Truth is not the logical, abstract truth, but the spiritual metaphysical. As Truth is the law that supports man and the universe, God is both the Law and the Law-giver. (2) God is Love itself. He is not a pure concept, but is affectional, affective, by nature. (3) Truth always prevails over falsity and falsehood in every conflict between the two sides. (4) One should stick to Truth. Then one will be supported by Truth or Being. Falsity leads to Non-being, non-existence. (5) As Truth, God, and Love are one and the same, one should stick to love. (6) One should, therefore, follow the path of non-violence. The opposite of love is violence, the destruction of what opposes us. (7) Man is finite, he is not God; his power, knowledge, and will are limited. He may be mistaken in his own convictions, to which he may stick. (8) In sticking to truth or to what one believes to be truth, one should not destroy another. For man, being finite, may take falsity for truth and may mistake the other to be wrong. Even then one should stick to his truth, until one is convinced that he himself is wrong and the other right. Conflicts thus are inevitable. But no conflict should lead to destruction. Truth will, however, ultimately prevail. If the parties really love each other and are earnest about truth, there will be no acrimony left, whoever be the winner. (9) When truth wins, falsity will be destroyed. If the two parties love each other, the destruction will only be the destruction of false convictions. But no party should try to destroy the other, even when afterwards it is shown to be wrong and not in earnest about truth. God alone has the right to destroy. In his infinite wisdom, he knows what is true and what is false, what is good and what is evil. When he destroys, he destroys in love, not in hatred. As finite beings, we not only cannot be certain of truth, but also cannot destroy in love. Generally in hate only can we destroy. Hate is easy, but love difficult for us. Our duty is to follow only the path of love; we shall then be like God, the law, ground, support of our being.

JIDDU KRISHNAMURTI Krishnamurti[21] (born 1895) was discovered by Mrs. Annie Besant, the founder of the Theosophical Society in India, considered by her as a spiritual genius, and even declared to be an incarnation[22] of God. But later, he not only declared himself to be an ordinary man, but also severed his connections with the Theosophical Society. But according to Bhagavan Das, he is still regarded as an incarnation of God by many theosophists. Krishnamurti was educated at Oxford. His teachings, which are found in many of his published talks, are a great inspiration to many men and women in different parts of the world.

One aspect of Krishnamurti's thought may be called anti-traditionalism. He is opposed to all traditions, to the idea of schools, dogmas, and creeds. True spiritual quest refuses to be associated with any school, dogma, or creed. To characterize it in terms of any is sheer thoughtlessness. It is spirit's relation to spirit and has nothing to do with any denomination. Every man should try the spiritual quest by himself. No teacher, no book, no specific practice can be the absolute guide. Schools, creeds, and dogmas encourage exclusiveness and intensify our egoity. They are based on illusion. Real search for truth begins when we are freed from the divisions they introduce. In Truth, there is no division between the I and the Thou.

Reality is pure life running its course. The individual who differentiates himself from other individuals is created in it through ignorance. True knowledge lies in catching reality in its living process. It is life itself, it is God himself. But it is not something other than ourselves; it runs through us, it is we. It is, therefore, ignorance to worship reality as other than we. Reality is non-dual. We do not realize our oneness with it, because we are not fully conscious of ourselves. Our I-consciousness is not full and complete consciousness. That is why it separates itself from reality. The separate I, or the ego is an illusion. We call it self-consciousness, but we do not have complete self-consciousness. Why and when does this illusion arise? Krishnamurti answers that it is beginningless, but can have an end. It ceases as soon as we realize our oneness with eternal life.

Krishnamurti believes that evolution naturally leads man to the realization of his oneness with eternal life. The drive of evolution is towards the realization of self-consciousness and it cannot stop with man's ego. The forces of evolution themselves will bring about universal salvation. But it is not clear whether Krishnamurti believes in the automatic salvation of all of us through the process of evolution, whether we want it or not. At times he says that man has to exert himself. But one may say that this exertion is a part of the evolutionary process when cosmically viewed, although the individual may think that he is making the exertion.

BHAGAVAN DAS[23] Bhagavan Das (1869–1957) is not so well known outside India as within India. Although he is a trained philosopher and taught the subject for some years, his contributions to technical philosophy are not so important as his contributions to a re-interpretation of India's ethical and social thought. By conviction, he is a theosophist; philosophically, he is an idealist of the Fichtian type, although he does not follow Fichte, but adapts him to a Vedānta of his own. His philosophical ideas are given in his *Science of Peace*. But the works for which he is better known are his *Essential Unity of All Religions*, *The Science of Social Organization*, and *The Ancient versus Modern Scientific Socialism*, to which class belongs his *Science of Emotions*.

In metaphysics, the basic categories, according to Bhagavan Das, are spirit, the non-spirit, and the nexus between the two. Spirit is found in three forms—the Infinite Spirit (Brahman), the finite spirit (*ātman*), and the embodied mind-body. All experience themselves as the "I," the ego. Thus we get the Infinite Ego, the finite ego, and the embodied ego. The embodied ego is a combination of the finite ego and the Non-ego, which is matter and which becomes the body. The ego knows the Non-ego as distinct from itself, yet identifies itself with it and wants to absorb it into itself. The three functions of the ego are cognition, action, and desire.

The Non-ego is the cosmic universe with its history. All the special sciences deal with it. It is the Prakṛti of the Sāṅkhya and the Vedānta. It has the three attributes, which Bhagavan Das calls cognizability, desirability, and movability (*sattva*, *rajas* and *tamas*), and explains them as luminosity, activity, and immobility.[24] The relation between the ego and the Non-ego is not what we call a logical relation, which is static, but the dynamic relation of energy (*śakti*). It has two aspects, the negative and the positive. The negative appears as space, time, and motion. The positive appears as causal energy in the form of action, reaction, and causal connection. The three—the ego, the Non-ego, and their relation—are found in the logian, "I am That."

Bhagavan Das bases his ethics and social organization on the three Attributes of Prakṛti and analysis of emotions. The three Attributes determine the character of the individual man. The Brahmin is the wise man in whom the Attribute, Luminosity, dominates. The Kṣatriya (warrior) is he in whom Activity dominates; and the Śūdra (the fourth caste) is he in whom immobility dominates. The class structure of society, which needs economic organization, brings in the third caste, the trader (*vaiśya*), who takes care of the wealth of society. Perhaps in him the Attributes, Activity and Immobility, dominate equally and predominate over Luminosity.

In social organization, we have four branches. (1) Educational organization needs the class of wise men, who are Brahmins and in whom Luminosity dominates. (2) Defensive organization needs the class of warriors in which Activity dominates. (3) Economic organization needs the traders and other professional men (*vaiśyas*) to manage and supervise over the production and distribution of wealth. (4) Industrial and labour organization needs the worker (*śūdra*), in whom immobility dominates and who needs to be guided and made to work. Thus Bhagavan Das justifies the four caste divisions accepted by Manu and other Indian law-givers. But he does not accept that these divisions are or should be based on birth. They are based only on character and profession, as the *Bhagavadgītā* teaches. We find a somewhat similar division of social classes in the philosophy of Plato.

The life of the individual also has to be organized into the four stages (*āśramas*). In the first, he should study about the world; in the second, earn, enjoy, and perform his duties; in the third, practice contemplation and reflect over his experiences; and in the fourth, give up all worldly connections, immerse himself in spiritual practices, and pray for the well-being of the world. Man's aim in the last stage is to give up all connections with Prakṛti and treat it as unreality. Then he becomes one with the Supreme Ego.

The two primary emotions are love and hate. Love has the three attitudes towards its object—superiority, equality, and inferiority. It appears, therefore, in three forms—respect, affection, and compassion. Hate also has the three attitudes and appears as fear, anger, and scorn. All the other emotions are permutations and combinations of the six, the three forms of love and the three of hate. These six are the internal enemies of man, and may take very perverted forms by being attached to wrong objects and by drawing the ego out of itself. The spiritual man conquers his own internal enemies. When he is no longer drawn towards Prakṛti (Non-ego), his ego becomes one with the Supreme Ego. As mentioned already, the contribution of

Bhagavan Das to the ethical thought of India is quite significant, but his contributions to metaphysics, have not attracted the attention of the academic circles.

MOHAMMAD IQBAL Although Iqbal[25] (1877–1948) is now called the philosopher of Pakistan, upto 1947 he was a philosopher or a poet-philosopher of India. His only philosophical work is *The Reconstruction of Religious Thought in Islam* and is not well-known. But his poetical works are better known and more widely read. His thought is particularly influenced by the Sufism of Persia, the Koran, some mystic elements of India, Nietzsche, and Bergson. He is opposed to the ideas of quietism, self-surrender, and desirelessness found in some Sufi philosophers like Gazzali and some Indian teachings. He is opposed also to the idea of merging in God, who, for Iqbal, is personal. He believes in the reality of time and the world. His ideal man is God's vice-regent[26] on earth, conquering, ruling, and enjoying it in the name of God.

Iqbal thinks that it is a mistake of Gazzali, Kant, and Bergson that they did not notice a deeper aspect of thought. Thought can reach the immanent Infinite, to whose unfolding movement all the finite concepts belong. That is, unlike Bergson, Iqbal would say that it is not necessary to transcend thought for catching reality and that, instead of deriving thought and intellect from intuition, intuition can be derived[27] from thought. The whole then would be, in the words of Koran, a kind of "Preserved Tablet," which holds together all the undetermined possibilities as a present reality, revealing in time all of them in serial succession. Reality is pure duration and the consciousness that reveals it to us in intuition. But this intuition is for us a deeper aspect of thought.

The self has two aspects—the external which enters into relation with the things of space and the internal, called the apperceptive, reached in moments of profound meditation. In the processes of the internal ego, all states of consciousness melt into one another. The unity of the ego is like a seed out of which a variety of forms germinates. There is no numerical distinctness within the plurality in it. We may compare this ideal with the Sāṅkhya conception of the ego. In it, according to Iqbal, all is a single "now," an eternal present as in the philosophies of Royce and the Vijñānavāda of Śāntarakṣita and Kamalaśīla.

For Iqbal, as for Bergson, evolution is a constant forward movement without any turning back. He differs, therefore, from Nietzsche, who accepted eternal recurrence. The final reality is the ego. The world consists of only egos, a view held by Leibniz and McTaggart. Yet a particle of dust is not an ego. We have to distinguish a particle of dust, a worm, man, and God. However, material nature is not an unreality. No self is thinkable without a character; God also is unthinkable without it. Nature is the character of God or, as the Koran puts it, it is the "habit of Allah." But in truth, there is no duality of mind and matter. Matter is spirit in space-time reference. Although reality is spirit, Iqbal does not accept pantheism. God's infinity does not mean his omnipresence; it means only the infinity of his inner possibilities.

Iqbal does not believe that the evil in the world will be conquered by God for man. Man himself has to work for it. He can and should never be inactive. He has to conquer the world for God and in the name of God, and rule it as his vice-regent.[28] Here is the old Hebraic idea that the world is created by God for man to enjoy it according to the divine law. In and for the conquest of the world, man has to be of strong character and be a tyrant, ignoring everything except God. This teaching is an echo of Nietzsche's doctrine of the Superman, with of course the difference that God is not dead for Iqbal. But we do not know what God does, except that he gives a free hand to such tyrants. Iqbal's philosophy is a philosophy of self-assertion, not of self-surrender even to God. Iqbal teaches only duty to God and love of God; but neither duty nor love seems to involve self-surrender. The love of God is a self-asserting love that forces the object into union. Expressions like "self-affirmation brings not-self to light," "the fountain of Life is Love's flashing sword," and "keep desire in thy heart, lest they little dust become a tomb," seem to justify the view of life as an aggressive drive for power and enjoyment, tolerating nothing in the way. It seems unnecessary to live such a life in the name of God; for even rejecting the reality of God, such an ideal of life has been taught particularly by Nietzsche. We cannot understand what important role God plays in the philosophy of Iqbal. It seems that the vice-regent tyrant of man does everything, and God receives only respect and prayers. It is perhaps doubtful whether Iqbal's teaching is in full accord with Islam, which believes in predestination (*Qismat*) and according to which God determines everything. Iqbal does not believe in pre-destination; for it conflicts with the idea of unceasing forward drive of the self, which keeps its desire ever burning alive and whose activity, like that of a tyrant, brooks nothing in the way. To oppose quietism of life, Iqbal seems to have gone to the opposite extreme.

CONCLUSION We see a great change in the attitude of contemporary philosophers to the world. The traditional classical opposition[29] between the life of action and the life of contemplation or no-action—which the *Bhagavadgītā* attempted to solve—is reconciled now by treating each as a complement of the other or by ignoring the life of contemplation as in the philosophy of Iqbal. But all the philosophers agree that life of action is important. Furthermore, the general trend is towards not treating the world of action as unreal. Māyā, in the extreme sense in which some interpretations of Śaṅkara indulged, is no longer accepted. Not even Radhakrishnan accepts it, in spite of his strong sympathies with Śaṅkara's philosophy. In fact, it was he who showed first to the western world that Śaṅkara's Māyā did not mean the unreality of the world for the individual.

We see also that both the Indian and Islamic philosophers now desire to join the line of western thinkers and are not merely expounding their traditional philosophies, but are also developing them along western lines with western terminologies, thereby accepting, both openly and tacitly, that the march of philosophical thought in the future will no longer be merely eastern or merely western. Even if in the ancient times the philosophical centres of the world thought in isolation—isolation was only relative even then, as there were many contacts between the East and the West even in antiquity—their thoughts are human thoughts and can, therefore, be incorporated into one another, contributing thereby to the richness of world-thought.

We observe also that, for all the important thinkers of India, philosophy is a philosophy of life. The problems of logic and epistemology have not attracted their attention much, except that of Radhakrishnan. The problem of life is more important than logic, as even Bertrand Russell lately realized. In one's youth one may be attracted largely by disciplines like logic, epistemology, linguistics, and analysis. One then comes across numerous doctrines, concepts, criticisms, and defences, all of which can be exciting. But for a mind sobered and made mature by experience and demands of reality, they lead nowhere by themselves. Life comes from somewhere and goes somewhere. It is more important to know life's nature, direction, and destiny than merely to be trained in logic and linguistics. That is why the philosophies of many of the contemporary thinkers in India are salvation philosophies. Even regarding logic and linguistics, one may say that the nature and function we attribute to them depends in a large measure on what we think of life's nature and destiny, whether the destiny is only this-worldly or extends to a world beyond and whether it is higher or lower than what it is now. For Marxism, for instance, the destiny is here in this world. For spiritual philosophies, it extends beyond. For the leaders of Indian thought, it still extends beyond. That is why all of them are, in one way or another, idealists and spiritualists.

NOTES

[1]Even now many Indian philosophy professors occupying important places in Indian universities watch which ways the philosophical movements of Oxford and Cambridge and recently Harvard go to be recognized as original thinkers.

[2]See Bhagavan Das: *The Essential Unity of All Religions.*

[3]See his *Subject as Freedom.*

[4]It seems that it is the idea of some of them that it is the moral duty of England and the rest of the West to save the Indians from their traditional philosophy. But there are some in the West, who pity the Indians for their incapability to develop anything out of their traditional philosophies.

[5]It is painful to think that, for some of these people, philosophical circles may become somewhat like small town clubs, where people meet to enjoy gossip and some light-hearted criticisms of others, without of course any earnestness. The circles in India where earnestness has not yet vanished are those of religious philosophies. One such circle may make fun of another, but is still earnest about its own doctrines.

[6]Contemporary events in Iran perhaps contradict this interpretation.

[7]It is a definite mistake to think that philosophical mysticism and Vedāntic (and Buddhistic) non-dualism are due to the advent of Islamic Sufism in India. I believe that these trends had their centres of origin all over the world. But there seems to be no check on the thinking of philosopher-politicians.

[8]See D. S. Sharma: *Hindu Renaissance*; P. T. Raju: "Research in Indian Philosophy: A Survey" in *The Journal of the Ganganatha Jha Research Institute*, February, May, August, 1944, Allahabad; and "Contemporary Indian Thought" in *History of Philosophy: Eastern and Western*; J. H. Muirhead: *Contemporary Indian Thought.*

[9]See D. S. Robinson: *The Story of Scottish Philosophy.*

[10]See Helmuth von Glassenapp: *Das Indienbild deutscher Denker.*

[11]The most important of his works are: *Indian Philosophy*, 2 Vols., *An Idealist View of Life*, *Religion and Society*, *Eastern Religions and Western Thought*, *The Philosophy of Rabindranath Tagore*, and *Reign of Religion in Contemporary Philosophy*. For works on Radhakrishnan, see C. E. M. Joad: *Counter Attack From the East*, and P. A. Schilpp: *The Philosophy of Sarvapalli Radhakrishnan.*

[12]P. A. Schipp: *The Philosophy of Sarvapalli Radhakrishnan*, p. 47.

[13]His main work is *The Life Divine*. See his *Essays on the Gītā*, and also P. T. Raju: *Idealistic Thought of India.*

[14]*The Life Divine*, pp. 243 and 259. [15]Ibid., pp. 260–61.

[16]His philosophical works are *The Religion of Man*, *Sādhana*, *Creative Unity*, and *Personality*. The poem for which he got his Nobel Prize is *Gītāñjali*. For a detailed study of his philosophy, see S. Radhakrishnan: *The Philosophy of Rabindranath Tagore*, D. S. Sharma: *Hindu Renaissance*, J. E. Thompson: *Rabindranath Tagore.*

[17]This seems to be a misunderstanding of the Advaita position. The Absolute is not away from the world, but is within the being of man, giving him the opportunity, if he wants, for complete peace and

perfection. Just as the agitation of Becoming cannot be separated from Being, Being cannot be separated from Becoming, as it absorbs Becoming. Or Becoming is within Being.

[18]See Clifford Manshardt: *The Mahatma and the Missionary*. A large number of books have been published on Gandhi. The student may read C. F. Andrews: *Mahatma Gandhi's Ideas*; S. Radhakrishnaṇ: *Mahatma Gandhi*; Romain Rolland: *Mahatma Gandhi*; M. K. Gandhi: *My Experiments with Truth*; M. K. Gandhi: *Hind Swaraj*; and P. T. Raju: *Idealistic Thought of India.*

[19]Some Jainas were opposed to Gandhi's action, and said that the calf should have been allowed to suffer. This is a ticklish ethical question, which is, in principle, the same as that of mercy killing in the case of human beings.

[20]Such an analytic study has to be done from the point of view of psychology, ethics, social philosophy, politics, and international relations. But there seems to be a tendency on the part of some leading Indians to shun any academic study of Gandhian thought, lest his philosophy become pure academics. Only a few are eager to have such a study. But it cannot be avoided, as the Gandhian principle is important and may become the only hope for the world of the atomic age.

[21]See P. T. Raju: *Idealistic Thought of India*, pp. 304 fol.

[22]It is a common phenomenon in India to declare almost every spiritual leader as an incarnation of God. But the sacred literature of India asserts ten only to be God's incarnations.

[23]See P. T. Raju: *Idealistic Thought of India*, pp. 311 fol. Almost all the works of Bhagavan Das are published by the Theosophical Publishing House, Adyar, Madras.

[24]See Bhagavan Das's article in J. H. Muirhead: *Contemporary Indian Philosophy*.

[25]See P. T. Raju: *Idealistic Thought of India*, pp. 375–394.

[26]This seems to be the predominant Islamic view. See my paper, "The Logos and the Māhān Ātmā," in *Ohio Journal of Religious Studies*, Vol. I, No.2, July 1973.

[27]The justifiability of the idea depends on the meaning of the word "derive." If it means "springing, issuing," then intuition does not issue out of thought; but if it means "discovering the implications," then intuition is implied in thought.

[28]This idea seems to be very often abused in history.

[29]found in Christianity also as the opposition between salvation by works and salvation by faith.

Chapter XVII

Conclusion

(i) Width and Depth of Indian Thought

We have so far covered practically everything important in Indian philosophy, so that we may say that the reader who completes this book is exposed to every important idea and doctrine. And this book gives a new type of comparison and constructive criticism. The word "important" is a relative term. Many minor schools have not been discussed, and much has to be omitted in the doctrines of even the schools presented. For instance, we could mention here and there only a few ideas of the grammarian philosophers, who were really the first among the greatest philosophers of language in the world and whose work is still a source of inspiration to many in the field.[1] Researches into many minor schools and systems are still being carried on, showing their relationship and contributions to the major schools. But on the whole, one may say, the reader who goes through this book is fairly well acquainted with the concepts and doctrines of Indian philosophy, and should have come across new doctrines and gained new insights not found in earlier works. He can see also how metaphysics, epistemology, and the ideal of life are closely interrelated by important Indian thinkers and that logic is not new to India, although it was not as formalized all along as in the west.

(ii) India and the West: Mutual Influence

We can appreciate also Radhakrishnan's observation: "There is hardly any height of spiritual insight or rational philosophy attained in the world that has not its parallel in the vast stretch that lies between the early Vedic seers and the modern Naiyāyikas."[2] To this we may add E. von Hartman's observation that in the philosophies of India and China there are still unearthed treasurers that will surprise the two-thousand year old philosophy of the West.[3] But one should not infer that, when the Indians refer to such statements, they are too proud of themselves. Even if they have such pride, it may be appreciated as a reaction of nationalism and patriotism to the long cultural dominance by, and subjection to the colonial powers, and to the unsympathetic treatment and criticism they have faced. But what men like Radhakrishnan mean—and every one ought to mean—is that man, who is spiritual and rational, thinks in the same way, whether he is eastern or western. There are a great many common areas between eastern and western thought, in spite of differences. A critical study of differences within the field of basic experiences discloses surprisingly valuable truths that will make East and West more and more transparent to each other. In Indian thought, we have come across activism and quietism, realism and idealism, pluralism and monism, theism, non-theism, atheism, and supra-personal absolutism, and different kinds of epistemological theories, including those of language. Taking western philosophy up to the end of the 16th century, a comparison of it with the Indian will not be unfavourable to the latter. Even the philosophical ideas of western theology—particularly with reference to the nature of the soul, its freedom, immortality, and its relation to God—cannot be said to have far surpassed the Indian. Both have still much to learn from each other. But I think that no serious Indian thinker considers Indian philosophy to be as well developed in every branch as the western is in the 20th century.

The West has already incorporated many central and basic ideas of Indian thought both knowingly and unknowingly, and developed them in several of their aspects to stages far surpassing those of the Indian.[4] It is said that the West did not have only one Renaissance, but three. The first occurred in about the 13th century when the Arabs brought Plato and Aristotle in the Neo-Platonic and Arabic garb to the West, and Thomism was the result. Then occurred the 16th century Renaissance. Both were for the West a revival of learning that was lost. But that revival was a revival of a comparatively recent past of the Aryans of Europe. Their more remote past existed in India and it was revived in the 18th century through the discovery of Sanskrit, its literature and philosophy. The golden age of German idealism and romanticism was the result of the mixing up of the Kantian and Indian traditions. Idealistic absolutism and romanticism spread to England and America. In being incorporated, the Indian ideas did not remain what they were in India, but obtained new significance and content in new contexts. As reactions to the flights of idealism and romanticism and with reference to them and as protests against them, arose many forms of traditional thought with new derivations, elaborations, explications of methods, and a re-catching of what originally was lost sight of. Thus we have different forms of realism, Neo-Kantianism, Neo-Hegelianism, pragmatism, logical and linguistic analysis, phenomenology, and existentialism. Even a few decades ago, existentialism was thought to be oriental by some Americans. Should we trace these new developments to only Kant and some other western origins or to the Vedānta also? We can do both, provided we keep in mind that these developments are not straight but circuitous, following devious ways, branching off the main road and sometimes coming back and rejoining it at unexpected points, but other times not returning at all. In these new developments, much was gained; but much was lost sight of and ignored. One may say that, in one sense, contemporary western thought has nothing to do with the Indian; but also that, in another sense, it has much to do with it. We have to find out how much truth lies in either alternative. What the Indian thinker has to do now is to graft all that has taken place in the West on to his own grand tradition. Such a task should not be impossible in view of the fact that the roots of the modern western traditions lie in the Indian ideas also. It will go to show that man not only thought but also does and can think alike both in the East and the West.

(iii) Systematic Nature of Indian Thought

It is often said that Indian philosophy is spiritual in outlook. From this statement the conclusion is drawn that it is not systematic. But the discussions on epistemology and on the nature of controversy and logic go to show how and how far systematic thinking is consistent with spiritual philosophy. The Indian interest in the problems of validity and invalidity, valid cognition and invalid cognition, the nature of the illusory object, and the absence of any important place for intuition in the means of valid cognition show whether the Indian thinkers were logical or intuitive. The student can answer the question for himself. Intuition is not recognized as a valid means of cognition for philosophical controversies. It appears in the Nyāya-Vaiśeṣika as the contact of the sense with the universal present in the perceived individual. But such an intuition is not infallible. It appears also in this school and in some others like Jainism as yogic knowledge; but it is not accepted as a valid means of knowledge for philosophical discussion. It appears, again, as integral experience in the Advaita, Radhakrishnan, and Aurobindo. But it is not a means of knowledge, but knowledge or consciousness that is also Being. Its recognition is meant to show that knowing is an act of the spirit.

If knowing is an act of the spirit, then idealism and existentialism should be capable of reconciliation. The cue for such a reconciliation is found in the Vedāntic systems. That is why Radhakrishnan, although calling himself an idealistic Vedāntin, says that existentialism is not new to the Upaniṣads. Neither must idealism be opposed to epistemological realism. If it is opposed, it can have no criterion for differentiating truth from falsity.

(iv) Ethical Thought in India

It is often said that India has no ethical thought. This criticism is true in a sense. There is no book like Plato's *Republic* in classical times in India. That is why, compared to the metaphysical and epistemological discussions, those on ethics and politics are very few. They are found in an unsystematized form only in the epics. The acceptance of the caste structure and the later rationalization of a historical fact stood in the way of further thinking about the subject. Yet we should not think that the Indian society was unethical or its ethics of action lacked all metaphysical foundation. The ethics of the individual and his caste, so long as he remained in it—for very often men of all castes became kings and emperors and entered the warrior caste—was as rigorous as anywhere else, and all ethical action was related to the Mīmāmsā concept of *dharma*, as the law of action, raised to a metaphysical level. All the ethical and legal codes called themselves applications of the law of action (*dharma*). But the philosophy of applications was not philosophical enough. The defect was that a historical fact, viz., the caste division, was taken as the ideal. The question was raised: Do character and profession have a necessary relation to colour of skin and birth? It was sometimes answered in the negative, but only to condemn people who did not live up to their ideal, but not to recommend people to a higher caste even when they rose above the ideal, but did not have the power and influence to compel recognition. On the whole, there was a general philosophical indifference to ethical and social thought. The necessary material for building up ethical and social philosophies was present, but no super-structures were raised. The result was that Indian society remained static for a long time. But the philosophies of salvation, metaphysics, and epistemology received great development.

(v) History and Indian Philosophy

We may say that this overwhelming interest in metaphysics and epistemology and the conviction that the eternal structure of society is the caste system are responsible for the so-called lack of historical sense in the Indians. History concerns the progress of society, whether progress is understood as continuous improvement in the mundane world, overcoming occasional appearances of evil, but without end or as being directed towards the great event, viz., the appearance of the kingdom of God on earth. If man does not have either idea, he may care very little for history, except for drawing a lesson from past mistakes. But caste system was supposed to be the perfect order; if man could retain it, everything would be all right. The individual's future, it was thought, does not lie in history, but in the transcendence of history, as Reinhold Niebhur among contemporary theologians holds. Yet even for mundane uses, history is important. As the ancients did not see its importance, they did not devote much thought to it. It is strange that a definite logical conception of history was not evolved, in spite of the fact that there was a school of philosophers called historians (*paurāṇikas*), who accepted in epistemology memory (*smṛti*) and tradition (*aitihya*) as valid means of cognition. History needs the recognition of the two forms of knowing. Memories may be preserved in tablets. There may be a tradition—a story of what happened, which is not the memory of the person who saw the happenings—that some gods lived nearby and went down the earth, which had become full of evil. It is on the basis of such stories that archeologists experiment. It appears that archeology as a science was not known in India of the time. Yet we come across these two valid means of knowing in the writings of the Nyāya-Vaiśeṣika, the Sāṅkhya-Yoga, and the Vedānta, all of which reject them. But that we find their mention and their attribution to the historians is very intriguing: Did the historians write any books on historical knowledge? We do not know. We know that there are several works divided into two classes, *purāṇas* and *itihāsas*, both of which are classed together under the English name epics. *Purāṇa* is defined[5] as a description of the five—creation, dissolution, dynasties, the periods of the progenitors of mankind, and the activities of the dynasties. Thus *purāṇa* is a world-history or history of the cosmos with relevance to the human situations created by the law-givers (*manus* are the progenitors of mankind and also the law-givers)[6] and the activites of the imperial and royal dynasties. *Itihāsa* is defined as a narration of what happened in the past along with (directed to) the teaching of the four values of life—wealth, enjoyment, ethical merit, and salvation.[7] In spite of the presence of these divisions and classifications and also of the recognition of the distinctive means of historical knowledge, India has not produced strict histories and their theories. It becomes all the more intriguing when we see that the Indian linguists could produce some of the most profound philosophies of language and grammar, but the historians could not produce philosophies of history or methods of historiography. Besides the reasons above mentioned for lack of historical knowledge in India, we may give two other reasons. First, the conception of the world process was over-charged with a sense of the metaphysical ethical potency and a sense of the presence of the eternal in the ever-changing historical events. Second, the ethical ideal was always felt to the pointing to the eternal divine. These attitudes are not new to the western theologians and are particularly present in the Greek subordination of the historical to the metaphysical reality. The wonder, again, is that, in spite of the strong sense of the transience of the mundane, the historical sense of the Greeks, the Jews, and the Christians was quite strong. Indeed, it was stronger in the latter two than in the former.

(vi) Subjectivism a False Charge

Another criticism of Indian thought is that it is subject-centred, that it cares for the object only so far as it is useful to the subject, that in its scientific attitude it is pragmatic and utilitarian, and that it cannot, therefore, encourage science for science's sake and knowledge for knowledge's sake. One wonders whether the charges of pragmatism and utilitarianism, if they are bad, can be levelled only against Indian thought, for which all is for the sake of the spirit in man. It is not necessary also to point to the latest attitudes of scientific philosophers like Bertrand Russell, who stage civil disobedience for the sake of man against manufacture and use of atomic weapons. What else do their activities show than that science should be made an instrument of human values? But do they show that science should not be studied for science's sake? Even according to the Indian thinkers, spiritual realization is not possible, unless man leads a life according to reality. Such a life is not possible also, unless man understands reality as it is. Otherwise, man will live in a false reality and lead a false life.[8] The epistemological discussions of Indian thinkers show that they were not pragmatic and utilitarian in the vulgarized senses of the terms. This charge against Indian thought is an unexamined one.

(vii) Pantheism and Pessimism not True

The charges that Indian thought is pantheistic and pessimistic are too old and too many times answered that they do not need detailed discussion again. Does God's omniscience or omnipresence mean pantheism? If it does not, then Indian philosophy is not pantheistic. Should we define optimism in the words of F. H. Bradley as the doctrine that this world is the best of all possible worlds, in which everything is bad? Does it mean that the world, as it is, is perfect? And how many western philosophers and theologians have not asserted that the world cannot be perfect in and within history, that the kingdom of God cannot be an event in history, and that the end of history cannot be within history? Does faith in progress necessarily mean that the kingdom of God will be an event in historical time? I remember that in the East-West Philosophers Conference of 1959, when someone pointed out that Indian thought is pessimistic, H. W. Schneider said that for the Indians the world may be full of sorrow, but for the westerners it is full of anxiety and nausea. A divine sadness, a dissatisfaction with the imperfections of the world from the eternal point of view, is not pessimism in the bad sense of the term. It is at the root of all progress. It is present at the root of all great religions. When was the world without acute problems and when will it be without them? Is there a guarantee that, if one generation succeeds in solving its problems, new problems will not arise for the next? It seems to be a safer advice that each generation should solve its problems and that the next generation should be ready to face new ones than the one that all problems will be solved in some future for this world and for man through God or natural, dialectical, biological, psychological, or sociological evolution. The new generations will then be kept alert and do not think that the Utopia has been realized.[9]

(viii) Totalitarianism not Implied

More important than the above charges is a new one, viz., that India is not fit for democracy because it believes in the Absolute, the Brahman, which is all and more. If the Absolute is the truth in metaphysics, then the government, it is thought, must be totalitarian dictatorship. The critic here must have Hegel and Marx in mind. But first, the Indian philosophers never dreamed of applying the concept of the Brahman to politics. They never accepted that it could be identified or equated to any political structure. Even Śaṅkara dismissed everything in the world as self-contradictory and as not representing the Brahman; then how can any one say that a dictatorial government represents the Brahman? Secondly, even if we accept a theistic personal God different from all the souls; as God is omnipotent, one may draw the conclusion that the political form should be autocratic if it is to represent the relationship of God and souls. God then will be the autocrat and the souls his subjects or slaves. But is he the Louis XIV of the heavens? In the *third* place, since the Brahman is the Supreme Spirit and the Spirit of all, the subjects, the Indian thinkers may say, can each claim that he is as great and important as the ruler. For the Brahman is the Spirit of not only the ruler but also of the subject. Then democracy will be the best political structure that represents the relation between the Absolute and man. There will really be no king or ruler to represent the omnipotent personal God, unconditionally to obey whom is the duty of the subjects. This criticism of the charge is not meant to show that India is perfect, but that the charge is philosophically unexamined. Indeed, no application of metaphysical truths can be so direct as the charge implies. We should remind ourselves of Kant's warning that categories applicable to the world should not be applied to the Ideals of Reason. God's power is unlimited, but not that of kings. The Absolute may be the Supreme Spirit and, as some say, the only truth; but it is not true that the dictator's will is the only will and what is good for him is the good for all. That man is made in the image of God does not mean that man, like his prototype, has unlimited freedom to do whatever he likes. And even if the spirit of every man is the same Supreme Spirit, it is not meant that a particular man, the dictator, represents the Supreme Spirit and be its viceroy. Nor does the one-ness of the Brahman mean one-ness of culture and regimentation of all the activities of all men. We should not forget that the Brahman transcends all thought and speech and that Indian religion and philosophies repeatedly proclaimed the possibility of a plurality of approaches to the Brahman. Neither is this plurality the same as anarchy and political chaos. One has to be careful that such conclusions, when philosophically viewed, do not end up as sophisms.

It is really a hard task and a wrong one to interpret Indian culture in terms of any of its philosophies. We should always keep in mind Kant's warning that opposite conclusions can be drawn from metaphysical ideas,[10] if their function is not properly understood. On the basis of absolutism, theism, deism, or materialism, any kind of political philosophy can be developed. But India did not and does not have any one of these political philosophies. Then the problem of deducing a political theory from them becomes all the more complicated. No culture—except the communist—is based on a single philosophy. Even Marx is not understood in a single way, except when a government forces its own interpretation on its people. One will not be too mistaken in saying that in contemporary times a people choose or have been made to choose a particular political structure corresponding to which a philosophy is accepted or developed. One cannot be sure and prophesy what India will choose in the distant future; but if one is allowed to foresee on the basis of the past, India will not choose dictatorship and totalitarianism in the undesirable senses of the terms. So far as her past goes, the life of her people was guided by the activism of the Mīmāmsā and the ideas of social and legal life derived from it and by the spiritual philosophies of the Vedānta. Her culture was not as one-sidedly otherworldly as it is often represented, although during the tragic periods of her history she took refuge in the philosophies of the spirit. But as soon as the catastrophes passed over, her life became as this-worldly as anywhere else. The ups and downs of fortune coincided with the dominance—not merely the presence—of activistic and contemplative philosophies or philosophies in which the outwardness and inwardness of man were emphasized alternately. But the history of India does not show that the origin of such philosophies was the result of social or political prosperity or catastrophe. Once such philosophies are at hand, the individual, community, or nation takes recourse to them, according to the conditions, for support or consolation. Neither men nor nations nor even philosophy itself can be charged with too much consistency. Life uses, but is not used by philosophy. Man is creative, but is not merely a creature of culture, whether in India or the West.

It is true that the rational essence of a culture is expressed in its philosophy. But when a culture has many philosophies, the task of interpreting the culture from only one of its philosophies is a mistake. It is easier to develop a philosophy out of the ideas of a culture—for then we may and can omit many elements of the culture, if they do not suit the superstructure of that philosophy—than to derive that culture out of that philosophy. Bertrand Russell thought that pragmatism was dangerous, as it would lead to the Marxian doctrine of the identity of theory and action.[11] But it will be the wonder of wonders if the United States ever becomes Marxist. The methods for a philosophical interpretation of culture are more complicated than discovering this or that line of thought in this or that philosophy of a particular culture. But it is beyond our scope to discuss them.

(ix) Activism not Necessarily Opposed to the Vedānta

That the world is a world of action and is meant for action is implied by all the schools of Indian philosophy except perhaps by the Cārvākas and some allied schools.

We have shown that the theory that the judgment is true if the object referred to performs the function for which it is meant (*arthakriyākāritā*) is involved in various degrees in the epistemologies of the schools, whether they are realist or idealist. All schools which accept the doctrine of *karma* and the law of ethical action have to accept the doctrine in some way. For the potencies of *karma* reside in the soul (*jīva, ātman*) and produce for it the world of subject-object and subject-predicate for the sake of further action and enjoyment. And it cannot but be true that what is produced by action (*karma*) for the sake of action can be confirmed mainly, if not only, by action and enjoyment. But enjoyment is not bits of experience or self-divided experience, but unitary; it is the return of the self to itself in the sense of achievement or attainment. It is the self-unification after diversification. Achievement through action is occasioned only when first there is a sense of the lack of something, of some incompleteness in the self. Then the self pulls itself out of itself or branches itself out to the object. When the object is obtained, achievement produces the sense of self-completeness by a return of what is pulled out into the original unity, although the return and the sense of achievement are temporary in the mundane world or the world of time. They are only temporary self-realizations. Man goes after things, one after another, unendingly with the same sense of lack or incompleteness so long as he is finite. What is needed then for full enjoyment is the realization of the fulness and infinity of the self (*ātman, ahamtā*).

So far as action and self-realization, without which action cannot be understood, go, the two important terms are enjoyment and self-completion of the self. Enjoyment is the return of the self to itself, after experience of the lack is removed; it is the realization of the self's fullness and its self-identity. For the sense of lack is a kind self-estrangement, part of the self being painfully dragged out of the rest or a pulling out of the self out of itself out there to the object. Then the aim of action is not merely the possession of the object that is desired, but the realization of one-self as possessing the desired object and so as incorporating it into one's self. This may be called differently from different points of view as the realization of one's fullness (*pūrṇāhamtā*) or as the absolute unity of the self with the world (*ātmaiva idam sarvam*).

One sees opposition between action and self-realization (of the Vedānta), only if one does not grasp the essential, deeper aspect of action. Going to his school from his house by Jim does not lie merely in the movement of his legs, but in his being at the school in the end and not being there in the beginning. It is a transformation of Jim's conscious being, his consciousness coinciding with the environment of the school and his "I" (*aham*) identifying itself with that consciousness. Who can see the whole of any action? In fact, who can see any action? Even a simple movement of my hand in lifting something is not seen by my eye or any other sense as one single unitary action. It is often said that my lifting of my hand is a series of instantaneous sensations or static pictures interpreted by mind as a single action. But is this interpretation an inference, syllogistic or otherwise? It is the experience of something unitary from lack of fulfilment to its attainment. It is a unitary something or idea that urges Jim to act and it is again a unitary experience that produces the sense of attainment in him. In the first case, it is the experience of something without succession or sequence (*akrama*) expressing itself externally as a succession of actions (*sakrama*), one movement after another of each of his feet; in the second case, the succession of movements enters him and produces in him a unitary sense of fulfilment, stops him from further walking and makes him sit in his chair or at his table. That is, a new action starts to work. But it should be noted that it is not the succession of walking movements that start the new action; it is he himself in his freedom and with his purposes who starts the new movements. It should be noted further that the consciousness of moments of action is not the same as the consciousness of the action of sitting, or of listening to what the teacher says; but it is Jim, the "he" or the *aham* or the I, the first person in him, that is the same and relates together all the different consciousnesses. It is this "I" that is prompted by the different lacks and fulfilments[12] and is itself without a succession of moments. The urge has to be unitary and the achievement has to be unitary; they are not possible unless Jim is a unitary self. Because of the non-dual (*advaita*, undivided) self in him, these unitary experiences[13] are possible.

So to maintain that action is opposed to the realization of ultimate Truth is to take action at the mundane level and ultimate Truth at the transcendental level. But action also at the transcendental level is a self-conscious unity of plurality, the plurality being directed towards the unity. Thus, action, when properly understood, is as good a path to self-realization as cognition (*jñāna*). Action can rightly be interpreted, as the *Bhagavadgītā* does, in interpreting sacrifice as the sacrificial oblation (*homa*) of the whole plurality (the horse of the horse sacrifice, the world, and man's psycho-physical plurality) into the unity of the self (*ātman*). It may be said that the Vedānta's, particularly the Advaita's, opposition to the way of action (*karma-mārga*) is due to the degeneration of the Mīmāmsā theory of *karma* as sacrificial activity as purely ritualistic. It is said that Jaimini, the author of the *Mīmāmsā Aphorisms*, was originally the author of *Vedānta Aphorisms* also before Bādarāyaṇa. If he was, he must have reconciled action and self-realization there; but we do not have his work except in some references. We have only his *Mīmāmsā Aphorisms*.

Thus at the deepest levels, the structures of all the phenomena—action, time, cognition, space, causation and so on—end up in Being (*sattā*), the *sattā* of the Supreme Spirit, the great I-AM, which knows itself as inclusive of everything, as lying at its roots and supplying Being to it, and which knows itself not as facing anything which it is not, but as comprehending it and including it in its own Being.

NOTES

1See Mādhavāchārya: *Sarvadarśanasaṅgraha*, Chapter XV; Bhartṛhari: *Vākyapadīya*; Yāska: *Nirukta*; Jagadīśa; *Śabdaśaktiprakaśa*; K. Kunjunni Raja: *Indian Theories of Meaning*; B. Bhattacharya: *Language and Meaning*; Max Müller: *The Science of Thought*; W. D. Whitney: *Oriental and Linguistic Studies*.

2S. Radhakrishnan: *Indian Philosophy*, Vol. I, p. 8.

3E. von Hartman: *Philosophie des Unbewussten*, Part I, pp. 26–27.(I find this name spelt sometimes with two "ns").

4Helmuth von Glassenapp: *Das Indienbild deutscher Denker*, pp. 27 fol.

5*Sargaśca pratisargaśca vamśo manvantārani ca vamśānucaritam caiva purāṇam pañcalakṣaṇam.*

6They are like Moses and Adam combined in Judo-Christian mythology, and are said to be fourteen in number. When the law of one law-giver became weak in the succeeding generations, another rose to strengthen it. The word "man" is derived from the word *manu* (the progenitor of man), which itself is derived from the verbal root *man*, meaning "to think," to which the Latin word "*mens*" can be traced. But "to think" must have been understood by the historian philosophers of India as "to think rightly," right meaning both the logical and the ethical. Thus Manu came to mean the law-giver. A *manvantara* is the period between one Manu and the next, and is said to last for 4,320,000 years.

[7]*Dharmārthakāmamokṣāṇām upadeśasamanvitam Purvavṛttakathāyuktam itihāsah pracakṣyate*. The *Rāmāyaṇa* and *Mahābhārata* are said to be *itihāsas* and the *Bhāgavata* is said to be a *purāṇa*. In popular language, all are *purāṇas*.

[8]He may live in a world of his fantasy. Should we not say that there are cultural, national, political, and religious fantasies, which work for the miseries of man?

[9]The above defence is only philosophical. The author is not unaware of the vast and immense poverty of India and its contrast to the ancient account of the wealth and prosperity, which attracted many foreign invaders. But no philosophical idea should hastily be applied without examination to a historical fact. If at the time when these philosophical ideas were ruling, India was prosperous, they cannot be the direct causes of effect of its poverty.

[10]Cp. his transcendental dialectic.

[11]Bertrand Russell: *My Philosophical Development*, p. 179.

[12]Hegel in his *Phenomenology* would agree with this interpretation.

[13]These unitary experiences are similar to the *sphoṭas*, the unitary *Gestalts* of meaning of the grammarian philosophers. But they should have gone from the *sphoṭas* to the unitary self (*ātman*)—for it is the *ātman* that is the controller of the *sphoṭas*—which they have not done clearly. We cannot discuss the point further for want of space. Cp. the view of Kasmir Śaivism. See Abhinavagupta: *Tantrāloka*, Vol. I, I, 155, with the Commentary of Jayadratha (Kasmir Series of Texts and Studies, Srinagar, 1918).

Appendices

1. GLOSSARY OF IMPORTANT SANSKRIT TERMS

It is difficult to collect all the important philosophical terms and give their meanings, unless we are prepared to write a dictionary. The present list cannot claim to be exhaustive; it can only be called helpful. The reader should not take any meaning of the term in any context as he chooses. Even the technical uses of the terms are many. He should not rely on Sanskrit-English dictionaries only, not even on the Sanskrit lexicons. For obtaining the correct meanings of the terms in their contexts, commentaries are indispensable, particularly in all cases in which the terms do not have physical meanings.

abaddham: not bound (to reality), false; freed, liberated.
abhāva: absence, negation; the negative; nothing.
ābhāsa: appearance; falsity.
abhihitānvaya: relating the meanings of words of a sentence after they are uttered; opposed to *anvitābhidhāna*.
adharma: demerit; sin; crime.
adṛṣṭa: unseen, unobserved; merit and demerit as unseen; fate; *kārmic* potencies lying hidden and acting as determinants or fate. See *apūrva* and *niyati*.
advaita: non-dual, non-duality, non-dualism; one, monism.
advaitin: non-dualist; monist.
advaya: non-dual, one.
āgama: that which has come down by tradition; name of any of the texts of sectarian religious philosophies like the Pāñcarātra, Pāśupata and Śākta; occasionally it means the Veda also; any sacred text.
agraha: non-cognition, non-perception; see *anupalabdhi*.
ahamdhī: I-consciousness, to be differentiated from *ahaṁkāra* or ego.
ahamkāra: ego, different from *ahamdhī* in most of the systems. Only in works of Kasmir Śaivism the words are occasionally used like synonyms.
aitihya: historical evidence; tradition; belief handed down; rumour.
ajātivāda: the doctrine that the world and the individual are not there, have not been formed or created at all, and nothing—law, *karma*, sin, merit, etc., —is real. This view held only from the ultimate point of view is often misunderstood and misapplied.
ākāśa: space; sky; ether; room; the word does not mean necessarily physical space, but

also mental, intellectual, and spiritual space; even Māyā is called *ākāśa* in many places in the sense of *avyakta*, the unmanifest, for the manifest is that which has acquired a shape, a contour, the unmanifest is the opposite. The word has associations with both sound and room or space. (Here is a new significance of the idea of space.)

akhyāti: non-perception, non-cognition, absence of cognition, an element that is missed in any cognition, the missing of that element; although etymologically, it is akin to *anupalabdhi* and *agraha*, technically it is different from *anupalabdhi*, but sometimes used as a synonym for *agraha*.

akhyātivāda: the doctrine that the object of illusion is due to the non-perception (of the difference between the seen and the remembered objects).

akṣara: imperishable, non-transient; the imperishable, the non-transient; sometimes used in the neuter gender and other times in the masculine. In the masculine it nearly invariably means the Brahman as God. In the neuter it similarly means Māyā, Prakṛti, which is insentient. But the usage is not uniform. One has to depend on the commentator.

alaya: Buddhist term meaning the indissoluble, the imperishable, the unending; corresponds to *akṣara* in meaning; some Buddhists say that *alaya* is higher than *ālaya*, also called *ālaya-vijñāna*. Do not miss the difference between *a* and *ā*.

ālaya: receptacle, storehouse; same as *ālaya-vijñāna*.

ālaya-vijñāna: the source and the storehouse of all the empirical forms of consciousness (*vijñāna*); the repository of all; corresponds in function to the causal body (*kāraṇa-śarīra*, *bījātman*) of the Advaita; treated by some Buddhists as the ultimate metaphysical reality; akin in connotation to apperception, *citta* of the Vedāntins; compare its similarities and differences to *sākṣi-caitanya*.

ālocanā: a Jaina epistemological term meaning "looking at," "approach."

anekānta-vāda: the doctrine that reality is modal and that all modes of perception are true; the doctrine of tropes; the doctrine that all relative truths are true and have their absoluteness.

anirvacanīya: inexplicable, indefinable; used as a synonym for Māyā and Avidyā or Ajñāna in the Advaita and the Mahāyāna.

anirvacanīya-khyāti-vāda: the doctrine that the object of illusion is inexplicable in terms of Being and Non-being, reality and unreality, truth and falsity.

antahkaraṇa: inner instrument, inner sense, consisting of reason (*buddhi*), ego (*ahaṁkāra*), and mind (*manas*); often only *manas* or only *buddhi* is used in its place; see *manas*.

antarmukhatā: inwardness; inward-directedness as of the phenomenological consciousness.

antaryāmin: inner controller, the higher spirit within.

aṇu: atom, absolutely small.

anumāna: inference; syllogism; that which comes after the first measure, viz., perception.

anupalabdhi: non-cognition, non-apprehension, non-perception; name of one of the means of valid means of cognition; note the difference from *akhyāti* and *agraha*.

anuvyavasāya: reflective cognition as in "I know that I know *X*."

anvitābhidhāna: see *abhihitānvaya*.

anyathākhyāti-vāda: the doctrine that illusion is the perception of the object in front as determined by the form (universal) of a remembered object (advocated by the Nyāya).
aparokṣa: direct, immediate cognition like the cognition of the existence of one's self.
apavarga: liberation, salvation.
apūrva: the extraordinary; merit and merit in the form or state of latency or potency; another name for *adṛṣṭa*.
artha: meaning; object; wealth; purpose, aim.
arthakriyā: purposive action; action directed towards a purpose.
arthakriyā-kāritā: fulfillment through action of the purpose for which the perceived object is meant; the pragmatic criterion of truth.
arthāpatti: presumption, presupposition; one of the means of valid knowledge.
asat: non-being, non-existence; the non-existent, the unreal; false, untrue.
asatkārya-vāda: the doctrine that the effect is non-being before it is born.
asatkhyāti-vāda: the doctrine that the object of illusion is non-being; generally attributed by the rivals to Nāgārjuna.
asmitā: one of the impurities (*kleśas*) of personality in the form of clinging to being what one is; also "am-ness" or pure self-affirmation, the experience of "am" without the ego, equated to Mahat by the Sāṅkhya; note the difference between the two meanings.
āśarma: a stage of life such as that of the student, householder, forest dweller, and the monk.
āśrava: inflow of *karma* in Jainism.
ātman: spirit; self; soul; if it is identical with the Brahman, it means the Brahman also, which is now and then called the *Paramātman*, the Supreme Spirit; *ātman* and *jīva* are used indifferently in Jainism and a few of the Vedāntic systems, but *jīva* means necessarily the soul as an ethical personality. See *paramātman*; *ātman* is now and then used in the sense of mind (*manas*); lexicons give many meanings.
avadhi: limited knowledge (in Jainism); limit, boundary.
avagraha: (Jainism) approach (to the object).
āvaraṇa: veil, screen.
avicyuti: (Jainism) non-stopping.
avidyā: same as *ajñāna*; *karma* also according to Rāmānuja; a veil or screen making the soul forget its relationship with the Brahman, according to Madhva.
avyakta: unmanifest; the Unmanifest; used as a synonym for Prakṛti and Māyā also; in the sectarian *āgamas* and in the *Bhagavadgītā*, it is the name of God before he manifests the world.
āyatana: support; site; cause; basis.
bahirmukhatā: outward-directedness (e.g., of the phenomenological consciousness); cp. *antarmukhatā*.
baddha: bound; determined (e.g., perception, if true, is determined by the object perceived, it is bound to it).
bandha: bondage; determination; control.
bhakti: devotion; love (not sexual).
bhedābheda: identity-cum-difference; identity-in-difference.
bhramā: error, illusion, hallucination; opposite of *pramā*.

bījātman: same as *kāraṇa-śarīra*; cp. *prājna*, *ālaya-vijñāna*, *citta*, and apperception.

bodhisattva: a Buddhist term meaning a being whose being is enlightened or enlightenment itself; one who is about to attain Buddhahood, but does not enter Nirvāṇa so that he can work for the salvation and enlightenment of the rest of the world; a Mahāyāna ideal opposed to the Hīnayāna ideal of the *arhat* (the deserving one), one who works for his own salvation.

brahman: the ever-growing, the ever-expanding; the Absolute; the Supreme Spirit; the personal God according to many forms of Śaivism and Vaiṣṇavism.

buddhi: reason; mind; knowledge, cognition, consciousness; concept, idea; in the Sāṅkhya-Yoga and the Vedānta, it has ontological significance, as in the philosophy of Plato; in the Nyāya-Vaiśeṣika and the Mīmāmsā, it is the consciousness which arises when the self knows an object; see *sattva* and *vijñāna*; apperception.

cit: consciousness.

citta: apperception, apperceptive reason; that which gathers (*cinoti*) and integrates all knowledge in man and constitutes his apperceptive mind; in the Sāṅkhya-Yoga, it is a synonym for *buddhi*, *mahat*, *vijñāna*, and *sattva*; in the Advaita, *buddhi* is the asserting, assenting, deciding (decision-making) function and *citta* is the apperceptive function of *antahkaraṇa*. (cp. the philosophies of Madhva and Rāmānuja and the roles of Mahat, Mahān Ātmā, and Hiraṇyagarbha); that which makes a thing conscious (cetayati).

darśana: perception; view; vision; philosophy; system.

devas: light-givers; those which or who shine; senses; the presiding deities of the senses, etc.

dhāraṇa: stabilization, retention (in Jainism and Yoga).

dhārāvāhika-jñāna: cognitive flow as in "That is a rose, that is a rose, that is a rose" and so on. It is a repetition of the same cognition and has to be differentiated from *anuvyavasāya*.

dharma: that which supports; nature; the law of nature; virtue; ethical law; the "ought"; merit; the potency of ethical actions; the right action; the law or the body of the doctrines of any faith; quality; characteristic; the law of the universe; reality; element; category; the principle of motion in Jainism.

dharmabhūta-jñāna: attribute consciousness in Rāmānuja; phenomenological consciousness.

dhātu: ore; original element.

dhyāna: meditation, concentration.

dik: space; direction; see *ākāśa*.

dravya: that which flows; substance.

duhkha: pain, suffering, misery, grief, sorrow, unhappiness.

dvaita: duel; the dual; dualistic; duality; dualism.

guṇa: quality; property; attribute (in the sense of Spinoza's).

hetu: cause, reason, ground.

hetvābhāsa: fallacy; illusion of reason.

hīnayāna: the lower vehicle; the earlier Buddhism, considered to be the orthodox, original Buddhism; a name given to all the southern schools of Buddhism, as distinguished from the Mahāyāna.

Hiraṇyagarbha: the golden womb; the foetus which is golden or conscious; the first appearance of the life of consciousness; cp. the embryonic consciousness (*vijñāna*) in the Buddhist twelve-linked causation, at the cosmic level, but not at the individual's level; cp. also the *taijasa* of the *Māṇḍūkya Upaniṣad*. *Hiraṇyagarbha* is also called *sūtrātman*, the *ātman* cosmic in significance playing the role of the thread passing through all the beads of a necklace that is, interconnecting all the souls through their life-principle (*prāṇa*).

īha: expectation (Jaina epistemology).

indriya: sense; organ.

jaḍa: the insentient; the inorganic; matter.

jāti: genus; universal; see *sāmānya*; it means also one of the wrong ways of arguing, raising a futile objection to a position; birth; source; caste.

jīva: soul as the ethical person; in Jainism it is used as a synonym for the *ātman* also.

jñāna: consciousness; knowledge; cognition.

jnānātman: *buddhi*, rational consciousness; cp. *dharmabhūta-jñāna* and *sākṣi-caitanya*, apperception, *citta, mahat*; different from *śānta ātman*, which is pure peace, unagitated, unvibrating.

jñātā: the knower (*jñātṛ*)

jñeya: the knowable.

kalā: limited ability; a digit.

kāla: time.

kāma: desire; love; pleasure; enjoyment; passion (not in the sense of "passive").

karaṇam: instrument; the main instrument; the main cause.

kāraṇam: cause; reason; ground; support; occasion.

karma: action; activity; process; the result or potency created by ethical action; rite; past actions in their potential forms or states.

kaivalya: alone-ness; salvation.

kevala: alone; absolutely direct (knowledge) in Jainism.

khyāti-vādas: doctrines of illusory and hallucinatory perceptions; although *khyāti* means cognition or knowledge, in this context it means illusory or hallucinatory cognition.

kośas: sheaths; collections.

kṣaṇa: instant; moment.

kṣaṇika-vāda: doctrine of momentariness; *kṣaṇika* means momentary; a doctrine of Buddhism.

kūṭastha: the name of the consciousness or person that is present in the unity or knot of all the forces that constitute the Unconscious and that is stable and alive to everything which man does and experiences; the consciousness that is present in the unity of *buddhi*, *ahaṁkāra*, and *manas*, which together constitute the inner instrument, *antahkaraṇa*, called here the group (*kūṭa*); a higher or deeper level of the soul; a higher "I"; for some thinkers, it is God himself, who is present in every person.

lakṣaṇa: mark; character; definition.

mahat, *mahān ātmā*: see *buddhi*, Hiraṇyagarbha.

mahāsattā: the Great Being; the Logos; the Sound Brahman; the Word; see *sphoṭa*.

mahāyāna: the higher vehicle of Buddhism; a name for all the northern schools of Buddhism taken together.
māna: measure.
manana: reflecting.
manahparyāya: knowledge of other minds (Jainism).
manas: mind, to be distinguished from mind as understood in Anglo-American psychology; sometimes used in the very wide sense of *antahkaraṇa*, when it coincides with the Anglo-American usage. In any context interpreters have to be careful and should refer to the commentaries.
mārga: way, path; the path to salvation; often the word yoga is used in its place.
mata: opinion; view; doctrine; faith; religion; thought.
mati: thinking, thought opinion (Jainism).
māyā: illusion; a synonym for Prakṛti, Avyakta, Pradhāna, Avidyā, Ajñāna, and Avyākṛta; the measured; the determined; cp. *prameya*.
mīmāmsā: discussion; debate; criticism; critical interpretation; name of the school of Jaimini, based on the first two parts of the Veda.
mithyā: the illusory, false, non-existent; illusion; see *bhramā*.
mokṣa: liberation, salvation, emancipation.
mukti: same as *mokṣa*
nayavāda: doctrine of tropes, of modalities, of points of view.
nididhyāsana: meditation.
nigamana: conclusion (as in Q.E.D.)
nirguṇa: without qualities, without characteristics, without attributes.
nirvāṇa: the unagitated; peace; salvation.
nirvikalpa: indeterminate, formless, absolutely direct cognition; see *asamprajñāta*; according to the Nyāya-vaiśeṣika, it is neither *pramā* nor *bhrama*, neither true nor false; but according to the Vedānta, it is absolutely true in the case of the cognition of the Brahman; according to the Yoga also, it can be true, cp. *ṛtambharā*.
nirviśeṣa: without *viśeṣa* or form (note the new meaning of *viśeṣa*); same as *nirvikalpa*.
nirvṛtti: attainment, completion, perfection.
nivṛtti: withdrawal from outward activity; turning inwards.
niyama: vow; self-imposed and accepted restriction.
pakṣa: minor term.
para: higher.
paramārtha: ultimate, highest, absolute; the absolute reality or truth.
pāramārthika: adjective derived from *paramārtha*.
paramātman: the Supreme Spirit; see *ātman*.
pariṇāma: change, transformation; transformation in which the being of the material cause is changed into something else and cannot be regained.
parokṣa: knowledge beyond the senses, indirect knowledge; that which is not direct experience; sometimes sense knowledge is included as it is said to be knowledge mediated by the senses and mind.
paryāya: synonym; in Jainism, quality, mode; change.
phala: result, fruit; *Ergebnis* as in German epistemology.

pradhāna: the primary, the important, the basic; a synonym for Prakṛti.

prajñā: a synonym for *buddhi*; intense knowledge, intense consciousness; intense self-consciousness; consciousness; knowledge.

prājña: the name for the *ātman* in the state of deep sleep; cp. Iśvara in Śaṅkara's philosophy; one who has *prajñā*; note the difference in Sanskrit spellings, i.e., diacritical marks.

prajñapti: apperceptive force in Buddhism.

prakāra: form; universal; method.

prakṛti: synonym for Pradhāna, Māyā etc., the schools differing in their interpretations; literally, the original; personified will of the Supreme Spirit.

pramā: valid knowledge; valid cognition, obtained through measuring by senses, mind, and reason.

pramāna: means of valid cognition like perception and inference.

prāmānya: validity of knowledge.

prāmānyavāda: doctrine of the validity of knowledge in answer to the question whether cognition is valid by itself or made valid by something else.

prameya: the knowable; object of cognition or knowledge.

prāṇa: life, vital principle; in some places it means a sense or organ of action; called *jīvitendriya* or the sense of living and also *jīvanayoni-yatna* or the origin or the womb of the effort of living.

pratibhāsa: appearance.

prātibhāsika: apparent, seeming; false.

pratijñā: thesis; hypothesis.

pratītya-samutpāda: dependent origination; the doctrine that the cause is only an occasion for the effect; the Buddhist doctrine of causation.

pratiyogi: counter-part; in referential cognition and experience, that on which the term depends or that to which it has to refer for its meaning.

pratyabhijñā: recognition.

pratyakṣa: sense perception; perception.

pratyāsatti: contact.

pravṛtti: activity directed towards external objects; the life of action; opposed to *nivṛtti* which is the life of withdrawal from the external world (not in the sense of abnormal psychology, but as characterizing the life of the saint in meditation).

pudgala: the psycho-physical person in Buddhism; the physical body in literary language.

puruṣa: *ātman*; person; man; man as distinct from woman; spirit; soul.

rajas: one of the Attributes of Prakṛti, called the Active; the world of action, movement, process.

saguṇa: with qualities or characteristics.

sākṣi: witness; witness consciousness; cp. *dharmabhūta-jñāna*, apperception *citta*, etc., and note the similarities and differences; cp. witness in Husserl's philosophy.

sākṣi-caitanya: witness consciousness.

samādhi: trance, ecstacy (not the existentialist ecstacy); intense concentration of one's being; the final stage in Yoga.

sāmānya: the common; common characteristic; cp. *jāti* in the sense of the genus, which is not merely that which is common to a number of individuals, but also that which determines their nature. The common may be a superficial common characteristic; the universal; idea.

samāpatti: in Yoga, the state of becoming (one with the object of cognition, the instrument of cognition, and the subject or agent of cognition) in meditation; attainment; achievement.

saṁghāta: collection, aggregate.

saṁghātavāda: the doctrine in Buddhism that the effect is only an aggregate of the constituents forming the material cause.

samjñā: sign; idea, ideal form.

samsāra: the flux of the world; the flow of the world; world.

samskāra: impression; instinct; imprint; innate tendency; innate potency; innate formative force; trauma; mold; nature inborn.

samsthāna: structure; settlement.

samvara: in Jainism damming the inflow of action; stopping action.

samvṛti: in Buddhism the empirical world; that which is surrounded, limited; limit, boundary.

samyoga: contact; conjunction.

sannikarṣa: see *pratyāsatti*; contact; nearness; connection.

śānta-ātmā: the *ātman* without agitation, disturbance, activity; the highest *ātman*; cp. *jñānātman*.

sat: being, existence, reality; a being, an existent, a real; virtuous.

satkāraṇavāda: the doctrine that only the material cause, but not the effect is real; the doctrine that Being is real, its forms and shapes are not real.

satkārya-vāda: the doctrine that the effect is real or existent even before it is born; the doctrine that the effect exists in a latent form before it is born.

satkhyāti-vāda: the doctrine that the object of illusion also is real.

sattā: Being, Existence; derivation from *sat*; power, force.

sattva: an Attribute of Prakṛti and is called the Transparent; a being; a synonym for *buddhi* or *mahat* in the Sāṅkhya; that which makes the self-affirmation of I-am.

satya: truth, reality; the true, the real; a derivation from *sat*.

śabda: sound; word; in grammarian philosophy, the same as *sphoṭa*.

śakti: energy, power, force; potency; the energy aspect of the Godhead.

savikalpaka: determinate; with form or shape; cp. *samprajñāta*.

skandha: aggregate, group; see *saṁghāta*; name also of God Śiva.

smṛti: memory; what is remembered; remembered sacred text like the epics and ethical codes.

spanda: vibration, pulsation, activity, movement.

sphoṭa: the original seed state of the word before its letters are uttered in a sequence; at that time it is of the form of *buddhi* or cognition comprehending the object also.

śravaṇa: hearing.

śruta: the heard; verbal cognition in Jainism.

śruti: the sense of hearing; ear; what is heard; a synonym for the Veda.

śuddha-sattva: in Rāmānuja's philosophy, a substance called the Pure Transparent, which constitutes the medium of existence of God and the liberated souls and which is different from the *sattva*, an Attribute of Prakṛti, which is impure.

śuddhavidyā: pure knowledge or cognition in the Śaiva schools; distinct from impure and limited knowledge; it has much similarity to *śuddha-sattva*.

śūnya: void, empty; the zero; the Void, the Empty; the indeterminate, that which is devoid of all determinations like deep sleep, in which the *ātman* is called by some philosophers by the name *śūnya-dṛk*, the knower of the void.

śūnyatā: voidness, emptiness, vacuity.

sūtra: thread, string; aphorism.

sūtrātman: one of the stages of the Logos, at which the Logos acts like the thread in a necklace of beads in tying or binding together all the souls in their dream states, although each soul has its own dreams; see Hiraṇyagarbha.

svabhāva: own nature as characterizing one's being; distinct from *svarūpa*, which is one's own being.

svarūpa: own being (*sattā*), as distinct from *svabhāva*; in literary language, one's own form, appearance, but may not mean even structure or characteristic.

svarūpa-jñāna: existential consciousness; one's own knowledge of one's own existence.

syādvāda: the doctrine of conditioned predication; the doctrine that knowledge is relative, but still true.

tādātmya: identity of being; same-self-ness.

tejas: light; psychic energy; the light of the dream, which constitutes also the objects of the dream, including the dreamer.

taijasa: of psychic energy; name of the *ātman* in dream.

tamas: one of the Attributes of Prakṛti and is called the Dark; it has greater significance than being an Attribute of Prakriti, see the text; positive Non-being or Being as the unconscious (Avidyā) and Void (Śūnya, cp. *śūnyadṛk*) in the Advaita.

tanmātras: subtle elements; ultimately specific sense qualities as potential fields of sense cognition.

tarka: argument; logic; counter-factual conditional; pro-factual conditional also as "Had it been so, this would have been so"; permutations and combinations of both conditionals.

tathā: such, so, thus, in that way.

tathatā: suchness, thusness; terms describing the nature of ultimate reality in one school of Buddhism.

tathāgata: one who has gone thus, attained the simple thusness; a name of Buddha who has gone the way of reality.

tathāgata-garbha: the womb of the Tathāgata: reality; the source of the universe.

tathyam: truth.

udāharaṇa: example.

ūha: guess; in Jainism, *tarka* or inductive statement.

upādhi: condition; conditionality.

upamāna: similarity; comparison; cognition of similarity.

vaidika: of the Veda.

varṇa: colour; caste.

vaiśadyam: clarity.

vāsana: perfume, smell; impression, imprint, trace, vestige; see *samskāra*.

vidhi: injunction; law; rule; fate; creator god; ethical command.

vibhu: all-pervading; infinite; endless.
vairāgya: detachment; withdrawal from the world.
vidyā: knowledge, learning; education; consciousness; see *śuddha-vidyā* also.
vaisvānara: the individual in the waking state; the person in the waking state; also means fire; in all the three states, the *ātman* is considered to be fire manifesting its powers in different forms, cp. the Stoic Fire; Logos in the gross state.
vijñāna: consciousness; determinate consciousness; knowledge of empirical arts and sciences; a synonym for *buddhi*; idea, concept used in a loose sense in Buddhism; no very uniform usage in the other schools also.
vijñapti: the same as *vijñāna* in Buddhism; application or appeal; not used as a synonym for *buddhi* in literary language.
vikalpa: doubt; concept; conceptualization; empty verbal cognition without a corresponding object; idea, image; distortion.
vikṣepa: projection, throwing out.
viparītakhyāti-vāda: the doctrine that the object of illusion is a remembered individual object; the doctrine that illusion is the perception of the object in front as a remembered object.
viśeṣa: the particular as distinct from the individual and the universal; any distinguishing mark.
viśva: world; cosmos; the Logos corresponding to *natura naturata*; the Cosmic Person of the waking state; cp. *vaisvānara*.
viṣaya: object of cognition; subject of discourse; topic.
vivarta: transformation; transformation in which the nature of the material cause is not affected; distinguished from *pariṇāma*.
vyāpāra: activity of the instrumental cause.
vyāpti: major premise; concomitance of the major and middle terms in a syllogism.
vyavahāra: activity; custom; convention; business.
vyāvahārika: that which belongs to active life; the pragmatic (world); the empirical; the conventional, the customary.
vyūha: formation, form; maze.
yadṛcchā: accidental.
yama: self-control; control.
yoga: see *mārga*: in Jainism, the contact of actions with the *ātman*; etymologically, the word means "yoking," "binding," "tying."

2. A NOTE ON TRANSLITERATION AND PRONUNCIATION

The following are given to help the reader in pronouncing only the Sanskrit words used in this book. Other letters and their pronunciations are omitted.

a short as in *particular*.
ā long as in *father*.
i short as in *pit*.
ī long as in *police* or *seat*.
u short as in *put*.
ū long as in *rude*.

ṛ short as rr in *merrily*.
e as in *pet*.
ai as in *pain*; rather as in *sign*.
o as in *go*.
ou as in *house*.
g as in *go*.
ṅ as in *sing*.
c as ch in *chores*.
ch as chh in *churchhouse*.
ñ as in *sing*.
ṭ as in *true*.
ḍ as in *drum*.
ṇ as in *tent*, when n and t are pronounced with the same position of the tongue.
t as in *thermos* without the h-sound.
d as th in *this*.
dh as when another h is added to th in *this*.
ś as in *sure*.
ṣ as sh in *shine*.
s as in *sit*.

Bibliography

Here are given only some suggestions for extended reading. The author has been reading and writing for over fifty years. Many books have gone out of print. It is difficult to remember their publishers and dates. Many have been reprinted, copies of which are not now within reach for the author, who does not claim to exhaustive oriental scholarship, but wishes only to help the earnest thinker and researcher by indicating where he can find further assistance in discovering the deeper roots of man's being. The author depended mainly on the original Sanskrit works, and then on expositions and translations. The translations are not always helpful; and they are not dependable fully except when made by persons with intensive training in western philosophy. As the work is meant to help western philosophers through comparative estimates, a number of western philosophical works utilized have also been given; but they are not exhaustive.

GENERAL

B. G. Tilak: *The Arctic Home of the Vedas* (Tilak Bros., Poona, 1956).

W. Windelband: *History of Philosophy*, 2 vols. (Eng. tr. by J. H. Tufts, Harper Bros., New York, 1958).

S. P. Lamprecht: *Our Philosophical Traditions* (Appleton Century, New York, 1955).

Albert Schweitzer: *Indian Thought and Its Development* (Henry Holt, New York, 1936).

W. T. Caan, P. T. Raju, et al: *The Great Asian Religions* (Macmillan, New York, 1969).

P. V. Kane: *History of the Dharma Śāstra*, 5 vols. (Bhandarkar Oriental Research Institute, Poona, 1932–62).

Mortimer Wheeler: *The Indus Civilization* (Cambridge University Press, Cambridge, 1960).

Manu: *Dharma Śāstra* (any edition).

——: *The Laws of Manu* (Christian Literature Society, Madras, 1921).

F. W. Cornford: *From Religion to Philosophy* (Harper, New York, 1957).

——: *Principium Sapientiae* (Harper, New York, 1965).

W. E. Hocking: *Living Religions and World Faith* (George Allen and Unwin, London, 1940).

W. T. Marvin: *History of European Philosophy* (Macmillan, New York, 1930).

R. C. Mazumdar: *An Advanced History of India* (Macmillan, New York, 1961).

A. B. Keith: *Religion and Philosophy of the Vedas and the Upanishads*, (Harvard University Press, Cambridge, 1925).

H. D. Griswold: *The Religion of the Ṛgveda* (Oxford Univ. Press, Oxford, 1923).

S. Radhakrishnan: *Indian Philosophy*, 2 vols. (George Allen and Unwin Ltd., London, latest edition).

S. N. Dasgupta: *History of Indian Philosophy*, 5 vols. (Cambridge Univ. Press, Cambridge, latest edition).

Maurice Bloomfield: *The Religion of the Veda* (B. P. Putnam and Sons, New York, 1908).

P. T. Raju: *Idealistic Thought of India* (George Allen and Unwin Ltd., London, 1953, also Harvard University Press, Cambridge, 1953).

——: *The Philosophical Traditions of India* (George Allen and Unwin Ltd., London, 1971, Pittsburgh Univ. Press, Pittsburgh).
——: *Introduction to Comparative Philosophy* (University of Southern Illinois Press, Carbondale, 1971).
——: *Indian Idealism and Modern Challenges* (Punjab University, Chandigarh, 1961).
Bhagavan Das: *Sanātana Dharma* (Theosophical Publishing House, Adyar, Madras, 1930).
G. T. Garret: *The Legacy of India* (Clarenden Press, Oxford, 1933).
P. T. Raju: "The Principle of Four-cornered Negation," *The Review of Metaphysics*, June 1954.
Karl Potter: *Presuppositions of Indian Philosophy* (Prentice-Hall, Englewood Cliffs, 1963).
L. Lange: *History of Materialism*, 3 vols. (Kegan Paul, London, 1925).
E. Warbecke: *The Searching Mind of Greece* (F. S. Crofts, New York, 1930).
Madhavacharya: *Sarvadarśana-Saṁgraha* (Anandasrama, Poona, 1928).
P. T. Raju: "Being: How Known and How Expressed," *International Journal of Philosophy*, June 1975.
——: "Self and Body: How Known and Distinguished," *The Monist*, January, 1978.
Karl Popper: *The Open Society and Its Enemies*, 2 vols. (Princeton Univ. Press, Princeton, 1950).
P. T. Raju: "The Problem of the Individual," *The Review of Metaphysics*, September, 1963.
——: "The Logos and the Mahān Ātmā," *Ohio Journal of Religion*, July, 1957.
S. Radhakrishnan and C. A. Moore: *Source Book of Indian Philosophy* (Princeton, 1957).
King Bhoja: *Sringāraprakās*, 2 vols. (Coronation Press, Mysore, 1955 and 1963).
S. Radhakrishnan and P. T. Raju: *The Concept of Man*, 2nd ed. (George Allen and Unwin Ltd., London, 1966).
P. T. Raju and A. Castell: *The Problem of the Self* (Martinus Nijhoff, The Hague, 1968).
Kumar Kishore Mandal: *A Comprehensive Study of the Concepts of Space and Time in Indian Thought* (Chowkhamba, Banaras, 1968).
S. Radhakrishnan: *History of Philosophy: Eastern and Western*, 2 vols. (George Allen and Unwin Ltd., London, 1952–53).
F. Max Müller: *The Six Systems of Indian Philosophy* (Longmans, New York, 1928).
H. Zimmer: *Philosophies of India* (Routledge, London, 1951).
M. Hiriyanna: *Outlines of Indian Philosophy* (George Allen and Unwin Ltd., London, latest edition).
Haribhadra: *Shaḍdarśana-Samuccaya* (Muktabhai Jnanamandir, Ahmedabad, no date).

PHILOSOPHICAL ENCYCLOPEDIAS AND DICTIONARIES IN SANSKRIT

Bhimacharya Jhalakikar: *Nyāya-Kośa* (Bhandarkar Oriental Research Institute, Poona, latest edition).
Kevalananda: *Mīmāṁsākośa*, 7 vols. (Prajnapathasala Mandal, Wal, India, 1939–61).
Śabdakalpadruma (Chowkhamba, Banaras, 1961).
Vācaspatyam (Chowkhamba, Banaras, 1960).
Lakshmana Sastri Joshi: *Dharmakośa*, 7 vols. (Prajnapathasala Mandal, Wal, India, 1937).
Abhidhana-Rājendra (Jaina Encyclopedia, Abhidhanarajendra Pracharak Sabha, Rutlan, no date).

WORKS ON WESTERN PHILOSOPHY

Henri Bergson: *Matter and Memory* (tr. by Nancy Margaret, George Allen and Unwin Ltd., London, 1913).
——: *Creative Evolution* (tr. by G. A. Mitchell, Henry Holt, New York, 1938).
Gilbert Ryle: *The Concept of Mind* (Barnes and Nobles, New York, 1949).
John Dewey: *How We Think* (D. C. Heath, Boston, 1910).
——: *Common Faith* (Yale University Press, New Haven, 1934).
——: *Essays in Experimental Logic* (Dover, New York, 1953).
Sigmund Freud: *Complete Works* (ed. James Strachey, Hogarth Press, London, 1953–66).
Carl G. Jung: *Collected Works* (ed. by Herbert Read, etc., Pantheon Books, 1953–67).
Martin Heidegger: *Being and Time* (English translation by John Macquerrie, etc., Harper, New York, 1962).
J. P. Sartre: *Being and Nothingness* (tr. by Hazel E. Barnes, Philosophical Library, New York, 1956).
Karl Jaspers: *Philosophy of Existence* (English translation by Richard E. Grabau, University of Pennsylvania Press, Philadelphia, 1971).

A. Schopenhauer: *The World as Will and Idea* (tr. by R. B. Haldane, Kegan Paul, London, 1886).
H. J. Blackham: *Six Existentialist Thinkers* (Macmillan, N. Y., 1952).
Merleau-Ponty: *Phenomenology of Perception* (tr. by J. B. B. Colin Smith, Humanities Press, N. Y., 1962).
J. Joachim: *The Nature of Truth* (Clarendon Press, Oxford, 1906).
G. W. F. Hegel: *Phenomenology of Mind* (tr. by J. B. Baillie, George Allen and Unwin Ltd., London, 1931).
——: *Logic* with an Introduction by W. Wallace (Oxford Univ. Press, Oxford, 1874).
——: *Science of Logic* (tr. by W. Johnston, George Allen and Unwin Ltd., London, 1951).
Edmund Husserl: *Ideas* (tr. by W. R. Gibson, George Allen and Unwin Ltd., London, 1952).
——: *Cartesian Meditations* (tr. by David Cairns, Martinus Nijhoff, 1960).
F. H. Bradley: *Appearance and Reality* (George Allen and Unwin Ltd., London, 1920).
——: *Principles of Logic* (Oxford University Press, Oxford, 1922).
——: *Essays on Truth and Reality* (Clarendon Press, Oxford, 1914).
B. Bosanquet: *Logic*, 2 vols., (Oxford University Press, Oxford, 1911).
——: *Essentials of Logic* (Macmillan, London, 1914).
Immanuel Kant: *Critique of Pure Reason* (tr. by N. K. Smith, Macmillan, London, 1934).
N. K. Smith: *Commentary to Kant's Critique of Pure Reason* (Macmillan, London, 1918).
Edward von Hartmann: *The Philosophy of the Unconscious* (tr. by D. K. Danol Martinus Nijhoff, The Hague, 1968).
J. W. Dunne: *An Experiment with Time* (Faber and Faber, London, 1938).
G. F. Stout: *Analytic Psychology*, 2 vol. (George Allen and Unwin, London, 1918).
Plato: *The Dialogues of Plato*, 2 vols. (tr. by B. Jowett, Random House, N. Y., 1937).
Aristotle: *The Basic Works of Aristotle* (tr. by Richard Mckeon, Random House, N. Y., 1941).
Reginald E. Allen: *From Thales to Aristotle* (Free Press, N. Y., 1966).
Jason L. Saunders: *Greek and Roman Philosophy after Aristotle* (Free Press, N. Y., 1966).
John W. Wippel and Allan W. Wolter: *Medieval Philosophy* (Free Press, N. Y., 1969).
W. J. Oates: *The Stoic and Epicurean Philosophers* (Modern Library, N. Y., 1957).
T. V. Smith: *From Descartes to Locke* (University of Chicago Press, Chicago, 1957).
——: *Berkeley, Hume, and Kant* (University of Chicago Press, Chicago, 1957).
F. N. Magill and Ian P. McGreal: *Masterpieces of World Philosophy* (Harper, N. Y., 1961).
B. Spinoza: *Ethics* (any edition).

(The works of the above philosophers should be carefully studied and the depths of their thought should be unearthed for a fruitful comparison with the thoughts of Indian philosophers; and the reverse also should be done. It will be mere pedantry to give the names of even the important works of the great philosophers. Readers can find them easily.)

W. P. Montague: *Ways of Knowing* (George Allen and Unwin Ltd., London, 1925).
Alice Ambrose: *Ludwig Wittgenstein: Philosophy and Language* (George Allen and Unwin Ltd., London, 1972).
Ludwig Wittgenstein: *Tractatus Logico-Philosophicus* (any edition).
——: *Philosophical Investigations* (any edition).
Kurt Koffka: *Principles of Gestalt Psychology* (Harcourt and Brace and Co., N. Y., 1935).
Wolfgang Kohler: *Gestalt Psychology* (Liveright Publications Corp., N. Y., 1947).

(Some of the general and historical works given in this and the previous section contain chapters on the following sections and material useful for the interpretation of the ideas of the books.)

UPANIṢADS

Amaradasa: *Ekādaśopaniṣads* (Motilal Banarasi Das, Delhi, 1927).
Śaṅkara: *Commentary on Daśopaniṣads* (Vanivilas Sanskrit Pustakalaya, Banaras, no date).
Guaḍapāda: *Vārtikās on the Māṇḍūkya Upaniṣad* (included in the above).
Upaniṣad Brahmayogi: *Commentary on the Śaiva, Śākta, Yoga, Sāmānya Vedānta, Daśopaniṣads, and Viṣṇava Upaniṣads etc.*, (all together one hundred and eight in number, (Theosophical Publishing House, Adyar, Madras, 1920–60).
Raṅgarāmānuja: *Commentary on Śvetāsvatara Upaniṣad* (Tirupati-Tirupalai Devasthanam Press, Tirupati, 1955).

(For Viśiṣṭādvaita commentaries on the Upaniṣads, see the section on the Viśiṣṭādvaita.)

R. D. Ranade: *A Constructive Survey of Upaniṣadic Philosophy* (Oriental Book Agency, Poona, 1927).
S. K. Belvalkar and R. D. Ranade: *The Creative Period* (Bilvakunja Publication House, Poona, 1927).
P. T. Raju: *Indian Idealism and Modern Challenges* (Punjab University, Chandigarh, 1961).
S. Radhakrishnan: *The Principal Upaniṣads* (George Allen and Unwin, London, 1953).
F. Max Müller: *Upaniṣads* (Costable, London, 1926).
R. E. Hume: *Thirteen Principal Upaniṣads* (Oxford University Press, Oxford, 1923).
K. R. Potdar: *Sacrifice in the Ṛgveda* (Bharatiya Vidya Bhavan, Bombay, 1953).
A. B. Keith: *Religion and Philosophy of the Vedas and the Upaniṣads* (Harvard University Press, Cambridge, 1925).
Paul Deussen: *The Philosophy of the Upaniṣads* (tr. by A. S. Geden, T and T Clark, London, 1908).

THE MĪMĀMSĀ

G. V. Devasthali: *Mīmāmsā* (Booksellers Publishing Co., Bombay, 1959).
Āpadeva: *Mīmāmsānyāyaprakāśā* with commentaries (Chowkhamba, Banaras, 1920).
Laughākṣi Bhāskara: *Arthasaṁgraha* (ed. by A. B. Gajendraghadkar, Author, Eliphinstone College, Bombay, 1934).
G. N. Jha: *Pūrvamīmāmsā in Its Sources* (Banaras Hindu University, Banaras, 1942).
P. T. Raju: "Activism in Indian Thought" (Annals of the Bhandarker Oriental Research Institute, Vol. XXXIV, Parts iii–iv, 1959).
Madhusūdana: *Prasthānabheda* (at the end of *Sarvadarśansaṅgraha*, see above).
A. B. Keith: *Karmamīmāmsā* (Oxford University Press, Oxford, 1921).
N. V. Thadani: *The Mīmāmsā* (Bharati Research Institute, Delhi, 1952).
Pārthasārathi Miśra: *Nyāyaratnamāla* (Oriental Institute, Baroda, 1937).
Kṛṣṇa Yajvan: *Mīmāmsā Paribhāṣā* (tr. by Swami Madhavananda, Ramakrishna Mission, Howrah, 1948).
Nārāyaṇa Bhatta: *Mānameyodaya* (Theosophical Publishing House, Adyar, 1933).
Pasupatinath Sastri: *The Pūrva Mīmāmsā* (Ashoknath Bhattacharya, Calcutta, 1923).
Mandana Misra: *Mīmāmsā Darśana* (Ramesh Book Depot, Jaipur, 1954).
Kuruganti Srirama Sastry: *Pāribhāṣikārthasaṅgraha* (Sarada Press, Amalapur, year not given).
Gaurinath Sastri: *Mīmāmsāparibhāṣā* (Sarada Sanskrit Series, Banaras, 1936).
Jaimini: *Mīmāmsā Sūtras* (ed. by G. N. Jha, Gaekwad Oriental Series, Baroda, 1933–36).
Kumārila: *Ślokavārtikā* (tr. by G. N. Jha, Asiatic Society of Bengal, Calcutta, 1908).
Govardan P. Bhatt: *Epistemology of the Mīmāmsā School* (Chowkhamba, Banaras, 1962).
Rāmānuja: *Tantrarahaśya*, a Primer of Prabhakara Mīmāmsā (Oriental Institute, Baroda, 1956).
Jaimini: *Mīmāmsā Sūtras* with the commentaries of Sabara, Kumarila, Murari, etc. (Anandasrama, Poona, 1931–51).
Kumārila: *Slokavārtikā* (ed. by Dvaraka Prasad, 6 Parts, Tara Publications, Banaras, 1978).

THE CĀRVĀKA

Jayarāśi: *Tattvopaplavasimha* (Gaekvad Oriental Series, Baroda, 1930).
Dakshinaranjan Sastri: *A Short History of Indian Materialism* (Bookland Private Ltd., Calcutta, 1951).
S. Dasgupta: *Obscure Religious Cults* (K. L. Mukhopadhyaya, Calcutta, 1969).
Deviprasad Chattopadhaya: *Lokāyata* (Peoples Publishing House, Calcutta, 1959).
A. L. Bhasham: *Ājīvikas* (Luzac and Co., London, 1951).

JAINISM

Umāsvāti: *Tattvārthādhigamasūtra*, also called *Tattvārthasūtra* (Superindent, Govt. Branch Press, Mysore, 1944).
Mallisena: *Syādvādamanjari* (Bombay Sanskrit Series, Bombay, 1938).
Kuṇḍakuṇḍa Āchārya: *Nyāyasāra* (The Central Jaina Publishing House, Lucknow, 1931).
——: *Samayasāra* (The Central Jaina Publishing House, Lucknow, 1930).
Prabhāchandra: *Prameyakamalamārtāṇḍa* (Nirnayasagar, Bombay, 1941).

Yaśovijaya: *Jainatarkabhāṣa* (Singhi Jaina Jnanapitha, Calcutta, 1938).
Walther Schuberg: *The Doctrine of the Jainas* (Motilal Banarasi Das, Delhi, 1912).
Sāntisūri: *Nyāyavatārasūtra-vārtikā-vṛtti* (Singhi Jaina Series, Bombay, 1949).
Hemachandra: *pramāṇā-mīmāmsā* (Singhi Jaina Series, Bombay, 1939).
S. Mookerjee: *Jaina Philosophy of Non-absolutism* (Bharatiya Mahavidyalaya, Calcutta, 1944).
M. L. Mehta: *Outlines of Jaina Philosophy* (Jaina Misssion Society, Bangalore, 1954).
——: *Jaina Psychology* (Sohanlal Jaina Dharma Pracharak Samiti, Amritsar, 1957).
S. T. Stevenson: *The Heart of Jainism* (Oxford University Press, London, 1915).
Nathmal Tatia: *Studies in Jaina Philosophy* (Jaina Cultural Research Society, Banaras, 1951).
Guṇabhadra Āchārya: *Ātmānuśāsana* (The Central Jaina Publishing House, Lucknow, 1928).
Amulyachandra Sen: *Schools and Sects in Jaina Literature* (Visvabharati Bookshop, Calcutta, 1931).
Panditacharya: *Prameyaratnālaṅkāra* (Superindent, Govt. Branch Press, Mysore, 1948).

BUDDHISM

B. M. Barua: *History of Pre-Buddhist Indian Philosophy* (Calcutta University, Calcutta, 1921).
——: Prolegomena to a *History of Buddhist Philosophy* (Calcutta University, Calcutta, 1918).
P. V. Bapat: *2500 Years of Buddhism* (Publications Division, Govt of India, Delhi, 1957).
Bhikṣu Saṅgharakṣita: *A Survey of Buddhism* (Indian Institute of World Culture, Bangalore, 1959).
E. J. Thomas: *History of Buddhist Thought* (Barnes and Nobles, New York, 1951).
H. V. Guenther: *Philosophy and Psychology in the Abhidharma* (Random House, New York, 1976).
E. J. Thomas: *Mahāyānasūtras* or *Prajñāpāramitā-Sūtras* (J. Murray, London, 1952).
Aniruddha: *Abhidharmārthasaṅgraha* (Eng. tr. by S. Z. Aung, Pali Text Society, London, 1910).
Theodore de Bary: *The Buddhist Tradition* (Vintage Books, New York, 1972).
Yamakami Sogen: *Systems of Buddhist Thought* (Calcutta University Press, Calcutta, 1912).
Prajñākaramati: *Bodhicharyāvatāra-Pañchikā* (ed. by Louise la Vallé Poussin, Luzac, London, no date available).
D. T. Suzuki: *Aśvaghoṣa's Mahāyanā- Śraddhotpāda Śāstra* (Eng. tr. Open Court, Chicago, 1900).
Asaṅga: *Mahāyana-Sutrālaṅkāra* (ed. by Sylvan Devi, Librarie Honore Champion, Parïs, 1907).
D. T. Suzuki: *Laṅkāvatārasūtra* (George Routledge and Sons, London, 1932).
D. T. Suzuki: *Studies in Laṅkāvatārasūtra* (Routledge and Kegan Paul, London, 1957).
S. Mookerjee: *The Buddhist Philosophy of Universal Flux* (Calcutta University, Calcutta, 1930).
Christian Humphreys: *Buddhism* (Pelican Books, Hammondworth, 1949).
Nāgārjuna: *Mādhyamika-Kārikās* (ed. by la Valeë Poussin, St. Petersburg, 1903).
J. B. Pratt: *A Pilgrimage of Buddhism and a Buddhist Pilgrimage* (Macmillan, New York, 1928).
Th. Stcherbatsky: *Buddhist Logic*, 2 vols. (Dover Publications, London, 1962).
A. B. Keith: *Buddhist Philosophy in India and Ceylon* (Clarendon Press, Oxford, 1923).
C. A. F. Rhys Davids: *A Manual of Buddhism* (Sheldon Press, London, 1932).
Sir Charles Eliot: *Hinduism and Buddhism*, 3 vols. (E. Arnold and Co., London latest edition).
Edward Conze: *Buddhism: Its Essence and Development* (Philosophical Library, New York, 1954).
A. K. Coomaraswamy: *Buddha and the Gospel of Buddhism* (Harrap, London, 1928).
A. J. Bahm: *Philosophy of the Buddha* (Harper, N. Y., 1958).
F. J. Streng: *Emptiness* (Abingdon Press, Nashville, 1967).
J. Takakusu: *The Essentials of Buddhist Philosophy* (University of Hawaii, Honolulu, 1947).
The Expositor (tr. by Maung Tin, ed. by Mrs. Rhys Davids, Pali Text Society, London, 1920).
Vasubandhu: *Abhidharmakośa* (ed. by Rahula Sankṛtyana, Kasi Vidyapith, Banaras, year not given).
Points of Controversy (ed. by Aung and Mrs. Rhys Davids, Pali Text Society, London, 1915).
Rhys Davids: *Buddhist Psychological Ethics* (Royal Asiatic Society, London, 1923).
Th. Stcherbatsky: *The Conception of Buddhist Nirvāṇa* (Academy of Sciences, U. S. S. R., Leningrad, 1927).
Rhys Davids: *Buddhist Psychologist Ethics* (Royal Asiatic Society, London, 1923).
Th. Stcherbatsky: *The Conception of Buddhist Nirvāṇa* (Academy of Sciences, U. S. S. R., Leningrad, 1927).
Ryukan Kimura: *The Original and Developed Doctrines of Buddhism* (University of Calcutta, Calcutta, 1920).
Vdhusekhar Bhattacharya: *The Basic Conception of Buddhism* (Calcutta University, Calcutta, 1934).
M. N. Dutt: *Aspects of Mahāyāna Buddhism* (Luzac, London, 1930).
Herman Jacobi: *Trimsatikāvijñapti* (W. Kohlhammer, Stuttgart, 1932).

G. N. Jha: *Tattvasaṁgraha of Śāntarakṣita* (Gaekwad Oriental Series, Baroda, 1939).
H. Oldenberg: *Buddha* (J. A. Cotta, Stuttgart, 1914).
Prajñākaragupta: *Pramāṇavārtikābhāṣyam* (Kasiprasad Jayaswal Research Institutè, Patna, 1953).
Dharmakirti: *Pramāṇavārtikā* (Banaras Hindu University, Banaras, 1959).
Mādhyamika Dialectic and the Philosophy of Nāgārjuna (ed. by Samdhong Rimpoche and C. Mani; Central Institute of Higher Tibetan Studies, Sarnath, Banaras, 1977).

THE NYĀYA

Vidyabhushan: *History of Indian Logic* (Calcutta University, Calcutta, 1921).
Gautama: *The Nyāyasūtras with Viśvanātha's Commentary* (Gupta Book Depot, Banaras, 1919).
Vātsāyana: *Nyāyabhāṣya* (tr. by G. N. Jha, Oriental Book Depot, Poona, 1939).
Kesava Misra: *Tarkabhāṣā* (Medical Hall Press, Banaras, 1922).
Annam Bhatta: *Tarkasaṁgraha* (ed. and tr. by Y. V. Athalye and M. R. Bodas, Bombay Sanskrit Series, Bombay, 1930).
Jayanta: *Nyāyamañjary* (Chowkhamba, Banaras, 1936).
Gangeśa: *Tattvacintāmaṇi*, Part I, (Mathila Vidyapith, Darbhanga, 1951).
H. H. Ingalls: *Materials for a Study of Navyanyāya Logic* (Harvard University Press, Cambridge, 1951).
Karl Potter: *Padārtha-Tattva-Cintāmani of Raghunātha Śiromaṇi* (Harvard University Press, 1957).
C. Goekoop: *The Logic of Invariable Concomitance in Tattvacintāmaṇi*, (Humanities Press, New York, 1967).
Manilal: *The Navyanyāya Doctrine of Negation* (Harvard University Press, Cambridge, 1968).
P. T. Raju: *Arthāpatti: Its Logical Significance* (Proceedings of the All India Oriental Conference, Banaras, 1942).
Jagadīśa: *Śabdaśaktiprakāśa* (Chowkhamba, Banaras, 1934).
A. B. Keith: *Indian Logic and Atomism* (Clarendon Press, Oxford, 1921).
S. C. Chatterji: *The Nyāya Theory of Knowledge* (Calcutta University, Calcutta, 1941).
S. Kuppuswami Sastri: *A Primer of Indian Logic* (P. Varadachari and Co., Madras, 1932).
Madhavananda: *Bhaṣāpariccheda* (tr. Advaitasrama, Calcutta, 1940).
Udayana: *Kiraṇāvali* (The Asiatic Society, Calcutta, 1956).
Udayana: *Nyāyakusumānjali* (Chowkhamba, Banaras, no date).
Erich Frauwalner: *Raghunātha* (Wiener Zeitschrift, Vienna, 1966–67).
Erich Frauwalner: *Landmarks in the History of Indian Logic* (Vienna, 1961).
Viśvanātha: *Kārikāvali with Muktāvali* with the Commentaries Ramarudri and Dinakari (Chowkhamba, Banaras, 1951).
Viśvanātha: *Kārikāvali with Muktāvali* with six Commentaries (Balamanorama Press, Madras, 1923).
Mathurānātha: *Vyāptipañcakam* (Chowkhamba, Banaras, 1928).
Gautama: *Nyāyasūtras* (tr. by S. C. Vidyabhushan, Sacred Books of the Hindus, Allahabad, 1930).
Karl Potter: *Indian Metaphysics and Epistemology* (Princeton University Press, Princeton, 1977).

THE VAIŚEṢIKA

H. Ui: *Vaiśeṣika Philosophy* (Royal Asiatic Society, London, 1917).
Feddagon: *The Vaiśeṣika System* (K. Müller, Amsterdam, 1918).
Kaṇāda: *Vaiśeṣika Sūtras* (Chowkhamba, Banaras, 1924).
Kaṇāda: *Vaiśeṣika Sūtras* (tr. by Nandalal Sinha, The Sacred Books of the Hindus, Allahabad, 1923).
Praśastapāda: *Padārtha-Dharma-Sangraha* (tr. by G. N. Jha, E. J. Lazarus and Co., Allahabad, 1916).
U. Misra: *The Conception of Matter According to Nyāya-Vaiśeṣika* (M. N. Pandey, Allahabad, 1936).

THE SĀṄKHYA

G. N. Jha: *Tattvakaumudi on Īśvarakṛṣṇa's Sāṅkhyakārikās* (Sanskrit original with Eng. tr., Oriental Book Agency, Poona, 1934).
Vijñānabhikṣu: *Sāṅkhyasūtras with his Commentary* (Chowkhamba, Banaras, 1909).
Kapila: *Sāṅkhyapravacanasūtra* (tr. by Nandalal Sinha, Sacred Books of the Hindus, Allahabad, 1915).

Jagneswar Ghosh: *The Sāṅkhyasūtras of Pañcaśikha and Other Ancient Sages*, (Sanatkumar Ghosh, Calcutta, 1934).
A. B. Keith: *The Sāṅkhya System* (Y. M. C. A. Publishing House, Calcutta, 1949).

THE YOGA

Patañjali: *Yogasūtras* with the Commentaries of King Bhoja and Vyāsa (Anandasram, Poona, 1932).
Patañjali: *Yogasūtras* with the Commentaries of Vyasa and Vacaspati Misra (tr. by Ram Prasad, Oriental Books Reprint Corp., New Delhi, 1978).
G. N. Jha: *Yogadarśana* (Eng. tr. Bombay Theosophical Publication, Bombay, 1907).
S. N. Dasgupta: *Yoga as Philosophy and Religion* (Kegan Paul, London, 1924).
J. H. Woods: *The Yoga System of Patañjali* (Harvard Oriental Series, Cambridge, 1927).
P. V. Pathak: *Heyapakṣa of Yoga* (Motilal Banarasi Das, Delhi, 1932).
A. J. Bahm: *Yogasūtras* (Frederick Ungar Publishing House, New York, 1961).
S. N. Dasgupta: *A Study of Patañjali* (Calcutta University, Calcutta, 1920).
Hariharananda Aranya: *Yoga Philosophy of Patañjali* (tr. by P. N. Mukerji, Calcutta University, Calcutta, 1977).

THE ADVAITA

P. T. Raju: *Thought and Reality: Hegelianism and Advaita* (George Allen and Unwin Ltd., London, 1937).
D. M. Datta: *Six Ways of Knowing* (Calcutta University Press, Calcutta, latest edition).
Gauḍapāda: *Māṇḍūkyakārikās* (see under Upaniṣads).
Vidhusekhara Bhattacharya: *Āgamaśāstra of Gauḍapāda* (Calcutta University, Calcutta, 1943).
Vidyāraṇya: *Pañcadaśi* (Nirnayasagar Press, Bombay, 1949).
Sadananda: *Vedāntasāra* (Jvala Prasad Gaud, Banaras, 1958).
Dharmaraja: *Vedāntaparibhāṣa* ((Chowkhamba, Banaras, 1954).
Appaya Diksita: *Siddhāntaleśa-Saṁgraha* (Chowkhamba, Banaras, 1916).
P. T. Raju: *Indian Idealism and Modern Challenges* (Punjab University, Chandigarh, 1961).
Maṇḍana Miśra: *Brahmasiddhi* (Govt. Oriental Manuscript Series, Madras, 1937).
Sureśvara: *Naiṣkarmyasiddhi* (University of Mysore, Mysore, 1965).
Vimuktātman: *Iṣṭasiddhi* (Gaekwad Oriental Series, Baroda, 1933).
Madhusūdana: *Advaitasiddhi* (ed. by N. Anantakrishna Sastri, Nirnayasagar Press, Bombay, 1937).
Padmapāda: *Pañcapādika* (Vizianagaram Sanskrit Series, Banaras, 1891).
G. Thibaut: *The Vedānta Sūtras with the Commentary of Śaṅkara* (Clarendon Press, Oxford, latest edition).
Vidyāraṇya: *Vivaraṇa-Prameya-Saṁgraha* (Achyutagranthamala Karyalaya, Banaras, no date).
Asutosh Bhattacharya: *Studies in Post-Śaṅkara Dialectics* (Calcutta University, Calcutta, 1936).
V. A. Sharma: *Chitsukha's Contribution to Advaita* (Kavyalaya Publishers, Mysore, 1974).
Vidyāraṇya: *Anubhūtiprakāśa* (Nirnayasagar Press, Bombay, 1926).
Śaṅkara: *Commentary on Brahmasūtras* with the Commentaries of Appayadiksita Amalananda, Vacaspati Misra, etc., ed. by N. Anantakrishna Sastri (Nirnayasagar Press, Bombay, 1917).
Śrī Harṣa: *Khaṇḍanakhaṇḍakhādya* (Chowkhamba, Banaras, 1904).
Śrī Harṣa: *Khaṇḍanakhaṇḍakhādya* (tr. by G. N. Jha, *Indian Thought*, Allahabad, 1913 onwards).
S. S. Suryanarayana Sastri: *A Critique of Difference* (University of Madras, Madras, 1936).
Anandapurna: *Nyāyacandrikā* with the Commentary Nyāyaprakāśa (ed. by N. Anantakrishna Sastri, Govt. Oriental Manuscript Series, Madras, 1959).
Sarvajñātman: *Saṅkṣepaśārīraka* with Commentary (Chowkhamba, Banaras, 1915).
Śaṅkara: *Vākyavṛtti:* (Anandasrama, Poona, 1915).
Gauḍapāda: *Māṇḍūkya Upaniṣad* with his *Kārikās* (Anandasrama, Poona, 1950).

THE VIŚIṢṬĀDVAITA

L. Srinivasacharya: *Darśanodaya* (Superintendent, Govt. Branch Press, Mysore, 1933).
P. T. Raju: "The Existential and the Phenomenological Consciousness in the Philosophy of Rāmānuja ," *Journal of the American Oriental Society*, Oct.-Dec., 1964.

Rāmānuja: *Śrī Bhāṣya*, 2 vols., (Commentary on the *Vedānta Sūtras*, A. V. Co., Madras, 1909).
Rāmānuja: *Vedāntasāra* (ed. V. Krishnamacharya and M. B. Narasimha Ayyangar, Theosophical Publishing House, Adyar, Madras, 1953).
Rāmānuja: *Vedārthasaṅgraha* (Tirumalai-Tirupati Devasthanam, Tirupati, 1953).
Pillai Lokacharya: *Tattvatraya* (Chowkhamba, Banaras, 1938).
Srinivasacharya: *Yatīndramatadīpikā* (ed. and tr. by Adidevananda, Ramakrishnan Math, Madras, 1949).
S. M. S. Chari: *Advaita and Viśiṣṭādvaita* (Luzac, London, 1961).
P. N. Srinivasachari: *The Philosophy of Viśiṣṭādvaita* (Adyar Library, Madras, 1950).
Vedantacharya: *Tattvamuktakalāpa and Sarvārthasiddhi*, 3 vols. (Govt. Branch Press, Mysore, 1954).
Narayanarya: *Nītimāla* (Annamalai University, Annamalainagar, 1940).
Atreya Rāmānuja: *Nyāyakuliśa* (Annamalai University, Annamalainagar, 1938).
K. C. Varadachari: *Śrī Rāmānuja's Theory of Knowledge* (Devasthanam Press, Tirupati, 1943).
Meghanatha Suri: *Nayadyumaṇi* (Govt. Oriental Manuscripts Library, Madras, 1956).
Vedanta Desika: *Nyāyasiddhāñjanam* (Vaisnavasiddhanta Prachara Sabha, Madras, 1934).
Raṅgarāmānuja: *Commentary on Taittarīya and Aitareya Upaniṣads* (Kalyana Press, Trichy, 1951).
Raṅgarāmānuja: *Commentary on praśna, Muṇḍaka, and Māṇḍūkya Upaniṣads*, (Devasthanam Press, Tirupati, 1949).
Raṅgarāmānuja: *Commentary on Īśāvāsya Upaniṣad* (Srinivasa Press, Tanjore, 1933).

MADHVA

Madhva: *Commentary on the Vedāntasūtras* (tr. by S. Subbarao, Sri Vyasa Press, Tirupati, 1936).
Madhva: *Commentary on the Bhagavadgītā* (any edition).
B. N. K. Sarma: *A History of the Dvaita School of Vedānta and Its Literature*, 2 vols., (Booksellers Publishing Co., Bombay, 1960–61).
B. N. K. Sarma: *The Philosophy of Śrī Madhvāchārya* (Bharatiya Vidyabhavan, Bombay, 1962).
P. Nagarajarao: *Vādāvali* of Jayatirtha (tr. Theosophical Publishing House, Adyar, Madras, 1943).
H. N. Raghavendrachar: *Dvaita Philosophy and Its Place in the Vedānta* (Mysore University, Mysore, 1941).
C. R. Krishnarao: *Śrī Madhvāchārya* (Prabhakar Press, Udipi, 1929).
B. A. Krishnaswami Rao: *Śrī Madhvāchārya* (Author, University of Mysore, Mysore, 1951).
Nagaraja Sarma: *The Reign of Realism in Indian Philosophy* (National Press, Madras, 1937).
S. K. Maitra: *Madhva Logic* (Calcutta University, Calcutta, 1936).
Vyasatirtha: *Tarkatāṇḍavam*, 4 vols. (Govt. Branch Press, Mysore, 1932–43).
P. Nagarajarao: *Elements of Dvaita Vedānta* (Adyar Library, Madras, 1976).
Vadiraja: *Nyāyaratnāvali* (tr. by L. S. Betty, Motilal Banarasi Das, Delhi, 1978).

OTHER VEDĀNTINS, ETC.

K. C. Pandey: *Abhinavagupta* (Chowkhamba, Banaras, 1963).
Rajanaka Ramakanta: *Commentary on the Bhagavadgītā* (Kasmir Sanskrit Series, Srinagar, 1943).
P. N. Srinivasachari: *Philosophy of Bhedābheda* (Srinivasa Varadachari and Co., Madras, 1934).
Bhāskara: *Commentary on the Vedānta Sūtras* (latest edition).
Srikaṇṭha: *Commentary on the Vedānta Sūtras* (latest edition).
Nibārka: *Commentary on the Vedānta Sūtras* called *Vedānta-Parijata-Saurabha* (ed. by Roma Bose, Royal Asiatic Society of Bengal, Calcutta, 1940–43).
Baladeva: *Commentary on the Vedānta Sūtras* (Sacred Books of the Hindus, Allahabad, 1912).
Vallabha: *Commentary on the Vedānta Sūtras* called *Aṇubhāṣya*, 2 vols. (Bombay Sanskrit Series, Bombay, 1921–26).
Vallabha: *Nyāyalīlāvati* (Chowkhamba, Banaras, 1927–34).
Vijñānabhikṣu: *Commentary on the Vedānta Sūtras* (latest edition).
S. Radhakrishnan (ed): *History of Philosophy: Eastern and Western*, 2 vols. (George Allen and Unwin Ltd., London, 1952).
Bhoja: *Tattvaprakāśa* (latest edition).
Bhoja: *Sṛṅgāraprakāśa*, 2 vols. (Coronation Press, Mysore, 1963).

Maheswarananda (Gorakhnath): *Mahārthamañjari* (Kasmir Sanscrit Series, Srinagar, 1918).
Spandakārikās with the Commentary of Ramakanta (Kasmir Sanscrit Series, Srinagar, 1913).
Somanandanatha: *Śivadṛṣṭi* with the Commentary of Utpala (Kasmir Sanscrit Series, Srinagar, 1934).
Varadaraja: *Śivasūtravārtikā* (Kasmir Sanscrit Series, Srinagar, 1925).
Bhaskara: *Śivasūtravārtikā* (Kasmir Sanscrit Series, Srinagar, 1916).
Utpala: *Īśvara-Pratyabhijna-Vimarsinī* with the Commentary of Abhinavagupta (Kasmir Sanscrit Series, Srinagar, 1921).
Vijñānabhairava with the Commentary of Ksemaraja (Kasmir Sanscrit Series, Srinagar, 1918).
Abhinavagupta: *Paramārthasāra* (Kasmir Sanscrit Series, Srinagar, 1916).
Abhinavagupta: *Parā Trimsikā* (Kasmir Sanscrit Series, Srinagar, 1918).
Pāśupatasūtras: (ed. by R. Anantakrishna Sastri, University of Travancore, Trivandrum, 1940).
Śrīpati: *Śrīkarabhāṣya*, 2 vols., (ed. by C. Hayavadana Rao, Bangalore Press, Bangalore, 1936).

BHAGAVADGĪTĀ

A. Mahadeva Sastri: *Bhagavadgītā* (tr. Minerva Press, Madras, 1897).
B. G. Tilak: *Gītārahasya*, 2 vols., (tr. Tilak Bros., Poona, 1935–36).
B. Bühler: *The Laws of Manu* (Sacred Books of the East, Clarendon Press, Oxford, latest edition).
S. Radhakrishnan: *The Bhagavadgītā* (George Allen and Unwin Ltd., London, 1948).
Franklin Edgerton: *The Bhagavadgītā*, 2 vols., (Harvard Oriental Series, Cambridge, 1944).
Rāmānuja's Commentary on the Gītā (tr. by M. R. Sampatkumaran, M. Rangacharya Memorial Trust, Madras, 1969).
Śaṅkara: *Commentary on the Bhagavadgītā* (Oriental Book Depot, Poona, 1950).
Rajanaka Ramakanta: *Commentary on the Bhagavadgītā* (Kasmir Sanscrit Series, Srinagar, 1943).

CONTEMPORARY PHILOSOPHY

Aurobindo: *Life Divine* (Aurobindo Asram, Pondicherry, latest edition).
Haridas Chaudhury: *Sri Aurobindo* (Aurobindo Mandir, Calcutta, 1951).
S. K. Maitra: *Introduction to the Philosophy of Sri Aurobindo* (Banaras Hindu University, Banaras, 1945).
D. N. Sharma: *The Hindu Renaissance* (Banaras Hindu University, Banaras, latest edition).
P. T. Raju: *Idealistic Thought of India* (Johnson Reprints Corp., New York, 1973).
P. T. Raju: *Introduction to Comparative Philosophy* (University of Southern Illinois Press, Carbondale, 1970).
P. T. Raju: *The Concept of Man*, 2nd ed., along with S. Radhakrishnan (George Allen and Unwin Ltd., London, 1966).
P. T. Raju: *Indian Idealism and Modern Challenges* (Punjab University, Chandigarh, 1961).
S. Radhakrishnan: *Contemporary Indian Philosophy*, 2nd ed., (George Allen and Unwin Ltd., London, 1952).
M. K. Gandhi: *My Experiments with Truth* (tr. Mahadev Desai, Ministry of Information, Govt of India. 1958–60).
M. K. Gandhi: *Collected Works* (Public Affairs Press, Washington, D. C., 1948).
G. N. Dhavan: *The Political Philosophy of Mahatma Gandhi* (Popular Book Depot, Bombay, 1946).
Paul A. Schilpp: *Sarvapalli Radhakrishnan* (Tudor, New York, 1952).
C. E. Joad: *Counter Attack from the East* (George Allen and Unwin Ltd., London, 1933).
S. Radhakrishnan: *Eastern Religions and Western Thought* (Oxford University Press, Oxford, 1940).
S. Radhakrishnan: *Idealist View of Life* (George Allen and Unwin Ltd., London, 1932).
C. F. Andrews: *Mahatma Gandhi's Ideas* (George Allen and Unwin Ltd., London, 1930).
Rabindranath Tagore: *The Religion of Man* (George Allen and Unwin Ltd., 1953).
Rabindranath Tagore: *Creative Unity* (Macmillan, Calcutta, 1971).
Rabindranath Tagore: *Sadhana* (Macmillan and Co. Ltd., London, 1947).
Rabindranath Tagore: *Towards a Universal Man* (Asia Publishing House, New York, 1961).
J. E. Thompson: *Rabindranath Tagore* (Y. M. C. A., Calcutta, 1961).
Romain Rolland: *Mahatma Gandhi* (tr. by Catherine D. Groth, Century Co., New York, 1924).
J. Krishnamurty: *Awakening of Intelligence* (Avon Books, New York, 1976).
J. Krishnamurty: *Truth and Actuality* (Victor Gollancz, London, 1977).
Bhagavan Das: *The Essential Unity of All Religions* (Theosophical Press, Wheaton, Illinois, 1966).

Bhagavan Das: *Science of the Self* (Indian Bookshop, Banaras, 1954).
Bhagavan Das: *Science of Peace* (Theosophical Publishing House, Adyar, Madras, latest edition).
Bhagavan Das: *Science of Emotions* (Theosophical Publishing House, Adyar, Madras, latest edition).
Bhagavan Das: *Science of Social Organization* (Theosophical Publishing House, Adyar, Madras, latest edition).
Mohammad Iqbal: *The Reconstruction of Religious Thought in Islam* (Muhhammad Asraf, Lahore, 1962).
P. N. Srinivasachari: *Mystics and Mysticism* (Sri Krishna Library, Madras, 1951).
P. M. Srinivasachari: *The Philosophy of the Beautiful* (Thompson and Co., Madras, 1942).
K. C. Bhattacharya: *The Subject as Freedom* (The Indian Institute of Philosophy, Amalner, 1930).

Index

It is difficult to make the index of any book absolutely exhaustive; for it will then be too long to be called an index and will contain very many repetitions of almost everything in the contents, particularly when they are given in sufficient detail as in the present work. This book contains very many references, some of which may be repetitions and useful, but may be omitted. Besides, in Indian philosophy, the reference comes to the same thing whether it is made in general to the Nyāya, Naiyāyikas, or Nyāya-Vaiśeṣika. Similar is the case with the Advaita, Advaitins, and Advaita Vedānta, and so on. In such cases, the word Nyāya or Advaita is used, and the reader may look for any of the words.